CASES AND MATERIALS

FEDERAL COURTS

THIRTEENTH EDITION

by

CHARLES ALAN WRIGHT
Late Charles Alan Wright Chair in Federal Courts
The University of Texas

JOHN B. OAKLEY
Distinguished Professor of Law Emeritus
The University of California at Davis

DEBRA LYN BASSETT
Justice Marshall F. McComb Professor of Law
Southwestern Law School

FOUNDATION PRESS
2012

THOMSON REUTERS

© 1946, 1950, 1957, 1962, 1970, 1976, 1982, 1988, 1992, 1999 FOUNDATION PRESS

© 2005, 2008 By THOMSON REUTERS/FOUNDATION PRESS

© 2012 By THOMSON REUTERS/FOUNDATION PRESS

     1 New York Plaza, 34th Floor

     New York, NY 10004

     Phone Toll Free 1–877–888–1330

     Fax 646–424–5201

     foundation–press.com

Printed in the United States of America

ISBN 978–1–60930–072–2

Mat #41190466

IN MEMORIAM
CHARLES ALAN WRIGHT
1927–2000

The extraordinary life of Charles Alan Wright ended, quite prematurely, on July 7, 2000. His illness was brief, and his death unexpected. He wrote many volumes, and was always at work keeping each of them up to date. But this casebook—his only casebook—was especially important to him. Professor Wright was above all a teacher, and building towards the next edition of his casebook was an essential part of his life, and of his legacy. He was 72 when he died, and his work on the casebook began when he was 33.

There could hardly be a more daunting task than composing an adequate testimonial to the stature of Professor Wright as an authority, a presence, a personality, a leader, and above all an exemplar in the teaching of the law of federal courts. His colleagues at the University of Texas met this challenge, brilliantly, in the Memorial Resolution that may be found at <http://www.utexas.edu/faculty/council/2000–2001/memorials/Wright/wright.html>.

Professor Wright was universally known to his friends as Charlie. He was the dominant figure in his field. He had a commanding personality, dressed elegantly, and spoke authoritatively with perfect grammar and diction. The nature of his presence was somewhere between the regal and the divine. But Charlie was a remarkably friendly interlocutor and a tireless correspondent, not only willing but eager to respond to inquiries about the law of federal courts from any level of the social order. He took a letter from a prisoner as seriously as one from a Justice of the Supreme Court; he would engage in colloquy as freely and earnestly with a student, new lawyer, or novice professor as with a leading light of the academy, the bench, or the bar. Charlie took seriously the teachings of his faith that the meek were to be valued as highly as the mighty.

This casebook continues to embody Charlie's values. It seeks to instruct through engagement. Students should bear in mind that their views are important, that a healthy legal system is not static but rather maintains its vitality by being open to reform and improvement, and that ultimately what matters in legal advocacy is the merit of an argument, not the status of its proponent.

It was Charlie's hope, and remains ours, that you will be persuaded—and will seek to persuade—by reason rather than assertion. We seek herein to give you the tools to be persuasive in your understanding and exposition of the law of federal courts.

JOHN B. OAKLEY
DEBRA LYN BASSETT

Davis, California
Los Angeles, California
March 2012

FOREWORD TO THE THIRTEENTH EDITION

The First Edition of this casebook, by Charles T. McCormick and James H. Chadbourn, was published in 1946. The Judicial Code of 1948 changed dramatically the map of the federal courts and made necessary a Second Edition in 1950. Seven more editions followed. Professor Charles Alan Wright of the University of Texas joined the original authors in writing the Fourth Edition in 1962. Dean McCormick died in 1963 and Professor Chadbourn in 1982. Professor John B. Oakley began assisting Professor Wright with the casebook's annual supplements in 1995.

When the Tenth Edition appeared in 1999 it was clear that the distance from the early editions was so great that the time had come to remove the names of McCormick and Chadbourn from the title page. Professor Wright passed away in 2000, and Professor Oakley produced the Eleventh Edition in 2005. Professor Debra Lyn Bassett began assisting Professor Oakley with the casebook's annual supplements in 2006, and joined Professor Oakley as a full co-author of the casebook with the Twelfth Edition. Professor Wright's influence remains substantial, and we contemplate retaining his name on the casebook for many editions to come.

* * * * *

In a field as dynamic as Federal Courts, new court decisions are a given. Although we have reexamined every chapter and integrated new material where it seemed useful to do so, we have tried to continue Professor Wright's resistance to making changes merely for the sake of change. If a case has worked well in the classroom we have retained it rather than substitute a different case simply because it is more recent. With this precept firmly in mind, we have dropped thirteen of the principal cases from the Twelfth Edition, and have added six new principal cases.

With 136 principal cases in this edition, few will have the time or inclination to discuss every case, but the array provided should permit suitably detailed coverage of any area within the field of Federal Courts that an instructor deems worthy of especially close attention, while supporting more general coverage of the balance of the course.

We always welcome your comments and suggestions, preferably by e-mail to jboakley@ucdavis.edu or dbassett@swlaw.edu.

J.B.O.

D.L.B.

Davis, California
Los Angeles, California
March 2012

PREFACE TO THE FIRST EDITION

The evolution of the system and procedure of the Federal courts illustrates that acceleration of change which has marked the development of all our institutions in the last two decades. Between the creation of the Circuit Court of Appeals, in 1891, and the Act empowering the Supreme Court to make rules of procedure, in 1934, Federal practice was a comparatively placid pool. Most judges and practitioners accepted with equanimity such complexities as conformity "as near as may be", and the dominion of "general law", peculiarities which however strange to the tyro possessed a pleasurable element of the esoteric. There had always been a few doubters, however, and by the thirties their agitation in dissenting opinions, in bar meetings, and in law reviews, had stirred the pool to a moving current. In 1938 the new Rules of Civil Procedure abolished conformity "as near as may be" and the separation of law and equity. In the same year Erie Railway v. Tompkins washed away the entire structure, or nearly so, of "general law". These violent changes have brought in their wake considerable bodies of new law—the accumulating gloss of decisions interpreting the Rules, and the great series of opinions which trace out the consequences of the new declaration of dependence proclaimed in the Erie case. Naturally this casebook draws deeply from both of these sources.

A notable but more gradual change has been the increasing volume of cases arising under the Federal Constitution and laws, resulting in the lessened frequency and importance of litigation founded on diversity. A spate of new Federal regulatory laws, providing for enforcement by Federal suits, such as the Fair Labor Standards Act, contributed to the former result, whereas the Erie case removed a cherished, though not the only, advantage of resorting to the Federal courts under the diversity clause.

Under the Erie case the Federal courts have abdicated in large measure their considerable influence in the development of substantive rules of non-Federal private law. To balance this however, the Federal courts have for the first time assumed a position of conspicuous national leadership in the improvement of judicial procedure and administration.

The statesmanlike planning of the enabling legislation preliminary to the new rules was a model of wise strategy, in delegating to the Supreme Court the troublesome question of uniting law and equity, and providing that the rules should lie for a period before Congress prior to taking effect. Moreover, the inspired choice of the Chairman of the Advisory Committee and his versatile associates led to the most intelligent campaign of discussion and education in the history of procedural reform and, finally, to the formulation of a Code of rules as revolutionary as the Field Code or the English Rules of the Supreme Court had been. The same liberal temper and the continuing resolve to keep the rules alive by utilizing the results of experience are manifest in the pending Amendments to the Rules. Already the Rules have had a deep influence upon state procedural systems, and it may be predicted that this influence will be a widening one. Manifestly, the study of Federal procedure today is the study in large degree of the present and future of state procedures also.*

All these developments show, however, that the statutes and cases in this book are not to be studied as if they were a closed system. We may expect that, while its velocity may be retarded, change will not cease, and the Federal system of judicial administration of tomorrow will not be that of today. Accordingly, it is profitable for the student to attempt to project the lines of change. Will the doctrine of corporate citizenship, hardly more deeply rooted in the past than the doctrine of Swift v. Tyson and far more vulnerable in theory, succumb to the heavy artillery of Professor McGovney? Is it likely that a more sweeping change will make this unnecessary, namely the withdrawal by Congress of the jurisdiction over cases between citizens of different states? And finally, how soon will the profession and Congress lay the groundwork for a new Code of Federal Jurisdiction which can do as much for simplifying and rationalizing the Federal practice as the new Rules have done? Some beginning in this direction is made by the teacher who leads his class to consider which of the jurisdictional barriers and obstacles revealed by these pages are rational applications of the constitutional division of powers between state and nation and which are merely the vagaries of the process of incrusting successive amendments upon the jurisdictional legislation of different eras. An ordered reconsideration of the whole structure seems overdue.

CHARLES T. MCCORMICK
JAMES H. CHADBOURN

January 3, 1946

---

* In this book, however, the distinctly federal features of the Rules are stressed. Many questions of practice and procedure are common to both State and Federal courts; others are peculiar to the Federal courts as a result of their limited jurisdiction and restrictions on venue. To the extent that the Rules concern the former, the Editors believe they should be treated in general procedural courses. Emphasis is therefore placed on the application and operation of the Rules in those special situations which are characteristic of the Federal courts alone.

SUMMARY OF CONTENTS

TABLE OF CONTENTS

CHAPTER XII. Appellate Jurisdiction and Procedure 979

CHAPTER XIII. Original Jurisdiction of the Supreme Court 1040

TABLE OF CASES

Principal cases are in bold type. Non-principal cases are in roman type. References are to Pages.

TABLE OF STATUTES AND RULES

CASES AND MATERIALS

FEDERAL COURTS

THIRTEENTH EDITION

INTRODUCTORY NOTE

———

The most important primary sources, which will need to be consulted constantly, are Title 28, United States Code (Judiciary and Judicial Procedure) revised in 1948, and the Rules of Civil Procedure for the United States District Courts. Several publishers have issued these in pamphlet form. A recent publication is essential, for almost every session of Congress produces changes in the Judicial Code, and a complete stylistic revision of the Civil Rules took effect on December 1, 2007.

This is a subject in which parallel reading is essential to a useful orientation in the field. There are two major treatises. One is Wright and Miller's Federal Practice and Procedure, joined over the years by a host of co-authors as to particular volumes. The full text of that treatise is available on WESTLAW in the FPP database. The other treatise is Moore's Federal Practice, a loose-leaf publication that has been revised and extended by several new authors. In each of these works, which run to many volumes, there is a full discussion of federal jurisdiction as well as individual consideration of each of the Rules of Civil Procedure. There are also three one-volume works that may be more useful to the student than are the multivolume treatises. These are Chemerinsky, Federal Jurisdiction (5th ed.2007), Mullenix, Redish & Vairo, Understanding Federal Courts and Jurisdiction (1998), and Wright & Kane, Handbook of the Law of Federal Courts (6th ed.2002). The subject is covered more briefly in Currie, Federal Jurisdiction in a Nutshell (4th ed.1999). An excellent overview is provided by Teply & Whitten, Civil Procedure, at 55–177 (3d ed.2004).

An adequate history of the federal judicial system would be an enlightening contribution. It has yet to be written. Some helpful readings upon particular phases of this history are the following: John P. Frank, Historical Bases of the Federal Judicial System, 13 Law & Contemp.Probs. 1 (1948); Felix Frankfurter & James M. Landis, The Business of the Supreme Court; A Study in the Federal Judicial System (Frankfurter & Hart ed.1938); Felix Frankfurter, The Distribution of Judicial Power Between United States and State Courts, 13 Cornell L.Q. 499 (1928); Charles Evans Hughes, The Supreme Court of the United States (1938); Charles Warren, New Light on the History of the Federal Judiciary Act of 1789, 37 Harv.L.Rev. 49 (1923); Charles Warren, The Supreme Court in United States History (rev. ed.1947). William W. Crosskey, Politics and the Constitution in the History of the United States (1953), advances some unfashionable theories as to the meaning of the Constitution, and these have repercussions with regard to the scope of federal judicial power. His book stirred acrimonious debate among the other experts. An important new contribution to the history of the judiciary is Holt, "To Establish Justice": Politics, the Judiciary Act of 1789, and the Invention of the Federal Courts, 1989 Duke L.J. 1421. What had been traditional views are challenged in a posthumous book by Professor Wilfred I. Ritz, Rewriting the History of the Judiciary Act of 1789 (Holt & LaRue eds.1990).

Each year the Annual Report of the Director of the Administrative Office of the United States Courts is published in a pamphlet with the title, Judicial Business of the United States Courts. These reports are now easily accessed on the internet at http://www.uscourts.gov/judbususc/judbus.html. Together with the numerous charts and statistical tables that are annexed, they give a revealing picture of the federal-court system in action, the distribution of the different kinds of cases (federal question, diversity, bankruptcy, criminal, etc.), and the rate of flow and dispatch of business in the different judicial units. They are helpful if not essential to an understanding of the often overlooked questions of policy and expediency incident to problems of jurisdiction.

The general problems of the federal courts are provocatively examined by Judge Henry J. Friendly in his book, Federal Jurisdiction: A General View (1973), and by Martin H. Redish in his book, Federal Jurisdiction: Tensions in the Allocation of Judicial Power (2d ed.1990). There is also a useful volume in which 12 leading experts undertake to predict what the future will bring: Symposium, The Federal Courts: The Next 100 Years, 38 S.C.L.Rev. 363 (1987). More recent symposia of note include Restructuring Federal Courts, 78 Tex.L.Rev. 1399 (2000); Managing the Federal Courts, 34 U.C. Davis L.Rev. 315 (2000); The Future of the Federal Courts, 46 Am.U.L.Rev. 263 (1996); Federal Courts Symposium II, 1991 BYU L.Rev. 737; and Federal Courts Symposium, 1990 BYU L.Rev. 67. A comprehensive bibliography of writing on the federal courts is helpfully provided by Thomas E. Baker in Federal Court Practice and Procedure: A Third Branch Bibliography (2001).

In 1960 the American Law Institute, at the request of Chief Justice Warren, undertook a study of the appropriate jurisdiction of federal courts. That work culminated with American Law Institute, Study of the Division of Jurisdiction between State and Federal Courts (Official Draft 1969). This volume not only contains the recommendations of the Institute for new chapters of the Judicial Code to replace the present chapters on jurisdiction, venue, and removal of cases, but also has an extensive supporting Commentary discussing the recommendations and developing the reasons for the changes in existing law they would make. It is referred to many times in the present work—in the form "ALI Study"—and, though it is somewhat dated now, it has much to say that is still relevant.

In 1988 Congress authorized creation of a Federal Courts Study Committee, to examine the problems and issues currently facing the courts of the United States and to develop a long-range plan for the future of the federal judiciary. The Committee, of which Judge Joseph F. Weis, Jr., was chairman, submitted its final report on April 2, 1990. That report is a thoughtful examination of the problems confronting the federal courts, but many of its recommendations were highly controversial.

Title III of the Judicial Improvements Act of 1990 has its own title: the "Federal Courts Study Committee Implementation Act of 1990." Act of

Dec. 1, 1990, Pub.L. 101–650, Tit. 111, 104 Stat. 5104. The stated purpose of the Act was "to implement some of the more noncontroversial recommendations of the Federal Courts Study Committee." H.R.Rep. No. 734, at 15, 101st Cong., 2d Sess. (1990), reprinted in 1991 U.S.Code Cong. & Admin.News 6860, 6861. See the comprehensive article Oakley, Recent Statutory Changes in the Law of Federal Jurisdiction and Venue: The Judicial Improvements Acts of 1988 and 1990, 24 U.C.Davis L.Rev. 735 (1991).

In March 1995 the Committee on Long Range Planning of the Judicial Conference of the United States submitted to the Judicial Conference its Proposed Long Range Plan for the Federal Courts. This 176–page document has much interesting information about where the federal courts were in 1995 and where they are likely to be in 2020. It is cited here as "1995 Long Range Plan."

Between 1995 and 2004 the American Law Institute undertook a fresh examination of the jurisdiction of the federal district courts. The background of the ALI's Federal Judicial Code Revision Project is described by its Reporter in Oakley, Prospectus for the American Law Institute's Federal Judicial Code Revision Project, 31 U.C.Davis L.Rev. 855 (1998). The first unit of that project was an examination of 28 U.S.C. § 1367. This was the statute, adopted in the 1990 Act referred to above, dealing with "supplemental jurisdiction." The ALI's proposals for a comprehensive revision of that statute were approved by the Institute at its Annual Meeting in 1998. The new text, as proposed by ALI with editorial revisions, is set out in Oakley, Integrating Supplemental Jurisdiction and Diversity Jurisdiction: A Progress Report on the Work of the American Law Institute, 74 Ind.L.J. 25 (1998).

The American Law Institute published the final text of its Federal Judicial Code Revision Project as a single volume in February, 2004. Part I deals with supplemental jurisdiction, Part II with venue and transfer, and Part III with removal. References in the present work generally use a short-form citation: "ALI Judicial Code Project." Each part sets forth proposed statutes, accompanying commentary, and notes by the Reporter. The full text of the approximately 700–page Project has been reprinted in volume 19A of the Federal Practice and Procedure treatise as an appendix to the treatise's coverage of Jurisdiction and Related Matters, and is searchable online in Westlaw's FPP database.

The original authors of this casebook were closely involved in the work of the Federal Judicial Code Revision Project. Professor Wright was the President of the American Law Institute from the inception of the Project in 1995 until his death in 2000, and in that capacity served as an adviser to the Project. Professor Oakley was the sole Reporter for the Project throughout its duration.

CHAPTER I

"Judicial Power" Over "Cases and Controversies"

THE CONSTITUTION OF THE UNITED STATES
ARTICLE I.

Section 1. All legislative Powers herein granted shall be vested in a Congress of the United States, ...

Section 2. . . . The House of Representatives . . . shall have the sole Power of Impeachment.

Section 3. . . . The Senate shall have the sole Power to try all Impeachments. When sitting for that Purpose, they shall be on Oath or Affirmation. When the President of the United States is tried, the Chief Justice shall preside: And no person shall be convicted without the Concurrence of two thirds of the Members present.

Judgment in Cases of Impeachment shall not extend further than to removal from Office, and disqualification to hold and enjoy any Office of honor, Trust or Profit under the United States: but the Party convicted shall nevertheless be liable and subject to Indictment, Trial, Judgment and Punishment, according to Law.

Section 8. The Congress shall have Power . . .

To establish . . . uniform Laws on the subject of Bankruptcies throughout the United States; . . .

To constitute Tribunals inferior to the supreme Court; . . .

To define and punish Piracies and Felonies committed on the high Seas, and Offenses against the Law of Nations;

To declare War, grant Letters of Marque and Reprisal, and make Rules concerning Captures on Land and Water; . . .

To make Rules for the Government and Regulation of the land and naval Forces; . . .

To exercise exclusive Legislation in all Cases whatsoever, over such District (not exceeding ten Miles square) as may, by Cession of particular States, and the Acceptance of Congress, become the Seat of the Government of the United States, and to exercise like Authority over all Places purchased by the Consent of the Legislature of the State in which the Same shall be, for the Erection of Forts, Magazines, Arsenals, Dock–Yards, and other needful Buildings; . . .

Section 9. . . . The Privilege of the Writ of Habeas Corpus shall not be suspended, unless when in Cases of Rebellion or Invasion the public Safety may require it.

ARTICLE II.

Section 1. The executive Power shall be vested in a President of the United States of America. . . .

Section 2. . . . [H]e shall have Power to grant Reprieves and Pardons for Offenses against the United States, except in cases of impeachment.

He . . . shall nominate, and by and with the Advice and Consent of the Senate, shall appoint . . . Judges of the supreme Court, and all other Officers of the United States, whose Appointments are not herein otherwise provided for, and which shall be established by Law: but the Congress may by Law vest the Appointment of such inferior Officers, as they think proper, in the President alone, in the Courts of Law, or in the Heads of Departments. . . .

Section 4. The President, Vice President and all civil Officers of the United States, shall be removed from Office on Impeachment for, and Conviction of, Treason, Bribery, or other High Crimes and Misdemeanors.

ARTICLE III.

Section 1. The judicial Power of the United States, shall be vested in one supreme Court, and in such inferior Courts as the Congress may from time to time ordain and establish. The Judges, both of the supreme and inferior Courts, shall hold their Offices during good Behavior, and shall, at stated Times, receive for their Services, a Compensation, which shall not be diminished during their Continuance in Office.

Section 2. The judicial Power shall extend to all Cases, in Law and Equity, arising under this Constitution, the Laws of the United States, and Treaties made, or which shall be made, under their Authority;—to all Cases affecting Ambassadors, other public Ministers and Consuls;—to all Cases of admiralty and maritime Jurisdiction;—to Controversies to which the United States shall be a party;—to Controversies between two or more States;—between a State and Citizens of another State;—between Citizens of different States;—between Citizens of the same State claiming Lands under Grants of different States, and between a State, or the Citizens thereof, and foreign States, Citizens or Subjects.

In all Cases affecting Ambassadors, other public Ministers and Consuls, and those in which a State shall be Party, the supreme Court shall have original Jurisdiction. In all the other Cases before mentioned, the supreme Court shall have appellate Jurisdiction, both as to Law and Fact, with such Exceptions, and under such Regulations as the Congress shall make.

The Trial of all Crimes, except in Cases of Impeachment, shall be by Jury; and such Trial shall be held in the State where the said Crimes shall have been committed; but when not committed within any State, the Trial shall be at such Place or Places as the Congress may by Law have directed.

Section 3. Treason against the United States, shall consist only in levying War against them, or, in adhering to their Enemies, giving them Aid and Comfort. No Person shall be convicted of Treason unless on the Testimony of two Witnesses to the same covert Act, or on Confession in open Court.

ARTICLE IV.

Section 1. Full Faith and Credit shall be given in each State to the public Acts, Records, and judicial Proceedings of every other State. And Congress may by general Laws prescribe the Manner in which such Acts, Records and Proceedings shall be proved, and the Effect thereof.

. . . . .

Section 3.

. . . . .

The Congress shall have Power to dispose of and make all needful Rules and Regulations respecting the Territory or other Property belonging to the United States . . . .

Section 4. The United States shall guarantee to every State in this Union a Republican Form of Government . . . .

ARTICLE VI.

. . . . .

This Constitution, and the Laws of the United States which shall be made in Pursuance thereof; and all Treaties made, or which shall be made, under the Authority of the United States, shall be the supreme Law of the Land; and the Judges in every State shall be bound thereby, any Thing in the Constitution or Laws of any State to the Contrary notwithstanding.

. . . . .

AMENDMENTS.

. . . . .

Amendment IV.

The right of the people to be secure in their persons, houses, papers, and effects, against unreasonable searches and seizures, shall not be violated, and no Warrants shall issue, but upon probable cause, supported by Oath or affirmation, and particularly describing the place to be searched, and the persons or things to be seized.

Amendment V.

No person shall be held to answer for a capital, or otherwise infamous crime, unless on a presentment or indictment of a Grand Jury, except in cases arising in the land or naval forces, or in the Militia, when in actual service in time of War or public danger; nor shall any person be subject for the same offence to be twice put in jeopardy of life or limb; nor shall be compelled in any criminal case to be a witness against himself, nor be deprived of life, liberty, or property, without due process of law ....

Amendment VI.

In all criminal prosecutions, the accused shall enjoy the right to a speedy and public trial, by an impartial jury of the State and district wherein the crime shall have been committed, which district shall have been previously ascertained by law, and to be informed of the nature and cause of the accusation; to be confronted with the witnesses against him; to have compulsory process for obtaining witnesses in his favor, and to have the Assistance of Counsel for his defence.

Amendment VII.

In Suits at common law, where the value in controversy shall exceed twenty dollars, the right of trial by jury shall be preserved, and no fact tried by a jury shall be otherwise re-examined in any Court of the United States, than according to the rules of the common law.

Amendment VIII.

Excessive bail shall not be required, nor excessive fines imposed, nor cruel and unusual punishments inflicted.

. . . . .

Amendment XI.

The Judicial power of the United States shall not be construed to extend to any suit in law or equity, commenced or prosecuted against one of the United States by Citizens of another State, or by Citizens or Subjects of any Foreign State.

. . . . .

Amendment XIV.

Section 1. All persons born or naturalized in the United States, and subject to the jurisdiction thereof, are citizens of the United States and of the State wherein they reside. No State shall make or enforce any law which shall abridge the privileges or immunities of citizens of the United States; nor shall any State deprive any person of life, liberty, or property, without due process of law; nor deny to any person within its jurisdiction the equal protection of the laws.

. . . . .

Section 5. The Congress shall have the power to enforce, by appropriate legislation, the provisions of this article.

. . . . .

Hodgson v. Bowerbank

Supreme Court of the United States, 1809.
5 Cranch (9 U.S.) 303, 3 L.Ed. 108.

Error to the Circuit Court for the District of Maryland.

The defendants below were described in the record as "late of the district of Maryland, merchants," but were not stated to be citizens of the state of Maryland. The plaintiffs were described as "aliens and subjects of the king of the United Kingdom of Great Britain and Ireland."

Martin contended, that the courts of the United States had not jurisdiction, it not being stated that the defendants were citizens of any State.

C. Lee contra. The Judiciary Act gives jurisdiction to the circuit courts, in all suits in which an alien is a party. Laws U.S. vol. 1, p. 55, § 11.

■ MARSHALL, C.J. Turn to the article of the Constitution of the United States, for the statute cannot extend the jurisdiction beyond the limits of the Constitution.

(The words of the Constitution were found to be "between a State, or the citizens thereof, and foreign States, citizens, or subjects.")

The court said the objection was fatal.

The record was afterwards amended by consent.[1]

———

Sheldon v. Sill

Supreme Court of the United States, 1850.
8 How. (49 U.S.) 441, 12 L.Ed. 1147.

■ MR. JUSTICE GRIER delivered the opinion of the court:

The only question which it will be necessary to notice in this case is, whether the Circuit Court had jurisdiction.

Sill, the complainant below, a citizen of New York, filed his bill in the Circuit Court of the United States for Michigan, against Sheldon, claiming to recover the amount of a bond and mortgage, which had been assigned to him by Hastings, the President of the Bank of Michigan.

Sheldon in his answer, among other things, pleaded that "the bond and mortgage in controversy, having been originally given by a citizen of

---

[1. "It has been argued that *Hodgson* represented merely a narrow interpretation of § 11 of the Judiciary Act of 1789, rather than a holding that § 11 was unconstitutional insofar as it purported to give the federal courts jurisdiction of all suits to which an alien was a party. Mahoney, A Historical Note on *Hodgson v. Bowerbank*, 1982, 49 U.Chi.L.Rev. 725. The latter view is described, at 733, as '[t]he Hart–Wechsler–Wright revisionist interpretation of *Hodgson*'s significance . . . .' The important point of *Hodgson*, however, is its recognition that a statute cannot extend the jurisdiction beyond the limits of the Constitution. Whether the Court then interpreted the statute narrowly, because it would be unconstitutional if construed literally, or whether it held the statute *pro tanto* unconstitutional, seems to the present author a question of semantics." Wright & Kane, Federal Courts § 8, at 33 n. 3 (6th ed.2002).]

Michigan to another citizen of the same State, and the complainant being assignee of them, the Circuit Court had no jurisdiction."

The eleventh section of the Judiciary Act, which defines the jurisdiction of the circuit courts, restrains them from taking "cognizance of any suit to recover the contents of any promissory note, or other chose in action, in favor of an assignee, unless a suit might have been prosecuted in such court to recover the contents, if no assignment had been made, except in cases of foreign bills of exchange."

The third article of the Constitution declares that "the judicial power of the United States shall be vested in one Supreme Court, and such inferior courts as the Congress may, from time to time, ordain and establish." The second section of the same article enumerates the cases and controversies of which the judicial power shall have cognizance, and, among others, it specifies "controversies between citizens of different States."

It has been alleged, that this restriction of the Judiciary Act, with regard to assignees of choses in action, is in conflict with this provision of the Constitution, and therefore void.[2]

It must be admitted, that if the Constitution had ordained and established the inferior courts, and distributed to them their respective powers, they could not be restricted or divested by Congress. But as it has made no such distribution, one of two consequences must result—either that each inferior court created by Congress must exercise all the judicial powers not given to the Supreme Court, or that Congress, having the power to

---

[2. The following excerpt from the argument of Mr. Ashmun for the appellee, 8 How. (49 U.S.) at 446–447, shows his drift: "Now we would remark first, that the case before the Circuit Court was a controversy between citizens of different States, and to such a controversy the judicial power of the courts of the United States extends by the Constitution, and by the same Constitution that power is vested, except where the Supreme Court has original jurisdiction by the Constitution, in the inferior courts created by Congress. This judicial power, therefore, to take cognizance of this case, is, by the Constitution, vested in the Circuit Court, and the plaintiff claims the constitutional right to have his controversy with Mr. Sheldon, living in Michigan, decided by that court. Congress has said, by the provision above referred to, that there are certain controversies between citizens of different states which the United States courts shall not take cognizance of; yet the judicial power of the court extends to them by the Constitution, and citizens of the different States have the right to have that power exercised in their controversies. Where does Congress get the power or authority to deprive the courts of the United States of the judicial power with which the Constitution has invested them? Congress may create the courts, but they are clothed with their powers by the Constitution, and we submit that the provision of the act of Congress materially conflicts with the provisions of the Constitution, and is void. It has been settled, that an act of Congress, enlarging the jurisdiction of the Supreme Court beyond the terms of the Constitution, is void. Marbury v. Madison, 1 Cranch [5 U.S.] 137. Can it any more take away a constitutional power than it can confer an unconstitutional one? We submit that it cannot. The jurisdiction of this class of controversies is in the Circuit Court. The Constitution makes no such distinction as the act of Congress does, and we respectfully submit, that it is of the utmost importance to citizens of the different States that the whole judicial power granted by the Constitution to the courts of the United States should be exercised. We are aware that in some cases it has been assumed that this act of Congress is valid; but we submit that there has been no decision of this court to that effect, and even if there had, being erroneous, the court would reverse it."]

establish the courts, must define their respective jurisdictions. The first of these inferences has never been asserted, and could not be defended with any show of reason and if not, the latter would seem to follow, also, that, having a right to prescribe, Congress may withhold from any court of its creation jurisdiction of any of the enumerated controversies. Courts created by statute can have no jurisdiction but such as the statute confers. No one of them can assert a just claim to jurisdiction exclusively conferred on another, or withheld from all.

The Constitution has defined the limits of the judicial power of the United States, but has not prescribed how much of it shall be exercised by the Circuit Court; consequently, the statute which does prescribe the limits of their jurisdiction, cannot be in conflict with the Constitution, unless it confers powers not enumerated therein.

Such has been the doctrine held by this court since its first establishment. To enumerate all the cases in which it has been either directly advanced or tacitly assumed would be tedious and unnecessary.

In the case of Turner v. Bank of North America (4 Dall. [4 U.S.] 8, 10), it was contended, as in this case, that, as it was a controversy between citizens of different States, the Constitution gave the plaintiff a right to sue in the Circuit Court, notwithstanding he was an assignee within the restriction of the eleventh section of the Judiciary Act. But the court said: "The political truth is, that the disposal of the judicial power (except in a few specified instances) belongs to Congress; and Congress is not bound to enlarge the jurisdiction of the federal courts to every subject, in every form which the Constitution might warrant." This decision was made in 1799; since that time, the same doctrine has been frequently asserted by this court, as may be seen in McIntire v. Wood (7 Cranch [11 U.S.] 504, 506), Kendall v. United States (12 Pet. [37 U.S.] 524, 616), Cary v. Curtis (3 How. [44 U.S.] 236, 245).[3]

. . . . .

The complainant in this case is the purchaser and assignee of a sum of money, a debt, a chose in action, not of a tract of land. He seeks to recover

---

[3. But compare the language of Story, J., in Martin v. Hunter's Lessee, 1 Wheat. (14 U.S.) 304, 328–330 (1816):

"The language of the article throughout is manifestly designed to be mandatory upon the legislature. Its obligatory force is so imperative, that congress could not, without a violation of its duty have refused to carry it into operation. The judicial power of the United States *shall be vested* (not may be vested) in one supreme court, and in such inferior courts as congress may, from time to time, ordain and establish. Could congress have lawfully refused to create a supreme court, or to vest in it the constitutional jurisdiction? . . .

"The same expression, 'shall be vested,' occurs in other parts of the constitution, in defining the powers of the other co-ordinate branches of the government. . . .

"If, then, it is a duty of congress to vest the judicial power of the United States, it is a duty to vest the *whole judicial power*. The language, if imperative as to one part, is imperative as to all. If it were otherwise, this anomaly would exist, that congress might successively refuse to vest the jurisdiction in any one class of cases enumerated in the

by this action a debt assigned to him. He is therefore the "assignee of a chose in action," within the letter and spirit of the act of Congress under consideration, and cannot support this action in the Circuit Court of the United States, where his assignor could not.

The judgment of the Circuit Court must therefore be reversed, for want of jurisdiction.[4]

Knee v. Chemical Leaman Tank Lines, Inc.

United States District Court, E.D. Pennsylvania, 1968.
293 F.Supp. 1094.

■ WEINER, DISTRICT JUDGE. Plaintiff, a Pennsylvania citizen and resident, has filed suit for personal injuries sustained by the alleged negligence of

---

constitution, and thereby defeat the jurisdiction as to all; for the constitution has not singled out any class on which congress are bound to act in preference to others."]

[4. See Senate Select Committee on Presidential Campaign Activities v. Nixon, 366 F.Supp. 51, 55 (D.D.C.1973), where the court said: "For the federal courts, jurisdiction is not automatic and cannot be presumed. Thus, the presumption in each instance is that a federal court lacks jurisdiction until it can be shown that a specific grant of jurisdiction applies. Federal courts may exercise only that judicial power provided by the Constitution in Article III and conferred by Congress. All other judicial power or jurisdiction is reserved to the states. And although plaintiffs may urge otherwise, it seems settled that federal courts may assume only that portion of the Article III judicial power which Congress, by statute, entrusts to them. Simply stated, Congress may impart as much or as little of the judicial power as it deems appropriate and the Judiciary may not thereafter on its own motion recur to the Article III storehouse for additional jurisdiction. When it comes to jurisdiction of the federal courts, truly, to paraphrase the scripture, the Congress giveth, and the Congress taketh away."

See likewise Lockerty v. Phillips, 319 U.S. 182 (1943), upholding the provision depriving all federal courts but one of jurisdiction to enjoin the enforcement of the Emergency Price Control Act. And compare the majority and minority opinions in Bartlett v. Bowen, 816 F.2d 695 (D.C.Cir.1987).

There is an immense literature on the power of Congress to control the jurisdiction of the federal courts. The seminal article is Hart, The Power of Congress to Limit the Jurisdiction of Federal Courts: An Exercise in Dialectic, 66 Harv.L.Rev. 1362 (1953). See also Amar, A Neo–Federalist View of Article III: Separating the Two Tiers of Federal Jurisdiction, 65 B.U.L.Rev. 205 (1985); Friedman, A Different Dialogue: The Supreme Court, Congress and Federal Jurisdiction, 85 Nw.U.L.Rev. 1 (1990); Amar, Taking Article III Seriously: A Reply to Professor Friedman, 85 Nw.U.L.Rev. 442 (1991); Friedman, Federal Jurisdiction and Legal Scholarship: A (Dialogic) Reply, 85 Nw.U.L.Rev. 478 (1991). See also Wright & Kane, Federal Courts § 10 (6th ed.2002); Chemerinsky, Federal Jurisdiction §§ 3.3, 3.4 (5th ed.2007). A recent example of the congressional ability to control the jurisdiction of the federal courts was the 2005 Terri Schiavo Bill (S.686), in which Congress passed a bill for private relief authorizing the federal courts to hear a claim on behalf of Terri Schiavo by her parents, Robert and Mary Schindler. Ms. Schiavo, who was in a persistent vegetative state, had been removed from life support pursuant to a Florida court order at the request of her husband and guardian; the Schindlers sought an injunction on a variety of theories, all of which ultimately were rejected by both the state and federal courts. See Schiavo ex rel. Schindler v. Schiavo, 403 F.3d 1289 (11th Cir.2005).]

defendant, Chemical Leaman Tank Lines, Inc., which is a Delaware corporation. Defendant has filed a Motion to Dismiss, claiming that its principal place of business is in Pennsylvania and, therefore, the requisite diversity required by 28 U.S.C. § 1332(c) is lacking.

In 1958, Congress added subsection (c) to 28 U.S.C. § 1332 "for the apparent purpose of somewhat contracting the diversity jurisdiction in cases involving corporations." Eldridge v. Richfield Oil Corporation, 247 F.Supp. 407 (S.D.Cal.1965), aff'd, 364 F.2d 909 (9th Cir.1966). The added subsection (c) provides in relevant part as follows:

> (c) For the purposes of this section and section 1441 of this title, a corporation shall be deemed a citizen of any State by which it has been incorporated and of the State where it has its principal place of business.

Kelly v. United States Steel Corporation, 284 F.2d 850 (3d Cir.1960), is the controlling case in this circuit for the determination of a corporation's principal place of business. The headquarters of the corporation's day to day activities and management is deemed controlling of this determination.

The uncontradicted affidavit of defendant's president establishes that all billing, all computation and disbursement of payrolls, general supervision of sales and the executive office along with all executive officers take place and are located in Pennsylvania. Defendant maintains a number of branch terminals throughout the country and in Canada, however, Pennsylvania has the largest number of terminals and the general supervision of all of the terminals as well as central dispatching comes from the Pennsylvania office. A consideration of the combination of factors that point to one place as the principal place of business necessitates the conclusion that Pennsylvania is defendant's principal place of business and thus there is no diversity of jurisdiction pursuant to § 1332(c). See Mazer v. Coastal Tanklines, Inc., 232 F.Supp. 689 (E.D.Pa.1964); Alpha Portland Cement Co. v. MacDonald Engineering Co., 224 F.Supp. 714 (E.D.Pa.1963).

The real thrust of plaintiff's argument is not aimed at the question of whether or not defendant has its principal place of business in Pennsylvania, but rather to the gross unfairness that will result if this motion is granted. She argues that defendant filed an answer admitting plaintiff's allegation that the corporation is a corporation organized under the laws of the State of Delaware and maintains an office in Downingtown, Pennsylvania. That it did not contend that this Court was without jurisdiction nor that its principal office was in Pennsylvania until after the Statute of Limitations had run. Furthermore, she argues that these facts were actively concealed as evidenced by the fact that defendant even proceeded to serve interrogatories while waiting for the statute to run. Such action, she argues, is unfair and should not accrue to the benefit of defendant.

Defendant's failure to contest jurisdiction in its answer is not binding on it. It is a well settled principle that the question of subject-matter jurisdiction is always open. It cannot be conferred or supplied by consent of both parties or by estoppel, laches, or waiver of either party. *Eldridge v.*

Richfield Oil Corporation, supra; Page v. Wright, 116 F.2d 449 (7th Cir.1940); Brown v. Fennell, 155 F.Supp. 424 (E.D.Pa.1957). In fact, Judge Lord stated in *Brown:*

> "But even if it could be shown that deliberate deception had been practiced, the plaintiff has no cause to complain, since the admissions in the answer in no way worked to his legal prejudice. Jurisdiction cannot be conferred on the Federal Courts by waiver, estoppel or consent." (Supra at 426).

Finally, plaintiff cites the recent decision of the Third Circuit in McSparran v. Weist, 402 F.2d 867 (3d Cir. filed October 2, 1968) for the proposition that in cases where jurisdiction is artificially created, a case should not be dismissed if the Statute of Limitations has expired, but rather should be retained by the Court. These cases are inapposite to the instant situation for two reasons. First, this is not a case where jurisdiction is "manufactured" as where an out of state guardian is appointed solely for diversity purposes. Furthermore, the decision to retain certain cases dealt with the question of whether or not to declare the new rule enunciated in those cases retrospective or prospective. The Court did not want to "work great hardship on those who have relied on our prior recognition of artificial diversity jurisdiction." *McSparran*, supra, 402 F.2d, at 876.[5] In the instant situation, we are dealing with a statute which has been in effect since 1958 and thus the reliance aspect is not present at all.

We do not like to see a plaintiff deprived of his day in court in this manner, however, "absent federal jurisdiction, no judgment of a federal court can stand." Wymard v. McCloskey & Co., Inc., 342 F.2d 495 (3d Cir.1965).

ORDER

Defendant's Motion to Dismiss for lack of requisite diversity of citizenship is granted.

It is so ordered.[6]

[5. In Firestone Tire & Rubber Co. v. Risjord, 449 U.S. 368, 379 (1981), the Court said that "by definition, a jurisdictional ruling may never be made prospective only." But the Court relaxed its view the following year. In Northern Pipeline Const. Co. v. Marathon Pipe Line Co., 458 U.S. 50, 84 (1982), discussed infra p. 84, n. 62, the Court stayed the effect of a judgment holding unconstitutional certain jurisdictional provisions of the Bankruptcy Reform Act of 1978 in order to give Congress time to enact corrective legislation.]

[6. Is this harsh doctrine, which is productive of so many seemingly unjust results, one that the courts are required to adopt in order to maintain in fair integrity the boundaries between state and national functions, and the limitations upon the federal judicial power? See Dobbs, Beyond Bootstrap: Foreclosing the Issue of Subject–Matter Jurisdiction before Final Judgment, 51 Minn.L.Rev. 491 (1967); Stephens, Estoppel to Deny Federal Jurisdiction—*Klee* and *Di Frischia* Break Ground, 68 Dick.L.Rev. 47 (1963); Morse, Judicial Self Denial and Judicial Activism: The Personality of the Original Jurisdiction of the District Courts, 3 Clev.–Marshall L.Rev. 101, 112 (1954). The ALI thought not and proposed a statute foreclosing jurisdictional issues that are not promptly raised. ALI Study § 1386.]

Baker v. Carr

Supreme Court of the United States, 1962.
369 U.S. 186, 82 S.Ct. 691, 7 L.Ed.2d 663.

■ MR. JUSTICE BRENNAN delivered the opinion of the Court.

This civil action was brought under 42 U.S.C. §§ 1983 and 1988 to redress the alleged deprivation of federal constitutional rights. The com-

---

In one case, after an initial challenge of jurisdiction by defendant, the parties stipulated that federal jurisdiction existed. Twenty-three months later, after there had been extensive preparation for trial and the state statute of limitations had run, defendant moved to dismiss for want of jurisdiction, alleging that its citizenship was such as to defeat diversity. The court of appeals held that it was error to grant the motion, observing that "a defendant may not play fast and loose with the judicial machinery and deceive the courts." Di Frischia v. New York Cent. R. Co., 279 F.2d 141, 142 (C.A.3d 1960).

A view similar to that of the principal case is taken in note 13 of Owen Equipment & Erection Co. v. Kroger, 437 U.S. 365, 377 n. 21 (1978), as reprinted infra p. 269, and in Sadat v. Mertes, 615 F.2d 1176, 1189 (7th Cir.1980), where the court said: "The Di Frischia decision has received considerable attention from the commentators, ... but has been ignored, criticized, or limited to its facts and distinguished by the federal courts." The Third Circuit has disavowed its holding in Di Frischia on the ground that it cannot be reconciled with the Supreme Court's contrary holding in Kroger. See Mennen Co. v. Atlantic Mut. Ins. Co., 147 F.3d 287, 294 n. 9 (3d Cir.1998).

In its original answer defendant admitted an allegation in the complaint that it was an employer within the meaning of a federal statute. Shortly before trial it sought leave to file a second answer denying that the court had subject-matter jurisdiction because defendant was not an employer within the meaning of the statute. The trial judge refused to allow the second answer and the appellate court, in a lengthy dictum, concluded that he was right to do so, saying that while a party cannot consent to jurisdiction itself, it can admit a fact and the establishment of that fact creates federal subject-matter jurisdiction. Ferguson v. Neighborhood Housing Services of Cleveland, Inc., 780 F.2d 549, 550–551 (6th Cir.1986).

A similar view is advocated in Marshall, The "Facts" of Federal Subject Matter Jurisdiction, 35 DePaul L.Rev. 23 (1985). See also Wagman, Second Bites at the Jurisdictional Apple: A Proposal for Preventing False Assertions of Diversity of Citizenship, 41 Hastings L.J. 1417 (1990).

Various "claim processing" rules applicable to litigation, such as internal time limits and rules specifying required elements of a claim or defense, are sometimes called "jurisdictional." But this does not mean that objections based on such rules are nonwaivable and can be invoked at any time during the litigation. "Clarity would be facilitated if courts and litigants used the label 'jurisdictional' not for claim-processing rules, but only for prescriptions delineating the classes of cases (subject-matter jurisdiction) and the persons (personal jurisdiction) falling within a court's adjudicatory authority." Kontrick v. Ryan, 540 U.S. 443, 455 (2004) (upholding waiver of debtor's right to object to creditor's untimely complaint in bankruptcy proceeding). See also Scarborough v. Principi, 541 U.S. 401, 413–414 (2004) (relying on Kontrick to hold that required allegations in application for payment of attorneys' fees by United States may be added by amendment that relates back to the time of filing of the defective application).

The distinction between "two sometimes confused or conflated concepts: federal-court 'subject-matter' jurisdiction over a controversy; and the essential ingredients of a federal claim for relief" was the focus of the Supreme Court's decision in Arbaugh v. Y & H Corp., 546 U.S. 500 (2006). After a jury found for Arbaugh on her Title VII sex discrimination claim and related state-law claims, Y & H argued that the judgment was void for lack of subject-matter jurisdiction because Y & H did not have 15 full-time employees at the time of the incident, and thus did not qualify as a statutory employer under Title VII. Resolving a split among the circuit courts, the Court held that the 15–employee definition, as "the threshold number of employees for application of Title VII[,] is an element of a plaintiff's claim for relief, not a jurisdictional issue." 546 U.S., at 516. Creating a bright-line rule, the Court stated that "when Congress does not rank a statutory limitation on coverage as jurisdictional, courts should treat the restriction as nonjurisdictional in character." Id.]

plaint, alleging that by means of a 1901 statute of Tennessee apportioning the members of the General Assembly among the State's 95 counties, "these plaintiffs and others similarly situated, are denied the equal protection of the laws accorded them by the Fourteenth Amendment to the Constitution of the United States by virtue of the debasement of their votes," was dismissed by a three-judge court convened under 28 U.S.C. § 2281. The court held that it lacked jurisdiction of the subject matter and also that no claim was stated upon which relief could be granted....

. . . . .

I.

The District Court's Opinion and Order of Dismissal.

. . . . .

In light of the District Court's treatment of the case, we hold today only (a) that the court possessed jurisdiction of the subject matter; (b) that a justiciable cause of action is stated upon which appellants would be entitled to appropriate relief; and (c) because appellees raise the issue before this Court, that the appellants have standing to challenge the Tennessee apportionment statutes. Beyond noting that we have no cause at this stage to doubt the District Court will be able to fashion relief if violations of constitutional rights are found, it is improper now to consider what remedy would be most appropriate if appellants prevail at the trial.

II.

Jurisdiction of the Subject Matter.

The District Court was uncertain whether our cases withholding federal judicial relief rested upon a lack of federal jurisdiction or upon the inappropriateness of the subject matter for judicial consideration—what we have designated "nonjusticiability." The distinction between the two grounds is significant. In the instance of nonjusticiability, consideration of the cause is not wholly and immediately foreclosed; rather, the Court's inquiry necessarily proceeds to the point of deciding whether the duty asserted can be judicially identified and its breach judicially determined, and whether protection for the right asserted can be judicially molded. In the instance of lack of jurisdiction the cause either does not "arise under" the Federal Constitution, laws or treaties (or fall within one of the other enumerated categories of Art. III, § 2), or is not a "case or controversy" within the meaning of that section; or the cause is not one described by any jurisdictional statute. Our conclusion ... that this cause presents no nonjusticiable "political question" settles the only possible doubt that it is a case or controversy. Under the present heading of "Jurisdiction of the

Subject Matter" we hold only that the matter set forth in the complaint does arise under the Constitution and is within 28 U.S.C. § 1343.

. . . . .

III.

Standing.

A federal court cannot "pronounce any statute, either of a state or of the United States, void, because irreconcilable with the constitution, except as it is called upon to adjudge the legal rights of litigants in actual controversies." Liverpool, N.Y. & P. Steamship Co. v. Commissioners of Emigration, 113 U.S. 33. Have the appellants alleged such a personal stake in the outcome of the controversy as to assure that concrete adverseness which sharpens the presentation of issues upon which the court so largely depends for illumination of difficult constitutional questions? This is the gist of the question of standing. It is, of course, a question of federal law.

The complaint was filed by residents of Davidson, Hamilton, Knox, Montgomery, and Shelby Counties. Each is a person allegedly qualified to vote for members of the General Assembly representing his county. These appellants sued "on their own behalf and on behalf of all qualified voters of their respective counties, and further, on behalf of all voters of the State of Tennessee who are similarly situated . . . ." The appellees are the Tennessee Secretary of State, Attorney General, Coordinator of Elections, and members of the State Board of Elections; the members of the State Board are sued in their own right and also as representatives of the County Election Commissioners whom they appoint.

. . . . .

These appellants seek relief in order to protect or vindicate an interest of their own, and of those similarly situated. Their constitutional claim is, in substance, that the 1901 statute constitutes arbitrary and capricious state action, offensive to the Fourteenth Amendment in its irrational disregard of the standard of apportionment prescribed by the State's Constitution or of any standard, effecting a gross disproportion of representation to voting population. The injury which appellants assert is that this classification disfavors the voters in the counties in which they reside, placing them in a position of constitutionally unjustifiable inequality *vis-à-vis* voters in irrationally favored counties. A citizen's right to a vote free of arbitrary impairment by state action has been judicially recognized as a right secured by the Constitution, when such impairment resulted from dilution by a false tally, cf. United States v. Classic, 313 U.S. 299; or by a refusal to count votes from arbitrarily selected precincts, cf. United States v. Mosley, 238 U.S. 383, or by a stuffing of the ballot box, cf. Ex parte Siebold, 100 U.S. 371; United States v. Saylor, 322 U.S. 385.

It would not be necessary to decide whether appellants' allegations of impairment of their votes by the 1901 apportionment will, ultimately, entitle them to any relief, in order to hold that they have standing to seek it. If such impairment does produce a legally cognizable injury, they are among those who have sustained it. They are asserting "a plain, direct and adequate interest in maintaining the effectiveness of their votes," Coleman v. Miller, 307 U.S. [433,] 438, not merely a claim of "the right possessed by every citizen 'to require that the government be administered according to law ...'." Fairchild v. Hughes, 258 U.S. 126, 129; compare Leser v. Garnett, 258 U.S. 130. They are entitled to a hearing and to the District Court's decision on their claims. "The very essence of civil liberty certainly consists in the right of every individual to claim the protection of the laws, whenever he receives an injury." Marbury v. Madison, 1 Cranch [5 U.S.] 137, 163.

IV.

Justiciability.

In holding that the subject matter of this suit was not justiciable, the District Court relied on Colegrove v. Green [328 U.S. 549], and subsequent *per curiam* cases.... We understand the District Court to have read the cited cases as compelling the conclusion that since the appellants sought to have a legislative apportionment held unconstitutional, their suit presented a "political question" and was therefore nonjusticiable. We hold that this challenge to an apportionment presents no nonjusticiable "political question." The cited cases do not hold the contrary.

Of course the mere fact that the suit seeks protection of a political right does not mean it presents a political question. Such an objection "is little more than a play upon words." Nixon v. Herndon, 273 U.S. 536, 540. Rather, it is argued that apportionment cases, whatever the actual wording of the complaint, can involve no federal constitutional right except one resting on the guaranty of a republican form of government, and that complaints based on that clause have been held to present political questions which are nonjusticiable.

We hold that the claim pleaded here neither rests upon nor implicates the Guaranty Clause and that its justiciability is therefore not foreclosed by our decisions of cases involving that clause. The District Court misinterpreted *Colegrove v. Green* and other decisions of this Court on which it relied. Appellants' claim that they are being denied equal protection is justiciable, and if "discrimination is sufficiently shown, the right to relief under the equal protection clause is not diminished by the fact that the discrimination relates to political rights." Snowden v. Hughes, 321 U.S. 1, 11. To show why we reject the argument based on the Guaranty Clause, we must examine the authorities under it. But because there appears to be some uncertainty as to why those cases did present political questions, and specifically as to whether this apportionment case is like those cases, we deem it necessary first to consider the contours of the "political question" doctrine.

Our discussion, even at the price of extending this opinion, requires review of a number of political question cases, in order to expose the attributes of the doctrine—attributes which, in various settings, diverge, combine, appear, and disappear in seeming disorderliness. Since that review is undertaken solely to demonstrate that neither singly nor collective-ly do these cases support a conclusion that this apportionment case is nonjusticiable, we of course do not explore their implications in other contexts. That review reveals that in the Guaranty Clause cases and in the other "political question" cases, it is the relationship between the judiciary and the coordinate branches of the Federal Government, and not the federal judiciary's relationship to the States, which gives rise to the "political question."

We have said that "In determining whether a question falls within [the political question] category, the appropriateness under our system of gov-ernment of attributing finality to the action of the political departments and also the lack of satisfactory criteria for a judicial determination are dominant considerations." Coleman v. Miller, 307 U.S. 433, 454–455. The nonjusticiability of a political question is primarily a function of the separation of powers. Much confusion results from the capacity of the "political question" label to obscure the need for case-by-case inquiry. Deciding whether a matter has in any measure been committed by the Constitution to another branch of government, or whether the action of that branch exceeds whatever authority has been committed, is itself a delicate exercise in constitutional interpretation, and is a responsibility of this Court as ultimate interpreter of the Constitution. To demonstrate this requires no less than to analyze representative cases and to infer from them the analytical threads that make up the political question doctrine. We shall then show that none of those threads catches this case.

. . . . .

It is apparent that several formulations which vary slightly according to the settings in which the questions arise may describe a political question, although each has one or more elements which identify it as essentially a function of the separation of powers. Prominent on the surface of any case held to involve a political question is found a textually demonstrable constitutional commitment of the issue to a coordinate politi-cal department; or a lack of judicially discoverable and manageable stan-dards for resolving it; or the impossibility of deciding without an initial policy determination of a kind clearly for nonjudicial discretion; or the impossibility of a court's undertaking independent resolution without ex-pressing lack of the respect due coordinate branches of government; or an unusual need for unquestioning adherence to a political decision already made; or the potentiality of embarrassment from multifarious pronounce-ments by various departments on one question.

Unless one of these formulations is inextricable from the case at bar, there should be no dismissal for nonjusticiability on the ground of a political question's presence. The doctrine of which we treat is one of "political questions," not one of "political cases." The courts cannot reject as "no law suit" a bona fide controversy as to whether some action denominated "political" exceeds constitutional authority. The cases we have reviewed show the necessity for discriminating inquiry into the precise facts and posture of the particular case, and the impossibility of resolution by any semantic cataloguing.

But it is argued that this case shares the characteristics of decisions that constitute a category not yet considered, cases concerning the Constitution's guaranty, in Art. IV, § 4, of a republican form of government. A conclusion as to whether the case at bar does present a political question cannot be confidently reached until we have considered those cases with special care. We shall discover that Guaranty Clause claims involve those elements which define a "political question," and for that reason and no other, they are nonjusticiable. In particular, we shall discover that the nonjusticiability of such claims has nothing to do with their touching upon matters of state governmental organization.

Republican form of government: Luther v. Borden, 7 How. [48 U.S.] 1, though in form simply an action for damages for trespass was, as Daniel Webster said in opening the argument for the defense, "an unusual case." The defendants, admitting an otherwise tortious breaking and entering, sought to justify their action on the ground that they were agents of the established lawful government of Rhode Island, which State was then under martial law to defend itself from active insurrection; that the plaintiff was engaged in that insurrection; and that they entered under orders to arrest the plaintiff. The case arose "out of the unfortunate political differences which agitated the people of Rhode Island in 1841 and 1842," 7 How., at 34, and which had resulted in a situation wherein two groups laid competing claims to recognition as the lawful government. The plaintiff's right to recover depended upon which of the two groups was entitled to such recognition; but the lower court's refusal to receive evidence or hear argument on that issue, its charge to the jury that the earlier established or "charter" government was lawful, and the verdict for the defendants, were affirmed upon appeal to this Court.

. . . . .

Clearly, several factors were thought by the Court in *Luther* to make the question there "political" : the commitment to the other branches of the decision as to which is the lawful state government; the unambiguous action by the President, in recognizing the charter government as the lawful authority; the need for finality in the executive's decision; and the lack of criteria by which a court could determine which form of government was republican.

But the only significance that *Luther* could have for our immediate purposes is in its holding that the Guaranty Clause is not a repository of judicially manageable standards which a court could utilize independently in order to identify a State's lawful government. The Court has since refused to resort to the Guaranty Clause—which alone had been invoked for the purpose—as the source of a constitutional standard for invalidating state action. . . .

. . . . .

Just as the Court has consistently held that a challenge to state action based on the Guaranty Clause presents no justiciable question so has it held, and for the same reasons, that challenges to congressional action on the ground of inconsistency with that clause present no justiciable question. . . .

. . . . .

We come, finally, to the ultimate inquiry whether our precedents as to what constitutes a nonjusticiable "political question" bring the case before us under the umbrella of that doctrine. A natural beginning is to note whether any of the common characteristics which we have been able to identify and label descriptively are present. We find none: The question here is the consistency of state action with the Federal Constitution. We have no question decided, or to be decided, by a political branch of government coequal with this Court. Nor do we risk embarrassment of our government abroad, or grave disturbance at home if we take issue with Tennessee as to the constitutionality of her action here challenged. Nor need the appellants, in order to succeed in this action, ask the Court to enter upon policy determinations for which judicially manageable standards are lacking. Judicial standards under the Equal Protection Clause are well developed and familiar, and it has been open to courts since the enactment of the Fourteenth Amendment to determine, if on the particular facts they must, that a discrimination reflects *no* policy, but simply arbitrary and capricious action.

This case does, in one sense, involve the allocation of political power within a State, and the appellants might conceivably have added a claim under the Guaranty Clause. Of course, as we have seen, any reliance on that clause would be futile. But because any reliance on the Guaranty Clause could not have succeeded it does not follow that appellants may not be heard on the equal protection claim which in fact they tender. True, it must be clear that the Fourteenth Amendment claim is not so enmeshed with those political question elements which render Guaranty Clause claims nonjusticiable as actually to present a political question itself. But we have found that not to be the case here.

. . . . .

We conclude that the nonjusticiability of claims resting on the Guaranty Clause which arises from their embodiment of questions that were thought "political," can have no bearing upon the justiciability of the equal protection claim presented in this case. Finally, we emphasize that it is the involvement in Guaranty Clause claims of the elements thought to define "political questions," and no other feature, which could render them nonjusticiable. Specifically, we have said that such claims are not held nonjusticiable because they touch matters of state governmental organization. Brief examination of a few cases demonstrates this.

. . . . .

We conclude that the complaint's allegations of a denial of equal protection present a justiciable constitutional cause of action upon which appellants are entitled to a trial and a decision. The right asserted is within the reach of judicial protection under the Fourteenth Amendment.

The judgment of the District Court is reversed and the cause is remanded for further proceedings consistent with this opinion.

Reversed and remanded.

[Justice Whittaker did not participate in the decision. The concurring opinions of Justices Douglas, Clark, and Stewart are omitted.]

■ MR. JUSTICE FRANKFURTER, whom MR. JUSTICE HARLAN joins, dissenting.

. . . . .

II.

The *Colegrove* doctrine, in the form in which repeated decisions have settled it, was not an innovation. It represents long judicial thought and experience. From its earliest opinions this Court has consistently recognized a class of controversies which do not lend themselves to judicial standards and judicial remedies. To classify the various instances as "political questions" is rather a form of stating this conclusion than revealing of analysis. Some of the cases so labelled have no relevance here. But from others emerge unifying considerations that are compelling.

. . . . .

. . . The influence of these converging considerations—the caution not to undertake decision where standards meet for judicial judgment are lacking, the reluctance to interfere with matters of state government in the absence of an unquestionable and effectively enforceable mandate, the unwillingness to make courts arbiters of the broad issues of political organization historically committed to other institutions and for whose adjustment the judicial process is ill-adapted—has been decisive of the settled line of cases, reaching back more than a century, which holds that Art. IV, § 4, of the Constitution, guaranteeing to the States "a Republican Form of Government," is not enforceable through the courts. . . .

. . . . .

III.

The present case involves all of the elements that have made the Guarantee Clause cases non-justiciable. It is, in effect, a Guarantee Clause claim masquerading under a different label. But it cannot make the case more fit for judicial action that appellants invoke the Fourteenth Amendment rather than Art. IV, § 4, where, in fact, the gist of their complaint is the same—unless it can be found that the Fourteenth Amendment speaks with greater particularity to their situation. We have been admonished to avoid "the tyranny of labels." Snyder v. Massachusetts, 291 U.S. 97, 114. Art. IV, § 4, is not committed by express constitutional terms to Congress. It is the nature of the controversies arising under it, nothing else, which has made it judicially unenforceable. Of course, if a controversy falls within judicial power, it depends "on how he [the plaintiff] casts his action," Pan American Petroleum Corp. v. Superior Court, 366 U.S. 656, 662, whether he brings himself within a jurisdictional statute. But where judicial competence is wanting, it cannot be created by invoking one clause of the Constitution rather than another....

· · · · ·

... Certainly, "equal protection" is no more secure a foundation for judicial judgment of the permissibility of varying forms of representative government than is "Republican Form." Indeed since "equal protection of the laws" can only mean an equality of persons standing in the same relation to whatever governmental action is challenged, the determination whether treatment is equal presupposes a determination concerning the nature of the relationship. This, with respect to apportionment, means an inquiry into the theoretic base of representation in an acceptably republican state. For a court could not determine the equal-protection issue without in fact first determining the Republican–Form issue, simply because what is reasonable for equal-protection purposes will depend upon what frame of government, basically, is allowed. To divorce "equal protection" from "Republican Form" is to talk about half a question.

· · · · ·

IV.

· · · · ·

Although the District Court had jurisdiction in the very restricted sense of power to determine whether it could adjudicate the claim, the case is of that class of political controversy which, by the nature of its subject, is unfit for federal judicial action. The judgment of the District Court, in dismissing the complaint for failure to state a claim on which relief can be granted, should therefore be affirmed.

[Justice Harlan also wrote a dissenting opinion, in which Justice Frankfurter joined.][7]

[7. There is a fascinating account of the process of decision that led to Baker v. Carr in Anthony Lewis's memorial tribute to Justice William Brennan, 111 Harv.L.Rev. 29 (1997).

In Powell v. McCormack, 395 U.S. 486 (1969), the Court held that the "political question" doctrine did not bar the courts from considering a claim that the House of Representatives had improperly refused to seat a person elected to it. Art. I, § 5, of the Constitution provides that "Each House shall be the Judge of the Elections, Returns, and Qualifications of its own Members ...," but the Court concluded that this provision "is at most a 'textually demonstrable commitment' to Congress to judge only the qualifications expressly set forth in the Constitution. Therefore, the 'textual commitment' formulation of the political question doctrine does not bar federal courts from adjudicating petitioners' claims."

But in Gilligan v. Morgan, 413 U.S. 1 (1973), a suit challenging the pattern of training, weaponry, and orders of the Ohio National Guard was held to present a nonjusticiable

Craig v. Boren

Supreme Court of the United States, 1976.
429 U.S. 190, 97 S.Ct. 451, 50 L.Ed.2d 397.

■ MR. JUSTICE BRENNAN delivered the opinion of the Court.

The interaction of two sections of an Oklahoma statute, 37 Okla.Stat. §§ 241 and 245, prohibits the sale of "nonintoxicating" 3.2% beer to males under the age of 21 and to females under the age of 18. The question to be decided is whether such a gender-based differential constitutes a denial to males 18–20 years of age of the Equal Protection of the Laws in violation of the Fourteenth Amendment.

This action was brought in the District Court for the Western District of Oklahoma on December 20, 1972, by appellant Craig, a male then between 18 and 21 years of age, and by appellant Whitener, a licensed vendor of 3.2% beer. The complaint sought declaratory and injunctive relief

---

political question in view of Article I, § 8, cl. 16 of the Constitution reserving to the states "the Authority of training the Militia according to the discipline prescribed by Congress."

The argument that a law was a revenue measure and should have originated in the House of Representatives under Article I, § 7, is justiciable and is not a "political question." United States v. Munoz–Flores, 495 U.S. 385 (1990): And in United States Dept. of Commerce v. Montana, 503 U.S. 442 (1992), it was held that the validity of the method Congress chooses to apportion seats in the House of Representatives, as required by Article II, § 2, is not a "political question."

Relying both on the "textually demonstrable constitutional commitment" to the Senate of "the sole Power to try all Impeachments" and on the lack of judicially manageable standards for resolving the dispute, the Supreme Court held that a former federal judge's suit challenging the Senate procedures used to convict him of two articles of impeachment presented a nonjusticiable political question. Nixon v. United States, 506 U.S. 224 (1993).

Any doubt that political cases do not necessarily present nonjusticiable "political questions" must be considered to have died with the Supreme Court's decision to review and decide issues determining the outcome of the 2000 Presidential election. Arguably the most remarkable aspect of the Court's two decisions in Bush v. Palm Beach County Canvassing Bd., 531 U.S. 70 (2000), and Bush v. Gore, 531 U.S. 98 (2000), is the failure in either opinion to mention the political-question doctrine, let alone to explain its inapplicability to a dispute over the process of appointment of state electors, a dispute that has arguably been committed by Article II and Amendment XII to resolution by the legislative branch rather than the judiciary. See Pushaw, *Bush v. Gore*: Looking at *Baker v. Carr* in a Conservative Mirror, 18 Const.Comm. 359 (2001); Pushaw, Judicial Review and the Political Question Doctrine: Reviving the Federalist "Rebuttable Presumption" Analysis, 80 N.C.L.Rev. 1165 (2002).

In Vieth v. Jubelirer, 541 U.S. 267 (2004), a sharply divided Court dismissed as nonjusticiable a claim that a congressional districting plan was a political gerrymander. Justice Scalia's plurality opinion, joined by the Chief Justice and Justices O'Connor and Thomas, deemed political gerrymandering claims to be nonjusticiable for lack of any discernible and manageable judicial standards. Justice Kennedy concurred only in the judgment, leaving open the possibility that judicial relief might be appropriate in some redistricting cases. Justice Stevens, Justice Souter (joined by Justice Ginsburg), and Justice Breyer filed separate dissents, agreeing that the case was justiciable but each suggesting somewhat different standards for adjudicating it.

See generally 13A Wright, Miller & Cooper, Federal Practice and Procedure: Jurisdiction 2d §§ 3534–3534.3 (1984); Chemerinsky, Federal Jurisdiction § 2.6 (5th ed.2007); Mullenix, Redish & Vairo, Understanding Federal Courts and Jurisdiction § 2.09 (1998).]

against enforcement of the gender-based differential on the ground that it constituted invidious discrimination against males 18–20 years of age. A three-judge court convened under 28 U.S.C. § 2281 sustained the constitutionality of the statutory differential and dismissed the action. 399 F.Supp. 1304 (1975). . . . We reverse.

I

We first address a preliminary question of standing. Appellant Craig attained the age of 21 after we noted probable jurisdiction. Therefore, since only declaratory and injunctive relief against enforcement of the gender-based differential is sought, the controversy has been rendered moot as to Craig. See, e.g., DeFunis v. Odegaard, 416 U.S. 312 (1974).[8] The question thus arises whether appellant Whitener, the licensed vendor of 3.2% beer, who has a live controversy against enforcement of the statute, may rely upon the equal protection objections of males 18–20 years of age to establish her claim of unconstitutionality of the age-sex differential. We conclude that she may.

Initially, it should be noted that, despite having had the opportunity to do so, appellees never raised before the District Court any objection to Whitener's reliance upon the claimed unequal treatment to 18–20–year–old males as the premise of her equal protection challenge to Oklahoma's 3.2% beer law. See 399 F.Supp., at 1306 n. 1. Indeed, at oral argument Oklahoma acknowledged that appellees always "presumed" that the vendor, subject to sanctions and loss of license for violation of the statute, was a proper party-in-interest to object to the enforcement of the sex-based regulatory provision. Tr., at 41. While such a concession certainly would not be controlling upon the reach of this Court's constitutional authority to exercise jurisdiction under Art. III, see, e.g., Sierra Club v. Morton, 405 U.S. 727, 732 n. 3 (1972); cf. Association of Data Processing Service Organizations, Inc. v. Camp, 397 U.S. 150, 151 (1970), our decisions have settled that limitations on a litigant's assertion of *jus tertii* are not constitutionally mandated, but rather stem from a salutary "rule of self-restraint" designed to minimize unwarranted intervention into controversies where the applicable constitutional questions are ill-defined and speculative. See, e.g., Barrows v. Jackson, 346 U.S. 249, 255, 257 (1953); see also Singleton v. Wulff, 428 U.S. 106, 121 (1976) (Powell, J., dissenting). These prudential objectives thought to be enhanced by restrictions on third-party standing cannot be furthered here, where the lower court already has entertained the relevant constitutional challenge and the parties have sought—or at least have never resisted—an authoritative constitutional determination. In such circumstances, a decision by us to forego consideration of the constitutional merits in order to await the initiation of a new challenge to the statute by injured third parties would be impermissibly to foster repetitive and time-consuming litigation under the guise of caution and prudence. Moreover, insofar as

---

8. Appellants did not seek class certification of Craig as representative of other similarly situated males between 18–20 years of age. See, e.g., Sosna v. Iowa, 419 U.S. 393, 401 (1975).

the applicable constitutional questions have been and continue to be presented vigorously and "cogently," Holden v. Hardy, 169 U.S. 366, 397 (1898), the denial of *jus tertii* standing in deference to a direct class suit can serve no functional purpose. Our Brother BLACKMUN'S comment is pertinent: "[I]t may be that a class could be assembled, whose fluid membership always included some [males] with live claims. But if the assertion of the right is to be 'representative' to such an extent anyway, there seems little loss in terms of effective advocacy from allowing its assertion by" the present *jus tertii* champion. *Singleton v. Wulff*, supra, 428 U.S., at 117.

In any event, we conclude that appellant Whitener has established independently her claim to assert *jus tertii* standing. The operation of §§ 241 and 245 plainly have inflicted "injury in fact" upon appellant sufficient to guarantee her "concrete adverseness," Baker v. Carr, 369 U.S. 186, 204 (1962), and to satisfy the constitutional-based standing requirements imposed by Art. III. The legal duties created by the statutory sections under challenge are addressed directly to vendors such as appellant. She is obliged either to heed the statutory discrimination, thereby incurring a direct economic injury through the constriction of her buyers' market, or to disobey the statutory command and suffer, in the words of Oklahoma's Assistant Attorney General, "sanctions and perhaps loss of license." Tr., at 41. This Court repeatedly has recognized that such injuries establish the threshold requirements of a "case or controversy" mandated by Art. III. See, e.g., *Singleton v. Wulff*, supra, 428 U.S., at 112 (doctors who receive payments for their abortion services are "classically adverse" to government as payer); Sullivan v. Little Hunting Park, 396 U.S. 229, 237 (1969); *Barrows v. Jackson*, supra, 346 U.S., at 255–256.

As a vendor with standing to challenge the lawfulness of §§ 241 and 245, appellant is entitled to assert those concomitant rights of third parties that would be "diluted or adversely affected" should her constitutional challenge fail and the statutes remain in force. Griswold v. Connecticut, 381 U.S. 479, 481 (1965); see Note, Standing to Assert Constitutional Jus Tertii, 88 Harv.L.Rev. 423, 432 (1974). Otherwise, the threatened imposition of governmental sanctions might deter appellant and other similarly situated vendors from selling 3.2% beer to young males, thereby ensuring that "enforcement of the challenged restriction against the [vendor] would result indirectly in the violation of third parties' rights." Warth v. Seldin, 422 U.S. 490, 510 (1975). Accordingly, vendors and those in like positions have been uniformly permitted to resist efforts at restricting their operations by acting as advocates for the rights of third parties who seek access to their market or function. See, e.g., Eisenstadt v. Baird, 405 U.S. 438 (1972); *Sullivan v. Little Hunting Park*, supra; *Barrows v. Jackson*, supra.[9]

---

9. The standing question presented here is not answered by the principle stated in United States v. Raines, 362 U.S. 17, 21 (1960), that "one to whom application of a statute is constitutional will not be heard to attack the statute on the ground that impliedly it might also be taken as applying to other persons or other situations in which its application might be unconstitutional." In *Raines,* the Court refused to permit certain public officials of

Indeed, the *jus tertii* question raised here is answered by our disposition of a like argument in *Eisenstadt v. Baird*, supra. There, as here, a state statute imposed legal duties and disabilities upon the claimant, who was convicted of distributing a package of contraceptive foam to a third party.[10] Since the statute was directed at Baird and penalized his conduct, the Court did not hesitate—again as here—to conclude that the "case or controversy" requirement of Art. III was satisfied. 405 U.S., at 443. In considering Baird's constitutional objections, the Court fully recognized his standing to defend the privacy interests of third parties. Deemed crucial to the decision to permit *jus tertii* standing was the recognition of "the impact of the litigation on the third-party interests." Id., at 445. Just as the defeat of Baird's suit and the "[e]nforcement of the Massachusetts statute will materially impair the ability of single persons to obtain contraceptives," id., at 446, so too the failure of Whitener to prevail in this suit and the continued enforcement of §§ 241 and 245 will "materially impair the ability of" the males 18–20 years of age to purchase 3.2% beer despite their classification by an overt gender-based criterion. Similarly, just as the Massachusetts law in *Eisenstadt* "prohibit[ed] not use, but distribution," id., at 446, and consequently the least awkward challenger was one in Baird's position who was subject to that proscription, the law challenged here explicitly regulates the sale rather than use of 3.2% beer, thus leaving a vendor as the obvious claimant.

We therefore hold that Whitener has standing to raise relevant Equal Protection challenges to Oklahoma's gender-based law. We now consider those arguments.

. . . . .

[On the merits the Court found that the gender-based differential was a denial of equal protection to males aged 18–20 and reversed the judgment of the District Court.]

Georgia to defend against application of the Civil Rights Act to their official conduct on the ground that the statute also might be construed to encompass the "purely private actions" of others. The *Raines* rule remains germane in such a setting, where the interests of the litigant and the rights of the proposed third parties are in no way mutually interdependent. Thus, a successful suit against Raines did not threaten to impair or diminish the independent private rights of others, and consequently, consideration of those third-party rights properly was deferred until another day.

Of course, the *Raines* principle has also been relaxed where legal action against the claimant threatens to "chill" the First Amendment rights of third parties. See, e.g., Lewis v. City of New Orleans, 415 U.S. 130 (1974).

10. The fact that Baird chose to disobey the legal duty imposed upon him by the Massachusetts, anticontraception statute, resulting in his criminal conviction, 405 U.S., at 440, does not distinguish the standing inquiry from that pertaining to the anticipatory attack in this case. In both *Eisenstadt* and here, the challenged statutes compel the *jus tertii* claimant either to cease their proscribed activities or to suffer appropriate sanctions. The existence of Art. III "injury in fact" and the structure of the claimant's relationship to the third parties are not altered by the litigative posture of the suit. And, certainly, no suggestion will be heard that Whitener's anticipatory challenge offends the normal requirements governing such actions. See generally Steffel v. Thompson, 415 U.S. 452 (1974); Samuels v. Mackell, 401 U.S. 66 (1971); Younger v. Harris, 401 U.S. 37 (1971).

■ MR. CHIEF JUSTICE BURGER, dissenting.

I am in general agreement with MR. JUSTICE REHNQUIST's dissent, but even at the risk of compounding the obvious confusion created by those voting to reverse the District Court, I will add a few words.

At the outset I cannot agree that appellant Whitener has standing arising from her status as a saloonkeeper to assert the constitutional rights of her customers. In this Court "a litigant may only assert his own constitutional rights or immunities." United States v. Raines, 362 U.S. 17, 21 (1960). There are a few, but strictly limited exceptions to that rule; despite the most creative efforts, this case fits within none of them.

This is not Sullivan v. Little Hunting Park, 396 U.S. 229 (1969), or Barrows v. Jackson, 346 U.S. 249 (1953), for there is here no barrier whatever to Oklahoma males 18–20 years of age asserting, in an appropriate forum, any constitutional rights they may claim to purchase 3.2% beer. Craig's successful litigation of this very issue was prevented only by the advent of his 21st birthday. There is thus no danger of interminable dilution of those rights if appellant Whitener is not permitted to litigate them here. Cf. Eisenstadt v. Baird, 405 U.S. 438, 445–446 (1972).

Nor is this controlled by Griswold v. Connecticut, 381 U.S. 479 (1965). It borders on the ludicrous to draw a parallel between a vendor of beer and the intimate professional physician-patient relationship which undergirded relaxation of standing rules in that case.

Even in *Eisenstadt,* the Court carefully limited its recognition of third party standing to cases in which the relationship between the claimant and the relevant third party "was not simply the fortuitous connection between a vendor and potential vendees, but the relationship between one who acted to protect the rights of a minority and the minority itself." 405 U.S., at 445. This is plainly not the case here. See also McGowan v. Maryland, 366 U.S. 420, 429–430 (1961); Brown v. United States, 411 U.S. 223, 230 (1973).

In sum, permitting a vendor to assert the constitutional rights of vendees whenever those rights are arguably infringed introduces a new concept of constitutional standing to which I cannot subscribe.

. . . . .

With MR. JUSTICE REHNQUIST, I would affirm the judgment of the District Court.

■ MR. JUSTICE REHNQUIST, dissenting.

. . . . .[11]

[11. In Carey v. Population Services, Int'l, 431 U.S. 678 (1977), a mail-order seller of contraceptives was allowed to raise the privacy rights of potential customers in challenging a state statute that barred anyone except a physician from distributing contraceptives to

Village of Arlington Heights v. Metropolitan Housing Development Corp.

Supreme Court of the United States, 1977.
429 U.S. 252, 97 S.Ct. 555, 50 L.Ed.2d 450.

■ MR. JUSTICE POWELL delivered the opinion of the Court.

In 1971 respondent Metropolitan Housing Development Corporation (MHDC) applied to petitioner, the Village of Arlington Heights, Ill., for the rezoning of a 15–acre parcel from single-family to multiple-family classification. Using federal financial assistance, MHDC planned to build 190 clustered townhouse units for low-and moderate-income tenants. The Village denied the rezoning request. MHDC, joined by other plaintiffs who are also respondents here, brought suit in the United States District Court for the Northern District of Illinois. They alleged that the denial was racially discriminatory and that it violated, *inter alia*, the Fourteenth Amendment and the Fair Housing Act of 1968, 82 Stat. 81, 42 U.S.C. § 3601 et seq.

. . . . .

[Arlington Heights is a Chicago suburb in which most of the land is zoned for detached single-family homes. According to the 1970 census, only 27 of the Village's 64,000 residents were black. MHDC is a nonprofit developer organized to build housing in the Chicago area for persons of low and moderate incomes, using federal subsidies available for this purpose. It had contracted to buy a tract of land in Arlington Heights to build what was known as Lincoln Green. The arrangement was contingent on getting zoning changes and federal subsidies. The Village denied the zoning changes and suit followed.]

II

At the outset, petitioners challenge the respondents' standing to bring the suit. It is not clear that this challenge was pressed in the Court of

---

persons under the age of 16 and also barred anyone except a physician or a pharmacist from distributing to persons over 16.

Booksellers were allowed to assert the First Amendment rights of bookbuyers in Virginia v. American Booksellers Assn., Inc., 484 U.S. 383 (1988).

In Powers v. Ohio, 499 U.S. 400, 411 (1991), the Court said that a litigant seeking to assert the rights of another party must satisfy three interrelated criteria: "The litigant must have suffered an injury in fact, thus giving him or her a sufficiently concrete interest in the outcome of the issue in dispute; the litigant must have a close relation to the third party; and there must exist some hindrance to the third party's ability to protect his or her own interests."

Although no mention was made of the doctrine of third-party standing, the Court apparently relied upon it for its jurisdiction to decide Bush v. Gore, 531 U.S. 98 (2000). In that case the Court reversed a judgment of the Florida Supreme Court that it held violated the equal-protection rights not of petitioner Bush, but rather of Florida voters not party to the suit before it. See Pushaw, *Bush v. Gore*: Looking at *Baker v. Carr* in a Conservative Mirror, 18 Const.Comm. 359, 392 & n. 196 (2001).

See generally 13 Wright, Miller & Cooper, Federal Practice and Procedure: Jurisdiction 2d § 3531.9 (1984); Chemerinsky, Federal Jurisdiction § 2.3.4 (5th ed.2007); Elliott, The Functions of Standing, 61 Stan.L.Rev. 459 (2008).]

Appeals, but since our jurisdiction to decide the case is implicated, Jenkins v. McKeithen, 395 U.S. 411, 421 (1969) (plurality opinion), we shall consider it.[12]

In Warth v. Seldin, 422 U.S. 490 (1975), a case similar in some respects to this one, we reviewed the constitutional limitations and prudential considerations that guide a court in determining a party's standing, and we need not repeat that discussion here. The essence of the standing question, in its constitutional dimension, is "whether the plaintiff has 'alleged such a personal stake in the outcome of the controversy' [as] to warrant *his* invocation of federal-court jurisdiction and to justify exercise of the court's remedial powers on his behalf." Id., at 498–499, quoting Baker v. Carr, 369 U.S. 186, 204 (1962). The plaintiff must show that he himself is injured by the challenged action of the defendant. The injury may be indirect, see United States v. SCRAP, 412 U.S. 669, 688 (1973), but the complaint must indicate that the injury is indeed fairly traceable to the defendant's acts or omissions. Simon v. Eastern Ky. Welfare Rights Org., 426 U.S. 26, 41–42 (1976); O'Shea v. Littleton, 414 U.S. 488, 498 (1974); Linda R.S. v. Richard D., 410 U.S. 614, 617 (1973).

A

Here there can be little doubt that MHDC meets the constitutional standing requirements. The challenged action of the petitioners stands as an absolute barrier to constructing the housing MHDC had contracted to place on the Victorian site. If MHDC secures the injunctive relief it seeks, that barrier will be removed. An injunction would not, of course, guarantee that Lincoln Green will be built. MHDC would still have to secure financing, qualify for federal subsidies, and carry through with construction. But all housing developments are subject to some extent to similar uncertainties. When a project is as detailed and specific as Lincoln Green, a court is not required to engage in undue speculation as a predicate for finding that the plaintiff has the requisite personal stake in the controversy. MHDC has shown an injury to itself that is "likely to be redressed by a favorable decision." *Simon v. Eastern Ky. Welfare Rights Org.*, supra, 426 U.S., at 38.[13]

[12. In National Organization for Women v. Scheidler, 510 U.S. 249, 255 (1994), the Court declared: "Standing represents a jurisdictional requirement which remains open to review at all stages of the litigation."]

[13. The *Simon* case was a suit by several indigents and organizations composed of indigents against the Secretary of the Treasury and the Commissioner of Internal Revenue. They challenged a Revenue Ruling allowing a nonprofit hospital to be regarded as "charitable," so that contributions to it were deductible by its donors, even though the hospital did not offer service to indigents except in its emergency room. In an opinion by Justice Powell, the Court held that the plaintiffs lacked standing. The Court assumed that some of the plaintiffs and some members of the organizations had been denied hospital service because they could not pay for it. But it said that Article III requires "injury that can fairly be traced to the challenged action of the defendant, and not injury that results from the independent action of some third party not before the court." The Court thought that it was "purely speculative" whether the denials of service fairly could be traced to the Revenue Letter or instead resulted from decisions made by the hospitals without regard to the tax implications.

Petitioners nonetheless appear to argue that MHDC lacks standing because it has suffered no economic injury. MHDC, they point out, is not the owner of the property in question. Its contract of purchase is contingent upon securing rezoning.[14] MHDC owes the owners nothing if rezoning is denied.

We cannot accept petitioners' argument. In the first place, it is inaccurate to say that MHDC suffers no economic injury from a refusal to rezone, despite the contingency provisions in its contract. MHDC has expended thousands of dollars on the plans for Lincoln Green and on the studies submitted to the Village in support of the petition for rezoning. Unless rezoning is granted, many of these plans and studies will be worthless even if MHDC finds another site at an equally attractive price.

And it thought it equally speculative whether granting the relief sought by plaintiffs would result in the availability to them of hospital services. "[I]t is just as plausible that the hospitals to which [plaintiffs] may apply for service would elect to forgo favorable tax treatment to avoid the undetermined financial drain of an increase in the level of uncompensated services." The Solicitor General had presented in his brief figures showing that nationwide, private philanthropy accounts for only 4% of private hospital revenues.]

14. Petitioners contend that MHDC lacks standing to pursue its claim here because a contract purchaser whose contract is contingent upon rezoning cannot contest a zoning decision in the Illinois courts. Under the law of Illinois, only the owner of the property has standing to pursue such an action. Clark Oil & Refining Corp. v. City of Evanston, 23 Ill.2d 48, 177 N.E.2d 191 (1961); but see Solomon v. City of Evanston, 29 Ill.App.3d 782, 331 N.E.2d 380 (1975).

State law of standing, however, does not govern such determinations in the federal courts. The constitutional and prudential considerations canvassed at length in Warth v. Seldin, 422 U.S. 490 (1975), respond to concerns that are peculiarly federal in nature. Illinois may choose to close its courts to applicants for rezoning unless they have an interest more direct than MHDC's, but this choice does not necessarily disqualify MHDC from seeking relief in federal courts for an asserted injury to its federal rights.

["The state trial court found that appellant has standing to challenge the validity of the Law, and neither of the other state courts addressed this issue on appeal. Nonetheless, an independent determination of the question of standing is necessary in this Court, for the special limitations that Article III of the Constitution imposes on the jurisdiction of the federal courts are not binding on the state courts.... The States are thus left free as a matter of their own procedural law to determine whether their courts may issue advisory opinions or to determine matters that would not satisfy the more stringent requirement in the federal courts that an actual 'case' or 'controversy' be presented for resolution." New York State Club Ass'n, Inc. v. City of New York, 487 U.S. 1, 8 n. 2 (1988).

Although state courts are not bound to adhere to federal standing rules, they can render a binding judicial decision that rests on their interpretation of federal law, and the Supreme Court can review such a decision if it causes concrete injury to the party seeking review, even though the state court plaintiff lacked standing by federal principles. ASARCO Inc. v. Kadish, 490 U.S. 605 (1989).

ASARCO is discussed in Elmendorf, Note, State Courts, Citizen Suits, and the Enforcement of Federal Environmental Law by Non–Article III Plaintiffs, 110 Yale L.J. 1003 (2001). In Virginia v. Hicks, 539 U.S. 113 (2003), the Court applied its *ASARCO* doctrine to hold that the State of Virginia had standing to seek federal review of an adverse state-court judgment granting the plaintiff relief on federal constitutional grounds, notwithstanding that the plaintiff might have lacked standing had he commenced the litigation in federal rather than state court.]

Petitioners' argument also misconceives our standing requirements. It has long been clear that economic injury is not the only kind of injury that can support a plaintiff's standing. *United States v. SCRAP*, supra, 412 U.S., at 686–687; Sierra Club v. Morton, 405 U.S. 727, 734 (1972); Data Processing Service v. Camp, 397 U.S. 150, 154 (1970). MHDC is a nonprofit corporation. Its interest in building Lincoln Green stems not from a desire for economic gain, but rather from an interest in making suitable low-cost housing available in areas where such housing is scarce. This is not mere abstract concern about a problem of general interest. See *Sierra Club v. Morton*, supra, 405 U.S., at 739. The specific project MHDC intends to build, whether or not it will generate profits, provides that "essential dimension of specificity" that informs judicial decisionmaking. Schlesinger v. Reservists Committee to Stop the War, 418 U.S. 208, 221 (1974).

B

Clearly MHDC has met the constitutional requirements, and it therefore has standing to assert its own rights. Foremost among them is MHDC's right to be free of arbitrary or irrational zoning actions. See Euclid v. Ambler Realty Co., 272 U.S. 365 (1926); Nectow v. City of Cambridge, 277 U.S. 183 (1928); Village of Belle Terre v. Boraas, 416 U.S. 1 (1974). But the heart of this litigation has never been the claim that the Village's decision fails the generous *Euclid* test, recently reaffirmed in *Belle Terre*. Instead it has been the claim that the Village's refusal to rezone discriminates against racial minorities in violation of the Fourteenth Amendment. As a corporation, MHDC has no racial identity and cannot be the direct target of the petitioners' alleged discrimination. In the ordinary case, a party is denied standing to assert the rights of third persons. *Warth v. Seldin*, 422 U.S., at 499. But we need not decide whether the circumstances of this case would justify departure from that prudential limitation and permit MHDC to assert the constitutional rights of its prospective minority tenants. See Barrows v. Jackson, 346 U.S. 249 (1953); cf. Sullivan v. Little Hunting Park, 396 U.S. 229, 237 (1969); Buchanan v. Warley, 245 U.S. 60, 72–73 (1917). For we have at least one individual plaintiff who has demonstrated standing to assert these rights as his own.

Respondent Ransom, a Negro, works at the Honeywell factory in Arlington Heights and lives approximately 20 miles away in Evanston in a 5–room house with his mother and his son. The complaint alleged that he seeks and would qualify for the housing MHDC wants to build in Arlington Heights. Ransom testified at trial that if Lincoln Green were built he would probably move there, since it is closer to his job.

The injury Ransom asserts is that his quest for housing nearer his employment has been thwarted by official action that is racially discriminatory. If a court grants the relief he seeks, there is at least a "substantial probability," *Warth v. Seldin*, supra, 422 U.S., at 504, that the Lincoln Green project will materialize, affording Ransom the housing opportunity he desires in Arlington Heights. His is not a generalized grievance. Instead, as we suggested in *Warth*, supra, at 507, 508 n. 18, it focuses on a particular project and is not dependent on speculation about the possible actions of third parties not before the court. See id., at 505; *Simon v. Eastern Ky. Welfare Rights Org.*, 426 U.S., at 41–42. Unlike the individual plaintiffs in *Warth,* Ransom has adequately averred an "actionable causal relationship" between Arlington Heights' zoning practices and his asserted injury. *Warth v. Seldin*, supra, 422 U.S., at 507. We therefore proceed to the merits.

. . . . .

[On the merits the Court held that while the impact of the Village's decision not to rezone bore more heavily on racial minorities, the plaintiffs had failed to show that the Village acted with a discriminatory intent as required to state a claim under the Fourteenth Amendment. The case was remanded for further consideration of plaintiffs' statutory claims. Justice Marshall, joined by Justice Brennan, joined in the standing portions of the opinion but dissented in part on the merits. Justice White dissented on the merits. Justice Stevens did not participate in the case.][15]

───────

[15. On organizational standing, see Hunt v. Washington State Apple Advertising Com'n, 432 U.S. 333, 343 (1977), noted 64 Iowa L.Rev. 121 (1978), where Chief Justice Burger wrote for the Court: "Thus we have recognized that an association has standing to bring suit on behalf of its members when: (a) its members would otherwise have standing to sue in their own right; (b) the interests it seeks to protect are germane to the organization's purpose; and (c) neither the claim asserted nor the relief requested requires the participation of individual members in the lawsuit."

In United Food and Commercial Workers Union Local 751 v. Brown Group, Inc., 517 U.S. 544 (1996), the Court held that the third prong of the *Hunt* test for associational standing, which normally forbids an organization from litigating an action when "the relief requested requires the participation of individual members in the lawsuit," was merely a prudential limitation on standing that Congress was free to override.

Environmental organizations were denied standing where they failed to show that any of their members would be directly affected apart from the members' special interest in the subject. Lujan v. Defenders of Wildlife, 504 U.S. 555 (1992). The *Lujan* case is criticized in Nichol, Justice Scalia, Standing, and Public Law Litigation, 42 Duke L.J. 1141 (1993), and Sunstein, What's Standing After *Lujan*? Of Citizen Suits, "Injuries," and Article III, 91 Mich.L.Rev. 163 (1992), but discussed more favorably in Breger, Defending Defenders: Remarks on Nichol and Pierce, 42 Duke L.J. 1202 (1993).

Amid a welter of concurring opinions, six Justices joined in reaffirming the holding of *Lujan* that a "triad of injury in fact, causation, and redressability comprises the core of Article III's case-or-controversy requirement, and [that] the party invoking federal jurisdiction bears the burden of establishing its existence." Steel Co. v. Citizens for a Better Environment, 523 U.S. 83, 103–104 (1998). The Court also rejected, 5–3, the doctrine of "hypothetical jurisdiction" by which some courts of appeal had deemed it appropriate to deny relief on the merits without first resolving a difficult question of jurisdiction, provided that the party prevailing on the merits would also be the party prevailing were jurisdiction held to be lacking. But see the Court's decision the next year in Ruhrgas AG v. Marathon Oil Co., reprinted infra p. 457.

In a decision tying "mootness" doctrine to the Article III standing requirement of "actual injury redressable by the court," —see Simon v. Eastern Kentucky Welfare Rights Organization, 426 U.S. 26, 39 (1976), discussed supra p. 29, n. 13—the Court held, 8–1, in Spencer v.

Valley Forge Christian College v. Americans United for Separation of Church and State, Inc.

Supreme Court of the United States, 1982.
454 U.S. 464, 102 S.Ct. 752, 70 L.Ed.2d 700.

■ JUSTICE REHNQUIST delivered the opinion of the Court.

. . . . .

[Article IV, § 3, cl. 2 of the Constitution gives Congress "Power to dispose of and make all needful Rules and Regulations respecting the . . . Property belonging to the United States." By statute, property that has

---

Kemna, 523 U.S. 1 (1998), that a prisoner's habeas petition challenging his parole revocation became moot upon the expiration of the underlying sentence from which he had been paroled. Rejecting its previous "collateral consequences" jurisprudence, whereby it had accepted "the most generalized and hypothetical of consequences as sufficient to avoid mootness in challenges to conviction," 523 U.S., at 9–10, the Court held that the prisoner (already reincarcerated on a new conviction) had failed to demonstrate any concrete injury from the possible collateral consequences of the parole revocation, or that the alleged illegality of his parole revocation realistically presented a situation " 'capable of repetition, yet evading review,' " 523 U.S., at 17.

Texas sought a federal declaratory judgment that a new statewide scheme of legislative sanctions for deficient local school-board performance, which included the potential replacement of elected board members by a special master, an outside management team, or an independent contractor, did not require preclearance under § 5 of the Voting Rights Act of 1965. The Supreme Court held that the claim was not ripe for adjudication. It restated the governing principles of its "ripeness" doctrine: "[a] claim is not ripe for adjudication if it rests upon 'contingent future events that may not occur as anticipated, or indeed may not occur at all[,]' " and "[r]ipeness 'requir[es] us to evaluate both the fitness of the issues for judicial decision and the hardship to the parties of withholding court consideration.' " Texas v. United States, 523 U.S. 296, 300 (1998).

In a subsequent case, also decided unanimously, the Court propounded a three-prong test for applying ripeness principles to the specific type of litigation most closely associated with ripeness problems: a suit for judicial review of administrative action. "In deciding whether an agency's decision is, or is not, ripe for judicial review, . . . we must consider: (1) whether delayed review will cause hardship to the plaintiffs; (2) whether judicial intervention would inappropriately interfere with further administrative action; and (3) whether the courts would benefit from further factual development of the issues presented." Applying this test, the Court found a challenge to a new federal forestry management plan to be "not justiciable, because it is not ripe for court review" and would not become ripe until such time as the government began to issue specific logging permits under color of the new plan. Ohio Forestry Assn., Inc. v. Sierra Club, 523 U.S. 726, 732–733 (1998).

In National Park Hospitality Ass'n v. Department of the Interior, 538 U.S. 803, 807–808 (2003), the Court held that ripeness is a prudential justiciability doctrine "designed 'to prevent the courts, through avoidance of premature adjudication, from entangling themselves in abstract disagreements over administrative policies, and also to protect the agencies from judicial interference until an administrative decision has been formalized and its effects felt in a concrete way by the challenging parties.' "

In Friends of the Earth, Inc. v. Laidlaw Environmental Services (TOC), Inc., 528 U.S. 167 (2000), the Court took an expansive view of the standing of environmental-protection organizations to seek to redress past violations of anti-pollution laws, and to deter future violations. The Court also clarified the relationship between the stringent initial requirement that plaintiffs have Article III standing and the more prudential and pragmatic analysis that governs whether a defendant's voluntary cessation of illegal conduct renders moot an otherwise justiciable claim to relief.]

outlived its usefulness to the federal government is declared "surplus" and may be transferred to private or other public entities. The price to be paid may be discounted in whole or part on the basis of the benefits to the United States from the use to which the property will be put by its new owner. The Department of the Army had operated Valley Forge General Hospital to provide medical care for members of the armed forces. In 1973, as part of a reduction in the number of military installations, it was decided to close the hospital and to declare it "surplus." In August 1976 a part of the property was transferred to Valley Forge Christian College. Although the appraised value of the property was $577,500, the college was given a 100% public benefit allowance, which allowed it to acquire the property without making any financial payment for it. The college is a nonprofit educational institution operating under the supervision of a religious order known as the Assemblies of God. When suit was brought challenging the conveyance on the ground that it violated the Establishment Clause of the First Amendment, the District Court held that plaintiffs lacked standing and dismissed the complaint, but the Third Circuit reversed by a divided vote.]

II

Article III of the Constitution limits the "judicial power" of the United States to the resolution of "cases" and "controversies." The constitutional power of federal courts cannot be defined, and indeed has no substance, without reference to the necessity "to adjudge the legal rights of litigants in actual controversies." Liverpool Steamship Co. v. Commissioners of Emigration, 113 U.S. 33, 39 (1885). The requirements of Art. III are not satisfied merely because a party requests a court of the United States to declare its legal rights, and has couched that request for forms of relief historically associated with courts of law in terms that have a familiar ring to those trained in the legal process. The judicial power of the United States defined by Art. III is not an unconditioned authority to determine the constitutionality of legislative or executive acts. The power to declare the rights of individuals and to measure the authority of governments, this Court said 90 years ago, "is legitimate only in the last resort, and as a necessity in the determination of real, earnest and vital controversy." Chicago & Grand Trunk R. Co. v. Wellman, 143 U.S. 339, 345 (1892). Otherwise, the power "is not judicial . . . in the sense in which judicial power is granted by the Constitution to the courts of the United States." United States v. Ferreira, 13 How. [54 U.S.] 40, 48 (1852).

As an incident to the elaboration of this bedrock requirement, this Court has always required that a litigant have "standing" to challenge the action sought to be adjudicated in the lawsuit. The term "standing" subsumes a blend of constitutional requirements and prudential considerations, see Warth v. Seldin, 422 U.S. 490, 498 (1975), and it has not always been clear in the opinions of this Court whether particular features of the "standing" requirement have been required by Art. III *ex proprio vigore,* or whether they are requirements that the Court itself has erected and which were not compelled by the language of the Constitution. See *Flast v. Cohen*, 392 U.S. [83, 97 (1968)].

A recent line of decisions, however, has resolved that ambiguity, at least to the following extent: at an irreducible minimum, Art. III requires the party who invokes the court's authority to "show that he personally has suffered some actual or threatened injury as a result of the putatively illegal conduct of the defendant," Gladstone, Realtors v. Village of Bellwood, 441 U.S. 91, 99 (1979), and that the injury "fairly can be traced to the challenged action" and "is likely to be redressed by a favorable decision," Simon v. Eastern Kentucky Welfare Rights Org., 426 U.S. 26, 38, 41 (1976). In this manner does Art. III limit the federal judicial power "to those disputes which confine federal courts to a role consistent with a system of separated powers and which are traditionally thought to be capable of resolution through the judicial process." *Flast v. Cohen*, supra, 392 U.S., at 97.

The requirement of "actual injury redressable by the court," *Simon,* supra, 426 U.S., at 39, serves several of the "implicit policies embodied in Article III," *Flast,* supra, 392 U.S., at 96. It tends to assure that the legal questions presented to the court will be resolved, not in the rarified atmosphere of a debating society, but in a concrete factual context conducive to a realistic appreciation of the consequences of judicial action. The "standing" requirement serves other purposes. Because it assures an actual factual setting in which the litigant asserts a claim of injury in fact, a court may decide the case with some confidence that its decision will not pave the way for lawsuits which have some, but not all, of the facts of the case actually decided by the court.

The Art. III aspect of standing also reflects a due regard for the autonomy of those persons likely to be most directly affected by a judicial order. The federal courts have abjured appeals to their authority which would convert the judicial process into "no more than a vehicle for the vindication of the value interests of concerned bystanders." United States v. SCRAP, 412 U.S. 669, 687 (1973). Were the federal courts merely publicly funded forums for the ventilation of public grievances or the refinement of jurisprudential understanding, the concept of "standing" would be quite unnecessary. But the "cases and controversies" language of Art. III forecloses the conversion of courts of the United States into judicial versions of college debating forums. As we said in Sierra Club v. Morton, 405 U.S. 727, 740 (1972):

> "The requirement that a party seeking review must allege facts showing that he is himself adversely affected . . . does serve as at least a rough attempt to put the decision as to whether review will be sought in the hands of those who have a direct stake in the outcome."

The exercise of judicial power, which can so profoundly affect the lives, liberty, and property of those to whom it extends, is therefore restricted to litigants who can show "injury in fact" resulting from the action which they seek to have the Court adjudicate.

The exercise of the judicial power also affects relationships between the coequal arms of the national government. The effect is, of course, most vivid when a federal court declares unconstitutional an act of the Legislative or Executive branch. While the exercise of that "ultimate and supreme function," *Chicago & Grand Trunk R. Co. v. Wellman*, 143 U.S., at 345, is a formidable means of vindicating individual rights, when employed unwisely or unnecessarily it is also the ultimate threat to the continued effectiveness of the federal courts in performing that role. While the propriety of such action by a federal court has been recognized since Marbury v. Madison, 1 Cranch [5 U.S.] 137 (1803), it has been recognized as a tool of last resort on the part of the federal judiciary throughout its nearly 200 years of existence:

> "[R]epeated and essentially head-on confrontations between the life-tenured branch and the representative branches of government will not, in the long run, be beneficial to either. The public confidence essential to the former and the vitality critical to the latter may well erode if we do not exercise self-restraint in the utilization of our power to negative the actions of the other branches." United States v. Richardson, 418 U.S., at 188 (Powell, J., concurring).

Proper regard for the complex nature of our constitutional structure requires neither that the judicial branch shrink from a confrontation with the other two coequal branches of the federal government, nor that it hospitably accept for adjudication claims of constitutional violation by other branches of government where the claimant has not suffered cognizable injury. Thus this Court has "refrain[ed] from passing upon the constitutionality of an act [of the representative branches] unless obliged to do so in the proper performance of our judicial function, when the question is raised by a party whose interests entitle him to raise it." Blair v. United States, 250 U.S. 273, 279 (1919). The importance of this precondition should not be underestimated as a means of "defin[ing] the role assigned to the judiciary in a tripartite allocation of power." *Flast v. Cohen*, supra, 392 U.S., at 95.

Beyond the constitutional requirements, the federal judiciary has also adhered to a set of prudential principles that bear on the question of standing. Thus, this Court has held that "the plaintiff generally must assert his own legal rights and interests, and cannot rest his claim to relief on the legal rights or interests of third parties." *Warth v. Seldin*, 422 U.S., at 499. In addition, even when the plaintiff has alleged redressable injury sufficient to meet the requirements of Art. III, the Court has refrained from adjudicating "abstract questions of wide public significance" which amount to "generalized grievances," pervasively shared and most appropriately addressed in the representative branches. Id., at 499–500. Finally, the Court has required that the plaintiff's complaint fall within "the zone of interests to be protected or regulated by the statute or constitutional guarantee in question." Data Processing Service v. Camp, 397 U.S. 150, 153 (1970).

Merely to articulate these principles is to demonstrate their close relationship to the policies reflected in the Art. III requirement of actual or threatened injury amenable to judicial remedy. But neither the counsels of prudence nor the policies implicit in the "case or controversy" requirement should be mistaken for the rigorous Art. III requirements themselves. Satisfaction of the former cannot substitute for a demonstration of " 'distinct and palpable injury' . . . that is likely to be redressed if the requested relief is granted." *Gladstone, Realtors v. Village of Bellwood*, supra, 441 U.S., at 100 (quoting *Warth v. Seldin*, supra, 422 U.S., at 501). That requirement states a limitation on judicial power, not merely a factor to be balanced in the weighing of so-called "prudential" considerations.

We need not mince words when we say that the concept of "Art. III standing" has not been defined with complete consistency in all of the various cases decided by this Court which have discussed it, nor when we say that this very fact is probably proof that the concept cannot be reduced to a one-sentence or one-paragraph definition. But of one thing we may be sure: Those who do not possess Art. III standing may not litigate as suitors in the courts of the United States. Art. III, which is every bit as important in its circumscription of the judicial power of the United States as in its granting of that power, is not merely a troublesome hurdle to be overcome if possible so as to reach the "merits" of a lawsuit which a party desires to have adjudicated; it is a part of the basic charter promulgated by the framers of the Constitution at Philadelphia in 1787, a charter which created a general government, provided for the interaction between that government and the governments of the several States, and was later amended so as to either enhance or limit its authority with respect to both States and individuals.

III

The injury alleged by respondents in their amended complaint is the "depriv[ation] of the fair and constitutional use of [their] tax dollar." As a result, our discussion must begin with Frothingham v. Mellon, 262 U.S. 447 (1923) . . . .

Following the decision in *Frothingham,* the Court confirmed that the expenditure of public funds in an allegedly unconstitutional manner is not an injury sufficient to confer standing, even though the plaintiff contributes to the public coffers as a taxpayer. In Doremus v. Board of Education, 342 U.S. 429 (1952), plaintiffs brought suit as citizens and taxpayers, claiming that a New Jersey law which authorized public school teachers in the classroom to read passages from the Bible violated the Establishment Clause of the First Amendment. The Court dismissed the appeal for lack of standing . . . .

In short, the Court found that plaintiffs' grievance was "not a direct dollars-and-cents injury but is a religious difference." Id., at 434. A case or controversy did not exist, even though the "clash of interests [was] real and . . . ." Id., at 436 (Douglas, J., dissenting).

The Court again visited the problem of taxpayer standing in Flast v. Cohen, 392 U.S. 83 (1968) . . .[16]

. . . . .

Unlike the plaintiffs in *Flast,* respondents fail the first prong of the test for taxpayer standing. Their claim is deficient in two respects. First, the source of their complaint is not a congressional action, but a decision by HEW to transfer a parcel of federal property.[17] *Flast* limited taxpayer standing to challenges directed "only [at] exercises of congressional power." Id., at 102. See Schlesinger v. Reservists Committee to Stop the War, 418 U.S. 208, 228 (1974) (denying standing because the taxpayer plaintiffs "did not challenge an enactment under Art. I, § 8, but rather the action of the Executive Branch").

Second, and perhaps redundantly, the property transfer about which respondents complain was not an exercise of authority conferred by the taxing and spending clause of Art. I, § 8. The authorizing legislation, the

---

[**16.** In *Flast* the Court held that a federal taxpayer has standing to challenge the expenditure of federal funds if there was a sufficient logical nexus between the status asserted and the claim sought to be adjudicated. "First, the taxpayer must establish a logical link between that status and the type of legislative enactment attacked. Thus, a taxpayer will be a proper party to allege the unconstitutionality only of exercise of congressional power under the taxing and spending clause of Art. I, § 8, of the Constitution. It will not be sufficient to allege an incidental expenditure of tax funds in the administration of an essentially regulatory statute. . . . Secondly the taxpayer must establish a nexus between that status and the precise nature of the constitutional infringement alleged. Under this requirement, the taxpayer must show that the challenged enactment exceeds specific constitutional limitations imposed upon the exercise of the congressional taxing and spending power and not simply that the enactment is generally beyond the powers delegated to Congress by Art. I, § 8." 392 U.S., at 102.

The Court in *Flast* distinguished the earlier case of Frothingham v. Mellon, 262 U.S. 447 (1923), in which it was held that a federal taxpayer lacked standing to restrain payments from the Treasury to states that chose to participate in a program created by the Maternity Act of 1921. The *Flast* Court held that both the plaintiffs before it and Mrs. Frothingham met the first of the two tests it announced. The *Flast* plaintiffs met the second test as well, since the Establishment Clause of the First Amendment was regarded as "a specific constitutional limitation upon the exercise by Congress of the taxing and spending power . . .," 392 U.S., at 104, while the constitutional provisions on which Mrs. Frothingham relied, the Tenth Amendment and the Due Process Clause of the Fifth Amendment, are not specific limitations on taxing and spending.

The *Frothingham* case distinguished the cases in which municipal taxpayers had been allowed to sue to prevent misuse of municipal funds. It was said that the interest of a municipal taxpayer is "direct and immediate." Does a state taxpayer have standing to enjoin spending tax revenues for allegedly unconstitutional purposes? Compare Hoohuli v. Ariyoshi, 741 F.2d 1169 (9th Cir.1984), with Taub v. Commonwealth of Kentucky, 842 F.2d 912 (6th Cir.1988).

See 13 Wright, Miller & Cooper, Federal Practice and Procedure: Jurisdiction 2d § 3531.10 (1984); Davis, Standing, Taxpayers and Others, 35 U.Chi.L.Rev. 601 (1968); Bittker, The Case of the Fictitious Taxpayer: The Federal Taxpayer's Suit Twenty Years After *Flast v. Cohen*, 30 U.Chi.L.Rev. 364 (1968); Davis, The Case of the Real Taxpayer: A Reply to Professor Bittker, 36 U.Chi.L.Rev. 375 (1968).]

17. Respondents do not challenge the constitutionality of the Federal Property and Administrative Services Act itself, but rather a particular Executive branch action arguably authorized by the Act.

Federal Property and Administrative Services Act of 1949, was an evident exercise of Congress' power under the Property Clause, Art. IV, § 3, cl. 2. Respondents do not dispute this conclusion, see Brief for Respondents 10, and it is decisive of any claim of taxpayer standing under the *Flast* precedent.[18]

Any doubt that once might have existed concerning the rigor with which the *Flast* exception to the *Frothingham* principle ought to be applied should have been erased by this Court's recent decisions in United States v. Richardson, 418 U.S. 166 (1974), and Schlesinger v. Reservists Committee to Stop the War, 418 U.S. 208 (1974). In *Richardson,* the question was whether the plaintiff had standing as a federal taxpayer to argue that legislation which permitted the Central Intelligence Agency to withhold from the public detailed information about its expenditures violated the Accounts Clause of the Constitution. We rejected plaintiff's claim of standing because "his challenge [was] not addressed to the taxing or spending power, but to the statutes regulating the CIA." 418 U.S., at 175. The "mere recital" of those claims "demonstrate[d] how far he [fell] short of the standing criteria of *Flast* and how neatly he [fell] within the *Frothingham* holding left undisturbed." Id., at 174–175.

The claim in *Schlesinger* was marred by the same deficiency. Plaintiffs in that case argued that the Incompatibility Clause of Art. I prevented certain Members of Congress from holding commissions in the Armed Forces Reserve. We summarily rejected their assertion of standing as taxpayers because they "did not challenge an enactment under Art. I, § 8, but rather the action of the Executive Branch in permitting Members of Congress to maintain their Reserve status." 418 U.S., at 228.

Respondents, therefore, are plainly without standing to sue as taxpayers. The Court of Appeals apparently reached the same conclusion. It remains to be seen whether respondents have alleged any other basis for standing to bring this suit.

---

18. Although not necessary to our decision, we note that any connection between the challenged property transfer and respondents' tax burden is at best speculative and at worst nonexistent. Although public funds were expended to establish the Valley Forge General Hospital, the land was acquired and the facilities constructed thirty years prior to the challenged transfer. Respondents do not challenge this expenditure, and we do not immediately perceive how such a challenge might now be raised. Nor do respondents dispute the government's conclusion that the property has become useless for federal purposes and ought to be disposed of in some productive manner. In fact, respondents' only objection is that the government did not receive adequate consideration for the transfer, because petitioner's use of the property will not confer a public benefit. Assuming *arguendo* that this proposition is true, an assumption by no means clear, there is no basis for believing that a transfer to a different purchaser would have added to government receipts. As the government argues, "the ultimate purchaser would, in all likelihood, have been another non-profit institution or local school district rather than a purchaser for cash." Moreover, each year of delay in disposing of the property *depleted* the Treasury by the amounts necessary to maintain a facility that had lost its value to the government. Even if respondents had brought their claim within the outer limits of *Flast,* therefore, they still would have encountered serious difficulty in establishing that they "personally would benefit in a tangible way from the court's intervention." Warth v. Seldin, 422 U.S., at 508.

IV

Although the Court of Appeals properly doubted respondents' ability to establish standing solely on the basis of their taxpayer status, it considered their allegations of taxpayer injury to be "essentially an assumed role." 619 F.2d, at 261.

> "Plaintiffs have no reason to expect, nor perhaps do they care about, any personal tax saving that might result should they prevail. The crux of the interest at stake, the plaintiffs argue, is found in the Establishment Clause, not in the supposed loss of money as such. As a matter of primary identity, therefore, the plaintiffs are not so much taxpayers as separationists . . . ." Ibid.

In the court's view, respondents had established standing by virtue of an " 'injury in fact' to their shared individuated right to a government that 'shall make no law respecting the establishment of religion.' " Ibid. The court distinguished this "injury" from "the question of 'citizen standing' as such." Id., at 262. Although citizens generally could not establish standing simply by claiming an interest in governmental observance of the Constitution, respondents had "set forth instead a particular and concrete injury" to a "personal constitutional right." Id., at 265.

The Court of Appeals was surely correct in recognizing that the Art. III requirements of standing are not satisfied by "the abstract injury in nonobservance of the Constitution asserted by . . . citizens." *Schlesinger v. Reservists Committee to Stop the War*, 418 U.S., at 223, n. 13. This Court repeatedly has rejected claims of standing predicated on " 'the right, possessed by every citizen, to require that the Government be administered according to law . . . .' Fairchild v. Hughes, 258 U.S. 126, 129 [1922]." Baker v. Carr, 369 U.S. 186, 208 (1962). See *Schlesinger v. Reservists Committee to Stop the War*, supra, 418 U.S., at 216–222; Laird v. Tatum, 408 U.S. 1 (1972); Ex parte Levitt, 302 U.S. 633 (1937). Such claims amount to little more than attempts "to employ a federal court as a forum in which to air . . . generalized grievances about the conduct of government." *Flast v. Cohen*, 392 U.S., at 106.

In finding that respondents had alleged something more than "the generalized interest of all citizens in constitutional governance," *Schlesinger,* supra, 418 U.S., at 217, the Court of Appeals relied on factual differences which we do not think amount to legal distinctions. The court decided that respondents' claim differed from those in *Schlesinger* and *Richardson,* which were predicated, respectively, on the Incompatibility and Accounts Clauses, because "it is at the very least arguable that the Establishment Clause creates in each citizen a 'personal constitutional right' to a government that does not establish religion." 619 F.2d, at 265 (footnote omitted). The court found it unnecessary to determine whether this "arguable" proposition was correct, since it judged the mere allegation of a legal right sufficient to confer standing.

This reasoning process merely disguises, we think with a rather thin veil, the inconsistency of the court's results with our decisions in *Schlesin-*

ger and *Richardson*. The plaintiffs in those cases plainly asserted a "personal right" to have the government act in accordance with their views of the Constitution; indeed, we see no barrier to the *assertion* of such claims with respect to any constitutional provision. But assertion of a right to a particular kind of government conduct, which the government has violated by acting differently, cannot alone satisfy the requirements of Art. III without draining those requirements of meaning.

Nor can *Schlesinger* and *Richardson* be distinguished on the ground that the Incompatibility and Accounts Clauses are in some way less "fundamental" than the Establishment Clause. Each establishes a norm of conduct which the federal government is bound to honor—to no greater or lesser extent than any other inscribed in the Constitution. To the extent the Court of Appeals relied on a view of standing under which the Art. III burdens diminish as the "importance" of the claim on the merits increases, we reject that notion. The requirement of standing "focuses on the party seeking to get his complaint before a federal court and not on the issues he wishes to have adjudicated." *Flast v. Cohen*, supra, 392 U.S., at 99. Moreover, we know of no principled basis on which to create a hierarchy of constitutional values or a complementary "sliding scale" of standing which might permit respondents to invoke the judicial power of the United States.[19] "The proposition that all constitutional provisions are enforceable

---

19. JUSTICE BRENNAN'S dissent is premised on a revisionist reading of our precedents which leads to the conclusion that the Art. III requirement of standing is satisfied by any taxpayer who contends "that the federal government has exceeded the bounds of the law in allocating its largesse." "The concept of taxpayer injury necessarily recognizes the continuing stake of the taxpayer in the disposition of the Treasury to which he has contributed his taxes, and his right to have those funds put to lawful uses." On this novel understanding, the dissent reads cases such as *Frothingham* and *Flast* as decisions on the merits of the taxpayers' claims. *Frothingham* is explained as a holding that a taxpayer ordinarily has no legal right to challenge congressional expenditures. The dissent divines from *Flast* the holding that a taxpayer *does* have an enforceable right "to challenge a federal bestowal of largesse" for religious purposes. This right extends to "the Government as a whole, regardless of which branch is at work in a particular instance," and regardless of whether the challenged action was an exercise of the spending power.

However appealing this reconstruction of precedent may be, it bears little resemblance to the cases on which it purports to rest. *Frothingham* and *Flast* were decisions that plainly turned on *standing,* and just as plainly they rejected any notion that the Art. III requirement of direct injury is satisfied by a taxpayer who contends "that the federal government has exceeded the bounds of the law in allocating its largesse." Moreover, although the dissent's view may lead to a result satisfying to many in this case, it is not evident how its substitution of "legal interest," for "standing" enhances "our understanding of the meaning of rights under law." Logically, the dissent must shoulder the burden of explaining why taxpayers with standing have no "legal interest" in congressional expenditures except when it is possible to allege a violation of the Establishment Clause: yet it does not attempt to do so.

Nor does the dissent's interpretation of standing adequately explain cases such as *Schlesinger* and *Richardson*. According to the dissent, the taxpayer plaintiffs in those cases lacked standing, not because they failed to challenge an exercise of the spending power, but because they did not complain of "the distribution of government largesse." And yet if the standing of a taxpayer is established by his "continuing stake . . . in the disposition of the Treasury to which he has contributed his taxes," it would seem to follow that he can assert a right to

by any citizen simply because citizens are the ultimate beneficiaries of those provisions has no boundaries." *Schlesinger v. Reservists Committee to Stop the War*, supra, 418 U.S., at 227.

The complaint in this case shares a common deficiency with those in *Schlesinger* and *Richardson*. Although they claim that the Constitution has been violated, they claim nothing else. They fail to identify any personal injury suffered by the plaintiffs *as a consequence* of the alleged constitutional error, other than the psychological consequence presumably produced by observation of conduct with which one disagrees. That is not an injury sufficient to confer standing under Art. III, even though the disagreement is phrased in constitutional terms. It is evident that respondents are firmly committed to the constitutional principle of separation of church and State, but standing is not measured by the intensity of the litigant's interest or the fervor of his advocacy. "[T]hat concrete adverseness which sharpens the presentation of issues," *Baker v. Carr*, 369 U.S., at 204, is the anticipated consequence of proceedings commenced by one who has been injured in fact; it is not a permissible substitute for the showing of injury itself.

In reaching this conclusion, we do not retreat from our earlier holdings that standing may be predicated on noneconomic injury. See, e.g., *United States v. SCRAP*, 412 U.S., at 686–688; *Data Processing Service v. Camp*, 397 U.S., at 153–154. We simply cannot see that respondents have alleged an *injury* of *any* kind, economic or otherwise, sufficient to confer standing.[20] Respondents complain of a transfer of property located in Chester

---

examine the budget of the CIA, as in *Richardson,* see 418 U.S., at 211, and a right to argue that members of Congress cannot claim reserve pay from the government, as in *Schlesinger,* see 418 U.S., at 211. Of course, both claims have been rejected, precisely because Art. III requires a demonstration of redressable injury that is not satisfied by a claim that tax monies have been spent unlawfully.

20. Respondents rely on our statement in Data Processing Serv. v. Camp, 397 U.S. 150, 154 (1970), that "[a] person or family may have a spiritual stake in First Amendment values sufficient to give standing to raise issues concerning the Establishment Clause and the Free Exercise Clause. Abington School District v. Schempp, 374 U.S. 203 [1963]." Respondents apparently construe this language to mean that any person asserting an Establishment Clause violation possesses a "spiritual stake" sufficient to confer standing. The language will not bear that weight. First, the language cannot be read apart from the context of its accompanying reference to *Abington School District v. Schempp,* supra. In *Schempp,* the Court invalidated laws that required Bible reading in the public schools. Plaintiffs were children who attended the schools in question, and their parents. The Court noted:

"It goes without saying that the laws and practices involved here can be challenged only by persons having standing to complain.... The parties here are school children and their parents, who are directly affected by the laws and practices against which their complaints are directed. These interests surely suffice to give the parties standing to complain." Id., at 224, n. 9.

The Court also drew a comparison with Doremus v. Board of Education, 342 U.S. 429 (1952), in which the identical substantive issues were raised, but in which the appeal was "dismissed upon the graduation of the school child involved and because of the appellants' failure to establish standing as taxpayers." 374 U.S., at 224, n. 9. The Court's discussion of the standing issue is not extensive, but it is sufficient to show the error in respondents' broad reading of the phrase "spiritual stake." The plaintiffs in *Schempp* had standing, not

County, Pennsylvania. The named plaintiffs reside in Maryland and Virginia, their organizational headquarters are located in Washington, D.C. They learned of the transfer through a news release. Their claim that the government has violated the Establishment Clause does not provide a special license to roam the country in search of governmental wrongdoing and to reveal their discoveries in federal court. The federal courts were simply not constituted as ombudsmen of the general welfare.

V

The Court of Appeals in this case ignored unambiguous limitations on taxpayer and citizen standing. It appears to have done so out of the conviction that enforcement of the Establishment Clause demands special exceptions from the requirement that a plaintiff allege " 'distinct and palpable injury to himself,' ... that is likely to be redressed if the requested relief is granted." *Gladstone, Realtors v. Village of Bellwood*, 441 U.S., at 100 (quoting *Warth v. Seldin*, 422 U.S., at 501). The court derived precedential comfort from *Flast v. Cohen*, supra: "The underlying justification for according standing in *Flast* it seems, was the implicit recognition that the Establishment Clause does create in every citizen a personal constitutional right, such that any citizen including taxpayers, may contest under that clause the constitutionality of federal expenditures." 619 F.2d, at 262.[21] The concurring opinion was even more direct. In its view, "statutes alleged to violate the Establishment Clause may not have an individual impact sufficient to confer standing in the traditional sense." Id., at 268. To satisfy "the need for an available plaintiff," id., at 267, and thereby to assure a basis for judicial review, respondents should be granted standing because, "as a practical matter, no one is better suited to bring this lawsuit and thus vindicate the freedoms embodied in the Establishment Clause," id., at 266.

Implicit in the foregoing is the philosophy that the business of the federal courts is correcting constitutional errors, and that "cases and controversies" are at best merely convenient vehicles for doing so and at worst nuisances that may be dispensed with when they become obstacles to that transcendent endeavor. This philosophy has no place in our constitutional scheme. It does not become more palatable when the underlying merits concern the Establishment Clause. Respondents' claim of standing

---

because their complaint rested on the Establishment Clause—for as *Doremus* demonstrated, that is insufficient—but because impressionable schoolchildren were subjected to unwelcome religious exercises or were forced to assume special burdens to avoid them. Respondents have alleged no comparable injury.

21. The majority believed that the only thing which prevented this Court from openly acknowledging this position was the fact that the complaint in *Flast* had alleged no basis for standing other than the plaintiffs' taxpayer status. 619 F.2d, at 262. As the dissent below pointed out, this view is simply not in accord with the facts. See id., at 269–270. The *Flast* plaintiffs and several *amici* strongly urged the Court to adopt the same view of standing for which respondents argue in this case. The Court plainly chose not to do so. Even if respondents were correct in arguing that the Court in *Flast* was bound by a "perceived limitation in the pleadings," id., at 262, we are not so bound in this case, and we find no merit in respondents' vision of standing.

implicitly rests on the presumption that violations of the Establishment Clause typically will not cause injury sufficient to confer standing under the "traditional" view of Art. III. But "[t]he assumption that if respondents have no standing to sue, no one would have standing, is not a reason to find standing." *Schlesinger v. Reservists Committee to Stop the War*, 418 U.S., at 227. This view would convert standing into a requirement that must be observed only when satisfied. Moreover, we are unwilling to assume that injured parties are nonexistent simply because they have not joined respondents in their suit. The law of averages is not a substitute for standing.

Were we to accept respondents' claim of standing in this case, there would be no principled basis for confining our exception to litigants relying on the Establishment Clause. Ultimately, that exception derives from the idea that the judicial power requires nothing more for its invocation than important issues and able litigants.[22] The existence of injured parties who might not wish to bring suit becomes irrelevant. Because we are unwilling to countenance such a departure from the limits on judicial power contained in Art. III, the judgment of the Court of Appeals is reversed.

It is so ordered.

■ JUSTICE BRENNAN, with whom JUSTICE MARSHALL and JUSTICE BLACKMUN join, dissenting.

A plaintiff's standing is a jurisdictional matter for Article III courts, and thus a "threshold question" to be resolved before turning attention to more "substantive" issues. See Linda R.S. v. Richard D., 410 U.S. 614, 616 (1973). But in consequence there is an impulse to decide difficult questions of substantive law obliquely in the course of opinions purporting to do nothing more than determine what the Court labels "standing" ; this accounts for the phenomenon of opinions, such as the one today, that tend merely to obfuscate, rather than inform, our understanding of the meaning of rights under the law. The serious by-product of that practice is that the Court disregards its constitutional responsibility when, by failing to acknowledge the protections afforded by the Constitution, it uses "standing to slam the courthouse door against plaintiffs who are entitled to full consideration of their claims on the merits." [23]

The opinion of the Court is a stark example of this unfortunate trend of resolving cases at the "threshold" while obscuring the nature of the underlying rights and interests at stake. The Court waxes eloquent on the

---

22. Were we to recognize standing premised on an "injury" consisting solely of an alleged violation of a " 'personal constitutional right' to a government that does not establish religion," 619 F.2d, at 265, a principled consistency would dictate recognition of respondents' standing to challenge execution of every capital sentence on the basis of a personal right to a government that does not impose cruel and unusual punishment, or standing to challenge every affirmative action program on the basis of a personal right to a government that does not deny equal protection of the laws, to choose but two among as many possible examples as there are commands in the Constitution.

23. Barlow v. Collins, 397 U.S. 159, 178 (1970) (BRENNAN, J., concurring in the result and dissenting).

blend of prudential and constitutional considerations that combine to create our misguided "standing" jurisprudence. *But not one word is said about the Establishment Clause right that the plaintiff seeks to enforce.* And despite its pat recitation of our standing decisions, the opinion utterly fails, except by the sheerest form of *ipse dixit,* to explain why this case is unlike Flast v. Cohen, 392 U.S. 83 (1968), and is controlled instead by Frothingham v. Mellon, 262 U.S. 447 (1923).

I

. . . . .

. . . The Court makes a fundamental mistake when it determines that a plaintiff has failed to satisfy the two-pronged "injury-in-fact" test, or indeed any other test of "standing," without first determining whether the Constitution or a statute defines injury, and creates a cause of action for redress of that injury, in precisely the circumstance presented to the Court.

It may of course happen that a person believing himself injured in some obscure manner by government action will be held to have no legal right under the constitutional or statutory provision upon which he relies, and will not be permitted to complain of the invasion of another person's "rights." It is quite another matter to employ the rhetoric of "standing" to deprive a person, whose interest is clearly protected by the law, of the opportunity to prove that his own rights have been violated. It is in precisely that dissembling enterprise that the Court indulges today.

The "case and controversy" limitation of Article III overrides no other provision of the Constitution.[24] To construe that Article to deny standing "to the class for whose sake [a] constitutional protection is given," Jones v. United States, 362 U.S. 257, 261 (1960), quoting Hatch v. Reardon, 204 U.S. 152, 160 (1907), simply turns the Constitution on its head. Article III was designed to provide a hospitable forum in which persons enjoying rights under the Constitution could assert those rights. How are we to discern whether a particular person is to be afforded a right of action in the courts? The Framers did not, of course, employ the modern vocabulary of standing. But this much is clear: The drafters of the Bill of Rights surely intended that the particular beneficiaries of their legacy should enjoy rights legally enforceable in courts of law. See West Virginia State Bd. of Educ. v. Barnette, 319 U.S. 624, 638 (1943).

With these observations in mind, I turn to the problem of taxpayer standing in general, and this case in particular.

II

A

. . . . .

---

24. When the Constitution makes it clear that a particular person is to be protected from a particular form of government action, then that person has a "right" to be free of that action: when that right is infringed, then there is injury, and a personal stake, within the meaning of Article III.

Frothingham's reasoning remains obscure.[25] The principal interpretative difficulty lies in the manner in which *Frothingham* chose to blend the language of policy with seemingly absolute statements about jurisdiction. . . .

. . . . .

The *Frothingham* rule may be seen as founded solely on the prudential judgment by the Court that precipitate and unnecessary interference in the activities of a coequal branch of government should be avoided. Alternatively, *Frothingham* may be construed as resting upon an unarticulated, constitutionally established barrier between Congress' power to tax and its power to spend, which barrier makes it analytically impossible to mount an assault on the former through a challenge to the latter. But it is sufficient for present purposes to say that *Frothingham* held that the federal taxpayer has no continuing legal interest in the affairs of the Treasury analogous to a shareholder's continuing interest in the conduct of a corporation.

Whatever its provenance, the general rule of *Frothingham* displays sound judgment: Courts must be circumspect in dealing with the taxing power in order to avoid unnecessary intrusion into the functions of the legislative and executive branches. Congress' *purpose* in taxing will not ordinarily effect the validity of the tax. Unless the tax *operates* unconstitutionally, see e.g., Murdock v. Pennsylvania, 319 U.S. 105 (1943), the taxpayer may not object to the use of his funds. Mrs. Frothingham's argument, that the use of tax funds for purposes unauthorized by the Constitution amounted to a violation of due process, did not provide her with the required legal interest because the Due Process Clause of the Fifth Amendment does not protect taxpayers against increases in tax liability. See *Flast v. Cohen*, supra, at 105. Mrs. Frothingham's claim was thus reduced to an assertion of "the States' interest in their legislative prerogatives," ibid., a third-party claim that could properly be barred. But in *Flast* the Court faced a different sort of constitutional claim, and found itself compelled to retreat from the general assertion in *Frothingham* that taxpayers have *no* interest in the disposition of their tax payments. To understand why *Frothingham*'s bar necessarily gave way in the face of an Establishment Clause claim, we must examine the right asserted by a taxpayer making such a claim.

---

25. The question apparently remains open whether *Frothingham* stated a prudential limitation or identified an Article III barrier. See Duke Power Co. v. Carolina Environmental Study Group, Inc., 438 U.S., at 79, n. 25; United States v. Richardson, 418 U.S. 166, 181, 196, n. 18 (1974) (POWELL, J., concurring). It was generally agreed at the time of *Flast,* 392 U.S., at 92, n. 6, 101, and clearly the view of Justice Harlan in dissent, id., at 130, that the rule stated reflected prudential and policy considerations, not constitutional limitations. Perhaps the case is most usefully understood as a "substantive" declaration of the legal rights of a taxpayer with respect to government spending, coupled with a prudential restriction on the taxpayer's ability to raise the claims of third parties. Under any construction, however, *Frothingham* must give way to a taxpayer's suit brought under the Establishment Clause.

B

In 1947, nine Justices of this Court recognized that the Establishment Clause does impose a very definite restriction on the power to tax. The Court held in Everson v. Board of Education, 330 U.S. 1, 15, that the " 'establishment of religion' clause of the First Amendment means at least this:"

> "No tax in any amount, large or small, can be levied to support any religious activities or institutions, whatever they may be called, or whatever form they may adopt, to teach or practice religion." Id., at 16.

.   .   .   .   .

It is clear in the light of this history, that one of the primary purposes of the Establishment Clause was to prevent the use of tax monies for religious purposes. *The taxpayer was the direct and intended beneficiary of the prohibition on financial aid to religion.* This basic understanding of the meaning of the Establishment Clause explains why the Court in *Everson,* while rejecting appellant's claim on the merits, perceived the issue presented there as it did. The appellant sued "in his capacity as a district taxpayer," 330 U.S., at 3, challenging the actions of the Board of Education in passing a resolution providing reimbursement to parents for the cost of transporting their children to parochial schools, and seeking to have that resolution "set aside." Appellant's Establishment Clause claim was precisely that the "statute ... forced inhabitants to pay taxes to help support and maintain" church schools. Id., at 5. It seems obvious that all the Justices who participated in *Everson* would have agreed with Justice Jackson's succinct statement of the question presented: "Is it constitutional to tax this complainant to pay the cost of carrying pupils to Church schools of one specified denomination?" Id., at 21 (Jackson, J., dissenting). Given this view of the issues, could it fairly be doubted that this taxpayer alleged injury in precisely the form that the Establishment Clause sought to make actionable?[26]

---

26. Justice Jackson, writing for the Court in Doremus v. Board of Education, 342 U.S. 429 (1952), explored the limitations of taxpayer standing under the Establishment Clause. In that case two New Jersey taxpayers challenged a New Jersey law that directed public school teachers to read selected passages from the Bible, seeking a declaratory judgment that such a law violated the Establishment Clause. The Court concluded that the taxpayer lacked standing:

> "There is no allegation that this activity is supported by any separate tax or paid for from any particular appropriation or that it adds any sum whatever to the cost of conducting the school. No information is given as to what kind of taxes are paid by appellants and there is no averment that the Bible reading increases any tax they do pay or that as taxpayers they are, will, or possibly can be out of pocket because of it." Id., at 433.

The Court had no difficulty distinguishing *Everson:*

> "Everson showed a measurable appropriation or disbursement of school-district funds occasioned solely by the activities complained of. This complaint does not." Id., at 434.

The difference between the two cases is relevant to the "standing" of taxpayers generally and most especially to taxpayers asserting claims under the Establishment Clause, for it is clear that even under the Establishment Clause the taxpayer's protection was against the use of

C

. . . . .

The Justices who participated in *Flast* were not unaware of the Court's continued recognition of a federally cognizable "case or controversy" when a *local* taxpayer seeks to challenge as unconstitutional the use of a *municipality*'s funds—the propriety of which had, of course, gone unquestioned in *Everson*.[27] The Court was aware as well of the rule stated in Doremus v. Board of Education, 342 U.S. 429 (1952), that the interest of a taxpayer, even one raising an Establishment Clause claim, was limited to the actions of a government involving the expenditure of funds. But in reaching its holding, it is also quite clear that the Court was responding, not only to *Everson*'s continued acceptance of municipal taxpayer actions but also to *Everson*'s exposition of the history and meaning of the Establishment Clause. See *Flast,* supra, 392 U.S., at 103–104.

It is at once apparent that the test of standing formulated by the Court in *Flast* sought to reconcile the developing doctrine of taxpayer "standing" with the Court's historical understanding that the Establishment Clause was intended to prohibit the Federal Government from using tax funds for the advancement of religion, and thus the constitutional imperative of taxpayer standing in certain cases brought pursuant to the Establishment Clause. The two-pronged "nexus" test offered by the Court, despite its general language, is best understood as "a determinant of standing of plaintiffs alleging only injury as taxpayers who challenge alleged violations of the Establishment and Free Exercise Clauses of the First Amendment," and not as a general statement of standing principles. . . .

. . . . .

It may be that Congress can tax for *almost* any reason, or for no reason at all. There is, so far as I have been able to discern, but one constitutionally imposed limit on that authority. Congress cannot use tax money to support a church, or to encourage religion. That is "*the* forbidden exaction." *Everson v. Board of Education*, 330 U.S., at 45 (Rutledge, J., dissenting) (emphasis added). See *Flast,* supra, 392 U.S., at 115–116 (Fortas, J., concurring). In absolute terms the history of the Establishment Clause of the First Amendment makes this clear. History also makes it clear that the federal taxpayer is a singularly "proper and appropriate party to invoke a federal court's jurisdiction" to challenge a federal bestowal of largesse as a violation of the Establishment Clause. Each, and indeed every, federal taxpayer suffers precisely the injury that the Estab-

---

his funds and not against the conduct of the government generally. The distinction between *Doremus* and *Everson* may be phrased alternatively: Everson was injured in a manner comprehended by the Establishment Clause, and Doremus was not.

27. The anomaly of allowing a municipality's actions to be challenged by a local taxpayer in federal court as a violation of the Establishment Clause, made applicable to the States by virtue of the Fourteenth Amendment, while exempting the Federal Government, whose use of the taxing power in aid of religion was the target of the Framers' adoption of the Establishment Clause, also must have been apparent to the Court.

lishment Clause guards against when the Federal Government directs that funds be taken from the pocketbooks of the citizenry and placed into the coffers of the ministry.

. . . . .

III

Blind to history, the Court attempts to distinguish this case from *Flast* by wrenching snippets of language from our opinions, and by perfunctorily applying that language under color of the first prong of *Flast's* two-part nexus test. The tortuous distinctions thus produced are specious, at best: at worst, they are pernicious to our constitutional heritage.

First, the Court finds this case different from *Flast* because here the "source of [plaintiff's] complaint is not a *congressional* action, but a decision by HEW to transfer a parcel of federal property." Ante, at 762 (emphasis added). . . .

More fundamentally, no clear division can be drawn in this context between actions of the legislative branch and those of the executive branch. To be sure, the First Amendment is phrased as a restriction on Congress' legislative authority; this is only natural since the Constitution assigns the authority to legislate and appropriate only to the Congress. But it is difficult to conceive of an expenditure for which the last governmental actor, either implementing directly the legislative will, or acting within the scope of legislatively delegated authority, is not an Executive Branch official. The First Amendment binds the Government as a whole, regardless of which branch is at work in a particular instance.

The Court's second purported distinction between this case and *Flast* is equally unavailing. The majority finds it "decisive" that the Federal Property and Administrative Services Act of 1949 "was an evident exercise of Congress' power under the Property Clause, Art. IV, § 3, cl. 2," while the government action in *Flast* was taken under the Art. I, § 8. The Court relies on United States v. Richardson, 418 U.S. 166 (1974), and Schlesinger v. Reservists Committee to Stop the War, 418 U.S. 208 (1974), to support the distinction between the two clauses, noting that those cases involved alleged deviations from the requirements of Art. I, § 9, cl. 7, and Art. I, § 6, cl. 2, respectively. The standing defect in each case was *not,* however, the failure to allege a violation of the Spending Clause; rather, the taxpayers in those cases had not complained of the distribution of government largesse, and thus failed to meet the essential requirement of taxpayer standing recognized in *Doremus.*

It can make no constitutional difference in the case before us whether the donation to the defendant here was in the form of a cash grant to build a facility, see Tilton v. Richardson, 403 U.S. 672 (1971), or in the nature of a gift of property including a facility already built. That this is a meaningless distinction is illustrated by *Tilton.* In that case, taxpayers were afforded standing to object to the fact that the Government had not received adequate assurance that if the property that it financed for use as an educational facility was later converted to religious uses, it would receive full value for the property, as the Constitution requires. The complaint here is precisely that, although the property at issue is actually being used for a sectarian purpose, the government has not received, nor demanded, full value payment. Whether undertaken pursuant to the Property Clause or the Spending Clause, the breach of the Establishment Clause, and the relationship of the taxpayer to that breach, is precisely the same.

IV

Plainly hostile to the Framers' understanding of the Establishment Clause, and *Flast*'s enforcement of that understanding, the Court vents that hostility under the guise of standing, "to slam the courthouse door against plaintiffs who [as the Framers intended] are entitled to full consideration of their [Establishment Clause] claims on the merits." Barlow v. Collins, 397 U.S. 159, 178 (1970) (BRENNAN, J., concurring in the result and dissenting). Therefore, I dissent.

■ JUSTICE STEVENS, dissenting.

In Parts I, II, and III of his dissenting opinion, JUSTICE BRENNAN demonstrates that respondent taxpayers have standing to mount an Establishment Clause challenge against the Federal Government's transfer of property worth $1,300,000 to the Assembly of God. For the Court to hold that plaintiffs' standing depends on whether the Government's transfer was an exercise of its power to spend money, on the one hand, or its power to dispose of tangible property, on the other, is to trivialize the standing doctrine.

One cannot read the Court's opinion and the concurring opinions of Justice Stewart and Justice Fortas in Flast v. Cohen, 392 U.S. 83, without forming the firm conclusion that the plaintiffs' invocation of the Establishment Clause was of decisive importance in resolving the standing issue in that case....

Today the Court holds, in effect, that the Judiciary has no greater role in enforcing the Establishment Clause than in enforcing other "norm[s] of conduct which the federal government is bound to honor," such as the Accounts Clause, United States v. Richardson, 418 U.S. 166, and the Incompatibility Clause, Schlesinger v. Reservists Committee to Stop the War, 418 U.S. 208. Ironically, however, its decision rests on the premise that the difference between a disposition of funds pursuant to the Spending Clause and a disposition of realty pursuant to the Property Clause is of fundamental jurisprudential significance. With all due respect, I am persuaded that the essential holding of *Flast v. Cohen* attaches special importance to the Establishment Clause and does not permit the drawing of a tenuous distinction between the Spending Clause and the Property Clause.

For this reason, and for the reasons stated in Parts I, II, and III of JUSTICE BRENNAN'S opinion, I would affirm the judgment of the Court of Appeals.[28]

[28. See Nichol, Standing on the Constitution: The Supreme Court and Valley Forge, 61 N.C.L.Rev. 798 (1983); Marshall & Flood, Establishment Clause Standing: The Not Very Revolutionary Decision at Valley Forge, 11 Hofstra L.Rev. 63 (1982). See generally Fletcher, The Structure of Standing, 98 Yale L.J. 221 (1988); Winter, The Metaphor of Standing and the Problem of Self–Governance, 40 Stan.L.Rev. 1371 (1988).

In Hein v. Freedom From Religion Foundation, Inc., 551 U.S. 587 (2007), the Supreme Court granted review to decide whether taxpayer standing under *Flast* extended to a suit that challenged the Executive Branch's use of federal funds to pay for conferences promoting "Faith–Based and Community Initiatives" that allegedly endorsed religious organizations and beliefs. The funds in question were not specifically appropriated by Congress to be spent in this fashion. They were taken out of the funds appropriated by Congress for the general operation of the Executive Branch. A divided Seventh Circuit panel had decided that *Flast* gave the plaintiffs standing to challenge the use of general Executive Branch funds to promote religious activity. The Supreme Court reversed in a plurality opinion. The plurality opinion of Justice Alito, joined by Chief Justice Roberts and Justice Kennedy, did not question the continuing authority of *Flast*, "But *Flast* focused on congressional action, and we must decline this invitation to extend its holding to encompass discretionary Executive Branch expenditures." Id. at 609. Justice Scalia, joined by Justice Thomas, denounced *Flast* and joined the plurality only in reversing the extension of *Flast* by the court below. "If this Court is to decide cases by rule of law rather than show of hands, we must surrender to logic and choose sides. Either Flast v. Cohen ... should be applied to (at a minimum) *all* challenges to the governmental expenditure of general tax revenues in a manner alleged to violate a constitutional provision specifically limiting the taxing and spending power, or *Flast* should be repudiated." Id. at 618. The plurality opinion replied that it was unnecessary in this case to consider overruling *Flast*, which suggested that *Flast* might not have long to live. But one member of the plurality, Justice Kennedy, filed his own concurring opinion in which he declared that "the result reached in *Flast* was correct and should not be called into question." Id. at 616. Justice Souter's dissenting opinion, joined by Justices Stevens, Ginsburg, and Breyer, pronounced *Flast* alive and well and properly applied by the court below. Thus five of the nine Justices indicated in *Hein* that *Flast* should not be overruled, two vehemently disagreed, and two Justices remained uncommitted.

Although Congress can create new interests, the invasion of which will confer standing, Congress cannot confer standing on persons who have suffered no concrete injury. Lujan v. Defenders of Wildlife, 504 U.S. 555 (1992).

Relying on the Line Item Veto Act's provision that "[a]ny Member of Congress or any individual adversely affected" by the Act could bring suit to challenge the constitutionality of the Act in the United States District Court for the District of Columbia, four members of the Senate and two members of the House of Representatives sought to have the Line Item Veto Act declared unconstitutional. The Supreme Court held that the plaintiffs lacked standing to sue. Relying principally on *Lujan* and *Valley Forge*, the Court disavowed any general doctrine of "legislative standing" and held that the plaintiffs' institutional interest in the constitutionality of the Act was too "abstract and widely dispersed" to constitute the " 'personal' " and " 'particularized' " injury required to satisfy the " 'bedrock requirement' " that federal courts may adjudicate only disputes amounting to a " 'case' or 'controversy' " within the meaning of Article III. Raines v. Byrd, 521 U.S. 811 (1997). The following Term, however, the Court struck down the Act after first finding that the plaintiffs—various entities that would have benefited from "cancelled items," i.e., particular provisions of a statute which the President specifically sought to nullify without vetoing the entirety of the statute—were "individual[s] adversely affected" within the meaning of the Act's special standing provision and had suffered the sort of actual and individualized injury required for standing under Article III. Clinton v. City of New York, 524 U.S. 417 (1998).

Summers v. Earth Island Institute

Supreme Court of the United States, 2009.
555 U.S. 488, 129 S.Ct. 1142, 173 L.Ed.2d 1.

■ JUSTICE SCALIA delivered the opinion of the Court.

Respondents are a group of organizations dedicated to protecting the environment. (We will refer to them collectively as "Earth Island.") They seek to prevent the United States Forest Service from enforcing regulations that exempt small fire-rehabilitation and timber-salvage projects from the notice, comment, and appeal process used by the Forest Service for more significant land management decisions. We must determine whether respondents have standing to challenge the regulations in the absence of a live dispute over a concrete application of those regulations.

See 13A Wright, Miller & Cooper, Federal Practice and Procedure: Jurisdiction 2d § 3531.11 (1984).

The Endangered Species Act has a broad provision allowing citizen suits to enforce the Act. 5 U.S.C. § 1540(g). Ranch operators and irrigation districts filed suit challenging a determination of the Fish and Wildlife Service that continued operation of the Klamath reclamation project was likely to jeopardize the continued existence of two endangered species of fish. Plaintiffs alleged that complying with the minimum water levels the Service thought required would irreparably damage their use of the reservoirs for recreational, aesthetic, and commercial purposes, as well as for their primary sources of irrigation water. The lower courts held that plaintiffs lacked standing, reasoning that only plaintiffs alleging an interest in the preservation of endangered species fell within the zone of interests protected by the Act. The Supreme Court unanimously reversed. It held that the prudential zone-of-interests test—see *Valley Forge*, reprinted supra p. 33, at p. 36—was negated by Congress when it provided that "any person may commence a civil suit." That language allows not only actions against the Secretary of the Interior asserting underenforcement of the Act, but also actions against the Secretary asserting overenforcement. Bennett v. Spear, 520 U.S. 154 (1997).

In McConnell v. Federal Election Comm'n, 540 U.S. 93, 224–229 (2003), the Court upheld the dismissal of objections to two sections of the Bipartisan Campaign Reform Act of 2002 on the ground that the relevant plaintiffs lacked standing to challenge these sections. Senator McConnell's interest in challenging the restrictions of § 305 on negative campaign advertisements was deemed too remote because he did not face reelection until 2008. Various citizen plaintiffs challenging the restrictions of § 307 on campaign contributions were held to allege injuries that were not "fairly traceable" to § 307 or could be remedied only by the special review procedures specified in the Federal Election Campaign Act—procedures left undisturbed by § 307's amendment of that Act.

[Does the assignee of a claim, pursuant to an assignment solely for purposes of collection that obligates the assignee to tender any recovery to the assignor, have Article III standing to bring suit on the assigned claim? In Sprint Communications Co., L.P. v. APCC Servs., Inc., 554 U.S. 269 (2008), a closely divided Supreme Court answered "yes." Justice Breyer's opinion, joined by Justices Stevens, Kennedy, Souter, and Ginsburg, relied on "history and tradition" to determine that collection suits had long been allowed in federal courts and found no compelling reason to depart from this "clear historical answer." Id. at 274, 275. Writing for the four dissenters, Chief Justice Roberts declared that common sense should trump history, and invoked a new source of Article III inspiration: "The absence of any right to the substantive recovery means that respondents cannot benefit from the judgment they seek and thus lack Article III standing. 'When you got nothing, you got nothing to

I

In 1992, Congress enacted the Forest Service Decisionmaking and Appeals Reform Act (Appeals Reform Act or Act), Pub.L. 102–381, Tit. III, § 322, 106 Stat. 1419, note following 16 U.S.C. § 1612. Among other things, this required the Forest Service to establish a notice, comment, and appeal process for "proposed actions of the Forest Service concerning projects and activities implementing land and resource management plans developed under the Forest and Rangeland Renewable Resources Planning Act of 1974." Ibid.

The Forest Service's regulations implementing the Act provided that certain of its procedures would not be applied to projects that the Service considered categorically excluded from the requirement to file an environmental impact statement (EIS) or environmental assessment (EA). 36 C.F.R. §§ 215.4(a) (notice and comment), 215.12(f) (appeal) (2008). Later amendments to the Forest Service's manual of implementing procedures, adopted by rule after notice and comment, provided that fire-rehabilitation activities on areas of less than 4,200 acres, and salvage-timber sales of 250 acres or less, did not cause a significant environmental impact and thus would be categorically exempt from the requirement to file an EIS or EA. 68 Fed.Reg. 33824 (2003) (Forest Service Handbook (FSH) 1909.15, ch. 30, § 31.2(11)); 68 Fed.Reg. 44607 (FSH 1909.15, ch. 30, § 31.2(13)). This had the effect of excluding these projects from the notice, comment, and appeal process.

In the summer of 2002, fire burned a significant area of the Sequoia National Forest. In September 2003, the Service issued a decision memo approving the Burnt Ridge Project, a salvage sale of timber on 238 acres damaged by that fire. Pursuant to its categorical exclusion of salvage sales of less than 250 acres, the Forest Service did not provide notice in a form consistent with the Appeals Reform Act, did not provide a period of public comment, and did not make an appeal process available.

In December 2003, respondents filed a complaint in the Eastern District of California, challenging the failure of the Forest Service to apply to the Burnt Ridge Project § 215.4(a) of its regulations implementing the Appeals Reform Act (requiring prior notice and comment), and § 215.12(f) of the regulations (setting forth an appeal procedure). The complaint also challenged six other Forest Service regulations implementing the Act that were not applied to the Burnt Ridge Project. They are irrelevant to this appeal.

The District Court granted a preliminary injunction against the Burnt Ridge salvage-timber sale. Soon thereafter, the parties settled their dispute over the Burnt Ridge Project and the District Court concluded that "the Burnt Ridge timber sale is not at issue in this case." Earth Island Inst. v. Pengilly, 376 F.Supp.2d 994, 999 (E.D.Cal.2005). The Government argued that, with the Burnt Ridge dispute settled, and with no other project before

---

lose.' Bob Dylan, Like a Rolling Stone, on Highway 61 Revisited (Columbia Records 1965)." Id. at 301. He predicted that the Court would change its tune in the future. Id. at 315.]

the court in which respondents were threatened with injury in fact, respondents lacked standing to challenge the regulations; and that absent a concrete dispute over a particular project a challenge to the regulations would not be ripe. The District Court proceeded, however, to adjudicate the merits of Earth Island's challenges. It invalidated five of the regulations (including §§ 215.4(a) and 215.12(f)), id., at 1011, and entered a nationwide injunction against their application, Earth Island Inst. v. Ruthenbeck, No. CIV F–03–6386 JKS, 2005 WL 5280466 *2 (Sept. 20, 2005).

The Ninth Circuit held that Earth Island's challenges to regulations not at issue in the Burnt Ridge Project were not ripe for adjudication because there was "not a sufficient 'case or controversy' " before the court to sustain a facial challenge. Earth Island Inst. v. Ruthenbeck, 490 F.3d 687, 696 (2007) (amended opinion). It affirmed, however, the District Court's determination that §§ 215.4(a) and 215.12(f), which were applicable to the Burnt Ridge Project, were contrary to law, and upheld the nationwide injunction against their application.

The Government sought review of the question whether Earth Island could challenge the regulations at issue in the Burnt Ridge Project, and if so whether a nationwide injunction was appropriate relief. We granted certiorari.

II

In limiting the judicial power to "Cases" and "Controversies," Article III of the Constitution restricts it to the traditional role of Anglo–American courts, which is to redress or prevent actual or imminently threatened injury to persons caused by private or official violation of law. Except when necessary in the execution of that function, courts have no charter to review and revise legislative and executive action. See Lujan v. Defenders of Wildlife, 504 U.S. 555, 559–560 (1992); Los Angeles v. Lyons, 461 U.S. 95, 111–112 (1983). This limitation "is founded in concern about the proper— and properly limited—role of the courts in a democratic society." Warth v. Seldin, 422 U.S. 490, 498 (1975). See United States v. Richardson, 418 U.S. 166, 179 (1974).

The doctrine of standing is one of several doctrines that reflect this fundamental limitation. It requires federal courts to satisfy themselves that "the plaintiff has 'alleged such a personal stake in the outcome of the controversy' as to warrant his invocation of federal-court jurisdiction." 422 U.S., at 498–499. He bears the burden of showing that he has standing for each type of relief sought. See *Lyons*, supra, at 105. To seek injunctive relief, a plaintiff must show that he is under threat of suffering "injury in fact" that is concrete and particularized; the threat must be actual and imminent, not conjectural or hypothetical; it must be fairly traceable to the challenged action of the defendant; and it must be likely that a favorable judicial decision will prevent or redress the injury. Friends of Earth, Inc. v. Laidlaw Environmental Services (TOC), Inc., 528 U.S. 167, 180–181 (2000). This requirement assures that "there is a real need to exercise the power of judicial review in order to protect the interests of the complaining party,"

Schlesinger v. Reservists Comm. to Stop the War, 418 U.S. 208, 221 (1974). Where that need does not exist, allowing courts to oversee legislative or executive action "would significantly alter the allocation of power ... away from a democratic form of government," *Richardson*, supra, at 188 (Powell, J., concurring).

The regulations under challenge here neither require nor forbid any action on the part of respondents. The standards and procedures that they prescribe for Forest Service appeals govern only the conduct of Forest Service officials engaged in project planning. "[W]hen the plaintiff is not himself the object of the government action or inaction he challenges, standing is not precluded, but it is ordinarily 'substantially more difficult' to establish." *Defenders of Wildlife*, supra, at 562. Here, respondents can demonstrate standing only if application of the regulations by the Government will affect them in the manner described above.

It is common ground that the respondent organizations can assert the standing of their members. To establish the concrete and particularized injury that standing requires, respondents point to their members' recreational interests in the National Forests. While generalized harm to the forest or the environment will not alone support standing, if that harm in fact affects the recreational or even the mere esthetic interests of the plaintiff, that will suffice. Sierra Club v. Morton, 405 U.S. 727, 734–736 (1972).

Affidavits submitted to the District Court alleged that organization member Ara Marderosian had repeatedly visited the Burnt Ridge site, that he had imminent plans to do so again, and that his interests in viewing the flora and fauna of the area would be harmed if the Burnt Ridge Project went forward without incorporation of the ideas he would have suggested if the Forest Service had provided him an opportunity to comment. The Government concedes this was sufficient to establish Article III standing with respect to Burnt Ridge. Brief for Petitioners 28. Marderosian's threatened injury with regard to that project was originally one of the bases for the present suit. After the District Court had issued a preliminary injunction, however, the parties settled their differences on that score. Marderosian's injury in fact with regard to that project has been remedied, and it is, as the District Court pronounced, "not at issue in this case." 376 F.Supp.2d, at 999. We know of no precedent for the proposition that when a plaintiff has sued to challenge the lawfulness of certain action or threatened action but has settled that suit, he retains standing to challenge the basis for that action (here, the regulation in the abstract), apart from any concrete application that threatens imminent harm to his interests. Such a holding would fly in the face of Article III's injury-in-fact requirement. See *Lyons*, supra, at 111.

Respondents have identified no other application of the invalidated regulations that threatens imminent and concrete harm to the interests of their members. The only other affidavit relied on was that of Jim Bensman.[1] He asserted, first, that he had suffered injury in the past from development on Forest Service land. That does not suffice for several reasons: because it was not tied to application of the challenged regulations, because it does not identify any particular site, and because it relates to past injury rather than imminent future injury that is sought to be enjoined.

Bensman's affidavit further asserts that he has visited many National Forests and plans to visit several unnamed National Forests in the future. Respondents describe this as a mere failure to "provide the name of each timber sale that affected [Bensman's] interests," Brief for Respondents 44. It is much more (or much less) than that. It is a failure to allege that *any* particular timber sale or other project claimed to be unlawfully subject to the regulations will impede a specific and concrete plan of Bensman's to enjoy the National Forests. The National Forests occupy more than 190 million acres, an area larger than Texas. See Meet the Forest Service, http:// www. fs. fed. us/ aboutus/ meetfs. shtml (as visited Feb. 27, 2009, and available in Clerk of Court's case file). There may be a chance, but is hardly a likelihood, that Bensman's wanderings will bring him to a parcel about to be affected by a project unlawfully subject to the regulations. Indeed, without further specification it is impossible to tell *which* projects are (in respondents' view) unlawfully subject to the regulations. The allegations here present a weaker likelihood of concrete harm than that which we found insufficient in *Lyons*, 461 U.S. 95, where a plaintiff who alleged that he had been injured by an improper police chokehold sought injunctive relief barring use of the hold in the future. We said it was "no more than conjecture" that Lyons would be subjected to that chokehold upon a later encounter. Id., at 108. Here we are asked to assume not only that Bensman will stumble across a project tract unlawfully subject to the regulations, but also that the tract is about to be developed by the Forest Service in a way that harms his recreational interests, and that he would have commented on the project but for the regulation. Accepting an intention to visit the National Forests as adequate to confer standing to challenge any Government action affecting any portion of those forests would be tantamount to eliminating the requirement of concrete, particularized injury in fact.

The Bensman affidavit does refer specifically to a series of projects in the Allegheny National Forest that are subject to the challenged regulations. It does not assert, however, any firm intention to visit their locations, saying only that Bensman " 'want[s] to' " go there. Brief for Petitioners 6. This vague desire to return is insufficient to satisfy the requirement of imminent injury: "Such 'some day' intentions—without any description of concrete plans, or indeed any specification of *when* the some day will be—

---

1. After the District Court had entered judgment, and after the Government had filed its notice of appeal, respondents submitted additional affidavits to the District Court. We do not consider these. If respondents had not met the challenge to their standing at the time of judgment, they could not remedy the defect retroactively.

do not support a finding of the 'actual or imminent' injury that our cases require." *Defenders of Wildlife*, 504 U.S., at 564.

Respondents argue that they have standing to bring their challenge because they have suffered procedural injury, namely that they have been denied the ability to file comments on some Forest Service actions and will continue to be so denied. But deprivation of a procedural right without some concrete interest that is affected by the deprivation—a procedural right *in vacuo*—is insufficient to create Article III standing. Only a "person who has been accorded a procedural right to protect *his concrete interests* can assert that right without meeting all the normal standards for redressability and immediacy." Id., at 572, n.7 (emphasis added). Respondents alleged such injury in their challenge to the Burnt Ridge Project, claiming that but for the allegedly unlawful abridged procedures they would have been able to oppose the project that threatened to impinge on their concrete plans to observe nature in that specific area. But Burnt Ridge is now off the table.

It makes no difference that the procedural right has been accorded by Congress. That can loosen the strictures of the redressability prong of our standing inquiry—so that standing existed with regard to the Burnt Ridge Project, for example, despite the possibility that Earth Island's allegedly guaranteed right to comment would not be successful in persuading the Forest Service to avoid impairment of Earth Island's concrete interests. See ibid. Unlike redressability, however, the requirement of injury in fact is a hard floor of Article III jurisdiction that cannot be removed by statute.

> "[I]t would exceed [Article III's] limitations if, at the behest of Congress and in the absence of any showing of concrete injury, we were to entertain citizen suits to vindicate the public's nonconcrete interest in the proper administration of the laws. . . . [T]he party bringing suit must show that the action injures him in a concrete and personal way." Id., at 580–581 (Kennedy, J., concurring in part and concurring in judgment).

III

The dissent proposes a hitherto unheard-of test for organizational standing: whether, accepting the organization's self-description of the activities of its members, there is a statistical probability that some of those members are threatened with concrete injury. Since, for example, the Sierra Club asserts in its pleadings that it has more than " '700,000 members nationwide, including thousands of members in California' " who " 'use and enjoy the Sequoia National Forest,' " post (opinion of Breyer, J.), it is probable (according to the dissent) that some (unidentified) members have planned to visit some (unidentified) small parcels affected by the Forest Service's procedures and will suffer (unidentified) concrete harm as a result. This novel approach to the law of organizational standing would make a mockery of our prior cases, which have required plaintiff-organizations to make specific allegations establishing that at least one identified member had suffered or would suffer harm. In *Defenders of Wildlife*, supra, at 563, we held that the organization lacked standing because it failed to "submit affidavits ... showing, through specific facts ... that one or more of [its] members would ... be 'directly' affected" by the allegedly illegal activity. *Morton*, 405 U.S. 727, involved the same Sierra Club that is a party in the present case, and a project in the Sequoia National Forest. The principal difference from the present case is that the challenged project was truly massive, involving the construction of motels, restaurants, swimming pools, parking lots, and other structures on 80 acres of the Forest, plus ski lifts, ski trails, and a 20–mile access highway. We did not engage in an assessment of statistical probabilities that one of the Sierra Club's members would be adversely affected, but held that the Sierra Club lacked standing. We said:

> "The Sierra Club failed to allege that it or its members would be affected in any of their activities or pastimes by the Disney development. Nowhere in the pleadings or affidavits did the Club state that its members use Mineral King for any purpose, much less that they use it in any way that would be significantly affected by the proposed actions of the respondents." Id., at 735.

And in FW/PBS, Inc. v. Dallas, 493 U.S. 215, 235 (1990), we noted that the affidavit provided by the city to establish standing would be insufficient because it did not name the individuals who were harmed by the challenged license-revocation program. This requirement of naming the affected members has never been dispensed with in light of statistical probabilities, but only where all the members of the organization are affected by the challenged activity. See, e.g., NAACP v. Alabama ex rel. Patterson, 357 U.S. 449, 459 (1958) (all organization members affected by release of membership lists).

A major problem with the dissent's approach is that it accepts the organizations' self-descriptions of their membership, on the simple ground that "no one denies" them. But it is well established that the court has an independent obligation to assure that standing exists, regardless of whether it is challenged by any of the parties. Bender v. Williamsport Area School Dist., 475 U.S. 534, 541 (1986). Without individual affidavits, how is the court to assure itself that the Sierra Club, for example, has " 'thousands of members' " who " 'use and enjoy the Sequoia National Forest' " ? And, because to establish standing plaintiffs must show that they "use the area affected by the challenged activity and not an area roughly in the vicinity of" a project site, *Defenders of Wildlife*, 504 U.S., at 566 (internal quotation marks omitted), how is the court to assure itself that some of these members plan to make use of the specific sites upon which projects may take place? Or that these same individuals will find their recreation burdened by the Forest Service's use of the challenged procedures? While it is certainly possible—perhaps even likely—that one individual will meet all of these criteria, that speculation does not suffice. "Standing," we have said, "is not 'an ingenious academic exercise in the conceivable' ... [but] requires ... a factual showing of perceptible harm." Ibid. In part because of the difficulty of verifying the facts upon which such probabilistic standing depends, the Court has required plaintiffs claiming an organizational standing to identify members who have suffered the requisite harm—surely not a difficult task here, when so many thousands are alleged to have been harmed.

The dissent would have us replace the requirement of " 'imminent' " harm, which it acknowledges our cases establish, with the requirement of " 'a *realistic* threat' that reoccurrence of the challenged activity would cause [the plaintiff] harm 'in the reasonably near future.' " That language is taken, of course, from an opinion that did *not* find standing, so the seeming expansiveness of the test made not a bit of difference. The problem for the dissent is that the timely affidavits no more meet that requirement than they meet the usual formulation. They fail to establish that the affiants' members will ever visit one of the small parcels at issue.

The dissent insists, however, that we should also have considered the late-filed affidavits. It invokes Federal Rule of Civil Procedure 15(d) (West 2008 rev.ed.), which says that "[t]he court may permit supplementation even though the original pleading is defective in stating of a claim or defense." So also does Rule 21 permit joinder of parties "at any time." But the latter no more permits joinder of parties, than the former permits the supplementation of the record, in the circumstances here: *after the trial is over, judgment has been entered, and a notice of appeal has been filed*. The dissent cites no instance in which "supplementation" has been permitted to resurrect and alter the outcome in a case that has gone to judgment, and indeed after notice of appeal had been filed. If Rule 15(b) allows additional facts to be inserted into the record after appeal has been filed, we are at the threshold of a brave new world of trial practice in which Rule 60 has been swallowed whole by Rule 15(b).

* * *

Since we have resolved this case on the ground of standing, we need not reach the Government's contention that plaintiffs have not demonstrated that the regulations are ripe for review under the Administrative Procedure Act. We likewise do not reach the question whether, if respondents prevailed, a nationwide injunction would be appropriate. And we do not disturb the dismissal of respondents' challenge to the remaining regulations, which has not been appealed.

The judgment of the Court of Appeals is reversed in part and affirmed in part.

It is so ordered.

■ JUSTICE KENNEDY, concurring.

I join in full the opinion of the Court. As the opinion explains, "deprivation of a procedural right without some concrete interest that is affected by the deprivation—a procedural right *in vacuo*—is insufficient to create Article III standing." The procedural injury must "impair a separate concrete interest." Lujan v. Defenders of Wildlife, 504 U.S. 555, 572 (1992).

This case would present different considerations if Congress had sought to provide redress for a concrete injury "giv[ing] rise to a case or controversy where none existed before." Id., at 580 (Kennedy, J., concurring in part and concurring in judgment). Nothing in the statute at issue here, however, indicates Congress intended to identify or confer some interest separate and apart from a procedural right.

■ JUSTICE BREYER, with whom JUSTICE STEVENS, JUSTICE SOUTER, and JUSTICE GINSBURG join, dissenting.

The Court holds that the Sierra Club and its members (along with other environmental organizations) do not suffer any " 'concrete injury' " when the Forest Service sells timber for logging on "many thousands" of small (250–acre or less) woodland parcels without following legally required procedures—procedures which, if followed, could lead the Service to cancel or to modify the sales. Nothing in the record or the law justifies this counterintuitive conclusion.

I

A

The plaintiffs, respondents in this case, are five environmental organizations. The Earth Island Institute, a California organization, has over 15,000 members in the United States, over 3,000 of whom "use and enjoy the National Forests of California for recreational, educational, aesthetic, spiritual and other purposes." Corrected Complaint for Declaratory and Injunctive Relief in Case No. CIV–F–03–630 REC DLB (ED Cal.) ¶ 8, App. 31 (hereinafter Complaint). The Sequoia ForestKeeper, a small organization, has "100 plus" members who "use the forests of the Southern Sierra Nevada for activities such as hiking, bird and animal watching, esthetic enjoyment, quiet contemplation, fishing and scientific study." Id., ¶ 9, at 32. Heartwood, Inc., located in Illinois and Indiana, is a coalition of environmental organizations with "members' who "continually use the National Forests for the purposes of ecological health, recreation, esthetic enjoyment, and other purposes." Id., ¶ 10, at 33. The Center for Biological Diversity, located in Arizona, California, New Mexico, and Washington, has over 5,000 members who "use Forest Service lands," and who are "dedicated to the preservation, protection, and restoration of biological diversity, native species and ecosystems in the Western United States and elsewhere." Ibid., ¶ 11. The Sierra Club has more than "700,000 members nationwide, including thousands of members in California" who "use and enjoy the Sequoia National Forest," for "outdoor recreation and scientific study of various kinds, including nature study, bird-watching, photography, fishing, canoeing, hunting, backpacking, camping, solitude, and a variety of other activities." Id., ¶ 12, at 34.

These five organizations point to a federal law that says the Forest Service "shall establish a notice and comment process," along with a procedure for filing administrative "appeals," for "proposed actions ... concerning projects and activities implementing land and resource management plans...." § 322, 106 Stat. 1419, note following 16 U.S.C. § 1612.

They add that the Service has exempted from "notice, comment, and appeal" processes its decisions that allow, among other things, salvage-timber sales on burned forest lands of less than 250 acres in size. 36 C.F.R. §§ 215.4(a), 215.12(f) (2008); see also 68 Fed.Reg. 44607–44608 (2003) (describing projects exempted). And they claim that the Service's refusal to provide notice, comment, and appeal procedures violates the statute. Complaint ¶ ¶ 105–106, App. 61.

B

The majority says that the plaintiffs lack *constitutional* standing to raise this claim. It holds that the dispute between the five environmental groups and the Forest Service consists simply of an abstract challenge; it does not amount to the concrete "Cas[e]" or "Controvers[y]" that the Constitution grants federal courts the power to resolve. Art. III, § 2, cl. 1. I cannot agree that this is so.

To understand the *constitutional* issue that the majority decides, it may prove helpful to imagine that Congress enacted a *statutory* provision that expressly permitted environmental groups like the respondents here to bring cases just like the present one, provided (1) that the group has members who have used salvage-timber parcels in the past and are likely to do so in the future, and (2) that the group's members have opposed Forest Service timber sales in the past (using notice, comment, and appeal procedures to do so) and will likely use those procedures to oppose salvage-timber sales in the future. The majority cannot, and does not, claim that such a statute would be unconstitutional. See Massachusetts v. EPA, 549 U.S. 497, 516–518 (2007); Sierra Club v. Morton, 405 U.S. 727, 734–738 (1972). How then can it find the present case constitutionally unauthorized?

I believe the majority answers this question as follows: It recognizes, as this Court has held, that a plaintiff has constitutional standing if the plaintiff demonstrates (1) an " 'injury in fact,' " (2) that is "fairly traceable" to the defendant's "challenged action," and which (3) a "favorable [judicial] decision" will likely prevent or redress. Friends of Earth, Inc. v. Laidlaw Environmental Services (TOC), Inc., 528 U.S. 167, 180–181 (2000). The majority does not deny that the plaintiffs meet the latter two requirements. It focuses only upon the first, the presence of "actual," as opposed to "conjectural or hypothetical," injury. Id., at 180. In doing so, it properly agrees that the "organizations" here can "assert the standing of their members." It points out that injuries to the "members' recreational" or even "mere esthetic interests . . . will suffice." Ibid. It does not claim that the *procedural* nature of the plaintiffs' claim makes the difference here, for it says only that "deprivation of a procedural right *without some concrete interest*" thereby affected, i.e., "a procedural right *in vacuo*" would prove "insufficient to create Article III standing." Ante (emphasis added); see also *EPA*, 549 U.S., at 517–518. The majority assumes, as do I, that these unlawful Forest Service procedures will lead to substantive actions, namely the sales of salvage timber on burned lands, that might not take place if the proper procedures were followed. But the majority then finds that the plaintiffs have not sufficiently demonstrated that these salvage-timber sales cause plaintiffs an actual injury, that is, harm to the recreational, esthetic, or other environmental interests of organization members. To put the matter in terms of my hypothetical statute, the majority holds that the plaintiff organizations, while showing that they have members who have used salvage-timber sale parcels in the past (i.e., parcels that the Service does not subject to the notice, comment, and appeal procedures required by law), have failed to show that they have members likely to use such parcels in the future.

II

How can the majority credibly claim that salvage-timber sales, and similar projects, are unlikely to harm the asserted interests of the members of these environmental groups? The majority apparently does so in part by arguing that the Forest Service actions are not "imminent" —a requirement more appropriately considered in the context of ripeness or the necessity of injunctive relief. See Ohio Forestry Ass'n, Inc. v. Sierra Club, 523 U.S. 726, 734 (1998). I concede that the Court has sometimes used the word "imminent" in the context of constitutional standing. But it has done so primarily to emphasize that the harm in question—the harm that was not "imminent" —was merely "conjectural" or "hypothetical" or otherwise speculative. Lujan v. Defenders of Wildlife, 504 U.S. 555, 560 (1992). Where the Court has directly focused upon the matter, i.e., where, as here, a plaintiff has already been subject to the injury it wishes to challenge, the Court has asked whether there is a *realistic likelihood* that the challenged future conduct will, in fact, recur and harm the plaintiff. That is what the Court said in Los Angeles v. Lyons, 461 U.S. 95 (1983), a case involving a plaintiff's attempt to enjoin police use of chokeholds. The Court wrote that the plaintiff, who had been subject to the unlawful chokehold in the past, would have had standing had he shown "a *realistic* threat" that reoccurrence of the challenged activity would cause him harm "in the reasonably near future." Id., at 107, n.7, 108 (emphasis added). Precedent nowhere suggests that the "realistic threat" standard contains identification requirements more stringent than the word "realistic" implies. See Blum v. Yaretsky, 457 U.S. 991, 1000 (1982).

How could the Court impose a stricter criterion? Would courts deny *standing* to a holder of a future interest in property who complains that a life tenant's waste of the land will almost inevitably hurt the value of his interest—though he will have no personal interest for several years into the future? Would courts deny *standing* to a landowner who complains that a neighbor's upstream dam constitutes a nuisance—even if the harm to his downstream property (while bound to occur) will not occur for several years? Would courts deny *standing* to an injured person seeking a protection order from future realistic (but nongeographically specific) threats of further attacks?

To the contrary, a threat of future harm may be realistic even where the plaintiff cannot specify precise times, dates, and GPS coordinates. Thus, we recently held that Massachusetts has *standing* to complain of a procedural failing, namely, EPA's failure properly to determine whether to restrict carbon dioxide emissions, even though that failing would create Massachusetts-based harm which (though likely to occur) might not occur for several decades. *EPA*, 549 U.S., at 522–523.

The Forest Service admits that it intends to conduct thousands of further salvage-timber sales and other projects exempted under the challenged regulations "in the reasonably near future." See Defendants' Motion to Clarify and Amend Judgment in No. CIV–F–03–6386–JKS–DLB (ED Cal.), pp. 13–14. How then can the Court deny that the plaintiffs have shown a "realistic" threat that the Forest Service will continue to authorize (without the procedures claimed necessary) salvage-timber sales, and other Forest Service projects, that adversely affect the recreational, esthetic, and environmental interests of the plaintiffs' members?

. . . . .

The Bensman affidavit does not say *which particular* sites will be affected by future Forest Service projects, but the Service itself has conceded that it will conduct thousands of exempted projects in the future. Why is more specificity needed to show a "realistic" threat that a project will impact land Bensman uses? To know, virtually for certain, that snow will fall in New England this winter is not to know the name of each particular town where it is bound to arrive. The law of standing does not require the latter kind of specificity. How could it? And Sierra Club v. Morton, 405 U.S. 727, on which the majority so heavily relies, involved plaintiffs who challenged (true, a "massive") development, but only on a single previously determined site, about 80 acres in size, in a portion of the forest with a "limited ... number of visitors." Id., at 728. The Court's unwillingness to infer harm to the Sierra Club's members there does not demand a similar unwillingness here, where the challenge is to procedures affecting "thousands" of sites, involving hundreds of times as much acreage, where the precise location of each may not yet be known. In *Sierra Club*, ibid., it may have been unreasonable simply to assume that members would suffer an "injury in fact." But here, given the very different factual circumstances, it is unreasonable to believe they would not.

Whatever doubt may remain is settled by the affidavits the plaintiffs submitted after the Burnt Ridge dispute was settled (while the other claims in the Complaint remained alive). The majority says it will not consider those affidavits because they were submitted "[a]fter the District Court had entered judgment." But the plaintiffs submitted the affidavits after judgment (in opposition to the Government's motion for a stay) because the Burnt Ridge dispute on which they had relied to show standing at the outset of suit had by that point been settled. No longer wishing to rely solely on evidence of their members' interest in that particular project, the plaintiff organizations submitted several other affidavits. Why describe this perfectly sensible response to the settlement of some of the Complaint's claims as a "retroactiv[e]" attempt to "me[e]t the challenge to their standing at the time of judgment" ? Ibid. In fact, the Government did not challenge standing until that point, so of course respondents (who all agree had standing at the outset) did not respond with affidavits until later—when their standing was challenged. This can hardly be characterized as an attempt to "resurrect and alter the outcome" in the case. Regardless, the Constitution does not bar the filing of further affidavits, nor does any statute. The Federal Rules of Civil Procedure contain no such bar. Indeed, those Rules provide a judge with liberal discretion to permit a plaintiff to amend a complaint—even after one dispute (of several) is settled. So why would they not permit the filing of affidavits—at least with the judge's permission? See Fed. Rule Civ. Proc. 15(d) ("The court may permit supplementation even though the original pleading is defective in stating a claim or defense").

The affidavits in question describe a number of then-pending Forest Service projects, all excluded from notice, comment, and appeal under the Forest Service regulations and all scheduled to take place on parcels that the plaintiff organizations' members use. . . .

These allegations and affidavits more than adequately show a "realistic threat" of injury to plaintiffs brought about by reoccurrence of the challenged conduct—conduct that the Forest Service thinks lawful and admits will reoccur. Many years ago the Ninth Circuit warned that a court should not "be blind to what must be necessarily known to every intelligent person." In re Wo Lee, 26 F. 471, 475 (1886). Applying that standard, I would find standing here.

* * *

I recognize that the Government raises other claims and bases upon which to deny standing or to hold that the case is not ripe for adjudication. I believe that these arguments are without merit. But because the majority does not discuss them here, I shall not do so either.

With respect, I dissent.

———

THE FEDERAL DECLARATORY JUDGMENT ACT
28 U.S.C. § 2201. Creation of remedy

(a) In a case of actual controversy within its jurisdiction, except with respect to Federal taxes other than actions brought under section 7428 of the Internal Revenue Code of 1986 . . ., any court of the United States, upon the filing of an appropriate pleading, may declare the rights and other legal relations of any interested party seeking such declaration, whether or not further relief is or could be sought. Any such declaration shall have the force and effect of a final judgment or decree and shall be reviewable as such.

. . . . .

28 U.S.C. § 2202. Further relief

Further necessary or proper relief based on a declaratory judgment or decree may be granted, after reasonable notice and hearing, against any adverse party whose rights have been determined by such judgment.[45]

Aetna Life Ins. Co. v. Haworth

Supreme Court of the United States, 1937.
300 U.S. 227, 57 S.Ct. 461, 81 L.Ed. 617.

Suit by the Aetna Life Insurance Company of Hartford, Connecticut, against Edwin P. Haworth and another.

■ MR. CHIEF JUSTICE HUGHES delivered the opinion of the Court.

The question presented is whether the District Court had jurisdiction of this suit under the Federal Declaratory Judgment Act.

.   .   .   .   .

The question arises upon the plaintiff's complaint which was dismissed by the District Court upon the ground that it did not set forth a "controversy" in the constitutional sense and hence did not come within the legitimate scope of the statute....

From the complaint it appears that plaintiff is an insurance company which had issued to the defendant Edwin P. Haworth five policies of insurance upon his life, the defendant Cora M. Haworth being named as beneficiary. The complaint set forth the terms of the policies. They contained various provisions which for the present purpose it is unnecessary fully to particularize. It is sufficient to observe that they all provided for certain benefits in the event that the insured became totally and permanently disabled. In one policy, for $10,000, issued in 1911, the company agreed, upon receiving the requisite proof of such disability and without further payment of premiums, to pay the sum insured, and dividend additions, in twenty annual installments, or a life annuity as specified, in full settlement. In four other policies issued in 1921, 1928, and 1929, respectively, for amounts aggregating $30,000, plaintiff agreed upon proof of such disability to waive further payment of premiums, promising in one of the policies to pay a specified amount monthly and in the other three to continue the life insurance in force. By these four policies the benefits to be payable at death, and the cash and loan values to be available, were to be the same whether the premiums were paid or were waived by reason of the described disability.

The complaint alleges that in 1930 and 1931 the insured ceased to pay premiums on the four policies last mentioned and claimed the disability benefits as stipulated. He continued to pay premiums on the first mentioned policy until 1934 and then claimed disability benefits. These claims,

---

45. [See also Civil Rule 57.]

which were repeatedly renewed, were presented in the form of affidavits accompanied by certificates of physicians. . . .

. . . . .

Plaintiff alleges that consistently and at all times it has refused to recognize these claims of the insured and has insisted that all the policies had lapsed according to their terms by reason of the nonpayment of premiums, the insured not being totally and permanently disabled at any of the times to which his claims referred. Plaintiff further states that taking loans into consideration four of the policies have no value and the remaining policy (the one first mentioned) has a value of only $45 as extended insurance. If, however, the insured has been totally and permanently disabled as he claims, the five policies are in full force, the plaintiff is now obliged to pay the accrued installments of cash disability benefits for which two of the policies provide, and the insured has the right to claim at any time cash surrender values accumulating by reason of the provisions for waiver of premiums, or at his death, Cora M. Haworth, as beneficiary, will be entitled to receive the face of the policies less the loans thereon.

Plaintiff thus contends that there is an actual controversy with defendants as to the existence of the total and permanent disability of the insured and as to the continuance of the obligations asserted despite the nonpayment of premiums. Defendants have not instituted any action wherein the plaintiff would have an opportunity to prove the absence of the alleged disability and plaintiff points to the danger that it may lose the benefit of evidence through disappearance, illness, or death of witnesses; and meanwhile, in the absence of a judicial decision with respect to the alleged disability, the plaintiff in relation to these policies will be compelled to maintain reserves in excess of $20,000.

The complaint asks for a decree that the four policies be declared to be null and void by reason of lapse for nonpayment of premiums and that the obligation upon the remaining policy be held to consist solely in the duty to pay the sum of $45 upon the death of the insured, and for such further relief as the exigencies of the case may require.

First. The Constitution (article 3, § 2) limits the exercise of the judicial power to "cases" and "controversies." "The term 'controversies,' if distinguishable at all from 'cases,' is so in that it is less comprehensive than the latter, and includes only suits of a civil nature." Per Mr. Justice Field In Re Pacific Railway Commission (C.C.), 32 F. 241, 255, citing Chisholm v. Georgia, 2 Dall. [2 U.S.] 419, 431. See Muskrat v. United States, 219 U.S. 346, 356, 357; Old Colony Trust Co. v. Commissioner, 279 U.S. 716, 723, 724. The Declaratory Judgment Act of 1934, in its limitation to "cases of actual controversy," manifestly has regard to the constitutional provision and is operative only in respect to controversies which are such in the constitutional sense. The word "actual" is one of emphasis rather than of definition. Thus the operation of the Declaratory Judgment Act is procedural only. In providing remedies and defining procedure in relation to cases and controversies in the constitutional sense the Congress is acting within its delegated power over the jurisdiction of the federal courts which the Congress is authorized to establish. Turner v. Bank of North America, 4 Dall. [4 U.S.] 8, 10; Kline v. Burke Construction Co., 260 U.S. 226, 234. Exercising this control of practice and procedure the Congress is not confined to traditional forms or traditional remedies. The judiciary clause of the Constitution "did not crystallize into changeless form the procedure of 1789 as the only possible means for presenting a case or controversy otherwise cognizable by the federal courts." Nashville, Chattanooga & St. Louis R. Co. v. Wallace, 288 U.S. 249, 264. In dealing with methods within its sphere of remedial action the Congress may create and improve as well as abolish or restrict. The Declaratory Judgment Act must be deemed to fall within this ambit of congressional power, so far as it authorizes relief which is consonant with the exercise of the judicial function in the determination of controversies to which under the Constitution the judicial power extends.

A "controversy" in this sense must be one that is appropriate for judicial determination. Osborn v. Bank of United States, 9 Wheat. [22 U.S.] 738, 819. A justiciable controversy is thus distinguished from a difference or dispute of a hypothetical or abstract character; from one that is academic or moot. United States v. Alaska S.S. Co., 253 U.S. 113, 116.[46] The controversy must be definite and concrete, touching the legal relations of parties having adverse legal interests. South Spring Hill Gold Min. Co. v. Amador Medean Gold Min. Co., 145 U.S. 300, 301;[47] Fairchild v. Hughes, 258 U.S. 126, 129; Massachusetts v. Mellon, 262 U.S. 447, 487, 488. It must be a real and substantial controversy admitting of specific relief through a decree of a conclusive character, as distinguished from an opinion advising what the law would be upon a hypothetical state of facts. See *Muskrat v. United States*, supra;[48] Texas v. Interstate Commerce Commission, 258 U.S.

[46. Appeal from an injunction against the enforcement of an order of the Interstate Commerce Commission prescribing the terms of carriers' bills of lading. It appeared that pending the appeal new legislation required changes in the form of the bills of lading; held, the appeal is dismissed as "moot," however convenient it might be to both parties to have decided the question of power of the Commission to make such orders.]

[47. Dispute between two corporations over title to mining property; after appeal, the two corporations came under control of same majority stockholders; held, the Supreme Court would not decide the appeal; litigation has ceased to be a "controversy" despite fact that the parties desire decision so that rights of minority stockholders may be ascertained.]

[48. Suit in the Court of Claims, authorized by a special Act of Congress, by certain Indians to test the validity of legislation purporting to increase the number of Indians entitled to share in the distribution of certain lands and funds. The Court held that there was no "case" or "controversy," saying that the United States, though made defendant to the action as provided in the authorizing legislation, had no interest adverse to the claimants. The Court also observed that "in a legal sense the judgment could not be executed, and amounts in fact to no more than an expression of opinion upon the validity of the acts in question."

The requirement set forth in *Aetna*—that a declaratory-judgment case be one in which the controversy would admit "of specific relief through a decree of a conclusive character" — was not met where a condemned inmate sought a declaratory judgment as to which of two provisions of AEDPA (discussed infra pp. 658, 702–706 would govern his as-yet unfiled

158, 162; New Jersey v. Sargent, 269 U.S. 328, 339, 340; Liberty Warehouse Co. v. Grannis, 273 U.S. 70; New York v. Illinois, 274 U.S. 488, 490; Willing v. Chicago Auditorium Association, 277 U.S. 274, 289, 290;[49] Arizona v. California, 283 U.S. 423, 463, 464; Alabama v. Arizona, 291 U.S. 286, 291; United States v. West Virginia, 295 U.S. 463, 474, 475;[50] Ashwander v. Tennessee Valley Authority, 297 U.S. 288, 324. Where there is such a concrete case admitting of an immediate and definitive determination of the legal rights of the parties in an adversary proceeding upon the facts alleged, the judicial function may be appropriately exercised although the adjudication of the rights of the litigants may not require the award of process or the payment of damages. Nashville, Chattanooga & St. Louis R. Co. v. Wallace, [288 U.S. 249,] 263;[51] Tutun v. United States, 270 U.S. 568, 576, 577;[52] Fidelity National Bank & Trust Co. v. Swope, 274 U.S. 123, 132;

---

habeas petition, and the suit was held nonjusticiable under Article III. Calderon v. Ashmus, 523 U.S. 740 (1998).

The "actual controversy" requirement of the Declaratory Judgment Act does not require a licensee under a patent to breach or terminate the license agreement before seeking a declaratory judgment that the underlying patent is invalid, unenforceable, or not infringed. MedImmune, Inc. v. Genentech, Inc., 549 U.S. 118, 127 S.Ct. 764 (2007).]

[**49.** Bill by lessee of real estate, on which it has erected an auditorium, seeking to establish that it has the right under lease to tear down the auditorium and replace it with a modern office building. Held, no federal jurisdiction. Court says that suit is not a bill to remove a cloud upon title, since the doubt as to plaintiff's right under the lease arises on the face of the instruments by which the plaintiff derives title. Brandeis, J.: "It is true that the plight of which the association complains cannot be remedied by an action at law. But it does not follow that the association may have relief in equity in a federal court. What the plaintiff seeks is simply a declaratory judgment. To grant that relief is beyond the power conferred upon the federal judiciary."

Stone, J., concurring in the result: "There is certainly no 'case or controversy' before us requiring an opinion on the power of Congress to incorporate the declaratory judgment into our federal jurisprudence. And the determination now made seems to me very similar itself to a declaratory judgment to the effect that we could not constitutionally be authorized to give such judgments—but is, in addition, prospective, unasked, and unauthorized under any statute."]

[**50.** Suit by United States to enjoin West Virginia, which had issued a license to a power company to build the Hawks' Nest Dam across the New River, from interfering with Federal power over a navigable stream. Dismissed for want of a justiciable controversy. Stone, J.: "The control of navigation by the United States may be threatened by the imminent construction of the dam, but not by permission to construct it.

"No effort is made by the government to sustain the bill under the Declaratory Judgment Act of June 14, 1934, c. 512, 48 Stat. 955. It is enough that that act is applicable only 'in cases of actual controversy.' It does not purport to alter the character of the controversies which are the subject of the judicial power under the Constitution."]

[**51.** Appeal to United States Supreme Court from judgment in taxpayer's proceeding in state court under Tennessee Declaratory Judgments Act to have tax on gasoline declared invalid, held to present a "case or controversy" within Federal appellate jurisdiction; opinion by Stone, J., reviewing the cases.]

[**52.** Held, a naturalization proceeding in the Federal court is a "case or controversy," to which "the United States is always a possible adverse party," although a certificate granted may be canceled in subsequent proceedings, and a denial of the petition may not preclude another application.]

Old Colony Trust Company v. Commissioner, [279 U.S. 716,] 725.[53] And as it is not essential to the exercise of the judicial power that an injunction be sought, allegations that irreparable injury is threatened are not required. Nashville, Chattanooga & St. Louis R. Co. v. Wallace, [288 U.S. 249,] 264.

With these principles governing the application of the Declaratory Judgment Act, we turn to the nature of the controversy, the relation and interests of the parties, and the relief sought in the instant case.

Second. There is here a dispute between parties who face each other in an adversary proceeding. The dispute relates to legal rights and obligations arising from the contracts of insurance. The dispute is definite and concrete, not hypothetical or abstract. Prior to this suit, the parties had taken adverse positions with respect to their existing obligations. Their contentions concerned the disability benefits which were to be payable upon prescribed conditions. On the one side, the insured claimed that he had become totally and permanently disabled and hence was relieved of the obligation to continue the payment of premiums and was entitled to the stipulated disability benefits and to the continuance of the policies in force. The insured presented this claim formally, as required by the policies. It was a claim of a present, specific right. On the other side, the company made an equally definite claim that the alleged basic fact did not exist, that the insured was not totally and permanently disabled and had not been relieved of the duty to continue the payment of premiums that in consequence the policies had lapsed, and that the company was thus freed from its obligation either to pay disability benefits or to continue the insurance in force. Such a dispute is manifestly susceptible of judicial determination. It calls, not for an advisory opinion upon a hypothetical basis, but for an adjudication of present right upon established facts.

[53. Certified question from the Circuit Court of Appeals to determine its jurisdiction to entertain, as required by Act of Congress, a petition to review a decision of the Board of Tax Appeals.

"The Board of Tax Appeals is not a court. It is an executive or administrative board, upon the decision of which the parties are given an opportunity to base a petition for review to the courts after the administrative inquiry of the Board has been had and decided.

"It is next suggested that there is no adequate finality provided in respect to the action of these courts. In the first place, it is not necessary, in order to constitute a judicial judgment, that there should be both a determination of the rights of the litigants and also power to issue formal execution to carry the judgment into effect, in the way that judgments for money or for the possession of land usually are enforced. A judgment is sometimes regarded as properly enforceable through the executive departments instead of through an award of execution by this Court, where the effect of the judgment is to establish the duty of the department to enforce it. La Abra Silver Mining Co. v. United States, 175 U.S. 423. The case of Fidelity National Bank & Trust Co. v. Swope, 274 U.S. 123, 132, shows clearly that there are instances where the award of execution is not an indispensable element of a constitutional case or controversy. In that decision there are collected familiar examples of judicial proceedings resulting in a final adjudication of the rights of litigants without it.

"But, even if a formal execution be required, we think power to resort to it is clearly shown with respect to the enforcement of the action of the courts here involved by sections 1001 to 1005 ...."]

That the dispute turns upon questions of fact does not withdraw it, as the respondent seems to contend, from judicial cognizance. The legal consequences flow from the facts and it is the province of the courts to ascertain and find the facts in order to determine the legal consequences. That is everyday practice. Equally unavailing is respondent's contention that the dispute relates to the existence of a "mutable fact" and a "changeable condition—the state of the insured's health." The insured asserted a total and permanent disability occurring prior to October, 1930, and continuing thereafter. Upon that ground he ceased to pay premiums. His condition at the time he stopped payment, whether he was then totally and permanently disabled so that the policies did not lapse, is not a "mutable" but a definite fact. It is a controlling fact which can be finally determined and which fixes rights and obligations under the policies. If it were found that the insured was not totally and permanently disabled when he ceased to pay premiums and hence was in default, the effect of that default and the consequent right of the company to treat the policies as lapsed could be definitely and finally adjudicated. If it were found that he was totally and permanently disabled as he claimed, the duty of the company to pay the promised disability benefits and to maintain the policies in force could likewise be adjudicated. There would be no difficulty in either event in passing a conclusive decree applicable to the facts found and to the obligations of the parties corresponding to those facts. If the insured made good his claim, the decree establishing his right to the disability benefits, and the continuance of the policies in force during the period of the proved disability, would be nonetheless final and conclusive as to the matters thus determined even though a different situation might later arise in the event of his recovery from that disability and his failure after that recovery to comply with the requirements of the policies. Such a contention would present a distinct subject matter.

If the insured had brought suit to recover the disability benefits currently payable under two of the policies there would have been no question that the controversy was of a justiciable nature, whether or not the amount involved would have permitted its determination in a federal court. Again, on repudiation by the insurer of liability in such a case and insistence by the insured that the repudiation was unjustified because of his disability, the insured would have "such an interest in the preservation of the contracts that he might maintain a suit in equity to declare them still in being." Burnet v. Wells, 289 U.S. 670, 680; Cohen v. New York Life Insurance Co., 50 N.Y. 610, 624, 10 Am.Rep. 522; *Fidelity National Bank & Trust Co. v. Swope*, supra. But the character of the controversy and of the issue to be determined is essentially the same whether it is presented by the insured or by the insurer. Whether the District Court may entertain such a suit by the insurer, when the controversy as here is between citizens of different States or otherwise is within the range of the federal judicial power, is for the Congress to determine. It is the nature of the controversy, not the method of its presentation or the particular party who presents it, that is determinative. See Gully v. Interstate Natural Gas Co. (C.C.A.Miss.) 82 F.2d 145, 149; Travelers Insurance Co. v. Helmer (D.C.Ga.) 15 F.Supp.

355, 356; New York Life Insurance Co. v. London (D.C.Mass.) 15 F.Supp. 586, 589.

We have no occasion to deal with questions that may arise in the progress of the cause, as the complaint has been dismissed in limine. Questions of burden of proof or mode of trial have not been considered by the courts below and are not before us.

Our conclusion is that the complaint presented a controversy to which the judicial power extends and that authority to hear and determine it has been conferred upon the District Court by the Declaratory Judgment Act. The decree is reversed and the cause is remanded for further proceedings in conformity with this opinion.

Reversed.

Golden v. Zwickler

Supreme Court of the United States, 1969.
394 U.S. 103, 89 S.Ct. 956, 22 L.Ed.2d 113.

■ Mr. Justice Brennan delivered the opinion of the Court.

This case was here before as Zwickler v. Koota, 389 U.S. 241 (1967). We there held that the three-judge District Court for the Eastern District of New York erred in abstaining from deciding whether Zwickler, appellee in the instant case, was entitled to a declaratory judgment respecting the constitutionality of New York Penal Law, McKinney's Consol.Laws, c. 40, § 781–b, now New York Election Law, McKinney's Consol.Laws, c. 17, § 457, and we remanded to the District Court for a determination of that question. Section 781–b made it a crime to distribute anonymous literature in connection with an election campaign. Zwickler had been convicted of violating this provision by distributing anonymous handbills in connection with the 1964 congressional election. That conviction was reversed, on state law grounds, by the New York Supreme Court, Appellate Term. The New York Court of Appeals affirmed in 1965 and filed a memorandum which stated that constitutional questions had not been reached. People v. Zwickler, 16 N.Y.2d 1069, 266 N.Y.S.2d 140, 213 N.E.2d 467. A few months thereafter, on April 22, 1966, Zwickler brought this suit.

The complaint sets forth the facts regarding the prosecution and its termination. A congressman standing for re-election in 1964 was criticized in the anonymous handbill for opposing two amendments to the 1964 Foreign Aid bill. The complaint alleged that the congressman "will become a candidate in 1966 for reelection ... and has been a political figure and public official for many years," and that Zwickler "desires and intends to distribute ... at the place where he had previously done so and at various places in said [Kings] county, the anonymous leaflet herein described ... and similar anonymous leaflets ... at any time during the election campaign of 1966 and in subsequent election campaigns or in connection with any election of party officials, nomination for public office and party position that may occur subsequent to said election campaign of 1966."

It was disclosed on the argument of *Zwickler v. Koota* in this Court that the congressman had left the House of Representatives for a place on the Supreme Court of New York. We deemed this development relevant to the question whether the prerequisites for the issuance of a declaratory judgment were present. We noted, however, that, probably because of the decision to abstain, the parties had not addressed themselves to, and the District Court had not adjudicated, that question. 389 U.S., at 244, n. 3. Therefore, we directed that on the remand "appellant [Zwickler] must establish the elements governing the issuance of a declaratory judgment." Id., at 252, n. 15; see also id., at 252–253, n. 16.

The District Court hearing on the remand was limited largely to the oral argument of counsel, and no testimony was taken concerning the existence of the elements governing the issuance of a declaratory judgment. The three-judge court held that the prerequisites of a declaratory judgment had been established by the facts alleged in the complaint, and that the fact that the congressman who was the original target of the handbills would not again stand for re-election did not affect the question. The Court said:

> "The attempt of defendant to moot the controversy and thus to abort a declaration of constitutional invalidity by citing the circumstance that the Congressman concerning whom the Zwickler handbill was published has since become a New York State Supreme Court Justice must fail. When this action was initiated the controversy was genuine, substantial and immediate, even though the date of the election to which the literature was pertinent had already passed.
>
>   . . . . .
>
> ... "The fortuitous circumstance that the candidate in relation to whose bid for office the anonymous handbill was circulated had, while vindication inched tediously forward, removed himself from the role of target of the 1964 handbill does not moot the plaintiff's further and far broader right to a general adjudication of unconstitutionality his complaint prays for. We see no reason to question Zwickler's assertion that the challenged statute currently impinges upon his freedom of speech by deterring him from again distributing anonymous handbills. His own interest as well as that of others who would with like anonymity practice free speech in a political environment persuade us to the justice of his plea." 290 F.Supp. 244, 248, 249 (1968).

We noted probable jurisdiction ... 393 U.S. 818 (1968). We reverse.

The District Court erred in holding that Zwickler was entitled to declaratory relief if the elements essential to that relief existed "[w]hen this action was initiated." The proper inquiry was whether a "controversy" requisite to relief under the Declaratory Judgment Act existed at the time of the hearing on the remand.[54] We now undertake that inquiry.

---

54. The Declaratory Judgment Act, 28 U.S.C. § 2201, expressly provides: "*In a case of actual controversy* within its jurisdiction ... any court of the United States, upon the filing of an

"[T]he federal courts established pursuant to Article III of the Constitution do not render advisory opinions. For adjudication of constitutional issues 'concrete legal issues, presented in actual cases, not abstractions' are requisite. This is as true of declaratory judgments as any other field." United Public Workers of America (C.I.O.) v. Mitchell, 330 U.S. 75, 89 (1947). "The difference between an abstract question and a 'controversy' contemplated by the Declaratory Judgment Act is necessarily one of degree, and it would be difficult, if it would be possible, to fashion a precise test for determining in every case whether there is such a controversy. Basically, the question in each case is whether the facts alleged, under all the circumstances, show that there is a substantial controversy, between parties having adverse legal interests, of sufficient immediacy and reality to warrant the issuance of a declaratory judgment." Maryland Casualty Co. v. Pacific Coal & Oil Co., 312 U.S. 270, 273 (1941).

We think that under all the circumstances of the case the fact that it was most unlikely that the congressman would again be a candidate for Congress precluded a finding that there was "sufficient immediacy and reality" here.[55] The allegations of the complaint focus upon the then forthcoming 1966 election when, it was alleged, the congressman would again stand for re-election. The anonymous handbills which the complaint identified as to be distributed in the 1966 and subsequent elections were the 1964 handbill and "similar anonymous leaflets." On the record therefore the only supportable conclusion was that Zwickler's sole concern was literature relating to the congressman and his record. Since the New York statute's prohibition of anonymous handbills applies only to handbills directly pertaining to election campaigns, and the prospect was neither real nor immediate of a campaign involving the congressman, it was wholly conjectural that another occasion might arise when Zwickler might be prosecuted for distributing the handbills referred to in the complaint. His assertion in his brief that the former congressman "can be a candidate for Congress again" is hardly a substitute for evidence that this is a prospect of "immediacy and reality." Thus the record is in sharp contrast to that in Evers v. Dwyer, 358 U.S. 202 (1958), relied upon by the District Court.

It was not enough to say, as did the District Court, that nevertheless Zwickler has a "further and far broader right to a general adjudication of unconstitutionality ... [in] [h]is own interest as well as that of others who would with like anonymity practice free speech in a political environment ...." The constitutional question, First Amendment or otherwise, must be presented in the context of a specific live grievance. In *United Public Workers of America (C.I.O.) v. Mitchell*, supra, at 89–90, we said:

> "The power of courts, and ultimately of this Court to pass upon the constitutionality of acts of Congress arises only when the interests

---

appropriate pleading, may declare the rights and other legal relations of any interested party seeking such declaration, whether or not further relief is or could be sought." (Emphasis added.)

55. The former congressman's term of office as a State Supreme Court Justice is 14 years.

of litigants require the use of this judicial authority for their protection against actual interference. A hypothetical threat is not enough."

The same is true of the power to pass upon the constitutionality of state statutes. No federal court, whether this Court or a District Court, has "jurisdiction to pronounce any statute, either of a state or of the United States, void, because irreconcilable with the constitution, *except as it is called upon to adjudge the legal rights of litigants in actual controversies.*" Liverpool, N.Y. and Phil. S.S. Co. v. Commissioners, 113 U.S. 33, 39 (1885). (Emphasis added.) See also United States v. Raines, 362 U.S. 17, 21 (1960). The express limitation of the Declaratory Judgment Act to cases "of actual controversy" is explicit recognition of this principle.

We conclude that Zwickler did not establish the existence at the time of the hearing on the remand of the elements governing the issuance of a declaratory judgment, and therefore that the District Court should have dismissed his complaint. We accordingly intimate no view upon the correctness of the District Court's holding as to the constitutionality of the New York statute. The judgment of the District Court is reversed, and the case is remanded with direction to enter a new judgment dismissing the complaint.

It is so ordered.

Judgment of District Court reversed and case remanded with direction.[56]

[56. See also Samuels v. Mackell, 401 U.S. 66 (1971), reprinted infra p. 618; Dickson, Declaratory Remedies and Constitutional Change, 24 Vand.L.Rev. 257 (1971); 10A Wright, Miller & Kane, Federal Practice and Procedure: Civil 3d § 2763 (1998).

A more hospitable attitude toward declaratory judgments is expressed in Steffel v. Thompson, 415 U.S. 452 (1974), reprinted infra p. 621.

In Wilton v. Seven Falls Co., 515 U.S. 277 (1995), reprinted infra p. 595, the Court held that the broad discretion vested in the district courts by the Declaratory Judgment Act, 28 U.S.C. § 2201, was not limited by the "exceptional circumstances" standard for *Colorado River* abstention. The Court thus upheld a district court's decision to stay a federal declaratory-judgment action in order to permit the dispute to be litigated to judgment in a parallel state-court action between the same parties.

On the question of mootness in general, compare Super Tire Engineering Co. v. McCorkle, 416 U.S. 115 (1974), with DeFunis v. Odegaard, 416 U.S. 312 (1974). See also County of Los Angeles v. Davis, 440 U.S. 625 (1979). See generally Lee, Deconstitutionalizing Justiciability: The Example of Mootness, 105 Harv.L.Rev. 605 (1992) Nichol, Moot Cases, Chief Justice Rehnquist, and the Supreme Court, 22 U.Conn.L.Rev. 703 (1990); 13A Wright, Miller & Cooper, Federal Practice and Procedure: Jurisdiction 2d §§ 3533–3533.11 (1984); Chemerinsky, Federal Jurisdiction § 2.5 (5th ed.2007).

In Spencer v. Kemna, 523 U.S. 1 (1998), discussed supra p. 32–33, n. 15, the Court reconceptualized the Article III nonjusticiability of a moot controversy in terms of the complaining party's lack of any continuing injury in fact, and hence lack of standing to sue.

In Arizonans for Official English v. Arizona, 520 U.S. 43, 67–75 (1997), the Court held that the litigation became moot upon the voluntary resignation from state employment of the individual who, as the sole plaintiff and without seeking to represent a class, had challenged the constitutionality of a state ballot initiative that might affect her performance of her

Palmore v. United States

Supreme Court of the United States, 1973.
411 U.S. 389, 93 S.Ct. 1670, 36 L.Ed.2d 342.

■ MR. JUSTICE WHITE delivered the opinion of the Court.

. . . [T]his case requires us to decide whether a defendant charged with a felony under the District of Columbia Code may be tried by a judge who does not have protection with respect to tenure and salary under Art. III of the Constitution. We hold that under its Art. I, § 8, cl. 17, power to legislate for the District of Columbia, Congress may provide for trying local criminal cases before judges who, in accordance with the District of Columbia Code, are not accorded life tenure and protection against reduction in salary. In this respect, the position of the District of Columbia defendant is similar to that of the citizen of any of the 50 States when charged with violation of a state criminal law: Neither has a federal constitutional right to be tried before judges with tenure and salary guarantees.

. . . . .

[Palmore was convicted in the Superior Court of the District of Columbia of carrying an unregistered pistol after having been convicted of a felony, in violation of the District of Columbia Code. The judges of the Superior Court are appointed by the President and serve for terms of 15 years. His conviction was affirmed by the District of Columbia Court of Appeals, a local court not to be confused with the United States Court of Appeals for the District of Columbia Circuit.]

III

Art. I, § 8, cl. 17, of the Constitution provides that Congress shall have power "[t]o exercise exclusive Legislation in all Cases whatsoever, over" the District of Columbia. The power is plenary. Not only may statutes of Congress of otherwise nationwide application be applied to the District of Columbia, but Congress may also exercise all the police and regulatory powers which a state legislature or municipal government would have in legislating for state or local purposes. Congress "may exercise within the District all legislative powers that the legislature of a state might exercise within the State, and may vest and distribute the judicial authority in and among courts and magistrates, and regulate judicial proceedings before them, as it may think fit, so long as it does not contravene any provision of the constitution of the United States." Capital Traction Co. v. Hof, 174 U.S. 1, 5 (1899). This has been the characteristic view in this Court of congressional powers with respect to the District. It is apparent that the power of Congress under Clause 17 permits it to legislate for the District in

duties as a state employee. In light of the serious federalism concerns posed by the course of the litigation below, in which novel state legislation had been construed by federal courts prior to its consideration by state courts, the Court decided that the mootness of the litigation required "vacatur down the line," wiping from the books even unappealed proceedings that had occurred before the case became moot.]

a manner with respect to subjects that would exceed its powers, or at least would be very unusual, in the context of national legislation enacted under other powers delegated to it under Art. I, § 8. See Gibbons v. District of Columbia, 116 U.S. 404, 408 (1886).

Pursuant to its Clause 17 authority, Congress has from time to time enacted laws that compose the District of Columbia Code. The 1970 Reorganization Act amended the Code by creating the Superior Court of the District of Columbia and the District of Columbia Court of Appeals, the courts being expressly "established pursuant to article I of the Constitution." D.C.Code Ann. §§ 11–101(2) (Supp. V, 1972). . . .

. . . . .

It was under the judicial power conferred on the Superior Court by the 1970 Reorganization Act that Palmore was convicted of violation of § 22–3204 of the District of Columbia Code (1967). The conviction was clearly within the authority granted Congress by Art. I, § 8, cl. 17, unless, as Palmore contends, Art. III of the Constitution requires that prosecutions for District of Columbia felonies must be presided over by a judge having the tenure and salary protections provided by Art. III. Palmore's argument is straightforward: Art. III vests the "judicial Power" of the United States in courts with judges holding office during good behavior and whose salary cannot be diminished; the "judicial Power" that these courts are to exercise "shall extend to all Cases, in Law and Equity, arising under this Constitution, the Laws of the United States, and Treaties made, or which shall be made, under their Authority . . ." ; the District of Columbia Code, having been enacted by Congress, is a law of the United States; his prosecution for violation of § 22–3204 of the Code is therefore a case arising under the laws of the United States, involves an exercise of the "judicial Power" of the United States, and must therefore be tried by an Art. III judge.

This position ultimately rests on the proposition that an Art. III judge must preside over every proceeding in which a charge, claim, or defense is based on an Act of Congress or a law made under its authority. At the very least, it asserts that criminal offenses under the laws passed by Congress may not be prosecuted except in courts established pursuant to Art. III. In our view, however, there is no support for this view in either constitutional text or in constitutional history and practice.

Article III describes the judicial power as extending to all cases, among others, arising under the laws of the United States; but, aside from this Court, the power is vested "in such inferior Courts as the Congress may from time to time ordain and establish." The decision with respect to inferior federal courts, as well as the task of defining their jurisdiction, was left to the discretion of Congress. That body was not constitutionally required to create inferior Art. III courts to hear and decide cases within the judicial power of the United States, including those criminal cases arising under the laws of the United States. Nor, if inferior federal courts were created, was it required to invest them with all the jurisdiction it was authorized to bestow under Art. III. "[T]he judicial power of the United

States . . . is (except in enumerated instances, applicable exclusively to this court) dependent for its distribution and organization, and for the modes of its exercise, entirely upon the action of Congress, who possess the sole power of creating the tribunals (inferior to the Supreme Court) . . . and of investing them with jurisdiction either limited, concurrent, or exclusive, and of withholding jurisdiction from them in the exact degrees and character which to Congress may seem proper for the public good." Cary v. Curtis, 3 How. [44 U.S.] 236, 245 (1845). Congress plainly understood this, for until 1875 Congress refrained from providing the lower federal courts with general federal-question jurisdiction. Until that time, the state courts provided the only forum for vindicating many important federal claims. Even then, with exceptions, the state courts remained the sole forum for the trial of federal cases not involving the required jurisdictional amount, and for the most part retained concurrent jurisdiction of federal claims properly within the jurisdiction of the lower federal courts.

It was neither the legislative nor judicial view, therefore, that trial and decision of all federal questions were reserved for Art. III judges. Nor, more particularly has the enforcement of federal criminal law been deemed the exclusive province of federal Art. III courts. Very early in our history, Congress left the enforcement of selected federal criminal laws to state courts and to state court judges who did not enjoy the protections prescribed for federal judges in Art. III. See Warren, Federal Criminal Laws and the State Courts, 38 Harv.L.Rev. 545, 551–553, 570–572 (1925); F. Frankfurter & J. Landis, The Business of the Supreme Court 293 (1927); Note, Utilization of State Courts to Enforce Federal Penal and Criminal Statutes: Development in Judicial Federalism, 60 Harv.L.Rev. 966 (1947). More recently, this Court unanimously held that Congress could constitutionally require state courts to hear and decide Emergency Price Control Act cases involving the enforcement of federal penal laws; the fact "that Rhode Island has an established policy against enforcement by its courts of statutes of other states and the United States which it deems penal, cannot be accepted as a 'valid excuse.'" Testa v. Katt, 330 U.S. 386, 392 (1947). Although recognizing the contrary sentiments expressed in Prigg v. Pennsylvania, 16 Pet. [41 U.S.] 539, 615–616 (1842), and other cases, the sense of the *Testa* opinion was that it merely reflected longstanding constitutional decision and policy represented by such cases as Claflin v. Houseman, 93 U.S. 130 (1876), and Mondou v. New York, N.H. & H.R. Co., 223 U.S. 1 (1912).

It is also true that throughout our history, Congress has exercised its power under Art. IV to "make all needful Rules and Regulations respecting the Territory or other Property belonging to the United States" by creating territorial courts and manning them with judges appointed for a term of years. These courts have not been deemed subject to the strictures of Art. III, even though they characteristically enforced not only the civil and criminal laws of Congress applicable throughout the United States, but also the laws applicable only within the boundaries of the particular territory. Speaking for a unanimous Court in American Ins. Co. v. Canter, 1 Pet. [26 U.S.] 511 (1828), Mr. Chief Justice Marshall held that the territorial courts of Florida, although not Art. III courts, could hear and determine cases governed by the admiralty and maritime law that ordinarily could be heard only by Art. III judges. "[T]he same limitation does not extend to the territories. In legislating for them, Congress exercises the combined powers of the general, and of a state government." Id., at 546. This has been the consistent view of this Court. Territorial courts, therefore, have regularly tried criminal cases arising under the general laws of Congress, as well as those brought under territorial laws.

There is another context in which criminal cases arising under federal statutes are tried, and defendants convicted, in non-Art. III courts. Under its Art. I, § 8, cl. 14, power "[t]o make Rules for the Government and Regulation of the land and naval Forces," Congress has declared certain behavior by members of the Armed Forces to be criminal and provided for the trial of such cases by court-martial proceedings in the military mode, not by courts ordained and established under Art. III. Within their proper sphere, courts-martial are constitutional instruments to carry out congressional and executive will. Dynes v. Hoover, 20 How. [61 U.S.] 65, 79, 82 (1857). The "exigencies of military discipline require the existence of a special system of military courts in which not all of the specific procedural protections deemed essential in Art. III trials need apply," O'Callahan v. Parker, 395 U.S. 258, 261 (1969); and "the Constitution does not provide life tenure for those performing judicial functions in military trials," U.S. ex rel. Toth v. Quarles, 350 U.S. 11, 17 (1955).

"The same confluence of practical considerations that dictated the result in [*American Ins. Co. v. Canter*, supra], has governed the decision in later cases sanctioning the creation of other courts with judges of limited tenure," Glidden Co. v. Zdanok, 370 U.S. 530, 547 (1962), such as the Court of Private Land Claims, United States v. Coe, 155 U.S. 76, 85–86 (1894); the Choctaw and Chickasaw Citizenship Court, Stephens v. Cherokee Nation, 174 U.S. 445 (1899); Ex parte Joins, 191 U.S. 93 (1903); Wallace v. Adams, 204 U.S. 415 (1907); courts created in unincorporated districts outside the mainland, Downes v. Bidwell, 182 U.S. 244, 266–267 (1901); Balzac v. Porto Rico, 258 U.S., at 312–313, and the Consular Courts established by concessions from foreign countries, In re Ross, 140 U.S. 453, 464–465, 480 (1891).

IV

Whatever may be true in other instances, however, it is strongly argued that O'Donoghue v. United States, 289 U.S. 516 (1933), constrains us to hold that all of the courts of the District of Columbia must be deemed Art. III courts and that the judges presiding over them must be appointed to serve during their good behavior in accordance with the requirements of Art. III. *O'Donoghue* involved the question whether the judges of the District of Columbia's Supreme Court and Court of Appeals were constitutionally protected from having their salaries reduced by an Act of Congress. This Court, over three dissents and contrary to extensive prior dicta, see Ex parte Bakelite Corp., 279 U.S. 438, 450 (1929); Butterworth v. Hoe, 112

U.S. 50 (1884); Keller v. Potomac Electric Power Co., 261 U.S. 428 (1923); Federal Radio Comm'n v. General Electric Co., 281 U.S. 464 (1930), held that the two courts under consideration were constitutional courts exercising the judicial power of the United States and that the judges in question were not subject to the salary reduction legislation as they would have been had they been judges of legislative courts.

We cannot agree that *O'Donoghue* governs this case.[57] The District of Columbia courts there involved, the Supreme Court and the Court of Appeals, had authority not only in the District, but also over all those controversies, civil and criminal, arising under the Constitution and the statutes of the United States and having nationwide application. These courts, as this Court noted in its opinion, were "of equal rank and power with those of other inferior courts of the federal system...." *O'Donoghue*, supra, 289 U.S., at 534. Relying heavily on congressional intent, the Court considered that Congress, by consistently providing the judges of these courts with lifetime tenure, had indicated a "congressional practice from the beginning [which] recognize[d] a complete parallelism between the courts of the District [of Columbia] and the District and Circuit Courts of Appeals of the United States." Id., at 549. Moreover, these courts, constituted as they were, and being closer to the legislative department, "exercise a more extensive jurisdiction in cases affecting the operations of the general government and its various departments," id., at 535, and were the only courts within the District in which District inhabitants could exercise their "right to have their cases arising under the Constitution heard and determined by federal courts created under, and vested with the judicial power conferred by, Art. III." Id., at 540.

The case before us is a far cry from *O'Donoghue*. Here Congress has expressly created two systems of courts in the District. One of them is made up of the United States District Court for the District of Columbia and the United States Court of Appeals for the District of Columbia Circuit, which are constitutional courts manned by Art. III judges to which the citizens of the District must or may resort for consideration of those constitutional and statutory matters of general concern which so moved the Court in *O'Donoghue*. The other system is made up of strictly local courts, the Superior Court and the District of Columbia Court of Appeals. These courts were expressly created pursuant to the plenary Art. I power to

---

57. We should note here that in *Glidden Co. v. Zdanok*, supra, it was urged that Art. III forbade the assignment of a judge of the Court of Customs and Patent Appeals to try a criminal case arising under the District of Columbia Code. The Court of Appeals ruled that even if the judge in question was not an Art. III judge, Art. I, § 8, cl. 17, was sufficient authority for his assignment to try cases in the District. The United States there urged that this was true at least with respect to laws arising under the District of Columbia Code rather than under a law of national application. MR. JUSTICE HARLAN, for himself and JUSTICES BRENNAN and STEWART, found it unnecessary to reach this question, but considered it an open one, for he expressly reserved "intimating any view as to the correctness of the holding below ...." 370 U.S., at 538. Apparently, for him, *O'Donoghue* had not foreclosed the issue with respect to the trial of the criminal case under the District of Columbia Code. Mr. Justice Clark, for himself and the Chief Justice, also thought the question open. See id., at 589 n. 4.

legislate for the District of Columbia. D.C.Code Ann. § 11–101(2) (Supp. V, 1972), and to exercise the "powers of . . . a state government in all cases where legislation is possible." Stoutenburgh v. Hennick, 129 U.S. 141, 147 (1889).

The *O'Donoghue* Court had before it District of Columbia courts in which the consideration of "purely local affairs [was] obviously subordinate and incidental." *O'Donoghue,* supra, 289 U.S., at 539. Here, on the other hand, we have courts the focus of whose work is primarily upon cases arising under the District of Columbia Code and to other matters of strictly local concern. They handle criminal cases only under statutes that are applicable to the District of Columbia alone. *O'Donoghue* did not concern itself with courts like these, and it is not controlling here.

V

It is apparent that neither this Court nor Congress has read the Constitution as requiring every federal question arising under the federal law, or even every criminal prosecution for violating an Act of Congress, to be tried in an Art. III court before a judge enjoying lifetime tenure and protection against salary reduction. Rather, both Congress and this Court have recognized that state courts are appropriate forums in which federal questions and federal crimes may at times be tried; and that the requirements of Art. III, which are applicable where laws of national applicability and affairs of national concern are at stake, must in proper circumstances give way to accommodate plenary grants of power to Congress to legislate with respect to specialized areas having particularized needs and warranting distinctive treatment. Here, Congress reorganized the court system in the District of Columbia and established one set of courts in the District with Art. III characteristics and devoted to matters of national concern. It also created a wholly separate court system designed primarily to concern itself with local law and to serve as a local court system for a large metropolitan area.

From its own studies, Congress had concluded that there was a crisis in the judicial system of the District of Columbia, that case loads had become unmanageable, and that neither those matters of national concern nor those of strictly local cognizance were being promptly tried and disposed of by the existing court system. See, e.g., 115 Cong.Rec. 25538 (1969); 116 Cong.Rec. 8091–8092 (1970). The remedy in part, was to relieve the regular Art. III courts, that is, the United States District Court for the District of Columbia and the United States Court of Appeals for the District of Columbia Circuit, from the smothering responsibility for the great mass of litigation, civil and criminal, that inevitably characterizes the court system in a major city and to confine the work of those courts to that which, for the most part, they were designed to do, namely, to try cases arising under the Constitution and the nationally applicable laws of Congress. The other part of the remedy, equally essential, was to establish an entirely new court system with functions essentially similar to those of the local courts found in the 50 States of the Union with responsibility for trying and deciding those distinctively local controversies that arise under local law, including local criminal laws having little, if any, impact beyond the local jurisdiction. S.Rep. No. 91–405, pp. 1–3, 5, 18; H.R.Rep. No. 91–907, pp. 23–24, 33.

Furthermore, Congress, after careful consideration, determined that it preferred, and had the power to utilize, a local court system staffed by judges without lifetime tenure. S.Rep. No. 91–405, supra, at 17–18; H.R.Rep. No. 91–907, supra, at 44. Congress made a deliberate choice to create judgeships with terms of 15 years, D.C.Code Ann. § 11–1502 (Supp. V, 1972), and to subject judges in those positions to removal or suspension by a judicial commission under certain established circumstances. Id., §§ 11–1502, 11–1521 et seq. It was thought that such a system would be more workable and efficient in administering and discharging the work of a multifaceted metropolitan court system. See S.Rep. No. 91–405, supra, at 8–11; H.R.Rep. No. 91–907, supra, at 35–39.

In providing for fixed terms of office, Congress was cognizant of the fact that "virtually no State has provided" for tenure during good behavior, S.Rep. No. 91–405, supra, at 8, see H.R.Rep. No. 91–907, supra, at 38, the District of Columbia Court of Appeals noting that 46 of the 50 States have not provided life tenure for trial judges who hear felony cases, 290 A.2d, at 578 n. 12, and the provisions of the Act, with respect to court administration and to judicial removal and suspension, were considered by some as a model for the States. 115 Cong.Rec. 25538 (1969). See Hearings on H.R. 13689 and 12854 before Subcommittee No. 1 of the House Committee on the District of Columbia, 91st Cong., 1st Sess., pt. 1, pp. 69, 71 (1969).

We do not discount the importance attached to the tenure and salary provisions of Art. III, but we conclude that Congress was not required to provide an Art. III court for the trial of criminal cases arising under its laws applicable only within the District of Columbia. Palmore's trial in the Superior Court was authorized by Congress' Art. I power to legislate for the District in all cases whatsoever. Palmore was no more disadvantaged and no more entitled to an Art. III judge than any other citizen of any of the 50 States who is tried for a strictly local crime. Nor did his trial by a nontenured judge deprive him of due process of law under the Fifth Amendment any more than the trial of the citizens of the various States for local crimes by judges without protection as to tenure deprives them of due process of law under the Fourteenth Amendment.

The judgment of the District of Columbia Court of Appeals is affirmed.

So ordered.

Affirmed.

■ Mr. Justice Douglas, dissenting.

Appellant, indicted for carrying a dangerous weapon in violation of D.C.Code Ann. § 22–3204, was tried and convicted in the Superior Court of the District of Columbia, an Art. I court created by Congress under the District of Columbia Court Reform and Criminal Procedure Act of 1970, 84

Stat. 473. His timely objection is that he was tried, convicted, and sentenced by a court not established under Art. III.

The judges of the court that convicted him

—hold office for a term of fifteen years, not for life as do Art. III judges;

—unlike Art. III judges, their salaries are not protected from diminishment during their continuance in office;

—unlike Art. III judges, they can be removed from office by a five-member Commission through less formidable means of procedure than impeachment. While two of the five members must be lawyers (one a member of the District Bar in active practice for at least five of the ten years prior to his appointment and one an active or retired federal judge serving in the District) the other three may be laymen. One of the three must be a layman. D.C.Code Ann. § 11–1522 (Supp. V, 1972).

In other words, these Superior Court judges are not members of the independent judiciary which has been one of our proudest boasts, by reason of Art. III. The safeguards accorded Art. III judges were designed to protect litigants with unpopular or minority causes or litigants who belong to despised or suspect classes. The safeguards surround the judge and give him a measure of protection against the hostile press, the leftist or rightist demands of the party in power, the glowering looks of those in the top echelon in whose hands rest the power of reappointment.

In the Constitutional Convention of 1787 it was proposed that judges "may be removed by the Executive on the application by the Senate and House of Representatives." The proposal was defeated, only Connecticut voting for it. Wilson apparently expressed the common sentiment: "The Judges would be in a bad situation if made to depend on any gust of faction which might prevail in the two branches of our Government." [58]

Without the independence granted and enjoyed by Art. III judges, a federal judge could more easily become the tool of a ravenous Executive Branch. This idea was reflected in Reports by Congress in 1965 and 1966,[59] sponsoring a law that would give lifetime tenure to federal judges in Puerto Rico. The House Report stated:[60]

"... Federal litigants in Puerto Rico should not be denied the benefit of judges made independent by life tenure from the pressures of those who might influence his chances of reappointment, which benefits the Constitution guarantees to the litigants in all other Federal courts."

Art. I, § 8, cl. 17, of the Constitution provides: "The Congress shall have Power ... To exercise exclusive Legislation ... over such District ...

---

58. Madison, 2 Journal of the Federal Convention 257 (G. Hunt ed.1908). [The speaker was James Wilson of Pennsylvania.]

59. H.R.Rep. No. 135, 89th Cong., 1st Sess.; S.Rep. No. 1504, 89th Cong., 2d Sess.

60. H.R.Rep. No. 135, supra, at 2.

as may ... become the Seat of the Government of the United States ...."
This legislative power is plenary, giving Congress authority to establish the
method by which the District of Columbia will be governed, and to alter
from time to time the form of that government. District of Columbia v.
Thompson Co., 346 U.S. 100, 104–110.

Legislative courts may be given executive and administrative duties,
the examples being well known. But if they are given "judicial Power," as
are the judges of the present Superior Court of the District, those trials
have guarantees that are prescribed by the Constitution and Bill of
Rights....

Few, if any, of these guarantees, I assume, would be applicable to Art. I
tribunals exercising legislative or administrative functions. But are any of
them inapplicable in criminal prosecutions where the "judicial Power" of
the United States is exercised?

I have been unable to see how that is possible. Yet if those aspects of
"judicial Power," as the term is used in Art. III, are all applicable, how can
the requirements for an independent judiciary be made an exception? For it
is as clearly required by Art. III for any exercise of "judicial Power" as are
the other guarantees.

. . . . .

In O'Donoghue v. United States, 289 U.S. 516, the Court held unconstitutional an Act of Congress reducing the salaries of trial and appellate
judges in the District of Columbia. It held that inherent in the separation of
powers was the idea that "the acts of each shall never be controlled by, or
subjected, directly or indirectly, to, the coercive influence of either of the
other departments." Id., at 530. Since the District was formed of portions
of two of the original States, the Court concluded it was "not reasonable to
assume that the cession stripped them of these [rights, guarantees and
immunities of the Constitution], and that it was intended that at the very
seat of the national government the people should be less fortified by the
guaranty of an independent judiciary than in other parts of the Union." Id.,
at 540. The Court concluded that while Congress could not confer administrative or legislative functions on Art. III courts, it could grant such
functions to District courts by reason of Art. I. Id., at 546. But that power,
it held, may not be used "to destroy the operative effect of the judicial
clause within the District." Ibid. The present Act does precisely that. Hence
today we make a major retreat from O'Donoghue.

Much is made of the fact that many States (about three-fourths of
them) have their judges at all levels elected by the people. That was one of
the basic Jacksonian principles. But the principle governing federal judges
is strongly opposed.[61] ...

---

61. See Brown, The Rent in Our Judicial Armor, 10 Geo.Wash.L.Rev. 127 (1941); Hyde,
   Judges: Their Selection and Tenure, 22 N.Y.U.L.Q.Rev. 389 (1947); E. Haynes, Selection
   and Tenure of Judges (1944); Kurland, The Constitution and the Tenure of Federal Judges:
   Some Notes from History, 36 U.Chi.L.Rev. 665 (1969).

James Bryce, writing in 1888, said:

We take a great step backward today when we deprive our federal regime in the District of that judicial independence which helps insure fearless and even-handed dispensation of justice. No federal court exercising Art. III judicial power should be made a minion of any cabal that from accidents of politics comes into the ascendancy as an overlord of the District of Columbia. That effort unhappily succeeds today and is in disregard of one of our most cherished constitutional provisions.

. . . . . .

Manipulated judiciaries are common across the world, especially in Communist and fascist nations. The faith in freedom which we profess and which is opposed to those ideologies assumes today an ominous cast. It is ominous because it indirectly associates the causes of crime with the Bill of Rights rather than with the sociological factors of poverty caused by unemployment and disemployment, the abrasive political tactics used against minorities, the blight of narcotics and the like. Those who hold the gun at the heads of Superior Court judges can retaliate against those who respect the spirit of the Fourth Amendment and the Fifth Amendment and who stand firmly against the ancient practice of using the third degree to get confessions and who fervently believe that the end does not justify the means.

I would reverse the judgment below.[62]

————

"Any one of the three phenomena I have described—popular elections, short terms, and small salaries—would be sufficient to lower the character of the judiciary. Popular elections throw the choice into the hands of political parties, that is to say, of knots of wirepullers inclined to use every office as a means of rewarding political services, and garrisoning with grateful partisans posts which may conceivably become of political importance. Short terms ... oblige the judge to remember and keep on good terms with those who have made him what he is, and in whose hands his fortunes lie. They induce timidity, they discourage independence." 1 American Commonwealth, c. 42, p. 507 (3d ed.1905).

[62. See generally Wright & Kane, Federal Courts § 11 (6th ed.2002); Chemerinsky, Federal Jurisdiction §§ 4.1–4.5 (5th ed.2007).

In Northern Pipeline Const. Co. v. Marathon Pipe Line Co., 458 U.S. 50 (1982), a badly-fragmented Court held that 28 U.S.C. § 1471(b), as provided by the Bankruptcy Act of 1978, was unconstitutional insofar as it purported to allow bankruptcy judges, who served 14–year terms, were removable by the judicial council of the circuit, and whose salaries were not protected against diminution, to hear a state-created claim for damages for breach of contract and warranty brought on behalf of a company that had earlier filed a petition for reorganization under the Bankruptcy Act. See Wright & Kane, Federal Courts, at 58–61.

In United States v. Canel, 708 F.2d 894, 896 (3d Cir.1983), the court said that the *Northern Pipeline* decision "must realistically be read as a disavowal by the majority of some of the more expansive statements in Justice White's *Palmore* opinion respecting congressional power to dispense with Article III judges in sanctioning contexts," but held that it did not disturb the settled principle that in the territories Article I judges can sentence violators of federal criminal statutes. See generally Bator, The Constitution as Architecture: Legislative and Administrative Courts Under Article III, 65 Ind.L.J. 233 (1990); Brown, Article III as a Fundamental Value—The Demise of *Northern Pipeline* and Its Implications for Congression-

Boumediene v. Bush

Supreme Court of the United States, 2008.
553 U.S. 723, 128 S.Ct. 2229, 171 L.Ed.2d 41.

■ JUSTICE KENNEDY delivered the opinion of the Court.

Petitioners are aliens designated as enemy combatants and detained at the United States Naval Station at Guantanamo Bay, Cuba. There are others detained there, also aliens, who are not parties to this suit.

Petitioners present a question not resolved by our earlier cases relating to the detention of aliens at Guantanamo: whether they have the constitutional privilege of habeas corpus, a privilege not to be withdrawn except in conformance with the Suspension Clause, Art. I, § 9, cl. 2. We hold these petitioners do have the habeas corpus privilege. Congress has enacted a statute, the Detainee Treatment Act of 2005 (DTA), 119 Stat. 2739, that provides certain procedures for review of the detainees' status. We hold that those procedures are not an adequate and effective substitute for habeas corpus. Therefore § 7 of the Military Commissions Act of 2006 (MCA), 28 U.S.C. § 2241(e) (Supp.2007), operates as an unconstitutional suspension of the writ. We do not address whether the President has authority to detain these petitioners nor do we hold that the writ must issue. These and other questions regarding the legality of the detention are to be resolved in the first instance by the District Court.

I

Under the Authorization for Use of Military Force (AUMF), § 2(a), 115 Stat. 224, note following 50 U.S.C. § 1541 (2000 ed., Supp. V), the President is authorized "to use all necessary and appropriate force against those nations, organizations, or persons he determines planned, authorized, com-

---

al Power, 49 Ohio St.L.J. 55 (1988); Fallon, Of Legislative Courts, Administrative Agencies, and Article III, 101 Harv.L.Rev. 915 (1988).

It is not inconsistent with either the Federal Magistrates Act, 28 U.S.C. § 636(b)(1)(B) or with Article III for a district court to decide a motion for suppression of evidence on the basis of the record developed before a United States magistrate and the magistrate's proposed findings of fact and recommendations. United States v. Raddatz, 447 U.S. 667 (1980).

A magistrate may not preside over selection of a jury in a felony trial. Gomez v. United States, 490 U.S. 858 (1989). But the magistrate—or "magistrate judge," as those officers have been called since 1990—may preside if the parties consent. Peretz v. United States, 501 U.S. 923 (1991).

The validity of the 1979 amendment of the Magistrates Act, 28 U.S.C. § 636(c), allowing magistrates to conduct civil trials with the consent of all parties, was upheld in Pacemaker Diagnostic Clinic of America v. Instromedix, 725 F.2d 537 (9th Cir.1984), and in Wharton–Thomas v. United States, 721 F.2d 922 (3d Cir.1983). See Comment, The Boundaries of Article III: Delegation of Final Decisionmaking Authority to Magistrates, 52 U.Chi.L.Rev. 1032 (1985); Note, Federal Magistrates and the Principles of Article III, 97 Harv.L.Rev. 1947 (1984).

In Nguyen v. United States, 539 U.S. 69 (2003), a closely divided Court did not reach Article III issues in holding that 28 U.S.C. § 292(a) prohibited the temporary assignment of judges of the territorial courts of Guam and the Northern Mariana Islands to serve on panels of the United States Court of Appeals for the Ninth Circuit.]

mitted, or aided the terrorist attacks that occurred on September 11, 2001, or harbored such organizations or persons, in order to prevent any future acts of international terrorism against the United States by such nations, organizations or persons."

In Hamdi v. Rumsfeld, 542 U.S. 507 (2004), five Members of the Court recognized that detention of individuals who fought against the United States in Afghanistan "for the duration of the particular conflict in which they were captured, is so fundamental and accepted an incident to war as to be an exercise of the 'necessary and appropriate force' Congress has authorized the President to use." Id., at 518 (plurality opinion of O'Connor, J.), id., at 588–589 (Thomas, J., dissenting). After *Hamdi*, the Deputy Secretary of Defense established Combatant Status Review Tribunals (CSRTs) to determine whether individuals detained at Guantanamo were "enemy combatants," as the Department defines that term. A later memorandum established procedures to implement the CSRTs. The Government maintains these procedures were designed to comply with the due process requirements identified by the plurality in *Hamdi*.

Interpreting the AUMF, the Department of Defense ordered the detention of these petitioners, and they were transferred to Guantanamo. Some of these individuals were apprehended on the battlefield in Afghanistan, others in places as far away from there as Bosnia and Gambia. All are foreign nationals, but none is a citizen of a nation now at war with the United States. Each denies he is a member of the al Qaeda terrorist network that carried out the September 11 attacks or of the Taliban regime that provided sanctuary for al Qaeda. Each petitioner appeared before a separate CSRT; was determined to be an enemy combatant; and has sought a writ of habeas corpus in the United States District Court for the District of Columbia.

The first actions commenced in February 2002. The District Court ordered the cases dismissed for lack of jurisdiction because the naval station is outside the sovereign territory of the United States. See Rasul v. Bush, 215 F.Supp.2d 55 (2002). The Court of Appeals for the District of Columbia Circuit affirmed. See Al Odah v. United States, 321 F.3d 1134, 1145 (2003). We granted certiorari and reversed, holding that 28 U.S.C. § 2241 extended statutory habeas corpus jurisdiction to Guantanamo. See Rasul v. Bush, 542 U.S. 466, 473 (2004). The constitutional issue presented in the instant cases was not reached in *Rasul*. Id., at 476.

After *Rasul*, petitioners' cases were consolidated and entertained in two separate proceedings. In the first set of cases, Judge Richard J. Leon granted the Government's motion to dismiss, holding that the detainees had no rights that could be vindicated in a habeas corpus action. In the second set of cases Judge Joyce Hens Green reached the opposite conclusion, holding the detainees had rights under the Due Process Clause of the Fifth Amendment. See Khalid v. Bush, 355 F.Supp.2d 311, 314 (DDC 2005); In re Guantanamo Detainee Cases, 355 F.Supp.2d 443, 464 (DDC 2005).

While appeals were pending from the District Court decisions, Congress passed the DTA. Subsection (e) of § 1005 of the DTA amended 28

U.S.C. § 2241 to provide that "no court, justice, or judge shall have jurisdiction to hear or consider ... an application for a writ of habeas corpus filed by or on behalf of an alien detained by the Department of Defense at Guantanamo Bay, Cuba." 119 Stat. 2742. Section 1005 further provides that the Court of Appeals for the District of Columbia Circuit shall have "exclusive" jurisdiction to review decisions of the CSRTs. Ibid.

In Hamdan v. Rumsfeld, 548 U.S. 557, 576–577 (2006), the Court held this provision did not apply to cases (like petitioners') pending when the DTA was enacted. Congress responded by passing the MCA, 10 U.S.C. § 948a et seq. (Supp.2007), which again amended § 2241. The text of the statutory amendment is discussed below. See Part II, infra. (Four Members of the *Hamdan* majority noted that "[n]othing prevent[ed] the President from returning to Congress to seek the authority he believes necessary." 548 U.S., at 636 (Breyer, J., concurring). The authority to which the concurring opinion referred was the authority to "create military commissions of the kind at issue" in the case. Ibid. Nothing in that opinion can be construed as an invitation for Congress to suspend the writ.)

Petitioners' cases were consolidated on appeal, and the parties filed supplemental briefs in light of our decision in *Hamdan*. The Court of Appeals' ruling, 476 F.3d 981 (CADC 2007), is the subject of our present review and today's decision.

The Court of Appeals concluded that MCA § 7 must be read to strip from it, and all federal courts, jurisdiction to consider petitioners' habeas corpus applications, id., at 987; that petitioners are not entitled to the privilege of the writ or the protections of the Suspension Clause, id., at 990–991; and, as a result, that it was unnecessary to consider whether Congress provided an adequate and effective substitute for habeas corpus in the DTA.

We granted certiorari.

II

As a threshold matter, we must decide whether MCA § 7 denies the federal courts jurisdiction to hear habeas corpus actions pending at the time of its enactment. We hold the statute does deny that jurisdiction, so that, if the statute is valid, petitioners' cases must be dismissed.

As amended by the terms of the MCA, 28 U.S.C. § 2241(e) (Supp.2007) now provides:

"(1) No court, justice, or judge shall have jurisdiction to hear or consider an application for a writ of habeas corpus filed by or on behalf of an alien detained by the United States who has been determined by the United States to have been properly detained as an enemy combatant or is awaiting such determination.

"(2) Except as provided in [§§ 1005(e)(2) and (e)(3) of the DTA] no court, justice, or judge shall have jurisdiction to hear or consider any other action against the United States or its agents relating to any aspect of the detention, transfer, treatment, trial, or conditions of confinement of an alien who is or was detained by the United States and has been determined by the United States to have been properly detained as an enemy combatant or is awaiting such determination."

Section 7(b) of the MCA provides the effective date for the amendment of § 2241(e). It states:

"The amendment made by [MCA § 7(a)] shall take effect on the date of the enactment of this Act, and shall apply to all cases, without exception, pending on or after the date of the enactment of this Act which relate to any aspect of the detention, transfer, treatment, trial, or conditions of detention of an alien detained by the United States since September 11, 2001." 120 Stat. 2636.

There is little doubt that the effective date provision applies to habeas corpus actions. Those actions, by definition, are cases "which relate to ... detention." See Black's Law Dictionary 728 (8th ed.2004) (defining habeas corpus as "[a] writ employed to bring a person before a court, most frequently to ensure that the party's imprisonment or detention is not illegal"). Petitioners argue, nevertheless, that MCA § 7(b) is not a sufficiently clear statement of congressional intent to strip the federal courts of jurisdiction in pending cases. See Ex parte Yerger, 8 Wall. 85, 102–103 (1869). We disagree.

. . . . .

... In *Hamdan* the Court found it unnecessary to address the petitioner's Suspension Clause arguments but noted the relevance of the clear statement rule in deciding whether Congress intended to reach pending habeas corpus cases. See 548 U.S., at 575 (Congress should "not be presumed to have effected such denial [of habeas relief] absent an unmistakably clear statement to the contrary"). This interpretive rule facilitates a dialogue between Congress and the Court.... If the Court invokes a clear statement rule to advise that certain statutory interpretations are favored in order to avoid constitutional difficulties, Congress can make an informed legislative choice either to amend the statute or to retain its existing text. If Congress amends, its intent must be respected even if a difficult constitutional question is presented. The usual presumption is that Members of Congress, in accord with their oath of office, considered the constitutional issue and determined the amended statute to be a lawful one; and the Judiciary, in light of that determination, proceeds to its own independent judgment on the constitutional question when required to do so in a proper case.

If this ongoing dialogue between and among the branches of Government is to be respected, we cannot ignore that the MCA was a direct response to *Hamdan*'s holding that the DTA's jurisdiction-stripping provision had no application to pending cases. The Court of Appeals was correct to take note of the legislative history when construing the statute, see 476 F.3d, at 986, n.2 (citing relevant floor statements); and we agree with its conclusion that the MCA deprives the federal courts of jurisdiction to entertain the habeas corpus actions now before us.

III

In deciding the constitutional questions now presented we must determine whether petitioners are barred from seeking the writ or invoking the protections of the Suspension Clause either because of their status, i.e., petitioners' designation by the Executive Branch as enemy combatants, or their physical location, i.e., their presence at Guantanamo Bay. The Government contends that noncitizens designated as enemy combatants and detained in territory located outside our Nation's borders have no constitutional rights and no privilege of habeas corpus. Petitioners contend they do have cognizable constitutional rights and that Congress, in seeking to eliminate recourse to habeas corpus as a means to assert those rights, acted in violation of the Suspension Clause.

We begin with a brief account of the history and origins of the writ. Our account proceeds from two propositions. First, protection for the privilege of habeas corpus was one of the few safeguards of liberty specified in a Constitution that, at the outset, had no Bill of Rights. In the system conceived by the Framers the writ had a centrality that must inform proper interpretation of the Suspension Clause. Second, to the extent there were settled precedents or legal commentaries in 1789 regarding the extraterritorial scope of the writ or its application to enemy aliens, those authorities can be instructive for the present cases.

A

The Framers viewed freedom from unlawful restraint as a fundamental precept of liberty, and they understood the writ of habeas corpus as a vital instrument to secure that freedom. Experience taught, however, that the common-law writ all too often had been insufficient to guard against the abuse of monarchial power. That history counseled the necessity for specific language in the Constitution to secure the writ and ensure its place in our legal system.

Magna Carta decreed that no man would be imprisoned contrary to the law of the land. Art. 39, in Sources of Our Liberties 17 (R. Perry & J. Cooper eds.1959) ("No free man shall be taken or imprisoned or dispossessed, or outlawed, or banished, or in any way destroyed, nor will we go upon him, nor send upon him, except by the legal judgment of his peers or by the law of the land"). Important as the principle was, the Barons at Runnymede prescribed no specific legal process to enforce it. Holdsworth tells us, however, that gradually the writ of habeas corpus became the means by which the promise of Magna Carta was fulfilled. 9 W. Holdsworth, A History of English Law 112 (1926) (hereinafter Holdsworth).

. . . . .

Still, the writ proved to be an imperfect check. Even when the importance of the writ was well understood in England, habeas relief often was denied by the courts or suspended by Parliament. Denial or suspension occurred in times of political unrest, to the anguish of the imprisoned and the outrage of those in sympathy with them.

A notable example from this period was Darnel's Case, 3 How. St. Tr. 1 (K.B.1627). The events giving rise to the case began when, in a display of the Stuart penchant for authoritarian excess, Charles I demanded that Darnel and at least four others lend him money. Upon their refusal, they were imprisoned. The prisoners sought a writ of habeas corpus; and the King filed a return in the form of a warrant signed by the Attorney General. Ibid. The court held this was a sufficient answer and justified the subjects' continued imprisonment. Id., at 59.

There was an immediate outcry of protest. The House of Commons promptly passed the Petition of Right, 3 Car. 1, ch. 1 (1627), 5 Statutes of the Realm 23, 24 (reprint 1963), which condemned executive "imprison[ment] without any cause" shown, and declared that "no freeman in any such manner as is before mencioned [shall] be imprisoned or deteined." Yet a full legislative response was long delayed. The King soon began to abuse his authority again, and Parliament was dissolved. See W. Hall & R. Albion, A History of England and the British Empire 328 (3d ed.1953) (hereinafter Hall & Albion). When Parliament reconvened in 1640, it sought to secure access to the writ by statute. The Act of 1640, 16 Car. 1, ch. 10, 5 Statutes of the Realm, at 110, expressly authorized use of the writ to test the legality of commitment by command or warrant of the King or the Privy Council. Civil strife and the Interregnum soon followed, and not until 1679 did Parliament try once more to secure the writ, this time through the Habeas Corpus Act of 1679, 31 Car. 2, ch. 2, id., at 935. The Act, which later would be described by Blackstone as the "stable bulwark of our liberties," 1 W. Blackstone, Commentaries *137 (hereinafter Blackstone), established procedures for issuing the writ; and it was the model upon which the habeas statutes of the 13 American Colonies were based, see Collings, supra, at 338–339.

This history was known to the Framers. It no doubt confirmed their view that pendular swings to and away from individual liberty were endemic to undivided, uncontrolled power. The Framers' inherent distrust of governmental power was the driving force behind the constitutional plan that allocated powers among three independent branches. This design serves not only to make Government accountable but also to secure individual liberty. . . .

That the Framers considered the writ a vital instrument for the protection of individual liberty is evident from the care taken to specify the limited grounds for its suspension: "The Privilege of the Writ of Habeas Corpus shall not be suspended, unless when in Cases of Rebellion or Invasion the public Safety may require it." Art. I, § 9, cl. 2. . . .

Surviving accounts of the ratification debates provide additional evidence that the Framers deemed the writ to be an essential mechanism in the separation-of-powers scheme. In a critical exchange with Patrick Henry at the Virginia ratifying convention Edmund Randolph referred to the Suspension Clause as an "exception" to the "power given to Congress to regulate courts." See 3 Debates in the Several State Conventions on the Adoption of the Federal Constitution 460–464 (J. Elliot 2d ed.1876). . . .

Alexander Hamilton likewise explained that by providing the detainee a judicial forum to challenge detention, the writ preserves limited government. As he explained in The Federalist No. 84:

"[T]he practice of arbitrary imprisonments, have been, in all ages, the favorite and most formidable instruments of tyranny. The observations of the judicious Blackstone ... are well worthy of recital: 'To bereave a man of life ... or by violence to confiscate his estate, without accusation or trial, would be so gross and notorious an act of despotism as must at once convey the alarm of tyranny throughout the whole nation; but confinement of the person, by secretly hurrying him to jail, where his sufferings are unknown or forgotten, is a less public, a less striking, and therefore a *more dangerous engine* of arbitrary government.' And as a remedy for this fatal evil he is everywhere peculiarly emphatical in his encomiums on the *habeas corpus* act, which in one place he calls 'the BULWARK of the British Constitution.' " C. Rossiter ed., p. 512 (1961) (quoting 1 Blackstone *136, 4 id., at *438).

Post–1789 habeas developments in England, though not bearing upon the Framers' intent, do verify their foresight. Those later events would underscore the need for structural barriers against arbitrary suspensions of the writ. Just as the writ had been vulnerable to executive and parliamentary encroachment on both sides of the Atlantic before the American Revolution, despite the Habeas Corpus Act of 1679, the writ was suspended with frequency in England during times of political unrest after 1789. . . .

In our own system the Suspension Clause is designed to protect against these cyclical abuses. The Clause protects the rights of the detained by a means consistent with the essential design of the Constitution. It ensures that, except during periods of formal suspension, the Judiciary will have a time-tested device, the writ, to maintain the "delicate balance of governance" that is itself the surest safeguard of liberty. See *Hamdi*, 542 U.S., at 536 (plurality opinion). The Clause protects the rights of the detained by affirming the duty and authority of the Judiciary to call the jailer to account. . . . The separation-of-powers doctrine, and the history that influenced its design, therefore must inform the reach and purpose of the Suspension Clause.

B

The broad historical narrative of the writ and its function is central to our analysis, but we seek guidance as well from founding-era authorities addressing the specific question before us: whether foreign nationals, apprehended and detained in distant countries during a time of serious threats to our Nation's security, may assert the privilege of the writ and seek its protection. The Court has been careful not to foreclose the possibility that the protections of the Suspension Clause have expanded along with post–1789 developments that define the present scope of the writ. See INS v. St. Cyr, 533 U.S. 289, 300–301 (2001). But the analysis may begin with precedents as of 1789, for the Court has said that "at the absolute minimum" the Clause protects the writ as it existed when the Constitution was drafted and ratified. Id., at 301.

To support their arguments, the parties in these cases have examined historical sources to construct a view of the common-law writ as it existed in 1789–as have amici whose expertise in legal history the Court has relied upon in the past.... The Government argues the common-law writ ran only to those territories over which the Crown was sovereign. Petitioners argue that jurisdiction followed the King's officers.... Diligent search by all parties reveals no certain conclusions. In none of the cases cited do we find that a common-law court would or would not have granted, or refused to hear for lack of jurisdiction, a petition for a writ of habeas corpus brought by a prisoner deemed an enemy combatant, under a standard like the one the Department of Defense has used in these cases, and when held in a territory, like Guantanamo, over which the Government has total military and civil control.

. . . . .

In the end a categorical or formal conception of sovereignty does not provide a comprehensive or altogether satisfactory explanation for the general understanding that prevailed when Lord Mansfield considered issuance of the writ outside England. In 1759 the writ did not run to Scotland but did run to Ireland, even though, at that point, Scotland and England had merged under the rule of a single sovereign, whereas the Crowns of Great Britain and Ireland remained separate (at least in theory).... But there was at least one major difference between Scotland's and Ireland's relationship with England during this period that might explain why the writ ran to Ireland but not to Scotland. English law did not generally apply in Scotland (even after the Act of Union) but it did apply in Ireland. Blackstone put it as follows: "[A]s Scotland and England are now one and the same kingdom, and yet differ in their municipal laws; so England and Ireland are, on the other hand, distinct kingdoms, and yet in general agree in their laws." ... This distinction, and not formal notions of sovereignty, may well explain why the writ did not run to Scotland (and Hanover [a German principality where the English king was also by birth the titular sovereign]) but would run to Ireland.

The prudential barriers that may have prevented the English courts from issuing the writ to Scotland and Hanover are not relevant here. We have no reason to believe an order from a federal court would be disobeyed at Guantanamo. No Cuban court has jurisdiction to hear these petitioners' claims, and no law other than the laws of the United States applies at the naval station. The modern-day relations between the United States and Guantanamo thus differ in important respects from the 18th-century relations between England and the kingdoms of Scotland and Hanover....

. . . . .

IV

Drawing from its position that at common law the writ ran only to territories over which the Crown was sovereign, the Government says the

Suspension Clause affords petitioners no rights because the United States does not claim sovereignty over the place of detention.

Guantanamo Bay is not formally part of the United States. See DTA § 1005(g), 119 Stat. 2743. And under the terms of the lease between the United States and Cuba, Cuba retains "ultimate sovereignty" over the territory while the United States exercises "complete jurisdiction and control." ...

. . . . .

We therefore do not question the Government's position that Cuba, not the United States, maintains sovereignty, in the legal and technical sense of the term, over Guantanamo Bay. But this does not end the analysis. Our cases do not hold it is improper for us to inquire into the objective degree of control the Nation asserts over foreign territory.... Accordingly, for purposes of our analysis, we accept the Government's position that Cuba, and not the United States, retains *de jure* sovereignty over Guantanamo Bay. As we did in *Rasul*, however, we take notice of the obvious and uncontested fact that the United States, by virtue of its complete jurisdiction and control over the base, maintains *de facto* sovereignty over this territory....

Were we to hold that the present cases turn on the political question doctrine, we would be required first to accept the Government's premise that de jure sovereignty is the touchstone of habeas corpus jurisdiction. This premise, however, is unfounded. For the reasons indicated above, the history of common-law habeas corpus provides scant support for this proposition; and, for the reasons indicated below, that position would be inconsistent with our precedents and contrary to fundamental separation-of-powers principles.

A

The Court has discussed the issue of the Constitution's extraterritorial application on many occasions. These decisions undermine the Government's argument that, at least as applied to noncitizens, the Constitution necessarily stops where *de jure* sovereignty ends.

. . . . .

Practical considerations weighed heavily ... in Johnson v. Eisentrager, 339 U.S. 763 (1950), where the Court addressed whether habeas corpus jurisdiction extended to enemy aliens who had been convicted of violating the laws of war. The prisoners were detained at Landsberg Prison in Germany during the Allied Powers' post-war occupation. The Court stressed the difficulties of ordering the Government to produce the prisoners in a habeas corpus proceeding. It "would require allocation of shipping space, guarding personnel, billeting and rations" and would damage the prestige of military commanders at a sensitive time. Id., at 779. In considering these factors the Court sought to balance the constraints of military occupation with constitutional necessities. Id., at 769–779.

True, the Court in *Eisentrager* denied access to the writ, and it noted the prisoners "at no relevant time were within any territory over which the United States is sovereign, and [that] the scenes of their offense, their capture, their trial and their punishment were all beyond the territorial jurisdiction of any court of the United States." 339 U.S., at 778. The Government seizes upon this language as proof positive that the *Eisentrager* Court adopted a formalistic, sovereignty-based test for determining the reach of the Suspension Clause. We reject this reading for three reasons.

First, we do not accept the idea that the above-quoted passage from *Eisentrager* is the only authoritative language in the opinion and that all the rest is dicta. The Court's further determinations, based on practical considerations, were integral to Part II of its opinion and came before the decision announced its holding. See 339 U.S., at 781.

Second, because the United States lacked both *de jure* sovereignty and plenary control over Landsberg Prison, it is far from clear that the *Eisentrager* Court used the term sovereignty only in the narrow technical sense and not to connote the degree of control the military asserted over the facility. The Justices who decided *Eisentrager* would have understood sovereignty as a multifaceted concept....

Third, if the Government's reading of *Eisentrager* were correct, the opinion would have marked not only a change in, but a complete repudiation of, [earlier cases'] functional approach to questions of extraterritoriality. We cannot accept the Government's view. Nothing in *Eisentrager* says that *de jure* sovereignty is or has ever been the only relevant consideration in determining the geographic reach of the Constitution or of habeas corpus. Were that the case, there would be considerable tension between *Eisentrager*, on the one hand, and [earlier cases] on the other. Our cases need not be read to conflict in this manner. A constricted reading of *Eisentrager* overlooks what we see as a common thread uniting [these cases]: the idea that questions of extraterritoriality turn on objective factors and practical concerns, not formalism.

B

The Government's formal sovereignty-based test raises troubling separation-of-powers concerns as well. The political history of Guantanamo illustrates the deficiencies of this approach. The United States has maintained complete and uninterrupted control of the bay for over 100 years.... Yet the Government's view is that the Constitution had no effect there, at least as to noncitizens, because the United States disclaimed sovereignty in the formal sense of the term. The necessary implication of the argument is that by surrendering formal sovereignty over any unincorporated territory to a third party, while at the same time entering into a lease that grants total control over the territory back to the United States, it would be possible for the political branches to govern without legal constraint.

Our basic charter cannot be contracted away like this. The Constitution grants Congress and the President the power to acquire, dispose of, and govern territory, not the power to decide when and where its terms apply. Even when the United States acts outside its borders, its powers are not "absolute and unlimited" but are subject "to such restrictions as are expressed in the Constitution." ... Abstaining from questions involving formal sovereignty and territorial governance is one thing. To hold the political branches have the power to switch the Constitution on or off at will is quite another. The former position reflects this Court's recognition that certain matters requiring political judgments are best left to the political branches. The latter would permit a striking anomaly in our tripartite system of government, leading to a regime in which Congress and the President, not this Court, say "what the law is." Marbury v. Madison, 1 Cranch 137, 177 (1803).

These concerns have particular bearing upon the Suspension Clause question in the cases now before us, for the writ of habeas corpus is itself an indispensable mechanism for monitoring the separation of powers. The test for determining the scope of this provision must not be subject to manipulation by those whose power it is designed to restrain.

C

. . . . .

It is true that before today the Court has never held that noncitizens detained by our Government in territory over which another country maintains de jure sovereignty have any rights under our Constitution. But the cases before us lack any precise historical parallel. They involve individuals detained by executive order for the duration of a conflict that, if measured from September 11, 2001, to the present, is already among the longest wars in American history. See Oxford Companion to American Military History 849 (1999). The detainees, moreover, are held in a territory that, while technically not part of the United States, is under the complete and total control of our Government. Under these circumstances the lack of a precedent on point is no barrier to our holding.

We hold that Art. I, § 9, cl. 2, of the Constitution has full effect at Guantanamo Bay. If the privilege of habeas corpus is to be denied to the detainees now before us, Congress must act in accordance with the requirements of the Suspension Clause. Cf. *Hamdi*, 542 U.S., at 564 (Scalia, J., dissenting) ("[I]ndefinite imprisonment on reasonable suspicion is not an available option of treatment for those accused of aiding the enemy, absent a suspension of the writ"). This Court may not impose a de facto suspension by abstaining from these controversies. See *Hamdan*, 548 U.S., at 585, n.16 ("[A]bstention is not appropriate in cases ... in which the legal challenge 'turn[s] on the status of the persons as to whom the military asserted its power' " (quoting Schlesinger v. Councilman, 420 U.S. 738, 759 (1975))). The MCA does not purport to be a formal suspension of the writ; and the Government, in its submissions to us, has not argued that it is. Petitioners, therefore, are entitled to the privilege of habeas corpus to challenge the legality of their detention.

V

In light of this holding the question becomes whether the statute stripping jurisdiction to issue the writ avoids the Suspension Clause mandate because Congress has provided adequate substitute procedures for habeas corpus. The Government submits there has been compliance with the Suspension Clause because the DTA review process in the Court of Appeals, see DTA § 1005(e), provides an adequate substitute. Congress has granted that court jurisdiction to consider

"(i) whether the status determination of the [CSRT] . . . was consistent with the standards and procedures specified by the Secretary of Defense . . . and (ii) to the extent the Constitution and laws of the United States are applicable, whether the use of such standards and procedures to make the determination is consistent with the Constitution and laws of the United States." § 1005(e)(2)(C), 119 Stat. 2742.

The Court of Appeals, having decided that the writ does not run to the detainees in any event, found it unnecessary to consider whether an adequate substitute has been provided. In the ordinary course we would remand to the Court of Appeals to consider this question in the first instance. See Youakim v. Miller, 425 U.S. 231, 234 (1976) (per curiam). It is well settled, however, that the Court's practice of declining to address issues left unresolved in earlier proceedings is not an inflexible rule. Ibid. Departure from the rule is appropriate in "exceptional" circumstances. See Cooper Industries, Inc. v. Aviall Services, Inc., 543 U.S. 157, 169 (2004); Duignan v. United States, 274 U.S. 195, 200 (1927).

The gravity of the separation-of-powers issues raised by these cases and the fact that these detainees have been denied meaningful access to a judicial forum for a period of years render these cases exceptional. . . .

. . . . .

Under the circumstances we believe the costs of further delay substantially outweigh any benefits of remanding to the Court of Appeals to consider the issue it did not address in these cases.

A

Our case law does not contain extensive discussion of standards defining suspension of the writ or of circumstances under which suspension has occurred. This simply confirms the care Congress has taken throughout our Nation's history to preserve the writ and its function. Indeed, most of the major legislative enactments pertaining to habeas corpus have acted not to contract the writ's protection but to expand it or to hasten resolution of prisoners' claims. . . .

. . . . .

To the extent any doubt remains about Congress' intent, the legislative history confirms what the plain text strongly suggests: In passing the DTA Congress did not intend to create a process that differs from traditional habeas corpus process in name only. It intended to create a more limited procedure. . . .

It is against this background that we must interpret the DTA and assess its adequacy as a substitute for habeas corpus. . . .

B

. . . . .

Where a person is detained by executive order, rather than, say, after being tried and convicted in a court, the need for collateral review is most pressing. A criminal conviction in the usual course occurs after a judicial hearing before a tribunal disinterested in the outcome and committed to procedures designed to ensure its own independence. These dynamics are not inherent in executive detention orders or executive review procedures. In this context the need for habeas corpus is more urgent. The intended duration of the detention and the reasons for it bear upon the precise scope of the inquiry. Habeas corpus proceedings need not resemble a criminal trial, even when the detention is by executive order. But the writ must be effective. The habeas court must have sufficient authority to conduct a meaningful review of both the cause for detention and the Executive's power to detain.

To determine the necessary scope of habeas corpus review, therefore, we must assess the CSRT process, the mechanism through which petitioners' designation as enemy combatants became final. Whether one characterizes the CSRT process as direct review of the Executive's battlefield determination that the detainee is an enemy combatant—as the parties have and as we do—or as the first step in the collateral review of a battlefield determination makes no difference in a proper analysis of whether the procedures Congress put in place are an adequate substitute for habeas corpus. What matters is the sum total of procedural protections afforded to the detainee at all stages, direct and collateral.

Petitioners identify what they see as myriad deficiencies in the CSRTs. The most relevant for our purposes are the constraints upon the detainee's ability to rebut the factual basis for the Government's assertion that he is an enemy combatant. As already noted, see Part IV–C, supra, at the CSRT stage the detainee has limited means to find or present evidence to challenge the Government's case against him. He does not have the assistance of counsel and may not be aware of the most critical allegations that the Government relied upon to order his detention. . . . The detainee can confront witnesses that testify during the CSRT proceedings. . . . But given that there are in effect no limits on the admission of hearsay evidence—the only requirement is that the tribunal deem the evidence "relevant and helpful," . . . the detainee's opportunity to question witnesses is likely to be more theoretical than real.

The Government defends the CSRT process, arguing that it was designed to conform to the procedures suggested by the plurality in *Hamdi*. See 542 U.S., at 538. Setting aside the fact that the relevant language in

Hamdi did not garner a majority of the Court, it does not control the matter at hand. None of the parties in *Hamdi* argued there had been a suspension of the writ. Nor could they. The § 2241 habeas corpus process remained in place, id., at 525. Accordingly, the plurality concentrated on whether the Executive had the authority to detain and, if so, what rights the detainee had under the Due Process Clause. True, there are places in the Hamdi plurality opinion where it is difficult to tell where its extrapolation of § 2241 ends and its analysis of the petitioner's Due Process rights begins. But the Court had no occasion to define the necessary scope of habeas review, for Suspension Clause purposes, in the context of enemy combatant detentions. The closest the plurality came to doing so was in discussing whether, in light of separation-of-powers concerns, § 2241 should be construed to prohibit the District Court from inquiring beyond the affidavit *Hamdi*'s custodian provided in answer to the detainee's habeas petition. The plurality answered this question with an emphatic "no." Id., at 527 (labeling this argument as "extreme"); id., at 535–536.

Even if we were to assume that the CSRTs satisfy due process standards, it would not end our inquiry. Habeas corpus is a collateral process that exists, in Justice Holmes' words, to "cu[t] through all forms and g[o] to the very tissue of the structure. It comes in from the outside, not in subordination to the proceedings, and although every form may have been preserved opens the inquiry whether they have been more than an empty shell." Frank v. Mangum, 237 U.S. 309, 346 (1915) (dissenting opinion). Even when the procedures authorizing detention are structurally sound, the Suspension Clause remains applicable and the writ relevant....

Although we make no judgment whether the CSRTs, as currently constituted, satisfy due process standards, we agree with petitioners that, even when all the parties involved in this process act with diligence and in good faith, there is considerable risk of error in the tribunal's findings of fact. This is a risk inherent in any process that, in the words of the former Chief Judge of the Court of Appeals, is "closed and accusatorial." See Bismullah III, 514 F.3d, at 1296 (Ginsburg, C. J., concurring in denial of rehearing en banc). And given that the consequence of error may be detention of persons for the duration of hostilities that may last a generation or more, this is a risk too significant to ignore.

For the writ of habeas corpus, or its substitute, to function as an effective and proper remedy in this context, the court that conducts the habeas proceeding must have the means to correct errors that occurred during the CSRT proceedings. This includes some authority to assess the sufficiency of the Government's evidence against the detainee. It also must have the authority to admit and consider relevant exculpatory evidence that was not introduced during the earlier proceeding....

. . . . .

The extent of the showing required of the Government in these cases is a matter to be determined. We need not explore it further at this stage. We do hold that when the judicial power to issue habeas corpus properly is invoked the judicial officer must have adequate authority to make a determination in light of the relevant law and facts and to formulate and issue appropriate orders for relief, including, if necessary, an order directing the prisoner's release.

C

We now consider whether the DTA allows the Court of Appeals to conduct a proceeding meeting these standards. "[W]e are obligated to construe the statute to avoid [constitutional] problems" if it is " 'fairly possible' " to do so. *St. Cyr*, 533 U.S., at 299–300 (quoting Crowell v. Benson, 285 U.S. 22, 62 (1932)). There are limits to this principle, however. The canon of constitutional avoidance does not supplant traditional modes of statutory interpretation. See Clark v. Martinez, 543 U.S. 371, 385 (2005) ("The canon of constitutional avoidance comes into play only when, after the application of ordinary textual analysis, the statute is found to be susceptible of more than one construction; and the canon functions as a means of choosing between them "). We cannot ignore the text and purpose of a statute in order to save it.

The DTA does not explicitly empower the Court of Appeals to order the applicant in a DTA review proceeding released should the court find that the standards and procedures used at his CSRT hearing were insufficient to justify detention. This is troubling. Yet, for present purposes, we can assume congressional silence permits a constitutionally required remedy. In that case it would be possible to hold that a remedy of release is impliedly provided for. The DTA might be read, furthermore, to allow petitioners to assert most, if not all, of the legal claims they seek to advance, including their most basic claim: that the President has no authority under the AUMF to detain them indefinitely. (Whether the President has such authority turns on whether the AUMF authorizes—and the Constitution permits—the indefinite detention of "enemy combatants" as the Department of Defense defines that term. Thus a challenge to the President's authority to detain is, in essence, a challenge to the Department's definition of enemy combatant, a "standard" used by the CSRTs in petitioners' cases.) At oral argument, the Solicitor General urged us to adopt both these constructions, if doing so would allow MCA § 7 to remain intact.

The absence of a release remedy and specific language allowing AUMF challenges are not the only constitutional infirmities from which the statute potentially suffers, however. The more difficult question is whether the DTA permits the Court of Appeals to make requisite findings of fact. The DTA enables petitioners to request "review" of their CSRT determination in the Court of Appeals, DTA § 1005(e)(2)(B)(i), 119 Stat. 2742; but the "Scope of Review" provision confines the Court of Appeals' role to reviewing whether the CSRT followed the "standards and procedures" issued by the Department of Defense and assessing whether those "standards and procedures" are lawful, § 1005(e)(2)(C), ibid. Among these standards is "the requirement that the conclusion of the Tribunal be supported by a preponderance of the evidence ... allowing a rebuttable presumption in favor of the Government's evidence." § 1005(e)(2)(C)(i), ibid.

Assuming the DTA can be construed to allow the Court of Appeals to review or correct the CSRT's factual determinations, as opposed to merely certifying that the tribunal applied the correct standard of proof, we see no way to construe the statute to allow what is also constitutionally required in this context: an opportunity for the detainee to present relevant exculpatory evidence that was not made part of the record in the earlier proceedings.

. . . . .

Although we do not hold that an adequate substitute must duplicate § 2241 in all respects, it suffices that the Government has not established that the detainees' access to the statutory review provisions at issue is an adequate substitute for the writ of habeas corpus. MCA § 7 thus effects an unconstitutional suspension of the writ. In view of our holding we need not discuss the reach of the writ with respect to claims of unlawful conditions of treatment or confinement.

VI

A

In light of our conclusion that there is no jurisdictional bar to the District Court's entertaining petitioners' claims the question remains whether there are prudential barriers to habeas corpus review under these circumstances.

The Government argues petitioners must seek review of their CSRT determinations in the Court of Appeals before they can proceed with their habeas corpus actions in the District Court. As noted earlier, in other contexts and for prudential reasons this Court has required exhaustion of alternative remedies before a prisoner can seek federal habeas relief. Most of these cases were brought by prisoners in state custody, e.g., Ex parte Royall, 117 U.S. 241, and thus involved federalism concerns that are not relevant here. But we have extended this rule to require defendants in courts-martial to exhaust their military appeals before proceeding with a federal habeas corpus action. See *Schlesinger*, 420 U.S., at 758.

The real risks, the real threats, of terrorist attacks are constant and not likely soon to abate. The ways to disrupt our life and laws are so many and unforeseen that the Court should not attempt even some general catalogue of crises that might occur. Certain principles are apparent, however. Practical considerations and exigent circumstances inform the definition and reach of the law's writs, including habeas corpus. The cases and our tradition reflect this precept.

In cases involving foreign citizens detained abroad by the Executive, it likely would be both an impractical and unprecedented extension of judicial power to assume that habeas corpus would be available at the moment the prisoner is taken into custody. If and when habeas corpus jurisdiction applies, as it does in these cases, then proper deference can be accorded to reasonable procedures for screening and initial detention under lawful and proper conditions of confinement and treatment for a reasonable period of time. Domestic exigencies, furthermore, might also impose such onerous burdens on the Government that here, too, the Judicial Branch would be required to devise sensible rules for staying habeas corpus proceedings until the Government can comply with its requirements in a responsible way. . . .

The cases before us, however, do not involve detainees who have been held for a short period of time while awaiting their CSRT determinations. Were that the case, or were it probable that the Court of Appeals could complete a prompt review of their applications, the case for requiring temporary abstention or exhaustion of alternative remedies would be much stronger. These qualifications no longer pertain here. In some of these cases six years have elapsed without the judicial oversight that habeas corpus or an adequate substitute demands. And there has been no showing that the Executive faces such onerous burdens that it cannot respond to habeas corpus actions. To require these detainees to complete DTA review before proceeding with their habeas corpus actions would be to require additional months, if not years, of delay. The first DTA review applications were filed over two years ago, but no decisions on the merits have been issued. While some delay in fashioning new procedures is unavoidable, the costs of delay can no longer be borne by those who are held in custody. The detainees in these cases are entitled to a prompt habeas corpus hearing.

Our decision today holds only that petitioners before us are entitled to seek the writ; that the DTA review procedures are an inadequate substitute for habeas corpus; and that petitioners in these cases need not exhaust the review procedures in the Court of Appeals before proceeding with their habeas actions in the District Court. The only law we identify as unconstitutional is MCA § 7, 28 U.S.C. § 2241(e) (Supp.2007). Accordingly, both the DTA and the CSRT process remain intact. Our holding with regard to exhaustion should not be read to imply that a habeas court should intervene the moment an enemy combatant steps foot in a territory where the writ runs. The Executive is entitled to a reasonable period of time to determine a detainee's status before a court entertains that detainee's habeas corpus petition. The CSRT process is the mechanism Congress and the President set up to deal with these issues. Except in cases of undue delay, federal courts should refrain from entertaining an enemy combatant's habeas corpus petition at least until after the Department, acting via the CSRT, has had a chance to review his status.

B

Although we hold that the DTA is not an adequate and effective substitute for habeas corpus, it does not follow that a habeas corpus court may disregard the dangers the detention in these cases was intended to prevent. . . . [T]he Suspension Clause does not resist innovation in the field of habeas corpus. Certain accommodations can be made to reduce the burden habeas corpus proceedings will place on the military without impermissibly diluting the protections of the writ.

. . . . .

These and the other remaining questions are within the expertise and competence of the District Court to address in the first instance.

* * *

In considering both the procedural and substantive standards used to impose detention to prevent acts of terrorism, proper deference must be accorded to the political branches. See United States v. Curtiss–Wright Export Corp., 299 U.S. 304, 320 (1936). Unlike the President and some designated Members of Congress, neither the Members of this Court nor most federal judges begin the day with briefings that may describe new and serious threats to our Nation and its people. The law must accord the Executive substantial authority to apprehend and detain those who pose a real danger to our security.

Officials charged with daily operational responsibility for our security may consider a judicial discourse on the history of the Habeas Corpus Act of 1679 and like matters to be far removed from the Nation's present, urgent concerns. Established legal doctrine, however, must be consulted for its teaching. Remote in time it may be; irrelevant to the present it is not. Security depends upon a sophisticated intelligence apparatus and the ability of our Armed Forces to act and to interdict. There are further considerations, however. Security subsists, too, in fidelity to freedom's first principles. Chief among these are freedom from arbitrary and unlawful restraint and the personal liberty that is secured by adherence to the separation of powers. It is from these principles that the judicial authority to consider petitions for habeas corpus relief derives.

Our opinion does not undermine the Executive's powers as Commander in Chief. On the contrary, the exercise of those powers is vindicated, not eroded, when confirmed by the Judicial Branch. Within the Constitution's separation-of-powers structure, few exercises of judicial power are as legitimate or as necessary as the responsibility to hear challenges to the authority of the Executive to imprison a person. Some of these petitioners have been in custody for six years with no definitive judicial determination as to the legality of their detention. Their access to the writ is a necessity to determine the lawfulness of their status, even if, in the end, they do not obtain the relief they seek.

Because our Nation's past military conflicts have been of limited duration, it has been possible to leave the outer boundaries of war powers undefined. If, as some fear, terrorism continues to pose dangerous threats to us for years to come, the Court might not have this luxury. This result is not inevitable, however. The political branches, consistent with their independent obligations to interpret and uphold the Constitution, can engage in a genuine debate about how best to preserve constitutional values while protecting the Nation from terrorism. . . .

It bears repeating that our opinion does not address the content of the law that governs petitioners' detention. That is a matter yet to be determined. We hold that petitioners may invoke the fundamental procedural protections of habeas corpus. The laws and Constitution are designed to survive, and remain in force, in extraordinary times. Liberty and security can be reconciled; and in our system they are reconciled within the framework of the law. The Framers decided that habeas corpus, a right of first importance, must be a part of that framework, a part of that law.

The determination by the Court of Appeals that the Suspension Clause and its protections are inapplicable to petitioners was in error. The judgment of the Court of Appeals is reversed. The cases are remanded to the Court of Appeals with instructions that it remand the cases to the District Court for proceedings consistent with this opinion.

It is so ordered.

■ JUSTICE SOUTER, with whom JUSTICE GINSBURG and JUSTICE BREYER join, concurring.

I join the Court's opinion in its entirety and add this afterword only to emphasize two things one might overlook after reading the dissents.

Four years ago, this Court in Rasul v. Bush, 542 U.S. 466 (2004), held that statutory habeas jurisdiction extended to claims of foreign nationals imprisoned by the United States at Guantanamo Bay, "to determine the legality of the Executive's potentially indefinite detention" of them, id., at 485. Subsequent legislation eliminated the statutory habeas jurisdiction over these claims, so that now there must be constitutionally based jurisdiction or none at all. Justice Scalia is thus correct that here, for the first time, this Court holds there is (he says "confers") constitutional habeas jurisdiction over aliens imprisoned by the military outside an area of *de jure* national sovereignty. But no one who reads the Court's opinion in *Rasul* could seriously doubt that the jurisdictional question must be answered the same way in purely constitutional cases, given the Court's reliance on the historical background of habeas generally in answering the statutory question. . . .

A second fact insufficiently appreciated by the dissents is the length of the disputed imprisonments, some of the prisoners represented here today having been locked up for six years. Hence the hollow ring when the dissenters suggest that the Court is somehow precipitating the judiciary into reviewing claims that the military (subject to appeal to the Court of Appeals for the District of Columbia Circuit) could handle within some reasonable period of time. . . .

It is in fact the very lapse of four years from the time *Rasul* put everyone on notice that habeas process was available to Guantanamo prisoners, and the lapse of six years since some of these prisoners were captured and incarcerated, that stand at odds with the repeated suggestions of the dissenters that these cases should be seen as a judicial victory in a contest for power between the Court and the political branches. The several answers to the charge of triumphalism might start with a basic fact of Anglo–American constitutional history: that the power, first of the Crown and now of the Executive Branch of the United States, is necessarily limited by habeas corpus jurisdiction to enquire into the legality of executive detention. And one could explain that in this Court's exercise of responsibility to preserve habeas corpus something much more significant is involved than pulling and hauling between the judicial and political branches. Instead, though, it is enough to repeat that some of these petitioners have spent six years behind bars. After six years of sustained executive detentions in Guantanamo, subject to habeas jurisdiction but without any actual habeas scrutiny, today's decision is no judicial victory, but an act of perseverance in trying to make habeas review, and the obligation of the courts to provide it, mean something of value both to prisoners and to the Nation.

■ Chief Justice Roberts, with whom Justice Scalia, Justice Thomas, and Justice Alito join, dissenting.

Today the Court strikes down as inadequate the most generous set of procedural protections ever afforded aliens detained by this country as enemy combatants. The political branches crafted these procedures amidst an ongoing military conflict, after much careful investigation and thorough debate. The Court rejects them today out of hand, without bothering to say what due process rights the detainees possess, without explaining how the statute fails to vindicate those rights, and before a single petitioner has exhausted the procedures under the law. And to what effect? The majority merely replaces a review system designed by the people's representatives with a set of shapeless procedures to be defined by federal courts at some future date. One cannot help but think, after surveying the modest practical results of the majority's ambitious opinion, that this decision is not really about the detainees at all, but about control of federal policy regarding enemy combatants.

The majority is adamant that the Guantanamo detainees are entitled to the protections of habeas corpus—its opinion begins by deciding that question. I regard the issue as a difficult one, primarily because of the unique and unusual jurisdictional status of Guantanamo Bay. I nonetheless agree with Justice Scalia's analysis of our precedents and the pertinent history of the writ, and accordingly join his dissent. The important point for me, however, is that the Court should have resolved these cases on other grounds. Habeas is most fundamentally a procedural right, a mechanism for contesting the legality of executive detention. The critical threshold question in these cases, prior to any inquiry about the writ's scope, is whether the system the political branches designed protects whatever rights the detainees may possess. If so, there is no need for any additional process, whether called "habeas" or something else.

. . . . .

I believe the system the political branches constructed adequately protects any constitutional rights aliens captured abroad and detained as enemy combatants may enjoy. I therefore would dismiss these cases on that ground. With all respect for the contrary views of the majority, I must dissent.

. . . . .

■ JUSTICE SCALIA, with whom THE CHIEF JUSTICE, JUSTICE THOMAS, and JUSTICE ALITO join, dissenting.

Today, for the first time in our Nation's history, the Court confers a constitutional right to habeas corpus on alien enemies detained abroad by our military forces in the course of an ongoing war. . . . [T]he procedures prescribed by Congress in the Detainee Treatment Act provide the essential protections that habeas corpus guarantees; there has thus been no suspension of the writ, and no basis exists for judicial intervention beyond what the Act allows. My problem with today's opinion is more fundamental still: The writ of habeas corpus does not, and never has, run in favor of aliens abroad; the Suspension Clause thus has no application, and the Court's intervention in this military matter is entirely ultra vires.

. . . . .

II

. . . . .

C

What drives today's decision is neither the meaning of the Suspension Clause, nor the principles of our precedents, but rather an inflated notion of judicial supremacy. The Court says that if the extraterritorial applicability of the Suspension Clause turned on formal notions of sovereignty, "it would be possible for the political branches to govern without legal constraint" in areas beyond the sovereign territory of the United States. That cannot be, the Court says, because it is the duty of this Court to say what the law is. It would be difficult to imagine a more question-begging analysis. "The very foundation of the power of the federal courts to declare Acts of Congress unconstitutional lies in the power and duty of those courts to decide cases and controversies *properly before them*." United States v. Raines, 362 U.S. 17, 20–21 (1960) (citing Marbury v. Madison, 1 Cranch 137 (1803); emphasis added). Our power "to say what the law is" is circumscribed by the limits of our statutorily and constitutionally conferred jurisdiction. See Lujan v. Defenders of Wildlife, 504 U.S. 555, 573–578 (1992). And that is precisely the question in these cases: whether the Constitution confers habeas jurisdiction on federal courts to decide petitioners' claims. It is both irrational and arrogant to say that the answer must be yes, because otherwise we would not be supreme.

But so long as there are *some* places to which habeas does not run—so long as the Court's new "functional" test will not be satisfied in every case—then there will be circumstances in which "it would be possible for the political branches to govern without legal constraint." Or, to put it more impartially, areas in which the legal determinations of the *other* branches will be (shudder!) *supreme*. In other words, judicial supremacy is not really assured by the constitutional rule that the Court creates. The gap between rationale and rule leads me to conclude that the Court's ultimate, unexpressed goal is to preserve the power to review the confinement of enemy prisoners held by the Executive anywhere in the world. The "functional" test usefully evades the precedential landmine of *Eisentrager* but is so inherently subjective that it clears a wide path for the Court to traverse in the years to come.

III

. . . . .

In sum, *all* available historical evidence points to the conclusion that the writ would not have been available at common law for aliens captured and held outside the sovereign territory of the Crown. Despite three opening briefs, three reply briefs, and support from a legion of amici, petitioners have failed to identify a single case in the history of Anglo–American law that supports their claim to jurisdiction. The Court finds it significant that there is no recorded case *denying* jurisdiction to such prisoners either. But a case standing for the remarkable proposition that the writ could issue to a foreign land would surely have been reported, whereas a case denying such a writ for lack of jurisdiction would likely not. At a minimum, the absence of a reported case either way leaves unrefuted the voluminous commentary stating that habeas was confined to the dominions of the Crown.

What history teaches is confirmed by the nature of the limitations that the Constitution places upon suspension of the common-law writ. It can be suspended only "in Cases of Rebellion or Invasion." Art. I, § 9, cl. 2. The latter case (invasion) is plainly limited to the territory of the United States; and while it is conceivable that a rebellion could be mounted by American citizens abroad, surely the overwhelming majority of its occurrences would be domestic. If the extraterritorial scope of habeas turned on flexible, "functional" considerations, as the Court holds, why would the Constitution limit its suspension almost entirely to instances of domestic crisis? Surely there is an even greater justification for suspension in foreign lands where the United States might hold prisoners of war during an ongoing conflict. And correspondingly, there is less threat to liberty when the Government suspends the writ's (supposed) application in foreign lands, where even on the most extreme view prisoners are entitled to fewer constitutional rights. It makes no sense, therefore, for the Constitution generally to forbid suspension of the writ abroad if indeed the writ has application there.

. . . . .

* * *

Today the Court warps our Constitution in a way that goes beyond the narrow issue of the reach of the Suspension Clause, invoking judicially brainstormed separation-of-powers principles to establish a manipulable "functional" test for the extraterritorial reach of habeas corpus (and, no doubt, for the extraterritorial reach of other constitutional protections as well). It blatantly misdescribes important precedents, most conspicuously Justice Jackson's opinion for the Court in Johnson v. Eisentrager. It breaks a chain of precedent as old as the common law that prohibits judicial inquiry into detentions of aliens abroad absent statutory authorization. And, most tragically, it sets our military commanders the impossible task of proving to a civilian court, under whatever standards this Court devises in the future, that evidence supports the confinement of each and every enemy prisoner.

The Nation will live to regret what the Court has done today. I dissent.[2]

---

2. [In another habeas case decided the same day as *Boumediene*, the Court held that a federal district court could exercise habeas jurisdiction over U.S. citizens who were detained by U.S. forces in Iraq, rejecting the Government's argument that habeas jurisdiction was unavailable because the U.S. forces were part of a multi-national force. However, although jurisdiction was upheld, the Court withheld relief in the exercise of the equitable jurisdiction that colors the exercise of habeas jurisdiction. Munaf v. Green, 553 U.S. 674 (2008).]

CHAPTER II

CASES ARISING UNDER THE CONSTITUTION AND LAWS OF THE UNITED STATES[1]

STATUTE

28 U.S.C. § 1331. Federal question

The district courts shall have original jurisdiction of all civil actions arising under the Constitution, laws, or treaties of the United States.[2] As

---

[1. See 13B Wright, Miller & Cooper, Federal Practice and Procedure: Jurisdiction 2d §§ 3562–3566 (1984): Wright & Kane, Federal Courts §§ 17–18 (6th ed.2002); Mullenix, Redish & Vairo, Understanding Federal Courts and Jurisdiction §§ 4.01–4.04 (1998); 15 Moore's Federal Practice § 103 (3d ed.1998); Chemerinsky, Federal Jurisdiction § 5.2 (5th ed.2007); ALI Study § 1311, and Commentary at 162–187 and 477–488; ALI Judicial Code Project, Reporter's Memorandum at 636–651.]

[2. *"Prima facie* it would be reasonable to expect that the same considerations which impelled the framers of the Constitution to empower Congress to create inferior courts for the enforcement of rights arising out of the Constitution and laws of the United States would have motivated the same men sitting in their legislative capacities to exercise the power in their Judiciary Act of 1789. Yet not until 1875 did Congress make the presence of a federal question ground for original federal jurisdiction.

. . . . .

"A possible explanation may well lie in the fact that the possibilities of discrimination in diversity cases were most likely to be realized in the fact-finding aspects of the trial, beyond the reach of review. On the other hand, federal questions were likely to be questions of law, and hence state prejudice in handling them could more readily be corrected on review by the Supreme Court of the United States. It may well be, therefore, that the denial of diversity jurisdiction was the less easily remedied." Chadbourn and Levin, Original Jurisdiction of Federal Questions, 90 U.Pa.L.Rev. 639, 640–641 (1942).

For a summary of this development, see also Frankfurter, Distribution of Judicial Power between United States and State Courts, 13 Cornell L.Q. 499, 507 (1928). Early cases affirming the power of Congress to grant review in the Supreme Court of the United States of decisions of state courts of last resort on the ground of the denial of a right claimed under the Federal Constitution and laws were Martin v. Hunter's Lessee, 1 Wheat. (14 U.S.) 304 (1816) and Cohens v. Virginia, 6 Wheat. (19 U.S.) 264, 379 (1821).

While the general jurisdiction over cases "arising under" federal law is concurrent with state courts, some of the provisions giving special jurisdiction over particular kinds of cases under federal law confer exclusive jurisdiction upon the federal courts, e.g., bankruptcy (§ 1334), patents and copyrights (§ 1338), and actions for fines, penalties, and forfeitures (§ 1355). The tests for determining whether Congress has granted exclusive jurisdiction or concurrent jurisdiction, where the statute is not explicit, were applied, and it was held that state courts

amended Oct. 21, 1976, Pub.L. 94–574, § 2, 90 Stat. 2721; Dec. 1, 1980, Pub.L. 96–486, 94 Stat. 2369.[3]

. . . . .

Osborn v. Bank of the United States
Supreme Court of the United States, 1824.
9 Wheat. (22 U.S.) 738, 6 L.Ed. 204.

[The Legislature of Ohio, as a measure of relief from the prevailing financial distress, passed in 1819 an act to levy a tax of $50,000 on each branch in that state of the Bank of the United States. Shortly thereafter McCulloch v. Maryland, 4 Wheat. (17 U.S.) 316 (1819), held that a similar taxing statute was violative of the federal Constitution, but the decision was violently criticized in Ohio and in the West and South, and Ohio proceeded to enforce its Act. Thereupon the present suit was instituted by the Bank in the Circuit Court of the United States for an injunction against Osborn, the State Auditor, prohibiting him from collecting the tax. A temporary injunction was ordered by the court, but when the Bank's attorneys heard this, "wine was drank freely and mirth abounded." They neglected to have the writ itself issued. Osborn, who was hoping to collect the tax before the injunction could be issued, sent his assistant, Harper, to the office of the Bank to collect. Harper seized there $120,475 in specie and notes, loaded the money in a wagon and conveyed it to the State Treasurer. Thereafter a final decree was entered for the restoration of this sum, with interest, to the Bank. Appeal by the defendants. Henry Clay and Daniel Webster argued the case for the Bank.][4]

---

have concurrent jurisdiction of civil RICO actions under 18 U.S.C. §§ 1961–1968, in Tafflin v. Levitt, 493 U.S. 455 (1990).]

[**3.** Until 1976 § 1331 had purported to require an amount in controversy, at that time more than $10,000, for federal-question cases. This was almost wholly illusory, since most federal-question cases arise under particular Acts of Congress giving jurisdiction regardless of amount. It did create, however, what was called "an unfortunate gap in the statutory jurisdiction of the federal courts" in that many suits challenging the action of federal officers could not be heard because less than $10,000 was in controversy. The 1976 amendment of § 1331 removed the amount-in-controversy requirement for suits against the United States, any agency thereof, of any officer or employee in his official capacity. In 1980 the abolition of the amount in controversy was made complete, but at the same time Congress amended § 23(a) of the Consumer Product Safety Act, 15 U.S.C. § 2072(a), to require that more than $10,000 be in controversy in actions under that statute. In addition, a 1978 statute that was not changed in 1980 amended 28 U.S.C. § 1337 to require that more than $10,000 be in controversy in suits by shippers of goods against common carriers to recover for loss or damage to the goods under the Carmack Amendment, 49 U.S.C. § 11707.

Suit in federal court under the Magnuson–Moss Warranty Act requires that more than $50,000 be in controversy. 15 U.S.C. § 2310(d)(3)(B). For an interesting application of this, see Boelens v. Redman Homes, Inc., 748 F.2d 1058 (5th Cir.1984), rehearing denied with opinion 759 F.2d 504 (5th Cir.1985).]

[**4.** The foregoing statement is substituted for that in the report. The facts and setting of the case are given in 4 Beveridge, Life of John Marshall 327–333, 385–396 (1919), and 1 Warren, Supreme Court in United States History 526 et seq. (1922).]

■ MR. CHIEF JUSTICE MARSHALL delivered the opinion of the Court, and, after stating the case, proceeded as follows:

At the close of the argument, a point was suggested, of such vital importance, as to induce the Court to request that it might be particularly spoken to. That point is, the right of the Bank to sue in the Courts of the United States. It has been argued, and ought to be disposed of, before we proceed to the actual exercise of jurisdiction, by deciding on the rights of the parties.

The appellants contest the jurisdiction of the Court on two grounds:

1st. That the act of Congress has not given it.

2d. That, under the constitution, Congress cannot give it.

1. The first part of the objection depends entirely on the language of the act. The words are, that the Bank shall be "made able and capable in law," "to sue and be sued, plead and be impleaded, answer and be answered, defend and be defended in all State Courts having competent jurisdiction, and in any Circuit Court of the United States."

These words seem to the Court to admit of but one interpretation. They cannot be made plainer by explanation. They give, expressly, the right "to sue and be sued," "in every Circuit Court of the United States," and it would be difficult to substitute other terms which would be more direct and appropriate for the purpose. The argument of the appellants is founded on the opinion of this Court, in The Bank of the United States v. Deveaux (5 Cranch [9 U.S. 61, at] 85). In that case it was decided, that the former Bank of the United States was not enabled, by the act which incorporated it, to sue in the federal Courts. The words of the 3d section of that act are, that the Bank may "sue and be sued," etc. "in Courts of record, or any other place whatsoever." The Court was of opinion, that these general words, which are usual in all acts of incorporation, gave only a general capacity to sue, not a particular privilege to sue in the Courts of the United States.... Whether this decision be right or wrong, it amounts only to a declaration, that a general capacity in the Bank to sue, without mentioning the Courts of the Union, may not give a right to sue in those Courts. To infer from this, that words expressly conferring a right to sue in those Courts, do not give the right, is surely a conclusion which the premises do not warrant.

The act of incorporation, then, confers jurisdiction on the Circuit Courts of the United States, if Congress can confer it.

2. We will now consider the constitutionality of the clause in the act of incorporation, which authorizes the Bank to sue in the federal Courts.

In support of this clause, it is said, that the legislative, executive, and judicial powers, of every well constructed government, are co-extensive with each other; that is, they are potentially co-extensive. The executive department may constitutionally execute every law which the Legislature may constitutionally make, and the judicial department may receive from the Legislature the power of construing every such law. All governments which are not extremely defective in their organization, must possess, within themselves, the means of expounding, as well as enforcing, their own laws. If we examine the constitution of the United States, we find that its framers kept this great political principle in view. The 2d article vests the whole executive power in the President; and the 3d article declares, "that the judicial power shall extend to all cases in law and equity arising under this constitution, the laws of the United States, and treaties made, or which shall be made, under their authority."

This clause enables the judicial department to receive jurisdiction to the full extent of the constitution, laws, and treaties of the United States, when any question respecting them shall assume such a form that the judicial power is capable of acting on it. That power is capable of acting only when the subject is submitted to it by a party who asserts his rights in the form prescribed by law. It then becomes a case, and the constitution declares, that the judicial power shall extend to all cases arising under the constitution, laws, and treaties of the United States.

The suit of The Bank of the United States v. Osborn and others, is a case, and the question is, whether it arises under a law of the United States?

The appellants contend, that it does not, because several questions may arise in it, which depend on the general principles of the law, not on any act of Congress.

If this were sufficient to withdraw a case from the jurisdiction of the federal Courts, almost every case, although involving the construction of a law, would be withdrawn; and a clause in the constitution, relating to a subject of vital importance to the government, and expressed in the most comprehensive terms, would be construed to mean almost nothing. There is scarcely any case, every part of which depends on the constitution, laws, or treaties of the United States. The questions, whether the fact alleged as the foundation of the action, be real or fictitious; whether the conduct of the plaintiff has been such as to entitle him to maintain his action; whether his right is barred; whether he has received satisfaction, or has in any manner released his claims, are questions, some or all of which may occur in almost every case; and if their existence be sufficient to arrest the jurisdiction of the Court, words which seem intended to be as extensive as the constitution, laws, and treaties of the Union, which seem designed to give the Court of the government the construction of all its acts, so far as they affect the rights of individuals, would be reduced to almost nothing.

In those cases in which original jurisdiction is given to the Supreme Court, the judicial power of the United States cannot be exercised in its appellate form. In every other case, the power is to be exercised in its original or appellate form, or both, as the wisdom of Congress may direct. With the exception of these cases, in which original jurisdiction is given to this court, there is none to which the judicial power extends, from which the original jurisdiction of the inferior Courts is excluded by the constitution. Original jurisdiction, so far as the constitution gives a rule, is co-extensive with the judicial power. We find, in the constitution, no prohibition to its exercise, in every case in which the judicial power can be exercised. It would be a very bold construction to say, that this power could be applied in its appellate form only, to the most important class of cases to which it is applicable.

The constitution establishes the Supreme Court, and defines its jurisdiction. It enumerates cases in which its jurisdiction is original and exclusive; and then defines that which is appellate, but does not insinuate, that in any such case, the power cannot be exercised in its original form by Courts of original jurisdiction. It is not insinuated, that the judicial power, in cases depending on the character of the cause, cannot be exercised in the first instance, in the Courts of the Union, but must first be exercised in the tribunals of the State; tribunals over which the government of the Union has no adequate control, and which may be closed to any claim asserted under a law of the United States.

We perceive, then, no ground on which the proposition can be maintained, that Congress is incapable of giving the Circuit Courts original jurisdiction, in any case to which the appellate jurisdiction extends.

We ask, then, if it can be sufficient to exclude this jurisdiction, that the case involves questions depending on general principles? A cause may depend on several questions of fact and law. Some of these may depend on the construction of a law of the United States; others on principles unconnected with that law. If it be a sufficient foundation for jurisdiction, that the title or right set up by the party, may be defeated by one construction of the constitution or law of the United States, and sustained by the opposite construction, provided the facts necessary to support the action be made out, then all the other questions must be decided as incidental to this, which gives that jurisdiction. Those other questions cannot arrest the proceedings. Under this construction, the judicial power of the Union extends effectively and beneficially to that most important class of cases, which depend on the character of the cause. On the opposite construction, the judicial power never can be extended to a whole case, as expressed by the constitution, but to those parts of cases only which present the particular question involving the construction of the constitution or the law. We say it never can be extended to the whole case, because, if the circumstance that other points are involved in it, shall disable Congress from authorizing the Courts of the Union to take jurisdiction of the original cause, it equally disables Congress from authorizing those Courts to take jurisdiction of the whole cause, on an appeal, and thus will be restricted to a single question in that cause; and words obviously intended to secure to those who claim rights under the constitution, laws, or treaties of the United States, a trial in the federal Courts, will be restricted to the insecure remedy of an appeal upon an insulated point, after it has received that shape which may be given to it by another tribunal, into which he is forced against his will.

We think, then, that when a question to which the judicial power of the Union is extended by the constitution, forms an ingredient of the original cause, it is in the power of Congress to give the Circuit Courts jurisdiction of that cause, although other questions of fact or of law may be involved in it.

The case of the Bank is, we think, a very strong case of this description. The charter of incorporation not only creates it but gives it every faculty which it possesses. The power to acquire rights of any description, to transact business of any description, to make contracts of any description, to sue on those contracts, is given and measured by its charter, and that charter is a law of the United States. This being can acquire no right, make no contract, bring no suit, which is not authorized by a law of the United States. It is not only itself the mere creature of a law, but all its actions and all its rights are dependent on the same law. Can a being, thus constituted, have a case which does not arise literally, as well as substantially, under the law?

Take the case of a contract, which is put as the strongest against the Bank.

When a Bank sues, the first question which presents itself, and which lies at the foundation of the cause, is, has this legal entity a right to sue? Has it a right to come, not into this Court particularly, but into any Court? This depends on a law of the United States. The next question is, has this being a right to make this particular contract? If this question be decided in the negative, the cause is determined against the plaintiff; and this question, too, depends entirely on a law of the United States. These are important questions, and they exist in every possible case. The right to sue, if decided once, is decided forever; but the power of Congress was exercised antecedently to the first decision on that right, and if it was constitutional then, it cannot cease to be so, because the particular question is decided. It may be revived at the will of the party, and most probably would be renewed, were the tribunal to be changed. But the question respecting the right to make a particular contract, or to acquire a particular property, or to sue on account of a particular injury, belongs to every particular case, and may be renewed in every case. The question forms an original ingredient in every cause. Whether it be in fact relied on or not, in the defence, it is still a part of the cause, and may be relied on. The right of the plaintiff to sue, cannot depend on the defence which the defendant may choose to set up. His right to sue is anterior to that defence, and must depend on the state of things when the action is brought. The questions which the case involves, then, must determine its character, whether those questions be made in the cause or not.

The appellants say that the case arises on the contract; but the validity of the contract depends on a law of the United States and the plaintiff is compelled, in every case, to show its validity. The case arises emphatically under the law. The act of Congress is its foundation. The contract could never have been made, but under the authority of that act. The act itself is the first ingredient in the case, is its origin, is that from which every other part arises. That other questions may also arise, as the execution of the contract, or its performance, cannot change the case, or give it any other origin than the charter of incorporation. The action still originates in, and is sustained by, that charter.

The clause giving the Bank a right to sue in the Circuit Courts of the United States, stands on the same principle with the acts authorizing officers of the United States who sue in their own names, to sue in the Courts of the United States. The Postmaster General, for example, cannot sue under that part of the constitution which gives jurisdiction to the federal Courts, in consequence of the character of the party, nor is he authorized to sue by the Judiciary Act. He comes into the Courts of the Union under the authority of an act of Congress, the constitutionality of which can only be sustained by the admission that his suit is a case arising under a law of the United States. If it be said, that it is such a case, because a law of the United States authorizes the contract, and authorizes the suit, the same reasons exist with respect to a suit brought by the Bank. That, too, is such a case; because that suit, too, is itself authorized, and is brought on a contract authorized by a law of the United States. It depends absolutely on that law, and cannot exist a moment without its authority.

If it be said, that a suit brought by the Bank may depend in fact altogether on questions unconnected with any law of the United States, it is equally true, with respect to suits brought by the Postmaster General. The plea in bar may be payment, if the suit be brought on a bond, or non assumpsit, if it be brought on an open account, and no other question may arise than what respects the complete discharge of the demand. Yet the constitutionality of the act authorizing the Postmaster General to sue in the Courts of the United States, has never been drawn into question. It is sustained singly by an act of Congress, standing on that construction of the constitution which asserts the right of the Legislature to give original jurisdiction to the Circuit Courts, in cases arising under a law of the United States.

The clause in the patent law, authorizing suits in the Circuit Courts, stands, we think, on the same principle. Such a suit is a case arising under a law of the United States. Yet the defendant may not, at the trial, question the validity of the patent, or make any point which requires the construction of an act of Congress. He may rest his defence exclusively on the fact, that he has not violated the right of the plaintiff.

That this fact becomes the sole question made in the cause, cannot oust the jurisdiction of the Court, or establish the position, that the case does not arise under a law of the United States.

It is said, that a clear distinction exists between the party and the cause; that the party may originate under a law with which the cause has no connexion; and that Congress may, with the same propriety, give a naturalized citizen, who is the mere creature of a law, a right to sue in the Courts of the United States, as give that right to the Bank.

This distinction is not denied; and, if the act of Congress was a simple act of incorporation, and contained nothing more, it might be entitled to great consideration. But the act does not stop with incorporating the Bank.

It proceeds to bestow upon the being it has made, all the faculties and capacities which that being possesses. Every act of the Bank grows out of this law, and is tested by it. To use the language of the constitution, every act of the Bank arises out of this law.

A naturalized citizen is indeed made a citizen under an act of Congress, but the act does not proceed to give, to regulate, or to prescribe his capacities. He becomes a member of the society, possessing all the rights of a native citizen, and standing, in the view of the constitution, on the footing of a native. The constitution does not authorize Congress to enlarge or abridge those rights. The simple power of the national Legislature, is to prescribe a uniform rule of naturalization, and the exercise of this power exhausts it, so far as respects the individual. The constitution then takes him up, and, among other rights, extends to him the capacity of suing in the Courts of the United States, precisely under the same circumstances under which a native might sue. He is distinguishable in nothing from a native citizen, except so far as the constitution makes the distinction. The law makes none.

There is, then, no resemblance between the act incorporating the Bank, and the general naturalization law.

Upon the best consideration we have been able to bestow on this subject, we are of opinion, that the clause in the act of incorporation, enabling the Bank to sue in the Courts of the United States, is consistent with the constitution, and to be obeyed in all Courts.

We will now proceed to consider the merits of the cause.

[In its lengthy discussion of the merits, the Court considered, inter alia, whether the State of Ohio should be deemed an indispensable party given that the individual defendants were acting in their capacities as state officers, and seized and held the funds in question for the benefit of the State. Acceptance of this argument would have required dismissal of the suit, because the 11th Amendment barred the joinder of the State as a named party. The 11th Amendment, discussed infra pp. 503–576, was assumed by the Court to bar a suit brought in federal court against a State by a corporate plaintiff such as the Bank of the United States even when the basis for federal jurisdiction over the Bank's suit was not diversity of citizenship, but rather that the suit was one arising under federal law. The Court rejected this argument, declaring: "It may, we think, be laid down as a rule which admits of no exception, that, in all cases where jurisdiction depends on the party, it is the party named in the record. Consequently, the 11th amendment, which restrains the jurisdiction granted by the constitution over suits against States, is, of necessity, limited to those suits in which a State is a party on the record. The amendment has its full effect, if the constitution be construed as it would have been construed, had the jurisdiction of the Court never been extended to suits brought against a State, by the citizens of another State, or by aliens." The Court affirmed the judgment below insofar as it required the restitution of the Bank's money, but reversed that judgment insofar as it required the payment of interest, "it being the opinion of this Court, that, while the parties were restrained by the authority of the Circuit Court from using [the money], they ought not to be charged with interest."]

■ Mr. Justice Johnson [dissenting].

. . . . .

I have very little doubt, that the public mind will be easily reconciled to the decision of the court here rendered; for, whether necessary or unnecessary, originally, a state of things has now grown up, in some of the states, which renders all the protection necessary, that the general government can give to this bank.

[Justice Johnson first disputed the Court's broad reading of the Bank's Act of Incorporation as one conferring federal jurisdiction over all suits by or against the Bank of the United States. But he recognized that this issue of statutory construction was of secondary importance: "for if Congress can vest this jurisdiction, and the people will it, the act may be amended, and the jurisdiction vested. I next proceed to consider, more distinctly, the constitutional question, on the right to vest the jurisdiction to the extent here contended for."]

And here I must observe, that I altogether misunderstood the counsel, who argued the cause for the plaintiff in error, if any of them contended against the jurisdiction, on the ground, that the cause involved questions depending on general principles. No one can question, that the court which has jurisdiction of the principal question must exercise jurisdiction over every question. The argument went to deny the right to assume jurisdiction, on a mere hypothesis. It was one of description, identity, definition; they contended, that until a question involving the construction or administration of the laws of the United States did actually arise, the *casus federis* was not presented, on which the constitution authorized the government to take to itself the jurisdiction of the cause. That until such a question actually arose, until such a case was actually presented, *non constat*, but the cause depended upon general principles, exclusively cognizable in the state courts; that neither the letter nor the spirit of the constitution sanctioned the assumption of jurisdiction on the part of the United States, at any previous stage.

And this doctrine has my hearty concurrence in its general application. . . .

. . . . .

. . . It is not, therefore, because congress may not vest an *original* jurisdiction, where they can constitutionally vest in the circuit courts *appellate* jurisdiction, that I object to this general grant of the right to sue; but because that the peculiar nature of this jurisdiction is such, as to render it impossible to exercise it, in a strictly original form, and because the principle of a possible occurrence of a question, as a ground of jurisdiction, is transcending the bounds of the constitution, and placing it on a ground which will admit of an *enormous accession*, if not an *unlimited assumption*, of jurisdiction.

. . . . .

Upon the whole, I feel compelled to dissent from the Court, on the point of jurisdiction . . . .

Decree affirmed, except as to interest . . . .[5]

———

Albright v. Teas

Supreme Court of the United States, 1883.
106 U.S. 613, 1 S.Ct. 550, 27 L.Ed. 295.

Appeal from the Circuit Court of the United States for the District of New Jersey.

This was a suit in equity originally brought in the court of chancery of the state of New Jersey by Andrew Teas, the appellee, against the appellants, Andrew Albright, Edwin R. Cahoone, and Samuel E. Tompkins. The bill alleged that Teas was the inventor and patentee of certain improvements in coach-pads, harness-saddles, and saddle-trees, covered by three certain letters patent issued to him; that on February 1, 1876, he made an agreement in writing of that date with Albright and Cahoone, which was in substance as follows: Teas agreed on his part to make assignments of said letters patent to Albright and Cahoone, and also of certain other letters patent for which he had made application to the patent-office, and also of any other patents which he might obtain for improvements in gig-saddles and coach-pads for harness; in consideration whereof Albright and Cahoone agreed that they would "use their best endeavors to have the aforesaid inventions worked, goods manufactured and sold to the best advantage of themselves and said Teas," and to pay Teas certain specified royalties for

---

[5. In the companion case of Bank of the United States v. Planters' Bank of Georgia, 9 Wheat. (22 U.S.) 904 (1824), federal jurisdiction was held to exist over a suit by the Bank of the United States as the bearer of negotiable notes made by a state bank.

The Pacific Railroad Removal Cases, 115 U.S. 1 (1885), held that every case to which a corporation chartered by Act of Congress was a party fell within the 1875 Act giving jurisdiction over "suits arising under the laws of the United States." The Court has since referred to this as an "unfortunate decision," Romero v. International Terminal Operating Co., 358 U.S. 354, 379 n. 50 (1959). It was quickly limited, and is now virtually overruled, by statute. The present statute, 28 U.S.C. § 1349, provides that the district courts shall not have jurisdiction on the ground that a corporation was incorporated by Congress unless the United States owns more than half of the capital stock of the corporation. Another statute, 28 U.S.C. § 1348, grants jurisdiction of certain limited cases to which banks may be parties, and provides otherwise that national banking associations shall be deemed citizens of the states in which they are located.

The Supreme Court, reaffirming the basic holding in *Osborn*, has held that the statute, 36 U.S.C. § 12, which gives the American National Red Cross "the power to sue and be sued in courts of law and equity, State or Federal," is a grant of jurisdiction over all suits in which the Red Cross is a party. American Nat. Red Cross v. S.G., 505 U.S. 247 (1992).]

the use of the patented improvements, and pay "all just and necessary expenses for the purpose of procuring and sustaining all of said letters patent against infringers," provided it be for the mutual interests of and financial benefits to all the parties to the agreement.

The bill further alleged that Teas did assign the patents as stipulated in the agreement and that the agreement was in full force; that a large amount of goods, in which the improvements covered by the patents of the complainant were used, had been manufactured by Albright and Cahoone under the name of the Cahoone Manufacturing Company, and by Tompkins, Albright, and Cahoone, under the firm name of Samuel E. Tompkins, Cahoone & Co.; that the defendants had failed to render proper statements of the quantity of goods manufactured by them; that complainant believed there was a large amount due him under said contract for royalties; and that he had tried without success to obtain an inspection of the account books of defendants to ascertain what was so due him.

The bill prayed for discovery, for an account of the sums due the complainant for royalties under said contract, and for a decree against Albright and Cahoone for the amount found to be due from them to him on said account and for general relief.

.   .   .   .   .

. . . [T]he defendants filed a petition for the removal of the cause to the circuit court of the United States, in which they alleged that all the parties to the suit were citizens of the state of New Jersey, but that the suit was one arising under the patent laws of the United States, and exclusively within the cognizance of the courts of the United States, and removable under the act of March 3, 1875, (18 St. 470). Upon this petition the cause was removed to the circuit court of the United States for the district of New Jersey. By consent of parties an interlocutory order was made in the circuit court referring the cause to a master to report the amount due the complainant, if anything, for royalty upon the articles, enumerating them, in the manufacture of which the patented improvements of the complainant were used.

Upon final hearing, the testimony having been closed, the counsel for the complainant moved the circuit court to remand the cause to the state court of chancery, and the court declaring its opinion to be that the suit was not one arising under any of the laws of the United States, but was one over which the United States courts had no jurisdiction, and that it was a suit for an accounting and relief for the settlement of controversies under a contract of which the state courts had full cognizance, ordered the cause to be remanded to the state court. To obtain a review of this order the present appeal was taken by Tompkins, Albright, and Cahoone, defendants in the circuit court.

■ WOODS, J. The contention of the appellants is that the case is one "arising under the . . . laws of the United States," and was, therefore, properly removable from the state to the United States courts, and should not have been remanded. It is clear, from an inspection of the bill and answers, that the case is founded upon the agreement in writing between the appellee and the appellants Albright and Cahoone, by which the former, for a consideration therein specified, transferred to the latter his interest in certain letters patent. The suit was brought to recover the consideration for this transfer, and was not based on the letters patent. The appellants insist, however, that evidence was taken in the cause by the appellee for the purpose of proving that they were using his patented improvements in the manufacture of goods for which they paid him no royalty, and which they contended did not embody the improvements covered by his patents; that the testimony developed a controversy between the parties on the question whether the goods manufactured by the appellants under the Tompkins and other patents owned by them, were or were not infringements on the patents of appellee; consequently that questions of infringement and of the construction of the claims of appellee's patents were necessarily involved in the case, and therefore it was one arising under the patent laws of the United States. We search the bill of complaint in vain to find any averments raising these questions. It makes no issue touching the construction of the patents granted the appellee, or their validity or their infringement. The only complaint made in the bill is that the appellants were fraudulently excluding the appellee from an inspection of their books of account, and refusing to pay him the sums due for royalties under his contract. And the prayer of the bill was for a discovery, an account of what was due appellee under his contract, and a decree for the amount found to be due him. On the face of the bill, therefore, the case is not one arising under the patent laws of the United States. Wilson v. Sandford, 10 How. [51 U.S.] 99.

The testimony on which appellants rely to show the jurisdiction of the circuit court is not before us, but conceding that it discloses the controversy which appellants assert it does, the question arises, does this fact give the courts of the United States jurisdiction of the case? Tompkins is the only one of the appellants who questions the validity of the appellee's patents. But he is not a party to the contract between appellee and Albright and Cahoone, and no relief is prayed against him by the bill; and though he says in his answer that he had always disputed the value and validity of the patents of appellee, he raises no issues thereon. The fact that he is made a party defendant to the bill can, therefore, have no effect on the question in hand.

In passing on the question of jurisdiction the case is to be considered as if Albright and Cahoone were the only defendants. The appellee, before the commencement of the suit, sold and transferred to Albright and Cahoone all his title and interest in the inventions covered by his patents. The transfer was absolute and unconditional. No right, therefore, secured to the appellee in the patent by any act of Congress remained in him. He had no right to prosecute any one for infringements of his patents, or to demand damages therefor or an account of profits. He was entitled to the royalties secured by his contract and nothing more. And the only question raised by the bill of complaint and the answer of Albright and Cahoone was simply this: What is the sum due the appellee from Albright and Cahoone for his royalties under this contract? In ascertaining this amount, it, of course, became necessary to inquire what goods were manufactured by the appellants under the patents of the appellee. In prosecuting this inquiry an incidental question might arise, namely, what goods were manufactured by the appellants under other patents of which they were the owners or licensees? But this incidental and collateral inquiry does not change the nature of the litigation. The fact that Albright and Cahoone had licenses to use other patents under which they were manufacturing goods, does not give them the right to litigate their cause in the United States courts because certain goods, which they asserted were made under the other patents, the appellee asserted were really made under his. The suit, notwithstanding the collateral inquiry, still remains a suit on the contract to recover royalties, and not a suit upon the letters patent. It arises solely upon the contract and not upon the patent laws of the United States. In fact, it does not appear that there is any dispute whatever between the parties in reference to the construction of the patents of the appellee. The controversy between them, as stated by the appellants themselves, is whether certain goods manufactured by them embody the invention covered by the appellee's patents. This does not necessarily involve a construction of the patents. Both parties may agree as to what the patented invention is, and yet disagree on the question whether the invention is employed in the manufacture of certain specified goods. The controversy between the parties in this case is clearly of the latter kind. The case cannot, therefore, be said to be one which grows out of the legislation of congress. Neither party asserts any right, privilege, claim, protection, or defense founded, in whole or in part, on any law of the United States. We are, therefore, of opinion that, even if we go outside the pleadings and look into the testimony, the case is not one arising under the laws of the United States, and, consequently, that the courts of the United States had no jurisdiction to entertain it.

. . . . .

From the conclusions reached by us, it follows that the decree of the circuit court remanding the cause to the state court must be affirmed.[6]

Feibelman v. Packard

Supreme Court of the United States, 1883.
109 U.S. 421, 3 S.Ct. 289, 27 L.Ed. 984.

In Error to the Circuit Court of the United States for the District of Louisiana.

[**6.** The distinction taken in the principal case between cases under the patent laws and cases involving contracts about patents is frequently applied. See, e.g., Luckett v. Delpark, Inc., 270 U.S. 496 (1926); Jim Arnold Corp. v. Hydrotech Systems, Inc., 109 F.3d 1567 (Fed.Cir. 1997). 13B Wright, Miller & Cooper, Federal Practice and Procedure: Jurisdiction 2d § 3582 (1984).]

■ MATTHEWS, J. This action was originally brought by Nathan Feibelman, since deceased, and revived by his administrator, the plaintiff in error, by petition filed April 24, 1873, in the fourth district court for the parish of Orleans, in the state of Louisiana. Its object was to recover damages for unlawfully seizing and taking forcible possession of a stock of merchandise alleged by the plaintiff to have been his property and in his possession. The defendant Packard was alleged to be the marshal of the United States for the district of Louisiana, and the seizure and taking of the property is stated to have been under a claim of authority based upon a writ or warrant issued by the judge of the district court of the United States for the district of Louisiana in certain proceedings in bankruptcy instituted in that court by D. Valentine & Co. as creditors against E. Dreyfus & Co., but it is averred that the writ did not justify the acts complained of. The other defendants below were sureties on the official bond of Packard as marshal, and by an amendment to the original petition it is alleged "that all the acts charged and complained of in said original petition by which the petitioners suffered the damages therein set forth were done by said Packard in his capacity of marshal aforesaid, and are breaches of the conditions of said bond, and give unto your petitioner this right of action on said bond against said marshal and his sureties." On April 7, 1875, the defendants filed in the state court their petition for the removal of the cause to the circuit court of the United States for that district, accompanied by a sufficient bond, conditioned according to law, upon the ground that the suit arose under a law of the United States, but the application was denied; and thereafter, on April 22, 1875, they filed in the circuit court a petition for a writ of certiorari to remove the same into that court, which was granted. Thereafter the cause proceeded to final judgment in favor of the defendants in that court.

The action of the circuit court in the removal of the cause from the state court is assigned for error, and is first to be considered. The suit was pending in the state court, but was not at issue, when the removal act of March 3, 1875, took effect, and the right of removal is regulated by its provisions. The ground of the removal was that the suit, being one of a civil nature at law, in which the matter in dispute, exclusive of costs, exceeded $500 in value, arose under the constitution and laws of the United States. It is clear that the circuit court did not err in directing the removal of the suit from the state court; for, if we look at the nature of the plaintiff's cause of action and the grounds of the defense, as set forth in his petition, it is apparent that the suit arose under a law of the United States. The action, as we have seen, was founded on the official bond of Packard as marshal of the United States for that district, his sureties being joined as codefendants, and the acts complained of as illegal and injurious being charged to be breaches of its condition. The bond was required to be given by section 783, Rev.St., and section 784 expressly gives the right of action as follows:

> "In the case of a breach of the condition of a marshal's bond, any person thereby injured may institute, in his own name and for his sole use, a suit on said bond and thereupon recover such damages as shall

be legally assessed, with costs of suit, for which execution may issue for him in due form. If such party fails to recover in the suit, judgment shall be rendered and execution may issue against him for costs in favor of the defendant; and the United States shall in no case be liable for the same."

Section 785 and 786 contain provisions regulating the suit, the latter prescribing the limitation of six years after the cause of action has accrued, after which no such suit shall be maintained, with the usual saving in behalf of persons under disabilities.

The counsel for plaintiff in error assumes in argument that the suit was to recover damages for alleged trespasses. It was plainly upon the bond itself, and therefore arose directly under the provisions of an act of congress. Gwin v. Breedlove, 2 How. [43 U.S.] 29; Gwin v. Barton, 6 How. [47 U.S.] 7.

. . . . .

Affirmed.

Joy v. St. Louis

Supreme Court of the United States, 1906.
201 U.S. 332, 26 S.Ct. 478, 50 L.Ed. 776.

In Error to the Circuit Court of the United States for the Eastern District of Missouri to review a judgment dismissing, for want of jurisdiction, the petition in an action of ejectment.

[The action was brought to recover land bordering on the Mississippi River in St. Louis. The plaintiff in his complaint deraigned title from a patent of the United States pursuant to an Act of Congress.]

■ MR. JUSTICE PECKHAM . . . delivered the opinion of the court:

There is no diversity of citizenship in this case, and the only ground of jurisdiction claimed is that the action arises under the laws of the United States. The case is a pure action of ejectment, and the general rule in such actions, as to the complaint, is that the only facts necessary to be stated therein are, that plaintiff is the owner of the premises described, and entitled to the possession, and that defendant wrongfully withholds such possession, to plaintiff's damage in an amount stated. Setting out the source of the plaintiff's title, as was done with so much detail in this case, was unnecessary, but it does not alter the case, because a claim that the title comes from the United States does not, for that reason merely, raise a Federal question.

It is a long-settled rule, evidenced by many decisions of this court, that the plaintiff cannot make out a case as arising under the Constitution or the laws of the United States unless it necessarily appears by the complaint or petition or bill in stating plaintiff's cause of action. In Little York Gold–

Washing & Water Co. v. Keyes, 96 U.S. 199–203, it was said that before the circuit court can be required to retain a cause under its jurisdiction, under § 5, act of 1875 [18 Stat. at L. 472, chap. 137], it must in some form appear upon the record, by a statement of facts, in legal and logical form, such as is required in good pleading, that the suit is one which really and substantially involves a dispute or controversy as to a right which depends upon the construction or effect of the Constitution, or some law or treaty of the United States.... This original jurisdiction, it has been frequently held, must appear by the plaintiff's statement of his own claim, and it cannot be made to appear by the assertion in the plaintiff's pleading that the defense raises or will raise a Federal question. As has been stated, the rule is a reasonable and just one that the complainant, in the first instance, shall be confined to a statement of his cause of action, leaving to the defendant to set up in his answer what his defense is, and, if anything more than a denial of plaintiff's cause of action, imposing upon the defendant the burden of proving such defense. This principle was given effect to in Tennessee v. Union & Planters' Bank, 152 U.S. 454; ... The mere fact that the title of plaintiff comes from a patent or under an act of Congress does not show that a Federal question arises. It was said in Blackburn v. Portland Gold Min. Co., 175 U.S. 571, that "this court has frequently been vainly asked to hold that controversies in respect to lands, one of the parties to which had derived his title directly from an act of Congress, for that reason alone presented a Federal question." ...

To say that there is a dispute between the parties as to the construction of the patent or of the several acts of Congress referred to does not raise a Federal question, because a statement that there is such dispute is entirely unnecessary in averring or proving plaintiff's cause of action. His source of title, as set forth in the petition, might not be disputed, and the defense might rest upon the defense of adverse possession, as set up in the answer. If defendants contented themselves on the trial with proof of such defense, then no question of a Federal nature would have been tried or decided.

In those cases where the dispute necessarily appears in the course of properly alleging and proving the plaintiff's cause of action, the situation is entirely different. In this case the real dispute, as stated by the plaintiff, is whether plaintiff is entitled to the land formed by accretion, which has taken place many years since the patent was issued and since the acts of Congress were passed. There is no dispute as to the terms of the patent or of the acts of Congress. The language of the averment in the petition ... shows that the controversy in dispute is not at all in regard to the land covered by the letters patent or by the acts of Congress, and no dispute is alleged to exist as to such land, but the dispute relates to land, "which land is a portion of the land formed by accretions or gradual deposits from said river, along said west bank thereof, between said north and south lines of said outlot, confirmation, and surveys, and which thereby became a portion of the land granted by said letters patent and acts of Congress approved June 13th, 1812, and June 6th, 1874, respectively."

Now, whether the land contained in the original patent reached to the Mississippi river as its eastern boundary, under the distances called for by the patent, would be a question of fact, as was stated in Sweringen v. St. Louis, 185 U.S. 38, and whether the plaintiff is, upon the facts set forth, entitled to the accretion, is a question of local or state law, and is not one of a Federal nature. St. Anthony Falls Water–Power Co. v. St. Paul Water Comrs., 168 U.S. 349–359, and cases cited. In Packer v. Bird, 137 U.S. 661, it was held that while the Federal court would construe grants of the general government without reference to the rules of construction adopted by the states for grants by them, yet whatever incidents or rights attached to the ownership of the property conveyed by the United States bordering on a navigable stream would be determined by the states in which it is situated, subject to the limitation that their rules do not impair the efficacy of the grant, or the use and enjoyment of the property by the grantee....

As this land in controversy is not the land described in the letters patent or the acts of Congress, but, as is stated in the petition, is formed by accretions or gradual deposits from the river, whether such land belongs to the plaintiff is, under the case just cited, a matter of local or state law, and not one arising under the laws of the United States.

The question before us is wholly different from the case of a writ of error to a state court founded upon § 709 of the Revised Statutes of the United States. A Federal question may appear in the course of the trial, and some right specially claimed or set up under a Federal statute may have been denied, and the party against whom the decision was made can have the question reviewed by this court under that section.

. . . . .

In any aspect in which this case may be viewed, we think it was not one over which the Circuit Court had jurisdiction, and for that reason its order dismissing the petition is affirmed.[7]

———

[7. "[W]here title to land is in doubt because of some matter of federal law, there is federal jurisdiction to entertain a bill to remove a cloud on title, Hopkins v. Walker, 244 U.S. 486 (1917), but not a suit to quiet title, Shulthis v. McDougal, 225 U.S. 561 (1912), since allegations as to the nature of the cloud are proper in the first kind of action but improper in the second. Again, an action to enjoin another from using land which, by federal law, is asserted to be plaintiff's raises a proper federal question, Lancaster v. Kathleen Oil Co., 241 U.S. 551 (1916), but if plaintiff is out of possession, he has an adequate legal remedy in an action for ejectment, in which allegations as to the title of land are not proper, and he cannot invoke federal question jurisdiction. White v. Sparkill Realty Corp., 280 U.S. 500 (1930)." ALI Study 170.

In Oneida Indian Nation of New York State v. County of Oneida, 464 F.2d 916 (2d Cir.1972), application of the well-pleaded complaint rule led to the result that an Indian tribe had no forum in any court to press their claim that they had been deprived of their lands in violation of federal law. A unanimous Supreme Court was able to avoid this unpalatable result, while adhering to the well-pleaded complaint rule, by finding that Indian title is always a matter of federal law and thus that the tribe was asserting a current right to

Louisville & Nashville R.R. v. Mottley

Supreme Court of the United States, 1908.
211 U.S. 149, 29 S.Ct. 42, 53 L.Ed. 126.

Statement by MR. JUSTICE MOODY: The appellees (husband and wife), being residents and citizens of Kentucky, brought this suit in equity in the circuit court of the United States for the western district of Kentucky against the appellant, a railroad company and a citizen of the same state. The object of the suit was to compel the specific performance of the following contract:

"Louisville, Ky., Oct. 2d, 1871.

"The Louisville & Nashville Railroad Company, in consideration that E.L. Mottley and wife, Annie E. Mottley, have this day released company from all damages or claims for damages for injuries received by them on the 7th of September, 1871, in consequence of a collision of trains on the railroad of said company at Randolph's Station, Jefferson County, Kentucky, hereby agrees to issue free passes on said railroad and branches now existing or to exist, to said E.L. & Annie E. Mottley for the remainder of the present year, and thereafter to renew said passes annually during the lives of said Mottley and wife or either of them."

The bill alleged that in September, 1871, plaintiffs, while passengers upon the defendant railroad, were injured by the defendant's negligence, and released their respective claims for damages in consideration of the agreement for transportation during their lives, expressed in the contract. It is alleged that the contract was performed by the defendant up to January 1, 1907, when the defendant declined to renew the passes. The bill then alleges that the refusal to comply with the contract was based solely upon that part of the act of Congress of June 29, 1906 (34 Stat. at L. 584, chap. 3591), which forbids the giving of free passes or free transportation. The bill further alleges: First, that the act of Congress referred to does not prohibit the giving of passes under the circumstances of this case; and, second, that, if the law is to be construed as prohibiting such passes, it is in conflict with the 5th Amendment of the Constitution, because it deprives the plaintiffs of their property without due process of law. The defendant demurred to the bill. The judge of the circuit court overruled the demurrer, entered a decree for the relief prayed for, and the defendant appealed directly to this court.

■ MR. JUSTICE MOODY, after making the foregoing statement, delivered the opinion of the court:

---

possession conferred by federal law wholly independent of state law. Oneida Indian Nation of New York State v. County of Oneida, 414 U.S. 661 (1974).

Fifteen years after the Supreme Court first passed on this case the matter came to an end when the Supreme Court refused to review a decision that the purchase of the land from the Oneida Indians by New York in 1785 and 1788 was valid. Oneida Indian Nation of New York v. New York, 860 F.2d 1145 (2d Cir.1988), cert. denied, 493 U.S. 871 (1989).]

Two questions of law were raised by the demurrer to the bill, were brought here by appeal, and have been argued before us. They are, first, whether that part of the act of Congress of June 29, 1906 (34 Stat. at L. 584, chap. 3591), which forbids the giving of free passes or the collection of any different compensation for transportation of passengers than that specified in the tariff filed, makes it unlawful to perform a contract for transportation of persons who, in good faith, before the passage of the act, had accepted such contract in satisfaction of a valid cause of action against the railroad; and, second, whether the statute, if it should be construed to render such a contract unlawful, is in violation of the 5th Amendment of the Constitution of the United States. We do not deem it necessary, however, to consider either of these questions, because, in our opinion, the court below was without jurisdiction of the cause. Neither party has questioned that jurisdiction, but it is the duty of this court to see to it that the jurisdiction of the circuit court, which is defined and limited by statute, is not exceeded. This duty we have frequently performed of our own motion. Mansfield, C. & L.M.R. Co. v. Swan, 111 U.S. 379, 382; King Iron Bridge & Mfg. Co. v. Otoe County, 120 U.S. 225; Blacklock v. Small, 127 U.S. 96, 105; Cameron v. Hodges, 127 U.S. 322; Continental Nat. Bank v. Buford, 191 U.S. 119.

There was no diversity of citizenship, and it is not and cannot be suggested that there was any ground of jurisdiction, except that the case was a "suit ... arising under the Constitution or laws of the United States." 25 Stat. at L. 434, chap. 866. It is the settled interpretation of these words, as used in this statute, conferring jurisdiction, that a suit arises under the Constitution and laws of the United States only when the plaintiff's statement of his own cause of action shows that it is based upon those laws or that Constitution. It is not enough that the plaintiff alleges some anticipated defense to his cause of action, and asserts that the defense is invalidated by some provision of the Constitution of the United States. Although such allegations show that very likely, in the course of the litigation, a question under the Constitution would arise, they do not show that the suit, that is, the plaintiff's original cause of action, arises under the Constitution....

. . . . .

It is ordered that the judgment be reversed and the case remitted to the circuit court with instructions to dismiss the suit for want of jurisdiction.[8]

[8. After dismissal of the federal action in the principal case, suit was brought in the state court and the Supreme Court ultimately decided the case on the merits on appeal from the state court. The Mottleys lost. Louisville & N.R. Co. v. Mottley, 219 U.S. 467 (1911).

In Vaden v. Discover Bank, 556 U.S. 49, 129 S.Ct. 1262 (2009), the Supreme Court explained that because federal courts must apply the well-pleaded complaint rule to ensure that federal jurisdiction exists, the complaint—and not merely the counterclaim—in the state

American Well Works Co. v. Layne & Bowler Co.

Supreme Court of the United States, 1916.
241 U.S. 257, 36 S.Ct. 585, 60 L.Ed. 987.

■ Mr. Justice Holmes delivered the opinion of the court.

This is a suit begun in a state court, removed to the United States court, and then, on motion to remand by the plaintiff, dismissed by the latter court, on the ground that the cause of action arose under the patent laws of the United States, that the state court had no jurisdiction, and that therefore, the one to which it was removed had none. There is a proper certificate and the case comes here direct from the district court.

Of course the question depends upon the plaintiff's declaration. The Fair v. Kohler Die & Specialty Co., 228 U.S. 22, 25. That may be summed up in a few words. The plaintiff alleges that it owns, manufactures, and sells a certain pump, has or has applied for a patent for it, and that the pump is known as the best in the market. It then alleges that the defendants have falsely and maliciously libeled and slandered the plaintiff's title to the pump by stating that the pump and certain parts thereof are infringements upon the defendant's pump and certain parts thereof, and that without probable cause they have brought suits against some parties who are using the plaintiff's pump, and that they are threatening suits against all who use it. The allegation of the defendants' libel or slander is repeated in slightly varying form, but it all comes to statements to various people that the plaintiff was infringing the defendants' patent, and that the defendant would sue both seller and buyer if the plaintiff's pump was used. Actual damage to the plaintiff in its business is alleged to the extent of $50,000, and punitive damages to the same amount are asked.

It is evident that the claim for damages is based upon conduct; or, more specifically, language, tending to persuade the public to withdraw its custom from the plaintiff, and having that effect to its damage. Such conduct, having such effect, is equally actionable whether it produces the result by persuasion, by threats, or by falsehood (Moran v. Dunphy, 177 Mass. 485, 487, 59 N.E. 125), and it is enough to allege and prove the conduct and effect, leaving the defendant to justify if he can. If the conduct complained of is persuasion, it may be justified by the fact that the defendant is a competitor, or by good faith and reasonable grounds. If it is a statement of fact, it may be justified, absolutely or with qualifications, by proof that the statement is true. But all such justifications are defenses, and raise issues that are no part of the plaintiff's case. In the present instance it is part of the plaintiff's case that it had a business to be damaged; whether built up by patents or without them does not matter. It is no part of it to prove anything concerning the defendants' patent, or that the plaintiff did not infringe the same—still less to prove anything concerning any patent of its own. The material statement complained of is that the plaintiff infringes,—which may be true notwithstanding the plaintiff's

---

action must establish a basis for federal jurisdiction in order for the federal court to exercise jurisdiction over a petition to compel arbitration of litigation that is pending in state court.]

patent. That is merely a piece of evidence. Furthermore, the damage alleged presumably is rather the consequence of the threat to sue than of the statement that the plaintiff's pump infringed the defendants' rights.

A suit for damages to business caused by a threat to sue under the patent law is not itself a suit under the patent law. And the same is true when the damage is caused by a statement of fact,—that the defendant has a patent which is infringed. What makes the defendants' act a wrong is its manifest tendency to injure the plaintiff's business; and the wrong is the same whatever the means by which it is accomplished. But whether it is a wrong or not depends upon the law of the state where the act is done, not upon the patent law, and therefore the suit arises under the law of the state. A suit arises under the law that creates the cause of action. The fact that the justification may involve the validity and infringement of a patent is no more material to the question under what law the suit is brought than it would be in an action of contract. If the state adopted for civil proceedings the saying of the old criminal law: the greater the truth, the greater the libel, the validity of the patent would not come in question at all. In Massachusetts the truth would not be a defense if the statement was made from disinterested malevolence. Rev.Laws, chap. 173, § 91. The state is master of the whole matter, and if it saw fit to do away with actions of this type altogether, no one, we imagine, would suppose that they still could be maintained under the patent laws of the United States.

Judgment reversed.

■ Mr. Justice McKenna dissents, being of opinion that the case involves a direct and substantial controversy under the patent laws.

Bell v. Hood

Supreme Court of the United States, 1946.
327 U.S. 678, 66 S.Ct. 773, 90 L.Ed. 939.

■ Mr. Justice Black delivered the opinion of the Court.

Petitioners brought this suit in a federal district court to recover damages in excess of $3,000 from the respondents who are agents of the Federal Bureau of Investigation. The complaint alleges that the Court's jurisdiction is founded upon federal questions arising under the Fourth and Fifth Amendments. It is alleged that the damages were suffered as a result of the defendants imprisoning the petitioners in violation of their Constitutional right to be free from deprivation of their liberty without due process of law, and subjecting their premises to search and their possessions to seizure, in violation of their Constitutional right to be free from unreasonable searches and seizures. Respondents moved to dismiss the complaint for failure to state a cause of action for which relief could be granted and for summary judgment on the grounds that the federal agents acted within the scope of their authority as officers of the United States and that the searches and seizures were incidental to lawful arrests and were therefore

valid. Respondents filed affidavits in support of their motions and petitioners filed counter-affidavits. After hearing the motions the district judge did
not pass on them but, on his own motion, dismissed the suit for want of
federal jurisdiction on the ground that this action was not one that "...
arises under the Constitution or laws of the United States ..." as required
by 28 U.S.C. § 41(1). The Circuit Court of Appeals affirmed on the same
ground. 9 Cir., 150 F.2d 96. At the same time it denied a motion made by
petitioners asking it to direct the district court to give petitioners leave to
amend their complaint in order to make it still more clearly appear that the
action was directly grounded on violations of rights alleged to stem from
the Fourth and Fifth Amendments. We granted certiorari because of the
importance of the jurisdictional issue involved.

Respondents make the following argument in support of the district
court's dismissal of the complaint for want of federal jurisdiction. First,
they urge that the complaint states a cause of action for the common law
tort of trespass made actionable by state law and that it therefore does not
raise questions arising "under the Constitution or laws of the United
States." Second, to support this contention, respondents maintain that
petitioners could not recover under the Constitution or laws of the United
States, since the Constitution does not expressly provide for recovery in
money damages for violations of the Fourth and Fifth Amendments and
Congress has not enacted a statute that does so provide. A mere reading of
the complaint refutes the first contention and, as will be seen, the second
one is not decisive on the question of jurisdiction of the federal court.

Whether or not the complaint as drafted states a common law action in
trespass made actionable by state law, it is clear from the way it was drawn
that petitioners seek recovery squarely on the ground that respondents
violated the Fourth and Fifth Amendments. It charges that the respondents
conspired to do acts prohibited by these amendments and alleges that
respondents' conduct pursuant to the conspiracy resulted in damages in
excess of $3,000. It cannot be doubted therefore that it was the pleaders'
purpose to make violation of these Constitutional provisions the basis of
this suit. Before deciding that there is no jurisdiction, the district court
must look to the way the complaint is drawn to see if it is drawn so as to
claim a right to recover under the Constitution and laws of the United
States. For to that extent "the party who brings a suit is master to decide
what law he will rely upon, and ... does determine whether he will bring a
'suit arising under' the ... [Constitution or laws] of the United States by
his declaration or bill." The Fair v. Kohler Die & Specialty Co., 228 U.S. 22,
25. Though the mere failure to set out the federal or Constitutional claims
as specifically as petitioners have done would not always be conclusive
against the party bringing the suit, where the complaint, as here, is so
drawn as to seek recovery directly under the Constitution or laws of the
United States, the federal court, but for two possible exceptions later noted,
must entertain the suit. Thus allegations far less specific than the ones in
the complaint before us have been held adequate to show that the matter in
controversy arose under the Constitution of the United States. Wiley v.
Sinkler, 179 U.S. 58, 64, 65; Swafford v. Templeton, 185 U.S. 487, 491, 492.
The reason for this is that the court must assume jurisdiction to decide

whether the allegations state a cause of action on which the court can grant relief as well as to determine issues of fact arising in the controversy.

Jurisdiction, therefore, is not defeated as respondents seem to contend, by the possibility that the averments might fail to state a cause of action on which petitioners could actually recover. For it is well settled that the failure to state a proper cause of action calls for a judgment on the merits and not for a dismissal for want of jurisdiction. Whether the complaint states a cause of action on which relief could be granted is a question of law and just as issues of fact it must be decided after and not before the court has assumed jurisdiction over the controversy. If the court does later exercise its jurisdiction to determine that the allegations in the complaint do not state a ground for relief, then dismissal of the case would be on the merits, not for want of jurisdiction. Swafford v. Templeton, 185 U.S. 487, 493, 494; Binderup v. Pathe Exchange, 263 U.S. 291, 305–308. The previously carved out exceptions are that a suit may sometimes be dismissed for want of jurisdiction where the alleged claim under the Constitution or federal statutes clearly appears to be immaterial and made solely for the purpose of obtaining jurisdiction or where such a claim is wholly insubstantial and frivolous. The accuracy of calling these dismissals jurisdictional has been questioned. The *Fair v. Kohler Die & Specialty Co.*, supra, 228 U.S., at p. 25. But cf. *Swafford v. Templeton*, supra.

But as we have already pointed out the alleged violations of the Constitution here are not immaterial but form rather the sole basis of the relief sought. Nor can we say that the cause of action alleged is so patently without merit as to justify, even under the qualifications noted, the court's dismissal for want of jurisdiction. The Circuit Court of Appeals correctly stated that "the complaint states strong cases, and if the allegations have any foundation in truth, the plaintiffs' legal rights have been ruthlessly violated." [150 F.2d 98.] Petitioners' complaint asserts that the Fourth and Fifth Amendments guarantee their rights to be free from unauthorized and unjustified imprisonment and from unreasonable searches and seizures. They claim that respondents' invasion of these rights caused the damages for which they seek to recover and point further to 28 U.S.C. § 41(1), which authorizes the federal district courts to try "suits of a civil nature" where the matter in controversy "arises under the Constitution or laws of the United States," whether these are suits in "equity" or at "law." Petitioners argue that this statute authorizes the Court to entertain this action at law and to grant recovery for the damages allegedly sustained. Respondents contend that the Constitutional provisions here involved are prohibitions against the federal government as a government and that 28 U.S.C. § 41(1) does not authorize recovery in money damages in suits against unauthorized officials who according to respondents are in the same position as individual trespassers.

Respondents' contention does not show that petitioners' cause is insubstantial or frivolous, and the complaint does in fact raise serious questions, both of law and fact, which the district court can decide only after it has assumed jurisdiction over the controversy. The issue of law is whether federal courts can grant money recovery for damages said to have been suffered as a result of federal officers violating the Fourth and Fifth

Amendments. That question has never been specifically decided by this Court. That the issue thus raised has sufficient merit to warrant exercise of federal jurisdiction for purposes of adjudicating it can be seen from the cases where this Court has sustained the jurisdiction of the district courts in suits brought to recover damages for depriving a citizen of the right to vote in violation of the Constitution. And it is established practice for this Court to sustain the jurisdiction of federal courts to issue injunctions to protect rights safeguarded by the Constitution and to restrain individual state officers from doing what the 14th Amendment forbids the state to do. Moreover, where federally protected rights have been invaded, it has been the rule from the beginning that courts will be alert to adjust their remedies so as to grant the necessary relief. And it is also well settled that where legal rights have been invaded, and a federal statute provides for a general right to sue for such invasion, federal courts may use any available remedy to make good the wrong done. Whether the petitioners are entitled to recover depends upon an interpretation of 28 U.S.C. § 41(1), and on a determination of the scope of the Fourth and Fifth Amendments' protection from unreasonable searches and deprivations of liberty without due process of law. Thus, the right of the petitioners to recover under their complaint will be sustained if the Constitution and laws of the United States are given one construction and will be defeated if they are given another. For this reason the district court has jurisdiction. Gully v. First National Bank, 299 U.S. 109, 112, 113; Smith v. Kansas City Title & Trust Co., 255 U.S. 180, 199, 200.

Reversed.

■ MR. JUSTICE REED joins in the opinion and the result.

. . . . .

■ MR. JUSTICE JACKSON took no part in the consideration or decision of this case.

■ MR. CHIEF JUSTICE STONE and MR. JUSTICE BURTON dissenting.

The district court is without jurisdiction as a federal court unless the complaint states a cause of action arising under the Constitution or laws of the United States. Whether the complaint states such a cause of action is for the court, not the pleader, to say. When the provision of the Constitution or federal statute affords a remedy which may in some circumstances be availed of by a plaintiff, the fact that his pleading does not bring him within that class as one entitled to the remedy, goes to the sufficiency of the pleading and not to the jurisdiction. The Fair v. Kohler Die & Specialty Co., 228 U.S. 22, 25; Binderup v. Pathe Exchange, 263 U.S. 291, 306–308, and cases cited. But where as here, neither the constitutional provision nor any act of Congress affords a remedy to any person, the mere assertion by a plaintiff that he is entitled to such a remedy cannot be said to satisfy jurisdictional requirements. Hence we think that the courts below rightly decided that the district court was without jurisdiction because no cause of action under the Constitution or laws of the United States was stated.

The only effect of holding, as the Court does, that jurisdiction is conferred by the pleader's unfounded assertion that he is one who can have a remedy for damages arising under the Fourth and Fifth Amendments is to transfer to the federal court the trial of the allegations of trespass to person and property, which is a cause of action arising wholly under state law. For even though it be decided that petitioners have no right to damages under the Constitution, the district court will be required to pass upon the question whether the facts stated by petitioners give rise to a cause of action for trespass under state law. See Hurn v. Oursler, 289 U.S. 238.[9]

Thurston Motor Lines, Inc. v. Jordan K. Rand, Ltd.

Supreme Court of the United States, 1983.
460 U.S. 533, 103 S.Ct. 1343, 75 L.Ed.2d 260.

■ PER CURIAM. Petitioner is a common carrier authorized by the Interstate Commerce Commission to transport commodities. When respondent alleg-

---

[9. In a dissent from the denial of certiorari in Yazoo County Industrial Development Corp. v. Suthoff, 454 U.S. 1157 (1982), Justice Rehnquist questioned the soundness of *Bell v. Hood* and whether its doctrine can be reconciled with Civil Rule 12.

See also Hagans v. Lavine, 415 U.S. 528, 536–538 (1974), where the Court said: "Over the years this Court has repeatedly held that the federal courts are without power to entertain claims otherwise within their jurisdiction if they are 'so attenuated and unsubstantial as to be absolutely devoid of merit,' Newburyport Water Co. v. Newburyport, 193 U.S. 561, 579 (1904); 'wholly insubstantial,' Bailey v. Patterson, 369 U.S. 31, 33 (1962); 'obviously frivolous,' Hannis Distilling Co. v. Baltimore, 216 U.S. 285, 288 (1910); 'plainly unsubstantial,' Levering & Garrigues Co. v. Morrin, 289 U.S. 103, 105 (1933); or 'no longer open to discussion,' McGilvra v. Ross, 215 U.S. 70, 80 (1909).... The substantiality doctrine as a statement of jurisdictional principles affecting the power of a federal court to adjudicate constitutional claims has been questioned, Bell v. Hood, 327 U.S. 678, 683 (1946), and characterized as 'more ancient than analytically sound,' Rosado v. Wyman, [397 U.S. 397, 404 (1970)]. But it remains the federal rule and needs no re-examination here, for we are convinced that within accepted doctrine petitioners' complaint alleged a constitutional claim sufficient to confer jurisdiction on the District Court to pass on the controversy."

In Duke Power Co. v. Carolina Environmental Study Group, 438 U.S. 59 (1978), the Court was able to use the principle of *Bell v. Hood* to avoid a difficult jurisdictional issue. It read the plaintiffs' complaint as asserting a right, implied from the Constitution, to vindicate plaintiffs' claimed rights of due process and equal protection by suing the Nuclear Regulatory Commission, the agency charged with the enforcement and administration of the challenged statute. The Court held it need not decide whether such a right of action against the NRC could actually be implied from the Constitution. Under *Bell v. Hood* it was "enough for present purposes that the claimed cause of action to vindicate appellees' constitutional rights is sufficiently substantial and colorable to sustain jurisdiction under § 1331(a)." 438 U.S. at 71–72.

The Supreme Court has tended of late to cite to the tail rather than the head of the body of precedent created by *Bell v. Hood* and successor cases. The Court's current favorite proxy is Steel Co. v. Citizens for a Better Environment, 523 U.S. 83, 89 (1998), which in turn refers back to *Bell v. Hood*.

The circumstances in which a right to sue federal officers for damages can be implied from constitutional provisions are considered in Correctional Services Corp. v. Malesko, 534 U.S. 61 (2001), reprinted infra p. 835.

edly failed to pay $661.41 in motor freight charges, petitioner filed suit in United States District Court. Its complaint alleged that respondent failed to pay for transport services as required by petitioner's tariffs on file with the Commission. The complaint also alleged that the action arose under the Interstate Commerce Act, 49 U.S.C. § 10741(a), and that the District Court had jurisdiction pursuant to 28 U.S.C. § 1337.

The District Court dismissed the matter for want of subject matter jurisdiction and the Court of Appeals for the Ninth Circuit affirmed. 682 F.2d 811 (1982). Characterizing the suit as a "simple contract-collection action," the court could not "discern any proposition of federal law that a court need confront in deciding what, it anything, can be recovered." Id., at 812.

Under the Interstate Commerce Act, as construed by this Court, the Court of Appeals was in error. In Louisville & Nashville R. v. Rice, 247 U.S. 201 (1918), this Court squarely held that federal-question jurisdiction existed over a suit to recover $145 allegedly due the carrier for an interstate shipment under tariffs regulated by the Interstate Commerce Act.

> "The Interstate Commerce Act requires carrier to collect and consignee to pay all lawful charges duly prescribed by the tariff in respect of every shipment. Their duty and obligation grow out of and depend upon that act." 247 U.S., at 202.

Other federal courts have had no difficulty in following the clear import of *Rice.* See Madler v. Artoe, 494 F.2d 323 (CA7 1974); Bernstein Bros. Pipe & Machinery Co. v. Denver & R.G.W.R. Co., 193 F.2d 441 (CA10 1951); Maritime Service v. Sweet Brokerage De Puerto Rico, 537 F.2d 560 (CA1 1976).

The Court of Appeals' attempt to distinguish this "most troublesome precedent" is wholly unconvincing. In its view, *Rice* turned upon the fact that the carrier billed the shipper for an additional amount that, while authorized by lawful tariffs, was contrary to the parties' understanding.[10] Unlike petitioner's complaint, the complaint in *Rice* could not have alleged that the shipper agreed to pay the amount sought; the carrier there had to rely exclusively on the Act to override the parties' understanding. There is no support for this novel interpretation in *Rice* or elsewhere. That the consignee attempted to avoid payment by invoking an estoppel defense is an accurate enough portrayal of the facts, but does not obscure that the claim arose under federal law. "As to interstate shipments," the Court stated, "the parties are held to the responsibilities imposed by the federal law, to the exclusion of all other rules of obligation." 247 U.S., as 202. A carrier's claim is, of necessity, predicated on the tariff—not an understand-

---

10. In *Rice,* the parties had an understanding requiring the carrier to assess all charges immediately upon the delivery of livestock. This arrangement allowed the shipper to include the transportation costs in the price at which the livestock was sold. The dispute resulted from the carrier billing the shipper after the delivery and sale of the livestock for an additional $145 to cover disinfecting the freight cars. This additional charge complied with lawful tariffs.

ing with the shipper. This was true in *Rice* and is equally true here. Under the Court of Appeals' approach, the question of federal jurisdiction would depend upon the defenses pleaded by the shipper—but we have long ago settled that it is the character of the action and not the defense which determines whether there is federal question jurisdiction. Public Serv. Comm'n of Utah v. Wycoff Co., 344 U.S. 237, 248 (1952); Phillips Petr. Co. v. Texaco, Inc., 415 U.S. 125, 127 (1974). In short the Court of Appeals has simply confused the factual contours of *Rice* for its unmistakable holding.

Perhaps unsure of its distinction of *Rice,* the Court of Appeals went on to "doubt that *Rice* is still good law." Needless to say, only this Court may overrule one of its precedents. Until that occurs, *Rice* is the law, and the decision below cannot be reconciled with it. The petition for certiorari is granted, the judgment of the Court of Appeals is reversed, and the case is remanded to that court for further proceedings consistent with this opinion.

So ordered.

———

Grable & Sons Metal Products, Inc. v. Darue Engineering & Manufacturing

Supreme Court of the United States, 2005.
545 U.S. 308, 125 S.Ct. 2363, 162 L.Ed.2d 257.

■ JUSTICE SOUTER delivered the opinion of the Court.

The question is whether want of a federal cause of action to try claims of title to land obtained at a federal tax sale precludes removal to federal court of a state action with non-diverse parties raising a disputed issue of federal title law. We answer no, and hold that the national interest in providing a federal forum for federal tax litigation is sufficiently substantial to support the exercise of federal question jurisdiction over the disputed issue on removal, which would not distort any division of labor between the state and federal courts, provided or assumed by Congress.

I

In 1994, the Internal Revenue Service seized Michigan real property belonging to petitioner Grable & Sons Metal Products, Inc., to satisfy Grable's federal tax delinquency. Title 26 U.S.C. § 6335 required the IRS to give notice of the seizure, and there is no dispute that Grable received actual notice by certified mail before the IRS sold the property to respondent Darue Engineering & Manufacturing. Although Grable also received notice of the sale itself, it did not exercise its statutory right to redeem the property within 180 days of the sale, § 6337(b)(1), and after that period had passed, the Government gave Darue a quitclaim deed. § 6339.

Five years later, Grable brought a quiet title action in state court, claiming that Darue's record title was invalid because the IRS had failed to notify Grable of its seizure of the property in the exact manner required by

§ 6335(a), which provides that written notice must be "given by the Secretary to the owner of the property [or] left at his usual place of abode or business." Grable said that the statute required personal service, not service by certified mail.

Darue removed the case to Federal District Court as presenting a federal question, because the claim of title depended on the interpretation of the notice statute in the federal tax law. The District Court declined to remand the case at Grable's behest after finding that the "claim does pose a significant question of federal law," and ruling that Grable's lack of a federal right of action to enforce its claim against Darue did not bar the exercise of federal jurisdiction. On the merits, the court granted summary judgment to Darue, holding that although § 6335 by its terms required personal service, substantial compliance with the statute was enough. 207 F.Supp.2d 694 (W.D.Mich.2002).

The Court of Appeals for the Sixth Circuit affirmed. 377 F.3d 592 (2004). On the jurisdictional question, the panel thought it sufficed that the title claim raised an issue of federal law that had to be resolved, and implicated a substantial federal interest (in construing federal tax law). The court went on to affirm the District Court's judgment on the merits. We granted certiorari on the jurisdictional question alone, to resolve a split within the Courts of Appeals on whether Merrell Dow Pharmaceuticals, Inc. v. Thompson, 478 U.S. 804 (1986), always requires a federal cause of action as a condition for exercising federal-question jurisdiction. We now affirm.

II

Darue was entitled to remove the quiet title action if Grable could have brought it in federal district court originally, 28 U.S.C. § 1441(a), as a civil action "arising under the Constitution, laws, or treaties of the United States," § 1331. This provision for federal-question jurisdiction is invoked by and large by plaintiffs pleading a cause of action created by federal law (e.g., claims under 42 U.S.C. § 1983). There is, however, another long-standing, if less frequently encountered, variety of federal "arising under" jurisdiction, this Court having recognized for nearly 100 years that in certain cases federal question jurisdiction will lie over state-law claims that implicate significant federal issues. E.g., Hopkins v. Walker, 244 U.S. 486, 490–491 (1917). The doctrine captures the commonsense notion that a federal court ought to be able to hear claims recognized under state law that nonetheless turn on substantial questions of federal law, and thus justify resort to the experience, solicitude, and hope of uniformity that a federal forum offers on federal issues, see ALI, Study of the Division of Jurisdiction Between State and Federal Courts 164–166 (1968).

The classic example is Smith v. Kansas City Title & Trust Co., 255 U.S. 180 (1921), a suit by a shareholder claiming that the defendant corporation could not lawfully buy certain bonds of the National Government because their issuance was unconstitutional. Although Missouri law provided the cause of action, the Court recognized federal-question jurisdiction because the principal issue in the case was the federal constitutionality of the bond issue. *Smith* thus held, in a somewhat generous statement of the scope of the doctrine, that a state-law claim could give rise to federal-question jurisdiction so long as it "appears from the [complaint] that the right to relief depends upon the construction or application of [federal law]." Id., at 199.

The *Smith* statement has been subject to some trimming to fit earlier and later cases recognizing the vitality of the basic doctrine, but shying away from the expansive view that mere need to apply federal law in a state-law claim will suffice to open the "arising under" door. As early as 1912, this Court had confined federal-question jurisdiction over state-law claims to those that "really and substantially involv[e] a dispute or controversy respecting the validity, construction or effect of [federal] law." Shulthis v. McDougal, 225 U.S. 561, 569 (1912). This limitation was the ancestor of Justice Cardozo's later explanation that a request to exercise federal-question jurisdiction over a state action calls for a "common-sense accommodation of judgment to [the] kaleidoscopic situations" that present a federal issue, in "a selective process which picks the substantial causes out of the web and lays the other ones aside." Gully v. First Nat. Bank in Meridian, 299 U.S. 109, 117–118 (1936). It has in fact become a constant refrain in such cases that federal jurisdiction demands not only a contested federal issue, but a substantial one, indicating a serious federal interest in claiming the advantages thought to be inherent in a federal forum. E.g., Chicago v. International College of Surgeons, 522 U.S. 156, 164 (1997); *Merrell Dow*, supra, at 814, and n. 12; Franchise Tax Bd. of Cal. v. Construction Laborers Vacation Trust for Southern Cal., 463 U.S. 1, 28 (1983).

But even when the state action discloses a contested and substantial federal question, the exercise of federal jurisdiction is subject to a possible veto. For the federal issue will ultimately qualify for a federal forum only if federal jurisdiction is consistent with congressional judgment about the sound division of labor between state and federal courts governing the application of § 1331. Thus, *Franchise Tax Bd.* explained that the appropriateness of a federal forum to hear an embedded issue could be evaluated only after considering the "welter of issues regarding the interrelation of federal and state authority and the proper management of the federal judicial system." Id., at 8. Because arising-under jurisdiction to hear a state-law claim always raises the possibility of upsetting the state-federal line drawn (or at least assumed) by Congress, the presence of a disputed federal issue and the ostensible importance of a federal forum are never necessarily dispositive; there must always be an assessment of any disruptive portent in exercising federal jurisdiction. See also *Merrell Dow*, supra, at 810.

These considerations have kept us from stating a "single, precise, all-embracing" test for jurisdiction over federal issues embedded in state-law claims between nondiverse parties. Christianson v. Colt Industries Operating Corp., 486 U.S. 800, 821 (1988) (Stevens, J., concurring). We have not kept them out simply because they appeared in state raiment, as Justice Holmes would have done, see *Smith*, supra, at 214 (1921) (dissenting opinion), but neither have we treated "federal issue" as a password opening federal courts to any state action embracing a point of federal law. Instead, the question is, does a state-law claim necessarily raise a stated federal issue, actually disputed and substantial, which a federal forum may entertain without disturbing any congressionally approved balance of federal and state judicial responsibilities.

III

A

This case warrants federal jurisdiction. Grable's state complaint must specify "the facts establishing the superiority of [its] claim," Mich. Ct. Rule 3.411(B)(2)(c) (West 2005), and Grable has premised its superior title claim on a failure by the IRS to give it adequate notice, as defined by federal law. Whether Grable was given notice within the meaning of the federal statute is thus an essential element of its quiet title claim, and the meaning of the federal statute is actually in dispute; it appears to be the only legal or factual issue contested in the case. The meaning of the federal tax provision is an important issue of federal law that sensibly belongs in a federal court. The Government has a strong interest in the "prompt and certain collection of delinquent taxes," United States v. Rodgers, 461 U.S. 677, 709 (1983), and the ability of the IRS to satisfy its claims from the property of delinquents requires clear terms of notice to allow buyers like Darue to satisfy themselves that the Service has touched the bases necessary for good title. The Government thus has a direct interest in the availability of a federal forum to vindicate its own administrative action, and buyers (as well as tax delinquents) may find it valuable to come before judges used to federal tax matters. Finally, because it will be the rare state title case that raises a contested matter of federal law, federal jurisdiction to resolve genuine disagreement over federal tax title provisions will portend only a microscopic effect on the federal-state division of labor . . . .

. . . . .

B

Merrell Dow Pharmaceuticals, Inc. v. Thompson, 478 U.S. 804 (1986), on which Grable rests its position, is not to the contrary. *Merrell Dow* considered a state tort claim resting in part on the allegation that the defendant drug company had violated a federal misbranding prohibition, and was thus presumptively negligent under Ohio law. Id., at 806. The Court assumed that federal law would have to be applied to resolve the claim, but after closely examining the strength of the federal interest at stake and the implications of opening the federal forum, held federal jurisdiction unavailable. Congress had not provided a private federal cause of action for violation of the federal branding requirement, and the Court found "it would ... flout, or at least undermine, congressional intent to conclude that federal courts might nevertheless exercise federal-question jurisdiction and provide remedies for violations of that federal statute solely because the violation . . . is said to be a 'proximate cause' under state law.'' Id., at 812.

Because federal law provides for no quiet title action that could be brought against Darue, Grable argues that there can be no federal jurisdiction here, stressing some broad language in *Merrell Dow* (including the passage just quoted) that on its face supports Grable's position . . . . But an opinion is to be read as a whole, and *Merrell Dow* cannot be read whole as overturning decades of precedent, as it would have done by effectively adopting the Holmes dissent in *Smith*, and converting a federal cause of action from a sufficient condition for federal-question jurisdiction into a necessary one.

In the first place, *Merrell Dow* disclaimed the adoption of any bright-line rule, as when the Court reiterated that "in exploring the outer reaches of § 1331, determinations about federal jurisdiction require sensitive judgments about congressional intent, judicial power, and the federal system.'' 478 U.S., at 810. The opinion included a lengthy footnote explaining that questions of jurisdiction over state-law claims require "careful judgments,'' id., at 814, about the "nature of the federal interest at stake,'' id., at 814, n. 12 (emphasis deleted). And as a final indication that it did not mean to make a federal right of action mandatory, it expressly approved the exercise of jurisdiction sustained in *Smith*, despite the want of any federal cause of action available to *Smith*'s shareholder plaintiff. 478 U.S., at 814, n. 12. *Merrell Dow* then, did not toss out, but specifically retained the contextual enquiry that had been *Smith*'s hallmark for over 60 years. At the end of *Merrell Dow*, Justice Holmes was still dissenting.

Accordingly, *Merrell Dow* should be read in its entirety as treating the absence of a federal private right of action as evidence relevant to, but not dispositive of, the "sensitive judgments about congressional intent'' that § 1331 requires. The absence of any federal cause of action affected *Merrell Dow*'s result in two ways. The Court saw the fact as worth some consideration in the assessment of substantiality. But its primary importance emerged when the Court treated the combination of no federal cause of action and no preemption of state remedies for misbranding as an important clue to Congress's conception of the scope of jurisdiction to be exercised under § 1331. The Court saw the missing cause of action not as a missing federal door key, always required, but as a missing welcome mat, required in the circumstances, when exercising federal jurisdiction over a state misbranding action would have attracted a horde of original filings and removal cases raising other state claims with embedded federal issues. For if the federal labeling standard without a federal cause of action could get a state claim into federal court, so could any other federal standard without a federal cause of action. And that would have meant a tremendous number of cases.

One only needed to consider the treatment of federal violations generally in garden variety state tort law. "The violation of federal statutes and regulations is commonly given negligence per se effect in state tort proceedings." 6 Restatement (Third) of Torts (proposed final draft) § 14, Comment a. See also W. Keeton, D. Dobbs, R. Keeton, & D. Owen, Prosser and Keeton on Torts, § 36, p. 221, n. 9 (5th ed.1984) ("[T]he breach of a federal statute may support a negligence per se claim as a matter of state law" (collecting authority)). A general rule of exercising federal jurisdiction over state claims resting on federal mislabeling and other statutory violations would thus have heralded a potentially enormous shift of traditionally state cases into federal courts. Expressing concern over the "increased volume of federal litigation," and noting the importance of adhering to "legislative intent," *Merrell Dow* thought it improbable that the Congress, having made no provision for a federal cause of action, would have meant to welcome any state-law tort case implicating federal law "solely because the violation of the federal statute is said to [create] a rebuttable presumption [of negligence] ... under state law." 478 U.S., at 811–812 (internal quotation marks omitted). In this situation, no welcome mat meant keep out. *Merrell Dow*'s analysis thus fits within the framework of examining the importance of having a federal forum for the issue, and the consistency of such a forum with Congress's intended division of labor between state and federal courts.

As already indicated, however, a comparable analysis yields a different jurisdictional conclusion in this case. Although Congress also indicated ambivalence in this case by providing no private right of action to Grable, it is the rare state quiet title action that involves contested issues of federal law .... Consequently, jurisdiction over actions like Grable's would not materially affect, or threaten to affect, the normal currents of litigation. Given the absence of threatening structural consequences and the clear interest the Government, its buyers, and its delinquents have in the availability of a federal forum, there is no good reason to shirk from federal jurisdiction over the dispositive and contested federal issue at the heart of the state-law title claim.

IV

The judgment of the Court of Appeals, upholding federal jurisdiction over Grable's quiet title action, is affirmed.

It is so ordered.

[The concurring opinion of Justice Thomas is omitted.][11]

[11. Would there have been federal-question jurisdiction in *Merrell Dow* had the plaintiffs not conceded, and the Supreme Court therefore assumed, that there was no private right of action under federal law to recover damages caused by violation of the FDCA? See In re Bendectin Litigation, 857 F.2d 290 (6th Cir.1988), in which the court of appeals held that the affirmative pleading of such a private right of action did assert a substantial federal question within the jurisdiction conferred by 28 U.S.C. § 1331. See generally Alleva, Prerogative Lost: The Trouble With Statutory Federal Question Jurisdiction After *Merrell Dow*, 52 Ohio S.L.J. 1477 (1991).

Empire Healthchoice Assurance, Inc. v. McVeigh

Supreme Court of the United States, 2006.
547 U.S. 677, 126 S. Ct. 2121, 165 L.Ed.2d 131.

■ JUSTICE GINSBURG delivered the opinion of the Court.

The Federal Employees Health Benefits Act of 1959 (FEHBA), 5 U.S.C. § 8901 et seq. (2000 ed. and Supp. III), establishes a comprehensive program of health insurance for federal employees. The Act authorizes the Office of Personnel Management (OPM) to contract with private carriers to offer federal employees an array of health-care plans. See § 8902(a) (2000 ed.). Largest of the plans for which OPM has contracted, annually since 1960, is the Blue Cross Blue Shield Service Benefit Plan (Plan), administered by local Blue Cross Blue Shield companies. This case concerns the proper forum for reimbursement claims when a plan beneficiary, injured in an accident, whose medical bills have been paid by the plan administrator, recovers damages (unaided by the carrier-administrator) in a state-court tort action against a third party alleged to have caused the accident.

FEHBA contains a preemption clause, § 8902(m)(1), displacing state law on issues relating to "coverage or benefits" afforded by health-care plans. The Act contains no provision addressing the subrogation or reimbursement rights of carriers. Successive annual contracts between OPM and the Blue Cross Blue Shield Association (BCBSA) have obligated the carrier to make "a reasonable effort" to recoup amounts paid for medical care. The statement of benefits distributed by the carrier alerts enrollees that all recoveries they receive "must be used to reimburse the Plan for benefits paid."

The instant case originated when the administrator of a Plan beneficiary's estate pursued tort litigation in state court against parties alleged to have caused the beneficiary's injuries. The carrier had notice of the state-

---

In City of Chicago v. International College of Surgeons, 522 U.S. 156 (1997), the Supreme Court regarded it as uncontroversial that a state-court suit on a state-created right to judicial review of a local administrative order was a suit arising under federal law for purposes of 28 U.S.C. § 1331, and hence was removable under 28 U.S.C. § 1441, when the plaintiff sought to overturn the administrative order on various alternative grounds, some founded not on state law but on alleged violations of the federal Constitution that could have been (but were not) asserted as the basis for relief under 42 U.S.C. § 1983. The plaintiff's reliance on violations of federal law for which Congress had provided a private right of action was deemed sufficient to make the plaintiff's right to relief under state law depend upon the resolution of substantial questions of federal law.

The various strands of pre-*Grable* doctrine dealing with federal-question jurisdiction under 28 U.S.C. § 1331 were reviewed and critically evaluated in Oakley, Federal Jurisdiction and the Problem of the Litigative Unit: When Does What "Arise Under" Federal Law?, 76 Texas L.Rev. 1829 (1998), and in ALI Judicial Code Project, Reporter's Memorandum at 636–651.

Does the phrase "arising under" mean the same thing in a statute of limitations as it does in a jurisdictional statute? A unanimous Court agreed that "the meaning of the term 'arising under' is not so clear," and that "our expositions of the 'arising under' concept in [the jurisdictional context, although] helpful in interpreting the term as it is used in [the limitations context,] do not point the way to an obvious answer." Jones v. R.R. Donnelley & Sons Co., 541 U.S. 369, 375 (2004).]

court action, but took no part in it. When the tort action terminated in a settlement, the carrier filed suit in federal court seeking reimbursement of the full amount it had paid for the beneficiary's medical care. The question presented is whether 28 U.S.C. § 1331 (authorizing jurisdiction over "civil actions arising under the ... laws ... of the United States") encompasses the carrier's action. We hold it does not.

FEHBA itself provides for federal-court jurisdiction only in actions against the United States. Congress could decide and provide that reimbursement claims of the kind here involved warrant the exercise of federal-court jurisdiction. But claims of this genre, seeking recovery from the proceeds of state-court litigation, are the sort ordinarily resolved in state courts. Federal courts should await a clear signal from Congress before treating such auxiliary claims as "arising under" the laws of the United States.

I

FEHBA assigns to OPM responsibility for negotiating and regulating health benefit plans for federal employees. See 5 U.S.C. § 8902(a). OPM contracts with carriers, FEHBA instructs, "shall contain a detailed statement of benefits offered and shall include such maximums, limitations, exclusions, and other definitions of benefits as [OPM] considers necessary or desirable." § 8902(d). Pursuant to FEHBA, OPM entered into a contract in 1960 with the BCBSA to establish a nationwide fee-for-service health plan, the terms of which are renegotiated annually. As FEHBA prescribes, the Federal Government pays about 75% of the premiums; the enrollee pays the rest. § 8906(b) (2000 ed.). Premiums thus shared are deposited in a special Treasury Fund, the Federal Employees Health Benefits Fund, § 8909(a). Carriers draw against the Fund to pay for covered health-care benefits. Ibid.; see also 48 C.F.R. § 1632.170(b) (2005).

The contract between OPM and the BCBSA provides: "By enrolling or accepting services under this contract, [enrollees and their eligible dependents] are obligated to all terms, conditions, and provisions of this contract." An appended brochure sets out the benefits the carrier shall provide, and the carrier's subrogation and recovery rights. Each enrollee, as FEHBA directs, receives a statement of benefits conveying information about the Plan's coverage and conditions. 5 U.S.C. § 8907(b). Concerning reimbursement and subrogation, matters FEHBA itself does not address, the BCBSA Plan's statement of benefits reads in part:

"If another person or entity ... causes you to suffer an injury or illness, and if we pay benefits for that injury or illness, you must agree to the following:

"All recoveries you obtain (whether by lawsuit, settlement, or otherwise), no matter how described or designated, must be used to reimburse us in full for benefits we paid. Our share of any recovery extends only to the amount of benefits we have paid or will pay to you or, if applicable, to your heirs, administrators, successors, or assignees."

. . . . .

"If you do not seek damages for your illness or injury, you must permit us to initiate recovery on your behalf (including the right to bring suit in your name). This is called subrogation.

"If we pursue a recovery of the benefits we have paid, you must cooperate in doing what is reasonably necessary to assist us. You must not take any action that may prejudice our rights to recover." [12]

If the participant does not voluntarily reimburse the Plan, the contract requires the carrier to make a "reasonable effort to seek recovery of amounts . . . it is entitled to recover in cases . . . brought to its attention." Pursuant to the OPM–BCBSA master contract, reimbursements obtained by the carrier must be returned to the Treasury Fund.

FEHBA contains a preemption provision, which originally provided:

"The provisions of any contract under this chapter which relate to the nature or extent of coverage or benefits (including payments with respect to benefits) shall supersede and preempt any State or local law, or any regulation issued thereunder, which relates to health insurance or plans to the extent that such law or regulation is inconsistent with such contractual provisions." 5 U.S.C. § 8902(m)(1) (1994 ed.).

To assure uniform coverage and benefits under plans OPM negotiates for federal employees, see H.R. Rep. No. 95–282, p. 1 (1977), § 8902(m)(1) preempted "State laws or regulations which specify types of medical care, providers of care, extent of benefits, coverage of family members, age limits for family members, or other matters relating to health benefits or coverage," id. at 4–5 (noting that some States mandated coverage for services not included in federal plans, for example, chiropractic services). In 1998, Congress amended § 8902(m)(1) by deleting the words "to the extent that such law or regulation is inconsistent with such contractual provisions." Thus, under § 8902(m)(1) as it now reads, state law—whether consistent or inconsistent with federal plan provisions—is displaced on matters of "coverage or benefits."

FEHBA contains but one provision addressed to federal-court jurisdiction. That provision vests in federal district courts "original jurisdiction, concurrent with the United States Court of Federal Claims, of a civil action or claim against the United States founded on this chapter." § 8912. The purpose of this provision—evident from its reference to the Court of

---

12. The statement of benefits further provides:

"You must tell us promptly if you have a claim against another party for a condition that we have paid or may pay benefits for, and you must tell us about any recoveries you obtain, whether in or out of court. We may seek a lien on the proceeds of your claim in order to reimburse ourselves to the full amount of benefits we have paid or will pay.

"We may request that you assign to us (1) your right to bring an action or (2) your right to the proceeds of a claim for your illness or injury. We may delay processing of your claims until you provide the assignment.

"*Note*: We will pay the costs of any covered services you receive that are in excess of any recoveries made."

Federal Claims—was to carve out an exception to the statutory rule that claims brought against the United States and exceeding $10,000 must originate in the Court of Federal Claims. See 28 U.S.C. § 1346(a)(2) (establishing district courts' jurisdiction, concurrent with the Court of Federal Claims, over claims against the United States that do not exceed $10,000); see also S. Rep. No. 1654, 83d Cong., 2d Sess., pp. 4–5 (1954) (commenting, with respect to an identical provision in the Federal Employees Group Life Insurance Act, 5 U.S.C. § 8715, that the provision "would extend the jurisdiction of United States district courts above the $10,000 limitation now in effect").

Under a 1995 OPM regulation, suits contesting final OPM action denying health benefits "must be brought against OPM and not against the carrier or carrier's subcontractors." 5 C.F.R. § 890.107(c) (2005). While this regulation channels disputes over coverage or benefits into federal court by designating a United States agency (OPM) sole defendant, no law opens federal courts to carriers seeking reimbursement from beneficiaries or recovery from tortfeasors. Cf. 29 U.S.C. § 1132(e)(1) (provision of the Employee Retirement Income Security Act (ERISA) vesting in federal district courts "exclusive jurisdiction of civil actions under this subchapter"). And nothing in FEHBA's text prescribes a federal rule of decision for a carrier's claim against its insured or an alleged tortfeasor to share in the proceeds of a state-court tort action.

II

Petitioner Empire Healthchoice Assurance, Inc., doing business as Empire Blue Cross Blue Shield (Empire), is the entity that administers the BCBSA Plan as it applies to federal employees in New York State. Respondent Denise Finn McVeigh (McVeigh) is the administrator of the estate of Joseph E. McVeigh (Decedent), a former enrollee in the Plan. The Decedent was injured in an accident in 1997. Plan payments for the medical care he received between 1997 and his death in 2001 amounted to $157,309. McVeigh, on behalf of herself, the Decedent, and a minor child, commenced tort litigation in state court against parties alleged to have caused Decedent's injuries. On learning that the parties to the state-court litigation had agreed to settle the tort claims, Empire sought to recover the $157,309 it had paid out for the Decedent's medical care.[13] Of the $3,175,000 for which the settlement provided, McVeigh, in response to Empire's asserted reimbursement right, agreed to place $100,000 in escrow.

Empire then filed suit in the United States District Court for the Southern District of New York, alleging that McVeigh was in breach of the reimbursement provision of the Plan. As relief, Empire demanded $157,309, with no offset for attorney's fees or other litigation costs McVeigh incurred in pursuing the state-court settlement. McVeigh moved to dismiss on various grounds, among them, lack of subject-matter jurisdic-

---

13. At oral argument, counsel for respondent McVeigh represented that "most of the [reimbursement claims] are not of th[is] magnitude" ; "[m]ost of the cases involve [amounts like] $5,500 and $6,500."

tion. See 396 F.3d 136, 139 (CA2 2005). Answering McVeigh's motion, Empire urged that the District Court had jurisdiction under 28 U.S.C. § 1331 because federal common law governed its reimbursement claim. In the alternative, Empire asserted that the Plan itself constituted federal law. See 396 F.3d, at 140. The District Court rejected both arguments and granted McVeigh's motion to dismiss for want of subject-matter jurisdiction. Ibid.

A divided panel of the Court of Appeals for the Second Circuit affirmed, holding that "Empire's clai[m] arise[s] under state law." Id., at 150. FEHBA's text, the court observed, contains no authorization for carriers "to vindicate [in federal court] their rights [against enrollees] under FEHBA-authorized contracts" ; therefore, the court concluded, "federal jurisdiction exists over this dispute only if federal common law governs Empire's claims." Id., at 140. Quoting Boyle v. United Technologies Corp., 487 U.S. 500, 507, 508 (1988), the appeals court stated that courts may create federal common law only when "the operation of state law would (1) 'significant[ly] conflict' with (2) 'uniquely federal interest[s].' " 396 F.3d, at 140.

Empire maintained that its contract-derived claim against McVeigh implicated "uniquely federal interest[s]," because (1) reimbursement directly affects the United States Treasury and the cost of providing health benefits to federal employees; and (2) Congress had expressed its interest in maintaining uniformity among the States on matters relating to federal health-plan benefits. Id., at 141. The court acknowledged that the case involved distinctly federal interests, but found that Empire had not identified "specific ways in which the operation of state contract law, or indeed of other laws of general application, would conflict materially with the federal policies underlying FEHBA in the circumstances presented." Id., at 150 (Sack, J., concurring); see id., at 142.

The Court of Appeals next considered and rejected Empire's argument that FEHBA's preemption provision, 5 U.S.C. § 8902(m)(1), independently conferred federal jurisdiction. 396 F.3d, at 145–149. That provision, the court observed, is "a limited preemption clause that the instant dispute does not trigger." Id., at 145. Unlike § 8912, which "authoriz[es] federal jurisdiction over FEHBA-related ... claims 'against the United States,' " the court noted, § 8902(m)(1) "makes no reference to a federal right of action [in] or to federal jurisdiction [over]" the contract-derived reimbursement claim here at issue. 396 F.3d, at 145, and n. 7.

Judge Raggi dissented. Id., at 151. In her view, FEHBA's preemption provision, § 8902(m)(1), as amended in 1998, both calls for the application of uniform federal common law to terms in a FEHBA plan and establishes federal jurisdiction over Empire's complaint.

We granted certiorari to resolve a conflict among lower federal courts concerning the proper forum for claims of the kind Empire asserts. Compare Blue Cross & Blue Shield of Illinois v. Cruz, 396 F.3d 793, 799–800 (CA7 2005) (upholding federal jurisdiction), Caudil v. Blue Cross & Blue Shield of North Carolina, 999 F.2d 74, 77 (CA4 1993) (same), and Medcenters Health Care v. Ochs, 854 F. Supp. 589, 593, and n. 3 (Minn. 1993) (same), aff'd, 26 F.3d 865 (CA8 1994), with Goepel v. Nat. Postal Mail Handlers Union, 36 F.3d 306, 314–315 (CA3 1994) (rejecting federal jurisdiction), and 396 F.3d, at 139 (decision below) (same).

III

Title 28 U.S.C. § 1331 vests in federal district courts "original jurisdiction" over "all civil actions arising under the Constitution, laws, or treaties of the United States." A case "arise[s] under" federal law within the meaning of § 1331, this Court has said, if "a well-pleaded complaint establishes either that federal law creates the cause of action or that the plaintiff's right to relief necessarily depends on resolution of a substantial question of federal law." Franchise Tax Bd. of Cal. v. Construction Laborers Vacation Trust for Southern Cal., 463 U.S. 1, 27–28 (1983).

Empire and the United States, as amicus curiae, present two principal arguments in support of federal-question jurisdiction. Emphasizing our opinion in Jackson Transit Authority v. Transit Union, 457 U.S. 15, 22 (1982), and cases cited therein, they urge that Empire's complaint raises a federal claim because it seeks to vindicate a contractual right contemplated by a federal statute, a right that Congress intended to be federal in nature. FEHBA's preemption provision, Empire and the United States contend, demonstrates Congress' intent in this regard. The United States argues, alternatively, that there is federal jurisdiction here, as demonstrated by our recent decision in Grable & Sons Metal Products, Inc. v. Darue Engineering & Mfg., 545 U.S. 308 (2005), because "federal law is a necessary element of [Empire's] claim." We address these arguments in turn. But first, we respond to the dissent's view that Empire and the United States have engaged in unnecessary labor, for Clearfield Trust Co. v. United States, 318 U.S. 363 (1943), provides "a basis for federal jurisdiction in this case."

A

Clearfield is indeed a pathmarking precedent on the authority of federal courts to fashion uniform federal common law on issues of national concern. See Friendly, In Praise of *Erie*—and of the New Federal Common Law, 39 N.Y.U. L. Rev. 383, 409–410 (1964). But the dissent is mistaken in supposing that the *Clearfield* doctrine covers this case. *Clearfield* was a suit by the United States to recover from a bank the amount paid on a Government check on which the payee's name had been forged. 318 U.S., at 365. Because the United States was the plaintiff, federal-court jurisdiction was solidly grounded. See ibid. ("This suit was instituted ... by the United States ..., the jurisdiction of the federal District Court being invoked pursuant to the provisions of § 24(1) of the Judicial Code, 28 U.S.C. § 41(1)," now contained in 28 U.S.C. §§ 1332, 1345, 1359). The case presented a vertical choice-of-law issue: Did state law under Erie R. Co. v. Tompkins, 304 U.S. 64 (1938), or a court-fashioned federal rule of decision (federal common law) determine the merits of the controversy? The Court held that "[t]he rights and duties of the United States on commercial paper which it issues are governed by federal rather than [state] law." 318 U.S., at 366.

In post-*Clearfield* decisions, and with the benefit of enlightened commentary, see, e.g., Friendly, supra, at 410, the Court has "made clear that uniform federal law need not be applied to all questions in federal government litigation, even in cases involving government contracts," R. Fallon, D. Meltzer, & D. Shapiro, Hart and Wechsler's The Federal Courts and the Federal System 700 (5th ed.2003) (hereinafter Hart and Wechsler).[14] "[T]he prudent course," we have recognized, is often "to adopt the ready-made body of state law as the federal rule of decision until Congress strikes a different accommodation." United States v. Kimbell Foods, Inc., 440 U.S. 715, 740 (1979).

Later, in *Boyle*, the Court telescoped the appropriate inquiry, focusing it on the straightforward question whether the relevant federal interest warrants displacement of state law. See 487 U.S., at 507, n. 3. Referring simply to "the displacement of state law," the Court recognized that prior cases had treated discretely (1) the competence of federal courts to formulate a federal rule of decision, and (2) the appropriateness of declaring a federal rule rather than borrowing, incorporating, or adopting state law in point. The Court preferred "the more modest terminology," questioning whether "the distinction between displacement of state law and displacement of federal law's incorporation of state law ever makes a practical difference." Ibid. *Boyle* made two further observations here significant. First, *Boyle* explained, the involvement of "an area of uniquely federal interest ... establishes a necessary, not a sufficient, condition for the displacement of state law." Id., at 507. Second, in some cases, an "entire body of state law" may conflict with the federal interest and therefore require replacement. Id., at 508. But in others, the conflict is confined, and "only particular elements of state law are superseded." Ibid.

The dissent describes this case as pervasively federal, and "the provisions ... here [as] just a few scattered islands in a sea of federal contractual provisions." But there is nothing "scattered" about the provisions on reimbursement and subrogation in the OPM–BCBSA master contract. Those provisions are linked together and depend upon a recovery from a third party under terms and conditions ordinarily governed by state law.[15] The Court of Appeals, whose decision we review, trained on the matter of

---

14. The United States, in accord with the dissent in this regard, several times cites United States v. County of Allegheny, 322 U.S. 174 (1944), maintaining that the construction of a federal contract "necessarily present[s] questions of 'federal law not controlled by the law of any State,' " id., at 26 (quoting 322 U.S., at 183). *Allegheny* does not stretch as widely as the United States suggests. That case concerned whether certain property belonged to the United States and, if so, whether the incidence of a state tax was on the United States or on a Government contractor. See id., at 181–183, 186–189. Neither the United States nor any United States agency is a party to this case, and the auxiliary matter here involved scarcely resembles the controversy in *Allegheny*.

15. The dissent nowhere suggests that uniform, court-declared federal law would govern the carrier's subrogation claim against the tortfeasor. Nor does the dissent explain why the two linked provisions—reimbursement and subrogation—should be decoupled.

reimbursement, not, as the dissent does, on FEHBA-authorized contracts at large. So focused, the appeals court determined that Empire has not demonstrated a "significant conflict ... between an identifiable federal policy or interest and the operation of state law." 396 F.3d, at 140–141. Unless and until that showing is made, there is no cause to displace state law, much less to lodge this case in federal court.

B

We take up next Empire's *Jackson Transit*-derived argument, which is, essentially, a more tailored variation of the theme sounded in the dissent. It is undisputed that Congress has not expressly created a federal right of action enabling insurance carriers like Empire to sue health-care beneficiaries in federal court to enforce reimbursement rights under contracts contemplated by FEHBA. Empire and the United States nevertheless argue that, under our 1982 opinion in *Jackson Transit*, Empire's claim for reimbursement, arising under the contract between OPM and BCBSA, "states a federal claim" because Congress intended all rights and duties stemming from that contract to be "federal in nature." We are not persuaded by this argument.

The reliance placed by Empire and the United States on *Jackson Transit* is surprising, for that decision held there was no federal jurisdiction over the claim in suit. The federal statute there involved, § 13(c) of the Urban Mass Transportation Act of 1964 (UMTA), 78 Stat. 307 (then codified at 49 U.S.C. § 1609(c) (1976 ed.)), conditioned a governmental unit's receipt of federal funds to acquire a privately owned transit company on preservation of collective-bargaining rights enjoyed by the acquired company's employees. 457 U.S., at 17–18. The city of Jackson, Tennessee, with federal financial assistance, acquired a failing private bus company and turned it into a public entity, the Jackson Transit Authority. Id., at 18. To satisfy the condition on federal aid, the transit authority entered into a "§ 13(c) agreement" with the union that represented the private company's employees, and the Secretary of Labor certified that agreement as "fair and equitable." Ibid. (internal quotation marks omitted).

For several years thereafter, the transit authority covered its unionized workers in a series of collective-bargaining agreements. Eventually, however, the Authority notified the union that it would no longer adhere to collective-bargaining undertakings. Id., at 19. The union commenced suit in federal court alleging breach of the § 13(c) agreement and of the latest collective-bargaining agreement. Ibid. This Court determined that the case did not arise under federal law, but was instead "governed by state law [to be] applied in state cour[t]." Id., at 29.

The Court acknowledged in *Jackson Transit* that "on several occasions [we had] determined that a plaintiff stated a federal claim when he sued to vindicate contractual rights set forth by federal statutes, [even though] the relevant statutes lacked express provisions creating federal causes of action." Id., at 22 (emphasis added) (citing Machinists v. Central Airlines, Inc., 372 U.S. 682 (1963) (union had a federal right of action to enforce an airline-adjustment-board award included in a collective-bargaining contract pursuant to a provision of the Railway Labor Act); Norfolk & Western R. Co. v. Nemitz, 404 U.S. 37 (1971) (railroad's employees stated federal claims when they sought to enforce assurances made by the railroad to secure Interstate Commerce Commission approval of a consolidation under a provision of the Interstate Commerce Act); Transamerica Mortgage Advisors, Inc. v. Lewis, 444 U.S. 11, 18–19 (1979) (permitting federal suit for rescission of a contract declared void by a provision of the Investment Advisers Act of 1940)). But prior decisions, we said, "d[id] not dictate the result in [the *Jackson Transit*] case," for in each case, "the critical factor" in determining "the scope of rights and remedies under a federal statute . . . is the congressional intent behind the particular provision at issue." 457 U.S., at 22.

"In some ways," the *Jackson Transit* Court said, the UMTA "seem[ed] to make § 13(c) agreements and collective-bargaining contracts creatures of federal law." Id., at 23. In this regard, the Court noted, § 13(c)

> "demand[ed] 'fair and equitable arrangements' as prerequisites for federal aid; it require[d] the approval of the Secretary of Labor for those arrangements; it specifie[d] five different varieties of protective provisions that must be included among the § 13(c) arrangements; and it expressly incorporate[d] the protective arrangements into the grant contract between the recipient and the Federal Government." Ibid. (quoting 49 U.S.C. § 1609(c) (1976 ed.)).

But there were countervailing considerations. The Court observed that "labor relations between local governments and their employees are the subject of a long-standing statutory exemption from the National Labor Relations Act." 457 U.S., at 23. "Section 13(c)," the Court continued, "evince[d] no congressional intent to upset the decision in the [NLRA] to permit state law to govern the relationships between local governmental entities and the unions representing their employees." Id., at 23–24. Legislative history was corroborative. "A consistent theme," the Court found, "[ran] throughout the consideration of § 13(c): Congress intended that labor relations between transit workers and local governments would be controlled by state law." Id., at 24. We therefore held that the union had come to the wrong forum. Congress had indeed provided for § 13(c) agreements and collective-bargaining contracts stemming from them, but in the Court's judgment, the union's proper recourse for enforcement of those contracts was a suit in state court.

Measured against the Court's discussion in *Jackson Transit* about when a claim arises under federal law, Empire's contract-derived claim for reimbursement is not a "creatur[e]" of federal law." Id., at 23. True, distinctly federal interests are involved. Principally, reimbursements are credited to a federal fund, and the OPM–BCBSA master contract could be described as "federal in nature" because it is negotiated by a federal agency and concerns federal employees. But, as in *Jackson Transit*, countervailing considerations control. Among them, the reimbursement right in question, predicated on a FEHBA-authorized contract, is not a prescription of federal law. And, of prime importance, "Congress considered jurisdictional issues in enacting FEHBA[,] . . . confer[ring] federal jurisdiction where it found it necessary to do so." 396 F.3d, at 145, n. 7.

FEHBA's jurisdictional provision, 5 U.S.C. § 8912, opens the federal district-court door to civil actions "against the United States." OPM's regulation, 5 C.F.R. § 890.107(c) (2005), instructs enrollees who seek to challenge benefit denials to proceed in court against OPM "and not against the carrier or carrier's subcontractors." Read together, these prescriptions "ensur[e] that suits brought by beneficiaries for denial of benefits will land in federal court." 396 F.3d, at 145, n. 7. Had Congress found it necessary or proper to extend federal jurisdiction further, in particular, to encompass contract-derived reimbursement claims between carriers and insured workers, it would have been easy enough for Congress to say so. Cf. 29 U.S.C. § 1132(a)(3) (authorizing suit in federal court "by a participant, beneficiary, or fiduciary" of a pension or health plan governed by ERISA to gain redress for violations of "this subchapter or the terms of the plan"). We have no warrant to expand Congress' jurisdictional grant "by judicial decree." See Kokkonen v. Guardian Life Ins. Co. of America, 511 U.S. 375, 377 (1994).

Jackson Transit, Empire points out, referred to decisions "demonstrat[ing] that . . . private parties in appropriate cases may sue in federal court to enforce contractual rights created by federal statutes." 457 U.S., at 22. This case, however, involves no right created by federal statute. As just reiterated, while the OPM–BCBSA master contract provides for reimbursement, FEHBA's text itself contains no provision addressing the reimbursement or subrogation rights of carriers.

Nor do we read 5 U.S.C. § 8902(m)(1), FEHBA's preemption provision, as a jurisdiction-conferring provision. That choice-of-law prescription is unusual in that it renders preemptive contract terms in health insurance plans, not provisions enacted by Congress. See 396 F.3d, at 143–145; id. at 151 (Sack, J., concurring). A prescription of that unusual order warrants cautious interpretation.

Section 8902(m)(1) is a puzzling measure, open to more than one construction, and no prior decision seems to us precisely on point. Reading the reimbursement clause in the master OPM–BCBSA contract as a condition or limitation on "benefits" received by a federal employee, the clause could be ranked among "[contract] terms . . . relat[ing] to . . . coverage or benefits" and "payments with respect to benefits," thus falling within § 8902(m)(1)'s compass. On the other hand, a claim for reimbursement ordinarily arises long after "coverage" and "benefits" questions have been resolved, and corresponding "payments with respect to benefits" have been made to care providers or the insured. With that consideration in view, § 8902(m)(1)'s words may be read to refer to contract terms relating to the beneficiary's entitlement (or lack thereof) to Plan payment for certain health-care services he or she has received, and not to terms relating to the carrier's post-payments right to reimbursement.

To decide this case, we need not choose between those plausible constructions. If contract-based reimbursement claims are not covered by FEHBA's preemption provision, then federal jurisdiction clearly does not exist. But even if FEHBA's preemption provision reaches contract-based reimbursement claims, that provision is not sufficiently broad to confer federal jurisdiction. If Congress intends a preemption instruction completely to displace ordinarily applicable state law, and to confer federal jurisdiction thereby, it may be expected to make that atypical intention clear. Cf. Columbus v. Ours Garage & Wrecker Service, Inc., 536 U.S. 424, 432–433 (2002) (citing Wisconsin Public Intervenor v. Mortier, 501 U.S. 597, 605 (1991)). Congress has not done so here.

Section 8902(m)(1)'s text does not purport to render inoperative any and all State laws that in some way bear on federal employee-benefit plans. Cf. 29 U.S.C. § 1144(a) (portions of ERISA "supersede any and all State laws insofar as they may now or hereafter relate to any employee benefit plan"). And, as just observed, given that § 8902(m)(1) declares no federal law preemptive, but instead, terms of an OPM–BCBSA negotiated contract, a modest reading of the provision is in order. Furthermore, a reimbursement right of the kind Empire here asserts stems from a personal-injury recovery, and the claim underlying that recovery is plainly governed by state law. We are not prepared to say, based on the presentations made in this case, that under § 8902(m)(1), an OPM–BCBSA contract term would displace every condition state law places on that recovery.

As earlier observed, the BCBSA Plan's statement of benefits links together the carrier's right to reimbursement from the insured and its right to subrogation. Empire's subrogation right allows the carrier, once it has paid an insured's medical expenses, to recover directly from a third party responsible for the insured's injury or illness. See 16 G. Couch, Cyclopedia of Insurance Law § 61:1 (2d ed.1982). Had Empire taken that course, no access to a federal forum could have been predicated on the OPM–BCBSA contract right. The tortfeasors' liability, whether to the insured or the insurer, would be governed not by an agreement to which the tortfeasors are strangers, but by state law, and § 8902(m)(1) would have no sway.

In sum, the presentations before us fail to establish that § 8902(m)(1) leaves no room for any state law potentially bearing on federal employee-benefit plans in general, or carrier-reimbursement claims in particular. Accordingly, we extract from § 8902(m)(1) no prescription for federal-court jurisdiction.

C

We turn finally to the argument that Empire's reimbursement claim, even if it does not qualify as a "cause of action created by federal law," nevertheless arises under federal law for § 1331 purposes, because federal law is "a necessary element of the [carrier's] claim for relief." This case, we are satisfied, does not fit within the special and small category in which the United States would place it. We first describe *Grable*, a recent decision that the United States identifies as exemplary,[16] and then explain why this case does not resemble that one.

Grable involved real property belonging to Grable & Sons Metal Products, Inc. (Grable), which the Internal Revenue Service (IRS) seized to satisfy a federal tax deficiency. 545 U.S., at 310. Grable received notice of the seizure by certified mail before the IRS sold the property to Darue Engineering & Manufacturing (Darue). Ibid. Five years later, Grable sued Darue in state court to quiet title. Grable asserted that Darue's record title was invalid because the IRS had conveyed the seizure notice improperly. Id., at 311. The governing statute, 26 U.S.C. § 6335(a), provides that "notice in writing shall be given ... to the owner of the property ... or shall be left at his usual place of abode or business ...." Grable maintained that § 6335(a) required personal service, not service by certified mail. 545 U.S., at 311.

Darue removed the case to federal court. Alleging that Grable's claim of title depended on the interpretation of a federal statutory provision, i.e., § 6335(a) of the Internal Revenue Code, Darue invoked federal-question jurisdiction under 28 U.S.C. § 1331. We affirmed lower court determinations that the removal was proper. "The meaning of the federal tax provision," we said, "is an important issue of federal law that sensibly belongs in a federal court." 545 U.S., at 315. Whether Grable received notice adequate under § 6335(a), we observed, was "an essential element of [Grable's] quiet title claim" ; indeed, "it appear[ed] to be the only ... issue contested in the case." Ibid.

This case is poles apart from *Grable*. The dispute there centered on the action of a federal agency (IRS) and its compatibility with a federal statute, the question qualified as "substantial," and its resolution was both dispositive of the case and would be controlling in numerous other cases. See id., at 313. Here, the reimbursement claim was triggered, not by the action of any federal department, agency, or service, but by the settlement of a personal-injury action launched in state court, and the bottom-line practical issue is the share of that settlement properly payable to Empire.

Grable presented a nearly "pure issue of law," one "that could be settled once and for all and thereafter would govern numerous tax sale cases." Hart and Wechsler 65 (2005 Supp.). In contrast, Empire's reimbursement claim, McVeigh's counsel represented without contradiction, is fact-bound and situation-specific. McVeigh contends that there were overcharges or duplicative charges by care providers, and seeks to determine whether particular services were properly attributed to the injuries caused by the 1997 accident and not rendered for a reason unrelated to the accident.

The United States observes that a claim for reimbursement may also involve as an issue "[the] extent, if any, to which the reimbursement

---

16. As the Court in *Grable* observed, 545 U.S., at 312, the classic example of federal-question jurisdiction predicated on the centrality of a federal issue is Smith v. Kansas City Title & Trust Co., 255 U.S. 180 (1921).

should take account of attorney's fees expended ... to obtain the tort recovery." Indeed it may. But it is hardly apparent why a proper "federal-state balance" would place such a nonstatutory issue under the complete governance of federal law, to be declared in a federal forum. The state court in which the personal-injury suit was lodged is competent to apply federal law, to the extent it is relevant, and would seem best positioned to determine the lawyer's part in obtaining, and his or her fair share in, the tort recovery.

The United States no doubt "has an overwhelming interest in attracting able workers to the federal workforce," and "in the health and welfare of the federal workers upon whom it relies to carry out its functions." Id., at 10. But those interests, we are persuaded, do not warrant turning into a discrete and costly "federal case" an insurer's contract-derived claim to be reimbursed from the proceeds of a federal worker's state-court-initiated tort litigation.

In sum, *Grable* emphasized that it takes more than a federal element "to open the 'arising-under' door." 545 U.S., at 313. This case cannot be squeezed into the slim category *Grable* exemplifies.

* * *

For the reasons stated, the judgment of the Court of Appeals for the Second Circuit is affirmed.

■ JUSTICE BREYER, with whom JUSTICE KENNEDY, JUSTICE SOUTER, and JUSTICE ALITO join, dissenting.

This case involves a dispute about the meaning of terms in a federal health insurance contract. The contract, between a federal agency and a private carrier, sets forth the details of a federal health insurance program created by federal statute and covering 8 million federal employees. In all this the Court cannot find a basis for federal jurisdiction. I believe I can. See Clearfield Trust Co. v. United States, 318 U.S. 363 (1943).

I

A

There is little about this case that is not federal. The comprehensive federal health insurance program at issue is created by a federal statute, the Federal Employees Health Benefits Act of 1959 (FEHBA), 5 U.S.C. § 8901 et seq. (2000 ed. and Supp. III). This program provides insurance for Federal Government employees and their families. That insurance program today covers approximately 8 million federal employees, retirees, and dependents, at a total cost to the Government of about $22 billion a year.

To implement the statute, the Office of Personnel Management (OPM), the relevant federal agency, enters into contracts with a handful of major insurance carriers. These agency/carrier contracts follow a standard agency form of about 38,000 words, and contain the details of the plan offered by the carrier. See § 8902(d) (2000 ed.) (requiring contract between carrier and agency to contain a detailed statement of the terms of the plan); see also Federal Employees Health Benefits Program Standard Contract (CR–2003) (2005). http://www.opm.gov/insure/carriers/samplecontract.doc (sample form agency/carrier contract) .... The contract lists, for example, the benefits provided to the employees who enroll. It provides a patient's bill of rights. It makes clear that the Government, not the carrier, will receive the premiums and will pay the benefits. It specifies that the carrier will administer the program that the contract sets forth, for which the carrier will receive an adjustable fee. The contract also states, "By enrolling or accepting services under this contract, [enrollees] are obligated to all terms, conditions, and provisions of this contract."

As the statute requires, § 8907(b), the agency/carrier contract also provides that the carrier will send each enrolled employee a brochure that explains the terms of the plan, as set forth in the contract. The brochure explains that it "describes the benefits of the ... [p]lan under [the carrier's] contract ... with [the federal agency], as authorized by the [federal statute]." The terms of the brochure are incorporated into the agency/carrier contract. The carrier distributes the brochure with a seal attached to the front stating, "Authorized for distribution by the United States Office of Personnel Management Retirement and Insurance Service."

The program is largely funded by the Federal Government. More specifically, the Federal Government pays about 75% of the plan premiums; the enrollee pays the rest. § 8906(b). These premiums are deposited into a special fund in the United States Treasury. § 8909(a). The carrier typically withdraws money from the fund to pay for covered health care services, ibid.; however, the fund's money belongs, not to the carrier, but to the federal agency that administers the program. After benefits are paid, any surplus in the fund can be used at the agency's discretion to reduce premiums, to increase plan benefits, or to make a refund to the Government and enrollees. § 8909(b); 5 C.F.R. § 890.503(c)(2) (2005). The carrier is not at risk. Rather, it earns a profit, not from any difference between plan premiums and the cost of benefits, but from a negotiated service charge that the federal agency pays directly.

Federal regulations provide that the federal agency will resolve disputes about an enrolled employee's coverage. § 890.105(a)(1); see also 5 U.S.C. § 8902(j) (requiring carrier to provide health benefit if OPM concludes that enrollee is entitled to the benefit under the contract). The agency's resolution is judicially reviewable under the Administrative Procedure Act in federal court. 5 C.F.R. § 890.107 (2005).

In sum, the statute is federal, the program it creates is federal, the program's beneficiaries are federal employees working throughout the country, the Federal Government pays all relevant costs, and the Federal Government receives all relevant payments. The private carrier's only role in this scheme is to administer the health benefits plan for the federal agency in exchange for a fixed service charge.

. . . . .

II

A

I have explained the nature of the program and have set forth the terms of the agency/carrier contract in some detail because, once understood, their federal nature brings this case well within the scope of the relevant federal jurisdictional statute, 28 U.S.C. § 1331, which provides jurisdiction for claims "arising under" federal law. For purposes of this statute, a claim arises under federal law if federal law creates the cause of action. Merrell Dow Pharmaceuticals Inc. v. Thompson, 478 U.S. 804, 808 (1986); see also American Well Works Co. v. Layne & Bowler Co., 241 U.S. 257, 260 (1916) (opinion of Holmes, J.) (A "suit arises under the law that creates the cause of action"). And this Court has explained that § 1331's "statutory grant of 'jurisdiction will support claims founded upon federal common law as well as those of a statutory origin.' " National Farmers Union Ins. Cos. v. Crow Tribe, 471 U.S. 845, 850 (1985); see also Illinois v. Milwaukee, 406 U.S. 91 (1972); C. Wright, A. Miller & E. Cooper, Federal Practice and Procedure § 4514, p. 455 (2d ed.1996) ("A case 'arising under' federal common law presents a federal question and as such is within the original subject-matter jurisdiction of the federal courts"). In other words, "[f]ederal common law as articulated in rules that are fashioned by court decisions are 'laws' as that term is used in § 1331." *National Farmers*, supra, at 850.

It seems clear to me that the petitioner's claim arises under federal common law. The dispute concerns the application of terms in a federal contract. This Court has consistently held that "obligations to and rights of the United States under its contracts are governed exclusively by federal law." Boyle v. United Technologies Corp., 487 U.S. 500, 504 (1988). This principle dates back at least as far as *Clearfield Trust*, 318 U.S., at 366, where the Court held that the "rights and duties of the United States on [federal] commercial paper," namely a federal employee's paycheck, "are governed by federal rather than local law." The Court reasoned that "[w]hen the United States disburses its funds or pays its debts, it is exercising a constitutional function or power," a power "in no way dependent on the laws of Pennsylvania or of any other state." Ibid. Accordingly, "[i]n [the] absence of an applicable Act of Congress it is for the federal courts to fashion the governing rule of law." Id., at 367.

This Court has applied this principle, the principle embodied in *Clearfield Trust*, to Government contracts of all sorts. See, e.g., West Virginia v. United States, 479 U.S. 305, 308–309 (1987) (contract regarding federal disaster relief efforts); United States v. Kimbell Foods, Inc., 440 U.S. 715, 726 (1979) (contractual liens arising from federal loan programs); United States v. Little Lake Misere Land Co., 412 U.S. 580, 592 (1973) (agreements to acquire land under federal conservation program); United States v. Seckinger, 397 U.S. 203, 209 (1970) (Government construction contracts); United States v. County of Allegheny, 322 U.S. 174, 183 (1944) (Government procurement contracts).

In this case, the words that provide the right to recover are contained in the brochure, which in turn explains the provisions of the contract between the Government and the carrier, provisions that were written by a federal agency acting pursuant to a federal statute that creates a federal benefit program for federal employees. At bottom, then, the petitioner's claim is based on the interpretation of a federal contract, and as such should be governed by federal common law. And because the petitioner's claim is based on federal common law, the federal courts have jurisdiction over it pursuant to § 1331. The lower federal courts have similarly found § 1331 jurisdiction over suits between private parties based on Federal Government contracts. See, e.g., Downey v. State Farm Fire & Casualty Co., 266 F.3d 675, 680–681 (CA7 2001) (Easterbrook, J.) (National Flood Insurance Program contracts); Almond v. Capital Properties, Inc., 212 F.3d 20, 22–24 (CA1 2000) (Boudin, J.) (Federal Railroad Administration contract); Price v. Pierce, 823 F.2d 1114, 1119–1120 (CA7 1987) (Posner, J.) (Dept. of Housing and Urban Development contracts).

.   .   .   .   .

C

The Court adds that, in spite of the pervasively federal character of this dispute, state law should govern it because the petitioner has not demonstrated a " 'significant conflict ... between an identifiable federal policy or interest and the operation of state law.' " But ... the Federal Government has two such interests: (1) the uniform operation of a federal employee health insurance program, and (2) obtaining reimbursement under a uniform set of legal rules. These interests are undermined if the amount a federal employee has to reimburse the FEHBA United States Treasury fund in cases like this one varies from State to State in accordance with state contract law. We have in the past recognized that this sort of interest in uniformity is sufficient to warrant application of federal common law. See, e.g., *Boyle*, 487 U.S., at 508 ("[W]here the federal interest requires a uniform rule, the entire body of state law applicable to the area conflicts and is replaced by federal rules"); *Clearfield Trust*, supra, at 367 (applying federal common law because "application of state law ... would subject the rights and duties of the United States to exceptional uncertainty" and "would lead to great diversity in results by making identical transactions subject to the vagaries of the laws of the several states," and therefore "[t]he desirability of a uniform rule is plain").

But even if the Court is correct that " '[t]he prudent course' is 'to adopt the readymade body of state law as the federal rule of decision until Congress strikes a different accommodation' " (quoting *Kimbell Foods*, supra, at 740), there would still be federal jurisdiction over this case. That is because, as *Clearfield Trust*, *Kimbell Foods*, and other cases make clear, the decision to apply state law "as the federal rule of decision" is itself a matter of federal common law. See, e.g., *Kimbell Foods*, supra, at 728, n. 21 (" 'Whether state law is to be incorporated as a matter of federal common law ... involves the ... problem of the relationship of a particular issue to a going federal program' " (emphasis added)); *Clearfield Trust*, supra, at 367 ("In our choice of the applicable federal rule we have occasionally selected state law" (emphasis added)); see also R. Fallon, D. Meltzer, & D. Shapiro, Hart and Wechsler's The Federal Courts and the Federal System 700 (5th ed.2003) ("[T]he current approach, as reflected in [*Kimbell Foods*, supra], suggests that ... while under *Clearfield* federal common law governs, in general it will incorporate state law as the rule of decision"); C. Wright, A. Miller, & E. Cooper, Federal Practice and Procedure § 4518, at 572–573 ("In recent years, the Supreme Court has put increasing emphasis on the notion that when determining what should be the content of federal common law, the law of the forum state should be adopted absent some good reason to displace it" (emphasis added; citing *Kimbell Foods*, supra, and *Clearfield Trust*, supra)).

On this view, the *Clearfield Trust* inquiry involves two questions: (1) whether federal common law governs the plaintiff's claim; (2) if so, whether, as a matter of federal common law, the Court should adopt state law as the proper " 'federal rule of decision' " (emphasis added). See, e.g., *Kimbell Foods*, supra, at 727 (deciding that "[f]ederal law therefore controls" the dispute but concluding that state law gives "content to this federal rule"); United States v. Little Lake Misere Land Co., 412 U.S., at 593–594 (The "first step of the *Clearfield* analysis" is to decide whether " 'the courts of the United States may formulate a rule of decision,' " and the "next step in our analysis is to determine whether" the federal rule of decision should " 'borro[w]' state law"); see also Friendly, In Praise of *Erie*—and of the New Federal Common Law, 39 N.Y.U.L.Rev. 383, 410 (1964) ("*Clearfield* decided not one issue but two. The first ... is that the right of the United States to recover for conversion of a Government check is a federal right, so that the courts of the United States may formulate a rule of decision. The second ... is whether, having this opportunity, the federal courts should adopt a uniform nation-wide rule or should follow state law" (footnote omitted)). Therefore, even if the Court is correct that state law applies to claims involving the interpretation of some provisions of this contract, the decision whether and when to apply state law should be made by the federal courts under federal common law. Accordingly, for jurisdictional purposes those claims must still arise under federal law, for federal common law determines the rule of decision.

. . . . .

With respect, I dissent.

———

E.   Edelmann & Co. v. Triple–A Specialty Co.

United States Court of Appeals, Seventh Circuit, 1937.
88 F.2d 852.

Suit by the Triple–A Specialty Company against E. Edelmann & Company. From a decree for plaintiff, defendant appeals.

■ Before EVANS, CIRCUIT JUDGE, and LINDLEY and BRIGGLE, DISTRICT JUDGES.

■ LINDLEY, DISTRICT JUDGE. Appellee brought suit in the District Court to secure a declaratory judgment, averring that appellant had wrongfully charged appellee with infringement of appellant's patent for a hydrometer to Edelmann No. 1,800,139 and had notified the trade of such untrue charges, and asking the court, first, to decide whether the patent is valid and, if so, whether it is infringed by appellee; and, second, to enjoin appellant from publication of such charges. The court found that it had jurisdiction of the parties and subject-matter, despite lack of diversity of citizenship. It did not pass upon the validity of the patent but declared appellee's device noninfringing and awarded an accounting for such damages, if any, as had accrued because of circulation of wrongful charges of infringement.

Appellant's first contention is that the court was without jurisdiction, because, there being no diversity of citizenship, no federal question was involved; that the suit is not one arising under the patent laws but under general jurisdiction in equity; and that the Declaratory Judgment Act is ineffective to confer jurisdiction.

The act (Jud.Code § 274d, 28 U.S.C. § 400) provides in part that: "In cases of actual controversy ... the courts of the United States shall have power upon petition, declaration, complaint, or other appropriate pleadings to declare rights and other legal relations of any interested party petitioning for such declaration."

Obviously the language does not create new substantive rights or legal relationships but adds, to remedies previously existing, an additional one for relief in the form of a judgment declaring in cases of actual controversy, the rights of the parties. Equally as clearly, prior to the passage of the act, no one had a right under the patent laws to initiate suits for affirmative relief in the form of an adjudication that another's patent was invalid or was not infringed. Therefore, appellant contends, the remedy provided by the act does not arise under the patent laws and the court was without jurisdiction.

It is clear that there is an actual controversy between the parties, whether appellee infringes the Edelmann patent. Appellant so charged, stating to appellee's customers and prospective customers that unless the infringement should be discontinued, suit would be entered against appellee and dealers.

Was the controversy one arising under the patent laws?

.   .   .   .   .

... Jurisdiction of the court was properly invoked in the present case. The cause arose under the patent laws of the United States; consequently jurisdiction existed, irrespective of diversity of citizenship.

The Declaratory Judgment Act merely introduced additional remedies. It modified the law only as to procedure and, though the right to such relief has been in some cases inherent, the statute extended greatly the situations under which such relief may be claimed. It was the congressional intent to avoid accrual of avoidable damages to one not certain of his rights and to afford him an early adjudication without waiting until his adversary should see fit to begin suit, after damage had accrued. But the controversy is the same as previously. Heretofore the owner of the patent might sue to enjoin infringement; now the alleged infringer may sue. But the controversy between the parties as to whether a patent is valid, and whether infringement exists is in either instance essentially one arising under the patent laws of the United States. It is of no moment, in the determination of the character of the relief sought, that the suit is brought by the alleged infringer instead of by the owner. Consequently we are unable to agree with the conclusions of Judge Davis of the Eighth Circuit in the case of International Harvest Hat Company v. Caradine Hat Company (D.C.Mo.), 17 F.Supp. 79.

Appellant urges, however, that the prayer for damages because of circulation of charges of infringement among dealers and potential customers, stamps appellee's suit as one to enforce a common-law remedy, namely, recovery of damages for unfair competition. If this were the only end sought and the jurisdiction of the court invoked to secure only that relief, the contention would necessarily prevail. But appellee relies upon two remedies: First, the determination of whether the patent is valid and infringed; and, second, if either of these questions is answered in the negative, whether it is also entitled to damages for violation of its common-law rights arising out of the same facts, plus the additional fact that appellant has wrongfully circulated, among the trade, false charges of infringement. The relief sought upon the second branch is upon a footing entirely apart from that prayed upon the first. Appellee included, as a basis for one sort of relief, facts pertinent only under the patent laws of the United States, over cases arising under which the federal courts have exclusive jurisdiction. It included also a prayer for another sort of relief of which any state court might have jurisdiction, and which the federal court, in the absence of another basis for jurisdiction, might not entertain except in case of diversity of citizenship.

In Hurn v. Oursler, 289 U.S. 238, the plaintiff charged that an act of the defendant constituted both infringement of a copyright and unfair competition. The District Court dismissed the bill, so far as relief under the copyright laws was concerned, thus disposing of that branch of the case upon the merits. It then proceeded to dismiss the case, so far as it involved unfair competition, for want of jurisdiction; there being no diversity of citizenship. The Supreme Court reversed this decree, holding that the trial court, having acquired jurisdiction under the copyright laws took jurisdiction of the remainder of the controversy. Here appellee might have sought relief from unfair competition in the state court, but it could not there obtain relief declaring the patent invalid or not infringed. Under Hurn v. Oursler, 289 U.S. 238, the court was endowed with jurisdiction also to determine the issues as to fair competition.

. . . . .

The decree is affirmed.[17]

———

Skelly Oil Co. v. Phillips Petroleum Co.

Supreme Court of the United States, 1950.
339 U.S. 667, 70 S.Ct. 876, 94 L.Ed. 1194.

■ MR. JUSTICE FRANKFURTER delivered the opinion of the Court.

In 1945, Michigan–Wisconsin Pipe Line Company sought from the Federal Power Commission a certificate of public convenience and necessity, required by § 7(c) of the Natural Gas Act, 52 Stat. 825, as amended, 15 U.S.C. § 717f(c), for the construction and operation of a pipe line to carry natural gas from Texas to Michigan and Wisconsin. A prerequisite for such a certificate is adequate reserves of gas. To obtain these reserves Michigan–Wisconsin entered into an agreement with Phillips Petroleum Company on December 11, 1945, whereby the latter undertook to make available gas from the Hugoton Gas Field, sprawling over Kansas, Oklahoma and Texas, which it produced or purchased from others. Phillips had contracted with petitioners, Skelly Oil Company, Stanolind Oil and Gas Company, and Magnolia Petroleum Company, to purchase gas produced by them in the Hugoton Field for resale to Michigan–Wisconsin. Each contract provided that "in the event Michigan–Wisconsin Pipe Line Company shall fail to secure from the Federal Power Commission on or before [October 1, 1946] a certificate of public convenience and necessity for the construction and operation of its pipe line, Seller [a petitioner] shall have the right to terminate this contract by written notice to Buyer [Phillips] delivered to Buyer at any time after December 1, 1946, but before the issuance of such certificate." The legal significance of this provision is at the core of this litigation.

The Federal Power Commission, in response to the application of Michigan–Wisconsin, on November 30, 1946, ordered that "A certificate of public convenience and necessity be and it is hereby issued to applicant [Michigan–Wisconsin], upon the terms and conditions of this order," listing among the conditions that there be no transportation or sale of natural gas by means of the sanctioned facilities until all necessary authorizations were obtained from the State of Wisconsin and the communities proposed to be

---

[17. Certiorari denied 300 U.S. 680 (1937).

The *Edelmann* case is cited approvingly, and the proposition for which it stands expressly stated, in Franchise Tax Bd. v. Construction Laborers Vacation Trust, 463 U.S. 1, 19 n. 19 (1983).

Even when a patent holder initiates litigation by suing for infringement, an *Edelmann*-style declaratory-judgment claim seeking to establish the invalidity of the patent will typically be asserted by the patent-infringement defendant as a compulsory counterclaim. Such a counterclaim is not mooted by successful assertion of the defense of noninfringement, and even if the appellate court upholds the noninfringement defense on appeal, it should generally also rule on the merits of the invalidity issue if it too has been raised on appeal. See Cardinal Chemical Co. v. Morton Int'l, Inc., 508 U.S. 83 (1993).]

served, that Michigan–Wisconsin should have the approval of the Securities and Exchange Commission for its plan of financing, that the applicant should file for the approval of the Commission a schedule of reasonable rates, and that the sanctioned facilities should not be used for the transportation of gas to Detroit and Ann Arbor except with due regard for the rights and duties of Panhandle Eastern Pipe Line Company, which had intervened before the Federal Power Commission, in its established service for resale in these areas, such rights and duties to be set forth in a supplemental order. It was also provided that Michigan–Wisconsin should have fifteen days from the issue of the supplemental order to notify the Commission whether the certificate "as herein issued is acceptable to it." Finally, the Commission's order provided that for purposes of computing the time within which applications for rehearing could be filed, "the date of issuance of this order shall be deemed to be the date of issuance of the opinions, or of the supplemental order referred to herein, whichever may be later." 5 F.P.C. 953, 954, 956.

News of the Commission's action was released on November 30, 1946, but the actual content of the order was not made public until December 2, 1946. Petitioners severally, on December 2, 1946, gave notice to Phillips of termination of their contracts on the ground that Michigan–Wisconsin had not received a certificate of public convenience and necessity. Thereupon Michigan–Wisconsin and Phillips brought suit against petitioners in the District Court for the Northern District of Oklahoma. Alleging that a certificate of public convenience and necessity, "within the meaning of said Natural Gas Act and said contracts" had been issued prior to petitioners' attempt at termination of the contracts, they invoked the Federal Declaratory Judgment Act for a declaration that the contracts were still "in effect and binding upon the parties thereto." Motions by petitioners to have Michigan–Wisconsin dropped as a party plaintiff were sustained, but motions to dismiss the complaint for want of jurisdiction were denied. The case then went to the merits, and the District Court decreed that the contracts between Phillips and petitioners have not been "effectively terminated and that each of such contracts remain [sic] in full force and effect." The Court of Appeals for the Tenth Circuit affirmed, 174 F.2d 89, and we brought the case here, 338 U.S. 846, because it raises in sharp form the question whether a suit like this "arises under the Constitution, laws or treaties of the United States," 28 U.S.C. § 1331, so as to enable District Courts to give declaratory relief under the Declaratory Judgment Act. 48 Stat. 955, as amended, now 28 U.S.C. § 2201.

"[T]he operation of the Declaratory Judgment Act is procedural only." Aetna Life Ins. Co. of Hartford, Conn. v. Haworth, 300 U.S. 227, 240. Congress enlarged the range of remedies available in the federal courts but did not extend their jurisdiction. When concerned as we are with the power of the inferior federal courts to entertain litigation within the restricted area to which the Constitution and Acts of Congress confine them, "jurisdiction" means the kinds of issues which give right of entrance to federal courts. Jurisdiction in this sense was not altered by the Declaratory Judgment Act. Prior to that Act, a federal court would entertain a suit on a contract only if the plaintiff asked for an immediately enforceable remedy like money damages or an injunction, but such relief could only be given if the requisites of jurisdiction, in the sense of a federal right or diversity, provided foundation for resort to the federal courts. The Declaratory Judgment Act allowed relief to be given by way of recognizing the plaintiff's right even though no immediate enforcement of it was asked. But the requirements of jurisdiction—the limited subject matters which alone Congress had authorized the District Courts to adjudicate—were not impliedly repealed or modified. See Great Lakes Dredge & Dock Co. v. Huffman, 319 U.S. 293, 300; Colegrove v. Green, 328 U.S. 549, 551–552.

If Phillips sought damages from petitioners or specific performance of their contracts, it could not bring suit in a United States District Court on the theory that it was asserting a federal right. And for the simple reason that such a suit would "arise" under the State law governing the contracts. Whatever federal claim Phillips may be able to urge would in any event be injected into the case only in anticipation of a defense to be asserted by petitioners. "Not every question of federal law emerging in a suit is proof that a federal law is the basis of the suit." Gully v. First National Bank in Meridian, 299 U.S. 109, 115; compare 28 U.S.C. § 1257 with 28 U.S.C. § 1331. Ever since Metcalf v. City of Watertown, 128 U.S. 586, 589, it has been settled doctrine that where a suit is brought in the federal courts "upon the sole ground that the determination of the suit depends upon some question of a federal nature, it must appear, at the outset, from the declaration or the bill of the party suing, that the suit is of that character." But "a suggestion of one party that the other will or may set up a claim under the Constitution or laws of the United States does not make the suit one arising under that Constitution or those laws." State of Tennessee v. Union & Planters' Bank, 152 U.S. 454, 464. The plaintiff's claim itself must present a federal question "unaided by anything alleged in anticipation of avoidance of defenses which it is thought the defendant may interpose." Taylor v. Anderson, 234 U.S. 74, 75–76; Louisville & Nashville R. Co. v. Mottley, 211 U.S. 149, 152.

These decisions reflect the current of jurisdictional legislation since the Act of March 3, 1875, 18 Stat. 470, first entrusted to the lower federal courts wide jurisdiction in cases "arising under this Constitution, the Laws of the United States, and Treaties." U.S. Const.Art. III, § 2. "The change is in accordance with the general policy of these acts, manifest upon their face, and often recognized by this court, to contract the jurisdiction of the circuit courts [which became the District Courts] of the United States." *State of Tennessee v. Union & Planters' Bank*, supra, 152 U.S., at p. 462. See also State of Arkansas v. Kansas & Texas Coal Co., 183 U.S. 185, 188, and *Gully v. First National Bank in Meridian*, supra, 299 U.S., at pp. 112–114. With exceptions not now relevant, Congress has narrowed the opportunities for entrance into the federal courts, and this Court has been more careful than in earlier days in enforcing these jurisdictional limitations. See *Gully v. First National Bank in Meridian*, supra, 299 U.S., at p. 113.

To be observant of these restrictions is not to indulge in formalism or sterile technicality. It would turn into the federal courts a vast current of litigation indubitably arising under State law, in the sense that the right to be vindicated was State-created, if a suit for a declaration of rights could be brought into the federal courts merely because an anticipated defense derived from federal law. Not only would this unduly swell the volume of litigation in the District Courts but it would also embarrass those courts—and this Court on potential review—in that matters of local law may often be involved and the District Courts may either have to decide doubtful questions of State law or hold cases pending disposition of such State issues by State courts. To sanction suits for declaratory relief as within the jurisdiction of the District Courts merely because, as in this case, artful pleading anticipates a defense based on federal law would contravene the whole trend of jurisdictional legislation by Congress, disregard the effective functioning of the federal judicial system and distort the limited procedural purpose of the Declaratory Judgment Act. See Developments in the Law—Declaratory Judgments—1941–1949, 62 Harv.L.Rev. 787, 802–803 (1949). Since the matter in controversy as to which Phillips asked for a declaratory judgment is not one that "arises under the ... laws ... of the United States" and since as to Skelly and Stanolind jurisdiction cannot be sustained on the score of diversity of citizenship, the proceedings against them should have been dismissed.

As to Magnolia, a Texas corporation, a different situation is presented. Since Phillips was a Delaware corporation, there is diversity of citizenship. Magnolia had qualified to do business in Oklahoma and appointed an agent for service of process in accordance with the prevailing Oklahoma statute. Okl.Stat.Ann. tit. 18, § 452. Magnolia claimed that the subject matter of this proceeding did not arise in Oklahoma within the meaning of its consent to be sued. This contention was rejected below, and we do not reexamine the local law as applied by the lower courts. Under the doctrine of Neirbo Co. v. Bethlehem Shipbuilding Corp., 308 U.S. 165, venue was properly laid in Oklahoma; that the declaratory remedy which may be given by the federal courts may not be available in the State courts is immaterial.

Therefore, in the case of Magnolia we must reach the merits.

. . . . .

In respect to Magnolia, the judgment of the Court of Appeals is vacated and the cause remanded for further proceedings not inconsistent with this opinion. As to Skelly and Stanolind, we reverse the judgment with directions that the cause be dismissed.

It is so ordered.

Judgment of Court of Appeals vacated in respect to Magnolia and cause remanded with directions; judgment as to Skelly and Stanolind reversed with directions.

■ MR. JUSTICE BLACK agrees with the Court of Appeals and would affirm its judgment.

■ MR. JUSTICE DOUGLAS took no part in the consideration or disposition of this case.

■ MR. CHIEF JUSTICE VINSON, with whom MR. JUSTICE BURTON joins, dissenting in part.

I concur in that part of the Court's judgment that directs dismissal of the cause as to Skelly and Stanolind. I have real doubts as to whether there is a federal question here at all, even though interpretation of the contract between private parties requires an interpretation of a federal statute and the action of a federal regulatory body. But the Court finds it unnecessary to reach that question because it holds that the federal question, if any, is not a part of the plaintiff's claim and that jurisdiction does not, therefore, attach. While this result is not a necessary one, I am not prepared to dissent from it at this time.

But I am forced to dissent from the vacation and remand of the cause in respect to Magnolia. I think that, as to this petitioner, the judgment of the Court of Appeals should be affirmed.[18]

[18.   See Wright & Kane, Federal Courts § 18 (6th ed.2002); ALI Study 170–172.

The limitations of the *Skelly* case on federal-question jurisdiction over declaratory-judgment actions were affirmed in Franchise Tax Board v. Construction Laborers Vacation Trust, 463 U.S. 1, 15–19 (1983).

The Supreme Court cast further darkness on the jurisdictional status of suits for declaratory relief in Textron Lycoming Reciprocating Engine Div. v. United Automobile Workers, 523 U.S. 653, 659 (1998), by questioning whether "facts which were the *converse* of *Skelly Oil*— *i.e.,* a declaratory-judgment complaint raising a *nonfederal* defense to an anticipated *federal* claim—*would* confer § 1331 jurisdiction."

But see Doernberg & Mushlin, The Trojan Horse: How the Declaratory Judgment Act Created a Cause of Action and Expanded Federal Jurisdiction While the Supreme Court Wasn't Looking, 36 UCLA L.Rev. 529 (1989). This article concludes, at 588: "The legislative history of the Declaratory Judgment Act cannot, and should not, be ignored. Although the courts have honored that history in the limited area of mirror-image patent cases, they have been unwilling to do so for the full range of cases that Congress intended the Act to affect. Candor in dealing with that legislative history requires recognition of the fact that Congress expanded federal courts' jurisdiction when it created the cause of action embodied in the Declaratory Judgment Act. Moreover, as the extensive testimony of the proponents of the new device shows, Congress could not have done so inadvertently. Though the courts may be uncomfortable with the policy expressed in the Act, as they have so often instructed, it is not their function to pass on the wisdom of legislation. It is time to recognize the Trojan Horse's contents in the light of day." These authors argue that it is not possible to reconcile *American Well Works*, *Edelmann*, and *Skelly*. The complaints in *American Well Works* and *Edelmann* are set out as an Appendix to that article. 36 UCLA L.Rev. at 590–596.

See also Doernberg & Mushlin, History Comes Calling: Dean Griswold Offers New Evidence about the Jurisdictional Debate Surrounding the Enactment of the Declaratory Judgment Act, 37 UCLA L.Rev. 139 (1989).

Plaintiff alleges in a well-pleaded complaint for declaratory relief that there is an actual controversy between the parties that the defendant could bring to federal court by asserting non-frivolous claims for coercive relief arising under federal law. Is this sufficient under the rule of the *Skelly* case to bring the declaratory-judgment within § 1331's grant of federal-question jurisdiction, even if the defendant need not necessarily invoke federal grounds for

Verlinden B.V. v. Central Bank of Nigeria

Supreme Court of the United States, 1983.
461 U.S. 480, 103 S.Ct. 1962, 76 L.Ed.2d 81.

■ CHIEF JUSTICE BURGER delivered the opinion of the Court.

We granted certiorari to consider whether the Foreign Sovereign Immunities Act of 1976, by authorizing a foreign plaintiff to sue a foreign state in a United States district court on a nonfederal cause of action, violates Article III of the Constitution.

. . . . .

[Verlinden B.V., a Dutch corporation, contracted to sell 240,000 metric tons of cement to the Federal Republic of Nigeria. The contract provided that Nigeria was to establish a confirmed letter of credit for the purchase price. Subsequently, Verlinden sued the Central Bank of Nigeria, an instrumentality of Nigeria, in the United States District Court for the Southern District of New York, alleging that certain actions by the bank constituted an anticipatory breach of the letter of credit. Jurisdiction was claimed to exist under the provision of the Federal Sovereign Immunities Act, 28 U.S.C. § 1330(a), granting district courts jurisdiction without regard to amount in controversy of "any nonjury civil action against a foreign state . . . as to any claim for relief in personam with respect to which the foreign state is not entitled to immunity either under sections 1605–1607 of this title or under any applicable international agreement." The District Court dismissed, finding that none of the exceptions to sovereign immunity specified in the statute were applicable. The Second Circuit affirmed the dismissal, but on the ground that neither the Diversity Clause nor the "Arising Under" Clause of Article III is broad enough to support jurisdiction over actions by foreign plaintiffs against foreign sovereigns.]

IV

We now turn to the core question presented by this case: whether Congress exceeded the scope of Art. III of the Constitution by granting federal courts subject-matter jurisdiction over certain civil actions by foreign plaintiffs against foreign sovereigns where the rule of decision may be provided by state law.

This Court's cases firmly establish that Congress may not expand the jurisdiction of the federal courts beyond the bounds established by the Constitution. See, e.g., Hodgson v. Bowerbank, 5 Cranch [9 U.S.] 303 (1809); Kline v. Burke Construction Co., 260 U.S. 226, 234 (1922). Within Art. III of the Constitution, we find two sources authorizing the grant of jurisdiction in the Foreign Sovereign Immunities Act: the Diversity Clause

---

coercive relief, and could instead seek coercive relief solely as a matter of state law? Agreeing with seven other circuits, the Eleventh Circuit has held that the declaratory-judgment plaintiff may invoke federal-question jurisdiction merely by showing that the declaratory-judgment defendant *could* bring a reciprocal coercive action that would arise under federal law. See Household Bank v. JFS Group, 320 F.3d 1249 (11th Cir.2003).]

and the "Arising Under" Clause.[19] The Diversity Clause, which provides that the judicial power extends to controversies between "a State, or the Citizens thereof, and foreign States," covers actions by citizens of States. Yet diversity jurisdiction is not sufficiently broad to support a grant of jurisdiction over actions by foreign plaintiffs, since a foreign plaintiff is not "a State, or [a] Citize[n] thereof." See Mossman v. Higginson, 4 Dall. [4 U.S.] 12 (1800). We conclude, however, that the "Arising Under" Clause of Art. III provides an appropriate basis for the statutory grant of subject-matter jurisdiction to actions by foreign plaintiffs under the Act.

The controlling decision on the scope of Art. III "arising under" jurisdiction is Chief Justice Marshall's opinion for the Court in Osborn v. Bank of United States, 9 Wheat. [22 U.S.] 738 (1824) . . . .

Osborn thus reflects a broad conception of "arising under" jurisdiction, according to which Congress may confer on the federal courts jurisdiction over any case or controversy that might call for the application of federal law. The breadth of that conclusion has been questioned. It has been observed that, taken at its broadest, *Osborn* might be read as permitting "assertion of original federal jurisdiction on the remote possibility of presentation of a federal question." Textile Workers v. Lincoln Mills, 353 U.S. 448, 482 (1957) (Frankfurter, J., dissenting). See, e.g., P. Bator, P. Mishkin, D. Shapiro, & H. Wechsler, Hart & Wechsler's The Federal Courts and the Federal System 866–867 (2d ed.1973). We need not now resolve that issue or decide the precise boundaries of Art. III jurisdiction, however, since the present case does not involve a mere speculative possibility that a federal question may arise at some point in the proceeding. Rather, a suit against a foreign state under this Act necessarily raises questions of

---

19.   In view of our conclusion that proper actions by foreign plaintiffs under the Foreign Sovereign Immunities Act are within Art. III "arising under" jurisdiction, we need not consider petitioner's alternative argument that the Act is constitutional as an aspect of so-called "protective jurisdiction." See generally Note, The Theory of Protective Jurisdiction, 57 N.Y.U.L.Rev. 933 (1982).

[The theory of "protective jurisdiction" is that with regard to subjects for which Congress has legislative power, a statute granting federal jurisdiction would be itself a "law of the United States" within the meaning of Article III, § 2, even though Congress had not enacted any substantive rule of decision. Wright & Kane, Federal Courts § 20 (6th ed.2002); Mullenix, Redish & Vairo, Understanding Federal Courts and Jurisdiction § 4.02[5] (1998). See Wechsler, Federal Jurisdiction and the Revision of the Judicial Code, 13 L. & Contemp.Prob. 216, 224–225 (1948), and Mishkin, The Federal "Question" Jurisdiction of the District Courts, 53 Colum.L.Rev. 157, 184–186 (1953) both supporting the theory. Two Justices were prepared to accept the theory in Textile Workers Union of America v. Lincoln Mills of Alabama, 353 U.S. 448, 459–460 (1957), but Justice Frankfurter, dissenting in that case, argued at length that " '[p]rotective jurisdiction,' once the label is discarded, cannot be justified under any view of the allowable scope to be given to Article III." 353 U.S., at 474–475.

The Price–Anderson Act, which establishes federal jurisdiction over "public liability actions" relating to nuclear incidents, though rules of decision are derived from state law, did not go beyond Article III as there were important federal questions to be resolved that were indispensable incidents of those actions. In re TMI Litigation Cases Consolidated II, 940 F.2d 832 (3d Cir.1991).]

substantive federal law at the very outset, and hence clearly "arises under" federal law, as that term is used in Art. III.

By reason of its authority over foreign commerce and foreign relations, Congress has the undisputed power to decide, as a matter of federal law, whether and under what circumstances foreign nations should be amenable to suit in the United States. Actions against foreign sovereigns in our courts raise sensitive issues concerning the foreign relations of the United States, and the primacy of federal concerns is evident. See, e.g., Banco Nacional de Cuba v. Sabbatino, 376 U.S. 398, 423–425 (1964); Zschernig v. Miller, 389 U.S. 429, 440–441 (1968).

To promote these federal interests, Congress exercised its Art. I powers[20] by enacting a statute comprehensively regulating the amenability of foreign nations to suit in the United States. The statute must be applied by the district courts in every action against a foreign sovereign, since subject-matter jurisdiction in any such action depends on the existence of one of the specified exceptions to foreign sovereign immunity, 28 U.S.C. § 1330(a).[21] At the threshold of every action in a district court against a foreign state, therefore, the court must satisfy itself that one of the exceptions applies—and in doing so it must apply the detailed federal law standards set forth in the Act. Accordingly, an action against a foreign sovereign arises under federal law, for purposes of Art. III jurisdiction.

In reaching a contrary conclusion, the Court of Appeals relied heavily upon decisions construing 28 U.S.C. § 1331, the statute which grants district courts general federal-question jurisdiction over any case that "arises under" the laws of the United States. The court placed particular emphasis on the so-called "well-pleaded complaint" rule, which provides, for purposes of *statutory* "arising under" jurisdiction, that the federal question must appear on the face of a well-pleaded complaint and may not enter in anticipation of a defense. See, e.g., Louisville & Nashville R. Co. v. Mottley, 211 U.S. 149 (1908); Gully v. First National Bank, 299 U.S. 109 (1936); 13 C. Wright, A. Miller, & E. Cooper, Federal Practice and Procedure § 3562 (1975) (hereinafter Wright, Miller, & Cooper). In the view of the Court of Appeals, the question of foreign sovereign immunity in this case arose solely as a defense, and not on the face of Verlinden's well-pleaded complaint.

Although the language of § 1331 parallels that of the "Arising Under" Clause of Art. III, this Court never has held that statutory "arising under"

---

20. In enacting the legislation, Congress relied specifically on its powers to prescribe the jurisdiction of federal courts, Art. I, § 8, cl. 9; to define offenses against the "Law of Nations," Art. I, § 8, cl. 10; to regulate commerce with foreign nations, Art. I, § 8, cl. 3; and to make all laws necessary and proper to execute the Government's powers, Art. I, § 8, cl. 18.

21. The House Report on the Act states that "sovereign immunity is an affirmative defense which must be specially pleaded," H.R.Rep. No. 941487, p. 17 (1976). Under the Act, however, subject-matter jurisdiction turns on the existence of an exception to foreign sovereign immunity, 28 U.S.C. § 1330(a). Accordingly, even if the foreign state does not enter an appearance to assert an immunity defense, a district court still must determine that immunity is unavailable under the Act.

jurisdiction is identical to Art. III "arising under" jurisdiction. Quite the contrary is true. Section 1331, the general federal-question statute, although broadly phrased,

> "has been continuously construed and limited in the light of the history that produced it, the demands of reason and coherence, and the dictates of sound judicial policy which have emerged from the [statute's] function as a provision in the mosaic of federal judiciary legislation. *It is a statute, not a Constitution, we are expounding.*" Romero v. International Terminal Operating Co., 358 U.S. 354, 379 (1959) (emphasis added).

In an accompanying footnote, the Court further observed: "Of course the many limitations which have been placed on jurisdiction under § 1331 are not limitations on the constitutional power of Congress to confer jurisdiction on the federal courts." Id., at 379, n. 51. We reiterated that conclusion in Powell v. McCormack, 395 U.S. 486, 515 (1969). See also Shoshone Mining Co. v. Rutter, 177 U.S. 505, 506 (1900). As these decisions make clear, Art. III "arising under" jurisdiction is broader than federal-question jurisdiction under § 1331, and the Court of Appeals' heavy reliance on decisions construing that statute was misplaced.[22]

In rejecting "arising under" jurisdiction, the Court of Appeals also noted that 28 U.S.C. § 1330 is a jurisdictional provision. Because of this, the court felt its conclusion compelled by prior cases in which this Court has rejected congressional attempts to confer jurisdiction on federal courts simply by enacting jurisdictional statutes. In Mossman v. Higginson, 4 Dall. [4 U.S.] 12 (1800), for example, this Court found that a statute purporting to confer jurisdiction over actions "where an alien is a party" would exceed the scope of Art. III if construed to allow an action solely between two aliens. And in The Propeller Genesee Chief v. Fitzhugh, 12 How. [53 U.S.] 443, 451–453 (1852), the Court, while upholding a statute granting jurisdiction over vessels on the Great Lakes as an exercise of maritime jurisdiction, rejected the view that the jurisdictional statute itself constituted a federal regulation of commerce upon which "arising under" jurisdiction could be based.

From these cases, the Court of Appeals apparently concluded that a jurisdictional statute can never constitute the federal law under which the action arises, for Art. III purposes. Yet the statutes at issue in these prior cases sought to do nothing more than grant jurisdiction over a particular class of cases. As the Court stated in *The Propeller Genesee Chief:* "The law ... contains no regulations of commerce.... *It merely confers a new jurisdiction on the district courts; and this is its only object and purpose....* It is evident ... that Congress, in passing [the law], did not intend to exercise their power to regulate commerce...." 12 How., at 451–452 (emphasis added).

---

22. Citing only Shoshone Mining Co. v. Rutter, 177 U.S. 505 (1900), the Court of Appeals recognized that this Court "has implied" that Art. III jurisdiction is broader than that under § 1331. The court nevertheless placed substantial reliance on decisions construing § 1331.

In contrast, in enacting the Foreign Sovereign Immunities Act, Congress expressly exercised its power to regulate foreign commerce, along with other specified Art. I powers. See n. [20], supra. As the House Report clearly indicates, the primary purpose of the Act was to "se[t] forth comprehensive rules governing sovereign immunity," H.R.Rep. No. 94-1487, p. 12 (1976); the jurisdictional provisions of the Act are simply one part of this comprehensive scheme. The Act thus does not merely concern access to the federal courts. Rather, it governs the types of actions for which foreign sovereigns may be held liable in a court in the United States, federal or state. The Act codifies the standards governing foreign sovereign immunity as an aspect of substantive federal law, see Ex parte Peru, 318 U.S. [578, 588 (1943)]; Mexico v. Hoffman, 324 U.S. [30, 36 (1945)]; and applying those standards will generally require interpretation of numerous points of federal law. Finally, if a court determines that none of the exceptions to sovereign immunity applies, the plaintiff will be barred from raising his claim in any court in the United States—manifestly, "the title or right set up by the party, may be defeated by one construction of the ... laws of the United States, and sustained by the opposite construction." *Osborn v. Bank of United States*, 9 Wheat., at 822. That the inquiry into foreign sovereign immunity is labeled under the Act as a matter of jurisdiction does not affect the constitutionality of Congress' action in granting federal courts jurisdiction over cases calling for application of this comprehensive regulatory statute.

Congress, pursuant to its unquestioned Art. I powers, has enacted a broad statutory framework governing assertions of foreign sovereign immunity. In so doing, Congress deliberately sought to channel cases against foreign sovereigns away from the state courts and into federal courts, thereby reducing the potential for a multiplicity of conflicting results among the courts of the 50 States. The resulting jurisdictional grant is within the bounds of Art. III, since every action against a foreign sovereign necessarily involves application of a body of substantive federal law, and accordingly "arises under" federal law, within the meaning of Art. III.

V

A conclusion that the grant of jurisdiction in the Foreign Sovereign Immunities Act is consistent with the Constitution does not end the case. An action must not only satisfy Art. III but must also be supported by a statutory grant of subject-matter jurisdiction. As we have made clear, deciding whether statutory subject-matter jurisdiction exists under the Foreign Sovereign Immunities Act entails an application of the substantive terms of the Act to determine whether one of the specified exceptions to immunity applies.

In the present case, the District Court, after satisfying itself as to the constitutionality of the Act, held that the present action does not fall within any specified exception. The Court of Appeals, reaching a contrary conclusion as to jurisdiction under the Constitution, did not find it necessary to address this statutory question. Accordingly, on remand the Court of

Appeals must consider whether jurisdiction exists under the Act itself. If the Court of Appeals agrees with the District Court on that issue, the case will be at an end. If, on the other hand, the Court of Appeals concludes that jurisdiction does exist under the statute, the action may then be remanded to the District Court for further proceedings.

It is so ordered.[23]

[23. See also Goldberg–Ambrose, The Protective Jurisdiction of the Federal Courts, 30 U.C.L.A. L.Rev. 542 (1983); Note, Over–Protective Jurisdiction: A State Sovereignty Theory of Federal Questions, 102 Harv.L.Rev. 1948 (1989).

In Bellia, Article III and the Cause of Action, 89 Iowa L.Rev. 777 (2004), the author criticizes *Verlinden*'s construction of *Osborn* and advocates a substantially narrower view of the *Osborn* "ingredient" test for when a cause of action arises under federal law within the meaning of Article III.

The immunity provisions of the FSIA were held in Republic of Austria v. Altmann, 541 U.S. 677 (2004), to apply retroactively to an alleged expropriation of valuable art works by the Austrian government in the aftermath of World War II. The effect of the ruling was to disallow a defense of foreign sovereign immunity that would have been applicable under federal law at the time of the alleged expropriation, but was abrogated by the 1976 enactment of the FSIA and its "expropriation exception" to foreign sovereign immunity.]

CHAPTER III

DIVERSITY OF CITIZENSHIP[1]

STATUTE

28 U.S.C. § 1332. Diversity of citizenship; amount in controversy; costs

(a) The district court shall have original jurisdiction of all civil actions[2] where the amount in controversy exceeds the sum or value of $75,000,[3] exclusive of interest and costs, and is between—

[1. See Friendly, Historic Basis of Diversity Jurisdiction, 41 Harv.L.Rev. 483 (1928); Yntema & Jaffin, Preliminary Analysis of Concurrent Jurisdiction, 79 U.Pa.L.Rev. 869 (1931); Frank, Historical Bases of the Federal Judicial System, 13 Law & Contemp.Prob. 3, 22–28 (1948); 13B Wright, Miller & Cooper, Federal Practice and Procedure: Jurisdiction 2d § 3601 (1984); 15 Moore's Federal Practice § 102 (3d ed.1998); Chemerinsky, Federal Jurisdiction § 5.3 (5th ed.2007); Mullenix, Redish & Vairo, Understanding Federal Courts and Jurisdiction §§ 3.01–3.17 (1998); Wright & Kane, Federal Courts § 23 (6th ed.2002); ALI Study 99–110, 458–464; ALI Judicial Code Project 613–628, 652–656.

Diversity cases are a large part of the business of the federal courts. In fiscal 2010—the year ending September 30, 2010—of the "private cases" commenced in federal court 138,655 were federal-question cases and 101,202 were diversity cases. Judicial Business of the United States Courts, Table C–2 (2010).

As explained at the beginning of Chapter II, unless Congress otherwise specifies, federal and state courts are assumed to have concurrent jurisdiction. In Gottlieb v. Carnival Corp., 436 F.3d 335 (2d Cir.2006), the Second Circuit analyzed the Telephone Consumer Protection Act (TCPA), which makes it unlawful to send unsolicited advertisements to a telephone facsimile machine. The Act provides that "[a] person or entity may, if otherwise permitted by the laws or rules of court of a State, bring in an appropriate court of that State" an action for monetary or injunctive relief. 47 U.S.C. § 227(b)(3). The Second Circuit held that Congress intended to divest federal courts of arising-under jurisdiction over private TCPA claims, but found no evidence that Congress intended to eliminate diversity jurisdiction over such claims. Adopting a presumption that § 1332 applies to all causes of action, whether created by federal or state law, unless Congress expresses a clear intent to the contrary, the court concluded that the Act confers federal diversity jurisdiction and state court jurisdiction over private claims.]

[2. The Supreme Court has recognized the existence of a domestic-relations exception to the diversity statute, but held that it is limited to divorce, alimony, and child custody. Ankenbrandt v. Richards, 504 U.S. 689 (1992). See Cahn, Family Law, Federalism, and the Federal Courts, 79 Iowa L.Rev. 1073 (1994); Stein, The Domestic Relations Exception to Federal Jurisdiction: Rethinking an Unsettled Federal Courts Doctrine, 36 B.C.L.Rev. 669 (1995).

Taking a narrow view of the domestic-relations exception, the Eleventh Circuit has held that a wife's fraudulent diversion of certain assets of her disabled husband—discovered but not pursued during the divorce proceedings, even though the diversion could have been asserted as grounds for increasing alimony—could be adjudicated by a federal court in a diversity action brought by the disabled husband's guardian against the former wife after the divorce proceedings had been completed. Dunn v. Cometa, 238 F.3d 38 (1st Cir.2001).

(1) citizens of different States;[4]

(2) citizens of a State and citizens or subjects of a foreign state, except that the district courts shall not have original jurisdiction under this subsection of an action between citizens of a State and citizens or subjects of a foreign state who are lawfully admitted for permanent residence in the United States and are domiciled in the same State;[5]

(3) citizens of different States and in which citizens or subjects of a foreign state are additional parties,[6] and

Cases involving probate administration have also generally been deemed by the courts to be beyond the scope of diversity jurisdiction. Vestal & Foster, Implied Limitations on the Diversity Jurisdiction of the Federal Courts, 41 Minn.L.Rev. 1 (1956); 13B Wright, Miller & Cooper, Federal Practice and Procedure: Jurisdiction 2d §§ 3609, 3610 (1984); Wright & Kane, Federal Courts § 25 (6th ed.2002); ALI Study 111–112.

Storm v. Storm, 328 F.3d 941 (7th Cir.2003), applied the probate exception to diversity jurisdiction to affirm the district court's dismissal of a suit alleging tortious interference with an inheritance expectancy based on an inter vivos trust. "Given the growth in recent years of various 'will substitutes,' we are loath to throw open the doors of the federal courts to disputes over testamentary intent simply because a decedent chose to use a will substitute rather than a traditional will to dispose of his or her estate." Id., at 947.

In Marshall v. Marshall, 547 U.S. 293 (2006), the Supreme Court affirmed the probate exception to federal diversity jurisdiction, but held that the exception had a "distinctly limited scope." Accordingly, the probate exception did not deprive a federal bankruptcy court of jurisdiction over a claim by Vickie Lynn Marshall (also known as Anna Nicole Smith) that her stepson had tortiously interfered with her expectancy of a gift or inheritance from her deceased husband. The Court noted that Ms. Marshall's claim did not involve the probate or annulment of a will, the administration of an estate, a res in a state court's custody, or any other purely probate matter.]

[3.   The stipulated amount was increased from $50,000 to $75,000 in 1996.]

[4.   The Judiciary Act of 1789 granted jurisdiction over suits "between a citizen of the State where the suit is brought, and a citizen of another State." The phrase "between citizens of different States" was substituted in 1875, and has been used ever since.]

[5.   JPMorgan Chase Bank v. Traffic Stream (BVI) Infrastructure Limited, 536 U.S. 88 (2002), provides a helpful overview of the history of and justification for federal alienage jurisdiction. A unanimous Court held that a corporation organized under the laws of the British Virgin Islands, a dependency of the United Kingdom, was a "citize[n] or subjec[t] of a foreign state" for purposes of 28 U.S.C. § 1332(a)(2).

Plaintiff, a United States citizen with his residence in Mexico, sues a Delaware corporation in district court, claiming that he is a "subject" of Mexico within 28 U.S.C. § 1332(a)(2). What result? Van Der Schelling v. United States News & World Report, Inc., 213 F.Supp. 756 (E.D.Pa.1963), affirmed 324 F.2d 956 (3d Cir.1963). See also Newman–Green, Inc. v. Alfonzo–Larrain, 490 U.S. 826 (1989); Johnson, Why Alienage Jurisdiction? Historical Foundations and Modern Justifications for Federal Jurisdiction Over Disputes Involving Noncitizens, 21 Yale J.Int'l.L. 1 (1996).]

[6.   Subsection (a)(3) was intended to remove doubt that an action involving a mixture of domestic and foreign citizens could draw jointly on both diversity jurisdiction under subsection (a)(1) and alienage jurisdiction under subsection (a)(2). See Goar v. Compania Peruana de Vapores, 688 F.2d 417, 421 (5th Cir.1982). The settled view is that subsection (a)(3) confers jurisdiction only when the mixture of parties includes domestic citizens on both sides of the dispute, and when, as between the domestic parties, there is the complete

(4) a foreign state, defined in section 1603(a) of this title, as plaintiff and citizens of a State or of different States.[7]

(b) Except when express provision therefor is otherwise made in a statute of the United States, where the plaintiff who files the case originally in the Federal courts is finally adjudged to be entitled to recover less than the sum or value of $75,000, computed without regard to any setoff or counterclaim to which the defendant may be adjudged to be entitled, and exclusive of interest and costs, the district court may deny costs to the plaintiff and, in addition, may impose costs on the plaintiff.

(c) For the purposes of this section and section 1441 of this title—

(1) a corporation shall be deemed to be a citizen of every State and foreign state by which it has been incorporated and of the State or foreign state where it has its principal place of business, except that in any direct action against the insurer of a policy or contract of liability insurance, whether incorporated or unincorporated, to which action the insured is not joined as a party-defendant, such insurer shall be deemed a citizen[8]—

---

diversity of state citizenship that is always required under subsection (a)(1) pursuant to Strawbridge v. Curtiss, 7 U.S. (3 Cranch) 267 (1806), reprinted infra p. 178. If there is complete diversity between citizens of different states as opposing parties to the dispute, aliens can be joined as parties to either or both sides, even if that results in aliens opposing each other—indeed even if the opposing aliens are citizens of the same foreign country. But if one set of parties consists of aliens only, the presence of any alien as an opposing party destroys jurisdiction, even if the other opposing parties are domestic citizens—because jurisdiction under subsection (a)(3) always requires the condition precedent of subsection (a)(1) jurisdiction between domestic parties before aliens can be joined as "additional parties." See Dresser Industries, Inc. v. Underwriters at Lloyd's of London, 106 F.3d 494 (3d Cir.1997); Bank of New York v. Bank of America, 861 F.Supp. 225, 228–229 (S.D.N.Y.1994).]

[7. Subsection (a)(4) was one of the provisions adopted in 1976 as part of the Foreign Sovereign Immunities Act (FSIA). See also § 1330(a), which purports to grant original jurisdiction without regard to amount in controversy of any nonjury civil action against a foreign state as to any claim for relief in personam with respect to which the foreign state is not entitled to immunity. The constitutionality of § 1330(a) was upheld in Verlinden B.V. v. Central Bank of Nigeria, 461 U.S. 480 (1983), reprinted supra p. 164. Resolving a deep circuit split, the Supreme Court has held that foreign-state status under the FSIA does not extend to the wholly-owned subsidiary of a corporation that is deemed to be an instrumentality of foreign state—notwithstanding that the parent corporation is itself entitled to foreign-sovereign status under the FSIA because a majority of its shares are owned by the foreign state. See Dole Food Co. v. Patrickson, 538 U.S. 468 (2003), reprinted infra p. 369.]

[8. Subsection (c)(1) was originally enacted in 1958 as part of a package of amendments intended to restrict diversity, including, among other things, raising the jurisdictional amount from $3,000 to $10,000. The proviso in (c)(1) was added in 1964 to change the result in cases such as Lumbermen's Mut. Cas. Co. v. Elbert, 348 U.S. 48 (1954), reprinted infra p. 231. The amendment is criticized in Weckstein, The 1964 Diversity Amendment: Congressional Indirect Action against State "Direct Action" Laws, 1965 Wis.L.Rev. 268. The proviso does not apply to a suit brought in federal court by an insurer. Northbrook Nat. Ins. Co. v. Brewer, 493 U.S. 6 (1989). The subsection was most recently amended in 2011 to add references to "foreign states."

The citizenship status of national banks is determined not by § 1332(c)(1), but by § 1348. In addition to conferring a special grant of federal-question jurisdiction on the district courts to

(A) every State and foreign state of which the insured is a citizen;

(B) every State and foreign state by which the insurer has been incorporated; and

(C) the State or foreign state where the insurer has its principal place of business; and

(2) the legal representative of the estate of a decedent shall be deemed to be a citizen only of the same State as the decedent, and the legal representative of an infant or incompetent shall be deemed to be a citizen only of the same State as the infant or incompetent.[9]

(d)(1) In this subsection—

(A) the term "class" means all of the class members in a class action;

(B) the term "class action" means any civil action filed under rule 23 of the Federal Rules of Civil Procedure or similar State statute or rule of judicial procedure authorizing an action to be brought by 1 or more representative persons as a class action;

(C) the term "class certification order" means an order issued by a court approving the treatment of some or all aspects of a civil action as a class action; and

(D) the term "class members" means the persons (named or unnamed) who fall within the definition of the proposed or certified class in a class action.

---

hear certain receivership disputes between national banks and federal regulators, § 1348 concludes by providing: "All national banking associations shall, for the purposes of all other actions by or against them, be deemed citizens of the states in which they are respectively located." The Supreme Court addressed the citizenship of national banks for diversity purposes in Wachovia Bank, N.A. v. Schmidt, 546 U.S. 303 (2006), confirming that, under § 1348, a national bank is a citizen of the state in which its main office, as set forth in its articles of association, is located.]

[9. Subsection (c)(2) was added by the 1988 amendments. It is taken in large part from § 1301(a)(4) of the ALI Study. The new subsection was intended to resolve a question that had caused great confusion among the circuits on whether, and if so how, 28 U.S.C. § 1359 applied to appointments of representatives of decedents and incompetents. See Mullenix, Creative Manipulation of Federal Jurisdiction: Is There Diversity After Death?, 70 Cornell L.Rev. 1011 (1985). Section 1359, which was adopted in 1948 to replace the infamous "assignee clause" —see Sheldon v. Sill, 49 U.S. (8 How.) 441 (1850), reprinted supra p. 8— says: "A district court shall not have jurisdiction of a civil action in which any party, by assignment or otherwise, has been improperly or collusively made or joined to invoke the jurisdiction of such court." For the application of the statute to wrongful-death cases, see Tank v. Chronister, 160 F.3d 597 (10th Cir.1998), reprinted infra p. 222.

The leading case on § 1359, Kramer v. Caribbean Mills, 394 U.S. 823 (1969), is discussed in Gentle v. Lamb–Weston, Inc., 302 F.Supp. 161 (D.Me.1969), reprinted infra p. 379. Taking an expansive view of Kramer and § 1359 as qualifying the famous precedent of Black & White Taxicab & Transfer Co. v. Brown & Yellow Taxicab & Transfer Co., 276 U.S. 518 (1928)—which permitted the assertion of diversity jurisdiction over a corporation that dissolved itself and reincorporated in a different state solely for jurisdictional purposes—the First Circuit has held that § 1359 bars diversity jurisdiction when diversity results from a corporate merger designed primarily to manufacture federal jurisdiction. Toste Farm Corp. v. Hadbury, Inc., 70 F.3d 640 (1st Cir.1995).]

(2) The district courts shall have original jurisdiction of any civil action in which the matter in controversy exceeds the sum or value of $5,000,000, exclusive of interest and costs, and is a class action in which—

(A) any member of a class of plaintiffs is a citizen of a State different from any defendant;

(B) any member of a class of plaintiffs is a foreign state or a citizen or subject of a foreign state and any defendant is a citizen of a State; or

(C) any member of a class of plaintiffs is a citizen of a State and any defendant is a foreign state or a citizen or subject of a foreign state.

(3) A district court may, in the interests of justice and looking at the totality of the circumstances, decline to exercise jurisdiction under paragraph (2) over a class action in which greater than one-third but less than two-thirds of the members of all proposed plaintiff classes in the aggregate and the primary defendants are citizens of the State in which the action was originally filed based on consideration of—

(A) whether the claims asserted involve matters of national or interstate interest;

(B) whether the claims asserted will be governed by laws of the State in which the action was originally filed or by the laws of other States;

(C) whether the class action has been pleaded in a manner that seeks to avoid Federal jurisdiction;

(D) whether the action was brought in a forum with a distinct nexus with the class members, the alleged harm, or the defendants;

(E) whether the number of citizens of the State in which the action was originally filed in all proposed plaintiff classes in the aggregate is substantially larger than the number of citizens from any other State, and the citizenship of the other members of the proposed class is dispersed among a substantial number of States; and

(F) whether, during the 3–year period preceding the filing of that class action, 1 or more other class actions asserting the same or similar claims on behalf of the same or other persons have been filed.

(4) A district court shall decline to exercise jurisdiction under paragraph (2)—

(A)(i) over a class action in which—

(I) greater than two-thirds of the members of all proposed plaintiff classes in the aggregate are citizens of the State in which the action was originally filed;

(II) at least 1 defendant is a defendant—

(aa) from whom significant relief is sought by members of the plaintiff class;

(bb) whose alleged conduct forms a significant basis for the claims asserted by the proposed plaintiff class; and

(cc) who is a citizen of the State in which the action was originally filed; and

(III) principal injuries resulting from the alleged conduct or any related conduct of each defendant were incurred in the State in which the action was originally filed; and

(ii) during the 3–year period preceding the filing of that class action, no other class action has been filed asserting the same or similar factual allegations against any of the defendants on behalf of the same or other persons; or

(B) two-thirds or more of the members of all proposed plaintiff classes in the aggregate, and the primary defendants, are citizens of the State in which the action was originally filed.

(5) Paragraphs (2) through (4) shall not apply to any class action in which—

(A) the primary defendants are States, State officials, or other governmental entities against whom the district court may be foreclosed from ordering relief; or

(B) the number of members of all proposed plaintiff classes in the aggregate is less than 100.

(6) In any class action, the claims of the individual class members shall be aggregated to determine whether the matter in controversy exceeds the sum or value of $5,000,000, exclusive of interest and costs.

(7) Citizenship of the members of the proposed plaintiff classes shall be determined for purposes of paragraphs (2) through (6) as of the date of filing of the complaint or amended complaint, or, if the case stated by the initial pleading is not subject to Federal jurisdiction, as of the date of service by plaintiffs of an amended pleading, motion, or other paper, indicating the existence of Federal jurisdiction.

(8) This subsection shall apply to any class action before or after the entry of a class certification order by the court with respect to that action.

(9) Paragraph (2) shall not apply to any class action that solely involves a claim—

(A) concerning a covered security as defined under 16(f)(3) of the Securities Act of 1933 (15 U.S.C. 78p(f)(3)) and section 28(f)(5)(E) of the Securities Exchange Act of 1934 (15 U.S.C. 78bb(f)(5)(E));

(B) that relates to the internal affairs or governance of a corporation or other form of business enterprise and that arises under or by virtue of the laws of the State in which such corporation or business enterprise is incorporated or organized; or

(C) that relates to the rights, duties (including fiduciary duties), and obligations relating to or created by or pursuant to any security (as defined under section 2(a)(1) of the Securities Act of 1933 (15 U.S.C. 77b(a)(1)) and the regulations issued thereunder).

(10) For purposes of this subsection and section 1453, an unincorporated association shall be deemed to be a citizen of the State where it has its principal place of business and the State under whose laws it is organized.

(11)(A) For purposes of this subsection and section 1453, a mass action shall be deemed to be a class action removable under paragraphs (2) through (10) if it otherwise meets the provisions of those paragraphs.

(B)(i) As used in subparagraph (A), the term "mass action" means any civil action (except a civil action within the scope of section 1711(2)) in which monetary relief claims of 100 or more persons are proposed to be tried jointly on the ground that the plaintiffs' claims involve common questions of law or fact, except that jurisdiction shall exist only over those plaintiffs whose claims in a mass action satisfy the jurisdictional amount requirements under subsection (a).[10]

(ii) As used in subparagraph (A), the term "mass action" shall not include any civil action in which—

(I) all of the claims in the action arise from an event or occurrence in the State in which the action was filed, and that allegedly resulted in injuries in that State or in States contiguous to that State;

(II) the claims are joined upon motion of a defendant;

(III) all of the claims in the action are asserted on behalf of the general public (and not on behalf of individual claimants or members of a purported class) pursuant to a State statute specifically authorizing such action; or

(IV) the claims have been consolidated or coordinated solely for pretrial proceedings.

(C)(i) Any action(s) removed to Federal court pursuant to this subsection shall not thereafter be transferred to any other court pursuant to section 1407, or the rules promulgated thereunder, unless a majority of the plaintiffs in the action request transfer pursuant to section 1407.

(ii) This subparagraph will not apply—

[**10.** Although this section defines a "mass action" as one in which "monetary relief claims of 100 or more persons are proposed to be tried jointly . . . ," the Seventh Circuit has adopted a broad construction of this provision, whereby the court deemed a tort complaint in which 144 plaintiffs joined in suing four defendants to be a mass action immediately upon filing, even though the complaint did not expressly propose a joint trial. Bullard v. Burlington N. Santa Fe Ry. Co., 535 F.3d 759 (7th Cir.2008). Although the plaintiffs argued that until the entry of a final pretrial order, it was unknown how many of the plaintiffs' claims would be tried together, the Seventh Circuit rejected this construction as essentially reading mass actions out of the Class Action Fairness Act.]

(I) to cases certified pursuant to rule 23 of the Federal Rules of Civil Procedure; or

(II) if plaintiffs propose that the action proceed as a class action pursuant to rule 23 of the Federal Rules of Civil Procedure.

(D) The limitations periods on any claims asserted in a mass action that is removed to Federal court pursuant to this subsection shall be deemed tolled during the period that the action is pending in Federal court.[11]

(e) The word "States," as used in this section, includes the Territories, the District of Columbia, and the Commonwealth of Puerto Rico.[12]

[11. New subsection (d) was added to § 1332 by the Class Action Fairness Act of 2005, Pub. L. 109–2, § 4(a), 119 Stat. 9 (Feb. 18, 2005), which also redesignated former 28 U.S.C. § 1332(d) as new subsection (e). The same legislation enacted a new removal statute, 28 U.S.C. § 1453, reprinted infra p. 389. New §§ 1332(d) and 1453 both "apply to any civil action commenced on or after the date of enactment of this Act." i.e., on or after February 18, 2005. Pub. L. 109–2, § 9, 119 Stat. 14.

New § 1332(d) has many unusual and potentially problematic features. It manifests a clear intention to make federal diversity jurisdiction, unencumbered by the complete-diversity rule or the usual restrictions as to the amount in controversy, the predicate for federal procedural control of the litigation of most major class actions even when based solely on alleged violations of state substantive law. To an unprecedented extent it makes the exercise of this expanded grant of federal jurisdiction discretionary, and it is likely to require a great deal of litigation to settle just what the governing standards are, how they should be applied, and the effects of their application or misapplication. What is the status, for instance, of a district court's judgment in a putative class action in which it is later determined, on appeal, that the district court should have declined jurisdiction, or that the action was improperly deemed to be a "class action" or a "mass action"? Is such a mistake mere error, subject to the harmless-error rule, or does it invalidate the proceedings below for lack of jurisdiction? What is the status and proper treatment of individual claims in an action that was brought in or removed to federal court as a class action, if it was properly brought as a putative class action but class certification was denied for pragmatic reasons? Is federal supplemental jurisdiction sufficient to permit adjudication of these lingering individual claims in federal court, should the individual plaintiffs have the means and will to continue the litigation? Lurking in the background of these and many other operational questions are serious workload issues posed for the federal courts in their new role as magnet courts for group litigation.

The Class Action Fairness Act is already generating litigation. See, e.g., Braud v. Transport Service Co. of Ill., 445 F.3d 801 (5th Cir.2006) (by amending class action complaint to add a new defendant after the enactment of the Act, a "new window" for removal was created); accord Knudsen v. Liberty Mut. Ins. Co., 411 F.3d 805 (7th Cir.2005); see also Pfizer v. Lott, 417 F.3d 725 (7th Cir.2005) (a state court class action filed one day before the Class Action Fairness Act was enacted may not be removed to federal court under the Act; the Act's language expressly applies only to suits "commenced on or after" the date of enactment); Berry v. American Express Pub. Corp., 381 F.Supp.2d 1118 (C.D.Cal.2005) (in assessing whether a class action satisfies the $5 million amount-in-controversy prerequisite for diversity jurisdiction under the Class Action Fairness Act, a court may look to either the aggregate value to the class members or the aggregate cost to the defendant). The circuit courts are split as to whether a removing defendant must show to a legal certainty that the amount in controversy exceeds $5 million, or must merely show a "reasonable probability" (a preponderance standard). Compare Lowdermilk v. U.S. Bank Nat'l Ass'n, 479 F.3d 994 (9th Cir. 2007) (legal certainty standard) with Amoche v. Guarantee Trust Life Ins. Co., 556 F.3d 41 (1st Cir. 2009) and Bell v. Hershey Co., 557 F.3d 953 (8th Cir. 2009) (reasonable probability standard).]

Strawbridge v. Curtiss

Supreme Court of the United States, 1806.
3 Cranch (7 U.S.) 267, 2 L.Ed. 435.

This was an appeal from a decree of the circuit court for the district of Massachusetts, which dismissed the complainants' bill in chancery, for want of jurisdiction.

Some of the complainants were alleged to be citizens of the state of Massachusetts. The defendants were also stated to be citizens of the same state, excepting Curtiss, who was averred to be a citizen of the state of Vermont, and upon whom the subpoena was served in that state.

The question of jurisdiction was submitted to the court without argument, by P.B. Key, for the appellants, and Harper, for the appellees.

On a subsequent day,

■ MARSHALL, CH.J., delivered the opinion of the court.

The court has considered this case, and is of opinion that the jurisdiction cannot be supported.

The words of the act of congress are, "where an alien is a party, or the suit is between a citizen of a state where the suit is brought, and a citizen of another state."

The court understands these expressions to mean, that each distinct interest should be represented by persons, all of whom are entitled to sue, or may be sued, in the federal courts. That is, that where the interest is joint, each of the persons concerned in that interest must be competent to sue, or liable to be sued, in those courts.

But the court does not mean to give an opinion in the case where several parties represent several distinct interests, and some of those parties are, and others are not, competent to sue, or liable to be sued, in the courts of the United States.

Decree affirmed.[13]

[12.   The validity of extending diversity to suits between citizens of a state and citizens of the District of Columbia was upheld by a bizarrely fragmented court in National Mutual Insurance Co. of District of Columbia v. Tidewater Transfer Co., 337 U.S. 582 (1949). The validity of extending jurisdiction to a suit between a citizen of a state and a citizen of the Commonwealth of Puerto Rico was upheld, on the authority of the National Mutual Insurance case, in Americana of Puerto Rico, Inc. v. Kaplus, 368 F.2d 431 (3d Cir.1966).]

[13.   It was asserted by Justice Wayne that Chief Justice Marshall later expressed regret that this decision had ever been made. Louisville, C. & C.R. Co. v. Letson, 2 How. (43 U.S.) 497, 555 (1844).

Seyler v. Steuben Motors, Inc.

United States Court of Appeals, Third Circuit, 1972.
462 F.2d 181.

■ Before STALEY, ALDISERT, and HUNTER, CIRCUIT JUDGES.

■ PER CURIAM.

In this diversity action the district court found that plaintiff-appellants and Steuben Motors, Inc., one of the two named defendants, were citizens of Pennsylvania, thus destroying the requirement of "complete diversity" necessitated by Strawbridge v. Curtiss, 3 Cranch. (7 U.S.) 267 (1806). See 1 Moore's Federal Practice ¶ 0.60 [8.–4]. The finding by the court that Steuben's principal place of business was in York, Pennsylvania, was not clearly erroneous.

Appellants' reliance on the doctrines of pendent or ancillary jurisdiction is misplaced. This is not a commingling of a state claim with one based on a federal question, United Mine Workers of America v. Gibbs, 383 U.S. 715 (1966); nor do the claims come within the ambit of Borror v. Sharon Steel Co., 327 F.2d 165 (3d Cir.1964). Wilson v. American Chain & Cable Co., 364 F.2d 558 (3d Cir.1966), and Jacobson v. Atlantic City Hospital, 392 F.2d 149 (3d Cir.1968), also relied upon by appellant, dealt with amounts in controversy and not the doctrine of complete diversity.

The judgment of the district court will be affirmed.[14]

––––––––

It has been held that this decision is a construction of the diversity statute and that complete diversity is not required by the diversity clause in Art. III. State Farm Fire & Cas. Co. v. Tashire, 386 U.S. 523, 530–531 (1967), reprinted infra p. 895.]

The Multiparty, Multiforum Trial Jurisdiction Act of 2002 enacted a new jurisdictional statute, 28 U.S.C. § 1369. Like the Class Action Fairness Act of 2005, the 2002 Act relies on the constitutional holding of *Tashire* to extend federal diversity jurisdiction close to the outer limits of that permitted by Article III. Under § 1369(a), district courts have original jurisdiction over "any civil action involving minimal diversity between adverse parties that arises from a single accident, where at least 75 natural persons have died in the accident at a discrete location," qualified under § 1369(b) by a vague statutory duty to abstain in cases involving localized mass torts. The Multiparty, Multiforum Trial Jurisdiction Act also enacted related amendments to the basic venue and removal statutes. See 28 U.S.C. § 1391(g), reprinted infra p. 414, and 28 U.S.C. § 1441(e), reprinted infra p. 329.

The *Strawbridge* rule has long been held not to apply with full force to class actions. Under Supreme Tribe of Ben–Hur v. Cauble, 255 U.S. 356 (1921), only the citizenship of the named representatives of a class is considered in determining the existence of diversity jurisdiction.

[14.   The supplemental jurisdiction statute enacted in 1990 was expressly drafted to preserve the rule of complete diversity. See 28 U.S.C. § 1367(b), reprinted infra p. 263. But while § 1367(b) bars supplemental jurisdiction over claims by plaintiffs against persons made parties under Civil Rule 20, the rule on permissive joinder of parties, it is silent about the use of supplemental jurisdiction to add nondiverse plaintiffs. The drafters of the statute say: "Original filing of a diversity complaint by two plaintiffs, one of them not of diverse citizenship from a defendant, remains barred by the complete diversity interpretation of the requirements for original diversity jurisdiction. Literally, though, section 1367(b) does not bar an original complete diversity filing and subsequent amendment to add a nondiverse co-plaintiff under Rule 20, taking advantage of supplemental jurisdiction over the claim of the

Morris v. Gilmer

Supreme Court of the United States, 1889.
129 U.S. 315, 9 S.Ct. 289, 32 L.Ed. 690.

[The present plaintiff had brought a suit against the present defendants, arising out of the same transaction and seeking similar relief, in the state court in Alabama and that suit had gone against the plaintiff on the ground that it was barred by the statute of limitations.]

.　.　.　.　.

The present suit was instituted, September 20, 1886, in the Circuit Court of the United States by Gilmer, claiming to be a citizen of Tennessee, against Morris and Billing.... Subsequently, December 16, 1887, the defendant Morris filed in the cause the affidavit of A.S. Gerald to the effect that, in a conversation held by him with the plaintiff on or about November 14, 1887, the latter informed him "that he had returned to the city of Montgomery to reside permanently, and had been living here with that intent some time previous to said conversation;" and also his own affidavit to the effect that he had been informed and believed that the plaintiff returned to the city of Montgomery "some time in the latter part of May or early part of June, 1887, with the purpose and intent of permanently residing in the State of Alabama, and has continuously resided in said State of Alabama ever since said time." On the 17th of November, 1887, before the final hearing of the cause, the defendants, with leave of court, filed a written motion for the dismissal of the suit upon the ground that it did not really and substantially involve a controversy within the jurisdiction of the Circuit Court; basing his motion upon the above affidavits of Gerald and Morris, and upon the depositions of the plaintiff, and of his father, F.M. Gilmer, taken in this cause in behalf of the plaintiff. The father, in his

new plaintiff against the existing defendant. We can only hope that the federal courts will plug that potentially gaping hole in the complete diversity requirement—either by regarding it as an unacceptable circumvention of original diversity jurisdiction requirements, or by reference to the intent not to abandon the complete diversity rule that is clearly expressed in the legislative history of section 1367." Rowe, Burbank & Mengler, Compounding or Creating Confusion about Supplemental Jurisdiction: A Reply to Professor Freer, 40 Emory L.J. 945, 961 n. 91 (1991). The Supreme Court addressed both the complete diversity and the amount-in-controversy components of diversity jurisdiction in the context of Rule 20 and supplemental jurisdiction in Exxon Mobil Corp. v. Allapattah Services, Inc., 545 U.S. 546 (2005), reprinted infra p. 289. Supplemental jurisdiction is fully covered in Chapter V, infra p. 263 et seq.

A court of appeals has the authority to grant a motion to dismiss a dispensable nondiverse party and need not remand the case to the district court for dismissal in that court's discretion. Newman–Green, Inc. v. Alfonzo–Larrain, 490 U.S. 826 (1989). For an unconventional interpretation of *Strawbridge v. Curtiss* that elaborates its neglected distinction between suits involving parties with "several" rather than "joint" interests and concludes in light of *Tashire* and *Newman–Green* that the rule of complete diversity is best understood as a restriction on the exercise of supplemental jurisdiction in diversity cases, see Oakley, Integrating Supplemental Jurisdiction and Diversity Jurisdiction: A Progress Report on the Work of the American Law Institute, 74 Ind.L.J. 25 (1998). This argument is repeated in ALI Judicial Code Project, Reporter's Memorandum at 613–624.]

deposition taken *de bene esse,* October 27, 1886, makes the following statements on cross-examination:

. . . . .

"Q. I ask you if you didn't advise him to move for the purpose of bringing this suit in the United States court? A. I did."

. . . . .

The plaintiff, in his deposition, taken April 26, 1887, made these statements on cross-examination:

"Q. Where do you reside now? A. In Memphis.

"Q. What State? A. The State of Tennessee.

"Q. How long have you resided there? A. One year.

"Q. Did you not go there, Mr. Gilmer, for the purpose of getting jurisdiction to the Federal court of this State? A. I did, sir.

"Q. Is it your purpose to return to Montgomery if you gain this suit? A. That depends altogether upon circumstances."

. . . . .

■ MR. JUSTICE HARLAN, after stating the case, delivered the opinion of the court.

. . . . .

The case presents no question of a Federal nature, and the jurisdiction of the Circuit Court was invoked solely upon the ground that the plaintiff was a citizen of Tennessee, and the defendants citizens of Alabama. But if the plaintiff, who was a citizen of Alabama when the suit in the state court was determined, had not become, in fact a citizen of Tennessee when the present suit was instituted, then, clearly, the controversy between him and the defendants was not one of which the Circuit Court could properly take cognizance; in which case, it became the duty of that court to dismiss it. It is true that, by the words of the statute, this duty arose only when it appeared to the satisfaction of the court that the suit was not one within its jurisdiction. But if the record discloses a controversy of which the court cannot properly take cognizance, its duty is to proceed no further and to dismiss the suit; and its failure or refusal to do what, under the law applicable to the facts proved, it ought to do, is an error which this court, upon its own motion, will correct, when the case is brought here for review.

. . . . .

We are thus brought to the question whether the plaintiff was entitled to sue in the Circuit Court. Was he, at the commencement of this suit, a citizen of Tennessee? It is true, as contended by the defendant, that a citizen of the United States can instantly transfer his citizenship from one State to another, Cooper v. Galbraith, 3 Wash. C.C. 546, 554, and that his right to sue in the courts of the United States is none the less because his change of domicil was induced by the purpose, whether avowed or not, of invoking, for the protection of his rights, the jurisdiction of a Federal court.

As said by Mr. Justice Story, in Briggs v. French, 2 Sumner, 251, 256, "if the new citizenship is really and truly acquired, his right to sue is a legitimate, constitutional and legal consequence, not to be impeached by the motive of his removal." Manhattan Ins. Co. v. Broughton, 109 U.S. 121, 125; Jones v. League, 18 How. [59 U.S.] 76. There must be an actual, not pretended, change of domicil; in other words, the removal must be "a real one, animo manendi, and not merely ostensible." Case v. Clarke, 5 Mason, 70. The intention and the act must concur in order to effect such a change of domicil as constitutes a change of citizenship. In Ennis v. Smith, 14 How. [55 U.S.] 400, 423, it was said that "a removal which does not contemplate an absence from the former domicile for an indefinite and uncertain time is not a change of it," and that while it was difficult to lay down any rule under which every instance of residence could be brought which may make a domicil of choice, "there must be, to constitute it, actual residence in the place, with the intention that it is to be a principal and permanent residence."

Upon the evidence in this record, we cannot resist the conviction that the plaintiff had no purpose to acquire a domicil or settled home in Tennessee, and that his sole object in removing to that State was to place himself in a situation to invoke the jurisdiction of the Circuit Court of the United States. He went to Tennessee without any present intention to remain there permanently or for an indefinite time, but with a present intention to return to Alabama as soon as he could do so without defeating the jurisdiction of the Federal court to determine his new suit. He was, therefore, a mere sojourner in the former State when this suit was brought. He returned to Alabama almost immediately after giving his deposition. The case comes within the principle announced in Butler v. Farnsworth, 4 Wash.C.C. 101, 103, where Mr. Justice Washington said: "If the removal be for the purpose of committing a fraud upon the law, and to enable the party to avail himself of the jurisdiction of the Federal courts, and that fact be made out by his acts, the court must pronounce that his removal was not with a bona fide intention of changing his domicil, however frequent and public his declarations to the contrary may have been."

The decree is reversed, with costs to the appellant in this court, and the cause remanded, with a direction to dismiss the suit without costs in the court below.[15]

Mas v. Perry

United States Court of Appeals, Fifth Circuit, 1974.
489 F.2d 1396.

■ Before WISDOM, AINSWORTH and CLARK, CIRCUIT JUDGES.

■ AINSWORTH, CIRCUIT JUDGE:

This case presents questions pertaining to federal diversity jurisdiction under 28 U.S.C. § 1332, which, pursuant to Article III, section II of the

---

[15. See, however, Williamson v. Osenton, 232 U.S. 619 (1914), where it is held that a genuine intention to remain in the new home indefinitely will give "citizenship," though the motive in moving was to create diversity jurisdiction, for a federal suit. Intention to remain "permanently" in the new home is not the test. Hardin v. McAvoy, 216 F.2d 399 (5th Cir.1954).]

Constitution, provides for original jurisdiction in federal district courts of all civil actions that are between, inter alia, citizens of different States or citizens of a State and citizens of foreign states and in which the amount in controversy is more than $10,000.

Appellees Jean Paul Mas, a citizen of France, and Judy Mas were married at her home in Jackson, Mississippi. Prior to their marriage, Mr. and Mrs. Mas were graduate assistants, pursuing coursework as well as performing teaching duties, for approximately nine months and one year, respectively, at Louisiana State University in Baton Rouge, Louisiana. Shortly after their marriage, they returned to Baton Rouge to resume their duties as graduate assistants at LSU. They remained in Baton Rouge for approximately two more years, after which they moved to Park Ridge, Illinois. At the time of the trial in this case, it was their intention to return to Baton Rouge while Mr. Mas finished his studies for the degree of Doctor of Philosophy. Mr. and Mrs. Mas were undecided as to where they would reside after that.

Upon their return to Baton Rouge after their marriage, appellees rented an apartment from appellant Oliver H. Perry, a citizen of Louisiana. This appeal arises from a final judgment entered on a jury verdict awarding $5,000 to Mr. Mas and $15,000 to Mrs. Mas for damages incurred by them as a result of the discovery that their bedroom and bathroom contained "two-way" mirrors and that they had been watched through them by the appellant during three of the first four months of their marriage.

At the close of the appellees' case at trial, appellant made an oral motion to dismiss for lack of jurisdiction. The motion was denied by the district court. Before this Court, appellant challenges the final judgment below solely on jurisdictional grounds, contending that appellees failed to prove diversity of citizenship among the parties and that the requisite jurisdictional amount is lacking with respect to Mr. Mas. Finding no merit to these contentions, we affirm. Under section 1332(a)(2), the federal judicial power extends to the claim of Mr. Mas, a citizen of France, against the appellant, a citizen of Louisiana. Since we conclude that Mrs. Mas is a citizen of Mississippi for diversity purposes, the district court also properly had jurisdiction under section 1332(a)(1) of her claim.

It has long been the general rule that complete diversity of parties is required in order that diversity jurisdiction obtain; that is, no party on one side may be a citizen of the same State as any party on the other side. Strawbridge v. Curtiss, 7 U.S. (3 Cranch) 267 (1806); see cases cited in 1 W. Barron & A. Holtzoff, Federal Practice and Procedure § 26, at 145 n. 95 (Wright ed.1960). This determination of one's State citizenship for diversity purposes is controlled by federal law, not by the law of any State. 1 J. Moore, Moore's Federal Practice ¶ 0.74[1], at 707.1 (1972). As is the case in other areas of federal jurisdiction, the diverse citizenship among adverse parties must be present at the time the complaint is filed. Mollan v.

Torrance, 22 U.S. (9 Wheat.) 537, 539 (1824); Slaughter v. Toye Bros. Yellow Cab Co., 5 Cir., 1966, 359 F.2d 954, 956. Jurisdiction is unaffected by subsequent changes in the citizenship of the parties.[16] Morgan's Heirs v. Morgan, 15 U.S. (2 Wheat.) 290, 297 (1817); Clarke v. Mathewson, 37 U.S. (12 Pet.) 164, 171 (1838); Smith v. Sperling, 354 U.S. 91, 93 n. 1 (1957). The burden of pleading the diverse citizenship is upon the party invoking federal jurisdiction, see Cameron v. Hodges, 127 U.S. 322 (1888); and if the diversity jurisdiction is properly challenged, that party also bears the burden of proof, McNutt v. General Motors Acceptance Corp., 298 U.S. 178 (1936); Welsh v. American Surety Co. of New York, 5 Cir., 1951, 186 F.2d 16, 17.

To be a citizen of a State within the meaning of section 1332, a natural person must be both a citizen of the United States, see Sun Printing & Publishing Association v. Edwards, 194 U.S. 377, 383 (1904); U.S. Const. Amend. XIV, § 1, and a domiciliary of that State. See Williamson v. Osenton, 232 U.S. 619, 624 (1914); Stine v. Moore, 5 Cir., 1954, 213 F.2d 446, 448. For diversity purposes, citizenship means domicile; mere residence in the State is not sufficient. See Wolfe v. Hartford Life & Annuity Ins. Co., 148 U.S. 389 (1893); Stine v. Moore, 5 Cir., 1954, 213 F.2d 446, 448.

A person's domicile is the place of "his true, fixed, and permanent home and principal establishment, and to which he has the intention of returning whenever he is absent therefrom . . . ." Stine v. Moore, 5 Cir., 1954, 213 F.2d 446, 448. A change of domicile may be effected only by a combination of two elements: (a) taking up residence in a different domicile with (b) the intention to remain there. Mitchell v. United States, 88 U.S. (21 Wall.) 350 (1875); Sun Printing & Publishing Association v. Edwards, 194 U.S. 377 (1904).

It is clear that at the time of her marriage, Mrs. Mas was a domiciliary of the State of Mississippi. While it is generally the case that the domicile of the wife—and, consequently, her State citizenship for purposes of diversity jurisdiction—is deemed to be that of her husband, 1 J. Moore, Moore's Federal Practice ¶ 0.74[6.–1], at 708.51 (1972), we find no precedent for extending this concept to the situation here, in which the husband is a citizen of a foreign state but resides in the United States. Indeed, such a fiction would work absurd results on the facts before us. If Mr. Mas were considered a domiciliary of France—as he would be since he had lived in Louisiana as a student-teaching assistant prior to filing this suit, see

[16. In Freeport–McMoRan, Inc. v. K N Energy, Inc., 498 U.S. 426, 428 (1991) (per curiam), the Court peremptorily reaffirmed this "well-established rule that diversity of citizenship is assessed at the time the action is filed. We have consistently held that if jurisdiction exists at the time an action is commenced, such jurisdiction may not be divested by subsequent events." In *Freeport–McMoRan*, this rule was invoked to sustain continued diversity jurisdiction in a contract case in which the original plaintiff assigned its contractual rights to a non-diverse successor in interest, who was then added to the litigation as an additional plaintiff under Rule 25(c). The time-of-filing rule limits as well as expands federal jurisdiction. See Grupo Dataflux v. Atlas Global Group, L.P., 541 U.S. 567 (2004), reprinted infra p. 209.]

Chicago & Northwestern Railway Co. v. Ohle, 117 U.S. 123 (1886); Bell v. Milsak, W.D.La., 1952, 106 F.Supp. 219—then Mrs. Mas would also be deemed a domiciliary, and thus, fictionally at least, a citizen of France. She would not be a citizen of any State and could not sue in a federal court on that basis; nor could she invoke the alienage jurisdiction to bring her claim in federal court, since she is not an alien. See C. Wright, Federal Courts 80 (1970). On the other hand, if Mrs. Mas's domicile were Louisiana, she would become a Louisiana citizen for diversity purposes and could not bring suit with her husband against appellant, also a Louisiana citizen, on the basis of diversity jurisdiction. These are curious results under a rule arising from the theoretical identity of person and interest of the married couple. See Linscott v. Linscott, S.D.Iowa, 1951, 98 F.Supp. 802, 804; Juneau v. Juneau, 227 La. 921, 80 So.2d 864, 867 (1955).

An American woman is not deemed to have lost her United States citizenship solely by reason of her marriage to an alien. 8 U.S.C. § 1489. Similarly, we conclude that for diversity purposes a woman does not have her domicile or State citizenship changed solely by reason of her marriage to an alien.

Mrs. Mas's Mississippi domicile was disturbed neither by her year in Louisiana prior to her marriage nor as a result of the time she and her husband spent at LSU after their marriage, since for both periods she was a graduate assistant at LSU. See Chicago & Northwestern Railway Co. v. Ohle, 117 U.S. 123 (1886). Though she testified that after her marriage she had no intention of returning to her parents' home in Mississippi, Mrs. Mas did not effect a change of domicile since she and Mr. Mas were in Louisiana only as students and lacked the requisite intention to remain there. See Hendry v. Masonite Corp., 5 Cir., 1972, 455 F.2d 955, cert. denied, 409 U.S. 1023. Until she acquires a new domicile, she remains a domiciliary, and thus a citizen, of Mississippi. See Mitchell v. United States, 88 U.S. (21 Wall.) 350, 352 (1875); Sun Printing & Publishing Association v. Edwards, 194 U.S. 377, 383 (1904); Welsh v. American Security Co. of New York, 5 Cir., 1951, 186 F.2d 16, 17.[17]

Appellant also contends that Mr. Mas's claim should have been dismissed for failure to establish the requisite jurisdictional amount for diversity cases of more than $10,000. In their complaint Mr. and Mrs. Mas alleged that they had each been damaged in the amount of $100,000. As we have noted, Mr. Mas ultimately recovered $5,000.

It is well settled that the amount in controversy is determined by the amount claimed by the plaintiff in good faith. KVOS, Inc. v. Associated Press, 299 U.S. 269 (1936); 1 J. Moore, Moore's Federal Practice ¶ 0.92[1]

---

17. The original complaint in this case was filed within several days of Mr. and Mrs. Mas's realization that they had been watched through the mirrors, quite some time before they moved to Park Ridge, Illinois. Because the district court's jurisdiction is not affected by actions of the parties subsequent to the commencement of the suit, see C. Wright, Federal Courts 93 (1970), . . . the testimony concerning Mr. and Mrs. Mas's moves after that time is not determinative of the issue of diverse citizenship, though it is of interest insofar as it supports their lack of intent to remain permanently in Louisiana.

(1972). Federal jurisdiction is not lost because a judgment of less than the jurisdictional amount is awarded. Jones v. Landry, 5 Cir., 1967, 387 F.2d 102; C. Wright, Federal Courts 111 (1970). That Mr. Mas recovered only $5,000 is, therefore, not compelling. . . .

. . . . .

Having heard the evidence presented at the trial, the district court concluded that the appellees properly met the requirements of section 1332 with respect to jurisdictional amount. Upon examination of the record in this case, we are also satisfied that the requisite amount was in controversy. See Jones v. Landry, 5 Cir., 1967, 387 F.2d 102.

. . . . .

Affirmed.[18]

Hertz Corp. v. Friend

Supreme Court of the United States, 2010.
559 U.S. ___, 130 S.Ct. 1181, 175 L.Ed.2d 1029.

■ JUSTICE BREYER delivered the opinion of the Court.

The federal diversity jurisdiction statute provides that "a corporation shall be deemed to be a citizen of any State by which it has been

---

[18. Certiorari denied 419 U.S. 842 (1974).

A husband and wife from Missouri leased their home there for one year and moved to Ohio, where the husband participated in a one-year educational program. He testified that when he finished his studies he would obtain the best position available and that he never intended Ohio to be his permanent home. He also testified that he had no specific intent to return to Missouri. Held, in a suit in Missouri against a citizen of Missouri, no jurisdiction. Holmes v. Sopuch, 639 F.2d 431 (8th Cir.1981). "Although the authorities sometime contain imprecise language, a change in domicile requires only the concurrence of (1) physical presence at the new location with (2) an intention to remain there indefinitely, or the absence of any intention to go elsewhere. . . . A person must intend to reside somewhere indefinitely with no present or fixed intent to move on upon the happening of a reasonably certain event." 639 F.2d, at 433–434.

Mas v. Perry was followed, and it was held that a Georgia woman who went to the University of South Carolina to do graduate work, and who clearly intended to leave Washington, Georgia, but had not positively decided on her residence after graduation, remained a citizen of Georgia and could not bring a diversity action against other Georgia citizens. Scoggins v. Pollock, 727 F.2d 1025 (11th Cir.1984).

But see Bair v. Peck, 738 F.Supp. 1354 (D.Kan.1990). A part-time college student who was born and raised in Kansas suffered an illness while living in Kansas. After moving to Colorado to attend college, he brought a diversity suit against his Kansas doctors. He later moved back to Kansas for unrelated medical reasons. Held, jurisdiction existed since plaintiff's domicile was in Colorado at the time of the suit. "Though the lives of young adults are sometimes viewed as transient by those of us who are more settled in our ways, it would be unfair to generalize that they lack the intent to make their own residence their domicile because they have only so soon left the comforts of their parent's home. When a young adult has taken those steps which objectively show a commitment for an indefinite period of time to become a member of the community in which he or she resides, the courts should not be reluctant to infer a domicile. Reliance on parents during this time for medical exigencies and a permanent medical address is understandable and does not significantly detract from the weight of the other objective factors." 738 F.Supp., at 1357–1358.]

incorporated and of the State where it has its principal place of business."
28 U.S.C. § 1332(c)(1) (emphasis added). We seek here to resolve different
interpretations that the Circuits have given this phrase. In doing so, we
place primary weight upon the need for judicial administration of a jurisdictional statute to remain as simple as possible. And we conclude that the
phrase "principal place of business" refers to the place where the corporation's high level officers direct, control, and coordinate the corporation's
activities. Lower federal courts have often metaphorically called that place
the corporation's "nerve center." See, e.g., Wisconsin Knife Works v.
National Metal Crafters, 781 F.2d 1280, 1282 (CA7 1986); Scot Typewriter
Co. v. Underwood Corp., 170 F.Supp. 862, 865 (SDNY 1959) (Weinfeld, J.).
We believe that the "nerve center" will typically be found at a corporation's headquarters.

I

In September 2007, respondents Melinda Friend and John Nhieu, two
California citizens, sued petitioner, the Hertz Corporation, in a California
state court. They sought damages for what they claimed were violations of
California's wage and hour laws. And they requested relief on behalf of a
potential class composed of California citizens who had allegedly suffered
similar harms.

Hertz filed a notice seeking removal to a federal court. 28 U.S.C.
§§ 1332(d)(2), 1441(a). Hertz claimed that the plaintiffs and the defendant
were citizens of different States. §§ 1332(a)(1), (c)(1). Hence, the federal
court possessed diversity-of-citizenship jurisdiction. Friend and Nhieu, however, claimed that the Hertz Corporation was a California citizen, like
themselves, and that, hence, diversity jurisdiction was lacking.

To support its position, Hertz submitted a declaration by an employee
relations manager that sought to show that Hertz's "principal place of
business" was in New Jersey, not in California. The declaration stated,
among other things, that Hertz operated facilities in 44 States; and that
California—which had about 12% of the Nation's population—accounted
for 273 of Hertz's 1,606 car rental locations; about 2,300 of its 11,230 full-
time employees; about $811 million of its $4.371 billion in annual revenue;
and about 3.8 million of its approximately 21 million annual transactions,
i.e., rentals. The declaration also stated that the "leadership of Hertz and
its domestic subsidiaries" is located at Hertz's "corporate headquarters" in
Park Ridge, New Jersey; that its "core executive and administrative
functions ... are carried out" there and "to a lesser extent" in Oklahoma
City, Oklahoma; and that its "major administrative operations ... are
found" at those two locations.

The District Court of the Northern District of California accepted
Hertz's statement of the facts as undisputed. But it concluded that, given
those facts, Hertz was a citizen of California. In reaching this conclusion,
the court applied Ninth Circuit precedent, which instructs courts to identi-

fy a corporation's "principal place of business" by first determining the amount of a corporation's business activity State by State. If the amount of activity is "significantly larger" or "substantially predominates" in one State, then that State is the corporation's "principal place of business." If there is no such State, then the "principal place of business" is the corporation's " 'nerve center,' " i.e., the place where " 'the majority of its executive and administrative functions are performed.' " Friend v. Hertz, No. C–07–5222 MMC, 2008 WL 7071465 (ND Cal., Jan. 15, 2008), p. 3 (hereinafter Order); Tosco Corp. v. Communities for a Better Environment, 236 F.3d 495, 500–502 (CA9 2001) (per curiam).

Applying this test, the District Court found that the "plurality of each of the relevant business activities" was in California, and that "the differential between the amount of those activities" in California and the amount in "the next closest state" was "significant." Hence, Hertz's "principal place of business" was California, and diversity jurisdiction was thus lacking. The District Court consequently remanded the case to the state courts.

Hertz appealed the District Court's remand order. 28 U.S.C. § 1453(c). The Ninth Circuit affirmed in a brief memorandum opinion. 297 Fed.Appx. 690 (2008). Hertz filed a petition for certiorari. And, in light of differences among the Circuits in the application of the test for corporate citizenship, we granted the writ. Compare *Tosco Corp.*, supra, at 500–502, and Capitol Indemnity Corp. v. Russellville Steel Co., 367 F.3d 831, 836 (CA8 2004) (applying "total activity" test and looking at "all corporate activities"), with *Wisconsin Knife Works*, supra, at 1282 (applying "nerve center" test).

II

At the outset, we consider a jurisdictional objection. Respondents point out that the statute permitting Hertz to appeal the District Court's remand order to the Court of Appeals, 28 U.S.C. § 1453(c), constitutes an exception to a more general jurisdictional rule that remand orders are "not reviewable on appeal." § 1447(d). They add that the language of § 1453(c) refers only to "court[s] of appeals," not to the Supreme Court. The statute also says that if "a final judgment on the appeal" in a court of appeals "is not issued before the end" of 60 days (with a possible 10–day extension), "the appeal shall be denied." And respondents draw from these statutory circumstances the conclusion that Congress intended to permit review of a remand order only by a court of appeals, not by the Supreme Court (at least not if, as here, this Court's grant of certiorari comes after § 1453(c)'s time period has elapsed).

This argument, however, makes far too much of too little. We normally do not read statutory silence as implicitly modifying or limiting Supreme Court jurisdiction that another statute specifically grants. Felker v. Turpin, 518 U.S. 651, 660–661 (1996); Ex parte Yerger, 8 Wall. [75 U.S.] 85, 104–105 (1869). Here, another, pre-existing federal statute gives this Court jurisdiction to "revie[w] ... [b]y writ of certiorari" cases that, like this case, are "in the courts of appeals" when we grant the writ. 28 U.S.C.

§ 1254. This statutory jurisdictional grant replicates similar grants that yet older statutes provided. See, e.g., § 1254, 62 Stat. 928; § 1, 43 Stat. 938–939 (amending § 240, 36 Stat. 1157); § 240, 36 Stat. 1157; Evarts Act, § 6, 26 Stat. 828. This history provides particularly strong reasons not to read § 1453(c)'s silence or ambiguous language as modifying or limiting our pre-existing jurisdiction.

We thus interpret § 1453(c)'s "60–day" requirement as simply requiring a court of appeals to reach a decision within a specified time—not to deprive this Court of subsequent jurisdiction to review the case. See Aetna Casualty & Surety Co. v. Flowers, 330 U.S. 464, 466–467 (1947); Gay v. Ruff, 292 U.S. 25, 28–31 (1934).

III

We begin our "principal place of business" discussion with a brief review of relevant history. The Constitution provides that the "judicial Power shall extend" to "Controversies . . . between Citizens of different States." Art. III, § 2. This language, however, does not automatically confer diversity jurisdiction upon the federal courts. Rather, it authorizes Congress to do so and, in doing so, to determine the scope of the federal courts' jurisdiction within constitutional limits. Kline v. Burke Constr. Co., 260 U.S. 226, 233–234 (1922); Mayor v. Cooper, 6 Wall. [73 U.S.] 247, 252 (1868).

Congress first authorized federal courts to exercise diversity jurisdiction in 1789 when, in the First Judiciary Act, Congress granted federal courts authority to hear suits "between a citizen of the State where the suit is brought, and a citizen of another State." § 11, 1 Stat. 78. The statute said nothing about corporations. In 1809, Chief Justice Marshall, writing for a unanimous Court, described a corporation as an "invisible, intangible, and artificial being" which was "certainly not a citizen." Bank of United States v. Deveaux, 5 Cranch [9 U.S.] 61, 86 (1809). But the Court held that a corporation could invoke the federal courts' diversity jurisdiction based on a pleading that the corporation's shareholders were all citizens of a different State from the defendants, as "the term citizen ought to be understood as it is used in the constitution, and as it is used in other laws. That is, to describe the real persons who come into court, in this case, under their corporate name." Id., at 91–92.

In Louisville, C. & C.R. Co. v. Letson, 2 How. [43 U.S.] 497 (1844), the Court modified this initial approach. It held that a corporation was to be deemed an artificial person of the State by which it had been created, and its citizenship for jurisdictional purposes determined accordingly. Id., at 558–559. Ten years later, the Court in Marshall v. Baltimore & Ohio R. Co., 16 How. [57 U.S.] 314 (1854), held that the reason a corporation was a citizen of its State of incorporation was that, for the limited purpose of determining corporate citizenship, courts could conclusively (and artificially) presume that a corporation's shareholders were citizens of the State of incorporation. Id., at 327–328. And it reaffirmed *Letson*. 16 How., at 325–326. Whatever the rationale, the practical upshot was that, for diversity purposes, the federal courts considered a corporation to be a citizen of the State of its incorporation. 13F C. Wright, A. Miller, & E. Cooper, Federal Practice and Procedure § 3623, pp. 1–7 (3d ed.2009) (hereinafter Wright & Miller).

In 1928 this Court made clear that the "state of incorporation" rule was virtually absolute. It held that a corporation closely identified with State A could proceed in a federal court located in that State as long as the corporation had filed its incorporation papers in State B, perhaps a State where the corporation did no business at all. See Black and White Taxicab & Transfer Co. v. Brown and Yellow Taxicab & Transfer Co., 276 U.S. 518, 522–525 (refusing to question corporation's reincorporation motives and finding diversity jurisdiction). Subsequently, many in Congress and those who testified before it pointed out that this interpretation was at odds with diversity jurisdiction's basic rationale, namely, opening the federal courts' doors to those who might otherwise suffer from local prejudice against out-of-state parties. See, e.g., S.Rep. No. 530, 72d Cong., 1st Sess., 2, 4–7 (1932). Through its choice of the State of incorporation, a corporation could manipulate federal-court jurisdiction, for example, opening the federal courts' doors in a State where it conducted nearly all its business by filing incorporation papers elsewhere. Id., at 4 ("Since the Supreme Court has decided that a corporation is a citizen . . . it has become a common practice for corporations to be incorporated in one State while they do business in another. And there is no doubt but that it often occurs simply for the purpose of being able to have the advantage of choosing between two tribunals in case of litigation"). See also Hearings on S. 937 et al. before a Subcommittee of the Senate Committee on the Judiciary, 72d Cong., 1st Sess., 4–5 (1932) (Letter from Sen. George W. Norris to Attorney General William D. Mitchell (May 24, 1930)) (citing a "common practice for individuals to incorporate in a foreign State simply for the purpose of taking litigation which may arise into the Federal courts"). Although various legislative proposals to curtail the corporate use of diversity jurisdiction were made, see, e.g., S. 937, S. 939, H.R. 11508, 72d Cong., 1st Sess. (1932), none of these proposals were enacted into law.

At the same time as federal dockets increased in size, many judges began to believe those dockets contained too many diversity cases. A committee of the Judicial Conference of the United States studied the matter. See Reports of the Proceedings of the Regular Annual Meeting and Special Meeting (Sept. 24–26 & Mar. 19–20, 1951), in H.R. Doc. No. 365, 82d Cong., 2d Sess., pp. 26–27 (1952). And on March 12, 1951, that committee, the Committee on Jurisdiction and Venue, issued a report (hereinafter Mar. Committee Rept.).

Among its observations, the committee found a general need "to prevent frauds and abuses" with respect to jurisdiction. Id., at 14. The committee recommended against eliminating diversity cases altogether. Id., at 28. Instead it recommended, along with other proposals, a statutory amendment that would make a corporation a citizen both of the State of its incorporation and any State from which it received more than half of its gross income. Id., at 14–15 (requiring corporation to show that "less than fifty per cent of its gross income was derived from business transacted within the state where the Federal court is held"). If, for example, a citizen of California sued (under state law in state court) a corporation that received half or more of its gross income from California, that corporation would not be able to remove the case to federal court, even if Delaware was its State of incorporation.

During the spring and summer of 1951 committee members circulated their report and attended circuit conferences at which federal judges discussed the report's recommendations. Reflecting those criticisms, the committee filed a new report in September, in which it revised its corporate citizenship recommendation. It now proposed that " 'a corporation shall be deemed a citizen of the state of its original creation ... [and] shall also be deemed a citizen of a state where it has its principal place of business.' " Judicial Conference of the United States, Report of the Committee on Jurisdiction and Venue 4 (Sept. 24, 1951) (hereinafter Sept. Committee Rept.)—the source of the present-day statutory language. See Hearings on H.R. 2516 et al. before Subcommittee No. 3 of the House Committee on the Judiciary, 85th Cong., 1st Sess., 9 (1957) (hereinafter House Hearings). The committee wrote that this new language would provide a "simpler and more practical formula" than the "gross income" test. Sept. Committee Rept. 2. It added that the language "ha[d] a precedent in the jurisdictional provisions of the Bankruptcy Act." Id., at 2–3.

In mid–1957 the committee presented its reports to the House of Representatives Committee on the Judiciary. House Hearings 9–27; see also H. Rep. No. 1706, 85th Cong., 2d Sess., 27–28 (1958) (hereinafter H.R. Rep. 1706) (reprinting Mar. and Sept. Committee Repts.); S.Rep. No. 1830, 85th Cong., 2d Sess., 15–31 (1958) (hereinafter S. Rep. 1830) (same). Judge Albert Maris, representing Judge John Parker (who had chaired the Judicial Conference Committee), discussed various proposals that the Judicial Conference had made to restrict the scope of diversity jurisdiction. In respect to the "principal place of business" proposal, he said that the relevant language "ha[d] been defined in the Bankruptcy Act." House Hearings 37. He added:

"All of those problems have arisen in bankruptcy cases, and as I recall the cases—and I wouldn't want to be bound by this statement because I haven't them before me—I think the courts have generally taken the view that where a corporation's interests are rather widespread, the principal place of business is an actual rather than a theoretical or legal one. It is the actual place where its business operations are coordinated, directed, and carried out, which would ordinarily be the place where its officers carry on its day-to-day business, where its accounts are kept, where its payments are made, and not necessarily a State in which it may have a plant, if it is a big corporation, or something of that sort."

"But that has been pretty well worked out in the bankruptcy cases, and that law would all be available, you see, to be applied here without having to go over it again from the beginning." Ibid.

The House Committee reprinted the Judicial Conference Committee Reports along with other reports and relevant testimony and circulated it to the general public "for the purpose of inviting further suggestions and comments." Id., at III. Subsequently, in 1958, Congress both codified the courts' traditional place of incorporation test and also enacted into law a slightly modified version of the Conference Committee's proposed "principal place of business" language. A corporation was to "be deemed a citizen of any State by which it has been incorporated and of the State where it has its principal place of business." § 2, 72 Stat. 415.

IV

The phrase "principal place of business" has proved more difficult to apply than its originators likely expected. Decisions under the Bankruptcy Act did not provide the firm guidance for which Judge Maris had hoped because courts interpreting bankruptcy law did not agree about how to determine a corporation's "principal place of business." Compare Burdick v. Dillon, 144 F. 737, 738 (CA1 1906) (holding that a corporation's "principal office, rather than a factory, mill, or mine . . . constitutes the 'principal place of business' "), with Continental Coal Corp. v. Roszelle Bros., 242 F. 243, 247 (CA6 1917) (identifying the "principal place of business" as the location of mining activities, rather than the "principal office"); see also Friedenthal, New Limitations on Federal Jurisdiction, 11 Stan. L.Rev. 213, 223 (1959) ("The cases under the Bankruptcy Act provide no rigid legal formula for the determination of the principal place of business").

After Congress' amendment, courts were similarly uncertain as to where to look to determine a corporation's "principal place of business" for diversity purposes. If a corporation's headquarters and executive offices were in the same State in which it did most of its business, the test seemed straightforward. The "principal place of business" was located in that State. See, e.g., Long v. Silver, 248 F.3d 309, 314–315 (CA4 2001); Pinnacle Consultants, Ltd. v. Leucadia Nat. Corp., 101 F.3d 900, 906–907 (CA2 1996).

But suppose those corporate headquarters, including executive offices, are in one State, while the corporation's plants or other centers of business activity are located in other States? In 1959 a distinguished federal district judge, Edward Weinfeld, relied on the Second Circuit's interpretation of the Bankruptcy Act to answer this question in part:

"Where a corporation is engaged in far-flung and varied activities which are carried on in different states, its principal place of business is the nerve center from which it radiates out to its constituent parts and from which its officers direct, control and coordinate all activities without regard to locale, in the furtherance of the corporate objective. The test applied by our Court of Appeals, is that place where the corporation has an 'office from which its business was directed and controlled'—the place where 'all of its business was under the supreme direction and control of its officers.' " Scot Typewriter Co., 170 F.Supp., at 865.

Numerous Circuits have since followed this rule, applying the "nerve center" test for corporations with "far-flung" business activities. See, e.g., Topp v. CompAir Inc., 814 F.2d 830, 834 (CA1 1987); see also 15 J. Moore et al., Moore's Federal Practice § 102.54[2], p. 102–112.1 (3d ed.2009) (hereinafter Moore's).

Scot's analysis, however, did not go far enough. For it did not answer what courts should do when the operations of the corporation are not "far-flung" but rather limited to only a few States. When faced with this question, various courts have focused more heavily on where a corporation's actual business activities are located. See, e.g., Diaz–Rodriguez v. Pep Boys Corp., 410 F.3d 56, 60–61 (CA1 2005); R.G. Barry Corp. v. Mushroom Makers, Inc., 612 F.2d 651, 656–657 (CA2 1979); see also 15 Moore's § 102.54, at 102–112.1.

Perhaps because corporations come in many different forms, involve many different kinds of business activities, and locate offices and plants for different reasons in different ways in different regions, a general "business activities" approach has proved unusually difficult to apply. Courts must decide which factors are more important than others: for example, plant location, sales or servicing centers; transactions, payrolls, or revenue generation. See, e.g., *R.G. Barry Corp.*, supra, at 656–657 (place of sales and advertisement, office, and full-time employees); *Diaz-Rodriguez*, supra, at 61–62 (place of stores and inventory, employees, income, and sales).

The number of factors grew as courts explicitly combined aspects of the "nerve center" and "business activity" tests to look to a corporation's "total activities," sometimes to try to determine what treatises have described as the corporation's "center of gravity." See, e.g., Gafford v. General Elec. Co., 997 F.2d 150, 162–163 (CA6 1993); Amoco Rocmount Co. v. Anschutz Corp., 7 F.3d 909, 915 (CA10 1993); 13F Wright & Miller § 3625, at 100. A major treatise confirms this growing complexity, listing Circuit by Circuit, cases that highlight different factors or emphasize similar factors differently, and reporting that the "federal courts of appeals have employed various tests" —tests which "tend to overlap" and which are sometimes described in "language" that "is imprecise." 15 Moore's § 102.54[2], at 102–112. See also id., §§ 102.54[2], [13], at 102–112 to 102–122 (describing, in 14 pages, major tests as looking to the "nerve center," "locus of operations," or "center of corporate activities"). Not surprisingly, different circuits (and sometimes different courts within a single circuit) have applied these highly general multifactor tests in different ways. Id., §§ 102.54[3]-[7], [11]-[13] (noting that the First Circuit "has never explained a basis for choosing between 'the center of corporate activity' test and the 'locus of operations' test" ; the Second Circuit uses a "two-part test" similar to that of the Fifth, Ninth, and Eleventh Circuits involving an initial determination as to whether "a corporation's activities are centralized or decentralized" followed by an application of either the "place of operations" or "nerve center" test; the Third Circuit applies the "center of corporate activities" test searching for the "headquarters of a corporation's day-to-day activity" ; the Fourth Circuit has "endorsed neither [the 'nerve center' or 'place of operations'] test to the exclusion of the other" ; the Tenth Circuit directs consideration of the "total activity of the company considered as a whole"). See also 13F Wright & Miller § 3625 (describing, in 73 pages, the "nerve center," "corporate activities," and "total activity" tests as part of an effort to locate the corporation's "center of gravity," while specifying different ways in which different circuits apply these or other factors).

This complexity may reflect an unmediated judicial effort to apply the statutory phrase "principal place of business" in light of the general purpose of diversity jurisdiction, i.e., an effort to find the State where a corporation is least likely to suffer out-of-state prejudice when it is sued in a local court, Pease v. Peck, 18 How. [56 U.S.] 595, 599 (1856). But, if so, that task seems doomed to failure. After all, the relevant purposive concern—prejudice against an out-of-state party—will often depend upon factors that courts cannot easily measure, for example, a corporation's image, its history, and its advertising, while the factors that courts can more easily measure, for example, its office or plant location, its sales, its employment, or the nature of the goods or services it supplies, will sometimes bear no more than a distant relation to the likelihood of prejudice. At the same time, this approach is at war with administrative simplicity. And it has failed to achieve a nationally uniform interpretation of federal law, an unfortunate consequence in a federal legal system.

V

A

In an effort to find a single, more uniform interpretation of the statutory phrase, we have reviewed the Courts of Appeals' divergent and increasingly complex interpretations. Having done so, we now return to, and expand, Judge Weinfeld's approach, as applied in the Seventh Circuit. See, e.g., *Scot Typewriter Co.*, 170 F.Supp., at 865; *Wisconsin Knife Works*, 781 F.2d, at 1282. We conclude that "principal place of business" is best read as referring to the place where a corporation's officers direct, control, and coordinate the corporation's activities. It is the place that Courts of Appeals have called the corporation's "nerve center." And in practice it should normally be the place where the corporation maintains its headquarters—provided that the headquarters is the actual center of direction, control, and coordination, i.e., the "nerve center," and not simply an office where the corporation holds its board meetings (for example, attended by directors and officers who have traveled there for the occasion).

Three sets of considerations, taken together, convince us that this approach, while imperfect, is superior to other possibilities. First, the statute's language supports the approach. The statute's text deems a corporation a citizen of the "State where it has its principal place of business." 28 U.S.C. § 1332(c)(1). The word "place" is in the singular, not the plural. The word "principal" requires us to pick out the "main, prominent" or "leading" place. 12 Oxford English Dictionary 495 (2d ed. 1989) (def.(A)(I)(2)). Cf. Commissioner v. Soliman, 506 U.S. 168, 174 (1993) (interpreting "principal place of business" for tax purposes to require an assessment of "whether any one business location is the 'most important, consequential, or influential' one"). And the fact that the word "place" follows the words "State where" means that the "place" is a place within a State. It is not the State itself.

A corporation's "nerve center," usually its main headquarters, is a single place. The public often (though not always) considers it the corporation's main place of business. And it is a place within a State. By contrast, the application of a more general business activities test has led some courts, as in the present case, to look, not at a particular place within a State, but incorrectly at the State itself, measuring the total amount of business activities that the corporation conducts there and determining whether they are "significantly larger" than in the next-ranking State. 297 Fed.Appx. 690.

This approach invites greater litigation and can lead to strange results, as the Ninth Circuit has since recognized. Namely, if a "corporation may be deemed a citizen of California on th[e] basis" of "activities [that] roughly reflect California's larger population . . . nearly every national retailer—no matter how far flung its operations—will be deemed a citizen of California for diversity purposes." Davis v. HSBC Bank Nev., N. A., 557 F.3d 1026, 1029–1030 (2009). But why award or decline diversity jurisdiction on the basis of a State's population, whether measured directly, indirectly (say proportionately), or with modifications?

Second, administrative simplicity is a major virtue in a jurisdictional statute. Sisson v. Ruby, 497 U.S. 358, 375 (1990) (Scalia, J., concurring in judgment) (eschewing "the sort of vague boundary that is to be avoided in the area of subject-matter jurisdiction wherever possible"). Complex jurisdictional tests complicate a case, eating up time and money as the parties litigate, not the merits of their claims, but which court is the right court to decide those claims. Cf. Navarro Savings Assn. v. Lee, 446 U.S. 458, 464, n. 13 (1980). Complex tests produce appeals and reversals, encourage gamesmanship, and, again, diminish the likelihood that results and settlements will reflect a claim's legal and factual merits. Judicial resources too are at stake. Courts have an independent obligation to determine whether subject-matter jurisdiction exists, even when no party challenges it. Arbaugh v. Y & H Corp., 546 U.S. 500, 514 (2006) (citing Ruhrgas AG v. Marathon Oil Co., 526 U.S. 574, 583 (1999)). So courts benefit from straightforward rules under which they can readily assure themselves of their power to hear a case. *Arbaugh*, supra, at 514.

Simple jurisdictional rules also promote greater predictability. Predictability is valuable to corporations making business and investment decisions. Cf. First Nat. City Bank v. Banco Para El Comercio Exterior de Cuba, 462 U.S. 611, 621 (1983) (recognizing the "need for certainty and predictability of result while generally protecting the justified expectations of parties with interests in the corporation"). Predictability also benefits plaintiffs deciding whether to file suit in a state or federal court.

A "nerve center" approach, which ordinarily equates that "center" with a corporation's headquarters, is simple to apply comparatively speaking. The metaphor of a corporate "brain," while not precise, suggests a single location. By contrast, a corporation's general business activities more often lack a single principal place where they take place. That is to say, the corporation may have several plants, many sales locations, and employees located in many different places. If so, it will not be as easy to determine which of these different business locales is the "principal" or most important "place."

Third, the statute's legislative history, for those who accept it, offers a simplicity-related interpretive benchmark. The Judicial Conference provided an initial version of its proposal that suggested a numerical test. A corporation would be deemed a citizen of the State that accounted for more than half of its gross income. Mar. Committee Rept. 14–15; see supra, at 1189. The Conference changed its mind in light of criticism that such a test would prove too complex and impractical to apply. Sept. Committee Rept. 2; see also H. Rep. 1706, at 28; S. Rep. 1830, at 31. That history suggests that the words "principal place of business" should be interpreted to be no more complex than the initial "half of gross income" test. A "nerve center" test offers such a possibility. A general business activities test does not.

B

We recognize that there may be no perfect test that satisfies all administrative and purposive criteria. We recognize as well that, under the "nerve center" test we adopt today, there will be hard cases. For example, in this era of telecommuting, some corporations may divide their command and coordinating functions among officers who work at several different locations, perhaps communicating over the Internet. That said, our test nonetheless points courts in a single direction, towards the center of overall direction, control, and coordination. Courts do not have to try to weigh corporate functions, assets, or revenues different in kind, one from the other. Our approach provides a sensible test that is relatively easier to apply, not a test that will, in all instances, automatically generate a result.

We also recognize that the use of a "nerve center" test may in some cases produce results that seem to cut against the basic rationale for 28 U.S.C. § 1332, see supra, at 1188. For example, if the bulk of a company's business activities visible to the public take place in New Jersey, while its top officers direct those activities just across the river in New York, the "principal place of business" is New York. One could argue that members of the public in New Jersey would be less likely to be prejudiced against the corporation than persons in New York—yet the corporation will still be entitled to remove a New Jersey state case to federal court. And note too that the same corporation would be unable to remove a New York state case to federal court, despite the New York public's presumed prejudice against the corporation.

We understand that such seeming anomalies will arise. However, in view of the necessity of having a clearer rule, we must accept them.

Accepting occasionally counterintuitive results is the price the legal system must pay to avoid overly complex jurisdictional administration while producing the benefits that accompany a more uniform legal system.

The burden of persuasion for establishing diversity jurisdiction, of course, remains on the party asserting it. Kokkonen v. Guardian Life Ins. Co. of America, 511 U.S. 375, 377 (1994); McNutt v. General Motors Acceptance Corp., 298 U.S. 178, 189 (1936); see also 13E Wright & Miller § 3602.1, at 119. When challenged on allegations of jurisdictional facts, the parties must support their allegations by competent proof. *McNutt*, supra, at 189; 15 Moore's § 102.14, at 102–32 to 102–32.1. And when faced with such a challenge, we reject suggestions such as, for example, the one made by petitioner that the mere filing of a form like the Securities and Exchange Commission's Form 10–K listing a corporation's "principal executive offices" would, without more, be sufficient proof to establish a corporation's "nerve center." See, e.g., SEC Form 10–K, online at http:// www. sec. gov/ about/ forms/ form10–k.pdf. (as visited Feb. 19, 2010, and available in Clerk of Court's case file). Cf. Dimmitt & Owens Financial, Inc. v. United States, 787 F.2d 1186, 1190–1192 (CA7 1986) (distinguishing "principle executive office" in the tax lien context, see 26 U.S.C. § 6323(f)(2), from "principal place of business" under 28 U.S.C. § 1332(c)). Such possibilities would readily permit jurisdictional manipulation, thereby subverting a major reason for the insertion of the "principal place of business" language in the diversity statute. Indeed, if the record reveals attempts at manipulation—for example, that the alleged "nerve center" is nothing more than a mail drop box, a bare office with a computer, or the location of an annual executive retreat—the courts should instead take as the "nerve center" the place of actual direction, control, and coordination, in the absence of such manipulation.

VI

Petitioner's unchallenged declaration suggests that Hertz's center of direction, control, and coordination, its "nerve center," and its corporate headquarters are one and the same, and they are located in New Jersey, not in California. Because respondents should have a fair opportunity to litigate their case in light of our holding, however, we vacate the Ninth Circuit's judgment and remand the case for further proceedings consistent with this opinion.

It is so ordered.

Carden v. Arkoma Associates

Supreme Court of the United States, 1990.
494 U.S. 185, 110 S.Ct. 1015, 108 L.Ed.2d 157.

■ JUSTICE SCALIA delivered the opinion of the Court.

The question presented in this case is whether, in a suit brought by a limited partnership, the citizenship of the limited partners must be taken into account to determine diversity of citizenship among the parties.

I

Respondent Arkoma Associates (Arkoma), a limited partnership organized under the laws of Arizona, brought suit on a contract dispute in the United States District Court for the Eastern District of Louisiana, relying upon diversity of citizenship for federal jurisdiction. The defendants, C. Tom Carden and Leonard L. Limes, citizens of Louisiana, moved to dismiss, contending that one of Arkoma's limited partners was also a citizen of Louisiana. The District Court denied the motion but certified the question for interlocutory appeal, which the Fifth Circuit declined. Thereafter Magee Drilling Company intervened in the suit and, together with the original defendants, counterclaimed against Arkoma under Texas law. Following a bench trial, the District Court awarded Arkoma a money judgment plus interest and attorney's fees; it dismissed Carden and Limes' counterclaim and as well as Magee's intervention and counterclaim. Carden, Limes, and Magee (petitioners here) appealed and the Fifth Circuit affirmed. 874 F.2d 226 (CA5 1988). With respect to petitioners' jurisdictional challenge, the Court of Appeals found complete diversity, reasoning that Arkoma's citizenship should be determined by reference to the citizenship of the general, but not the limited, partners....

II

Article III of the Constitution provides, in pertinent part, that "The judicial Power shall extend to ... Controversies ... between Citizens of different States." Congress first authorized the federal courts to exercise diversity jurisdiction in the Judiciary Act of 1789, ch. 20, § 11, 1 Stat. 78. In its current form, the diversity statute provides that "[t]he district courts shall have original jurisdiction of all civil actions where the matter in controversy exceeds ... $50,000 ..., and is between ... citizens of different States ...." 28 U.S.C. § 1332(a) (Oct. 1989 Supp.). Since its enactment, we have interpreted the diversity statute to require "complete diversity" of citizenship. See Strawbridge v. Curtiss, 3 Cranch [7 U.S.] 267 (1806). The District Court erred in finding complete diversity in this case unless (1) a limited partnership may be considered in its own right a "citizen" of the State that created it, or (2) a federal court must look to the citizenship of only its general, but not its limited, partners to determine whether there is complete diversity of citizenship. We consider these questions in turn.

A

We have often had to consider the status of artificial entities created by state law insofar as that bears upon the existence of federal diversity jurisdiction. The precise question posed under the terms of the diversity statute is whether such an entity may be considered a "citizen" of the State under whose laws it was created.[19] A corporation is the paradigmatic

---

19. The dissent reaches a conclusion different from ours primarily because it poses, and then answers, an entirely different question. It "do[es] not consider" "whether the limited partnership is a 'citizen,'" but simply "assum[es] it is a citizen," because even if we hold

artificial "person," and the Court has considered its proper characterization under the diversity statute on more than one occasion—not always reaching the same conclusion. Initially, we held that a corporation "is certainly not a citizen," so that to determine the existence of diversity jurisdiction the Court must "look to the character of the individuals who compose [it]." Bank of United States v. Deveaux, 5 Cranch [9 U.S.] 61, 86, 91–92 (1809). We overruled *Deveaux* 35 years later in Louisville, C. & C.R. Co. v. Letson, 2 How. [43 U.S.] 497, 558 (1844), which held that a corporation is "capable of being treated as a citizen of [the State which created it], as much as a natural person." Ten years later, we reaffirmed the result of *Letson,* though on the somewhat different theory that "those who use the corporate name, and exercise the faculties conferred by it," should be presumed conclusively to be citizens of the corporation's State of incorporation. Marshall v. Baltimore & Ohio R. Co., 16 How. [57 U.S.] 314, 329 (1854).

While the rule regarding the treatment of corporations as "citizens" has become firmly established, we have (with an exception to be discussed presently) just as firmly resisted extending that treatment to other entities. For example, in Chapman v. Barney, 129 U.S. 677 (1889), a case involving an unincorporated "joint stock company," we raised the question of jurisdiction on our own motion, and found it to be lacking:

> "On looking into the record we find no satisfactory showing as to the citizenship of the plaintiff. The allegation of the amended petition is, that the United States Express Company is a joint stock company organized under a law of the State of New York, and is a citizen of that State. But the express company cannot be a *citizen* of New York, within the meaning of the statutes regulating jurisdiction, unless it be a corporation. The allegation that the company was *organized* under the laws of New York is not an allegation that it is a corporation. In fact the allegation is, that the company is *not* a corporation, but a joint stock company—that is, a mere partnership." Id., at 682.

---

that it is, "we are still required to consider which, if any, of the *other citizens before the Court* as members of Arkoma Associates are real parties to the controversy." (emphasis added). Furthermore, "[t]he only potentially nondiverse *party* in this case is a limited partner" because "[a]ll *other parties,* including the general partners and the limited partnership itself, assuming it is a citizen, are diverse." Ibid. (emphasis added).

That is the central fallacy from which, for the most part, the rest of the dissent's reasoning logically follows. The question presented today is not which of various parties before the Court should be considered for purposes of determining whether there is complete diversity of citizenship, a question that will generally be answered by application of the "real party to the controversy" test. There are *not,* as the dissent assumes, multiple respondents before the Court, but only *one:* the artificial entity called Arkoma Associates, a limited partnership. And what we must decide is the quite different question of how the citizenship of that single artificial entity is to be determined—which in turn raises the question whether it can (like a corporation) assert its own citizenship, or rather is deemed to possess the citizenship of its members, and, if so, which members. The dissent fails to cite a single case in which the citizenship of an artificial entity, the issue before us today, has been decided by application of the "real party to the controversy" test that it describes.

Similarly, in Great Southern Fire Proof Hotel Co. v. Jones, 177 U.S. 449 (1900), we held that a "limited partnership association" —although possessing "some of the characteristics of a corporation" and deemed a "citizen" by the law creating it—may not be deemed a "citizen" under the jurisdictional rule established for corporations. Id., at 456. "That rule must not be extended." Id., at 457. As recently as 1965, our unanimous opinion in Steelworkers v. R.H. Bouligny, Inc., 382 U.S. 145, reiterated that "the doctrinal wall of *Chapman v. Barney*," id., 129 U.S., at 151, would not be breached.

The one exception to the admirable consistency of our jurisprudence on this matter is Puerto Rico v. Russell & Co., 288 U.S. 476 (1933), which held that the entity known as a *sociedad en comandita,* created under the civil law of Puerto Rico, could be treated as a citizen of Puerto Rico for purposes of determining federal court jurisdiction. The *sociedad's* juridical personality, we said, "is so complete in contemplation of the law of Puerto Rico that we see no adequate reason for holding that the *sociedad* has a different status for purposes of federal jurisdiction than a corporation organized under that law." Id., at 482. Arkoma fairly argues that this language, and the outcome of the case, "reflec[t] the Supreme Court's willingness to look beyond the incorporated/unincorporated dichotomy and to study the internal organization, state law requirements, management structure, and capacity or lack thereof to act and/or sue, to determine diversity of citizenship." The problem with this argument lies not in its logic, but in the fact that the approach it espouses was proposed and specifically rejected in *Bouligny.* There, in reaffirming "the doctrinal wall of *Chapman v. Barney*," we explained *Russell* as a case resolving the distinctive problem "of fitting an exotic creation of the civil law ... into a federal scheme which knew it not." 382 U.S., at 151. There could be no doubt, after *Bouligny,* that at least common-law entities (and likely all entities beyond the Puerto Rican *sociedad en comandita*) would be treated for purposes of the diversity statute pursuant to what *Russell* called "[t]he tradition of the common law," which is "to treat as legal persons only incorporated groups and to assimilate all others to partnerships." 288 U.S., at 480.[20]

---

20.   The dissent correctly observes that *"Russell* tells us nothing about whether the citizenship of the *sociedad's* members, unlimited or limited, should be considered for purposes of diversity jurisdiction." Rather, as is evident from our discussing the case here instead of in Part B below, *Russell* (according to respondent) tells us something about whether an artificial entity other than a corporation can be considered a "citizen" in its own right. That "[t]he issue in *Russell* was not diversity, but whether the suit against the *sociedad en comandita* could be removed from the Insular Court to the United States District Court for Puerto Rico," does not affect *Russell's* arguable relevance to that question because the operative word in both the diversity statute and the removal statute at issue in *Russell* is "citizens."

The dissent goes on to criticize as "seriously flawed," our attempt to distinguish *Russell* in connection with the issue we do address, whether a partnership can be considered a "citizen." We point out, not by way of complaint but to prevent confusion, that the criticism is gratuitous, inasmuch as the dissent itself takes no position on this issue, announcing at the very outset that it "do[es] not consider" the question "whether the limited partnership is a 'citizen.'" In any event, the dissent's evidence bearing on the historical pedigree of

Arkoma claims to have found another exception to our *Chapman* tradition in Navarro Savings Assn. v. Lee, 446 U.S. 458 (1980). That case, however, did not involve the question whether a party that is an artificial entity other than a corporation can be considered a "citizen" of a State, but the quite separate question whether parties that were undoubted "citizens" (viz., natural persons) were the real parties to the controversy. The plaintiffs in *Navarro* were eight individual trustees of a Massachusetts business trust, suing in their own names. The defendant, Navarro Savings Association, disputed the existence of complete diversity, claiming that the trust beneficiaries rather than the trustees were the real parties to the controversy, and that the citizenship of the former and not the latter should therefore control. In the course of rejecting this claim, we did indeed discuss the characteristics of a Massachusetts business trust—not at all, however, for the purpose of determining whether the trust had attributes making it a "citizen," but only for the purpose of establishing that the respondents were "active trustees whose control over the assets held in their names is real and substantial," thereby bringing them under the rule, "more than 150 years" old, which permits such trustees "to sue in their own right, without regard to the citizenship of the trust beneficiaries." Id., at 465–466. *Navarro,* in short, has nothing to do with the *Chapman* question, except that it makes available to respondent the argument by analogy that, just as business reality is taken into account for purposes of determining whether a trustee is the real party to the controversy, so also it should be taken into account for purposes of determining whether an artificial entity is a citizen. That argument is, to put it mildly, less than compelling.

B

As an alternative ground for finding complete diversity, Arkoma asserts that the Fifth Circuit correctly determined its citizenship solely by reference to the citizenship of its general partners, without regard to the citizenship of its limited partners. Only the general partners, it points out, "manage the assets, control the litigation, and bear the risk of liability for the limited partnership's debts," and, more broadly, "have exclusive and complete management and control of the operations of the partnership." This approach of looking to the citizenship of only some of the members of the artificial entity finds even less support in our precedent than looking to the State of organization (for which one could at least point to *Russell*). We have never held that an artificial entity, suing or being sued in its own name, can invoke the diversity jurisdiction of the federal courts based on the citizenship of some but not all of its members. No doubt some members of the joint stock company in *Chapman,* the labor union in *Bouligny,* and the limited partnership association in *Great Southern* exercised greater control over their respective entities than other members. But such considerations have played no part in our decisions.

---

partnerships comes to our attention at least 25 years too late. For the reasons stated in the text, *Bouligny* considered and rejected applying *Russell* beyond its facts.

To support its approach, Arkoma seeks to press *Navarro* into service once again, arguing that just as that case looked to the trustees to determine the citizenship of the business trust, so also here we should look to the general partners, who have the management powers, in determining the citizenship of this partnership. As we have already explained, however, *Navarro* had nothing to do with the citizenship of the "trust," since it was a suit by the trustees in their own names.

The dissent supports Arkoma's argument on this point, though, as we have described, under the rubric of determining which parties supposedly before the Court are the real parties, rather than under the rubric of determining the citizenship of the limited partnership. The dissent asserts that "[t]he real party to the controversy approach," —by which it means an approach that looks to "control over the conduct of the business and the ability to initiate or control the course of litigation," —"has been implemented by the Court both in its oldest and in its most recent cases examining diversity jurisdiction with respect to business associations." Not a single case the dissent discusses, neither old nor new, supports that assertion. *Deveaux,* which was in any event overruled by *Letson,* seems to be applying not a "real party to the controversy" test, but rather the principle that for jurisdictional purposes the corporation has no substance, and merely "represents" its shareholders, see 5 Cranch, at 90–91; but even if it can be regarded as applying a "real party to the controversy" test, it deems that test to be met by *all* the shareholders of the corporation, without regard to their "control over the operation of the business." *Marshall,* which as we have discussed re-rationalized *Letson*'s holding that a corporation was a "citizen" in its own right, contains language quite clearly adopting a "real party to the controversy" approach, and arguably even adopting a "control" test for that status. ("[T]he court ... will look behind the corporate or collective name ... to find the persons who act *as the representatives, curators, or trustees* ..." 16 How., at 328–329 (emphasis added). "The presumption arising from the habitat of a corporation in the place of its creation [is] conclusive as to the residence or citizenship *of those who use the corporate name and exercise the faculties conferred by it* ...." Id., at 329 (emphasis added).) But as we have also discussed, and as the last quotation shows, that analysis was a complete fiction; the real citizenship of the shareholders (or the controlling shareholders) was not consulted at all.[21] From the fictional *Marshall,* the dissent must leap almost a century and a third to *Navarro* to find a "real party to the controversy" analysis that discusses "control." That case, as we have said, is irrelevant, since it involved not a juridical person but the distinctive common-law institution of trustees.

---

21. *Marshall*'s fictional approach appears to have been abandoned. Later cases revert to the formulation of Louisville, C. & C.R. Co. v. Letson, 2 How. [43 U.S.] 497 (1844), that the corporation has its own citizenship. See Great Southern Fire Proof Hotel v. Jones, 177 U.S. 449, 456 (1900) ("for purposes of jurisdiction ... a corporation was to be deemed a citizen of the State creating it") (citing *Letson*); Chapman v. Barney, 129 U.S. 677, 682 (1889) ("express company cannot be a *citizen* of New York, within the meaning of the statutes regulating jurisdiction, unless it be a corporation").

The dissent finds its position supported, rather than contradicted, by the trilogy of *Chapman, Great Southern,* and *Bouligny*—cases that did involve juridical persons but that did not apply "real party to the controversy" analysis, much less a "control" test as the criterion for that status. In those cases, the dissent explains, "the members of each association held equivalent power and control over the association's assets, business, and litigation." It seeks to establish this factual matter, however, not from the text of the opinions (where not the slightest discussion of the point appears) but, for *Chapman,* by citation of scholarly commentary dealing with the general characteristics of joint stock company agreements, with no reference to (because the record does not contain) the particular agreement at issue in the case, for *Great Southern,* by citation of scholarly commentary dealing with the general characteristics of Pennsylvania limited partnership associations, and citation of Pennsylvania statutes; and, for *Bouligny,* by nothing more than the observation that "[t]here was no indication that any of the union members had any greater power over the litigation or the union's business and assets than any other member, and, therefore, as in *Chapman* and *Great Southern,* the Court was not called upon to decide" the issue. This will not do. Since diversity of citizenship is a jurisdictional requirement, the Court is always "called upon to decide" it. As the Court said in *Great Southern* itself:

> "[T]he failure of parties to urge objections [to diversity of citizenship] cannot relieve this court from the duty of ascertaining from the record whether the Circuit Court could properly take jurisdiction of this suit ... 'The rule ... is inflexible and without exception, which requires this court, of its own motion, to deny its own jurisdiction, and, in the exercise of its appellate power, that of all other courts of the United States, in all cases where such jurisdiction does not affirmatively appear in the record on which, in the exercise of that power, it is called to act.' " 177 U.S., at 453 (quoting Mansfield, C. & L.M.R. Co. v. Swan, 111 U.S. 379, 382 (1884)).

If, as the dissent contends, these three cases were applying a "real party to the controversy" test governed by "control" over the associations, so that the citizenship of all members would be consulted only if all members had equivalent control, it is inconceivable that the existence of equivalency, *or at least the absence of any reason to suspect nonequivalency,* would not have been mentioned in the opinions. Given what 180 years of cases have said and done, as opposed to what they might have said, it is difficult to understand how the dissent can characterize as "newly formulated" the "rule that the Court will, without analysis of the particular entity before it, count every member of an unincorporated association for purposes of diversity jurisdiction."

In sum, we reject the contention that to determine, for diversity purposes, the citizenship of an artificial entity, the court may consult the citizenship of less than all of the entity's members. We adhere to our oft-repeated rule that diversity jurisdiction in a suit by or against the entity depends on the citizenship of "all the members," *Chapman,* 129 U.S., at

682, "the several persons composing such association," *Great Southern,* 177 U.S., at 456, "each of its members," *Bouligny,* 382 U.S., at 146.

C

The resolutions we have reached above can validly be characterized as technical, precedent-bound, and unresponsive to policy considerations raised by the changing realities of business organization. But, as must be evident from our earlier discussion, that has been the character of our jurisprudence in this field after *Letson.* See Currie, The Federal Courts and the American Law Institute, 36 U.Chi.L.Rev. 1, 35 (1968). Arkoma is undoubtedly correct that limited partnerships are functionally similar to "other types of organizations that have access to federal courts," and is perhaps correct that "[c]onsiderations of basic fairness and substance over form require that limited partnerships receive similar treatment." Brief for Respondent 33. Similar arguments were made in *Bouligny.* The District Court there had upheld removal because it could divine " 'no common sense reason for treating an unincorporated national labor union differently from a corporation,' " 382 U.S., at 146, and we recognized that that contention had "considerable merit," id., at 150. We concluded, however, that "[w]hether unincorporated labor unions ought to be assimilated to the status of corporations for diversity purposes," id., at 153, is "properly a matter for legislative consideration which cannot adequately or appropriately be dealt with by this Court," id., at 147. In other words, having entered the field of diversity policy with regard to artificial entities once (and forcefully) in *Letson,* we have left further adjustments to be made by Congress.

Congress has not been idle. In 1958 it revised the rule established in *Letson,* providing that a corporation shall be deemed a citizen not only of its State of incorporation but also "of the State where it has its principal place of business." 28 U.S.C. § 1332(c) (Oct.1989 Supp.). No provision was made for the treatment of artificial entities other than corporations, although the existence of many new, post-*Letson* forms of commercial enterprises, including at least the sort of joint stock company at issue in *Chapman,* the sort of limited partnership association at issue in *Great Southern,* and the sort of Massachusetts business trust at issue in *Navarro,* must have been obvious.

Thus, the course we take today does not so much disregard the policy of accommodating our diversity jurisdiction to the changing realities of commercial organization, as it honors the more important policy of leaving that to the people's elected representatives. Such accommodation is not only performed more legitimately by Congress than by courts, but it is performed more intelligently by legislation than by interpretation of the statutory word "citizen." The fifty States have created, and will continue to create, a wide assortment of artificial entities possessing different powers and characteristics, and composed of various classes of members with varying degrees of interest and control. Which of them is entitled to be considered a "citizen" for diversity purposes, and which of their members' citizenship is to be consulted, are questions more readily resolved by legislative prescription than by legal reasoning, any questions whose complexity is particularly unwelcome at the threshold stage of determining whether a court has jurisdiction. We have long since decided that, having established special treatment for corporations, we will leave the rest to Congress; We adhere to that decision.

. . . . .

˗ Reversed and remanded.

■ JUSTICE O'CONNOR, with whom JUSTICE BRENNAN, JUSTICE MARSHALL, and JUSTICE BLACKMUN join, dissenting.

The only potentially nondiverse party in this case is a limited partner. All other parties, including the general partners and the limited partnership itself, assuming it is a citizen, are diverse. Thus, the Court has before it a single question—whether the citizenship of a limited partner must be counted for purposes of diversity jurisdiction. The Court first addresses whether the limited partnership is a "citizen." I do not consider that issue, because even if we were to hold that a limited partnership is a citizen, we are still required to consider which, if any, of the other citizens before the Court as members of Arkoma Associates are real parties to the controversy, i.e., which parties have control over the subject of and litigation over the controversy. See Marshall v. Baltimore & Ohio R. Co., 16 How. [57 U.S.] 314, 328 (1854). Application of that test leads me to conclude that limited partners are not real parties to the controversy and, therefore, should not be counted for purposes of diversity jurisdiction.

I

The Court asserts that "[w]e have long since decided" to leave to Congress the issue of the proper treatment of unincorporated associations for diversity purposes, because the issue of which business association "is entitled to be considered a 'citizen' for diversity purposes, and which of their members' citizenship is to be consulted, are questions more readily resolved by legislative prescription than by legal reasoning." That assertion is insupportable in light of Navarro Savings Assn. v. Lee, 446 U.S. 458 (1980) (determination of which members of unincorporated business trust must be considered for purposes of diversity jurisdiction) and even Steel-workers v. R.H. Bouligny, Inc., 382 U.S. 145 (1965) (determination of proper treatment of union for diversity jurisdiction purposes according to settled law; Congress has power to change result), on which the Court relies. Indeed, the Court in this case does not leave the issue to Congress, but rather decides the issue and then invokes deference to Congress to justify its newly formulated rule that the Court will, without analysis of the particular entity before it, count every member of an unincorporated association for purposes of diversity jurisdiction. In my view, the Court properly tackles the issue, because "application of statutes to situations not anticipated by the legislature is a pre-eminently judicial function." Currie, Federal Courts and the American Law Institute, 36 U.Chi.L.Rev. 1, 35

(1968); see also Bank of United States v. Deveaux, 5 Cranch [9 U.S.] 61, 87 (1809) ("The duties of this [C]ourt, to exercise jurisdiction where it is conferred, and not to usurp it where it is not conferred, are of equal obligation. The constitution, therefore, and the law, are to be expounded, without a leaning the one way or the other, according to those general principles which usually govern in the construction of fundamental or other laws").

II

The starting point for any analysis of who must be counted for purposes of diversity jurisdiction is Strawbridge v. Curtiss, 3 Cranch [7 U.S.] 267 (1806), in which the Court held that "complete diversity" is required among "citizens" of different States. Complete diversity, however, is not constitutionally mandated. See State Farm Fire & Casualty Co. v. Tashire, 386 U.S. 523, 530–531 (1967) (statutory interpleader need not satisfy complete diversity requirement as long as there is diversity between two or more claimants); see also American Law Institute, Study of the Division of Jurisdiction Between State and Federal Courts § 1301(b)(2), Supporting Memorandum A, pp. 426–436 (1969). For example, in a class action authorized pursuant to Federal Rule of Civil Procedure 23, only the citizenship of the named representatives of the class is considered, without regard to whether the citizenship of other members of the class would destroy complete diversity or to the class members' particular stake in the controversy. See Snyder v. Harris, 394 U.S. 332, 340 (1969); C. Wright, Law of Federal Courts 314–315 (2d ed.1970); see also Owen Equipment & Erection Co. v. Kroger, 437 U.S. 365, 375, and n. 18 (1978) (citizenship of parties joined under ancillary jurisdiction not taken into account for purposes of determining diversity jurisdiction); Wright, supra, at 19 (same).

Since the early 19th century, one of the benchmarks for determining whether a particular party among those involved in the litigation must be counted for purposes of diversity jurisdiction has been whether the party has a "real interest" in the suit or, in other words, is a "real party" to the controversy. See 6 C. Wright & A. Miller, Federal Practice and Procedure § 1556, p. 711 (1971) (well settled "citizenship rule testing diversity in terms of the real party in interest is grounded in notions of federalism"). See generally Note, Diversity Jurisdiction over Unincorporated Business Entities: The Real Party in Interest as a Jurisdictional Rule, 56 Texas L.Rev. 243, 247–250 (1978)....

. . . . .

In Steelworkers v. R.H. Bouligny, Inc., 382 U.S. 145 (1965), the Court addressed whether a labor union could be treated as an entity for purposes of diversity jurisdiction. The Court held that a labor union is not a juridical person, and therefore, not a citizen for purposes of diversity jurisdiction. See Mesa Operating Limited Partnership v. Louisiana Intrastate Gas Corp., 797 F.2d 238, 240–241 (CA5 1986) (union in *Bouligny* failed to meet party to controversy test). There was no indication that any of the union members had any greater power over the litigation or the union's business and assets than any other member, and therefore, as in Chapman [v. Barney, 129 U.S. 677 (1889),] and Great Southern [Fire Proof Hotel Co. v. Jones, 177 U.S. 449 (1900)], the Court was not called upon to decide which of the citizens before it were real parties to the controversy.

In the next case, in which application of the real party to the controversy test was appropriate, the Court unanimously applied it. See *Navarro Savings Assn. v. Lee*, 446 U.S., at 460, 464–465 (BLACKMUN, J., dissenting). In that case, the Court addressed the question whether the beneficiaries' citizenship must be counted when the trustees brought suit involving the assets of the trust. See id., at 458. Because the trust beneficiaries lacked both control over the conduct of the business and the ability to initiate or control the course of litigation, the Court held that the citizenship of the trust beneficiaries should not be counted. Id., at 464–465.

As *Navarro* makes clear, the nature of the named party does not settle the question of who are the real parties to the controversy. In fact, if the Court's characterization of the issue before us were correct, ante, at n. 1, then we seriously erred in *Navarro Savings Assn. v. Lee*, supra, at 464–466, when we considered whether the trust beneficiaries were the real parties to the controversy, in light of the fact that they were not named parties to the litigation.

The Court attempts to distinguish *Navarro* on the ground that it involved not a juridical person, but rather the "distinctive common-law institution of trustees." Such a view is consonant with the Court's new diversity jurisdiction analysis announced in this case, but fails to take into account the actual language and analysis in *Navarro*. If the nature of the institution of trustees was sufficient to answer the question of which parties to count for diversity jurisdiction purposes in that case, the Court's discussion of whether the trust beneficiaries were real parties to the controversy would have been wholly superfluous. Given that the Court granted certiorari in that case on the very issue whether the citizenship of trust beneficiaries must be counted, and then unanimously applied the real parties to the controversy test, the discussion clearly was not superfluous.

Application of the parties to the controversy test to the limited partnership yields the conclusion that limited partners should not be considered for purposes of diversity jurisdiction. Like the trust beneficiary in *Navarro*, the limited partner "can neither control the disposition of this action nor intervene in the affairs of the trust except in the most extraordinary situations." *Navarro*, supra, at 464–465 . . . .

The concern perhaps implicit in the Court's holding today is that failure to consider the citizenship of all the members of an unincorporated business association will expand diversity jurisdiction at a time when our federal courts are already seriously overburdened. This concern is more illusory than real in the context of unincorporated business associations. For, despite the Court's holding today, unincorporated associations may gain access to the federal courts by bringing or defending suit as a Rule 23 class action, in which case the citizenship of the members of the class would not be considered. See Federal Diversity Jurisdiction—Citizenship for Unincorporated Associations, 19 Vand.L.Rev. 984, 991–992 (1966). Thus, I see little reason to depart in this case from our long settled practice of applying the real parties to the controversy test.

Because there is complete diversity between petitioners and the limited partnership (assuming that it should be considered a citizen) and each of the general partners, the issue presented by this case is fully resolved by application of the parties to the controversy test.

III

Even though the case does not directly relate to the issue before us, the Court takes pains to address and distinguish Puerto Rico v. Russell & Co., 288 U.S. 476 (1933). The issue in *Russell* was not diversity, but whether the suit against the *sociedad en comandita* could be removed from the Insular Court to the United States District Court for Puerto Rico on the ground that no party on one side was a citizen of or domiciled in Puerto Rico. See 288 U.S., at 478. None of the partners were citizens of Puerto Rico, but the Court determined that the *sociedad* was and, therefore, removal was precluded. Thus, *Russell* tells us nothing about whether the citizenship of the *sociedad*'s members, unlimited or limited, should be considered for purposes of diversity jurisdiction.

In any event, the Court's attempts to distinguish *Russell* are seriously flawed. In *Russell,* the Court examined the Puerto Rican *sociedad en comandita,* which is the civil law version of the modern limited partnership. The Court delineated a series of factors and concluded that, under civil law, the *sociedad* was a "juridical person." Id., at 481. Ironically, the Court in this case endorses the holding of *Russell,* despite the fact that virtually all of the factors listed are equally applicable to the modern limited partnership. . . . It is hardly an answer to the history of the limited partnership in this country and abroad to assert that it appears 25 years after Steelworkers v. R.H. Bouligny, Inc., 382 U.S. 145 (1965). The "admirable consistency of our jurisprudence," ante, at p. [200] is not blemished by distinguishing between unions and limited partnerships. It is, however, severely marred by holding that an association within the continental United States is not afforded the same treatment as its virtually identical Puerto Rican counterpart. See also ante, at n. [20] ("operative word in both the diversity statute and the removal statute at issue in *Russell* is 'citizens' "). The Court's decision today, endorsing treatment of a Puerto Rican business association as an entity while refusing to treat as an entity its virtually identical stateside counterpart, is justified neither by our precedents nor by historical and commercial realities.

For the foregoing reasons, I respectfully dissent.[22]

[22. See the case on remand, 904 F.2d 5 (5th Cir.1990).

Grupo Dataflux v. Atlas Global Group, L.P.

Supreme Court of the United States, 2004.
541 U.S. 567, 124 S.Ct. 1920, 158 L.Ed.2d 866.

■ JUSTICE SCALIA delivered the opinion of the Court.

This case presents the question whether a party's post-filing change in citizenship can cure a lack of subject-matter jurisdiction that existed at the time of filing in an action premised upon diversity of citizenship. See 28 U.S.C. § 1332.

I

Respondent Atlas Global Group, L.P., is a limited partnership created under Texas law. In November 1997, Atlas filed a state-law suit against petitioner Grupo Dataflux, a Mexican corporation, in the United States District Court for the Southern District of Texas. The complaint contained claims for breach of contract and *in quantum meruit,* seeking over $1.3 million in damages. It alleged that "[f]ederal jurisdiction is proper based upon diversity jurisdiction pursuant to 28 U.S.C. § 1332(a), as this suit is between a Texas citizen [Atlas] and a citizen or subject of Mexico [Grupo Dataflux]." Pretrial motions and discovery consumed almost three years. In October 2000, the parties consented to a jury trial presided over by a

---

See Comment, Carden v. Arkoma Associates: The Citizenship of Limited Partnerships, Associations, and Juridical Entities—A Chilling Future for Diversity Jurisdiction, 27 N.Eng.L.Rev. 505 (1992).

A circuit split has developed regarding the diversity status under *Carden* of individual "names" or investors in insurance syndicates organized by Lloyd's of London. Rejecting the contrary reasoning of the Sixth Circuit in Certain Interested Underwriters at Lloyd's v. Layne, 26 F.3d 39 (6th Cir.1994), the Seventh Circuit has held that each name is a limited partner of the syndicate. Thus, in a suit against a Lloyd's syndicate by an Indiana corporation, the Indiana citizenship of just one of the syndicate's names was sufficient to defeat diversity jurisdiction. Indiana Gas Co. v. Home Ins. Co., 141 F.3d 314 (7th Cir.1998), certiorari denied 525 U.S. 931. The Second and Fifth Circuits have oscillated between these positions, depending on whether the suit is brought by or against a Lloyd's "name" in an individual or in a representative capacity. See Corfield v. Dallas Glen Hills LP, 355 F.3d 853 (5th Cir.2003); E.R. Squibb & Sons, Inc. v. Lloyd's & Cos., 241 F.3d 154 (2d Cir.2001).

The *Carden* rule, by which a partnership is transparent for diversity purposes and has the citizenship status of each member regardless of that partner's "general" or "limited" status, applies as well to a complex, multitiered partnership combining individual and corporate partners in both general and limited capacities at each of three levels. See Cerberus Partners, L.P. v. Gadsby & Hannah, 976 F.Supp. 119 (D.R.I.1997). A limited-liability company created under Michigan law was deemed to have the diversity status of a partnership rather than a corporation in International Flavors & Textures, LLC v. Gardner, 966 F.Supp. 552 (W.D.Mich.1997). Another district court reluctantly reached the same conclusion regarding a limited-liability partnership created under Delaware law. "This Court is particularly troubled that a Big Six accounting firm which operates offices within every state in the United States has effectively immunized itself from the reach of the diversity jurisdiction of the federal courts simply by organizing itself as a limited liability partnership rather than a corporation. Nevertheless, until Congress addresses the jurisdictional implications of this new class of business entities, this Court can reach no other result." Reisman v. KPMG Peat Marwick LLP, 965 F.Supp. 165, 176 (D.Mass.1997).]

Magistrate Judge. On October 27, after a 6–day trial, the jury returned a verdict in favor of Atlas awarding $750,000 in damages.

On November 18, before entry of the judgment, Dataflux filed a motion to dismiss for lack of subject-matter jurisdiction because the parties were not diverse at the time the complaint was filed. See Fed. Rules Civ. Proc. 12(b)(1), (h)(3). The Magistrate Judge granted the motion. The dismissal was based upon the accepted rule that, as a partnership, Atlas is a citizen of each state or foreign country of which any of its partners is a citizen. See Carden v. Arkoma Associates, 494 U.S. 185, 192–195 (1990). Because Atlas had two partners who were Mexican citizens at the time of filing, the partnership was a Mexican citizen. (It was also a citizen of Delaware and Texas based on the citizenship of its other partners.) And because the defendant, Dataflux, was a Mexican corporation, aliens were on both sides of the case, and the requisite diversity was therefore absent. See Mossman v. Higginson, 4 Dall. [4 U.S.] 12, 14 (1800).

On appeal, Atlas did not dispute the finding of no diversity at the time of filing. It urged the Court of Appeals to disregard this failure and reverse dismissal because the Mexican partners had left the partnership in a transaction consummated the month before trial began. Atlas argued that, since diversity existed when the jury rendered its verdict, dismissal was inappropriate. The Fifth Circuit agreed. 312 F.3d 168, 174 (2002). It acknowledged the general rule that, for purposes of determining the existence of diversity jurisdiction, the citizenship of the parties is to be determined with reference to the facts as they existed at the time of filing. Id., at 170. However, relying on our decision in Caterpillar Inc. v. Lewis, 519 U.S. 61 (1996), it held that the conclusiveness of citizenship at the time of filing was subject to exception when the following conditions are satisfied:

> "(1) [A]n action is filed or removed when constitutional and/or statutory jurisdictional requirements are not met, (2) neither the parties nor the judge raise the error until after a jury verdict has been rendered, or a dispositive ruling has been made by the court, and (3) before the verdict is rendered, or ruling is issued, the jurisdictional defect is cured." 312 F.3d, at 174.

The opinion strictly limited the exception as follows: "If at any point prior to the verdict or ruling, the issue is raised, the court must apply the general rule and dismiss regardless of subsequent changes in citizenship." Ibid.

The jurisdictional error in the present case not having been identified until after the jury returned its verdict; and the postfiling change in the composition of the partnership having (in the Court [of Appeal]'s view) cured the jurisdictional defect; the Court [of Appeals] reversed and remanded with instructions to the District Court to enter judgment in favor of Atlas. Ibid. We granted certiorari. 540 U.S. 944 (2003).

II

It has long been the case that "the jurisdiction of the Court depends upon the state of things at the time of the action brought." Mollan v.

Torrance, 9 Wheat. [22 U.S.] 537, 539 (1824). This time-of-filing rule is hornbook law (quite literally[23]) taught to first-year law students in any basic course on federal civil procedure. It measures all challenges to subject-matter jurisdiction premised upon diversity of citizenship against the state of facts that existed at the time of filing—whether the challenge be brought shortly after filing, after the trial, or even for the first time on appeal. (Challenges to subject-matter jurisdiction can of course be raised at any time prior to final judgment. See Capron v. Van Noorden, 2 Cranch [6 U.S.] 126 (1804).)

We have adhered to the time-of-filing rule regardless of the costs it imposes. For example, in Anderson v. Watt, 138 U.S. 694 (1891), two executors of an estate, claiming to be New York citizens, had brought a diversity-based suit in federal court against defendants alleged to be Florida citizens. When it later developed that two of the defendants were New York citizens, the plaintiffs sought to save jurisdiction by revoking the letters testamentary for one executor and alleging that the remaining executor was in fact a British citizen. The Court rejected this attempted postfiling salvage operation, because at the time of filing the executors included a New Yorker. Id., at 708. It dismissed the case for want of jurisdiction, even though the case had been filed about 5 1/2 years earlier, the trial court had entered a decree ordering land to be sold 4 years earlier, the sale had been made, exceptions had been filed and overruled, and the case had come to the Court on appeal from the order confirming the land sale. Id., at 698. Writing for the Court, Chief Justice Fuller adhered to the principle set forth in Conolly v. Taylor, 2 Pet. [27 U.S.] 556, 565 (1829), that "jurisdiction depending on the condition of the party is governed by that condition, as it was at the commencement of the suit." "[J]urisdiction," he reasoned, "could no more be given . . . by the amendment than if a citizen of Florida had sued another in that court and subsequently sought to give it jurisdiction by removing from the State." 138 U.S., at 708.[24]

It is uncontested that application of the time-of-filing rule to this case would require dismissal, but Atlas contends that this Court "should accept the very limited exception created by the Fifth Circuit to the time-of-filing principle." The Fifth Circuit and Atlas rely on our statement in *Caterpillar,* supra, at 75, that "[o]nce a diversity case has been tried in federal court . . . considerations of finality, efficiency, and economy become overwhelming." This statement unquestionably provided the *ratio decidendi* in *Cater-*

---

23. See, *e.g.,* J. Friedenthal, M. Kane, & A. Miller, Civil Procedure 27 (3d ed.1999); C. Wright & M. Kane, Law of Federal Courts 173 (6th ed.2002). See also 13B C. Wright, A. Miller, & E. Cooper, Federal Practice and Procedure § 3608, p. 452 (1984).

24. The dissent asserts that *Anderson* is "not altogether in tune with *Caterpillar* and *Newman–Green,*" but the cases can easily be harmonized. *Anderson* did not, as the dissent suggests, refuse to give diversity-perfecting effect to the dismissal of an independent severable party; it refused to give that effect to the alteration of a coexecutorship into a lone executorship—much as we decline to give diversity-perfecting effect to the alteration of a partnership with diversity-destroying partners into a partnership without diversity-destroying partners.

pillar, but it did not augur a new approach to deciding whether a jurisdictional defect has been cured.

Caterpillar broke no new ground, because the jurisdictional defect it addressed had been cured by the dismissal of the party that had destroyed diversity. That method of curing a jurisdictional defect had long been an exception to the time-of-filing rule. "[T]he question always is, or should be, when objection is taken to the jurisdiction of the court by reason of the citizenship of some of the parties, whether . . . they are indispensable parties, for if their interests are severable and a decree without prejudice to their rights may be made, the jurisdiction of the court should be retained and the suit dismissed as to them." Horn v. Lockhart, 17 Wall. [84 U.S.] 570, 579 (1873). Federal Rule of Civil Procedure 21 provides that "[p]arties may be dropped or added by order of the court on motion of any party or of its own initiative at any stage of the action and on such terms as are just." By now, "it is well settled that Rule 21 invests district courts with authority to allow a dispensable nondiverse party to be dropped at any time, even after judgment has been rendered." Newman–Green, Inc. v. Alfonzo–Larrain, 490 U.S. 826, 832 (1989). Indeed, the Court held in *Newman–Green* that courts of appeals also have the authority to cure a jurisdictional defect by dismissing a dispensable nondiverse party. Id., at 837.

Caterpillar involved an unremarkable application of this established exception. Complete diversity had been lacking at the time of removal to federal court, because one of the plaintiffs shared Kentucky citizenship with one of the defendants. Almost three years after the District Court denied a motion to remand, but before trial, the diversity-destroying defendant settled out of the case and was dismissed. The case proceeded to a 6–day jury trial, resulting in judgment for the defendant, Caterpillar, against Lewis. This Court unanimously held that the lack of complete diversity at the time of removal did not require dismissal of the case.

The sum of *Caterpillar*'s jurisdictional analysis was an approving acknowledgment of Lewis's admission that there was "complete diversity, and therefore federal subject-matter jurisdiction, at the time of trial and judgment." 519 U.S., at 73. The failure to explain *why* this solved the problem was not an oversight, because there was nothing novel to explain. The postsettlement dismissal of the diversity-destroying defendant cured the jurisdictional defect just as the dismissal of the diversity-destroying party had done in *Newman–Green*. In both cases, the less-than-complete diversity which had subsisted throughout the action had been converted to complete diversity between the remaining parties to the final judgment. See also *Horn,* supra, at 579.

While recognizing that *Caterpillar* is "technically" distinguishable because the defect was cured by the dismissal of a diversity-destroying party, the Fifth Circuit reasoned that "this factor was not at the heart of the Supreme Court's analysis . . . ." 312 F.3d, at 172–173. The crux of the analysis, according to the Fifth Circuit, was *Caterpillar's* statement that "[o]nce a diversity case has been tried in federal court . . . considerations of finality, efficiency, and economy become overwhelming." 519 U.S., at 75. This was indeed the crux of analysis in *Caterpillar,* but analysis of a different issue. It related not to cure of the *jurisdictional* defect, but to cure of a *statutory* defect, namely failure to comply with the requirement of the removal statute, 28 U.S.C. § 1441(a), that there be complete diversity at the time of removal.[25] The argument to which the statement was directed took as its *starting point* that subject-matter jurisdiction had been satisfied: "ultimate satisfaction of the subject-matter jurisdiction requirement ought not swallow up antecedent *statutory* violations." 519 U.S., at 74 (emphasis added). The resulting holding of *Caterpillar,* therefore, is only that a statutory defect—"Caterpillar's failure to meet the § 1441(a) requirement that the case be fit for federal adjudication at the time the removal petition is filed" id., at 73—did not require dismissal once there was no longer any jurisdictional defect.

III

To our knowledge, the Court has never approved a deviation from the rule articulated by Chief Justice Marshall in 1829 that "[w]here there is *no* change of party, a jurisdiction depending on the condition of the party is governed by that condition, as it was at the commencement of the suit." *Conolly,* 2 Pet., at 556 (emphasis added). Unless the Court is to manufacture a brand-new exception to the time-of-filing rule, dismissal for lack of subject-matter jurisdiction is the only option available in this case. The purported cure arose not from a change in the parties to the action, but from a change in the citizenship of a continuing party. Withdrawal of the Mexican partners from Atlas did not change the fact that Atlas, the single artificial entity created under Texas law, remained a party to the action. True, the composition of the partnership, and consequently its citizenship, changed. But allowing a citizenship change to cure the jurisdictional defect that existed at the time of filing would contravene the principle articulated by Chief Justice Marshall in *Conolly.*[26] We decline to do today what the Court has refused to do for the past 175 years.

---

25.   28 U.S.C. § 1441(a) provides, in relevant part:

"Except as otherwise expressly provided by Act of Congress, any civil action brought in a State court of which the district courts of the United States have original jurisdiction, may be removed by the defendant or the defendants, to the district court of the United States for the district and division embracing the place where such action is pending."

26.   The dissent acknowledges that "[t]he Court has long applied [Chief Justice] Marshall's time-of-filing rule categorically to post-filing changes that otherwise would *destroy* diversity jurisdiction," but asserts that "[i]n contrast, the Court has not adhered to a similarly steady rule for post-filing changes in the party line-up, alterations that *perfect* previously defective statutory subject-matter jurisdiction." The authorities relied upon by the dissent do not call into question the particular aspect of the time-of-filing rule that is at issue in this case—the principle (quoted in text) that "[w]here there is *no* change of party, a jurisdiction depending on the condition of the party is governed by that condition, as it was at the commencement of the suit." *Conolly,* 2 Pet., at 556 (emphasis added). The dissent identifies five cases in which the Court permitted a postfiling change to cure a jurisdictional defect. Every one of them involved a *change of party.* The dissent does not identify a single case in which the

Apart from breaking with our longstanding precedent, holding that "finality, efficiency, and judicial economy" can justify suspension of the time-of-filing rule would create an exception of indeterminate scope. The Court of Appeals sought to cabin the exception with the statement that "[i]f at any point prior to the verdict or ruling, the [absence of diversity at the time of filing] is raised, the court must apply the general rule and dismiss regardless of subsequent changes in citizenship." 312 F.3d, at 174. This limitation is unsound in principle and certain to be ignored in practice.

It is unsound in principle because there is no basis in reason or logic to dismiss preverdict if in fact the change in citizenship has eliminated the jurisdictional defect. Either the court has jurisdiction at the time the defect is identified (because the parties are diverse at that time) or it does not (because the postfiling citizenship change is irrelevant). If the former, then dismissal is inappropriate; if the latter, then retention of jurisdiction postverdict is inappropriate.

Only two escapes from this dilemma come to mind, neither of which is satisfactory. First, one might say that it is not *any* change in party citizenship that cures the jurisdictional defect, but only a change that remains unnoticed until the end of trial. That is not so much a logical explanation as a restatement of the illogic that produces the dilemma. There is no conceivable reason why the jurisdictional deficiency which continues despite the citizenship change should suddenly disappear upon the rendering of a verdict. Second, one might say that there never was a cure, but that the party who failed to object before the end of trial forfeited his objection. This is logical enough, but comes up against the established principle, reaffirmed earlier this Term, that "a court's subject-matter jurisdiction cannot be expanded to account for the parties' litigation conduct." Kontrick v. Ryan, 540 U.S. 443, 456 (2004). "A litigant generally may raise a court's lack of subject-matter jurisdiction at any time in the same civil action, even initially at the highest appellate instance." Id., at 455. Because the Fifth Circuit's attempted limitation upon its new exception makes a casualty either of logic or of this Court's jurisprudence, there is no principled way to defend it.

And principled or not, the Fifth Circuit's artificial limitation is sure to be discarded in practice. Only 8% of diversity cases concluded in 2003 actually went to trial, and the median time from filing to trial disposition was nearly two years. See Administrative Office of the United States Courts, Statistics on Diversity Filings and Terminations in District Courts for Calendar Year 2003 (on file with the Clerk of Court). In such a litigation environment, an approach to jurisdiction that focuses on efficiency and judicial economy cannot possibly be held to the line drawn by the Court of Appeals. As Judge Garza observed in his dissent:

Court held that a single party's postfiling change of citizenship cured a previously existing jurisdictional defect.

"[T]here is no difference in efficiency terms between the jury verdict and, for example, the moment at which the jury retires. Nor, for that matter, is there a large difference between the verdict and mid-way through the trial.... Indeed, in complicated cases requiring a great deal of discovery, the parties and the court often expend tremendous resources long before the case goes to trial." 312 F.3d, at 177.

IV

The dissenting opinion rests on two principal propositions: (1) the jurisdictional defect in this case was cured by a change in the composition of the partnership; and (2) refusing to recognize an exception to the time-of-filing rule in this case wastes judicial resources, while creating an exception does not. We discuss each in turn.

A

Unlike the dissent, our opinion does not turn on whether the jurisdictional defect here contained at least "minimal diversity." [27] Regardless of how one characterizes the acknowledged jurisdictional defect, it was never cured. The only two ways in which one could conclude that it had been cured would be either (1) to acknowledge that a party's postfiling change of citizenship *can* cure a time-of-filing jurisdictional defect, or (2) to treat a change in the composition of a partnership like a change in the parties to the action. The Court has never, to our knowledge, done the former; and not even the dissent suggests that it ought to do so in this case.[28] The dissent diverges from our analysis by adopting the latter approach, stating that "this case seems ... indistinguishable from one in which there is a change in the parties to the action."

---

27. The answer to the "minimal diversity" question is not as straightforward as the dissent's analysis suggests. We understand "minimal diversity" to mean the existence of at least *one* party who is diverse in citizenship from one party on the other side of the case, even though the extraconstitutional "complete diversity" required by our cases is lacking. It is possible, though far from clear, that one can have opposing parties in a two-party case who are co-citizens, and yet have minimal Article III jurisdiction because of the multiple citizenship of one of the parties. Although the Court has previously said that minimal diversity requires "two adverse parties [who] are not co-citizens," State Farm Fire & Casualty Co. v. Tashire, 386 U.S. 523, 531 (1967), the Court did not have before it a multiple-citizenship situation.

The dissent contends that the existence of minimal diversity was clear because the rule of Carden v. Arkoma Associates, 494 U.S. 185 (1990), is not required by the Constitution. But neither is the rule that a corporation is "a citizen of any State by which it has been incorporated and of the State where it has its principal place of business." 28 U.S.C. § 1332(c)(1). We do not understand the inquiry into minimal diversity to proceed by hypothetically rewriting, to whatever the Constitution might allow that would support Article III jurisdiction in the particular case, all laws bearing upon the diversity question. Whether the Constitution requires it or not, *Carden* is the subconstitutional rule by which we determine the citizenship of a partnership—and in this case it leads to the conclusion that there were *no* opposing parties who were not co-citizens.

28. The dissent appears to leave open the possibility that this line could be crossed in a future case, contrasting Caterpillar Inc. v. Lewis, 519 U.S. 61 (1996), not with all cases involving a party's change of citizenship, but with the polar extreme of "a plaintiff who moves to another State to create diversity not even minimally present when the complaint was filed."

This equation of a dropped partner with a dropped party is flatly inconsistent with *Carden*. The dissent in *Carden* sought to apply a "real party to the controversy" approach to determine which partners counted for purposes of jurisdictional analysis. The *Carden* majority rejected that approach, reasoning that "[t]he question presented today is not which of various parties before the Court should be considered for purposes of determining whether there is complete diversity of citizenship.... There are *not* ... multiple respondents before the Court, but only *one*: the artificial entity called Arkoma Associates, a limited partnership." 494 U.S., at 188, n. 1. Today's dissent counters that "[w]hile a partnership may be characterized as a single artificial entity, a district court determining whether diversity jurisdiction exists looks to the citizenship of the several persons composing [the entity]." It is true that the court "looks to" the citizenship of the several persons composing the entity, but it does so for the purpose of determining the citizenship of the entity that is a party, not to determine which citizens who compose the entity are to be treated as parties. See *Carden*, 494 U.S., at 188, n. 1 ("[W]hat we must decide is the ... question of how the citizenship of that single artificial entity is to be determined"); id., at 195 ("[W]e reject the contention that to determine, for diversity purposes, the citizenship of an artificial entity, the court may consult the citizenship of less than all of the entity's members").[29]

There was from the beginning of this action a single plaintiff (Atlas), which, under *Carden*, was not diverse from the sole defendant (Dataflux). Thus, this case fails to present "two adverse parties [who] are not co-citizens." State Farm Fire & Casualty Co. v. Tashire, 386 U.S. 523, 531 (1967). Contrary to the dissent's characterization, then, this is not a case like *Caterpillar* or *Newman–Green* in which "party line-up changes ... simply trimmed the litigation down to an ever present core that met the statutory requirement." Rather, this is a case in which a single party changed its citizenship by changing its internal composition.

The incompatibility with prior law of the dissent's attempt to treat a change in partners like a change in parties is revealed by a curious anomaly: It would produce a case unlike every other case in which dropping a party has cured a jurisdictional defect, in that no judicial action (such as granting a motion to dismiss) was necessary to get the jurisdictional spoilers out of the case. Indeed, judicial action to that end was not even *possible:* The court could hardly have "dismissed" the partners from the partnership to save jurisdiction.[30]

---

29. These statements from *Carden* rebut the dissent's assertion that "an association whose citizenship, for diversity purposes, is determined by aggregating the citizenships of each of its members" could "[w]ith equal plausibility ... be characterized as an 'aggregation' composed of its members, or an 'entity' comprising its members." We think it evident that *Carden* decisively adopted an understanding of the limited partnership as an "entity," rather than an "aggregation," for purposes of diversity jurisdiction. See 494 U.S., at 188, n. 1.

30. An additional anomaly, under the particular facts of the present case, is that the two individual Mexican partners, whom the dissent treats *like parties* for purposes of enabling

B

We now turn from consideration of the conceptual difficulties with the dissent's disposition to consideration of its practical consequences. The time-of-filing rule is what it is precisely because the facts determining jurisdiction are subject to change, and because constant litigation in response to that change would be wasteful. The dissent would have it that the time-of-filing rule applies to establish that a court has jurisdiction (and to protect that jurisdiction from later destruction), but does *not* apply to establish that a court lacks jurisdiction (and to prevent post-filing changes that perfect jurisdiction). But whether destruction or perfection of jurisdiction is at issue, the policy goal of minimizing litigation over jurisdiction is thwarted whenever a new exception to the time-of-filing rule is announced, arousing hopes of further new exceptions in the future. Cf. Dretke v. Haley, 541 U.S. 386, 395–396 (2004) (recognizing that the creation of exceptions to judge-made procedural rules will enmesh the federal courts in litigation testing the boundaries of each new exception). That litigation-fostering effect would be particularly strong for a new exception derived from such an expandable concept as the "efficiency" rationale relied upon by the dissent.

The dissent argues that it is essential to uphold jurisdiction in this and similar cases because dismissal followed by refiling condemns the parties to "an almost certain replay of the case, with, in all likelihood, the same ultimate outcome." But if the parties expect "the same ultimate outcome," they will not waste time and resources slogging through a new trial. They will settle, with the jury's prior verdict supplying a range for the award. Indeed, settlement instead of retrial will probably occur even if the parties do *not* expect the same ultimate outcome. When the stakes remain the same and the players have been shown each other's cards, they will not likely play the hand all the way through just for the sake of the game. And finally, even if the parties run the case through complete "relitigation in the very same District Court in which it was first filed in 1997," the "waste" will not be great. Having been through three years of discovery and pretrial motions in the current case, the parties would most likely proceed promptly to trial.

Looked at in its overall effect, and not merely in its application to the sunk costs of the present case, it is the dissent's proposed rule that is wasteful. Absent uncertainty about jurisdiction (which the dissent's readiness to change settled law would preserve for the future), the obvious course, for a litigant whose suit was dismissed as Atlas's was, would have been immediately to file a new action. That is in fact what Atlas did, though it later dismissed the new case without prejudice. Had that second suit been pursued instead of this one, there is little doubt that the dispute

---

their withdrawal to perfect jurisdiction, were brought into the litigation personally by the court's granting of Dataflux's motion to add them as parties for purposes of Dataflux's counterclaim. The motion was made and granted under Federal Rule of Civil Procedure 13(h), which applies only to "[p]ersons *other than* those made parties to the original action." (Emphasis added.)

would have been resolved on the merits by now. Putting aside the time that has passed between the Fifth Circuit's decision and today, there were two years of wasted time between dismissal of the action and the Fifth Circuit's reversal of that dismissal—time that the parties could have spent litigating the merits (or engaging in serious settlement talks) instead of litigating jurisdiction.

Atlas and Dataflux have thus far litigated this case for more than 6½ years, including 3½ years over a conceded jurisdictional defect. Compared with the *one month* it took the Magistrate Judge to apply the time-of-filing rule and *Carden* when the jurisdictional problem was brought to her attention, this waste counsels strongly against any course that would impair the certainty of our jurisdictional rules and thereby encourage similar jurisdictional litigation.

* * *

We decline to endorse a new exception to a time-of-filing rule that has a pedigree of almost two centuries. Uncertainty regarding the question of jurisdiction is particularly undesirable, and collateral litigation on the point particularly wasteful. The stability provided by our time-tested rule weighs heavily against the approval of any new deviation. The judgment of the Fifth Circuit is reversed.

It is so ordered.

■ JUSTICE GINSBURG, with whom JUSTICE STEVENS, JUSTICE SOUTER, and JUSTICE BREYER join, dissenting.

When this lawsuit was filed in the United States District Court for the Southern District of Texas in 1997, diversity of citizenship was incomplete among the adverse parties: The plaintiff partnership, Atlas Global Group (Atlas), had five members, including a general partner of Delaware citizenship and two limited partners of Mexican citizenship; the defendant, Grupo Dataflux (Dataflux), was a Mexican corporation with its principal place of business in Mexico. In a transaction completed in September 2000 unrelated to this lawsuit, all Mexican-citizen partners withdrew from Atlas. Thus, before trial commenced in October 2000, complete diversity existed. Only after the jury returned a verdict favorable to Atlas did Dataflux, by moving to dismiss the case, draw the initial jurisdictional flaw to the District Court's attention. The Court today holds that the initial flaw "still burden[s] and run[s] with the case," Caterpillar Inc. v. Lewis, 519 U.S. 61, 70 (1996); consequently, the entire trial and jury verdict must be nullified. In my view, the initial defect here—the original absence of complete diversity—"is not fatal to the ensuing adjudication." *Caterpillar,* 519 U.S., at 64. In accord with the Court of Appeals for the Fifth Circuit, I would leave intact the results of the six-day trial between completely diverse citizens, and would not expose Atlas and the courts to the "exorbitant cost" of relitigation.

. . . . .

Caterpillar and *Newman–Green* [, Inc. v. Alfonzo–Larrain, 490 U.S. 826 (1989),] are indeed the decisions most closely on point. In *Caterpillar,* plaintiff Lewis, a Kentucky citizen, filed a civil action in state court against two corporate defendants—Caterpillar Inc., a citizen of both Delaware and Illinois, and Whayne Supply Company, a Kentucky citizen. 519 U.S., at 64–65. Several months later, Liberty Mutual, a Massachusetts corporation, intervened as a plaintiff, asserting claims against both defendants. Id., at 65. After Lewis settled with Whayne Supply, Caterpillar filed a notice of removal. Ibid. Lewis moved to remand the case to the state court on the ground that Liberty Mutual had not settled its claim against Whayne Supply, and that Whayne Supply's continuing presence as a defendant in the lawsuit defeated complete diversity. Id., at 65–66. The District Court denied Lewis' motion to remand. Id., at 66. Liberty Mutual and Whayne Supply subsequently settled, and the District Court dismissed Whayne Supply from the suit. Ibid.

The case proceeded to a jury trial, which yielded a verdict and corresponding judgment for Caterpillar. Id., at 66–67. On appeal to the Court of Appeals for the Sixth Circuit, Lewis prevailed. Id., at 67. Observing that, at the time of removal, diversity was incomplete, the appellate court accepted Lewis' argument that dismissal of the case for want of subject-matter jurisdiction was obligatory. Ibid. In turn, this Court reversed the Court of Appeals' judgment: "[A] district court's error in failing to remand a case improperly removed," this Court held unanimously, "is not fatal to the ensuing adjudication if federal jurisdictional requirements are met at the time judgment is entered." Id., at 64.

Newman–Green concerned a state-law action filed in Federal District Court by an Illinois corporation against a Venezuelan corporation, four Venezuelan citizens, and a United States citizen domiciled in Venezuela. 490 U.S., at 828. After the District Court granted partial summary judgment for the defendants, the plaintiff appealed. Ibid. *Sua sponte*, the Court of Appeals for the Seventh Circuit inquired into the basis for federal jurisdiction over the case, and concluded that the presence of the Venezuela-domiciled United States citizen spoiled complete diversity. Id., at 828–829.[31] To cure the defect, the three-judge panel granted the plaintiff's motion to drop the nondiverse party, citing Federal Rule of Civil Procedure 21. *Newman–Green,* 490 U.S., at 829.[32] But the full Circuit Court, empan-

---

31. A United States citizen with no domicile in any State ranks as a stateless person for purposes of 28 U.S.C. § 1332(a)(3), providing for suits between "citizens of different States and in which citizens or subjects of a foreign state are additional parties," and § 1332(a)(2), authorizing federal suit when "citizens of a State" sue "citizens or subjects of a foreign state." See *Newman–Green,* 490 U.S., at 828.

[As observed in Swiger v. Allegheny Energy, Inc., 2007 WL 442383 (E.D. Pa., Feb. 7, 2007), this particular anomaly means that when a law firm is organized as a partnership, it cannot be sued in federal court on the basis of diversity when one of the firm's partners is domiciled outside the United States.]

32. Rule 21, governing proceedings in district courts, provides in relevant part: "Parties may be dropped or added by order of the court on motion of any party or of its own initiative at any stage of the action and on such terms as are just."

eled en banc, concluded that an appellate court lacks such authority. Id., at 830–831. This Court reversed that determination. Federal appellate courts, the Court held, "posses[s] the authority to grant motions to dismiss dispensable nondiverse parties." Id., at 836.[33]

As in *Caterpillar* and *Newman–Green,* minimal diversity within Article III's compass existed in this case from the start. See U.S. Const., Art. III, § 2, cl. 1 ("The judicial Power shall extend to all Cases ... between a State, or the Citizens thereof, and foreign States, Citizens or Subjects."); State Farm Fire & Casualty Co. [v. Tashire, 386 U.S. 523, 531 (1967)] ("Article III poses no obstacle to the legislative extension of federal jurisdiction, founded on diversity, so long as any two adverse parties are not co-citizens."). The jurisdictional flaw—in *Caterpillar, Newman–Green,* and this case—was the absence of complete diversity, required by the governing statute, § 1332(a), when the action commenced, a flaw eliminated at a later stage of the proceedings. . . .

It bears clarification why this case, in common with *Caterpillar* and *Newman–Green,* met the constitutional requirement of minimal diversity at the onset of the litigation. True, Atlas' case involves a partnership, while the diversity spoiler in *Caterpillar* was a corporation and in *Newman–Green,* an individual. In Carden v. Arkoma Associates, [494 U.S. 185 (1990),] this Court held that, in determining a partnership's qualification to sue or be sued under § 1332, the citizenship of each partner, whether general or limited, must be attributed to the partnership. See 494 U.S., at 195–196.

Notably, however, the Court did not suggest in *Carden* that minimal diversity, which is adequate for Article III purposes, would be absent when some, but not all, partners composing the "single artificial entity," id., at 188, n. 1, share the opposing party's citizenship. To the contrary, the Court emphasized in *Carden* that Congress could, "by legislation," determine which of the "wide assortment of artificial entities possessing different powers and characteristics ... is entitled to be considered a 'citizen' for diversity purposes, and which of their members' citizenship is to be consulted." Id., at 197. Congress would be disarmed from making such determinations—for example, from legislating that only the citizenship of general partners counts for § 1332 purposes—if Article III itself commanded that each partner's citizenship, limited and general partner's alike, inescapably adheres to the partnership entity. See ibid.; cf. United Steelworkers v. R.H. Bouligny, Inc., 382 U.S. 145, 153 (1965) (assimilating unincorporated labor unions to the status of corporations for diversity purposes, instead of counting each member's citizenship, is a matter "suited to the legislative and not the judicial branch"). Just as Article III did not dictate the *Carden* decision, so the question here is plainly sub-constitutional in character.

. . . . .

---

33. After our decision, the Seventh Circuit dismissed the nondiverse defendant and remanded the case to the District Court. Newman–Green, Inc. v. Alfonzo–Larrain, 734 F.Supp. 1470, 1472 (N.D.Ill.1990).

In short, the Fifth Circuit correctly comprehended the essential teaching of *Caterpillar* and *Newman–Green:* The generally applicable time-of-filing rule is displaced when (1) a "jurisdictional requiremen[t] [is] not met, (2) neither the parties nor the judge raise the error until after a jury verdict has been rendered, or a dispositive ruling [typically, a grant of summary judgment] has been made by the court, and (3) before the verdict is rendered, or [the dispositive] ruling is issued, the jurisdictional defect is cured." 312 F.3d, at 174.[34]

. . . . .

The "considerations of finality, efficiency, and economy" the Court found "overwhelming" in *Caterpillar* and *Newman–Green* have undiluted application here. *Caterpillar,* 519 U.S., at 75; see *Newman–Green,* 490 U.S., at 836–837. See also Friends of Earth, Inc. v. Laidlaw Environmental Services (TOC), Inc., 528 U.S. 167, 191–192 (2000) (noting stricter approach to standing than to mootness in view of "sunk costs" once a "case has been brought and litigated"). In *Newman–Green,* this Court observed that rigid insistence on the time-of-filing rule, rather than allowing elimination of the jurisdictional defect by dropping a dispensable party, would mean an almost certain replay of the case, with, in all likelihood, the same ultimate outcome. 490 U.S., at 837. Similarly here, given the October 2000 jury verdict of $750,000 and the unquestioned current existence of complete diversity, Atlas can be expected "simply [to] refile in the District Court" and rerun the proceedings. See ibid. No legislative prescription, nothing other than this Court's readiness to cut loose a court-made rule from common sense, accounts for waste of this large order.

. . . . .

The Court invokes "175 years" of precedent endorsing a time-of-filing rule that, generally, is altogether sound. On that point, the Court is united. For the class of cases over which we divide—cases involving a post-filing

---

34. According to the majority, it would be "unsound in principle and certain to be ignored in practice" to decline to apply the time-of-filing rule only in those cases where the flaw is drawn to a court's attention after a full adjudication of the case, whether through trial or by a dispositive court ruling. Declining to apply the time-of-filing rule only in those cases, the Court suggests, can be justified only on the theory that "the party who failed to object before the end of trial [or dispositive court ruling] forfeited his objection." Ibid. (citing Kontrick v. Ryan, 540 U.S. 443, 455–456). The time-of-filing rule, however, is a court-created rule; it is therefore incumbent on the Court to define the contours of that rule's application. The Fifth Circuit's decision rested not on a forfeiture theory; rather, the decision accurately reflected the judicial economy underpinnings of the time-of-filing rule. True, as the Court observes, judicial economy concerns might be pressing even when a case is not fully adjudicated through trial or summary pretrial disposition. When a district court has so fully adjudicated the case, however, there can be no doubt that the "sunk costs to the judicial system," Friends of Earth, Inc. v. Laidlaw Environmental Services (TOC), Inc., 528 U.S. 167, 192, n. 5 (2000), have become "overwhelming," Caterpillar Inc. v. Lewis, 519 U.S. 61, 75 (1996). That the rule advanced by the Court of Appeals is underinclusive does not make it "illogic[al]" ; instead, the limitation makes the rule readily manageable. To hold the time-of-filing rule developed by this Court inapplicable here merely abjures mechanical extension of the rule in favor of responding sensibly to the rule's underlying justifications when those justifications are indisputably present.

change in the composition of a multimember association such as a partnership—the Court presents no authority impelling the waste today's judgment approves. Even if precedent could provide a basis for the Court's disposition, rules fashioned by this Court for "the just, speedy, and inexpensive determination [of cases]," Fed. Rule Civ. Proc. 1, should not become immutable at the instant of their initial articulation. Rather, they should remain adjustable in light of experience courts constantly gain in handling the cases that troop before them. See Great–West Life & Annuity Ins. Co. v. Knudson, 534 U.S. 204, 233 (2002) (GINSBURG, J., dissenting); Grupo Mexicano de Desarrollo, S.A. v. Alliance Bond Fund, Inc., 527 U.S. 308, 336–337, and n. 4 (1999) (GINSBURG, J., concurring in part and dissenting in part) (recognizing, in line with contemporary English decisions, dynamic quality of equity jurisprudence in response to evolving social and commercial needs). I would affirm the judgment of the Fifth Circuit, which faithfully and sensibly followed the path the Court marked in *Newman–Green* and *Caterpillar*.

———

Tank v. Chronister

United States Court of Appeals, Tenth Circuit, 1998.
160 F.3d 597

■ Before HENRY, McKAY, and BRISCOE, CIRCUIT JUDGES.

■ BRISCOE, CIRCUIT JUDGE.

. . . . .

I.

Plaintiff filed a wrongful death action in United States District Court for the District of Kansas, asserting defendants' negligent conduct contributed to the death of his mother, Kathleen Tank. Plaintiff is a resident of Wisconsin. Decedent was a resident of Kansas at the time of her death. Her husband and an adult daughter were also Kansas residents at the time of her death and at the time this action was filed. Defendants are residents of Kansas.

Defendants filed a motion to dismiss, asserting complete diversity of jurisdiction was not present because, pursuant to 28 U.S.C. § 1332(c)(2), a wrongful death plaintiff in Kansas is deemed to be a citizen of the same state as the decedent. Section 1332(c)(2) provides in part that "[t]he legal representative of the estate of a decedent shall be deemed to be a citizen of the same State as the decedent." In initially granting defendants' motion to dismiss, the district court concluded "one who brings a wrongful death action under Kansas law is a 'legal representative of a decedent's estate' for purposes of § 1332(c)(2) and is therefore deemed to be a citizen of the same state as the decedent." Appendix I at 124. It logically followed from this determination that complete diversity did not exist as decedent and defendants were all residents of Kansas. However, plaintiff moved for reconsideration and the district court reversed its ruling, holding § 1332(c)(2) did not apply to individuals who are authorized by state statute to pursue—in their individual capacities and not on behalf or for the benefit of decedent's estate—a claim for wrongful death. Thus, the court granted plaintiff's motion for reconsideration and certified its decision for interlocutory appeal pursuant to 28 U.S.C. § 1292(b).

II.

. . . . .

Diversity jurisdiction

In Kansas, there are two separate and distinct actions that may arise out of a person's death caused by another's negligence. A survival action may be brought only by the estate administrator pursuant to Kan. Stat. Ann. § 60–1901, and only for the purpose of recovering damages suffered by the decedent prior to death. See Mason v. Gerin Corp., 231 Kan. 718, 647 P.2d 1340, 1343 (1982). In contrast, a wrongful death action may be brought only by the decedent's heirs-at-law pursuant to Kan. Stat. Ann. § 60–1902, and only for their "exclusive benefit" for damages suffered by them as a result of the wrongful death. See id.; Hembree v. Tinnin, 807 F.Supp. 109, 110 (D.Kan.1992). The claim for wrongful death is brought neither on behalf or for the benefit of the estate, but only on behalf and for the benefit of the heirs. On appeal, defendants contend Congress intended § 1332(c)(2) to apply to all wrongful death actions in which the decedent and defendant were residents of the same state. Plaintiff responds that § 1332(c)(2) does not apply to him because he is not, pursuant to § 60–1902, acting as "the legal representative" of his mother's estate.

Section 1332 was added to the diversity statute as part of the Judicial Improvements Act of 1988. The purpose of the Act was to reduce substantially the diversity jurisdiction of the federal courts. See H.R.Rep. No. 100–889, reprinted in 1988 U.S.C.C.A.N. 5982. Section 1332(c)(2) contributed to this effort by discouraging, in cases involving a decedent's estate, the appointment of out-of-state personal representatives solely for the purpose of creating diversity of citizenship where it would otherwise not exist. See David D. Siegel, Changes in Federal Jurisdiction and Practice Under the New Judicial Improvements and Access to Justice Act, reprinted in 123 F.R.D. 399, 409 (1989). This tactic was most often utilized to gain access to the federal courts where decedent and defendants were residents of the same state. See id. Section 1332(c)(2), which does not define "legal representative of the estate," was premised on the following 1969 proposal of the American Law Institute:

> An executor, administrator, or any person representing the estate of a decedent or appointed pursuant to statute with authority to bring an action for wrongful death is deemed to be a citizen only of the same state as the decedent.... The purpose is to prevent either the creation or destruction of diversity jurisdiction by the appointment of a repre-

sentative of different citizenship from that of the decedent or person represented.

Richard H. Field, Jurisdiction of Federal Courts, reprinted in 46 F.R.D. 141, 143 (1969).

Under the proposal, plaintiff, as a person appointed pursuant to statute with authority to bring a wrongful death action, would be deemed to be a citizen of the same state as decedent. However, Congress did not adopt the ALI proposal wholesale, but instead deleted all references to executors, administrators, and the like in favor of the designation "legal representative of the estate of a decedent." By its plain terms, § 1332(c)(2) is more narrow than the ALI proposal and excludes from its coverage those who are not representing the estate of a decedent, even if the individual is "appointed pursuant to statute with authority to bring an action for wrongful death." Section 1332(c)(2) therefore is not triggered, as defendants suggest, by the fact that under Kansas law a wrongful death plaintiff acts in a "representative capacity." Although the named plaintiff does serve as a representative, the plaintiff represents only the other heirs and not the estate itself. See Kan. Stat. Ann. § 60–1902 ("The action shall be for the exclusive benefit of all of the heirs who ha[ve] sustained a loss regardless [of] whether they all join or intervene therein."). Defendants' proposed interpretation ignores that part of § 1332(c)(2) requiring that representation be on behalf "of the estate of a decedent."

We decline defendants' invitation to ignore the plain statutory language and assume Congress "merely substituted the single term 'legal representative' for the ALI's enumerated fiduciaries." Green v. Lake of the Woods County, 815 F.Supp. 305, 308 (D.Minn.1993). There is no basis either in the text of the statute or in the limited legislative history to support that conclusion. See H.R.Rep. No. 100–889 (making no reference to or comment upon addition of subsection (c)(2)). In the absence of such evidence, we will not speculate that Congress meant what it did not say. See [F.D.I.C. v.] Canfield, 967 F.2d [443, 445 (10th Cir.1992)] (" 'Absent a clearly expressed legislative intent to the contrary, [the plain language of a law] must ordinarily be regarded as conclusive.' ") (quoting Kaiser Aluminum & Chem. Corp. v. Bonjorno, 494 U.S. 827, 835 (1990)).[40]

We also find inapposite James v. Three Notch Medical Center, 966 F.Supp. 1112 (M.D.Ala.1997), and Liu v. Westchester County Medical Center, 837 F.Supp. 82 (S.D.N.Y.1993). In both cases, the plaintiffs were proceeding under statutory schemes significantly different from § 60–1902. The wrongful death statutes in those cases involved court or statutory appointment of an individual, not necessarily a person related to the decedent, to represent the *estate* in a wrongful death action. Thus, although the claims were brought for the exclusive benefit of the heirs as opposed to the estate, they nonetheless were brought on *behalf* of the estate. See

---

40. It bears mention that had Congress so desired, it could have eliminated federal court jurisdiction in all wrongful death cases except where the decedent and defendant were diverse.

James, 966 F.Supp., at 1114 ("right to bring a wrongful death action is vested only in the person who has been appointed to represent the decedent's estate, not a person acting on behalf of one or all of the distributees"); *Liu*, 837 F.Supp., at 83.

The decision in Milam v. State Farm Mutual Auto. Ins. Co., 972 F.2d 166 (7th Cir.1992), is more persuasive authority in these circumstances. There, the wife of a motorist killed in a traffic accident brought suit against the defendant insurance company. The decedent and the insurer both were citizens of Illinois; at the time of suit, plaintiff was a citizen of Louisiana. On appeal, the court raised sua sponte the issue of diversity jurisdiction, specifically citing § 1332(c)(2). Although that provision was not in effect when plaintiff filed her suit, it nonetheless was embodied in preexisting Seventh Circuit law. The court upheld the exercise of jurisdiction, based on what it described as "an oddity of Louisiana law." Id., at 168. As the court explained:

> Louisiana apparently does not regard a decedent's estate as an entity on behalf of which a lawsuit can be brought. So [plaintiff] brought this suit not as the legal representative of her husband's estate but in her own behalf and as the guardian of her children.... [S]he is not suing as a representative of her husband's estate, and therefore the main objection to basing diversity jurisdiction on the representative's own citizenship—that it facilitates spurious invocations of the diversity jurisdiction (the estate of a state resident could sue another state resident in federal court by appointing a nonresident executor)—is absent.

Id., at 168. This reasoning is equally applicable here: An "oddity" of Kansas law precludes a wrongful death suit from being pursued by or on behalf of the estate. Hence, any such suit is not within the ambit of § 1332(c)(2). Compare *James*, 966 F.Supp., at 1114 (distinguishing *Milam* based on differences in Louisiana statute and statute at issue); and *Liu*, 837 F.Supp., at 84 n. 3 (same), with Marler v. Hiebert, 960 F.Supp. 253 (D.Kan.1997) (under Kansas law a wrongful death plaintiff is not the "legal representative of the estate of a decedent" under § 1332(c)(2)).

Our decision is bolstered significantly by the ALI's own explanatory comment to its proposal suggesting decedent's citizenship is not adopted when the plaintiff is not randomly appointed by the court or pursuant to statute, but is of a designated relationship to the decedent which by statute is given a right to sue in his or her own name because of decedent's death:

> The phrasing "any person representing the estate of a decedent or appointed pursuant to statute with authority to bring an action because of the death of a decedent" is couched so as to include any person, regardless of the form of statutory designation, who is appointed with authority to bring an action for wrongful death. *It does not include a person given by statute a right to bring an action in his own name because of a decedent's death by reason of his relationship to the decedent (e.g., a widow or child of the decedent); such a person retains such right of access to a federal court as his own citizenship gives him.*

The imposition upon diversity jurisdiction has been the appointment of out-of-staters to create diversity, and there seems no sufficient reason to cover a person whose right to sue is because of his relationship rather than by appointment.

American Law Institute, Study of the Division of Jurisdiction between State and Federal Courts at 118 (1968) (emphasis added). The facts here fall squarely within this exception. A Kansas statute grants plaintiff, by virtue of his relationship to the decedent, the right to sue for wrongful death, and the plaintiff, by virtue of his independent citizenship status, is diverse from the defendant. See *Marler*, 960 F.Supp., at 254 (citing above comment in finding § 1332(c)(2) did not preclude Alabama citizen and heir-at-law of Kansas decedent from suing a Kansas defendant for wrongful death in federal district court). This interpretation gives effect to all of the provisions and comments embodied in the ALI proposal but does not dilute the effectiveness of § 1332(c)(2) as a deterrent to forum shopping. Indeed, subsection (c)(2) still accomplishes its primary goal—to discourage the random appointment of unrelated out-of-state legal or personal representatives either by the court or pursuant to statute where the representative is not of a specified relationship to the decedent.

Defendants note a majority of states require that wrongful death claims be brought by an appointed personal representative of the estate, even though the estate is not the beneficiary of any recovery. Defendants complain in those states § 1332 would sweep broader than in the small minority of states like Kansas where the estate does not, indeed cannot, bring the wrongful death claim. Defendants' argument is not without merit, but it exaggerates the extent of the problem, at least in Kansas where the wrongful death claimant is required by § 60–1902 to be an heir-at-law who brings the action for the exclusive benefit of all of the heirs who have sustained a loss by reason of the death. See Carter v. City of Emporia, 543 F.Supp. 354, 357 (D.Kan.1982) (construing "the term 'heirs at law' to be synonymous with the term 'heirs' as construed under the Kansas intestate succession statutes") (citing Johnson v. McArthur, 226 Kan. 128, 596 P.2d 148 (1979)). In states where access is denied, claimant is bringing the action on behalf of the estate and is more likely unknown and unrelated to decedent. Only in this latter scenario of the unrelated claimant is forum shopping a legitimate concern.

We hold that an individual bringing a wrongful death action under Kan. Stat. Ann. § 60–1902 is not the "legal representative of the estate of a decedent" under § 1332(c)(2), and is therefore not deemed to be a resident of the same state as the decedent for diversity of jurisdiction purposes.

Collusion

Defendants alternatively contend any heir-at-law who brings a wrongful death action in which that heir is diverse from the defendant should per se be considered to have improperly or collusively invoked diversity jurisdiction if other heirs-at-law are not diverse from the defendant. As previously stated, there were other heirs-at-law here who were Kansas residents.

"A district court shall not have jurisdiction of a civil action in which any party, by assignment or otherwise, has been improperly or collusively made or joined to invoke the jurisdiction of such court." 28 U.S.C. § 1359. Before enactment of § 1332(c)(2), numerous courts employed § 1359 to deter forum shopping in survival and wrongful death actions. See *Green*, 815 F.Supp., at 307–08. In fact, it was the inability of the various circuits to agree on a single test under § 1359 that led to the ALI proposal and the eventual enactment of § 1332(c)(2). See id. It is thus debatable whether the exercise of jurisdiction, once found to be proper under § 1332(c)(2), should be further scrutinized under § 1359.

Even if a § 1359 analysis is appropriate, defendants' arguments fail under prevailing Tenth Circuit law. In Hackney v. Newman Mem'l Hosp., Inc., 621 F.2d 1069, 1071 (10th Cir.1980), we held a party with a "real, substantive stake in the litigation" may not be the subject of a § 1359 jurisdictional challenge, "even if [the plaintiff] was appointed . . . simply to obtain diversity jurisdiction." . . . .

The reasoning of *Hackney* applies here. Tank has a real, beneficial interest in the lawsuit and, as one of decedent's heirs, is entitled to a share of any eventual recovery. It is therefore irrelevant that a local, non-diverse heir might more easily or logically serve as plaintiff. See Martinez v. United States Olympic Committee, 802 F.2d 1275, 1279 (10th Cir.1986) (holding inquiry into motive of appointment is necessary only if appointee has no personal economic stake in litigation).

AFFIRMED.

United States Fidelity and Guaranty Co. v. A & S Manufacturing Co.

United States Court of Appeals, Fourth Circuit, 1995.
48 F.3d 131.

■ Before Russell and Michael, Circuit Judges, and Butzner, Senior Circuit Judge.

■ Butzner, Senior Circuit Judge:

United States Fidelity and Guaranty Company (USF & G) appeals the district court's order realigning the parties and dismissing this action for lack of diversity. USF & G contends that the court applied the incorrect standard in deciding whether realignment of the parties was appropriate. In the alternative, USF & G argues that even if the court used the correct standard, the court improperly applied it. Affirming, we conclude that the district court properly selected and applied the "principal purpose" test, which is derived from Indianapolis v. Chase Nat'l Bank, 314 U.S. 63 (1941).

I

From 1972 to 1989, A & S Manufacturing Co. separately contracted with USF & G, Federal Insurance Company, and Hartford Accident and

Indemnity Company for primary liability insurance. Environmental contamination allegedly occurred at A & S sites covered by these contracts. The Environmental Protection Agency has sued A & S to recover costs for responding to the contamination. A & S called upon the three insurers for defense and indemnity.

USF & G filed this action against A & S, Federal, and Hartford. USF & G sought a declaration of the parties' rights and duties as they relate to A & S's claims for insurance coverage for environmental liabilities. Each insurer denies liability to A & S. Each also contends that if it were liable, one or both of the other insurers would be liable to it for reimbursement under various theories. As aligned in USF & G's complaint, complete diversity existed and the district court had jurisdiction pursuant to 28 U.S.C. § 1332.

One month later, A & S filed a virtually identical declaratory judgment action against USF & G, Federal, Hartford, and others in a New Jersey state court. A & S then moved to realign the parties in this federal action.

The district court applied the "principal purpose" standard and aligned the three insurers as plaintiffs and A & S as the sole defendant. Both A & S and Federal have their principal place of business in New Jersey. This identity of citizenship after realignment destroyed complete diversity, and the district court dismissed the action for lack of jurisdiction. United States Fidelity and Guar. Co. v. A & S Mfg. Co., 839 F.Supp. 347 (D.Md.1993).

II

The circuits are currently divided over the appropriate standard for deciding whether to realign. The district court applied the principal purpose test which has been adopted in the Third, Sixth, and Ninth circuits. See United States Fidelity and Guar. Co. v. Thomas Solvent Co., 955 F.2d 1085, 1088–91 (6th Cir.1992); Employers Ins. of Wausau v. Crown Cork & Seal Co., 942 F.2d 862, 864–67 (3d Cir.1991); Continental Airlines, Inc. v. Goodyear Tire & Rubber Co., 819 F.2d 1519, 1523 n. 2 (9th Cir.1987).

USF & G urges this court to join the Second and Seventh Circuits in adopting the substantial controversy test. See Maryland Casualty Co. v. W.R. Grace and Co., 23 F.3d 617, 621–24 (2d Cir.1993); American Motorists Ins. Co. v. Trane Co., 657 F.2d 146, 149–51 (7th Cir.1981). USF & G contends that the Supreme Court, the majority of the circuits, and this court have consistently applied a substantial controversy test in realignment cases. They also maintain that the principal purpose test cannot be reconciled with the language of either Article III or the diversity statute.

Both standards are derived from Indianapolis v. Chase Nat'l Bank, 314 U.S. 63 (1941).[41]

[41. The bank, a New York citizen, was trustee under a mortgage deed securing certain bonds issued by a defunct gas company. When that company became inactive, decades before the present suit, it had leased all of its assets to a competing gas company in exchange for a promise to service the bonds. The lessee itself became inactive when it was later taken over

Indianapolis outlines certain principles that govern realignment:

To sustain diversity jurisdiction there must exist an actual, substantial controversy between citizens of different states, all of whom on one side of the controversy are citizens of different states from all parties on the other side. Diversity jurisdiction cannot be conferred upon the federal courts by the parties' own determination of who are plaintiffs and who defendants. It is our duty, as it is that of the lower federal courts, to look beyond the pleadings and arrange the parties according to their sides in the dispute. Litigation is the pursuit of practical ends, not a game of chess. Whether the necessary collision of interests exists, is therefore not to be determined by mechanical rules. It must be ascertained from the principal purpose of the suit and the primary and controlling matter in dispute.

314 U.S., at 69 (citations and internal quotation marks omitted).

The substantial controversy test asks whether any actual and substantial conflict exists between the opposing parties. If a substantial conflict separates the opposing parties, regardless of whether the conflict is the principal dispute in the case, the court will not realign the parties. See *Maryland Casualty Co.*, 23 F.3d, at 622–23. This approach emphasizes the first sentence of *Indianapolis*'s governing principles, but it cannot be reconciled with the remainder of that opinion. *Indianapolis* specifically requires the district court to ascertain the "collision of interests" from the "principal purpose of the suit, and the primary and controlling matter in dispute" and to "arrange the parties according to their sides in the dispute." 314 U.S., at 69 (citations and internal quotation marks omitted). The requirement that a district court ascertain the "principal purpose of the suit and the primary and controlling matter in dispute" cannot be disregarded as mere surplusage.

Although the Court in *Indianapolis* considered additional controversies raised by the parties opposed to realignment, 314 U.S., at 73 n. 3, this does not validate a substantial controversy approach. The Court's examination of other controversies was simply to identify the principal purpose of the

---

by the city of Indianapolis, which defaulted on the interest owed on the bonds under the terms of the lease. The bank brought an action against both inactive gas companies and the city of Indianapolis, all Indiana citizens, for a determination that the city had succeeded to the obligation of the lessee gas company on the lease and that the lease was valid, and for overdue interest on the bonds. A bare majority of the Court held that in aligning parties it must look to the "primary and controlling matter in dispute," which in the case before it was whether the city was bound by the lease. Since on this issue the lessor gas company was united in interest with the bank, the majority held that the lessor gas company should be realigned as a plaintiff and ordered dismissal for want of jurisdiction. The four dissenters noted that the judgment below did hold the lessor gas company liable for more than a million dollars owed to its bondholders, though it fixed primary liability on the city. They found a real controversy between the bank as trustee and the lessor gas company as to the liability for interest on the bonds issued by that company, and rejected the notion that jurisdiction should turn on whether the court considers one issue to be more "actual" or "substantial" than the other.]

suit. The Court was confirming that the other controversies were not primary in the dispute.

The substantial controversy test allows parties to easily manipulate diversity jurisdiction. In many multiple party suits, some hypothetical adversity between diverse parties can be claimed as giving rise to a substantial controversy. Thus, the substantial controversy test allows diversity jurisdiction in a broad range of cases, limited only by the creative pleading of the plaintiff. The principal purpose standard, in contrast, allows parties to engage a federal forum in a narrower range of situations. This result comports with the mandate that courts carefully confine their diversity jurisdiction to the precise limits that the jurisdictional statute, pursuant to Article III, has defined. See *Crown Cork & Seal Co.*, 942 F.2d, at 867.

. . . . .

III

Application of the principal purpose test entails two steps. First, the court must determine the primary issue in the controversy. Next, the court should align the parties according to their positions with respect to the primary issue. If the alignment differs from that in the complaint, the court must determine whether complete diversity continues to exist.

USF & G asserts that the district court improperly applied the principal purpose test. USF & G claims that the court must look at USF & G's principal purpose for bringing the suit and then determine if the parties are properly aligned with respect to that purpose. It maintains that its principal purpose in bringing the suit was to resolve its obligations and rights with respect to A & S, Federal, and Hartford. It protests that the principal purpose test allows a district court to make arbitrary realignment decisions.

Antagonism between parties should be resolved by the pleadings and the nature of the controversy. Smith v. Sperling, 354 U.S. 91, 97 (1957). The pleadings and the nature of the suit clearly manifest the proper alignment of the dispute. The district court found that the primary issue in the case was whether the insurers owe A & S a duty to defend against the underlying environmental lawsuits and a duty to indemnify for any liability assessed against A & S. The court found that any disputes existing among the insurers regarding contribution are ancillary to the primary issue of the duty to indemnify. It arranged the parties around this primary dispute, placing the insurers as plaintiffs and the insured as the defendant.

Practicalities undergird the district court's reasoning. A court trying the merits of this controversy would first have to decide whether the insurers were under any obligation to defend and indemnify A & S. If none, or only one, provided coverage, the question of the insurers' liability to each other would be moot. Only if two or more were liable to A & S, would the court have to allocate liability and costs.

The district court's findings and conclusions with respect to realignment were proper. The dispute among the insurers is secondary to whether the insurers are liable to A & S and is hypothetical until the insurers' liability is determined. The potentially substantial, though not principal, controversies that USF & G raises are subsumed in the primary issue of the insurers' liability to A & S. The insurers share the primary goal of avoiding obligations to A & S, and the district court properly realigned them as plaintiffs opposite the defendant A & S. The Sixth and Third Circuits have come to similar conclusions under comparable facts. See United States Fidelity & Guar. Co. v. Thomas Solvent Co., 955 F.2d 1085, 1088–91 (6th Cir.1992); Employers Ins. of Wausau v. Crown Cork and Seal Co., 942 F.2d 862, 864–67 (3d Cir.1991). But see Maryland Casualty Co. v. W.R. Grace and Co., 23 F.3d 617, 621–24 (2d Cir.1993); American Motorists Ins. Co. v. Trane Co., 657 F.2d 146, 149–51 (7th Cir.1981).

The dismissal for lack of diversity jurisdiction is affirmed.

AFFIRMED.[42]

Lumbermen's Mutual Casualty Co. v. Elbert

Supreme Court of the United States, 1954.
348 U.S. 48, 75 S.Ct. 151, 99 L.Ed. 59.

■ Mr. CHIEF JUSTICE WARREN delivered the opinion of the Court.

[The Court here held that diversity existed in a suit by a Louisiana citizen under the Louisiana direct action statute against an Illinois insurance company that insured a citizen of Louisiana who allegedly had harmed plaintiff in a Louisiana accident. That particular result was changed by the 1964 amendment of 28 U.S.C. § 1332(c). See note 9 supra. The case is now of interest only because of the opinion of Justice Frankfurter.]

■ MR. JUSTICE FRANKFURTER, concurring.

Not deeming it appropriate now to question Meredith v. City of Winter Haven, 320 U.S. 228, I join the Court's opinion. But our holding results in

---

[42. See Wright & Kane, Federal Courts § 30 (6th ed.2002); Note, Janus Was Not a God of Justice: Realignment of Parties in Diversity Jurisdiction, 68 N.Y.U.L.Rev. 1072 (1993).

In a stockholders' derivative action, where the corporation is alleged to be under control antagonistic to the interests of the stockholders bringing suit, it will be aligned as a defendant for purposes of determining diversity, even though the ultimate interest of the corporation is the same as that of the plaintiffs. Smith v. Sperling, 354 U.S. 91 (1957).

Parties may be realigned, not only to defeat jurisdiction, but also to create jurisdiction. E.g., Bonell v. General Acc. Fire & Life Assur. Corp., 167 F.Supp. 384 (N.D.Cal.1958) (declaratory judgment action by insured against his insurer and person suing insured in tort: tort claimant realigned as plaintiff, since his interest and that of the insured were identical as against insurer, and diversity thus found).

In Reed v. Robilio, 376 F.2d 392 (6th Cir.1967), it was held error to realign an executor as plaintiff in a suit by a beneficiary to obtain relief for the benefit of the estate when the executor opposed the action and asserted affirmative defenses in it.]

such a glaring perversion of the purpose to which the original grant of diversity jurisdiction was directed that it ought not to go without comment, as further proof of the mounting mischief inflicted on the federal judicial system by the unjustifiable continuance of diversity jurisdiction.

The stuff of diversity jurisdiction is state litigation. The availability of federal tribunals for controversies concerning matters which in themselves are outside federal power and exclusively within state authority, is the essence of a jurisdiction solely resting on the fact that a plaintiff and a defendant are citizens of different States. The power of Congress to confer such jurisdiction was based on the desire of the Framers to assure out-of-state litigants courts free from susceptibility to potential local bias. That the supposed justification for this fear was not rooted in weighty experience is attested by the fact that so ardent a nationalist as Marshall gave that proposal of the Philadelphia Convention only tepid support in the Virginia Convention. 3 Elliot's Debates 556 (1891). But in any event, whatever "fears and apprehensions" were entertained by the Framers and ratifiers there was fear that parochial prejudice by the citizens of one State toward those of another, as well as toward aliens, would lead to unjust treatment of citizens of other States and foreign countries.

Such was the reason for enabling a citizen of one State to press a claim or stand on a defense, wholly state-created, against a citizen of another in a federal court of the latter's State. The abuses to which this opportunity was put when, more than a hundred years ago, corporations began their transforming influence on American economic and social life are familiar history. Their classic exposition in Gerard C. Henderson's Position of Foreign Corporations in American Constitutional Law has lost neither its vividness nor force during the intervening decades. The short of the matter is that by resorting to the federal courts the out-of-state corporation sought to gain, and much too frequently did, an advantage as against the local citizen. Instead of protecting out-of-state litigants against discrimination by state courts, the effect of diversity jurisdiction was discrimination against citizens of the State in favor of litigants from without the State.

Diversity jurisdiction aroused opposition from its very inception, but the modern manifestation of these evils through corporate litigation gathered increasing hostility and led to repeated congressional attempts at restriction and eventually of abolition. The proliferation of the doctrine of Swift v. Tyson, 16 Pet. [41 U.S.] 1, brought into lurid light the discriminatory distortions to which diversity jurisdiction could be subverted by judicial sanction of professional astuteness. The growing sense of the injustice of these developments and its serious hurt to the prestige of the federal courts in the exercise of their essential jurisdiction, came to a head with the decision in Black & White Taxicab & Transfer Co. v. Brown & Yellow Taxicab Co., 276 U.S. 518. The federal courts became the target of acrimonious political controversy. In the course of our history this was not the first time that diversity jurisdiction played the federal courts an ill turn. Again and again in the 60's and the 70's and the 80's such a conflict had flared up, but in the earlier periods it was by way of being a conflict between the financial East and the agrarian West. This time President Hoover's Attorney General and Senator George W. Norris of Nebraska united against the disclosed evils of diversity jurisdiction.

Attorney General Mitchell urged on Congress a measure whereby a corporation should be deemed, for diversity purposes, a citizen of any State in which it carries on business "as respect all suits brought within that State between itself and residents thereof and arising out of the business carried on in such State." Hearings before Subcommittee of Senate Committee on the Judiciary on S. 937, S. 939 and S. 3243, 72d Cong., 1st Sess. 4. At the same time, the Senate Judiciary Committee, under the leadership of Chairman Norris, went further. Twice it reported bills for the abolition of diversity jurisdiction. S.Rep. No. 691, 71st Cong., 2d Sess.; S.Rep. No. 530, 72d Cong., 1st Sess. Legislative attempts at correction have thus far failed. But by overruling the doctrine of *Swift v. Tyson*, despite its century-old credentials, this Court uprooted the most noxious weeds that had grown around diversity jurisdiction. What with the increasing permeation of national feeling and the mobility of modern life, little excuse is left for diversity jurisdiction, now that Erie Railroad Co. v. Tompkins, 304 U.S. 64, has put a stop to the unwarranted freedom of federal courts to fashion rules of local law in defiance of local law.

A legal device like that of federal diversity jurisdiction which is inherently, as I believe it to be, not founded in reason, offers constant temptation to new abuses. This case is an instance. Here we have not an out-of-state litigant resorting to a federal court to be sure of obtaining for himself the same treatment which state courts mete out to their own citizens. Here we have a Louisiana citizen resorting to the federal court in Louisiana in order to avoid consequences of the Louisiana law by which every Louisiana citizen is bound when suing another Louisiana citizen. If Florence R. Elbert, the present plaintiff, had to sue the owner of the offending automobile which caused her injury, or if she were suing an insurance company chartered by Louisiana, she would have no choice but to go, like every other Louisiana plaintiff who sues a fellow citizen of Louisiana, to a Louisiana state court and receive the law as administered by the Louisiana courts. But by the fortuitous circumstance that this Louisiana litigant could sue directly an out-of-state insurance company, she can avoid her amenability to Louisiana law. In concrete terms, she can cash in on the law governing jury trials in the federal courts, with its restrictive appellate review of jury verdicts, and escape the rooted jurisprudence of Louisiana law in reviewing jury verdicts. There is, to be sure, a kind of irony for corporate defendants to discover that two can play at the game of working, to use a colloquial term, the perverse potentialities of diversity jurisdiction. . . .

This case, however, stirs anew an issue that cuts deeper than the natural selfishness of litigants to exploit the law's weaknesses. My concern is with the bearing of diversity jurisdiction on the effective functioning of the federal judiciary. . . .

Diversity cases have long constituted a considerable portion of all civil cases filed in the federal courts. For the last ten years the proportion of diversity cases has greatly increased, so that it is safe to say that diversity cases are now taking at least half of the time that the District Courts are devoting to civil cases. (This is the conclusion of the Division of Procedural Studies and Statistics of the Administrative Office of the United States Courts.) The rise in motor-vehicle registration from 32 million in 1940 to 56 million in 1953 has inevitably been reflected in increasing resort to diversity jurisdiction in ordinary negligence suits. The consequences that this entails for the whole federal judicial system—for increase in the business of the District Courts means increase in the business of the Courts of Appeals and a swelling of the petitions for certiorari here—cannot be met by a steady increase in the number of federal judges. The business of courts, particularly of the federal courts, is drastically unlike the business of factories. The function and role of the federal courts and the nature of their judicial process involve impalpable factors, subtle but far-reaching, which cannot be satisfied by enlarging the judicial plant. A recent report of the House Committee on the Judiciary proposed an increase of the required amount in controversy for jurisdiction of the federal courts from $3,000 to $10,000. Referring to the consequences of "a tremendous increase in the number of cases filed," it felt that appointment of additional judges "has done much to alleviate the problem" but recognized that merely multiplying judges is no solution. See H.R.Rep. No. 1506, 82d Cong., 2d Sess. 1. In the farthest reaches of the problem a steady increase in judges does not alleviate; in my judgment, it is bound to depreciate the quality of the federal judiciary and thereby adversely to affect the whole system.

Since diversity jurisdiction is increasingly the biggest source of the civil business of the District Courts, the continuance of that jurisdiction will necessarily involve inflation of the number of the district judges. This in turn will result, by its own Gresham's law, in a depreciation of the judicial currency and the consequent impairment of the prestige and of the efficacy of the federal courts.... Can the state tribunals not yet be trusted to mete out justice to nonresident litigants; should resident litigants not be compelled to trust their own state tribunals? In any event, is it sound public policy to withdraw from the incentives and energies for reforming state tribunals, where such reform is needed, the interests of influential groups who through diversity litigation are now enabled to avoid state courts?

———

REPORT OF THE FEDERAL COURTS STUDY COMMITTEE (April 2, 1990), p. 38

Recommendation 2.B.1.a: Congress should limit federal jurisdiction based on diversity of citizenship to complex multi-state litigation, interpleader, and suits involving aliens. At the least, it should effect changes to curtail the most obvious problems of the current jurisdiction.[43]

[**43.** The Study Committee justifies its recommendation at pages 38–43 of its report. The literature is vast, and is cited in Wright & Kane, Federal Courts § 23 (6th ed.2002).

In 1978 the House of Representatives twice passed bills that would have abolished general diversity jurisdiction, though retaining alienage cases and interpleader actions. The matter never came to a vote in the Senate.

Recommendation 7 of the 1995 Long Range Plan, pp. 29–32, calls for the elimination of diversity "except in actions involving aliens, interpleader actions, and cases in which the petitioner can clearly demonstrate the need for a federal forum. Diversity jurisdiction should also be retained for some consolidated 'mass tort' litigation. . . ." As an alternative the Plan calls for barring in-state plaintiffs from invoking jurisdiction under § 1332(a) and for more rigorous rules about amount in controversy, discussed below in connection with p. 250, n. 1.

See also Report of the New York County Lawyers' Association Committee on the Federal Courts on the Recommendation of the Federal Courts Study Committee to Abolish Diversity Jurisdiction, 158 F.R.D. 185 (1995). This report is critical of proposals to abolish diversity jurisdiction. It supports eliminating the in-state plaintiff and, as now has been done, raising the jurisdictional amount in diversity cases to $75,000.]

CHAPTER IV

JURISDICTIONAL AMOUNT[1]

Vance v. W.A. Vandercook Co.

Supreme Court of the United States, 1898.
170 U.S. 468, 18 S.Ct. 645, 42 L.Ed. 1111.

The appellee, a corporation of the State of California, began this action against the present plaintiffs in error, citizens of the State of South Carolina, averring the alleged wrongful seizure by the defendants Bahr and Scott, at a railroad depot in the city of Charleston, South Carolina, of packages of wines and brandies, the property of the plaintiff. It was averred that at the time of the seizure the liquors were in the custody of a common carrier, under a shipment from San Francisco to the agent of the plaintiff at Charleston, who was to make delivery of each package to a particular

---

[1. See Baker, The History and Tradition of the Amount in Controversy Requirement: A Proposal to "Up the Ante" in Diversity Jurisdiction, 102 F.R.D. 299 (1984); 14A Wright, Miller & Cooper, Federal Practice and Procedure: Jurisdiction 3d §§ 3701–3712 (1998); 15 Moore's Federal Practice ¶¶ 102.100–102.109 (3d ed.1998); Mullenix, Redish & Vairo, Understanding Federal Courts and Jurisdiction § 3.18 (1998); Wright & Kane, Federal Courts §§ 32–37 (6th ed.2002).

As pointed out earlier, the requirement of an amount in controversy in federal-question cases under 28 U.S.C. § 1331, had been illusory in most cases and was abolished in 1980. See supra, p. 109, n. 3. In diversity more than $75,000, exclusive of interests and costs, must be in controversy. 28 U.S.C. § 1332(a), reprinted supra p. 171. The Judiciary Act of 1789 fixed the jurisdictional amount at $500. This was increased to $2,000 in 1887, to $3,000 in 1911, to $10,000 in 1958, to $50,000 in 1988, and to $75,000 in 1996. Congress has endeavored to set a figure "not so high as to convert the Federal courts into courts of big business nor so low as to fritter away their time in the trial of petty controversies." Sen.Rep. No. 1830, 85th Cong., 2d Sess. (1958). The 1958 increase in jurisdictional amount had only a "very slight" effect on the volume of federal litigation. Warren, Address to the American Law Institute, 25 F.R.D. 213 (1960). But the increase to $50,000 in 1988 is credited with a drop of 15% between 1989 and 1990 in the number of diversity cases filed. Annual Report of the Director of the Administrative Office 87–88 (1991).

The 1995 Long Range Plan, p. 126, says that if "caseload volume renders the courts of appeals and district courts unable to deliver timely, well-reasoned decisions and speedy trials with procedural fairness, the Judicial Conference should consider seeking more extensive reductions in federal court jurisdiction," including legislation to "[r]estore a minimum amount in controversy requirement for federal question cases, either generally or in specific categories."]

This Chapter addresses various issues concerning the amount-in-controversy requirement set forth in § 1332(a). The Supreme Court's decision in Exxon Mobil Corp. v. Allapattah Services, Inc., 545 U.S. 546 (2005), reprinted infra, p. 289, discusses the amount-in-controversy requirement in the context of supplemental jurisdiction for class actions pursuant to Fed. Rule Civ. Proc. 23 and permissive joinder of plaintiffs pursuant to Fed. Rule Civ. Proc. 20.

individual, who, prior to the shipment, had given an order for the same. Averring that the defendant Vance had subsequently to the seizure, and with knowledge of its wrongful nature, received said packages into his custody, it was further alleged that demand had been made for the return of the property seized, that it was still detained, and that plaintiff was entitled to the immediate possession thereof. Judgment was prayed against the defendants for the recovery of possession of the packages or their value, alleged to be one thousand dollars, in case delivery could not be had, and for damages in the sum of ten thousand dollars. There was an allegation of special damage, to wit: "That by said malicious trespass of said defendants and their continuation in the wrongful detention of said sixty-eight packages of wine the plaintiff has been greatly injured in its lawful trade and business with the citizens and residents of the State of South Carolina to its great hurt and damage in the breaking up of such trade and commerce."

. . .

■ Mr. Justice White, after making the foregoing statement, delivered the opinion of the court.

. . . . .

We shall dispose of the case upon the jurisdictional question, as it is manifest that the amount of recovery to which the plaintiff was entitled, upon the construction put upon the complaint by its counsel and acted upon by the trial court, could not equal the sum of two thousand dollars.

. . . . .

As by section 914 of the Revised Statutes of the United States the practice, pleadings and forms and modes of proceedings in actions at common law in a Circuit Court of the United States are required to conform, as near as may be, to those prevailing in the state court, and as by section 721 the laws of the several States are made rules of decision in trials at common law in the courts of the United States, in cases where they apply, Bauserman v. Blunt, 147 U.S. 647, we will examine the laws of South Carolina and the decisions of its courts, in order to ascertain the nature of the state statutory action to recover possession of personal property, and the rights of the parties thereunder.

. . . . .

Under the decisions to which we have referred, it is evident that, in the case at bar, the measure of damages for the detention was interest on the value of the property from the time of the wrong complained of ....

The courts of South Carolina, as we have seen, have held that in an action of trover consequential damages are not recoverable, and have also held that in the action of claim and delivery damages for the detention must have respect to the property and to a direct injury arising from the detention. Destruction of business not being of the latter character, it follows that the special damages averred in the complaint were not recoverable.

It results that as the plaintiff's action was solely one for claim and delivery of property alleged to have been unlawfully detained and for damages for the detention thereof, the amount of recovery depended first upon the alleged value of the property, which in the present case was one thousand dollars, and such damages as it was by operation of law allowed to recover in the action in question. As, however, by way of damages in an action of this character, recovery was only allowable for the actual damage caused by the detention, and could not embrace a cause of damage which was not in legal contemplation the proximate result of the wrongful detention, and such recovery was confined, as we have seen, to interest on the value of the property, it results that there was nothing in the damages alleged in the petition and properly recoverable adequate, when added to the value of the property, to have conferred upon the court jurisdiction to have entertained a consideration of the suit. Upon the face of the complaint, therefore, the Circuit Court was without jurisdiction over the action, and it erred in deciding to the contrary.

. . . . .[2]

[2. When a sufficient amount in controversy has been properly pleaded, jurisdiction is not lost because a defense to the plaintiff's claim appears on the face of the complaint, see Schunk v. Moline, Milburn & Stoddard Co., 147 U.S. 500 (1892), or because the defendant defaults or expressly admits liability, see In re Metropolitan Railway Receivership, 208 U.S. 90 (1907).

"When determining the amount in controversy, we scrutinize a claim for punitive damages more closely than a claim for actual damages to ensure that Congress's limits on diversity jurisdiction are properly observed." Missouri ex rel. Pemiscot County v. Western Sur. Co., 51 F.3d 170, 173 (8th Cir.1995).

Plaintiff in her ad damnum sought damages of "not more than $45,000." State law allowed the factfinder to give a plaintiff any relief she is entitled to, even if she asked for less. And plaintiff had refused to sign a stipulation precluding her from ever amending her claim to seek damages over $50,000. Held, the case was not removable. "The possibility that plaintiff may in the future seek or recover more damages is insufficient now." Burns v. Windsor Ins. Co., 31 F.3d 1092 (11th Cir.1994).

But compare De Aguilar v. Boeing Co., 47 F.3d 1404 (5th Cir.1995): "[W]e hold that if a defendant can show [by a preponderance of the evidence] that the amount in controversy actually exceeds the jurisdictional amount, the plaintiff must be able to show that, as a matter of law, it is certain that he will not be able to recover more than the damages for which he has prayed in the state court complaint. Such a rule is necessary to avoid the sort of manipulation that has occurred in the instant case." 47 F.3d, at 1411. See also Jackson v. American Bankers Ins. Co. of Florida, 976 F.Supp. 1450, 1455 (S.D.Ala.1997), in which the plaintiff's complaint demanded punitive and compensatory damages "not to exceed" $70,000. The district court acknowledged the binding authority of *Burns* but held that the Eleventh Circuit had there left open the possibility that a defendant might carry the "heavy burden of proving 'to a legal certainty' that more than $75,000 is in controversy." The district court sustained removal on this basis, the defendants having presented the affidavits of expert witnesses (including an eminent law professor) valuing the amount in controversy at substantially in excess of $75,000.

See generally Note, Pleading to Stay in State Court: Forum Control, Federal Removal Jurisdiction, and the Amount in Controversy Requirement, 56 Wash. & Lee L.Rev. 651 (1999).]

Burns v. Anderson

United States Court of Appeals, Fifth Circuit, 1974.
502 F.2d 970.

■ Before Brown, Chief Judge, and Thornberry and Ainsworth, Circuit Judges.

■ John R. Brown, Chief Judge:

The question on this appeal is whether a district court may dismiss a personal injury diversity suit where it appears "to a legal certainty" that the claim was "really for less than the jurisdictional amount." [3]

The suit grew out of an auto accident in which plaintiff Burns' automobile was struck amidships by that of defendant Anderson. Burns' principal injury was a broken thumb. He brought the action in the Eastern District of Louisiana, claiming $1,026.00 in lost wages and medical expenses and another $60,000.00 for pain and suffering. After a pre-trial conference and considerable discovery, the District Court dismissed for want of jurisdiction. Plaintiff appeals.

The test for jurisdictional amount was established by the Supreme Court in St. Paul Mercury Indemnity Co. v. Red Cab Co. [4] There, the Court held that the determinant is plaintiff's good faith claim and that to justify dismissal it must appear to a legal certainty that the claim is really for less than the jurisdictional amount. There is no question but that this is a test of liberality, [5] and it has been treated as such by this Court. [6] This does not mean, however, that Federal Courts must function as small claims courts. The test is an objective one and, once it is clear that as a matter of law the claim is for less than $10,000.00, the Trial Judge is required to dismiss.

In the instant case, the District Judge dismissed only after examination of an extensive record. This record included the testimony of three doctors who treated Burns, as well as his own deposition. The accident occurred on May 26. The evidence is without contradiction that by the middle of August only very minimal disability remained. By December, even this minor condition had disappeared. Burns' actions speak even more strongly than the medical testimony. In his deposition he testified that he took a job as a carpenter's assistant on June 21 or 22—less than a month after the accident. He did heavy manual labor for the remainder of the summer with

---

3. St. Paul Mercury Indemnity Co. v. Red Cab Co., 1938, 303 U.S. 283, 289.

4. Id.

5. See Bell v. Preferred Life Assurance Society, 1943, 320 U.S. 238; Horton v. Liberty Mutual Ins. Co., 1961, 367 U.S. 348.

6. E.g. Jones v. Landry, 5 Cir., 1967, 387 F.2d 102; Mas v. Perry, 5 Cir., 1974, 489 F.2d 1396; Miami Beach Yacht Corp. v. Terro Corp., 5 Cir., 1972, 461 F.2d 770; Anderson v. Moorer, 5 Cir., 1967, 372 F.2d 747; Burks v. Texas, 5 Cir., 1954, 211 F.2d 443. Of course there have been situations where the pain, suffering and other intangible factors were so slight that no substantial evidence could be offered to support a verdict for as much as the jurisdictional amount. Starks v. Louisville & Nashville R.R. Co., 5 Cir., 1972, 468 F.2d 896; Matthiesen v. Northwestern Mutual Ins. Co., 5 Cir., 1961, 286 F.2d 775; Leehans v. American Employers Ins. Co., 5 Cir., 1959, 273 F.2d 72.

absolutely no indication of any difficulty with his thumb. It is equally clear that any pain he suffered was not of very great magnitude or lasting duration. Burns admitted that by the end of July there was no pain whatsoever. As a matter of fact, the evidence reveals that the only medication he ever received was a single prescription on the day of the accident for Empirin, a mild aspirin compound. Nor did his special damages take him a significant way down the road to the $10,000.00 minimum. His total medical bills were less than $250.00. Although he claims $800.00 in lost wages, it is difficult to see how this could have amounted to even $300.00 at Burns' rate of pay that summer.[7]

The point of this fact recitation is that it really does appear to a legal certainty that the amount in controversy is less than $10,000. This is no *Plimsoll* case,[8] where dismissal was based on "bare bones pleadings" alone. The present situation differs from that case also in that this dismissal was for lack of subject matter jurisdiction not for failure to state a claim. Here the Trial Court examined an extensive record and determined as a matter of law that the requisite amount in controversy was not present. Indeed, had the case gone to trial and had the jury returned an award of $10,000, a *Gorsalitz*-girded Judge would have been compelled as a matter of law to order a remittitur. He would have inescapably found that the verdict was "so inordinately large as obviously to exceed the maximum of the reasonable range within which the jury may properly operate.[9]" Of course, we decline to make any more precise determination of plaintiff's loss since to do so might prejudice his right to a trial in another court.

Neither are we affected by plaintiff's plaintive plea that he is being deprived of a jury trial. The question in this case is not whether Burns is entitled to a trial by jury but rather where that trial is to be. We hold only that the case cannot be tried in the Federal Court because competence over it has not been granted to that Court by Congress.

Affirmed.[10]

---

7. Burns was making the minimum wage, $1.65 an hour. Four forty-hour work weeks at this wage grosses $264.00.

8. Cook & Nichol, Inc. v. Plimsoll Club, 5 Cir., 1971, 451 F.2d 505.

9. Gorsalitz v. Olin Mathieson Chemical Corp., 5 Cir., 1970, 429 F.2d 1033, 1046.

[10. Is the provision for costs in 28 U.S.C. § 1332(b), reprinted supra p. 172, added by amendment in 1958, likely to be of much use in borderline cases? See Cowen, Federal Jurisdiction Amended, 44 Va.L.Rev. 971, 978 (1958); Comment, 58 Colum.L.Rev. 1287, 1291–1294 (1958); ALI Study 120. Is Civil Rule 11, as amended in 1993, a more effective deterrent?

See generally Note, Trial by Jury of Preliminary Jurisdictional Facts in Federal Courts, 28 Iowa L.Rev. 471 (1963).

The one and only time for ascertaining the amount in controversy remains the time at which the action is filed in or removed to the district court. This cardinal feature of the *St. Paul Mercury* rule was not qualified by the emphasis in Caterpillar Inc. v. Lewis, 519 U.S. 61

Hoffman v. Vulcan Materials Co.

United States District Court, Middle District of North Carolina, 1998.
19 F.Supp.2d 475.

MEMORANDUM OPINION AND ORDER

■ ELIASON, UNITED STATE MAGISTRATE JUDGE.

Facts, Procedural History, and Contentions of the Parties

On February 9, 1998, plaintiffs, who are homeowners, filed a complaint in state court in Richmond County, North Carolina. They alleged that defendant committed nuisance and trespass against them through its operation of a quarry near their homes. The quarrying process allegedly creates excessive dust, flying rocks, noise, and blasting shocks. As a consequence, plaintiffs contended that their health, peace of mind, land, and homes have been damaged. In accordance with state law, plaintiffs listed their damages only as "in excess of $10,000." They each sought an amount in excess of $10,000 for damage to their homes and property from the blasting shocks, an amount in excess of $10,000 for the trespass and nuisance created by the dust and rocks which land on their property, and an amount in excess of $10,000 in punitive damages. They also asked for an injunction to prevent defendant's continuing trespass and nuisance.

Subsequently, defendant removed the case to this Court pursuant to 28 U.S.C. § 1441, contending that the case met the requirements for diversity jurisdiction as set out in 28 U.S.C. § 1332. Plaintiffs countered by seeking remand back to state court. They do not dispute that the parties are of diverse citizenship as required by 28 U.S.C. § 1332(a). However, they argue that defendant fails to show the jurisdictional amount of $75,000 because, on the face of the complaint, they only seek damages of in excess of $30,000 each.

Defendant argues that in determining the jurisdictional amount, the Court may look beyond the dollar amount of damages sought by plaintiffs and may consider as well the amount which plaintiffs' injunction request, if granted, would cost defendant. In support of its assertion, defendant has supplied an affidavit from Rodney Hobbs, an Area Production Manager for defendant. He states that closing the quarry near plaintiffs' homes would deprive defendant of at least $4,862,000 per year in pretax earnings, that

---

(1996), on the jurisdictional posture of a case at the end of the litigation. See Grinnell Mut. Reins. Co. v. Shierk, 121 F.3d 1114, 1117 (7th Cir.1997), where the court declared:

> A defect in diversity jurisdiction exists, if at all, only when a case is filed in federal court or removed to federal court from state court. If a jurisdictional defect in existence when a suit is filed remains uncured, then any judgment in the case must be vacated and the case must be dismissed. But events occurring subsequent to the filing or removal of a case— whether one party changes its residence, thereby destroying complete diversity, or the amount in controversy drops below the jurisdictional amount—are not "defects" in the court's jurisdiction; these subsequent events do not affect a federal court's diversity jurisdiction at all.

Any doubt about the continued vitality of this time-of-filing rule was removed by Grupo Dataflux v. Atlas Global Group, L.P., 541 U.S. 567, reprinted supra, p. 209.]

each lost hour of daily production would amount to an annual economic impact of more than $979,000, and that any restriction which measurably reduced defendant's output would have an annual economic impact on defendant in excess of $75,000. Plaintiffs reply that the Court should determine the amount in controversy only from plaintiffs' perspective and not consider the economic impact on defendant.

Discussion

The law used to determine jurisdictional amount in "diversity" cases is quite clear, up to a point. Federal courts "have original jurisdiction of all civil actions where the matter in controversy exceeds the sum or value of $75,000, exclusive of interest and costs, and is between citizens of different states." 28 U.S.C. § 1332(a). In addition, any matter which may have been originally brought in federal court, but is filed in a state court, may be removed by the defendant to federal district court. 28 U.S.C. § 1441.

"In either a case originally filed in, or one removed to, federal court, [t]he party seeking to invoke the jurisdiction of the federal courts has the burden of proving its existence by showing that it does not appear to a legal certainty that its claim is for less than the jurisdictional amount." 14A Charles Alan Wright, et al., Federal Practice and Procedure § 3702, at 19 (2d ed.1985). Accordingly, in a removal case, the defendant, rather than the plaintiff, has the burden of proving that the jurisdictional requirements for removal are met. Griffin v. Holmes, 843 F.Supp. 81 (E.D.N.C.1993) (citing Kirchner Gafford v. General Electric Co., 997 F.2d 150, 155 (6th Cir.1993)). For a removal, this means defendant must prove to a "legal certainty" that plaintiffs' claim exceeds $75,000. St. Paul Mercury Indemnity Co. v. Red Cab Co., 303 U.S. 283, 289 (1938); Burns v. Windsor Ins. Co., 31 F.3d 1092, 1095 (11th Cir.1994). However, a plaintiff's right to select the forum for its claim is stronger than a defendant's right to remove. Therefore, any doubts about removal must be resolved in favor of remand. *Griffin*, 843 F.Supp., at 84; *Burns*, 31 F.3d, at 1095. In this case, the jurisdictional dispute only involves the amount in controversy, and not diversity of citizenship.

The amount in controversy is normally determined from the face of the pleadings. *St. Paul*, 303 U.S., at 289–90, 293. In this case, no specific amount is alleged in the complaint. Therefore, it will not aid in determining whether the action meets the jurisdictional amount in controversy. This is because, under North Carolina pleading rules, in negligence actions, claims in excess of $10,000 may only so state.[11] That is how plaintiffs plead their

---

11. Rule 8. General rules of pleadings.

 . . . . .

   [(a)](2) A demand for judgment for the relief to which he deems himself entitled. Relief in the alternative or of several different types may be demanded. In all negligence actions, and in all claims for punitive damages in any civil action, wherein the matter in controversy exceeds the sum or value of ten thousand dollars ($10,000), the pleading shall not state the demand for monetary relief, but shall state that the relief demanded is for damages incurred or to be incurred in excess of ten thousand dollars ($10,000). However, at any time after service of the claim for relief, any party may request of the claimant a

demand for judgment.[12]

When federal jurisdiction is not plain from the face of a plaintiff's complaint, the defendant must offer evidence in support of its claim that the controversy satisfies the federal jurisdictional amount. The court makes its determination on the basis of the existing record. 14A Wright, supra, § 3725, at 417. This means pleadings, affidavits or other matters in the record. 14A Wright, supra, § 3702, at 26; 14A Wright, supra, § 3725, at 223 (Supp.1997).

In the instant case, plaintiffs' complaint only shows that the damages for each plaintiff exceeds $30,000. Defendant did not file a motion under Rule 8 of the North Carolina Rules of Civil Procedure in order to ascertain the exact amount in controversy as to each plaintiff. It, therefore, becomes incumbent on defendant to point to some evidence in the record or to submit independent evidence which would show that the plaintiffs' damage claims exceed $75,000. Defendant fails to do this.... Consequently, the Court finds that defendant has failed to meet its burden of proof as to the amount of damages sought by plaintiffs. However, this does not end the matter because not only have plaintiffs sought money damages, but they also seek injunctive and declaratory relief.

In an action such as this one where plaintiffs seek injunctive or declaratory relief, "the amount in controversy is measured by the value of the object of the litigation." Hunt v. Washington State Apple Advertising Commission, 432 U.S. 333, 347 (1977) (citations omitted). Some courts construe this to mean the value of the right to be enforced or protected. Ericsson GE Mobile Communications, Inc. v. Motorola Communications & Electronics, Inc., 120 F.3d 216, 219 (11th Cir.1997); Kheel v. Port of New York Authority, 457 F.2d 46, 49 (2d Cir.); Alfonso v. Hillsborough County Aviation Authority, 308 F.2d 724, 726 (5th Cir.1962); Seven–Up Company v. Blue Note, Inc., 260 F.2d 584, 585 (7th Cir.1958).

There is basic agreement among the courts concerning *what* must be valued. The seemingly never ending source of confusion concerns *how* to value it. The Supreme Court itself has never made one clear, definitive statement on how to go about placing a monetary value on the "object of the litigation." Consequently, lower courts, when faced with the myriad of fact patterns which arise in diversity cases, have formulated a number of

---

written statement of the monetary relief sought, and the claimant shall, within 30 days after such service, provide such statement, which shall not be filed with the clerk until the action has been called for trial or entry of default entered. Such statement may be amended in the manner and at times as provided by Rule 15.

N.C. Gen.Stat. § 1A–1, Rule 8 Rules Civ. Proc., Rule 8, G.S. § 1A–1

12. Because North Carolina complaints will not state the exact amount in controversy, this state pleading rule poses a special difficulty for the federal court and the parties in a removal situation. 14A Charles Alan Wright, et al., Federal Practice and Procedure § 3725, at 423–24 (2d ed.1985). [The Jurisdiction and Venue Clarification Act of 2011 addressed this issue by amending § 1446 to permit the notice of removal to assert the amount in controversy when the state practice does not permit a demand for a specific sum.]

different valuation rules, each with indirect support from various Supreme Court opinions.

One such rule is known as the "plaintiff-viewpoint" rule. See generally 14A Wright, supra, § 3703. Courts applying this rule look only to the benefit to be gained by the plaintiff in order to find the amount in controversy.[13] The main criticism of the viewpoint rule is that it is an imperfect way to realize the purpose behind the jurisdictional amount limit, which is to keep trivial cases out of the federal courts. 14A Wright, supra, § 3703, at 66–67. Unfortunately, the rule achieves this goal by also keeping out cases where great sums of money are involved on the part of the defendant, but not the plaintiff.

Courts which utilize the plaintiff-viewpoint rule are, of course, unable to cite to a Supreme Court decision that directly mandates it. Instead, they must rely on the case of Glenwood Light & Water Company v. Mutual Light, Heat, & Power Company, 239 U.S. 121 (1915), for support. However, that case is less than satisfactory for the purpose because of its unique fact situation.

In *Glenwood*, the town of Glenwood Springs, Colorado, had granted both parties the right to construct power plants and to supply the town with electricity. Defendant constructed its power lines so near to the pre-existing lines of the plaintiff that they interfered with the plaintiff's maintenance and operation of its lines. Plaintiff requested an injunction to restrain defendant's activities. 239 U.S., at 122–124. The district court found that the cost to defendant to move the offending lines would be less than the $3,000 jurisdictional amount and remanded the action. 239 U.S., at 124. The Supreme Court reversed, holding that the trial court erred by judging the amount in controversy using the lesser cost to the defendant rather than looking at the greater value of plaintiff's right to supply power without wrongful interference. There was no question but that this right was worth more than the jurisdictional amount. 239 U.S., at 126.

Courts relying on *Glenwood* tend to interpret it as forbidding using the cost to defendants when valuing injunction cases. That interpretation is strained because *Glenwood* does not cover the situation where the value to defendant, but not the plaintiff exceeds the jurisdictional amount. 14A Wright, supra, § 3703, at 64. Limiting *Glenwood* to its specific facts more fully reflects the policy goal that the amount in controversy limitation

---

13. The late Judge Armistead Dobie of the Fourth Circuit was a strong proponent of this rule which a number of courts have adopted. 14A Wright, supra, § 3703. In fact, it appears to be the clear rule in at least four federal circuits. See Ericsson GE Mobile Communications, Inc. v. Motorola Communications & Electronics, Inc., 120 F.3d 216, 219–220 (11th Cir.1997); Columbia Gas Transmission Corp. v. Tarbuck, 62 F.3d 538, 542 (3d Cir.1995); Kheel v. Port of New York Authority, 457 F.2d 46, 49 (2d Cir. 1972); Alfonso v. Hillsborough County Aviation Authority, 308 F.2d 724, 726–727 (5th Cir.1962). Other circuits seem to apply the plaintiff-viewpoint rule in limited circumstances such as certain class action lawsuits. See Snow v. Ford Motor Company, 561 F.2d 787, 790–791 (9th Cir.1977); Massachusetts State Pharmaceutical Association v. Federal Prescription Service, Inc., 431 F.2d 130, 132 (8th Cir.1970).

should allow federal courts to hear important cases while excluding trivial ones. See id., at 66–67.

An alternative rule, known as the either-viewpoint rule, has been adopted by a number of circuits and appears to be the more recent trend. Id., at 66; In re Brand Name Prescription Drugs Antitrust Litigation, 123 F.3d 599, 609 (7th Cir.1997); Oklahoma Retail Grocers Association v. Wal–Mart Stores, Incorporated, 605 F.2d 1155, 1159 (10th Cir.1979); Williams v. Kleppe, 539 F.2d 803, n. 1 (1st Cir.1976) (dicta); Tatum v. Laird, 444 F.2d 947, 951 (D.C.Cir.1971), rev'd on other grounds, 408 U.S. 1 (1972); Ridder Bros., Inc. v. Blethen, 142 F.2d 395, 399 (9th Cir.1944) (non-class action case).

Like the proponents of the plaintiff-viewpoint rule, the courts which use the either-viewpoint rule are also unable to point to a Supreme Court case which definitively establishes their test. Instead, they rely on Supreme Court cases decided both before and after *Glenwood* which use either-viewpoint language and require a narrow reading of *Glenwood* for purposes of consistency. See Smith v. Adams, 130 U.S. 167 (1889); and Thomson v. Gaskill, 315 U.S. 442 (1942).

In *Smith*, the Court, construing a statute with language similar to that found in 28 U.S.C. 1332(a), stated that,

> [i]t is conceded that the pecuniary value of the matter in dispute may be determined, not only by the money judgment prayed, where such is the case, but in some cases by the increased or diminished value of the property directly affected by the relief prayed, or by the *pecuniary result to one of the parties* immediately from the judgment.

Smith, 130 U.S., at 175 (emphasis added). This statement was echoed more than 50 years later in *Thomson* when the Court determined that "[i]n a diversity litigation the value of the 'matter in controversy' is measured not by the monetary result of determining the principle involved, but by its *pecuniary consequence to those involved* in the litigation." *Thomson*, 315 U.S., at 447 (emphasis added). Additional, albeit implicit, minimal support may be found in cases reaching the Supreme Court where lower courts relied on the value of the case to defendants to find the jurisdictional amount. See Tatum v. Laird, 444 F.2d 947; and Laird v. Tatum, 408 U.S. 1 (1972) (lower court relied on cost to defendant to find jurisdiction, Supreme Court failed to even discuss the issue).

Fourth Circuit law, which controls this case, appears to be somewhat unsettled....

The above review satisfies the Court that neither Supreme Court nor Fourth Circuit law commands it to follow the plaintiff-viewpoint rule, the either-viewpoint rule, or any "viewpoint" rule. Indeed, it would appear that adoption of "viewpoint" valuation has led to some distraction and a great deal of confusion. The Supreme Court's cases do not mention "viewpoint" value. Rather they state that "the amount in controversy is measured by the value of the object of the litigation" and that, generally, the value is measured by "pecuniary consequences to those involved in the litigation."

Hunt, 432 U.S., at 347; *Thomson*, 315 U.S., at 447. Any rule constructed for valuing the amount in controversy must take into account that diversity cases, like their appellation, present federal courts with endlessly diverse sets of facts and demands for relief beyond simple money judgments.

In order to take into account both the factual variances and the numerous types of relief, the Court feels it best to move away from "viewpoint" terminology and instead recognize that any one case may be legitimately valued in a number of different ways, no one of which may be said to inherently represent true value in every case. By "value" the Court understands that its duty is to find the economic worth of the "object in controversy." In a free market situation, any one object may have a different value to different individuals based on need, taste, etc. Nevertheless, appraisers and auditors often give opinions based on value to hypothetical willing sellers and buyers. Likewise, in a lawsuit seeking declaratory and injunctive relief, the relief will have both a cost and benefit to the parties, depending on whether relief is granted or denied. No one economic analysis will be right for all cases.

For example, in cases where injunctions or declaratory judgments are requested, the value of the relief could be determined by considering how much it would cost the plaintiff to purchase the given relief and how much the defendant would be willing to pay the plaintiff to be rid of the injunction. One federal court of appeals has suggested such an approach. See In re Brand Name Prescription Drugs Antitrust Litigation, 123 F.3d [599, 609 (7th Cir. 1997)]. There, the plaintiffs purposely did not allege damages exceeding the jurisdictional threshold as they had a right to do. However, they also asked for injunctive relief. The Seventh Circuit has adopted the either-viewpoint rule. It noted that while the value of an injunction to each plaintiff may not be easy to calculate, a defendant could show jurisdictional amount by measuring the costs defendant would face if it had to alter its method of business and/or if it had to forego a lucrative transaction. Id. If the object of the injunction does not normally have economic value, a court may allow consideration of defendant's clerical and ministerial costs of compliance. Id. However, the *Brand Name* court did not have to ultimately resolve the issue because defendants' failed to offer any proof.

A flexible approach better reflects the Supreme Court's mandate to consider the "pecuniary consequence to those involved in the litigation." *Thomson*, 315 U.S., at 447. It fulfills without favoritism to either side the original purpose of jurisdictional amounts by only keeping minor cases out of federal court. This broader approach to valuation will allow the court to make better reasoned decisions by demanding a better evidentiary record. Defendants will no longer need to make gross speculations concerning the value to plaintiff of the injunction. They can set their own value based on their knowledge of their own affairs and back the assertions with facts and reasoned opinions. The Court will be in a position to demand and get higher quality offers of proof.

Turning now to the case before the Court, the amount in controversy must be greater than $75,000 in order for the Court to have jurisdiction. The plaintiffs have each requested in excess of $30,000 in damages in addition to an injunction. Therefore, if defendant can show that the injunction is worth more than $45,000 to any one plaintiff, then plaintiffs' motion to remand must be denied.[14]

Plaintiffs have requested the injunction in order to protect their properties and their peace of mind. Plaintiffs have not put any information into the record concerning the value of their properties and the effect on property values of defendant's continued operations. Nor can the value of the injunction be determined based on plaintiffs' peace of mind. This is too subjective without more facts. That does not end the matter because defendant has offered evidence of the value of the injunction to itself.

Defendant runs a large-scale quarry. It has presented an affidavit showing a number of different ways of valuing the harm to it of any meaningful curtailing of its operations. The affidavit states:

(a) If the Rockingham Quarry were closed completely, Vulcan would lose at least $4,862,000.00 per year in pretax earnings, which is based upon conservative production and sales volumes for this facility.

(b) If the Rockingham Quarry operations were restricted by the hours of operation, the annual economic impact to Vulcan for each hour of lost production per day would exceed $979,000.

(c) The economic impact of any other restriction on the operation of the Rockingham Quarry would depend upon the nature of the restriction(s), but it is safe to predict that any restriction that causes a measurable reduction in the amount of crushed stone produced by this quarry would have an annual economic impact to Vulcan far in excess of $75,000.00....

Defendant also cites the loss of jobs to employees and harm to companies purchasing its materials. This does not constitute value to the defendant, except perhaps indirectly. The losses cited if quarry operations were curtailed is better evidence of the value of the injunction to defendant. And, because the defendant will sustain this loss even if only one plaintiff were to obtain the injunction, this is a case where plaintiffs have an undivided

---

14. In regard to the $45,000 amount, two matters need to be pointed out. First, because the parties have not raised the issue, the Court is making the assumption that if the injunction is valued at $45,000, this will not decrease the $30,000 amount claimed in damages, either by reducing future damages or punitive damages.

Second, the Supreme Court's nonaggregation rules require that the amount in controversy be determined for each defendant as to each plaintiff. 14A Wright, supra, § 3704; Brand Name Prescription Drugs Antitrust Litigation, 123 F.3d 599, 607–608 (7th Cir.1997). If each plaintiff has a separate right to be free from defendant's acts, then the value of the injunction is determined only in regard to that plaintiff. Id. However, if the plaintiffs have an undivided interest in the relief, this total, single amount is used. In *Brand Name*, each plaintiff was seeking relief from alleged collusion pricing. Consequently, it may have cost defendant very little to cease the activity with respect to any one plaintiff.

interest in the injunction so the loss will be attributed to each plaintiff. See n. [14], supra.

Plaintiffs have not disputed the figures. If the quarry were closed, the jurisdictional amount is clearly met merely on an income valuation. Alternatively, even if the value of lost production per hour actually represents lost sales, not net income, it seems clear that a restriction in quarrying of one hour per day over some reasonable time period will still have a value to defendant of over $45,000. Therefore, defendant has met its burden of proof and has shown that, between the money damages and the value of the injunction, the $75,000 amount in controversy requirement is met in this case. Because the necessary amount is present, the Court has jurisdiction over the matter and plaintiffs' motion to remand must be denied.

. . . . .[15]

[15. In Barry v. Mercein, 5 How. (46 U.S.) 103, it was held that a dispute between a mother and a father about custody of a child could not be heard by the Supreme Court, since the statute at that time required that more than $2,000 be in controversy to appeal to the Supreme Court and no pecuniary value could be put on the custody of a child. This has been applied to the statutes granting original jurisdiction to the district courts and it is a settled rule that if the right or matter in controversy cannot be translated into terms of money, there is no amount in controversy. E.g., Hague v. CIO, 307 U.S. 496 (1939) (free speech); Senate Select Committee on Presidential Campaign Activities v. Nixon, 366 F.Supp. 51 (D.D.C.1973) (presidential tapes).

"[I]t seems to this court that applying a cost to the defendant approach to injunctive relief is logically inconsistent with the law proscribing aggregation of legal damage claims. This court is not prepared to create a back door to the federal courthouse by using the cost to the defendant of plaintiff's requested injunctive relief as a basis for federal jurisdiction." Shelly v. Southern Bell Tel. & Tel. Co., 873 F.Supp. 613, 617 (M.D.Ala.1995).

The problem of determining the amount in controversy in consumer class actions seeking injunctive relief as well as damages is a recurrent one. The caselaw is ragged, but the balance of authority supports the approach of *Shelly* that Snyder v. Harris, 394 U.S. 332 (1969) and Zahn v. International Paper Co., 414 U.S. 291 (1973), prohibit application of the "either viewpoint" rule in a consumer class action so as to aggregate the cost to the defendant of classwide injunctive relief. See In re Ford Motor Company/Citibank (South Dakota), N.A., 264 F.3d 952 (9th Cir.2001), cert. granted sub nom. Ford Motor Co. v. McCauley, 534 U.S. 1126, cert. dismissed as improvidently granted sub nom. Ford Motor Co. v. McCauley, 537 U.S. 1 (2002).

The "either-viewpoint" rule was endorsed, and deemed consistent with the nonaggregation rule for determining the amount in controversy in class actions, in Comment, The $75,000.01 Question: What is the Value of Injunctive Relief, 6 Geo.Mason L.Rev. 1013 (1998).

The caselaw has been even more ragged with respect to a different issue of contemporary aggregation law posed by consumer class actions and other cases involving the joinder of multiple plaintiffs: whether the 1990 supplemental-jurisdiction statute, 28 U.S.C. § 1367, had the unintended effect of abrogating both the non-aggregation rule of *Zahn* as to additional plaintiffs joined as absent class members under Rule 23, and the parallel non-aggregation rule of Clark v. Paul Gray, Inc., 306 U.S. 583 (1939), as to additional plaintiffs joined individually under Rule 20. This is discussed below in Chapter V. See Exxon Mobil Corp. v. Allapattah Services, Inc., 545 U.S. 546 (2005), reprinted infra, p. 289, and Comment on 28 U.S.C. §§ 1367(b) & 1367(c), infra, p. 311.]

Barnes v. Parker

United States District Court, W.D.Mo.1954.
126 F.Supp. 649.

■ RIDGE, DISTRICT JUDGE.

Defendant Parker has perfected removal proceedings in both of the above causes which were originally filed in the Circuit Court of Douglas County, Missouri, on the alleged ground of diverse citizenship of the parties, and requisite jurisdictional amount being involved. [In Case No. 1255, the complaint alleged that Parker and a codefendant, Cron, were jointly liable for a debt of $4,063.62. This exceeded the jurisdictional threshold of $3,000 then required for federal diversity jurisdiction. As discussed in Pinel v. Pinel, 240 U.S. 594 (1916), reprinted infra, p. 257, the total amount of a liability that is "joint" rather than "several" determines the amount in controversy, even when asserted collectively by or against multiple parties. But defendant Cron had failed to join defendant Parker in removing the case, violating the "rule of unanimity" that ordinarily requires all properly joined and served defendants to act collectively in removing a case. See Mathews v. County of Fremont, Wyoming, 826 F. Supp. 1315 (D. Wyo. 1993), reprinted infra, p. 400.] Since defendant Cron has not joined in the present removal proceeding, Cause No. 1255 . . . must be remanded to the state court for all further proceedings.

Case No. 1256

In Case Number 1256, an action for breach of contract is alleged. The total damages prayed for in the petition, exclusive of interest and costs, is the sum of $2,161.30. While the cause was pending in the state court, the defendant, "for the sole purpose of establishing diversity of citizenship" and "establishing the requisite amount necessary to render the cause removable to the United States District Court," filed a counterclaim in the amount of $4,876.84. The petition for removal was submitted with such counterclaim.

We had thought that it was now established beyond all debate that, in determining the amount in controversy in actions sought to be removed, the Court to which removal is sought determines the question solely by looking to the amount in good faith prayed for as *damnum* in the complaint, St. Paul Mercury Indemnity Co. v. Red Cab Co., 303 U.S. 283, regardless of subsequent events in the action; Kirby v. American Soda Fountain Co., 194 U.S. 141, and that, accordingly, if the amount therein claimed was less than the jurisdictional requirement, amounts claimed by way of counterclaim could not be considered as increasing the amount of the required sum. Falls Wire Mfg. Co. v. Broderick, C.C.Mo., 6 F. 654; Gates v. Union Central Life Ins. Co., D.C., 56 F.Supp. 149; Stuart v. Creel, D.C., 90 F.Supp. 392.

However, there are decisions by other District Courts, Wheatley v. Martin, D.C.Ark., 62 F.Supp. 109; Lange v. Chicago, R.I. & P.R. Co., D.C.S.D.Iowa, 99 F.Supp. 1; Rosenblum v. Trullinger, D.C.Ark., 118 F.Supp. 394, which apparently create an exception to the above rule when a counterclaim is asserted and classified as "compulsory" under the local state practice. We can agree with neither the reasoning nor the confusion which would result if such holdings are followed. To recognize such an exception is to make the federal removal practice dependent on state court procedure and will, if extended, effectively preclude attaining that orderly procedure and uniformity of practice which has been the goal of all the removal acts and which was thought to be achieved by the present statute, 28 U.S.C. § 1441. To do so would make the removability of an action into the federal court dependent upon the practice with respect to counterclaims in use in the particular state wherein the federal court happened to be sitting and would soon create forty-eight different tests of removability. Each federal court would be called upon to decide whether the particular counterclaims with which it is faced would be described as "compulsory" or "permissive" under the local state practice.

The view taken in the decisions above referred to appears to arise from the mistaken application in the *Wheatley* case, supra, 62 F.Supp. at page 114, of the doctrine of Erie R. Co. v. Tompkins, 304 U.S. 64. We cannot agree that the various state practice codes dealing with counterclaims prescribe matters of substance binding on the federal courts, under the doctrine of the *Erie* case. Even if we did agree, we would soon be contradicted, for the controlling Missouri decisions expressly hold that the matter is one of procedure rather than substance. Zickel v. Knell, 357 Mo. 678, 210 S.W.2d 59. (This indicates the maze into which the exception recognized can lead.) Federal removal practice is purely a matter of federal law unaffected by conflicting state court decisions. Stoll v. Hawkeye Cas. Co., 8 Cir., 185 F.2d 96.

In addition, there is an even greater objection to following such holdings, for the practice could be used to effectively circumvent the expressed intent of Congress to restrict removability. A nonresident defendant would thus be able to bring a claim asserted against him, no matter how minute, within the jurisdiction of the federal court by merely filing a counterclaim to the claim asserted against him. The Federal Court would then be forced to consider the good-faith assertion of the counterclaim, before considering the merits of the cause, in order to ascertain whether it had jurisdiction to pass upon it. Thus, as long ago noted in the *Broderick* case, 1881, supra, 6 F. at page 655, "the door for removals is wide open" to intolerable practice. We do not feel that such a result should lightly be accepted.

We accordingly conclude that Cases Numbered 1255 and 1256 were improperly removed to this Court.

It is ordered that the above causes be, and the same are hereby, remanded to the Circuit Court of Douglas County, Missouri, for all further proceedings.[16]

[16. The case law on this point is divided, though most of the cases agree with the principal decision. Compare West Virginia State Bar v. Bostic, 351 F.Supp. 1118 (S.D.W.Va.1972)

Elgin v. Marshall

Supreme Court of the United States, 1883.
106 U.S. 578, 1 S.Ct. 484, 27 L.Ed. 249.

■ Mr. Justice Matthews delivered the opinion of the court.

This action was brought by Marshall and another, being citizens of Wisconsin, against the town of Elgin, Minn., to recover the amount due upon certain coupons or interest warrants, detached from municipal bonds, alleged to have been issued by it, in aid of a railroad company. The defence set up was that the bonds and coupons were void, the statute, under the assumed authority of which they had been issued, being, as was alleged, unconstitutional.... Judgment was given for the amount, $1,660.75, due thereon, being for the interest on fifteen bonds of $500 each. The town brought this writ of error.

. . . . .

It is true that the point actually litigated and determined in this action was the validity of the bonds, and as between these parties in any subsequent action upon other coupons, or upon the bonds themselves, this judgment, according to the principles stated in Cromwell v. County of Sac, 94 U.S. 351, might, and as to all questions actually adjudged would, be conclusive as an estoppel.

. . . In our opinion, sects. 691 and 692, Rev.Stat., which, as amended by sect. 3 of the act of Feb. 16, 1875, c. 77, limit the jurisdiction of this court, on writs of error and appeal, to review final judgments in civil actions, and

---

(denying removal), with National Upholstery Co. v. Corley, 144 F.Supp. 658 (M.D.N.C.1956) allowing removal (where claim was for $1,400 and counterclaim for $78,000). See Feinberg, Establishing Federal Jurisdictional Amount by a Counterclaim, 21 Mo.L.Rev. 243 (1956). The result in the principal case is defended in 16 Moore's Federal Practice ¶ 107 App. 110[2] (3d ed.1998), but criticized in 14B Wright, Miller & Cooper, Federal Practice and Procedure: Jurisdiction 3d § 3706, at 214–218 (1998).

Removal would be permitted in this situation by ALI Study § 1304(d).

One case has departed from the majority view and held that a diversity case was properly removed by defendant, though plaintiff's claim was for less than $50,000, where defendant had a counterclaim, compulsory under state law, for more than $50,000. Swallow & Associates v. Henry Molded Products, Inc., 794 F.Supp. 660 (E.D.Mich.1992). But four other district courts have specifically refused to follow the decision in the *Swallow* case. Independent Machine Co. v. International Tray Pads & Packaging, Inc., 991 F.Supp. 687 (D.N.J. 1998); Continental Ozark, Inc. v. Fleet Supplies, Inc., 908 F.Supp. 668, 670–672 (W.D.Ark. 1995); Meridian Aviation Service v. Sun Jet Int'l, 886 F.Supp. 613 (S.D.Tex.1995); Iowa Lamb Corp. v. Kalene Industries, Inc., 871 F.Supp. 1149 (N.D.Iowa 1994). Compare Spectacor Management Group v. Brown, 131 F.3d 120, 121 (3d Cir.1997), a questionable decision in which the Third Circuit relied upon a compulsory counterclaim to determine that there was a sufficient amount in controversy in a diversity action commenced in (rather than removed to) federal court.

In the related context of statutory federal-question jurisdiction rather than diversity jurisdiction, the Supreme Court has twice made clear that counterclaims are irrelevant for purposes of determining whether a case "arises under" federal law. See Vaden v. Discover Bank, 556 U.S. 49 (2009); Holmes Group, Inc. v. Vornado Air Circulation Systems, Inc., 535 U.S. 826 (2002).]

final decrees in cases of equity and of admiralty and maritime jurisdiction, to those where the matter in dispute, exclusive of costs, exceeds the sum or value of $5,000, have reference to the matter which is directly in dispute, in the particular cause in which the judgment or decree sought to be reviewed, has been rendered, and do not permit us, for the purpose of determining its sum or value, to estimate its collateral effect in a subsequent suit between the same or other parties.

. . . . .

... It would be, clearly, a violation of the rule, to add to the value of the matter determined any estimate in money, by reason of the probative force of the judgment itself in some subsequent proceeding. That would often depend upon contingencies, and might be mere conjecture and speculation, while the statute evidently contemplated an actual and present value in money, determined by a mere inspection of the record. . . . It is not the actual value of the judgment sought to be reviewed which confers jurisdiction, otherwise it might be required to hear evidence that it could not be collected; but it is the nominal or apparent sum or value of the subject-matter of the judgment. It is impossible to foresee into what mazes of speculation and conjecture we may not be led by a departure from the simplicity of the statutory provision.

. . . . .

... The writ of error is accordingly

Dismissed for want of jurisdiction.[17]

————

Aetna Casualty & Surety Co. v. Flowers

Supreme Court of the United States, 1947.
330 U.S. 464, 67 S.Ct. 798, 91 L.Ed. 1024.

Proceeding under the Workmen's Compensation Law of Tennessee by Mrs. Fannie M. Flowers, widow of Edward E. Flowers, deceased, employee, in her own right and in behalf of two minor children, opposed by the J.A. Jones Construction Company, a North Carolina corporation, employer, and

---

[17. In a suit to restrain collection of a tax the jurisdictional amount must be satisfied by the tax that will be levied during the period of litigation. Neither the capitalized value of the tax, nor the value of the right to conduct business free of the tax, is relevant. Healy v. Ratta, 292 U.S. 263 (1934).

In Hunt v. Washington State Apple Advertising Commission, 432 U.S. 333 (1977), the Court made a general recital of a variety of types of demonstrated and potential costs to Washington state apple growers challenging a North Carolina statute. It then said: "Both the substantial volume of sales in North Carolina—the record demonstrates that in 1974 alone, such sales were in excess of $2 million—and the continuing nature of the statute's interference with the business affairs of the Commission's constituents, preclude our saying 'to a legal certainty,' on this record, that such losses and expenses will not, over time, if they have not done so already, amount to the requisite $10,000 for at least some of the individual growers and dealers." 432 U.S., at 348.]

by the Aetna Casualty & Surety Company, a Connecticut corporation, insurance carrier. The proceeding was instituted in the state court and removed to the federal district court. An order dismissing [rather than remanding] the action was reversed by the Circuit Court of Appeals [which ordered the case remanded], 154 F.2d 881, and to review the judgment of the Circuit Court of Appeals, the employer and insurance carrier bring certiorari.

■ Mr. Justice Douglas delivered the opinion of the Court.

. . . . .

The complaint alleged that respondent's husband died as the result of an accident occurring in the course of his employment. Burial expenses plus benefits in the amount of $5,000, the maximum under the Tennessee statute,[18] were sought on behalf of respondent and her two minor children, aged twelve and fifteen. . . .

Second. We think that the jurisdictional amount of $3,000 was involved in this suit. The contrary conclusion of the Circuit Court of Appeals was based on the nature of the award under the Tennessee statute. The award may be paid in installments at regular intervals by the employer or by a trustee with whom the amount of the award, reduced to present value, has been deposited. Tenn.Code § 6893. Moreover, the death or remarriage of respondent, plus the death or attainment of the age of eighteen by the children, would terminate all payments. Tenn.Code § 6883. Since an award to respondent would be payable in installments, and by operation of conditions subsequent the total payments might never reach $3,000, the Circuit Court of Appeals concluded that the jurisdictional amount was lacking.

If this case were one where judgment could be entered only for the installments due at the commencement of the suit (cf. New York Life Ins. Co. v. Viglas, 297 U.S. 672, 678), future installments could not be considered in determining whether the jurisdictional amount was involved, even though the judgment would be determinative of liability for future installments as they accrued. Wright v. Mutual Life Ins. Co., 5 Cir., 19 F.2d 117, aff'd 276 U.S. 602. Cf. Button v. Mutual Life Ins. Co., D.C., 48 F.Supp. 168. But this is not that type of case. For the Tennessee statute which creates liability for the award contemplates a single action for the determination of claimant's right to benefits and a single judgment for the award granted. See Tenn.Code §§ 6880, 6881, 6890, 6891, 6893; Shockley v. Morristown Produce & Ice Co., 171 Tenn. 591, 106 S.W.2d 562.

---

18. Death benefits are provided in the amount of 60% of the average weekly wages of the employee (as computed in accordance with Tenn.Code § 6852(c)), but payments may not exceed $18 per week, nor continue for more than 400 weeks. § 6880; § 6883(17). In addition there is a ceiling of $5,000 on total benefits exclusive of burial and certain other expenses. § 6881. See Haynes v. Columbia Pictures Corp., 178 Tenn. 648, 162 S.W.2d 383. The complaint alleged that 60% of the average weekly wages for the statutory period would exceed $5,000.

Nor does the fact that it cannot be known as a matter of absolute certainty that the amount which may ultimately be paid, if respondent prevails, will exceed $3,000, mean that the jurisdictional amount is lacking. This Court has rejected such a restrictive interpretation of the statute creating diversity jurisdiction. It has held that a possibility that payments will terminate before the total reaches the jurisdictional minimum is immaterial if the right to all the payments is in issue. Brotherhood of Locomotive Firemen v. Pinkston, [293 U.S. 96]; Thompson v. Thompson, 226 U.S. 551. Future payments are not in any proper sense contingent, although they may be decreased or cut off altogether by the operation of conditions subsequent. *Thompson v. Thompson*, supra, 226 U.S., p. 560. And there is no suggestion that by reason of life expectancy or law of averages the maximum amount recoverable can be expected to fall below the jurisdictional minimum. Cf. *Brotherhood of Locomotive Firemen v. Pinkston*, supra, 293 U.S., p. 101. Moreover, the computation of the maximum amount recoverable is not complicated by the necessity of determining the life expectancy of respondent. Cf. *Thompson v. Thompson*, supra, 226 U.S., p. 559; *Brotherhood of Locomotive Firemen v. Pinkston*, 293 U.S., p. 100 . . . .

Reversed.[19]

Beaman v. Pacific Mutual Life Ins. Co.

United States Court of Appeals, Fourth Circuit, 1966.
369 F.2d 653.

■ Before HAYNSWORTH, CHIEF JUDGE, and BELL and WINTER, CIRCUIT JUDGES.

■ WINTER, CIRCUIT JUDGE.

The district judge, on the authority of Mutual Life Ins. Co. of New York v. Moyle, 116 F.2d 434 (4 Cir.1940), dismissed, for lack of jurisdiction, a complaint for a declaratory judgment in which appellant sought a declaration that he was permanently and totally disabled under the terms of a health and accident policy issued by appellee and also sought recovery of $69,884.00, based upon the monthly benefit under the policy times his claimed life expectancy, without discount. Lack of jurisdiction was predicated upon the determination that the amount in controversy was less than $10,000.00. The district judge was correct in his determination, and we affirm.

The policy was issued December 28, 1961. It provided indemnity of $200.00 per month, if appellant were involved in an accident which caused his total disability, for as long as appellant remained in that condition. In the event of partial disability from accident, the benefit was $100.00 per

[19. In Weinberger v. Wiesenfeld, 420 U.S. 636, 642 n. 10 (1975), it was held that the amount in controversy in a suit to determine the plaintiff's eligibility for social-security benefits is the present value of the potential future payments under the program and is not limited to the value of the benefits accrued at the time of filing suit.]

month for a like period. Total disability was defined as disability which prevented appellant from performing every duty pertaining to any gainful occupation. Partial disability was defined as disability which prevented the performance of one or more important daily duties pertaining to appellant's occupation.

On or about November 26, 1962, appellant was injured in an industrial accident while performing his usual occupation as an employee of a construction steel contractor. In his complaint, appellant alleged that as a result he "... suffered a total disability as a result of accident which has in the past and will in the future during the plaintiff's lifetime render him totally disabled and prevent him from performing every duty pertaining to any gainful occupation for which he is reasonably fitted as defined by the policy." For twenty-four months after the accident occurred, appellee paid appellant $200.00 per month. However, on October 21, 1964, upon obtaining a report from one of the appellant's attending physicians that he was then "able to do light work," appellee concluded that appellant was no longer totally disabled within the meaning of the policy and monthly disability payments were discontinued in January, 1965. Suit was filed July 27, 1965. At a pretrial conference it was stipulated that the appellant was born March 13, 1918, and that the life expectancy of a male of appellant's age on the anticipated date of trial was 25.27 years. Diversity of citizenship between the parties was alleged and admitted. The only issue on the merits raised by the pleadings was whether appellant was totally disabled and prevented from performing every duty pertaining to any gainful occupation for which he was reasonably fitted, as defined by the policy, on and after January 1, 1965.

In review of the motion granted, we must assume that appellant's allegations as to his total disability would be sustained by the proof. We must, therefore, determine the proper measure of recovery to which appellant would now be entitled, because that amount is determinative of whether appellant may maintain his action in a federal district court in the light of the jurisdictional requirement that, in an action for declaratory judgment, jurisdiction exists only where there is diversity of jurisdiction between the parties, and the amount in controversy exceeds $10,000.00, exclusive of interests and costs. 28 U.S.C. §§ 2201 and 1332. If appellant were entitled to recover only $200.00 per month for the period January 1, 1965 to July 27, 1965, manifestly, the amount in controversy was insufficient to sustain jurisdiction; but if appellant were entitled to recover that amount and also to treat appellee's failure to pay the benefits during that period as an anticipatory breach of appellee's obligation to pay benefits for total disability for the remainder of appellant's life, a sum in excess of $10,000.00 would be in controversy and the lower court would have jurisdiction.

The decided cases in the Supreme Court of the United States and in this and other circuits are clear that in a suit like the case at bar, the measure of recovery and, hence, the amount in controversy, is only the aggregate value of past benefits allegedly wrongly withheld. New York L.

Ins. Co. v. Viglas, 297 U.S. 672 (1936); Mobley v. New York Life Ins. Co., 295 U.S. 632 (1935); Keck v. Fidelity and Casualty Company of New York, 359 F.2d 840 (7 Cir.1966), and cases cited therein; Mutual Life Ins. Co. of New York v. Moyle, 116 F.2d 434 (4 Cir.1940). As we stated in the *Moyle* case:

> "... all that is in controversy is the right of the insured to the disability payments which had accrued at the time of suit. The company is obligated to make these payments only so long as the condition evidencing total and permanent disability continues; and, as this condition, theoretically at least, may change at any time, it is impossible to say that any controversy exists as to any disability payments except such as have accrued." (116 F.2d, at 435).

We added:

> "Such a case is to be distinguished from one where the controversy relates to the validity of the policy and not merely to liability for benefits accrued; for, in the latter case, the amount involved is necessarily the face of the policy in addition to the amount of such benefits." (116 F.2d, at 435).

An early decision in the Sixth Circuit held that a refusal to pay benefits because of a claim that the insured was not totally disabled could be treated as an anticipatory breach of the entire contract if the insured alleged, and was prepared to prove, total disability for her remaining life. The present value of the entire contract would thus constitute the amount in controversy. Federal Life Ins. Co. v. Rascoe, 12 F.2d 693 (6 Cir.1926). But that holding has been expressly disapproved by the Supreme Court of the United States in the *Viglas* case (297 U.S., at 678–679), and the *Mobley* case (295 U.S., at 639). Its result has been criticized in 5 Williston, Contracts (1937 Ed.) § 1330A, and its disapproval by the Supreme Court has brought about a revision of 2 Restatement of the Law of Contracts (1930 Ed.) § 318. See Restatement of the Law (Contracts), 1948 Supplement, § 318, and discussion following.

As summarized in the Restatement, there cannot be an anticipatory breach unless there is "an element of an exchange of values still unperformed." [20] See also, *Federal Life Insurance Co. v. Rascoe*, supra (dissenting opinion, 12 F.2d, pp. 697–698). In other words, the doctrine of anticipatory breach has no application to a unilateral contract like the insurance policy in this case, because the condition in the policy that the insured must be totally disabled to be entitled to a benefit is not an exchange of values so as to render the contract bilateral.

---

20. Restatement of the Law (Contracts), 1948 Supplement, § 318, Comment e:

"The doctrine of anticipatory breach is not extended to unilateral contracts unless the promisor's duty is conditional on receipt by him, at some time subsequent to the repudiation, of the agreed exchange for his promise or performance. The mere happening or performance of a condition is not enough, unless the performance is part of the agreed exchange of performances on the transaction, even though it is not promised .... There must be an element of an exchange of value still unperformed in order to make a breach by anticipatory repudiation possible."

Appellee relies upon Aetna Casualty & Surety Co. v. Flowers, 330 U.S. 464 (1947); Brotherhood of Locomotive Firemen & Enginemen v. Pinkston, 293 U.S. 96 (1934); and Thompson v. Thompson, 226 U.S. 551 (1913), to support a contrary result. But in each of these cases, the matter sought to be litigated was not a right to future payments contingent on a continuation of present status, but a basic right to receive unconditional payments in the future. In *Thompson,* a wife, separated from her husband, sought to have reinstated a decree for her support and maintenance. The issue was whether the decree, in its entirety, should be given full faith and credit; the wife's right to *all* future payments was thus jeopardized. In *Pinkston,* widow sought to prevent threatened dissolution of the fund from which her pension was payable and thus to enforce her entire right to that pension. In *Flowers,* a widow sought to enforce for herself and her minor children their right to death benefits, payable in installments, under a state workmen's compensation statute. The Court, in an opinion summarizing the law of this subject, and harmonizing many of the cases cited in this opinion, specifically stated that had the widow been suing merely for the installments due her at the time of the action, dismissal would have been proper. The crucial fact in that case was that "the Tennessee statute which creates liability for the award contemplates a single action for the determination of claimant's right to benefits and a single judgment for the award granted." (330 U.S., at 467–468.) Again, the entire right to the benefits was in issue.

In the case at bar, appellee was not alleged to have declared the policy void, nor to have refused its obligation to pay if appellant was in fact totally disabled. Appellee questions only the latter fact. The significance of the distinction between a contest over a basic right to payment and a contest over payment of certain installment payments, the basic right to payment upon the happening of certain conditions being unquestioned, is, as our quotation from the *Moyle* case, supra, demonstrates, that for jurisdictional purposes the value of the former is its present aggregate value, while the value of the latter is the aggregate of installments alleged to be past due.

Since the amount in controversy in this case is less than $10,000.00, the judgment of the district court is

Affirmed.[21]

Pinel v. Pinel

Supreme Court of the United States, 1916.
240 U.S. 594, 36 S.Ct. 416, 60 L.Ed. 817.

■ MR. JUSTICE PITNEY delivered the opinion of the court.

This is a direct appeal under § 238, Jud.Code, from an order dismissing a bill of complaint for want of jurisdiction. There are two complainants,

---

[21.   See also Keck v. Fidelity & Cas. Co. of New York, 359 F.2d 840 (7th Cir.1966); White v. North Am. Acc. Ins. Co., 316 F.2d 5 (10th Cir.1963).

The entire amount of potential benefits payable to a disability claimant in the future are in controversy in a suit by the insurer for rescission of the policy. Massachusetts Casualty Ins. Co. v. Harmon, 88 F.3d 415 (6th Cir.1996).]

and the jurisdictional questions certified are, (1) whether the amount in controversy is sufficient to give the court jurisdiction, and (2) whether the parties are collusively joined.

It is averred in the bill that complainants and defendants are the children of one Charles T. Pinel, a resident of the State of Michigan, who died June 26, 1888, possessed in fee simple of a tract of land situated in that State, and leaving a last will and testament which was afterwards duly admitted to probate there, by which he left his entire estate to the defendants, failing to provide for complainants, who are two of his children, and for another child, Charles W. Pinel; that their omission from the will was not intentional on the part of the said Charles T. Pinel, but was made by a mistake or accident; that the laws of the State of Michigan (Comp. Laws, 1897, § 9286), provide that when any testator shall omit to provide in his will for any of his children, and it shall appear that such omission was not intentional and was made by mistake or accident, such child shall have the same share in the estate of the testator as if he had died intestate; that by virtue of the statute complainants and the said Charles W. Pinel were severally entitled to the same shares in the estate of Charles T. Pinel, deceased, as if he had died intestate; that testator left a widow and nine children, one of whom is since deceased; that after testator's death Charles W. Pinel conveyed all his interest in the estate to the complainant Sarah Slyfield; and that, by reason of the premises, "complainant Herman Pinel is entitled to an undivided one-eighth interest, and complainant Sarah Slyfield to an undivided two-eighths interest, or in all both complainants together to an undivided three-eighths interest in the aforesaid property, which said interests are of the value of $4,500 and upwards over and above all encumbrances." The prayer is, in effect, that the title of complainants to an undivided three-eighths interest in the land may be established.

The settled rule is that when two or more plaintiffs having separate and distinct demands unite in a single suit, it is essential that the demand of each be of the requisite jurisdictional amount; but when several plaintiffs unite to enforce a single title or right in which they have a common and undivided interest, it is enough if their interests collectively equal the jurisdictional amount. Clay v. Field, 138 U.S. 464, 479; Troy Bank v. Whitehead, 222 U.S. 39. This case comes within the former class, since the title of each complainant is separate and distinct from that of the other; it being evident that the testator's omission to provide for one of his children by will, based upon mistake or accident, is independent of the question whether a like mistake was made with respect to another child.

The action having been brought in the District Court under the first paragraph of § 24, Jud.Code (act of March 3, 1911, ch. 231; 36 Stat. 1087, 1091), on the ground of diversity of citizenship, it is necessary that the matter in controversy exceed the sum or value of $3,000, and that this shall appear by distinct averment upon the face of the bill, or otherwise from the proofs. The averment that complainant Pinel is entitled to an undivided one-eighth interest, and complainant Slyfield to an undivided two-eighths interest, making together an undivided three-eighths interest in the property in question, "which said interests are of the value of $4,500 and upwards over and above all encumbrances," is not the legal equivalent of saying that the interest of either complainant is of the value of more than $3,000. It is not necessarily to be inferred that the value of an undivided two-eighths is two-thirds of the value of an undivided three-eighths. The probable cost and difficulty of partition, and other like considerations, prevent the application of a mere rule of proportion. . . .

Upon the whole, it does not satisfactorily appear that the interest claimed by either complainant is sufficient in value to confer jurisdiction, and hence the bill was properly dismissed. It is obvious that, in the view we take of the case, the question of collusive joinder becomes immaterial.

Decree affirmed.[22]

[22. *Pinel* did not disturb the long-standing rule that a single plaintiff suing a single defendant can aggregate all of his claims, whether they are related or unrelated. See, e.g., Griffin v. Red Run Lodge, Inc., 610 F.2d 1198 (4th Cir.1979). This rule persists by the sheer force of precedent unsupported by any apparent justification. See Wright & Kane, Federal Courts § 36 (6th ed.2002). See generally Rensberger, The Amount in Controversy: Understanding the Rules of Aggregation, 26 Ariz.St.L.J. 925 (1995).

Punitive damages can be aggregated for purposes of amount in controversy. Allen v. R & H Oil & Gas Co., 63 F.3d 1326 (5th Cir.1995) (applying Mississippi law); In re Norplant Contraceptive Products Liability Litigation, 907 F.Supp. 244 (E.D.Tex.1995) (applying Texas law).

Plaintiff joins in good faith several claims that total more than the required amount in controversy. Summary judgment is entered for defendant on one of the claims and the remaining claims taken together do not meet the statutory minimum. Does the federal court continue to have jurisdiction to hear the remaining claims without reliance on the discretionary exercise of supplemental jurisdiction, discussed below in Chapter V? Compare Stevenson v. Severs, 158 F.3d 1332 (D.C.Cir.1998), and Shanaghan v. Cahill, 58 F.3d 106 (4th Cir.1995) (treating the district court's jurisdiction over the remaining claims as supplemental and hence discretionary under 28 U.S.C. § 1367(c)), with Wolde–Meskel v. Vocational Instruction Project Community Services, Inc., 166 F.3d 59, 64 (2d Cir.1999) (rejecting the reasoning of *Stevenson* and *Shanaghan* as "confused"). See Note, *Shanaghan v. Cahill*: Supplementing Supplemental Jurisdiction, 1996 B.Y.U.L.Rev. 281. See also Grinnell Mut. Reins Co. v. Shierk, 121 F.3d 1114 (7th Cir.1997), discussed supra, p. 241, n. 10.

Note that the complaint in *Pinel* asserted the rights of three pretermitted heirs: the brothers Charles W. Pinel and Herman Pinel and their sister Sarah Slyfield, each claiming a one-eighth interest in the estate of their father, Charles T. Pinel. The estate consisted of a tract of land, and the complaint alleged that the matter in controversy was three-eighths of the value of that land: "$4,500 and upwards." Herman sought a one-eighth share, and his sister sought a two-eighths share (one-eighth on her own account and one-eighth as successor in interest to her brother Charles). Suppose that the Supreme Court had continued to disregard the "and upwards" part of the jurisdictional-amount allegation as too vague, but had been willing to apply "a mere rule of proportion" and had also resolved the unreached "collusive joinder" issue in favor of allowing Sarah to combine her claim with that assigned to her by her brother Charles. If this were the case, Sarah would have been deemed to have properly asserted a claim for exactly $3,000. Would that have sufficed to allow her, at least, to bring her case in federal court on the ground of diversity of citizenship? See the next case, *Brainin v. Melikian*.

Brainin v. Melikian

United States Court of Appeals, Third Circuit, 1968.
396 F.2d 153.

■ Before HASTIE, CHIEF JUDGE, and MCLAUGHLIN, KALODNER, GANEY, FREEDMAN, SEITZ, and VAN DUSEN, CIRCUIT JUDGES.

ON PETITION FOR REHEARING

■ KALODNER, CIRCUIT JUDGE.

On August 14, 1967, the plaintiff, Irving Brainin, instituted this diversity action in the District Court against the defendants, K. Cyrus Melikian and Lloyd K. Rudd, endorsers of a note of Rudd–Melikian, Inc. in the principal amount of $10,000.00 payable ten months after date with interest at 8% per annum. Between the date of the note's execution on March 21, 1967 and the date of its maturity, and before any payment had been made on it, Rudd–Melikian, Inc. filed bankruptcy proceedings causing plaintiff to accelerate the note's payment date. Upon demand and dishonor, plaintiff sued the endorsers of the note for $10,324.44, the principal amount of the note, plus the 8% interest therein fixed, to the date of the filing of the complaint.

On September 14, 1967, after defendant Melikian failed to answer within the required time, a default judgment was entered against him. Service was not perfected on Rudd.

Thereafter, on October 9, 1967, Melikian moved to vacate the default judgment, contending that the judgment was entered without jurisdiction because the amount in controversy did not exceed $10,000, "exclusive of interest and costs," as required by 28 U.S.C. § 1332(a), inasmuch as the face amount of the note was only $10,000. By Order of October 24, 1967, 285 F.Supp. 420, the District Court denied Melikian's motion, stating in its accompanying opinion:

"... [Melikian's] contention fails to draw the distinction which the cases recognize, between interest imposed as a penalty for delay in payment, and interest exacted as the agreed upon price for the hire of money. The former is the 'interest' which is excluded in determining jurisdictional

---

Now suppose that Sarah and Herman amended their complaint and alleged in good faith that Sarah's combined shares of the property in question each amounted to a separate and distinct interest of $1,600 while Herman's single share also amounted to a separate and distinct interest of $1,600. Assuming again that Sarah's joinder of a claim to her own share with her claim to the share acquired from her brother Charles was not deemed collusive, she would be able to aggregate her two claims to place in controversy a total of $3,200, thus satisfying the jurisdictional-amount requirement then in effect for diversity jurisdiction. But as a matter of aggregation law, Herman's $1,600 claim would have to be dismissed as jurisdictionally insufficient. Although a single party can aggregate multiple claims, multiple parties cannot (unless the claims are considered "joint" rather than "several"). But as noted previously, p. 248, n. 15, and discussed in Comment on 28 U.S.C. §§ 1367(b) & 1367(c), infra, p. 311, supplemental jurisdiction permits what aggregation law had traditionally forbidden: the adjudication of related "several" claims by additional plaintiffs provided some one plaintiff independently satisfies the jurisdictional amount. See Exxon Mobil Corp. v. Allapattah Services, Inc., 545 U.S. 546 (2005), reprinted infra, p. 289.]

amount; the latter is rightly computed as part of the amount to which the claimant is entitled. *The instant case involves the latter insofar as it claims interest at the rate specified in the note during the period before maturity.* [citing authorities]." (Emphasis supplied.)

On appeal to this Court, we affirmed per curiam for the reasons stated in the Opinion of the District Court.

In the instant Petition for Rehearing, Melikian cites cases which he claims are in "direct conflict" with our decision. All of the cases cited were previously brought to this Court's attention in Melikian's original brief and his present petition presents nothing new.

The cases relied on by Melikian are inapposite to the factual situation obtaining here inasmuch as they involved situations where the interest claimed was an incident arising solely by virtue of a delay in payment.[23] As the District Court stated, the interest claimed in the instant case involves not a charge for delay in the payment of money, but ". . . interest exacted as the agreed upon price for the hire of money . . . *insofar as it claims interest at the rate specified in the note during the period before maturity.*" (Emphasis supplied.)

Brown v. Webster, 156 U.S. 328 (1895);[24] Edwards v. Bates County, 163 U.S. 269 (1896); Intermela v. Perkins, 205 F. 603 (C.C.A. 9 Cir.1913), cert. den'd, 231 U.S. 757 (1914); and Continental Casualty Company v. Spradlin, 170 F. 322 (C.C.A. 4 Cir.1909), cited by Melikian, afford no nourishment to his position and indeed, support the District Court's disposition. They held that the "interest" there involved was *includable* in computing the jurisdictional amount on the theory that such interest was not merely incidental or "accessory" to the principal amount demanded, but was an integral part of the aggregate amount of damages claimed, *Brown v. Webster*, supra, 156 U.S., at 330; *Intermela v. Perkins*, supra, 205 F., at 606; *Continental Casualty Company*, supra, 170 F., at 323, or, was itself a "principal obligation." *Edwards v. Bates County*, supra, 163 U.S., at 272.[25] Similarly, the interest claimed here for the period before the maturity of the note is also not incidental or "accessory" to the main obligation,

---

23. Regan v. Marshall, 309 F.2d 677, 678 (1 Cir.1962); Moore v. Town Council of Edgefield, 32 F. 498 (Cir.Ct.D.S.C.1887); Albani v. D & R Truck Service, Inc., 248 F.Supp. 268 (D.Conn.1965); Fratto v. Northern Insurance Company of New York, 242 F.Supp. 262, 268–269 (W.D.Pa.1965) aff'd per curiam on other grounds, 359 F.2d 842 (3 Cir.1966); and Voorhees v. Aetna Life Insurance Co., 250 F. 484 (D.C.N.J.1918).

[24. In *Brown v. Webster* the distinction is drawn—though with very questionable application upon the facts—between interest "as damages" and interest "as such."]

25. Defendant's contention that *Intermela v. Perkins*, supra; *Continental Casualty Company v. Spradlin*, supra; *Albani v. D & R Truck Service, Inc.*, supra; and *Moore v. Town Council of Edgefield*, supra, "have specifically held that where interest has arisen by reason of a contractual promise, said interest may not be included in the amount in controversy," is utterly specious. Those cases do not "specifically" or implicitly stand for such a proposition. Moreover, such a result would be contrary to *Edwards v. Bates County*, supra, where the Supreme Court held that the amount of a matured bond interest coupon could be added to the amount of the bond in determining the jurisdictional amount.

but an integral part of the total obligation demanded from defendant by plaintiff.

As the plaintiff pointed out in his original brief, two of the cases relied on by Melikian, Alropa Corp. v. Myers, 55 F.Supp. 936 (D.Del.1944); and Fritchen v. Mueller, 27 F.2d 167 (D.Kan.1928), appear to be contrary to the present decision. Neither of those decisions is binding upon this Court, and insofar as they hold that the interest accruing on a promissory note *before* maturity is excludable in determining the jurisdictional amount, we disagree.

It should also be noted that *Alropa* and *Fritchen,* in failing to recognize the distinction between interest accruing *after* the maturity of a promissory note and that accruing *prior* to maturity, ignore Congress' purpose in excluding "interest" in determining the jurisdictional amount. Congress limited federal diversity jurisdiction to cases involving in excess of $10,000.00, "exclusive of interest . . . ," 28 U.S.C. § 1332(a), to prevent the delaying of a suit merely to accumulate the necessary amount for federal jurisdiction. 1 Moore's Federal Practice, ¶ 0.99, p. 903 (2d ed.1964).

For the reasons stated the petition for rehearing will be denied.[26]

[26.   Accord: Bailey Employment System, Inc. v. Hahn, 655 F.2d 473 (2d Cir.1981).

If a state statute permits recovery of an attorney's fee in an action, the fee demanded is included in measuring the amount in controversy, even though the statute describes the fee as part of the recoverable costs. Missouri State Life Ins. Co. v. Jones, 290 U.S. 199 (1933).

On more than one occasion unwary counsel have pegged their clients' diversity claims at exactly the amount specified in § 1332(a). The statute confers jurisdiction only when the amount in controversy "exceeds" the specified figure. There being no good-faith basis for counsel to revise the amount claimed once the insufficiency was revealed, the claims were each dismissed for lack of a penny—and thus for lack of jurisdiction. See Larkin v. Brown, 41 F.3d 387, 389 (8th Cir.1994); LeBlanc v. Spector, 378 F.Supp. 301, 307–308 (D.Conn. 1973).]

CHAPTER V

SUPPLEMENTAL JURISDICTION[1]

STATUTE[2]

28 U.S.C. § 1367. Supplemental jurisdiction

(a) Except as provided in subsections (b) and (c) or as expressly provided otherwise by Federal statute, in any civil action of which the district courts have original jurisdiction, the district courts shall have supplemental jurisdiction over all other claims that are so related to claims in the action within such original jurisdiction that they form part of the same case or controversy under Article III of the United States Constitution. Such supplemental jurisdiction shall include claims that involve the joinder or intervention of additional parties.

(b) In any civil action of which the district courts have original jurisdiction founded solely on section 1332 of this title, the district courts shall not have supplemental jurisdiction under subsection (a) over claims by plaintiffs against persons made parties under Rule 14, 19, 20, or 24 of the Federal Rules of Civil Procedure, or over claims by persons proposed to be joined as plaintiffs under Rule 19 of such rules, or seeking to intervene as plaintiffs under Rule 24 of such rules, when exercising supplemental jurisdiction over such claims would be inconsistent with the jurisdictional requirements of section 1332.

(c) The district courts may decline to exercise supplemental jurisdiction over a claim under subsection (a) if—

    (1) the claim raises a novel or complex issue of State law,

    (2) the claim substantially predominates over the claim or claims over which the district court has original jurisdiction,

    (3) the district court has dismissed all claims over which it has original jurisdiction, or

    (4) in exceptional circumstances, there are other compelling reasons for declining jurisdiction.

(d) The period of limitations for any claim asserted under subsection (a), and for any other claim in the same action that is voluntarily dismissed

---

[1. See generally ALI Judicial Code Project, Part I: Supplemental Jurisdiction, at 5–136; 13B Wright, Miller & Cooper, Federal Practice and Procedure: Jurisdiction 2d § 3567.3 (2004 Supp.); Teply & Whitten, Civil Procedure 116–148 (3d ed.2004); Mullenix, Redish & Vairo, Understanding Federal Courts and Jurisdiction § 5.04 (1998).]

[2. Act of Dec. 1, 1990, Pub.L. 101–650, Title III, § 310(a), 104 Stat. 5113.]

at the same time as or after the dismissal of the claim under subsection (a), shall be tolled while the claim is pending and for a period of 30 days after it is dismissed unless State law provides for a longer tolling period.

(e) As used in this section, the term "State" includes the District of Columbia, the Commonwealth of Puerto Rico, and any territory or possession of the United States.

INTRODUCTORY NOTE

The federal supplemental-jurisdiction statute was not written on a blank slate. The first three principal cases in this chapter provide essential background. The constitutional foundation for the statute is provided by the *Gibbs* case. The roots of the statute's attempt to preserve the restrictive effect of the rule of complete diversity within an otherwise global regime of supplemental jurisdiction lie in the *Kroger* case. The separation-of-powers concerns expressed in *Finley* were the predicate for the statute's codification and conceptual union—under the new rubric of "supplemental jurisdiction" —of the judge-made doctrines of ancillary and pendent jurisdiction that had flourished under *Gibbs* except as reined in by *Kroger*. The remaining principal cases of this chapter examine the scope and effect of the statute by which Congress sought to still the questions raised by *Finley* without fundamentally altering the jurisdictional terrain mapped by *Gibbs* and *Kroger*.

United Mine Workers of America v. Gibbs
Supreme Court of the United States, 1966.
383 U.S. 715, 86 S.Ct. 1130, 16 L.Ed.2d 218.

[Gibbs sued the union in federal court, asserting that the union had brought improper pressure on his employer, Grundy, to discharge him. He claimed the union had engaged in a secondary boycott, for which he was entitled to relief under § 303 of the Taft–Hartley Act, 29 U.S.C. § 187, and also alleged a state common-law claim of unlawful conspiracy to interfere with his contract of employment. After verdict for Gibbs, the district court held that the union pressure to discharge him was a primary dispute with his employer, not cognizable under § 303. It sustained an award to Gibbs on the verdict on the ground that interference with employment was cognizable as a state claim.]

■ MR. JUSTICE BRENNAN delivered the opinion of the Court.

. . . . .

I.

A threshold question is whether the District Court properly entertained jurisdiction of the claim based on Tennessee law. . . .

The fact that state remedies were not entirely preempted does not, however, answer the question whether the state claim was properly heard in the District Court absent diversity jurisdiction. The Court held in Hurn v. Oursler, 289 U.S. 238, that state law claims are appropriate for federal court determination if they form a separate but parallel ground for relief also sought in a substantial claim based on federal law. The Court distinguished permissible from nonpermissible exercise of federal judicial power over state law claims by contrasting "a case where two distinct grounds in support of a single cause of action are alleged, one only of which presents a federal question, and a case where two separate and distinct causes of action are alleged, one only of which is federal in character. In the former, where the federal question averred is not plainly wanting in substance, the federal court, even though the federal ground be not established, may nevertheless retain and dispose of the case upon the non-federal *ground;* in the latter, it may not do so upon the non-federal *cause of action.*" 289 U.S., at 246. The question is into which category the present action fell.

Hurn was decided in 1933, before the unification of law and equity by the Federal Rules of Civil Procedure. At the time, the meaning of "cause of action" was a subject of serious dispute; the phrase might "mean one thing for one purpose and something different for another." United States v. Memphis Cotton Oil Co., 288 U.S. 62, 67–68. The Court in *Hurn* identified what it meant by the term by citation of Baltimore S.S. Co. v. Phillips, 274 U.S. 316, a case in which "cause of action" had been used to identify the operative scope of the doctrine of res judicata. In that case the Court had noted that " 'the whole tendency of our decisions is to require a plaintiff to try his whole cause of action and his whole case at one time,' " 274 U.S., at 320, and stated its holding in the following language, quoted in part in the *Hurn* opinion:

> "Upon principle, it is perfectly plain that the respondent [a seaman suing for an injury sustained while working aboard ship] suffered but one actionable wrong and was entitled to but one recovery, whether his injury was due to one or the other of several distinct acts of alleged negligence or to a combination of some or all of them. In either view, there would be but a single wrongful invasion of a single primary right of the plaintiff, namely, the right of bodily safety, whether the acts constituting such invasion were one or many, simple or complex.

> "A cause of action does not consist of facts, but of the unlawful violation of a right which the facts show. The number and variety of the facts alleged do not establish more than one cause of action so long as their result, whether they be considered severally or in combination, is the violation of but one right by a single legal wrong. The mere multiplication of grounds of negligence alleged as causing the same injury does not result in multiplying the causes of action. 'The facts are merely the means, and not the end. They do not constitute the cause of action, but they show its existence by making the wrong appear.' " Id., at 321.

Had the Court found a jurisdictional bar to reaching the state claim in *Hurn*, we assume that the doctrine of res judicata would not have been applicable in any subsequent state suit. But the citation of *Baltimore S.S.* shows that the Court found that the weighty policies of judicial economy and fairness to parties reflected in res judicata doctrine were in themselves strong counsel for the adoption of a rule which would permit federal courts to dispose of the state as well as the federal claims.

With the adoption of the Federal Rules of Civil Procedure and the unified form of action, Fed.Rules Civ.Proc. 2, much of the controversy over "cause of action" abated. The phrase remained as the keystone of the *Hurn* test, however, and, as commentators have noted, has been the source of considerable confusion. Under the Rules, the impulse is toward entertaining the broadest possible scope of action consistent with fairness to the parties; joinder of claims, parties and remedies are strongly encouraged. Yet because the *Hurn* question involves issues of jurisdiction as well as convenience, there has been some tendency to limit its application to cases in which the state and federal claims are, as in *Hurn*, "little more than the equivalent of different epithets to characterize the same group of circumstances." 289 U.S., at 246.

This limited approach is unnecessarily grudging. Pendent jurisdiction, in the sense of judicial *power,* exists whenever there is a claim "arising under [the] Constitution, the Laws of the United States, and Treaties made, or which shall be made, under their Authority ...." U.S. Const., Art. III, § 2, and the relationship between that claim and the state claims made in the complaint permits the conclusion that the entire action before the court comprises but one constitutional "case." The federal claim must have substance sufficient to confer subject matter jurisdiction on the court. Levering & Garrigues Co. v. Morrin, 289 U.S. 103. The state and federal claims must derive from a common nucleus of operative fact. But if, considered without regard for their federal or state character, a plaintiff's claims are such that he would ordinarily be expected to try them all in one judicial proceeding, then, assuming substantiality of the federal issues, there is *power* in federal courts to hear the whole.

That power need not be exercised in every case in which it is found to exist. It has consistently been recognized that pendent jurisdiction is a doctrine of discretion, not of plaintiff's right. Its justification lies in considerations of judicial economy, convenience and fairness to litigants; if these are not present a federal court should hesitate to exercise jurisdiction over state claims, even though bound to apply state law to them, Erie R. Co. v. Tompkins, 304 U.S. 64. Needless decisions of state law should be avoided both as a matter of comity and to promote justice between the parties, by procuring for them a surer footed reading of applicable law. Certainly, if the federal claims are dismissed before trial, even though not insubstantial in a jurisdictional sense, the state claims should be dismissed as well. Similarly, if it appears that the state issues substantially predominate, whether in terms of proof, of the scope of the issues raised, or of the comprehensiveness of the remedy sought, the state claims may be dismissed without prejudice and left for resolution to state tribunals. There may, on the other hand, be situations in which the state claim is so closely tied to questions of federal policy that the argument for exercise of pendent jurisdiction is particularly strong. In the present case, for example, the allowable scope of the state claim implicates the federal doctrine of pre-emption; while this interrelationship does not create statutory federal question jurisdiction, Louisville & N.R. Co. v. Mottley, 211 U.S. 149, its existence is relevant to the exercise of discretion. Finally, there may be reasons independent of jurisdictional considerations, such as the likelihood of jury confusion in treating divergent legal theories of relief, that would justify separating state and federal claims for trial, Fed.Rules Civ.Proc. 42(b); if so, jurisdiction here, too, should ordinarily be refused.

The question of power will ordinarily be resolved on the pleadings. But the issue whether pendent jurisdiction has been properly assumed is one which remains open throughout the litigation. Pretrial procedures or even the trial may reveal a substantial hegemony of state law claims, or likelihood of jury confusion, which could not have been anticipated at the pleading stage. Although it will of course be appropriate to take account in this circumstance of the already completed course of the litigation, dismissal of the state claim might even then be merited. For example, it may appear that the plaintiff was well aware of the nature of his proofs and the relative importance of his claims; recognition of a federal court's wide latitude to decide ancillary questions of state law does not imply that it must tolerate a litigant's effort to impose upon it what is in effect only a state law case. Once it appears that a state claim constitutes the real body of a case, to which the federal claim is only an appendage, the state claim may fairly be dismissed.

We are not prepared to say that in the present case the District Court exceeded its discretion in proceeding to judgment on the state claim. We may assume for purposes of decision that the District Court was correct in its holding that the claim of pressure on Grundy to terminate the employment contract was outside the purview of § 303. Even so, the § 303 claims based on secondary pressures on Grundy relative to the haulage contract and on other coal operators generally were substantial. Although § 303 limited recovery to compensatory damages based on secondary pressures, ... and state law allowed both compensatory and punitive damages, and allowed such damages as to both secondary and primary activity, the state and federal claims arose from the same nucleus of operative fact and reflected alternative remedies. The jury was so instructed on its verdict sheet, which allowed no room for the award of double damages, one on the federal and one on the state claim.

It is true that the § 303 claims ultimately failed and that the only recovery allowed respondent was on the state claim. We cannot confidently say, however, that the federal issues were so remote or played such a minor role at the trial that in effect the state claim only was tried. Although the District Court dismissed as unproved the claims that petitioner's secondary activities included attempts to induce coal operators other than Grundy to cease doing business with respondent, the court submitted the § 303 claims relating to Grundy to the jury. The jury returned verdicts against petitioner on those claims, and it was only on petitioner's motion for a directed verdict and a judgment n.o.v. that they were set aside. The District Judge considered the claim as to the haulage contract proved as to liability, and held it failed only for lack of proof of damages. Although there was some risk of confusing the jury in joining the state and federal claims—especially since, as will be developed, differing standards of proof of UMW involvement applied—the possibility of confusion could be lessened by employing a special verdict form, as the District Court did. Moreover, the question whether the permissible scope of the state claim was limited by the doctrine of pre-emption afforded a special reason for the exercise of pendent jurisdiction; the federal courts are particularly appropriate bodies for the application of pre-emption principles. We thus conclude that although it may be that the District Court might, in its sound discretion, have dismissed the state claim, the circumstances show no error in refusing to do so.

[In Part II, the Court held that the trial court had improperly instructed the jury on the narrow circumstances—confined to acts of violence—in which state tort law can regulate union conduct without being substantively preempted by federal labor law. In Part III, the Court alternatively held that to the extent state tort law could be applied to the union conduct at issue in this case, it was procedurally qualified by a federal statute (§ 6 of the Norris–LaGuardia Act) imposing special proof requirements in suits against unions, and that as a matter of law the evidence of record failed to meet this "clear proof" standard for holding a union liable for strike-related violence.]

Reversed.

■ THE CHIEF JUSTICE took no part in the decision of this case.

■ MR. JUSTICE HARLAN, whom MR. JUSTICE CLARK joins, concurring.

I agree with and join in Part I of the Court's opinion relating to pendent jurisdiction. As to Part II, I refrain from joining the Court's speculations about the uses to which it may put the preemption doctrine in similar future cases. The holding in Part III that the Norris–LaGuardia Act requires reversal here seems to me correct, but my interpretation of the statute is different and somewhat narrower than that of the Court.

. . . . .[3]

[3. A federal court has discretion to decide a claim within its pendent jurisdiction after the claim that gave it jurisdiction of the case has become moot. Rosado v. Wyman, 397 U.S. 397 (1970).

In a case removed from state court to federal court, in which all of the federal-law claims that were the basis for removal have been eliminated from the case and only pendent state-law claims remain, the district court has discretion to remand the remaining claims to state

Owen Equipment and Erection Co. v. Kroger

Supreme Court of the United States, 1978.
437 U.S. 365, 98 S.Ct. 2396, 57 L.Ed.2d 274.

■ Mr. Justice Stewart delivered the opinion of the Court.

In an action in which federal jurisdiction is based on diversity of citizenship, may the plaintiff assert a claim against a third-party defendant when there is no independent basis for federal jurisdiction over that claim? The Court of Appeals for the Eighth Circuit held in this case that such a claim is within the ancillary jurisdiction of the federal courts. We granted certiorari ... because this decision conflicts with several recent decisions of other Courts of Appeals.

I

On January 18, 1972, James Kroger was electrocuted when the boom of a steel crane next to which he was walking came too close to a high tension electric power line. The respondent (his widow, who is the administratrix of his estate) filed a wrongful death action in the United States District Court for the District of Nebraska against the Omaha Public Power District (OPPD). Her complaint alleged that OPPD's negligent construction, maintenance and operation of the power line had caused Kroger's death. Federal jurisdiction was based on diversity of citizenship, since the respondent was a citizen of Iowa and OPPD was a Nebraska corporation.

OPPD then filed a third-party complaint pursuant to Fed.Rule Civ. Proc. 14(a) against the petitioner, Owen Equipment and Erection Company (Owen), alleging that the crane was owned and operated by Owen, and that Owen's negligence had been the proximate cause of Kroger's death. OPPD later moved for summary judgment on the respondent's complaint against it. While this motion was pending, the respondent was granted leave to file an amended complaint naming Owen as an additional defendant. Thereafter, the District Court granted OPPD's motion for summary judgment in an unreported opinion. The case thus went to trial between the respondent and the petitioner alone.

The respondent's amended complaint alleged that Owen was "a Nebraska corporation with its principal place of business in Nebraska." Owen's answer admitted that it was "a corporation organized and existing under the Laws of the State of Nebraska," and denied every other allegation of the complaint. On the third day of trial, however, it was disclosed that the petitioner's principal place of business was in Iowa, not Nebraska,[4]

---

court rather than dismissing them. Carnegie–Mellon University v. Cohill, 484 U.S. 343 (1988).

See generally 13A Wright, Miller & Cooper, Federal Practice and Procedure: Jurisdiction 2d §§ 3567, 3567.1 (1984 and Supp. 2005).]

4. The problem apparently was one of geography. Although the Missouri River generally marks the boundary between Iowa and Nebraska, Carter Lake, Iowa, where the accident occurred and where Owen had its main office, lies west of the river, adjacent to Omaha,

and that the petitioner and the respondent were thus both citizens of Iowa. The petitioner then moved to dismiss the complaint for lack of jurisdiction. The District Court reserved decision on the motion, and the jury thereafter returned a verdict in favor of the respondent. In an unreported opinion issued after the trial, the District Court denied the petitioner's motion to dismiss the complaint.

The judgment was affirmed on appeal. 558 F.2d 417. The Court of Appeals held that under this Court's decision in Mine Workers v. Gibbs, 383 U.S. 715, the District Court had jurisdictional power, in its discretion, to adjudicate the respondent's claim against the petitioner because that claim arose from the "core of 'operative facts' giving rise to both [respondent's] claim against OPPD and OPPD's claim against Owen." 558 F.2d, at 424. It further held that the District Court had properly exercised its discretion in proceeding to decide the case even after summary judgment had been granted to OPPD, because the petitioner had concealed its Iowa citizenship from the respondent. Rehearing en banc was denied by an equally divided court. 558 F.2d 417.

II

It is undisputed that there was no independent basis of federal jurisdiction over the respondent's state-law tort action against the petitioner, since both are citizens of Iowa. And although Fed.Rule Civ.Proc. 14(a) permits a plaintiff to assert a claim against a third-party defendant, ... it does not purport to say whether or not such a claim requires an independent basis of federal jurisdiction. Indeed, it could not determine that question, since it is axiomatic that the Federal Rules of Civil Procedure do not create or withdraw federal jurisdiction.

In affirming the District Court's judgment, the Court of Appeals relied upon the doctrine of ancillary jurisdiction, whose contours it believed were defined by this Court's holding in *Mine Workers v. Gibbs*, supra. The *Gibbs* case differed from this one in that it involved pendent jurisdiction, which concerns the resolution of a plaintiff's federal and state law claims against a single defendant in one action. By contrast, in this case there was no claim based upon substantive federal law, but rather state-law tort claims against two different defendants. Nonetheless, the Court of Appeals was correct in perceiving that *Gibbs* and this case are two species of the same generic problem: Under what circumstances may a federal court hear and decide a state-law claim arising between citizens of the same State?[5] But we believe that the Court of Appeals failed to understand the scope of the doctrine of the *Gibbs* case.

. . . . .

Neb. Apparently the river once avulsed at one of its bends, cutting Carter Lake off from the rest of Iowa.

5. No more than in Aldinger v. Howard, 427 U.S. 1, is it necessary to determine here "whether there are any 'principled' differences between pendent and ancillary jurisdiction; or, if there are, what effect *Gibbs* had on such differences." Id., at 13.

It is apparent that *Gibbs* delineated the constitutional limits of federal judicial power. But even if it be assumed that the District Court in the present case had constitutional power to decide the respondent's lawsuit against the petitioner,[6] it does not follow that the decision of the Court of Appeals was correct. Constitutional power is merely the first hurdle that must be overcome in determining that a federal court has jurisdiction over a particular controversy. For the jurisdiction of the federal courts is limited not only by the provisions of Art. III of the Constitution, but by Acts of Congress. Palmore v. United States, 411 U.S. 389, 401; Lockerty v. Phillips, 319 U.S. 182, 187; Kline v. Burke Constr. Co., 260 U.S. 226, 234; Cary v. Curtis, 3 How. [44 U.S.] 236, 245.

That statutory law as well as the Constitution may limit a federal court's jurisdiction over nonfederal claims[7] is well illustrated by two recent decisions of this Court, Aldinger v. Howard, 427 U.S. 1, and Zahn v. International Paper Co., 414 U.S. 291. In *Aldinger* the Court held that a federal district court lacked jurisdiction over a state-law claim against a county, even if that claim was alleged to be pendent to one against county officials under 42 U.S.C. § 1983. In *Zahn* the Court held that in a diversity class action under Fed.Rule Civ.Proc. 23(b)(3), the claim of each member of the plaintiff class must independently satisfy the minimum jurisdictional amount of $10,000 set by 28 U.S.C. § 1332(a), and rejected the argument that jurisdiction existed over those claims that involved less than $10,000 as ancillary to those that involved more. In each case, despite the fact that federal and nonfederal claims arose from a "common nucleus of operative fact," the Court held that the statute conferring jurisdiction over the federal claim did not allow the exercise of jurisdiction over the nonfederal claims.[8]

The *Aldinger* and *Zahn* cases thus make clear that a finding that federal and nonfederal claims arise from a "common nucleus of operative fact," the test of *Gibbs,* does not end the inquiry into whether a federal court has power to hear the nonfederal claims along with the federal ones. Beyond this constitutional minimum, there must be an examination of the

---

6. Federal jurisdiction in *Gibbs* was based upon the existence of a question of federal law. The Court of Appeals in the present case believed that the "common nucleus of operative fact" test also determines the outer boundaries of constitutionally permissible federal jurisdiction when that jurisdiction is based upon diversity of citizenship. We may assume without deciding that the Court of Appeals was correct in this regard. See also n. [9], infra.

7. As used in this opinion, the term "nonfederal claim" means one as to which there is no independent basis for federal jurisdiction. Conversely, a "federal claim" means one as to which an independent basis for federal jurisdiction exists.

8. In Monell v. New York City Dept. of Social Services, 436 U.S. 658, we have overruled Monroe v. Pape, 365 U.S. 167 insofar as it held that political subdivisions are never amenable to suit under 42 U.S.C. § 1983—the basis of the holding in *Aldinger* that 28 U.S.C. § 1343(3) does not allow pendent jurisdiction of a state-law claim against a county. But *Monell* in no way qualifies the holding of *Aldinger* that the jurisdictional questions presented in a case such as this one are statutory as well as constitutional, a point on which the dissenters in *Aldinger* agreed with the Court. See 427 U.S., at 22 n. 3 (BRENNAN, J., joined by BLACKMUN and MARSHALL, JJ., dissenting).

posture in which the nonfederal claim is asserted and of the specific statute that confers jurisdiction over the federal claim, in order to determine whether "Congress in [that statute] has . . . expressly or by implication negated" the exercise of jurisdiction over the particular nonfederal claim. *Aldinger v. Howard*, supra, 427 U.S., at 18.

III

The relevant statute in this case, 28 U.S.C. § 1332(a)(1), confers upon federal courts jurisdiction over "civil actions where the matter in controversy exceeds the sum or value of $10,000 . . . and is between . . . citizens of different States." This statute and its predecessors have consistently been held to require complete diversity of citizenship.[9] That is, diversity jurisdiction does not exist unless *each* defendant is a citizen of a different State from *each* plaintiff. Over the years Congress has repeatedly re-enacted or amended the statute conferring diversity jurisdiction, leaving intact this rule of complete diversity. Whatever may have been the original purposes of diversity of citizenship jurisdiction, this subsequent history clearly demonstrates a congressional mandate that diversity jurisdiction is not to be available when any plaintiff is a citizen of the same State as any defendant. Cf. Snyder v. Harris, 394 U.S. 332, 338–339.

Thus it is clear that the respondent could not originally have brought suit in federal court naming Owen and OPPD as codefendants, since citizens of Iowa would have been on both sides of the litigation. Yet the identical lawsuit resulted when she amended her complaint. Complete diversity was destroyed just as surely as if she had sued Owen initially. In either situation, in the plain language of the statute, the "matter in controversy" could not be "between . . . citizens of different States."

It is a fundamental precept that federal courts are courts of limited jurisdiction. The limits upon federal jurisdiction, whether imposed by the Constitution or by Congress, must be neither disregarded nor evaded. Yet under the reasoning of the Court of Appeals in this case, a plaintiff could defeat the statutory requirement of complete diversity by the simple expedient of suing only those defendants who were of diverse citizenship and waiting for them to implead nondiverse defendants.[10] If, as the Court

---

9.   E.g., Strawbridge v. Curtiss, 3 [3 U.S.] Cranch 267; Coal Company v. Blatchford, 11 Wall. [78 U.S.] 172; Indianapolis v. Chase National Bank, 314 U.S. 63, 69; American Fire & Cas. Co. v. Finn, 341 U.S. 6, 17. It is settled that complete diversity is not a constitutional requirement. State Farm Fire & Cas. Co. v. Tashire, 386 U.S. 523, 530–531.

10.   This is not an unlikely hypothesis, since a defendant in a tort suit such as this one would surely try to limit his liability by impleading any joint tortfeasors for indemnity or contribution. Some commentators have suggested that the possible abuse of third-party practice could be dealt with under 28 U.S.C. § 1359, which forbids collusive attempts to create federal jurisdiction. See, e.g., 3 Moore's Federal Practice ¶ 14.27[1], at 14–571 (2d ed.1974); 6 C. Wright & A. Miller, Federal Practice and Procedure § 1444, at 231–232 (1971); Note, Rule 14 Claims and Ancillary Jurisdiction, 57 Va.L.Rev. 265, 274–275 (1971). The dissenting opinion today also expresses this view. . . . But there is nothing necessarily collusive about a plaintiff selectively suing only those tortfeasors of diverse citizenship, or about the named defendants' desire to implead joint tortfeasors. Nonetheless, the requirement of complete diversity would be eviscerated by such a course of events.

of Appeals thought, a "common nucleus of operative fact" were the only requirement for ancillary jurisdiction in a diversity case, there would be no principled reason why the respondent in this case could not have joined her cause of action against Owen in her original complaint as ancillary to her claim against OPPD. Congress' requirement of complete diversity would thus have been evaded completely.

It is true, as the Court of Appeals noted, that the exercise of ancillary jurisdiction over nonfederal claims has often been upheld in situations involving impleader, cross-claims or counterclaims.[11] But in determining whether jurisdiction over a nonfederal claim exists, the context in which the nonfederal claim is asserted is crucial. See *Aldinger v. Howard*, 427 U.S., at 14. And the claim here arises in a setting quite different from the kinds of nonfederal claim that have been viewed in other cases as falling within the ancillary jurisdiction of the federal courts.

First, the nonfederal claim in this case was simply not ancillary to the federal one in the same sense that, for example, the impleader by a defendant of a third-party defendant always is. A third-party complaint depends at least in part upon the resolution of the primary lawsuit. . . . Its relation to the original complaint is thus not mere factual similarity but logical dependence. Cf. Moore v. New York Cotton Exchange, 270 U.S. 593, 610. The respondent's claim against the petitioner, however, was entirely separate from her original claim against OPPD, since the petitioner's liability to her depended not at all upon whether or not OPPD was also liable. Far from being an ancillary and dependent claim, it was a new and independent one.

Second, the nonfederal claim here was asserted by the plaintiff, who voluntarily chose to bring suit upon a state-law claim in a federal court. By contrast, ancillary jurisdiction typically involves claims by a defending party haled into court against his will, or by another person whose rights might be irretrievably lost unless he could assert them in an ongoing action in a federal court. A plaintiff cannot complain if ancillary jurisdiction does not encompass all of his possible claims in a case such as this one, since it is he who has chosen the federal rather than the state forum and must thus accept its limitations. "[T]he efficiency plaintiff seeks so avidly is available

---

11. The ancillary jurisdiction of the federal courts derives originally from cases such as Freeman v. Howe, 24 How. [65 U.S.] 450, which held that when federal jurisdiction "effectively controls the property or fund under dispute, other claimants thereto should be allowed to intervene in order to protect their interests, without regard to jurisdiction." *Aldinger v. Howard*, 427 U.S., at 11. More recently, it has been said to include cases that involve multiparty practice, such as compulsory counterclaims, e.g., Moore v. New York Cotton Exchange, 270 U.S. 593; impleader, e.g., H.L. Peterson Co. v. Applewhite, 383 F.2d 430, 433 (CA5); Dery v. Wyer, 265 F.2d 804 (CA2); crossclaims, e.g., LASA Per L'Industria Del Marmo Soc. Per Azioni v. Alexander, 414 F.2d 143 (CA6); Scott v. Fancher, 369 F.2d 842, 844 (CA5); Glens Falls Indemnity Co. v. United States ex rel. Westinghouse Electric Supply Co., 229 F.2d 370, 373–374 (CA9); or intervention as of right, e.g., Phelps v. Oaks, 117 U.S. 236, 241; Smith Petroleum Service, Inc. v. Monsanto Chemical Co., 420 F.2d 1103, 1113–1115 (CA5).

without question in the state courts." Kenrose Mfg. Co. v. Fred Whitaker Co., 512 F.2d 890, 894 (CA4).[12]

It is not unreasonable to assume that, in generally requiring complete diversity, Congress did not intend to confine the jurisdiction of federal courts so inflexibly that they are unable to protect legal rights or effectively to resolve an entire, logically entwined lawsuit. Those practical needs are the basis of the doctrine of ancillary jurisdiction. But neither the convenience of litigants nor considerations of judicial economy can suffice to justify extension of the doctrine of ancillary jurisdiction to a plaintiff's cause of action against a citizen of the same State in a diversity case. Congress has established the basic rule that diversity jurisdiction exists under 28 U.S.C. § 1332 only when there is complete diversity of citizenship. "The policy of the statute calls for its strict construction." Healy v. Ratta, 292 U.S. 263, 270; Indianapolis v. Chase National Bank, 314 U.S. 63, 76; Thomson v. Gaskill, 315 U.S. 442, 446; Snyder v. Harris, 394 U.S., at 340. To allow the requirement of complete diversity to be circumvented as it was in this case would simply flout the congressional command.[13]

Accordingly, the judgment of the Court of Appeals is reversed.

It is so ordered.

■ Mr. Justice White, with whom Mr. Justice Brennan joins, dissenting.

The Court today states that "[i]t is not unreasonable to assume that, in generally requiring complete diversity, Congress did not intend to confine the jurisdiction of federal courts so inflexibly that they are unable ... effectively to resolve an entire, logically entwined lawsuit." In spite of this recognition, the majority goes on to hold that in diversity suits federal courts do not have the jurisdictional power to entertain a claim asserted by a plaintiff against a third-party defendant, no matter how entwined it is with the matter already before the court, unless there is an independent basis for jurisdiction over that claim. Because I find no support for such a requirement in either Art. III of the Constitution or in any statutory law, I dissent from the Court's "unnecessarily grudging" approach.

The plaintiff below, Mrs. Kroger, chose to bring her lawsuit against the Omaha Public Power District (OPPD) in Federal District Court. No one questions the power of the District Court to entertain this claim, for Mrs. Kroger at the time was a citizen of Iowa, OPPD was a citizen of Nebraska, and the amount in controversy was greater than $10,000; jurisdiction therefore existed under 28 U.S.C. § 1332(a). As permitted by Fed.Rule Civ.Proc. 14(a), OPPD impleaded petitioner Owen Equipment & Erection

---

12. Whether Iowa's statute of limitations would now bar an action by the respondent in an Iowa court is, of course, entirely a matter of state law. See Iowa Code § 614.10. Compare 558 F.2d, at 420, with id., at 432 n. 42 (Bright, J., dissenting); cf. Burnett v. New York Central R. Co., 380 U.S. 424, 431–432, and n. 9.

13. Our holding is that the District Court lacked power to entertain the respondent's lawsuit against the petitioner. Thus, the asserted inequity in the respondent's alleged concealment of its citizenship is irrelevant. Federal judicial power does not depend upon "prior action or consent of the parties." *American Fire & Cas. Co. v. Finn*, 341 U.S., at 17–18.

Co. (Owen). Although OPPD's claim against Owen did not raise a federal question and although it was alleged that Owen was a citizen of the same State as OPPD, the parties and the court apparently believed that the District Court's ancillary jurisdiction encompassed this claim. Subsequently, Mrs. Kroger asserted a claim against Owen, everyone believing at the time that these two parties were citizens of different States. Because it later came to light that Mrs. Kroger and Owen were in fact both citizens of Iowa, the Court concludes that the District Court lacked jurisdiction over the claim.

In Mine Workers v. Gibbs, 383 U.S. 715, 725 (1966), we held that once a claim has been stated that is of sufficient substance to confer subject-matter jurisdiction on the federal district court, the court has judicial power to consider a nonfederal claim if it and the federal claim are derived from "a common nucleus of operative fact." Although the specific facts of that case concerned a state claim that was said to be pendent to a federal-question claim, the Court's language and reasoning were broad enough to cover the instant factual situation: "[I]f, considered without regard to their federal or state character, a plaintiff's claims are such that he would ordinarily be expected to try them all in one judicial proceeding, then, assuming substantiality of the federal issues, there is *power* in federal courts to hear the whole." Ibid. (footnote omitted). In the present case, Mrs. Kroger's claim against Owen and her claim against OPPD derived from a common nucleus of fact; this is necessarily so because in order for a plaintiff to assert a claim against a third-party defendant, Fed.Rule Civ. Proc. 14(a) requires that it "aris[e] out of the transaction or occurrence that is the subject matter of the plaintiff's claim against the third-party plaintiff ...." Furthermore, the substantiality of the claim Mrs. Kroger asserted against OPPD is unquestioned. Accordingly, as far as Art. III of the Constitution is concerned, the District Court had power to entertain Mrs. Kroger's claim against Owen.

The majority correctly points out, however, that the analysis cannot stop here. As Aldinger v. Howard, 427 U.S. 1 (1976), teaches, the jurisdictional power of the federal courts may be limited by Congress, as well as by the Constitution. In *Aldinger,* although the plaintiff's state claim against Spokane County was closely connected with her § 1983 claim against the county treasurer, the Court held that the District Court did not have pendent jurisdiction over the state claim, for, under the Court's precedents at that time, it was thought that Congress had specifically determined not to confer on the federal courts jurisdiction over civil rights claims against cities and counties. That being so, the Court refused to allow "the federal courts to fashion a jurisdictional doctrine under the general language of Art. III enabling them to circumvent this exclusion ...." Id., at 16.

In the present case, the only indication of congressional intent that the Court can find is that contained in the diversity jurisdictional statute, 28 U.S.C. § 1332(a), which states that "district courts shall have original jurisdiction of all civil actions where the matter in controversy exceeds the sum or value of $10,000 ... and is between ... citizens of different States ...." Because this statute has been interpreted as requiring complete diversity of citizenship between each plaintiff and each defendant, Straw-bridge v. Curtiss, 3 Cranch [7 U.S.] 267 (1806), the Court holds that the District Court did not have ancillary jurisdiction over Mrs. Kroger's claim against Owen. In so holding, the Court unnecessarily expands the scope of the complete-diversity requirement while substantially limiting the doctrine of ancillary jurisdiction.

The complete-diversity requirement, of course, could be viewed as meaning that in a diversity case, a federal district court may adjudicate only those claims that are between parties of different States. Thus, in order for a defendant to implead a third-party defendant, there would have to be diversity of citizenship; the same would also be true for cross-claims between defendants and for a third-party defendant's claim against a plaintiff. Even the majority, however, refuses to read the complete-diversity requirement so broadly; it recognizes with seeming approval the exercise of ancillary jurisdiction over nonfederal claims in situations involving impleader, cross-claims, and counterclaims. Given the Court's willingness to recognize ancillary jurisdiction in these contexts, despite the requirements of § 1332(a), I see no justification for the Court's refusal to approve the District Court's exercise of ancillary jurisdiction in the present case.

It is significant that a plaintiff who asserts a claim against a third-party defendant is not seeking to add a new party to the lawsuit. In the present case, for example, Owen had already been brought into the suit by OPPD, and, that having been done, Mrs. Kroger merely sought to assert against Owen a claim arising out of the same transaction that was already before the court. Thus the situation presented here is unlike that in *Aldinger* . . . .

Because in the instant case Mrs. Kroger merely sought to assert a claim against someone already a party to the suit, considerations of judicial economy, convenience, and fairness to the litigants—the factors relied upon in *Gibbs,* supra—support the recognition of ancillary jurisdiction here. Already before the court was the whole question of the cause of Mr. Kroger's death. Mrs. Kroger initially contended that OPPD was responsible; OPPD in turn contended that Owen's negligence had been the proximate cause of Mr. Kroger's death. In spite of the fact that the question of Owen's negligence was already before the District Court, the majority requires Mrs. Kroger to bring a separate action in state court in order to assert that very claim. Even if the Iowa statute of limitations will still permit such a suit, see n. [12], ante, considerations of judicial economy are certainly not served by requiring such duplicative litigation.[14]

The majority, however, brushes aside such considerations of convenience, judicial economy, and fairness because it concludes that recognizing

---

14. It is true that prior to trial OPPD was dismissed as a party to the suit and that, as we indicated in *Gibbs*, the dismissal prior to trial of the federal claim will generally require the dismissal of the nonfederal claim as well. See 383 U.S., at 726. Given the unusual facts of the present case, however—in particular, the fact that the actual location of Owen's principal place of business was not revealed until the third day of trial—fairness to the parties would lead me to conclude that the District Court did not abuse its discretion in retaining jurisdiction over Mrs. Kroger's claim against Owen. Under the Court's disposition, ancillary jurisdiction over a plaintiff's claim against a third-party defendant would permit the plaintiff to circumvent the complete-diversity requirement and thereby "flout the congressional command." Since the plaintiff in such a case does not bring the third-party defendant into the suit, however, there is no occasion for deliberate circumvention of the diversity requirement, absent collusion with the defendant. In the case of such collusion, of which there is absolutely no indication here,[15] the court can dismiss the action under the authority of 28 U.S.C. § 1359. In the absence of such collusion, there is no reason to adopt an absolute rule prohibiting the plaintiff from asserting those claims that he may properly assert against the third-party defendant pursuant to Fed.Rule Civ.Proc. 14(a). The plaintiff in such a situation brings suit against the defendant only with absolutely no assurance that the defendant will decide or be able to implead a particular third-party defendant. Since the plaintiff has no control over the defendant's decision to implead a third party, the fact that he could not have originally sued that party in federal court should be irrelevant. Moreover, the fact that a plaintiff in some cases may be able to foresee the subsequent chain of events leading to the impleader does not seem to me to be a sufficient reason to declare that a district court does not have the power to exercise ancillary jurisdiction over the plaintiff's claims against the third-party defendant.[16]

We have previously noted that "[s]ubsequent decisions of this Court indicate that *Strawbridge* is not to be given an expansive reading." State Farm Fire & Cas. Co. v. Tashire, 386 U.S. 523, 531 n. 6 (1967). In light of this teaching, it seems to me appropriate to view § 1332 as requiring complete diversity only between the plaintiff and those parties he actually brings into the suit. Beyond that, I would hold that in a diversity case the District Court has power, both constitutional and statutory, to entertain all claims among the parties arising from the same nucleus of operative fact as the plaintiff's original, jurisdiction-conferring claim against the defendant. Accordingly, I dissent from the Court's disposition of the present case.[17]

———

of course, it would not matter whether or not the federal claim is tried, for in either situation the court would have no jurisdiction over the plaintiff's nonfederal claim against the third-party defendant.

15. When Mrs. Kroger brought suit, it was believed that Owen was a citizen of Nebraska, not Iowa. Therefore, had she desired at that time to make Owen a party to the suit, she would have done so directly by naming Owen as a defendant.

16. Under the *Gibbs* analysis, recognition of the District Court's power to hear a plaintiff's nonfederal claim against a third-party defendant in a diversity suit would not mean that the court would be required to entertain such claims in all cases. The District Court would have the discretion to dismiss the nonfederal claim if it concluded that the interests of judicial economy, convenience, and fairness would not be served by the retention of the claim in the federal lawsuit. See *Gibbs,* 383 U.S., at 726. Accordingly, the majority's concerns that lead it to conclude that ancillary jurisdiction should not be recognized in the present situation could be met on a case-by-case basis, rather than by the absolute rule it adopts.

[**17.** For a comprehensive account of the background facts and litigation history of the *Kroger* case, a critical analysis of the handling of the case by Mrs. Kroger's counsel, and an

Finley v. United States

Supreme Court of the United States, 1989.
490 U.S. 545, 109 S.Ct. 2003, 104 L.Ed.2d 593.

■ JUSTICE SCALIA delivered the opinion of the Court.

On the night of November 11, 1983, a twin-engine plane carrying petitioner's husband and two of her children struck electric transmission lines during its approach to a San Diego, California, airfield. No one survived the resulting crash. Petitioners brought a tort action in state court, claiming that San Diego Gas and Electric Company had negligently positioned and inadequately illuminated the transmission lines, and that the city of San Diego's negligent maintenance of the airport's runway lights had rendered them inoperative the night of the crash. When she later discovered that the Federal Aviation Administration (FAA) was in fact the party responsible for the runway lights, petitioner filed the present action against the United States in the United States District Court for the Southern District of California. The complaint based jurisdiction upon the Federal Tort Claims Act (FTCA), 28 U.S.C. § 1346(b), alleging negligence in the FAA's operation and maintenance of the runway lights and performance of air traffic control functions. Almost a year later, she moved to amend the federal complaint to include claims against the original state-court defendants, as to which no independent basis for federal jurisdiction existed. The District Court granted petitioner's motion and asserted "pendent" jurisdiction under Mine Workers v. Gibbs, 383 U.S. 715 (1966), finding it "clear" that "judicial economy and efficiency" favored trying the actions together, and concluding that they arose "from a common nucleus of operative facts." . . . The District Court certified an interlocutory appeal to the Court of Appeals for the Ninth Circuit under 28 U.S.C. § 1292(b). That court summarily reversed on the basis of its earlier opinion in Ayala v. United States, 550 F.2d 1196 (1977), cert. dism'd, 435 U.S. 982 (1978), which had categorically rejected pendent-party jurisdiction under the FTCA. We granted certiorari . . . to resolve a split among the Circuits on whether the FTCA permits an assertion of pendent jurisdiction over additional parties. Compare, e.g., *Ayala v. United States*, supra, with Lykins v. Pointer, Inc., 725 F.2d 645 (CA11 1984), and Stewart v. United States, 716 F.2d 755 (CA10 1982), cert. denied, 469 U.S. 1018 (1984).

The FTCA provides that "the district courts . . . shall have exclusive jurisdiction of civil actions on claims against the United States" for certain torts of federal employees acting within the scope of their employment. 28 U.S.C. § 1346(b). Petitioner seeks to append her claims against the city and the utility to her FTCA action against the United States, even though this would require the District Court to extend its authority to additional parties for whom an independent jurisdictional base—such as diversity of citizenship, 28 U.S.C. § 1332(a)(1)—is lacking.

---

evaluation of the Court's reasoning in historical perspective, see Oakley, The Story of *Owen Equipment v. Kroger*: A Change in the Weather of Federal Jurisdiction, in Clermont, ed., Civil Procedure Stories 81–134 (2d ed.2008). See also Wright & Kane, Federal Courts § 76 (6th ed.2002).]

In 1807 Chief Justice Marshall wrote for the Court that "courts which are created by written law, and whose jurisdiction is defined by written law, cannot transcend that jurisdiction. It is unnecessary to state the reasoning on which this opinion is founded, because it has been repeatedly given by this court; and with the decisions heretofore rendered on this point, no member of the bench has, even for an instant, been dissatisfied." Ex parte Bollman, 4 Cranch [8 U.S.] 75, 93 (1807). It remains rudimentary law that "[a]s regards all courts of the United States inferior to this tribunal, two things are necessary to create jurisdiction, whether original or appellate. The Constitution must have given to the court the capacity to take it, *and an act of Congress must have supplied it* .... To the extent that such action is not taken, the power lies dormant." The Mayor v. Cooper, 6 Wall. [73 U.S.] 247, 252 (1868) (emphasis added); ....

Despite this principle, in a line of cases by now no less well established we have held, without specific examination of jurisdictional statutes, that federal courts have "pendent" claim jurisdiction—that is, jurisdiction over nonfederal claims between parties litigating other matters properly before the court—to the full extent permitted by the Constitution. Mine Workers v. Gibbs, 383 U.S. 715 (1966); Hurn v. Oursler, 289 U.S. 238 (1933); Siler v. Louisville & Nashville R. Co., 213 U.S. 175 (1909). *Gibbs,* which has come to stand for the principle in question, held that "[p]endent jurisdiction, in the sense of judicial *power,* exists whenever there is a claim 'arising under [the] Constitution, the Laws of the United States, and Treaties made, or which shall be made, under their Authority ...,' U.S. Const., Art. III, § 2, and the relationship between that claim and the state claim permits the conclusion that the entire action before the court comprises but one constitutional 'case.' " 383 U.S., at 725 (emphasis in original). The requisite relationship exists, *Gibbs* said, when the federal and nonfederal claims "derive from a common nucleus of operative fact" and are such that a plaintiff "would ordinarily be expected to try them in one judicial proceeding." Ibid. Petitioner contends that the same criterion applies here, leading to the result that her state-law claims against San Diego Gas and Electric Company and the city of San Diego may be heard in conjunction with her FTCA action against the United States.

Analytically, petitioner's case is fundamentally different from *Gibbs* in that it brings into question what has become known as pendent-*party* jurisdiction, that is, jurisdiction over parties not named in any claim that is independently cognizable by the federal court.[18] We may assume, without deciding, that the constitutional criterion for pendent-party jurisdiction is analogous to the constitutional criterion for pendent-claim jurisdiction, and that petitioner's state-law claims pass that test. Our cases show, however, that with respect to the addition of parties, as opposed to the addition of

---

18. Justice Stevens is thus mistaken to rely upon ... this Court's decision in Moore v. New York Cotton Exchange, 270 U.S. 593 (1926). That case involved jurisdiction over a counterclaim brought by and against parties who were already properly before the court on other, federal-question grounds. His dissent generally ignores this distinction—a central distinction, as we shall later discuss—between new parties and parties already before the court.

only claims, we will not assume that the full constitutional power has been congressionally authorized, and will not read jurisdictional statutes broadly. In Zahn v. International Paper Co., 414 U.S. 291, 301 (1973), we refused to allow a plaintiff pursuing a diversity action worth less than the jurisdictional minimum of $10,000 to append his claim to the jurisdictionally adequate diversity claims of other members of a plaintiff class—even though all of the *claims* would together have amounted to a single "case" under *Gibbs,* see Owen Equipment & Erection Co. v. Kroger, 437 U.S. 365, 372 (1978). We based this holding upon "the statutes defining the jurisdiction of the District Court," 414 U.S., at 292, and did not so much as mention *Gibbs.*

Two years later, the nontransferability of *Gibbs* to pendent-party claims was made explicit. In Aldinger v. Howard, 427 U.S. 1 (1976), the plaintiff brought federal claims under 42 U.S.C. § 1983 against individual defendants, and sought to append to them a related state claim against Spokane County, Washington. (A federal § 1983 claim was unavailable against the county because of this Court's decision in Monroe v. Pape, 365 U.S. 167 (1961).)[19] We specifically disapproved application of the *Gibbs* mode of analysis, finding a "significant legal difference." 427 U.S., at 15. "[T]he addition of a completely new party," we said, "would run counter to the well-established principle that federal courts ... are courts of limited jurisdiction marked out by Congress." Ibid. "Resolution of a claim of pendent-party jurisdiction ... calls for careful attention to the relevant statutory language." Id., at 17. We held in *Aldinger* that the jurisdictional statute under which suit was brought, 28 U.S.C. § 1343, which conferred district court jurisdiction over civil actions of certain types "authorized by law to be commenced," did not mean to include as "authorized by law" a state-law claim against a party that had been statutorily insulated from similar federal suit. The county had been "*excluded* from liability in § 1983, and therefore by reference in the grant of jurisdiction under § 1343(3)." *Ibid.* (emphasis in original).

We reaffirmed and further refined our approach to pendent-party jurisdiction in *Owen Equipment & Erection Co. v. Kroger,* supra, 437 U.S., at 372–375—a case, like *Zahn,* involving the diversity statute, 28 U.S.C. § 1332(a)(1), but focusing on the requirement that the suit be "between ... citizens of different states," rather than the requirement that it "excee[d] the sum or value of $10,000." We held that the jurisdiction which § 1332(a)(1) confers over a "matter in controversy" between a plaintiff and defendant of diverse citizenship cannot be read to confer pendent jurisdiction over a different, nondiverse defendant, even if the *claim* involving that other defendant meets the *Gibbs* test. "*Gibbs,*" we said, "does not end the inquiry into whether a federal court has power to hear the nonfederal claims along with the federal ones. Beyond this constitutional minimum, there must be an examination of the posture in which the nonfederal claim

---

19. *Monroe v. Pape* was later overruled by Monell v. New York City Dept. of Social Services, 436 U.S. 658 (1978).

is asserted and of the specific statute that confers jurisdiction over the federal claim," 437 U.S., at 373.

The most significant element of "posture" or of "context," id., at 376, in the present case (as in *Zahn, Aldinger,* and *Kroger*) is precisely that the added claims involve added parties over whom no independent basis of jurisdiction exists. While in a narrow class of cases a federal court may assert authority over such a claim "ancillary" to jurisdiction otherwise properly vested—for example, when an additional party has a claim upon contested assets within the court's exclusive control, see, e.g., Krippendorf v. Hyde, 110 U.S. 276 (1884); Freeman v. Howe, 24 How. [65 U.S.] 450, 460 (1861), or when necessary to give effect to the court's judgment, see, e.g., Local Loan Co. v. Hunt, 292 U.S. 234, 239 (1934); Julian v. Central Trust Co., 193 U.S. 93, 112–114 (1904)—we have never reached such a result solely on the basis that the *Gibbs* test has been met. And little more basis than that can be relied upon by petitioner here. As in *Kroger,* the relationship between petitioner's added claims and the original complaint is one of "mere factual similarity," which is of no consequence since "neither the convenience of the litigants nor considerations of judicial economy can suffice to justify extension of the doctrine of ancillary jurisdiction," 437 U.S., at 376–377. It is true that here, unlike in *Kroger,* see id., at 376, the party seeking to bring the added claims had little choice but to be in federal rather than state court, since the FTCA permits the Federal Government to be sued only there. But that alone is not enough, since we have held that suits against the United States under the Tucker Act, 24 Stat. 505 (which can of course be brought only in federal court, see 28 U.S.C. §§ 1346(a)(2), 1491(a)(1)) cannot include private defendants. United States v. Sherwood, 312 U.S. 584 (1941).

The second factor invoked by *Kroger,* the text of the jurisdictional statute at issue, likewise fails to establish petitioner's case. The FTCA, § 1346(b), confers jurisdiction over "civil actions on claims against the United States." It does not say "civil actions on claims that include requested relief against the United States," nor "civil actions in which there is a claim against the United States"—formulations one might expect if the presence of a claim against the United States constituted merely a minimum jurisdictional requirement, rather than a definition of the permissible scope of FTCA actions. Just as the statutory provision "between . . . citizens of different States" has been held to mean citizens of different States and no one else, see *Kroger,* 437 U.S. 365 (1978), so also here we conclude that "against the United States" means against the United States and no one else. "Due regard for the rightful independence of state governments . . . requires that [federal courts] scrupulously confine their own jurisdiction to the precise limits which the statute has defined." Healy v. Ratta, 292 U.S. 263, 270 (1934), accord, Executive Jet Aviation, Inc. v. Cleveland, 409 U.S. 249, 272–273 (1972); Shamrock Oil & Gas Corp. v. Sheets, 313 U.S. 100, 108–109 (1941). The statute here defines jurisdiction in a manner that does not reach defendants other than the United States.

. . . . .

Because the FTCA permits the Government to be sued only in federal court, our holding that parties to related claims cannot necessarily be sued there means that the efficiency and convenience of a consolidated action will sometimes have to be forgone in favor of separate actions in state and federal courts. We acknowledged this potential consideration in *Aldinger,* 427 U.S., at 18, but now conclude that the present statute permits no other result.

. . . . .

As we noted at the outset, our cases do not display an entirely consistent approach with respect to the necessity that jurisdiction be explicitly conferred. The *Gibbs* line of cases was a departure from prior practice, and a departure that we have no intent to limit or impair. But *Aldinger* indicated that the *Gibbs* approach would not be extended to the pendent-party field, and we decide today to retain that line. Whatever we say regarding the scope of jurisdiction conferred by a particular statute can of course be changed by Congress. What is of paramount importance is that Congress be able to legislate against a background of clear interpretive rules, so that it may know the effect of the language it adopts. All our cases—*Zahn, Aldinger,* and *Kroger*—have held that a grant of jurisdiction over claims involving particular parties does not itself confer jurisdiction over additional claims by or against different parties. Our decision today reaffirms that interpretive rule; the opposite would sow confusion.

For the foregoing reasons, the judgment of the Court of Appeals is

Affirmed.

■ Justice Blackmun, dissenting.

. . . . .

In a case not controlled by any express intent to limit the scope of a constitutional "case," [Aldinger v. Howard, 427 U.S. 1 (1976),] suggests that the appropriateness of pendent-party jurisdiction might turn on the "alignmen[t] of parties and claims," and that one significant factor is whether "the grant of jurisdiction to [the] federal court is exclusive," 427 U.S., at 18, as is the situation here. Where, as here, Congress' preference for a federal forum for a certain category of claims makes the federal forum the *only* possible one in which the constitutional case may be heard as a whole, the sensible result is to permit the exercise of pendent-party jurisdiction. *Aldinger* imposes no obstacle to that result, and I would not reach out to create one. I therefore dissent.

■ Justice Stevens, with whom Justice Brennan and Justice Marshall join, dissenting.

The Court's holding is not faithful to our precedents and casually dismisses the accumulated wisdom of our best judges. As we observed more than 16 years ago, "numerous decisions throughout the courts of appeals since [United Mine Workers v. Gibbs, 383 U.S. 715 (1966)] have recognized the existence of judicial power to hear pendent claims involving pendent parties where 'the entire action before the court comprises but one constitutional "case" ' as defined in *Gibbs*." Moor v. County of Alameda, 411 U.S. 693, 713 (1973). I shall first explain why the position taken by the overwhelming consensus of federal judges is correct and then comment on major flaws in the opinion the Court announces today.

I

. . . . .

The case before us today is one in which the United States is a party. Given the plain language of Article III, there is not even an arguable basis for questioning the federal court's constitutional power to decide it. Moreover, by enacting the Federal Tort Claims Act (FTCA) in 1946, 28 U.S.C. § 1346(b), Congress unquestionably authorized the District Court to accept jurisdiction of "civil actions on claims against the United States." Thus, it is perfectly clear that the District Court has both constitutional and statutory power to decide this case.

. . . . .

Prior to the adoption of the Federal Rules of Civil Procedure in 1938, the federal courts routinely decided state-law claims in cases in which they had subject-matter jurisdiction, see, e.g., Hurn v. Oursler, 289 U.S. 238, 246 (1933); Siler v. Louisville & Nashville R. Co., 213 U.S. 175 (1909), and granted relief against nondiverse parties on state claims as to which there was no independent basis for federal jurisdiction, see, e.g., Moore v. New York Cotton Exchange, 270 U.S. 593 (1926); Julian v. Central Trust Co., 193 U.S. 93, 112–114 (1904); Freeman v. Howe, 65 U.S. (24 How.) 450, 460 (1861). Although the contours of the federal cause of action—or "case"— were then more narrowly defined than they are today, see, e.g., *Hurn v. Oursler*, supra, the doctrine of "pendent" or "ancillary" jurisdiction had long been firmly established. The relevant change that was effectuated by the adoption of the Rules in 1938 was, in essence, a statutory broadening of the dimensions of the cases that federal courts may entertain.

The Court's unanimous opinion in *Gibbs* highlights the modern conception of a "civil action" and a "constitutional case." . . .

Immediately after *Gibbs* was decided, federal judges throughout the nation recognized that its reasoning applied to cases in which it was necessary to add an additional party on a pendent nonfederal claim in order to grant complete relief. For example, Judge Henry Friendly considered this precise question in three separate opinions. Because he is universally recognized not only as one of our wisest judges,[20] but also as one with special learning and expertise in matters of federal jurisdiction,[21] a reference to each of those opinions is appropriate.

---

20. In 1963, Justice Frankfurter regarded him "as the best judge now writing opinions on the American scene," see Freund, In Memoriam: Henry J. Friendly, 99 Harv.L.Rev. 1709, 1720 (1986); Erwin Griswold has described him as "the ablest lawyer of my generation," ibid., and Judge Posner called him "the greatest federal appellate judge of his time," id., at 1724.

21. See H. Friendly, Federal Jurisdiction: A General View (1973); see also, Paul Freund's comments in 99 Harv.L.Rev., at 1716–1718, and David Currie's comments in On Blazing

[JUSTICE STEVENS here discussed Leather's Best, Inc. v. S.S. Morma-clynx, 451 F.2d 800 (2d Cir.1971); Almenares v. Wyman, 453 F.2d 1075 (2d Cir.1971), and Weinberger v. Kendrick, 698 F.2d 61 (2d Cir.1982).]

In the *Weinberger* case the circumstances were "about as powerful for the exercise of pendent-party jurisdiction as can be imagined" because Congress had vested the federal courts with exclusive jurisdiction over claims arising under the Securities Exchange Act. The federal district court was therefore the only forum in which the entire constitutional case could be tried at one time. That powerful circumstance is also present in cases arising under the FTCA. In fact, in dicta, the *Aldinger* Court suggested that pendent-party jurisdiction might be available under the FTCA for precisely this reason. 427 U.S., at 18.

I would thus hold that the grant of jurisdiction to hear "civil actions on claims against the United States" authorizes the federal courts to hear state-law claims against a pendent party. As many other judges have recognized,[22] the fact that such claims are within the exclusive federal jurisdiction, together with the absence of any evidence of congressional disapproval of the exercise of pendent-party jurisdiction in FTCA cases, provides a fully sufficient justification for applying the holding in *Gibbs* to this case.

II

The Court's contrary conclusion rests on an insufficient major premise, a failure to distinguish between diversity and federal question cases, and an implicit reliance on a narrow view of the waiver of sovereign immunity in the Federal Tort Claims Act.

. . . . .

The Court's reliance on cases within the diversity jurisdiction also loses sight of the purpose behind the principle of pendent jurisdiction.[23]

Trails: Judge Friendly and The Federal Jurisdiction, 133 U.Pa.L.Rev. 5 (1984). The authors of Hart & Wechsler's The Federal Courts and The Federal System, who dedicated the first two editions of the book to Justice Frankfurter and Professor Henry M. Hart, Jr., respectively, dedicate the third edition to Judge Friendly whom they describe as "man for all seasons in the law; master of this subject." P. Bator, D. Meltzer, P. Mishkin, & D. Shapiro, Hart and Wechsler's The Federal Courts and The Federal System xix (3d ed.1988).

22. In *Moor,* 411 U.S., at 713–714, in 1973, we noted that the Ninth Circuit rule denying pendent-party jurisdiction "stands virtually alone against this post-*Gibbs* trend in the courts of appeals." An overwhelming number of judges adhered to that view after *Aldinger* was decided....

23. The unwisdom of having "lumped together indiscriminately cases involving each of the three different contexts in which the question of pendent parties has been litigated" has been sufficiently criticised by Professors Wright, Miller, and Cooper. See their treatise on Federal Practice and Procedure § 3567.2, pp. 152–153 (2d ed.1984). They explain:

"The distinctions are there and do not become less real because they are not mentioned. The meaning of 'amount in controversy' in § 1332 raises one question, the meaning of 'between citizens of different states' in the same statute raises a different question, and the permissible scope of cases 'arising under' federal law within the Constitution and § 1331 raises still a third question. The considerations for allowing

The doctrine of pendent jurisdiction rests in part on a recognition that forcing a federal plaintiff to litigate his or her case in both federal and state courts impairs the ability of the federal court to grant full relief, Supreme Tribe of Ben–Hur v. Cauble, 255 U.S. 356, 367 (1921), and "imparts a fundamental bias against utilization of the federal forum owing to the deterrent effect imposed by the needless requirement of duplicate litigation if the federal forum is chosen." *Aldinger,* 427 U.S., at 36 (BRENNAN, J., dissenting). "The courts, by recognizing pendent jurisdiction, are effectuating Congress' decision to provide the plaintiff with a federal forum for litigating a jurisdictionally sufficient claim." Miller, Ancillary and Pendent Jurisdiction, 26 So.Tex.L.Rev. 1, 4 (1985). This is especially the case when, by virtue of the grant of exclusive federal jurisdiction, "*only* in a federal court may all of the claims be tried together." *Aldinger,* 427 U.S., at 18. In such circumstances, in which Congress has unequivocally indicated its intent that the federal right be litigated in a federal forum, there is reason to believe that Congress did not intend that the substance of the federal right be diminished by the increased costs in efficiency and convenience of litigation in two forums. Cf. Moses H. Cone Memorial Hospital v. Mercury Construction Corp., 460 U.S. 1, 25 (1983); Will v. Calvert Fire Insurance Co., 437 U.S. 655, 673–675 (1978) (BRENNAN, J., dissenting).[24] No such special federal interest is present when federal jurisdiction is invoked on the basis of the diverse citizenship of the parties and the state-law claims may be litigated in a state forum. See Owen Equipment & Erection Co. v. Kroger, 437 U.S. [365, 376 (1978)]; Currie, The Federal Courts and the American Law Institute, 36 U.Chi.L.Rev. 1, 21 (1968). To be sure "[w]hatever we say regarding the scope of jurisdiction conferred by a particular statute can ... be changed by Congress," ... but that does not relieve us of our responsibility to be faithful to the congressional design. The Court is quite incorrect to presume that because Congress did not sanction the exercise of pendent-party jurisdiction in the diversity context, it has not permitted its exercise with respect to claims within the exclusive federal jurisdiction.

. . . . .

Today we should be guided by the wisdom of Cardozo and Friendly rather than by the "unnecessarily grudging" approach that was unanimously rebuffed in *Gibbs.* See 383 U.S., at 725.

I respectfully dissent.

————

'pendent parties' in a federal question case may well be more compelling than for doing so when the only effect is to broaden the scope—and attractiveness—of diversity jurisdiction."

24. See also Musher Foundation v. Alba Trading Co., 127 F.2d 9, 11 (CA2 1942) (Clark, J., dissenting) ("If the roast must be reserved exclusively for the federal bench, it is anomalous to send the gravy across the street to the state court house").

REPORT OF THE FEDERAL COURTS STUDY COMMITTEE (APRIL 2, 1990), P. 47

Recommendation 2.B.2.b: Congress should expressly authorize federal courts to assert pendent jurisdiction over parties without an independent federal jurisdictional basis.

———

NOTE ON THE ENACTMENT OF 28 U.S.C. § 1367

Section 1367, like the other provisions of the Judicial Improvements Act of 1990, was passed in the middle of a busy night at the end of the 101st Congress and had little public or professional attention prior to its passage. For a detailed account of the legislative process that saw the proposal made by the Federal Courts Study Committee on April 2, 1990, become law—but in greatly modified form—on December 1st of that year, see Wolf, Codification of Supplemental Jurisdiction: Anatomy of a Legislative Proposal, 14 W.New Eng.L.Rev. 1 (1992). For highlights of the rush to enactment, see Oakley, Recent Statutory Changes in the Law of Federal Jurisdiction and Venue: The Judicial Improvements Acts of 1988 and 1990, 24 U.C.Davis L.Rev. 735, 736 n. 2 (1991).

For analysis of the substance of the statute and the problems of construction it poses, see Oakley, supra, 24 U.C.Davis L.Rev., at 757–769; McLaughlin, The Federal Supplemental Jurisdiction Statute—A Constitutional and Statutory Analysis, 24 Ariz.St.L.J. 849 (1992); Fairman, Abdication to Academia: The Case of the Supplemental Jurisdiction Statute, 28 U.S.C. § 1367, 19 Seton Hall Legis.J. 157 (1994); Note, The "Noncontroversial" Statute: Have Expressed Concerns of 28 U.S.C. § 1367 Come to Light?, 72 U.Det.Mercy L.Rev. 397 (1995); Comment, Pandora's Box or Treasure Chest?: Circuit Courts Face 28 U.S.C. § 1367's Effect on Multi-Plaintiff Diversity Actions, 27 Seton Hall L.Rev. 1497 (1997); Comment, Plugging the "Gaping Hole" : The Effect of 28 U.S.C. § 1367 on the Complete Diversity Requirement of 28 U.S.C. § 1332, 49 Baylor L.Rev. 1069 (1997); Pfander, Supplemental Jurisdiction and Section 1367: The Case for Sympathetic Textualism, 148 U.Pa.L.Rev. 107 (1999).

Three academics who were instrumental in the drafting of the statute undertook to explain it in Mengler, Burbank & Rowe, Congress Accepts Supreme Court's Invitation to Codify Supplemental Jurisdiction, 74 Judicature 213 (1991). The statute was criticized in Freer, Compounding Confusion and Hampering Diversity: Life After Finley and the Supplemental Jurisdiction Statute, 40 Emory L.J. 445 (1991). This led to an extraordinary series of spirited, and often ad hominem, exchanges: Rowe, Burbank & Mengler, Compounding or Creating Confusion about Supplemental Jurisdiction? A Reply to Professor Freer, 40 Emory L.J. 943 (1991); Arthur & Freer, Grasping at Burnt Straws: The Disaster of the Supplemental Jurisdiction Statute, 40 Emory L.J. 963 (1991); Rowe, Burbank & Mengler, A Coda on Supplemental Jurisdiction, 40 Emory L.J. 993 (1991); Arthur &

Freer, Close Enough for Government Work: What Happens When Congress Doesn't Do Its Job, 40 Emory L.J. 1007 (1991).

These exchanges led five other scholars to express their views on the new statute in Colloquy: Perspectives on Supplemental Jurisdiction, 41 Emory L.J. (1992). Another excellent set of articles, some looking back at experience to date under § 1367 and others looking forward to consider various proposed amendments of § 1367, has been published as Symposium: A Reappraisal of the Supplemental–Jurisdiction Statute: Title 28 U.S.C. § 1367, 74 Ind.L.J. 1 (1998).

———

COMMENT ON 28 U.S.C. § 1367(a)

In City of Chicago v. International College of Surgeons, 522 U.S. 156 (1997), the Supreme Court held that the "supplemental" jurisdiction conferred by § 1367(a) was not necessarily confined to "original" jurisdiction. Justice O'Connor's opinion for the Court sustained the district court's jurisdiction over all claims for relief in a suit for judicial review of a local administrative order. Although the right to relief was state-created, those claims seeking such relief on federal grounds were deemed to arise under federal law. Because the district court had original jurisdiction under 28 U.S.C. § 1331 of these claims arising under federal law, it also had supplemental jurisdiction under 28 U.S.C. § 1367 of the parallel claims for on-the-record judicial review of the validity of the administrative order as a matter of state law. Over the vigorous dissent of Justice Ginsburg, joined by Justice Stevens, Justice O'Connor's majority opinion deemed it irrelevant that the exercise of such supplemental jurisdiction might require the exercise of "appellate" rather than "original" jurisdiction, since the supplemental jurisdiction conferred by § 1367 was not expressly limited to original jurisdiction. The Court did not decide whether the district court should have abstained or otherwise declined to exercise its supplemental jurisdiction as permitted by § 1367(c), leaving these issues open for further consideration upon remand of the case to the court of appeals. See Note, City of Chicago v. International College of Surgeons: The Interplay Between Supplemental Jurisdiction and Cross–System Appeals, and the Impact on Federalism, 50 Mercer L.Rev. 1137 (1999).

The American Law Institute recommended enactment of a revised version of § 1367 that would moot the effect of City of Chicago by expressly declaring supplemental jurisdiction to be a form of original jurisdiction, thus rendering supplemental jurisdiction inapplicable to any claim that would require the exercise of appellate jurisdiction. See Judicial Code Project, Part I, § 1367(b), and the accompanying Commentary and Reporter's Notes at 71–78.

The ALI's project coined a new term, "freestanding claim," to refer to a claim within the original jurisdiction of a district court without reliance on supplemental jurisdiction. See Judicial Code Project, Part I, § 1367(a)(1). This would allow claims asserted by pleadings in the federal district courts to be divided into three jurisdictional categories: "freestanding" claims qualifying for original jurisdiction independently of any other claims, "supplemental" claims qualifying for original jurisdiction based on their relationship to one or more freestanding claims in the same civil action, and "orphan" claims that must be dismissed because they are beyond the original jurisdiction of the district courts. This classificatory scheme would allow claims that are within the jurisdiction of the district courts—a jurisdiction historically limited by statute to original rather than appellate jurisdiction—to be distinguished as either freestanding or supplemental without invoking a false dichotomy between "original" (meaning independent) and "supplemental" (meaning dependent) jurisdiction.

For further discussion of the conceptual basis and fundamental structure of the ALI's approach to supplemental jurisdiction, see Comment on 28 U.S.C. §§ 1367(b) & 1367(c), infra p. 311.

The Fourth Circuit has held that when supplemental jurisdiction over state-law claims is based on a federal claim as to which nationwide service of process is authorized, such as a civil RICO claim, there is "pendent personal jurisdiction" to adjudicate the state-law claims in the same state as that in which the federal claim is being litigated even though the defendants lack minimum contacts with that state and could not otherwise be subject to its personal jurisdiction with respect to the state-law claims. ESAB Group, Inc. v. Centricut, Inc., 126 F.3d 617 (4th Cir.1997).

The Supreme Court has twice indicated that the enactment of § 1367 did not deprive courts of their traditional power to exercise nonstatutory supplemental jurisdiction, at least in narrowly limited circumstances. In Kokkonen v. Guardian Life Ins. Co. of America, 511 U.S. 375, 378 (1994), Justice Scalia declared for a unanimous Court that nonstatutory ancillary jurisdiction may properly be invoked "to enable a court to function successfully, that is, to manage its proceedings, vindicate its authority, and effectuate its decrees." In Peacock v. Thomas, 516 U.S. 349, 359 (1996), the Court elaborated on *Kokkonen*, stressing that "[a]ncillary enforcement jurisdiction is, at its core, a creature of necessity" to be invoked "only in extraordinary circumstances." In both cases the circumstances were held, however, *not* to justify the exercise of nonstatutory supplemental jurisdiction.

Section 1367(a)'s grant of supplemental jurisdiction is sweeping. It extends to the limits of Article III, thus ratifying and incorporating the constitutional analysis of *Gibbs*. Subsection (a) thus removes any *statutory* doubt about the propriety of courts exercising supplemental jurisdiction of claims by or against additional parties, provided that such claims are part of the same "case or controversy under Article III" as claims independently within the original jurisdiction of the district courts. Does any *constitutional* doubt remain?

In *Finley*, the Court was prepared only to "assume, without deciding, that the constitutional criterion for pendent-party jurisdiction is analogous to the constitutional criterion for pendent-claim jurisdiction." Section 1367(a) merely restates this assumption in the new terminology of supplemental jurisdiction. Just how expansively the concept of a single "case or controversy" may be applied in multiparty litigation cannot be determined until the Supreme Court revisits the constitutional issue left dangling in *Finley*—and the Court appears to be in no hurry to do so.

Exxon Mobil Corp. v. Allapattah Services, Inc.

Supreme Court of the United States, 2005.
545 U.S. 546, 125 S.Ct. 2611, 162 L.Ed.2d 502.

■ JUSTICE KENNEDY delivered the opinion of the Court.

These consolidated cases present the question whether a federal court in a diversity action may exercise supplemental jurisdiction over additional plaintiffs whose claims do not satisfy the minimum amount-in-controversy requirement, provided the claims are part of the same case or controversy as the claims of plaintiffs who do allege a sufficient amount in controversy. Our decision turns on the correct interpretation of 28 U.S.C. § 1367. The question has divided the Courts of Appeals, and we granted certiorari to resolve the conflict.

We hold that, where the other elements of jurisdiction are present and at least one named plaintiff in the action satisfies the amount-in-controversy requirement, § 1367 does authorize supplemental jurisdiction over the claims of other plaintiffs in the same Article III case or controversy, even if those claims are for less than the jurisdictional amount specified in the statute setting forth the requirements for diversity jurisdiction. We affirm the judgment of the Court of Appeals for the Eleventh Circuit in No. 04–70, and we reverse the judgment of the Court of Appeals for the First Circuit in No. 04–79.

I

In 1991, about 10,000 Exxon dealers filed a class-action suit against the Exxon Corporation in the United States District Court for the Northern District of Florida. The dealers alleged an intentional and systematic scheme by Exxon under which they were overcharged for fuel purchased from Exxon. The plaintiffs invoked the District Court's § 1332(a) diversity jurisdiction. After a unanimous jury verdict in favor of the plaintiffs, the District Court certified the case for interlocutory review, asking whether it had properly exercised § 1367 supplemental jurisdiction over the claims of class members who did not meet the jurisdictional minimum amount in controversy.

The Court of Appeals for the Eleventh Circuit upheld the District Court's extension of supplemental jurisdiction to these class members. Allapattah Services, Inc. v. Exxon Corp., 333 F.3d 1248 (2003). "[W]e find," the court held, "that § 1367 clearly and unambiguously provides district courts with the authority in diversity class actions to exercise supplemental jurisdiction over the claims of class members who do not meet the minimum amount in controversy as long as the district court has original jurisdiction over the claims of at least one of the class representatives." Id., at 1256. This decision accords with the views of the Courts of Appeals for the Fourth, Sixth, and Seventh Circuits. See Rosmer v. Pfizer, Inc., 263 F.3d 110 (CA4 2001); Olden v. LaFarge Corp., 383 F.3d 495 (CA6 2004); Stromberg Metal Works, Inc. v. Press Mechanical, Inc., 77 F.3d 928 (CA7 1996); In re Brand Name Prescription Drugs Antitrust Litigation, 123 F.3d 599 (CA7 1997). The Courts of Appeals for the Fifth and Ninth Circuits, adopting a similar analysis of the statute, have held that in a diversity class action the unnamed class members need not meet the amount-in-controversy requirement, provided the named class members do. These decisions, however, are unclear on whether all the named plaintiffs must satisfy this requirement. In re Abbott Labs., 51 F.3d 524 (CA5 1995); Gibson v. Chrysler Corp., 261 F.3d 927 (CA9 2001).

In the other case now before us the Court of Appeals for the First Circuit took a different position on the meaning of § 1367(a). 370 F.3d 124 (2004). In that case, a 9–year-old girl sued Star–Kist in a diversity action in the United States District Court for the District of Puerto Rico, seeking damages for unusually severe injuries she received when she sliced her finger on a tuna can. Her family joined in the suit, seeking damages for emotional distress and certain medical expenses. The District Court granted summary judgment to Star–Kist, finding that none of the plaintiffs met the minimum amount-in-controversy requirement. The Court of Appeals for the First Circuit, however, ruled that the injured girl, but not her family members, had made allegations of damages in the requisite amount.

The Court of Appeals then addressed whether, in light of the fact that one plaintiff met the requirements for original jurisdiction, supplemental jurisdiction over the remaining plaintiffs' claims was proper under § 1367. The court held that § 1367 authorizes supplemental jurisdiction only when the district court has original jurisdiction over the action, and that in a diversity case original jurisdiction is lacking if one plaintiff fails to satisfy the amount-in-controversy requirement. Although the Court of Appeals claimed to "express no view" on whether the result would be the same in a class action, id., at 143, n.19, its analysis is inconsistent with that of the Court of Appeals for the Eleventh Circuit. The Court of Appeals for the First Circuit's view of § 1367 is, however, shared by the Courts of Appeals for the Third, Eighth, and Tenth Circuits, and the latter two Courts of Appeals have expressly applied this rule to class actions. See Meritcare, Inc. v. St. Paul Mercury Ins. Co., 166 F.3d 214 (CA3 1999); Trimble v. Asarco, Inc., 232 F.3d 946 (CA8 2000); Leonhardt v. Western Sugar Co., 160 F.3d 631 (CA10 1998).

II

A

. . . . . As the jurisdictional statutes existed in 1989, then, here is how matters stood: First, the diversity requirement in § 1332(a) required complete diversity; absent complete diversity, the district court lacked original jurisdiction over all of the claims in the action. *Strawbridge*, 3 Cranch, at 267–268; *Kroger*, 437 U.S., at 373–374. Second, if the district court had original jurisdiction over at least one claim, the jurisdictional statutes implicitly authorized supplemental jurisdiction over all other claims between the same parties arising out of the same Article III case or controversy. *Gibbs*, 383 U.S., at 725. Third, even when the district court had original jurisdiction over one or more claims between particular parties, the jurisdictional statutes did not authorize supplemental jurisdiction over additional claims involving other parties. *Clark*, supra, at 590; *Zahn*, supra, at 300–301; *Finley*, supra, at 556.

B

In *Finley* we emphasized that "[w]hatever we say regarding the scope of jurisdiction conferred by a particular statute can of course be changed by Congress." 490 U.S., at 556. In 1990, Congress accepted the invitation. It passed the Judicial Improvements Act, 104 Stat. 5089, which enacted § 1367, the provision which controls these cases.

Section 1367 provides, in pertinent part:

"(a) Except as provided in subsections (b) and (c) or as expressly provided otherwise by Federal statute, in any civil action of which the district courts have original jurisdiction, the district courts shall have supplemental jurisdiction over all other claims that are so related to claims in the action within such original jurisdiction that they form part of the same case or controversy under Article III of the United States Constitution. Such supplemental jurisdiction shall include claims that involve the joinder or intervention of additional parties.

"(b) In any civil action of which the district courts have original jurisdiction founded solely on section 1332 of this title, the district courts shall not have supplemental jurisdiction under subsection (a) over claims by plaintiffs against persons made parties under Rule 14, 19, 20, or 24 of the Federal Rules of Civil Procedure, or over claims by persons proposed to be joined as plaintiffs under Rule 19 of such rules, or seeking to intervene as plaintiffs under Rule 24 of such rules, when exercising supplemental jurisdiction over such claims would be inconsistent with the jurisdictional requirements of section 1332."

All parties to this litigation and all courts to consider the question agree that § 1367 overturned the result in *Finley*. There is no warrant, however, for assuming that § 1367 did no more than to overrule *Finley* and otherwise to codify the existing state of the law of supplemental jurisdiction. We must not give jurisdictional statutes a more expansive interpretation than their text warrants, 490 U.S., at 549, 556; but it is just as important not to adopt an artificial construction that is narrower than what the text provides. No sound canon of interpretation requires Congress to speak with extraordinary clarity in order to modify the rules of federal jurisdiction within appropriate constitutional bounds. Ordinary principles of statutory construction apply. In order to determine the scope of supplemental jurisdiction authorized by § 1367, then, we must examine the statute's text in light of context, structure, and related statutory provisions.

Section 1367(a) is a broad grant of supplemental jurisdiction over other claims within the same case or controversy, as long as the action is one in which the district courts would have original jurisdiction. The last sentence of § 1367(a) makes it clear that the grant of supplemental jurisdiction extends to claims involving joinder or intervention of additional parties. The single question before us, therefore, is whether a diversity case in which the claims of some plaintiffs satisfy the amount-in-controversy requirement, but the claims of other plaintiffs do not, presents a "civil action of which the district courts have original jurisdiction." If the answer is yes, § 1367(a) confers supplemental jurisdiction over all claims, including those that do not independently satisfy the amount-in-controversy requirement, if the claims are part of the same Article III case or controversy. If the answer is no, § 1367(a) is inapplicable and, in light of our holdings in *Clark* and *Zahn*, the district court has no statutory basis for exercising supplemental jurisdiction over the additional claims.

We now conclude that the answer must be yes. When the well-pleaded complaint contains at least one claim that satisfies the amount-in-controversy requirement, and there are no other relevant jurisdictional defects, the district court, beyond all question, has original jurisdiction over that claim. The presence of other claims in the complaint, over which the district court may lack original jurisdiction, is of no moment. If the court has original jurisdiction over a single claim in the complaint, it has original jurisdiction over a "civil action" within the meaning of § 1367(a), even if the civil action over which it has jurisdiction comprises fewer claims than were included in the complaint. Once the court determines it has original jurisdiction over the civil action, it can turn to the question whether it has a constitutional and statutory basis for exercising supplemental jurisdiction over the other claims in the action.

Section 1367(a) commences with the direction that §§ 1367(b) and (c), or other relevant statutes, may provide specific exceptions, but otherwise § 1367(a) is a broad jurisdictional grant, with no distinction drawn between pendent-claim and pendent-party cases. In fact, the last sentence of § 1367(a) makes clear that the provision grants supplemental jurisdiction over claims involving joinder or intervention of additional parties. The terms of § 1367 do not acknowledge any distinction between pendent jurisdiction and the doctrine of so-called ancillary jurisdiction. Though the doctrines of pendent and ancillary jurisdiction developed separately as a historical matter, the Court has recognized that the doctrines are "two species of the same generic problem," [Owen Equipment & Erection Co. v.] Kroger, [437 U.S. 365,] at 370 [(1978)]. Nothing in § 1367 indicates a congressional intent to recognize, preserve, or create some meaningful, substantive distinction between the jurisdictional categories we have historically labeled as pendent and ancillary.

If § 1367(a) were the sum total of the relevant statutory language, our holding would rest on that language alone. The statute, of course, instructs us to examine § 1367(b) to determine if any of its exceptions apply, so we proceed to that section. While § 1367(b) qualifies the broad rule of § 1367(a), it does not withdraw supplemental jurisdiction over the claims of the additional parties at issue here. The specific exceptions to § 1367(a) contained in § 1367(b), moreover, provide additional support for our conclusion that § 1367(a) confers supplemental jurisdiction over these claims. Section 1367(b), which applies only to diversity cases, withholds supplemental jurisdiction over the claims of plaintiffs proposed to be joined as indispensable parties under Federal Rule of Civil Procedure 19, or who seek to intervene pursuant to Rule 24. Nothing in the text of § 1367(b), however, withholds supplemental jurisdiction over the claims of plaintiffs permissively joined under Rule 20 (like the additional plaintiffs in No. 04–79) or certified as class-action members pursuant to Rule 23 (like the additional plaintiffs in No. 04–70). The natural, indeed the necessary, inference is that § 1367 confers supplemental jurisdiction over claims by Rule 20 and Rule 23 plaintiffs. This inference, at least with respect to Rule 20 plaintiffs, is strengthened by the fact that § 1367(b) explicitly excludes supplemental jurisdiction over claims against defendants joined under Rule 20.

We cannot accept the view, urged by some of the parties, commentators, and Courts of Appeals, that a district court lacks original jurisdiction over a civil action unless the court has original jurisdiction over every claim in the complaint. As we understand this position, it requires assuming either that all claims in the complaint must stand or fall as a single, indivisible "civil action" as a matter of definitional necessity—what we will refer to as the "indivisibility theory"—or else that the inclusion of a claim or party falling outside the district court's original jurisdiction somehow contaminates every other claim in the complaint, depriving the court of original jurisdiction over any of these claims—what we will refer to as the "contamination theory."

The indivisibility theory is easily dismissed, as it is inconsistent with the whole notion of supplemental jurisdiction. If a district court must have original jurisdiction over every claim in the complaint in order to have "original jurisdiction" over a "civil action," then in *Gibbs* there was no civil action of which the district court could assume original jurisdiction under § 1331, and so no basis for exercising supplemental jurisdiction over any of the claims. The indivisibility theory is further belied by our practice—in both federal-question and diversity cases—of allowing federal courts to cure jurisdictional defects by dismissing the offending parties rather than dismissing the entire action. *Clark*, for example, makes clear that claims that are jurisdictionally defective as to amount in controversy do not destroy original jurisdiction over other claims. 306 U.S., at 590 (dismissing parties who failed to meet the amount-in-controversy requirement but retaining jurisdiction over the remaining party). If the presence of jurisdictionally problematic claims in the complaint meant the district court was without original jurisdiction over the single, indivisible civil action before it, then the district court would have to dismiss the whole action rather than particular parties.

We also find it unconvincing to say that the definitional indivisibility theory applies in the context of diversity cases but not in the context of federal-question cases. The broad and general language of the statute does not permit this result. The contention is premised on the notion that the phrase "original jurisdiction of all civil actions" means different things in § 1331 and § 1332. It is implausible, however, to say that the identical phrase means one thing (original jurisdiction in all actions where at least one claim in the complaint meets the following requirements) in § 1331 and something else (original jurisdiction in all actions where every claim in the complaint meets the following requirements) in § 1332.

The contamination theory, as we have noted, can make some sense in the special context of the complete diversity requirement because the presence of nondiverse parties on both sides of a lawsuit eliminates the justification for providing a federal forum. The theory, however, makes little sense with respect to the amount-in-controversy requirement, which is meant to ensure that a dispute is sufficiently important to warrant federal-court attention. The presence of a single nondiverse party may eliminate the fear of bias with respect to all claims, but the presence of a claim that falls short of the minimum amount in controversy does nothing to reduce the importance of the claims that do meet this requirement.

It is fallacious to suppose, simply from the proposition that § 1332 imposes both the diversity requirement and the amount-in-controversy requirement, that the contamination theory germane to the former is also relevant to the latter. There is no inherent logical connection between the amount-in-controversy requirement and § 1332 diversity jurisdiction. After all, federal-question jurisdiction once had an amount-in-controversy requirement as well. If such a requirement were revived under § 1331, it is clear beyond peradventure that § 1367(a) provides supplemental jurisdiction over federal-question cases where some, but not all, of the federal-law claims involve a sufficient amount in controversy. In other words, § 1367(a) unambiguously overrules the holding and the result in *Clark*. If that is so, however, it would be quite extraordinary to say that § 1367 did not also overrule *Zahn*, a case that was premised in substantial part on the holding in *Clark*.

In addition to the theoretical difficulties with the argument that a district court has original jurisdiction over a civil action only if it has original jurisdiction over each individual claim in the complaint, we have already considered and rejected a virtually identical argument in the closely analogous context of removal jurisdiction. In Chicago v. International College of Surgeons, 522 U.S. 156 (1997), the plaintiff brought federal-and state-law claims in state court. The defendant removed to federal court. The plaintiff objected to removal, citing the text of the removal statute, § 1441(a). That statutory provision, which bears a striking similarity to the relevant portion of § 1367, authorizes removal of "any civil action ... of which the district courts of the United States have original jurisdiction ...." The *College of Surgeons* plaintiff urged that, because its state-law claims were not within the District Court's original jurisdiction, § 1441(a) did not authorize removal. We disagreed. The federal law claims, we held, "suffice to make the actions 'civil actions' within the 'original jurisdiction' of the district courts .... Nothing in the jurisdictional statutes suggests that the presence of related state law claims somehow alters the fact that [the plaintiff's] complaints, by virtue of their federal claims, were 'civil actions' within the federal courts' 'original jurisdiction.' " Id., at 166. Once the case was removed, the District Court had original jurisdiction over the federal law claims and supplemental jurisdiction under § 1367(a) over the state-law claims. Id., at 165.

The dissent in *College of Surgeons* argued that because the plaintiff sought on-the-record review of a local administrative agency decision, the review it sought was outside the scope of the District Court's jurisdiction. Id., at 177 (opinion of GINSBURG, J.). We rejected both the suggestion that state-law claims involving administrative appeals are beyond the scope of § 1367 supplemental jurisdiction, id., at 168–172 (opinion of the Court), and the claim that the administrative review posture of the case deprived the District Court of original jurisdiction over the federal-law claims in the case, id., at 163–168. More importantly for present purposes, *College of Surgeons* stressed that a district court has original jurisdiction of a civil action for purposes of § 1441(a) as long as it has original jurisdiction over a subset of the claims constituting the action. Even the *College of Surgeons* dissent, which took issue with the Court's interpretation of § 1367, did not appear to contest this view of § 1441(a).

Although *College of Surgeons* involved additional claims between the same parties, its interpretation of § 1441(a) applies equally to cases involving additional parties whose claims fall short of the jurisdictional amount. If we were to adopt the contrary view that the presence of additional parties means there is no "civil action ... of which the district courts ... have original jurisdiction," those cases simply would not be removable. To our knowledge, no court has issued a reasoned opinion adopting this view of the removal statute. It is settled, of course, that absent complete diversity a case is not removable because the district court would lack original jurisdiction. Caterpillar, Inc. v. Lewis, 519 U.S. 61, 73 (1996). This, however, is altogether consistent with our view of § 1441(a). A failure of complete diversity, unlike the failure of some claims to meet the requisite amount in controversy, contaminates every claim in the action.

We also reject the argument, similar to the attempted distinction of *College of Surgeons* discussed above, that while the presence of additional claims over which the district court lacks jurisdiction does not mean the civil action is outside the purview of § 1367(a), the presence of additional parties does. The basis for this distinction is not altogether clear, and it is in considerable tension with statutory text. Section 1367(a) applies by its terms to any civil action of which the district courts have original jurisdiction, and the last sentence of § 1367(a) expressly contemplates that the court may have supplemental jurisdiction over additional parties. So it cannot be the case that the presence of those parties destroys the court's original jurisdiction, within the meaning of § 1367(a), over a civil action otherwise properly before it. Also, § 1367(b) expressly withholds supplemental jurisdiction in diversity cases over claims by plaintiffs joined as indispensable parties under Rule 19. If joinder of such parties were sufficient to deprive the district court of original jurisdiction over the civil action within the meaning of § 1367(a), this specific limitation on supplemental jurisdiction in § 1367(b) would be superfluous. The argument that the presence of additional parties removes the civil action from the scope of § 1367(a) also would mean that § 1367 left the *Finley* result undisturbed. *Finley*, after all, involved a Federal Tort Claims Act suit against a federal defendant and state-law claims against additional defendants not otherwise subject to federal jurisdiction. Yet all concede that one purpose of § 1367 was to change the result reached in *Finley*.

Finally, it is suggested that our interpretation of § 1367(a) creates an anomaly regarding the exceptions listed in § 1367(b): It is not immediately obvious why Congress would withhold supplemental jurisdiction over plaintiffs joined as parties "needed for just adjudication" under Rule 19 but would allow supplemental jurisdiction over plaintiffs permissively joined under Rule 20. The omission of Rule 20 plaintiffs from the list of exceptions in § 1367(b) may have been an "unintentional drafting gap," *Meritcare*, 166 F.3d, at 221 and n.6. If that is the case, it is up to Congress rather than the courts to fix it. The omission may seem odd, but it is not absurd. An alternative explanation for the different treatment of Rule 19 and Rule 20 is that Congress was concerned that extending supplemental jurisdiction to Rule 19 plaintiffs would allow circumvention of the complete diversity rule: A nondiverse plaintiff might be omitted intentionally from the original action, but joined later under Rule 19 as a necessary party. See *Stromberg Metal Works*, 77 F.3d, at 932. The contamination theory described above, if applicable, means this ruse would fail, but Congress may have wanted to make assurance double sure. More generally, Congress may have concluded that federal jurisdiction is only appropriate if the district court would have original jurisdiction over the claims of all those plaintiffs who are so essential to the action that they could be joined under Rule 19.

To the extent that the omission of Rule 20 plaintiffs from the list of § 1367(b) exceptions is anomalous, moreover, it is no more anomalous than the inclusion of Rule 19 plaintiffs in that list would be if the alternative view of § 1367(a) were to prevail. If the district court lacks original jurisdiction over a civil diversity action where any plaintiff's claims fail to comply with all the requirements of § 1332, there is no need for a special § 1367(b) exception for Rule 19 plaintiffs who do not meet these requirements. Though the omission of Rule 20 plaintiffs from § 1367(b) presents something of a puzzle on our view of the statute, the inclusion of Rule 19 plaintiffs in this section is at least as difficult to explain under the alternative view.

And so we circle back to the original question: When the well-pleaded complaint in district court includes multiple claims, all part of the same case or controversy, and some, but not all, of the claims are within the court's original jurisdiction, does the court have before it "any civil action of which the district courts have original jurisdiction" ? It does. Under § 1367, the court has original jurisdiction over the civil action comprising the claims for which there is no jurisdictional defect. No other reading of § 1367 is plausible in light of the text and structure of the jurisdictional statute. Though the special nature and purpose of the diversity requirement mean that a single nondiverse party can contaminate every other claim in the lawsuit, the contamination does not occur with respect to jurisdictional defects that go only to the substantive importance of individual claims.

It follows from this conclusion that the threshold requirement of § 1367(a) is satisfied in cases, like those now before us, where some, but not all, of the plaintiffs in a diversity action allege a sufficient amount in controversy. We hold that § 1367 by its plain text overruled *Clark* and *Zahn* and authorized supplemental jurisdiction over all claims by diverse parties arising out of the same Article III case or controversy, subject only to enumerated exceptions not applicable in the cases now before us.

C

The proponents of the alternative view of § 1367 insist that the statute is at least ambiguous and that we should look to other interpretive tools, including the legislative history of § 1367, which supposedly demonstrate Congress did not intend § 1367 to overrule *Zahn*. We can reject this argument at the very outset simply because § 1367 is not ambiguous. For the reasons elaborated above, interpreting § 1367 to foreclose supplemental jurisdiction over plaintiffs in diversity cases who do not meet the minimum amount in controversy is inconsistent with the text, read in light of other statutory provisions and our established jurisprudence. Even if we were to stipulate, however, that the reading these proponents urge upon us is textually plausible, the legislative history cited to support it would not alter our view as to the best interpretation of § 1367.

Those who urge that the legislative history refutes our interpretation rely primarily on the House Judiciary Committee Report on the Judicial Improvements Act, H.R. Rep. No. 101–734 (1990) (House Report or Report). This Report explained that § 1367 would "authorize jurisdiction in a case like *Finley*, as well as essentially restore the pre-*Finley* understandings of the authorization for and limits on other forms of supplemental jurisdiction." House Report, at 28. The Report stated that § 1367(a) "generally authorizes the district court to exercise jurisdiction over a supplemental claim whenever it forms part of the same constitutional case or controversy as the claim or claims that provide the basis of the district court's original jurisdiction," and in so doing codifies *Gibbs* and fills the statutory gap recognized in *Finley*. House Report, at 28–29, and n.15. The Report then remarked that § 1367(b) "is not intended to affect the jurisdictional requirements of [§ 1332] in diversity-only class actions, as those requirements were interpreted prior to *Finley*," citing, without further elaboration, *Zahn* and Supreme Tribe of Ben–Hur v. Cauble, 255 U.S. 356 (1921). House Report, at 29, and n.17. The Report noted that the "net effect" of

§ 1367(b) was to implement the "principal rationale" of *Kroger*, House Report, at 29, at n.16, effecting only "one small change" in pre-*Finley* practice with respect to diversity actions: § 1367(b) would exclude "Rule 23(a) plaintiff-intervenors to the same extent as those sought to be joined as plaintiffs under Rule 19." House Report, at 29. (It is evident that the report here meant to refer to Rule 24, not Rule 23.)

As we have repeatedly held, the authoritative statement is the statutory text, not the legislative history or any other extrinsic material. Extrinsic materials have a role in statutory interpretation only to the extent they shed a reliable light on the enacting Legislature's understanding of otherwise ambiguous terms. Not all extrinsic materials are reliable sources of insight into legislative understandings, however, and legislative history in particular is vulnerable to two serious criticisms. First, legislative history is itself often murky, ambiguous, and contradictory. Judicial investigation of legislative history has a tendency to become, to borrow Judge Leventhal's memorable phrase, an exercise in "looking over a crowd and picking out your friends." See Wald, Some Observations on the Use of Legislative History in the 1981 Supreme Court Term, 68 Iowa L.Rev. 195, 214 (1983). Second, judicial reliance on legislative materials like committee reports, which are not themselves subject to the requirements of Article I, may give unrepresentative committee members—or, worse yet, unelected staffers and lobbyists—both the power and the incentive to attempt strategic manipulations of legislative history to secure results they were unable to achieve through the statutory text. We need not comment here on whether these problems are sufficiently prevalent to render legislative history inherently unreliable in all circumstances, a point on which Members of this Court have disagreed. It is clear, however, that in this instance both criticisms are right on the mark.

First of all, the legislative history of § 1367 is far murkier than selective quotation from the House Report would suggest. The text of § 1367 is based substantially on a draft proposal contained in a Federal Court Study Committee working paper, which was drafted by a Subcommittee chaired by Judge Posner. Report of the Subcommittee on the Role of the Federal Courts and Their Relationship to the States 567–568 (Mar. 12, 1990), reprinted in Judicial Conference of the United States, 1 Federal Courts Study Committee, Working Papers and Subcommittee Reports (July 1, 1990). See also Judicial Conference of the United States, Report of the Federal Courts Study Committee 47–48 (Apr. 2, 1990) (Study Committee Report) (echoing, in brief summary form, the Subcommittee Working Paper proposal and noting that the Subcommittee Working Paper "contains additional material on this subject"); House Report, at 27 ("[Section 1367] implements a recommendation of the Federal Courts Study Committee found on pages 47 and 48 of its report"). While the Subcommittee explained, in language echoed by the House Report, that its proposal "basically restores the law as it existed prior to *Finley*," Subcommittee Working Paper, at 561, it observed in a footnote that its proposal would overrule *Zahn* and that this would be a good idea, Subcommittee Working Paper, at 561, n.33. Although the Federal Courts Study Committee did not expressly adopt the Subcommittee's specific reference to *Zahn*, it neither explicitly disagreed with the Subcommittee's conclusion that this was the best reading of the proposed text nor substantially modified the proposal to avoid this result. Study Committee Report, at 47–48. Therefore, even if the House Report could fairly be read to reflect an understanding that the text of § 1367 did not overrule *Zahn*, the Subcommittee Working Paper on which § 1367 was based reflected the opposite understanding. The House Report is no more authoritative than the Subcommittee Working Paper. The utility of either can extend no further than the light it sheds on how the enacting Legislature understood the statutory text. Trying to figure out how to square the Subcommittee Working Paper's understanding with the House Report's understanding, or which is more reflective of the under-standing of the enacting legislators, is a hopeless task.

Second, the worst fears of critics who argue legislative history will be used to circumvent the Article I process were realized in this case. The telltale evidence is the statement, by three law professors who participated in drafting § 1367, see House Report, at 27, n.13, that § 1367 "on its face" permits "supplemental jurisdiction over claims of class members that do not satisfy section 1332's jurisdictional amount requirement, which would overrule [*Zahn*]. [There is] a disclaimer of intent to accomplish this result in the legislative history.... It would have been better had the statute dealt explicitly with this problem, and the legislative history was an attempt to correct the oversight." Rowe, Burbank, & Mengler, Compound-ing or Creating Confusion About Supplemental Jurisdiction? A Reply to Professor Freer, 40 Emory L.J. 943, 960, n.90 (1991). The professors were frank to concede that if one refuses to consider the legislative history, one has no choice but to "conclude that section 1367 has wiped *Zahn* off the books." Ibid. So there exists an acknowledgment, by parties who have detailed, specific knowledge of the statute and the drafting process, both that the plain text of § 1367 overruled *Zahn* and that language to the contrary in the House Report was a *post hoc* attempt to alter that result. One need not subscribe to the wholesale condemnation of legislative history to refuse to give any effect to such a deliberate effort to amend a statute through a committee report.

In sum, even if we believed resort to legislative history were appropri-ate in these cases—a point we do not concede—we would not give signifi-cant weight to the House Report. The distinguished jurists who drafted the Subcommittee Working Paper, along with three of the participants in the drafting of § 1367, agree that this provision, on its face, overrules *Zahn*. This accords with the best reading of the statute's text, and nothing in the legislative history indicates directly and explicitly that Congress understood the phrase "civil action of which the district courts have original jurisdic-tion" to exclude cases in which some but not all of the diversity plaintiffs meet the amount in controversy requirement.

No credence, moreover, can be given to the claim that, if Congress understood § 1367 to overrule *Zahn*, the proposal would have been more controversial. We have little sense whether any Member of Congress would have been particularly upset by this result. This is not a case where one can plausibly say that concerned legislators might not have realized the possible effect of the text they were adopting. Certainly, any competent legislative aide who studied the matter would have flagged this issue if it were a matter of importance to his or her boss, especially in light of the Subcommittee Working Paper. There are any number of reasons why legislators did not spend more time arguing over § 1367, none of which are relevant to our interpretation of what the words of the statute mean.

D

Finally, we note that the Class Action Fairness Act (CAFA), Pub. L. 109–2, 119 Stat. 4, enacted this year, has no bearing on our analysis of these cases. Subject to certain limitations, the CAFA confers federal diversity jurisdiction over class actions where the aggregate amount in controversy exceeds $5 million. It abrogates the rule against aggregating claims, a rule this Court recognized in *Ben-Hur* and reaffirmed in *Zahn*. The CAFA, however, is not retroactive, and the views of the 2005 Congress are not relevant to our interpretation of a text enacted by Congress in 1990. The CAFA, moreover, does not moot the significance of our interpretation of § 1367, as many proposed exercises of supplemental jurisdiction, even in the class-action context, might not fall within the CAFA's ambit. The CAFA, then, has no impact, one way or the other, on our interpretation of § 1367.

* * *

The judgment of the Court of Appeals for the Eleventh Circuit is affirmed. The judgment of the Court of Appeals for the First Circuit is reversed, and the case is remanded for proceedings consistent with this opinion.

It is so ordered.

■ JUSTICE STEVENS, with whom JUSTICE BREYER joins, dissenting.

JUSTICE GINSBURG'S carefully reasoned opinion demonstrates the error in the Court's rather ambitious reading of this opaque jurisdictional statute. She also has demonstrated that "ambiguity" is a term that may have different meanings for different judges, for the Court has made the remarkable declaration that its reading of the statute is so obviously correct—and JUSTICE GINSBURG'S so obviously wrong—that the text does not even qualify as "ambiguous." Because ambiguity is apparently in the eye of the beholder, I remain convinced that it is unwise to treat the ambiguity *vel non* of a statute as determinative of whether legislative history is consulted. Indeed, I believe that we as judges are more, rather than less, constrained when we make ourselves accountable to *all* reliable evidence of legislative intent. . . .

The legislative history of 28 U.S.C. § 1367 provides powerful confirmation of JUSTICE GINSBURG'S interpretation of that statute. . . .

Not only does the House Report specifically say that § 1367 was not intended to upset Zahn v. International Paper Co., 414 U.S. 291 (1973), but its entire explanation of the statute demonstrates that Congress had in mind a very specific and relatively modest task—undoing this Court's 5-to-4 decision in Finley v. United States, 490 U.S. 545 (1989). In addition to overturning that unfortunate and much-criticized decision, the statute, according to the Report, codifies and preserves "the pre-*Finley* understandings of the authorization for and limits on other forms of supplemental jurisdiction," House Report, at 28, with the exception of making "one small change in pre-*Finley* practice," id., at 29, which is not relevant here.

The sweeping purpose that the Court's decision imputes to Congress bears no resemblance to the House Report's description of the statute. But this does not seem to trouble the Court, for its decision today treats statutory interpretation as a pedantic exercise, divorced from any serious attempt at ascertaining congressional intent. Of course, there are situations in which we do not honor Congress' apparent intent unless that intent is made "clear" in the text of a statute—in this way, we can be certain that Congress considered the issue and intended a disfavored outcome, see, e.g., Landgraf v. USI Film Products, 511 U.S. 244 (1994) (requiring clear statement for retroactive civil legislation). But that principle provides no basis for discounting the House Report, given that our cases have never recognized a presumption in *favor* of expansive diversity jurisdiction.

The Court's reasons for ignoring this virtual billboard of congressional intent are unpersuasive. That a subcommittee of the Federal Courts Study Committee believed that an earlier, substantially similar version of the statute overruled *Zahn* ... only highlights the fact that the statute is ambiguous. What is determinative is that the House Report explicitly rejected that broad reading of the statutory text. Such a report has special significance as an indicator of legislative intent. In Congress, committee reports are normally considered the authoritative explication of a statute's text and purposes, and busy legislators and their assistants rely on that explication in casting their votes. . . .

The Court's second reason—its comment on the three law professors who participated in drafting § 1367—is similarly off the mark. In the law review article that the Court refers to, the professors were merely saying that the text of the statute was susceptible to an overly broad (and simplistic) reading, and that clarification in the House Report was therefore appropriate. See Rowe, Burbank & Mengler, Compounding or Creating Confusion About Supplemental Jurisdiction? A Reply to Professor Freer, 40 Emory L.J. 943, 960 n.90 (1991). Significantly, the reference to *Zahn* in the House Report does not at all appear to be tacked-on or out of place; indeed, it is wholly consistent with the Report's broader explanation of Congress' goal of overruling *Finley* and preserving pre-*Finley* law. . . .

After nearly 20 pages of complicated analysis, which explores subtle doctrinal nuances and coins various neologisms, the Court announces that § 1367 could not reasonably be read another way. . . . That conclusion is difficult to accept. . . . Given JUSTICE GINSBURG'S persuasive account of the statutory text and its jurisprudential backdrop, and given the uncommonly clear legislative history, I am confident that the majority's interpretation of § 1367 is mistaken. I respectfully dissent.

——

■ JUSTICE GINSBURG, with whom JUSTICE STEVENS, JUSTICE O'CONNOR, and JUSTICE BREYER join, dissenting.

These cases present the question whether Congress, by enacting 28 U.S.C. § 1367, overruled this Court's decisions in Clark v. Paul Gray, Inc., 306 U.S. 583, 589 (1939) (reaffirming the holding of Troy Bank v. G.A. Whitehead & Co., 222 U.S. 39, 40 (1911)), and Zahn v. International Paper Co., 414 U.S. 291 (1973). . . .

. . . . .

The Court adopts a plausibly broad reading of § 1367, a measure that is hardly a model of the careful drafter's art. There is another plausible reading, however, one less disruptive of our jurisprudence regarding supplemental jurisdiction. If one reads § 1367(a) to instruct, as the statute's text suggests, that the district court must first have "original jurisdiction" over a "civil action" before supplemental jurisdiction can attach, then *Clark* and *Zahn* are preserved, and supplemental jurisdiction does not open the way for joinder of plaintiffs, or inclusion of class members, who do not independently meet the amount-in-controversy requirement. For the reasons that follow, I conclude that this narrower construction is the better reading of § 1367.

I

A

Section 1367, captioned "Supplemental jurisdiction," codifies court-recognized doctrines formerly labeled "pendent" and "ancillary" jurisdiction. Pendent jurisdiction involved the enlargement of federal-question litigation to include related state-law claims. Ancillary jurisdiction evolved primarily to protect defending parties, or others whose rights might be adversely affected if they could not air their claims in an ongoing federal-court action. Given jurisdiction over the principal action, federal courts entertained certain matters deemed ancillary regardless of the citizenship of the parties or the amount in controversy.

Mine Workers v. Gibbs, 383 U.S. 715 (1966), the leading pendent jurisdiction case, involved a claim against a union for wrongfully inducing the plaintiff's discharge. The plaintiff stated a federal claim under the Taft–Hartley Act, and an allied state-law claim of unlawful conspiracy to interfere with his employment contract. This Court upheld the joinder of federal and state claims. "[T]here is *power* in federal courts to hear the whole," the Court said, when the state and federal claims "derive from a common nucleus of operative fact" and are so linked that the plaintiff "would ordinarily be expected to try them all in one judicial proceeding." Id., at 725.

Gibbs involved the linkage of federal and state claims against the same defendant. In Finley v. United States, 490 U.S. 545, the Court contained *Gibbs*. Without congressional authorization, the Court admonished, the pendent jurisdiction umbrella could not be stretched to cover the joinder of additional parties. *Gibbs* had departed from earlier decisions recognizing that "jurisdiction [must] be explicitly conferred," the Court said. 490 U.S., at 556.... While the *Finley* Court did not "limit or impair" *Gibbs* itself, 490 U.S., at 556, for further development of pendent jurisdiction, the Court made it plain, the initiative would lie in Congress' domain. Id., at 555–556.

Ancillary jurisdiction, which evolved as a more sprawling doctrine than pendent jurisdiction, was originally rooted in "the notion that [when] federal jurisdiction in [a] principal suit effectively controls the property or fund under dispute, other claimants thereto should be allowed to intervene in order to protect their interests, without regard to jurisdiction." *Aldinger*, 427 U.S., at 11 .... In Owen Equipment & Erection Co. v. Kroger, 437 U.S. 365 (1978), the Court addressed the permissible scope of the doctrine in relation to the liberal provisions of the Federal Rules of Civil Procedure for joinder of parties and claims.

Kroger commenced as a suit between a citizen of Iowa and a Nebraska corporation. When the Nebraska defendant impleaded an Iowa corporation as a third-party defendant under Rule 14(a), the plaintiff asserted state-law claims against the impleaded party. No independent basis of federal jurisdiction existed over the newly asserted claims, for both plaintiff and impleaded defendant were citizens of Iowa. 437 U.S., at 370. The Court held that the plaintiff could not draw in a co-citizen defendant in this manner. Id., at 377. Federal courts, by the time of *Kroger*, were routinely exercising ancillary jurisdiction over compulsory counterclaims, impleader claims, cross-claims among defendants, and claims of parties who intervened "of right." See id., at 375, n.18 (collecting cases). In *Kroger*, however,

> "the nonfederal claim ... was asserted by the plaintiff, who voluntarily chose to bring suit upon a state-law claim in a federal court. By contrast, ancillary jurisdiction typically involve[d] claims by a defending party haled into court against his will, or by another person whose rights might be irretrievably lost unless he could assert them in an ongoing action in a federal court." Id., at 376.

Having "chosen the federal rather than the state forum," the Court said, the plaintiff had to "accept its limitations." Ibid.

In sum, in federal-question cases before § 1367's enactment, the Court recognized pendent-claim jurisdiction, *Gibbs*, 383 U.S., at 725, but not pendent-party jurisdiction, *Finley*, 490 U.S., at 555–556. As to ancillary jurisdiction, the Court adhered to the limitation that in diversity cases, throughout the litigation, all plaintiffs must remain diverse from all defendants. See *Kroger*, 437 U.S., at 374.

Although pendent jurisdiction and ancillary jurisdiction evolved discretely, the Court has recognized that they are "two species of the same generic problem: Under what circumstances may a federal court hear and decide a state-law claim arising between citizens of the same State?" Id., at 370. *Finley* regarded that question as one properly addressed to Congress. . . .

B

Shortly before the Court decided *Finley*, Congress had established the Federal Courts Study Committee to take up issues relating to "the federal courts' congestion, delay, expense, and expansion." Judicial Conference of the United States, Report of the Federal Courts Study Committee 3 (Apr. 2, 1990) (hereinafter Committee Report). The Committee's charge was to conduct a study addressing the "crisis" in federal courts caused by the "rapidly growing" caseload. Id., at 6 (internal quotation marks omitted).

Among recommendations, the Committee urged Congress to "authorize federal courts to assert pendent jurisdiction over parties without an independent federal jurisdictional base." Id., at 47. If adopted, this recommendation would overrule *Finley*. Earlier, a subcommittee had recommended that Congress overrule both *Finley* and *Zahn*. Report of the Subcommittee on the Role of the Federal Courts and Their Relationship to the States 547, 561, n.33 (Mar. 12, 1990), reprinted in 1 Judicial Conference of the United States, Federal Courts Study Committee, Working Papers and Subcommittee Reports (July 1, 1990) (hereinafter Subcommittee Report). In the subcommittee's view, "[f]rom a policy standpoint," *Zahn* "ma[de] little sense." Subcommittee Report 561, n.33.[25] The full Committee, however, urged only the overruling of *Finley* and did not adopt the recommendation to overrule *Zahn*. Committee Report, 47–48.

As a separate matter, a substantial majority of the Committee "strongly recommend[ed]" the elimination of diversity jurisdiction, save for "complex multi-state litigation, interpleader, and suits involving aliens." Id., at 38–39; accord Subcommittee Report, 454–458. "[N]o other step," the Committee's Report maintained, "will do anywhere nearly as much to reduce federal caseload pressures and contain the growth of the federal judiciary." Committee Report, 39.

Congress responded by adopting, as part of the Judicial Improvements Act of 1990, 104 Stat. 5089, recommendations of the Federal Courts Study Committee ranked by the House Committee on the Judiciary as "modest" and "noncontroversial." H.R. Rep. No. 101–734, pp. 15–16 (1990) (hereinafter H.R. Rep.); see also 136 Cong. Rec. 36288 (1990). Congress did not take up the Study Committee's immodest proposal to curtail diversity jurisdic-

---

25. Anomalously, in holding that each class member "must satisfy the jurisdictional amount," Zahn v. International Paper Co., 414 U.S. 291, 301 (1973), the *Zahn* Court did not refer to Supreme Tribe of Ben–Hur v. Cauble, 255 U.S. 356, 366 (1921), which established that in a class action, the citizenship of the named plaintiff is controlling. But see *Zahn*, 414 U.S., at 309–310 (Brennan, J., dissenting) (urging *Zahn*'s inconsistency with *Ben–Hur*).

tion. It did, however, enact a supplemental jurisdiction statute, codified as 28 U.S.C. § 1367.

II

A

Section 1367, by its terms, operates only in civil actions "of which the district courts have original jurisdiction." The "original jurisdiction" relevant here is diversity-of-citizenship jurisdiction, conferred by § 1332. The character of that jurisdiction is the essential backdrop for comprehension of § 1367.

The Constitution broadly provides for federal-court jurisdiction in controversies "between Citizens of different States." Art. III, § 2, cl. 1. This Court has read that provision to demand no more than "minimal diversity," i.e., so long as one party on the plaintiffs' side and one party on the defendants' side are of diverse citizenship, Congress may authorize federal courts to exercise diversity jurisdiction. See State Farm Fire & Casualty Co. v. Tashire, 386 U.S. 523, 530–531 (1967). Further, the Constitution includes no amount-in-controversy limitation on the exercise of federal jurisdiction. But from the start, Congress, as its measures have been construed by this Court, has limited federal court exercise of diversity jurisdiction in two principal ways. First, unless Congress specifies otherwise, diversity must be "complete," i.e., all parties on plaintiffs' side must be diverse from all parties on defendants' side. Strawbridge v. Curtiss, 3 Cranch [7 U.S.] 267 (1806); see 13B Wright & Miller § 3605 (2d ed.1984). Second, each plaintiff's stake must independently meet the amount-in-controversy specification: "When two or more plaintiffs, having separate and distinct demands, unite for convenience and economy in a single suit, it is essential that the demand of each be of the requisite jurisdictional amount." *Troy Bank*, 222 U.S., at 40.

The statute today governing federal court exercise of diversity jurisdiction in the generality of cases, § 1332, like all its predecessors, incorporates both a diverse-citizenship requirement and an amount-in-controversy specification.[26] As to the latter, the statute reads: "The district courts shall have original jurisdiction [in diversity-of-citizenship cases] where the matter in controversy exceeds the sum ... of $75,000." § 1332(a). This Court has

---

26. Endeavoring to preserve the "complete diversity" rule first stated in Strawbridge v. Curtiss, 3 Cranch [7 U.S.] 267 (1806), the Court's opinion drives a wedge between the two components of 28 U.S.C. § 1332, treating the diversity-of-citizenship requirement as essential, the amount-in-controversy requirement as more readily disposable. Section 1332 itself, however, does not rank order the two requirements. What "[o]rdinary principl[e] of statutory construction" or "sound canon of interpretation," allows the Court to slice up § 1332 this way? In partial explanation, the Court asserts that amount in controversy can be analyzed claim-by-claim, but the diversity requirement cannot. It is not altogether clear why that should be so. The cure for improper joinder of a nondiverse party is the same as the cure for improper joinder of a plaintiff who does not satisfy the jurisdictional amount. In both cases, original jurisdiction can be preserved by dismissing the nonqualifying party. See Caterpillar Inc. v. Lewis, 519 U.S. 61, 64 (1996) (diversity); Newman–Green, Inc. v. Alfonzo–Larrain, 490 U.S. 826, 836–838 (1989) (same); *Zahn*, 414 U.S., at 295, 300 (amount in controversy); Clark v. Paul Gray, Inc., 306 U.S. 583, 590 (1939) (same).

long held that, in determining whether the amount-in-controversy requirement has been satisfied, a single plaintiff may aggregate two or more claims
against a single defendant, even if the claims are unrelated. See, e.g.,
Edwards v. Bates County, 163 U.S. 269, 273 (1896). But in multiparty
cases, including class actions, we have unyieldingly adhered to the
nonaggregation rule stated in *Troy Bank*. See *Clark*, 306 U.S., at 589
(reaffirming the "familiar rule that when several plaintiffs assert separate
and distinct demands in a single suit, the amount involved in each separate
controversy must be of the requisite amount to be within the jurisdiction of
the district court, and that those amounts cannot be added together to
satisfy jurisdictional requirements"); Snyder v. Harris, 394 U.S. 332, 339–
340 (1969) (abandonment of the nonaggregation rule in class actions would
undercut the congressional "purpose . . . to check, to some degree, the
rising caseload of the federal courts").

This Court most recently addressed "[t]he meaning of [§ 1332's]
'matter in controversy' language" in *Zahn*, 414 U.S., at 298. *Zahn*, like
Snyder decided four years earlier, was a class action. In *Snyder*, no class
member had a claim large enough to satisfy the jurisdictional amount. But
in *Zahn*, the named plaintiffs had such claims. 414 U.S., at 292. Nevertheless, the Court declined to depart from its "longstanding construction of
the 'matter in controversy' requirement of § 1332." Id., at 301. The *Zahn*
Court stated:

> "*Snyder* invoked the well-established rule that each of several plain-
> tiffs asserting separate and distinct claims must satisfy the jurisdic-
> tional-amount requirement if his claim is to survive a motion to
> dismiss. This rule plainly mandates not only that there may be no
> aggregation and that the entire case must be dismissed where none of
> the plaintiffs' claims [meets the amount-in-controversy requirement]
> but also requires that any plaintiff without the jurisdictional amount
> must be dismissed from the case, even though others allege jurisdic-
> tionally sufficient claims." Id., at 300.

The rule that each plaintiff must independently satisfy the amount-in-
controversy requirement, unless Congress expressly orders otherwise, was
thus the solidly established reading of § 1332 when Congress enacted the
Judicial Improvements Act of 1990, which added § 1367 to Title 28.

B

These cases present the question whether Congress abrogated the
nonaggregation rule long tied to § 1332 when it enacted § 1367. In
answering that question, "context [should provide] a crucial guide." Rosario Ortega v. Star–Kist Foods, Inc., 370 F.3d 124, 135 (2004). The Court
should assume, as it ordinarily does, that Congress legislated against a
background of law already in place and the historical development of that
law. See National Archives and Records Admin. v. Favish, 541 U.S. 157,
169 (2004). Here, that background is the statutory grant of diversity
jurisdiction, the amount-in-controversy condition that Congress, from the

start, has tied to the grant, and the nonaggregation rule this Court has long applied to the determination of the "matter in controversy."

Section 1367(a) provides . . . .

The Court is unanimous in reading § 1367(a) to permit pendent-party jurisdiction in federal-question cases, and thus, to overrule *Finley*. The basic jurisdictional grant, § 1331, provides that "[t]he district courts shall have original jurisdiction of all civil actions arising under the Constitution, laws, or treaties of the United States." Since 1980, § 1331 has contained no amount-in-controversy requirement. See 94 Stat. 2369 (eliminating § 1331's amount-in-controversy requirement). Once there is a civil action presenting a qualifying claim arising under federal law, § 1331's sole requirement is met. District courts, we have held, may then adjudicate, additionally, state-law claims "deriv[ing] from a common nucleus of operative fact." *Gibbs*, 383 U.S., at 725. Section 1367(a) enlarges that category to include not only state-law claims against the defendant named in the federal claim, but also "[state-law] claims that involve the joinder or intervention of additional parties."

The Court divides, however, on the impact of § 1367(a) on diversity cases controlled by § 1332. Under the majority's reading, § 1367(a) permits the joinder of related claims cut loose from the nonaggregation rule that has long attended actions under § 1332. Only the claims specified in § 1367(b) would be excluded from § 1367(a)'s expansion of § 1332's grant of diversity jurisdiction. And because § 1367(b) contains no exception for joinder of plaintiffs under Rule 20 or class actions under Rule 23, the Court concludes, *Clark* and *Zahn* have been overruled.[27]

The Court's reading is surely plausible, especially if one detaches § 1367(a) from its context and attempts no reconciliation with prior interpretations of § 1332's amount-in-controversy requirement. But § 1367(a)'s text, as the First Circuit held, can be read another way, one that would involve no rejection of *Clark* and *Zahn*.

As explained by the First Circuit in *Ortega*, and applied to class actions by the Tenth Circuit in *Leonhardt*, . . . § 1367(a) addresses "civil action[s] of which the district courts have original jurisdiction," a formulation that, in diversity cases, is sensibly read to incorporate the rules on joinder and aggregation tightly tied to § 1332 at the time of § 1367's enactment. On this reading, a complaint must first meet that "original jurisdiction" measurement. If it does not, no supplemental jurisdiction is authorized. If it does, § 1367(a) authorizes "supplemental jurisdiction" over related

---

27. Under the Court's construction of § 1367, . . . Beatriz Ortega's family members can remain in the action because their joinder is merely permissive, see Fed. Rule Civ. Proc. 20. If, however, their presence was "needed for just adjudication," Rule 19, their dismissal would be required. The inclusion of those who may join, and exclusion of those who should or must join, defies rational explanation, . . . and others adopting the interpretation the Court embraces have so acknowledged, see Stromberg Metal Works, Inc. v. Press Mechanical, Inc., 77 F.3d 928, 932 (CA7 1996) (recognizing the anomaly and inquiring: "What sense can this make?"); cf. 14B Wright & Miller § 3704, p. 168 (3d ed.1998) (distinction between Rule 19 and Rule 20 "seems incongruous, and serves no apparent public policy purpose").

claims. In other words, § 1367(a) would preserve undiminished, as part and parcel of § 1332 "original jurisdiction" determinations, both the "complete diversity" rule and the decisions restricting aggregation to arrive at the amount in controversy.[28] Section 1367(b)'s office, then, would be "to prevent the erosion of the complete diversity [and amount-in-controversy] requirement[s] that might otherwise result from an expansive application of what was once termed the doctrine of ancillary jurisdiction." See Pfander, Supplemental Jurisdiction and Section 1367: The Case for a Sympathetic Textualism, 148 U.Pa.L.Rev. 109, 114 (1999) . . . . In contrast to the Court's construction of § 1367, which draws a sharp line between the diversity and amount-in-controversy components of § 1332, . . . the interpretation presented here does not sever the two jurisdictional requirements.

The more restrained reading of § 1367 just outlined would yield affirmance of the First Circuit's judgment in *Ortega*, and reversal of the Eleventh Circuit's judgment in *Exxon*. It would not discard entirely, as the Court does, the judicially developed doctrines of pendent and ancillary jurisdiction as they existed when *Finley* was decided.[29] Instead, it would recognize § 1367 essentially as a codification of those doctrines, placing them under a single heading, but largely retaining their substance, with overriding *Finley* the only basic change: Supplemental jurisdiction, once the district court has original jurisdiction, would now include "claims that involve the joinder or intervention of additional parties." § 1367(a).

Pendent jurisdiction, as earlier explained, applied only in federal-question cases and allowed plaintiffs to attach nonfederal claims to their jurisdiction-qualifying claims. Ancillary jurisdiction applied primarily, although not exclusively, in diversity cases and "typically involve[d] claims *by a defending party* haled into court against his will." *Kroger*, 437 U.S., at 376 (emphasis added) . . . . As the First Circuit observed, neither doctrine permitted a plaintiff to circumvent the dual requirements of § 1332 (diversity of citizenship and amount in controversy) "simply by joining her [jurisdictionally inadequate] claim in an action brought by [a] jurisdictionally competent diversity plaintiff." *Ortega*, 370 F.3d, at 138.

Not only would the reading I find persuasive "alig[n] statutory supplemental jurisdiction with the judicially developed doctrines of pendent and ancillary jurisdiction," ibid., it would also synchronize § 1367 with the removal statute, 28 U.S.C. § 1441. As the First Circuit carefully explained:

> "Section 1441, like § 1367, applies only if the 'civil action' in question is one 'of which the district courts . . . have original jurisdiction.' § 1441(a). Relying on that language, the Supreme Court has interpreted § 1441 to prohibit removal unless the entire action, as it stands at

---

28. On this reading of § 1367(a), it is immaterial that § 1367(b) "does not withdraw supplemental jurisdiction over the claims of the additional parties at issue here." . . . Because those claims would not come within § 1367(a) in the first place, Congress would have had no reason to list them in § 1367(b). . . .

29. The Court's opinion blends the two doctrines, according no significance to their discrete development.

the time of removal, could have been filed in federal court in the first instance.... Section 1441 has thus been held to incorporate the well-pleaded complaint rule, see City of Chicago [v. International College of Surgeons, 522 U.S. 156, 163 (1997)];[30] the complete diversity rule, see Caterpillar, Inc. v. Lewis, 519 U.S. 61, 73 (1996); and rules for calculating the amount in controversy, see St. Paul Mercury Indem. Co. v. Red Cab Co., 303 U.S. 283, 291–292 (1938)." *Ortega*, 370 F.3d, at 138 (citations omitted and footnote added).

The less disruptive view I take of § 1367 also accounts for the omission of Rule 20 plaintiffs and Rule 23 class actions in § 1367(b)'s text. If one reads § 1367(a) as a plenary grant of supplemental jurisdiction to federal courts sitting in diversity, one would indeed look for exceptions in § 1367(b). Finding none for permissive joinder of parties or class actions, one would conclude that Congress effectively, even if unintentionally, overruled *Clark* and *Zahn*. But if one recognizes that the nonaggregation rule delineated in *Clark* and *Zahn* forms part of the determination whether "original jurisdiction" exists in a diversity case, ... then plaintiffs who do not meet the amount-in-controversy requirement would fail at the § 1367(a) threshold. Congress would have no reason to resort to a § 1367(b) exception to turn such plaintiffs away from federal court, given that their claims, from the start, would fall outside the court's § 1332 jurisdiction. See Pfander, 148 U.Pa.L.Rev., at 148.

Nor does the more moderate reading assign different meanings to "original jurisdiction" in diversity and federal-question cases.... As the First Circuit stated:

" '[O]riginal jurisdiction' in § 1367(a) has the same meaning in every case: [An] underlying statutory grant of original jurisdiction must be satisfied. What differs between federal question and diversity cases is not the meaning of 'original jurisdiction' but rather the [discrete] requirements of sections 1331 and 1332. Under § 1331, the sole issue is whether a federal question appears on the face of the plaintiff's well-pleaded complaint; the [citizenship] of the parties and the amounts they stand to recover [do not bear on that determination]. Section 1332, by contrast, predicates original jurisdiction on [satisfaction of the amount-in-controversy specification]. [In short,] the 'original jurisdiction' language in § 1367 operates differently in federal-question and diversity cases not because the meaning of that term varies, but because the [jurisdiction-granting] statutes are different." *Ortega*, 370 F.3d, at 139–140.

---

30. The point of the Court's extended discussion of Chicago v. International College of Surgeons, 522 U.S. 156 (1997), in the instant cases, slips from my grasp. There was no disagreement in that case, and there is none now, that 28 U.S.C. § 1367(a) is properly read to authorize the exercise of supplemental jurisdiction in removed cases. *International College of Surgeons* was unusual in that the federal court there was asked to review a decision of a local administrative agency. Such review, it was unsuccessfully argued, was "appellate" in character, and therefore outside the ken of a court empowered to exercise "original" jurisdiction. Compare 522 U.S., at 166–168, with id., at 176–177 (GINSBURG, J., dissenting).

What is the utility of § 1367(b) under my reading of § 1367(a)? Section 1367(a) allows parties other than the plaintiff to assert *reactive* claims once entertained under the heading ancillary jurisdiction [, such as] compulsory counterclaims and impleader claims, over which federal courts routinely exercised ancillary jurisdiction.... As earlier observed, § 1367(b) stops plaintiffs from circumventing § 1332's jurisdictional requirements by using another's claim as a hook to add a claim that the plaintiff could not have brought in the first instance. *Kroger* is the paradigm case. There, the Court held that ancillary jurisdiction did not extend to a plaintiff's claim against a nondiverse party who had been impleaded by the defendant under Rule 14. Section 1367(b), then, is corroborative of § 1367(a)'s coverage of claims formerly called ancillary, but provides exceptions to assure that accommodation of added claims would not fundamentally alter "the jurisdictional requirements of section 1332." See Pfander, supra, at 135–137.

While § 1367's enigmatic text[31] defies flawless interpretation,[32] the precedent-preservative reading, I am persuaded, better accords with the historical and legal context of Congress' enactment of the supplemental jurisdiction statute, . . . and the established limits on pendent and ancillary jurisdiction . . . . It does not attribute to Congress a jurisdictional enlargement broader than the one to which the legislators adverted, . . . and it follows the sound counsel that "close questions of [statutory] construction should be resolved in favor of continuity and against change." Shapiro, Continuity and Change in Statutory Interpretation, 67 N.Y.U.L.Rev. 921, 925 (1992).[33]

* * *

---

31. The Court notes the passage this year of the Class Action Fairness Act (CAFA), Pub. L. 109–2, 119 Stat. 4, only to dismiss that legislation as irrelevant. Subject to several exceptions and qualifications, CAFA provides for federal-court adjudication of state-law-based class actions in which diversity is "minimal" (one plaintiff's diversity from one defendant suffices), and the "matter in controversy" is an aggregate amount in excess of $5,000,000. Significant here, CAFA's enlargement of federal-court diversity jurisdiction was accomplished, "clearly and conspicuously," by amending § 1332 . . . .

32. If § 1367(a) itself renders unnecessary the listing of Rule 20 plaintiffs and Rule 23 class actions in § 1367(b), then it is similarly unnecessary to refer, as § 1367(b) does, to "persons proposed to be joined as plaintiffs under Rule 19." On one account, Congress bracketed such persons with persons "seeking to intervene as plaintiffs under Rule 24" to modify pre-§ 1367 practice. Before enactment of § 1367, courts entertained, under the heading of ancillary jurisdiction, claims of Rule 24(a) intervenors "of right," see Owen Equipment & Erection Co. v. Kroger, 437 U.S. 365, 375, n.18 (1978), but denied ancillary jurisdiction over claims of "necessary" Rule 19 plaintiffs, see 13 Wright & Miller § 3523, p. 127 (2d ed.Supp. 2005). Congress may have sought simply to underscore that those seeking to join as plaintiffs, whether under Rule 19 or Rule 24, should be treated alike, i.e., denied joinder when "inconsistent with the jurisdictional requirements of § 1332." See *Ortega*, 370 F.3d, at 140, and n.15 (internal quotation marks omitted); H.R. Rep., at 29 ("Subsection (b) makes one small change in pre-*Finley* practice," i.e., it eliminates the Rule 19/Rule 24 anomaly.).

33. While the interpretation of § 1367 described in this opinion does not rely on the measure's legislative history, that history, as JUSTICE STEVENS has shown, is corroborative of the statutory reading set out above.

For the reasons stated, I would hold that § 1367 does not overrule *Clark* and *Zahn*. I would therefore affirm the judgment of the Court of Appeals for the First Circuit and reverse the judgment of the Court of Appeals for the Eleventh Circuit.[34]

———

COMMENT ON 28 U.S.C. §§ 1367(b) & 1367(c)

Subsection (b) reflects obvious Congressional endorsement of the concern expressed in *Kroger* that freewheeling supplemental jurisdiction over additional parties might undermine the policy goals of § 1332's nonconstitutional rule of complete diversity. See House Committee Report, as reprinted infra p. 878. But merely being told to codify "the rule of the *Kroger* case" presents the drafter of a supplemental-jurisdiction statute with two perplexing problems. First, just what is that rule: does it merely codify the result in *Kroger* (no supplemental jurisdiction in a diversity case over an amended complaint's assertion of a claim against an additional, nondiverse defendant after impleader of that defendant under the seventh sentence of Federal Rule of Civil Procedure 14(a))? Or does it more broadly limit supplemental jurisdiction in diversity cases, with the incidental and perhaps intended effect of discouraging diversity litigation? Second, how should the restriction of supplemental jurisdiction in diversity cases be legislatively implemented? Should there be a functional exclusion of certain claims? Or should § 1367(b) seek to foresee and identify, rule by rule, particular instances of disfavored joinder of additional claims and parties in diversity cases and by a prohibitory checklist exclude those and only instances of joinder from § 1367(a)'s otherwise global grant of supplemental jurisdiction?

With respect to both of these problems, § 1367(b) fatefully adopted the second alternative, going substantially beyond the four corners of the *Kroger* case in prohibiting the use of supplemental jurisdiction in diversity cases, and doing so by a "blacklist" approach that attempts to identify and disqualify disfavored claims according to their status under the Federal Rules of Civil Procedure. The interpretation of § 1367(b) resulted in a circuit split, leading to the *Allapattah* decision reprinted supra p. 289. See generally Pfander, The Simmering Debate Over Supplemental Jurisdiction, 2002 U.Ill.L.Rev. 1209; Freer, The Cauldron Boils: Supplemental Jurisdic-

---

[**34.** The circuit courts have followed *Exxon Mobil*'s plain text approach in addressing other supplemental jurisdiction issues. In Global NAPS, Inc. v. Verizon New England, Inc., 603 F.3d 71 (1st Cir. 2010), the First Circuit observed that judge-made law predating the enactment of § 1367 had distinguished between compulsory and permissive counterclaims, finding jurisdiction only for counterclaims classified as compulsory. The court held that § 1367 superseded that case law: "The statute does not use the terminology of 'permissive' or 'compulsory.' It gives federal courts supplemental jurisdiction over all claims that are part of the same Article III case or controversy." Declining to define the statute's phrase "so related . . . that [the claims] form part of the same case or controversy under Article III," the court stated, "In this case we need only decide that supplemental jurisdiction is somewhat broader than the transaction-or-occurrence test."]

tion, Amount in Controversy, and Diversity of Citizenship Class Actions, 53 Emory L.J. 55 (2004); Greitzer, Developments in the Law: Federal Jurisdiction and Forum Selection, Part IV: Supplemental Jurisdiction, 37 Loy. L.A.L.Rev. 1501 (2004).

The American Law Institute completed work on a new supplemental-jurisdiction statute in 1998, when it adopted Tentative Draft No. 2 of its Federal Judicial Code Revision Project. These recommendations for reform of § 1367 constitute Part I of the report of the Judicial Code Project as published in final form in 2004, together with recommended reforms of federal venue law (Part II) and removal law (Part III). The Judicial Code Project proposes a fundamental reconceptualization of federal jurisdiction as attaching primarily to particular claims between parties rather than to the cluster of claims and parties that may constitute a given civil action. This "claim-specific" rather than "action-specific" approach to federal jurisdiction leads to important changes in how a broad grant of supplemental jurisdiction is reconciled with the traditionally narrow scope of statutory diversity jurisdiction. See ALI, Federal Judicial Code Revision Project, Part I: Supplemental Jurisdiction, Commentary, at 29–31 & Reporter's Notes, at 41–42; id., App. A, Reporter's Memorandum on the Claim–Specific Nature of the Original Jurisdiction of the District Courts, at 599–656 (2004). See generally Oakley, Integrating Supplemental Jurisdiction and Diversity Jurisdiction: A Progress Report on the Work of the American Law Institute, 74 Ind.L.J. 25 (1998), which reprints the full text of the ALI's proposed revision of § 1367.

Although the ALI sought to preserve the rule of the *Kroger* case, its interpretation and codification of that rule have been criticized as insufficiently protective of the underlying rule of complete diversity. See Colloquy: Supplemental Jurisdiction, the ALI, and the Rule of *Kroger* Case, 51 Duke L.J. 647 (2001), a four-part exchange between Professor Edward A. Hartnett and the ALI's Reporter, Professor Oakley. Other views, both favoring and criticizing the ALI's approach, appear in Symposium: A Reappraisal of the Supplemental–Jurisdiction Statute: Title 28 U.S.C. § 1367, 74 Ind.L.J. 1 (1998).

By the juxtaposition of subsections (a) and (c) Congress appeared to create a strong presumption in favor of the exercise of supplemental jurisdiction, but the issue has split the circuits. Subsection (a) grants the jurisdiction in mandatory terms ("shall have supplemental jurisdiction") subject to subsection (c)'s rather strict standards for when the district courts may decline to exercise supplemental jurisdiction. These standards combine the language of discretion found in *Gibbs* with the language of abstention. Abstention doctrines have never been understood to be a plenary grant of discretion to the district courts, but rather have functioned to permit the district courts to decline to exercise their otherwise mandatory jurisdiction for extraordinary reasons of respect for state authority or to avoid unnecessary adjudication of federal constitutional issues. Importing abstention considerations into the standards governing district courts' discretion to decline to exercise supplemental jurisdiction would appear substantially to curtail that discretion.

The Ninth Circuit and the Seventh Circuit have adopted divergent views of the scope of a district court's discretion under subsection (c) to decline to exercise the supplemental jurisdiction otherwise conferred upon it by subsection (a). The Ninth Circuit expressly agreed with the view stated above (as set forth in 13B Wright, Miller & Cooper, Federal Practice and Procedure: Jurisdiction 2d § 3567.3 (1992 Supp.)) that the discretion to decline supplemental jurisdiction under subsection (c) is narrower than that previously existing under the principles of *Gibbs*. Executive Software North America, Inc. v. United States District Court, 24 F.3d 1545, 1556 (9th Cir.1994). The Ninth Circuit acknowledged the Seventh Circuit's contrary view that "the new statute is intended to codify rather than alter the judge-made principles of pendent . . . jurisdiction," Brazinski v. Amoco Petroleum Additives Co., 6 F.3d 1176, 1182 (7th Cir.1993), but declared this to be merely "broad dicta." 24 F.3d, at 1559, n. 12. The First, Third, and D.C. Circuits have adopted the Seventh Circuit's approach, while the Second, Eighth, and Eleventh Circuits have aligned themselves with the Ninth Circuit's reading of § 1367(c). See Itar–Tass Russian News Agency v. Russian Kurier, Inc., 140 F.3d 442, 446–447 (2d Cir.1998). See also Malkani, Upside Down and Inside Out: Appellate Review of Discretion Under the Supplemental Jurisdiction Statute, 28 U.S.C. § 1367, 1997 Ann.Surv.Am. Law 661; Comment, The Discretionary Exercise of Supplemental Jurisdiction Under the Supplemental Jurisdiction Statute, 1995 B.Y.U.L.Rev. 1263.

On a related issue, however, the Seventh and Ninth Circuits are in agreement. If supplemental jurisdiction exists and no party objects to its exercise, the district court need not undertake sua sponte to consider declining to exercise that jurisdiction, and the court of appeals will not undertake sua sponte to decide whether the district court abused the discretion that neither party asked it to exercise. See Acri v. Varian Associates, Inc., 114 F.3d 999 (9th Cir.1997) (en banc); Myers v. County of Lake, 30 F.3d 847 (7th Cir.1994).

Supplemental jurisdiction of related state-law claims is not lost when the jurisdictionally self-sufficient claim upon which supplemental jurisdiction depends is dismissed for nonjurisdictional reasons, although such a dismissal may justify a discretionary declination of supplemental jurisdiction over still-pending state-law claims under § 1367(c)(3). It has been held, however, that when the complaint is formally *amended* to delete the jurisdiction-conferring claim after it has been voluntarily dismissed, the amended complaint alone is determinative of the subject-matter jurisdiction of the district court. Wellness Community–National v. Wellness House, 70 F.3d 46 (7th Cir.1995). But compare another decision of the Seventh Circuit, Grinnell Mut. Reins. Co. v. Shierk, 121 F.3d 1114 (7th Cir.1997), holding that diversity jurisdiction (rather than the supplemental jurisdiction at issue in *Wellness*) attaches conclusively at the time of the filing or removal of an action and is unaffected by later litigative developments. See also Angus v. Shiley Inc., 989 F.2d 142, 145 (3d Cir.1993), noting that giving jurisdictional effect to an amended complaint would allow a plaintiff desirous of undoing a successful removal to destroy federal jurisdiction by filing an amended complaint lowering the prayer for damages to less than the jurisdictional amount.

In all circuits, regardless of the circuit law on whether § 1367(c) merely codified or narrowed the scope of the discretion afforded to district courts under *Gibbs,* the exercise of that discretion is largely sheltered from case-by-case oversight by the deferential standard of appellate review for abuse of discretion. District courts are understandably prone to reduce docket pressure by dismissing supplemental claims when they have discretion to do so, especially when all claims independently within federal jurisdiction have previously been dismissed. But even in this circumstance there may be countervailing concerns of overall judicial efficiency, and if federal claims remain to be litigated, the relegation of related state claims to state court may have the effect of unfairly burdening a party's choice of federal forum for viable federal claims.

Smith v. Amedisys, Inc.

United States Court of Appeals, Fifth Circuit, 2002.
298 F.3d 434.

■ Before: JONES, EMILIO M. GARZA and CARL E. STEWART, CIRCUIT JUDGES.

■ CARL E. STEWART, CIRCUIT JUDGE.

Lori Smith ("Smith") appeals the district court's grant of summary judgment for her former employer and three former supervisors on her claims under Title VII, Louisiana employment discrimination statutes, and Louisiana tort law. For the reasons that follow, we affirm the decision of the district court.

. . . . .

In light of our conclusion that the trial court correctly granted summary judgment in favor of Amedisys on Smith's Title VII claims, we must next address Smith's challenge to the trial court's election to exercise supplemental jurisdiction over Smith's state law claims under 28 U.S.C. § 1367 after dismissing all of Smith's federal claims.

After dismissing Smith's Title VII claims, the trial court appropriately considered whether it could properly exercise supplemental jurisdiction over Smith's remaining state law claims. Concluding that Smith's state law claims did not involve novel or complex issues of law, that extensive discovery had been completed and the case had been pending for almost three years, that the parties had exhaustively briefed the issues in the case, and that the court was intimately familiar with the merits of Smith's claims, the trial court held that retaining the state law claims was appropriate. Smith argues that her state law claims predominate, that virtually all discovery was conducted at the state level, that the case was close to trial in state court, and the state court was equally if not more familiar with the case.

The trial court's decision to retain jurisdiction over pendent state law claims is reviewed for abuse of discretion. McClelland v. Gronwaldt, 155 F.3d 507, 519 (5th Cir.1998). Our review is guided by "both the statutory provisions of 28 U.S.C. § 1367(c) and the balance of the relevant factors of judicial economy, convenience, fairness, and comity." Batiste v. Island Records, Inc., 179 F.3d 217, 227 (1999). "Although we have stated that our 'general rule' is to decline to exercise jurisdiction over pendent state-law claims when all federal claims are dismissed or otherwise eliminated from a case prior to trial, this rule is neither mandatory nor absolute." Id.

We review the trial court's decision beginning with the factors enumerated in 28 U.S.C. § 1367(c).[35] Regarding the first factor, the remaining claims do not involve any "novel or complex" issues of state law. Considering the second and third factors, our analysis above affirms the trial court's dismissal of the only federal claims alleged. Thus, the state law claims now predominate over the nonexistent federal claims. Turning to the fourth factor, we find no "exceptional circumstances" for refusing to retain jurisdiction. Thus, our § 1367(c) analysis results in the conclusion that two factors weigh toward retaining jurisdiction over the remaining claims, and two factors point toward declining jurisdiction.

We next consider the factors of judicial economy, convenience, fairness, and comity. The instant case has been pending for almost three years, the parties have taken numerous depositions, and the matter had progressed to the advanced stages of litigation with little left to do before trial. Further, as the trial court noted, it "devoted many hours to reviewing [the parties'] memoranda, the attached exhibits and the record in this case; researching the legal issues involved; and reaching the decisions" in its comprehensive summary judgment ruling. Thus, the trial court had "substantial familiarity with the merits of the case." Parker & Parsley Petroleum Co. v. Dresser Indus., 972 F.2d 580, 587 (5th Cir.1992); see also *Batiste*, 179 F.3d, at 228 ("The familiarity of the district court with the merits of the Batistes' claims demonstrates that further proceedings in the district court would prevent redundancy and conserve scarce judicial resources ...."). We therefore determine that the principles of judicial economy, convenience, and fairness to the parties weigh heavily toward retaining jurisdiction.

---

35. 28 U.S.C. § 1367(c) provides that

[t]he district courts may decline to exercise supplemental jurisdiction over a claim under subsection (a) if—

(1) the claim raises a novel or complex issue of State law,

(2) the claim substantially predominates over the claim or claims over which the district court has original jurisdiction,

(3) the district court has dismissed all claims over which it has original jurisdiction, or

(4) in exceptional circumstances, there are other compelling reasons for declining jurisdiction.

After balancing all of the factors in this case, we conclude that the trial court did not abuse its discretion in exercising supplemental jurisdiction over Smith's remaining state law claims.

Smith next contends that the trial court erred by granting summary judgment on her claims against the individual Defendants under Louisiana employment discrimination statutes. . . . We disagree.

. . . . .

For the foregoing reasons, we AFFIRM the trial court's grant of summary judgment in favor of Amedisys and the individual Defendants.

AFFIRMED.

Wasserman v. Potamkin Toyota, Inc.

United States District Court, E.D. Pennsylvania, 1998
1998 WL 744090

MEMORANDUM AND ORDER

■ HERBERT J. HUTTON, DISTRICT JUDGE.

Presently before the Court are Defendants' Motion to Dismiss Count III and Count IV of Plaintiff's Complaint pursuant to Rule 12(b)(6) or 28 U.S.C. § 1367(c) . . . .

I. BACKGROUND

The Plaintiff alleges the following facts in her complaint. Plaintiff, Rachel Wasserman ("Wasserman" or Plaintiff), worked for Potamkin Toyota from October 19, 1994 until August 12, 1996. Plaintiff was an executive assistant. Defendants Weisen and Parrilla were Managers and Defendant Hyman was Vice President.

During her employment at Toyota, she alleges that Defendants David Hyman ("Hyman"), Robert Weisen ("Weisen"), and Santi Parrilla ("Parrilla") subjected her to a continuous pattern of sexually hostile and offensive conduct. This included sexually offensive gestures and comments. Plaintiff also alleges that these acts created a hostile and offensive work environment which interfered with the performance of her employment.

Plaintiff repeatedly objected to the conduct of Defendants Weisen and Parrilla. When her objections fell on deaf ears, Plaintiff brought her objections to Defendant Hyman. Defendant Hyman failed to cease the acts of sexual harassment and sex discrimination, and thus, added to the already hostile and offensive work environment. Defendant Hyman also subjected Plaintiff to sexually offensive conduct. On August 12, 1996, realizing that the Defendants would not cease this behavior, Plaintiff involuntarily resigned her position.

Plaintiff subsequently filed a complaint and alleged four causes of actions. The four counts are: (1) Count I—Title VII claim against Potamkin

Toyota; (2) Count II—Pennsylvania Human Relations Act ("PHRA") claim against Potamkin Toyota; (3) Count III—PHRA claim against Weisen, Parrilla, and Hyman; (4) Count IV—intentional infliction of emotional distress claim against all Defendants. Defendants now move to dismiss Counts III and IV.

. . . . .

III. DISCUSSION

[The court dismissed Count IV under Federal Rule of Civil Procedure 12(b)(6) for failure to state a claim upon which relief could be granted, but also granted leave to the plaintiff to file an amended complaint if she could legitimately plead the outrageous conduct necessary to state a claim for intentional infliction of emotional distress under Pennsylvania law.]

B. Declining Supplemental Jurisdiction Under 28 U.S.C. § 1367(c)

Finally, Defendants argue that this Court should decline the exercise of supplemental jurisdiction over Plaintiff's PHRA claims. Defendants contend that these claims present a novel and complex issue of state law because Pennsylvania courts have not concluded whether the PHRA imposes personal liability on individual employees. This Court does not agree.

Section 1367 states that the federal courts "shall have supplemental jurisdiction" over claims which are "part of the same case or controversy" as a claim over which the court exercises original jurisdiction. 28 U.S.C. § 1367(a) (1994). Thus, in order to properly exercise supplemental jurisdiction, there are three requirements. First, the " 'federal claim must have substance sufficient to confer subject matter jurisdiction on the court.' " Lyon v. Whisman, 45 F.3d 758, 760 (3d Cir.1995) (quoting [United Mine Workers v. Gibbs, 383 U.S. 715, 725 (1966)]). Plaintiff's Title VII claim satisfies that standard. Second, the state and federal claims must derive from a common nucleus of operative fact. See id. Plaintiff's Title VII and PHRA claims are derived from the same set of facts concerning the sexual harassment of three supervisors.... Third and finally, Plaintiff must ordinarily expect to try all claims in one judicial proceeding. See *Lyon*, 45 F.3d, at 760. Here, Plaintiff should have expected to try both her Title VII claim and PHRA claim together because: (1) these claims mirror one another and (2) she would save on litigation expenses....

Thus, the Court concludes that it has supplemental jurisdiction over Plaintiff's PHRA claim. Nevertheless, Section 1367(c) provides that a district court may, in its discretion, decline to exercise jurisdiction if any of four conditions are met. These four conditions are:

(1) the claim raises a novel or complex issue of State law,

(2) the claim substantially predominates over the claim or claims over which the district court has original jurisdiction,

(3) the district court has dismissed all claims over which it has original jurisdiction, or

(4) in exceptional circumstances, there are other compelling reasons for declining jurisdiction.

... The Court may properly decline to exercise supplemental jurisdiction and dismiss the state claims if any one of these conditions apply.... In making its determination, the district court should take into account generally accepted principles of "judicial economy, convenience, and fairness to the litigants." United Mine Workers v. Gibbs, 383 U.S. 715, 726 (1966).

In this case, Defendants urge this Court to exercise its discretion and deny supplemental jurisdiction because Plaintiff's PHRA claim[s] present a novel and complex state law issue. Defendants argue that Pennsylvania courts have not concluded whether individual employees may be liable under § 955(e) of the PHRA, and therefore, this Court should dismiss that claim under 28 U.S.C. § 1367(c)(1). In support of this argument, Defendants cite Goodwin v. Seven–Up Bottling Co. of Phila., No. CIV.A.96–2301, 1996 WL 601683 (E.D.Pa. Oct.18, 1996). In *Goodwin*, the court dismissed the plaintiff's PHRA claim against the individual defendants because the Pennsylvania state courts had yet to decide whether § 955 imposes personal liability on individual employees.... Based on comity, federalism, and 28 U.S.C. § 1367(c)(1), the court dismissed that part of the plaintiff's case....

In the case at bar, the Court declines to exercise its discretion to refuse supplemental jurisdiction and retains jurisdiction over Plaintiff's PHRA claim. The situation presented to the court in *Goodwin* is distinguishable from the present case. In *Goodwin*, the court also dismissed the Title VII case against the individual employees.... Thus, the *Goodwin* court declined supplemental jurisdiction pursuant to § 1367(c)(1), which authorizes dismissal when presented with a novel state issue, and § 1367(c)(3), which authorizes dismissal when the federal claim against the defendant is dismissed.... Therefore, the court in *Goodwin* found that it would not prejudice the plaintiffs if the Court dismissed this claim and forced them to file their PHRA claim in state court....

The situation in *Goodwin* is not presented in this case. The Title VII claim is still viable against the [employer based on the conduct of the] individual employees. Thus, if this Court were to dismiss Plaintiff's PHRA claim, she would have to maintain a separate action involving the same exact set of facts in state court. The Plaintiff would have to expend a substantial amount of time, effort, and money to prepare a claim that could just as easily be argued in federal court. See *Gibbs*, 383 U.S., at 726 (noting that the district court should take into account generally accepted principles of "judicial economy, convenience, and fairness to the litigants" in making its determination of whether to exercise or decline supplemental jurisdiction); see also Hargest v. Smithkline Beecham Corp., No. CIV.A.91–6981, 1993 WL 62752, at *2 (E.D.Pa. Mar.9, 1993) ("This Court, in exercising its discretion pursuant to § 1367(c), determines that it would not be in the interest of justice to decline supplemental jurisdiction over plaintiff's PHRA claims based on the same alleged wrongful conduct [as plaintiff's Title VII claims]. As pointed out above ... it would create duplication and waste.").

Moreover, this Court finds that Plaintiff's PHRA claim no longer presents a novel or complex state law issue. In *Goodwin*, the Third Circuit had just issued the then recent *Dici* opinion [Dici v. Commonwealth of Pennsylvania, 91 F.3d 542 (3d Cir.1996)], which found that individual employees may be liable under § 955(e) of the PHRA.... Many courts have since concluded that individual employees may be liable under § 955(e) of the PHRA.... While the Supreme Court of Pennsylvania has yet to rule on this issue, the Court is confident that the Supreme Court would agree with the numerous courts that have concluded that individual employee liability is possible under § 955 of the PHRA. Therefore, this Court rejects Defendants' invitation to decline supplemental jurisdiction on this ground.

. . . . .[36]

COMMENT ON 28 U.S.C. § 1367(d)

Subsection (d)'s tolling provision gives litigants a minimum of 30 days to file a timely action in state court on any claim asserted under § 1367 that is dismissed by the district court. The tolling provision also applies to "any other claim in the same action that is voluntarily dismissed at the same time as or after the dismissal of the claim [that was dependent on the exercise of supplemental jurisdiction]." This seems to address the situation presented in Aldinger v. Howard, discussed in *Finley*, supra p. 278. There the Court observed that the plaintiff had available to her a state forum with jurisdiction to adjudicate in a single action all her claims against a group of defendants, some of whom were not then deemed subject to suit on a claim arising under federal law. As of December 1, 1990, a litigant in the position of Monica Aldinger could sue in federal court, invoking supplemental jurisdiction under § 1367 to permit adjudication of a transactionally related claim under state law against an additional party not otherwise subject to suit in federal court. If the district court thought that the state law claim was novel and complex, or substantially predominated over the federal claims, or for some other exceptional reason dismissed the state law claim without dismissing the federal claims, the tolling provision would allow a plaintiff such as Ms. Aldinger to dismiss voluntarily the still-pending federal claims and refile the entire suit for unitary adjudication in state court free of limitations problems.

This tolling provision would not, however, relieve the plaintiff in the *Kroger* case from potential prejudice under the state statute of limitations applicable to her dismissed claim against the Owen Equipment & Erection Co. Although § 1367(d) tolls the period of limitations applicable under state law to "any claim asserted under subsection (a) ... while the claim is pending and for a period of 30 days after it is dismissed," a close reading of

---

[36. To like effect see Judge Keeton's discussion of his decision to exercise supplemental jurisdiction in Part IV of McLaughlin v. Liberty Mutual Ins. Co., 224 F.R.D. 304, reprinted in Chapter XI as a principal case on Rule 23, infra p. 914.]

the legislative history of the statute establishes that this tolling provision was intended to apply only to claims that validly invoked federal supplemental jurisdiction under subsections (a) and (b), yet were dismissed on *discretionary* grounds under subsection (c). Geraldine Kroger's claim against Owen Equipment was dismissed because it did not qualify for pendent or ancillary jurisdiction, not for discretionary reasons. Were her case to be litigated today, her claim against Owen Equipment would clearly run afoul of present § 1367(b) because it would be a claim by a plaintiff against a party joined under Rule 14. Section 1367(b) specifies that "the district courts shall not have supplemental jurisdiction under subsection (a)" of any such disqualified claim. That claim would therefore not be a "claim asserted under subsection (a)" within the meaning of § 1367(d).

This arguable inequity would be corrected should Congress enact the ALI's proposed new supplemental-jurisdiction statute. That statute's counterpart to present § 1367(d) is proposed new § 1367(f). It expressly extends the tolling provision to "any supplemental claim dismissed because the district court *lacks* or declines to exercise supplemental jurisdiction." ALI Judicial Code Project, Part I, § 1367(f)(1) (emphasis added). In Commentary the ALI makes clear that this language was intended to "protect future Mrs. Krogers." Id., Comment f–2, at 132.

The constitutionality of § 1367(d) had distinguished support from the ALI, which in its 1969 Study had proposed an even broader federal tolling provision. See § 1386(b); Commentary at 374; Supporting Memorandum E at 453–457. But it was not a foregone conclusion. See Note, Pushing the Limits of the Judicial Power: Tolling State Statutes of Limitations Under 28 U.S.C. § 1367(d), 77 Texas L.Rev. 1049 (1999). When it first considered § 1367(d), in a case brought in state court against the state itself that had previously been dismissed from federal court on Eleventh Amendment grounds, the Supreme Court sidestepped the constitutional issue by narrowly construing § 1367(d) to be inapplicable to suits against states. See Raygor v. Regents of Univ. of Minn., 534 U.S. 533 (2002). But the Court returned to the issue the very next term, this time resolving it without rewriting the statute.

Jinks v. Richland County, South Carolina

Supreme Court of the United States, 2003.
538 U.S. 456, 123 S.Ct. 1667, 155 L.Ed.2d 631.

■ JUSTICE SCALIA delivered the opinion of the Court.

The Supreme Court of South Carolina dismissed petitioner's lawsuit against respondent as time-barred. In doing so it held that 28 U.S.C. § 1367(d), which required the state statute of limitation to be tolled for the period during which petitioner's cause of action had previously been pending in federal court, is unconstitutional as applied to lawsuits brought against a State's political subdivisions. The issue before us is the validity of that constitutional determination.

I

A

When a federal district court has original jurisdiction over a civil cause of action, § 1367 determines whether it may exercise supplemental jurisdiction over other claims that do not independently come within its jurisdiction, but that form part of the same Article III "case or controversy." Section 1367(a) provides:

> "Except as provided in subsections (b) and (c) or as expressly provided otherwise by Federal statute, in any civil action of which the district courts have original jurisdiction, the district courts shall have supplemental jurisdiction over all other claims that are so related to claims in the action within such original jurisdiction that they form part of the same case or controversy under Article III of the United States Constitution. Such supplemental jurisdiction shall include claims that involve the joinder or intervention of additional parties."

As the introductory clause suggests, not every claim within the same "case or controversy" as the claim within the federal courts' original jurisdiction will be decided by the federal court; §§ 1367(b) and (c) describe situations in which a federal court may or must decline to exercise supplemental jurisdiction. Section 1367(c), for example, states:

> "The district courts may decline to exercise supplemental jurisdiction over a claim under subsection (a) if—
>
> "(1) the claim raises a novel or complex issue of State law,
>
> "(2) the claim substantially predominates over the claim or claims over which the district court has original jurisdiction,
>
> "(3) the district court has dismissed all claims over which it has original jurisdiction, or
>
> "(4) in exceptional circumstances, there are other compelling reasons for declining jurisdiction."

Thus, some claims asserted under § 1367(a) will be dismissed because the district court declines to exercise jurisdiction over them and, if they are to be pursued, must be refiled in state court. To prevent the limitations period on such supplemental claims from expiring while the plaintiff was fruitlessly pursuing them in federal court, § 1367(d) provides a tolling rule that must be applied by state courts:

> "The period of limitations for any claim asserted under subsection (a), and for any other claim in the same action that is voluntarily dismissed at the same time as or after the dismissal of the claim under subsection (a), shall be tolled while the claim is pending and for a period of 30 days after it is dismissed unless State law provides for a longer tolling period."

B

On October 14, 1994, Carl H. Jinks was arrested and jailed for failure to pay child support. Four days later, while confined at respondent Richland County's detention center, he died of complications associated with alcohol withdrawal. In 1996, within the applicable statute of limitations, petitioner Susan Jinks, Carl Jinks's widow, brought an action in the United States District Court for the District of South Carolina against respondent, its detention center director, and its detention center physician. She asserted a cause of action under Rev. Stat. § 1979, 42 U.S.C. § 1983, and also supplemental claims for wrongful death and survival under the South Carolina Tort Claims Act. See S.C.Code Ann. § 15–78–10 et seq. (West Supp.2002). On November 20, 1997, the District Court granted the defendants' motion for summary judgment on the § 1983 claim, and two weeks later issued an order declining to exercise jurisdiction over the remaining state-law claims, dismissing them without prejudice pursuant to 28 U.S.C. § 1367(c)(3).

On December 18, 1997, petitioner filed her wrongful death and survival claims in state court. After the jury returned a verdict of $80,000 against respondent on the wrongful-death claim, respondent appealed to the South Carolina Supreme Court, which reversed on the ground that petitioner's state-law claims were time-barred. Although they would not have been time-barred under § 1367(d)'s tolling rule, the state supreme court held that § 1367(d) was unconstitutional as applied to claims brought in state court against a State's political subdivisions, because it "interferes with the State's sovereign authority to establish the extent to which its political subdivisions are subject to suit." 349 S.C. 298, 304, 563 S.E.2d 104, 107 (2002).

We granted certiorari, 537 U.S. 972 (2002).

II

A

Respondent and its amici first contend that § 1367(d) is facially invalid because it exceeds the enumerated powers of Congress. We disagree. Although the Constitution does not expressly empower Congress to toll limitations periods for state-law claims brought in state court, it does give Congress the authority "[t]o make all Laws which shall be necessary and proper for carrying into Execution [Congress's Article I, § 8,] Powers and all other Powers vested by this Constitution in the Government of the United States. . . ." Art. I, § 8, cl. 18. The enactment of § 1367(d) was not the first time Congress prescribed the alteration of a state-law limitations period;[37] nor is this the first case in which we have ruled on its authority to

---

37. See, *e.g.,* Soldiers' and Sailors' Civil Relief Act of 1940, 50 U.S.C. App. § 525 ("The period of military service shall not be included in computing any period now or hereafter to be limited by any law, regulation, or order for the bringing of any action or proceeding in any court . . . by or against any person in military service"); 42 U.S.C. § 9658(a)(1) ("In the case of any action brought under State law for personal injury, or property damages, which are caused or contributed to by exposure to any hazardous substance, or pollutant or

do so. In Stewart v. Kahn, 11 Wall. [78 U.S.] 493 (1871), we upheld as constitutional a federal statute that tolled limitations periods for state-law civil and criminal cases for the time during which actions could not be prosecuted because of the Civil War. We reasoned that this law was both necessary and proper to carrying into effect the Federal Government's war powers, because it "remed[ied] the evils" that had arisen from the war. "It would be a strange result if those in rebellion, by protracting the conflict, could thus rid themselves of their debts, and Congress, which had the power to wage war and suppress the insurrection, had no power to remedy such an evil, which is one of its consequences." Id., at 507.

Of course § 1367(d) has nothing to do with the war power. We agree with petitioner and amicus United States, however, that § 1367(d) is necessary and proper for carrying into execution Congress's power "[t]o constitute Tribunals inferior to the supreme Court," U.S. Const., Art. I, § 8, cl. 9, and to assure that those tribunals may fairly and efficiently exercise "[t]he judicial Power of the United States," Art. III, § 1. As to "necessity" : The federal courts can assuredly exist and function in the absence of § 1367(d), but we long ago rejected the view that the Necessary and Proper Clause demands that an Act of Congress be " '*absolutely* necessary' " to the exercise of an enumerated power. See McCulloch v. Maryland, 4 Wheat. [17 U.S.] 316, 414–415 (1819). Rather, it suffices that § 1367(d) is "conducive to the due administration of justice" in federal court,[38] and is "plainly adapted" to that end, id., at 417, 421. Section 1367(d) is conducive to the administration of justice because it provides an alternative to the unsatisfactory options that federal judges faced when they decided whether to retain jurisdiction over supplemental state-law claims that might be time barred in state court. In the pre-§ 1367(d) world, they had three basic choices: First, they could condition dismissal of the state-law claim on the defendant's waiver of any statute-of-limitations defense in state court. See, e.g., Duckworth v. Franzen, 780 F.2d 645, 657 (CA7 1985); Financial General Bankshares, Inc. v. Metzger, 680 F.2d 768, 778 (CADC 1982). That waiver could be refused, however, in which case one of the remaining two choices would have to be pursued. Second, they could retain jurisdiction over the state-law claim even though it would

---

contaminant, released into the environment from a facility, if the applicable limitations period for such action (as specified in the State statute of limitations or under common law) provides a commencement date which is earlier than the federally required commencement date, such period shall commence at the federally required commencement date in lieu of the date specified in such State statute"); 11 U.S.C. § 108(c) ("Except as provided in section 524 of this title, if applicable nonbankruptcy law ... fixes a period for commencing or continuing a civil action in a court other than a bankruptcy court on a claim against the debtor ... and such period has not expired before the date of the filing of the petition, then such period does not expire until the later of—(1) the end of such period, including any suspension of such period occurring on or after the commencement of the case; or (2) 30 days after notice of the termination or expiration of the stay under section 362, 922, 1201, or 1301 of this title, as the case may be, with respect to such claim").

38. This was Chief Justice Marshall's description in *McCulloch* of why—by way of example— legislation punishing perjury in the federal courts is valid under the Necessary and Proper Clause. See 4 Wheat. [17 U.S.], at 417.

more appropriately be heard in state court. See Newman v. Burgin, 930 F.2d 955, 963–964 (CA1 1991) (collecting cases). That would produce an obvious frustration of statutory policy. And third, they could dismiss the state-law claim but allow the plaintiff to reopen the federal case if the state court later held the claim to be time barred. See, e.g., Rheaume v. Texas Dept. of Public Safety, 666 F.2d 925, 932 (CA5 1982). That was obviously inefficient. By providing a straightforward tolling rule in place of this regime, § 1367(d) unquestionably promotes fair and efficient operation of the federal courts and is therefore conducive to the administration of justice.

And it is conducive to the administration of justice for another reason: It eliminates a serious impediment to access to the federal courts on the part of plaintiffs pursuing federal-and state-law claims that "derive from a common nucleus of operative fact," Mine Workers v. Gibbs, 383 U.S. 715, 725 (1966). Prior to enactment of § 1367(d), they had the following unattractive options: (1) They could file a single federal-court action, which would run the risk that the federal court would dismiss the state-law claims after the limitations period had expired; (2) they could file a single state-law action, which would abandon their right to a federal forum; (3) they could file separate, timely actions in federal and state court and ask that the state-court litigation be stayed pending resolution of the federal case, which would increase litigation costs with no guarantee that the state court would oblige. Section 1367(d) replaces this selection of inadequate choices with the assurance that state-law claims asserted under § 1367(a) will not become time barred while pending in federal court.

We are also persuaded, and respondent does not deny, that § 1367(d) is "plainly adapted" to the power of Congress to establish the lower federal courts and provide for the fair and efficient exercise of their Article III powers. There is no suggestion by either of the parties that Congress enacted § 1367(d) as a "pretext" for "the accomplishment of objects not entrusted to the [federal] government," McCulloch, supra, at 423, nor is the connection between § 1367(d) and Congress's authority over the federal courts so attenuated as to undermine the enumeration of powers set forth in Article I, § 8, cf. United States v. Lopez, 514 U.S. 549, 567–568 (1995); United States v. Morrison, 529 U.S. 598, 615 (2000).

Respondent and its amici further contend, however, that § 1367(d) is not a "proper" exercise of Congress's Article I powers because it violates principles of state sovereignty. See Printz v. United States, 521 U.S. 898, 923–924 (1997). Respondent views § 1367(d)'s tolling rule as a regulation of state-court "procedure," and contends that Congress may not, consistent with the Constitution, prescribe procedural rules for state courts' adjudication of purely state-law claims. See, e.g., Bellia, Federal Regulation of State Court Procedures, 110 Yale L.J. 947 (2001); Congressional Authority to Require State Courts to Use Certain Procedures in Products Liability Cases, 13 Op. Off. Legal Counsel 372, 373–374 (1989) (stating that "potential constitutional questions" arise when Congress "attempts to prescribe directly the state court procedures to be followed in products liability cases"). Assuming for the sake of argument that a principled dichotomy can be drawn, for purposes of determining whether an Act of Congress is "proper," between federal laws that regulate state-court "procedure" and laws that change the "substance" of state-law rights of action, we do not think that state-law limitations periods fall into the category of "procedure" immune from congressional regulation. Respondent's reliance on Sun Oil Co. v. Wortman, 486 U.S. 717 (1988), which held state statute of limitations to be "procedural" for purposes of the Full Faith and Credit Clause, is misplaced. As we noted in that very case, the meaning of " 'substance' " and " 'procedure' " in a particular context is "largely determined by the purposes for which the dichotomy is drawn." Id., at 726. For *Erie* purposes, see Erie R. Co. v. Tompkins, 304 U.S. 64 (1938), for example, statutes of limitation are treated as substantive. Guaranty Trust Co. v. York, 326 U.S. 99 (1945). *Stewart v. Kahn*, 11 Wall., at 506–507, provides ample support for the proposition that—if the substance-procedure dichotomy posited by respondent is valid—the tolling of limitation periods falls on the "substantive" side of the line. To sustain § 1367(d) in this case, we need not (and do not) hold that Congress has unlimited power to regulate practice and procedure in state courts.

We therefore reject respondent's contention that § 1367(d) is facially unconstitutional.

B

Respondent next maintains that § 1367(d) should not be interpreted to apply to claims brought against a State's political subdivisions. We find this contention also to be without merit.

The South Carolina Tort Claims Act, S.C.Code Ann. § 15–78–10 et seq. (West Supp.2002), confers upon respondent an immunity from tort liability for any claim brought more than two years after the injury was or should have been discovered. In respondent's view, § 1367(d)'s extension of the time period in which a State's political subdivisions may be sued constitutes an impermissible abrogation of "sovereign immunity." That is not so. Although we have held that Congress lacks authority under Article I to override a *State's* immunity from suit in its own courts, see Alden v. Maine, 527 U.S. 706 (1999), it may subject a *municipality* to suit in state court if that is done pursuant to a valid exercise of its enumerated powers, see id., at 756. Section 1367(d) tolls the limitations period with respect to *state-law* causes of action brought against municipalities, but we see no reason why that represents a greater intrusion on "state sovereignty" than the undisputed power of Congress to override state-law immunity when subjecting a municipality to suit under a federal cause of action. In either case, a State's authority to set the conditions upon which its political subdivisions are subject to suit in its own courts must yield to the enactments of Congress. This is not an encroachment on "state sovereignty," but merely the consequence of those cases (which respondent does not ask us to overrule) which hold that municipalities, unlike States, do not enjoy a constitutionally protected immunity from suit.

Nor do we see any reason to construe § 1367(d) not to apply to claims brought against a State's political subdivisions absent an "unmistakably clear" statement of the statute's applicability to such claims. Although we held in Raygor v. Regents of Univ. of Minn., 534 U.S. 533 (2002), that § 1367(d) does not apply to claims filed in federal court against *States* but subsequently dismissed on sovereign immunity grounds, we did so to avoid interpreting the statute in a manner that would raise "serious constitutional doubt" in light of our decisions protecting a *State's* sovereign immunity from congressional abrogation, id., at 543. As we have just explained, however, no such constitutional doubt arises from holding that petitioner's claim against respondent—which is not a State, but a political subdivision of a State—falls under the definition of "*any claim* asserted under subsection (a)." (Emphasis added.) In any event, the idea that an "unmistakably clear" statement is required before an Act of Congress may expose a *local* government to liability cannot possibly be reconciled with our holding in Monell v. New York City Dept. of Social Servs., 436 U.S. 658 (1978), that municipalities are subject to suit as "persons" under § 1983.

* * *

The judgment of the Supreme Court of South Carolina is reversed, and the case is remanded for proceedings not inconsistent with this opinion.

It is so ordered.

■ Justice Souter, concurring.

In joining the Court today, I do not signal any change of opinion from my dissent in Alden v. Maine, 527 U.S. 706 (1999).

CHAPTER VI

REMOVAL LAW[1]

COMMENT ON REMOVAL STATUTES

It is a common misnomer to refer to the basic removal statutes as conferring "removal jurisdiction." In fact, these statutes confer only a *right of removal*, contingent on the case being one that is within the original jurisdiction conferred on the district courts by some other statute. By contrast, statutes such as 28 U.S.C. §§ 1442–1443 are true grants of *removal jurisdiction* that permit district courts to adjudicate removed cases that would not otherwise be within their original jurisdiction. See ALI Judicial Code Project, Commentary on New § 1441, at 347–348. In addition to statutes conferring rights of removal and true removal jurisdiction, federal removal law consists of statutes prescribing *removal procedure*. See 28 U.S.C. §§ 1446–1447 & 1453, reprinted infra pp. 385–390.

[1. See generally ALI Judicial Code Project, Part III: Removal, at 325–597 (2004); ALI Study §§ 1381–1384; 14B Wright, Miller & Cooper, Federal Practice and Procedure: Jurisdiction 2d §§ 3721–3740 (1998); 16 Moore's Federal Practice ch. 107 (3d ed.1998); Wright & Kane, Federal Courts §§ 38–41 (6th ed.2002); Mullenix, Redish & Vairo, Understanding Federal Courts and Jurisdiction §§ 6.01–6.08 (1998); Miller, An Empirical Study of Forum Choices in Removal Cases Under Diversity and Federal Question Jurisdiction, 41 Am.U.L.Rev. 369 (1992).

In fiscal 2010, 31,341 actions were removed from state court to federal court as against 190,543 actions commenced in federal court. Judicial Business of the United States Courts, Table S–7 (2010).

After a series of conflicting holdings upon the question, it has been decided that a state may not, as a condition of admitting a foreign corporation to do business, exact a waiver of the right to remove to the federal court nor cancel the permit to do business because of the exercise of the right of removal. Terral v. Burke Const. Co., 257 U.S. 529. But a party may waive its statutory right of removal by a contractual provision agreeing to suit in the courts of a state so long as the provision is not unreasonable nor procured under duress. Wm. H. Muller & Co., Inc. v. Swedish American Line Ltd., 224 F.2d 806 (2d Cir.1955); Perini Corp. v. Orion Ins. Co., 331 F.Supp. 453 (E.D.Cal.1971). See generally ALI Judicial Code Project, Part III, at 579–589 (Reporter's Note J: Waiver and Revival of the Right of Removal.)

The application of the 1990 supplemental-jurisdiction statute, 28 U.S.C. § 1367, reprinted supra p. 263, to removed actions is examined in Steinman, Supplemental Jurisdiction in § 1441 Removed Cases: An Unsurveyed Frontier of Congress' Handiwork, 35 Ariz.L.Rev. 306 (1993).

For a fascinating study of the apparent "removal effect" whereby successful removal of a case from a state court to a federal district court significantly reduces the probability that the plaintiff will prevail on the merits, see Clermont & Eisenberg, Do Case Outcomes Really Reveal Anything About the Legal System? Win Rates and Removal Jurisdiction, 83 Cornell L.Rev. 581 (1998).]

STATUTES CONFERRING AND RESTRICTING RIGHTS OF REMOVAL

28 U.S.C. § 1441. Removal of Civil Actions

(a) GENERALLY.—Except as otherwise expressly provided by Act of Congress, any civil action[2] brought in a State court of which the district courts of the United States have original jurisdiction,[3] may be removed by the defendant or the defendants, to the district court of the United States for the district and division embracing the place where such action is pending.

(b) REMOVAL BASED ON DIVERSITY OF CITIZENSHIP.—

(1) In determining whether a civil action is removable on the basis of the jurisdiction under section 1332(a) of this title, the citizenship of defendants sued under fictitious names shall be disregarded.

(2) A civil action otherwise removable solely on the basis of the jurisdiction under section 1332(a) of this title may not be removed if any of the parties in interest properly joined and served as defendants is a citizen of the State in which such action is brought.

(c) JOINDER OF FEDERAL LAW CLAIMS AND STATE LAW CLAIMS.—

(1) If a civil action includes—

(A) a claim arising under the Constitution, laws, or treaties of the United States (within the meaning of section 1331 of this title), and

(B) a claim not within the original or supplemental jurisdiction of the district court or a claim that has been made nonremovable by statute,

the entire action may be removed if the action would be removable without the inclusion of the claim described in subparagraph (B).

[2. There is a difficult question as to the point at which a state condemnation proceeding, begun before an administrative tribunal, becomes a civil action and subject to removal. See Chicago, R.I. & P.R. Co. v. Stude, 346 U.S. 574 (1954); Note, 64 Yale L.J. 600 (1955); 12 Wright, Miller & Marcus, Federal Practice and Procedure: Civil 2d § 3055 (2d ed.1997).]

[3. In most instances it would be futile for an individual as plaintiff to sue a state in federal court—the state will assert its sovereign immunity under the Eleventh Amendment. But the consequence of such a mistake is simply dismissal of the state as a defendant, without prejudice to the continuation of the action against any defendants not shielded by the state's sovereign immunity. The Seventh Circuit thought that a different rule pertained in the removal context when faced with the unusual circumstance of a federal-question suit brought against a state in its own courts and removed by the state itself to a federal district court. Reasoning that if part of the case (the claim by the plaintiff against the state) was beyond the district court's jurisdiction then the case as a whole was not one "of which the district courts have original jurisdiction" and hence did not qualify for removal under § 1441(a), the court of appeals ruled that the district court should have remanded the entire case for lack of subject-matter jurisdiction. The Supreme Court disagreed, holding that the state's sovereign immunity was merely a potential bar to the exercise of the district court's jurisdiction and thus at the time of the state's removal the entire case was within the original jurisdiction of the district court and as such eligible for removal under § 1441(a). See Wisconsin Dept. of Corrections v. Schacht, 524 U.S. 381 (1998).]

(2) Upon removal of an action described in paragraph (1), the district court shall sever from the action all claims described in paragraph (1)(B) and shall remand the severed claims to the State court from which the action was removed. Only defendants against whom a claim described in paragraph (1)(A) has been asserted are required to join in or consent to the removal under paragraph (1).

(d) ACTIONS AGAINST FOREIGN STATES.—Any civil action brought in a State court against a foreign state as defined in section 1603(a) of this title may be removed by the foreign state to the district court of the United States for the district and division embracing the place where such action is pending. Upon removal the action shall be tried by the court without jury. Where removal is based upon this subsection, the time limitations of section 1446(b) of this chapter may be enlarged at any time for cause shown.

(e) MULTIPARTY, MULTIFORUM JURISDICTION.—(1) Notwithstanding the provisions of subsection (b) of this section, a defendant in a civil action in a State court may remove the action to the district court of the United States for the district and division embracing the place where the action is pending if—

(A) the action could have been brought in a United States district court under section 1369[4] of this title; or

(B) the defendant is a party to an action which is or could have been brought, in whole or in part, under section 1369 in a United States district court and arises from the same accident as the action in State court, even if the action to be removed could not have been brought in a district court as an original matter.

The removal of an action under this subsection shall be made in accordance with section 1446 of this title, except that a notice of removal may also be filed before trial of the action in State court within 30 days after the date on which the defendant first becomes a party to an action under section 1369 in a United States district court that arises from the same accident as the action in State court, or at a later time with leave of the district court.

(2) Whenever an action is removed under this subsection and the district court to which it is removed or transferred under section 1407(j) has made a liability determination requiring further proceedings as to damages, the district court shall remand the action to the State court from which it had been removed for the determination of damages, unless the court finds that, for the convenience of parties and witnesses and in the interest of justice, the action should be retained for the determination of damages.

(3) Any remand under paragraph (2) shall not be effective until 60 days after the district court has issued an order determining liability and

---

[4. 28 U.S.C. § 1369 is a minimal-diversity grant of federal jurisdiction in single-accident mass-tort cases that, together with §§ 1441(e)–(f), was enacted by the Multiparty, Multiforum Trial Jurisdiction Act of 2002. It is discussed supra p. 179, n. 13.]

has certified its intention to remand the removed action for the determination of damages. An appeal with respect to the liability determination of the district court may be taken during that 60–day period to the court of appeals with appellate jurisdiction over the district court. In the event a party files such an appeal, the remand shall not be effective until the appeal has been finally disposed of. Once the remand has become effective, the liability determination shall not be subject to further review by appeal or otherwise.

(4) Any decision under this subsection concerning remand for the determination of damages shall not be reviewable by appeal or otherwise.

(5) An action removed under this subsection shall be deemed to be an action under section 1369 and an action in which jurisdiction is based on section 1369 of this title for purposes of this section and sections 1407, 1697, and 1785 of this title.

(6) Nothing in this subsection shall restrict the authority of the district court to transfer or dismiss an action on the ground of inconvenient forum.[5]

(f) DERIVATIVE REMOVAL JURISDICTION.—The court to which a civil action is removed under this section is not precluded from hearing and determining any claim in such civil action because the State court from which such civil action is removed did not have jurisdiction over that claim.[6]

28 U.S.C. § 1445. Nonremovable actions

(a) A civil action in any State court against a railroad or its receivers or trustees, arising under sections 1–4 and 5–10 of the Act of April 22, 1908 (45 U.S.C. 51–54, 55–60), may not be removed to any district court of the United States.

[5. Subsection (e) was added by the Multiparty, Multiforum Trial Jurisdiction Act of 2002, discussed supra p. 179, n. 13.]

[6. Former § 1441(e), added in 1986, abolished the "rule of derivative jurisdiction" —the strange notion that if a case were removed from a state court that lacked subject-matter jurisdiction over it, the federal court also lacked jurisdiction—even if the case was one that could have been brought originally in federal court. Thus, if a suit properly within the exclusive jurisdiction of the federal courts was brought in state court and removed to a federal court, that court could not hear the case. It could not even remand the case. Dismissal was required. General Inv. Co. v. Lake Shore & M.S. Ry. Co., 260 U.S. 261 (1922). See also American Well Works Co. v. Layne & Bowler Co., reprinted supra p. 127.

When it died, the rule of derivative jurisdiction had no known mourners. See generally 14 Wright, Miller & Cooper, Federal Practice and Procedure: Jurisdiction 3d § 3722, at 480– 489 (1998). But it now threatens to crawl out of its grave. Former § 1441(e) was redesignated § 1441(f) by the Multiparty, Multiforum Trial Jurisdiction Act of 2002, discussed above at p. 179, n. 13. In the process it was modified: the words "The court to which such civil action is removed . . ." were replaced with the words "The court to which a civil action is removed *under this section . . . .*" (Emphasis added.) This change, wholly unmentioned in the legislative history of the 2002 Act, is unfortunate. Read literally, it limits the applicability of § 1441(f) to civil actions removed *under 28 U.S.C. § 1441*, the basic removal statute. This may have the unwelcome effect of bringing the rule of derivative jurisdiction back to life in cases within the exclusive jurisdiction of the federal courts that are mistakenly brought in state court and then are removed to federal court under some special removal statute other than § 1441.]

(b) A civil action in any State court against a carrier or its receivers or trustees to recover damages for delay, loss, or injury of shipments, arising under section 11706 or 14706 of title 49, may not be removed to any district court of the United States unless the matter in controversy exceeds $10,000, exclusive of interest and costs.

(c) A civil action in any State court arising under the workmen's compensation laws of such State may not be removed to any district court of the United States.[7]

STATUTES CONFERRING REMOVAL JURISDICTION

28 U.S.C. § 1442. Federal officers or agencies sued or prosecuted

(a) A civil action or criminal prosecution commenced in a State court against any of the following may be removed by them to the district court of the United States for the district and division embracing the place wherein it is pending:

> (1) The United States or any agency thereof or any officer (or any person acting under that officer) of the United States or of any agency thereof, sued in an official or individual capacity for any act under color of such office or on account of any right, title or authority claimed under any Act of Congress for the apprehension or punishment of criminals or the collection of the revenue.[8]

. . . . .

28 U.S.C. § 1443. Civil rights cases

Any of the following civil actions or criminal prosecutions, commenced in a State court may be removed by the defendant to the district court of

------

[7. 28 U.S.C. § 1445 concludes with subsection (d), which provides: "A civil action in any State court arising under section 40302 of the Violence Against Women Act of 1994 may not be removed to any district court of the United States." It has been rendered moot by United States v. Morrison, 529 U.S. 598 (2000), which held that the Violence Against Women Act (VAWA) was unconstitutional.]

[8. In Mesa v. California, 489 U.S. 121 (1989), it was held that removal by a federal officer under § 1442(a)(1) must be predicated on the allegation of a colorable federal defense. To allow removal by a federal officer without the assertion of a federal defense would, the Court said, "unnecessarily present grave constitutional problems." 489 U.S., at 136.

In Winters v. Diamond Shamrock Chemical Co., 149 F.3d 387 (5th Cir.1998), the court held that the defendant corporations, which had manufactured Agent Orange under government contracts that included detailed chemical specifications, were "persons" who, in following the government's specifications, had been "acting under" federal officers and hence were entitled to remove a state-court products-liability suit under § 1442(a)(1) on the basis of their colorable "government contractor" defense.

In Watson v. Philip Morris Cos., Inc., 551 U.S. 142, 127 S.Ct. 2301 (2007), the Court held that cigarette manufacturer Philip Morris did not "act under" a federal officer or agency within the meaning of § 1442 simply by complying with federal regulations concerning the testing of cigarettes.]

the United States for the district and division embracing the place wherein it is pending:

(1) Against any person who is denied or cannot enforce in the courts of such State a right under any law providing for the equal civil rights of citizens of the United States, or of all persons within the jurisdiction thereof;

(2) For any act under color of authority derived from any law providing for equal rights, or for refusing to do any act on the ground that it would be inconsistent with such law.[9]

. . . . .

Beneficial National Bank v. Anderson

Supreme Court of the United States, 2003.
539 U.S. 1, 123 S.Ct. 2058, 156 L.Ed.2d 1.

■ JUSTICE STEVENS delivered the opinion of the Court.

The question in this case is whether an action filed in a state court to recover damages from a national bank for allegedly charging excessive interest in violation of both "the common law usury doctrine" and an Alabama usury statute may be removed to a federal court because it actually arises under federal law. We hold that it may.

I

Respondents are 26 individual taxpayers who made pledges of their anticipated tax refunds to secure short-term loans obtained from petitioner Beneficial National Bank, a national bank chartered under the National Bank Act. Respondents brought suit in an Alabama court against the bank and the two other petitioners that arranged the loans, seeking compensatory and punitive damages on the theory, among others, that the bank's interest rates were usurious. Their complaint did not refer to any federal law.

[9. As demonstrated in Mathews v. County of Fremont, Wyoming, reprinted infra p. 400, § 1443 is of very little utility because of the strict construction put on it by the Supreme Court. See Georgia v. Rachel, 384 U.S. 780 (1966); City of Greenwood v. Peacock, 384 U.S. 808 (1966); Johnson v. Mississippi, 421 U.S. 213 (1975).

Another specialized removal statute, 28 U.S.C. § 1452, is much more frequently invoked. It permits removal of claims related to bankruptcy cases, but subsection (b) of § 1452 confers on the district court (generally operating through its adjunct, the bankruptcy court) a near-plenary discretion to remand even properly removed claims "on any equitable ground." For a thorough survey by a federal bankruptcy judge, see Bennett, Removal, Remand, and Abstention Related to Bankruptcies: Yet Another Litigation Quagmire!, 27 Cumb.L.Rev. 1037 (1997).

There are many specialized removal provisions enacted outside of Title 28 of the U.S. Code. In general they expand rather than restrict the right of removal provided by the general removal statute, 28 U.S.C. § 1441. See, e.g., the Securities Litigation Uniform Standards Act of 1998, discussed infra p. 940, n. 49.]

Petitioners removed the case to the United States District Court for the Middle District of Alabama. In their notice of removal they asserted that the National Bank Act, Rev. Stat. § 5917, as amended, 12 U.S.C. § 85,[10] is the exclusive provision governing the rate of interest that a national bank may lawfully charge, that the rates charged to respondents complied with that provision, that § 86 provides the exclusive remedies available against a national bank charging excessive interest,[11] and that the removal statute, 28 U.S.C. § 1441, therefore applied. The District Court denied respondents' motion to remand the case to state court but certified the question whether it had jurisdiction to proceed with the case to the Court of Appeals pursuant to 28 U.S.C. § 1292(b).

A divided panel of the Eleventh Circuit reversed. Anderson v. H & R Block, Inc., 287 F.3d 1038 (2002). The majority held that under our "well-pleaded complaint" rule, removal is generally not permitted unless the complaint expressly alleges a federal claim and that the narrow exception from that rule known as the "complete preemption doctrine" did not apply because it could "find no clear congressional intent to permit removal under §§ 85 and 86." Id., at 1048. Because this holding conflicted with an

---

10. Title 12 U.S.C. § 85 provides:

"Rate of interest on loans, discounts and purchases

"Any association may take, receive, reserve, and charge on any loan or discount made, or upon any notes, bills of exchange, or other evidences of debt, interest at the rate allowed by the laws of the State, Territory, or District where the bank is located, or at a rate of 1 per centum in excess of the discount rate on ninety-day commercial paper in effect at the Federal reserve bank in the Federal reserve district where the bank is located, whichever may be the greater, and no more, except that where by the laws of any State a different rate is limited for banks organized under state laws, the rate so limited shall be allowed for associations organized or existing in any such State under title 62 of the Revised Statutes. When no rate is fixed by the laws of the State, or Territory, or District, the bank may take, receive, reserve, or charge a rate not exceeding 7 per centum, or 1 per centum in excess of the discount rate on ninety day commercial paper in effect at the Federal reserve bank in the Federal reserve district where the bank is located, whichever may be the greater, and such interest may be taken in advance, reckoning the days for which the note, bill, or other evidence of debt has to run. The maximum amount of interest or discount to be charged at a branch of an association located outside of the States of the United States and the District of Columbia shall be at the rate allowed by the laws of the country, territory, dependency, province, dominion, insular possession, or other political subdivision where the branch is located. And the purchase, discount, or sale of a bona fide bill of exchange, payable at another place than the place of such purchase, discount, or sale, at not more than the current rate of exchange for sight drafts in addition to the interest, shall not be considered as taking or receiving a greater rate of interest."

11. Section 86 provides:

"Usurious interest; penalty for taking; limitations

"The taking, receiving, reserving, or charging a rate of interest greater than is allowed by section 85 of this title, when knowingly done, shall be deemed a forfeiture of the entire interest which the note, bill, or other evidence of debt carries with it, or which has been agreed to be paid thereon. In case the greater rate of interest has been paid, the person by whom it has been paid, or his legal representatives, may recover back, in an action in the nature of an action of debt, twice the amount of the interest thus paid from the association taking or receiving the same: *Provided,* That such action is commenced within two years from the time the usurious transaction occurred."

Eighth Circuit decision, Krispin v. May Dept. Stores Co., 218 F.3d 919 (2000), we granted certiorari. 537 U.S. 1169 (2003).

II

A civil action filed in a state court may be removed to federal court if the claim is one "arising under" federal law. § 1441(b). To determine whether the claim arises under federal law, we examine the "well pleaded" allegations of the complaint and ignore potential defenses: "a suit arises under the Constitution and laws of the United States only when the plaintiff's statement of his own cause of action shows that it is based upon those laws or that Constitution. It is not enough that the plaintiff alleges some anticipated defense to his cause of action and asserts that the defense is invalidated by some provision of the Constitution of the United States." Louisville & Nashville R. Co. v. Mottley, 211 U.S. 149, 152 (1908); see Taylor v. Anderson, 234 U.S. 74 (1914). Thus, a defense that relies on the preclusive effect of a prior federal judgment, Rivet v. Regions Bank of La., 522 U.S. 470 (1998), or the pre-emptive effect of a federal statute, Franchise Tax Bd. of Cal. v. Construction Laborers Vacation Trust for Southern Cal., 463 U.S. 1 (1983), will not provide a basis for removal. As a general rule, absent diversity jurisdiction, a case will not be removable if the complaint does not affirmatively allege a federal claim.

Congress has, however, created certain exceptions to that rule. For example, the Price–Anderson Act contains an unusual pre-emption provision, 42 U.S.C. § 2014(hh), that not only gives federal courts jurisdiction over tort actions arising out of nuclear accidents but also expressly provides for removal of such actions brought in state court even when they assert only state-law claims. See El Paso Natural Gas Co. v. Neztsosie, 526 U.S. 473, 484–485 (1999).

We have also construed § 301 of the Labor Management Relations Act, 1947 (LMRA), 29 U.S.C. § 185, as not only preempting state law but also authorizing removal of actions that sought relief only under state law. Avco Corp. v. Machinists, 390 U.S. 557 (1968). We later explained that holding as resting on the unusually "powerful" pre-emptive force of § 301:

> "The Court of Appeals held, 376 F.2d, at 340, and we affirmed, 390 U.S., at 560, that the petitioner's action 'arose under' § 301, and thus could be removed to federal court, although the petitioner had undoubtedly pleaded an adequate claim for relief under the state law of contracts and had sought a remedy available *only* under state law. The necessary ground of decision was that the pre-emptive force of § 301 is so powerful as to displace entirely any state cause of action 'for violation of contracts between an employer and a labor organization.' Any such suit is purely a creature of federal law, notwithstanding the fact that state law would provide a cause of action in the absence of § 301. *Avco* stands for the proposition that if a federal cause of action completely pre-empts a state cause of action any complaint that comes within the scope of the federal cause of action necessarily 'arises under' federal law." *Franchise Tax Bd.*, 463 U.S., at 23–24 (footnote omitted).

Similarly, in Metropolitan Life Ins. Co. v. Taylor, 481 U.S. 58 (1987), we considered whether the "complete pre-emption" approach adopted in *Avco* also supported the removal of state common-law causes of action asserting improper processing of benefit claims under a plan regulated by the Employee Retirement Income Security Act of 1974 (ERISA), 29 U.S.C. § 1001 *et seq.* For two reasons, we held that removal was proper even though the complaint purported to raise only state-law claims. First, the statutory text in § 502(a), 29 U.S.C. § 1132, not only provided an express federal remedy for the plaintiffs' claims, but also in its jurisdiction subsection, § 502(f), used language similar to the statutory language construed in *Avco,* thereby indicating that the two statutes should be construed in the same way. 481 U.S., at 65. Second, the legislative history of ERISA unambiguously described an intent to treat such actions "as arising under the laws of the United States in similar fashion to those brought under section 301 of the Labor–Management Relations Act of 1947." Id., at 65–66 (internal quotation marks and emphasis omitted).

Thus, a state claim may be removed to federal court in only two circumstances—when Congress expressly so provides, such as in the Price–Anderson Act, supra, at 2062, or when a federal statute wholly displaces the state-law cause of action through complete pre-emption.[12] When the federal statute completely pre-empts the state-law cause of action, a claim which comes within the scope of that cause of action, even if pleaded in terms of state law, is in reality based on federal law. This claim is then removable under 28 U.S.C. § 1441(b), which authorizes any claim that "arises under" federal law to be removed to federal court. In the two categories of cases[13] where this Court has found complete pre-emption—certain causes of action under the LMRA and ERISA—the federal statutes at issue provided the exclusive cause of action for the claim asserted and also set forth procedures and remedies governing that cause of action. See 29 U.S.C. § 1132 (setting forth procedures and remedies for civil claims under ERISA); § 185 (describing procedures and remedies for suits under the LMRA).

III

Count IV of respondents' complaint sought relief for "usury violations" and claimed that petitioners "charged . . . excessive interest in violation of the common law usury doctrine" and violated "Alabama Code. § 8–8–1, et seq. by charging excessive interest." Respondents' complaint thus expressly charged petitioners with usury. *Metropolitan Life, Avco,* and *Franchise Tax*

---

12. Of course, a state claim can also be removed through the use of the supplemental jurisdiction statute, 28 U.S.C. § 1367(a), provided that another claim in the complaint is removable.

13. This Court has also held that federal courts have subject-matter jurisdiction to hear possessory land claims under state law brought by Indian tribes because of the uniquely federal "nature and source of the possessory rights of Indian tribes." Oneida Indian Nation of N.Y. v. County of Oneida, 414 U.S. 661, 667 (1974). Because that case turned on the special historical relationship between Indian tribes and the Federal Government, it does not assist the present analysis.

Board provide the framework for answering the dispositive question in this case: Does the National Bank Act provide the exclusive cause of action for usury claims against national banks? If so, then the cause of action necessarily arises under federal law and the case is removable. If not, then the complaint does not arise under federal law and is not removable.

Sections 85 and 86 serve distinct purposes. The former sets forth the substantive limits on the rates of interest that national banks may charge. The latter sets forth the elements of a usury claim against a national bank, provides for a 2–year statute of limitations for such a claim, and prescribes the remedies available to borrowers who are charged higher rates and the procedures governing such a claim. If, as petitioners asserted in their notice of removal, the interest that the bank charged to respondents did not violate § 85 limits, the statute unquestionably pre-empts any common-law or Alabama statutory rule that would treat those rates as usurious. The section would therefore provide the petitioners with a complete federal defense. Such a federal defense, however, would not justify removal. Caterpillar Inc. v. Williams, 482 U.S. 386, 393 (1987). Only if Congress intended § 86 to provide the exclusive cause of action for usury claims against national banks would the statute be comparable to the provisions that we construed in the *Avco* and *Metropolitan Life* cases.[14]

In a series of cases decided shortly after the Act was passed, we endorsed that approach. In Farmers' and Mechanics' Nat. Bank v. Dearing, 91 U.S. 29, 32–33 (1875), we rejected the borrower's attempt to have an entire debt forfeited, as authorized by New York law, stating that the various provisions of §§ 85 and 86 "form a system of regulations ... [a]ll the parts [of which] are in harmony with each other and cover the entire subject," so that "the State law would have no bearing whatever upon the case." We also observed that "[i]n any view that can be taken of [§ 86], the power to supplement it by State legislation is conferred neither expressly nor by implication." Id., at 35. In Evans v. National Bank of Savannah, 251 U.S. 108, 114 (1919), we stated that "federal law ... completely defines what constitutes the taking of usury by a national bank, referring to the state law only to determine the maximum permitted rate." See also Barnet v. National Bank, 98 U.S. 555, 558 (1879) (the "statutes of Ohio and Indiana upon the subject of usury ... cannot affect the case" because the Act "creates a new right" that is "exclusive"); Haseltine v. Central Bank of Springfield, 183 U.S. 132, 134 (1901) ("[T]he definition of usury and the penalties affixed thereto must be determined by the National Banking Act and not by the law of the State").

In addition to this Court's longstanding and consistent construction of the National Bank Act as providing an exclusive federal cause of action for usury against national banks, this Court has also recognized the special

---

14. Because the proper inquiry focuses on whether Congress intended the federal cause of action to be exclusive rather than on whether Congress intended that the cause of action be removable, the fact that these sections of the National Bank Act were passed in 1864, 11 years prior to the passage of the statute authorizing removal, is irrelevant, contrary to respondents' assertions.

nature of federally chartered banks. Uniform rules limiting the liability of national banks and prescribing exclusive remedies for their overcharges are an integral part of a banking system that needed protection from "possible unfriendly State legislation." Tiffany v. National Bank of Mo., 18 Wall. [85 U.S.] 409, 412 (1874). The same federal interest that protected national banks from the state taxation that Chief Justice Marshall characterized as the "power to destroy," McCulloch v. Maryland, 4 Wheat. [17 U.S.] 316, 431 (1819), supports the established interpretation of §§ 85 and 86 that gives those provisions the requisite pre-emptive force to provide removal jurisdiction. In actions against national banks for usury, these provisions supersede both the substantive and the remedial provisions of state usury laws and create a federal remedy for overcharges that is exclusive, even when a state complainant, as here, relies entirely on state law. Because §§ 85 and 86 provide the exclusive cause of action for such claims, there is, in short, no such thing as a state-law claim of usury against a national bank. Even though the complaint makes no mention of federal law, it unquestionably and unambiguously claims that petitioners violated usury laws. This cause of action against national banks only arises under federal law and could, therefore, be removed under § 1441.

The judgment of the Court of Appeals is reversed.

It is so ordered.

■ JUSTICE SCALIA, with whom JUSTICE THOMAS joins, dissenting.

Today's opinion takes the view that because § 30 of the National Bank Act, 12 U.S.C. §§ 85, 86, provides the exclusive cause of action for claims of usury against a national bank, all such claims—even if explicitly pleaded under state law—are to be construed as "aris[ing] under" federal law for purposes of our jurisdictional statutes. This view finds scant support in our precedents and no support whatever in the National Bank Act or any other Act of Congress. I respectfully dissent.

Unless Congress expressly provides otherwise, the federal courts may exercise removal jurisdiction over state-court actions "of which the district courts of the United States have original jurisdiction." 28 U.S.C. § 1441(a). In this case, petitioners invoked as the predicate for removal the district courts' original jurisdiction over "all civil actions arising under the Constitution, laws, or treaties of the United States." § 1331.

This so-called "arising under" or "federal question" jurisdiction has long been governed by the well-pleaded-complaint rule, which provides that "federal jurisdiction exists only when a federal question is presented on the face of the plaintiff's properly pleaded complaint." Caterpillar Inc. v. Williams, 482 U.S. 386, 392 (1987). A federal question "is presented" when the complaint invokes federal law as the basis for relief. It does not suffice that the facts alleged in support of an asserted state-law claim would *also* support a federal claim. "The [well-pleaded-complaint] rule makes the plaintiff the master of the claim; he or she may avoid federal jurisdiction by exclusive reliance on state law." Ibid. See also The Fair v. Kohler Die & Specialty Co., 228 U.S. 22, 25 (1913) ("Of course the party who brings a suit is master to decide what law he will rely upon"). Nor does it even suffice that the facts alleged in support of an asserted state-law claim *do not support* a state-law claim and would *only* support a federal claim. "Jurisdiction may not be sustained on a theory that the plaintiff has not advanced." Merrell Dow Pharmaceuticals Inc. v. Thompson, 478 U.S. 804, 809, n. 6 (1986).

Under the well-pleaded-complaint rule, "a federal court does not have original jurisdiction over a case in which the complaint presents a state-law cause of action, but also asserts that federal law deprives the defendant of a defense he may raise, . . . or that a federal defense the defendant may raise is not sufficient to defeat the claim." Franchise Tax Bd. of Cal. v. Construction Laborers Vacation Trust for Southern Cal., 463 U.S. 1, 10 (1983). Of critical importance here, the rejection of a federal defense as the basis for original federal-question jurisdiction applies with equal force when the defense is one of federal pre-emption. "By unimpeachable authority, a suit brought upon a state statute does not arise under an act of Congress or the Constitution of the United States because prohibited thereby." Gully v. First Nat. Bank in Meridian, 299 U.S. 109, 116 (1936). "[A] case may *not* be removed to federal court on the basis of . . . the defense of pre-emption . . . ." *Caterpillar*, supra, at 393. To be sure, pre-emption requires a state court to *dismiss* a particular claim that is filed under state law, but it does not, as a general matter, provide grounds for *removal*.

This Court has twice recognized exceptions to the well-pleaded-complaint rule, upholding removal jurisdiction notwithstanding the absence of a federal question on the face of the plaintiff's complaint. First, in Avco Corp. v. Machinists, 390 U.S. 557 (1968), we allowed removal of a state-court action to enforce a no-strike clause in a collective-bargaining agreement. The complaint concededly did not advance a federal claim, but was subject to a defense of pre-emption under § 301 of the Labor Management Relations Act, 1947 (LMRA), 29 U.S.C. § 185. The well-pleaded-complaint rule notwithstanding, we treated the plaintiff's state-law contract claim as one arising under § 301, and held that the case could be removed to federal court. *Avco*, supra, at 560.

The only support mustered by the *Avco* Court for its conclusion was a statement wrenched out of context from our decision in Textile Workers v. Lincoln Mills of Ala., 353 U.S. 448, 457 (1957), that "[a]ny state law applied [in a § 301 case] will be absorbed as federal law and will not be an independent source of private rights." To begin with, this statement is entirely unnecessary to the landmark holding in *Lincoln Mills*—that § 301 not only gives federal courts jurisdiction to decide labor relations cases but also supplies them with authority to create the governing substantive law. Id., at 456. More importantly, understood in the context of that holding, the quoted passage in no way supports the proposition for which it is relied upon in *Avco*—that state-law claims relating to labor relations necessarily *arise under* § 301. If one reads *Lincoln Mills* with any care, it is clear beyond doubt that the relevant passage merely confirms that when, in deciding cases arising under § 301, courts employ legal rules that overlap with, or are even explicitly borrowed from, state law, such rules are nevertheless rules of federal law. It is in this sense that "[a]ny state law applied [in a § 301 case] will be absorbed as federal law" —in the sense that federally adopted state rules become federal rules, not in the sense that a state-law claim becomes a federal claim.

Other than its entirely misguided reliance on *Lincoln Mills,* the opinion in *Avco* failed to clarify the analytic basis for its unprecedented act of jurisdictional alchemy. The Court neglected to explain *why* state-law claims that are pre-empted by § 301 of the LMRA are exempt from the strictures of the well-pleaded-complaint rule, nor did it explain *how* such a state-law claim can plausibly be said to "arise under" federal law. Our subsequent opinion in *Franchise Tax Board,* struggled to prop up *Avco*'s puzzling holding:

> "The necessary ground of decision [in *Avco*] was that the pre-emptive force of § 301 is so powerful as to displace entirely any state cause of action 'for violation of contracts between an employer and a labor organization.' Any such suit is purely a creature of federal law, notwithstanding the fact that state law would provide a cause of action in the absence of § 301. *Avco* stands for the proposition that if a federal cause of action completely pre-empts a state cause of action any complaint that comes within the scope of the federal cause of action necessarily 'arises under' federal law." 463 U.S., at 23–24 (footnote omitted).

This passage has repeatedly been relied upon by the Court as an explanation for its decision in *Avco*. See, e.g., ante, *Caterpillar,* supra, at 394; Metropolitan Life Ins. Co. v. Taylor, 481 U.S. 58, 64 (1987). Of course it is not an explanation at all. It provides nothing more than an account of what *Avco* accomplishes, rather than a justification (unless *ipse dixit* is to count as justification) for the radical departure from the well-pleaded-complaint rule, which demands rejection of the defense of federal pre-emption as a basis for federal jurisdiction. *Gully,* supra, at 116. Neither the excerpt quoted above, nor any other fragment of the decision in *Franchise Tax,* explains how or why the nonviability (due to pre-emption) of the state-law contract claim in *Avco* magically transformed that claim into one "arising under" federal law.

Metropolitan Life Ins. Co. v. Taylor, supra, was our second departure from the prohibition against resting federal "arising under" jurisdiction upon the existence of a federal defense. In that case, Taylor sued his former employer and its insurer, alleging breach of contract and seeking, *inter alia*, reinstatement of certain disability benefits and insurance coverages. Id., at 61. Though Taylor invoked no federal law in his complaint, we treated his case as one arising under § 502 of the Employee Retirement Income Security Act of 1974 (ERISA) and upheld the District Court's exercise of removal jurisdiction. Id., at 66–67.

In reaching this conclusion, the *Taylor* Court broke no new analytic ground; its opinion follows the exception established in *Avco* and described in *Franchise Tax Board,* but says nothing to commend that exception to logic or reason. Instead, *Taylor* simply relies on the "clos[e] parallels," 481 U.S., at 65, between the language of the pre-emptive provision in ERISA and the language of the LMRA provision deemed in *Avco* to be so dramatically pre-emptive as to summon forth a federal claim where none had been asserted. "No more specific reference to the *Avco* rule can be expected," we said, than what was found in § 502(a); and we accordingly concluded that "Congress has clearly manifested an intent to make causes of action within the scope of the civil enforcement provisions of § 502(a) removable to federal court." 481 U.S., at 66. As in *Avco* and *Franchise Tax Board,* no explanation was provided for *Avco's* abrogation of the rule that "[f]ederal pre-emption is ordinarily a federal defense to the plaintiff's suit[, and as such] it does not appear on the face of a well-pleaded complaint, [nor does it] authorize removal to federal court." [15] 481 U.S., at 63.

It is noteworthy that the straightforward (though similarly unsupported) rule announced in today's opinion—under which (1) removal is permitted "[w]hen [a] federal statute completely pre-empts a state-law cause of action," ante, and (2) a federal statute is completely pre-emptive when it "provide[s] the exclusive cause of action for the claim asserted," ibid.—is nowhere to be found in either *Avco* or *Taylor.* To the contrary, the analysis in today's opinion implicitly contradicts (by rendering inexplicable) *Taylor's* discussion of pre-emption and removal. (*Avco,* as I observed earlier, has no discussion to be contradicted.) Had it thought that today's decision was the law, the *Taylor* Court need not have taken pains to emphasize the "clos[e] parallels" between § 502(a)(1)(B) of ERISA and § 301 of the LMRA and need not have pored over the legislative history of § 502(a) to show that Congress expected ERISA to be treated like the LMRA. See *Taylor,* supra, at 65–66 (citing H.R. Conf. Rep. No. 93–1280, p. 327, (1974), U.S.Code Cong. & Admin.News 1974, pp. 4639, 5107; 120 Cong. Rec. 29933 (1974) (remarks of Sen. Williams); *id.,* at 29942 (remarks of Sen. Javits)). Instead, it could have rested after noting the "unique pre-emptive force of ERISA," *Taylor,* supra, at 65. Indeed, it could even have spared itself the trouble of adding the adjective "unique." While there is something unique about statutes whose pre-emptive force is closely patterned after that of the LMRA (which we had held to support removal), there is nothing whatever unique about a federal cause of action that displaces state causes of action. Displacement alone, if today's opinion is to be believed, would have sufficed to establish the existence of removal jurisdiction.

The best that can be said, from a precedential perspective, for the rule of law announced by the Court today is that variations on it have twice appeared in our cases in the purest dicta. Rivet v. Regions Bank of La., 522 U.S. 470, 476 (1998) ("[O]nce an area of state law has been completely pre-

---

15. This is not to say that *Taylor* was wrongly decided. Having been informed through the Avco Corp. v. Machinists, 390 U.S. 557 (1968), decision that the language of § 301 triggered "arising under" jurisdiction even with respect to certain state-law claims, Congress' subsequent decision to insert language into ERISA that "closely parallels" the text of § 301 can be viewed to be, as we said, a "specific reference to the *Avco* rule." 481 U.S., at 65–66. *Taylor,* in other words, rests upon a sort of statutory incorporation of *Avco. Avco* itself, on the other hand, continues to rest upon nothing.

empted, any claim purportedly based on that pre-empted state-law claim is considered, from its inception, a federal claim, and therefore arises under federal law" (internal quotation marks omitted)); *Caterpillar,* 482 U.S., at 393 ("[I]f a federal cause of action completely pre-empts a state cause of action any complaint that comes within the scope of the federal cause of action necessarily 'arises under' federal law" (some internal quotation marks omitted)). Dicta of course have no precedential value, see U.S. Bancorp Mortgage Co. v. Bonner Mall Partnership, 513 U.S. 18, 24 (1994), even when they do not contradict, as they do here, prior holdings of the Court.

The difficulty with today's holding, moreover, is not limited to the flimsiness of its precedential roots. As has been noted already, the holding cannot be squared with bedrock principles of removal jurisdiction. One or another of two of those principles must be ignored: Either (1) the principle that merely setting forth in state court facts that would support a federal cause of action—indeed, even facts that would support a federal cause of action and would *not* support the claimed state cause of action—does not produce a federal question supporting removal, *Caterpillar,* 482 U.S., at 391, or (2) the principle that a federal defense to a state cause of action does not support federal-question jurisdiction, see *id.,* at 393. Relatedly, today's holding also represents a sharp break from our long tradition of respect for the autonomy and authority of state courts. For example, in Healy v. Ratta, 292 U.S. 263, 270 (1934), we explained that "[d]ue regard for the rightful independence of state governments, which should actuate federal courts, requires that they scrupulously confine their own jurisdiction to the precise limits which the statute has defined." And in Shamrock Oil & Gas Corp. v. Sheets, 313 U.S. 100, 108 (1941), we insisted on a "strict construction" of the federal removal statutes.[16] Today's decision ignores these venerable principles and effectuates a significant shift in decisional authority from state to federal courts.

In an effort to justify this shift, the Court explains that "[b]ecause §§ 85 and 86 [of the National Bank Act] provide the exclusive cause of action for such claims, there is ... no such thing as a state-law claim of usury against a national bank." But the mere fact that a state-law claim is invalid no more deprives it of its character as a state-law claim which does not raise a federal question, than does the fact that a federal claim is invalid deprive it of its character as a federal claim which does raise a federal question. The proper response to the presentation of a nonexistent claim to a state court is *dismissal,* not the "federalize-and-remove" dance authorized by today's opinion. For even if the Court is correct that the National Bank Act obliterates entirely any state-created right to relief for usury against a national bank, that does not explain how or why the claim

---

16. Our traditional regard for the role played by state courts in interpreting and enforcing federal law has other doctrinal manifestations. We indulge, for example, a "presumption of concurrent [state and federal] jurisdiction," which can be rebutted only "by an explicit statutory directive, by unmistakable implication from legislative history, or by a clear incompatibility between state-court jurisdiction and federal interests." Gulf Offshore Co. v. Mobil Oil Corp., 453 U.S. 473, 478 (1981).

of such a right is transmogrified into the claim of a federal right. Congress's mere act of creating a federal right and eliminating all state-created rights *in no way* suggests an expansion of federal jurisdiction so as to wrest from state courts the authority to decide questions of pre-emption under the National Bank Act.

Petitioners seek to justify their end-run around the well-pleaded-complaint rule by insisting that, in determining whether federal jurisdiction exists, we are required to " 'look beyond the pleadings.' " Brief for Petitioners 18 (quoting Indianapolis v. Chase Nat. Bank, 314 U.S. 63, 69 (1941)). They point out:

> "[A] long line of cases disallow[s] manipulations by plaintiffs designed to create or avoid diversity jurisdiction, such as misaligning the interests of the parties, naming parties (whether plaintiffs or defendants) who have no real interest in or relationship to the controversy, misstating the citizenship of a party (whether plaintiffs or defendants), or misstating the amount in controversy."

Petitioners insist that, like the "manipulative" complaints in these diversity cases, "[r]espondents' complaint is disingenuously pleaded, not 'well pleaded' in any respect, for it purports to raise a state law claim that does not exist." Accordingly, the argument continues, just as federal courts may assert jurisdiction where a plaintiff seeks to hide the true citizenship of the parties, so too they may assert jurisdiction where a plaintiff cloaks a necessarily federal claim in state-law garb.

To begin with, the cases involving diversity jurisdiction are probably distinguishable on the ground that there is a crucial difference between, on the one hand, "looking beyond the pleadings" to determine whether a factual assertion is true, and, on the other hand, doing so in order to determine whether the plaintiff has proceeded on the basis of the "correct" legal theory. But even assuming that the analogy to the diversity cases is apt, petitioners can derive no support from it in this case. Their argument proceeds from the faulty premise that if one looks behind the pleadings in this case, one discovers that the plaintiffs have, in fact, presented a federal claim. But that begs the question—that is, it assumes the answer to the very question presented. It assumes that whenever a claim of usury is brought against a national bank, that claim is a federal one. As I have discussed above, neither logic nor precedent supports that conclusion; they support, at best, the proposition that the only *viable* claim against a national bank for usury is a federal one. Federal jurisdiction is ordinarily determined—invariably determined, except for *Avco* and *Taylor*—on the basis of what claim is pleaded, rather than on the basis of what claim can prevail.

There may well be good reasons to favor the expansion of removal jurisdiction that petitioners urge and that the Court adopts today. As the United States explains in its *amicus* brief:

> "Absent removal, the state court would have only two legitimate options—to recharacterize the claim in federal-law terms or to dismiss

the claim altogether. Any plaintiff who truly seeks recovery on that claim would prefer the first option, which would make the propriety of removal crystal clear. A third possibility, however, is that the state court would err and allow the claim to proceed under state law notwithstanding Congress's decision to make the federal cause of action exclusive. The complete pre-emption rule avoids that potential error." Brief for United States as Amicus Curiae 17–18.

True enough, but inadequate to render today's decision either rational or properly within the authority of this Court. Inadequate for rationality, because there is no more reason to fear state-court error with respect to federal pre-emption accompanied by creation of a federal cause of action than there is with respect to federal pre-emption unaccompanied by creation of a federal cause of action—or, for that matter, than there is with respect to *any* federal defense to a state-law claim. The rational response to the United States' concern is to eliminate the well-pleaded-complaint rule entirely. And inadequate for judicial authority, because it is up to Congress, not the federal courts, to decide when the risk of state-court error with respect to a matter of federal law becomes so unbearable as to justify divesting the state courts of authority to decide the federal matter. Unless and until we receive instruction from Congress that claims pre-empted under the National Bank Act—in contrast to almost all other claims that are subject to federal pre-emption—"arise under" federal law, we simply lack authority to "avoi[d] ... potential errors," id., at 18, by permitting removal.

* * *

Today's opinion has succeeded in giving to our *Avco* decision a theoretical foundation that neither *Avco* itself nor *Taylor* provided. Regrettably, that theoretical foundation is itself without theoretical foundation. That is to say, the more general proposition that (1) the existence of a pre-emptive federal cause of action causes the invalid assertion of a state cause of action to raise a federal question, has no more logic or precedent to support it than the very narrow proposition that (2) the LMRA *(Avco)* and statutes modeled after the LMRA *(Taylor)* cause invalid assertions of state causes of action pre-empted by those particular statutes to raise federal questions. Since I believe that, as between an inexplicable narrow holding and an inexplicable broad one, the former is the lesser evil, I would adhere to the approach taken by *Taylor* and on the basis of stare decisis simply affirm, without any real explanation, that the LMRA and statutes modeled after it have a "unique pre-emptive force" that (quite illogically) suspends the normal rules of removal jurisdiction. Since no one asserts that the National Bank Act is modeled after the LMRA, the state-law claim pleaded here cannot be removed, and it is left to the state courts to dismiss it. From the Court's judgment to the contrary, I respectfully dissent.[17]

[17. See generally 13B Wright, Miller & Cooper, Federal Practice & Procedure: Jurisdiction 2d § 3566 (1984 & 2005 Supp.).

Syngenta Crop Protection, Inc. v. Henson

Supreme Court of the United States, 2002.
537 U.S. 28, 123 S.Ct. 366, 154 L.Ed.2d 368.

■ CHIEF JUSTICE REHNQUIST delivered the opinion of the Court.

Respondent Hurley Henson filed suit in state court in Iberville Parish, Louisiana, against petitioner Syngenta Crop Protection, Inc. (then known as Ciba–Geigy Corp.) asserting various tort claims related to petitioners' manufacture and sale of a chlordimeform-based insecticide. A similar action, Price v. Ciba–Geigy Corp., was already underway in the United States District Court for the Southern District of Alabama. The Louisiana court stayed respondent's action when respondent successfully intervened in the *Price* suit and participated in the ensuing settlement. That settlement included a stipulation that the *Henson* action, "including any and all claims ... against [petitioners], shall be dismissed, with prejudice," as of the approval date.

Following the approval of the settlement, the Louisiana state court conducted a hearing to determine whether the *Henson* action should be dismissed. Counsel for respondent told the court that the *Price* settlement required dismissal of only some of the claims raised in *Henson*. Although this representation appeared to be contrary to the terms of the settlement agreement, the Louisiana court relied upon it and invited respondent to amend the complaint and proceed with the action.

Counsel for petitioners did not attend the hearing. Upon learning of the state court's action, however, petitioners promptly removed the action to the Middle District of Louisiana relying on 28 U.S.C. § 1441(a). The

---

In Vaden v. Discover Bank, 556 U.S. 49 (2009), the Supreme Court took a similar approach, explaining that when federal courts are determining whether they have jurisdiction to compel arbitration, the courts should "look through" the petition to compel arbitration in order to examine the entirety of the parties' underlying controversy. The Court also observed that federal courts must apply the well-pleaded complaint rule to ensure that federal jurisdiction exists, and thus the complaint, and not merely the counterclaim, in the state action must establish a basis for federal jurisdiction in order for the federal court to exercise jurisdiction over a petition to compel arbitration of litigation that is pending in state court. *Vaden* was premised on arising-under jurisdiction. In determining whether *diversity* jurisdiction exists in such cases, the circuit courts have looked only at the citizenship of the parties to the federal action to compel arbitration. See Northport Health Servs. of Ark., LLC v. Rutherford, 605 F.3d 483 (8th Cir.2010).

The completely preemptive effect of ERISA's § 502(a)(1)(B) permits removal of state-law tort claims based on denial-of-coverage claims against an employer-sponsored HMO. Aetna Health Inc. v. Davila, 542 U.S. 200 (2004). The effect of the unanimous ruling is to bar recovery of compensatory or punitive damages that would otherwise be available under state law, and to limit the liability of an HMO to prospective "make-whole" relief—provision of the wrongfully denied medical services—free and clear of liability for damages suffered by a plan beneficiary as a consequence of the HMO's wrongful denial of proper coverage in the first instance. Justice Ginsburg, joined by Justice Breyer, called in a concurring opinion for Congress to amend ERISA. "Because the Court has coupled an encompassing interpretation of ERISA's preemptive force with a cramped construction of the 'equitable relief' allowed under § 502(a)(3), a 'regulatory vacuum' exists: '[V]irtually all state law remedies are preempted but very few federal substitutes are provided.'" 542 U.S., at 222 (concurring opn.) (quoting DiFelice v. Aetna U.S. Healthcare, 346 F.3d 442, 456 (3d Cir.2003)).]

notice of removal asserted federal jurisdiction under the All Writs Act, § 1651, and under the supplemental jurisdiction statute, § 1367. The Middle District of Louisiana granted a transfer to the Southern District of Alabama pursuant to § 1404(a), and the Alabama court then dismissed *Henson* as barred by the *Price* settlement and sanctioned respondent's counsel for his misrepresentation to the Louisiana state court.

The Court of Appeals for the Eleventh Circuit affirmed the sanctions but vacated the District Court's order dismissing the *Henson* action. Henson v. Ciba–Geigy Corp., 261 F.3d 1065 (2001). The court reasoned that § 1441 by its terms authorizes removal only of actions over which the district courts have original jurisdiction. But the All Writs Act authorizes writs "in aid of [the courts'] respective jurisdictions" without providing any federal subject-matter jurisdiction in its own right, see, e.g., Clinton v. Goldsmith, 526 U.S. 529, 534–535 (1999). Therefore, the Court of Appeals concluded, the All Writs Act could not support removal of the *Henson* action from state to federal court.

In so holding, the Court of Appeals recognized that several Circuits have held that the All Writs Act gives a federal court the authority to remove a state-court case in order to prevent the frustration of orders the federal court has previously issued. See, e.g., Xiong v. Minnesota, 195 F.3d 424, 426 (CA8 1999); Bylinski v. Allen Park, 169 F.3d 1001, 1003 (CA6 1999); In re Agent Orange Product Liability Litigation, 996 F.2d 1425, 1431 (CA2 1993). It noted, however, that other Circuits have agreed with its conclusion that the All Writs Act does not furnish removal jurisdiction. See, e.g., Hillman v. Webley, 115 F.3d 1461, 1469 (CA10 1997). We granted certiorari to resolve this controversy, 534 U.S. 1126 (2002), and now affirm.

The All Writs Act, 28 U.S.C. § 1651(a), provides that "[t]he Supreme Court and all courts established by Act of Congress may issue all writs necessary or appropriate in aid of their respective jurisdictions and agreeable to the usages and principles of law." Petitioners advance two arguments in support of their claim that removal of the *Henson* action was proper under the All Writs Act: (1) The All Writs Act authorized removal of the *Henson* action, and (2) the All Writs Act in conjunction with the doctrine of ancillary enforcement jurisdiction authorized the removal. We address these contentions in turn.

First, petitioners, like the courts that have endorsed "All Writs removal," rely upon our statement in United States v. New York Telephone Co., 434 U.S. 159, 172 (1977), that the Act authorizes a federal court "to issue such commands . . . as may be necessary or appropriate to effectuate and prevent the frustration of orders it has previously issued in its exercise of jurisdiction otherwise obtained." Petitioners also cite Pennsylvania Bureau of Correction v. United States Marshals Service, 474 U.S. 34, 41 (1985), for the proposition that the All Writs Act "fill[s] the interstices of federal judicial power when those gaps threate[n] to thwart the otherwise proper exercise of federal courts' jurisdiction." They argue that the Act comes into play here because maintenance of the *Henson* action in state court in

Louisiana frustrated the express terms of the *Price* settlement, which required that "any and all claims" in *Henson* be dismissed.

But *Pennsylvania Bureau* made clear that "[w]here a statute specifically addresses the particular issue at hand, it is that authority, and not the All Writs Act, that is controlling." 474 U.S., at 43. The right of removal is entirely a creature of statute and "a suit commenced in a state court must remain there until cause is shown for its transfer under some act of Congress." Great Northern R. Co. v. Alexander, 246 U.S. 276, 280 (1918) (citing GoldWashing and Water Co. v. Keyes, 96 U.S. 199, 201 (1878)). These statutory procedures for removal are to be strictly construed. See, e.g., Shamrock Oil & Gas Corp. v. Sheets, 313 U.S. 100, 108–109 (1941) (noting that policy underlying removal statutes "is one calling for the strict construction of such legislation"); Healy v. Ratta, 292 U.S. 263, 270 (1934) ("Due regard for the rightful independence of state governments ... requires that [federal courts] scrupulously confine their own jurisdiction to the precise limits which the statute has defined"); Matthews v. Rodgers, 284 U.S. 521, 525 (1932); Kline v. Burke Constr. Co., 260 U.S. 226, 233–234 (1922). Petitioners may not, by resorting to the All Writs Act, avoid complying with the statutory requirements for removal. See *Pennsylvania Bureau,* supra, at 43 (All Writs Act "does not authorize [federal courts] to issue ad hoc writs whenever compliance with statutory procedures appears inconvenient or less appropriate").

Petitioners' question presented to this Court suggests a variation on this first argument, asking whether the All Writs Act "vests federal district courts with authority to exercise removal jurisdiction *under 28 U.S.C. § 1441.*" Pet. for Cert. i (emphasis added). The general removal statute, 28 U.S.C. § 1441, provides that "any civil action brought in a State court of which the district courts of the United States have original jurisdiction, may be removed by the defendant or the defendants, to the district court of the United States for the district and division embracing the place where such action is pending," unless Congress specifically provides otherwise. § 1441(a). Under the plain terms of § 1441(a), in order properly to remove the *Henson* action pursuant to that provision, petitioners must demonstrate that original subject-matter jurisdiction lies in the federal courts. They concede that the All Writs Act "does not, by its specific terms, provide federal courts with an independent grant of jurisdiction." Brief for Petitioners 9; see also *Clinton,* 526 U.S., at 534–535 (express terms of the All Writs Act confine a court "to issuing process 'in aid of' its existing statutory jurisdiction; the Act does not enlarge that jurisdiction"). Because the All Writs Act does not confer jurisdiction on the federal courts, it cannot confer the original jurisdiction required to support removal pursuant to § 1441.

Second, petitioners contend that some combination of the All Writs Act and the doctrine of ancillary enforcement jurisdiction support the removal of the *Henson* action. As we explained in Peacock v. Thomas, 516 U.S. 349, 355 (1996), "[a]ncillary jurisdiction may extend to claims having a factual and logical dependence on 'the primary lawsuit.' " Petitioners emphasize that the Southern District of Alabama retained jurisdiction over the *Price* settlement, thus distinguishing Kokkonen v. Guardian Life Ins. Co. of America, 511 U.S. 375 (1994), in which we found ancillary jurisdiction lacking. They argue that respondent's maintenance of the *Henson* action undermined the *Price* settlement and that, in light of the Alabama court's retained jurisdiction, ancillary enforcement jurisdiction was necessary and appropriate.[18] But they fail to explain how the Alabama District Court's retention of jurisdiction over the *Price* settlement authorized *removal* of the *Henson* action. Removal is governed by statute, and invocation of ancillary jurisdiction, like invocation of the All Writs Act, does not dispense with the need for compliance with statutory requirements.

Read in light of the question presented in the petition for certiorari, perhaps petitioners' argument is that ancillary jurisdiction authorizes removal under 28 U.S.C. § 1441. As we explained in *Peacock,* however, a "court must have jurisdiction over a case or controversy before it may assert jurisdiction over ancillary claims." 516 U.S., at 355. Ancillary jurisdiction, therefore, cannot provide the original jurisdiction that petitioners must show in order to qualify for removal under § 1441.

Section 1441 requires that a federal court have original jurisdiction over an action in order for it to be removed from a state court. The All Writs Act, alone or in combination with the existence of ancillary jurisdiction in a federal court, is not a substitute for that requirement. Accordingly, the judgment of the Court of Appeals is

Affirmed.

■ JUSTICE STEVENS, concurring.

As the Court acknowledges, the decisions of the Courts of Appeal that we disapprove today have relied in large part on our decision in United States v. New York Telephone Co., 434 U.S. 159 (1977). Because the overly expansive interpretation given to the All Writs Act in *New York Telephone* may produce further mischief, I would expressly overrule that misguided decision.

. . . . .

Lincoln Property Co. v. Roche

Supreme Court of the United States, 2005.
546 U.S. 81, 126 S.Ct. 606, 163 L.Ed.2d 415.

■ JUSTICE GINSBURG delivered the opinion of the Court.

This case concerns 28 U.S.C. § 1441, which authorizes the removal of civil actions from state court to federal court when the action initiated in

---

18. Petitioners' assertion that removal was "necessary" is unpersuasive on its own bottom. One in petitioners' position may apply to the court that approved a settlement for an injunction requiring dismissal of a rival action. Petitioners could also have sought a determination from the Louisiana state court that respondent's action was barred by the judgment of the Alabama District Court.

state court is one that could have been brought, originally, in a federal district court. § 1441(a). When federal-court jurisdiction is predicated on the parties' diversity of citizenship, see § 1332, removal is permissible "only if none of the parties in interest properly joined and served as defendants is a citizen of the State in which [the] action [was] brought." § 1441(b).

Christophe and Juanita Roche, plaintiffs below, respondents here, are citizens of Virginia. They commenced suit in state court against diverse defendants, including Lincoln Property Company (Lincoln), a corporation chartered and having its principal place of business in Texas. The defendants removed the litigation to a Federal District Court where, after discovery proceedings, they successfully moved for summary judgment. Holding the removal improper, the Court of Appeals instructed remand of the action to state court. 373 F.3d 610, 620–622 (CA4 2004). The appellate court so ruled on the ground that the Texas defendant failed to show the nonexistence of an affiliated Virginia entity that was the "real party in interest." Id., at 622.

We reverse the judgment of the Court of Appeals. Defendants may remove an action on the basis of diversity of citizenship if there is complete diversity between all named plaintiffs and all named defendants, and no defendant is a citizen of the forum State. It is not incumbent on the named defendants to negate the existence of a potential defendant whose presence in the action would destroy diversity.[19]

I

Christophe and Juanita Roche leased an apartment in the Westfield Village complex in Fairfax County, Virginia. About a year after moving in, they discovered evidence of toxic mold in their apartment. Expert inspection confirmed the presence of mold, which the inspection report linked to hair loss, headaches, irritation of the respiratory tract, fatigue, and dermatitis. The report stated that spores from toxigenic mold species were airborne in the apartment and had likely contaminated the carpeting and fabric surfaces throughout the dwelling. The Roches moved out of their apartment for the remediation process, leaving their personal belongings in the care of Lincoln, the designated property manager of Westfield Village, and the mold treatment firm. 373 F.3d, at 612.

---

19. Defendants below, petitioners here, presented a second question in their petition for certiorari: Can a limited partnership be deemed a citizen of a State on the sole ground that the partnership's business activities bear a "very close nexus" with the State? Because no partnership is or need be a party to this action, that question is not live for adjudication. We note, however, that our prior decisions do not regard as relevant to subject-matter jurisdiction the locations at which partnerships conduct business. See Carden v. Arkoma Associates, 494 U.S. 185, 189, 192–197 (1990) (for diversity purposes, a partnership entity, unlike a corporation, does not rank as a citizen; to meet the complete diversity requirement, all partners, limited as well as general, must be diverse from all parties on the opposing side).

Some months later, the Roches commenced suit, filing two substantially similar complaints in the Circuit Court for Fairfax County, Virginia. Both complaints asserted serious medical ailments from the Roches' year-long exposure to toxic mold, and sought damages under multiple headings, including negligence, breach of contract, actual fraud, constructive fraud, and violations of Virginia housing regulations. In addition, the Roches alleged loss, theft, or destruction of their personal property (including irreplaceable family keepsakes) during the remediation process. Regarding these losses, they sought damages for conversion and infliction of emotional distress.

In state court, the Roches' complaints named three defendants: Lincoln; INVESCO Institutional, an investment management group; and State of Wisconsin Investment Board, the alleged owner of Westfield Village. The complaints described Lincoln as "a developer and manager of residential communities, including . . . Westfield Village." "[A]cting by and through [its] agents," the Roches alleged, Lincoln caused the personal injuries of which they complained.

Defendants timely removed the twin cases to the United States District Court for the Eastern District of Virginia, invoking that court's diversity-of-citizenship jurisdiction. See 28 U.S.C. §§ 1332(a)(1), 1441(a). The notice of removal described Lincoln as a Texas corporation with its principal place of business in Texas, INVESCO as a Delaware corporation with its principal place of business in Georgia, and State of Wisconsin Investment Board as an independent agency of Wisconsin. In their consolidated federal-court complaint, the Roches identified themselves as citizens of Virginia and Lincoln as a corporation headquartered in Texas, just as they did in their state-court complaints.[20] Further, they stated affirmatively that the federal court "has jurisdiction of this matter." Lincoln, in its answer to the complaint, admitted that, through its regional offices, "it manages Westfield Village." Lincoln did not seek to avoid liability by asserting that some other entity was responsible for managing the property.

In both their state- and federal-court complaints, the Roches stated that, "[u]pon further discovery in the case," they would "determine if additional defendant or defendants will be named." Although they engaged in some discovery concerning Lincoln's affiliates, their efforts in this regard were not extensive, and at no point did they seek to join any additional defendant.

After discovery, the parties cross-moved for summary judgment. The District Court granted defendants' motion and denied plaintiffs' motion, noting that it would set forth its reasons in a forthcoming memorandum order. The promised memorandum order issued a few months later, and the District Court entered final judgment for the defendants the same day.

---

20. Some weeks after the removal, the District Court dismissed INVESCO as a defendant. Nothing turns on the presence or absence of INVESCO as a defending party. State of Wisconsin Investment Board, alleged owner of Westfield Village, remains a defendant-petitioner. Its status as a Wisconsin citizen for diversity purposes is not currently contested.

Six days after the District Court granted defendants' motion for summary judgment, but before final judgment was entered, the Roches moved to remand the case to the state court, alleging for the first time the absence of federal subject-matter jurisdiction. Specifically, the Roches alleged that Lincoln "is not a Texas Corporation, but a Partnership with one of its partners residing in the Commonwealth of Virginia." The District Court denied the remand motion, concluding that Lincoln is a Texas corporation and that removal was proper because the requisite complete diversity existed between all plaintiffs and all defendants.

The Court of Appeals for the Fourth Circuit reversed and instructed the District Court to remand the case to the state court. 373 F.3d, at 622. Although recognizing that Lincoln is a Texas citizen and a proper party to the action, id., at 620–621, the Court of Appeals observed that "Lincoln operates under many different structures," id., at 617. Describing Lincoln as "the nominal party and ultimate parent company," the appellate court suspected that an unidentified "Virginia subsidiary, be it a partnership, corporation or otherwise, rather than the Texas parent," was "the real and substantial party in interest." Id., at 620–621. Lincoln, the party invoking federal-court jurisdiction, had not demonstrated the nonexistence of "the Virginia sub-'partnership,' " the Court of Appeals reasoned, id., at 621, and therefore had not met its burden of establishing diversity, id., at 621–622.

We granted certiorari to resolve a division among the Circuits on the question whether an entity not named or joined as a defendant can nonetheless be deemed a real party in interest whose presence would destroy diversity. Compare 373 F.3d, at 620–622, with Plains Growers, Inc. v. Ickes–Braun Glasshouses, Inc., 474 F.2d 250, 252 (CA5 1973) ("The citizenship of one who has an interest in the lawsuit but who has not been made a party . . . by plaintiff cannot be used by plaintiff on a motion to remand to defeat diversity jurisdiction."), and Simpson v. Providence Washington Ins. Group, 608 F.2d 1171, 1173–1175 (CA9 1979) (KENNEDY, J.) (upholding removal where Alaska plaintiff sued Rhode Island parent company without joining as well potentially liable Alaska subsidiary, and the parties did not act collusively to create diversity jurisdiction).

II

The Court of Appeals correctly identified Lincoln as a proper party to the action, but it erred in insisting that some other entity affiliated with Lincoln should have been joined as a codefendant, and that it was Lincoln's obligation to name that entity and show that its joinder would not destroy diversity.

We stress, first, that, at this stage of the case, the existence of complete diversity between the Roches and Lincoln is not in doubt. The Roches, both citizens of Virginia, acknowledge that Lincoln is indeed a corporation, not a partnership, and that Lincoln is chartered in and has its principal place of business in Texas. 373 F.3d, at 620. Accordingly, for jurisdictional purposes, Lincoln is a citizen of Texas and of no other State. 28 U.S.C. § 1332(c)(1) ("a corporation shall be deemed to be a citizen of any State by which it has been incorporated and of the State where it has its principal place of business").

We turn now to the reasons why the Fourth Circuit erred in determining that diversity jurisdiction was not proved by the removing parties. 373 F.3d, at 612 (concluding that "Defendants failed to carry their burden of proof with respect to their allegedly diverse citizenship"). The principal federal statute governing diversity jurisdiction, 28 U.S.C. § 1332, gives federal district courts original jurisdiction of all civil actions "between ... citizens of different States" where the amount in controversy exceeds $75,000. § 1332(a)(1). Since Strawbridge v. Curtiss, 3 Cranch [7 U.S.] 267 (1806), we have read the statutory formulation "between ... citizens of different States" to require complete diversity between all plaintiffs and all defendants. Caterpillar Inc. v. Lewis, 519 U.S. 61, 68 (1996); cf. State Farm Fire & Casualty Co. v. Tashire, 386 U.S. 523, 530–531 (1967) (explaining that complete diversity is not constitutionally required and upholding interpleader under § 1335 based on minimal diversity, i.e., diversity between two or more adverse parties).

While § 1332 allows plaintiffs to invoke the federal courts' diversity jurisdiction, § 1441 gives defendants a corresponding opportunity. Section 1441(a) states: "Except as otherwise expressly provided by Act of Congress, any civil action brought in a State court of which the district courts of the United States have original jurisdiction, may be removed by the defendant or the defendants, to the district court of the United States for the district and division embracing the place where such action is pending." The scales are not evenly balanced, however. An in-state plaintiff may invoke diversity jurisdiction, but § 1441(b) bars removal on the basis of diversity if any "part[y] in interest properly joined and served as [a] defendan[t] is a citizen of the State in which [the] action is brought." In the instant case, Virginia plaintiffs Christophe and Juanita Roche joined and served no Virginian as a party defendant. Hence the action qualified for the removal defendants effected.

Neither Federal Rule of Civil Procedure 17(a), captioned "Real Party in Interest," nor Federal Rule 19, captioned "Joinder of Persons Needed for Just Adjudication," requires plaintiffs or defendants to name and join any additional parties to this action. Both Rules, we note, address party joinder, not federal-court subject-matter jurisdiction. See Rule 82 ("[The Federal Rules of Civil Procedure] shall not be construed to extend or limit the jurisdiction of the United States district courts ...."); Advisory Committee's Notes on Fed. Rule Civ. Proc. 19, 28 U.S.C. App., pp. 696–698. Rule 17(a) directs that "[e]very action shall be *prosecuted* in the name of the real party in interest." (Emphasis added.) That Rule, as its text displays, speaks to joinder of *plaintiffs*, not defendants.

Rule 19 provides for the joinder of parties who should or must take part in the litigation to achieve a "[j]ust [a]djudication." See Provident Tradesmens Bank & Trust Co. v. Patterson, 390 U.S. 102, 118–123 (1968). The Roches place no reliance on Rule 19 and maintain that the Rule "played no part, explicitly or implicitly, in the Court of Appeals' conclusion." Given Lincoln's admission that it managed Westfield Village when mold contaminated the Roches' apartment, it does indeed appear that no absent person, formally or practically, was "[n]eeded for [j]ust [a]djudication." Fed. Rule Civ. Proc. 19; cf. *Simpson*, 608 F.2d, at 1174 (diverse corporate defendant accepted full liability for any eventual adverse judgment; nondiverse subsidiary need not be joined as a defendant, although arguably it had joint liability with its parent); 16 J. Moore et al., Moore's Federal Practice ¶ 107.14[2][c], p. 107–67 (3d ed.2005) ("In general, the plaintiff is the master of the complaint and has the option of naming only those parties the plaintiff chooses to sue, subject only to the rules of joinder [of] necessary parties.").

While Rule 17(a) applies only to joinder of parties who assert claims, the Court of Appeals and the Roches draw from decisions of this Court a jurisdictional "real parties to the controversy" rule applicable in diversity cases to complaining and defending parties alike. See Navarro Savings Assn. v. Lee, 446 U.S. 458, 462, n.9 (1980) (citing Note, Diversity Jurisdiction over Unincorporated Business Entities: The Real Party in Interest as a Jurisdictional Rule, 56 Texas L.Rev. 243, 247–250 (1978)). But no decision called to our attention supports the burden the Court of Appeals placed on a properly joined defendant to negate the existence of a potential codefendant whose presence in the action would destroy diversity.

III

Our decisions employing "real party to the controversy" terminology in describing or explaining who counts and who can be discounted for diversity purposes bear scant resemblance to the action the Roches have commenced. No party here has been "improperly or collusively" named solely to create federal jurisdiction, see 28 U.S.C. § 1359 ("A district court shall not have jurisdiction of a civil action in which any party, by assignment or otherwise, has been improperly or collusively made or joined to invoke the jurisdiction of such court."); Kramer v. Caribbean Mills, Inc., 394 U.S. 823, 830 (1969) (assignment for collection only, motivated by desire to make diversity jurisdiction available, falls within the "very core" of § 1359); Little v. Giles, 118 U.S. 596, 600–607 (1886) (where land was purportedly sold to out-of-state farmer but no money or deed changed hands, quiet title action could not be maintained based on farmer's diverse citizenship), nor to defeat it, see Cheaspeake & Ohio R. Co. v. Cockrell, 232 U.S. 146, 152 (1914) (diverse defendants, upon showing that joinder of nondiverse party was "without right and made in bad faith," may successfully remove the action to federal court).

Nor are the Roches aided by cases in which actions against a state agency have been regarded as suits against the State itself. See, e.g., State Highway Comm'n of Wyo. v. Utah Constr. Co., 278 U.S. 194, 199–200 (1929) ("[S]tate Commission was but the arm or alter ego of the State with no funds or ability to respond in damages."). Decisions of this genre are bottomed on this Court's recognition of a State's asserted Eleventh Amendment right not to be haled into federal court. See, e.g., Federal Maritime

Comm'n v. South Carolina Ports Authority, 535 U.S. 743, 769 (2002). They are not pertinent to suits between private parties.

Unlike cases in which a party was named to satisfy state pleading rules, e.g., McNutt ex rel. Leggett, Smith, & Lawrence v. Bland, 2 How. [43 U.S.] 9, 14 (1844), or was joined only as designated performer of a ministerial act, e.g., Walden v. Skinner, 101 U.S. 577, 589 (1880), or otherwise had no control of, impact on, or stake in the controversy, e.g., Wood v. Davis, 18 How. [59 U.S.] 467, 469–470 (1856), Lincoln has a vital interest in this case.[21] Indeed, Lincoln accepted responsibility, in the event that the Roches prevailed on the merits of their claims, by admitting that, "[since 1996,] it has managed Westfield Village Apartments." A named defendant who admits involvement in the controversy and would be liable to pay a resulting judgment is not "nominal" in any sense except that it is named in the complaint. Cf. Knapp v. Railroad Co., 20 Wall. [87 U.S.] 117, 122 (1874).

In any event, we emphasize, the Fourth Circuit had no warrant in this case to inquire whether some other person might have been joined as an additional or substitute defendant. See id., at 122 (federal courts should not "inquir[e] outside of the case in order to ascertain whether some other person may not have an equitable interest in the cause of action"); *Little*, 118 U.S., at 603 (if named party's interest is real, the fact that other interested parties are not joined "will not affect the jurisdiction of the [federal courts]"); 16 Moore, supra, ¶ 107.14[2][c], p. 107–67 ("Ordinarily, a court will not interfere with the consequences of a plaintiff's selection in naming parties, unless the plaintiff has impermissibly manufactured diversity or used an unacceptable device to defeat diversity.").

Congress, empowered to prescribe the jurisdiction of the federal courts, sometimes has specified that a named party's own citizenship does not determine its diverse status. Thus, as a procedural matter, executors, administrators, and guardians "may sue in [their] own name[s] without joining the party for whose benefit the action is brought." Rule 17(a). As to diversity jurisdiction, however, § 1332(c)(2) directs that "the legal representative of [a decedent's] estate ... shall be deemed to be a citizen only of the same State as the decedent, and the legal representative of an infant or incompetent shall be deemed to be a citizen only of the same State as the infant or incompetent." Congress has also provided that in direct action suits against insurers to which the insured is not made a party, the "insurer shall be deemed a citizen of the State of which the insured is a citizen, as well as of any State by which the insurer has been incorporated and of the State where it has its principal place of business." § 1332(c)(1).

But Congress surely has not directed that a corporation, for diversity-of-citizenship purposes, shall be deemed to have acquired the citizenship of

---

21. The Roches' complaint cast Lincoln as the primary tortfeasor, alleging that Lincoln engaged in "a conscious and predetermined plan" to conceal the hazards of mold from apartment residents. Further, the Roches alleged that Lincoln ignored numerous mold-related maintenance requests they "personally" made to Lincoln, inquiries that, if followed up, might have prevented or lessened their injuries.

all or any of its affiliates. For cases of the kind the Roches have instituted, Congress has provided simply and only this instruction: "[A] corporation shall be deemed to be a citizen of any State by which it has been incorporated and of the State where it has its principal place of business." Ibid. The jurisdictional rule governing here is unambiguous and it is not amenable to judicial enlargement. Under § 1332(c)(1), Lincoln is a citizen of Texas alone, and under § 1441(a) and (b), this case was properly removed.

* * *

The Roches sued the entity they thought responsible for managing their apartment. Lincoln affirmed that it was so responsible. Complete diversity existed. The potential liability of other parties was a matter plaintiffs' counsel might have assiduously explored through discovery devices. It was not incumbent on Lincoln to propose as additional defendants persons the Roches, as masters of their complaint, permissively might have joined.

For the reasons stated, the judgment of the United States Court of Appeals for the Fourth Circuit is reversed, and the case is remanded for further proceedings consistent with this opinion.

It is so ordered.[22]

Borough of West Mifflin v. Lancaster

United States Court of Appeals, Third Circuit, 1995.
45 F.3d 780.

■ Before Stapleton, Garth, and Pratt,[23] Circuit Judges.

■ Pratt, Circuit Judge:

FACTS AND BACKGROUND

[In September 1991 Alan D. Lindsey and Randall Coughanour were involved with security guards at an indoor shopping mall in West Mifflin Borough, near Pittsburgh, Pa. They had gone to the mall to shop, but allege that they were "harassed, threatened, and assaulted by the security guards." West Mifflin Police Officer Evan came in response to a call from Lindsey and Coughanour. He refused to arrest or admonish the guards, but

---

[22. What if a defendant seeks diversity-based removal and although the parties' diversity of citizenship is clear, the amount in controversy is not? The federal courts are divided as to whether the defendant may undertake jurisdictional discovery after removal in order to prove the requisite amount in controversy exists. Although some courts have permitted such discovery, see Shaw v. Dow Brands, Inc., 994 F.2d 364 (7th Cir. 1993), others have required that the defendant already have in its possession the evidence necessary for establishing diversity jurisdiction at the moment of removal, see May v. Wal–Mart Stores, Inc., 751 F.Supp.2d 946 (E.D.Ky.2010).]

23. Honorable George C. Pratt, United States Circuit Judge for the Second Circuit, sitting by designation.

told Lindsey and Coughanour to leave the mall and never come back, or they would be arrested. The following day Lindsey returned to the mall in an attempt to talk to someone from the DeBartolo organization, which owned the mall, to find out why he had been accosted. Over the next three weeks he repeatedly tried without success to contact the mall manager. He then consulted a lawyer, who advised him that the law permitted his entrance to the mall as long as the mall was open to the public.

[Lindsey and Coughanour then returned to the mall to shop. They were accosted and handcuffed in the mall men's room and dragged through the corridor to the mall office. Officer Evan arrived and wrote out citations for disorderly conduct and defiant trespass. The handcuffs were then removed and Lindsey and Coughanour were ordered to leave the mall separately, which they did. They were convicted in Common Pleas Court on charges stemming from the incidents at the mall, but those convictions were vacated by an appellate court, which ordered them discharged.

[Lindsey and Coughanour then filed a seven-count complaint in state court. As defendants, they named the Borough of West Mifflin and Officer Evan ("the municipal defendants"), as well as the owners, supervisors, and security officers of the mall ("the DeBartolo defendants"). Lindsey and Coughanour alleged: (1) state-law claims of malicious prosecution, malicious abuse of process, assault, and conspiracy against all defendants; (2) a negligence claim against the municipal defendants; (3) a negligence claim against the DeBartolo defendants; and (4) a federal claim under 42 U.S.C. § 1983 that alleged that the municipal defendants and the DeBartolo defendants conspired to deprive Lindsey and Coughanour of their civil rights through harassment, assault, false arrest, malicious prosecution, and abuse of process in violation of the 4th, 5th, and 14th amendments.

[Relying on the federal civil-rights claim, the municipal defendants filed a notice of removal from the state court to the United States District Court for the Western District of Pennsylvania. Lindsey and Coughanour then moved to remand the case back to state court. On the recommendation of a United States magistrate judge, District Judge Gary L. Lancaster ordered the case remanded under 28 U.S.C. § 1441(c), finding that the issues of state law clearly predominated, not only with respect to the state-law claims but also with respect to the § 1983 claim. The municipal defendants then petitioned the Third Circuit for mandamus to require Judge Lancaster to accept jurisdiction of the action. They contend that it was properly removed under § 1441(a) and (b) and that by remanding the entire case under § 1441(c), the district judge exceeded his authority.]

. . . . .

DISCUSSION

Preliminarily, it is clear that we have jurisdiction to review the district court's remand order. While appellate review of remands is somewhat restricted (see 28 U.S.C. § 1447(d); Aliota v. Graham, 984 F.2d 1350, 1354–55 (3d Cir.1993)), this case, which was removed because it included a

§ 1983 civil rights claim brought under 28 U.S.C. §§ 1331 and 1343, falls within the specific exception to § 1447(d), which states that

> an order remanding a case to the State court from which it was removed pursuant to section 1443 ["civil rights cases"] of this title shall be reviewable by appeal or otherwise.

28 U.S.C. § 1447(d). Thus, Congress has demonstrated a special concern to preserve our power to review remand orders in civil rights cases.[24]

A. *Federal Jurisdiction Generally.*

Removal and remand issues must be considered in light of the general principles of federal subject matter jurisdiction. There are several sources for original jurisdiction in the federal courts: federal question jurisdiction of civil actions arising under the Constitution, laws, or treaties of the United States, 28 U.S.C. § 1331; diversity of citizenship jurisdiction of civil actions where the matter in controversy exceeds $50,000, and is between citizens of different states, 28 U.S.C. § 1332; and other specific jurisdictional statutes, such as RICO, 18 U.S.C. § 1962, et seq.; Civil Rights Cases, 28 U.S.C. § 1443; ERISA, 29 U.S.C. § 1002, et seq.; and FELA, 45 U.S.C. §§ 51–60.

In addition,

> ... in any civil action of which the district courts have original jurisdiction [except diversity cases], the district courts shall have supplemental jurisdiction over all other claims that are so related to claims in the action within such original jurisdiction that they form part of the same case or controversy under Article III of the United States Constitution.

28 U.S.C. § 1367. Section 1367 also grants jurisdiction over claims that involve the joinder or intervention of additional parties, thereby codifying what had been dubbed "pendent-party" jurisdiction as well as some forms of "ancillary" jurisdiction. Thus § 1367 provides federal courts with statutory authority to hear some claims that lack an independent basis for federal subject matter jurisdiction.

[**24.** The text of § 1447(d) is reprinted infra p. 388 and the text of § 1443 is reprinted supra p. 331. As will be seen, § 1447(d) does not make an exception to the usual rule of nonreviewability of remand orders for all civil-rights cases, but only for those removed pursuant to § 1443. Was this such a case? See 14B Wright, Miller & Cooper, Federal Practice & Procedure: Jurisdiction 3d § 3728 (1998). See also Mathews v. County of Fremont, Wyoming, reprinted infra p. 400.

It has since been established, however, that § 1447(d) bars appellate review only when a remand is ordered on one of the two grounds specified by § 1447(c): lack of subject-matter jurisdiction or a procedural defect in the removal of the case. See Quackenbush v. Allstate Insurance Co., 517 U.S. 706 (1996). Under the construction of § 1447(d) announced in *Quackenbush*, § 1447(d) clearly did not bar the Third Circuit's review in *Borough of West Mifflin* of a remand ordered by the district court under § 1441(c) rather than § 1447(c). As discussed infra, p. 388, n. 49, *Quackenbush* also held that reviewable remand orders are appealable as of right under 28 U.S.C. § 1291, obviating the need to resort to a petition for a writ of mandamus.]

B. *Removal Jurisdiction Generally.*

Cases begun in state court over which a federal court may also have jurisdiction can be removed by the defendants under 28 U.S.C. § 1441 ("Actions removable generally"). Section 1441(a) reads in relevant part:

. . . . .

Under (a), therefore, unless otherwise barred by Congress, any civil action brought in a state court (plaintiff's choice) over which a federal district court would have original jurisdiction may be removed by the defendant (defendant's choice) to a district court. This would include both federal question and diversity cases as well as the miscellaneous federal jurisdiction cases. In the case now before us, Lindsey's and Coughanour's state court action included a claim under 42 U.S.C. § 1983, over which the federal court has jurisdiction under 28 U.S.C. §§ 1331 and 1343, plus a variety of state law claims arising out of the same events and circumstances, over which the federal court has supplemental jurisdiction under § 1367. Because the district court had subject matter jurisdiction, the action was properly removed from state court under § 1441(a).

Under § 1441(b) diversity cases have an additional obstacle to removal: a resident defendant is barred from removing to federal court. If jurisdiction is based on a federal question, however, there is no residency restriction. This shows an added concern of Congress that cases such as this one—civil rights claims raising federal questions—should be permitted to be heard in federal courts.

C. *Application of § 1441(c).*

The dispute on this mandamus application focuses on the effect of subdivision (c) of § 1441. That provision, prior to 1990, read:

> Whenever a separate and independent claim or cause of action, which would have been removable if sued upon alone, is joined with one or more otherwise nonremovable claims or causes of action, the entire case may be removed and the district court may determine all issues therein, or, in its discretion, remand all matters not otherwise within its original jurisdiction.

In 1990, Congress amended § 1441(c) in a manner which the parties contend affects our decision in this case. See Judicial Improvements Act of 1990, Pub.L. No. 101–650 § 312, 104 Stat. 5089, 5114 (1990). Section 1441(c) now reads:

> Whenever a separate and independent claim or cause of action within the jurisdiction of 1331 of this title is joined with one or more otherwise non-removable claims or causes of action, the entire case may be removed and the district court may determine all issues therein, or, in its discretion, may remand all matters in which State law predominates.

In enacting the amendment to § 1441(c), Congress altered two provisions of the statute. First, it replaced the phrase "a separate and independent claim or cause of action, *which would have been removable if sued upon alone*" with "a separate and independent claim or cause of action *within the jurisdiction of 1331 of this title.*" Second, it replaced the phrase "the district court may ... remand all matters *not otherwise in its original jurisdiction*" with "the district court may ... remand all matters *in which State law predominates.*"

A fair reading of the Congressional intent in enacting the amendment to § 1441(c) is that it was designed to restrict removal to only those cases falling within the court's federal question jurisdiction and to bring the remand provisions into harmony with 28 U.S.C. § 1367, thereby possibly avoiding piecemeal litigation. See David D. Siegel, Commentary on 1988 and 1990 Revisions to Section 1441, 28 U.S.C. § 1441 (1994).

In the present case, the district court relied upon the addition which reads "the district court may ... remand all matters in which State law predominates" to remand the entire case, including the § 1983 claim, to state court. It did so without regard for the requirement, which the Congress left unchanged when it amended § 1441(c), that the federal cause of action removed by the municipal defendants had to be "separate and independent" from the state causes of action.

Thus, § 1441(c) provides for removal or remand *only* where the federal question claims are "separate and independent" from the state law claims with which they are joined in the complaint. However, where there is a single injury to plaintiff for which relief is sought, arising from an interrelated series of events or transactions, there is no separate or independent claim or cause of action under § 1441(c). American Fire & Casualty Co. v. Finn, 341 U.S. 6 (1951). Suits involving pendent (now "supplemental") state claims that "derive from a common nucleus of operative fact," see United Mine Workers v. Gibbs, 383 U.S. 715, 725 (1966), do not fall within the scope of § 1441(c), since pendent claims are not "separate and independent." Carnegie–Mellon University v. Cohill, 484 U.S. 343, 354 (1988).

It is apparent, then, that "§ 1441(c) grants the district court only a limited authority to remand a case." Kabealo v. Davis, 829 F.Supp. 923, 926 (S.D.Ohio 1993) (citing to Buchner v. F.D.I.C., 981 F.2d 816 (5th Cir.1993)). In *Kabealo*, the plaintiff had brought a federal claim under the Racketeer Influenced and Corrupt Organizations Act, 18 U.S.C. § 1962, et seq., along with state law claims of engaging in a pattern of corrupt activity under Ohio law, breach of fiduciary duty, breach of contract, and fraud. Defendant filed a notice of removal, and the plaintiffs moved for remand under 28 U.S.C. § 1441(c). The district court of Ohio concluded that some cases had analyzed § 1441(c) too broadly, and held, as petitioners have argued here, that:

> Even if it is assumed that § 1441(c) would authorize the remand of an entire case, including federal claims, plaintiff must establish that remand of this case would be appropriate under 1441(c). That section provides for removal or remand only where the federal claims are "separate and independent" from the state law claims with which they are joined in the complaint [citing authorities]. Where there is a single

injury to plaintiff for which relief is sought, arising from an interrelated series of events or transactions, there is no separate and independent claim or cause of action under 1441(c). American Fire & Casualty Co. v. Finn, 341 U.S. 6 (1951). The use of different counts to plead different legal theories or multiple theories of recovery does not automatically make those counts separate and independent.

Kabealo, 829 F.Supp., at 926. The court then found that because the plaintiff in that case relied on the same set of facts for all counts of the complaint, including the RICO count, § 1441(c) did not authorize remand, because the federal claims were not separate and independent under that section.

Kabealo, drawing heavily upon *Buchner*, stands alone among the district courts in having reached the same conclusion as *Buchner* reached and as we reach here. Other district courts have apparently read the 1990 amendments as broadening rather than narrowing the scope of their discretion to remand. We cannot agree.

For instance, in Moore v. DeBiase, 766 F.Supp. 1311 (D.N.J.1991), the complaint presented allegations similar to the allegations found in the present case. Moore had accused DeBiase, a police supervisor, of malicious abuse of authority, abuse of police procedure, a conspiracy to terminate Moore, defamation, and violation of § 1983 by depriving him of his "rights, privileges, and immunities secured by the United States Constitution and New Jersey Law." Id., at 1314. Moore also sought damages against the Borough of Dunnellen and the Dunnellen Police Department under conspiracy and respondeat superior theories. Id.

Without determining that Moore's § 1983 claim was "separate and independent" from his state law claims, the district court remanded all of Moore's claims, including his § 1983 claim. It did so in the belief that the phrase "all matters in which State law predominates" in § 1441(c) permits the remand of even federal claims within the district court's original federal jurisdiction if, in the discretion of the district court, state law predominated in the action as a whole.

As we have pointed out, however, unless the federal question claims removed by the defendant were "separate and independent" from the state law claims, § 1441(c) cannot apply and the district court must retain the federal claim. Hence, the district court's discretion to remand under § 1441(c) can pertain only to those *state law claims* which the district court could decline to hear under 28 U.S.C. § 1367. (See "Application of § 1367(c)"). Thus, we reject the reasoning of *Moore v. DeBiase* and those courts which have adopted its rationale. See, e.g. Holland v. World Omni Leasing, Inc., 764 F.Supp. 1442 (N.D.Ala.1991); Martin v. Drummond Coal Co., Inc., 756 F.Supp. 524 (N.D.Ala.1991).

Similarly in the present case, Lindsey and Coughanour rely on the same series of events for all counts of their complaint, including the federal § 1983 count; therefore, the federal claim is not separate and independent under § 1441(c), and the district court had no authority to remand the case under that section.

D.   *Application of § 1367(c).*

The plaintiffs insist that, even if the district court was not authorized to remand this entire case under § 1441(c), its action should be sustained under the authority of 28 U.S.C. § 1367(c) which gives a district court discretion to decline to hear certain state claims it would have supplemental jurisdiction to entertain under § 1367(a). We disagree for two reasons. First, nothing in § 1367(c) authorizes a district court to decline to entertain a claim over which it has original jurisdiction and, accordingly, that section clearly does not sanction the district court's remand of this entire case, including the civil rights claims, to the state court.

Further, § 1367(c) cannot legitimately be invoked to affirm even the district court's remand of the state claims to the state court. While we agree with plaintiffs that the discretion bestowed by § 1367(c) exists with respect to removed claims as well as claims filed initially in the district court, it is apparent that the district court has not exercised that discretion in this case. The magistrate judge's opinion, adopted by the district court, refers only to § 1441(c) and it is apparent from that opinion that the court remanded the entire case based solely on the authority of that section. Moreover, the result of an exercise of discretion under § 1367(c) in circumstances like those before the district court would have been two parallel proceedings, one in federal court and one in the state system, and a district court cannot properly exercise its discretion under § 1367(c) without taking that fact into account. The district court's § 1441(c) analysis accordingly cannot serve as a surrogate for a § 1367(c) analysis that was not conducted.

As we have indicated, § 1367(c) is potentially applicable in a removed case involving federal claims and state claims over which the district court has supplemental jurisdiction. A district court may thus be called upon to exercise its discretion at any time during the course of such a proceeding in light of the circumstances that then exist. *Gibbs*, 383 U.S., at 727. Because the district court in this case may hereafter be called upon to exercise its discretion under § 1367(c), we offer the following guidance.

Subsection (a) of § 1367 directs that "in any civil action of which the district courts have original jurisdiction, the district courts shall have supplemental jurisdiction over all other claims that are so related to [the original jurisdiction claims] that they form part of the same case or controversy." Subsection (c) goes on to describe four categories of such claims which the district courts may nevertheless decline to adjudicate:

(c) The district courts may decline to exercise supplemental jurisdiction over a claim under subsection (a) if—

(1) the claim raises a novel or complex issue of State law,

(2) the claim substantially predominates over the claim or claims over which the district court has original jurisdiction,

(3) the district court has dismissed all claims over which it has original jurisdiction, or

(4) in exceptional circumstances, there are other compelling reasons for declining jurisdiction.

While § 1367(c) does not specify what disposition the district court is to make of state claims it decides not to hear, based on the teachings of *Carnegie-Mellon*, 484 U.S. at 343, we believe that in a case that has been removed from a state court, a remand to that court is a viable alternative to a dismissal without prejudice. See Balazik v. County of Dauphin, 44 F.3d 209, 216–17 (3d Cir.1995).

Section 1367(a)'s grant of "supplemental" jurisdiction was intended to broaden the preexisting scope of what had previously been termed "pendent" jurisdiction to include claims involving the addition of parties. H.R.Rep. No. 416, 101st Cong., 2d Sess. 29 (1990), reprinted in 1990 U.S.C.C.A.N. 6802, 6875. Section 1367(c), on the other hand, was intended simply to codify the preexisting pendent jurisdiction law, enunciated in *Gibbs* and its progeny, concerning those instances in which a district court is authorized to decline to hear a state claim it would have the power to hear because of its relationship to an original federal jurisdiction claim. H.R.Rep. No. 416, 1990 U.S.C.C.A.N. at 6875 (Subsection 1367(c) "codifies the factors that the Supreme Court has recognized as providing legitimate bases upon which a district court may decline jurisdiction over a supplemental claim, even though it is empowered to hear the claim."). It is of particular importance in the present context to note that the "substantially predominates" standard found in § 1367(c)(2) comes directly from the Supreme Court's opinion in *Gibbs* and should be understood in that context....[25]

Under *Gibbs* jurisprudence, where the claim over which the district court has original jurisdiction is dismissed before trial, the district court must decline to decide the pendent state claims unless considerations of judicial economy, convenience, and fairness to the parties provide an affirmative justification for doing so. Lovell Mfg. v. Export–Import Bank of the United States, 843 F.2d 725 (3d Cir.1988); Growth Horizons, Inc. v. Delaware County, 983 F.2d 1277 (3d Cir.1993). Where the original federal jurisdiction claim is proceeding to trial, however, such considerations will normally counsel an exercise of district court jurisdiction over state claims based on the same nucleus of operative facts unless the district court can point to some substantial countervailing consideration. This is the teaching of our opinion in Sparks v. Hershey, 661 F.2d 30 (3d Cir.1981), where the complaint asserted a civil rights claim under § 1983, a state wrongful death claim, and a state survival act claim, all based on the same jailhouse suicide. We there observed:

[25. The circuits are split on the issue of whether § 1367(c) indeed codified without alteration the *Gibbs* standards of judicial discretion to decline to exercise supplemental jurisdiction, or by its express terms narrowed the scope of that discretion. The issue is discussed supra p. ___.]

We do not hold that where there is a common nucleus of operative facts, state claims must always be appended to the federal claim; but where, as here, the district court does not set forth a persuasive, reasoned elaboration for dismissing the state claims, we are inclined to believe that the dictates of "judicial economy, convenience, fairness to the parties, and comity" ... are better served by recognizing pendent jurisdiction. This is especially true where it is desirable to avoid the possibility of duplicating the recovery of damages. Here it is preferable for a single fact finder, under proper instruction from the court, to consider the varying elements of damages recoverable under the federal § 1983 claim and the state wrongful death and survival actions.... We will therefore reverse the district court's order dismissing the pending state claims and direct that court to exercise jurisdiction over them.

Sparks, 661 F.2d, at 33–34 (citations omitted).

Plaintiffs do not suggest that subparagraphs (1), (3), or (4) of § 1367(c) are applicable here. They do maintain that their state claims substantially predominate over their federal claims and, accordingly, that this case falls within subparagraph (2). The district court is in a better position than we to pass upon this contention. Moreover, even if § 1367(c) does not authorize a refusal to hear the state claims based on the current record, it might provide that authority at some later stage in the proceeding. Accordingly, the following observations concerning § 1367(c)(2) are offered solely by way of guidance and are not intended to foreclose the district court from hereafter exercising its discretion under § 1367(c) upon appropriate application.

As we have noted, the "substantially predominates" standard of § 1367(c)(2) comes from *Gibbs*. It is important to recognize that this standard was fashioned as a limited exception to the operation of the doctrine of pendent jurisdiction—a doctrine that seeks to promote judicial economy, convenience, and fairness to litigants by litigating in one case all claims that arise out of the same nucleus of operative fact. When a district court exercises its discretion not to hear state claims under § 1367(c)(2), the advantages of a single suit are lost. For that reason, § 1367(c)(2)'s authority should be invoked only where there is an important countervailing interest to be served by relegating state claims to the state court. This will normally be the case only where "a state claim constitutes the real body of a case, to which the federal claim is only an appendage," *Gibbs*, 383 U.S., at 727—only where permitting litigation of all claims in the district court can accurately be described as allowing a federal tail to wag what is in substance a state dog.

Given the origin of the "substantially predominate" standard, a district court's analysis under § 1367(c)(2) should track the Supreme Court's explication of that standard in *Gibbs*. We do not understand plaintiffs to suggest that there is a substantial quantity of evidence supporting their state claims that would not be relevant to the federal claims that the defendants, acting under color of state law, conspired to violate plaintiffs' constitutional rights by assaulting, wrongfully arresting, and maliciously prosecuting them. Thus, in the terminology of *Gibbs*, the state issues would not appear to "substantially predominate ... in terms of proof." 383 U.S., at 726. Nor would they appear to "substantially predominate ... in terms of ... the comprehensiveness of the remedy sought." Id. The remedy sought based on the state claims is the same remedy sought based on the federal claims—damages for the same set of injuries to the plaintiffs. As we observed in *Sparks*, 661 F.2d, at 33–34, the difficulty of avoiding duplicative recoveries is a factor tending to weigh against litigating related federal and state claims in different fora.

This leaves the issue of whether the state claims can be said to "substantially predominate ... in terms of ... the scope of the issues raised." Id. It is true that the state claims here outnumber the federal claims. The "substantially predominate" standard, however, is not satisfied simply by a numerical count of the state and federal claims the plaintiff has chosen to assert on the basis of the same set of facts. An analysis more sensitive to the relevant interests is required.

While federal constitutional tort law under § 1983 derives much of its content from the general common law of torts, plaintiffs' civil rights claims based on the alleged assault, arrest, and prosecution are nevertheless governed exclusively by federal law. Heck v. Humphrey, 512 U.S. 477, 483–84 (1994). While the claims based upon the arrest and the prosecution may require an inquiry into whether the defendants had probable cause to believe a crime had been committed and this may in part require some reference to the state criminal law, the probable cause issue and the other issues raised by these claims are nevertheless issues of federal law and concern. E.g. id.; Rose v. Bartle, 871 F.2d 331 (3d Cir.1989); Lee v. Mihalich, 847 F.2d 66 (3d Cir.1988); Losch v. Borough of Parkesburg, 736 F.2d 903 (3d Cir.1984).

There are, to be sure, a complementary set of state law issues arising out of the state claims based on the alleged assault, arrest, and prosecution. But these state issues do not appear from our vantage point to substantially predominate over the comparable but distinct federal issues. Plaintiffs do not suggest that these state issues are more important, more complex, more time consuming to resolve, or in any other way more significant than their federal counterparts. The only other state issues are those which may arise from the plaintiffs' negligence claims against the municipal defendants and the DeBartolo defendants. The dimensions of those claims are not clear at this stage of the case, but it seems unlikely to us that they will cause the state issues to "substantially predominate" within the meaning of § 1367(c)(2). If the factual allegations of the complaint are accepted at face value, as we are required to do at this point, this case involves several substantial claims that the plaintiffs' constitutional rights have been infringed. In such circumstances, we believe it will be the rare case, at least, where the addition of straightforward negligence claims based on the same facts as the constitutional claims will cause the state issues to substantially predominate.

In short, while we do not foreclose the parties from hereafter arguing, and the district court from hereafter considering, the issue posed by § 1367(c)(2), we think it unlikely that either will be able to point to a countervailing interest that would justify bifurcating this case into a federal and a state suit that will essentially duplicate each other.

SUMMARY AND CONCLUSION

The district court had subject matter jurisdiction over the § 1983 claim and supplemental jurisdiction over the other claims, which arose out of the same incidents and addressed the same course of conduct by the defendants; therefore, the federal and nonfederal claims were not "separate and independent", and the district court had no authority under § 1441(c) to remand either part or all of the case.

Accordingly, the petition for a writ of mandamus is granted.[26]

———

Breuer v. Jim's Concrete of Brevard, Inc.

Supreme Court of the United States, 2003.
538 U.S. 691, 123 S.Ct. 1882, 155 L.Ed.2d 923.

■ JUSTICE SOUTER delivered the opinion of the Court.

The question is whether the provision of the Fair Labor Standards Act of 1938 (FLSA or Act), that suit under the Act "may be maintained . . . in

---

[26. Congress amended § 1441(c) in 1990 and again in 2011. The version of § 1441(c) discussed in *Borough of West Mifflin* (the 1990 version) was declared to be unconstitutional in Salei v. Boardwalk Regency Corp., 913 F.Supp. 993 (E.D.Mich.1996), insofar as it purported to authorize the removal to federal court of state-law claims between nondiverse parties solely because those claims were joined to a "separate and independent" federal-law claim. The court instead construed § 1441(a) as permitting the constructive severance of a federal-law claim that has been joined in state litigation to a separate and independent state-law claim, so that the federal-law claim may be removed to federal court on its own without any purported assertion of federal jurisdiction over the state-law claim. The court did not address the considerable administrative problems that would arise were a defendant indeed to attempt to remove only part of a civil action pending in a state court.

Given the well-established principle that the limited jurisdiction of the federal courts does not divest them of the jurisdiction to determine their jurisdiction, see Chapter VIII, infra p. 440 et seq., the better view is that Congress may constitutionally authorize the removal of the entire case under § 1441(c), subject to the constitutional obligation (rather than the merely discretionary prerogative articulated in the text of present § 1441(c)) promptly to remand to state court any claims that are indeed separate and independent from those claims that are within the original jurisdiction of the district court. This allows the severance of claims subject to federal jurisdiction from those that are not to occur in an orderly fashion, and avoids the possibility of the conflicting exercise of jurisdiction over different parts of the same putative case by preserving the current law of § 1446(d), which cuts off any power of the state court to act with respect to a removed case—even when the case has been removed improperly or without any basis for federal jurisdiction—until a remand order has been issued by the federal court to which the case has been removed. This is the approach adopted by the ALI's proposed new § 1441(c). See ALI Judicial Code Project, § 1441(c); id., Commentary at 372–378. Compare the 2011 amendment of § 1441(c) at p. 328, supra. Is this amendment consistent with the ALI's proposal?]

any Federal or State court of competent jurisdiction," 52 Stat. 1069, as amended, 29 U.S.C. § 216(b), bars removal of a suit from state to federal court. We hold there is no bar.

I

Petitioner, Phillip T. Breuer, sued respondent, his former employer, Jim's Concrete of Brevard, Inc., in a state court of Florida for unpaid wages, liquidated damages, prejudgment interest, and attorney's fees. Section 216(b) provides not only that an employer who violates its minimum wage and overtime provisions is liable to an employee, but that "[a]n action to recover the liability prescribed . . . may be maintained against any employer (including a public agency) in any Federal or State court of competent jurisdiction."

Jim's Concrete removed the case to the United States District Court for the Middle District of Florida under 28 U.S.C. § 1441(a), which reads that "[e]xcept as otherwise expressly provided by Act of Congress, any civil action brought in a State court of which the district courts of the United States have original jurisdiction, may be removed by the defendant or the defendants, to the district court of the United States for the district and division embracing the place where such action is pending." Breuer sought an order remanding the case to state court, arguing that removal was improper owing to the FLSA's provision that an action "may be maintained" in any state court, a provision that Breuer put forward as an express exception to the general authorization of removal under § 1441(a). Though the District Court denied Breuer's motion, it certified the issue for interlocutory appeal under § 1292(b). The Eleventh Circuit affirmed, saying that Congress had expressly barred removal in "direct, unequivocal language" in other statutes, 292 F.3d 1308, 1310 (2002), but was not comparably prohibitory in § 216(b). The Eleventh Circuit thus joined the First, see Cosme Nieves v. Deshler, 786 F.2d 445 (1986), but placed itself at odds with the Eighth, see Johnson v. Butler Bros., 162 F.2d 87 (1947) (denying removability under FLSA). We granted certiorari to resolve the conflict, 537 U.S. 1099 (2003) and now affirm.

II

A

There is no question that Breuer could have begun his action in the District Court. The FLSA provides that an action "may be maintained . . . in any Federal or State court of competent jurisdiction," § 216(b), and the district courts would in any event have original jurisdiction over FLSA claims under 28 U.S.C. § 1331, as "arising under the Constitution, laws, or treaties of the United States," and § 1337(a), as "arising under any Act of Congress regulating commerce." Removal of FLSA actions is thus prohibited under § 1441(a) only if Congress expressly provided as much.

Nothing on the face of 29 U.S.C. § 216(b) looks like an express prohibition of removal, there being no mention of removal, let alone of prohibition. While § 216(b) provides that an action "may be maintained

... in any ... State court of competent jurisdiction," the word "maintain" enjoys a breadth of meaning that leaves its bearing on removal ambiguous at best. "To maintain an action" may mean "to continue" to litigate, as opposed to "commence" an action.[27] Black's Law Dictionary 1143 (3d ed.1933). But "maintain" in reference to a legal action is often read as "bring" or "file" ; "[t]o maintain an action or suit may mean to commence or institute it; the term imports the existence of a cause of action." Ibid.; see 1A J. Moore et al., Moore's Federal Practice ¶ 0.167[5], p. 472 (2d ed.1996) (calling the " 'may be maintained' " language an "ambiguous phrase" and "certainly not an express provision against removal within the meaning of § 1441"); 14C C. Wright, A. Miller, & E. Cooper, Federal Practice and Procedure § 3729, p. 235 (1998)(referring to "use of the ambiguous term 'maintain' in the statute"). The most, then, that Breuer can claim simply from the use of the term "maintain" is that any text, even when ambiguous, that might be read as inconsistent with removal is an "express" prohibiting provision under the statute. But if an ambiguous term like "maintain" qualified as an express provision for purposes of 28 U.S.C. § 1441(a), then the requirement of an "expres[s] provi[sion]" would call for nothing more than a "provision," pure and simple, leaving the word "expressly" with no consequence whatever. "[E]xpres[s] provi[sion]" must mean something more than any verbal hook for an argument.

The need to take the express exception requirement seriously is underscored by examples of indisputable prohibitions of removal in a number of other statutes. Section 1445, for example, provides that

> "(a) A civil action in any State court against a railroad or its receivers or trustees ... may not be removed to any district court of the United States.
>
> "(b) A civil action in any State court against a carrier or its receivers or trustees to recover damages for delay, loss, or injury of shipments ... may not be removed to any district court of the United States unless the matter in controversy exceeds $10,000, exclusive of interest and costs.
>
> "(c) A civil action in any State court arising under the workmen's compensation laws of such State may not be removed to any district court of the United States.

---

27. Actually, there is reason to think that this sense of "maintain" was intended. Under the FLSA, the Secretary of Labor may file a suit on behalf of an employee to recover unpaid wages or overtime compensation, and when the Secretary files such a suit, an employee's right to bring a comparable action terminates, see, e.g., 29 U.S.C. § 216(c). Congressional reports suggest that although an employee may no longer initiate a new action once the Secretary has sued, an employee may continue to litigate, *i.e.,* "maintain," an action already pending. See H.R. Conf. Rep. No. 327, 87th Cong., 1st Sess., p. 20 (1961) (filing of the Secretary's complaint would "not, however, operate to terminate any employee's right to maintain such a private suit to which he had become a party plaintiff before the Secretary's action"); S.Rep. No. 145, 87th Cong., 1st Sess., p. 39 (1961) (Secretary's filing of complaint "terminates the rights of individuals to later file suit"); cf. Smallwood v. Gallardo, 275 U.S. 56, 61 (1927) ("To maintain a suit is to uphold, continue on foot and keep from collapse a suit already begun"). Seen in this light, Congress's use of the term "maintain" is easy to understand, carrying no implication for removal.

"(d) A civil action in any State court arising under ... the Violence Against Women Act of 1994 may not be removed to any district court of the United States."

See also 15 U.S.C. § 77v(a) ("[N]o case arising under [the Securities Act of 1933] and brought in any State court of competent jurisdiction shall be removed to any court of the United States"); § 1719 ("No case arising under [the Interstate Land Sales Full Disclosure Act] and brought in any State court of competent jurisdiction shall be removed to any court of the United States, except where the United States or any officer or employee of the United States in his official capacity is a party"); § 3612 ("No case arising under [the Condominium and Cooperative Abuse Relief Act of 1980] and brought in any State court of competent jurisdiction shall be removed to any court of the United States, except where any officer or employee of the United States in his official capacity is a party"). When Congress has "wished to give plaintiffs an absolute choice of forum, it has shown itself capable of doing so in unmistakable terms." *Cosme Nieves,* 786 F.2d, at 451. It has not done so here.

B

None of Breuer's refinements on his basic argument from the term "maintain" puts him in a stronger position. He goes on to say, for example, that interpretation does not stop at the dictionary, and he argues that the statutory phrase "may be maintained" shows up as sufficiently prohibitory once it is coupled with a federal policy of construing removal jurisdiction narrowly. Breuer relies heavily on our statement in Shamrock Oil & Gas Corp. v. Sheets, 313 U.S. 100 (1941), that "the policy of the successive acts of Congress regulating the jurisdiction of federal courts is one calling for the strict construction of [removal legislation].... 'Due regard for the rightful independence of state governments, which should actuate federal courts, requires that they scrupulously confine their own jurisdiction to the precise limits ... the statute has defined.' " Id., at 108–109 (quoting Healy v. Ratta, 292 U.S. 263, 270 (1934)). But whatever apparent force this argument might have claimed when *Shamrock* was handed down has been qualified by later statutory development. At the time that case was decided, § 1441 provided simply that any action within original federal subject-matter jurisdiction could be removed. Fourteen years later, however, it was amended into its present form, requiring any exception to the general removability rule to be express. See Act of June 25, 1948, § 1441(a), 62 Stat. 937 (authorizing removal over civil suits within the district courts' original jurisdiction "[e]xcept as otherwise expressly provided by Act of Congress"); see also 28 U.S.C. § 1441 (historical and revision notes). Since 1948, therefore, there has been no question that whenever the subject matter of an action qualifies it for removal, the burden is on a plaintiff to find an express exception. As *Shamrock* itself said, "the language of the Act ... evidence[s] the Congressional purpose," 313 U.S., at 108, and congressional insistence on express exception is hardly satisfied by the malleability of the term "maintain" in the text Breuer relies upon.

Nor does it do Breuer any good to emphasize a sense of "maintain" as implying continuation of an action to final judgment, so as to give a plaintiff who began an action the statutory right under 29 U.S.C. § 216(b) to see it through. We may concede that it does, and the concession leaves the term "maintain" just as ambiguous as ever on the issue before us. The right to maintain an action may indeed be a right to fight to the finish, but removal does nothing to defeat that right; far from concluding a case before final judgment, removal just transfers it from one forum to another. As between a state and a federal forum, the statute seems to betray an indifference, with its provision merely for maintaining action "in any Federal or State Court." Ibid.

But even if the text of § 216(b) were not itself reason enough to doubt that the provision conveys any right to remain in the original forum, the implication of Breuer's position would certainly raise misgivings about his point. For if the phrase "[a]n action ... may be maintained" meant that a plaintiff could insist on keeping an FLSA case wherever he filed it in the first place, it would seem that an FLSA case brought in a federal district court could never be transferred to a different one over the plaintiff's objection, a result that would plainly clash with the provision for change of venue, 28 U.S.C. § 1404(a) ("For the convenience of parties and witnesses, in the interest of justice, a district court may transfer any civil action to any other district or division where it might have been brought").

It is, finally, a like concern about consequences that leaves us with fatal reservations about Breuer's pragmatic appeal that many claims under the FLSA are for such small amounts that removal to a sometimes distant federal court may make it less convenient and more expensive for employees to vindicate their rights effectively. This may often be true, but even if its truth somehow justified winking at the ambiguity of the term "maintain," the implications would keep us from going Breuer's way. A number of other statutes incorporate or use the same language as § 216(b), see 29 U.S.C. § 626(b)(providing that the Age Discrimination in Employment Act of 1967 "shall be enforced in accordance with the powers, remedies, and procedures provided in" § 216(b) and other sections of the FLSA); § 2005(c)(2) ("An action to recover the liability prescribed [under the Employee Polygraph Protection Act of 1988] in paragraph (1) may be maintained against the employer in any Federal or State court of competent jurisdiction"); § 2617(a)(2)("An action to recover the damages or equitable relief [under the Family and Medical Leave Act of 1993] prescribed in paragraph (1) may be maintained against any employer (including a public agency) in any Federal or State court of competent jurisdiction by any one or more employees"). Breuer, then, cannot have a removal exception for the FLSA without entailing exceptions for other statutory actions, to the point that it becomes just too hard to believe that a right to "maintain" an action was ever meant to displace the right to remove.[28]

---

28.   Breuer points to two nonjudicial authorities that do nothing to assuage our skepticism. He calls our attention to the position taken by the Administrator of the Wage and Hour Division, United States Department of Labor, in an amicus brief filed before the Eighth

III

Breuer's case was properly removed under 28 U.S.C. § 1441, and the judgment of the Eleventh Circuit is affirmed.

It is so ordered.

Dole Food Company v. Patrickson

Supreme Court of the United States, 2003.
538 U.S. 468, 123 S.Ct. 1655, 155 L.Ed.2d 643.

■ Justice Kennedy delivered the opinion of the Court.

Foreign states may invoke certain rights and immunities in litigation under the Foreign Sovereign Immunities Act of 1976 (FSIA or Act), Pub.L. 94–583, 90 Stat. 2891. Some of the Act's provisions also may be invoked by a corporate entity that is an "instrumentality" of a foreign state as defined by the Act. Republic of Argentina v. Weltover, Inc., 504 U.S. 607, 611 (1992); Verlinden B.V. v. Central Bank of Nigeria, 461 U.S. 480, 488 (1983). The corporate entities in this action claim instrumentality status to invoke the Act's provisions allowing removal of state-court actions to federal court. As the action comes to us, it presents two questions. The first is whether a corporate subsidiary can claim instrumentality status where the foreign state does not own a majority of its shares but does own a majority of the shares of a corporate parent one or more tiers above the subsidiary. The second question is whether a corporation's instrumentality status is defined as of the time an alleged tort or other actionable wrong occurred or, on the other hand, at the time suit is filed. We granted certiorari, 536 U.S. 956 (2002).

I

The underlying action was filed in a state court in Hawaii in 1997 against Dole Food Company and other companies (Dole petitioners). Plaintiffs in the action were a group of farm workers from Costa Rica, Ecuador, Guatemala, and Panama who alleged injury from exposure to dibromochloropropane, a chemical used as an agricultural pesticide in their home countries. The Dole petitioners impleaded petitioners Dead Sea Bromine

---

Circuit in Johnson v. Butler Bros., 162 F.2d 87 (1947), arguing that the text of the FLSA and the policies motivating its passage demonstrate that FLSA actions may not be removed to federal court. But this brief is not persuasive authority. The Secretary has no responsibility for applying the removal statute and no particular authority to interpret it; the Secretary's opinion cannot make up for the absence of express statutory language. Breuer also points to a Senate Report accompanying the 1958 enactment of 28 U.S.C. § 1445, a provision barring removal of workers' compensation actions under state law. Referring to actions brought under the FLSA, the report states "[i]f filed in the State courts the law prohibits removal to the Federal court." S.Rep. No. 1830, 85th Cong., 2d Sess., p. 9 (1958). But a stray comment in a congressional report stands a long way from an express statutory provision.

Co., Ltd., and Bromine Compounds, Ltd. (collectively, the Dead Sea Companies). The merits of the suit are not before us.

The Dole petitioners removed the action to the United States District Court for the District of Hawaii under 28 U.S.C. § 1441(a), arguing that the federal common law of foreign relations provided federal-question jurisdiction under § 1331. The District Court agreed there was federal subject-matter jurisdiction under the federal common law of foreign relations but, nevertheless, dismissed the case on grounds of forum non conveniens.

The Dead Sea Companies removed under a separate theory. They claimed to be instrumentalities of a foreign state as defined by the FSIA, entitling them to removal under § 1441(d). The District Court held that the Dead Sea Companies are not instrumentalities of a foreign state for purposes of the FSIA and are not entitled to removal on that basis. Civ. No. 97–01516HG (D.Haw., Sept. 9, 1998).

The Court of Appeals reversed. Addressing the ground relied on by the Dole petitioners, it held removal could not rest on the federal common law of foreign relations. 251 F.3d 795, 800 (CA9 2001). In this Court the Dole petitioners did not seek review of that portion of the Court of Appeals' ruling, and we do not address it. Accordingly, the writ of certiorari in No. 01–593 is dismissed.

The Court of Appeals also reversed the order allowing removal at the instance of the Dead Sea Companies, who alleged they were instrumentalities of the State of Israel. The Court of Appeals noted, but declined to answer, the question whether status as an instrumentality of a foreign state is assessed at the time of the alleged wrongdoing or at the time suit is filed. It went on to hold that the Dead Sea Companies, even at the earlier date, were not instrumentalities of Israel because they did not meet the Act's definition of instrumentality.

In order to prevail here, the Dead Sea Companies must show both that instrumentality status is determined as of the time the alleged tort occurred and that they can claim instrumentality status even though they were but subsidiaries of a parent owned by the State of Israel. We address each question in turn. In No. 01–594, the case in which the Dead Sea Companies are petitioners, we now affirm.

II

A

Title 28 U.S.C. § 1441(d) governs removal of actions against foreign states. It provides that "[a]ny civil action brought in a State court against a foreign state as defined in [28 U.S.C. § 1603(a)] may be removed by the foreign state to the district court of the United States for the district and division embracing the place where such action is pending." See also 28 U.S.C. § 1330 (governing original jurisdiction). Section 1603(a), part of the FSIA, defines "foreign state" to include an "agency or instrumentality of a foreign state." "[A]gency or instrumentality of a foreign state" is defined, in turn, as:

"[A]ny entity—

"(1) which is a separate legal person, corporate or otherwise, and

"(2) which is an organ of a foreign state or political subdivision thereof, or a majority of whose shares or other ownership interest is owned by a foreign state or political subdivision thereof, and

"(3) which is neither a citizen of a State of the United States ... nor created under the laws of any third country." § 1603(b).

B

The Court of Appeals resolved the question of the FSIA's applicability by holding that a subsidiary of an instrumentality is not itself entitled to instrumentality status. Its holding was correct.

The State of Israel did not have direct ownership of shares in either of the Dead Sea Companies at any time pertinent to this suit. Rather, these companies were, at various times, separated from the State of Israel by one or more intermediate corporate tiers. For example, from 1984–1985, Israel wholly owned a company called Israeli Chemicals, Ltd.; which owned a majority of shares in another company called Dead Sea Works, Ltd.; which owned a majority of shares in Dead Sea Bromine Co., Ltd.; which owned a majority of shares in Bromine Compounds, Ltd.

The Dead Sea Companies, as indirect subsidiaries of the State of Israel, were not instrumentalities of Israel under the FSIA at any time. Those companies cannot come within the statutory language which grants status as an instrumentality of a foreign state to an entity a "majority of whose shares or other ownership interest is owned by a foreign state or political subdivision thereof." § 1603(b)(2). We hold that only direct ownership of a majority of shares by the foreign state satisfies the statutory requirement.

Section 1603(b)(2) speaks of ownership. The Dead Sea Companies urge us to ignore corporate formalities and use the colloquial sense of that term. They ask whether, in common parlance, Israel would be said to own the Dead Sea Companies. We reject this analysis. In issues of corporate law structure often matters. It is evident from the Act's text that Congress was aware of settled principles of corporate law and legislated within that context. The language of § 1603(b)(2) refers to ownership of "shares," showing that Congress intended statutory coverage to turn on formal corporate ownership. Likewise, § 1603(b)(1), another component of the definition of instrumentality, refers to a "separate legal person, corporate or otherwise." In light of these indicia that Congress had corporate formalities in mind, we assess whether Israel owned shares in the Dead Sea Companies as a matter of corporate law, irrespective of whether Israel could be said to have owned the Dead Sea Companies in everyday parlance.

A basic tenet of American corporate law is that the corporation and its shareholders are distinct entities. See, e.g., First Nat. City Bank v. Banco

Para El Comercio Exterior de Cuba, 462 U.S. 611, 625 (1983) ("Separate legal personality has been described as 'an almost indispensable aspect of the public corporation'"); Burnet v. Clark, 287 U.S. 410, 415 (1932) ("A corporation and its stockholders are generally to be treated as separate entities"). An individual shareholder, by virtue of his ownership of shares, does not own the corporation's assets and, as a result, does not own subsidiary corporations in which the corporation holds an interest. See 1 Fletcher Cyclopedia of the Law of Private Corporations § 31 (rev. ed.1999). A corporate parent which owns the shares of a subsidiary does not, for that reason alone, own or have legal title to the assets of the subsidiary; and, it follows with even greater force, the parent does not own or have legal title to the subsidiaries of the subsidiary. See id., § 31, at 514 ("The properties of two corporations are distinct, though the same shareholders own or control both. A holding corporation does not own the subsidiary's property"). The fact that the shareholder is a foreign state does not change the analysis. See *First Nat. City Bank,* supra, at 626–627 ("[G]overnment instrumentalities established as juridical entities distinct and independent from their sovereign should normally be treated as such").

Applying these principles, it follows that Israel did not own a majority of shares in the Dead Sea Companies. The State of Israel owned a majority of shares, at various times, in companies one or more corporate tiers above the Dead Sea Companies, but at no time did Israel own a majority of shares in the Dead Sea Companies. Those companies were subsidiaries of other corporations.

The veil separating corporations and their shareholders may be pierced in some circumstances, and the Dead Sea Companies essentially urge us to interpret the FSIA as piercing the veil in all cases. The doctrine of piercing the corporate veil, however, is the rare exception, applied in the case of fraud or certain other exceptional circumstances, see, e.g., *Burnet,* supra, at 415; 1 Fletcher, supra, §§ 41 to 41.20, and usually determined on a case-by-case basis. The Dead Sea Companies have referred us to no authority for extending the doctrine so far that, as a categorical matter, all subsidiaries are deemed to be the same as the parent corporation. The text of the FSIA gives no indication that Congress intended us to depart from the general rules regarding corporate formalities.

Where Congress intends to refer to ownership in other than the formal sense, it knows how to do so. Various federal statutes refer to "direct and indirect ownership." See, e.g., 5 U.S.C. § 8477(a)(4)(G)(iii) (referring to an interest "owned directly or indirectly"); 12 U.S.C. § 84(c)(5) (referring to "any corporation wholly owned directly or indirectly by the United States"); 15 U.S.C. § 79b(a)(8)(A) (referring to securities "which are directly or indirectly owned, controlled, or held with power to vote"); § 1802(3) ("The term 'newspaper owner' means any person who owns or controls directly, or indirectly through separate or subsidiary corporations, one or more newspaper publications"). The absence of this language in 28 U.S.C. § 1603(b) instructs us that Congress did not intend to disregard structural ownership rules.

The FSIA's definition of instrumentality refers to a foreign state's majority ownership of "shares or other ownership interest." § 1603(b)(2). The Dead Sea Companies would have us read "other ownership interest" to include a state's "interest" in its instrumentality's subsidiary. The better reading of the text, in our view, does not support this argument. The words "other ownership interest," when following the word "shares," should be interpreted to refer to a type of interest other than ownership of stock. The statute had to be written for the contingency of ownership forms in other countries, or even in this country, that depart from conventional corporate structures. The statutory phrase "other ownership interest" is best understood to accomplish this objective. Reading the term to refer to a state's interest in entities lower on the corporate ladder would make the specific reference to "shares" redundant. Absent a statutory text or structure that requires us to depart from normal rules of construction, we should not construe the statute in a manner that is strained and, at the same time, would render a statutory term superfluous. See Mertens v. Hewitt Associates, 508 U.S. 248, 258 (1993) ("We will not read the statute to render the modifier superfluous"); United States v. Nordic Village, Inc., 503 U.S. 30, 36 (1992) (declining to adopt a construction that would violate the "settled rule that a statute must, if possible, be construed in such fashion that every word has some operative effect").

The Dead Sea Companies say that the State of Israel exercised considerable control over their operations, notwithstanding Israel's indirect relationship to those companies. They appear to think that, in determining instrumentality status under the Act, control may be substituted for an ownership interest. Control and ownership, however, are distinct concepts. See, e.g., United States v. Bestfoods, 524 U.S. 51, 64–65 (1998) (distinguishing between "operation" and "ownership" of a subsidiary's assets for purposes of Comprehensive Environmental Response, Compensation, and Liability Act of 1980 liability). The terms of § 1603(b)(2) are explicit and straightforward. Majority ownership by a foreign state, not control, is the benchmark of instrumentality status. We need not delve into Israeli law or examine the extent of Israel's involvement in the Dead Sea Companies' operations. Even if Israel exerted the control the Dead Sea Companies describe, that would not give Israel a "majority of [the companies'] shares or other ownership interest." The statutory language will not support a control test that mandates inquiry in every case into the past details of a foreign nation's relation to a corporate entity in which it does not own a majority of the shares.

The better rule is the one supported by the statutory text and elementary principles of corporate law. A corporation is an instrumentality of a foreign state under the FSIA only if the foreign state itself owns a majority of the corporation's shares.

We now turn to the second question before us, which provides an alternative reason for affirming the Court of Appeals. See Woods v. Interstate Realty Co., 337 U.S. 535, 537 (1949).

C

To be entitled to removal under § 1441(d), the Dead Sea Companies must show that they are entities "a majority of whose shares or other ownership interest is owned by a foreign state." § 1603(b)(2). We think the plain text of this provision, because it is expressed in the present tense, requires that instrumentality status be determined at the time suit is filed.

Construing § 1603(b) so that the present tense has real significance is consistent with the "longstanding principle that 'the jurisdiction of the Court depends upon the state of things at the time of the action brought.'" Keene Corp. v. United States, 508 U.S. 200, 207 (1993) (quoting Mollan v. Torrance, 9 Wheat. [22 U.S.] 537, 539 (1824)). It is well settled, for example, that federal-diversity jurisdiction depends on the citizenship of the parties at the time suit is filed. See, e.g., Anderson v. Watt, 138 U.S. 694, 702–703 (1891) ("And the [jurisdictional] inquiry is determined by the condition of the parties at the commencement of the suit"); see also Minneapolis & St. Louis R. Co. v. Peoria & Pekin Union R. Co., 270 U.S. 580, 586 (1926) ("The jurisdiction of the lower court depends upon the state of things existing at the time the suit was brought"). The Dead Sea Companies do not dispute that the time suit is filed is determinative under § 1332(a)(4), which provides for suits between "a foreign state, defined in section 1603(a) ..., as plaintiff and citizens of a State or of different States." It would be anomalous to read § 1441(d)'s words, "foreign state as defined in section 1603(a)," differently.

The Dead Sea Companies urge us to administer the FSIA like other status-based immunities, such as the qualified immunity accorded a state actor, that are based on the status of an officer at the time of the conduct giving rise to the suit. We think its comparison is inapt. Our cases applying those immunities do not involve the interpretation of a statute. See, e.g., Spalding v. Vilas, 161 U.S. 483, 493–499 (1896) (basing a decision regarding official immunity on common law and considerations of "convenience and public policy"); Scheuer v. Rhodes, 416 U.S. 232, 239–242 (1974).

The reason for the official immunities in those cases does not apply here. The immunities for government officers prevent the threat of suit from "crippl[ing] the proper and effective administration of public affairs." *Spalding,* supra, at 498 (discussing immunity for executive officers); see also Pierson v. Ray, 386 U.S. 547, 554 (1967) (judicial immunity serves the public interest in judges who are "at liberty to exercise their functions with independence and without fear of consequences" (internal quotation marks omitted)). Foreign sovereign immunity, by contrast, is not meant to avoid chilling foreign states or their instrumentalities in the conduct of their business but to give foreign states and their instrumentalities some protection from the inconvenience of suit as a gesture of comity between the United States and other sovereigns. *Verlinden,* 461 U.S., at 486.

For the same reason, the Dead Sea Companies' reliance on Nixon v. Fitzgerald, 457 U.S. 731 (1982), is unavailing. There, we recognized that the President was immune from liability for official actions taken during his time in office, even against a suit filed when he was no longer serving in that capacity. The immunity served the same function that the other official immunities serve. See id., at 751 ("Because of the singular importance of the President's duties, diversion of his energies by concern with private lawsuits would raise unique risks to the effective functioning of government"). As noted above, immunity under the FSIA does not serve the same purpose.

The immunity recognized in *Nixon* was also based on a further rationale, one not applicable here: the constitutional separation of powers. See id., at 749 ("We consider this immunity a functionally mandated incident of the President's unique office, rooted in the constitutional tradition of the separation of powers and supported by our history"). That rationale is not implicated by the statutory immunity Congress created for actions such as the one before us.

Any relationship recognized under the FSIA between the Dead Sea Companies and Israel had been severed before suit was commenced. As a result, the Dead Sea Companies would not be entitled to instrumentality status even if their theory that instrumentality status could be conferred on a subsidiary were accepted.

* * *

For these reasons, we hold first that a foreign state must itself own a majority of the shares of a corporation if the corporation is to be deemed an instrumentality of the state under the provisions of the FSIA; and we hold second that instrumentality status is determined at the time of the filing of the complaint.

The judgment of the Court of Appeals in No. 01–594 is affirmed, and the writ of certiorari in No. 01–593 is dismissed.

It is so ordered.

■ JUSTICE BREYER, with whom JUSTICE O'CONNOR joins, concurring in part and dissenting in part.

I join Parts I, II–A, and II–C, and dissent only from Part II–B, of the Court's opinion. Unlike the majority, I believe that the statutory phrase "other ownership interest . . . owned by a foreign state," 28 U.S.C. § 1603(b)(2), covers a Foreign Nation's legal interest in a Corporate Subsidiary, where that interest consists of the Foreign Nation's ownership of a Corporate Parent that owns the shares of the Subsidiary.

. . . . .

The majority's "veil piercing" argument is beside the point. So is the majority's reiteration of the separateness of a corporation and its shareholders, a formal separateness that this statute explicitly sets aside. See 28 U.S.C. §§ 1603(a), (b) (acknowledging the separateness of a corporate entity but nevertheless deliberately conferring the "foreign state" status of the shareholder upon the corporation itself); H.R.Rep. No. 94–1487, p. 15 (1976), U.S.Code Cong. & Admin.News 1976, pp. 6604, 6613–6614 (same). See also Working Group of the American Bar Association, Reforming the Foreign Sovereign Immunities Act, 40 Colum. J. Transnat'l L. 489, 517–518 (2002) (hereinafter ABA Working Group) (FSIA rejects the "separate-entity" rule that courts had often applied to deny immunity to state-owned corporations).

Statutory interpretation is not a game of blind man's bluff. Judges are free to consider statutory language in light of a statute's basic purposes. And here, ... an examination of those purposes sheds considerable light. The statute itself makes clear that it seeks: (1) to provide a foreign-state defendant in a legal action the right to have its claim of a sovereign immunity bar decided by the "courts of the United States," i.e., the federal courts, 28 U.S.C. § 1604; see § 1441(d); and (2) to make certain that the merits of unbarred claims against foreign states, say, states engaging in commercial activities, see § 1605(a)(2), will be decided "in the same manner" as similar claims against "a private individual," § 1606; but (3) to guarantee a foreign state defending an unbarred claim certain protections, including a prohibition of punitive damages, the right to removal to federal court, a trial before a judge, and other procedural rights (related to service of process, venue, attachment, and execution of judgments). §§ 1330, 1391(f), 1441(d), 1606, 1608–1611. See Verlinden B.V. v. Central Bank of Nigeria, 461 U.S. 480, 497 (1983) ("Congress deliberately sought to channel cases against foreign sovereigns away from the state courts and into federal courts"); H.R.Rep. No. 94–1487, at 32, U.S.Code Cong. & Admin.News 1976, at pp. 6604, 6631 ("giv[ing] foreign states clear authority to remove to a Federal forum actions brought against them in the State courts" in light of "the potential sensitivity of actions against foreign states and the importance of developing a uniform body of law in this area"); id., at 13, U.S.Code Cong. & Admin.News 1976, at pp. 6604, 6611 ("Such broad jurisdiction in the Federal courts should be conducive to uniformity in decision, which is desirable since a disparate treatment of cases involving foreign governments may have adverse foreign relations consequences").

Most important for present purposes, the statute seeks to guarantee these protections to the foreign nation not only when it acts directly in its own name but also when it acts through separate legal entities, including corporations and other "organ[s]." 28 U.S.C. § 1603(b).

Given these purposes, what might lead Congress to grant protection to a Foreign Nation acting through a Corporate Parent but deny the same protection to the Foreign Nation acting through, for example, a wholly owned Corporate Subsidiary? The answer to this question is: In terms of the statute's purposes, *nothing at all* would lead Congress to make such a distinction.

.   .   .   .   .

Dodd v. Fawcett Publications, Inc.

United States Court of Appeals, Tenth Circuit, 1964.
329 F.2d 82.

■ Before PICKETT and LEWIS, CIRCUIT JUDGES, and KERR, DISTRICT JUDGE.

■ LEWIS, CIRCUIT JUDGE.

This appeal, taken pursuant to 28 U.S.C. § 1292(b), is from an interlocutory order of the district court denying plaintiff-appellant's motion to remand the cause to the Oklahoma state court. The dispositive question is whether the decision of the Oklahoma Supreme Court in Fawcett Publications, Inc. v. Morris, 377 P.2d 42, has made the joinder of the co-defendant Mid–Continent News Company fraudulent in law so as to now vest complete diversity jurisdiction in the federal court. The *Morris* case, the case at bar, and eleven other pending cases all arise from a single identical factual incident.

In March, 1958, Fawcett Publications, Inc., published in its magazine *True* an article entitled "The Pill That Can Kill Sports" wherein reference was made to the 1956 University of Oklahoma varsity football team. Alleging the article to be libelous per se, thirteen members of the Oklahoma team, each being a citizen of that state, filed separate actions for damages in the Oklahoma state court naming Fawcett, a foreign corporation, and Mid–Continent as co-defendants. Mid–Continent is a Delaware corporation with principal place of business located in Oklahoma City and is a distributor of *True* and other magazines. An attempt at that time by the co-defendants to remove the actions to federal court failed, it appearing that each plaintiff and the defendant Mid–Continent, since its principal place of business was at Oklahoma City, were citizens of Oklahoma, 28 U.S.C. § 1332(c), and that plaintiffs were each seeking a joint judgment against the co-defendants. The orders of remand were entered and the actions were severally returned to the jurisdiction of the state court.

The *Morris* case proceeded to trial before a state district court sitting with a jury. At the conclusion of the evidence the trial judge instructed the jury to return a verdict against Fawcett leaving only the amount of damages to be determined. The trial court also directed a verdict in favor of the co-defendant Mid–Continent. The jury returned a verdict for $75,000[29] in favor of plaintiff Morris and against defendant Fawcett. Both Fawcett and Morris appealed the judgment to the Oklahoma Supreme Court, Morris' appeal being limited to a claim of error in the trial judge's directed verdict in favor of Mid–Continent. The Oklahoma high court affirmed the judgment in all respects, 377 P.2d 42, and its judgment is now final as it affects Mid–Continent. It is against this background of the *Morris* case that the co-defendants in the case at bar bottomed their instant petition for removal and upon which, after pertinent inquiries made of counsel at a hearing, the federal district court based its denial of remand.

Plaintiff's counsel were also plaintiff's counsel in the *Morris* case. As indicated by ... colloquy between court and counsel occurring at the hearing on motion to remand, the court concluded that plaintiff Dodd's evidence affecting the liability of Mid–Continent would have the same legal

---

29. Morris was an alternate fullback on the 1956 team. Present plaintiff Dodd was the first-string quarterback.

substance as that given in the *Morris* case and that the non-liability of Mid–Continent had thus been judicially established to that extent. . . .

The determination of the non-liability of Mid–Continent made in the *Morris* case cannot be applied in the case at bar under either the doctrine of res judicata or estoppel, for, as plaintiff Dodd properly asserts, the cases lack identity of parties. In fact, the judgment in the *Morris* case, as such, is in no way binding upon the parties in this action. However, the law of Oklahoma as determined in the *Morris* case is binding upon the federal court not only in this case but in any diversity case. Erie R.R. v. Tompkins, 304 U.S. 64. And, although, as plaintiff Dodd again correctly contends, the opinion in *Morris* does not spell out the liability of a distributor of magazines containing libelous matter, nevertheless the case does determine that Mid–Continent was not liable under the evidence produced in that case. Whatever the liability of a magazine distributor may be in Oklahoma such liability is not established by evidence having only the legal substance contained in *Morris*. To such extent *Morris* is pertinent to and binding upon the federal court in the instant case and the trial court did not err in so holding.

In many cases, removability can be determined by the original pleadings and normally the statement of a cause of action against the resident defendant will suffice to prevent removal. But upon specific allegations of fraudulent joinder the court may pierce the pleadings, Chesapeake & O. Ry. v. Cockrell, 232 U.S. 146; Nunn v. Feltinton, 5 Cir., 294 F.2d 450; Morris v. E.I. DuPont De Nemours & Co., 8 Cir., 68 F.2d 788, consider the entire record, and determine the basis of joinder by any means available, McLeod v. Cities Serv. Gas Co., 10 Cir., 233 F.2d 242. The joinder of a resident defendant against whom no cause of action is stated is patent sham, Parks v. New York Times Co., 5 Cir., 308 F.2d 474, and though a cause of action be stated, the joinder is similarly fraudulent if in fact no cause of action exists, Lobato v. Pay Less Drug Stores, Inc., 10 Cir., 261 F.2d 406. This does not mean that the federal court will pre-try, as a matter of course, doubtful issues of fact to determine removability; the issue must be capable of summary determination and be proven with complete certainty. *McLeod v. Cities Serv. Gas Co.*, supra.

Applying these rules to the case at bar it seems clear that the trial court properly refused to remand. The Oklahoma Supreme Court has judicially determined that unrecited but specific proof occurring in the *Morris* case was insufficient to impose liability upon Mid–Continent. Without material addition that same proof appears with complete certainty to be the sole basis of present plaintiff's claim against the same defendant in a case having identical origin. Mid–Continent's non-liability is thus established as both a matter of fact and law, and its continued joinder serves only to frustrate federal jurisdiction. In such case the joinder is fraudulent.

Finally, appellant contends that to retain jurisdiction in the federal court is, in effect, "saying that this Appellant, or plaintiffs in companion cases, cannot *possibly* produce sufficient evidence on trial of the cases to establish liability against [Mid–Continent] . . . ." (Emphasis added.) This court is, of course, not concerned with possibilities that discord with the record. The trial court had the power to compel appellant to disclose his evidence affecting Mid–Continent's liability, see Berger v. Brannan, 10 Cir., 172 F.2d 241, cert. denied, 337 U.S. 941; Holcomb v. Aetna Life Insurance Co., 10 Cir., 255 F.2d 577, and we consider the legal effect of such evidence only.

The judgment is affirmed.[30]

Gentle v. Lamb–Weston, Inc.

United States District Court, District of Maine, 1969.
302 F.Supp. 161.

■ GIGNOUX, DISTRICT JUDGE.

This matter is before the Court on plaintiffs' motion for remand to the Aroostook County, Maine Superior Court. The pertinent facts may be briefly stated. On September 30, 1968, nine plaintiffs, all Maine citizens and potato farmers residing in Aroostook County, commenced an action for breach of contract in the Aroostook County Superior Court against Snow Flake Canning Co., a Maine corporation engaged in the canning and processing of various foods. Several months prior thereto, unbeknownst to plaintiffs' counsel, Snow Flake had merged with Lamb–Weston, Inc., an Oregon corporation, the latter surviving. Upon being appraised of this, plaintiffs' counsel brought the present action in the same court on December 23, 1968 naming Lamb–Weston as defendant. The second action seeks the same relief and differs only in that there are three additional plaintiffs, one of whom is George O. Tamblyn, an Oregon citizen. Shortly before the filing of the second action, Tamblyn, who was a law school classmate of an attorney in the law firm representing plaintiffs, took an assignment of

---

[30. Claims of fraudulent joinder are not uncommon but usually removal is denied. See Wright & Kane, Federal Courts § 31 (6th ed.2002).

An evidentiary hearing on whether joinder is fraudulent is ordinarily improper. The court must resolve all disputed questions of fact from the pleadings and affidavits in favor of plaintiff and then determine whether there could possibly be a valid claim under state law against the defendant in question. B., Inc. v. Miller Brewing Co., 663 F.2d 545 (5th Cir.1981). See also Carriere v. Sears, Roebuck & Co., 893 F.2d 98 (5th Cir.1990).

The removal of the suit by Pete Rose against the Commissioner of Baseball was based on a finding that the Cincinnati Reds and Major League Baseball were at most nominal parties and that their joinder was "fraudulent" in the sense in which that term is used in connection with removal. Rose v. Giamatti, 721 F.Supp. 906 (S.D.Ohio 1989). The decision is criticized in Note, Maintaining the Home Field Advantage: *Rose vs. Federal Court*, 10 Loy.Ent.L.J. 695 (1990).

See Blumenkopf, Pett & Metta, Fighting Fraudulent Joinder: Proving the Impossible and Preserving Your Corporate Client's Right to a Federal Forum, 24 Am.J. Trial Advocacy 297 (2000); Note, Reintroducing "Fraud" to the Doctrine of Fraudulent Joinder, 78 Va.L.Rev. 1377 (1992). See generally ALI, Judicial Code Project at 515–518 (Reporter's Note C: The "Voluntary/Involuntary" Rule and "Fraudulent Joinder," Part IV, "Fraudulent Joinder" Issues).]

1/100 of each plaintiff's claim.[31] It is undisputed that Tamblyn had no previous interest in the litigation and agreed to take the assignments at the request of, and as an accommodation to, his classmate.[32] The conceded purpose of the assignments was to defeat an anticipated removal to this Court by defendant under 28 U.S.C. § 1441(a) (1964) by destroying the complete diversity of citizenship required for federal jurisdiction under 28 U.S.C. § 1332(a)(1) (1964). See Hyde v. Ruble, 104 U.S. 407 (1882).[33] Nevertheless, on January 13, 1969 defendant removed the action to this Court, and on February 3, 1969 plaintiffs filed the pending motion for remand, on the ground that this Court lacks subject matter jurisdiction "in that George O. Tamblyn, plaintiff and Lamb–Weston, Inc., defendant, are both citizens of the State of Oregon...."

Through this cynical device, plaintiffs seek to benefit from whatever local prejudice a trial against a foreign corporation before an Aroostook County jury might afford them. The central issue[34] then is whether this Court is powerless to protect its jurisdiction and the constitutional (Art. III, § 2, cl. 1) and statutory (28 U.S.C. § 1332 (1964)) right of a defendant of diverse citizenship to have a federal forum free from the potentiality of local bias. The Court concludes that it is not.

Congress has provided that a federal district court shall not have jurisdiction of an action in which a party has been "improperly or collusive-

---

31. As a 1/100 assignee of these claims, Tamblyn stands to recover 1/100 of any net recovery in this case and will be liable, absent an adequate recovery, for the same proportion of any disbursements. In addition, he is to be compensated for any time expended by him at the rate of $20 per hour and is to be reimbursed for any out-of-pocket expenses he may incur. As consideration for the assignments, Tamblyn paid each assignor $1, or a total of $9.

32. As plaintiffs assert, it may be that Tamblyn was also motivated by the hope of making a quick and easy profit, since plaintiffs' claims are alleged to be worth a total of $300,000.

33. Plaintiffs' counsel have been unembarrassedly frank about their objective at every step. In their petition for remand, they "admit that the principal object of the bona fide assignment for a valuable consideration of 1/100th of all the causes of action herein sued upon to George O. Tamblyn was to prevent the invoking of federal diversity jurisdiction." With even greater candor, this admission is repeated in a letter from one of plaintiffs' attorneys to one of defendant's attorneys, quoted in part in plaintiffs' brief:

Again so that there can be no mistake, we have admitted both orally and in writing that George O. Tamblyn ... who practices law and resides in Portland, Oregon, has been brought into this case solely for the purposes of destroying diversity jurisdiction.

34. Another question briefed and argued by the parties is whether a partial assignment, otherwise valid under Maine law (see National Exchange Bank of Boston v. McLoon, 73 Me. 498, 504–505 (1882); Shiro v. Drew, 174 F.Supp. 495, 497, n. 2 (D.Me.1959); and see 11 M.R.S.A. § 2–210(2) (1964)), is void under these circumstances as violative of the Maine champerty statute, 17 M.R.S.A. § 801 (1964) which provides:

Whoever ... gives ... any valuable consideration ... with intent thereby to procure any account, note or other demand for the profit arising from its collection by a civil action ... shall be punished....

See Hinckley v. Giberson, 129 Me. 308, 151 A. 542 (1930). Although the question is not entirely free from doubt, the Court is satisfied that, despite the literal wording of the Maine statute, the assignments are not champertous since they do not promote additional litigation and since the assignee had no "improper intention." See Plummer v. Noble, 6 Me. 285, 288 (1830); *National Exchange Bank of Boston v. McLoon,* supra.

ly made or joined" for the purpose of creating federal jurisdiction. 28 U.S.C. § 1359 (1964). There is no similar statutory provision, however, barring collusive action to defeat federal jurisdiction. While conceding that remedial legislation is called for, plaintiffs say it is for Congress, and not the courts, to correct this evil, and that controlling authority has sanctioned the type of arrangement present in this case.

In support of their position plaintiffs place principal reliance on Provident Savings Life Assurance Society v. Ford, 114 U.S. 635 (1885) and Mecom v. Fitzsimmons Drilling Co., 284 U.S. 183 (1931). *Provident* was a case in which a judgment was assigned to plaintiff for the purpose of preventing removal from the state to the federal court. The Supreme Court affirmed the state court's refusal to grant removal, observing:

"[I]t, may, perhaps, be a good defence to an action in a state court to show that a colorable assignment has been made to deprive the United States court of jurisdiction; but, as before said, it would be a defence to the action, and not a ground of removing that cause into the federal court."

114 U.S., at 641. Accord, Oakley v. Goodnow, 118 U.S. 43 (1886); Leather Manufacturers' Nat. Bank v. Cooper, 120 U.S. 778 (1887); Carson v. Dunham, 121 U.S. 421 (1887).

In *Mecom* an administrator was selected for the sole purpose of defeating diversity jurisdiction. The Supreme Court there held that the administrator's motion to remand to the state court should have been granted, stating:

"[I]t is clear that the motive or purpose that actuated any or all of these parties in procuring a lawful and valid appointment is immaterial upon the question of identity or diversity of citizenship. To go behind the decree of the probate court would be collaterally to attack it, not for lack of jurisdiction of the subject-matter or absence of jurisdictional facts, but to inquire into purposes and motives of the parties before that court when, confessedly, they practiced no fraud upon it.... It has been uniformly held that, where there is a prima facie joint liability, averment and proof that resident and nonresident tortfeasors are jointly sued for the purpose of preventing removal does not amount to an allegation that the joinder was fraudulent, and will not justify a removal from the state court (citations omitted). The facts disclosed in this record fall far short of proof of actual fraud such as was held sufficient to justify removal in ... (citations omitted)."

284 U.S., at 189–190.

Plaintiffs assert that in light of the *Provident* line of cases and of *Mecom,* federal courts must unquestioningly honor the most colorable attempts to deprive them of their jurisdiction, at least until Congress provides otherwise. However, *Provident* and its progeny all involved assignments of entire claims, not partial assignments. As defendant aptly points out, "It is one thing to say that diversity may be destroyed by an assignment of the assignor's entire claim and quite another to say that diversity may be destroyed by the assignment of a mere one per cent of a claim." The Supreme Court has never spoken on the effectiveness of a partial assignment to destroy diversity. And a fractional assignment, where the assignor remains a party for the purpose of profiting from local prejudice, is manifestly less defensible. Nor is *Mecom* compelling authority for plaintiffs' position. That case involved, not a colorable assignment, but the appointment of an administrator for the purpose of defeating removal. The Court was quite obviously reluctant to permit a collateral attack on the lawful and valid decree of the state court which appointed the administrator. See Wright, Federal Courts 88 (1963). In Kramer v. Caribbean Mills, Inc., [394 U.S. 823 (1969)], the Supreme Court itself has recognized the distinction between cases of appointment and cases of assignment:

> "Cases involving representatives vary in several respects from those in which jurisdiction is based on assignments: (1) in the former situation, some representative must be appointed before suit can be brought, while in the latter the assignor normally is himself capable of suing in state court; (2) under state law, different kinds of guardians and administrators may possess discrete sorts of powers; and (3) all such representatives owe their appointment to the decree of a state court, rather than solely to an action of the parties. 394 U.S., at 827. See also Ferrara v. Philadelphia Laboratories, Inc., 272 F.Supp. 1000, 1015–1016 n. 7 (D.Vt.1967), aff'd mem., 393 F.2d 934 (2d Cir.1968)."

In assessing the present weight of Supreme Court precedent, it must be borne in mind that the Court has not spoken on the effectiveness of assignments to destroy diversity jurisdiction since 1887 and that it has never spoken on the effectiveness of partial assignments to destroy diversity. Moreover, in the years since 1887 the Court has condemned similar practices in a way which makes it clear that the federal courts should be alert to protect their jurisdiction against cleverly-designed maneuvers designed by ingenious counsel to defeat it. Thus, in Ex parte Nebraska, 209 U.S. 436 (1908), the Court refused to accept the appearance of the State of Nebraska as a party plaintiff and its allegation of an interest in the action as conclusive. Instead, the Court held that the federal circuit court properly refused to remand the case to the state court because, on an examination of the entire record, it was apparent that the State of Nebraska was a mere nominal party plaintiff with no substantial interest in the controversy. Likewise, in Wecker v. National Enameling and Stamping Co., 204 U.S. 176 (1907), the plaintiff, in a tort action, joined a co-defendant for the express purpose of destroying diversity. Since the sham was apparent (because the codefendant could not conceivably have been liable), the Supreme Court affirmed the circuit court's refusal to remand to the state court. The Court concludes its opinion with the following words of admonition, applicable here:

> "While the plaintiff, in good faith, may proceed in the state courts upon a cause of action which he alleges to be joint, *it is equally true that the Federal courts should not sanction devices intended to prevent a removal to a Federal court where one has that right, and should be*

equally vigilant to protect the right to proceed in the Federal court as to permit the state courts, in proper cases, to retain their own jurisdiction."

204 U.S., at 185–186 (emphasis added). Accord, Wilson v. Republic Iron & Steel Co., 257 U.S. 92 (1921).[35] See also Pullman Co. v. Jenkins, 305 U.S. 534, 541 (1939); Alabama Great Southern Railway Co. v. Thompson, 200 U.S. 206, 218 (1906); Updike v. West, 172 F.2d 663, 665 (10th Cir.), cert. denied, 337 U.S. 908 (1949).

This Court is aware that many,[36] though not all,[37] federal courts have sustained the use of assignments to defeat diversity. On the other hand, the commentators have been uniformly critical of, and alarmed by, the increasing use of this device. 3A Moore, Federal Practice ¶ 17.05[2], at 156 (2d ed.1968); Wright, supra, at 88; Field, Proposals on Federal Diversity Jurisdiction, 17 S.Car.L.Rev. 669, 671 (1965); ALI, Study of the Division of Jurisdiction Between State and Federal Courts, Commentary on Proposed § 1307, at 104–05 (September 25, 1965 Official Draft); see also 44 Harv. L.Rev. 97, 100 (1930); 40 Va.L.Rev. 803, 804 (1954); 34 Tex.L.Rev. 476, 477 (1956); Note, The Assignment Device in Diversity Cases: The Illusory Right of Removal, 35 U.Cin.L.Rev. 33, 40 (1966). The American Law Institute has proposed federal legislation which would foreclose this abuse.[38] See ALI,

---

35. In *Wilson*, plaintiff attempted the same device as in *Wecker*. In an apparent extension of *Wecker*, the Court affirmed the federal district court's retention of jurisdiction without regard to whether the codefendant could have been technically liable, since the device was obviously a sham.

36. See, e.g., Rosecrans v. William S. Lozier, Inc., 142 F.2d 118 (8th Cir.1944); King v. McMillan, 252 F.Supp. 390 (D.S.C.1966); Heape v. Sullivan, 233 F.Supp. 127 (E.D.S.C.1964); Leshem v. Continental American Life Ins. Co., 219 F.Supp. 504 (S.D.N.Y.1963); Hair v. Savannah Steel Drum Corp., 161 F.Supp. 654 (E.D.S.C.1955); Krenzien v. United Services Life Ins. Co. of Washington, D.C., 121 F.Supp. 243 (D.Kan.1954); Ridgeland Box Mfg. Co. v. Sinclair Refining Co., 82 F.Supp. 274 (E.D.S.C.1949); Bernblum v. Travelers' Ins. Co., 9 F.Supp. 34 (W.D.Mo.1934); Verschell v. Fireman's Fund Ins. Co., 257 F.Supp. 153 (S.D.N.Y. 1966) (dictum). However, only the South Carolina District Court has countenanced the use of a partial assignment to defeat diversity. See *King v. McMillan*, supra; *Heape v. Sullivan*, supra; *Ridgeland Box Mfg. Co. v. Sinclair Refining Co.*, supra, all involving, as here, the assignment of a ¹⁄₁₀₀ interest in a plaintiff's claim for the sole purpose of defeating the jurisdiction of the federal court. In Lisenby v. Patz, 130 F.Supp. 670, 672 (E.D.S.C.1955), Judge Hoffman, sitting as a visiting judge, adverted to the widespread use of this device throughout the State of South Carolina and noted that in fact a member of the bar had written a book promoting the practice.

37. See Phoenix Mutual Life Ins. Co. of Hartford, Conn. v. England, 22 F.Supp. 284 (W.D.Mo.1938); *Lisenby v. Patz*, supra. In a frequently quoted passage, Judge Collett, in Phoenix, stated:

The facts showing that the assignment was a mere pretext and that its execution was fraudulent, as that term is used without opprobrium, it must be ignored. To do otherwise would make federal procedure a game in which the statutory rights of parties might be blocked by an adroit and cleverly designed maneuver of his adversary.

22 F.Supp., at 286. In *Lisenby* Judge Hoffman denied remand on the ground that personal injury claims were not assignable under South Carolina law. In *Hair v. Savannah Steel Drum Corp.*, supra, Chief Judge Timmerman in the same district reached a contrary result, holding that Judge Hoffman had misconstrued South Carolina law.

38. In support of its proposals, the American Law Institute points out:

Study, supra, at 21–22. However, this Court is inclined to agree with Professor Moore's observation:

> "The proposals in this respect are good ones. But we respectfully suggest that the federal courts should not await legislative action to cure an erroneous doctrine which had been evolved by the federal courts."

Moore, supra, at 156; see also id. ¶ 17.05[3.–3], at 166.

Only one further comment is necessary. Plaintiffs strenuously argue that the state court is the proper forum to determine whether the assignments are invalid because they were made to defeat federal jurisdiction, citing, inter alia, *Provident Savings Life Assurance Society v. Ford*, supra and Leshem v. Continental American Life Ins. Co., [219 F.Supp. 504 (S.D.N.Y. 1963)]. However, as the Supreme Court noted in *Kramer v. Caribbean Mills, Inc.*, supra, 395 U.S., at 829, "The existence of federal jurisdiction is a matter of federal, not state, law." Since all the facts relating to the assignments are before this Court, there is no necessity for a remand to the state court for a determination as to their effect upon this Court's jurisdiction. See *Wilson v. Republic Iron & Steel Co.*, supra, 257 U.S., at 97; Phoenix Mutual Life Ins. Co. v. England, [22 F.Supp. 284, 286 (W.D. Mo. 1938)]; see also Lisenby v. Patz, [130 F.Supp. 670 (E.D.S.C. 1955)]. As Professor Moore has observed, "[I]f the federal courts will not protect their jurisdiction from fraudulent evasion it is not likely that state courts will do it for them." Moore, supra, ¶ 17.05[2], at 154.[39]

In accordance with the foregoing views then, the Court conceives it to be both its prerogative and its duty to pierce the appearance of plaintiff Tamblyn's interest in this case. Having done so, it concludes that the essential diversity of citizenship of the parties at bar has not been vitiated by plaintiffs' sham transaction. Were the Court to hold otherwise, it would be by acquiescence a party to the fraudulent avoidance of its jurisdiction and the substantial frustration of defendant's constitutional and statutory rights. This it declines to be.

Plaintiffs' motion for remand is denied.

It is so ordered.[40]

So long as federal diversity jurisdiction exists ... the need for its assertion may well be greatest when the plaintiff tries hardest to defeat it. The plaintiff who chooses to sue a noncitizen defendant in a state court may be motivated by the hope that the out-of-state defendant will be at a substantial disadvantage in that court, and the likelihood of such motivation increases with the lengths to which the plaintiff will go to prevent removal to a federal forum.

ALI, Study, supra, at 104.

39. In a footnote to the quoted passage Professor Moore lists several cases in which state courts have in fact refused to give effect to the defense that a claim was assigned to prevent removal to a federal court. Moore, supra, ¶ 17.05[2], at 154 n. 5.

[40. Accord: Grassi v. Ciba–Geigy, Ltd., 894 F.2d 181 (5th Cir.1990); Smilgin v. New York Life Ins. Co., 854 F.Supp. 464 (S.D.Tex.1994); Carter v. Seaboard Coast Line R. Co., 318 F.Supp. 368 (D.S.C.1970); McClanahan v. Snodgrass, 319 F.Supp. 913 (N.D.Miss.1970).

STATUTES ON REMOVAL PROCEDURE

28 U.S.C. § 1446. Procedure for removal[41]

(a) GENERALLY.—A defendant or defendants desiring to remove any civil action from a State court shall file in the district court of the United States[42] for the district and division within which such action is pending a notice of removal signed pursuant to Rule 11 of the Federal Rules of Civil Procedure and containing a short and plain statement of the grounds for removal, together with a copy of all process, pleadings, and orders served upon such defendant or defendants in such action.

(b) REQUIREMENTS; GENERALLY.—(1) The notice of removal of a civil action or proceeding shall be filed within 30 days after the receipt by the defendant, through service or otherwise, of a copy of the initial pleading setting forth the claim for relief upon which such action or proceeding is based, or within 30 days after the service of summons upon the defendant if such initial pleading has then been filed in court and is not required to be served on the defendant, whichever period is shorter.

A Kansas corporation owns certain leases that are disputed by Mobil Oil, a New York corporation. The sole stockholder of the Kansas corporation creates his own New York corporation and has his Kansas corporation assign the leases to it. A few minutes later the New York corporation sues Mobil in state court in New York. Can the suit be removed? See Douglas Energy of New York, Inc. v. Mobil Oil Corp., 585 F.Supp. 546 (D.Kan.1984).

Neither assignment of part or all of the claim nor appointment of a cocitizen as administrator would be effective to defeat removal under the proposals in ALI Study §§ 1307(b), 1301(b)(4).]

[**41.**   See Wright & Kane, Federal Courts § 70 (6th ed.2002); Mullenix, Redish & Vairo, Understanding Federal Courts and Jurisdiction §§ 6.09, 6.10 (1998); ALI Study 336–357; Powell & Pearce–Reggio, The Ins and Outs of Federal Court: A Practitioner's Guide to Removal and Remand, 17 Miss.Coll.L.Rev. 227 (1997). See generally Bassett & Perschbacher, The Roots of Removal, 77 Brook.L.Rev. 1 (2011).

Recent cases are in conflict as to whether the right to remove is waived if the defendant files a motion to dismiss in state court before filing the notice of removal. In Somoano v. Ryder Systems, Inc., 985 F.Supp. 1476 (S.D.Fla.1998), the court held that there was no waiver when the motion to dismiss was filed within the 20 days required for a responsive pleading under state law, and the notice of removal was filed within the longer 30–day period permitted by § 1446(b). But other reported cases have held that filing a motion to dismiss may indicate clear and unequivocal intent to litigate in state court. See Heafitz v. Interfirst Bank of Dallas, 711 F.Supp. 92 (S.D.N.Y.1989); Scholz v. RDV Sports, Inc., 821 F.Supp. 1469 (M.D.Fla.1993). Merely filing an answer, however, does not waive the right of removal. See, e.g., Gore v. Stenson, 616 F.Supp. 895 (S.D.Tex.1984); Miami Herald Publishing Co. v. Ferre, 606 F.Supp. 122 (S.D.Fla.1984). In Jacko v. Thorn Americas, Inc., 121 F.Supp.2d 574 (E.D.Tex.2000), the right of removal was held to have been waived by the filing and argument of a motion for summary judgment. See also Johnson, Removal and the Special Appearance—Which to Do First?, 19 Rev.Litig. 25 (2000); Musalli, Tick, Tock: Rules on the Removal Clock, 19 Rev.Litig. 47 (2000). See also ALI Judicial Code Project 584–588 (Reporter's Note J: Waiver and Revival of the Right of Removal, Part II, Waiver of the Right of Removal by Litigation Conduct).]

[**42.**   Prior to 1948 a petition for removal was filed in the first instance in the state court. If the state court refused to allow removal, defendant had three courses of action, none of which was very reassuring. See Metropolitan Cas. Ins. Co. v. Stevens, 312 U.S. 563 (1941).]

(2) (A) When a civil action is removed solely under section 1441(a), all defendants who have been properly joined and served must join in or consent to the removal of the action.

(B) Each defendant shall have 30 days after receipt by or service on that defendant of the initial pleading or summons described in paragraph (1) to file the notice of removal.

(C) If defendants are served at different times, and a later-served defendant files a notice of removal, any earlier-served defendant may consent to the removal even though that earlier-served defendant did not previously initiate or consent to removal.

(3) Except as provided in subsection (c), if the case stated by the initial pleading is not removable, a notice of removal may be filed within thirty days after receipt by the defendant, through service or otherwise, of a copy of an amended pleading, motion, order or other paper from which it may first be ascertained that the case is one which is or has become removable.

(c) Requirements; Removal Based on Diversity of Citizenship.—

(1) A case may not be removed under subsection (b)(3) on the basis of jurisdiction conferred by section 1332 more than 1 year after commencement of the action, unless the district court finds that the plaintiff has acted in bad faith in order to prevent a defendant from removing the action.

(2) If removal of a civil action is sought on the basis of the jurisdiction conferred by section 1332(a), the sum demanded in good faith in the initial pleading shall be deemed to be the amount in controversy, except that—

(A) the notice of removal may assert the amount in controversy if the initial pleading seeks—

(i) nonmonetary relief; or

(ii) a money judgment, but the State practice either does not permit demand for a specific sum or permits recovery of damages in excess of the amount demanded; and

(B) removal of the action is proper on the basis of an amount in controversy asserted under subparagraph (A) if the district court finds, by the preponderance of the evidence, that the amount in controversy exceeds the amount specified in section 1332(a).

(3) (A) If the case stated by the initial pleading is not removable solely because the amount in controversy does not exceed the amount specified in section 1332(a), information relating to the amount in controversy in the record of the State proceeding, or in responses to discovery, shall be treated as an "other paper" under subsection (b)(3).

(B) If the notice of removal is filed more than 1 year after commencement of the action and the district court finds that the plaintiff deliberately failed to disclose the actual amount in controversy to prevent removal, that finding shall be deemed bad faith under paragraph (1).

(d) NOTICE TO ADVERSE PARTIES AND STATE COURT.—Promptly after the filing of such notice of removal of a civil action the defendant or defendants shall give written notice thereof to all adverse parties and shall file a copy of the notice with the clerk of such State court, which shall effect the removal and the State court shall proceed no further unless and until the case is remanded.[43]

28 U.S.C. § 1447. Procedure after removal generally[44]

(a) In any case removed from a State court, the district court may issue all necessary orders and process to bring before it all proper parties whether served by process issued by the State court or otherwise.

(b) It may require the removing party to file with its clerk copies of all records and proceedings in such State court or may cause the same to be brought before it by writ of certiorari issued to such State court.

(c) A motion to remand the case on the basis of any defect other than lack of subject matter jurisdiction must be made within 30 days after the filing of the notice of removal under section 1446(a).[45] If at any time before

[43. It is well settled that once removal is effected any proceedings by the state court are void even though the action is ultimately remanded. E.g., Hopson v. North American Ins. Co., 71 Idaho 461, 233 P.2d 799, (1951); State v. Francis, 261 N.C. 358, 134 S.E.2d 681 (1964). Can defendant abort a state court trial that is going badly for him by filing an untenable notice of removal just before the case is to go to the jury? Is there any solution for such an abuse? See ALI Study § 1383(a).

In Heniford v. American Motors Sales Corp., 471 F.Supp. 328 (D.S.C.1979), it was held that the statement of plaintiffs' counsel in closing argument, "I don't want you to give a verdict against" the nondiverse defendant, made the case removable, and the verdict of the state jury was a nullity, although defendant's removal papers were not filed with the state court until after the jury had begun deliberating.

In Davis v. Veslan Enterprises, 765 F.2d 494 (5th Cir.1985), it was held that Rule 11 of the Federal Rules of Civil Procedure, as amended in 1983, authorized imposition of sanctions against a defendant that in bad faith filed a petition for removal the day before plaintiff's motion for entry of judgment on a jury verdict was to have been heard. The plaintiff was awarded $5,855 for attorney's fees and $32,988.99 as the amount of interest lost because of the delay in entering the state judgment.]

[44. See Rule 81(c), Federal Rules of Civil Procedure; Granny Goose Foods, Inc. v. Brotherhood of Teamsters & Auto Truck Drivers Local No. 70, 415 U.S. 423 (1974); 14C Wright, Miller & Cooper, Federal Practice and Procedure: Jurisdiction 3d § 3738 (1998); Mullenix, Redish & Vairo, Understanding Federal Courts and Jurisdiction §§ 6.11–6.13 (1998).]

[45. As adopted in 1988 § 1447(c) put a 30–day limit on motions to remand "on the basis of any defect in removal procedure." The courts held that this 30–day rule applied to all motions for remand except where the federal court lacks subject-matter jurisdiction. It applied to a motion to remand based on the fact that some defendants in a diversity case were citizens of the forum state. In re Shell Oil Co., 932 F.2d 1523 (5th Cir.1991). It applied also to an objection that a case was not removable although it could have been commenced in federal court and the federal courts would have had subject-matter jurisdiction. Baris v.

final judgment it appears that the district court lacks subject matter jurisdiction, the case shall be remanded.[46] An order remanding the case may require payment of just costs and any actual expenses, including attorney fees, incurred as a result of the removal. A certified copy of the order of remand shall be mailed by the clerk to the clerk of the State court. The State court may thereupon proceed with such case.[47]

(d) An order remanding a case to the State court from which it was removed is not reviewable on appeal or otherwise, except that an order remanding a case to the State court from which it was removed pursuant to section 1443[48] of this title shall be reviewable by appeal or otherwise.[49]

Sulpicio Lines, Inc., 932 F.2d 1540 (5th Cir.1991); Western Securities Co. v. Derwinski, 937 F.2d 1276 (7th Cir.1991). But see Foster v. Chesapeake Ins. Co., 933 F.2d 1207 (3d Cir.1991). The Supreme Court denied certiorari in both the *Baris* and *Foster* cases. 502 U.S. 908 (1991). The interpretation put on § 1447(c) in the *Baris* and *Western Securities* cases was written into the statute by amendment of § 1447(c) in 1996.

Section 1447(c)'s 30–day time limit for motions to remand on the basis of "any defect other than lack of subject matter jurisdiction" also limits the power of the district court to remand sua sponte, and an untimely sua sponte remand order is not insulated from appellate review by § 1447(d). See In re Bethesda Memorial Hospital, Inc., 123 F.3d 1407 (11th Cir.1997) (collecting and following cases from the Third, Fifth, and Ninth Circuits as to both points).]

[46. The Supreme Court has approved an additional, nonstatutory category of quasi-jurisdictional remand when, in a removed case, the district court discretionarily decides not to exercise supplemental jurisdiction over one or more claims in the removed action. Although the Court declared that the district court has discretion whether to dismiss or to remand supplemental claims incident to a discretionary declination of jurisdiction, it strongly implied that when dismissal would foreclose relitigation of the claims on statute-of-limitations grounds, it would be an abuse of discretion to dismiss rather than to remand such claims. See Carnegie–Mellon University v. Cohill, 484 U.S. 343 (1988). The ALI would codify the duty to remand rather than dismiss supplemental claims that were joined to a removed action before its removal. See ALI Judicial Code Project § 1367(f) and Commentary, at 131.]

[47. In a case of first impression in the federal appellate courts, the Fourth Circuit addressed § 1447(c), which provides, in part, that "[a]n order remanding [an erroneously-removed] case may require payment of just costs and any actual expenses, including attorney fees, incurred as a result of the removal." In re Crescent City Estates, LLC, 588 F.3d 822 (4th Cir. 2009). After a case was removed from Maryland state court to federal bankruptcy court, the plaintiffs sought remand and also requested attorney fees for improper removal from both the removing parties and their defense counsel. The Fourth Circuit concluded that § 1447(c) gives the trial court discretion to award costs and expenses, but that, consistent with the American Rule presumption that parties must pay their own legal costs regardless of the litigation's outcome, the costs and expenses of an improper removal can be imposed only against the parties that removed the lawsuit, and not against their lawyers. The court of appeals observed in its conclusion, however, that attorneys are not wholly immune from liability for improper removals that result from egregious misconduct rather than merely poor legal judgment. An attorney's "particularly blameworthy" decision to remove a nonremovable case can be sanctioned under Federal Rule 11, 28 U.S.C. § 1927, and the court's inherent powers. 588 F.3d at 831.]

[48. The text of 28 U.S.C. § 1443 is set out supra p. 331.]

[49. The exception to this subsection, added by amendment in 1964, is criticized as "inartistic drafting" in New York v. Galamison, 342 F.2d 255, 257 (2d Cir.1965).

For application of the subsection itself see Thermtron Products, Inc. v. Hermansdorfer, 423 U.S. 336 (1976). In Quackenbush v. Allstate Insurance Co., 517 U.S. 706 (1996), the Court

(e) If after removal the plaintiff seeks to join additional defendants whose joinder would destroy subject matter jurisdiction, the court may deny joinder, or permit joinder and remand the action to the State court.[50]

§ 1453. Removal of class actions

(a) **Definitions.**—In this section, the terms "class" , "class action" , "class certification order" , and "class member" shall have the meanings given such terms under section 1332(d)(1).

(b) **In general.**—A class action may be removed to a district court of the United States in accordance with section 1446 (except that the 1–year limitation under section 1446(c)(1) shall not apply), without regard to whether any defendant is a citizen of the State in which the action is

---

reaffirmed the reasoning of *Thermtron* and of Things Remembered, Inc. v. Petrarca, 516 U.S. 124 (1995), that only remands on the grounds specified in 28 U.S.C. § 1447(c) are withdrawn from appellate jurisdiction by 28 U.S.C. § 1447(d). But the *Quackenbush* Court went on to "disavow" *Thermtron* insofar as that case held that the means of review of a remand ordered on non-§ 1447(c) grounds was by petition for a writ of mandamus. This aspect of *Thermtron* was deemed incompatible with the later holding of Moses H. Cone Memorial Hospital v. Mercury Construction Corp., 460 U.S. 1 (1983), that an abstention-based stay order was appealable as of right as either a "final decision" or a "collateral order" under 28 U.S.C. § 1291. Since the abstention-based remand order at issue in *Quackenbush* was functionally identical to the abstention-based stay order reviewed under § 1291 in *Moses H. Cone Memorial Hospital*, the remand order was also subject to review by appeal under § 1291 rather than by petition for a writ of mandamus.

In an opinion by Judge Posner, the Seventh Circuit denied preclusive effect to remand orders premised on a lack of federal subject-matter jurisdiction that are nonreviewable under § 1447(d). See Health Cost Controls of Illinois, Inc. v. Washington, 187 F.3d 703 (7th Cir.1999).

Disapproving a line of contrary cases from the district courts, the only circuit to rule on the issue has held that a magistrate judge whose exercise of civil jurisdiction is not based on the parties' consent under 28 U.S.C. § 636(c)(1), and whose authority is thus limited to "nondispositive pretrial orders" under § 636(b), has no authority to remand a removed case. Such an unauthorized remand order is equivalent to a dismissal and is appealable notwithstanding § 1447(d). See In re U.S. Healthcare, 159 F.3d 142 (3d Cir.1998).

See generally Hrdlick, Appellate Review of Remand Orders in Removed Cases: Are They Losing a Certain Appeal?, 82 Marq.L.Rev. 535 (1999).]

[**50.** This provision, added in 1988, can cause hardship when cases have been removed from the courts of states that liberally permit amendment of the complaint to add additional defendants. One state, California, notoriously employs such amendments, together with the use of "Doe" defendants and generous standards for "relation back" of amended complaints, to mitigate the effect of its unusually short statute of limitations for suits for personal injury or wrongful death. Under § 1447(e) there is a standing potential for diversity jurisdiction to be used to cause substantive harm to a plaintiff whose California state-court case is removed to federal court. When the plaintiff seeks to add new nondiverse defendants, as would routinely be allowed in state court, the district court must either remand the case or deny leave to amend. If it does the former, a great deal of time may be wasted. If it does the latter, it immunizes the proposed new defendants from liability because it is too late for the plaintiff to commence a fresh suit against them in state court. The ALI would give the district court the third option of permitting the amendment and exercising a special grant of supplemental jurisdiction to retain jurisdiction over the entire case. See ALI Judicial Code Project § 1367(e); id., Commentary, at 126–127 and Reporter's Note, at 128–131.]

brought, except that such action may be removed by any defendant without the consent of all defendants.

(c) Review of remand orders.—

(1) In general.—Section 1447 shall apply to any removal of a case under this section, except that notwithstanding section 1447(d), a court of appeals may accept an appeal from an order of a district court granting or denying a motion to remand a class action to the State court from which it was removed if application is made to the court of appeals not more than 10 days after entry of the order.

(2) Time period for judgment.—If the court of appeals accepts an appeal under paragraph (1), the court shall complete all action on such appeal, including rendering judgment, not later than 60 days after the date on which such appeal was filed, unless an extension is granted under paragraph (3).

(3) Extension of time period.—The court of appeals may grant an extension of the 60–day period described in paragraph (2) if—

(A) all parties to the proceeding agree to such extension, for any period of time; or

(B) such extension is for good cause shown and in the interests of justice, for a period not to exceed 10 days.

(4) Denial of appeal.—If a final judgment on the appeal under paragraph (1) is not issued before the end of the period described in paragraph (2), including any extension under paragraph (3), the appeal shall be denied.

(d) Exception.—This section shall not apply to any class action that solely involves—

(1) a claim concerning a covered security as defined under section 16(f)(3) of the Securities Act of 1933 (15 U.S.C. 78p(f)(3)) and section 28(f)(5)(E) of the Securities Exchange Act of 1934 (15 U.S.C. 78bb(f)(5)(E));

(2) a claim that relates to the internal affairs or governance of a corporation or other form of business enterprise and arises under or by virtue of the laws of the State in which such corporation or business enterprise is incorporated or organized; or

(3) a claim that relates to the rights, duties (including fiduciary duties), and obligations relating to or created by or pursuant to any security (as defined under section 2(a)(1) of the Securities Act of 1933 (15 U.S.C. 77b(a)(1)) and the regulations issued thereunder).[51]

[51. Added by the Class Action Fairness Act of 2005, Pub.L. 109–2, § 5(a), 119 Stat. 12 (Feb. 18, 2005). The Class Action Fairness Act is discussed supra p. 177, n. 11.]

Murphy Bros., Inc. v. Michetti Pipe Stringing, Inc.

Supreme Court of the United States, 1999.
526 U.S. 344, 119 S.Ct. 1322, 143 L.Ed.2d 448.

■ JUSTICE GINSBURG delivered the opinion of the Court.

This case concerns the time within which a defendant named in a state-court action may remove the action to a federal court. The governing provision is 28 U.S.C. § 1446(b), which specifies, in relevant part, that the removal notice "shall be filed within thirty days after the receipt by the defendant, through service or otherwise, of a copy of the [complaint]." The question presented is whether the named defendant must be officially summoned to appear in the action before the time to remove begins to run. Or, may the 30–day period start earlier, on the named defendant's receipt, before service of official process, of a "courtesy copy" of the filed complaint faxed by counsel for the plaintiff?

We read Congress' provisions for removal in light of a bedrock principle: An individual or entity named as a defendant is not obliged to engage in litigation unless notified of the action, and brought under a court's authority, by formal process. Accordingly, we hold that a named defendant's time to remove is triggered by simultaneous service of the summons and complaint, or receipt of the complaint, "through service or otherwise," after and apart from service of the summons, but not by mere receipt of the complaint unattended by any formal service.

I

On January 26, 1996, respondent Michetti Pipe Stringing, Inc. (Michetti), filed a complaint in Alabama state court seeking damages for an alleged breach of contract and fraud by petitioner Murphy Bros., Inc. (Murphy). Michetti did not serve Murphy at that time, but three days later it faxed a "courtesy copy" of the file-stamped complaint to one of Murphy's vice presidents. The parties then engaged in settlement discussions until February 12, 1996, when Michetti officially served Murphy under local law by certified mail.

On March 13, 1996 (30 days after service but 44 days after receiving the faxed copy of the complaint), Murphy removed the case under 28 U.S.C. § 1441 to the United States District Court for the Northern District of Alabama.[52] Michetti moved to remand the case to the state court on the ground that Murphy filed the removal notice 14 days too late. The notice of removal had not been filed within 30 days of the date on which Murphy's vice president received the facsimile transmission. Consequently, Michetti asserted, the removal was untimely under 28 U.S.C. § 1446(b), which provides:

---

52. Murphy invoked the jurisdiction of the Federal District Court under 28 U.S.C. § 1332 based on diversity of citizenship. Michetti is a Canadian company with its principal place of business in Alberta, Canada; Murphy is an Illinois corporation with its principal place of business in that State.

"The notice of removal of a civil action or proceeding shall be filed within thirty days after the receipt by the defendant, *through service or otherwise*, of a copy of the initial pleading setting forth the claim for relief upon which such action or proceeding is based, or within thirty days after the service of summons upon the defendant if such initial pleading has then been filed in court and is not required to be served on the defendant, whichever period is shorter." (Emphasis added.)

The District Court denied the remand motion on the ground that the 30–day removal period did not commence until Murphy was officially served with a summons. The court observed that the phrase "or otherwise" was added to § 1446(b) in 1949 to govern removal in States where an action is commenced merely by the service of a summons, without any requirement that the complaint be served or even filed contemporaneously. Accordingly, the District Court said, the phrase had "no field of operation" in States such as Alabama, where the complaint must be served along with the summons.

On interlocutory appeal permitted pursuant to 28 U.S.C. § 1292(b), the Court of Appeals for the Eleventh Circuit reversed and remanded, instructing the District Court to remand the action to state court. 125 F.3d 1396, 1399 (1997). The Eleventh Circuit held that "the clock starts to tick upon the defendant's receipt of a copy of the filed initial pleading." Id., at 1397. "By and large," the appellate court wrote, "our analysis begins and ends with" the words "receipt . . . or otherwise." Id., at 1397–1398 (emphasis deleted). Because lower courts have divided on the question whether service of process is a prerequisite for the running of the 30–day removal period under § 1446(b), we granted certiorari. . . .

II

Service of process, under longstanding tradition in our system of justice, is fundamental to any procedural imposition on a named defendant. At common law, the writ of capias ad respondendum directed the sheriff to secure the defendant's appearance by taking him into custody. See 1 J. Moore, Moore's Federal Practice ¶ 0.6[2.–2], p. 212 (2d ed.1996) ("[T]he three royal courts, Exchequer, Common Pleas, and King's Bench . . . obtained an *in personam* jurisdiction over the defendant in the same manner through the writ of *capias ad respondendum*."). The requirement that a defendant be brought into litigation by official service is the contemporary counterpart to that writ. See International Shoe Co. v. Washington, 326 U.S. 310, 316 (1945) ("[T]he *capias ad respondendum* has given way to personal service of summons or other form of notice.").

In the absence of service of process (or waiver of service by the defendant), a court ordinarily may not exercise power over a party the complaint names as defendant. See Omni Capital Int'l, Ltd. v. Rudolf Wolff & Co., 484 U.S. 97, 104 (1987) ("Before a . . . court may exercise personal jurisdiction over a defendant, the procedural requirement of service of summons must be satisfied."); Mississippi Publishing Corp. v. Murphree, 326 U.S. 438, 444–445 (1946) ("[S]ervice of summons is the procedure by which a court ... asserts jurisdiction over the person of the party served."). Accordingly, one becomes a party officially, and is required to take action in that capacity, only upon service of a summons or other authority-asserting measure stating the time within which the party served must appear and defend. See Fed. Rule Civ. Proc. 4(a) ("[The summons] shall ... state the time within which the defendant must appear and defend, and notify the defendant that failure to do so will result in a judgment by default against the defendant."); Fed. Rule Civ. Proc. 12(a)(1)(A) (a defendant shall serve an answer within 20 days of being served with the summons and complaint). Unless a named defendant agrees to waive service, the summons continues to function as the *sine qua non* directing an individual or entity to participate in a civil action or forgo procedural or substantive rights.

III

When Congress enacted § 1446(b), the legislators did not endeavor to break away from the traditional understanding. Prior to 1948, a defendant could remove a case any time before the expiration of her time to respond to the complaint under state law. See, e.g., 28 U.S.C. § 72 (1940 ed.). Because the time limits for responding to the complaint varied from State to State, however, the period for removal correspondingly varied. To reduce the disparity, Congress in 1948 enacted the original version of § 1446(b), which provided that "[t]he petition for removal of a civil action or proceeding may be filed within twenty days after commencement of the action or service of process, whichever is later." Act of June 25, 1948, 62 Stat. 939, as amended, 28 U.S.C. § 1446(b). According to the relevant House Report, this provision was intended to "give adequate time and operate uniformly throughout the Federal jurisdiction." H.R.Rep. No. 308, 80th Cong., 1st Sess., A135 (1947).

Congress soon recognized, however, that § 1446(b), as first framed, did not "give adequate time and operate uniformly" in all States. In States such as New York, most notably, service of the summons commenced the action, and such service could precede the filing of the complaint. Under § 1446(b) as originally enacted, the period for removal in such a State could have expired before the defendant obtained access to the complaint.

To ensure that the defendant would have access to the complaint before commencement of the removal period, Congress in 1949 enacted the current version of § 1446(b): "The petition for removal of a civil action or proceeding shall be filed within twenty days [now thirty days][53] after the receipt by the defendant, through service or otherwise, of a copy of the initial pleading setting forth the claim for relief upon which such action or proceeding is based." Act of May 24, 1949, § 83(a), 63 Stat. 101. The accompanying Senate Report explained:

---

53. Congress extended the period for removal from 20 days to 30 days in 1965. See Act of September 29, 1965, 79 Stat. 887.

"In some States suits are begun by the service of a summons or other process without the necessity of filing any pleading until later. As the section now stands, this places the defendant in the position of having to take steps to remove a suit to Federal court before he knows what the suit is about. As said section is herein proposed to be rewritten, a defendant is not required to file his petition for removal until 20 days after he has received (or it has been made available to him) a copy of the initial pleading filed by the plaintiff setting forth the claim upon which the suit is based and the relief prayed for. It is believed that this will meet the varying conditions of practice in all the States." S.Rep. No. 303, 81st Cong., 1st Sess., 6 (1949).

See also H.R.Rep. No. 352, 81st Cong., 1st Sess., 14 (1949) ("The first paragraph of the amendment to subsection (b) corrects [the New York problem] by providing that the petition for removal need not be filed until 20 days after the defendant has received a copy of the plaintiff's initial pleading.").[54] Nothing in the legislative history of the 1949 amendment so much as hints that Congress, in making changes to accommodate atypical state commencement and complaint filing procedures, intended to dispense with the historic function of service of process as the official trigger for responsive action by an individual or entity named defendant.[55]

IV

The Eleventh Circuit relied on the "plain meaning" of § 1446(b) that the panel perceived. See 125 F.3d, at 1398. In the Eleventh Circuit's view, because the term " '[r]eceipt' is the nominal form of 'receive,' which means broadly 'to come into possession of' or to 'acquire,' 'the phrase' '[receipt] through service or otherwise' opens a universe of means besides service for putting the defendant in possession of the complaint." Ibid. What are the dimensions of that "universe" ? The Eleventh Circuit's opinion is uninformative. Nor can one tenably maintain that the words "or otherwise" provide a clue. Cf. Potter v. McCauley, 186 F.Supp. 146, 149 (D.Md.1960) ("It is not possible to state definitely in general terms the precise scope and

---

54. The second half of the revised § 1446(b), providing that the petition for removal shall be filed "within twenty days after the service of summons upon the defendant if such initial pleading has then been filed in court and is not required to be served on the defendant, whichever period is shorter," § 83(b), 63 Stat. 101, was added to address the situation in States such as Kentucky, which required the complaint to be filed at the time the summons issued, but did not require service of the complaint along with the summons. See H.R.Rep. No. 352, 81st Cong., 1st Sess., 14 (1949) ("Th[e first clause of revised § 1446(b)], however, without more, would create further difficulty in those States, such as Kentucky, where suit is commenced by the filing of the plaintiff's initial pleading and the issuance and service of a summons without any requirement that a copy of the pleading be served upon or otherwise furnished to the defendant. Accordingly . . . the amendment provides that in such cases the petition for removal shall be filed within 20 days after the service of the summons.").

55. It is evident, too, that Congress could not have foreseen the situation posed by this case, for, as the District Court recognized, "[i]n 1949 Congress did not anticipate use of facsmile [sic] transmissions." Indeed, even the photocopy machine was not yet on the scene at that time. See 9 New Encyclopedia Britannica 400 (15th ed.1985) (noting that photocopiers "did not become available for commercial use until 1950").

effect of the word 'otherwise' in its context here because its proper application in particular situations will vary with state procedural requirements."); Apache Nitrogen Products, Inc. v. Harbor Ins. Co., 145 F.R.D. 674, 679 (D.Ariz.1993) ("[I]f in fact the words 'service or otherwise' had a plain meaning, the cases would not be so hopelessly split over their proper interpretation.").

The interpretation of § 1446(b) adopted here adheres to tradition, makes sense of the phrase "or otherwise," and assures defendants adequate time to decide whether to remove an action to federal court. As the court in *Potter* observed, the various state provisions for service of the summons and the filing or service of the complaint fit into one or another of four main categories. See *Potter*, 186 F.Supp., at 149. In each of the four categories, the defendant's period for removal will be no less than 30 days from service, and in some categories, it will be more than 30 days from service, depending on when the complaint is received.

As summarized in *Potter*, the possibilities are as follows. First, if the summons and complaint are served together, the 30–day period for removal runs at once. Second, if the defendant is served with the summons but the complaint is furnished to the defendant sometime after, the period for removal runs from the defendant's receipt of the complaint. Third, if the defendant is served with the summons and the complaint is filed in court, but under local rules, service of the complaint is not required, the removal period runs from the date the complaint is made available through filing. Finally, if the complaint is filed in court prior to any service, the removal period runs from the service of the summons. See ibid.

Notably, Federal Rule of Civil Procedure 81(c), amended in 1949, uses the identical "receipt through service or otherwise" language in specifying the time the defendant has to answer the complaint once the case has been removed:

> "In a removed action in which the defendant has not answered, the defendant shall answer or present the other defenses or objections available under these rules within 20 days after the receipt through service or otherwise of a copy of the initial pleading setting forth the claim for relief upon which the action or proceeding is based."

Rule 81(c) sensibly has been interpreted to afford the defendant at least 20 days after service of process to respond. See Silva v. Madison, 69 F.3d 1368, 1376–1377 (CA7 1995). In *Silva*, the Seventh Circuit Court of Appeals observed that "nothing ... would justify our concluding that the drafters, in their quest for evenhandedness and promptness in the removal process, intended to abrogate the necessity for something as fundamental as service of process." Id., at 1376. In reaching this conclusion, the court distinguished an earlier decision, Roe v. O'Donohue, 38 F.3d 298 (CA7 1994), which held that a defendant need not receive service of process before his time for removal under § 1446(b) begins to run. See 69 F.3d, at 1376. But, as the United States maintains in its amicus curiae brief, the *Silva* court "did not adequately explain why one who has not yet lawfully been made a party to an action should be required to decide in which court system the case should be heard." If, as the Seventh Circuit rightly determined, the "service or otherwise" language was not intended to abrogate the service requirement for purposes of Rule 81(c), that same language also was not intended to bypass service as a starter for § 1446(b)'s clock. The fact that the Seventh Circuit could read the phrase "or otherwise" differently in *Silva* and *Roe*, moreover, undercuts the Eleventh Circuit's position that the phrase has an inevitably "plain meaning." [56]

Furthermore, the so-called "receipt rule" —starting the time to remove on receipt of a copy of the complaint, however informally, despite the absence of any formal service—could, as the District Court recognized, operate with notable unfairness to individuals and entities in foreign nations. Because facsimile machines transmit instantaneously, but formal service abroad may take much longer than 30 days, plaintiffs "would be able to dodge the requirements of international treaties and trap foreign opponents into keeping their suits in state courts."

* * *

In sum, it would take a clearer statement than Congress has made to read its endeavor to extend removal time (by adding receipt of the complaint) to effect so strange a change—to set removal apart from all other responsive acts, to render removal the sole instance in which one's procedural rights slip away before service of a summons, i.e., before one is subject to any court's authority. Accordingly, for the reasons stated in this opinion, the judgment of the United States Court of Appeals for the Eleventh Circuit is reversed, and the case is remanded for further proceedings consistent with this opinion.

It is so ordered.

■ CHIEF JUSTICE REHNQUIST, with whom JUSTICE SCALIA and JUSTICE THOMAS join, dissenting.

Respondent faxed petitioner a copy of the file-stamped complaint in its commenced state-court action, and I believe that the receipt of this facsimile triggered the 30–day removal period under the plain language of 28 U.S.C. § 1446(b). The Court does little to explain why the plain language of the statute should not control, opting instead to superimpose a judicially created service of process requirement onto § 1446(b). In so doing, it departs from this Court's practice of strictly construing removal and

---

56. Contrary to a suggestion made at oral argument, 28 U.S.C. § 1448 does not support the Eleventh Circuit's position. That section provides that "[i]n all cases removed from any State court to any district court of the United States in which any one or more of the defendants has not been served with process or in which the service has not been perfected prior to removal ... such process or service may be completed or new process issued in the same manner as in cases originally filed in such district court." Nothing in § 1448 requires the defendant to take any action. The statute simply allows the plaintiff to serve an unserved defendant or to perfect flawed service once the action has been removed. In fact, the second paragraph of § 1448, which provides that "[t]his section shall not deprive any defendant upon whom process is served after removal of his right to move to remand the case," explicitly reserves the unserved defendant's right to take action (move to remand) *after* service is perfected.

similar jurisdictional statutes. See Shamrock Oil & Gas Corp. v. Sheets, 313 U.S. 100, 108–109 (1941). Because I believe the Eleventh Circuit's analysis of the issue presented in this case was cogent and correct, see 125 F.3d 1396, 1397–1398 (1997), I would affirm the dismissal of petitioner's removal petition for the reasons stated by that court.

Burroughs v. Palumbo

United States District Court, Eastern District of Virginia, 1994.
871 F.Supp. 870.

■ BRINKEMA, DISTRICT JUDGE.

I.

The relevant facts of this case are not in dispute. Plaintiff is an attorney in Northern Virginia who brought this action against a former client for unpaid legal fees. The case was filed in the Arlington Circuit Court on August 18, 1994. William S. Burroughs, Jr. v. P.M. Palumbo, Jr., At Law 94–1042 (Arlington Circuit Court, August 18, 1994). Defendant is a citizen of Florida and was served in accordance with the Virginia long-arm statute. Va.Code Ann. § 8.01–329 (Michie 1992). Service was made on the Secretary of the Commonwealth on August 24, 1994. On August 30, 1994, the Secretary mailed the Motion for Judgment to the defendant. A certificate of compliance was filed with the state court on September 1, 1994, making service effective. Under Virginia law, the defendant had twenty-one days from the date of service to file an answer in the state court. Va.S.Ct.R. 3:5.

Defendant filed a notice of removal with this Court on September 29, 1994. Defendant's notice of removal was within the time allowed by federal law for filing a removal petition. 28 U.S.C. § 1446(b) (1994)("The notice of removal of a civil action or proceeding shall be filed within thirty days after receipt by the defendant . . . of the initial pleading.") However, defendant was out of time for filing his answer in state court. The state court entered a default judgment against the defendant on September 30, 1994. Later that same day, defendant filed the notice of removal with the clerk of the state court. Defendant now seeks to have this Court set aside the state court default judgment on the grounds that the state court lacked jurisdiction at the time that the default judgment was entered because the notice of removal had already been filed in federal court.

This case presents a "prickly little technical problem" which few courts have addressed. Berberian v. Gibney, 514 F.2d 790, 792 (1st Cir. 1975). During the period between the filing of the notice of removal in federal court and the filing in state court, which court had jurisdiction? For the reasons discussed below, we find that jurisdiction was concurrent and that this case was properly removed with the default judgment intact.

II.

The Federal Rules of Civil Procedure [sic] establish a two-step procedure for removal. First, the defendant must file a notice of removal in the United States district court for the district and division in which the state court action is pending. 28 U.S.C. § 1446(a) (1994). Second, promptly after filing the notice of removal, the defendant must give written notice to adverse parties and must file a copy of the notice of removal with the clerk of the state court. 28 U.S.C. § 1446(d) (1994). Filing the notice of removal with the state court "shall *effect* the removal and *the State court shall proceed no further* unless and until the case is remanded." Id. (emphasis added).

It is clear that the filing of the notice of removal in the state court terminates the state court's jurisdiction. A plain reading of the removal statute leads us to this conclusion. 28 U.S.C. § 1446(d) (1994) (providing that state court proceedings shall cease upon filing of removal notice with state court). In addition, the Fourth Circuit has held that the state court loses all jurisdiction immediately upon completion of the two-step removal process. State of South Carolina v. Moore, 447 F.2d 1067, 1073 (4th Cir.1971)(holding that proceedings after filing of notice of removal in state court are void because state court loses all jurisdiction after filing of notice in federal court *and* in state court).

The obvious inference from the statute and the Fourth Circuit holding is that the state court maintains jurisdiction over the action until the state court receives actual notice of removal. This reading of the statute furthers the underlying purpose behind requiring that notice of removal be filed with the state court. That purpose is to notify the state court of the removal so that it can stay its proceedings, avoid duplicitous actions, and conserve judicial resources. See Delavigne v. Delavigne, 530 F.2d 598, 601 n. 5 (4th Cir.1976) (noting that other courts have relied on the purpose of the requirement in finding substantial compliance with the statute) citing United States ex rel. Echevarria v. Silberglitt, 441 F.2d 225, 227 (2d Cir.1971). A finding that state court jurisdiction was severed sometime before filing of the notice with the state court would subvert this purpose. Indeed, it would be "unfair to a state court to hold that it can be stripped of jurisdiction though it has no notice of this fact." Charles A. Wright, Law of Federal Courts 247 (1994). Furthermore, such a conclusion would frustrate the requirement that notice to the state court be made "promptly" by eliminating the incentive for quick action. 28 U.S.C. § 1446(d) (1994).

On the other hand, a finding that the state court had exclusive jurisdiction until the completion of the two-step removal procedure would undermine the federal rules regarding removal. The federal rules allow a defendant thirty days from receipt of the initial pleading in which to file a notice of removal with the federal court. In Virginia, and in other states that allow less than thirty days for the filing of an answer, a finding of exclusive state court jurisdiction during the period in question would cut short the time for filing the notice of removal.[57] The time for filing a notice of removal would therefore be dependent on state law and would defeat Congress' effort to create a rule of uniform application. See Grubbs v. General Electric Credit Corp., 405 U.S. 699, 705 (1972) ("[T]he removal statutes ... are intended to have uniform nationwide application.") We cannot countenance such a result.

Accordingly, we find that federal jurisdiction attached when the notice of removal was filed in federal court on September 29, 1994 and that state court jurisdiction continued until the notice was filed in state court on September 30, 1994. In other words, there was concurrent state and federal jurisdiction during the period between the filing of the notice of removal in federal court and the filing in state court. See Berberian v. Gibney, 514 F.2d 790, 792 (1st Cir.1975) (citing 1A Moore ¶ 0.168[3.–8], at 509–11).

During the period of concurrent jurisdiction, the state court entered a default judgment. This judgment was properly entered, and must be treated as if entered by this Court. See id., at 793, citing Butner v. Neustadter, 324 F.2d 783, 785 (9th Cir.1963) (stating that the federal court takes the case as it finds it on removal and that state court default judgment must be treated as if entered in federal court); Munsey v. Testworth Lab., 227 F.2d 902, 903 (6th Cir.1955) (affirming district court decision to set aside state court default judgment and stating that federal court takes removed case as though everything done in state court had been done in federal court). Therefore, this Court may vacate the default judgement upon an adequate showing by the defendant.

On December 16, 1994, defendant presented evidence explaining his failure to file an answer in state court within twenty-one days of service. Defendant testified that he was out of town at the time that the Secretary of the Commonwealth mailed the motion for judgment to his Florida address and that he did not return until September 23, 1994. The Court finds that this is sufficient grounds to set aside the default judgment. Therefore, defendant's Motion to Set Aside Default Judgment is hereby GRANTED.

Defendant's Motion to Dismiss is hereby DENIED.[58]

---

57. In fact, a holding of exclusive state jurisdiction would require a defendant to complete both steps of the removal process with the 21 day period. This result clearly conflicts with the federal rules which allow 30 days for filing the notice with the federal court and additional time for filing with the state court. 28 U.S.C. § 1446(b) (1994) (allowing 30 days for filing with federal court); 28 U.S.C. § 1446(d) (1994) (requiring that notice be filed with state court "promptly after" filing with federal court).

[58. It was held in Lawrence v. Chancery Court of Tennessee, 188 F.3d 687 (6th Cir.1999), that after the removal of a case the state court retains the power to assess costs incurred prior to the removal of the litigation.

The determination of precisely when the federal court acquires jurisdiction of a removed case, and of precisely when the state court from which it was removed loses jurisdiction, has long troubled federal removal law. Confusion and uncertainty are hard to avoid under present

Mathews v. County of Fremont, Wyoming

United States District Court, D. Wyoming, 1993.
826 F.Supp. 1315.

ORDER GRANTING MOTIONS TO REMAND

■ ALAN B. JOHNSON, CHIEF JUDGE.

The Motions to remand filed by Defendant Fremont County and Plaintiff came on for hearing on May 27, 1993. The Court, having considered the motions, the arguments of counsel, and being fully advised in the premises, FINDS and ORDERS as follows:

Background

The complaint in this case was originally filed by plaintiff in the District Court of Fremont County, Wyoming, Ninth Judicial District, Civil Number 27605 on March 26, 1993. The record now before the Court does not reflect when the defendants were served with process in the state court proceeding. That record also discloses that the defendant Fremont County filed an answer in that proceeding on April 7, 1993 and that defendant Lucero filed an answer on April 20, 1993 and an amended answer on April 26, 1993. Defendant Joseph Lucero filed a Notice of Removal to federal court on April 26, 1993, pursuant to 28 U.S.C. § 1446(a).

The complaint includes the following allegations: Plaintiff was employed as a Deputy Sheriff in Fremont County since 1977. Lucero is the elected Sheriff of Fremont County .... Plaintiff's complaint asserts a claim for wrongful termination of employment....

The complaint seeks a declaration that the defendants are in violation of the First Amendment, 42 U.S.C. § 1983, and the Wyoming Constitution. In it, Plaintiff also seeks reinstatement to active employment as a deputy sheriff, back wages, benefits, seniority, and all other terms and conditions of employment as a deputy sheriff from March 18, 1992, to the present, as well as compensatory, punitive, and exemplary damages, costs and attorneys' fees.

---

§ 1446(d), which conditions the effectiveness of removal on three distinct acts—filing of the notice of removal, service of notice of the removal on adverse parties, and filing of a copy of the notice of removal with the state court—that rarely if ever will occur with near simultaneity. See generally ALI Judicial Code Project, Part III, Reporter's Note I: The Effective Time of Removal and Other Problems of Removal Procedure Under § 1446.

The ALI's solution follows that of *Burroughs v. Palumbo* by authorizing both the federal and the state court to exercise concurrent jurisdiction between the time of the filing of the notice of removal in federal court and the time of the filing of a copy of the notice of removal in state court. ALI Judicial Code Project § 1446(c). The ALI would impose on the removing party a duty of prompt notification of both the state court and adverse parties. See id., § 1446(a)(5). To discourage footdragging in the discharge of this duty of notification, the ALI would toll the 30-day time-limit otherwise imposed on the making of a motion to remand on procedural grounds until the removing party has complied with this duty of notification. Thus delay in giving notice works to the disadvantage of the removing party by prolonging the period of time in which procedural defects can result in undoing the removal. See id., § 1447(c)(1).]

The factual disputes in the case concern matters relating to plaintiff's employment with and subsequent dismissal from the Fremont County Sheriff's Department. The sheriff's department had a manual with policies and procedures regarding discipline and discharge of employees, provided to deputy sheriffs with the expectation that they would rely upon the manual. Plaintiff claims the manual's policies and procedures were not followed. Additionally, during the 1990 election, plaintiff supported the reelection of incumbent Sheriff McKinney. That election race was won by defendant Sheriff Lucero.

Plaintiff was a Captain in the department from 1982 until January 1991. Plaintiff claims Lucero had informed plaintiff that he would no longer hold the position of Captain if Lucero won the election and that Coppack would hold the position of undersheriff. Plaintiff was also informed if there was a patrol position available, he could have that position. After the election, plaintiff's rank was lowered to patrol deputy and he received a decrease in salary. Plaintiff asserts that after Lucero took office, he became the subject of a continuing course of harassment, which ended up in his written employee records as written reprimands....

. . . . .

Defendant Lucero generally denies the allegations, asserts governmental immunity under the Wyoming Governmental Claims Act, qualified immunity, failure to state a claim, plaintiff has failed to mitigate his claims, defendant's acts are authorized by law or privileged, and that "extraordinary circumstances" exist in this case, under which defendant neither knew nor should have known of the relevant legal standard.

. . . . .

Fremont County now seeks an order remanding the case back to the Ninth Judicial District Court for the State of Wyoming. The County argues that there is a procedural defect in defendant Lucero's notice of removal which requires this Court to remand the case back to the state district court. Specifically, Fremont County argues that remand is appropriate because it has not joined in the petition for removal, nor has it consented to the removal.

Plaintiff Larry Mathews also has filed a motion for remand on the grounds that the action was improperly removed to the federal court and is not within the jurisdiction of this Court, again for the reason that all of the defendants named in the complaint and properly served in the action did not join in the notice of removal.

Defendant Lucero did not offer a written response to the motion to remand, but responded to the motion orally at the hearing. He argued that, because the complaint asserts claims against him under 42 U.S.C. § 1983, he has an absolute right to remove the case to federal court, relying on 28 U.S.C. § 1443. Defendant Coppack agreed with the arguments asserted by Lucero, and joined with Lucero's request that the case not be remanded to state court.

Discussion

The right to litigate federal questions in federal courts is not absolute or unlimited. Resident Advisory Bd. v. Tate, 329 F.Supp. 427, 432 (E.D.Pa. 1971). The issue before the Court now is whether the federal court must accept removal of the case from state court when a well-pleaded complaint asserts a claim under 42 U.S.C. § 1983. This is significant, of course, because Section 1983 claims are claims over which the federal and state courts exercise concurrent jurisdiction. Howlett By and Through Howlett v. Rose, 496 U.S. 356, 357 (1990). The removal statutes permit a federal court to "encroach upon a state court's right to determine cases properly brought before that state court only with the express authority of Congress." Resident Advisory Bd. v. Tate, 329 F.Supp. 427, 431 (E.D.Pa.1971).

It has long been the general federal rule that all defendants must join in or consent to removal. See e.g., Brown v. Demco, Inc., 792 F.2d 478, 481 (5th Cir.1986); Gallagher v. Mitsubishi, 1990 WL 129611, 7 (N.D.Ill.1990) (unpublished opinion); Hewitt v. City of Stanton, 798 F.2d 1230, 1232 (9th Cir.1986). The rule requiring unanimity of defendants is the rule that continues to obtain in the Tenth Circuit as well. In Cornwall v. Robinson, 654 F.2d 685, 686 (10th Cir.1981), the Tenth Circuit stated that where "a co-defendant [. . .] did not join in the petition for removal [. . .] the petition was thus procedurally defective[,]" citing Tri–Cities Newspapers, Inc. v. Tri–Cities Pressmen Local 349, 427 F.2d 325 (5th Cir.1970). In the *Cornwall v. Robinson* case, as in this one, a non-consenting co-defendant and plaintiff both objected to the removal to federal court. See also FDIC v. OKC Partners, Ltd., 961 F.2d 219 (10th Cir.1992) (unpublished disposition, text in Westlaw).

Removal statutes are to be "strictly construed to limit the federal court's authority to that expressly provided by Congress and to protect the states' judicial powers." First Nat. Bank & Trust Co. v. Nicholas, 768 F.Supp. 788, 790 (D.Kan.1991) (quoting Cohen v. Hoard, 696 F.Supp. 564, 565 (D.Kan.1988)). Further, the party seeking removal always has the burden of showing the propriety of removal. Id.; Emrich v. Touche Ross & Co., 846 F.2d 1190, 1193 n. 1, 1195 (9th Cir.1988) (citing Wilson v. Republic Iron & Steel Co., 257 U.S. 92, 97 (1921)).

There are exceptions to the general rule requiring unanimity of all served defendants. For example, when a nonjoined or non-consenting defendant is merely a nominal party, removal may be appropriate, notwithstanding the failure to consent to removal. *Hewitt v. City of Stanton*, 798 F.2d, at 1232; First Nat. Bank & Trust Co. v. Nicholas, 768 F.Supp. 788, 790 (D.Kan.1991). Indeed, defendant Lucero has argued that Fremont County is only a nominal defendant in this case and that removal to federal court is appropriate.

Nominal parties may be disregarded for removal purposes. The burden of establishing a party's nominal status rests with the party seeking removal. Norman v. Cuomo, 796 F.Supp. 654, 658 (N.D.N.Y.1992). This burden may be satisfied by demonstrating that "the non-consenting defendants, despite their presence in the suit, simply cannot afford the desired

relief to the plaintiffs." Id. Courts have described nominal parties variously: "[A] party is considered nominal if 'no cause of action or claim for relief
is or could be stated against him or on his behalf ....' " Id. A nominal
party has also been described as one that has no interest in the outcome of
the litigation other than as a stakeholder or depository. *Hewitt v. City of
Stanton*, 798 F.2d, at 1233.

In this case, plaintiffs are asserting specific relief against Fremont
County, a defendant who has not consented to nor joined in the removal to
federal court. Fremont County argues that unquestionably it is more than a
nominal party, contrary to the assertions of defendant Lucero at the
hearing. This Court agrees with Fremont County. Plaintiff seeks relief
against all of the defendants, including Fremont County, in the form of
damages, among other relief. Fremont County has more than a casual
interest in protecting the public purse. It cannot be gainsaid that Fremont
County is a mere stakeholder, depository or a nominal party with no
interest in the outcome of the instant litigation.

Another exception to the general rule requiring unanimity of defendants for removal are cases where federal jurisdiction of a party is based on
a separate and independent jurisdictional grant. These cases involve parties
with statutory grants of party-based jurisdiction, examples being those
cases involving the American National Red Cross or the F.D.I.C. See, e.g.,
American National Red Cross v. S.G. & A.E., 505 U.S. 247 (1992); Roe v.
Little Co. of Mary Hosp., 815 F.Supp. 241 (N.D.Ill.1992). In the instant
case, however, this exception has no application, as there is no party with
an independent, party-based jurisdictional grant with a substantive right to
remove to federal court.

Finally, this Court must consider whether the fact that plaintiff's
complaint asserts claims under 42 U.S.C. § 1983 requires removal in the
absence of complete unanimity among defendants. The Court was unable to
locate any caselaw which requires that Section 1983 claims be treated, for
removal purposes, differently than any other federal statute giving the
district court federal question jurisdiction. Hewitt v. City of Stanton, 798
F.2d 1230 (9th Cir.1986), was a case involving an appeal of an order of the
district court imposing sanctions for a petition for removal found to be
frivolous and interposed for the improper purpose of delay. The complaint
in that case was one in which the plaintiff had asserted against the city a
42 U.S.C. § 1983 civil rights and state wrongful death action. Removal had
been sought pursuant to 28 U.S.C. § 1441(b), federal question jurisdiction
removal, and 28 U.S.C. § 1443. The defendant city had not been joined in
the petition for removal.

In the case, it was argued that the City was a nominal party because
its liability was derivative and dependent on the police officer's liability.
That court stated the argument was frivolous, because "as a municipality,
the City could be held liable even if the good faith qualified immunity
defense would shield [the defendant] from liability[,]" 798 F.2d, at 1233,
among other reasons.

Additionally, the court noted that even if the city had joined in the removal petition,

> removal under section 1443 would nevertheless have been frivolous. To remove a civil rights case under section 1443, it must appear that the right allegedly denied arises under a federal law "providing for specific civil rights stated in terms of racial equality," and that the removal petitioner is denied or cannot enforce the specific federal right in state court.

Id. The court found the claim presented no basis for removal under section 1443. The Court believes this case represents a well reasoned approach for resolving the issues which are now before the Court. Because there are no allegations in the complaint asserting specific civil rights stated in terms of racial equality, removal under section 1443 in this case is not appropriate.

The Court has been unable to discern any reason why the prevailing Tenth Circuit rules regarding removal should not be applied in the instant case. Because there is no unanimity among defendants, the case should be remanded to the District Court of Fremont County, Wyoming, Ninth Judicial District, Civil Number 27605. Accordingly, and for the foregoing reasons, it is therefore

ORDERED that the Motion to Remand filed by the County of Fremont, Wyoming, by and through its Board of Commissioners, shall be, and is, GRANTED. It is further

ORDERED that the Motion for Remand filed by Plaintiff Larry M. Mathews shall be, and is, GRANTED.[59]

Carlsbad Technology, Inc. v. HIF Bio, Inc.

Supreme Court of the United States, 2009.
556 U.S. 635, 129 S.Ct. 1862, 173 L.Ed.2d 843.

■ JUSTICE THOMAS delivered the opinion of the Court.

In this case, we decide whether a federal court of appeals has jurisdiction to review a district court's order that remands a case to state court after declining to exercise supplemental jurisdiction over state-law claims under 28 U.S.C. § 1367(c). The Court of Appeals for the Federal Circuit held that appellate review of such an order is barred by § 1447(d) because it viewed the remand order in this case as resting on the District Court's lack of subject-matter jurisdiction over the state-law claims. We disagree and reverse the judgment of the Court of Appeals.

[59. When unanimity is required, the wisest course to follow to avoid the risk of a procedurally defective removal is for all defendants formally to join in and to sign the notice of removal. When the notice of removal is filed unilaterally, some courts have refused to accept a mere representation by the removing defendant, even though it is accurate and undisputed, that the notice of removal has been filed with the consent of all other defendants required to join in the removal. See, e.g., Stonewall Jackson Memorial Hospital v. American United Life Ins. Co., 963 F.Supp. 553 (N.D.W.Va.1997).]

I

In 2005, respondents filed a complaint against petitioner and others in California state court, alleging that petitioner had violated state and federal law in connection with a patent dispute. Petitioner removed the case to the United States District Court for the Central District of California pursuant to § 1441(c), which allows removal of an "entire case" when it includes at least one claim over which the federal district court has original jurisdiction. Petitioner then filed a motion to dismiss the only federal claim in the lawsuit, which arose under the Racketeer Influenced and Corrupt Organizations Act (RICO), 18 U.S.C. §§ 1961–1968, for failure to adequately allege a pattern of racketeering. HIF Bio, Inc. v. Yung Shin Pharmaceuticals Indus. Co., 508 F.3d 659, 662 (C.A.Fed.2007). The District Court agreed that respondents had failed to state a RICO claim upon which relief could be granted and dismissed the claim pursuant to Federal Rule of Civil Procedure 12(b)(6). The District Court also declined to exercise supplemental jurisdiction over the remaining state-law claims pursuant to 28 U.S.C. § 1367(c)(3), which provides that a district court "may decline to exercise supplemental jurisdiction over a claim" if "the district court has dismissed all claims over which it has original jurisdiction." The District Court then remanded the case to state court. . . .

Petitioner appealed to the United States Court of Appeals for the Federal Circuit, arguing that the District Court should have exercised supplemental jurisdiction over the state-law claims because they implicate federal patent-law rights. 508 F.3d, at 663. The Court of Appeals dismissed the appeal, finding that the remand order could "be colorably characterized as a remand based on lack of subject matter jurisdiction" and, therefore, could not be reviewed under §§ 1447(c) and (d), which provide in part that remands for "lack of subject matter jurisdiction" are "not reviewable on appeal or otherwise." See id., at 667.

This Court has not yet decided whether a district court's order remanding a case to state court after declining to exercise supplemental jurisdiction is a remand for lack of subject-matter jurisdiction for which appellate review is barred by §§ 1447(c) and (d). . . . We granted certiorari to resolve this question, and now hold that such remand orders are not based on a lack of subject-matter jurisdiction. Accordingly, we reverse the judgment of the Court of Appeals and remand for further proceedings.

II

Appellate review of remand orders is limited by 28 U.S.C. § 1447(d), which states:

> "An order remanding a case to the State court from which it was removed is not reviewable on appeal or otherwise, except that an order remanding a case to the State court from which it was removed pursuant to section 1443 of this title shall be reviewable by appeal or otherwise."

This Court has consistently held that § 1447(d) must be read in pari materia with § 1447(c), thus limiting the remands barred from appellate review by § 1447(d) to those that are based on a ground specified in § 1447(c). See Thermtron Products, Inc. v. Hermansdorfer, 423 U.S. 336, 345–346 (1976); see also *Powerex*, supra, at 229; Quackenbush v. Allstate Ins. Co., 517 U.S. 706, 711–712; Things Remembered, Inc. v. Petrarca, 516 U.S. 124, 127 (1995).[60]

One type of remand order governed by § 1447(c)—the type at issue in this case—is a remand order based on a lack of "subject matter jurisdiction." § 1447(c) (providing, in relevant part, that "[i]f at any time before final judgment it appears that the district court lacks subject matter jurisdiction, the case shall be remanded"). The question presented in this case is whether the District Court's remand order, which rested on its decision declining to exercise supplemental jurisdiction over respondents' state-law claims, is a remand based on a "lack of subject matter jurisdiction" for purposes of §§ 1447(c) and (d). It is not.

"Subject matter jurisdiction defines the court's authority to hear a given type of case," United States v. Morton, 467 U.S. 822, 828 (1984); it represents "the extent to which a court can rule on the conduct of persons or the status of things." Black's Law Dictionary 870 (8th ed.2004). This Court's precedent makes clear that whether a court has subject-matter jurisdiction over a claim is distinct from whether a court chooses to exercise that jurisdiction. See, e.g., *Quackenbush*, supra, at 712 (holding that an abstention-based remand is not a remand for "lack of subject matter jurisdiction" for purposes of §§ 1447(c) and (d)); Ankenbrandt v. Richards, 504 U.S. 689, 704 (1992) (questioning whether, "even though subject matter jurisdiction might be proper, sufficient grounds exist to warrant abstention from the exercise of that jurisdiction"); Iowa Mut. Ins. Co. v. LaPlante, 480 U.S. 9, 16, n.8 (1987) (referring to exhaustion requirement as "a matter of comity" that does "not deprive the federal courts of subject-matter jurisdiction" but does "rende[r] it appropriate for the federal courts to decline jurisdiction in certain circumstances").

With respect to supplemental jurisdiction in particular, a federal court has subject-matter jurisdiction over specified state-law claims, which it may (or may not) choose to exercise. See §§ 1367(a), (c). A district court's decision whether to exercise that jurisdiction after dismissing every claim over which it had original jurisdiction is purely discretionary. See § 1367(c) ("The district courts may decline to exercise supplemental jurisdiction over a claim . . . if . . . the district court has dismissed all claims over which it has original jurisdiction" (emphasis added)); Osborn v. Haley, 549 U.S. 225, 245 (2007) ("Even if only state-law claims remained after resolution of the federal question, the District Court would have discretion, consistent with Article III, to retain jurisdiction"); Arbaugh v. Y & H Corp., 546 U.S. 500, 514 (2006) ("[W]hen a court grants a motion to dismiss for failure to state

---

60. We do not revisit today whether *Thermtron* was correctly decided. Neither the brief for petitioner nor the brief for respondents explicitly asked the Court to do so here, and counsel for both parties clearly stated at oral argument that they were not asking for *Thermtron* to be overruled. . . . We also note that the parties in *Powerex*, *Quackenbush*, and *Things Remembered* did not ask for *Thermtron* to be overruled.

a federal claim, the court generally retains discretion to exercise supplemental jurisdiction, pursuant to 28 U.S.C. § 1367, over pendent state-law claims"); see also 13D C. Wright, A. Miller, E. Cooper, & R. Freer, Federal Practice and Procedure § 3567.3, pp. 428–432 (3d ed.2008) ("Once it has dismissed the claims that invoked original bases of subject matter jurisdiction, all that remains before the federal court are state-law claims.... The district court retains discretion to exercise supplemental jurisdiction [over them]"). As a result, "the [district] court's exercise of its discretion under § 1367(c) is not a jurisdictional matter. Thus, the court's determination may be reviewed for abuse of discretion, but may not be raised at any time as a jurisdictional defect." 16 J. Moore et al., Moore's Federal Practice § 106.05[4], p. 106–27 (3d ed.2009).

It is undisputed that when this case was removed to federal court, the District Court had original jurisdiction over the federal RICO claim pursuant to 28 U.S.C. § 1331 and supplemental jurisdiction over the state-law claims because they were "so related to claims in the action within such original jurisdiction that they form[ed] part of the same case or controversy under Article III of the United States Constitution." § 1367(a). Upon dismissal of the federal claim, the District Court retained its statutory supplemental jurisdiction over the state-law claims. Its decision declining to exercise that statutory authority was not based on a jurisdictional defect but on its discretionary choice not to hear the claims despite its subject-matter jurisdiction over them. See Chicago v. International College of Surgeons, 522 U.S. 156, 173 (1997) ("Depending on a host of factors, then-including the circumstances of the particular case, the nature of the state law claims, the character of the governing state law, and the relationship between the state and federal claims—district courts may decline to exercise jurisdiction over supplemental state law claims"). The remand order, therefore, is not based on a "lack of subject matter jurisdiction" for purposes of the bar to appellate review created by §§ 1447(c) and (d).

The Court of Appeals held to the contrary based on its conclusion that "every § 1367(c) remand necessarily involves a predicate finding that the claims at issue lack an independent basis of subject matter jurisdiction." 508 F.3d at 667. But, as explained above, §§ 1367(a) and (c) provide a basis for subject-matter jurisdiction over any properly removed state claim. See *Osborn*, supra, at 245; *Arbaugh*, supra, at 514. We thus disagree with the Court of Appeals that the remand at issue here "can be colorably characterized as a lack of subject matter jurisdiction." 508 F.3d at 667.

* * *

When a district court remands claims to a state court after declining to exercise supplemental jurisdiction, the remand order is not based on a lack of subject-matter jurisdiction for purposes of §§ 1447(c) and (d). The judgment of the Court of Appeals for the Federal Circuit is reversed, and the case is remanded for further proceedings consistent with this opinion.

It is so ordered.

[The concurring opinions of Justice Stevens, Justice Scalia, and Justice Breyer are omitted.]

CHAPTER VII

VENUE[1]

INTRODUCTORY NOTE

Although the concept of venue—that there is a particular court or courts in which an action should be brought—is of ancient common-law lineage, it was not until 1887 that the federal courts had any significant venue requirements for civil actions. Until that time the relevant statute, with origins going back to the First Judiciary Act, permitted suit in any district where the defendant "is an inhabitant, or in which he shall be found ...." The latter clause meant that venue was proper in ordinary cases wherever service could be made on the defendant.

Although there were changes in detail, the framework created by the 1887 statute continued until a major revision was made in 1990. The general plan, as it stood under the 1948 Judicial Code until the statutes were thoroughly overhauled in 1990, was that if jurisdiction was founded "only" on diversity of citizenship, suit could be brought only "in the district where all plaintiffs or all defendants reside," 28 U.S.C. § 1391(a), while if jurisdiction was based in whole or in part on the presence of a federal question, suit had to be brought in the district "where all defendants reside." 28 U.S.C. § 1391(b). If defendants resided in different districts of the same state, suit could be brought in any of those districts. 28 U.S.C. § 1392(a). A useful addition, written into the statutes in 1966 but given a grudgingly narrow construction by the Supreme Court, provided an alternative in both diversity and federal-question cases. Suit could be brought in the district "in which the claim arose." From 1948 to 1988 it was provided that a corporation could be sued in any district "in which it is incorporated or licensed to do business or is doing business." There was much disagreement on the interpretation of that section, and a new and broader definition of corporate residence was written into 28 U.S.C. § 1391(c) in 1988.

The classic explanation of the significance of venue was by Justice Frankfurter in Neirbo Co. v. Bethlehem Shipbuilding Corp., 308 U.S. 165, 167–168 (1939):

> The jurisdiction of the federal courts—their power to adjudicate—is a grant of authority to them by Congress and thus beyond the scope of

[1. See generally, ALI Judicial Code Project, Part II: Venue and Transfer, at 137–323; Wright & Kane, Federal Courts, § 42 (6th ed.2002); National Legal Center for the Public Interest, Venue at the Crossroads (1982); Clermont, Restating Territorial Jurisdiction and Venue for State and Federal Courts, 66 Cornell L.Rev. 411 (1981).]

litigants to confer. But the locality of a law suit—the place where judicial authority may be exercised—though defined by legislation relates to the convenience of litigants and as such is subject to their disposition. This basic difference between the court's power and the litigant's convenience is historic in the federal courts.... Section 51 "merely accords to the defendant a personal privilege respecting the venue, or place of suit, which he may assert, or may waive, at his election." Commercial Cas. Ins. Co. v. Stone, 278 U.S. 177, 179 [(1929)].

> Being a privilege, it may be lost. It may be lost by failure to assert it seasonably, by formal submission in a cause, or by submission through conduct.... Whether such surrender of a personal immunity be conceived negatively as a waiver or positively as a consent to be sued, is merely an expression of literary preference.

———

COMMENT ON THE PROBLEMATICS OF FEDERAL VENUE LAW[2]

The complications of allocating venue among the federal district courts arise from conceptual doubt as well as doctrinal conflict. They present many interesting issues of principle. Not first-order principles, to be sure. The place of suit should not be unduly inconvenient, either to the involuntary parties or to the involuntary agents of adjudication—judges, courts more generally, jurors, witnesses. But second-order principles, that determine how cases are to be allocated in the way that the familiar first-order principles demand. If the residence of defending parties is an appropriate venue criterion, because it guards against their inconvenience, what conception of residence should be determinative? Should it matter whether those parties are individuals or entities, and if entities, whether they are incorporated? If the nature of the litigation rather than the circumstances of the parties is determinative, how far should venue law go in permitting claims to be aggregated, even if some of these claims could not be litigated in the chosen forum if sued upon alone? And what account should be taken of the strategic impact of venue on the probable outcome of the litigation— an impact more fundamental than such matters of tactical advantage as differences in local culture or the practical burden of presenting an effective case in an inconvenient location?

As these questions suggest, venue law is a polymorphic topic. This results in part from its sources—the usual mélange of law inherited, discovered, construed, and created from history, statute, and the felt imperatives of the time. But since form follows function, this results also from two distinct functions that venue law performs. One is personal to affected parties, whose convenience may be affected and whose rights may

---

2. This text is reprinted from Professor Oakley's introduction, as Reporter, to the new and revised venue statutes proposed by the Judicial Code Project. ALI, Federal Judicial Code Revision Project, Part II: Venue and Transfer, Reporter's Summary at 137–140 (2004).

be waived. The other is institutional, and serves the interest of the court system in allocating cases efficiently among the various available venues. The tension between these two functions is most apparent in the law of interdistrict transfer. Venue rights may be waived, but waiver is not permitted to enlarge the range of potential transferee districts.

Lurking in the background is a third function that venue law serves, indirectly if not intrinsically, and that accounts for the great importance that parties attach to their venue options quite apart from any genuine inconvenience that may or may not result from being forced to litigate a case in one district rather than another. Where a case is litigated will often determine what law will be applied to key issues in that case. Much of the energy devoted to contests over venue is derived from the fact that the choice of the venue of a civil action will, if successfully defended, control the choice of the substantive law to be applied in that civil action.

Strategic choice-of-law concerns may drive choice of venue, and lead to hard-fought venue contests, even as to issues of federal law. Despite the nominal uniformity of federal law, divisions among the circuits on issues of federal law may control the likely outcome of litigation, with slim prospects that the split in authority will soon be resolved by the Supreme Court. But it is with respect to issues of state law that the most palpable differences arise between the law applied in one district as opposed to another in a different state.

Choice of law by state courts is unruly and, in all but the rarest cases, essentially unregulated by the United States Supreme Court. The default tends to be the application of the law of the forum, and there are dramatic differences among states on frequently litigated issues of substantive liability. When litigation takes place in federal court, the *Erie* doctrine compels the federal court to follow the choice-of-law rules of the state in which the case was properly commenced, even if it has since been transferred on convenience grounds to a district in another state. And while *Erie* is associated with diversity litigation, its choice-of-law rules and their link to initial venue may significantly impact the adjudication of state-law claims that are within the now-generous supplemental jurisdiction of the federal district courts.

A related wrinkle is the concurrent jurisdiction of state courts over most cases that are within federal subject-matter jurisdiction. When a plaintiff chooses to sue in state court notwithstanding the availability of a federal forum, defendants may have a right of removal—although where federal jurisdiction is based only on diversity of citizenship, this right is relatively easy to frustrate by a plaintiff alert to that unwelcome possibility. But even where the right of removal is properly exercised, issues of state law remain linked by *Erie* to the plaintiff's initial choice of the state in which to bring suit.

This means that forum-shopping for favorable state law cannot be controlled by narrow federal venue statutes. No lawsuit can proceed in a court without territorial jurisdiction over a defendant anxious to avoid suit there rather than in some other forum where law more favorable to the defendant will be applied. In choosing among potential state forums, a plaintiff is constrained by considerations of territorial jurisdiction whether suit is brought in state or federal court. Thus, territorial jurisdiction acts as an initial filter for choice of forum and hence choice of law. Venue constraints are meaningful only when they demand something more than territorial jurisdiction to make a particular forum one in which venue may properly be laid. But if federal venue law is made highly discriminating, restricting a plaintiff's choice of a federal forum to the district courts of just one or two states, the plaintiff has the standing option to sue instead in state court in some other state with territorial jurisdiction over the defendant whose law favors the plaintiff. And the defendant will often be able to remove that suit to a federal court in which it could not originally have been commenced. Removal law thus acts as a trump of narrow federal venue provisions.

Abolishing or limiting removal would attack the symptom, not its cause. Concurrent state-court jurisdiction and liberal state-court territorial jurisdiction are what fuel interstate forum shopping for favorable choices of law. Restricting removal would simply close the federal courts to many cases more appropriately litigated there than in state court, magnifying rather than minimizing the tactical burdens that accompany strategic forum-shopping within the joint system of state and federal courts.

————

REPORT OF FEDERAL COURTS STUDY COMMITTEE (April 2, 1990), p. 94

Recommendation 5.B.2: Congress should clarify 28 U.S.C. §§ 1391(a) & (b), the general venue statute.

The general venue statute includes "the judicial district ... in which the claim arose" as one of the districts where civil actions may be brought. The implication that there can be only one such district encourages litigation over which of the possibly several districts involved in a multi-forum transaction is the one "in which the claim arose." We suggest that Congress replace that phrase with: "any judicial district in which a substantial part of the events or omissions giving rise to the claim occurred, or a substantial part of property that is the subject of the action is situated." Congress used the same phrasing in a 1976 amendment designating venue in actions against foreign states.

Congress should also eliminate the century-old anomaly, now codified in the venue in diversity but not federal question cases "in the judicial district where all plaintiffs ... reside." There is no good historical or functional reason for this distinction, which perversely favors home-state plaintiffs in diversity cases. The American Law Institute's 1969 Study of the Division of Jurisdiction Between State and Federal Courts proposed eliminating plaintiffs' residence as a basis for venue and providing for venue in a judicial district in which "any defendant resides, if all defendants reside in the same State." The moderate broadening of venue suggested immediately above means that if a litigation has a significant relation to a plaintiff's home state, it may be brought there; if it has no such relation, the plaintiff's residence alone should not suffice for venue.

———

VENUE STATUTES

28 U.S.C. § 1390. Scope[3]

(a) VENUE DEFINED.—As used in this chapter, the term "venue" refers to the geographic specification of the proper court or courts for the litigation of a civil action that is within the subject-matter jurisdiction of the district courts in general, and does not refer to any grant or restriction of subject-matter jurisdiction providing for a civil action to be adjudicated only by the district court for a particular district or districts.

(b) EXCLUSION OF CERTAIN CASES.—Except as otherwise provided by law, this chapter shall not govern the venue of a civil action in which the district court exercises the jurisdiction conferred by section 1333, except that such civil actions may be transferred between district courts as provided in this chapter.

(c) CLARIFICATION REGARDING CASES REMOVED FROM STATE COURTS.—This chapter shall not determine the district court to which a civil action pending in a State court may be removed, but shall govern the transfer of an action so removed as between districts and divisions of the United States district courts.

28 U.S.C. § 1391. Venue generally

(a) APPLICABILITY OF SECTION.—Except as otherwise provided by law—

(1) this section shall govern the venue of all civil actions brought in district courts of the United States; and

(2) the proper venue for a civil action shall be determined without regard to whether the action is local or transitory in nature.

(b) VENUE IN GENERAL.—A civil action may be brought in—

(1) a judicial district in which any defendant resides, if all defendants are residents of the State in which the district is located;

(2) a judicial district in which a substantial part of the events or omissions giving rise to the claim occurred, or a substantial part of the property that is the subject of the action is situated; or

(3) if there is no district in which an action may otherwise be brought as provided in this section, any judicial district in which any defendant is subject to the court's personal jurisdiction with respect to such action.

(c) RESIDENCY.—For all venue purposes—

---

3. Section 1390 was added as part of the Jurisdiction and Venue Clarification Act of 2011, which also amended sections 1391 and 1404.

(1) a natural person, including an alien lawfully admitted for permanent residence in the United States, shall be deemed to reside in the judicial district in which that person is domiciled;

(2) an entity with the capacity to sue and be sued in its common name under applicable law, whether or not incorporated, shall be deemed to reside, if a defendant, in any judicial district in which such defendant is subject to the court's personal jurisdiction with respect to the civil action in question and, if a plaintiff, only in the judicial district in which it maintains its principal place of business; and

(3) a defendant not resident in the United States may be sued in any judicial district, and the joinder of such a defendant shall be disregarded in determining where the action may be brought with respect to other defendants.

(d) Residency of Corporations in States With Multiple Districts.—For purposes of venue under this chapter, in a State which has more than one judicial district and in which a defendant that is a corporation is subject to personal jurisdiction at the time an action is commenced, such corporation shall be deemed to reside in any district in that State within which its contacts would be sufficient to subject it to personal jurisdiction if that district were a separate State, and, if there is no such district, the corporation shall be deemed to reside in the district within which it has the most significant contacts.

(e) Actions Where Defendant is Officer or Employee of the United States.—

(1) In General.—A civil action in which a defendant is an officer or employee of the United States or any agency thereof acting in his official capacity or under color of legal authority, or an agency of the United States, may, except as otherwise provided by law, be brought in any judicial district in which:

(A) a defendant in the action resides;

(B) a substantial part of the events or omissions giving rise to the claim occurred, or a substantial part of property that is the subject of the action is situated, or

(C) the plaintiff resides if no real property is involved in the action.

Additional persons may be joined as parties to any such action in accordance with the Federal Rules of Civil Procedure and with such other venue requirements as would be applicable if the United States or one of its officers, employees, or agencies were not a party.

(2) Service.—The summons and complaint in such an action shall be served as provided by the Federal Rules of Civil Procedure except that the delivery of the summons and complaint to the officer or agency as required by the rules may be made by certified mail beyond the territorial limits of the district in which the action is brought.

(f) CIVIL ACTIONS AGAINST A FOREIGN STATE.—A civil action against a foreign state as defined in section 1603(a) of this title may be brought—

(1) in any judicial district in which a substantial part of the events or omissions giving rise to the claim occurred, or a substantial part of property that is the subject of the action is situated;

(2) in any judicial district in which the vessel or cargo of a foreign state is situated, if the claim is asserted under section 1605(b) of this title;

(3) in any judicial district in which the agency or instrumentality is licensed to do business or is doing business, if the action is brought against an agency or instrumentality of a foreign state as defined in section 1603(b) of this title; or

(4) in the United States District Court for the District of Columbia if the action is brought against a foreign state or political subdivision thereof.[4]

(g) MULTIPARTY, MULTIFORM LITIGATION.—A civil action in which jurisdiction of the district court is based upon section 1369 of this title may be brought in any district in which any defendant resides or in which a substantial part of the accident giving rise to the action took place.[5]

[4. Subsection (f) was added by the Foreign Sovereign Immunities Act of 1976, Pub.L. 94–583, § 5, 90 Stat. 2897. This Act is discussed in Verlinden, B.V. v. Central Bank of Nigeria, reprinted supra p. 164.]

[5. Subsection (g) was added by the Multiparty, Multiforum Trial Jurisdiction Act of 2002, discussed supra p. 179, n. 13.

There are many specialized venue provisions, scattered in and out of Title 28. Many of those existing in 1969 were listed in ALI Study, Appendix F, at 498–501. That list has been revised and greatly extended in ALI, Federal Judicial Code Revision Project, Part II, Reporter's Note B: Special Venue Statutes, at 253–304 (2004). With the broadening of the definition of corporate residence in § 1391(c) in 1988 and the general broadening of venue choices by the rewriting of subsections (a) and (b) of § 1391 in 1990, it is difficult to believe that there is any utility in these special statutes. Although the ALI's 2004 project did not undertake a general weeding of redundant special-venue statutes, it did propose to repeal one especially troublesome one: the patent-venue statute, 28 U.S.C. § 1400. See ALI Judicial Code Project, Commentary on Repeal of § 1400, at 212–214.

A standing question posed by any special venue provision is whether it is restrictive (specifying venue exclusive of the general venue statute, 28 U.S.C. § 1391) or permissive (supplementing the venue options provided by the general venue statute). In Cortez Byrd Chips, Inc. v. Bill Harbert Construction Co., 529 U.S. 193 (2000), the Court determined that the special venue provisions of the Federal Arbitration Act, 9 U.S.C. §§ 9–11, were permissive rather than restrictive. Thus the venue of an action to vacate or modify an arbitration award was held to have properly been laid in the district in which the relevant contract was to have been performed—a district in which venue was proper under 28 U.S.C. § 1391(a)(2)—even though it was not a district specified by 9 U.S.C. §§ 10–11, which specify that an action to vacate (§ 10) or modify (§ 11) an arbitration award may be brought in the district in which the award was made.

When different venue statutes apply to multiple claims joined in a single complaint, difficult questions of "pendent venue" may arise. See Corn, Comment, Pendent Venue: A Doctrine in Search of a Theory, 68 U.Chi.L.Rev. 931 (2001). The ALI would allow "pendent-claim" but not "pendent-party" venue. See Judicial Code Project, Commentary on § 1406(b), at 224; id., § 1406(d) and Commentary at 231–234.]

28 U.S.C. § 1404. Change of venue

(a) For the convenience of parties and witnesses, in the interest of justice, a district court may transfer any civil action to any other district or division where it might have been brought or to any district or division to which all parties have consented.[6]

(b) Upon motion, consent or stipulation of all parties, any action, suit or proceeding of a civil nature or any motion or hearing thereof, may be transferred, in the discretion of the court, from the division in which pending to any other division in the same district. Transfer of proceedings in rem brought by or on behalf of the United States may be transferred under this section without the consent of the United States where all other parties request transfer.

(c) A district court may order any civil action to be tried at any place within the division in which it is pending.

(d) Transfers from a district court of the United States to the District Court of Guam, the District Court for the Northern Mariana Islands, or the District Court of the Virgin Islands shall not be permitted under this section. As otherwise used in this section, the term "district court" includes the District Court of Guam, the District Court for the Northern Mariana Islands, and the District Court of the Virgin Islands, and the term "district" includes the territorial jurisdiction of each such court.

28 U.S.C. § 1406. Cure or waiver of defects

(a) The district court of a district in which is filed a case laying venue in the wrong division or district shall *dismiss, or if it be in the interest of justice,*[7] transfer such case to any district or division in which it could have been brought.

(b) Nothing in this chapter shall impair the jurisdiction of a district court of any matter involving a party who does not interpose timely and sufficient objection to the venue.[8]

[6. See Wright & Kane, Federal Courts § 44 (6th ed.2002).]

[7. The italicized words were added by amendment May 24, 1949. The Senate Report observes that without such amendment the "provision may be subject to abuse in that a plaintiff might deliberately bring a suit in the wrong division or district where he could get service on the defendant, and when the question of venue is raised the court is required to transfer the case to the court where 'it could have been brought.' However, in the meantime, service has been perfected on a defendant in the wrong venue and it will carry over into the new (and proper) venue. Rather than promote justice, it can be seen that this section may be subject to abuse." Senate Report No. 303, April 26, 1949.]

[8. The ALI's proposed reforms would alter the language of present §§ 1404 and 1406 but would leave substantially unchanged the transfer mechanisms presently in place under those statutes. A number of new features would be added to these statutes, however. Two of these innovations are of particular importance. Proposed new § 1404(c) would allow discretionary transfer between districts within a multi-district state, making unnecessary the tortuous "significant contacts" language of present § 1391(c). Proposed new § 1406(d) would provide comprehensively for the enforcement of forum-selection clauses that alter the venue choices otherwise available to the parties. make significant changes in language but

28 U.S.C. § 1407. Multidistrict litigation

(a) When civil actions involving one or more common questions of fact are pending in different districts, such actions may be transferred to any district for coordinated or consolidated pretrial proceedings. Such transfers shall be made by the judicial panel on multidistrict litigation authorized by this section upon its determination that transfers for such proceedings will be for the convenience of parties and witnesses and will promote the just and efficient conduct of such actions. Each action so transferred shall be remanded by the panel at or before the conclusion of such pretrial proceedings to the district from which it was transferred unless it shall have been previously terminated: *Provided, however,* That the panel may separate any claim, cross-claim, counter-claim, or third-party claim and remand any of such claims before the remainder of the action is remanded.

. . . . .[9]

28 U.S.C. § 1631. Transfer to cure want of jurisdiction

Whenever a civil action is filed in a court as defined in section 610 of this title or an appeal, including a petition for review of administrative action, is noticed for or filed with such a court and that court finds that there is a want of jurisdiction, the court shall, if it is in the interest of justice, transfer such action or appeal to any other such court in which the action or appeal could have been brought at the time it was filed or noticed, and the action or appeal shall proceed as if it had been filed in or noticed for the court to which it is transferred on the date upon which it was actually filed in or noticed for the court from which it is transferred.[10]

---

would leave the substance of largely unaltered. See Judicial Code Revision Project, § 1404 and Commentary at 215–218; id., § 1406 and Commentary at 220–235.]

[9. This is only the first of eight subsections of § 1407, a complex and important provision added in 1968 by Pub.L. 90–296, § 1, 82 Stat. 109. See Comment, The Judicial Panel on Multidistrict Litigation: Time for Rethinking, 140 U.Pa.L.Rev. 711 (1991). See generally Kyle, The Mechanics of Motion Practice Before the Judicial Panel on Multidistrict Litigation, 175 F.R.D. 589 (1998). The ALI Judicial Code Project does not address possible reform of § 1407, which might well merit a project in its own right. Some aspects of § 1407 were considered in ALI, Complex Litigation: Statutory Recommendations and Analysis (1994).

In Lexecon, Inc. v. Milberg Weiss Bershad Hynes & Lerach, 523 U.S. 26 (1998), the Supreme Court rejected contrary authority in the lower courts to rule that § 1407 mandates retransfer of an action back to its original district if trial is required after pretrial proceedings have ended, and that § 1404 cannot properly be used to subvert this mandate. Despite considerable attention, in and out of Congress, *Lexecon* has yet to be overruled. See, e.g., Note, Congress and the Multiparty, Multiforum Trial Jurisdiction Act of 2002: Meaningful Reform or a Comedy of Errors?, 54 Duke L.J. 255, 277–279 (2004).]

[10. This transfer statute was added to the Judicial Code in 1982, at the same time as the creation of two courts of specialized subject-matter jurisdiction: the United States Court of Appeals for the Federal Circuit, and the United States Claims Court (renamed in 1992 the United States Court of Federal Claims). In permitting transfer rather than dismissal when a civil action or appeal has been filed in a court in which "there is a want of jurisdiction," § 1631 was undoubtedly intended to apply only to defects of *subject-matter jurisdiction*

Gregory v. Pocono Grow Fertilizer Corp.

United States District Court, Western District of New York, 1999.
35 F.Supp.2d 295.

■ LARIMER, CHIEF JUDGE.

. . . . .

FACTUAL BACKGROUND

Waste Stream is a New York corporation with its principal place of business in Weedsport, New York. Waste Stream recycles biosolids and sells products and services to the wastewater treatment industry in the Northeast United States. All the shares of Waste Stream were owned by Gregory, who resides in New York, Junior, who resides in Massachusetts, and Gordon, who resides in Maryland.

Pocono Grow is a Pennsylvania corporation with its principal place of business in Stroudsberg, Pennsylvania. Pocono Grow owns the permits and licenses necessary to construct and operate a waste treatment and recycling facility in East Stroudsberg, Pennsylvania. All the shares of Pocono Grow are owned by Bruce and Karen Ecke, who reside in Pennsylvania.

The undisputed facts on this motion establish that the parties began discussing a potential business relationship in February 1997. They conducted these negotiations between New York and Pennsylvania by telephone, facsimile, and mail. Additionally, one face-to-face meeting occurred between Gregory and the Eckes in Pennsylvania during the summer or fall of 1997.

On March 12, 1998, Gregory prepared and executed a letter of intent in New York, which proposed that Waste Stream become a 50% equity owner of Pocono Grow's stock and execute an operation and maintenance agreement for the facility. This letter of intent was delivered to Bruce Ecke in Pennsylvania, signed by him on March 13, 1998, and then returned to Gregory in New York.

---

arising from the filing in the wrong federal court of an action or appeal that is within the subject-matter jurisdiction of some other federal court. The imprecise wording of § 1631 has led some courts, however, to treat it as a general transfer provision that may be used to cure a lack of personal jurisdiction or even venue. See generally Oakley, Prospectus for the American Law Institute's Judicial Code Revision Project, 31 U.C.Davis L.Rev. 855, 979–981 (1998). The ALI's proposed new § 1631 would be limited to transfers between federal courts to cure a lack of subject-matter jurisdiction. See Judicial Code Project § 1631 and Commentary at 236–238.

One clearly proper (if perhaps unintended) application of present § 1631 is to preserve appellate jurisdiction of an appeal when the notice of appeal has been timely filed in the wrong judicial circuit. The circuits are divided, however, as to whether the court of appeals in which the notice of appeal has been timely but otherwise erroneously filed must actually transfer the appeal to the proper circuit, or whether the mere potential for such a transfer is sufficient to give the proper circuit jurisdiction when an untimely notice of appeal has later been filed in that circuit. Compare, e.g., Rodriguez–Roman v. Immigration and Naturalization Service, 98 F.3d 416 (9th Cir.1996) (actual transfer not required), with Howitt v. U.S. Dep't of Commerce, 897 F.2d 583, 584 (1st Cir.1990) (Breyer, J.) (contra, but on distinguishable facts).]

In April 1998, Gregory informed Pocono Grow that all the stock of Waste Stream and Earth Blends, Inc., a company affiliated with Waste Stream, had been acquired by U.S. Liquids, Inc. and U.S. Liquids Northeast, Inc. Gregory assured Pocono Grow that this stock acquisition would not have any adverse effect on Waste Stream's commitment to the facility. Gregory also indicated that in the event U.S. Liquids declined to undertake the project, the individual partners would assume Waste Stream's obligations.

On May 22, 1998, U.S. Liquids informed Pocono Grow that it did not intend to provide equity for the facility. Waste Stream's individual partners also decided that they did not want to pursue the transaction contemplated by the letter of intent.

On June 4, 1998, defendants advised the plaintiffs that they were prepared to commence litigation against Waste Stream and the individual plaintiffs for breach of the letter of intent. Plaintiffs immediately commenced this action for a declaratory judgment that there is no enforceable agreement between the parties. Defendants now move to dismiss plaintiffs' complaint for improper venue or, in the alternative, to transfer this action to the Middle District of Pennsylvania.

DISCUSSION

A. *Defendants' Motion to Dismiss Pursuant to 28 U.S.C. § 1406(a)*

Defendants move to dismiss plaintiffs' complaint for improper venue pursuant to 28 U.S.C. § 1406(a). Section 1406(a) provides that "[t]he district court of a district in which is filed a case laying venue in the wrong division or district shall dismiss, or if it be in the interest of justice, transfer such case to any district or division in which it could have been brought."

Venue in this case is governed by 28 U.S.C. § 1391, which states:

(a) A civil action wherein jurisdiction is founded only on diversity of citizenship may, except as otherwise provided by law, be brought only in (1) a judicial district where any defendant resides, if all defendants reside in the same State, (2) a judicial district in which a substantial part of the events or omissions giving rise to the claim occurred, or a substantial part of property that is the subject of the action is situated, or (3) a judicial district in which any defendant is subject to personal jurisdiction at the time the action is commenced, if there is no district in which the action may otherwise be brought.

At the outset, I must determine whether subsections (a)(1) and (a)(2) provide two independent and alternative bases for venue or whether subsection (a)(2) can be used to establish venue only if subsection (a)(1) does not apply. One court has described the issue as whether the statute should be read conjunctively or disjunctively. School Dist. of Philadelphia v. Pennsylvania Milk Mktg. Bd., 877 F.Supp. 245, 249 (E.D.Pa.1995).

There is some authority that the language of § 1391(a) is to be read disjunctively or hierarchically. In other words, when venue is proper in a particular district pursuant to subsection (a)(1) because all the defendants reside in the same state, venue does not lie elsewhere pursuant to subsection (a)(2). See, e.g., Dashman v. Peter Letterese & Assocs., Inc., 999 F.Supp. 553 (S.D.N.Y.1998); Cobra Partners L.P. v. Liegl, 990 F.Supp. 332 (S.D.N.Y.1998); Welch Foods, Inc. v. Packer, 1994 WL 665399 (W.D.N.Y. Nov.22, 1994). These courts have essentially distilled this proposition from the history of the statute and from certain language found in the Supreme Court's decision in Leroy v. Great Western United Corp., 443 U.S. 173 (1979).

Prior to 1966, the statute provided that venue would be proper "only in the judicial district where all plaintiffs or all defendants reside." Act of June 25, 1948, ch. 646, 62 Stat. 935. If there was no district where all the plaintiffs or all the defendants resided, then a "venue gap" resulted, and the case could not be brought in federal court. In 1966, Congress amended the statute to authorize venue "in the judicial district where all plaintiffs or all defendants reside, or in which the claim arose." Pub.L. No. 89–714, 80 Stat. 1111 (1966). In 1990, the statute was again amended to eliminate the plaintiffs' residence as a proper venue and to change the language from a district "in which the claim arose" to a district "in which a substantial part of the events or omissions giving rise to the claim occurred." Pub.L. No. 101–650, 104 Stat. 5114 (1990).

In *Leroy*, the Supreme Court stated that "the amendment of § 1391 to provide for venue where the claim arose was designed to close the 'venue gaps' that existed under earlier versions of the statute in situations in which ... multiple defendants who contributed to a single injurious act, could not be sued jointly because they resided in different districts." Id., at 184 n. 17. According to the Court, "[s]o long as the plain language of the statute does not open the severe type of 'venue gap' that the amendment giving plaintiffs the right to proceed in the district where the claim arose was designed to close, there is no reason to read it more broadly on behalf of plaintiffs." Id., at 184.

District courts in this Circuit have relied on the history of the statute and the language from *Leroy* for the conclusion that suits may be brought in the district where a substantial part of the events occurred only if all the defendants do not reside in the same state. In my opinion, this conclusion is inconsistent with the plain language of the statute as well as with its legislative history.

The plain language of § 1391(a) indicates that venue is proper either in a district within the state where all the defendants reside or in a district in which a substantial part of the events or omissions giving rise to the claim occurred. Additionally, the legislative history of § 1391 states that "H.R.7382 amends subsections 1391(a) and 1391(b) of Title 28, United States Code, to enlarge venue authority so as to authorize any civil action to be brought in the judicial district where the claim arose. Under [subsection 1391(a)], as amended, a civil action wherein jurisdiction is founded only on diversity of citizenship, unless otherwise provided by law, may be brought in the judicial district in which the claim arose, as well as in the judicial districts where all plaintiffs or defendants reside." Committee Note to 1966 Amendment to Section 1391 (emphasis added), reprinted in 17 Moore's Federal Practice § 110 App. 05[2] (3d ed.1998). There is simply nothing in the language of the statute or its legislative history to suggest that the statute is to be read disjunctively or hierarchically. If Congress had, in fact, intended that result, it certainly could have drafted the language of the statute to that end.

I, therefore, adopt the reasoning of those courts that have held that the language of the statute—which clearly provides alternative bases for venue—controls. See, e.g., Northern Kentucky Welfare Rights Ass'n v. Wilkinson, 1991 WL 86267, at *3 (6th Cir.1991) ("[T]he statute is phrased in the alternative."); Market Transition Facility v. Twena, 941 F.Supp. 462, 465 (D.N.J.1996) ("[T]he plain language of § 1391(a) indicates that venue in diversity cases is proper, regardless of circumstances, in either a district within the state where all defendants reside or in a district where a substantial part of the events or omissions giving rise to the claim occurred. There is nothing on the face of the statute to support [defendant's] interpretation that venue must be in a district where a defendant resides, when all defendants reside in the same state."); *School Dist. of Philadelphia*, 877 F.Supp., at 249 ("Accordingly, we find that even though venue would be appropriate in the Middle District based on (b)(1), it can also be proper here if the requirements of (b)(2) are met."); Merchants Nat'l Bank v. Safrabank, 776 F.Supp. 538, 541 (D.Kan.1991) ("The defendants' argument fails to give effect to the plain language of the statute.... We believe that the language of the statute must control and it provides for alternative bases of venue. Accordingly, we reject the defendants' argument that venue is improper here because all of the defendants reside in the Central District of California.").

I also note that this "alternative" approach has been approved by a leading commentator. According to Wright, Miller & Cooper, "[t]he provision for residential venue, in paragraph (1) ..., and the provision for transactional venue, in paragraph (2) ..., are in the alternative. Venue is proper if either one of those conditions is met." 15 Charles A. Wright et al., Federal Practice and Procedure § 3804, at 16 (2d ed. Supp.1998). This same commentator stated further that it is "clearer than ever that [§ 1391(a)(2)] may be used in any case and is not limited to cases in which defendants could not be sued jointly because they resided in different districts." Id. § 3806, at 17 (2d ed. Supp.1998).

I find, therefore, that both (a)(1) and (a)(2) provide alternative bases for venue. Accordingly, although venue would be proper under (a)(1) in the Middle District of Pennsylvania because all the defendants reside there, venue also would be proper in this District if a substantial part of the events giving rise to plaintiffs' claim occurred here. I turn now to that inquiry.

The standard set forth in § 1391(a)(2) does not require that plaintiffs establish that the Western District of New York has "the most substantial contacts to the dispute; rather it is sufficient that a substantial part of the events occurred [here], even if a greater part of the events occurred elsewhere." Neufeld v. Neufeld, 910 F.Supp. 977, 986 (S.D.N.Y.1996) (quoting Leucadia Nat'l Corp. v. FPL Group Capital, Inc., 1993 WL 464691, at *6 (S.D.N.Y. Nov.9, 1993)). As Professor Seigel explains, "[t]he fact that substantial activities took place in district B does not disqualify district A as proper venue as long as 'substantial' activities took place in A, too. Indeed, district A should not be disqualified even if it is shown that the activities in B were more substantial, or even the most substantial." 28 U.S.C.A. § 1391, David D. Seigel, Commentary on 1988 and 1990 Revisions of Section 1391, at 9.

Courts in this Circuit have held that the substantial activities' standard "may be satisfied by a communication transmitted to or from the district in which the cause of action was filed, given a sufficient relationship between the communication and the cause of action." Constitution Reinsurance Corp. v. Stonewall Ins. Co., 872 F.Supp. 1247, 1249 (S.D.N.Y. 1995) (quoting Sacody Techs., Inc. v. Avant, Inc., 862 F.Supp. 1152, 1157 (S.D.N.Y.1994)).

I find that plaintiffs have alleged sufficient facts to establish that a substantial part of the events giving rise to their claim occurred within this District. There is no dispute that defendants' dealings with plaintiffs regarding the letter of intent occurred by telephone calls, facsimile transmissions, and correspondence between defendants in Pennsylvania and plaintiffs in New York. Further, Gregory prepared and executed the letter of intent in this District and transmitted it to defendants in Pennsylvania. Defendants then transmitted the letter back to plaintiffs in this District. Additionally, any alleged breach of the letter of intent by plaintiffs occurred in this District.

Some important events did occur outside this District in the Middle District of Pennsylvania. For example, a meeting did take place there between Gregory and the Eckes concerning a facility to be constructed in Pennsylvania. "However, as referenced above, a plaintiff does not have to prove that his or her chosen venue is the best forum for the action; a plaintiff need only demonstrate that the choice is a permissible one." *Leucadia Nat'l Corp.*, 1993 WL 464691, at *6. I find that plaintiffs have done so. Accordingly, defendants' motion to dismiss plaintiffs' complaint for improper venue pursuant to § 1406(a) is denied.

B. *Defendants' Motion to Transfer Pursuant to 28 U.S.C. § 1404(a)*

Defendants also move, in the alternative, to transfer this action to the Middle District of Pennsylvania pursuant to § 1404(a). Section 1404(a) permits a district court to transfer an action that is otherwise properly venued to another district where it might have been brought "[f]or the convenience of parties and witnesses, in the interest of justice."

A defendant moving for a change of venue must make out a strong case for transfer. Cerasoli v. Xomed, Inc., 952 F.Supp. 152, 154 (W.D.N.Y.1997). "To prevail on the motion, defendant must make a 'clear showing' that the litigation in the proposed transferee district would be more convenient and would better serve the interests of justice." Id., at 155. I find that defendants have not made any showing in their motion papers why this case should be transferred. Accordingly, defendants' motion to transfer this action pursuant to § 1404 is denied.

. . . . .

Gulf Insurance Co. v. Glasbrenner

United States Court of Appeals, Second Circuit, 2005.
417 F.3d 353.

■ Before MESKILL, JACOBS AND STRAUB, Circuit Judges.

■ MESKILL, Circuit Judge.

In 1990, Congress amended the statute that dictates where venue lies in federal civil suits, 28 U.S.C. § 1391. Although those amendments are not particularly complicated, they are significant and we have previously addressed them only briefly. We do so at length now, and conclude that venue may properly lie in *any* judicial district in which significant events or omissions material to the plaintiff's claim have occurred. Because the United States District Court for the Southern District of New York, Stanton, J.—which dismissed this suit for improper venue—seemingly misapplied this standard, we vacate and remand.

I

The history of this case—spanning eleven years and involving four separate civil actions as well as one non-binding arbitration—is tortuous, but the details are ultimately irrelevant to the appeal before us. We recapitulate only the important facts.

In April 1994, Susan Glasbrenner was injured in a Caldor store in New Jersey. She and her husband David (the appellants here) sued Caldor in New Jersey state court in February of the following year. But by that time, Caldor had filed for bankruptcy and the Glasbrenners' suit was stayed pending proceedings before the bankruptcy court in the Southern District of New York. The bankruptcy court required the Glasbrenners to arbitrate their claim, but ultimately permitted the New Jersey state suit to proceed. The bankruptcy court imposed one caveat, however: any judgment against Caldor could not be held against the bankrupt estate, but would instead have to be satisfied by Caldor's insurers, which included Gulf Insurance Co.

In April 2003, nine years after the injury, a New Jersey jury returned a verdict of approximately $2.6 million for the Glasbrenners. By then, Caldor's bankruptcy proceedings were long over, the bankruptcy court having ordered Caldor to wind down in late 2001.

Once the jury returned its verdict against Caldor, Gulf immediately filed this suit in the Southern District of New York seeking a declaration that, under the terms of the applicable insurance policy, it is not liable to pay the New Jersey judgment. The Glasbrenners promptly moved to dismiss the suit for improper venue, among other things, arguing that venue lies in New Jersey. Simultaneously, they filed a suit in New Jersey state court—since removed to federal court in the District of New Jersey—seeking to compel Gulf to pay the judgment.

The district court in New York dismissed Gulf's declaratory judgment action for improper venue pursuant to Federal Rule of Civil Procedure 12(b)(3), and this appeal followed. We understand that the New Jersey enforcement action has been stayed pending the outcome of this appeal.

II

[The Second Circuit concluded that its review of a motion to dismiss for improper venue is de novo.]

III

We turn now to the civil venue statute itself. *See* 28 U.S.C. § 1391. It provides, in pertinent part:

> A civil action wherein jurisdiction is not founded solely on diversity of citizenship may, except as otherwise provided by law, be brought only in (1) a judicial district where any defendant resides, if all defendants reside in the same State, (2) a judicial district in which a substantial part of the events or omissions giving rise to the claim occurred, or a substantial part of property that is the subject of the action is situated, or (3) a judicial district in which any defendant may be found, if there is no district in which the action may otherwise be brought.

28 U.S.C. § 1391(b).[11] Caldor was a Delaware corporation doing business out of Connecticut. The Glasbrenners reside in Pennsylvania. The defendants thus reside in different states, and subsection (1) does not apply. And because the parties concede that the action could have been brought in New Jersey—indeed, the Glasbrenners' New Jersey enforcement action is nothing but the mirror-image of this declaratory judgment action—subsection (3) does not apply. Thus, our question is whether the Southern District of New York is "a judicial district in which a substantial part of the events or omissions giving rise to the claim occurred." Id.

A

Prior to its amendment in 1990, however, the civil venue statute required a different inquiry. It provided that "a civil action wherein jurisdiction is not founded solely on diversity of citizenship may be brought only in *the* judicial district ... *in which the claim arose*." 28 U.S.C. § 1391(b) (1989) (emphasis added). See generally Colleen McMahon, *Venue*, in Federal Civil Practice 61, 67–68 (Georgene M. Vairo ed., 1989). The

---

[11. The separate, although substantively identical, venue provisions for diversity versus arising-under cases were merged into a single provision as part of the Jurisdiction and Venue Clarification Act of 2011.]

emphasized language left considerable doubt as to whether, under this provision, venue could plausibly lie in more than one jurisdiction, see, e.g., Cheeseman v. Carey, 485 F.Supp. 203, 210–11 (S.D.N.Y.1980), although the Supreme Court supposed that it could, at least in an "unusual case," Leroy v. Great Western United Corp., 443 U.S. 173, 185 (1979).

In any event, in 1990 Congress revamped the venue statute and enacted the current language, which is clearer. See Judicial Improvements Act of 1990, Pub. L. No. 101–650, § 311, 104 Stat. 5089 (1990); see also Report of the House Committee on the Judiciary, H.R. Rep. No. 101–734 (1990), reprinted in 1990 U.S.C.C.A.N. 6860, 6869 (expressing the view that the former statute's reference to the district "in which the claim arose" was "litigation breeding," because it failed to address the situation "in which substantial parts of the underlying events have occurred in several districts"). By laying venue in "a" —not "the" —"judicial district in which a *substantial part* of the events or omissions giving rise to the claim occurred," 28 U.S.C. § 1391(b)(2) (emphasis added), Congress removed much of the ambiguity of the former statute. The new language contemplates that venue can be appropriate in more than one district.

We thus join several other circuits in holding that the civil venue statute permits venue in multiple judicial districts as long as "a substantial part" of the underlying events took place in those districts, a conclusion that we alluded to in Bates v. C & S Adjusters, 980 F.2d 865, 867 (2d Cir. 1992) (holding that the revised statute "does not, as a general matter, require the District Court to determine the best venue"). See, e.g., Jenkins Brick Co. v. Bremer, 321 F.3d 1366, 1371 (11th Cir.2003); Uffner v. La Reunion Francaise, S.A., 244 F.3d 38, 42 (1st Cir.2001); First of Mich. Corp. v. Bramlet, 141 F.3d 260, 263 (6th Cir.1998); Setco Enters. v. Robbins, 19 F.3d 1278, 1281 (8th Cir.1994).

In doing so, however, we caution district courts to take seriously the adjective "substantial." We are required to construe the venue statute strictly. See Olberding v. Illinois Cent. R.R., 346 U.S. 338, 340 (1953). That means for venue to be proper, *significant* events or omissions *material* to the plaintiff's claim must have occurred in the district in question, even if other material events occurred elsewhere. It would be error, for instance, to treat the venue statute's "substantial part" test as mirroring the minimum contacts test employed in personal jurisdiction inquiries. See *Jenkins Brick*, 321 F.3d, at 1372; Cottman Transmission Sys. v. Martino, 36 F.3d 291, 294 (3d Cir.1994); cf. United States ex rel. Rudick v. Laird, 412 F.2d 16, 20 (2d Cir.1969) ("The concepts of personal jurisdiction and venue are closely related but nonetheless distinct.").

B

Against this background, we examine the events underlying Gulf's claims. But first, it is important to appreciate the nature of those claims. At its core, Gulf's suit sounds in contract. Gulf seeks a declaration that it is not liable for the personal injury judgment against Caldor and in favor of the Glasbrenners, principally because Gulf was not timely notified of the

Glasbrenners' claims. Indeed, at oral argument, the Glasbrenners conceded that "this dispute is about whether an insurance contract applies to provide coverage for a judgment and . . . an injury that occurred in the state of New Jersey." (Emphasis added). The essence of the suit, therefore, is whether the defendants below (both Caldor and the Glasbrenners) were in breach of or complied with that insurance contract.

The next, and last, question is whether significant events material to those claims occurred in the Southern District of New York. The answer is "probably." Courts making venue determinations in contract disputes have looked to such factors as "where the contract was negotiated or executed, where it was to be performed, and where the alleged breach occurred." Matera v. Native Eyewear, 355 F.Supp.2d 680, 686 (E.D.N.Y.2005) (quoting PI, Inc. v. Quality Prods., 907 F.Supp. 752, 757–58 (S.D.N.Y.1995)).

Gulf's complaint alleges that the insurance policy "was submitted, approved and issued by Gulf in the State of New York." We believe that the submission, approval, and issuance of the policy constituted a "substantial part of the events" underlying Gulf's claims, at least in combination with one other important (and undisputed) fact: that the Glasbrenners requested and received a lift of the automatic stay from the bankruptcy court in the Southern District of New York that specifically authorized them to file their suit in New Jersey, and which in turn influenced the form of the state court judgment.[12]

However, Gulf's allegations are not enough: New York State encompasses four judicial districts, but the complaint does not specify in which one the policy was issued. At oral argument, Gulf's counsel indicated that the policy was "negotiated, approved, and executed" at Gulf's headquarters, which the complaint places squarely within the Southern District. But neither the complaint nor the policy itself (incorporated by reference into the complaint) unambiguously lays venue in the Southern District. Nevertheless, if Gulf can prove these facts, venue would be appropriate in the Southern District. We believe that Gulf should have the opportunity to do so.[13]

This is not to say that venue is not also appropriate in New Jersey. As the district court correctly observed, a number of relevant events occurred in New Jersey—the original injury, the trial, and the underlying judgment

---

12. We therefore explicitly decline to decide, because that question is not before us, whether the negotiation and issuance of a contract in a given judicial district, standing alone, is sufficient to lay venue in that district.

13. We would not ordinarily give Gulf a second chance to submit evidence of key facts. In this case, however, the Glasbrenners have not seriously disputed that the policy originated in the Southern District of New York, and the complaint's reference to New York State rather than to the Southern District seems to us to have been an inadvertence. Because to do so will not prejudice the Glasbrenners and will permit an accurate venue ruling, we will allow Gulf to submit new evidence to the district court.

Moreover, Gulf's counsel indicated that he is in possession of a document—a letter associated with the policy—unambiguously attesting that the policy was negotiated, approved, and issued in the Southern District (although he conceded that it was not part of the record). Gulf's proof that venue is proper should therefore not require extensive discovery.

that Gulf is seeking to avoid all happened in New Jersey. This does not mean, as the district court concluded, that "no substantial part of the events giving rise to the present claim occurred in New York." Rather, substantial events giving rise to the claim occurred in *both* the Southern District of New York (assuming Gulf can produce the necessary documentation) and the District of New Jersey, and venue was proper in either district. That being so, because Gulf chose to file suit in the Southern District of New York, the Glasbrenners' Rule 12(b)(3) motion should have been rejected.

IV

For the reasons just supplied, we vacate the judgment of the district court and remand for further proceedings consistent with this opinion. Specifically, the district court should permit Gulf to submit evidence that the policy was submitted, approved, or issued in the Southern District of New York. Whether these documents actually do so, of course, is for the district court to decide.

Ferens v. John Deere Co.

Supreme Court of the United States, 1990.
494 U.S. 516, 110 S.Ct. 1274, 108 L.Ed.2d 443.

■ JUSTICE KENNEDY delivered the opinion of the Court.

Section 1404(a) of Title 28 states: "For the convenience of parties and witnesses, in the interest of justice, a district court may transfer any civil action to any other district or division where it might have been brought." 28 U.S.C. § 1404(a) (1982 ed.). In Van Dusen v. Barrack, 376 U.S. 612 (1964), we held that, following a transfer under § 1404(a) initiated by a defendant, the transferee court must follow the choice of law rules that prevailed in the transferor court. We now decide that, when a plaintiff moves for the transfer, the same rule applies.

I

Albert Ferens lost his right hand when, the allegation is, it became caught in his combine harvester, manufactured by Deere & Company. The accident occurred while Ferens was working with the combine on his farm in Pennsylvania. For reasons not explained in the record, Ferens delayed filing a tort suit and Pennsylvania's 2–year limitations period expired. In the third year, he and his wife sued Deere in the United States District Court for the Western District of Pennsylvania, raising contract and warranty claims as to which the Pennsylvania limitations period had not yet run. The District Court had diversity jurisdiction, as Ferens and his wife are Pennsylvania residents, and Deere is incorporated in Delaware with its principal place of business in Illinois.

Not to be deprived of a tort action, the Ferenses in the same year filed a second diversity suit against Deere in the United States District Court for the Southern District of Mississippi, alleging negligence and products liability. Diversity jurisdiction and venue were proper. The Ferenses sued Deere in the District Court in Mississippi because they knew that, under Klaxon Co. v. Stentor Electric Mfg. Co., 313 U.S. 487, 496 (1941), the federal court in the exercise of diversity jurisdiction must apply the same choice of law rules that Mississippi state courts would apply if they were deciding the case. A Mississippi court would rule that Pennsylvania substantive law controls the personal injury claim but that Mississippi's own law governs the limitation period.

Although Mississippi has a borrowing statute which, on its face, would seem to enable its courts to apply statutes of limitations from other jurisdictions, see Miss.Code Ann. § 15–1–65 (1972), the State Supreme Court has said that the borrowing statute "only applies where a nonresident [defendant] in whose favor the statute has accrued afterwards moves into this state." Louisiana & Mississippi R. Transfer Co. v. Long, 159 Miss. 654, 667, 131 So. 84, 88 (1930). The borrowing statute would not apply to the Ferenses' action because, as the parties agree, Deere was a corporate resident of Mississippi before the cause of action accrued. The Mississippi courts, as a result, would apply Mississippi's 6–year statute of limitations to the tort claim arising under Pennsylvania law and the tort action would not be time-barred under the Mississippi statute. See Miss.Code Ann. § 15–1–49 (1972).

The issue now before us arose when the Ferenses took their forum shopping a step further: having chosen the federal court in Mississippi to take advantage of the State's limitations period, they next moved, under § 1404(a), to transfer the action to the federal court in Pennsylvania on the ground that Pennsylvania was a more convenient forum. The Ferenses acted on the assumption that, after the transfer, the choice of law rules in the Mississippi forum, including a rule requiring application of the Mississippi statute of limitations, would continue to govern the suit.

Deere put up no opposition, and the District Court in Mississippi granted the § 1404(a) motion. The Court accepted the Ferenses' arguments that they resided in Pennsylvania; that the accident occurred there; that the claim had no connection to Mississippi; that a substantial number of witnesses resided in the Western District of Pennsylvania but none resided in Mississippi; that most of documentary evidence was located in the Western District of Pennsylvania but none was located in Mississippi; and that the warranty action pending in the Western District of Pennsylvania presented common questions of law and fact.

The District Court in Pennsylvania consolidated the transferred tort action with the Ferenses' pending warranty action but declined to honor the Mississippi statute of limitations as the District Court in Mississippi would have done. It ruled instead that, because the Ferenses had moved for transfer as plaintiffs, the rule in *Van Dusen* did not apply. Invoking the 2–year limitations period set by Pennsylvania law, the District Court dismissed their tort action. Ferens v. Deere & Co., 639 F.Supp. 1484 (W.D.Pa. 1986).

The Court of Appeals for the Third Circuit affirmed, but not, at first, on grounds that the Ferenses had lost their entitlement to Mississippi choice of law rules by their invoking § 1404(a). The Court of Appeals relied at the outset on the separate theory that applying Mississippi's statute of limitations would violate due process because Mississippi had no legitimate interest in the case. Ferens v. Deere & Co., 819 F.2d 423 (1987). We vacated this decision and remanded in light of Sun Oil Co. v. Wortman, 486 U.S. 717 (1988), in which we held that a State may choose to apply its own statute of limitations to claims governed by the substantive laws of another State without violating either the Full Faith and Credit Clause or the Due Process Clause. Ferens v. Deere & Co., 487 U.S. 1212 (1988). On remand, the Court of Appeals again affirmed, this time confronting the *Van Dusen* question and ruling that a transferor court's choice of law rules do not apply after a transfer under § 1404(a) on a motion by a plaintiff. 862 F.2d 31 (CA3 1988).

II

Section 1404(a) states only that a district court may transfer venue for the convenience of the parties and witnesses when in the interest of justice. It says nothing about choice of law, and nothing about affording plaintiffs different treatment from defendants. We touched upon these issues in *Van Dusen,* but left open the question presented in this case. See 376 U.S., at 640. In *Van Dusen,* an airplane flying from Boston to Philadelphia crashed into Boston Harbor soon after take-off. The personal representatives of the accident victims brought more than 100 actions in the District Court for the District of Massachusetts and more than 40 actions in the District Court for the Eastern District of Pennsylvania. When the defendants moved to transfer the actions brought in Pennsylvania to the federal court in Massachusetts, a number of the Pennsylvania plaintiffs objected because they lacked capacity under Massachusetts law to sue as representatives of the decedents. The plaintiffs also averred that the transfer would deprive them of the benefits of Pennsylvania's choice of law rules because the transferee forum would apply to their wrongful death claims a different substantive rule. The plaintiffs obtained from the Court of Appeals a writ of mandamus ordering the District Court to vacate the transfer. See id., at 613–615.

We reversed. After considering issues not related to the present dispute, we held that the Court of Appeals erred in its assumption that Massachusetts law would govern the action following transfer. The legislative history of § 1404(a) showed that Congress had enacted the statute because broad venue provisions in federal acts often resulted in inconvenient forums and that Congress had decided to respond to this problem by permitting transfer to a convenient federal court under § 1404(a). 376 U.S., at 634–636. We said:

"This legislative background supports the view that § 1404(a) was not designed to narrow the plaintiff's venue privilege or to defeat the state-law advantages that might accrue from the exercise of this venue privilege but rather the provision was simply to counteract the inconveniences that flowed from the venue statutes by permitting transfer to a convenient federal court. The legislative history of § 1404(a) certainly does not justify the rather startling conclusion that one might 'get a change of a law as a bonus for a change of venue.' Indeed, an interpretation accepting such a rule would go far to frustrate the remedial purposes of § 1404(a). If a change in the law were in the offing, the parties might well regard the section primarily as a forum-shopping instrument. And, more importantly, courts would at least be reluctant to grant transfers, despite considerations of convenience, if to do so might conceivably prejudice the claim of a plaintiff who initially selected a permissible forum. We believe, therefore, that both the history and purposes of § 1404(a) indicate that it should be regarded as a federal judicial housekeeping measure, dealing with the placement of litigation in the federal courts and generally intended, on the basis of convenience and fairness, simply to authorize a change of court-rooms." Id., at 635–637 (footnotes omitted).

We thus held that the law applicable to a diversity case does not change upon a transfer initiated by a defendant.

III

The quoted part of *Van Dusen* reveals three independent reasons for our decision. First, § 1404(a) should not deprive parties of state law advantages that exist absent diversity jurisdiction. Second, § 1404(a) should not create or multiply opportunities for forum shopping. Third, the decision to transfer venue under § 1404(a) should turn on considerations of convenience and the interest of justice rather than on the possible prejudice resulting from a change of law. Although commentators have questioned whether the scant legislative history of § 1404(a) compels reliance on these three policies, see Note, Choice of Law after Transfer of Venue, 75 Yale L.J. 90, 123 (1965), we find it prudent to consider them in deciding whether the rule in *Van Dusen* applies to transfers initiated by plaintiffs. We decide that, in addition to other considerations, these policies require a transferee forum to apply the law of the transferor court, regardless of who initiates the transfer. A transfer under § 1404(a), in other words, does not change the law applicable to a diversity case.

A

The policy that § 1404(a) should not deprive parties of state law advantages, although perhaps discernible in the legislative history, has its real foundation in Erie R. Co. v. Tompkins, 304 U.S. 64 (1938). See *Van Dusen,* 376 U.S., at 637. The *Erie* rule remains a vital expression of the federal system and the concomitant integrity of the separate States. We explained *Erie* in Guaranty Trust Co. v. York, 326 U.S. 99, 109, as follows:

> "In essence, the intent of [the *Erie*] decision was to insure that, in all cases where a federal court is exercising jurisdiction solely because of the diversity of citizenship of the parties, the outcome of the litigation in the federal court should be substantially the same, so far as legal rules determine the outcome of a litigation, as it would be if tried in a State court. The nub of the policy that underlies *Erie R. Co. v. Tompkins* is that for the same transaction the accident of a suit by a non-resident litigant in a federal court instead of in a State court a block away should not lead to a substantially different result."

In Hanna v. Plumer, 380 U.S. 460, 473 (1965), we held that Congress has the power to prescribe procedural rules that differ from state law rules even at the expense of altering the outcome of litigation. This case does not involve a conflict. As in *Van Dusen,* our interpretation of § 1404(a) is in full accord with the *Erie* rule.

The *Erie* policy had a clear implication for *Van Dusen.* The existence of diversity jurisdiction gave the defendants the opportunity to make a motion to transfer venue under § 1404(a), and if the applicable law were to change after transfer, the plaintiff's venue privilege and resulting state-law advantages could be defeated at the defendant's option. 376 U.S., at 638. To allow the transfer and at the same time preserve the plaintiff's state-law advantages, we held that the choice of law rules should not change following a transfer initiated by a defendant. Id., at 639.

Transfers initiated by a plaintiff involve some different considerations, but lead to the same result. Applying the transferor law, of course, will not deprive the plaintiff of any state law advantages. A defendant, in one sense, also will lose no legal advantage if the transferor law controls after a transfer initiated by the plaintiff; the same law, after all, would have applied if the plaintiff had not made the motion. In another sense, however, a defendant may lose a nonlegal advantage. Deere, for example, would lose whatever advantage inheres in not having to litigate in Pennsylvania, or, put another way, in forcing the Ferenses to litigate in Mississippi or not at all.

We, nonetheless, find the advantage that the defendant loses slight. A plaintiff always can sue in the favorable state court or sue in diversity and not seek a transfer. By asking for application of the Mississippi statute of limitations following a transfer to Pennsylvania on grounds of convenience, the Ferenses are seeking to deprive Deere only of the advantage of using against them the inconvenience of litigating in Mississippi. The text of § 1404(a) may not say anything about choice of law, but we think it not the purpose of the section to protect a party's ability to use inconvenience as a shield to discourage or hinder litigation otherwise proper. The section exists to eliminate inconvenience without altering permissible choices under the venue statutes. See *Van Dusen,* supra, at 634–635. This interpretation should come as little surprise. As in our previous cases, we think that "[t]o construe § 1404(a) this way merely carries out its design to protect litigants, witnesses and the public against unnecessary inconvenience and expense, not to provide a shelter for . . . proceedings in costly and inconvenient forums." Continental Grain Co. v. Barge FBL–585, 364 U.S. 19, 27 (1960). By creating an opportunity to have venue transferred between courts in different States on the basis of convenience, an option that does not exist absent federal jurisdiction, Congress, with respect to diversity, retained the *Erie* policy while diminishing the incidents of inconvenience.

Applying the transferee law, by contrast, would undermine the *Erie* rule in a serious way. It would mean that initiating a transfer under § 1404(a) changes the state law applicable to a diversity case. We have held, in an isolated circumstance, that § 1404(a) may pre-empt state law. See Stewart Organization, Inc. v. Ricoh Corp., 487 U.S. 22 (1988) (holding that federal law determines the validity of a forum selection clause). In general, however, we have seen § 1404(a) as a housekeeping measure that should not alter the state law governing a case under *Erie*. See *Van Dusen,* supra, 376 U.S., at 636–637; see also *Stewart Organization,* supra, 487 U.S., at 37 (SCALIA, J., dissenting) (finding the language of § 1404(a) "plainly insufficient" to work a change in the applicable state law through pre-emption). The Mississippi statute of limitations, which everyone agrees would have applied if the Ferenses had not moved for a transfer, should continue to apply in this case.

In any event, defendants in the position of Deere would not fare much better if we required application of the transferee law instead of the transferor law. True, if the transferee law were to apply, some plaintiffs would not sue these defendants for fear that they would have no choice but to litigate in an inconvenient forum. But applying the transferee law would not discourage all plaintiffs from suing. Some plaintiffs would prefer to litigate in an inconvenient forum with favorable law than to litigate in a convenient forum with unfavorable law or not to litigate at all. The Ferenses, no doubt, would have abided by their initial choice of the District Court in Mississippi had they known that the District Court in Pennsylvania would dismiss their action. If we were to rule for Deere in this case we would accomplish little more than discouraging the occasional motions by plaintiffs to transfer inconvenient cases. Other plaintiffs would sue in an inconvenient forum with the expectation that the defendants themselves would seek transfer to a convenient forum, resulting in application of the transferor law under *Van Dusen*. See Note, Choice of Law in Federal Court After Transfer of Venue, 63 Cornell L.Rev. 149, 156 (1977). In this case, for example, Deere might have moved for a transfer if the Ferenses had not.

B

Van Dusen also sought to fashion a rule that would not create opportunities for forum shopping. Some commentators have seen this policy as the most important rationale of *Van Dusen,* see e.g., 19 C. Wright, A. Miller, & E. Cooper, Federal Practice and Procedure § 4506, p. 79 (1982), but few attempt to explain the harm of forum shopping when the plaintiff initiates a transfer. An opportunity for forum shopping exists whenever a party has a choice of forums that will apply different laws. The *Van Dusen* policy against forum shopping simply requires us to interpret § 1404(a) in a way that does not create an opportunity for obtaining a more favorable law by selecting a forum through a transfer of venue. In the *Van Dusen* case itself, this meant that we could not allow defendants to use a transfer to change the law. 376 U.S., at 636.

No interpretation of § 1404(a), however, will create comparable opportunities for forum shopping by a plaintiff because, even without § 1404(a), a plaintiff already has the option of shopping for a forum with the most favorable law. The Fereneses, for example, had an opportunity for forum shopping in the state courts because both the Mississippi and Pennsylvania courts had jurisdiction and because they each would have applied a different statute of limitations. Diversity jurisdiction did not eliminate these forum shopping opportunities; instead, under *Erie*, the federal courts had to replicate them. See *Klaxon Co. v. Stentor Electric Mfg. Co., Inc.*, 313 U.S., at 496 ("Whatever lack of uniformity [*Erie*] may produce between federal courts in different states is attributable to our federal system, which leaves to a state, within the limits permitted by the Constitution, the right to pursue local policies diverging from those of its neighbors"). Applying the transferor law would not give a plaintiff an opportunity to use a transfer to obtain a law that he could not obtain through his initial forum selection. If it does make selection of the most favorable law more convenient, it does no more than recognize a forum shopping choice that already exists. This fact does not require us to apply the transferee law. Section 1404(a), to reiterate, exists to make venue convenient and should not allow the defendant to use inconvenience to discourage plaintiffs from exercising the opportunities that they already have.

Applying the transferee law, by contrast, might create opportunities for forum shopping in an indirect way. The advantage to Mississippi's personal injury lawyers that resulted from the State's then applicable 6–year statute of limitations has not escaped us; Mississippi's long limitation period no doubt drew plaintiffs to the State. Although *Sun Oil* held that the federal courts have little interest in a State's decision to create a long statute of limitations or to apply its statute of limitations to claims governed by foreign law, we should recognize the consequences of our interpretation of § 1404(a). Applying the transferee law, to the extent that it discourages plaintiff-initiated transfers, might give States incentives to enact similar laws to bring in out-of-state business that would not be moved at the instance of the plaintiff.

C

Van Dusen also made clear that the decision to transfer venue under § 1404(a) should turn on considerations of convenience rather than on the possibility of prejudice resulting from a change in the applicable law. See 376 U.S., at 636; Piper Aircraft Co. v. Reyno, 454 U.S. 235, 253–254, and n. 20 (1981). We reasoned in *Van Dusen* that, if the law changed following a transfer initiated by the defendant, a district court "would at least be reluctant to grant transfers, despite considerations of convenience, if to do so might conceivably prejudice the claim of a plaintiff." 376 U.S., at 636.

The court, to determine the prejudice, might have to make an elaborate survey of the law, including statutes of limitations, burdens of proof, presumptions, and the like. This would turn what is supposed to be a statute for convenience of the courts into one expending extensive judicial time and resources. Because this difficult task is contrary to the purpose of the statute, in *Van Dusen* we made it unnecessary by ruling that a transfer of venue by the defendant does not result in a change of law. This same policy requires application of the transferor law when a plaintiff initiates a transfer.

If the law were to change following a transfer initiated by a plaintiff, a district court in a similar fashion would be at least reluctant to grant a transfer that would prejudice the defendant. Hardship might occur because plaintiffs may find as many opportunities to exploit application of the transferee law as they would find opportunities for exploiting application of the transferor law. See Note, 63 Cornell L.Rev., at 156. If the transferee law were to apply, moreover, the plaintiff simply would not move to transfer unless the benefits of convenience outweighed the loss of favorable law.

Some might think that a plaintiff should pay the price for choosing an inconvenient forum by being put to a choice of law versus forum. But this assumes that § 1404(a) is for the benefit only of the moving party. By the statute's own terms, it is not. Section 1404(a) also exists for the benefit of the witnesses and the interest of justice, which must include the convenience of the court. Litigation in an inconvenient forum does not harm the plaintiff alone.... The desire to take a punitive view of the plaintiff's actions should not obscure the systemic costs of litigating in an inconvenient place.

D

This case involves some considerations to which we perhaps did not give sufficient attention in *Van Dusen*. Foresight and judicial economy now seem to favor the simple rule that the law does not change following a transfer of venue under § 1404(a). Affording transfers initiated by plaintiffs different treatment from transfers initiated by defendants may seem quite workable in this case, but the simplicity is an illusion. If we were to hold that the transferee law applies following a § 1404(a) motion by a plaintiff, cases such as this would not arise in the future. Although applying the transferee law, no doubt, would catch the Ferenses by surprise, in the future no plaintiffs in their position would move for a change of venue.

Other cases, however, would produce undesirable complications. The rule would leave unclear which law should apply when both a defendant and a plaintiff move for a transfer of venue or when the court transfers venue on its own motion. See Note, 63 Cornell L.Rev., at 158. The rule also might require variation in certain situations, such as when the plaintiff moves for a transfer following a removal from state court by the defendant, or when only one of several plaintiffs requests the transfer, or when circumstances change through no fault of the plaintiff making a once convenient forum inconvenient. True, we could reserve any consideration of these questions for a later day. But we have a duty, in deciding this case, to consider whether our decision will create litigation and uncertainty. On the basis of these considerations, we again conclude that the transferor law should apply regardless who makes the § 1404(a) motion.

IV

Some may object that a district court in Pennsylvania should not have to apply a Mississippi statute of limitations to a Pennsylvania cause of action. This point, although understandable, should have little to do with the outcome of this case. Congress gave the Ferenses the power to seek a transfer in § 1404(a) and our decision in *Van Dusen* already could require a district court in Pennsylvania to apply the Mississippi statute of limitations to Pennsylvania claims. Our rule may seem too generous because it allows the Ferenses to have both their choice of law and their choice of forum, or even to reward the Ferenses for conduct that seems manipulative. We nonetheless see no alternative rule that would produce a more acceptable result. Deciding that the transferee law should apply, in effect, would tell the Ferenses that they should have continued to litigate their warranty action in Pennsylvania and their tort action in Mississippi. Some might find this preferable, but we do not. We have made quite clear that "[t]o permit a situation in which two cases involving precisely the same issues are simultaneously pending in different District Courts leads to the wastefulness of time, energy and money that § 1404(a) was designed to prevent." *Continental Grain*, 364 U.S., at 26.

From a substantive standpoint, two further objections give us pause but do not persuade us to change our rule. First, one might ask why we require the Ferenses to file in the District Court in Mississippi at all. Efficiency might seem to dictate a rule allowing plaintiffs in the Ferenses' position not to file in an inconvenient forum and then to return to a convenient forum through a transfer of venue, but instead simply to file in the convenient forum and ask for the law of the inconvenient forum to apply. Although our rule may invoke certain formality, one must remember that § 1404(a) does not provide for an automatic transfer of venue. The section, instead, permits a transfer only when convenient and "in the interest of justice." Plaintiffs in the position of the Ferenses must go to the distant forum because they have no guarantee, until the court there examines the facts, that they may obtain a transfer. No one has contested the justice of transferring this particular case, but the option remains open to defendants in future cases. Although a court cannot ignore the systemic costs of inconvenience, it may consider the course that the litigation already has taken in determining the interest of justice.

Second, one might contend that, because no *per se* rule requiring a court to apply either the transferor law or the transferee law will seem appropriate in all circumstances, we should develop more sophisticated federal choice of law rules for diversity actions involving transfers. See

Note, 75 Yale L.J., at 130–135. To a large extent, however, state conflicts of law rules already ensure that appropriate laws will apply to diversity cases. Federal law, as a general matter, does not interfere with these rules. See *Sun Oil,* 486 U.S., at 727–729. In addition, even if more elaborate federal choice of law rules would not run afoul of *Klaxon* and *Erie,* we believe that applying the law of the transferor forum effects the appropriate balance between fairness and simplicity. Cf. R. Leflar, American Conflicts Law § 143, p. 293 (3d ed.1977) (arguing against a federal common law of conflicts).

For the foregoing reasons, we conclude that Mississippi's statute of limitations should govern the Ferenses' action. We reverse and remand for proceedings consistent with this opinion.

It is so ordered.

■ JUSTICE SCALIA, with whom JUSTICE BRENNAN, JUSTICE MARSHALL, and JUSTICE BLACKMUN join, dissenting.

. . . . .

The question we must answer today is whether 28 U.S.C. § 1404(a) and the policies underlying [Klaxon Co. v. Stentor Electric Mfg. Co., 313 U.S. 487 (1941)]—namely, uniformity within a State and the avoidance of forum shopping—produce a result different from *Klaxon* when the suit in question was not filed in the federal court initially, but was transferred there under § 1404(a) on plaintiff's motion. In Van Dusen v. Barrack, 376 U.S. 612 (1964), we held that a result different from *Klaxon* is produced when a suit has been transferred under § 1404(a) on defendant's motion. . . . The goal of *Erie* and *Klaxon,* we reasoned, was to prevent "forum shopping" as between state and federal systems; the plaintiff makes a choice of forum-law by filing the complaint, and that choice must be honored in federal court, just as it would have been honored in state court, where the defendant would not have been able to transfer the case to another State.

We left open in *Van Dusen* the question presented today, viz., whether "the same considerations would govern" if a plaintiff sought a § 1404(a) transfer. 376 U.S., at 640. In my view, neither of those considerations is served—and indeed both are positively defeated—by a departure from *Klaxon* in that context. First, just as it is unlikely that Congress, in enacting § 1404(a), meant to provide the defendant with a vehicle by which to manipulate in his favor the substantive law to be applied in a diversity case, so too is it unlikely that Congress meant to provide the *plaintiff* with a vehicle by which to appropriate the law of a distant and inconvenient forum in which he does not intend to litigate, and to carry that prize back to the State in which he wishes to try the case. Second, application of the transferor court's law in this context would encourage forum-shopping between federal and state courts in the same jurisdiction on the basis of differential substantive law. It is true, of course, that the plaintiffs here did not select the *Mississippi* federal court in preference to the Mississippi state courts because of any differential substantive law; the former, like the latter, would have applied Mississippi choice-of-law rules, and thus the Mississippi statute of limitations. But one must be blind to reality to say that it is the *Mississippi* federal court in which these plaintiffs have chosen to sue. That was merely a way station en route to suit in the *Pennsylvania* federal court. The plaintiffs were seeking to achieve exactly what *Klaxon* was designed to prevent: the use of a Pennsylvania federal court instead of a Pennsylvania state court in order to obtain application of a different substantive law. Our decision in *Van Dusen* compromised "the principle of uniformity within a state," *Klaxon,* 313 U.S., at 496, only in the abstract, but today's decision compromises it precisely in the respect that matters– i.e., insofar as it bears upon the plaintiff's choice between a state and a federal forum. The significant federal judicial policy expressed in *Erie* and *Klaxon* is reduced to a laughingstock if it can so readily be evaded through filing-and-transfer.

The Court is undoubtedly correct that applying the *Klaxon* rule after a plaintiff-initiated transfer would deter a plaintiff in a situation such as exists here from seeking a transfer, since that would deprive him of the favorable substantive law. But that proves only that this disposition achieves what *Erie* and *Klaxon* are designed to achieve: preventing the plaintiff from using "the accident of diversity of citizenship," *Klaxon,* 313 U.S., at 496, to obtain the application of a different law within the State where he wishes to litigate. In the context of the present case, he must either litigate in the State of Mississippi under Mississippi law, or in the Commonwealth of Pennsylvania under Pennsylvania law.

The Court expresses concern . . . that if normal *Erie–Klaxon* principles were applied a district judge might be reluctant to order a transfer, even when faced with the prospect of a trial that would be manifestly inconvenient to the parties, for fear that in doing so he would be ordering what is tantamount to a dismissal on the merits. But where the plaintiff himself has moved for a transfer, surely the principle of *volenti non fit injuria* suffices to allay that concern. The Court asserts that in some cases it is the defendant who will be prejudiced by a transfer-induced change in the applicable law. That seems likely to be quite rare, since it assumes that the plaintiff has gone to the trouble of bringing the suit in a *less* convenient forum, where the law is *less* favorable to him. But where the defendant is disadvantaged by a plaintiff-initiated transfer, I do not see how it can reasonably be said that he has been "prejudiced," since the plaintiff could have brought the suit in the "plaintiff's-law forum" with the law more favorable to him (and the more convenient forum) in the first place. Prejudice to the defendant, it seems to me, occurs only when the plaintiff is enabled to have his cake and eat it too—to litigate in the more convenient forum that he desires, but with the law of the distant forum that he desires.

The Court suggests that applying the choice-of-law rules of the forum court to a transferred case ignores the interest of the federal courts themselves in avoiding the "systemic costs of litigating in an inconvenient place," quoting Justice Jackson's eloquent remarks on that subject in Gulf

Oil Corp. v. Gilbert, 330 U.S. 501, 509 (1947). . . . The point, apparently, is that these systemic costs will increase because the change in law attendant to transfer will not only deter the plaintiff from moving to transfer but will also deter the court from ordering sua sponte a transfer that will harm the plaintiff's case. Justice Jackson's remarks were addressed, however, not to the operation of § 1404(a), but to "those rather rare cases where the doctrine [of *forum non conveniens*] should be applied." 330 U.S., at 509. Where the systemic costs are that severe, transfer ordinarily will occur whether the plaintiff moves for it or not; the district judge can be expected to order it sua sponte. I do not think that the prospect of depriving the plaintiff of favorable law will any more deter a district judge from transfer-ring[14] than it would have deterred a district judge, under the prior regime, from ordering a dismissal *sua sponte* pursuant to the doctrine of *forum non conveniens*. In fact the deterrence to *sua sponte* transfer will be consider-ably less, since transfer involves no risk of statute-of-limitations bars to refiling.

Thus, it seems to me that a proper calculation of systemic costs would go as follows: Saved by the Court's rule will be the incremental cost of trying in forums that are inconvenient (but not so inconvenient as to prompt the court's *sua sponte* transfer) those suits that are now filed in such forums for choice-of-law purposes. But incurred by the Court's rule will be the costs of considering and effecting transfer, not only in those suits but in the indeterminate number of additional suits that will be filed in inconvenient forums now that filing-and-transfer is an approved form of shopping for law; plus the costs attending the necessity for transferee courts to figure out the choice-of-law rules (and probably the substantive law) of distant States much more often than our *Van Dusen* decision would require. It should be noted that the file-and-transfer ploy sanctioned by the Court today will be available not merely to achieve the relatively rare (and generally unneeded) benefit of a longer statute of limitations, but also to bring home to the desired state of litigation all sorts of favorable choice-of-law rules regarding substantive liability—in an era when the diversity among the States in choice-of-law principles has become kaleidoscopic.

The Court points out, apparently to deprecate the prospect that filing-and-transfer will become a regular litigation strategy, that there is "no guarantee" that a plaintiff will be accorded a transfer; that while "[n]o one has contested the justice of transferring this particular case," that option "remains open to defendants in future cases" ; and that "[a]lthough a court cannot ignore the systemic costs of inconvenience, it may consider the course that the litigation already has taken in determining the interest of justice." I am not sure what this means—except that it plainly does not

---

14. The prospective transferor court would not be deterred at all, of course, if we simply extended the *Van Dusen* rule to court-initiated transfers. In my view that would be inappropriate, however, since court-initiated transfer, like plaintiff-initiated transfer, does not confer upon the defendant the advantage of forum-shopping for law, Van Dusen v. Barrack, 376 U.S. 612, 636 (1964), and does not enable the defendant "to utilize a transfer to achieve a result in federal court which could not have been achieved in the courts of the State where the action was filed," id., at 638.

mean what it must mean to foreclose the filing-and-transfer option, name-ly, that transfer can be denied because the plaintiff was law-shopping. The whole theory of the Court's opinion is that it is not in accord with the policy of § 1404(a) to deprive the plaintiff of the "state-law advantages" to which his "venue privilege" entitles him. The Court explicitly repudiates "[t]he desire to take a punitive view of the plaintiff's actions," and to make him "pay the price for choosing an inconvenient forum by being put to a choice of law versus forum." Thus, all the Court is saying by its "no guarantee" language is that the plaintiff must be careful to choose a *really inconvenient* forum if he wants to be sure about getting a transfer. That will often not be difficult. In sum, it seems to me quite likely that today's decision will cost the federal courts more time than it will save them.

Thus, even as an exercise in giving the most extensive possible scope to the policies of § 1404(a), the Court's opinion seems to me unsuccessful. But as I indicated by beginning this opinion with the Rules of Decision Act, that should not be the object of the exercise at all. The Court and I reach different results largely because we approach the question from different directions. For the Court, this case involves an "interpretation of § 1404(a)," and the central issue is whether *Klaxon* stands in the way of the policies of that statute. For me, the case involves an interpretation of the Rules of Decision Act, and the central issue is whether § 1404(a) alters the "principle of uniformity within a state" which *Klaxon* says that Act embodies. I think my approach preferable, not only because the Rules of Decision Act does, and § 1404(a) does not, address the specific subject of which law to apply, but also because, as the Court acknowledges, our jurisprudence under that statute is "a vital expression of the federal system and the concomitant integrity of the separate States." To ask, as in effect the Court does, whether *Erie* gets in the way of § 1404(a), rather than whether § 1404(a) requires adjustment of *Erie,* seems to me the expression of a mistaken sense of priorities.

For the foregoing reasons, I respectfully dissent.[15]

[15. See Note, The Plaintiff's Forum Shopping Gold Card: Choice of Law in Federal Courts after Transfer of Venue under Section 1404(a), 110 Wake Forest L.Rev. 809 (1991). What the author of the Note saw as a "gold card" has been described as a "Ferens coupon." Oakley, Recent Statutory Changes in the Law of Federal Jurisdiction and Venue: The Judicial Improvements Act of 1988 and 1990, 24 U.C.Davis L.Rev. 735, 781 n. 186 (1991).

See Stewart Organization, Inc. v. Ricoh Corp., 487 U.S. 22 (1988), described below at p. 777, note 44. This case arose out of a contract that contained a clause providing that any disputes could be brought only in a court in New York. A diversity action was brought in federal court in Alabama. Alabama was a proper venue but defendant, relying on the forum-selection clause, moved to transfer the suit to the Southern District of New York. The Eleventh Circuit was sharply divided on whether, in a diversity case, a federal court should look to Alabama law, which regards forum-selection clauses as unenforceable, or to federal law, which was thought to enforce such clauses if they are not unreasonable. The Supreme Court thought that this was not the correct question. It held that 28 U.S.C. § 1404(a) governs whether to transfer a case, and that in the exercise of discretion under § 1404(a) the district court must consider the forum-selection clause along with all other factors.

If a case is transferred for pretrial proceedings under 28 U.S.C. § 1407, what effect should the transferee court give to the views on a question of federal law taken in the transferor forum? See In re Korean Air Lines Disaster of Sept. 1, 1983, 829 F.2d 1171 (D.C.Cir.1987).

The doctrine of *forum non conveniens*, allowing dismissal where the more convenient forum is a foreign court, is considered in Piper Aircraft Co. v. Reyno, 454 U.S. 235 (1981). The court has a broader discretion to transfer under § 1404(a) than to dismiss under *forum non conveniens*. Norwood v. Kirkpatrick, 349 U.S. 29 (1955).

In Posner v. Essex Insurance Co., Ltd., 178 F.3d 1209 (11th Cir.1999), the court ostensibly invoked the novel doctrine of "international abstention," but the authority to dismiss the suit in question would appear far more conventionally rooted in the power to dismiss on *forum non conveniens* grounds, as established in the *Piper Aircraft* case.

Conversely, there is a "first-to-file" rule that generally leads the second court in which related litigation is pending to defer to the first court. This rule may be expressed as a venue rule, but appears to function as a form of abstention. See Cadle Co. v. Whataburger of Alice, Inc., 174 F.3d 599 (5th Cir.1999).

The practical consequences of a § 1404(a) transfer have been demonstrated by Clermont & Eisenberg, Exorcising the Evil of Forum Shopping, 80 Cornell L.Rev. 1507 (1995): "Utilizing a database of the three million federal cases terminated over thirteen recent years, we take a closer look. Most importantly, we see that the plaintiffs' rate of winning drops from 58% in cases in which there is no transfer to 29% in transferred cases. This dramatic effect prevails over the range of substantively different types of cases. A big part of the most probable explanation for this drop is that plaintiffs are indeed forum-shopping, but that courts are transferring cases to more just courts, so that the decrease in the win rate reflects the fact that courts are stripping plaintiffs of unjust forum advantages. Statistical analysis supports this explanation and, at long last, demonstrates that forum does affect outcome."]

CHAPTER VIII

JURISDICTION TO DETERMINE JURISDICTION

United States v. United Mine Workers of America

Supreme Court of the United States, 1947.
330 U.S. 258, 67 S.Ct. 677, 91 L.Ed. 884.

[In a Federal District Court, a union and its president were adjudged guilty of criminal and civil contempt and fined for violation of a temporary restraining order issued in a suit by the Government in a labor dispute arising while the coal mines were in the possession of, and were being operated by, the Government pursuant to Executive Order 9728, 11 F.R. 5593, issued under the President's constitutional authority as Commander in Chief of the Army and Navy and authority conferred upon him by the War Labor Disputes Act, 57 Stat. 163. 70 F.Supp. 42. While an appeal to the United States Court of Appeals for the District of Columbia was pending, the Court granted certiorari pursuant to § 240(a) of the Judicial Code.[1]]

. . . . .

■ MR. CHIEF JUSTICE VINSON delivered the opinion of the Court.

In October, 1946, the United States was in possession of, and operating, the major portion of the country's bituminous coal mines. Terms and conditions of employment were controlled "for the period of Government possession" by an agreement entered into on May 29, 1946, between Secretary of Interior Krug, as Coal Mines Administrator, and John L. Lewis, as President of the United Mine Workers of America. The Krug–Lewis agreement embodied far reaching changes favorable to the miners; and, except as amended and supplemented therein, the agreement carried forward the terms and conditions of the National Bituminous Coal Wage Agreement of April 11, 1945.

[1. This statute permitting review by certiorari *before* judgment in the court of appeals, now embodied in 28 U.S.C. § 1254(1), is reprinted infra p. 1009. Supreme Court Rule 11 states: "A petition for a writ of certiorari to review a case pending in a United States court of appeals, before judgment is entered in that court, will be granted only upon a showing that the case is of such imperative public importance as to justify deviation from normal appellate practice and to require immediate determination in this Court." For the social and political background of the events described in the *United Mine Workers* case, and insight into their "imperative public importance," see McCullough, Truman 492–529 (1992).]

On October 21, 1946, the defendant Lewis directed a letter to Secretary Krug and presented issues which led directly to the present controversy. According to the defendant Lewis, the Krug–Lewis agreement carried forward § 15 of the National Bituminous Coal Wage Agreement of April 11, 1945. Under that section either party to the contract was privileged to give ten days' notice in writing of a desire for a negotiating conference which the other party was required to attend; fifteen days after the beginning of the conference either party might give notice in writing of the termination of the agreement, effective five days after receipt of such notice. Asserting authority under this clause, the defendant Lewis in his letter of October 21 requested that a conference begin November 1 for the purpose of negotiating new arrangements concerning wages, hours, practices, and other pertinent matters appertaining to the bituminous coal industry.

. . . . .

Conferences were scheduled and began in Washington on November 1, both the union and the Government adhering to their opposing views regarding the right of either party to terminate the contract. At the fifth meeting, held on November 11, the union for the first time offered specific proposals for changes in wages and other conditions of employment. On November 13 Secretary Krug requested the union to negotiate with the mine owners. This suggestion was rejected. On November 15 the union, by John L. Lewis, notified Secretary Krug that "Fifteen days having now elapsed since the beginning of said conference, the United Mine Workers of America, exercising its option hereby terminates said Krug–Lewis Agreement as of 12:00 o'clock P.M., Midnight, Wednesday, November 20, 1946."

Secretary Krug again notified the defendant Lewis that he had no power under the Krug–Lewis agreement or under the law to terminate the contract by unilateral declaration. The President of the United States announced his strong support of the Government's position and requested reconsideration by the union in order to avoid a national crisis. However, the defendant Lewis, as union president, circulated to the mine workers copies of the November 15 letter to Secretary Krug. This communication was for the "official information" of union members.

The United States on November 18 filed a complaint in the District Court for the District of Columbia against the United Mine Workers of America and John L. Lewis, individually and as president of the union. The suit was brought under the Declaratory Judgment Act and sought judgment to the effect that the defendants had no power unilaterally to terminate the Krug–Lewis agreement. And alleging that the November 15 notice was in reality a strike notice, the United States, pending the final determination of the cause, requested a temporary restraining order and preliminary injunctive relief.

The court, immediately and without notice to the defendants, issued a temporary order restraining the defendants from continuing in effect the notice of November 15, from encouraging the mine workers to interfere with the operation of the mines by strike or cessation of work, and from taking any action which would interfere with the court's jurisdiction and its determination of the case. The order by its terms was to expire at 3:00 p.m. on November 27 unless extended for good cause shown. A hearing on the preliminary injunction was set for 10:00 a.m. on the same date. The order and complaint were served on the defendants on November 18.

A gradual walkout by the miners commenced on November 18, and, by midnight of November 20, consistent with the miners' "no contract, no work" policy, a full-blown strike was in progress. Mines furnishing the major part of the nation's bituminous coal production were idle.

On November 21 the United States filed a petition for a rule to show cause why the defendants should not be punished as and for contempt, alleging a willful violation of the restraining order. The rule issued, setting November 25 as the return day and, if at that time the contempt was not sufficiently purged, setting November 27 as the day for trial on the contempt charge.

On the return day, defendants, by counsel, informed the court that no action had been taken concerning the November 15 notice, and denied the jurisdiction of the court to issue the restraining order and rule to show cause. Trial on the contempt charge was thereupon ordered to begin as scheduled on November 27. On November 26 the defendants filed a motion to discharge and vacate the rule to show cause. Their motion challenged the jurisdiction of the court, and raised the grave question of whether the Norris–LaGuardia Act prohibited the granting of the temporary restraining order at the instance of the United States.

After extending the temporary restraining order on November 27, and after full argument on November 27 and November 29, the court, on the latter date, overruled the motion and held that its power to issue the restraining order in this case was not affected by either the Norris–LaGuardia Act or the Clayton Act.

The defendants thereupon pleaded not guilty and waived an advisory jury. Trial on the contempt charge proceeded. The Government presented eight witnesses, the defendants none. At the conclusion of the trial on December 3, the court found that the defendants had permitted the November 15 notice to remain outstanding, had encouraged the miners to interfere by a strike with the operation of the mines and with the performance of governmental functions, and had interfered with the jurisdiction of the court. Both defendants were found guilty beyond reasonable doubt of both criminal and civil contempt dating from November 18. The court entered judgment on December 4, fining the defendant Lewis $10,000, and the defendant union $3,500,000. On the same day a preliminary injunction, effective until a final determination of the case, was issued in terms similar to those of the restraining order.

On December 5 the defendants filed notices of appeal from the judgments of contempt. The judgments were stayed pending the appeals. The United States on December 6 filed a petition for certiorari in both cases. Section 240(a) of the Judicial Code authorizes a petition for certiorari by any party and the granting of certiorari prior to judgment in the Circuit Court of Appeals. Prompt settlement of this case being in the public interest, we granted certiorari on December 9, and subsequently, for similar reasons, granted petitions for certiorari filed by the defendants, 329 U.S. 708, 709, 710. The cases were consolidated for argument.

I

Defendants' first and principal contention is that the restraining order and preliminary injunction were issued in violation of the Clayton and Norris–LaGuardia Acts. We have come to a contrary decision.

It is true that Congress decreed in § 20 of the Clayton Act that "no such restraining order or injunction shall prohibit any person or persons ... from recommending, advising, or persuading others ..." to strike. But by the Act itself this provision was made applicable only to cases "between an employer and employees, or between employers and employees, or between employees, or between persons employed and persons seeking employment ...." For reasons which will be explained at greater length in discussing the applicability of the Norris–LaGuardia Act, we cannot construe the general term "employer" to include the United States, where there is no express reference to the United States and no evident affirmative grounds for believing that Congress intended to withhold an otherwise available remedy from the Government as well as from a specified class of private persons.

.   .   .   .   .

II

Although we have held that the Norris–LaGuardia Act did not render injunctive relief beyond the jurisdiction of the District Court, there are alternative grounds which support the power of the District Court to punish violations of its orders as criminal contempt.

Attention must be directed to the situation obtaining on November 18. The Government's complaint sought a declaratory judgment in respect to the right of the defendants to terminate the contract by unilateral action. What amounted to a strike call, effective at midnight on November 20, had been issued by the defendant Lewis as an "official notice." Pending a determination of defendants' right to take this action, the Government requested a temporary restraining order and injunctive relief. The memorandum in support of the restraining order seriously urged the inapplicability of the Norris–LaGuardia Act to the facts of this case, and the power of the District Court to grant the ancillary relief depended in great part upon the resolution of this jurisdictional question. In these circumstances, the District Court unquestionably had the power to issue a restraining order for the purpose of preserving existing conditions pending a decision upon its own jurisdiction.

The temporary restraining order was served on November 18. This was roughly two and one-half days before the strike was to begin. The defendants filed no motion to vacate the order. Rather they ignored it, and allowed a nationwide coal strike to become an accomplished fact. This Court has used unequivocal language in condemning such conduct,[2] and has in United States v. Shipp, 203 U.S. 563 (1906), provided protection for judicial authority in situations of this kind. In that case this Court had allowed an appeal from a denial of a writ of habeas corpus by the Circuit Court of Tennessee. The petition had been filed by Johnson, then confined under a sentence of death imposed by a state court. Pending the appeal, this Court issued an order staying all proceedings against Johnson. However, the prisoner was taken from jail and lynched. Shipp, the sheriff having custody of Johnson, was charged with conspiring with others for the purpose of lynching Johnson, with intent to show contempt for the order of this Court. Shipp denied the jurisdiction of this Court to punish for contempt on the ground that the stay order was issued pending an appeal over which this Court had no jurisdiction because the constitutional questions alleged were frivolous and only a pretense. The Court, through Mr. Justice Holmes, rejected the contention as to want of jurisdiction, and in ordering the contempt to be tried, stated:

> "We regard this argument as unsound. It has been held, it is true, that orders made by a court having no jurisdiction to make them may be disregarded without liability to process for contempt. In re Sawyer, 124 U.S. 200; Ex parte Fisk, 113 U.S. 713, Ex parte Rowland, 104 U.S. 604. But even if the Circuit Court had no jurisdiction to entertain Johnson's petition, and if this court had no jurisdiction of the appeal, this court, and this court alone, could decide that such was the law. It and it alone necessarily had jurisdiction to decide whether the case was properly before it. On that question, at least, it was its duty to permit argument, and to take the time required for such consideration as it might need. See Mansfield, Coldwater & Lake Michigan Ry. Co. v. Swan, 111 U.S. 379, 387. Until its judgment declining jurisdiction should be announced, it had authority, from the necessity of the case, to make orders to preserve the existing conditions and the subject of the petition, just as the state court was bound to refrain from further proceedings until the same time. Rev.Stat. § 766, act of March 3, 1893, c. 226, 27 Stat. 751. The fact that the petitioner was entitled to argue his case shows what needs no proof, that the law contemplates the possibility of a decision either way, and therefore must provide for it." 203 U.S. 573.

If this Court did not have jurisdiction to hear the appeal in the *Shipp* case, its order would have had to be vacated. But it was ruled that only the Court itself could determine that question of law. Until it was found that the Court had no jurisdiction, "... it had authority, from the necessity of the case, to make orders to preserve the existing conditions and the subject of the petition ...."

---

2. "If a party can make himself a judge of the validity of orders which have been issued, and by his own act of disobedience set them aside, then are the courts impotent, and what the Constitution now fittingly calls the 'judicial power of the United States' would be a mere mockery." Gompers v. Buck's Stove & Range Co., 1911, 221 U.S. 418, 450.

Application of the rule laid down in *United States v. Shipp*, supra, is apparent in Carter v. United States, 135 F.2d 858 ([CA5] 1943). There a district court, after making the findings required by the Norris–LaGuardia Act, issued a temporary restraining order. An injunction followed after a hearing in which the court affirmatively decided that it had jurisdiction and overruled the defendants' objections based upon the absence of diversity and the absence of a case arising under a statute of the United States. These objections of the defendants prevailed on appeal, and the injunction was set aside. Brown v. Coumanis, 135 F.2d 163 ([CA5] 1943). But in *Carter*, a companion case, violations of the temporary restraining order were held punishable as criminal contempt. Pending a decision on a doubtful question of jurisdiction, the District Court was held to have power to maintain the status quo and punish violations as contempt.[3]

In the case before us, the District Court had the power to preserve existing conditions while it was determining its own authority to grant injunctive relief. The defendants, in making their private determination of the law, acted at their peril. Their disobedience is punishable as criminal contempt.

Although a different result would follow were the question of jurisdiction frivolous and not substantial, such contention would be idle here. The applicability of the Norris–LaGuardia Act to the United States in a case such as this had not previously received judicial consideration, and both the language of the Act and its legislative history indicated the substantial nature of the problem with which the District Court was faced.

Proceeding further, we find impressive authority for the proposition that an order issued by a court with jurisdiction over the subject matter and person must be obeyed by the parties until it is reversed by orderly and proper proceedings. This is true without regard even for the constitutionality of the Act under which the order is issued. In Howat v. Kansas, 258 U.S. 181, 18–90 (1922), this Court said:

> "An injunction duly issuing out of a court of general jurisdiction with equity powers, upon pleadings properly invoking its action, and served upon persons made parties therein and within the jurisdiction, must be obeyed by them, however erroneous the action of the court may be, even if the error be in the assumption of the validity of a seeming, but void law going to the merits of the case. It is for the court of first instance to determine the question of the validity of the law, and until its decision is reversed for error by orderly review, either by

---

3. "It cannot now be broadly asserted that a judgment is always a nullity if jurisdiction of some sort or other is wanting. It is now held that, except in case of plain usurpation, a court has jurisdiction to determine its own jurisdiction, and if it be contested and on due hearing it is upheld, the decision unreversed binds the parties as a thing adjudged. Treinies v. Sunshine Mining Co., 308 U.S. 66; Sunshine Anthracite Coal Co. v. Adkins, 310 U.S. 381, 403; Stoll v. Gottlieb, 305 U.S. 165. So in the matter of federal jurisdiction, which is often a close question, the federal court may either have to determine the facts, as in contested citizenship, or the law, as whether the case alleged arises under a law of the United States."

itself or by a higher court, its orders based on its decision are to be respected, and disobedience of them is contempt of its lawful authority, to be punished."

Violations of an order are punishable as criminal contempt even though the order is set aside on appeal, Worden v. Searls, 121 U.S. 14 (1887), or though the basic action has become moot. Gompers v. Buck's Stove & Range Co., 221 U.S. 418 (1911).

We insist upon the same duty of obedience where, as here, the subject matter of the suit, as well as the parties, was properly before the court; where the elements of federal jurisdiction were clearly shown; and where the authority of the court of first instance to issue an order ancillary to the main suit depended upon a statute, the scope and applicability of which were subject to substantial doubt. The District Court on November 29 affirmatively decided that the Norris–LaGuardia Act was of no force in this case and that injunctive relief was therefore authorized. Orders outstanding or issued after that date were to be obeyed until they expired or were set aside by appropriate proceedings, appellate or otherwise. Convictions for criminal contempt intervening before that time may stand.

It does not follow, of course, that simply because a defendant may be punished for criminal contempt for disobedience of an order later set aside on appeal, that the plaintiff in the action may profit by way of a fine imposed in a simultaneous proceeding for civil contempt based upon a violation of the same order. The right to remedial relief falls with an injunction which events prove was erroneously issued, *Worden v. Searls*, supra, 121 U.S., at pages 25, 26; Salvage Process Corp. v. Acme Tank Cleaning Process Corp., 86 F.2d 727 ([CA2] 1936); S. Anargyros v. Anargyros & Co., 191 F. 208 ([C.C.N.D.Cal.] 1911); and *a fortiori* when the injunction or restraining order was beyond the jurisdiction of the court. Nor does the reason underlying *United States v. Shipp*, supra, compel a different result. If the Norris–LaGuardia Act were applicable in this case, the conviction for civil contempt would be reversed in its entirety.

Assuming, then, that the Norris–LaGuardia Act applied to this case and prohibited injunctive relief at the request of the United States, we would set aside the preliminary injunction of December 4 and the judgment for civil contempt; but we would, subject to any infirmities in the contempt proceedings or in the fines imposed, affirm the judgments for criminal contempt as validly punishing violations of an order then outstanding and unreversed.

[The Court rejected the defendants' arguments that the trial court had committed reversible error in conducting the trial, and that the Government was not legally entitled in a case such as this to a judgment for civil as opposed to criminal contempt.]

V.

It is urged that, in any event, the amount of the fine of $10,000 imposed on defendant Lewis and of the fine of $3,500,000 imposed on the defendant Union were arbitrary, excessive, and in no way related to the evidence adduced at the hearing.

. . . . .

In the light of these principles, we think the record clearly warrants a fine of $10,000 against defendant Lewis for criminal contempt. A majority of the Court, however, does not think that it warrants the unconditional imposition of a fine of $3,500,000 against the defendant union. A majority feels that, if the court below had assessed a fine of $700,000 against the defendant union, this, under the circumstances, would not be excessive as punishment for the criminal contempt theretofore committed; and feels that, in order to coerce the defendant union into a future compliance with the court's order, it would have been effective to make the other $2,800,000 of the fine conditional on the defendant's failure to purge itself within a reasonable time. Accordingly, the judgment against the defendant union is held to be excessive. It will be modified so as to require the defendant union to pay a fine of $700,000, and further, to pay an additional fine of $2,800,000 unless the defendant union, within five days after the issuance of the mandate herein, shows that it has fully complied with the temporary restraining order issued November 18, 1946, and the preliminary injunction issued December 4, 1946. The defendant union can effect full compliance only by withdrawing unconditionally the notice given by it, signed John L. Lewis, President, on November 15, 1946, to J.A. Krug, Secretary of the Interior, terminating the Krug–Lewis agreement as of twelve o'clock midnight, Wednesday, November 20, 1946, and by notifying, at the same time, its members of such withdrawal in substantially the same manner as the members of the defendant union were notified of the notice to the Secretary of the Interior above-mentioned; and by withdrawing and similarly instructing the members of the defendant union of the withdrawal of any other notice to the effect that the Krug–Lewis agreement is not in full force and effect until the final determination of the basic issues arising under the said agreement.

. . . . .

We have examined the other contentions advanced by the defendants but have found them to be without merit. The temporary restraining order and the preliminary injunction were properly issued, and the actions of the District Court in these respects are affirmed. The judgment against the defendant Lewis is affirmed. The judgment against the defendant union is modified in accordance with this opinion, and, as modified, that judgment is affirmed.

So ordered.

■ MR. JUSTICE JACKSON joins in this opinion except as to the Norris–LaGuardia Act which he thinks relieved the courts of jurisdiction to issue injunctions in this class of case.

[MR. JUSTICE FRANKFURTER concurred in the judgment. He thought the Norris–LaGuardia Act applied but agreed with Part II of the opinion.]

[MR. JUSTICE BLACK and MR. JUSTICE DOUGLAS concurred in part and dissented in part. They thought Norris–LaGuardia inapplicable but thought a fine for criminal contempt was improper and would have made the entire amount of the fines payable conditionally.]

■ MR. JUSTICE MURPHY, dissenting.

[MR. JUSTICE MURPHY was certain that the Norris–LaGuardia Act applied to this case and prohibited the orders in question.]

Since in my view the restraining order and the temporary injunction in this case were void and without effect, there remains for me only the contention that the defendants are guilty of criminal contempt for having willfully ignored the void restraining order. . . .

.   .   .   .   .

Congress was well aware of this use of restraining orders to break strikes. After full consideration it intentionally and specifically prohibited their use, with certain exceptions not here relevant. We are not free to disregard that prohibition. Hence the doctrine of [United States v. Shipp, 203 U.S. 563 (1906)] has no relation whatever to our present problem. That case dealt with an order of this Court staying the execution of a convicted felon, an order which lay within the recognized power of this Court and which had not been validly prohibited by Congress. Naturally, no man could violate that order with impunity. But we are acting here in the unique field of labor relations, dealing with a type of order which Congress has definitely proscribed. If we are to hold these defendants in contempt for having violated a void restraining order, we must close our eyes to the expressed will of Congress and to the whole history of equitable restraints in the field of labor disputes. We must disregard the fact that to compel one to obey a void restraining order in a case involving a labor dispute and to require that it be tested on appeal is to sanction the use of the restraining order to break strikes—which was precisely what Congress wanted to avoid. Every reason supporting the salutary principle of the *Shipp* case breaks down when that principle is applied in this setting. I would therefore reverse the judgment of the District Court in toto.

.   .   .   .   .

■ MR. JUSTICE RUTLEDGE, dissenting.

.   .   .   .   .

MR. JUSTICE FRANKFURTER has shown conclusively, I think, that the policy of the Norris–LaGuardia Act, 47 Stat. 70, applies to this situation. The legislative history he marshals so accurately and cogently compels the conclusion that the War Labor Disputes Act of 1943, 57 Stat. 163, not only confirms the applicability of the earlier statute, but itself excludes resort to injunctive relief for enforcement of its own provisions in situations of this sort.

.   .   .   .   .

This conclusion substantially compels the further one that United States v. Shipp, 203 U.S. 563, has no valid application to the situation presented by this case.

This Court has not yet expressly denied, rather it has repeatedly confirmed Congress' power to control the jurisdiction of the inferior federal courts and its own appellate jurisdiction. Const., Art. III, § 2, Ex parte McCardle, 7 Wall. [74 U.S.] 506; Lockerty v. Phillips, 319 U.S. 182, 187 and authorities cited. See Warren, New Light on the History of the Federal Judiciary Act of 1789 (1923), 37 Harv.L.Rev. 49, 67ff. That power includes the power to deny jurisdiction as well as to confer it. Ibid. And where Congress has acted expressly to exclude particular subject matter from the jurisdiction of any court, except this Court's original jurisdiction, I know of no decision here which holds the exclusion invalid, or that a refusal to obey orders or judgments contravening Congress' mandate is criminal or affords cause for punishment as for contempt.

If that were the law, the result could only be to nullify the congressional power over federal jurisdiction for a great volume of cases. And if it should become the law, for every case raising a question not frivolous concerning the court's jurisdiction to enter an order or judgment, that punishment for contempt may be imposed irrevocably simply upon a showing of violation, the consequences would be equally or more serious. The force of such a rule, making the party act on pain of certain punishment regardless of the validity of the order violated or the court's jurisdiction to enter it as determined finally upon review, would be not only to compel submission. It would be also in practical effect for many cases to terminate the litigation, foreclosing the substantive rights involved without any possibility for their effective appellate review and determination.

This would be true, for instance, wherever the substantive rights asserted or the opportunity for exercising them would vanish with obedience to the challenged order. Cf. Ex parte Fisk, 113 U.S. 713. The First Amendment liberties especially would be vulnerable to nullification by such control. Thus, the constitutional rights of free speech and free assembly could be brought to naught and censorship established widely over those areas merely by applying such a rule to every case presenting a substantial question concerning the exercise of those rights. This Court has refused to countenance a view so destructive of the most fundamental liberties. Thomas v. Collins, 323 U.S. 516. These and other constitutional rights would be nullified by the force of invalid orders issued in flat violation of the constitutional provisions securing them, and void for that reason. The same thing would be true also in other cases involving doubt, where statutory or other rights asserted or the benefit of asserting them would vanish, for any practical purpose, with obedience.

Indeed it was because these were so often the effects, not simply of final orders entered after determination upon the merits, but of interlocutory injunctions and ex parte restraining orders, that the Norris–LaGuardia Act became law and, as I think, the War Labor Disputes Act continued in force its policy. For in labor disputes the effect of such orders, it was pointed out officially and otherwise, is generally not merely failure to maintain the status quo pending final decision on the merits. It is also most often to break the strike, without regard to its legality or any conclusive determination on that account, and thus to render moot and abortive the substantive controversy.

It is not every case therefore where substantial doubt appears, concerning either the issues in the main cause or the court's jurisdiction to issue interlocutory or other orders, in which violation will bring the so-called *Shipp* doctrine into play. If that were true then indeed would a way have been found to nullify the constitutional limitations placed upon the powers of courts, including the control of Congress over their jurisdiction. Then also the liberties of our people would be placed largely at the mercy of invalid orders issued without power given by the Constitution and in contravention of power constitutionally withheld by Congress. Ex parte Fisk, 113 U.S. 713; *Thomas v. Collins*, supra.

. . . . .

■ MR. JUSTICE MURPHY joins in this opinion.[4]

[4. See 13A Wright, Miller & Cooper, Federal Practice and Procedure: Jurisdiction 2d § 3537 (1984); Chafee, Some Problems of Equity 364–380 (1950); Rendleman, More on Void Orders, 7 Ga.L.Rev. 246 (1973).

In one case the Supreme Court set aside a state-court contempt conviction for violation of an injunction where the subject matter was arguably within the exclusive jurisdiction of the National Labor Relations Board. The *United Mine Workers* case was distinguished on the ground that it "involved a restraining order of a federal court and presented no question of pre-emption of a field by Congress where, if the federal policy is to prevail, federal power must be complete." Petition of Green, 369 U.S. 689, 692 n. 1 (1962).

But in Walker v. City of Birmingham, 388 U.S. 307 (1967), the Court upheld a contempt conviction for violation of a state-court injunction though the ordinance on which the injunction was based and the terms of the injunction itself were of doubtful constitutionality. The *Green* case was distinguished on the ground that Green had attempted to challenge the validity of the injunction by moving to have it vacated before violating it and that the claim in *Green* was that the state court was "without jurisdiction" to issue the injunction.

In United States v. Ryan, 402 U.S. 530, 532 n. 4 (1971), the Court explained that in *Walker v. City of Birmingham* its "holding that the claims there sought to be asserted were not open on review of petitioners' contempt convictions was based upon the availability of review of those claims at an earlier stage." See United States v. Dickinson, 465 F.2d 496, 509–514 (5th Cir.1972).

The *Walker* case was distinguished in Matter of Providence Journal Co., 820 F.2d 1342, 1354 (1st Cir.1986), certiorari dismissed 485 U.S. 693 (1988), where it was held that a party subject to an order that constitutes a transparently invalid prior restraint on pure speech may challenge the order by violating it.

In International Union, United Mine Workers of America v. Bagwell, 512 U.S. 821, 830 (1994), the Court elaborated upon the standards of the 1947 *Mine Workers* case for distinguishing criminal from civil contempt. Because the "somewhat elusive distinction" controls whether alleged contemnors have a right to jury trial—applicable only to criminal contempt—the Court emphasized the need for careful attention to the nature and circumstances of particular contempt citations in relation to the policies and values served by the right to jury trial.

Baldwin v. Iowa State Traveling Men's Assn.

Supreme Court of the United States, 1931.
283 U.S. 522, 51 S.Ct. 517, 75 L.Ed. 1244.

■ MR. JUSTICE ROBERTS delivered the opinion of the Court.

A writ of certiorari was granted herein to review the affirmance by the Circuit Court of Appeals of a judgment for respondent rendered by the District Court for Southern Iowa. The action was upon the record of a judgment rendered in favor of the petitioner against the respondent in the United States District Court for Western Missouri.

The defense was lack of jurisdiction of the person of the respondent in the court which entered the judgment. After hearing, in which a jury was waived, this defense was sustained and the action dismissed. The first suit was begun in a Missouri state court and removed to the District Court. Respondent appeared specially and moved to quash and dismiss for want of service. The court quashed the service, but refused to dismiss. An alias summons was issued and returned served whereupon it again appeared specially, moved to set aside the service, quash the return, and dismiss the case for want of jurisdiction of its person. After a hearing on affidavits and briefs, the motion was overruled, with leave to plead within thirty days. No plea having been filed within that period, the cause proceeded, and judgment was entered for the amount claimed. Respondent did not move to set aside the judgment nor sue out a writ of error.

The ground of the motion made in the first suit is the same as that relied on as a defense to this one, namely, that the respondent is an Iowa corporation, that it never was present in Missouri, and that the person served with process in the latter state was not such an agent that service on him constituted a service on the corporation. The petitioner objected to proof of these matters, asserting that the defense constituted a collateral attack and a retrial of an issue settled in the first suit. The overruling of this objection and the resulting judgment for respondent are assigned as error.

The petitioner suggests that article 4, section 1, of the Constitution, forbade the retrial of the question determined on respondent's motion in the Missouri District Court; but the full faith and credit required by that clause is not involved, since neither of the courts concerned was a state court. Compare Cooper v. Newell, 173 U.S. 555, 567; Supreme Lodge, Knights of Pythias v. Meyer, 265 U.S. 30, 33. The respondent, on the other hand, insists that to deprive it of the defense which it made in the court

---

Under 18 U.S.C. § 3742(a)(1), a defendant may appeal the sentence received for a crime if the sentence "was imposed in violation of law." The Ninth Circuit held that the sentence in question was illegal. Reversing the Ninth Circuit on this point, the Supreme Court paused to explain why this reversal did not abrogate its appellate jurisdiction. "Although we ultimately conclude that respondent's sentence was not 'imposed in violation of law' and therefore that § 3742(a)(1) does not authorize an appeal in a case of this kind, it is familiar law that a federal court always has jurisdiction to determine its own jurisdiction. United States v. United Mine Workers, 330 U.S. 258, 291 (1947)." United States v. Ruiz, 536 U.S. 622, 628 (2002).]

below, of lack of jurisdiction over it by the Missouri District Court, would be to deny the due process guaranteed by the Fourteenth Amendment; but there is involved in that doctrine no right to litigate the same question twice. Chicago Life Ins. Co. v. Cherry, 244 U.S. 25; compare York v. Texas, 137 U.S. 15.

The substantial matter for determination is whether the judgment amounts to res judicata on the question of the jurisdiction of the court which rendered it over the person of the respondent. It is of no moment that the appearance was a special one expressly saving any submission to such jurisdiction. That fact would be important upon appeal from the judgment, and would save the question of the propriety of the court's decision on the matter, even though, after the motion had been overruled, the respondent had proceeded, subject to a reserved objection and exception, to a trial on the merits. Harkness v. Hyde, 98 U.S. 476; Goldey v. Morning News, 156 U.S. 518; Toledo Rys. & Light Co. v. Hill, 244 U.S. 49; Hitchman Coal & Coke Co. v. Mitchell, 245 U.S. 229; Morris & Co. v. Skandinavia Ins. Co., 279 U.S. 405. The special appearance gives point to the fact that the respondent entered the Missouri court for the very purpose of litigating the question of jurisdiction over its person. It had the election not to appear at all. If, in the absence of appearance, the court had proceeded to judgment, and the present suit had been brought thereon, respondent could have raised and tried out the issue in the present action, because it would never have had its day in court with respect to jurisdiction. Thompson v. Whitman, 18 Wall. (85 U.S.) 457; Pennoyer v. Neff, 95 U.S. 714; Hart v. Sansom, 110 U.S. 151; Wetmore v. Karrick, 205 U.S. 141; Bigelow v. Old Dominion Copper Co., 225 U.S. 111; McDonald v. Mabee, 243 U.S. 90. It had also the right to appeal from the decision of the Missouri District Court, as is shown by *Harkness v. Hyde*, supra, and the other authorities cited. It elected to follow neither of those courses, but, after having been defeated upon full hearing in its contention as to jurisdiction, it took no further steps, and the judgment in question resulted.

Public policy dictates that there be an end of litigation; that those who have contested an issue shall be bound by the result of the contest; and that matters once tried shall be considered forever settled as between the parties. We see no reason why this doctrine should not apply in every case where one voluntarily appears, presents his case and is fully heard, and why he should not, in the absence of fraud, be thereafter concluded by the judgment of the tribunal to which he has submitted his cause.

. . . . .

The judgment is reversed and the cause remanded for further proceedings in conformity with this opinion.[5]

[5. See American Surety Co. v. Baldwin, 287 U.S. 156 (1932), where a judgment was rendered in the trial court against a surety on an appeal bond without notice. The effect of the judgment was to make the surety liable upon a judgment against one defendant though

Chicot County Drainage Dist. v. Baxter State Bank

Supreme Court of the United States, 1940.
308 U.S. 371, 60 S.Ct. 317, 84 L.Ed. 329.

Action by the Baxter State Bank and another against Chicot County Drainage District to recover on bonds issued by the defendant. A judgment for plaintiff was affirmed by the Circuit Court of Appeals, 103 F.2d 847, and the defendant brings certiorari.

■ MR. CHIEF JUSTICE HUGHES delivered the opinion of the Court.

Respondents brought this suit in the United States District Court for the Western Division of the Eastern District of Arkansas to recover on fourteen bonds of $1,000 each, which had been issued in 1924 by the petitioner, Chicot County Drainage District, organized under statutes of Arkansas, and had been in default since 1932.

In its answer, petitioner pleaded a decree of the same District Court in a proceeding instituted by petitioner to effect a plan of readjustment of its indebtedness under the Act of May 24, 1934, providing for "Municipal–Debt Readjustments." The decree recited that a plan of readjustment had been accepted by the holders of more than two-thirds of the outstanding indebtedness and was fair and equitable; that to consummate the plan and with the approval of the court petitioner had issued and sold new serial bonds to the Reconstruction Finance Corporation in the amount of $193,500 and that these new bonds were valid obligations; that, also with the approval of the court, the Reconstruction Finance Corporation had purchased outstanding obligations of petitioner to the amount of $705,087.06 which had been delivered in exchange for new bonds and canceled; that certain proceeds had been turned over to the clerk of the court and that the disbursing agent had filed its report showing that the Reconstruction Finance Corporation had purchased all the old bonds of petitioner other than the amount of $57,449.30. The decree provided for the application of the amount paid into court to the remaining old obligations of petitioner, that such obligations might be presented within one

---

it had signed the bond presumably only on behalf of another defendant. The surety moved to vacate the judgment against it and the trial court denied the motion on the ground that it had jurisdiction to enter the judgment. It was decided that this holding was res judicata on the question of jurisdiction in a later suit in the federal court to enjoin the enforcement of the judgment.

See also Stoll v. Gottlieb, 305 U.S. 165 (1938). In that case an adjudication of a federal court in a bankruptcy proceeding that canceled the guaranty upon a bond of the bankrupt corporation was pleaded as res judicata in a suit in a state court on the guaranty, brought by the holder of the bond. The holder had been notified of the proceedings in the federal court but he did not appear. After the decree, however, he did appear and moved to vacate it for want of jurisdiction. The motion was denied. Could he question in the state court the federal court's jurisdiction to release the liability of the guarantor? See the comments on the *Stoll* case of Chafee, Some Problems of Equity 319 n. 42 (1950).

If the court of State B erroneously fails to give conclusive effect to a previous judgment of a court in State A upon the fallacious view that State A was without jurisdiction, is the second judgment entitled to full faith and credit? See Treinies v. Sunshine Mining Co., 308 U.S. 66, 74 (1939).]

year, and that unless so presented they should be forever barred from participating in the plan of readjustment or in the fund paid into court. Except for the provision for such presentation, the decree canceled the old bonds and the holders were enjoined from thereafter asserting any claim thereon.

Petitioner pleaded this decree, which was entered in March, 1936, as res judicata. Respondents demurred to the answer. Thereupon the parties stipulated for trial without a jury.

The evidence showed respondents' ownership of the bonds in suit and that respondents had notice of the proceeding for debt readjustment. The record of that proceeding, including the final decree, was introduced. The District Court ruled in favor of respondents and the Circuit Court of Appeals affirmed. 8 Cir., 103 F.2d 847. The decision was placed upon the ground that the decree was void because, subsequent to its entry, this Court in a proceeding relating to a municipal district in Texas had declared the statute under which the District Court had acted to be unconstitutional. Ashton v. Cameron County District, 298 U.S. 513. In view of the importance of the question we granted certiorari. . . .

The courts below have proceeded on the theory that the Act of Congress, having been found to be unconstitutional, was not a law; that it was inoperative, conferring no rights and imposing no duties, and hence affording no basis for the challenged decree. Norton v. Shelby County, 118 U.S. 425, 442; Chicago, Indianapolis & Louisville Rwy. Co. v. Hackett, 228 U.S. 559, 566. It is quite clear, however, that such broad statements as to the effect of a determination of unconstitutionality must be taken with qualifications. The actual existence of a statute, prior to such a determination, is an operative fact and may have consequences which cannot justly be ignored. The past cannot always be erased by a new judicial declaration. The effect of the subsequent ruling as to invalidity may have to be considered in various aspects,—with respect to particular relations, individual and corporate, and particular conduct, private and official. Questions of rights claimed to have become vested, of status, or prior determinations deemed to have finality and acted upon accordingly, of public policy in the light of the nature both of the statute and of its previous application, demand examination. These questions are among the most difficult of those which have engaged the attention of courts, state and federal, and it is manifest from numerous decisions that an all-inclusive statement of a principle of absolute retroactive invalidity cannot be justified.[6] Without attempting to review the different classes of cases in which the consequences of a ruling against validity have been determined in relation to the particular circumstances of past transactions, we appropriately confine our consideration to the question of res judicata as it now comes before us.

First. Apart from the contention as to the effect of the later decision as to constitutionality, all the elements necessary to constitute the defense of

---

6. See Field, "The Effect of an Unconstitutional Statute" ; 42 Yale L.J. 779; 45 Yale L.J. 1533; 48 Harv.L.Rev. 1271; 25 Va.L.Rev. 210.

res judicata are present. It appears that the proceedings in the District Court to bring about a plan of readjustment were conducted in complete conformity to the statute. The Circuit Court of Appeals observed that no question had been raised as to the regularity of the court's action. The answer in the present suit alleged that the plaintiffs (respondents here) had notice of the proceeding and were parties, and the evidence was to the same effect, showing compliance with the statute in that respect. As parties, these bondholders had full opportunity to present any objections to the proceeding, not only as to its regularity, or the fairness of the proposed plan of readjustment, or the propriety of the terms of the decree, but also as to the validity of the statute under which the proceeding was brought and the plan put into effect. Apparently no question of validity was raised and the cause proceeded to decree on the assumption by all parties and the court itself that the statute was valid. There was no attempt to review the decree. If the general principles governing the defense of res judicata are applicable, these bondholders, having the opportunity to raise the question of invalidity, were not the less bound by the decree because they failed to raise it. Cromwell v. County of Sac, 94 U.S. 351, 352; Case v. Beauregard, 101 U.S. 688, 692; Baltimore Steamship Co. v. Phillips, 274 U.S. 316, 319, 325; Grubb v. Public Utilities Commission, 281 U.S. 470, 479.

Second. The argument is pressed that the District Court was sitting as a court of bankruptcy, with the limited jurisdiction conferred by statute, and that, as the statute was later declared to be invalid, the District Court was without jurisdiction to entertain the proceeding and hence its decree is open to collateral attack. We think the argument untenable. The lower federal courts are all courts of limited jurisdiction, that is, with only the jurisdiction which Congress has prescribed. But none the less they are courts with authority, when parties are brought before them in accordance with the requirements of due process, to determine whether or not they have jurisdiction to entertain the cause and for this purpose to construe and apply the statute under which they are asked to act. Their determinations of such question, while open to direct review, may not be assailed collaterally.

In the early case of McCormick v. Sullivant, 10 Wheat. [23 U.S.] 192, where it was contended that the decree of the federal district court did not show that the parties to the proceedings were citizens of different States and hence that the suit was *coram non judice* and the decree void, this Court said: "But this reason proceeds upon an incorrect view of the character and jurisdiction of the inferior courts of the United States. They are all of limited jurisdiction; but they are not, on that account, inferior courts, in the technical sense of those words, whose judgments, taken alone, are to be disregarded. If the jurisdiction be not alleged in the proceedings, their judgments and decrees are erroneous, and may, upon a writ of error or appeal, be reversed for that cause. But they are not absolute nullities." Id., 10 Wheat. page 199. See, also, Skillern's Executors v. May's Executors, 6 Cranch [10 U.S.] 267; Des Moines Navigation Co. v. Iowa Homestead Co., 123 U.S. 552, 557, 559; Dowell v. Applegate, 152 U.S. 327, 340; Evers v. Watson, 156 U.S. 527, 533; Cutler v. Huston, 158 U.S.

423, 430, 431. This rule applies equally to the decrees of the District Court sitting in bankruptcy, that is, purporting to act under a statute of Congress passed in the exercise of the bankruptcy power. The court has the authority to pass upon its own jurisdiction and its decree sustaining jurisdiction against attack, while open to direct review, is res judicata in a collateral action. Stoll v. Gottlieb, 305 U.S. 165, 171, 172.

Whatever the contention as to jurisdiction may be, whether it is that the boundaries of a valid statute have been transgressed, or that the statute itself is invalid, the question of jurisdiction is still one for judicial determination. If the contention is one as to validity, the question is to be considered in the light of the standing of the party who seeks to raise the question and of its particular application. In the present instance it is suggested that the situation of petitioner, Chicot County Drainage District, is different from that of the municipal district before the court in the *Ashton* case. Petitioner contends that it is not a political subdivision of the State of Arkansas but an agent of the property owners within the District. See Drainage District No. 7 of Poinsett County v. Hutchins, 184 Ark. 521, 42 S.W.2d 996. We do not refer to that phase of the case as now determinative but merely as illustrating the sort of question which the District Court might have been called upon to resolve had the validity of the Act of Congress in the present application been raised. As the question of validity was one which had to be determined by a judicial decision, if determined at all, no reason appears why it should not be regarded as determinable by the District Court like any other question affecting its jurisdiction. There can be no doubt that if the question of the constitutionality of the statute had actually been raised and decided by the District Court in the proceeding to effect a plan of debt readjustment in accordance with the statute, that determination would have been final save as it was open to direct review upon appeal. *Stoll v. Gottlieb*, supra.

The remaining question is simply whether respondents having failed to raise the question in the proceeding to which they were parties and in which they could have raised it and had it finally determined, were privileged to remain quiet and raise it in a subsequent suit. Such a view is contrary to the well-settled principle that res judicata may be pleaded as a bar, not only as respects matters actually presented to sustain or defeat the right asserted in the earlier proceeding, "but also as respects any other available matter which might have been presented to that end." *Grubb v. Public Utilities Commission*, supra; *Cromwell v. County of Sac*, supra.

The judgment is reversed and the cause is remanded to the District Court with direction to dismiss the complaint.[7]

[7. See Wright & Kane, Federal Courts § 16 (6th ed.2002).

After full litigation the Nebraska Supreme Court held that certain land was in Nebraska, that the courts of that state had jurisdiction of the subject matter, and that title to the land was in a particular party. Held, that this judgment precluded the losing party in the Nebraska proceedings from contending in a diversity action in a federal court in Missouri that the

Ruhrgas AG v. Marathon Oil Co.

Supreme Court of the United States, 1999.
526 U.S. 574, 119 S.Ct. 1563, 143 L.Ed.2d 760.

■ JUSTICE GINSBURG delivered the opinion of the Court.

This case concerns the authority of the federal courts to adjudicate controversies. Jurisdiction to resolve cases on the merits requires both authority over the category of claim in suit (subject-matter jurisdiction) and authority over the parties (personal jurisdiction), so that the court's decision will bind them. In Steel Co. v. Citizens for Better Environment, 523 U.S. 83 (1998), this Court adhered to the rule that a federal court may not hypothesize subject-matter jurisdiction for the purpose of deciding the merits. *Steel Co.* rejected a doctrine, once approved by several Courts of Appeals, that allowed federal tribunals to pretermit jurisdictional objections "where (1) the merits question is more readily resolved, and (2) the prevailing party on the merits would be the same as the prevailing party were jurisdiction denied." Id., at 93. Recalling "a long and venerable line of our cases," id., at 94, *Steel Co.* reiterated: "The requirement that jurisdiction be established as a threshold matter ... is 'inflexible and without exception,' " id., at 94–95 (quoting Mansfield, C. & L.M.R. Co. v. Swan, 111 U.S. 379, 382 (1884)); for "[j]urisdiction is power to declare the law," and " '[w]ithout jurisdiction the court cannot proceed at all in any cause,' " 523 U.S., at 94 (quoting Ex parte McCardle, 7 Wall. [74 U.S.] 506, 514 (1868)). The Court, in *Steel Co.*, acknowledged that "the absolute purity" of the jurisdiction-first rule had been diluted in a few extraordinary cases, 523 U.S., at 101, and JUSTICE O'CONNOR, joined by JUSTICE KENNEDY, joined the majority on the understanding that the Court's opinion did not catalog "an exhaustive list of circumstances" in which exceptions to the solid rule were appropriate, id., at 110.

Steel Co. is the backdrop for the issue now before us: If, as *Steel Co.* held, jurisdiction generally must precede merits in dispositional order, must subject-matter jurisdiction precede personal jurisdiction on the decisional line? Or, do federal district courts have discretion to avoid a difficult question of subject-matter jurisdiction when the absence of personal jurisdiction is the surer ground? The particular civil action we confront was

land was in fact in Missouri and that the Nebraska courts lacked jurisdiction. Durfee v. Duke, 375 U.S. 106 (1963), noted 18 Sw.L.J. 500 (1964).

Once a judgment has become final, Congress lacks the power to compel the reopening of the judgment. In Plaut v. Spendthrift Farm, Inc., 514 U.S. 211 (1995), the Court held unconstitutional a 1991 amendment adding § 27A(b) to the Securities Exchange Act of 1934, 15 U.S.C. § 78aa–1. Section 27A(b) required the reopening of final judgments in securities-fraud actions that had been dismissed as time-barred on the authority of Lampf, Pleva, Lipkind, Prupis & Petigrow v. Gilbertson, 501 U.S. 350 (1991), which had announced a new and retroactively applicable period of limitations for such actions. The intent of Congress was to limit the retroactivity of *Lampf.* The *Plaut* Court acknowledged that Congress could change the law applicable to pending actions, but held that it was exclusively a judicial function to reopen a final judgment in order to apply a change of law enacted after the judgment became final on appeal or for lack of a timely appeal. Section 27A(b) thus violated the Constitution's separation of the judicial and legislative powers.]

commenced in state court and removed to federal court. The specific question on which we granted certiorari asks "[w]hether a federal district court is absolutely barred in all circumstances from dismissing a removed case for lack of personal jurisdiction without first deciding its subject-matter jurisdiction." ....

We hold that in cases removed from state court to federal court, as in cases originating in federal court, there is no unyielding jurisdictional hierarchy. Customarily, a federal court first resolves doubts about its jurisdiction over the subject matter, but there are circumstances in which a district court appropriately accords priority to a personal jurisdiction inquiry. The proceeding before us is such a case.

I

The underlying controversy stems from a venture to produce gas in the Heimdal Field of the Norwegian North Sea. In 1976, respondents Marathon Oil Company and Marathon International Oil Company acquired Marathon Petroleum Company (Norway) (MPCN) and respondent Marathon Petroleum Norge (Norge)....[8] Before the acquisition, Norge held a license to produce gas in the Heimdal Field; following the transaction, Norge assigned the license to MPCN.... In 1981, MPCN contracted to sell 70% of its share of the Heimdal gas production to a group of European buyers, including petitioner Ruhrgas AG.... The parties' agreement was incorporated into the Heimdal Gas Sales Agreement (Heimdal Agreement), which is "governed by and construed in accordance with Norwegian Law," ...; disputes thereunder are to be "exclusively and finally ... settled by arbitration in Stockholm, Sweden, in accordance with" International Chamber of Commerce rules....

II

Marathon Oil Company, Marathon International Oil Company, and Norge (collectively, Marathon) filed this lawsuit against Ruhrgas in Texas state court on July 6, 1995, asserting state-law claims of fraud, tortious interference with prospective business relations, participation in breach of fiduciary duty, and civil conspiracy.... Marathon Oil Company and Marathon International Oil Company alleged that Ruhrgas and the other European buyers induced them with false promises of "premium prices" and guaranteed pipeline tariffs to invest over $300 million in MPCN for the development of the Heimdal Field and the erection of a pipeline to Ruhrgas' plant in Germany.... Norge alleged that Ruhrgas' effective monopolization of the Heimdal gas diminished the value of the license Norge had assigned to MPCN.... Marathon asserted that Ruhrgas had furthered its plans at three meetings in Houston, Texas, and through a stream of correspondence directed to Marathon in Texas....

---

8.   Ruhrgas is a German corporation; Norge is a Norwegian corporation.... Marathon Oil Company, an Ohio corporation, and Marathon International Oil Company, a Delaware corporation, moved their principal places of business from Ohio to Texas while the venture underlying this case was in formation....

Ruhrgas removed the case to the District Court for the Southern District of Texas. See 145 F.3d 211, 214 (CA5 1998). In its notice of removal, Ruhrgas asserted three bases for federal jurisdiction: diversity of citizenship, see 28 U.S.C. § 1332 (1994 ed.and Supp. III), on the theory that Norge, the only nondiverse plaintiff, had been fraudulently joined;[9] federal question, see § 1331, because Marathon's claims "raise[d] substantial questions of foreign and international relations, which are incorporated into and form part of the federal common law," ...; and 9 U.S.C. § 205, which authorizes removal of cases "relat[ing] to" international arbitration agreements.[10] See 145 F.3d, at 214–215, 115 F.3d 315, 319–321 (CA5), vacated and rehearing en banc granted, 129 F.3d 746 (1997). Ruhrgas moved to dismiss the complaint for lack of personal jurisdiction. Marathon moved to remand the case to the state court for lack of federal subject-matter jurisdiction. See 145 F.3d, at 215.

After permitting jurisdictional discovery, the District Court dismissed the case for lack of personal jurisdiction.... In so ruling, the District Court relied on Fifth Circuit precedent allowing district courts to adjudicate personal jurisdiction without first establishing subject-matter jurisdiction.... Texas' long-arm statute, see Tex. Civ. Prac. & Rem.Code Ann. § 17.042 (1997), authorizes personal jurisdiction to the extent allowed by the Due Process Clause of the Federal Constitution. See ... Kawasaki Steel Corp. v. Middleton, 699 S.W.2d 199, 200 (Tex.1985). The District Court addressed the constitutional question and concluded that Ruhrgas' contacts with Texas were insufficient to support personal jurisdiction.... Finding "no evidence that Ruhrgas engaged in any tortious conduct in Texas," ... the court determined that Marathon's complaint did not present circumstances adequately affiliating Ruhrgas with Texas....

A panel of the Court of Appeals for the Fifth Circuit concluded that "respec[t]" for "the proper balance of federalism" impelled it to turn first to "the formidable subject matter jurisdiction issue presented." 115 F.3d, at 318. After examining and rejecting each of Ruhrgas' asserted bases of federal jurisdiction, see id., at 319–321,[11] the Court of Appeals vacated the

---

9. A suit between "citizens of a State and citizens or subjects of a foreign state" lies within federal diversity jurisdiction. 28 U.S.C. § 1332(a)(2). Section 1332 has been interpreted to require "complete diversity." See Strawbridge v. Curtiss, 3 Cranch [7 U.S.] 267 (1806); R. Fallon, D. Meltzer, & D. Shapiro, Hart and Wechsler's The Federal Courts and the Federal System 1528–1531 (4th ed.1996). The foreign citizenship of defendant Ruhrgas, a German corporation, and plaintiff Norge, a Norwegian corporation, rendered diversity incomplete.

10. Title 9 U.S.C. § 205 allows removal "[w]here the subject matter of an action or proceeding pending in a State court relates to an arbitration agreement or award falling under the Convention [on the Recognition and Enforcement of Foreign Arbitral Awards of June 10, 1958]."

11. The Court of Appeals concluded that whether Norge had a legal interest in the Heimdal license notwithstanding its assignment to MPCN likely turned on difficult questions of Norwegian law; Ruhrgas therefore could not show, at the outset, that Norge had been fraudulently joined as a plaintiff to defeat diversity. See 115 F.3d 315, 319–320 (CA5), vacated and rehearing en banc granted, 129 F.3d 746 (1997). The appeals court also determined that Marathon's claims did not "strike at the sovereignty of a foreign nation," so as to raise a federal question on that account. 115 F.3d, at 320. Finally, the court

judgment of the District Court and ordered the case remanded to the state court, see id., at 321. This Court denied Ruhrgas' petition for a writ of certiorari, which was limited to the question whether subject-matter jurisdiction existed under 9 U.S.C. § 205. See 522 U.S. 967 (1997).

The Fifth Circuit, on its own motion, granted rehearing en banc, thereby vacating the panel decision. See 129 F.3d 746 (CA5 1997). In a 9-to-7 decision, the en banc court held that, in removed cases, district courts must decide issues of subject-matter jurisdiction first, reaching issues of personal jurisdiction "only if subject-matter jurisdiction is found to exist." 145 F.3d, at 214. Noting *Steel Co.*'s instruction that subject-matter jurisdiction must be " 'established as a threshold matter,' " 145 F.3d, at 217 (quoting 523 U.S., at 94), the Court of Appeals derived from that decision "counsel against" recognition of judicial discretion to proceed directly to personal jurisdiction. 145 F.3d, at 218. The court limited its holding to removed cases; it perceived in those cases the most grave threat that federal courts would "usur[p] . . . state courts' residual jurisdiction." Id., at 219.[12]

Writing for the seven dissenters, Judge Higginbotham agreed that subject-matter jurisdiction ordinarily should be considered first. See id., at 231. If the challenge to personal jurisdiction involves no complex state-law questions, however, and is more readily resolved than the challenge to subject-matter jurisdiction, the District Court, in the dissenters' view, should take the easier route. See ibid. Judge Higginbotham regarded the District Court's decision dismissing Marathon's case as illustrative and appropriate: While Ruhrgas' argument under 9 U.S.C. § 205 presented a difficult issue of first impression, its personal jurisdiction challenge raised "[n]o substantial questions of purely state law," and "could be resolved relatively easily in [Ruhrgas'] favor." 145 F.3d, at 232–233.

We granted certiorari, 525 U.S. 1039 (1998), to resolve a conflict between the Circuits[13] and now reverse.

III

Steel Co. held that Article III generally requires a federal court to satisfy itself of its jurisdiction over the subject matter before it considers the merits of a case. "For a court to pronounce upon [the merits] when it has no jurisdiction to do so," *Steel Co.* declared, "is . . . for a court to act

---

concluded that Marathon asserted claims independent of the Heimdal Agreement and that the case therefore did not "relat[e] to" an international arbitration agreement under 9 U.S.C. § 205. See 115 F.3d, at 320–321.

12. The Fifth Circuit remanded the case to the District Court for it to consider the "nove[l]" subject-matter jurisdiction issues presented. 145 F.3d 211, 225 (CA5 1998). The appeals court "express[ed] no opinion" on the vacated panel decision which had held that the District Court lacked subject-matter jurisdiction. Id., at 225, n.23.

13. The Court of Appeals for the Second Circuit has concluded that district courts have discretion to dismiss a removed case for want of personal jurisdiction without reaching the issue of subject-matter jurisdiction. See Cantor Fitzgerald, L.P. v. Peaslee, 88 F.3d 152, 155 (1996).

ultra vires." 523 U.S., at 101–102. The Fifth Circuit incorrectly read *Steel Co.* to teach that subject-matter jurisdiction must be found to exist, not only before a federal court reaches the merits, but also before personal jurisdiction is addressed. See 145 F.3d, at 218.

A

The Court of Appeals accorded priority to the requirement of subject-matter jurisdiction because it is nonwaivable and delimits federal-court power, while restrictions on a court's jurisdiction over the person are waivable and protect individual rights. See id., at 217–218. The character of the two jurisdictional bedrocks unquestionably differs. Subject-matter limitations on federal jurisdiction serve institutional interests. They keep the federal courts within the bounds the Constitution and Congress have prescribed. Accordingly, subject-matter delineations must be policed by the courts on their own initiative even at the highest level. See *Steel Co.*, 523 U.S., at 94–95; Fed. Rule Civ. Proc. 12(h)(3) ("Whenever it appears . . . that the court lacks jurisdiction of the subject matter, the court shall dismiss the action."); 28 U.S.C. § 1447(c) (1994 ed., Supp. III) ("If at any time before final judgment [in a removed case] it appears that the district court lacks subject matter jurisdiction, the case shall be remanded.").

Personal jurisdiction, on the other hand, "represents a restriction on judicial power . . . as a matter of individual liberty." Insurance Corp. of Ireland v. Compagnie des Bauxites de Guinee, 456 U.S. 694, 702 (1982). Therefore, a party may insist that the limitation be observed, or he may forgo that right, effectively consenting to the court's exercise of adjudicatory authority. See Fed. Rule Civ. Proc. 12(h)(1) (defense of lack of jurisdiction over the person waivable); *Insurance Corp. of Ireland*, 456 U.S., at 703 (same).

These distinctions do not mean that subject-matter jurisdiction is ever and always the more "fundamental." Personal jurisdiction, too, is "an essential element of the jurisdiction of a district . . . court," without which the court is "powerless to proceed to an adjudication." Employers Reinsurance Corp. v. Bryant, 299 U.S. 374, 382 (1937). In this case, indeed, the impediment to subject-matter jurisdiction on which Marathon relies—lack of complete diversity—rests on statutory interpretation, not constitutional command. Marathon joined an alien plaintiff (Norge) as well as an alien defendant (Ruhrgas). If the joinder of Norge is legitimate, the complete diversity required by 28 U.S.C. § 1332 (1994 ed.and Supp. III), but not by Article III, see State Farm Fire & Casualty Co. v. Tashire, 386 U.S. 523, 530–531 (1967), is absent. In contrast, Ruhrgas relies on the constitutional safeguard of due process to stop the court from proceeding to the merits of the case. See *Insurance Corp. of Ireland*, 456 U.S., at 702 ("The requirement that a court have personal jurisdiction flows . . . from the Due Process Clause.").

While *Steel Co.* reasoned that subject-matter jurisdiction necessarily precedes a ruling on the merits, the same principle does not dictate a sequencing of jurisdictional issues. "[A] court that dismisses on . . . non-merits grounds such as ... personal jurisdiction, before finding subject-matter jurisdiction, makes no assumption of law-declaring power that violates the separation of powers principles underlying *Mansfield* and *Steel Company*." In re Papandreou, 139 F.3d 247, 255 (CADC 1998). It is hardly novel for a federal court to choose among threshold grounds for denying audience to a case on the merits. Thus, as the Court observed in *Steel Co.*, district courts do not overstep Article III limits when they decline jurisdiction of state-law claims on discretionary grounds without determining whether those claims fall within their pendent jurisdiction, see Moor v. County of Alameda, 411 U.S. 693, 715–716 (1973), or abstain under Younger v. Harris, 401 U.S. 37 (1971), without deciding whether the parties present a case or controversy, see Ellis v. Dyson, 421 U.S. 426, 433–434 (1975). See *Steel Co.*, 523 U.S., at 100–101, n. 3; cf. Arizonans for Official English v. Arizona, 520 U.S. 43, 66–67 (1997) (pretermitting challenge to appellants' standing and dismissing on mootness grounds).

B

Maintaining that subject-matter jurisdiction must be decided first even when the litigation originates in federal court, ... Marathon sees removal as the more offensive case, on the ground that the dignity of state courts is immediately at stake. If a federal court dismisses a removed case for want of personal jurisdiction, that determination may preclude the parties from relitigating the very same personal jurisdiction issue in state court. See Baldwin v. Iowa State Traveling Men's Assn., 283 U.S. 522, 524–527 (1931) (personal jurisdiction ruling has issue-preclusive effect).

Issue preclusion in subsequent state-court litigation, however, may also attend a federal court's subject-matter determination. Ruhrgas hypothesizes, for example, a defendant who removes on diversity grounds a state-court suit seeking $50,000 in compensatory and $1 million in punitive damages for breach of contract.... If the district court determines that state law does not allow punitive damages for breach of contract and therefore remands the removed action for failure to satisfy the amount in controversy, see 28 U.S.C. § 1332(a) (1994 ed., Supp. III) ($75,000), the federal court's conclusion will travel back with the case. Assuming a fair airing of the issue in federal court, that court's ruling on permissible state-law damages may bind the parties in state court, although it will set no precedent otherwise governing state-court adjudications. See Chicot County Drainage Dist. v. Baxter State Bank, 308 U.S. 371, 376 (1940) ("[Federal courts'] determinations of [whether they have jurisdiction to entertain a case] may not be assailed collaterally."); Restatement (Second) of Judgments § 12, p. 115 (1980) ("When a court has rendered a judgment in a contested action, the judgment [ordinarily] precludes the parties from litigating the question of the court's subject matter jurisdiction in subsequent litigation."). Similarly, as Judge Higginbotham observed, our "dualistic ... system of federal and state courts" allows federal courts to make issue-preclusive rulings about state law in the exercise of supplemental jurisdiction under 28 U.S.C. § 1367. 145 F.3d, at 231, and n. 7.

Most essentially, federal and state courts are complementary systems for administering justice in our Nation. Cooperation and comity, not competition and conflict, are essential to the federal design. A State's dignitary interest bears consideration when a district court exercises discretion in a case of this order. If personal jurisdiction raises "difficult questions of [state] law," and subject-matter jurisdiction is resolved "as eas[ily]" as personal jurisdiction, a district court will ordinarily conclude that "federalism concerns tip the scales in favor of initially ruling on the motion to remand." Allen v. Ferguson, 791 F.2d 611, 616 (CA7 1986). In other cases, however, the district court may find that concerns of judicial economy and restraint are overriding. See, e.g., Asociacion Nacional de Pescadores v. Dow Quimica, 988 F.2d 559, 566–567 (CA5 1993) (if removal is nonfrivolous and personal jurisdiction turns on federal constitutional issues, "federal intrusion into state courts' authority . . . is minimized"). The federal design allows leeway for sensitive judgments of this sort. " 'Our Federalism' "

> "does not mean blind deference to 'States' Rights' any more than it means centralization of control over every important issue in our National Government and its courts. The Framers rejected both these courses. What the concept does represent is a system in which there is sensitivity to the legitimate interests of both State and National Governments." Younger [v. Harris, 401 U.S. 37, 44 (1971)].

The Fifth Circuit and Marathon posit that state-court defendants will abuse the federal system with opportunistic removals. A discretionary rule, they suggest, will encourage manufactured, convoluted federal subject-matter theories designed to wrench cases from state court. See 145 F.3d, at 219 . . . . This specter of unwarranted removal, we have recently observed, "rests on an assumption we do not indulge—that district courts generally will not comprehend, or will balk at applying, the rules on removal Congress has prescribed. . . . The well-advised defendant . . . will foresee the likely outcome of an unwarranted removal—a swift and nonreviewable remand order, see 28 U.S.C. §§ 1447(c), (d), attended by the displeasure of a district court whose authority has been improperly invoked." Caterpillar Inc. v. Lewis, 519 U.S. 61, 77–78 (1996).

C

In accord with Judge Higginbotham, we recognize that in most instances subject-matter jurisdiction will involve no arduous inquiry. See 145 F.3d, at 229 ("engag[ing]" subject-matter jurisdiction "at the outset of a case . . . [is] often . . . the most efficient way of going"). In such cases, both expedition and sensitivity to state courts' coequal stature should impel the federal court to dispose of that issue first. See Cantor Fitzgerald, L.P. v. Peaslee, 88 F.3d 152, 155 (CA2 1996) (a court disposing of a case on personal jurisdiction grounds "should be convinced that the challenge to the court's subject-matter jurisdiction is not easily resolved"). Where, as here, however, a district court has before it a straightforward personal jurisdiction issue presenting no complex question of state law, and the alleged defect in subject-matter jurisdiction raises a difficult and novel question, the court does not abuse its discretion by turning directly to personal jurisdiction.

For the reasons stated, the judgment of the Court of Appeals is reversed, and the case is remanded for proceedings consistent with this opinion.

It is so ordered.[14]

Kalb v. Feuerstein

Supreme Court of the United States, 1940.
308 U.S. 433, 60 S.Ct. 343, 84 L.Ed. 370.

Action by Ernest Newton Kalb and Margaret Kalb, his wife, for restoration of possession of a farm, for cancellation of a sheriff's deed, and

---

[14. In Lolavar v. de Santibanes, 430 F.3d 221 (4th Cir.2005), the Fourth Circuit, citing *Ruhrgas AG*, held that the district court had acted within its discretion in electing to address a straightforward issue of personal jurisdiction without first addressing subject-matter jurisdiction where personal jurisdiction over the nonresident defendant was lacking.

The Supreme Court has extended this general concept from *Ruhrgas AG*—that there is no jurisdictional hierarchy requiring that subject-matter jurisdiction always be addressed before turning to personal jurisdiction—to *forum non conveniens*. A unanimous Court, although observing that federal courts typically will address jurisdictional issues first, stated that "where subject-matter or personal jurisdiction is difficult to determine, and *forum non conveniens* considerations weigh heavily in favor of dismissal, the court properly takes the less burdensome course." Sinochem International Co. v. Malaysia International Shipping Corp., 549 U.S. 422 (2007).

In Willy v. Coastal Corporation, 503 U.S. 131 (1992), the Supreme Court upheld the power of a district court to impose sanctions under Federal Rule of Civil Procedure 11 against a plaintiff who acted improperly in the further conduct of a lawsuit that had been wrongfully removed from state court. The plaintiff first moved to remand the action. When that motion was erroneously denied, the plaintiff wantonly filed a blizzard of carelessly drafted and haphazardly organized papers in response to the defendant's motion to dismiss on the merits. The Supreme Court sustained the Fifth Circuit's judgment on appeal that not only remanded the action for lack of subject-matter jurisdiction but also upheld the sanctions imposed by the district court for the plaintiff's conduct during the continued litigation of the action over which the district court lacked jurisdiction.

On sanctions generally, and Rule 11 in particular, see Wright & Kane, Federal Courts § 69A (6th ed.2002); Leiferman, The 1993 Rule 11 Amendments: The Transformation of the Venomous Viper into the Toothless Tiger?, 29 Tort & Ins.L.J. 497 (1994).

The circuits are divided as to whether a case may be dismissed with prejudice as a procedural sanction if the district court lacks subject-matter jurisdiction of the case. Two circuits have said no. Hernandez v. Conriv Realty Associates, 182 F.3d 121 (2d Cir.1999); In re Orthopedic Bone Screw Products Liability Litigation, 132 F.3d 152 (3d Cir.1997). The Ninth Circuit has ruled otherwise, deeming a dismissal ordered as a procedural sanction to be collateral to the merits. In re Exxon Valdez, 102 F.3d 429 (9th Cir.1996).

In Calderon v. Ashmus, 523 U.S. 740, 745 n. 2 (1998), the Court held that a challenge to the judicial power of a federal court under Article III must be resolved before considering whether the court lacks jurisdiction under the Eleventh Amendment. See generally Steinman, After *Steel Co.*: Hypothetical Jurisdiction in the Federal Appellate Courts, 58 Wash. & Lee L.Rev. 855 (2001).]

for removal of defendants from the farm, and action by Ernest Newton Kalb against Roscoe R. Luce and others to recover damages for conspiracy to deprive plaintiff of possession of his farm, for assault and battery, and for false imprisonment. Judgments dismissing the complaints were affirmed by the Supreme Court of Wisconsin, 285 N.W. 431, and plaintiffs appeal.

■ Mr. Justice Black delivered the opinion of the Court.

Appellants are farmers. Two of appellees, as mortgagees, began foreclosure on appellants' farm March 7, 1933, in the Walworth (Wisconsin) County Court; judgment of foreclosure was entered April 21, 1933; July 20, 1935, the sheriff sold the property under the judgment; September 16, 1935, while appellant Ernest Newton Kalb had duly pending in the bankruptcy court a petition for composition and extension of time to pay his debts under section 75 of the Bankruptcy Act (Frazier–Lemke Act), the Walworth County Court granted the mortgagees' motion for confirmation of the sheriff's sale; no stay of the foreclosure or of the subsequent action to enforce it was ever sought or granted in the State or bankruptcy court; December 16, 1935, the mortgagees, who had purchased at the sheriff's sale, obtained a writ of assistance from the State court; and March 12, 1936, the sheriff executed the writ by ejecting appellants and their family from the mortgaged farm.

The question in both No. 120 and No. 121 are whether the Wisconsin County Court had jurisdiction, while the petition under the Frazier–Lemke Act was pending in the bankruptcy court, to confirm the sheriff's sale and order appellants dispossessed, and, if it did not, whether its action in the absence of direct appeal is subject to collateral attack.

But if appellants are right in their contention that the Federal Act of itself, from the moment the petition was filed and so long as it remained pending, operated, in the absence of the bankruptcy court's consent, to oust the jurisdiction of the State court so as to stay its power to proceed with foreclosure, to confirm a sale, and to issue an order ejecting appellants from their farm, the action of the Walworth County Court was not merely erroneous but was beyond its power, void, and subject to collateral attack. And the determination whether the Act did so operate is a construction of that Act and a Federal question.

It is generally true that a judgment by a court of competent jurisdiction bears a presumption of regularity and is not, thereafter subject to collateral attack. But Congress, because its power over the subject of bankruptcy is plenary, may by specific bankruptcy legislation create an exception to that principle and render judicial acts taken with respect to the person or property of a debtor whom the bankruptcy law protects nullities and vulnerable collaterally. Although the Walworth County Court had general jurisdiction over foreclosures under the law of Wisconsin, a peremptory prohibition by Congress in the exercise of its supreme power over bankruptcy that no State court have jurisdiction over a petitioning farmer-debtor or his property would have rendered the confirmation of sale and its enforcement beyond the County Court's power and nullities subject to collateral attack. The States cannot, in the exercise of control over local laws and practice, vest State courts with power to violate the supreme law of the land. The Constitution grants Congress exclusive power to regulate bankruptcy and under this power Congress can limit the jurisdiction which courts, State or Federal, can exercise over the person and property of a debtor who duly invokes the bankruptcy law. If Congress has vested in the bankruptcy courts exclusive jurisdiction over farmer-debtors and their property, and has by its Act withdrawn from all other courts all power under any circumstances to maintain and enforce foreclosure proceedings against them, its Act is the supreme law of the land which all courts—State and Federal—must observe. The wisdom and desirability of an automatic statutory ouster of jurisdiction of all except bankruptcy courts over farmer-debtors and their property were considerations for Congress alone.

We think the language and broad policy of the Frazier–Lemke Act conclusively demonstrate that Congress intended to, and did deprive the Wisconsin County Court of the power and jurisdiction to continue or maintain in any manner the foreclosure proceedings against appellants without the consent after hearing of the bankruptcy court in which the farmer's petition was then pending.

The Act expressly provided:

"(n) The filing of a petition . . . shall immediately subject the farmer and all his property, wherever located, . . . to the exclusive jurisdiction of the court, including . . . the right or the equity of redemption where the period of redemption has not or had not expired, . . . or where the sale has not or had not been confirmed," and "In all cases where, at the time of filing the petition, the period of redemption has not or had not expired, . . . or where the sale has not or had not been confirmed, . . . the period of redemption shall be extended or the confirmation of sale withheld for the period necessary for the purpose of carrying out the provisions of this section"; and

"(*o*) Except upon petition made to and granted by the judge after hearing and report by the conciliation commissioner, the following proceedings *shall not be instituted,* or if instituted at any time prior to the filing of a petition under this section, *shall not be maintained, in any court or otherwise,* against the farmer or his property, *at any time after the filing* of the petition under this section, and *prior to the confirmation* or other disposition of the composition or extension proposal by the court: . . . .

"(2) *Proceedings for foreclosure of a mortgage on land,* or for cancellation, rescission, or specific performance of an agreement for sale of land *or for recovery of possession of land;* . . . .

"(6) Seizures, distress, sale, or other proceedings under an execution or under any lease, lien, chattel mortgage, conditional sale agreement, crop payment agreement, or mortgage.

"(p) *The prohibitions . . . shall apply to all judicial or official proceedings in any court or under the direction of any official,* and *shall apply to all creditors, public or private,* and *to all of the debtor's property, wherever located. All such property shall be* under *the sole jurisdiction and control of the court in bankruptcy,* and subject to the payment of the debtor farmer's creditors, as provided for in [this section] section 75 of this Act." (Italics supplied.)

Thus Congress repeatedly stated its unequivocal purpose to prohibit—in the absence of consent by the bankruptcy court in which a distressed farmer has a pending petition—a mortgagee or any court from instituting, or maintaining if already instituted, any proceeding against the farmer to sell under mortgage foreclosure, to confirm such a sale, or to dispossess under it.

. . . . .

Congress set up in the Act an exclusive and easily accessible statutory means for rehabilitating distressed farmers who, as victims of a general economic depression, were without means to engage in formal court litigation. To this end, a referee or Conciliation Commissioner was provided for every county in which fifteen prospective farmer-debtors requested an appointment; and express provision was made that these Commissioners should "upon request assist any farmer in preparing and filing a petition under this section and in all matters subsequent thereto arising under this section and farmers shall not be required to be represented by an attorney in any proceeding under this section." In harmony with the general plan of giving the farmer an opportunity for rehabilitation, he was relieved—after filing a petition for composition and extension—of the necessity of litigation elsewhere and its consequent expense. This was accomplished by granting the bankruptcy court exclusive jurisdiction of the petitioning farmer and all his property with complete and self-executing statutory exclusion of all other courts.

The mortgagees who sought to enforce the mortgage after the petition was duly filed in the bankruptcy court, the Walworth County Court that attempted to grant the mortgagees relief, and the sheriff who enforced the court's judgment, were all acting in violation of the controlling Act of Congress. Because that State court had been deprived of all jurisdiction or power to proceed with the foreclosure, the confirmation of the sale, the execution of the sheriff's deed, the writ of assistance, and the ejection of appellants from their property—to the extent based upon the court's actions—were all without authority of law.

. . . . .

Congress manifested its intention that the issue of jurisdiction in the foreclosing court need not be contested or even raised by the distressed farmer-debtor. The protection of the farmers was left to the farmers themselves or to the Commissioners who might be laymen, and considerations as to whether the issue of jurisdiction was actually contested in the County Court, or whether it could have been contested, are not applicable where the plenary power of Congress over bankruptcy has been exercised as in this Act.

The judgments in both cases are reversed and the causes are remanded to the Supreme Court of Wisconsin for further proceedings not inconsistent with this opinion.

Reversed and remanded.[15]

[**15.** See also United States v. U.S. Fidelity & Guaranty Co., 309 U.S. 506, 514 (1940) (government immunity from suit).

Exceptions to the rule that a judgment in a contested action precludes a party from litigating the question of the court's subject matter jurisdiction are stated in Restatement (Second) of Judgments § 12 (1982). Although a valid and final judgment of a state court normally has the same effects in a subsequent action in federal court as it has by the law of the state in which the judgment was rendered, the state judgment has no preclusive effect if a scheme of federal remedies permits assertion of the federal claim notwithstanding the state adjudication or leaves the federal court free to make an independent determination of the issue in question. Id., § 86. See Moore, Collateral Attack on Subject Matter Jurisdiction: A Critique of the Restatement (Second) of Judgments, 66 Cornell L.Rev. 534 (1981).

"Federal law determines the effects under the rules of res judicata of a judgment of a federal court." Restatement (Second) of Judgments § 87 (1982). See also Degnan, Federalized Res Judicata, 85 Yale L.J. 741 (1976); 18 Wright, Miller & Cooper, Federal Practice and Procedure: Jurisdiction 2d §§ 4468–4472 (2002); Wright & Kane, Federal Courts § 100A (6th ed.2002); Symposium, Preclusion in a Federal System, 70 Cornell L.Rev. 599 (1985).

It was held in Semtek Int'l Inc. v. Lockheed Martin Corp., 531 U.S. 497 (2001), reprinted infra p. 802, that federal rules of res judicata determine the effect to be given the judgment of a federal court in a diversity case. This view is supported by Erickson, Interjurisdictional Preclusion, 96 Mich.L.Rev. 945 (1998). The contrary view is argued in Burbank, Interjurisdictional Preclusion, Full Faith and Credit and Federal Common Law: A General Approach, 71 Cornell L.Rev. 733 (1986).]

CHAPTER IX

CONFLICTS BETWEEN STATE AND NATIONAL JUDICIAL SYSTEMS

SECTION 1. STATE ENFORCEMENT OF FEDERAL LAW

Howlett by Howlett v. Rose

Supreme Court of the United States, 1990.
496 U.S. 356, 110 S.Ct. 2430, 110 L.Ed.2d 332.

■ JUSTICE STEVENS delivered the opinion of the Court.

Section 1 of the Civil Rights Act of 1871, Rev.Stat. § 1979, now codified as 42 U.S.C. § 1983, creates a remedy for violations of federal rights committed by persons acting under color of state law.[1] State courts as well as federal courts have jurisdiction over § 1983 cases. The question in this case is whether a state law defense of "sovereign immunity" is available to a school board otherwise subject to suit in a Florida court even though such a defense would not be available if the action had been brought in a federal forum.

[A former high school student sued in state court against a school board and three school officials. He claimed that an assistant principal made an illegal search of his car when it was parked on school grounds and that he was wrongfully suspended from classes for five days without due process. He claimed that the search and suspension violated his rights under the Fourth and Fourteenth Amendments and similar provisions of the Florida constitution. He sued for damages and for an order expunging any reference to the suspension from the school records. The state district court dismissed the claim against the school board. It read the decision of

---

1. 42 U.S.C. § 1983 provides in relevant part:

    "Every person who, under color of any statute, ordinance, regulation, custom, or usage of any State ..., subjects, or causes to be subjected, any citizen of the United States or other person within the jurisdiction thereof to the deprivation of any rights, privileges, or immunities secured by the Constitution and laws, shall be liable to the party injured in an action at law, suit in equity, or other proper proceeding for redress."

the Florida Supreme Court in Hill v. Department of Corrections, 513 So.2d 129 (1987), as meaning that Florida's statutory waiver of sovereign immunity applied only to tort actions and conferred a blanket immunity on state governmental entities from federal civil rights actions under 42 U.S.C. § 1983 in state court. The Florida District Court of Appeals affirmed and the Florida Supreme Court denied review.]

II

. . . . .

On its facts, the disposition of the *Hill* case would appear to be unexceptional. The defendant in *Hill* was a state agency protected from suit in a federal court by the Eleventh Amendment. . . .

The language and reasoning of the State Supreme Court, if not its precise holding, however, went further. That further step was completed by the District Court of Appeal in this case. As it construed the law, Florida has extended absolute immunity from suit, not only to the State and its arms but also to municipalities, counties, and school districts who might otherwise be subject to suit under § 1983 in federal court. That holding raises the concern that the state court may be evading federal law and discriminating against federal causes of action. The adequacy of the state law ground to support a judgment precluding litigation of the federal question is itself a federal question which we review de novo. . . .

III

Federal law is enforceable in state courts not because Congress has determined that federal courts would otherwise be burdened or that state courts might provide a more convenient forum—although both might well be true—but because the Constitution and laws passed pursuant to it are as much laws in the States as laws passed by the state legislature. The Supremacy Clause makes those laws "the supreme Law of the Land," and charges state courts with a coordinate responsibility to enforce that law according to their regular modes of procedure. "The laws of the United States are laws in the several States, and just as much binding on the citizens and courts thereof as the State laws are. . . . The two together form one system of jurisprudence, which constitutes the law of the land for the State; and the courts of the two jurisdictions are not foreign to each other, nor to be treated by each other as such, but as courts of the same country, having jurisdiction partly different and partly concurrent." Claflin v. Houseman, 93 U.S. 130, 136–137 (1876); see Minneapolis & St. Louis R. Co. v. Bombolis, 241 U.S. 211, 222 (1916) ("the governments and courts of both the Nation and the several States [are not] strange or foreign to each other in the broad sense of that word, but [are] all courts of a common country, all within the orbit of their lawful authority being charged with the duty to safeguard and enforce the right of every citizen without reference to the particular exercise of governmental power from which the right may have arisen, if only the authority to enforce such right comes generally within the scope of the jurisdiction conferred by the government creating them"); Hart, The Relations Between State and Federal Law, 54 Colum.L.Rev. 489 (1954) ("The law which governs daily living in the United States is a single system of law"); see also Tafflin v. Levitt, 493 U.S. 455, 468 (1990) (SCALIA, J., concurring). . . .

Three corollaries follow from the proposition that "federal" law is part of the "Law of the Land" in the State:

1. A state court may not deny a federal right, when the parties and controversy are properly before it, in the absence of "valid excuse." Douglas v. New York, N.H. & H. R. Co., 279 U.S. 377, 387–388 (1929) (Holmes, J.).[2] "The existence of the jurisdiction creates an implication of duty to exercise it." Mondou v. New York, N.H. & H. R. Co., 223 U.S. 1, 58 (1912); see Testa v. Katt, 330 U.S. 386 (1947); Missouri ex rel. St. Louis, B. & M. R. Co. v. Taylor, 266 U.S. 200, 208 (1924); Robb v. Connolly, 111 U.S. 624, 637 (1884).[3]

---

2. See Hathorn v. Lovorn, 457 U.S. 255, 263 (1982); Barr v. City of Columbia, 378 U.S. 146, 149 (1964); *NAACP v. Alabama ex rel. Patterson*, 357 U.S., at 455; Rogers v. Alabama, 192 U.S. 226, 230–231 (1904); Eustis v. Bolles, 150 U.S. 361 (1893); Hill, The Inadequate State Ground, 65 Colum.L.Rev. 943, 954–957 (1965).

To understand why this is so, one need only imagine a contrary system in which the Supremacy Clause operated as a constraint on the activity of state court judges like that imposed on other state actors, rather than as a rule of decision. On that hypothesis, state courts would be subject to the ultimate superintendence of federal courts which would vacate judgments entered in violation of federal law, just as they might overturn unconstitutional state legislative or executive decisions. Federal courts would exercise a superior authority to enforce and apply the Constitution and laws passed pursuant to it. See Wechsler, The Appellate Jurisdiction of the Supreme Court: Reflections on the Law and the Logistics of Direct Review, 34 Wash. & Lee L.Rev. 1043, 1047 (1977) (describing, and rejecting, alternative view of Supremacy Clause, as intrusion on state autonomy).

The language of the Supremacy Clause—which directs that "the Judges in every State shall be bound thereby, any Thing in the Constitution or Laws of any state to the Contrary notwithstanding," —and our cases confirm that state courts have the coordinate authority and consequent responsibility to enforce the Supreme Law of the Land. Early in our history, in support of the Court's power of review over state courts, Justice Story anticipated that such courts "in the exercise of their ordinary jurisdiction . . . would incidentally take cognizance of cases arising under the constitution, the laws, and treaties of the United States," Martin v. Hunter's Lessee, 1 Wheat [14 U.S. 304], at 342, and would decide federal questions even when, pleaded in replication, they were necessary to the plaintiff's case. Id., at 340. The adequate state ground doctrine accords respect to state courts as decisionmakers by honoring their modes of procedure. The structure of our system of judicial review, the requirement that a federal question arising from a state case must first be presented to the state courts for decision, see, e.g., Cardinale v. Louisiana, 394 U.S. 437 (1969); State Farm Mutual Automobile Ins. Co. v. Duel, 324 U.S. 154, 160–161 (1945); McGoldrick v. Compagnie Generale Transatlantique, 309 U.S. 430, 434 (1940), and the rule that a federal district court cannot entertain an original action alleging that a state court violated the Constitution by giving effect to an unconstitutional state statute, see Rooker v. Fidelity Trust Co., 263 U.S. 413, 415–416 (1923) ("If the constitutional questions stated in the bill actually arose in the cause, it was the province and duty of the state courts to decide them; and their decision, whether right or wrong, was an exercise of jurisdiction. . . . Unless and until so reversed or modified, it would be an effective and conclusive adjudication"); see also District of Columbia Court of Appeals v. Feldman, 460 U.S. 462, 476, 483–484, n. 16 (1983), all also presuppose that state courts presumptively have the obligation to apply federal law to a dispute before them and may not deny a federal right in the absence of a valid excuse.

3. Amici argue that the obligation of state courts to enforce federal law rests, not on the Supremacy Clause, but on a presumption about congressional intent and that Congress

2.   An excuse that is inconsistent with or violates federal law is not a valid excuse: the Supremacy Clause forbids state courts to dissociate themselves from federal law because of disagreement with its content or a refusal to recognize the superior authority of its source. "The suggestion that the act of Congress is not in harmony with the policy of the State, and therefore that the courts of the State are free to decline jurisdiction, is quite inadmissible because it presupposes what in legal contemplation does not exist. When Congress, in the exertion of the power confided to it by the Constitution, adopted that act, it spoke for all the people and all the States, and thereby established a policy for all. That policy is as much the policy of [the State] as if the act had emanated from its own legislature, and should be respected accordingly in the courts of the State." *Mondou,* 223 U.S., at 57; see Miles v. Illinois Central R. Co., 315 U.S. 698, 703–704 (1942) ("By virtue of the Constitution, the courts of the several states must remain open to such litigants on the same basis that they are open to litigants with causes of action springing from a different source"); McKnett v. St. Louis & San Francisco R. Co., 292 U.S. 230, 233–234 (1934); Minneapolis & St. Louis R. Co. v. Bombolis, 241 U.S. 211 (1916); cf. FERC v. Mississippi, 456 U.S. 742, 776, n. 1 (1982) (opinion of O'Connor, J.) (State may not discriminate against federal causes of action).

3.   When a state court refuses jurisdiction because of a neutral state rule regarding the administration of the courts, we must act with utmost caution before deciding that it is obligated to entertain the claim. See Missouri ex rel. Southern R. Co. v. Mayfield, 340 U.S. 1 (1950); Georgia Railroad & Banking Co. v. Musgrove, 335 U.S. 900 (1949); Herb v. Pitcairn, 324 U.S. 117 (1945); Douglas v. New York, N.H. & H.R. Co., 279 U.S. 377 (1929). The requirement that a state court of competent jurisdiction treat federal law as the law of the land does not necessarily include within it a requirement that the State create a court competent to hear the case in which the federal claim is presented. The general rule "bottomed deeply in belief in the importance of state control of state judicial procedure, is that federal law takes the state courts as it finds them." Hart, 54 Colum.L.Rev., at 508; see also Southland Corp. v. Keating, 465 U.S. 1, 33 (1984) (O'Connor, J., dissenting); *FERC v. Mississippi,* 456 U.S., at 774 (opinion of Powell, J.). The States thus have great latitude to establish the structure and jurisdiction of their own courts. See *Herb,* supra; *Bombolis,* supra; Missouri v. Lewis, 101 U.S. 22, 30–31 (1880). In addition, States may apply their own neutral procedural rules to federal claims, unless those rules are

should be explicit when it intends to make federal claims enforceable in state court. Brief for Washington Legal Foundation et al. as Amici Curiae 8–9, 13. The argument is strikingly similar to the argument that we addressed in Minneapolis & St. Louis R. Co. v. Bombolis, 241 U.S. 211 (1916), when we held that state courts need not comply with the Seventh Amendment in hearing a federal statutory claim. We rejected the argument that "state courts [had] become courts of the United States exercising a jurisdiction conferred by Congress, whenever the duty was cast upon them to enforce a Federal right." Id., at 222. We reject it again today. . . .

pre-empted by federal law. See Felder v. Casey, 487 U.S. 131 (1988); James v. Kentucky, 466 U.S. [341, 348 (1984)].

These principles are fundamental to a system of federalism in which the state courts share responsibility for the application and enforcement of federal law. In *Mondou,* for example, we held that rights under the Federal Employers' Liability Act (FELA) "may be enforced, as of right, in the courts of the States when their jurisdiction, as prescribed by local laws, is adequate to the occasion." 223 U.S., at 59. The Connecticut courts had declined cognizance of FELA actions because the policy of the federal act was "not in accord with the policy of the State" and it was "inconvenient and confusing" to apply federal law. Id., at 55–56. We noted, as a matter of some significance, that Congress had not attempted "to enlarge or regulate the jurisdiction of state courts or to control or affect their modes of procedure," id., at 56, and found from the fact that the state court was a court of general jurisdiction with cognizance over wrongful death actions that the court's jurisdiction was "appropriate to the occasion," id., at 57. "The existence of the jurisdiction creat[ed] an implication of duty to exercise it," id., at 58, which could not be overcome by disagreement with the policy of the federal act, id., at 57.

In *McKnett,* the state court refused to exercise jurisdiction over a FELA cause of action against a foreign corporation for an injury suffered in another State. We held "[w]hile Congress has not attempted to compel states to provide courts for the enforcement of the Federal Employers' Liability Act, the Federal Constitution prohibits state courts of general jurisdiction from refusing to do so solely because the suit is brought under a federal law." 292 U.S., at 233–234 (citation omitted). Because the state court had "general jurisdiction of the class of actions to which that here brought belongs, in cases between litigants situated like those in the case at bar," id., at 232, the refusal to hear the FELA action constituted discrimination against rights arising under federal laws, id., at 234, in violation of the Supremacy Clause.

We unanimously reaffirmed these principles in *Testa v. Katt.* We held that the Rhode Island courts could not decline jurisdiction over treble damages claims under the federal Emergency Price Control Act when their jurisdiction was otherwise "adequate and appropriate under established local law." 330 U.S., at 394. The Rhode Island court had distinguished our decisions in *McKnett* and *Mondou* on the grounds that the federal act was a "penal statute," which would not have been enforceable under the Full Faith and Credit Clause if passed by another State. We rejected that argument. We observed that the Rhode Island court enforced the "same type of claim" arising under state law and claims for double damages under federal law. 330 U.S., at 394. We therefore concluded that the court had "jurisdiction adequate and appropriate under established local law to adjudicate this action." Ibid.[4] The court could not decline to exercise this

---

4. We cited for this proposition the section of the Rhode Island code authorizing the State District Court and Superior Court to entertain actions for fines, penalties and forfeitures. See 330 U.S., at 394, n.13 (citing R.I.Gen.Laws ch. 631, § 4 (1938)).

jurisdiction to enforce federal law by labeling it "penal." The policy of the Federal Act was to be considered "the prevailing policy in every state" which the state court could not refuse to enforce " 'because of conceptions of impolicy or want of wisdom on the part of Congress in having called into play its lawful powers.' " Id., at 393 (quoting *Minneapolis & St. Louis R. Co. v. Bombolis,* 241 U.S., at 222).

On only three occasions have we found a valid excuse for a state court's refusal to entertain a federal cause of action. Each of them involved a neutral rule of judicial administration. In Douglas v. New York, N.H. & H.R. Co., 279 U.S. 377 (1929), the state statute permitted discretionary dismissal of both federal and state claims where neither the plaintiff nor the defendant was a resident of the forum state.[5] In *Herb,* the city court denied jurisdiction over a FELA action on the grounds that the cause of action arose outside its territorial jurisdiction. Although the state court was not free to dismiss the federal claim "because it is a federal one," we found no evidence that the state courts "construed the state jurisdiction and venue laws in a discriminatory fashion." 324 U.S., at 123. Finally, in *Mayfield,* we held that a state court could apply the doctrine of *forum non conveniens* to bar adjudication of a FELA case if the State "enforces its policy impartially so as not to involve a discrimination against Employers' Liability Act suits." 340 U.S., at 4 (citation omitted).

IV

The parties disagree as to the proper characterization of the District Court of Appeal's decision. Petitioner argues that the court adopted a substantive rule of decision that state agencies are not subject to liability under § 1983. Respondents, stressing the court's language that it had not "opened its own courts for federal actions against the state," 537 So.2d, at 708, argue that the case simply involves the court's refusal to take cognizance of § 1983 actions against state defendants. We conclude that whether the question is framed in pre-emption terms, as petitioner would have it, or in the obligation to assume jurisdiction over a "federal" cause of action, as respondents would have it, the Florida court's refusal to entertain one discrete category of § 1983 claims, when the court entertains similar state law actions against state defendants, violates the Supremacy Clause.

If the District Court of Appeal meant to hold that governmental entities subject to § 1983 liability enjoy an immunity over and above those already provided in § 1983, that holding directly violates federal law. The elements of, and the defenses to, a federal cause of action are defined by federal law. See, e.g., Monessen Southwestern R. Co. v. Morgan, 486 U.S. 330, 335 (1988); Chesapeake & Ohio R. Co. v. Kuhn, 284 U.S. 44, 46–47 (1931). A State may not, by statute or common law, create a cause of action

---

5. We wrote: "It may very well be that if the Supreme Court of New York were given no discretion, being otherwise competent, it would be subject to a duty. But there is nothing in the Act of Congress that purports to force a duty upon such Courts as against an otherwise valid excuse. Second Employers' Liability Cases, 223 U.S. 1, 56, 57." 279 U.S., at 387–388.

under § 1983 against an entity whom Congress has not subjected to liability. Moor v. County of Alameda, 411 U.S. 693, 698–710 (1973). Since this Court has construed the word "person" in § 1983 to exclude States, neither a federal court nor a state court may entertain a § 1983 action against such a defendant. Conversely, since the Court has held that municipal corporations and similar governmental entities are "persons," see Monell v. New York City Dept. of Social Services, 436 U.S. 658, 663 (1978); cf. Will, 491 U.S., at 69, n.9; Mt. Healthy City Board of Education v. Doyle, 429 U.S. 274, 280–281 (1977), a state court entertaining a § 1983 action must adhere to that interpretation. . . .

In Martinez v. California, 444 U.S. 277 (1980), we unanimously concluded that a California statute that purported to immunize public entities and public employees from any liability for parole release decisions, was preempted by § 1983 "even though the federal cause of action [was] being asserted in the state courts." Id., at 284. . . .

In *Felder v. Casey*, we followed *Martinez* and held that a Wisconsin notice-of-claim statute that effectively shortened the statute of limitations and imposed an exhaustion requirement on claims against public agencies and employees was preempted insofar as it was applied to § 1983 actions. After observing that the lower federal courts, with one exception, had determined that notice of claim statutes were inapplicable to § 1983 actions brought in federal courts, we stated that such a consensus also demonstrated that "enforcement of the notice-of-claim statute in § 1983 actions brought in state court . . . interfer[ed] with and frustrat[ed] the substantive right Congress created." 487 U.S., at 151. We concluded, "The decision to subject state subdivisions to liability for violations of federal rights . . . was a choice that Congress, not the Wisconsin Legislature, made, and it is a decision that the State has no authority to override." Id., at 143.

While the Florida Supreme Court's actual decision in *Hill* is consistent with the foregoing reasoning, the Court of Appeal's extension of *Hill* to persons subject by § 1983 to liability is flatly inconsistent with that reasoning and the holdings in both *Martinez* and *Felder*. Federal law makes governmental defendants that are not arms of the State, such as municipalities, liable for their constitutional violations. See St. Louis v. Praprotnik, 485 U.S. 112, 121–122 (1988); Monell v. New York City Dept. of Social Services, 436 U.S. 658 (1978). Florida law, as interpreted by the District Court of Appeal, would make all such defendants absolutely immune from liability under the federal statute. To the extent that the Florida law of sovereign immunity reflects a substantive disagreement with the extent to which governmental entities should be held liable for their constitutional violations, that disagreement cannot override the dictates of federal law. "Congress surely did not intend to assign to state courts and legislatures a conclusive role in the formative function of defining and characterizing the essential elements of a federal cause of action." Wilson v. Garcia, 471 U.S. 261, 269 (1985).

If, on the other hand, the District Court of Appeal meant that § 1983 claims are excluded from the category of tort claims that the Circuit Court could hear against a school board, its holding was no less violative of federal law. Cf. Atlantic Coast Line R. Co. v. Burnette, 239 U.S. 199, 201 (1915). This case does not present the questions whether Congress can require the States to create a forum with the capacity to enforce federal statutory rights or to authorize service of process on parties who would not otherwise be subject to the court's jurisdiction.[6] The State of Florida has constituted the Circuit Court for Pinellas County as a court of general jurisdiction. It exercises jurisdiction over tort claims by private citizens against state entities (including school boards), of the size and type of petitioner's claim here, and it can enter judgment against them. That court also exercises jurisdiction over § 1983 actions against individual officers and is fully competent to provide the remedies the federal statute requires. Cf. Sullivan v. Little Hunting Park, Inc., 396 U.S. 229, 238 (1969). Petitioner has complied with all the state law procedures for invoking the jurisdiction of that court.

. . . . .

Respondents have offered no neutral or valid excuse for the Circuit Court's refusal to hear § 1983 actions against state entities. The Circuit Court would have had jurisdiction if the defendant were an individual officer and the action was based on § 1983. It would also have had jurisdiction over the defendant school board if the action were based on established state common law or statutory law. A state policy that permits actions against state agencies for the failure of their officials to adequately police a parking lot and for the negligence of such officers in arresting a person on a roadside, but yet declines jurisdiction over federal actions for constitutional violations by the same persons can be based only on the rationale that such persons should not be held liable for § 1983 violations in the courts of the State. That reason, whether presented in terms of direct disagreement with substantive federal law or simple refusal to take cognizance of the federal cause of action, flatly violates the Supremacy Clause.

V

Respondents offer two final arguments in support of the judgment of the District Court of Appeal. First, at oral argument—but not in its brief—they argued that a federal court has no power to compel a state court to entertain a claim over which the state court has no jurisdiction as a matter of state law. Second, respondents argue that sovereign immunity is not a

---

6. Virtually every State has expressly or by implication opened its courts to § 1983 actions and there are no state court systems that refuse to hear § 1983 cases. See Steinglass, Section 1983 Litigation in State Courts 1–3, and App. E (1989) (listing cases). We have no occasion to address in this case the contentions of respondents' amici, see Brief for National Association of Counties et al. as Amici Curiae 16–25; Brief for Washington Legal Foundation et al. as Amici Curiae 9–15, that the States need not establish courts competent to entertain § 1983 claims. See Maine v. Thiboutot, 448 U.S. 1, 3, n.1 (1980); Martinez v. California, 444 U.S. 277, 283, n.7 (1980).

creature of state law, but of long-established legal principles which have not been set aside by § 1983. We find no merit in these contentions.

. . . . .

The judgment of the Court of Appeal is reversed and the case is remanded for further proceedings not inconsistent with this opinion.

It is so ordered.[7]

———

[7. See Note, Separate but Not Sovereign: Reconciling Federal Commandeering of State Courts, 52 Vand.L.Rev. 143 (1999).

An Illinois statute barred suit in the courts of that state to recover damages for deaths occurring outside Illinois. Later Supreme Court decisions held that, in view of the full-faith-and-credit clause, Illinois could not refuse to entertain actions brought under the death acts of other states. Held, that "by the interplay of judicial decisions, instead of the direct language of the statute," a discrimination against federal law existed, and that Illinois was constitutionally required to entertain a Federal Employers' Liability Act suit for a death occurring in Indiana. Allendorf v. Elgin, J. & E.R. Co., 8 Ill.2d 164, 133 N.E.2d 288 (1956).

In Johnson v. Fankell, 520 U.S. 911 (1997), the Court held unanimously that Idaho's state-court standard for determining when a trial-court order was sufficiently "final" to be eligible for mandatory appellate review qualified as a "neutral state rule" under *Howlett* and as such was not preempted by federal law. The plaintiff had filed a § 1983 action in state court. The defendant state officials moved to dismiss her action on qualified-immunity grounds. The state trial court denied the motion, and the Supreme Court of Idaho dismissed the defendants' purported appeal as-of-right as premature. The defendants made no effort to invoke state procedures permitting discretionary interlocutory review in extraordinary cases. Instead, they relied on the undisputed fact that if the trial court had been a federal district court, a ruling rejecting the defense of qualified official immunity would have been immediately appealable as of right under the federal "collateral order" doctrine, discussed at pp. 984–986 of the *Gulfstream* case as reprinted infra p. 983. But state courts were held to be under no duty to provide a right of immediate appellate review when a parallel situation arises in the course of state-court litigation of a § 1983 claim.

The scope of the liability to which governments below the state level are exposed by 42 U.S.C. § 1983 has been much debated in the decisions of the Supreme Court. It was held in Monroe v. Pape, 365 U.S. 167 (1961), that municipalities were not "persons" within the meaning of § 1983. This construction of § 1983 was overruled by Monell v. New York City Dept. of Social Services, 436 U.S. 658 (1978), subject to the proviso that municipal liability under § 1983 may not be based on the traditional theory of respondeat superior. The wrongful act of a municipal agent must be tied to municipal "policy" in order for the municipality itself to be liable under § 1983. The general trend of recent authority has been to narrow the scope of municipal liability under § 1983 by rigorous application of this requirement of a showing that the harm suffered resulted from municipal "policy" rather than individual misconduct that was neither sanctioned nor encouraged by the defendant municipality. See, e.g., McMillian v. Monroe County, Alabama, 520 U.S. 781 (1997) (Alabama sheriffs are policymakers for the state, but not for the county, hence county not liable to innocent man released after six years on Death Row for unlawful law-enforcement policy of county sheriff in suppressing exculpatory evidence); Board of County Commissioners of Bryan County, Oklahoma v. Brown, 520 U.S. 397 (1997) (isolated wrongful act by county policymaker insufficient to subject county to § 1983 liability).

How broad is the power of Congress, incident to its regulation of commerce, to regulate the procedural rules applied by state courts in civil litigation that might affect commerce? And is such power as Congress may possess limited to state-court adjudication of claims for relief

Section 2. Federal Injunctions Against State Court Proceedings[8]

ANTI–INJUNCTION ACT

28 U.S.C. § 2283. Stay of State court proceedings

A court of the United States may not grant an injunction to stay proceedings in a State court except as expressly authorized by Act of Congress, or where necessary in aid of its jurisdiction, or to protect or effectuate its judgments.

Reviser's Notes: Section 2283—Section Revised

Based on title 28, U.S.C., 1940 ed., § 379 (Mar. 3, 1911, ch. 231, § 265, 36 Stat. 1162).

An exception as to Acts of Congress relating to bankruptcy was omitted and the general exception substituted to cover all exceptions.

The phrase "in aid of its jurisdiction" was added to conform to section 1651 of this title and to make clear the recognized power of the Federal courts to stay proceedings in State cases removed to the district courts.

The exceptions specifically include the words "to protect or effectuate its judgments," for lack of which the Supreme Court held that the Federal courts are without power to enjoin relitigation of cases and controversies fully adjudicated by such courts. (See Toucey v. New York Life Insurance Co., 314 U.S. 118. A vigorous dissenting opinion (314 U.S., at 141) notes that at the time of the 1911 revision of the Judicial Code, the power of the courts of the United States to protect their judgments was unquestioned and that the revisers of that code noted no change and Congress intended no change).

Therefore the revised section restores the basic law as generally understood and interpreted prior to the *Toucey* decision.

Changes were made in phraseology.[9]

---

grounded in federal law, or does it extend even to state-court litigation of claims arising solely under state law? See Bellia, Federal Regulation of State Court Procedures, 110 Yale L.J. 947 (2001).]

[8.　7 Wright, Miller & Cooper, Federal Practice and Procedure: Jurisdiction 2d §§ 4221–4226 (1988); 17 Moore's Federal Practice ch. 121 (3d ed.1998); Wright & Kane, Federal Courts § 47 (6th ed.2002); ALI Study 299–312; Wood, Fine–Tuning Judicial Federalism: A Proposal for Reform of the Anti–Injunction Act, 1990 B.Y.U.L.Rev. 298.]

[9.　Barrett, Federal Injunctions Against Proceedings in State Courts, 35 Cal.L.Rev. 545, 563 (1947), said of the statute that became § 2283 in the 1948 Judicial Code: "... any amendment should properly solve more questions than it raises. The proposed revision does not appear to have this virtue."

Compare ALI Study § 1372.

The prohibition against "staying proceedings" does not bar injunctions against the institution of future suits. Dombrowski v. Pfister, 380 U.S. 479, 484 n. 2 (1965).

A proceeding may be in a state court and still not be within § 2283. See Lynch v. Household Finance Corp., 405 U.S. 538 (1972) (prejudgment garnishment); Roudebush v. Hartke, 405 U.S. 15 (1972) (election recount by a state court).

The Anti–Injunction Act bars the issuance of a declaratory judgment that would have the same effect as an injunction. "To allow declaratory relief in these circumstances would be to transform section 2283 from a pillar of federalism reflecting the fundamental constitutional independence of the states and their courts, to an anachronistic, minor technicality, easily avoided by mere nomenclature or procedural sleight of hand." Texas Employers' Ins. Ass'n v. Jackson, 862 F.2d 491, 505 (5th Cir.1988).

Has the doctrine of Wells Fargo & Co. v. Taylor, 254 U.S. 175 (1920), that a federal court may enjoin a party from enforcing a state court judgment obtained by fraud, survived the 1948 revision of the statute? It is held that it has not in Warriner v. Fink, 307 F.2d 933 (5th Cir.1962); Furnish v. Board of Medical Examiners, 257 F.2d 520 (9th Cir.1958), certiorari denied 358 U.S. 882 (1958); Norwood v. Parenteau, 228 F.2d 148 (8th Cir.1955). See also ALI Study 311–312; Comment, 40 N.Y.U.L.Rev. 987 (1965). But see Comment, 32 U.Chi. L.Rev. 471, 486–488 (1965).

Does the Anti–Injunction Act apply if the federal action was commenced before there was any state proceeding but a state proceeding has begun before the federal court acts on the request to enjoin action in the state court? Compare Roth v. Bank of the Commonwealth, 583 F.2d 527 (6th Cir.1978), certiorari dismissed 442 U.S. 925 (1979), with National City Lines, Inc. v. LLC Corp., 687 F.2d 1122 (8th Cir.1982).

In a state-court action a county obtained an injunction enforcing the condition in a conditional-use permit that the owner of land could not sell water from the land outside of the county. Persons from Mexico who expected to buy water from the land owner then sued in federal court to enjoin the county from enforcing the condition on the ground that it violated the Commerce Clause. Held, that the federal suit was within the Anti–Injunction Act even though the state proceedings had been concluded, and the plaintiffs in the federal suit could not have injunctive relief unless they could show that they were "strangers to the state court proceeding." County of Imperial v. Munoz, 449 U.S. 54 (1980). See also the same case on remand, 510 F.Supp. 879 (S.D.Cal.1981), affirmed 667 F.2d 811 (9th Cir.1982), certiorari denied 474 U.S. 825 (1982).

A federal district court that approved a class action settlement involving a home siding manufacturer violated the Anti–Injunction Act by enjoining a state judgment in favor of a middleman who used the siding product in his business and was not a party to the class action. The "necessary in aid of jurisdiction" exception was inapplicable "because the state court action did not threaten the district court's jurisdiction over the [class] litigation." Similarly, the relitigation exception was inapplicable because the state lawsuit did not challenge the res judicata effect of the class settlement. See Sandpiper Village Condominium Ass'n v. Louisiana–Pacific Corp., 428 F.3d 831 (9th Cir.2005).

In Doernberg, What's Wrong with This Picture?: Rule Interpleader, the Anti–Injunction Act, In Personam Jurisdiction, and M.C. Escher, 67 U.Colo.L.Rev. 551, 591–594 (1996), the author calls for amendment of either the Anti–Injunction Act or the Federal Interpleader Act to make it clear that federal courts may enjoin conflicting state-court litigation incident to the exercise of their interpleader jurisdiction under Rule 22 of the Federal Rules of Civil Procedure as well as under the Federal Interpleader Act, 28 U.S.C. § 1335.

Responding to a circuit split regarding the Anti–Injunction Act's relitigation exception, the Supreme Court unanimously held that a federal court exceeded its authority in enjoining similar class actions from proceeding in state court where the class was never certified in federal court and the class certification standards in the federal and state courts differed,

Vendo Co. v. Lektro–Vend Corp.

Supreme Court of the United States, 1977.
433 U.S. 623, 97 S.Ct. 2881, 53 L.Ed.2d 1009.

■ MR. JUSTICE REHNQUIST announced the judgment of the Court and delivered an opinion in which MR. JUSTICE STEWART and MR. JUSTICE POWELL join.

I

After nine years of litigation in the Illinois state courts, the Supreme Court of Illinois affirmed a judgment in favor of petitioner and against respondents in the amount of $7,363,500. Shortly afterwards the United States District Court for the Northern District of Illinois enjoined, at the behest of respondents, state proceedings to collect the judgment. 403 F.Supp. 527 (1975). The order of the United States District Court was affirmed by the Court of Appeals for the Seventh Circuit, 545 F.2d 1050 (1976), and we granted certiorari to consider the important question of the relationship between state and federal courts which such an injunction raises. 429 U.S. 815 (1976).

II

The Illinois state court litigation arose out of commercial dealings between petitioner and respondents. In 1959 petitioner Vendo Company, a vending machine manufacturer located in Kansas City, Mo., acquired most of the assets of Stoner Manufacturing, which was thereupon reorganized as respondent Stoner Investment, Inc. Respondent Harry H. Stoner and members of his family owned all of the stock of Stoner Manufacturing, and that of Stoner Investments. Stoner Manufacturing had engaged in the manufacture of vending machines which dispensed candy, and as a part of the acquisition agreement it undertook to refrain from owning or managing any business engaged in the manufacture or sale of vending machines. Pursuant to an employment contract, respondent Harry Stoner was employed by petitioner as a consultant for five years at a salary of $50,000, and he agreed that during the term of his contract and for five years thereafter he would not compete with petitioner in the business of manufacturing vending machines.

In 1965, petitioner sued respondents[10] in state court for breach of these noncompetition covenants. Shortly thereafter, respondents sued petitioner in the United States District Court for the Northern District of Illinois, complaining that petitioner had violated §§ 1 and 2 of the Sherman Act, 15 U.S.C. §§ 1 and 2. Respondents alleged that the covenants against competition were unreasonable restraints of trade because they were not reasonably limited as to time and place, and that the purpose of petitioner's state

---

and thus the prerequisites for preclusion did not exist. Smith v. Bayer Corp., 564 U.S. ___, 131 S.Ct. 2368 (2011).]

10. In addition to respondents Stoner and Stoner Manufacturing, petitioner also sued respondent Lektro–Vend Corporation. Lektro–Vend had developed a radically new vending machine, and it was Stoner's relationship with Lektro–Vend that formed the basis of the lawsuit.

court lawsuit was to "unlawfully harass" respondents and to "eliminate the competition" of respondents. App. 22, 25.

Respondents set up this federal antitrust claim as an affirmative defense to petitioner's state court suit. Id., at 31–32. However, prior to any ruling by the state courts on the merits of this defense, respondents voluntarily withdrew it. Id., at 82.

The state court litigation ran its protracted course, including two trials, two appeals to the State Appellate Court, and an appeal to the Supreme Court of Illinois. In September 1974, the latter court affirmed a judgment in favor of petitioner and against respondents in an amount exceeding seven million dollars. Vendo Co. v. Stoner, 58 Ill.2d 289, 321 N.E.2d 1 (1974). The Supreme Court of Illinois predicated its judgment on its holding that Stoner had breached a fiduciary duty owed to petitioner, rather than upon any breach of the noncompetitive covenants. This Court denied respondents' petition for a writ of certiorari. 420 U.S. 975 (1975).

During the entire nine-year course of the state court litigation, respondents' antitrust suit in the District Court was, in the words of the Court of Appeals, allowed to lie "dormant." 545 F.2d, at 1055. But the day after a Circuit Justice of this Court had denied a stay of execution pending petition for certiorari to the Supreme Court of Illinois, respondents moved in the District Court for a preliminary injunction against collection of the Illinois judgment. The District Court in due course granted this motion.

The court found that it "appear[ed] that the non-competition covenants were overly broad," 403 F.Supp., at 533, and that there was "persuasive evidence that Vendo's activities in its litigation against the Stoner interests in Illinois state court were not a genuine attempt to use the adjudicative process legitimately." Id., at 534–535. Recognizing that there is a "paucity of authority" on the issue, id., at 536, the District Court held that the injunctive relief provision of the Clayton Act, 15 U.S.C. § 26, constitutes an express exception to 28 U.S.C. § 2283, the "Anti–Injunction Act." The court further found that collection efforts would eliminate two of the three plaintiffs and thus that the injunction was necessary to protect the jurisdiction of the court, within the meaning of that exception to § 2283.

The Court of Appeals affirmed, finding that § 16 of the Clayton Act was an express exception to 28 U.S.C. § 2283. The court did not reach the issue of whether injunction was necessary to protect the jurisdiction of the District Court.

In this Court, petitioner renews its contention that principles of equity, comity, and federalism, as well as the Anti–Injunction Act, barred the issuance of the injunction by the District Court. Petitioner also asserts in its brief on the merits that the United States District Court was required to give full faith and credit to the judgment entered by the Illinois courts. Because we agree with petitioner that the District Court's order violated the Anti–Injunction Act, we reach none of its other contentions.

III

The Anti–Injunction Act, 28 U.S.C. § 2283, provides:

"A court of the United States may not grant an injunction to stay proceedings in a State court except as expressly authorized by Act of Congress, or where necessary in aid of its jurisdiction, or to protect or effectuate its judgments."

The origins and development of the present Act, and of the statutes which preceded it, have been amply described in our prior opinions and need not be restated here. The most recent of these opinions are Mitchum v. Foster, 407 U.S. 225 (1972), and Atlantic Coast Line R. Co. v. Brotherhood of Locomotive Engineers, 398 U.S. 281 (1970). Suffice it to say that the Act is an absolute prohibition against any injunction of any state court proceedings, unless the injunction falls within one of the three specifically defined exceptions in the Act. The Act's purpose is to forestall the inevitable friction between the state and federal courts that ensues from the injunction of state judicial proceedings by a federal court. Oklahoma Packing Co. v. Oklahoma Gas & Electric Co., 309 U.S. 4, 9 (1940). Respondents' principal contention is that, as the Court of Appeals held, § 16 of the Clayton Act, which authorizes a private action to redress violations of the antitrust laws, comes within the "expressly authorized" exception to § 2283.

We test this proposition mindful of our admonition that:

"[a]ny doubts as to the propriety of a federal injunction against state court proceedings should be resolved in favor of permitting the state courts to proceed in an orderly fashion to finally determine the controversy." *Atlantic Coast Line R. Co.*, supra, 398 U.S., at 297.

This cautious approach is mandated by the "explicit wording of Section 2283" and the "fundamental principle of a dual system of courts." Ibid. We have no occasion to construe the section more broadly:

"[It is] clear beyond cavil that the prohibition is not to be whittled away by judicial improvisation." Amalgamated Clothing Workers of America v. Richman Bros. Co., 348 U.S. 511, 514 (1955).

Our inquiry of course begins with the language of § 16 of the Clayton Act, which is the statute claimed to "expressly authorize" the injunction issued here. It provides, in pertinent part:

"[A]ny person ... shall be entitled to sue for and have injunctive relief, in any court of the United States having jurisdiction over the parties, against threatened loss or damage by violation of the antitrust laws ... when and under the same conditions and principles as injunctive relief against threatened conduct that will cause loss or damage is granted by courts of equity, under the rules governing such proceedings ...." 38 Stat. 737, 15 U.S.C. § 26.

On its face, the language merely authorizes private injunctive relief for antitrust violations. Not only does the statute not mention § 2283 or the enjoining of state court proceedings, but the granting of injunctive relief under § 16 is by the terms of that section limited to "the same conditions and principles" employed by courts of equity, and by "the rules governing such proceedings." In 1793 the predecessor to § 2283 was enacted specifically to limit the general equity powers of a federal court. Smith v. Apple, 264 U.S. 274, 279 (1924); Toucey v. N.Y. Life Insurance, 314 U.S. 118, 130 n. 2 (1941). When § 16 was enacted in 1914 the bar of the Anti–Injunction Act had long constrained the equitable power of federal courts to issue injunctions. Thus, on its face, § 16 is far from an express exception to the Anti–Injunction Act, and may be fairly read as virtually incorporating the prohibitions of the Anti–Injunction Act with restrictive language not found, for example, in 42 U.S.C. § 1983. See discussion of *Mitchum v. Foster*, infra.

Respondents rely, as did the Court of Appeals and the District Court, on the following language from *Mitchum:*

"... [I]t is clear that, in order to qualify as an 'expressly authorized' exception to the anti-injunction statute, an Act of Congress must have created a specific and uniquely federal right or remedy, enforceable in a federal court of equity, that could be frustrated if the federal court were not empowered to enjoin a state court proceeding. This is not to say that in order to come within the exception an Act of Congress must, on its face and in every one of its provisions, be totally incompatible with the prohibition of the anti-injunction statute. *The test, rather, is whether an Act of Congress, clearly creating a federal right or remedy enforceable in a federal court of equity, could be given its intended scope only by the stay of a state court proceeding.*" 407 U.S. 225, 237–238. (Emphasis added.)

But we think it is clear that neither this language from *Mitchum* nor *Mitchum*'s ratio decidendi supports the result contended for by respondents.

The private action for damages conferred by the Clayton Act is a "uniquely federal right or remedy," in that actions based upon it may be brought only in the federal courts. See General Investment Company v. Lake Shore & Mich. So. R. Co., 260 U.S. 261, 287 (1922). It thus meets the first part of the test laid down in the quoted language from *Mitchum.*

But that authorization for private actions does not meet the second part of the *Mitchum* test; it is not an "Act of Congress [which] could be given its intended scope only by the stay of a state court proceeding," id., 407 U.S., at 238. Crucial to our determination in *Mitchum* that 42 U.S.C. § 1983 fulfilled this requirement—but wholly lacking here—was our recognition that one of the clear congressional concerns underlying the enactment of § 1983 was the possibility that state courts, as well as other branches of state government, might be used as instruments to deny citizens their rights under the federal constitution. This determination was based on our review of the legislative history of § 1983; similar review of the legislative history underlying § 16 demonstrates that that section does not meet this aspect of the *Mitchum* test.

Section 1983 on its face, of course, contains no reference to § 2283, nor does it expressly authorize injunctions against state court proceedings. But, as *Mitchum* recognized, such language need not invariably be present in order for a statute to come within the "expressly authorized" exception if there exists sufficient evidence in the legislative history demonstrating that Congress recognized and intended the statute to authorize injunction of state court proceedings. In Part IV of our opinion in *Mitchum* we examined in extenso the purpose and legislative history underlying § 1983, originally § 1 of the Civil Rights Act of 1871. We recounted in detail that statute's history which made it abundantly clear that by its enactment Congress demonstrated its direct and explicit concern to make available the federal courts to protect civil rights against unconstitutional actions of state courts.

We summarized our conclusion in these words:

"This legislative history makes evident that Congress clearly conceived that it was altering the relationship between the States and the Nation with respect to the protection of federally created rights; it was concerned that state instrumentalities could not protect those rights; it realized that state officers might, in fact, be antipathetic to the vindication of those rights; and it believed that these failings extended to the state courts." *Mitchum,* 407 U.S., at 242.

Thus, in *Mitchum,* absence of express language authorization for enjoining state court proceedings in § 1983 actions was cured by the presence of relevant legislative history. In this case, however, neither the respondents nor the courts below have called to our attention any similar legislative history in connection with the enactment of § 16 of the Clayton Act. It is not suggested that Congress was concerned with the possibility that state court proceedings would be used to violate the Sherman or Clayton Acts. Indeed, it seems safe to say that of the many and varied anticompetitive schemes which § 16 was intended to combat, Congress in no way focused upon a scheme using litigation in the state courts. The relevant legislative history of § 16 simply suggests that in enacting § 16 Congress was interested in extending the right to enjoin antitrust violations to private citizens. The critical aspects of the legislative history recounted in *Mitchum* which led us to conclude that § 1983 was within the "expressly authorized" exception to § 2283 are wholly absent from the relevant history of § 16 of the Clayton Act. This void is not filled by other evidence of congressional authorization.

Section 16 undoubtedly embodies congressional policy favoring private enforcement of the antitrust laws, and undoubtedly there exists a strong national interest in antitrust enforcement.[11] However, contrary to certain

---

11.   In California Motor Transport Co. v. Trucking Unlimited, 404 U.S. 508 (1972), this Court held that harassing and sham state-court proceedings of a repetitive nature could be part of an anticompetitive scheme or conspiracy. In Otter Tail Power Co. v. United States, 410 U.S. 366 (1973), one of the allegations was that the federal court defendant had instituted and supported state court litigation for anticompetitive purposes in violation of the anti-trust laws. The District Court had enjoined the defendant from "instituting, supporting, or

language in the opinion of the District Court, 403 F.Supp., at 536, the importance of the federal policy to be "protected" by the injunction is not the focus of the inquiry. Presumptively, all federal policies enacted into law by Congress are important, and there will undoubtedly arise particular situations in which a particular policy would be fostered by the granting of an injunction against a pending state court action. If we were to accept respondents' contention that § 16 could be given its "intended scope" only by allowing such injunctions, then § 2283 would be completely eviscerated since the ultimate logic of this position can mean no less than that virtually *all* federal statutes authorizing injunctive relief are exceptions to § 2283. Certainly all federal injunctive statutes are enacted to provide for the suspension of activities antithetical to the federal policies underlying the injunctive statute or related statutes. If the injunction would issue under the general rules of equity practice—requiring, inter alia, a showing of irreparable injury—but for the bar of § 2283, then clearly § 2283 in some sense may be viewed as frustrating or restricting federal policy since the activity inconsistent with the federal policy may not be enjoined because of § 2283's bar.[12] Thus, were we to accede to respondent's interpretation of

---

engaging in litigation, directly or indirectly against cities and towns, and officials thereof, which have voted to establish municipal power systems...." Jurisdictional Statement ... at A–115. This Court vacated and remanded to the District Court for consideration, in light of the intervening decision of *California Motor Transport*, of whether the state court litigation came within the "mere sham" exception announced in Eastern Railroad Conference v. Noerr Motor Freight, Inc., 365 U.S. 127 (1961). Those cases together may be cited for the proposition that repetitive, sham litigation in state courts may constitute an antitrust violation and that an injunction may lie to enjoin future state court litigation. However, neither of those cases involved the injunction of a pending state-court proceeding, and thus the bar of § 2283 was not brought into play.

Nothing that we say today cuts back in any way on the holdings of these two cases; what we must here decide is whether such a lawsuit may be enjoined by a federal court *after* it has been commenced, notwithstanding the bar of the Anti–Injunction Act. While we conclude that it may not, nothing in our opinion today prevents a federal court in the proper exercise of its jurisdiction to enjoin the commencement of additional state court proceedings if it concludes from the course and outcome of the first one that such proceedings would constitute a violation of the antitrust laws. With respect to this future litigation, the injunction will prevent even the commencement of a second such action, and the principles of federalism do not require the bar of § 2283. This distinction is totally consistent with the realization that the true bona fides of the initial state-court litigation is often not apparent:

"One claim, which a court or agency may think baseless, may go unnoticed; but a pattern of baseless, repetitive claims may emerge which leads the factfinder to conclude that the administrative and judicial processes have been abused." *California Motor Transport,* supra, at 513.

Any "disadvantage" to which the federal plaintiff is put in the initial proceeding is diminished by his ability to set up the federal antitrust claim as an affirmative defense, reviewable by this Court under 28 U.S.C. § 1257(3), and his ability to sue for treble damages resulting from the vexatious prosecution of that state-court litigation.

12. MR. JUSTICE STEVENS in his dissent ... would conclude that since certain types of state-court litigation may violate the antitrust laws, an injunction of such litigation while pending is "expressly authorized" under the provisions of the Anti–Injunction Act. But this conclusion does not at all follow from the premise that judicial decisions have construed the prohibition of the antitrust laws to include sham and frivolous state-court proceedings—a premise with which we do not at all disagree, see n. [11] supra. The conclusion is

the "intended scope" language, an exception to § 2283 would always be found to be "necessary" to give the injunctive act its full intended scope, and § 2283 would place no additional limitation on the right to enjoin state proceedings. The Anti–Injunction Act, a fixture in federal law since 1793, would then be a virtual dead letter whenever the plaintiff seeks an injunction under a federal injunctive statute. Whether or not the state proceeding could be enjoined would rest solely upon the traditional principles of equity and comity. However, as we emphasized in *Mitchum,* 407 U.S., at 243, the prohibitions of § 2283 exist separate and apart from these traditional principles, and we cannot read the "intended scope" language as rendering this specific and longstanding statutory provision inoperative simply because important federal policies are fostered by the statute under which the injunction is sought. Congress itself has found that these policies, in the ordinary case, must give way to the policies underlying § 2283. Given the clear prohibition of § 2283, the courts will not sit to balance and weigh the importance of various federal policies in seeking to determine which are sufficiently important to override historical concepts

supportable only as a matter of policy preference, and not of statutory construction. Under MR. JUSTICE STEVENS' view, all a federal court need do is find a violation of the federal statute, then by the very force of that finding "express authorization" for the statute would be presumed. But this approach flies in the face of our past decisions. For example, in Mitchum v. Foster, 407 U.S. 225, 227 (1972), the petitioner had alleged that the state courts "were depriving him of rights protected by the First and Fourteenth Amendments." 407 U.S., at 227. Under MR. JUSTICE STEVENS' syllogistic formulation, since the state-court action is a violation of § 1983, the express authorization would be readily found on the face of the statute. However, the Court in *Mitchum* found no such ipso facto shortcut to the explicit prohibition of § 2283, but resorted to careful analysis of the legislative history in order to find evidence of congressional authorization. In short, MR. JUSTICE STEVENS' approach, which removes the bar of § 2283 from all federal injunctive statutes, is totally inconsistent with this Court's longstanding recognition that "[l]egislative policy is here expressed in a clear-cut prohibition qualified only by specifically defined exceptions." Clothing Workers v. Richmond Bros. Co., 348 U.S. 511, 516 (1955).

In reaching this conclusion, MR. JUSTICE STEVENS argues that the Anti–Injunction Act should be "considered wholly inapplicable to later enacted federal statutes that are enforceable exclusively in federal litigation." But this view is inconsistent with the approach adopted by the Court in *Clothing Workers,* supra. In that case an employer had sought an injunction against a union in state court. This Court found that the action before the state court was "outside state authority," 348 U.S., at 514, and that jurisdiction was vested solely in the National Labor Relations Board. But the Court found that the exclusive federal jurisdiction was not sufficient to render § 2283 inapplicable. See also Atlantic Coast Line R. Co. v. Locomotive Engineers, 398 U.S. 281 (1970).

We think MR. JUSTICE STEVENS' view tends to confuse the jurisdiction granted to federal courts by § 16 of the Clayton Act with the separate question of whether a court having such jurisdiction has also been "expressly authorize[d]" to enjoin state-court proceedings. But the question of whether an injunction against state-court proceedings has been "expressly authorized" under § 2283 never arises unless the federal court asked to issue the injunction has subject matter jurisdiction of the case in which the injunction is sought. Here the District Court is entirely free to proceed with the litigation on the merits of respondents' antitrust claim against petitioner, and to grant damages and such other relief as may be appropriate if it determines the issues in favor of respondents. All that we conclude is that it may not include as a part of that relief an injunction against an already pending state-court proceeding.

of federalism underlying § 2283; by its statutory scheme it has enacted, Congress has clearly reserved this judgment unto itself.[13]

Our conclusion that the "importance," or the potential restriction in scope, of the federal injunction statute does not control for § 2283 purposes is consistent with the analysis of those very few statutes which we have in the past held to be exceptions to the Anti–Injunction Act. See *Mitchum*, supra, 234–235, and nn. 12–16. The original version of the Anti–Injunction Act itself was amended in 1874 to allow federal courts to enjoin state court proceedings which interfere with the administration of a federal bankruptcy proceeding. Rev.Stat. § 720 (1874). The Interpleader Act of 1926, 28 U.S.C. § 2361, the Frazier–Lemke Act, 11 U.S.C. § 203, and the Federal Habeas Corpus Act, 28 U.S.C. § 2251, while not directly referring to § 2283, have nonetheless explicitly authorized injunctive relief against state court proceedings. The Act of 1851 limiting liability to shipowners, 46 U.S.C. § 185, provided that, after deposit for certain funds in the court by the shipowner, "all claims and proceedings against the owner with respect to the matter in question shall cease." The statutory procedures for removal of a case from state court to federal court provide that the removal acts as a stay of the state court proceedings. 28 U.S.C. § 1446(e).

By limiting the statutory exceptions to § 2283 and its predecessors to these few instances, we have clearly recognized that the act countenancing the federal injunction must necessarily interact with, or focus upon, a state judicial proceeding.[14] Section 16 of the Clayton Act, which does not by its very essence contemplate or envision any necessary interaction with state judicial proceedings, is clearly not such an act.

---

13. Much of Mr. Justice Stevens' dissenting opinion is an able brief for the conceded importance of the Sherman and Clayton Acts. But however persuasive it might be in inducing Congress to lift the bar of § 2283 with respect to injunctions issued under § 16, we do not believe it is persuasive in determining whether, under the present state of the law, Congress has in fact "expressly authorized" the injunction issued by the District Court here. For example, Mr. Justice Stevens laments that state-court proceedings may now become the vehicles by which an anti-trust violator may put one independent businessman after another out of business. Federal courts are able to enjoin future repetitive litigation, see discussion of *California Motor Transport* and *Otter Tail Power*, n. [11] supra. But even if one were to agree with this broad speculation, the solution is simple and straightforward. If Congress determines that the use of state-court proceedings to foster anticompetitive schemes is of sufficient gravity, it may simply conclude that the need for greater antitrust enforcement outweighs the need to prevent friction in our federal system and amend § 16 to expressly authorize an injunction of state-court proceedings.

No desire for more vigorous antitrust enforcement should cause us to lose sight of our role as judges in interpreting explicit command of a congressional statute; for notwithstanding the rhetoric of the dissenting opinion, the conclusion that § 16 is an "expressly authorized" exception to § 2283 is no more than an ipse dixit. The "explicit wording of Section 2283," *Atlantic Coast Line R. Co.,* supra, at 297, is lost on the dissent; the dissent's approach is the clearest form of judicial improvisation which the Court counseled against in *Clothing Workers of America v. Richman Bros. Co.,* supra, 348 U.S., at 514.

14. A possible exception is Porter v. Dicken, 328 U.S. 252 (1946), regarding § 205(a) of the Emergency Price Control Act of 1942. This Act, enacted in response to wartime exigencies, expired in 1947.

IV

Although the Court of Appeals did not reach the issue, the District Court found that, in addition to being "expressly authorized," the injunction was "necessary in aid of its jurisdiction," a separate exception to § 2283. The rationale of the District Court was as follows:

"The Court also holds that § 2283 authorizes an injunction here because further collection efforts would eliminate two plaintiffs, Stoner Investments and Lektro–Vend Corp., as parties under the case or controversy provisions of Article III since they would necessarily be controlled by Vendo. Vendo's offer to place the Stoner Investment and Lektro–Vend stock under control of the Court does not meet this problem because as a matter of substance Vendo would control both plaintiff and defendant, requiring dismissal under Article III. Thus the injunction is also necessary to protect the jurisdiction of the Court." 403 F.Supp., at 536–537.

In *Toucey v. New York Life Insurance Company*, 314 U.S., at 134–135 (1945), we acknowledged the existence of an historical exception to the Anti–Injunction Act in cases where the federal court has obtained jurisdiction over the res, prior to the state court action. Although the "necessary in aid of" exception to § 2283 may be fairly read as incorporating this historical in rem exception, see C. Wright, Law of Federal Courts, § 47, at 204 (3d ed.), the federal and state actions here are simply in personam. The traditional notion is that in personam actions in federal and state court may proceed concurrently, without interference from either court, and there is no evidence that the exception to § 2283 was intended to alter this balance. We have never viewed parallel in personam actions as interfering with the jurisdiction of either court; as we stated in Kline v. Burke Construction Co., 260 U.S. 226 (1922):

"[A]n action brought to enforce [a personal liability] *does not tend to impair or defeat the jurisdiction* of the court in which a prior action for the same cause is pending. Each court is free to proceed in its own way and in its own time, without reference to the proceedings in the other court. Whenever a judgment is rendered in one of the courts and pleaded in the other, the effect of that judgment is to be determined by the application of the principles of res adjudicata...." Id., at 230 (emphasis added).

No case of this Court has ever held that an injunction to "preserve" a case or controversy fits within the "necessary in aid of its jurisdiction" exception; neither have the parties directed us to any other federal-court decisions so holding.

The District Court's legal conclusion is not only unsupported by precedent, but the factual premises upon which it rests are not persuasive. First, even if the two corporate plaintiffs would cease to litigate the case after execution of the state court judgment, there is no indication that Harry Stoner himself would lose his standing to vindicate his rights, or that the case could not go forward. Nor does it appear that two corporate plaintiffs would necessarily be removed from the lawsuit. As far as the record indicates, there are currently minority shareholders in those corporations whose ownership interests would not be affected by petitioner's acquisition of majority stock control of the corporations. Under the applicable rules for shareholder derivative actions, see Fed.Rule Civ.Proc. 23.1, the shareholders could presumably pursue the corporate rights of action, which would inure to their benefit, even if the corporations themselves chose not to do so. Finally, petitioner offered to enter a consent decree which assuredly would eliminate any possibility of petitioners acquiring control of the corporation. See App. 209, 258. The injunction in this case was therefore even under the District Courts' legal theory not *necessary* in aid of that court's jurisdiction.

Our conclusion that neither of the bases relied upon by the District Court constitutes an exception to § 2283 is more than consistent with the recognition that any doubt must be resolved *against* the finding of an exception to § 2283, *Atlantic Coast Line R. Co.,* 398 U.S., at 297, a holding that there is an exception present in this case would demonstrably involve "judicial improvisation." *Clothing Workers,* 348 U.S., at 514.

Reversed and remanded.

■ MR. JUSTICE BLACKMUN, with whom THE CHIEF JUSTICE joins, concurring in the result.

Although I agree that the decision of the Court of Appeals should be reversed, I do so for reasons that differ significantly from those expressed by the plurality. According to the plurality's analysis, § 16 of the Clayton Act, 15 U.S.C. § 26, is not an expressly authorized exception to the Anti–Injunction Act, 28 U.S.C. § 2283, because it is not "an 'Act of Congress [which] could be given its intended scope only by the stay of a state court proceeding.' [Mitchum v. Foster, 407 U.S. 225, 238 (1972)]." I do not agree that this is invariably the case; since I am of the opinion, however, that the state-court proceeding in this case should not have been enjoined by the federal court, I concur in the result.

In my opinion, application of the *Mitchum* test for deciding whether a statute is an "expressly authorized" exception to the Anti–Injunction Act shows that § 16 is such an exception under narrowly limited circumstances. Nevertheless, consistently with the decision in California Motor Transport Co. v. Trucking Unlimited, 404 U.S. 508 (1972),[15] I would hold

---

15. I cannot agree with MR. JUSTICE STEVENS that the examples given in the quoted portion of *California Motor Transport Co. v. Trucking Unlimited,* necessarily involve the use of the adjudicatory process in the same way that the state courts were being used in this case. For example, there is no reason to believe that the Court's reference to the use of a patent obtained by fraud to exclude a competitor contemplated only one lawsuit. The case cited in connection with that reference, Walker Process Equipment, Inc. v. Food Machinery & Chemical Corp., 382 U.S. 172 (1965), held only that the enforcement of a patent procured by fraud on the Patent Office could state a claim under § 2 of the Sherman Act, where the monopolistic acts alleged included use of the fraudulent patent through a course of action involving both threats of suit and prosecution of an infringement suit.

that no injunction may issue against currently pending state-court proceedings unless those proceedings are themselves part of a "pattern of baseless, repetitive claims" that are being used as an anticompetitive device, all the traditional prerequisites for equitable relief are satisfied, and the only way to give the antitrust laws their intended scope is by staying the state proceedings. Cf. *California Motor Transport Co. v. Trucking Unlimited*, 404 U.S., at 513. See also Otter Tail Power Co. v. United States, 410 U.S. 366, 380 (1973).

In my view, the District Court failed properly to apply the *California Motor Transport* rule. The court believed that it was enough that Vendo's activities in the single state-court proceeding involved in this case were not genuine attempts to use the state adjudicative process legitimately. In reaching this conclusion, the court looked to Vendo's purpose in conducting the state litigation and to several negative effects that the litigation had upon respondent. The court, however, did not find a "pattern of baseless, repetitive claims," nor could it have done so under the circumstances. Only one state-court proceeding was involved in this case, and it resulted in the considered affirmance by the Illinois Supreme Court of a judgment for more than $7 million. In my opinion, therefore, it cannot be said on this record that Vendo was using the state-court proceeding as an anti-competitive device in and of itself. Thus, I believe that § 16 itself did not authorize the injunction below, and on this ground, I would reverse.

■ MR. JUSTICE STEVENS, with whom MR. JUSTICE BRENNAN, MR. JUSTICE WHITE, and MR. JUSTICE MARSHALL join, dissenting.

.   .   .   .   .

Judge McLaren found substantial evidence that petitioner intended to monopolize the relevant market; that one of the overt acts performed in furtherance thereof was the use of litigation as a method of harassing and eliminating competition; that two of the corporate plaintiffs in the case, respondents here, would be eliminated by collection of the Illinois judgment; and that the state litigation had already severely hampered, and collection of the judgment would prevent, the marketing of a promising, newly developed machine which would compete with petitioner's products. 403 F.Supp. 527, 534–535, 538 (N.D.Ill.1975). The Court of Appeals implic-

---

MR. JUSTICE STEVENS' quotation from *California Motor Transport* stops just short of the language that I consider critical to the instant case. The Court's opinion continues:

"... Misrepresentations, condoned in the political arena, are not immunized when used in the adjudicatory process. Opponents before agencies or courts often think poorly of the other's tactics, motions, or defenses and may readily call them baseless. One claim, which a court or agency may think baseless, may go unnoticed; but a pattern of baseless, repetitive claims may emerge which leads the factfinder to conclude that the administrative and judicial processes have been abused. That may be a difficult line to discern and draw." 404 U.S., at 513.

Since I believe that federal courts should be hesitant indeed to enjoin on-going state-court proceedings, I am of the opinion that a pattern of baseless, repetitive claims or some equivalent showing of grave abuse of the state courts must exist before an injunction would be proper. No such finding was made by the District Court in this case.

itly endorsed these findings when it noted that "[h]ere Vendo seeks to thwart a federal antitrust suit by the enforcement of state court judgments which are alleged to be the very object of antitrust violations." 545 F.2d 1050, 1057 (CA7 1976).

The question which is therefore presented is whether the anti-injunction statute deprives the federal courts of power to stay state court litigation which is being prosecuted in direct violation of the Sherman Act. I cannot believe that any of the members of Congress who unanimously enacted that basic charter of economic freedom in 1890 would have answered that question the way the plurality does today.

I

The plurality relies on the present form of a provision of the Judiciary Act of 1793. In the ensuing century, there were changes in our economy which persuaded the Congress that the state courts could not adequately deal with contracts in restraint of trade that affected commerce in more than one jurisdiction. The Sherman Act was enacted unanimously in 1890 to protect the national economy from the pernicious effects of regulation by private cartel and to vest the federal courts with jurisdiction adequate to "exert such remedies as would fully accomplish the purposes intended."

Between 1890 and 1914, although private litigants could recover treble damages, only the United States could invoke the jurisdiction of the federal courts to prevent and restrain violations of the Sherman Act. When Congress authorized the federal courts to grant injunctive relief in private antitrust litigation, it conferred the same broad powers that the courts possess in cases brought by the Government. Section 16 of the Clayton Act expressly authorizes injunctions against "a violation of the antitrust laws."

The scope of the jurisdictional grant is just as broad as the definition of a violation of the antitrust laws. That definition was deliberately phrased in general language to be sure that "every conceivable act which could possibly come within the spirit or purpose of the prohibition" would be covered by the statute, regardless of whether or not the particular form of restraint was actually foreseen by Congress. In the decades following the formulation of the Rule of Reason in 1911, this Court has made it perfectly clear that the prosecution of litigation in a state court may itself constitute a form of violation of the federal statute.

Thus, the attempt to enforce a patent obtained by fraud, or a patent known to be invalid for other reasons, may constitute an independent violation of the Sherman Act; and such litigation may be brought in a state court. The prosecution of frivolous claims and objections before regulatory bodies, including state agencies, may violate the antitrust laws. The enforcement of restrictive provisions in a license to use a patent or a trademark may violate the Sherman Act; such enforcement may, of course, be sought in the state courts. Similarly, the provisions of a lease, or a fair trade agreement, may become the focus of enforcement litigation which has a purpose or effect of frustrating rights guaranteed by the antitrust laws, either in a state or federal court. Indeed, the enforcement of a covenant not to compete—the classic example of a contract in restraint of trade—typically takes place in a state court.

These examples are sufficient to demonstrate that "litigation in state courts may constitute an antitrust violation . . . ." Since the judicial construction of a statute is as much a part of the law as the words written by the legislature, the illegal use of state court litigation as a method of monopolizing or restraining trade is as plainly a violation of the antitrust laws as if Congress had specifically described each of the foregoing cases as an independent violation. The language in § 16 of the Clayton Act which expressly authorizes injunctions against violations of the antitrust laws is therefore applicable to this species of violation as well as to other kinds of violations.

Since § 16 of the Clayton Act is an Act of Congress which expressly authorizes an injunction against a state court proceeding which violates the antitrust laws, the plain language of the anti-injunction statute excepts this kind of injunction from its coverage.

II

There is nothing in this Court's precedents which is even arguably inconsistent with this rather obvious reading of the statutory language. On at least three occasions the Court has held that general grants of federal jurisdiction which make no mention of either state court proceedings, or of the anti-injunction statute, are within the "expressly authorized" exception. Providence & N.Y.S.S. Co. v. Hill Mfg. Co., 109 U.S. 578, 599–601; Porter v. Dicken, 328 U.S. 252; Mitchum v. Foster, 407 U.S. 225.

In *Mitchum* the Court made it clear that a statute may come within the "expressly authorized" exception to § 2283 even though it does not mention the anti-injunction statute or contain any reference to state court proceedings, provided that it creates a uniquely federal right or remedy that could be frustrated if the federal court was not empowered to enjoin the state proceeding. The Court then formulated and applied this test: "The test . . . is whether an Act of Congress, clearly creating a federal right or remedy enforceable in a federal court of equity, could be given its intended scope only by the stay of a state court proceeding." 407 U.S., at 238.

Section 16 of the Clayton Act created a federal remedy which can only be given its intended scope if it includes the power to stay state court proceedings in appropriate cases. As one of the sponsors of the statute explained, under "this most excellent provision a man does not have to wait until he is ruined in his business before he has his remedy." But if the plurality's interpretation of the legislation were correct, a private litigant might indeed be "ruined in his business before he has his remedy" against state court litigation seeking enforcement of an invalid patent, a covenant not to compete, or an executory merger agreement, to take only a few obvious examples of antitrust violations that might be consummated by state court litigation.

The plurality assumes that Congress intended to distinguish between illegal state proceedings which are already pending and those which have not yet been filed at the time of a federal court's determination that a violation of the antitrust laws has been consummated; the federal court may enjoin the latter, but is powerless to restrain the former. Nothing in the history of the anti-injunction statute suggests any such logic-chopping distinction.[16] Indeed, it is squarely at odds with Senator Sherman's own explanation of the intended scope of the statutory power "... to issue all remedial process or writs proper and necessary to enforce its provisions ...." It would demean the legislative process to construe the eloquent rhetoric which accompanied the enactment of the antitrust laws as implicitly denying federal courts the power to restrain illegal state court litigation simply because it was filed before the federal case was concluded. A faithful application of the rationale of *Mitchum v. Foster* requires a like result in this case.

III

The plurality expresses the fear that if the Clayton Act is given its intended scope, the anti-injunction statute "would be completely eviscerated" since there are 26 other federal statutes which may also be within the "expressly authorized" exception.... That fear, stated in its strongest terms, is that in the 184 years since the anti-injunction statute was originally enacted, there are 26 occasions on which Congress has qualified its prohibition to some extent. There are at least three reasons why this argument should not cause panic.

First, the early history of the anti-injunction statute indicates that it was primarily intended to prevent the federal courts from exercising a sort of appellate review function in litigation in which the state and federal courts had equal competence. The statute imposed a limitation on the general equity powers of the federal courts which existed in 1793, and which have been exercised subsequently in diversity and other private litigation. But the anti-injunction statute has seldom, if ever, been construed to interfere with a federal court's power to implement federal policy pursuant to an express statutory grant of federal jurisdiction. Although there is no need to resolve the question in this case, I must confess that I am not now persuaded that the concept of federalism is necessarily inconsistent with the view that the 1793 Act should be considered wholly inapplicable to later enacted federal statutes that are enforceable exclusive-

---

16. Thus, the 1851 act to limit the liability of shipowners, 9 Stat. 635, applied equally to "preventing or arresting the prosecution of separate suits," see Providence & N.Y. S.S. Co. v. Hill Mfg. Co., 109 U.S. 578, 596. The Interpleader Act, 28 U.S.C. § 2361, in terms, applies equally to the "instituting or prosecuting" of other litigation. In terms of the interest in federalism, since the injunction against litigation typically runs against the parties rather than the Court, there is little difference between denying a citizen access to the state forum and denying him the right to prosecute an existing case to its conclusion. In either situation, a federal injunction must rest on a determination that an important federal policy outweighs the interest in allowing a state court to resolve a particular controversy. But when the federal policy does justify that conclusion, the timing of the state court action should rarely be controlling.

ly in federal litigation. If a fair reading of the jurisdictional grant in any such statute does authorize an injunction against state court litigation frustrating the federal policy, nothing in our prior cases would foreclose the conclusion that it is within the "expressly authorized" exception to § 2283.

Second, in any event, the question whether the Packers and Stockyards Act of 1921, for example, gives the federal court the power to enjoin state litigation has little if any, relevance to the issues presented by this case. Whatever the answer to that question may be, that 56–year–old statute will not exacerbate federal-state relations and jeopardize the vitality of "our federalism." Indeed, even if all the statutes identified by the plurality are within the "expressly authorized" exception to § 2283, it is extremely doubtful that they would generate as much, or as significant, litigation as either the Civil Rights Act or the antitrust laws. The answer to the important question presented by this case should not depend on speculation about potential consequences for other statutes of relatively less importance to the economy and the Nation.

Third, concern about the Court's ability either to enlarge or to contain the exceptions from the anti-injunction statute, ... is disingenuous at best. As originally enacted in 1793, the statute contained no express exception at all. Those few that were recognized in the ensuing century and a half were the product of judicial interpretation of the statute's prohibition in concrete situations. The codification of the judicial code in 1948 restated the exceptions in statutory language, but was not intended to modify the Court's power to accommodate the terms of the statute to overriding expressions of national policy embodied in statutes like the Ku Klux Act of 1870 or the Sherman Law of 1890.

IV

Since the votes of THE CHIEF JUSTICE and MR. JUSTICE BLACKMUN are decisive, a separate comment on MR. JUSTICE BLACKMUN's opinion concurring in the result is required.

His agreement with the proposition that an injunction properly entered pursuant to § 16 of the Clayton Act is within the "expressly authorized" exception to the anti-injunction statute establishes that proposition as the law for the future. His view that § 16 did not authorize the preliminary injunction entered by Judge McLaren is dispositive of this litigation but, for reasons which may be briefly summarized, is not a view that finds any support in the law.

Unlike the plurality which would draw a distinction between on-going litigation and future litigation, MR. JUSTICE BLACKMUN differentiates between a violation committed by a multiplicity of lawsuits and a violation involving only one lawsuit. The very case on which he relies rejects that distinction. In California Motor Transport Co. v. Trucking Unlimited, 404 U.S. 508, 512–513, the Court stated:

> "Yet unethical conduct in the setting of the adjudicatory process often results in sanctions. Perjury of witnesses is one example. Use of a

patent obtained by fraud to exclude a competitor from the market may involve a violation of the antitrust laws, as we held in Walker Process Equipment v. Food Machinery & Chemical Corp., 382 U.S. 172, 175–177. Conspiracy with a licensing authority to eliminate a competitor may also result in an antitrust transgression. Continental Ore Co. v. Union Carbide & Carbon Corp., 370 U.S. 690, 707, Harman v. Valley National Bank, 339 F.2d 564 (CA9, 1964). Similarly, bribery of a public purchasing agent may constitute a violation of § 2(c) of the Clayton Act, as amended by the Robinson–Patman Act. Rangen, Inc. v. Sterling Nelson & Sons, 351 F.2d 851 (CA9, 1965).

"There are many other forms of illegal and reprehensible practice which may corrupt the administrative or judicial processes and which may result in antitrust violations."

Each of the examples given in this excerpt from the *California Motor Transport* opinion involves a single use of the adjudicatory process to violate the antitrust laws. Manifestly, when Mr. Justice Douglas wrote for the Court in that case and described "a pattern of baseless, repetitive claims," id., at 513, as an illustration of an antitrust violation, he did not thereby circumscribe the category to that one example. Nothing in his opinion even remotely implies that there would be any less reason to enjoin the "[u]se of a patent obtained by fraud to exclude a competitor from the market," id., at 512, for example, than to enjoin the particular violation before the Court in that case.

. . . . .

V

Apart from the anti-injunction statute, petitioner has argued that principles of equity, comity, and federalism create a bar to injunctive relief in this case. This argument is supported by three facts: The Illinois litigation was pending for a period of nine years; the Illinois Supreme Court concluded that respondents were guilty of a breach of fiduciary duty; and respondents withdrew their antitrust defense from the state action.

Unfortunately, in recent years long periods of delay have been a characteristic of litigation in the Illinois courts. That is not a reason for a federal court to show any special deference to state courts; quite the contrary, it merely emphasizes the seriousness of any decision by a federal court to abstain, on grounds of federalism, from the prompt decision of a federal question.

The Illinois Supreme Court's conclusion that respondents had violated a fiduciary obligation and that petitioner was entitled to a large damage recovery rested on that court's appraisal of the legality of a covenant in restraint of trade. The fact that the covenant not to compete is valid as a matter of state law is irrelevant to the federal antitrust issue. If, for example, instead of a contract totally excluding respondents from the relevant market, the parties had agreed on a lesser restraint which merely required respondents to sell at prices fixed by petitioner, the Illinois court might also have concluded that respondents were bound by the contract even though the federal courts would have found it plainly violative of the Sherman Act. The Illinois decision on the merits merely highlights the fact that state and federal courts apply significantly different standards in evaluating contracts in restraint of trade.

That fact provides the explanation for respondents' decision to withdraw their federal antitrust defense from the Illinois litigation and to present it to the federal courts. Congress has granted the federal courts exclusive jurisdiction over the prosecution of private antitrust litigation. Since the state courts do not have the power to award complete relief for an antitrust violation, since state judges are unfamiliar with the complexities of this area of the law, and since state procedures are sometimes unsatisfactory for cases of nationwide scope, no adverse inference should be drawn from a state court defendant's election to reserve his federal antitrust claim for decision by a federal court.

Indeed, since these respondents made that election, and since Congress has withheld jurisdiction of antitrust claims from the state courts, the plurality properly ignores the argument that principles of federalism require abstention in this case. For a ruling requiring the federal court to abstain from the decision of an antitrust issue that might have been raised in a state court proceeding would be tantamount to holding that the federal defense *must* be asserted in the state action. Such a holding could not be reconciled with the congressional decision to confer exclusive jurisdiction of the private enforcement of the antitrust laws on the federal courts. Quite plainly, therefore, this is not the kind of case in which abstention is even arguably proper.

. . . . .

I respectfully dissent.[17]

———

[17. Ultimately the federal injunction was dissolved but not until the case had been before the Supreme Court on two other occasions. Vendo Co. v. Lektro–Vend Corp., 434 U.S. 425 (1978); In re Vendo Co., 435 U.S. 994 (1978). On the merits it was eventually held that Vendo had not violated the antitrust laws. Lektro–Vend Corp. v. Vendo Co., 660 F.2d 255 (7th Cir.1981), certiorari denied, 455 U.S. 921 (1982).

A statute, 42 U.S.C. § 4332(2)(C) requires an environmental-impact statement before taking major actions that may affect environmental quality. It says nothing about injunctions, against state proceedings or any other. Does the Anti–Injunction Act bar a federal court from enjoining state condemnation proceedings that are part of a project for which arguably an environmental-impact statement is required? Stockslager v. Carroll Elec. Co-op. Corp., 528 F.2d 949 (8th Cir.1976).

Does § 2283 bar a federal court that has *certified* a class action from enjoining the continuation of pending state court proceedings by members of the class? Compare the majority and dissenting opinions in In re Federal Skywalk Cases, 680 F.2d 1175 (8th Cir.1982), certiorari denied 459 U.S. 988 (1982). See Sherman, Class Actions and Duplicative Litigation, 62 Ind.L.J. 507 (1987); Larimore, Exploring the Interface Between Rule 23 Class Actions and the Anti–Injunction Act, 18 Ga.L.Rev. 259 (1984).

SECTION 3. STATE INJUNCTIONS AGAINST FEDERAL COURT PROCEEDINGS OR FEDERAL OFFICERS

Donovan v. City of Dallas

Supreme Court of the United States, 1964.
377 U.S. 408, 84 S.Ct. 1579, 12 L.Ed.2d 409.

■ MR. JUSTICE BLACK delivered the opinion of the Court.

The question presented here is whether a state court can validly enjoin a person from prosecuting an action in personam in a district or appellate court of the United States which has jurisdiction both of the parties and of the subject matter.

The City of Dallas, Texas, owns Love Field, a municipal airport. In 1961, 46 Dallas citizens who owned or had interests in property near the airport filed a class suit in a Texas court to restrain the city from building an additional runway and from issuing and selling municipal bonds for that purpose. The complaint alleged many damages that would occur to the plaintiffs if the runway should be built and charged that issuance of the bonds would be illegal for any reasons. The case was tried, summary judgment was given for the city, the Texas Court of Civil Appeals affirmed, the Supreme Court of Texas denied review, and we denied certiorari. Later 120 Dallas citizens, including 27 of the plaintiffs in the earlier action, filed another action in the United States District Court for the Northern District of Texas seeking similar relief. A number of new defendants were named in addition to the City of Dallas, all the defendants being charged with taking part in plans to construct the runway and to issue and sell bonds in violation of state and federal laws. The complaint sought an injunction against construction of the runway, issuance of bonds, payment on bonds already issued, and circulation of false information about the bond issue, as well as a declaration that all the bonds were illegal and void. None of the bonds would be approved, and therefore under Texas law none could be issued, so long as there was pending litigation challenging their validity. The city filed a motion to dismiss and an answer to the complaint in the federal court. But at the same time the city applied to the Texas Court of Civil Appeals for a writ of prohibition to bar all the plaintiffs in the case in the United States District Court from prosecuting their case there. The

The Seventh Circuit has given nationwide, issue-preclusive effect to a federal court's order that *denied* certification of a nationwide class of consumers in a products-liability action. The court held the order to be binding on all members of the putative plaintiff class, named and unnamed, and on their counsel. Relying on the "protect or effectuate its judgments" exception to the Anti–Injunction Act, Judge Easterbrook's opinion ordered the court below to enter an injunction prohibiting the relitigation of the class-certification issue in any other court, state or federal. In re Bridgestone/Firestone, Inc., 333 F.3d 763 (7th Cir.2003).]

Texas Court of Civil Appeals denied relief, holding that it was without power to enjoin litigants from prosecuting an action in a federal court and that the defense of res judicata on which the city relied could be raised and adjudicated in the United States District Court. On petition for mandamus the Supreme Court of Texas took a different view, however, held it the duty of the Court of Civil Appeals to prohibit the litigants from further prosecuting the United States District Court case, and stated that a writ of mandamus would issue should the Court of Civil Appeals fail to perform this duty. The Court of Civil Appeals promptly issued a writ prohibiting all the plaintiffs in the United States District Court case from any further prosecution of that case and enjoined them "individually and as a class . . . from filing or instituting . . . any further litigation, law suits or actions in any court, the purpose of which is to contest the validity of the airport revenue bonds . . . or from in any manner interfering with . . . the proposed bonds . . . ." The United States District Court in an unreported opinion dismissed the case pending there. Counsel Donovan, who is one of the petitioners here, excepted to the dismissal and then filed an appeal from that dismissal in the United States Court of Appeals for the Fifth Circuit. The Texas Court of Civil Appeals thereupon cited Donovan and the other United States District Court claimants for contempt and convicted 87 of them on a finding that they had violated its "valid order." Donovan was sentenced to serve 20 days in jail, and the other 86 were fined $200 each, an aggregate of $17,200. These penalties were imposed upon each contemner for having either (1) joined as a party plaintiff in the United States District Court case; (2) failed to request and contested the dismissal of that case; (3) taken exceptions to the dismissal preparatory to appealing to the Court of Appeals; or (4) filed a separate action in the Federal District Court seeking to enjoin the Supreme Court of Texas from interfering with the original federal-court suit. After the fines had been paid and he had served his jail sentence, counsel Donovan appeared in the District Court on behalf of himself and all those who had been fined and moved to dismiss the appeal to the United States Court of Appeals. His motion stated that it was made under duress and that unless the motion was made "the Attorney for Defendant City of Dallas and the Chief Judge of the Court of Civil Appeals have threatened these Appellants and their Attorney with further prosecution for contempt resulting in additional fines and imprisonment." The United States District Court then dismissed the appeal.

We declined to grant certiorari to review the United States District Court's dismissal of the case before it or its dismissal of the appeal brought on by the state court's coercive contempt judgment, but we did grant certiorari to review the State Supreme Court's judgment directing the Civil Court of Appeals to enjoin petitioners from prosecuting their action in the federal courts and also granted certiorari to review the Civil Court of Appeals' judgment of conviction for contempt. 375 U.S. 878. We think the Texas Court of Civil Appeals was right in its first holding that it was without power to enjoin these litigants from prosecuting their federal-court action, and we therefore reverse the State Supreme Court's judgment upsetting that of the Court of Appeals. We vacate the later contempt judgment of the Court of Civil Appeals, which rested on the mistaken belief that the writ prohibiting litigation by the federal plaintiffs was "valid."

Early in the history of our country a general rule was established that state and federal courts would not interfere with or try to restrain each other's proceedings.[18] That rule has continued substantially unchanged to this time. An exception has been made in cases where a court has custody of property, that is, proceedings in rem or quasi in rem. In such cases this Court has said that the state or federal court having custody of such property has exclusive jurisdiction to proceed. Princess Lida v. Thompson, 305 U.S. 456, 465–468. In *Princess Lida* this Court said "where the judgment sought is strictly in personam, both the state court and the federal court, having concurrent jurisdiction, may proceed with the litigation at least until judgment is obtained in one of them which may be set up as res judicata in the other." Id., 305 U.S., at 466. See also Kline v. Burke Construction Co., 260 U.S. 226. It may be that a full hearing in an appropriate court would justify a finding that the state-court judgment in favor of Dallas in the first suit barred the issues raised in the second suit, a question as to which we express no opinion. But plaintiffs in the second suit chose to file that case in the federal court. They had a right to do this, a right which is theirs by reason of congressional enactments passed pursuant to congressional policy. And whether or not a plea of res judicata in the second suit would be good is a question for the federal court to decide. While Congress has seen fit to authorize courts of the United States to restrain state-court proceedings in some special circumstances, it has in no way relaxed the old and well-established judicially declared rule[19] that state courts are completely without power to restrain federal-court proceedings in in personam actions like the one here. And it does not matter that the prohibition here was addressed to the parties rather than to the federal court itself. . . .

Petitioners being properly in the federal court had a right granted by Congress to have the court decide the issues they presented, and to appeal to the Court of Appeals from the District Court's dismissal. They have been punished both for prosecuting their federal-court case and for appealing it. They dismissed their appeal because of threats to punish them more if they did not do so. The legal effect of such a coerced dismissal on their appeal is not now before us, but the propriety of a state court's punishment of a federal-court litigant for pursuing his right to federal-court remedies is. That right was granted by Congress and cannot be taken away by the State. The Texas courts were without power to take away this federal right by contempt proceedings or otherwise.[20]

---

18. See, e.g., M'Kim v. Voorhies, 7 Cranch [11 U.S.] 279; Diggs v. Wolcott, 4 Cranch [8 U.S.] 179.

19. See, e.g., United States ex rel. Moses v. Council of Keokuk, 6 Wall. [73 U.S.] 514, 517; Weber v. Lee County, 6 Wall. [73 U.S.] 210; Riggs v. Johnson County, 6 Wall. [73 U.S.] 166, 194–196; M'Kim v. Voorhies, 7 Cranch [11 U.S.] 279.

20. In Baltimore & O.R. Co. v. Kepner, 314 U.S. 44, the Court did not reach the question before us, since the decision there was rested on the special venue provisions of the Federal Employers' Liability Act. See 36 Stat. 291, as amended, 45 U.S.C. § 56.

It is argued here, however, that the Court of Civil Appeals' judgment of contempt should nevertheless be upheld on the premise that it was petitioners' duty to obey the restraining order whether that order was valid or invalid. The Court of Civil Appeals did not consider or pass upon this question, but acted on the assumption that petitioners were guilty of "willful disobedience of a *valid* order." 368 S.W.2d, at 244. (Emphasis supplied.) Since we hold the order restraining petitioners from prosecuting their case in the federal courts was not valid, but was invalid, petitioners have been punished for disobeying an invalid order. Whether the Texas court would have punished petitioners for contempt had it known that the restraining order petitioners violated was invalid, we do not know. However, since that question was neither considered nor decided by the Texas court, we leave it for consideration by that court on remand. We express no opinion on that question at this time.

The judgment of the Texas Supreme Court is reversed, the judgment of the Texas Court of Civil Appeals is vacated, and the case is remanded to the Court of Civil Appeals for further proceedings not inconsistent with this opinion.

■ MR. JUSTICE HARLAN, whom MR. JUSTICE CLARK and MR. JUSTICE STEWART join, dissenting.

The question presented by this case is not the general one stated by the Court at the outset of its opinion, but a much narrower one: May a state court enjoin resident state-court suitors from prosecuting in the federal courts vexatious, duplicative litigation which has the effect of thwarting a state-court judgment already rendered against them? Given the Texas Supreme Court's finding, amply supported by the record and in no way challenged by this Court, that this controversy "has reached the point of vexatious and harassing litigation," 365 S.W.2d 919, 927, I consider both the state injunction and the ensuing contempt adjudication to have been perfectly proper.

I.

The power of a court in equity to enjoin persons subject to its jurisdiction from conducting vexatious and harassing litigation in another forum has not been doubted until now. . . .

This Court, in 1941, expressly recognized the power of a state court to do precisely what the Texas court did here. In Baltimore & Ohio R. Co. v. Kepner, 314 U.S. 44, 51–52, the Court, although denying the state court's power to issue an injunction in that case, said:

> "The real contention of petitioner is that despite the admitted venue respondent is acting in a vexatious and inequitable manner in maintaining the federal court suit in a distant jurisdiction when a convenient and suitable forum is at respondent's doorstep. Under such circumstances petitioner asserts power, abstractly speaking, in the Ohio court to prevent a resident under its jurisdiction from doing

inequity. *Such power does exist.*" (Footnote omitted; emphasis supplied.)

Mr. Justice Frankfurter, dissenting because of disagreement with the particular basis for the Court's refusal to give effect to the general principle, ... observed that the opinion of the Court did "not deny the historic power of courts of equity to prevent a misuse of litigation by enjoining resort to vexatious and oppressive foreign suits," id., at 55, and that the decision did not "give new currency to the discredited notion that there is a general lack of power in the state courts to enjoin proceedings in federal courts," id., at 56.

Apart from these express statements in both the majority and dissenting opinions, the Court's reasoning in the *Baltimore & Ohio R. Co.* case clearly implies a view contrary to the one taken by the majority here. Kepner, an injured employee of the railroad, filed suit against it in the District Court for the Eastern District of New York. The accident out of which his injuries arose occurred in Ohio, which was also the State in which he resided. Jurisdiction was based on the provision of the Federal Employers' Liability Act which permitted an employee to bring suit in a district in which the defendant was doing business. The railroad brought a proceeding in the Ohio state courts to enjoin Kepner from continuing to prosecute his suit in the federal court in New York. It argued that more appropriate state and federal courts were open and that the large cost to itself of defending the suit in a distant forum was needless. Deciding solely on the basis that the venue provisions of the Federal Employers' Liability Act gave an injured employee a privilege which state legislative or judicial action could not override, the Court denied the power of the Ohio courts to issue an injunction. Quite evidently, this basis of decision would have been meaningless unless it was presumed that in the absence of the venue provisions of the statute the Ohio court would have had power to enjoin. Nor is it even necessary to resort to this obvious inference. For the Court made it express: "As courts of equity admittedly possessed this power [to enjoin improper resort to the courts of a foreign jurisdiction] before the enactment of § 6 [of the F.E.L.A.] ...." Id., at 53. See also Blanchard v. Commonwealth Oil Co., 294 F.2d 834, 841.

In light of the foregoing, there was no impropriety in the issuance of the state court's injunction in the present case.

II.

None of the cases on which the Court relies deals with, or in any way negatives, the power of a state court to enjoin federal litigation in circumstances such as those involved here. None of them was concerned with vexatious litigation.

The issue in M'Kim v. Voorhies, 7 Cranch [11 U.S.] 279, ... was whether a state court could stay proceedings on a federal court's judgment which had already been rendered when the state court acquired jurisdiction and which, therefore, involved no element of harassment at all. Similarly, in Diggs v. Wolcott, 4 Cranch [8 U.S.] 179 ..., in which the position of the courts was in reverse, suit was first commenced in the state court. Riggs v. Johnson County, 6 Wall. [73 U.S.] 166 ..., resembled *McKim,* supra; it involved the power of a state court to issue an injunction which had the effect of preventing a federal court from enforcing its judgment, entered before the state court ever got its hands on the case. The other two cases which the Court cites with *Riggs* ... are the same and were decided on the authority of *Riggs.* Weber v. Lee County, 6 Wall. [73 U.S.] 210, 212; United States ex rel. Ill. v. Council of Keokuk, 6 Wall. [73 U.S.] 514, 517.

. . . . .

There can be no dispute, therefore, that all the weight of authority, including that of a recent pronouncement of this Court, is contrary to the position which the Court takes in this case. It is not necessary to comment on the Court's assertion ... that the petitioners "had a right granted by Congress" to maintain their suit in the federal court, for that is the very question at issue. In any event, the statutory boundaries of federal jurisdiction are hardly to be regarded as a license to conduct litigation in the federal courts for the purpose of harassment.[21] The exception which the Court recognizes for in rem actions demonstrates that no such view of federal jurisdiction is tenable; for in those cases, too, the federal courts have statutory jurisdiction to proceed.

In short, today's decision rests upon confusion between two distinct lines of authority in this Court, one involving vexatious litigation and the other not.

I would affirm.[22]

————

21. As the cases cited in Part II of this opinion illustrate, this Court's power to review judgments of the state courts is available to prevent interference with the *legitimate* invocation of federal jurisdiction. The parallel development of the two distinct lines of cases which are now confused for the first time itself demonstrates that the possibility of abuse in some cases is no ground for denying altogether the traditional equitable power to prevent improper resort to the courts.

[**22.** See Hornstein & Magle, State Court Power to Enjoin Federal Judicial Proceedings: *Donovan v. City of Dallas Revisited,* 60 Wash.U.L.Q. 1 (1982); Arnold, State Power to Enjoin Federal Proceedings, 51 Va.L.Rev. 59 (1965); ALI Study § 1373.

It is explicitly held in General Atomic Co. v. Felter, 434 U.S. 12 (1977), that a state court may not enjoin commencement of a federal action in the future. See also General Atomic Co. v. Felter, 436 U.S. 493 (1978).

It has long been settled that state courts may entertain actions against federal officers for damages or for the recovery of specific property and that they have jurisdiction to try federal officers for crime (although the officer may remove to federal court, 28 U.S.C. § 1442, reprinted supra p. 331, or may seek federal habeas corpus, 28 U.S.C. § 2241(c)(2), reprinted infra p. 659). It is equally clear that a state court cannot issue a writ of mandamus against a federal officer and cannot grant habeas corpus for the discharge of a person held in federal custody. The uncertain was area was long whether a state court has power to enjoin a federal officer. See Arnold, The Power of State Courts to Enjoin Federal Officers, 73 Yale L.J. 1385 (1954). The question became moot in the light of 1976 legislation that waived sovereign immunity in suits in federal court against federal officers and agencies for other

SECTION 4. FEDERAL ACTIONS TO RESTRAIN STATE OFFICERS

Ex parte Young

Supreme Court of the United States, 1908.
209 U.S. 123, 28 S.Ct. 441, 52 L.Ed. 714.

■ [Statement by MR. JUSTICE PECKHAM:]

An original application was made to this court for leave to file a petition for writs of habeas corpus and certiorari in behalf of Edward T. Young, petitioner, as Attorney General of the State of Minnesota.

[In 1907 the Minnesota legislature passed a law reducing railroad rates and providing very severe criminal penalties for any railroad, or agent or representative of a railroad, that failed to comply. The day before this was to take effect stockholders of nine railroads brought suits in federal court to enjoin the companies of which they were stockholders from complying with the law. They claimed that the rates were confiscatory, and would deprive the companies of property without due process of law, but that the penalties were such that the railroads, if not restrained, would comply with it. Among other defendants they joined Attorney General Young and prayed that he be restrained from seeking to enforce the law. The federal court issued a preliminary injunction granting the relief the plaintiffs sought. The day after the injunction issued Young sued in state court for a writ of mandamus against the railroads to compel them to comply with the new law. He was adjudged guilty of contempt for this action, fined $100, and ordered to jail until he dismissed the state mandamus proceeding. This application to the Supreme Court for a writ of habeas corpus followed.]

■ MR. JUSTICE PECKHAM, after making the foregoing statement, delivered the opinion of the court:

We recognize and appreciate to the fullest extent the very great importance of this case, not only to the parties now before the court, but also to the great mass of the citizens of this country, all of whom are interested in the practical working of the courts of justice throughout the land, both Federal and state, and in the proper exercise of the jurisdiction of the Federal courts, as limited and controlled by the Federal Constitution and the laws of Congress.

That there has been room for difference of opinion with regard to such limitations the reported cases in this court bear conclusive testimony. It

---

than money damages. This means that if a citizen claims that a federal officer is proceeding against him or her illegally and should be enjoined, there is a federal forum available and there is no need to allow state injunctions, with all of their potential for conflict between the two systems. See 17 Wright, Miller & Cooper, Federal Practice and Procedure: Jurisdiction 2d § 4213 (1988).]

cannot be stated that the case before us is entirely free from any possible doubt nor that intelligent men may not differ as to the correct answer to the question we are called upon to decide.

The question of jurisdiction, whether of the Circuit Court or of this court, is frequently a delicate matter to deal with, and it is especially so in this case, where the material and most important objection to the jurisdiction of the Circuit Court is the assertion that the suit is in effect against one of the States of the Union. It is a question, however, which we are called upon, and which it is our duty, to decide....

. . . . .

We conclude that the Circuit Court had jurisdiction in the case before it, because it involved the decision of Federal questions arising under the Constitution of the United States.

Coming to the inquiry regarding the alleged invalidity of these acts, we take up the contention that they are invalid on their face on account of the penalties. For disobedience to the freight act the officers, directors, agents and employees of the company are made guilty of a misdemeanor, and upon conviction each may be punished by imprisonment in the county jail for a period not exceeding ninety days. Each violation would be a separate offense, and, therefore, might result in imprisonment of the various agents of the company who would dare disobey for a term of ninety days each for each offense. Disobedience to the passenger rate act renders the party guilty of a felony and subject to a fine not exceeding five thousand dollars or imprisonment in the state prison for a period not exceeding five years, or both fine and imprisonment. The sale of each ticket above the price permitted by the act would be a violation thereof. It would be difficult, if not impossible, for the company to obtain officers, agents or employees willing to carry on its affairs except in obedience to the act and orders in question. The company itself would also, in case of disobedience, be liable to the immense fines provided for in violating orders of the Commission. The company, in order to test the validity of the acts, must find some agent or employee to disobey them at the risk stated. The necessary effect and result of such legislation must be to preclude a resort to the courts (either state or Federal) for the purpose of testing its validity. The officers and employees could not be expected to disobey any of the provisions of the acts or orders at the risk of such fines and penalties being imposed upon them, in case the court should decide that the law was valid. The result would be a denial of any hearing to the company....

. . . . .

We have, therefore, upon this record the case of an unconstitutional act of the state legislature and an intention by the Attorney General of the State to endeavor to enforce its provisions, to the injury of the company, in compelling it, at great expense, to defend legal proceedings of a complicated and unusual character, and involving questions of vast importance to all employees and officers of the company, as well as to the company itself. The question that arises is whether there is a remedy that the parties interested may resort to, by going into a Federal court of equity, in a case involving a violation of the Federal Constitution . . . .

This inquiry necessitates an examination of the most material and most important objection made to the jurisdiction of the Circuit Court,— the objection being that the suit is, in effect, one against the State of Minnesota, and that the injunction issued against the Attorney General illegally prohibits state action, either criminal or civil, to enforce obedience to the statutes of the State. This objection is to be considered with reference to the Eleventh and Fourteenth Amendments to the Federal Constitution. The Eleventh Amendment prohibits the commencement or prosecution of any suit against one of the United States by citizens of another state or citizens or subjects of any foreign State. The Fourteenth Amendment provides that no State shall deprive any person of life, liberty or property without due process of law, nor shall it deny to any person within its jurisdiction the equal protection of the laws.

The case before the Circuit Court proceeded upon the theory that the orders and acts heretofore mentioned would, if enforced, violate rights of the complainants protected by the latter Amendment. We think that whatever the rights of complainants may be, they are largely founded upon that Amendment, but a decision of this case does not require an examination or decision of the question whether its adoption in any way altered or limited the effect of the earlier Amendment. We may assume that each exists in full force, and that we must give to the Eleventh Amendment all the effect it naturally would have, without cutting it down or rendering its meaning any more narrow than the language, fairly interpreted, would warrant. It applies to a suit brought against a State by one of its own citizens as well as to a suit brought by a citizen of another State. Hans v. Louisiana, 134 U.S. 1. It was adopted after the decision of this court in Chisholm v. Georgia (1793), 2 Dall. [2 U.S.] 419, where it was held that a State might be sued by a citizen of another State. Since that time there have been many cases decided in this court involving the Eleventh Amendment, among them being Osborn v. United States Bank (1824), 9 Wheat. [22 U.S.] 738, 846, 857, which held that the Amendment applied only to those suits in which the State was a party on the record. In the subsequent case of Governor of Georgia v. Madrazo (1828), 1 Pet. [26 U.S.] 110, 122, 123, that holding was somewhat enlarged, and Chief Justice Marshall, delivering the opinion of the court, while citing *Osborn v. United States Bank*, supra, said that where the claim was made, as in the case then before the court, against the Governor of Georgia as governor, and the demand was made upon him, not personally, but officially (for moneys in the treasury of the State and for slaves in possession of the state government) the State might be considered as the party on the record (page 123), and therefore the suit could not be maintained.

Davis v. Gray, 16 Wall. [83 U.S.] 203, 220, reiterates the rule of *Osborn v. United States Bank* so far as concerns the right to enjoin a state officer from executing a state law in conflict with the Constitution or a statute of the United States, when such execution will violate the right of the complainant.

In Virginia Coupon Cases, 114 U.S. 270, 296 (Poindexter v. Greenhow), it was adjudged that a suit against a tax collector who had refused coupons in payment of taxes, and, under color of a void law, was about to seize and sell the property of a taxpayer for non-payment of his taxes, was a suit against him personally as a wrongdoer and not against the State.

Hagood v. Southern, 117 U.S. 52, 67, decided that the bill was in substance a bill for the specific performance of a contract between the complainants and the State of South Carolina, and, although the State was not in name made a party defendant, yet being the actual party to the alleged contract the performance of which was sought and the only party by whom it could be performed, the State was, in effect, a party to the suit, and it could not be maintained for that reason. The things required to be done by the actual defendants were the very things which when done would constitute a performance of the alleged contract by the State.

The cases upon the subject were reviewed, and it was held, [In re] Ayers, 123 U.S. 443, that a bill in equity brought against officers of a State, who, as individuals, have no personal interest in the subject-matter of the suit, and defend only as representing the State, where the relief prayed for, if done, would constitute a performance by the State of the alleged contract of the State, was a suit against the State (page 504), following in this respect *Hagood v. Southern*, supra.

A suit of such a nature was simply an attempt to make the State itself, through its officers, perform its alleged contract, by directing those officers to do acts which constituted such performance. The State alone had any interest in the question, and a decree in favor of plaintiff would affect the treasury of the State.

On the other hand, United States v. Lee, 106 U.S. 196, determined that an individual in possession of real estate under the Government of the United States, which claimed to be its owner, was, nevertheless, properly sued by the plaintiff, as owner, to recover possession, and such suit was not one against the United States, although the individual in possession justified such possession under its authority. See also Tindal v. Wesley, 167 U.S. 204, to the same effect.

In Pennoyer v. McConnaughy, 140 U.S. 1, 9, a suit against land commissioners of the State was said not to be against the State, although the complainants sought to restrain the defendants, officials of the State, from violating, under an unconstitutional act, the complainants' contract with the State, and thereby working irreparable damage to the property rights of the complainants. *Osborn v. United States Bank*, supra, was cited, and it was stated: "But the general doctrine of *Osborn v. Bank of the United States* [supra], that the Circuit Courts of the United States will restrain a state officer from executing an unconstitutional statute of the State, when to execute it would violate rights and privileges of the complainant which had been guaranteed by the Constitution, and would work irreparable damage and injury to him, has never been departed from." The same principle is decided in Scott v. Donald, 165 U.S. 58, 67. And see Missouri & c. v. Missouri Railroad Commission, 183 U.S. 53.

The cases above cited do not include one exactly like this under discussion. They serve to illustrate the principles upon which many cases have been decided. We have not cited all the cases, as we have not thought it necessary. But the injunction asked for in the *Ayers Case*, 123 U.S. (supra), was to restrain the state officers from commencing suits under the act of May 12, 1887 (alleged to be unconstitutional), in the name of the State and brought to *recover taxes for its use*, on the ground that if such suits were commenced they would be a breach of a contract with the State. The injunction was declared illegal because the suit itself could not be entertained as it was one against the State to enforce its alleged contract. It was said, however, that if the court had power to entertain such a suit, it would have power to grant the restraining order preventing the commencement of suits. (Page 487). It was not stated that the suit or the injunction was necessarily confined to a case of a threatened direct trespass upon or injury to property.

Whether the commencement of a suit could ever be regarded as an actionable injury to another, equivalent in some cases to a trespass such as is set forth in some of the foregoing cases, has received attention in the rate cases, so called. Reagan v. Farmers' Loan & Trust Co., 154 U.S. 362 (a rate case), was a suit against the members of a railroad commission (created under an act of the State of Texas) and the Attorney General, all of whom were held suable, and that such suit was not one against the State. The Commission was enjoined from enforcing the rates it had established under the act, and the Attorney General was enjoined from instituting suits to recover penalties for failing to conform to the rates fixed by the Commission under such act. It is true the statute in that case creating the board provided that suit might be maintained by any dissatisfied railroad company, or other party in interest, in a court of competent jurisdiction in Travis County, Texas, against the Commission as defendant. This court held that such language permitted a suit in the United States Circuit Court for the Western District of Texas, which embraced Travis County, but it also held that, irrespective of that consent, the suit was not in effect a suit against the State (although the Attorney General was enjoined), and therefore not prohibited under the Amendment. . . .

     . . . . .

The various authorities we have referred to furnish ample justification for the assertion that individuals, who, as officers of the State, are clothed with some duty in regard to the enforcement of the laws of the State, and who threaten and are about to commence proceedings, either of a civil or criminal nature, to enforce against parties affected an unconstitutional act, violating the Federal Constitution, may be enjoined by a Federal court of equity from such action.

     . . . . .

In making an officer of the State a party defendant in a suit to enjoin the enforcement of an act alleged to be unconstitutional it is plain that such officer must have some connection with the enforcement of the act, or else it is merely making him a party as a representative of the State, and thereby attempting to make the State a party.

It has not, however, been held that it was necessary that such duty should be declared in the same act which is to be enforced. In some cases, it is true, the duty of enforcement has been so imposed (154 U.S. 362, 366, § 19 of the act), but that may possibly make the duty more clear; if it otherwise exists it is equally efficacious. The fact that the state officer by virtue of his office has some connection with the enforcement of the act is the important and material fact, and whether it arises out of the general law, or is specially created by the act itself, is not material so long as it exists.

. . . . .

It is also objected that as the statute does not specifically make it the duty of the Attorney General (assuming he has that general right) to enforce it, he has under such circumstances a full general discretion whether to attempt its enforcement or not, and the court cannot interfere to control him as Attorney General in the exercise of his discretion.

In our view there is no interference with his discretion under the facts herein. There is no doubt that the court cannot control the exercise of the discretion of an officer. . . .

The general discretion regarding the enforcement of the laws when and as he deems appropriate is not interfered with by an injunction which restrains the state officer from taking any steps towards the enforcement of an unconstitutional enactment to the injury of complainant. In such case no affirmative action of any nature is directed, and the officer is simply prohibited from doing an act which he had no legal right to do. An injunction to prevent him from doing that which he has no legal right to do is not an interference with the discretion of an officer.

It is also argued that the only proceeding which the Attorney General could take to enforce the statute, so far as his office is concerned, was one by mandamus, which would be commenced by the State in its sovereign and governmental character, and that the right to bring such action is a necessary attribute of a sovereign government. It is contended that the complainants do not complain and they care nothing about any action which Mr. Young might take or bring as an ordinary individual, but that he was complained of as an officer, to whose discretion is confided the use of the name of the State of Minnesota so far as litigation is concerned, and that when or how he shall use it is a matter resting in his discretion and cannot be controlled by any court.

The answer to all this is the same as made in every case where an official claims to be acting under the authority of the State. The act to be enforced is alleged to be unconstitutional, and if it be so, the use of the name of the State to enforce an unconstitutional act to the injury of complainants is a proceeding without the authority of and one which does not affect the State in its sovereign or governmental capacity. It is simply an illegal act upon the part of a state official in attempting by the use of the name of the State to enforce a legislative enactment which is void because unconstitutional. If the act which the state Attorney General seeks to enforce be a violation of the Federal Constitution, the officer in proceeding under such enactment comes into conflict with the superior authority of that Constitution, and he is in that case stripped of his official or representative character and is subjected in his person to the consequences of his individual conduct. The State has no power to impart to him any immunity from responsibility to the supreme authority of the United States. See [*In re*] *Ayers*, supra, [at p.] 507. . . .

The question remains whether the Attorney General had, by the law of the State, so far as concerns these rate acts, any duty with regard to the enforcement of the same. By his official conduct it seems that he regarded it as a duty connected with his office to compel the company to obey the commodity act, for he commenced proceedings to enforce such obedience immediately after the injunction issued, at the risk of being found guilty of contempt by so doing.

. . . . .

It is further objected (and the objection really forms part of the contention that the State cannot be sued) that a court of equity has no jurisdiction to enjoin criminal proceedings, by indictment or otherwise, under the state law. This, as a general rule, is true. But there are exceptions. When such indictment or proceeding is brought to enforce an alleged unconstitutional statute, which is the subject matter of inquiry in a suit already pending in a Federal court, the latter court having first obtained jurisdiction over the subject matter, has the right, in both civil and criminal cases, to hold and maintain such jurisdiction, to the exclusion of all other courts, until its duty is fully performed. Prout v. Starr, 188 U.S. 537, 544. But the Federal court cannot, of course, interfere in a case where the proceedings were already pending in a state court. Taylor v. Taintor, 16 Wall. [83 U.S.] 366, 370; Harkrader v. Wadley, 172 U.S. 148.

Where one commences a criminal proceeding who is already party to a suit then pending in a court of equity, if the criminal proceedings are brought to enforce the same right that is in issue before that court the latter may enjoin such criminal proceedings. Davis & [Farnum Mfg.] Co. v. Los Angeles, 189 U.S. 207. In Dobbins v. Los Angeles, 195 U.S. 223–241, it is remarked by Mr. Justice Day, in delivering the opinion of the court, that "it is well settled that where property rights will be destroyed, unlawful interference by criminal proceedings under a void law or ordinance may be reached and controlled by a court of equity." . . .

. . . . .

Finally it is objected that the necessary result of upholding this suit in the Circuit Court will be to draw to the lower Federal courts a great flood of litigation of this character, where one Federal judge would have it in his power to enjoin proceedings by state officials to enforce the legislative acts of the State, either by criminal or civil actions. To this it may be answered, in the first place, that no injunction ought to be granted unless in a case reasonably free from doubt. We think such rule is, and will be, followed by all the judges of the Federal courts.

And, again, it must be remembered that jurisdiction of this general character has, in fact, been exercised by Federal courts from the time of *Osborn v. United States Bank*, supra, up to the present; the only difference in regard to the case of *Osborn* and the case in hand being that in this case the injury complained of is the threatened commencement of suits, civil or criminal, to enforce the act, instead of, as in the *Osborn* case, an actual and direct trespass upon or interference with tangible property. A bill filed to prevent the commencement of suits to enforce an unconstitutional act, under the circumstances already mentioned, is no new invention, as we have already seen. The difference between an actual and direct interference with tangible property and the enjoining of state officers from enforcing an unconstitutional act, is not of a radical nature, and does not extend, in truth, the jurisdiction of the courts over the subject matter. In the case of the interference with property the person enjoined is assuming to act in his capacity as an official of the State, and justification for his interference is claimed by reason of his position as a state official. Such official cannot so justify when acting under an unconstitutional enactment of the legislature. So, where the state official, instead of directly interfering with tangible property, is about to commence suits, which have for their object the enforcement of an act which violates the Federal Constitution, to the great and irreparable injury of the complainants, he is seeking the same justification from the authority of the State as in other cases. The sovereignty of the State is, in reality, no more involved in one case than in the other. The State cannot in either case impart to the official immunity from responsibility to the supreme authority of the United States. See [*In re*] *Ayers*, supra, [at p.] 507.

This supreme authority, which arises from the specific provisions of the Constitution itself, is nowhere more fully illustrated than in the series of decisions under the Federal habeas corpus statute (§ 753, Rev.Stat.), in some of which cases persons in the custody of state officers for alleged crimes against the State have been taken from that custody and discharged by a Federal court or judge, because the imprisonment was adjudged to be in violation of the Federal Constitution. . . .

It is somewhat difficult to appreciate the distinction which, while admitting that the taking of such a person from the custody of the State by virtue of service of the writ on the state officer in whose custody he is found, is not a suit against the State, and yet service of a writ on the Attorney General to prevent his enforcing an unconstitutional enactment of a state legislature is a suit against the State.

There is nothing in the case before us that ought properly to breed hostility to the customary operation of Federal courts of justice in cases of this character.

The rule to show cause is discharged and the petition of writs of habeas corpus and certiorari is dismissed.

So ordered.

■ MR. JUSTICE HARLAN, dissenting:

. . . . .

Let it be observed that the suit instituted by Perkins and Shepard in the Circuit Court of the United States was, as to the defendant Young, one against him *as, and only because he was*, Attorney General of Minnesota. No relief was sought against him individually but only in his capacity as Attorney General. And the manifest, indeed the avowed and admitted, object of seeking such relief was *to tie the hands* of the *State* so that it could not in any manner or by any mode of proceeding, *in its own courts*, test the validity of the statutes and orders in question. It would therefore seem clear that within the true meaning of the Eleventh Amendment the suit brought in the Federal court was one, in legal effect, against the State,—as much so as if the State had been formally named on the record as a party,—and therefore it was a suit to which, under the Amendment, so far as the State or its Attorney General was concerned, the judicial power of the United States did not and could not extend. If this proposition be sound it will follow,—indeed, it is conceded that if, so far as relief is sought against the Attorney General of Minnesota, this be a suit against the State,—then the order of the Federal court enjoining that officer from taking any action, suit, step or proceeding to compel the railway company to obey the Minnesota statute was beyond the jurisdiction of that court and wholly void; in which case, that officer was at liberty to proceed in the discharge of his official duties as defined by the laws of the State, and the order adjudging him to be in contempt for bringing the mandamus proceeding in the state court was a nullity.

The fact that the Federal Circuit Court, had, prior to the institution of the mandamus suit in the state court, preliminarily (but not finally) held the statutes of Minnesota and the orders of its Railroad and Warehouse Commission in question to be in violation of the Constitution of the United States, was no reason why that court should have laid violent hands upon the Attorney General of Minnesota and by its orders have deprived the State of the services of its constitutional law officer in its own courts. Yet that is what was done by the Federal Circuit Court; for, the intangible thing, called a State, however extensive its powers, can never appear to be represented or known in any court in a litigated case, except by and through its officers. When, therefore, the Federal court forbade the defendant Young, as Attorney General of Minnesota, from taking any action, suit, step or proceeding whatever looking to the enforcement of the statutes in question, it said in effect to the State of Minnesota: "It is true that the powers not delegated to the United States by the Constitution, nor prohibited by it to the States, are reserved to the States respectively or to its people, and it is true that under the Constitution the judicial power of the United States does not extend to any suit brought against a State by a citizen of another State or by a citizen or subject of a foreign State, yet the Federal court adjudges that you, the State, although a sovereign for many important governmental purposes, shall not appear in your own courts, by your law officer, with the view of enforcing, or even for determining the validity of the state enactments which the Federal court has, upon a preliminary hearing, declared to be in violation of the Constitution of the United States.''

This principle, if firmly established, would work a radical change in our governmental system. It would inaugurate a new era in the American judicial system and in the relations of the National and state governments. It would enable the subordinate Federal courts to supervise and control the official action of the States as if they were "dependencies" or provinces. It would place the States of the Union in a condition of inferiority never dreamed of when the Constitution was adopted or when the Eleventh Amendment was made a part of the Supreme Law of the Land. I cannot suppose that the great men who framed the Constitution ever thought the time would come when a subordinate Federal court, having no power to compel a State, in its corporate capacity, to appear before it as a litigant, would yet assume to deprive a State of the right to be represented in its own courts by its regular law officer. That is what the court below did, as to Minnesota, when it adjudged that the appearance of the defendant Young *in the state court*, as the Attorney General of Minnesota, representing his State as its chief law officer, was a contempt of the authority of the Federal court, punishable by fine and imprisonment. Too little consequence has been attached to the fact that the courts of the States are under an obligation equally strong with that resting upon the courts of the Union to respect and enforce the provisions of the Federal Constitution as the Supreme Law of the Land, and to guard rights secured or guaranteed by that instrument. We must assume—a decent respect for the States requires us to assume—that the state courts will enforce every right secured by the Constitution. If they fail to do so, the party complaining has a clear remedy for the protection of his rights; for, he can come by writ of error, in an orderly, judicial way, from the highest court of the State to this tribunal for redress in respect of every right granted or secured by that instrument and denied by the state court. . . .

. . . . .

I dissent from the opinion and judgment.[23]

———

[23. See Wright & Kane, Federal Courts § 48 (6th ed.2002); 17 Moore's Federal Practice § 123.20 (3d ed.1998); 17 Wright, Miller & Cooper, Federal Practice and Procedure: Jurisdiction 2d §§ 4231–4232 (1988); Duker, Mr. Justice Rufus W. Peckham and the Case of *Ex Parte Young*: *Lochner*izing *Munn v. Illinois*, 1980 B.Y.U.L.Rev. 539.

If the action of the officer is regarded as "individual" for purposes of the Eleventh Amendment, can it be "state" action for purposes of the Fourteenth Amendment? See Home Telephone & Telegraph Co. v. City of Los Angeles, 227 U.S. 278 (1913). See also Davis, Suing the Government by Falsely Pretending to Sue An Officer, 29 U.Chi.L.Rev. (1962).

Seminole Tribe of Florida v. Florida

Supreme Court of the United States, 1996.
517 U.S. 44, 116 S.Ct. 1114, 134 L.Ed.2d 252.

■ CHIEF JUSTICE REHNQUIST delivered the opinion of the Court.

The Indian Gaming Regulatory Act provides that an Indian tribe may conduct certain gaming activities only in conformance with a valid compact between the tribe and the State in which the gaming activities are located. 102 Stat. 2475, 25 U.S.C. § 2710(d)(1)(C). The Act, passed by Congress under the Indian Commerce Clause, U.S. Const., Art. I, § 8, imposes upon the States a duty to negotiate in good faith with an Indian tribe toward the formation of a compact, § 2710(d)(3)(A), and authorizes a tribe to bring suit in federal court against a State in order to compel performance of that duty, § 2710(d)(7)....

I

. . . . .

When the case was decided on the merits, it was held that the rates required by the statute were valid. Minnesota Rate Cases (Simpson v. Shepard), 230 U.S. 352 (1913). Does this mean that Young was not acting unconstitutionally in enforcing the rates, that he was therefore not stripped of his state authority, and that the suit was indeed one against the state and barred by the Eleventh Amendment?

In a case decided a few months after *Ex parte Young*, it was held that an injunction would not lie against enforcement of a state rate order until the state administrative—or "legislative," as they were called by Justice Holmes—remedies had been exhausted. In that case the Virginia Supreme Court of Appeals had such broad powers in passing on orders of the State Corporation Commission that review in that court was required before an injunction could issue. Prentis v. Atlantic Coast Line Co., 211 U.S. 210 (1908). But in Bacon v. Rutland R. Co., 232 U.S. 134 (1914), it was held that the appeal under the Vermont statute was "judicial," and that it did not have to be exhausted.

When suit is brought, however, under the federal civil-rights statute, 42 U.S.C. § 1983, even state administrative remedies need not be first exhausted. Patsy v. Board of Regents of Florida, 457 U.S. 496 (1982).

In District of Columbia Court of Appeals v. Feldman, 460 U.S. 462 (1983), it was held that the refusal of the District of Columbia Court of Appeals to waive a bar-admission rule is a judicial, not a legislative or ministerial act, and that district courts therefore lack jurisdiction to review it. This is often referred to as "the *Rooker–Feldman* doctrine," discussed infra p. 652.

In a case that allowed an abortion clinic to proceed with its challenge to test the constitutionality of state antiabortion laws, the Eleventh Circuit held that a showing of imminent enforcement of an allegedly unconstitutional state law is not required in a suit seeking prospective injunctive relief against a state officer under the doctrine of *Ex parte Young*. Summit Medical Associates, P.C. v. Pryor, 180 F.3d 1326 (11th Cir.1999).

In undertaking an Ex Parte Young inquiry, the Supreme Court has observed that a court need only conduct a "straightforward inquiry into whether [the] complaint alleges an ongoing violation of federal law and seeks relief properly characterized as prospective." Applying this standard, the Supreme Court held that claims brought by the Virginia Office for Protection and Advocacy, seeking access to records related to the deaths of patients at state-run psychiatric hospitals, could proceed without violating the Eleventh Amendment. Virginia Office for Protection and Advocacy v. Stewart, 563 U.S. ___, 131 S.Ct. 1632 (2011).]

In September 1991, the Seminole Tribe of Indians, petitioner, sued the State of Florida and its Governor, Lawton Chiles, respondents. Invoking jurisdiction under 25 U.S.C. § 2710(d)(7)(A), as well as 28 U.S.C. §§ 1331 and 1362, petitioner alleged that respondents had "refused to enter into any negotiation for inclusion of [certain gaming activities] in a tribal-state compact," thereby violating the "requirement of good faith negotiation" contained in § 2710(d)(3).... Respondents moved to dismiss the complaint, arguing that the suit violated the State's sovereign immunity from suit in federal court. The District Court denied respondents' motion, 801 F.Supp. 655 (S.D.Fla.1992), and the respondents took an interlocutory appeal of that decision. See Puerto Rico Aqueduct and Sewer Authority v. Metcalf & Eddy, Inc., 506 U.S. 139 (1993) (collateral order doctrine allows immediate appellate review of order denying claim of Eleventh Amendment immunity).

The Court of Appeals for the Eleventh Circuit reversed the decision of the District Court, holding that the Eleventh Amendment barred petitioner's suit against respondents. 11 F.3d 1016 (1994)....

Petitioner sought our review of the Eleventh Circuit's decision, and we granted certiorari, 513 U.S. 1125 (1995), in order to consider two questions: (1) Does the Eleventh Amendment prevent Congress from authorizing suits by Indian tribes against States for prospective injunctive relief to enforce legislation enacted pursuant to the Indian Commerce Clause?; and (2) Does the doctrine of Ex parte Young [209 U.S. 123 (1908)] permit suits against a State's governor for prospective injunctive relief to enforce the good faith bargaining requirement of the Act? We answer the first question in the affirmative, the second in the negative, and we therefore affirm the Eleventh Circuit's dismissal of petitioner's suit.

The Eleventh Amendment provides:

> "The Judicial power of the United States shall not be construed to extend to any suit in law or equity, commenced or prosecuted against one of the United States by Citizens of another State, or by Citizens or Subjects of any Foreign State."

Although the text of the Amendment would appear to restrict only the Article III diversity jurisdiction of the federal courts, "we have understood the Eleventh Amendment to stand not so much for what it says, but for the presupposition ... which it confirms." Blatchford v. Native Village of Noatak, 501 U.S. 775, 779 (1991). That presupposition, first observed over a century ago in Hans v. Louisiana, 134 U.S. 1 (1890), has two parts: first, that each State is a sovereign entity in our federal system; and second, that " '[i]t is inherent in the nature of sovereignty not to be amenable to the suit of an individual without its consent.' " Id., at 13 (emphasis deleted), quoting The Federalist No. 81, p. 487 (C. Rossiter ed.1961)(A. Hamilton). See also *Puerto Rico Aqueduct and Sewer Authority*, supra, at 146 ("The Amendment is rooted in a recognition that the States, although a union, maintain certain attributes of sovereignty, including sovereign immunity"). For over a century we have reaffirmed that federal jurisdiction over suits against unconsenting States "was not contemplated by the Constitution when establishing the judicial power of the United States." *Hans*, supra, at 15.

Here, petitioner has sued the State of Florida and it is undisputed that Florida has not consented to the suit. See *Blatchford*, supra, at 782 (States by entering into the Constitution did not consent to suit by Indian tribes). Petitioner nevertheless contends that its suit is not barred by state sovereign immunity. First, it argues that Congress through the Act abrogated the States' sovereign immunity. Alternatively, petitioner maintains that its suit against the Governor may go forward under *Ex parte Young*, supra. We consider each of those arguments in turn.

II

Petitioner argues that Congress through the Act abrogated the States' immunity from suit. In order to determine whether Congress has abrogated the States' sovereign immunity, we ask two questions: first, whether Congress has "unequivocally expresse[d] its intent to abrogate the immunity," Green v. Mansour, 474 U.S. 64, 68 (1985); and second, whether Congress has acted "pursuant to a valid exercise of power." Ibid.

A

. . . . .

[W]e agree with the parties, with the Eleventh Circuit in the decision below, 11 F.3d, at 1024, and with virtually every other court that has confronted the question that Congress has in § 2710(d)(7) provided an "unmistakably clear" statement of its intent to abrogate.... [W]e think that the numerous references to the "State" in the text of § 2710(d)(7)(B) make it indubitable that Congress intended through the Act to abrogate the States' sovereign immunity from suit.[24]

B

Having concluded that Congress clearly intended to abrogate the States' sovereign immunity through § 2710(d)(7), we turn now to consider whether the Act was passed "pursuant to a valid exercise of power." *Green v. Mansour*, 474 U.S., at 68. Before we address that question here, however, we think it necessary first to define the scope of our inquiry.

Petitioner suggests that one consideration weighing in favor of finding the power to abrogate here is that the Act authorizes only prospective injunctive relief rather than retroactive monetary relief. But we have often

---

24. JUSTICE SOUTER, in his dissenting opinion, argues that in order to avoid a constitutional question, we should interpret the Act to provide only a suit against state officials rather than a suit against the State itself. But in light of the plain text of § 2710(d)(7)(B), we disagree with the dissent's assertion that the Act can reasonably be read in that way. "We cannot press statutory construction 'to the point of disingenuous evasion' even to avoid a constitutional question." See United States v. Locke, 471 U.S. 84, 96, (1985), quoting George Moore Ice Cream Co. v. Rose, 289 U.S. 373, 379 (1933) (Cardozo, J.). We already have found the clear statement rule satisfied, and that finding renders the preference for avoiding a constitutional question inapplicable.

made it clear that the relief sought by a plaintiff suing a State is irrelevant to the question whether the suit is barred by the Eleventh Amendment. See, e.g., Cory v. White, 457 U.S. 85, 90 (1982) ("It would be a novel proposition indeed that the Eleventh Amendment does not bar a suit to enjoin the State itself simply because no money judgment is sought"). We think it follows a fortiori from this proposition that the type of relief sought is irrelevant to whether Congress has power to abrogate States' immunity. The Eleventh Amendment does not exist solely in order to "preven[t] federal court judgments that must be paid out of a State's treasury," Hess v. Port Authority Trans–Hudson Corporation, 513 U.S. 30, 48 (1994); it also serves to avoid "the indignity of subjecting a State to the coercive process of judicial tribunals at the instance of private parties," *Puerto Rico Aqueduct and Sewer Authority*, 506 U.S., at 146 (internal quotation marks omitted).

Similarly, petitioner argues that the abrogation power is validly exercised here because the Act grants the States a power that they would not otherwise have, viz., some measure of authority over gaming on Indian lands. It is true enough that the Act extends to the States a power withheld from them by the Constitution. See California v. Cabazon Band of Mission Indians, 480 U.S. 202 (1987). Nevertheless, we do not see how that consideration is relevant to the question whether Congress may abrogate state sovereign immunity. The Eleventh Amendment immunity may not be lifted by Congress unilaterally deciding that it will be replaced by grant of some other authority. Cf. [Atascadero State Hospital v. Scanlon, 473 U.S. 246–247 (1985)] ("[T]he mere receipt of federal funds cannot establish that a State has consented to suit in federal court").

Thus our inquiry into whether Congress has the power to abrogate unilaterally the States' immunity from suit is narrowly focused on one question: Was the Act in question passed pursuant to a constitutional provision granting Congress the power to abrogate? See, e.g., Fitzpatrick v. Bitzer, 427 U.S. 445, 452–456 (1976). Previously, in conducting that inquiry, we have found authority to abrogate under only two provisions of the Constitution. In *Fitzpatrick*, we recognized that the Fourteenth Amendment, by expanding federal power at the expense of state autonomy, had fundamentally altered the balance of state and federal power struck by the Constitution. Id., at 455. We noted that § 1 of the Fourteenth Amendment contained prohibitions expressly directed at the States and that § 5 of the Amendment expressly provided that "The Congress shall have the power to enforce, by appropriate legislation, the provisions of this article." See id., at 453 (internal quotation marks omitted). We held that through the Fourteenth Amendment, federal power extended to intrude upon the province of the Eleventh Amendment and therefore that § 5 of the Fourteenth Amendment allowed Congress to abrogate the immunity from suit guaranteed by that Amendment.[25]

[25. It was held in *Fitzpatrick* that both retroactive payments and attorneys' fees could be
    ordered against a state since Congress, exercising its enforcement powers of § 5 of the

In only one other case has congressional abrogation of the States' Eleventh Amendment immunity been upheld. In Pennsylvania v. Union Gas Co., 491 U.S. 1 (1989), a plurality of the Court found that the Interstate Commerce Clause, Art. I, § 8, cl. 3, granted Congress the power to abrogate state sovereign immunity, stating that the power to regulate interstate commerce would be "incomplete without the authority to render States liable in damages." 491 U.S., at 19–20. Justice White added the fifth vote necessary to the result in that case, but wrote separately in order to express that he "[did] not agree with much of [the plurality's] reasoning." Id., at 57 (White, J., concurring in judgment in part and dissenting in part).

. . . . .

Both parties make their arguments from the plurality decision in *Union Gas*, and we, too, begin there. We think it clear that Justice Brennan's opinion finds Congress' power to abrogate under the Interstate Commerce Clause from the States' cession of their sovereignty when they gave Congress plenary power to regulate interstate commerce. . . .

Following the rationale of the *Union Gas* plurality, our inquiry is limited to determining whether the Indian Commerce Clause, like the Interstate Commerce Clause, is a grant of authority to the Federal Government at the expense of the States. The answer to that question is obvious. If anything, the Indian Commerce Clause accomplishes a greater transfer of power from the States to the Federal Government than does the Interstate Commerce Clause. This is clear enough from the fact that the States still exercise some authority over interstate trade but have been divested of virtually all authority over Indian commerce and Indian tribes. Under the rationale of *Union Gas*, if the States' partial cession of authority over a particular area includes cession of the immunity from suit, then their virtually total cession of authority over a different area must also include cession of the immunity from suit. . . . We agree with the petitioner that the plurality opinion in *Union Gas* allows no principled distinction in favor of the States to be drawn between the Indian Commerce Clause and the Interstate Commerce Clause.

Respondents argue, however, that we need not conclude that the Indian Commerce Clause grants the power to abrogate the States' sovereign immunity. Instead, they contend that if we find the rationale of the *Union Gas* plurality to extend to the Indian Commerce Clause, then "*Union Gas* should be reconsidered and overruled." . . . Generally, the principle of stare decisis, and the interests that it serves, viz., "the evenhanded, predictable, and consistent development of legal principles, . . . reliance on judicial decisions, and . . . the actual and perceived integrity of the judicial process," Payne v. Tennessee, 501 U.S. 808, 827 (1991), counsel strongly against reconsideration of our precedent. Nevertheless, we always have treated stare decisis as a "principle of policy," Helvering v. Hallock, 309 U.S. 106, 119 (1940), and not as an "inexorable command,"

Fourteenth Amendment, had so provided in a 1972 statute amending Title VII of the Civil Rights Act of 1964.]

Payne, 501 U.S., at 828. "[W]hen governing decisions are unworkable or are badly reasoned, 'this Court has never felt constrained to follow precedent.' " Id., at 827 (quoting Smith v. Allwright, 321 U.S. 649, 665 (1944)). Our willingness to reconsider our earlier decisions has been "particularly true in constitutional cases, because in such cases 'correction through legislative action is practically impossible.' " *Payne*, supra, at 828, (quoting Burnet v. Coronado Oil & Gas Co., 285 U.S. 393, 407 (1932) (Brandeis, J., dissenting)).

The Court in *Union Gas* reached a result without an expressed rationale agreed upon by a majority of the Court. We have already seen that Justice Brennan's opinion received the support of only three other Justices. See *Union Gas*, supra, at 5 (Marshall, Blackmun, and STEVENS, JJ., joined Justice Brennan). Of the other five, Justice White, who provided the fifth vote for the result, wrote separately in order to indicate his disagreement with the majority's rationale, id., at 57 (White, J., concurring in judgment and dissenting in part), and four Justices joined together in a dissent that rejected the plurality's rationale. Id., at 35–45 (SCALIA, J., dissenting, joined by REHNQUIST, C.J., and O'CONNOR and KENNEDY, JJ.). Since it was issued, *Union Gas* has created confusion among the lower courts that have sought to understand and apply the deeply fractured decision. See, e.g., [Chavez v. Arte Publico Press, 59 F.3d 539, 543–545 (CA5 1995)] ("Justice White's concurrence must be taken on its face to disavow" the plurality's theory); [and the opinion of the court below in this case,] 11 F.3d, at 1027 (Justice White's "vague concurrence renders the continuing validity of *Union Gas* in doubt").

The plurality's rationale also deviated sharply from our established federalism jurisprudence and essentially eviscerated our decision in *Hans*. See *Union Gas*, supra, at 36 ("If *Hans* means only that federal-question suits for money damages against the States cannot be brought in federal court unless Congress clearly says so, it means nothing at all") (SCALIA, J., dissenting). It was well established in 1989 when *Union Gas* was decided that the Eleventh Amendment stood for the constitutional principle that state sovereign immunity limited the federal courts' jurisdiction under Article III. The text of the Amendment itself is clear enough on this point: "The Judicial power of the United States shall not be construed to extend to any suit . . . ." And our decisions since *Hans* had been equally clear that the Eleventh Amendment reflects "the fundamental principle of sovereign immunity [that] limits the grant of judicial authority in Article III," Pennhurst State School and Hospital v. Halderman, 465 U.S. 89, 97–98 (1984); see *Union Gas*, supra, at 38, (" '[T]he entire judicial power granted by the Constitution does not embrace authority to entertain a suit brought by private parties against a State without consent given . . .' ") (SCALIA, J., dissenting) (quoting Ex parte New York, 256 U.S. 490, 497 (1921)) . . . . As the dissent in *Union Gas* recognized, the plurality's conclusion—that Congress could under Article I expand the scope of the federal courts' jurisdiction under Article III—"contradict[ed] our unvarying approach to Article III as setting forth the *exclusive* catalog of permissible federal court jurisdiction." *Union Gas*, supra, at 39.

Never before the decision in *Union Gas* had we suggested that the bounds of Article III could be expanded by Congress operating pursuant to any constitutional provision other than the Fourteenth Amendment. Indeed, it had seemed fundamental that Congress could not expand the jurisdiction of the federal courts beyond the bounds of Article III. Marbury v. Madison, 1 Cranch [5 U.S.] 137 (1803). The plurality's citation of prior decisions for support was based upon what we believe to be a misreading of precedent. See *Union Gas*, 491 U.S., at 40–41 (Scalia, J., dissenting). The plurality claimed support for its decision from a case holding the unremarkable, and completely unrelated, proposition that the States may waive their sovereign immunity, see id., at 14–15 (citing Parden v. Terminal Railway of Ala. State Docks Dept., 377 U.S. 184 (1964)), and cited as precedent propositions that had been merely assumed for the sake of argument in earlier cases, see 491 U.S., at 15 (citing [Welch v. Texas Dept. of Highways & Pub. Transp., 483 U.S. 468, 475–476, & n. 5 (1987)], and [County of Oneida v. Oneida Indian Nation of N.Y., 470 U.S. 226, 252 (1985)]).

The plurality's extended reliance upon our decision in Fitzpatrick v. Bitzer, 427 U.S. 445 (1976), that Congress could under the Fourteenth Amendment abrogate the States' sovereign immunity was also, we believe, misplaced. *Fitzpatrick* was based upon a rationale wholly inapplicable to the Interstate Commerce Clause, viz., that the Fourteenth Amendment, adopted well after the adoption of the Eleventh Amendment and the ratification of the Constitution, operated to alter the pre-existing balance between state and federal power achieved by Article III and the Eleventh Amendment. Id., at 454. As the dissent in *Union Gas* made clear, *Fitzpatrick* cannot be read to justify "limitation of the principle embodied in the Eleventh Amendment through appeal to antecedent provisions of the Constitution." *Union Gas*, 491 U.S., at 42 (Scalia, J., dissenting).

In the five years since it was decided, *Union Gas* has proven to be a solitary departure from established law. See Puerto Rico Aqueduct and Sewer Authority v. Metcalf & Eddy, Inc., 506 U.S. 139 (1993). Reconsidering the decision in *Union Gas*, we conclude that none of the policies underlying stare decisis require our continuing adherence to its holding. The decision has, since its issuance, been of questionable precedential value, largely because a majority of the Court expressly disagreed with the rationale of the plurality. See Nichols v. United States, 511 U.S. 738, 746 (1994) (the "degree of confusion following a splintered decision ... is itself a reason for reexamining that decision"). The case involved the interpretation of the Constitution and therefore may be altered only by constitutional amendment or revision by this Court. Finally, both the result in *Union Gas* and the plurality's rationale depart from our established understanding of the Eleventh Amendment and undermine the accepted function of Article III. We feel bound to conclude that *Union Gas* was wrongly decided and that it should be, and now is, overruled.

The dissent makes no effort to defend the decision in *Union Gas*, but nonetheless would find congressional power to abrogate in this case.[26] Contending that our decision is a novel extension of the Eleventh Amendment, the dissent chides us for "attend[ing]" to dicta. We adhere in this case, however, not to mere obiter dicta, but rather to the well-established rationale upon which the Court based the results of its earlier decisions. When an opinion issues for the Court, it is not only the result but also those portions of the opinion necessary to that result by which we are bound. Cf. Burnham v. Superior Court of Cal., County of Marin, 495 U.S. 604, 613 (1990) (exclusive basis of a judgment is not dicta) (plurality); Allegheny County v. American Civil Liberties Union, Greater Pittsburgh Chapter, 492 U.S. 573, 668 (1989) ("As a general rule, the principle of stare decisis directs us to adhere not only to the holdings of our prior cases, but also to their explications of the governing rules of law.") (KENNEDY, J., concurring and dissenting); Sheet Metal Workers v. EEOC, 478 U.S. 421, 490 (1986) ("Although technically dicta, . . . an important part of the Court's rationale for the result that it reache[s] . . . is entitled to greater weight . . .") (O'CONNOR, J., concurring). For over a century, we have grounded our decisions in the oft-repeated understanding of state sovereign immunity as an essential part of the Eleventh Amendment. In Principality of Monaco v. Mississippi, 292 U.S. 313 (1934), the Court held that the Eleventh Amendment barred a suit brought against a State by a foreign state. Chief Justice Hughes wrote for a unanimous Court:

> "[N]either the literal sweep of the words of Clause one of § 2 of Article III, nor the absence of restriction in the letter of the Eleventh Amendment, permits the conclusion that in all controversies of the sort described in Clause one, and omitted from the words of the Eleventh Amendment, a State may be sued without her consent. Thus Clause one specifically provides that the judicial power shall extend 'to all Cases, in Law and Equity, arising under this Constitution, the Laws of the United States, and Treaties made, or which shall be made, under their Authority.' But, although a case may arise under the Constitution and laws of the United States, the judicial power does not extend to it if the suit is sought to be prosecuted against a State, without her consent, by one of her own citizens . . . ."

> "Manifestly, we cannot rest with a mere literal application of the words of § 2 of Article III, or assume that the letter of the Eleventh Amendment exhausts the restrictions upon suits against non-consenting States. Behind the words of the constitutional provisions are postulates which limit and control. There is the essential postulate that the controversies, as contemplated, shall be found to be of a justiciable character. There is also the postulate that States of the Union, still possessing attributes of sovereignty, shall be immune from suits, without their consent, save where there has been a 'surrender of this immunity in the plan of the convention.' "

---

26. Unless otherwise indicated, all references to the dissent are to the dissenting opinion authored by JUSTICE SOUTER.

Id., at 321–323 (citations and footnote omitted); see id., at 329–330; see also *Pennhurst*, 465 U.S., at 98 ("In short, the principle of sovereign immunity is a constitutional limitation on the federal judicial power established in Art. III"); [Ex parte New York, 256 U.S. 490, 497 (1921)] ("[T]he entire judicial power granted by the Constitution does not embrace authority to entertain a suit brought by private parties against a State without consent given ..."). It is true that we have not had occasion previously to apply established Eleventh Amendment principles to the question whether Congress has the power to abrogate state sovereign immunity (save in *Union Gas*). But consideration of that question must proceed with fidelity to this century-old doctrine.

The dissent, to the contrary, disregards our case law in favor of a theory cobbled together from law review articles and its own version of historical events. The dissent cites not a single decision since *Hans* (other than *Union Gas*) that supports its view of state sovereign immunity, instead relying upon the now-discredited decision in Chisholm v. Georgia, 2 Dall. [2 U.S.] 419 (1793).... Its undocumented and highly speculative extralegal explanation of the decision in *Hans* is a disservice to the Court's traditional method of adjudication.

The dissent mischaracterizes the *Hans* opinion. That decision found its roots not solely in the common law of England, but in the much more fundamental " 'jurisprudence in all civilized nations.' " *Hans*, 134 U.S., at 17, quoting Beers v. Arkansas, 20 How. [61 U.S.] 527, 529 (1858); see also The Federalist No. 81, p. 487 (C. Rossiter ed.1961) (A. Hamilton) (sovereign immunity "is the general sense and the general practice of mankind"). The dissent's proposition that the common law of England, where adopted by the States, was open to change by the legislature, is wholly unexceptionable and largely beside the point: that common law provided the substantive rules of law rather than jurisdiction. Cf. *Monaco*, supra, at 323 (state sovereign immunity, like the requirement that there be a "justiciable" controversy, is a constitutionally grounded limit on federal jurisdiction). It also is noteworthy that the principle of state sovereign immunity stands distinct from other principles of the common law in that only the former prompted a specific constitutional amendment.

Hans—with a much closer vantage point than the dissent—recognized that the decision in *Chisholm* was contrary to the well-understood meaning of the Constitution. The dissent's conclusion that the decision in *Chisholm* was "reasonable," ... certainly would have struck the Framers of the Eleventh Amendment as quite odd: that decision created "such a shock of surprise that the Eleventh Amendment was at once proposed and adopted." *Monaco*, supra, at 325. The dissent's lengthy analysis of the text of the Eleventh Amendment is directed at a straw man—we long have recognized that blind reliance upon the text of the Eleventh Amendment is " 'to strain the Constitution and the law to a construction never imagined or dreamed of.' " *Monaco*, 292 U.S., at 326, quoting *Hans*, 134 U.S., at 15. The text dealt in terms only with the problem presented by the decision in *Chisholm*; in light of the fact that the federal courts did not have federal question jurisdiction at the time the Amendment was passed (and would not have it until 1875), it seems unlikely that much thought was given to the prospect of federal question jurisdiction over the States.

That same consideration causes the dissent's criticism of the views of Marshall, Madison, and Hamilton to ring hollow. The dissent cites statements made by those three influential Framers, the most natural reading of which would preclude all federal jurisdiction over an unconsenting State. Struggling against this reading, however, the dissent finds significant the absence of any contention that sovereign immunity would affect the new federal-question jurisdiction.... But the lack of any statute vesting general federal question jurisdiction in the federal courts until much later makes the dissent's demand for greater specificity about a then-dormant jurisdiction overly exacting.[27]

In putting forward a new theory of state sovereign immunity, the dissent develops its own vision of the political system created by the Framers, concluding with the statement that "[t]he Framer's principal objectives in rejecting English theories of unitary sovereignty ... would have been impeded if a new concept of sovereign immunity had taken its place in federal question cases, and would have been substantially thwarted if that new immunity had been held untouchable by any congressional effort to abrogate it." [28] ... This sweeping statement ignores the fact that the Nation survived for nearly two centuries without the question of the existence of such power ever being presented to this Court. And Congress itself waited nearly a century before even conferring federal-question jurisdiction on the lower federal courts.[29]

---

27. Although the absence of any discussion dealing with federal-question jurisdiction is therefore unremarkable, what is notably lacking in the Framers' statements is any mention of Congress' power to abrogate the States' immunity. The absence of any discussion of that power is particularly striking in light of the fact that the Framers virtually always were very specific about the exception to state sovereign immunity arising from a State's consent to suit. See, e.g., The Federalist No. 81, pp. 487–488 (C. Rossiter ed.1961) (A. Hamilton) ("It is inherent in the nature of sovereignty not to be amenable to the suit of an individual *without its consent*.... Unless, therefore, there is a surrender of this immunity in the plan of the convention, it will remain with the States and the danger intimated must be merely ideal") (emphasis in the original); 3 J. Elliot, [Debates on the Federal Constitution] 533 [(2d ed.1836)] (J. Madison) ("It is not in the power of individuals to call any state into court.... [The Constitution] can have no operation but this: ... if a state should condescend to be a party, this court may take cognizance of it").

28. This argument wholly disregards other methods of ensuring the States' compliance with federal law: the Federal Government can bring suit in federal court against a State, see, e.g., United States v. Texas, 143 U.S. 621, 644–645 (1892) (finding such power necessary to the "permanence of the Union"); an individual can bring suit against a state officer in order to ensure that the officer's conduct is in compliance with federal law, see, e.g., Ex parte Young, 209 U.S. 123 (1908); and this Court is empowered to review a question of federal law arising from a state-court decision where a State has consented to suit, see, e.g., Cohens v. Virginia, 6 Wheat. [19 U.S.] 264 (1821).

29. Justice Stevens, in his dissenting opinion, makes two points that merit separate response. First, he contends that no distinction may be drawn between state sovereign immunity and the immunity enjoyed by state and federal officials. But even assuming that the latter has no constitutional foundation, the distinction is clear: The Constitution specifically recog-

In overruling *Union Gas* today, we reconfirm that the background principle of state sovereign immunity embodied in the Eleventh Amendment is not so ephemeral as to dissipate when the subject of the suit is an area, like the regulation of Indian commerce, that is under the exclusive control of the Federal Government. Even when the Constitution vests in Congress complete law-making authority over a particular area, the Eleventh Amendment prevents congressional authorization of suits by private parties against unconsenting States.[30] The Eleventh Amendment restricts the judicial power under Article III, and Article I cannot be used to circumvent the constitutional limitations placed upon federal jurisdiction. Petitioner's suit against the State of Florida must be dismissed for a lack of jurisdiction.

III

Petitioner argues that we may exercise jurisdiction over its suit to enforce § 2710(d)(3) against the Governor notwithstanding the jurisdictional bar of the Eleventh Amendment. Petitioner notes that since our decision

---

nizes the States as sovereign entities, while government officials enjoy no such constitutional recognition. Second, JUSTICE STEVENS criticizes our prior decisions applying the "clear statement rule," suggesting that they were based upon an understanding that Article I allowed Congress to abrogate state sovereign immunity. His criticism, however, ignores the fact that many of those cases arose in the context of a statute passed under the Fourteenth Amendment, where Congress' authority to abrogate is undisputed. See, e.g., Quern v. Jordan, 440 U.S. 332 (1979). And a more fundamental flaw of the criticism is its failure to recognize that both the doctrine requiring avoidance of constitutional questions, and principles of federalism, require us always to apply the clear statement rule before we consider the constitutional question whether Congress has the power to abrogate.

30.   JUSTICE STEVENS understands our opinion to prohibit federal jurisdiction over suits to enforce the bankruptcy, copyright, and antitrust laws against the States. He notes that federal jurisdiction over those statutory schemes is exclusive, and therefore concludes that there is "no remedy" for state violations of those federal statutes.

That conclusion is exaggerated both in its substance and in its significance. First, JUSTICE STEVENS' statement is misleadingly overbroad. We have already seen that several avenues remain open for ensuring state compliance with federal law. Most notably, an individual may obtain injunctive relief under *Ex parte Young* in order to remedy a state officer's ongoing violation of federal law. Second, contrary to the implication of JUSTICE STEVENS' conclusion, it has not been widely thought that the federal antitrust, bankruptcy, or copyright statutes abrogated the States' sovereign immunity. This Court never has awarded relief against a State under any of those statutory schemes; in the decision of this Court that JUSTICE STEVENS cites (and somehow labels "incompatible" with our decision here), we specifically reserved the question whether the Eleventh Amendment would allow a suit to enforce the antitrust laws against a State. See Goldfarb v. Virginia State Bar, 421 U.S. 773, 792 n. 22 (1975). Although the copyright and bankruptcy laws have existed practically since our nation's inception, and the antitrust laws have been in force for over a century, there is no established tradition in the lower federal courts of allowing enforcement of those federal statutes against the States. Notably, both Court of Appeals decisions cited by JUSTICE STEVENS were issued last year and were based upon *Union Gas*. See Chavez v. Arte Publico Press, 59 F.3d 539 (CA5 1995); Matter of Merchants Grain, Inc. v. Mahern, 59 F.3d 630 (CA7 1995). Indeed, while the Court of Appeals in *Chavez* allowed the suit against the State to go forward, it expressly recognized that its holding was unprecedented. See *Chavez*, 59 F.3d, at 546 ("we are aware of no case that specifically holds that laws passed pursuant to the Copyright Clause can abrogate State immunity").

in Ex parte Young, 209 U.S. 123 (1908), we often have found federal jurisdiction over a suit against a state official when that suit seeks only prospective injunctive relief in order to "end a continuing violation of federal law." *Green v. Mansour*, 474 U.S., at 68. The situation presented here, however, is sufficiently different from that giving rise to the traditional *Ex parte Young* action so as to preclude the availability of that doctrine.

Here, the "continuing violation of federal law" alleged by petitioner is the Governor's failure to bring the State into compliance with § 2710(d)(3). But the duty to negotiate imposed upon the State by that statutory provision does not stand alone. Rather, as we have seen, ... Congress passed § 2710(d)(3) in conjunction with the carefully crafted and intricate remedial scheme set forth in § 2710(d)(7).[31]

Where Congress has created a remedial scheme for the enforcement of a particular federal right, we have, in suits against federal officers, refused to supplement that scheme with one created by the judiciary. Schweiker v. Chilicky, 487 U.S. 412, 423 (1988) ("When the design of a Government program suggests that Congress has provided what it considers adequate remedial mechanisms for constitutional violations that may occur in the course of its administration, we have not created additional ... remedies"). Here, of course, the question is not whether a remedy should be created, but instead is whether the Eleventh Amendment bar should be

---

[**31.** The Act discriminates between three different classes of gaming on Indian lands. Most heavily regulated is class III gaming, the type at issue in this suit. It is defined as "all forms of gaming that are not class I gaming or class II gaming," § 2703(8), and includes such things as slot machines, casino games, banking card games, dog racing, and lotteries. The Act provides that class III gaming is lawful only where it is: (1) authorized by an ordinance or resolution that (a) is adopted by the governing body of the Indian tribe, (b) satisfies certain statutorily prescribed requirements, and (c) is approved by the National Indian Gaming Commission; (2) located in a State that permits such gaming for any purpose by any person, organization, or entity; and (3) "conducted in conformance with a Tribal–State compact entered into by the Indian tribe and the State under paragraph (3) that is in effect." § 2710(d)(1). "Paragraph (3)" refers to § 2710(d)(3), which describes the permissible scope of a Tribal–State compact, provides that it is effective only upon publication in the Federal Register, and describes the process by which a State and an Indian tribe begin negotiations toward a Tribal–State compact:

Any Indian tribe having jurisdiction over the Indian lands upon which a class III gaming activity is being conducted, or is to be conducted, shall request the State in which such lands are located to enter into negotiations for the purpose of entering into a Tribal–State compact governing the conduct of gaming activities. Upon receiving such a request, the State shall negotiate with the Indian tribe in good faith to enter into such a compact.

The State's obligation to "negotiate with the Indian tribe in good faith," is made judicially enforceable by §§ 2710(d)(7)(A)(i) and (B)(i):

(A) The United States district courts shall have jurisdiction over—

(i) any cause of action initiated by an Indian tribe arising from the failure of a State to enter into negotiations with the Indian tribe for the purpose of entering into a Tribal–State compact under paragraph (3) or to conduct such negotiations in good faith....

(B)(i) An Indian tribe may initiate a cause of action described in subparagraph (A)(i) only after the close of the 180–day period beginning on the date on which the Indian tribe requested the State to enter into negotiations under paragraph (3)(A).]

lifted, as it was in *Ex parte Young*, in order to allow a suit against a state officer. Nevertheless, we think that the same general principle applies: therefore, where Congress has prescribed a detailed remedial scheme for the enforcement against a State of a statutorily created right, a court should hesitate before casting aside those limitations and permitting an action against a state officer based upon *Ex parte Young*.

Here, Congress intended § 2710(d)(3) to be enforced against the State in an action brought under § 2710(d)(7); the intricate procedures set forth in that provision show that Congress intended therein not only to define, but also significantly to limit, the duty imposed by § 2710(d)(3). For example, where the court finds that the State has failed to negotiate in good faith, the only remedy prescribed is an order directing the State and the Indian tribe to conclude a compact within 60 days. And if the parties disregard the court's order and fail to conclude a compact within the 60–day period, the only sanction is that each party then must submit a proposed compact to a mediator who selects the one which best embodies the terms of the Act. Finally, if the State fails to accept the compact selected by the mediator, the only sanction against it is that the mediator shall notify the Secretary of the Interior who then must prescribe regulations governing Class III gaming on the tribal lands at issue. By contrast with this quite modest set of sanctions, an action brought against a state official under *Ex parte Young* would expose that official to the full remedial powers of a federal court, including, presumably, contempt sanctions. If § 2710(d)(3) could be enforced in a suit under *Ex parte Young*, § 2710(d)(7) would have been superfluous; it is difficult to see why an Indian tribe would suffer through the intricate scheme of § 2710(d)(7) when more complete and more immediate relief would be available under *Ex parte Young*.[32]

Here, of course, we have found that Congress does not have authority under the Constitution to make the State suable in federal court under § 2710(d)(7). Nevertheless, the fact that Congress chose to impose upon the

---

32. Contrary to the claims of the dissent, we do not hold that Congress *cannot* authorize federal jurisdiction under *Ex parte Young* over a cause of action with a limited remedial scheme. We find only that Congress did not intend that result in the Indian Gaming Regulatory Act. Although one might argue that the text of § 2710(d)(7)(A)(i), taken alone, is broad enough to encompass both a suit against a State (under an abrogation theory) and a suit against a state official (under an *Ex parte Young* theory), subsection (A)(i) of § 2710(d)(7) cannot be read in isolation from subsections (B)(ii)–(vii), which repeatedly refers exclusively to "the State." ... In this regard, § 2710(d)(7) stands in contrast to the statutes cited by the dissent as examples where lower courts have found that Congress implicitly authorized suit under *Ex parte Young*. Compare 28 U.S.C. § 2254(e) (Federal court authorized to issue an "order directed to an appropriate State official"); 42 U.S.C. § 11001 (1988 ed.) (requiring "the Governor" of a State to perform certain actions and holding "the Governor" responsible for nonperformance); 33 U.S.C. § 1365(a) (authorizing a suit against "any person" who is alleged to be in violation of relevant water pollution laws). Similarly the duty imposed by the Act—to "negotiate . . . in good faith to enter into" a compact with another sovereign—stands distinct in that it is not of the sort likely to be performed by an individual state executive officer or even a group of officers. Cf. State ex rel Stephan v. Finney, 836 P.2d 1169, 251 Kan. 559 (1992) (Governor of Kansas may negotiate but may not enter into compact without grant of power from legislature).

State a liability which is significantly more limited than would be the liability imposed upon the state officer under *Ex parte Young* strongly indicates that Congress had no wish to create the latter under § 2710(d)(3). Nor are we free to rewrite the statutory scheme in order to approximate what we think Congress might have wanted had it known that § 2710(d)(7) was beyond its authority. If that effort is to be made, it should be made by Congress, and not by the federal courts. We hold that *Ex parte Young* is inapplicable to petitioner's suit against the Governor of Florida, and therefore that suit is barred by the Eleventh Amendment and must be dismissed for a lack of jurisdiction.

IV

The Eleventh Amendment prohibits Congress from making the State of Florida capable of being sued in federal court. The narrow exception to the Eleventh Amendment provided by the *Ex parte Young* doctrine cannot be used to enforce § 2710(d)(3) because Congress enacted a remedial scheme, § 2710(d)(7), specifically designed for the enforcement of that right. The Eleventh Circuit's dismissal of petitioner's suit is hereby affirmed.

It is so ordered.

■ JUSTICE STEVENS, dissenting.

This case is about power—the power of the Congress of the United States to create a private federal cause of action against a State, or its Governor, for the violation of a federal right. In Chisholm v. Georgia, 2 Dall. [2 U.S.] 419 (1793), the entire Court—including Justice Iredell whose dissent provided the blueprint for the Eleventh Amendment—assumed that Congress had such power. In Hans v. Louisiana, 134 U.S. 1 (1890)—a case the Court purports to follow today—the Court again assumed that Congress had such power. In Fitzpatrick v. Bitzer, 427 U.S. 445 (1976), and Pennsylvania v. Union Gas Co., 491 U.S. 1, 24 (1989) (STEVENS, J., concurring), the Court squarely held that Congress has such power. In a series of cases beginning with Atascadero State Hospital v. Scanlon, 473 U.S. 234, 238–239 (1985), the Court formulated a special "clear statement rule" to determine whether specific Acts of Congress contained an effective exercise of that power. Nevertheless, in a sharp break with the past, today the Court holds that with the narrow and illogical exception of statutes enacted pursuant to the Enforcement Clause of the Fourteenth Amendment, Congress has no such power.

The importance of the majority's decision to overrule the Court's holding in *Pennsylvania v. Union Gas Co.* cannot be overstated. The majority's opinion does not simply preclude Congress from establishing the rather curious statutory scheme under which Indian tribes may seek the aid of a federal court to secure a State's good faith negotiations over gaming regulations. Rather, it prevents Congress from providing a federal forum for a broad range of actions against States, from those sounding in copyright and patent law, to those concerning bankruptcy, environmental law, and the regulation of our vast national economy.[33]

There may be room for debate over whether, in light of the Eleventh Amendment, Congress has the power to ensure that such a cause of action may be enforced in federal court by a citizen of another State or a foreign citizen. There can be no serious debate, however, over whether Congress has the power to ensure that such a cause of action may be brought by a citizen of the State being sued. Congress' authority in that regard is clear.

As JUSTICE SOUTER has convincingly demonstrated, the Court's contrary conclusion is profoundly misguided. Despite the thoroughness of his analysis, supported by sound reason, history, precedent, and strikingly uniform scholarly commentary, the shocking character of the majority's affront to a coequal branch of our government merits additional comment.

.   .   .   .   .

While I am persuaded that there is no justification for permanently enshrining the judge-made law of sovereign immunity, I recognize that federalism concerns—and even the interest in protecting the solvency of the States that was at work in *Chisholm* and *Hans*—may well justify a grant of immunity from federal litigation in certain classes of cases. Such a grant, however, should be the product of a reasoned decision by the policymaking branch of our Government. For this Court to conclude that time-worn shibboleths iterated and reiterated by judges should take precedence over the deliberations of the Congress of the United States is simply irresponsible.

V

Fortunately, and somewhat fortuitously, a jurisdictional problem that is unmentioned by the Court may deprive its opinion of precedential significance. The Indian Gaming Regulatory Act establishes a unique set of procedures for resolving the dispute between the Tribe and the State. If each adversary adamantly adheres to its understanding of the law, if the

---

33.   See, e.g., Pennsylvania v. Union Gas Co., 491 U.S. 1 (1989) (holding that a federal court may order a State to pay clean-up costs pursuant to the Comprehensive Environmental Response, Compensation, and Liability Act of 1980); In re Merchants Grain, Inc., 59 F.3d 630 (CA7 1995) (holding that the Eleventh Amendment does not bar a bankruptcy court from issuing a money judgment against a State under the Bankruptcy Code); Chavez v. Arte Publico Press, 59 F.3d 539 (CA5 1995) (holding that a state university could be sued in federal court for infringing an author's copyright). The conclusion that suits against States may not be brought in federal court is also incompatible with our cases concluding that state entities may be sued for antitrust violations. See, e.g, Goldfarb v. Virginia State Bar, 421 U.S. 773, 791–792 (1975).

As federal courts have exclusive jurisdiction over cases arising under these federal laws, the majority's conclusion that the Eleventh Amendment shields States from being sued under them in federal court suggests that persons harmed by state violations of federal copyright, bankruptcy, and antitrust laws have no remedy. See Harris & Kenny, Eleventh Amendment Jurisprudence After *Atascadero*: The Coming Clash With Antitrust, Copyright, and Other Causes of Action Over Which the Federal Courts Have Exclusive Jurisdiction, 37 Emory L.J. 645 (1988).

District Court determines that the State's inflexibility constitutes a failure to negotiate in good faith, and if the State thereafter continues to insist that it is acting within its rights, the maximum sanction that the Court can impose is an order that refers the controversy to a member of the Executive Branch of the Government for resolution. 25 U.S.C. § 2710(d)(7)(B). As the Court of Appeals interpreted the Act, this final disposition is available even though the action against the State and its Governor may not be maintained. 11 F.3d 1016, 1029 (CA11 1994) (The Court does not tell us whether it agrees or disagrees with that disposition.) In my judgment, it is extremely doubtful that the obviously dispensable involvement of the judiciary in the intermediate stages of a procedure that begins and ends in the Executive Branch is a proper exercise of judicial power. See Gordon v. United States, 117 U.S. Appx. 697, 702–703 (1864) (opinion of Taney, C. J.); United States v. Ferreira, 13 How. [54 U.S.] 40, 48 (1852). It may well follow that the misguided opinion of today's majority has nothing more than an advisory character. Whether or not that be so, the better reasoning in JUSTICE SOUTER's far wiser and far more scholarly opinion will surely be the law one day.

For these reasons, as well as those set forth in JUSTICE SOUTER's opinion, I respectfully dissent.

■ JUSTICE SOUTER, with whom JUSTICE GINSBURG and JUSTICE BREYER join, dissenting.

In holding the State of Florida immune to suit under the Indian Gaming Regulatory Act, the Court today holds for the first time since the founding of the Republic that Congress has no authority to subject a State to the jurisdiction of a federal court at the behest of an individual asserting a federal right. Although the Court invokes the Eleventh Amendment as authority for this proposition, the only sense in which that amendment might be claimed as pertinent here was tolerantly phrased by JUSTICE STEVENS in his concurring opinion in Pennsylvania v. Union Gas, 491 U.S. 1, 23 (1989) (STEVENS, J., concurring). There, he explained how it has come about that we have two Eleventh Amendments, the one ratified in 1795, the other (so-called) invented by the Court nearly a century later in Hans v. Louisiana, 134 U.S. 1 (1890). JUSTICE STEVENS saw in that second Eleventh Amendment no bar to the exercise of congressional authority under the Commerce Clause in providing for suits on a federal question by individuals against a State, and I can only say that after my own canvass of the matter I believe he was entirely correct in that view, for reasons given below. His position, of course, was also the holding in *Union Gas*, which the Court now overrules and repudiates.

The fault I find with the majority today is not in its decision to reexamine *Union Gas*, for the Court in that case produced no majority for a single rationale supporting congressional authority. Instead, I part company from the Court because I am convinced that its decision is fundamentally mistaken, and for that reason I respectfully dissent.

I

It is useful to separate three questions: (1) whether the States enjoyed sovereign immunity if sued in their own courts in the period prior to ratification of the National Constitution; (2) if so, whether after ratification the States were entitled to claim some such immunity when sued in a federal court exercising jurisdiction either because the suit was between a State and a non-state litigant who was not its citizen, or because the issue in the case raised a federal question; and (3) whether any state sovereign immunity recognized in federal court may be abrogated by Congress.

The answer to the first question is not clear, although some of the Framers assumed that States did enjoy immunity in their own courts. The second question was not debated at the time of ratification, except as to citizen-state diversity jurisdiction;[34] there was no unanimity, but in due course the Court in Chisholm v. Georgia, 2 Dall. [2 U.S.] 419 (1793), answered that a state defendant enjoyed no such immunity. As to federal question jurisdiction, state sovereign immunity seems not to have been debated prior to ratification, the silence probably showing a general understanding at the time that the States would have no immunity in such cases.

The adoption of the Eleventh Amendment soon changed the result in *Chisholm*, not by mentioning sovereign immunity, but by eliminating citizen-state diversity jurisdiction over cases with state defendants. I will explain why the Eleventh Amendment did not affect federal question jurisdiction, a notion that needs to be understood for the light it casts on the soundness of *Hans*'s holding that States did enjoy sovereign immunity in federal question suits. The *Hans* Court erroneously assumed that a State could plead sovereign immunity against a noncitizen suing under federal question jurisdiction, and for that reason held that a State must enjoy the same protection in a suit by one of its citizens. The error of *Hans*'s reasoning is underscored by its clear inconsistency with the Founders' hostility to the implicit reception of common-law doctrine as federal law, and with the Founders' conception of sovereign power as divided between the States and the National Government for the sake of very practical objectives.

The Court's answer today to the third question is likewise at odds with the Founders' view that common law, when it was received into the new American legal systems, was always subject to legislative amendment. In ignoring the reasons for this pervasive understanding at the time of the ratification, and in holding that a nontextual common-law rule limits a clear grant of congressional power under Article I, the Court follows a

---

34. The two Citizen–State Diversity Clauses provide as follows: "The judicial Power shall extend ... to Controversies ... between a State and Citizens of another State; ... and between a State, or the Citizens thereof, and foreign States, Citizens or Subjects." U.S. Const., Art. III, § 2. In his opinion in *Union Gas*, JUSTICE STEVENS referred to these clauses as the "citizen-state" and "alien-state" clauses, respectively, Pennsylvania v. Union Gas Co., 491 U.S. 1, 24 (1989) (STEVENS, J., concurring). I have grouped the two as "Citizen–State Diversity Clauses" for ease in frequent repetition here.

course that has brought it to grief before in our history, and promises to do so again.

Beyond this third question that elicits today's holding, there is one further issue. To reach the Court's result, it must not only hold the *Hans* doctrine to be outside the reach of Congress, but must also displace the doctrine of Ex parte Young, 209 U.S. 123 (1908), that an officer of the government may be ordered prospectively to follow federal law, in cases in which the government may not itself be sued directly. None of its reasons for displacing *Young*'s jurisdictional doctrine withstand scrutiny.

. . . . .

IV

The Court's holding that the States' *Hans* immunity may not be abrogated by Congress leads to the final question in this case, whether federal question jurisdiction exists to order prospective relief enforcing IGRA against a state officer, respondent Chiles, who is said to be authorized to take the action required by the federal law. Just as with the issue about authority to order the State as such, this question is entirely jurisdictional, and we need not consider here whether petitioner Seminole Tribe would have a meritorious argument for relief, or how much practical relief the requested order (to bargain in good faith) would actually provide to the Tribe. Nor, of course, does the issue turn in any way on one's views about the scope of the Eleventh Amendment or *Hans* and its doctrine, for we ask whether the state officer is subject to jurisdiction only on the assumption that action directly against the State is barred. The answer to this question is an easy yes, the officer is subject to suit under the rule in Ex parte Young, 209 U.S. 123 (1908), and the case could, and should, readily be decided on this point alone.

. . . . .

V

Absent the application of *Ex parte Young*, I would, of course, follow *Union Gas* in recognizing congressional power under Article I to abrogate *Hans* immunity. Since the reasons for this position, as explained in Parts II–III, supra, tend to unsettle *Hans* as well as support *Union Gas*, I should add a word about my reasons for continuing to accept *Hans*'s holding as a matter of stare decisis.

The *Hans* doctrine was erroneous, but it has not previously proven to be unworkable or to conflict with later doctrine or to suffer from the effects of facts developed since its decision (apart from those indicating its original errors). I would therefore treat *Hans* as it has always been treated in fact until today, as a doctrine of federal common law. For, as so understood, it has formed one of the strands of the federal relationship for over a century now, and the stability of that relationship is itself a value that stare decisis aims to respect.

In being ready to hold that the relationship may still be altered, not by the Court but by Congress, I would tread the course laid out elsewhere in our cases. The Court has repeatedly stated its assumption that insofar as the relative positions of States and Nation may be affected consistently with the Tenth Amendment, they would not be modified without deliberately expressed intent. See [Gregory v. Ashcroft, 501 U.S. 452, 460–461 (1991)]. The plain statement rule, which "assures that the legislature has in fact faced, and intended to bring into issue, the critical matters involved in the judicial decision," [United States v. Bass, 404 U.S. 336, 349 (1971)], is particularly appropriate in light of our primary reliance on "[t]he effectiveness of the federal political process in preserving the States' interests." Garcia v. San Antonio Metropolitan Transit Authority, 469 U.S. 528, 552 (1985).[35] Hence, we have required such a plain statement when Congress pre-empts the historic powers of the States, Rice v. Santa Fe Elevator Corp., 331 U.S. 218, 230 (1947), imposes a condition on the grant of federal moneys, South Dakota v. Dole, 483 U.S. 203, 207 (1987), or seeks to regulate a State's ability to determine the qualifications of its own officials. *Gregory*, supra, at 464.

When judging legislation passed under unmistakable Article I powers, no further restriction could be required. Nor does the Court explain why more could be demanded. In the past, we have assumed that a plain statement requirement is sufficient to protect the States from undue federal encroachments upon their traditional immunity from suit. See, e.g., [Welch v. Texas Dept. of Highways & Pub. Transp., 483 U.S. 468, 475 (1987)]; *Atascadero State Hospital v. Scanlon*, 473 U.S., at 239–240. It is hard to contend that this rule has set the bar too low, for (except in *Union Gas*) we have never found the requirement to be met outside the context of laws passed under § 5 of the Fourteenth Amendment. The exception I would recognize today proves the rule, moreover, because the federal abrogation of state immunity comes as part of a regulatory scheme which is itself designed to invest the States with regulatory powers that Congress need not extend to them. This fact suggests to me that the political safeguards of federalism are working, that a plain statement rule is an adequate check on congressional overreaching, and that today's abandonment of that approach is wholly unwarranted.

There is an even more fundamental "clear statement" principle, however, that the Court abandons today. John Marshall recognized it over a century and a half ago in the very context of state sovereign immunity in federal question cases:

"The jurisdiction of the Court, then, being extended by the letter of the constitution to all cases arising under it, or under the laws of the United States, it follows that those who would withdraw any case of

---

35. See also The Federalist No. 46, at 319 (J. Madison) (explaining that the Federal Government "will partake sufficiently of the spirit [of the States], to be disinclined to invade the rights of the individual States, or the prerogatives of their governments"); Wechsler, The Political Safeguards of Federalism: The Role of the States in the Composition and Selection of the National Government, 54 Colum.L.Rev. 543 (1954).

this description from that jurisdiction, must sustain the exemption they claim on the spirit and true meaning of the constitution, which spirit and true meaning must be so apparent as to overrule the words which its framers have employed." Cohens v. Virginia, 6 Wheat. (19 U.S.), at 379–380.

Because neither text, precedent, nor history supports the majority's abdication of our responsibility to exercise the jurisdiction entrusted to us in Article III, I would reverse the judgment of the Court of Appeals.[36]

COMMENT ON DEVELOPMENTS IN THE LAW OF STATE SOVEREIGN IMMUNITY SINCE *SEMINOLE TRIBE*

In Idaho v. Coeur d'Alene Tribe of Idaho, 521 U.S. 261 (1997), a narrow majority of the Court again held that the Eleventh Amendment barred federal-court adjudication of a tribe's claim against a state or state officers. But this time the majority itself fractured, with only Chief Justice Rehnquist joining so much of Justice Kennedy's principal opinion as called for a fundamental reconceptualization of *Ex parte Young*. In general, Justice Kennedy would have limited the *Ex parte Young* "exception" to the Eleventh Amendment to cases in which no state forum is available to decide whether federal law entitles the plaintiff to injunctive relief to avoid prospective harm under color of state law. Justices O'Connor, Scalia, and Thomas joined Justice Kennedy and the Chief Justice to form a majority holding that the particular relief sought by the tribe—a nominally declaratory and injunctive decree that would have functioned as a decree quieting title to certain submerged lands—was too intrusive on the fundamental interests of the state as sovereign to be permissible under *Ex parte Young*. But to the evident relief of the four *Seminole Tribe* dissenters (who would have let the tribe's suit proceed under *Ex parte Young*), the O'Connor wing delivered a ringing endorsement of the traditional scope and function of *Ex parte Young* as a counterbalance to the Eleventh Amendment that is essential to maintaining the constitutional supremacy of federal law.

In California v. Deep Sea Research, Inc., 523 U.S. 491 (1998), the Court acknowledged the "general proposition" that under *Coeur d'Alene Tribe* "federal courts cannot adjudicate a State's claim of title to property," but held that "in the context of the federal courts' in rem admiralty jurisdiction," federal courts could "exercise jurisdiction over property that the State does not actually possess." 523 U.S., at 506.

In a seemingly casual statement for a surprisingly unanimous Court, Justice Breyer has potentially set Eleventh Amendment doctrine on a new tack by declaring that state sovereign immunity is essentially a defense to liability rather than a negation of federal judicial power (subject, perhaps, to the unstated qualification that the Eleventh Amendment does have

---

[**36.** See Meltzer, The *Seminole* Decision and State Sovereign Immunity, 1996 Sup.Ct.Rev. 1.]

jurisdictional force when applied according to its literal terms to bar diversity-based suits against states by citizens of other states). "The Eleventh Amendment ... does not automatically destroy original jurisdiction. Rather, the Eleventh Amendment grants the State a legal power to assert a sovereign immunity defense should it choose to do so. The State can waive the defense.... Nor need a court raise the defect on its own. Unless the State raises the matter, a court can ignore it." Wisconsin Dept. of Corrections v. Schacht, 524 U.S. 381, 389 (1998). For discussion of the precedent for and relative implications of immunity-based and other conceptions of the Eleventh Amendment, see Vazquez, What is Eleventh Amendment Immunity?, 106 Yale L.J. 1683 (1997).

The bloc of five Justices who formed the majority in *Seminole Tribe* extended the reasoning of that case three years later to hold that Congress lacks Article I power to required nonconsenting states to adjudicate in their own courts private federal suits to enforce concededly constitutional obligations imposed on states by federal law, notwithstanding that such obligations could be enforced—if far less efficiently—by suits in federal courts brought by the United States itself on behalf of the wronged individuals. Alden v. Maine, 527 U.S. 706 (1999).

Alden is uncompromising in its reaffirmation and extension of the reasoning of *Seminole Tribe*. It held that Congress lacked the power to compel state courts to entertain suits against a state by state employees, who had been denied the overtime pay to which they were entitled under the federal Fair Labor Standards Act (FLSA).

> We have ... sometimes referred to the States' immunity from suit as "Eleventh Amendment immunity." The phrase is convenient shorthand but something of a misnomer, for the sovereign immunity of the States neither derives from nor is limited by the terms of the Eleventh Amendment. Rather, as the Constitution's structure, and its history, and the authoritative interpretations by this Court make clear, the States' immunity from suit is a fundamental aspect of the sovereignty which the States enjoyed before the ratification of the Constitution, and which they retain today (either literally or by virtue of their admission into the Union upon an equal footing with the other States) except as altered by the plan of the Convention or certain constitutional Amendments.
>
> ... Any doubt regarding the constitutional role of the States as sovereign entities is removed by the Tenth Amendment, which, like the other provisions of the Bill of Rights, was enacted to allay lingering concerns about the extent of the national power.
>
> . . . . .
>
> ... The State of Maine has not questioned Congress' power to prescribe substantive rules of federal law to which it must comply. Despite an initial good-faith disagreement about the requirements of the FLSA, it is conceded by all that the State has altered its conduct so that its compliance with federal law cannot now be questioned. The Solicitor

General of the United States has appeared before this Court, however, and asserted that the federal interest in compensating the State's employees for alleged past violations of federal law is so compelling that sovereign State of Maine must be stripped of its immunity and subjected to suit in its own courts by its own employees. Yet, despite specific statutory authorization, 29 U.S.C. § 216(c), the United States apparently found the same interests insufficient to justify sending even a single attorney to Maine to prosecute this litigation. The difference between a suit by the United States on behalf of the employees and a suit by the employees implicates a rule that the National Government must itself deem the case of sufficient importance to take action against a State; and history, precedent, and the structure of the Constitution make clear that, under the plan of the Convention, the States have consented to suits of the first kind but not of the second.

527 U.S., at 713–714, 759–760.

By the same 5–4 majority, the Court held the same day in the two *College Savings Bank* cases that neither the express liability imposed on states by the Patent and Plant Variety Protection Remedy Clarification Act, nor that imposed by the Trademark Remedy Clarification Act (amending the Lanham Act), could be sustained despite the reliance of Congress on legislative power conferred by § 5 of the Fourteenth Amendment as well as the patent and commerce clauses of Article I. Florida Prepaid Postsecondary Education Expense Board v. College Savings Bank (*College Savings Bank I*), 527 U.S. 627 (1999); College Savings Bank v. Florida Prepaid Postsecondary Education Board (*College Savings Bank II*), 527 U.S. 666 (1999).

In *College Savings Bank I* the Court held that Congress had failed to show that stripping states of their sovereign immunity from patent-infringement suits was necessary to remedy the Fourteenth Amendment violation of depriving patentees of property without "due process of law," since "Congress itself said nothing about the existence or adequacy of state remedies . . . ." 527 U.S., at 644.

> The historical record and the scope of coverage therefore make it clear that the Patent Remedy Act cannot be sustained under § 5 of the Fourteenth Amendment. The examples of States avoiding liability for patent infringement by pleading sovereign immunity in a federal-court patent action are scarce enough, but any plausible argument that such action on the part of the State deprived patentees of property and left them without a remedy under state law is scarcer still. The statute's apparent and more basic aims were to provide a uniform remedy and to place States on the same footing as private parties under that regime. These are proper Article I concerns, but that Article does not give Congress the power to enact such legislation after *Seminole Tribe*.

527 U.S., at 647–648.

In *College Savings Bank II*, the Court reached a similar conclusion as to the Fourteenth Amendment argument, but on different grounds. The

Court held that a trademark, unlike a patent, confers no property right that the Due Process Clause protects. 527 U.S., at 672–673. The Court then held similarly unavailing the argument that by engaging in commercial activity that infringed the trademark of competitor, Florida had " 'impliedly' or 'constructively' waived its immunity from Lanham Act suit." 527 U.S., at 676. Calling the [Parden v. Terminal R. Co. of Ala. Docks Dept., 377 U.S. 184 (1964)], case "an elliptical opinion that stands at the nadir of our waiver (and, for that matter, sovereign immunity) jurisprudence," id., the Court declared that "the constructive-waiver experiment of *Parden* was ill conceived, and we see no merit in attempting to salvage any remnant of it." 527 U.S., at 680.

> Given how anomalous it is to speak of the "constructive waiver" of a constitutionally protected privilege, it is not surprising that the very cornerstone of the *Parden* opinion was the notion that state sovereign immunity is not constitutionally grounded.... Our more recent decision in *Seminole Tribe* expressly repudiates that proposition, and in formally overruling *Parden* we do no more than make explicit what that case implied.

527 U.S., at 682–683.

In its next two terms, the Court held that Congress lacked the power under § 5 of the Fourteenth Amendment to abrogate state sovereign immunity with respect to suits under the Age Discrimination in Employment Act, Kimel v. Florida Board of Regents, 528 U.S. 62 (2000), or the Americans with Disabilities Act, Board of Trustees of the University of Alabama v. Garrett, 531 U.S. 356 (2001). The Court continued its extension of the constitutional scope of state sovereign immunity in Federal Maritime Commission v. South Carolina State Ports Authority, 535 U.S. 743 (2002), reprinted infra p. 536, but softened its restrictions on congressional abrogation of that immunity in Nevada Dept. of Human Resources v. Hibbs, 538 U.S. 721 (2003), and Tennessee v. Lane, 541 U.S. 509 (2004), reprinted infra p. 560.

In Lapides v. Board of Regents of the University System of Georgia, 535 U.S. 613 (2002), a unanimous Court held that a state's sovereign immunity can be waived by its litigation conduct even if the official responsible for the conduct in question—here, the state attorney general, who joined with individual defendants in removing to federal court a case that had been brought against the state in a state court—is not expressly authorized by state law to waive the state's Eleventh Amendment immunity. In another unanimous decision, Frew v. Hawkins, 540 U.S. 431 (2004), the Court found it unnecessary to determine whether a state's entry into a consent decree effected a waiver of its Eleventh Amendment immunity from a suit to enforce the terms of the consent decree. Instead, the Court held that a valid federal consent decree—one that resolves a case within federal jurisdiction, is consistent with the general scope of the case as presented by the pleadings, and that furthers the objectives of the federal statute upon which the case was based—is enforceable against state officers under *Ex parte Young*.

Ex parte Young was also the basis for the Court's decision in Verizon Maryland, Inc. v. Public Service Comm'n of Maryland, 535 U.S. 635 (2002). There the Court first held that a challenge to a state regulatory commission's construction of a federally authorized agreement between telecommunications carriers at least arguably arose under federal law, and hence could be heard by a federal district court in the exercise of its original jurisdiction under 28 U.S.C. § 1331. The unanimous eight-member Court (Justice O'Connor not participating) then held that *Ex parte Young* trumped the state's claim that the Eleventh Amendment barred judicial review of the commission's ruling by the federal district court.

For criticism of the intellectual framework of the Court's Eleventh Amendment jurisprudence, see Noonan, Narrowing the Nation's Power: The Supreme Court Sides with the States (2002); Purcell, The Particularly Dubious Case of *Hans v. Louisiana*: An Essay on Law, Race, History, and "Federal Courts" , 81 N.C. L.Rev. 1927 (2003). See generally Symposium: State Sovereign Immunity and the Eleventh Amendment, 75 Notre Dame L.Rev. 817 (2000); Vázquez, Sovereign Immunity, Due Process, and the *Alden* Trilogy, 109 Yale L.J. 1927 (2000); Symposium, Shifting the Balance of Power? The Supreme Court, Federalism, and State Sovereign Immunity, 53 Stan. L.Rev. 1115 (2001); Fitzgerald, Comment, State Sovereign Immunity: Searching for Stability, 48 UCLA L.Rev. 1203 (2001); Zietlow, Federalism's Paradox: The Spending Power and Waiver of Sovereign Immunity, 37 Wake Forest L.Rev. 141 (2002).

Federal Maritime Commission v. South Carolina State Ports Authority

Supreme Court of the United States, 2002.
535 U.S. 743, 122 S.Ct. 1864, 152 L.Ed.2d 962.

■ JUSTICE THOMAS delivered the opinion of the Court.

This case presents the question whether state sovereign immunity precludes petitioner Federal Maritime Commission (FMC or Commission) from adjudicating a private party's complaint that a state-run port has violated the Shipping Act of 1984, 46 U.S.C.App. § 1701 et seq. (1994 ed.and Supp. V). We hold that state sovereign immunity bars such an adjudicative proceeding.

I

On five occasions, South Carolina Maritime Services, Inc. (Maritime Services), asked respondent South Carolina State Ports Authority (SCSPA) for permission to berth a cruise ship, the M/V *Tropic Sea,* at the SCSPA's port facilities in Charleston, South Carolina. Maritime Services intended to offer cruises on the M/V *Tropic Sea* originating from the Port of Charleston. Some of these cruises would stop in the Bahamas while others would merely travel in international waters before returning to Charleston with no intervening ports of call. On all of these trips, passengers would be permitted to participate in gambling activities while on board.

The SCSPA repeatedly denied Maritime Services' requests, contending that it had an established policy of denying berths in the Port of Charleston to vessels whose primary purpose was gambling. As a result, Maritime Services filed a complaint with the FMC, contending that the SCSPA's refusal to provide berthing space to the M/V *Tropic Sea* violated the Shipping Act. Maritime Services alleged in its complaint that the SCSPA had implemented its antigambling policy in a discriminatory fashion by providing berthing space in Charleston to two Carnival Cruise Lines vessels even though Carnival offered gambling activities on these ships. Maritime Services therefore complained that the SCSPA had unduly and unreasonably preferred Carnival over Maritime Services in violation of 46 U.S.C.App. § 1709(d)(4) (1994 ed., Supp. V), and unreasonably refused to deal or negotiate with Maritime Services in violation of § 1709(b)(10). App. 14–15. It further alleged that the SCSPA's unlawful actions had inflicted upon Maritime Services a "loss of profits, loss of earnings, loss of sales, and loss of business opportunities." Id., at 15.

To remedy its injuries, Maritime Services prayed that the FMC: (1) seek a temporary restraining order and preliminary injunction in the United States District Court for the District of South Carolina "enjoining [the SCSPA] from utilizing its discriminatory practice to refuse to provide berthing space and passenger services to Maritime Services;" [37] (2) direct the SCSPA to pay reparations to Maritime Services as well as interest and reasonable attorneys' fees;[38] (3) issue an order commanding, among other things, the SCSPA to cease and desist from violating the Shipping Act; and (4) award Maritime Services "such other and further relief as is just and proper." Id., at 16.

Consistent with the FMC's Rules of Practice and Procedure, Maritime Services' complaint was referred to an administrative law judge (ALJ) .... The SCSPA then filed an answer, maintaining, inter alia, that it had adhered to its antigambling policy in a nondiscriminatory manner. It also filed a motion to dismiss, asserting, as relevant, that the SCSPA, as an arm of the State of South Carolina, was "entitled to Eleventh Amendment

---

37. See § 1710(h)(1) (1994 ed.) ("In connection with any investigation conducted under this section, the Commission may bring suit in a district court of the United States to enjoin conduct in violation of this chapter. Upon a showing that standards for granting injunctive relief by courts of equity are met and after notice to the defendant, the court may grant a temporary restraining order or preliminary injunction for a period not to exceed 10 days after the Commission has issued an order disposing of the issues under investigation. Any such suit shall be brought in a district in which the defendant resides or transacts business").

38. See § 1710(g) (1994 ed., Supp. V) ("For any complaint filed within 3 years after the cause of action accrued, the Commission shall, upon petition of the complainant and after notice and hearing, direct payment of reparations to the complainant for actual injury (which, for purposes of this subsection, also includes the loss of interest at commercial rates compounded from the date of injury) caused by a violation of this chapter plus reasonable attorney's fees").

immunity" from Maritime Services' suit. App. 41. The SCSPA argued that "the Constitution prohibits Congress from passing a statute authorizing Maritime Services to file [this] Complaint before the Commission and, thereby, sue the State of South Carolina for damages and injunctive relief." Id., at 44.

The ALJ agreed, concluding that recent decisions of this Court "interpreting the Eleventh Amendment and State sovereign immunity from *private* suits ... require[d] that [Maritime Services'] complaint be dismissed." App. to Pet. for Cert. 49a (emphasis in original). Relying on Seminole Tribe of Fla. v. Florida, 517 U.S. 44 (1996), in which we held that Congress, pursuant to its Article I powers, cannot abrogate state sovereign immunity, the ALJ reasoned that "[i]f federal courts that are established under Article III of the Constitution must respect States' Eleventh Amendment immunity and Congress is powerless to override the States' immunity under Article I of the Constitution, it is irrational to argue that an agency like the Commission, created under an Article I statute, is free to disregard the Eleventh Amendment or its related doctrine of State immunity from *private* suits." App. to Pet. for Cert. 59a (emphasis in original). The ALJ noted, however, that his decision did not deprive the FMC of its "authority to look into [Maritime Services'] allegations of Shipping Act violations and enforce the Shipping Act." Id., at 60a. For example, the FMC could institute its own formal investigatory proceeding, see 46 CFR § 502.282 (2001), or refer Maritime Services' allegations to its Bureau of Enforcement, App. to Pet. for Cert. 60a–61a.

While Maritime Services did not appeal the ALJ's dismissal of its complaint, the FMC on its own motion decided to review the ALJ's ruling to consider whether state sovereign immunity from private suits extends to proceedings before the Commission. It concluded that "[t]he doctrine of state sovereign immunity ... is meant to cover proceedings before judicial tribunals, whether Federal or state, not executive branch administrative agencies like the Commission." Id., at 33a. As a result, the FMC held that sovereign immunity did not bar the Commission from adjudicating private complaints against state-run ports and reversed the ALJ's decision dismissing Maritime Services' complaint. Id., at 35a.

The SCSPA filed a petition for review, and the United States Court of Appeals for the Fourth Circuit reversed. Observing that "any proceeding where a federal officer adjudicates disputes between private parties and unconsenting states would not have passed muster at the time of the Constitution's passage nor after the ratification of the Eleventh Amendment," the Court of Appeals reasoned that "[s]uch an adjudication is equally as invalid today, whether the forum be a state court, a federal court, or a federal administrative agency." 243 F.3d 165, 173 (CA4 2001). Reviewing the "precise nature" of the procedures employed by the FMC for resolving private complaints, the Court of Appeals concluded that the proceeding "walks, talks, and squawks very much like a lawsuit" and that "[i]ts placement within the Executive Branch cannot blind us to the fact that the proceeding is truly an adjudication." Id., at 174. The Court of

Appeals therefore held that because the SCSPA is an arm of the State of South Carolina, sovereign immunity precluded the FMC from adjudicating Maritime Services' complaint, and remanded the case with instructions that it be dismissed. Id., at 179.

We granted the FMC's petition for certiorari, 534 U.S. 971 (2001), and now affirm.

II

Dual sovereignty is a defining feature of our Nation's constitutional blueprint. See Gregory v. Ashcroft, 501 U.S. 452, 457 (1991). States, upon ratification of the Constitution, did not consent to become mere appendages of the Federal Government. Rather, they entered the Union "with their sovereignty intact." Blatchford v. Native Village of Noatak, 501 U.S. 775, 779 (1991). An integral component of that "residuary and inviolable sovereignty," The Federalist No. 39, p. 245 (C. Rossiter ed.1961) (J. Madison), retained by the States is their immunity from private suits. Reflecting the widespread understanding at the time the Constitution was drafted, Alexander Hamilton explained,

> "It is inherent in the nature of sovereignty not to be amenable to the suit of an individual *without its consent.* This is the general sense and the general practice of mankind; and the exemption, as one of the attributes of sovereignty, is now enjoyed by the government of every State of the Union. Unless, therefore, there is a surrender of this immunity in the plan of the convention, it will remain with the States . . . ." Id., No. 81, at 487–488 (emphasis in original).

States, in ratifying the Constitution, did surrender a portion of their inherent immunity by consenting to suits brought by sister States or by the Federal Government. See Alden v. Maine, 527 U.S. 706, 755 (1999). Nevertheless, the Convention did not disturb States' immunity from private suits, thus firmly enshrining this principle in our constitutional framework. "The leading advocates of the Constitution assured the people in no uncertain terms that the Constitution would not strip the States of sovereign immunity." Id., at 716.

The States' sovereign immunity, however, fell into peril in the early days of our Nation's history when this Court held in Chisholm v. Georgia, 2 Dall. [2 U.S.] 419 (1793), that Article III authorized citizens of one State to sue another State in federal court. The "decision 'fell upon the country with a profound shock.' " *Alden,* supra, at 720, quoting 1 C. Warren, The Supreme Court in United States History 96 (rev. ed.1926). In order to overturn *Chisholm,* Congress quickly passed the Eleventh Amendment and the States ratified it speedily. The Amendment clarified that "[t]he judicial Power of the United States shall not be construed to extend to any suit in law or equity, commenced or prosecuted against one of the United States by Citizens of another State, or by Citizens or Subjects of any Foreign State." We have since acknowledged that the *Chisholm* decision was erroneous. See, e.g., *Alden,* 527 U.S., at 721–722.

Instead of explicitly memorializing the full breadth of the sovereign immunity retained by the States when the Constitution was ratified, Congress chose in the text of the Eleventh Amendment only to "address the specific provisions of the Constitution that had raised concerns during the ratification debates and formed the basis of the *Chisholm* decision." Id., at 723. As a result, the Eleventh Amendment does not define the scope of the States' sovereign immunity; it is but one particular exemplification of that immunity. Cf. *Blatchford*, supra, at 779 ("[W]e have understood the Eleventh Amendment to stand not so much for what it says, but for the presupposition of our constitutional structure which it confirms").

III

We now consider whether the sovereign immunity enjoyed by States as part of our constitutional framework applies to adjudications conducted by the FMC. Petitioner FMC and respondent United States[39] initially maintain that the Court of Appeals erred because sovereign immunity only shields States from exercises of "judicial power" and FMC adjudications are not judicial proceedings. As support for their position, they point to the text of the Eleventh Amendment and contend that "[t]he Amendment's reference to 'judicial Power' and 'to any suit in law or equity' clearly mark it as an immunity from judicial process." Brief for United States 15.

For purposes of this case, we will assume, arguendo, that in adjudicating complaints filed by private parties under the Shipping Act, the FMC does not exercise the judicial power of the United States. Such an assumption, however, does not end our inquiry as this Court has repeatedly held that the sovereign immunity enjoyed by the States extends beyond the literal text of the Eleventh Amendment.[40] See, e.g., *Alden*, supra (holding that sovereign immunity shields States from private suits in state courts pursuant to federal causes of action); *Blatchford*, supra (applying state sovereign immunity to suits by Indian tribes); Principality of Monaco v. Mississippi, 292 U.S. 313 (1934) (applying state sovereign immunity to suits by foreign nations); Ex parte New York, 256 U.S. 490 (1921) (applying state sovereign immunity to admiralty proceedings); Smith v. Reeves, 178 U.S. 436 (1900) (applying state sovereign immunity to suits by federal corporations); Hans v. Louisiana, 134 U.S. 1 (1890) (applying state sovereign immunity to suits by a State's own citizens under federal-question jurisdiction). Adhering to that well-reasoned precedent, see Part II, supra, we must

---

39. While the United States is a party to this case and agrees with the FMC that state sovereign immunity does not preclude the Commission from adjudicating Maritime Services' complaint against the SCSPA, it is nonetheless a respondent because it did not seek review of the Court of Appeals' decision below. See this Court's Rule 12.6. The United States instead opposed the FMC's petition for certiorari. See Brief for United States in Opposition.

40. To the extent that Justice Breyer, looking to the text of the Eleventh Amendment, suggests that sovereign immunity only shields States from the " 'the judicial power of the United States,' " post, (dissenting opinion), he "engage[s] in the type of a historical literalism we have rejected in interpreting the scope of the States' sovereign immunity since the discredited decision in *Chisholm*," Alden v. Maine, 527 U.S. 706, 730 (1999). Furthermore, it is ironic that Justice Breyer adopts such a textual approach in defending the conduct of an independent agency that itself lacks any textual basis in the Constitution.

determine whether the sovereign immunity embedded in our constitutional structure and retained by the States when they joined the Union extends to FMC adjudicative proceedings.

A

"[L]ook[ing] first to evidence of the original understanding of the Constitution," *Alden*, 527 U.S., at 741, as well as early congressional practice, see id., at 743–744, we find a relatively barren historical record, from which the parties draw radically different conclusions. Petitioner FMC, for instance, argues that state sovereign immunity should not extend to administrative adjudications because "[t]here is no evidence that state immunity from the adjudication of complaints by *executive officers* was an established principle at the time of the adoption of the Constitution." Brief for Petitioner 28 (emphasis in original). The SCSPA, on the other hand, asserts that it is more relevant that "Congress did not attempt to subject the States to private suits before federal administrative tribunals" during the early days of our Republic. Brief for Respondent SCSPA 19.

In truth, the relevant history does not provide direct guidance for our inquiry. The Framers, who envisioned a limited Federal Government, could not have anticipated the vast growth of the administrative state. See *Alden*, supra, at 807 (SOUTER, J., dissenting) ("The proliferation of Government, State and Federal, would amaze the Framers, and the administrative state with its reams of regulations would leave them rubbing their eyes"). Because formalized administrative adjudications were all but unheard of in the late 18th century and early 19th century, the dearth of specific evidence indicating whether the Framers believed that the States' sovereign immunity would apply in such proceedings is unsurprising.

This Court, however, has applied a presumption—first explicitly stated in *Hans v. Louisiana*, supra—that the Constitution was not intended to "rais[e] up" any proceedings against the States that were "anomalous and unheard of when the Constitution was adopted." Id., at 18. We therefore attribute great significance to the fact that States were not subject to private suits in administrative adjudications at the time of the founding or for many years thereafter. For instance, while the United States asserts that "state entities have long been subject to similar administrative enforcement proceedings," Reply Brief for United States 12, the earliest example it provides did not occur until 1918, see id., at 14 (citing California Canneries Co. v. Southern Pacific Co., 51 I.C.C. 500 (1918)).

B

To decide whether the *Hans* presumption applies here, however, we must examine FMC adjudications to determine whether they are the type of proceedings from which the Framers would have thought the States possessed immunity when they agreed to enter the Union.

In another case asking whether an immunity present in the judicial context also applied to administrative adjudications, this Court considered whether administrative law judges share the same absolute immunity from suit as do Article III judges. See Butz v. Economou, 438 U.S. 478 (1978). Examining in that case the duties performed by an ALJ, this Court observed:

> "There can be little doubt that the role of the modern federal hearing examiner or administrative law judge ... is 'functionally comparable' to that of a judge. His powers are often, if not generally, comparable to those of a trial judge: He may issue subpoenas, rule on proffers of evidence, regulate the course of the hearing, and make or recommend decisions. More importantly, the process of agency adjudication is currently structured so as to assure that the hearing examiner exercises his independent judgment on the evidence before him, free from pressures by the parties or other officials within the agency." Id., at 513 (citation omitted).

Beyond the similarities between the role of an ALJ and that of a trial judge, this Court also noted the numerous common features shared by administrative adjudications and judicial proceedings:

> "[F]ederal administrative law requires that agency adjudication contain many of the same safeguards as are available in the judicial process. The proceedings are adversary in nature. They are conducted before a trier of fact insulated from political influence. A party is entitled to present his case by oral or documentary evidence, and the transcript of testimony and exhibits together with the pleadings constitutes the exclusive record for decision. The parties are entitled to know the findings and conclusions on all of the issues of fact, law, or discretion presented on the record." Ibid. (citations omitted).

This Court therefore concluded in *Butz* that administrative law judges were "entitled to absolute immunity from damages liability for their judicial acts." Id., at 514.

Turning to FMC adjudications specifically, neither the Commission nor the United States disputes the Court of Appeals' characterization below that such a proceeding "walks, talks, and squawks very much like a lawsuit." 243 F.3d, at 174. Nor do they deny that the similarities identified in *Butz* between administrative adjudications and trial court proceedings are present here. See 46 CFR § 502.142 (2001).

A review of the FMC's Rules of Practice and Procedure confirms that FMC administrative proceedings bear a remarkably strong resemblance to civil litigation in federal courts. For example, the FMC's Rules governing pleadings are quite similar to those found in the Federal Rules of Civil Procedure. A case is commenced by the filing of a complaint.... The defendant then must file an answer, generally within 20 days of the date of service of the complaint, ... and may also file a motion to dismiss .... A defendant is also allowed to file counterclaims against the plaintiff.... If a defendant fails to respond to a complaint, default judgment may be entered on behalf of the plaintiff. Intervention is also allowed....

Likewise, discovery in FMC adjudications largely mirrors discovery in federal civil litigation.... In both types of proceedings, parties may conduct depositions, ... which are governed by similar requirements.... Parties may also discover evidence by: (1) serving written interrogatories ... ; (2) requesting that another party either produce documents ... or allow entry on that party's property for the purpose of inspecting the property or designated objects thereon ... ; and (3) submitting requests for admissions .... And a party failing to obey discovery orders in either type of proceeding is subject to a variety of sanctions, including the entry of default judgment....

Not only are discovery procedures virtually indistinguishable, but the role of the ALJ, the impartial officer designated to hear a case, see § 502.147, is similar to that of an Article III judge. An ALJ has the authority to "arrange and give notice of hearing." Ibid. At that hearing, he may

> "prescribe the order in which evidence shall be presented; dispose of procedural requests or similar matters; hear and rule upon motions; administer oaths and affirmations; examine witnesses; direct witnesses to testify or produce evidence available to them which will aid in the determination of any question of fact in issue; rule upon offers of proof ... and dispose of any other matter that normally and properly arises in the course of proceedings." Ibid.

The ALJ also fixes "the time and manner of filing briefs," § 502.221(a), which contain findings of fact as well as legal argument .... After the submission of these briefs, the ALJ issues a decision that includes "a statement of findings and conclusions, as well as the reasons or basis therefor, upon all the material issues presented on the record, and the appropriate rule, order, section, relief, or denial thereof." § 502.223. Such relief may include an order directing the payment of reparations to an aggrieved party.... The ALJ's ruling subsequently becomes the final decision of the FMC unless a party, by filing exceptions, appeals to the Commission or the Commission decides to review the ALJ's decision "on its own initiative." § 502.227(a)(3). In cases where a complainant obtains reparations, an ALJ may also require the losing party to pay the prevailing party's attorney's fees....

In short, the similarities between FMC proceedings and civil litigation are overwhelming. In fact, to the extent that situations arise in the course of FMC adjudications "which are not covered by a specific Commission rule," the FMC's own Rules of Practice and Procedure specifically provide that "the Federal Rules of Civil Procedure will be followed to the extent that they are consistent with sound administrative practice." [41] § 502.12.

C

The preeminent purpose of state sovereign immunity is to accord States the dignity that is consistent with their status as sovereign entities.

---

41. In addition, "[u]nless inconsistent with the requirements of the Administrative Procedure Act and [the FMC's Rules of Practice and Procedure], the Federal Rules of Evidence [are] applicable" in FMC adjudicative proceedings. 46 C.F.R. § 502.156 (2001).

See In re Ayers, 123 U.S. 443, 505 (1887). "The founding generation thought it 'neither becoming nor convenient that the several States of the Union, invested with that large residuum of sovereignty which had not been delegated to the United States, should be summoned as defendants to answer the complaints of private persons.'" *Alden*, 527 U.S., at 748 (quoting [In re Ayers, 123 U.S. 443, 505 (1887)]).

Given both this interest in protecting States' dignity and the strong similarities between FMC proceedings and civil litigation, we hold that state sovereign immunity bars the FMC from adjudicating complaints filed by a private party against a nonconsenting State. Simply put, if the Framers thought it an impermissible affront to a State's dignity to be required to answer the complaints of private parties in federal courts, we cannot imagine that they would have found it acceptable to compel a State to do exactly the same thing before the administrative tribunal of an agency, such as the FMC. Cf. *Alden*, supra, at 749 ("Private suits against nonconsenting States . . . present 'the indignity of subjecting a State to the coercive process of judicial tribunals at the instance of private parties,' *regardless of the forum*") (quoting *In re Ayers*, supra, at 505) (citations omitted; emphasis added). The affront to a State's dignity does not lessen when an adjudication takes place in an administrative tribunal as opposed to an Article III court.[42] In both instances, a State is required to defend itself in an adversarial proceeding against a private party before an impartial federal officer.[43] Moreover, it would be quite strange to prohibit Congress from exercising its Article I powers to abrogate state sovereign immunity in Article III judicial proceedings, see *Seminole Tribe*, 517 U.S., at 72, but permit the use of those same Article I powers to create court-like administrative tribunals where sovereign immunity does not apply.[44]

D

The United States suggests two reasons why we should distinguish FMC administrative adjudications from judicial proceedings for purposes of state sovereign immunity. Both of these arguments are unavailing.

---

42. One, in fact, could argue that allowing a private party to haul a State in front of such an administrative tribunal constitutes a greater insult to a State's dignity than requiring a State to appear in an Article III court presided over by a judge with life tenure nominated by the President of the United States and confirmed by the United States Senate.

43. Contrary to the suggestion contained in JUSTICE BREYER's dissenting opinion, our "basic analogy" is not "between a federal administrative proceeding triggered by a private citizen and a private citizen's lawsuit against a State" in a State's own courts. Rather, as our discussion above makes clear, the more apt comparison is between a complaint filed by a private party against a State with the FMC and a lawsuit brought by a private party against a State in federal court.

44. While JUSTICE BREYER asserts by use of analogy that this case implicates the First Amendment right of citizens to petition the Federal Government for a redress of grievances, the Constitution no more protects a citizen's right to litigate against a State in front of a federal administrative tribunal than it does a citizen's right to sue a State in federal court. Both types of proceedings were "anomalous and unheard of when the Constitution was adopted," Hans v. Louisiana, 134 U.S. 1, 18 (1890), and a private party plainly has no First Amendment right to haul a State in front of either an Article III court or a federal administrative tribunal.

1

The United States first contends that sovereign immunity should not apply to FMC adjudications because the Commission's orders are not self-executing.... Whereas a court may enforce a judgment through the exercise of its contempt power, the FMC cannot enforce its own orders. Rather, the Commission's orders can only be enforced by a federal district court....

The United States presents a valid distinction between the authority possessed by the FMC and that of a court. For purposes of this case, however, it is a distinction without a meaningful difference. To the extent that the United States highlights this fact in order to suggest that a party alleged to have violated the Shipping Act is not coerced to participate in FMC proceedings, it is mistaken. The relevant statutory scheme makes it quite clear that, absent sovereign immunity, States would effectively be required to defend themselves against private parties in front of the FMC.

A State seeking to contest the merits of a complaint filed against it by a private party must defend itself in front of the FMC or substantially compromise its ability to defend itself at all. For example, once the FMC issues a nonreparation order, and either the Attorney General or the injured private party seeks enforcement of that order in a federal district court,[45] the sanctioned party is *not* permitted to litigate the merits of its position in that court. See § 1713(c) (limiting district court review to whether the relevant order "was properly made and duly issued"). Moreover, if a party fails to appear before the FMC, it may not then argue the merits of its position in an appeal of the Commission's determination filed under 28 U.S.C. § 2342(3)(B)(iv). See United States v. L.A. Tucker Truck Lines, Inc., 344 U.S. 33, 37 (1952) ("Simple fairness to those who are engaged in the tasks of administration, and to litigants, requires as a general rule that courts should not topple over administrative decisions unless the administrative body not only has erred but has erred against objection made at the time appropriate under its practice").

Should a party choose to ignore an order issued by the FMC, the Commission may impose monetary penalties for each day of noncompliance. See 46 U.S.C.App. § 1712(a). The Commission may then request that the Attorney General of the United States seek to recover the amount assessed by the Commission in federal district court, see § 1712(e), and a State's sovereign immunity would not extend to that action, as it is one brought by the United States. Furthermore, once the FMC issues an order assessing a civil penalty, a sanctioned party may not later contest the merits of that order in an enforcement action brought by the Attorney General in federal district court. See ibid. (limiting review to whether the assessment of the civil penalty was "regularly made and duly issued"); United States v. Interlink Systems, Inc., 984 F.2d 79, 83 (CA2 1993) (holding that review of

---

45. A reparation order issued by the FMC, by contrast, may be enforced in a United States district court only in an action brought by the injured private party. See Part IV–B, infra. 46 U.S.C.App. § 1713(d).

whether an order was "regularly made and duly issued" does not include review of the merits of the FMC's order).

Thus, any party, including a State, charged in a complaint by a private party with violating the Shipping Act is faced with the following options: appear before the Commission in a bid to persuade the FMC of the strength of its position or stand defenseless once enforcement of the Commission's nonreparation order or assessment of civil penalties is sought in federal district court.[46] To conclude that this choice does not coerce a State to participate in an FMC adjudication would be to blind ourselves to reality.[47]

The United States and JUSTICE BREYER maintain that any such coercion to participate in FMC proceedings is permissible because the States have consented to actions brought by the Federal Government. See *Alden,* 527 U.S., at 755–756 ("In ratifying the Constitution, the States consented to suits brought by . . . the Federal Government"). The Attorney General's decision to bring an enforcement action against a State after the conclusion of the Commission's proceedings, however, does not retroactively convert an FMC adjudication initiated and pursued by a private party into one initiated and pursued by the Federal Government. The prosecution of a complaint filed by a private party with the FMC is plainly not controlled by the United States, but rather is controlled by that private party; the only duty assumed by the FMC, and hence the United States, in conjunction with a private complaint is to assess its merits in an impartial manner. Indeed, the FMC does not even have the discretion to refuse to adjudicate complaints brought by private parties. See, e.g., 243 F.3d, at 176 ("The FMC had no choice but to adjudicate this dispute"). As a result, the United States plainly does not "exercise . . . political responsibility" for such complaints, but instead has impermissibly effected "a broad delegation to private persons to sue nonconsenting States." [48] *Alden,* supra, at 756.

---

46. While JUSTICE BREYER argues that States' access to "full judicial review" of the Commission's orders mitigates any coercion to participate in FMC adjudicative proceedings, he earlier concedes that a State must appear before the Commission in order "to obtain full judicial review of an adverse agency decision in a court of appeals." This case therefore does not involve a situation where Congress has allowed a party to obtain full *de novo* judicial review of Commission orders without first appearing before the Commission, and we express no opinion as to whether sovereign immunity would apply to FMC adjudicative proceedings under such circumstances.

47. JUSTICE BREYER's observation that private citizens may pressure the Federal Government in a variety of ways to take *other* actions that affect States is beside the point. Sovereign immunity concerns are not implicated, for example, when the Federal Government enacts a rule opposed by a State. It is an entirely different matter, however, when the Federal Government attempts to coerce States into answering the complaints of private parties in an adjudicative proceeding. See Part III–C, supra.

48. Moreover, a State obviously will not know ex ante whether the Attorney General will choose to bring an enforcement action. Therefore, it is the mere prospect that he may do so that coerces a State to participate in FMC proceedings. For if a State does not present its arguments to the Commission, it will have all but lost any opportunity to defend itself in the event that the Attorney General later decides to seek enforcement of a Commission order or the Commission's assessment of civil penalties.

2

The United States next suggests that sovereign immunity should not apply to FMC proceedings because they do not present the same threat to the financial integrity of States as do private judicial suits. The Government highlights the fact that, in contrast to a nonreparation order, for which the Attorney General may seek enforcement at the request of the Commission, a reparation order may be enforced in a United States district court only in an action brought by the private party to whom the award was made. See 46 U.S.C.App. § 1713(d)(1). The United States then points out that a State's sovereign immunity would extend to such a suit brought by a private party.

This argument, however, reflects a fundamental misunderstanding of the purposes of sovereign immunity. While state sovereign immunity serves the important function of shielding state treasuries and thus preserving "the States' ability to govern in accordance with the will of their citizens," *Alden,* supra, at 750–751, the doctrine's central purpose is to "accord the States the respect owed them as" joint sovereigns. See Puerto Rico Aqueduct and Sewer Authority v. Metcalf & Eddy, Inc., 506 U.S. 139, 146 (1993); see Part III–C, supra. It is for this reason, for instance, that sovereign immunity applies regardless of whether a private plaintiff's suit is for monetary damages or some other type of relief. See *Seminole Tribe,* 517 U.S., at 58 ("[W]e have often made it clear that the relief sought by a plaintiff suing a State is irrelevant to the question whether the suit is barred by the Eleventh Amendment").

Sovereign immunity does not merely constitute a defense to monetary liability or even to all types of liability. Rather, it provides an immunity from suit. The statutory scheme, as interpreted by the United States, is thus no more permissible than if Congress had allowed private parties to sue States in federal court for violations of the Shipping Act but precluded a court from awarding them any relief.

It is also worth noting that an FMC order that a State pay reparations to a private party may very well result in the withdrawal of funds from that State's treasury. A State subject to such an order at the conclusion of an FMC adjudicatory proceeding would either have to make the required payment to the injured private party or stand in violation of the Commission's order. If the State were willfully and knowingly to choose noncompliance, the Commission could assess a civil penalty of up to $25,000 a day against the State. See 46 U.S.C.App. § 1712(a). And if the State then refused to pay that penalty, the Attorney General, at the request of the Commission, could seek to recover that amount in a federal district court; because that action would be one brought by the Federal Government, the State's sovereign immunity would not extend to it.

To be sure, the United States suggests that the FMC's statutory authority to impose civil penalties for violations of reparation orders is "doubtful." Reply Brief for United States 7. The relevant statutory provisions, however, appear on their face to confer such authority. For while reparation orders and nonreparation orders are distinguished in other parts of the statutory scheme, see, e.g., 46 U.S.C.App. § 1713(c) and (d), the provision addressing civil penalties makes no such distinction. See § 1712(a) ("Whoever violates ... a Commission order is liable to the United States for a civil penalty"). The United States, moreover, does not even dispute that the FMC could impose a civil penalty on a State for failing to obey a nonreparation order, which, if enforced by the Attorney General, would also result in a levy upon that State's treasury.

IV

Two final arguments raised by the FMC and the United States remain to be addressed. Each is answered in part by reference to our decision in *Seminole Tribe.*

A

The FMC maintains that sovereign immunity should not bar the Commission from adjudicating Maritime Services' complaint because "[t]he constitutional necessity of uniformity in the regulation of maritime commerce limits the States' sovereignty with respect to the Federal Government's authority to regulate that commerce." Brief for Petitioner 29. This Court, however, has already held that the States' sovereign immunity extends to cases concerning maritime commerce. See, e.g., Ex parte New York, 256 U.S. 490 (1921). Moreover, *Seminole Tribe* precludes us from creating a new "maritime commerce" exception to state sovereign immunity. Although the Federal Government undoubtedly possesses an important interest in regulating maritime commerce, see U.S. Const., Art. I, § 8, cl. 3, we noted in *Seminole Tribe* that "the background principle of state sovereign immunity embodied in the Eleventh Amendment is not so ephemeral as to dissipate when the subject of the suit is an area ... that is under the exclusive control of the Federal Government," [49] 517 U.S., at 72. Thus, "[e]ven when the Constitution vests in Congress complete lawmaking authority over a particular area, the Eleventh Amendment prevents congressional authorization of suits by private parties against unconsenting States." Ibid. Of course, the Federal Government retains ample means of ensuring that state-run ports comply with the Shipping Act and other valid federal rules governing ocean-borne commerce. The FMC, for example, remains free to investigate alleged violations of the Shipping Act, either upon its own initiative or upon information supplied by a private party, ... and to institute its own administrative proceeding against a state-run port .... Additionally, the Commission "may bring suit in a district court of the United States to enjoin conduct in violation of [the Act]." 46 U.S.C.App.

---

49. JUSTICE BREYER apparently does not accept this proposition, maintaining that it is not supported by the text of the Tenth Amendment. The principle of state sovereign immunity enshrined in our constitutional framework, however, is not rooted in the Tenth Amendment. See Part II, supra. Moreover, to the extent that JUSTICE BREYER argues that the Federal Government's Article I power "[t]o regulate Commerce with foreign Nations, and among the several States," U.S. Const., Art. I, § 8, cl. 3, allows it to authorize private parties to sue nonconsenting States, his quarrel is not with our decision today but with our decision in Seminole Tribe of Fla. v. Florida, 517 U.S. 44 (1996). See id., at 72.

§ 1710(h)(1).[50] Indeed, the United States has advised us that the Court of Appeals' ruling below "should have little practical effect on the FMC's enforcement of the Shipping Act," Brief for United States in Opposition 20, and we have no reason to believe that our decision to affirm that judgment will lead to the parade of horribles envisioned by the FMC.

B

Finally, the United States maintains that even if sovereign immunity were to bar the FMC from adjudicating a private party's complaint against a state-run port for purposes of issuing a reparation order, the FMC should not be precluded from considering a private party's request for other forms of relief, such as a cease-and-desist order.... As we have previously noted, however, the primary function of sovereign immunity is not to protect State treasuries, see Part III–C, supra, but to afford the States the dignity and respect due sovereign entities. As a result, we explained in *Seminole Tribe* that "the relief sought by a plaintiff suing a State is irrelevant to the question whether the suit is barred by the Eleventh Amendment." 517 U.S., at 58. We see no reason why a different principle should apply in the realm of administrative adjudications.

* * *

While some might complain that our system of dual sovereignty is not a model of administrative convenience, see, e.g., post (BREYER, J., dissenting), that is not its purpose. Rather, "[t]he 'constitutionally mandated balance of power' between the States and the Federal Government was adopted by the Framers to ensure the protection of 'our fundamental liberties.'" Atascadero State Hospital v. Scanlon, 473 U.S. 234, 242 (1985) (quoting Garcia v. San Antonio Metropolitan Transit Authority, 469 U.S. 528, 572 (1985) (Powell, J., dissenting)). By guarding against encroachments by the Federal Government on fundamental aspects of state sovereignty, such as sovereign immunity, we strive to maintain the balance of power embodied in our Constitution and thus to "reduce the risk of tyranny and abuse from either front." *Gregory v. Ashcroft*, 501 U.S., at 458. Although the Framers likely did not envision the intrusion on state sovereignty at issue in today's case, we are nonetheless confident that it is contrary to their constitutional design, and therefore affirm the judgment of the Court of Appeals.

It is so ordered.

■ JUSTICE STEVENS, dissenting.

JUSTICE BREYER has explained why the Court's recent sovereign immunity jurisprudence does not support today's decision. I join his opinion without reservation, but add these words to emphasize the weakness of the

---

50. For these reasons, private parties remain "perfectly free to complain to the Federal Government about unlawful State activity" and "the Federal Government [remains] free to take subsequent legal action." Post, (BREYER, J., dissenting). The only step the FMC may not take, consistent with this Court's sovereign immunity jurisprudence, is to adjudicate a dispute between a private party and a nonconsenting State.

two predicates for the majority's holding. Those predicates are, first, the Court's recent decision in Alden v. Maine, 527 U.S. 706 (1999), and second, the "preeminent" interest in according States the "dignity" that is their due.

JUSTICE SOUTER has already demonstrated that *Alden*'s creative "conception of state sovereign immunity . . . is true neither to history nor to the structure of the Constitution." 527 U.S., at 814 (dissenting opinion). And I have previously explained that the "dignity" rationale is " 'embarrassingly insufficient,' " Seminole Tribe of Fla. v. Florida, 517 U.S. 44 (1996) (dissenting opinion; citation omitted), in part because "Chief Justice Marshall early on laid to rest the view that the purpose of the Eleventh Amendment was to protect a State's dignity," id., at 96–97 (citing Cohens v. Virginia, 6 Wheat. [19 U.S.] 264, 406–407 (1821)).

This latter point is reinforced by the legislative history of the Eleventh Amendment. It is familiar learning that the Amendment was a response to this Court's decision in Chisholm v. Georgia, 2 Dall. [2 U.S.] 419 (1793). Less recognized, however, is that *Chisholm* necessarily decided two jurisdictional issues: that the Court had personal jurisdiction over the state defendant, and that it had subject-matter jurisdiction over the case.[51] The first proposed draft of a constitutional amendment responding to *Chisholm*—introduced in the House of Representatives in February, 1793, on the day after *Chisholm* was decided—would have overruled the first holding, but not the second.[52] That proposal was not adopted. Rather, a proposal introduced the following day in the Senate,[53] which was "cast in terms that we associate with subject matter jurisdiction," [54] provided the basis for the present text of the Eleventh Amendment.

This legislative history suggests that the Eleventh Amendment is best understood as having overruled *Chisholm*'s subject-matter jurisdiction

---

51. See Nelson, Sovereign Immunity as a Doctrine of Personal Jurisdiction, 115 Harv.L.Rev. 1561, 1565–1566 (2002).

52. The House proposal read: "[N]o state shall be liable to be made a party defendant, in any of the judicial courts, established, or which shall be established under the authority of the United States, at the suit of any person or persons, whether a citizen or citizens, or a foreigner or foreigners, or of any body politic or corporate, whether within or without the United States." Id., at 1602, and n. 211 (quoting Proceedings of the United States House of Representatives (Feb. 19, 1793), Gazette of the United States, Feb. 20, 1793, reprinted in 5 Documentary History of the Supreme Court of the United States, 1789–1800 pp. 605–606 (M. Marcus ed., 1994)) (internal quotation marks omitted).

53. The Senate proposal read: "The Judicial Power of the United States shall not extend to any Suits in Law or Equity commenced or prosecuted against any one of the United States by Citizens of another State or by Citizens or Subjects of any foreign State." Nelson, supra, at 1603, and n. 212 (quoting Resolution in the United States Senate (Feb. 20, 1793), reprinted in 5 Documentary History of the Supreme Court, supra, at 607–608) (internal quotation marks omitted). The Senate version closely tracked the ultimate language of the Eleventh Amendment. See U.S. Const., Amdt. 11 ("The Judicial power of the United States shall not be construed to extend to any suit in law or equity, commenced or prosecuted against one of the United States by Citizens of another State, or by Citizens or Subjects of any Foreign State").

54. Nelson, supra, at 1603.

holding, thereby restricting the federal courts' diversity jurisdiction. However, the Amendment left intact *Chisholm*'s personal jurisdiction holding: that the Constitution does not immunize States from a federal court's process. If the paramount concern of the Eleventh Amendment's framers had been protecting the so-called "dignity" interest of the States, surely Congress would have endorsed the first proposed amendment granting the States immunity from process, rather than the later proposal that merely delineates the subject matter jurisdiction of courts. Moreover, as Chief Justice Marshall recognized, a subject-matter reading of the Amendment makes sense, considering the states' interest in avoiding their creditors. See *Cohens v. Virginia,* 6 Wheat. [19 U.S.], at 406–407.

The reasons why the majority in *Chisholm* concluded that the "dignity" interests underlying the sovereign immunity of English Monarchs had not been inherited by the original 13 States remain valid today. See, e.g., *Seminole Tribe of Fla.*, 517 U.S., at 95–97 (Stevens, J., dissenting). By extending the untethered "dignity" rationale to the context of routine federal administrative proceedings, today's decision is even more anachronistic than *Alden.*

■ Justice Breyer, with whom Justice Stevens, Justice Souter, and Justice Ginsburg join, dissenting.

The Court holds that a private person cannot bring a complaint against a State to a federal administrative agency where the agency (1) will use an internal adjudicative process to decide if the complaint is well founded, and (2) if so, proceed to court to enforce the law. Where does the Constitution contain the principle of law that the Court enunciates? I cannot find the answer to this question in any text, in any tradition, or in any relevant purpose. In saying this, I do not simply reiterate the dissenting views set forth in many of the Court's recent sovereign immunity decisions. See, e.g., Kimel v. Florida Bd. of Regents, 528 U.S. 62 (2000); Alden v. Maine, 527 U.S. 706 (1999); College Savings Bank v. Florida Prepaid Postsecondary Ed. Expense Bd., 527 U.S. 666 (1999); Seminole Tribe of Fla. v. Florida, 517 U.S. 44 (1996). For even were I to believe that those decisions properly stated the law—which I do not—I still could not accept the Court's conclusion here.

I

At the outset one must understand the constitutional nature of the legal proceeding before us. The legal body conducting the proceeding, the Federal Maritime Commission, is an "independent" federal agency. Constitutionally speaking, an "independent" agency belongs neither to the Legislative Branch nor to the Judicial Branch of Government. Although Members of this Court have referred to agencies as a "fourth branch" of Government, FTC v. Ruberoid Co., 343 U.S. 470, 487 (1952) (Jackson, J., dissenting), the agencies, even "independent" agencies, are more appropriately considered to be part of the Executive Branch. See Freytag v. Commissioner, 501 U.S. 868, 910 (1991) (Scalia, J., concurring in part and concurring in judgment). The President appoints their chief administrators, typically a Chairman and Commissioners, subject to confirmation by the Senate. Cf. Bowsher v. Synar, 478 U.S. 714, 723 (1986). The agencies derive their legal powers from congressionally enacted statutes. And the agencies enforce those statutes, i.e., they "execute" them, in part by making rules or by adjudicating matters in dispute. Cf. Panama Refining Co. v. Ryan, 293 U.S. 388, 428–429 (1935).

The Court long ago laid to rest any constitutional doubts about whether the Constitution permitted Congress to delegate rulemaking and adjudicative powers to agencies.... That, in part, is because the Court established certain safeguards surrounding the exercise of these powers.... And the Court denied that those activities as safeguarded, however much they might *resemble* the activities of a legislature or court, fell within the scope of Article I or Article III of the Constitution.... Consequently, in exercising those powers, the agency is engaging in an Article II, Executive Branch activity. And the powers it is exercising are powers that the Executive Branch of Government must possess if it is to enforce modern law through administration.

This constitutional understanding explains why both commentators and courts have often attached the prefix "quasi" to descriptions of an agency's rulemaking or adjudicative functions.... The terms *"quasi* legislative" and *"quasi* adjudicative" indicate that the agency uses legislative *like* or court *like* procedures but that it is not, constitutionally speaking, either a legislature or a court....

The case before us presents a fairly typical example of a federal administrative agency's use of agency adjudication. Congress has enacted a statute, the Shipping Act of 1984 (Act or Shipping Act), 46 U.S.C.App. § 1701 et seq., which, among other things, forbids marine terminal operators to discriminate against terminal users. The Act grants the Federal Maritime Commission the authority to administer the Act. The law grants the Commission the authority to enforce the Act in a variety of ways, for example, by making rules and regulations, by issuing or revoking licenses, and by conducting investigations and issuing reports. It also permits a private person to file a complaint, which the Commission is to consider. Interestingly enough, it does not say that the Commission must determine the merits of the complaint through agency adjudication—though, for present purposes, I do not see that this statutory lacuna matters.

Regardless, the Federal Maritime Commission has decided to evaluate complaints through an adjudicative process. That process involves assignment to an administrative law judge, a hearing, an initial decision, Commission review, and a final Commission decision, followed by federal appellate court review, 28 U.S.C. § 2342(3)(B). The initial hearing, like a typical court hearing, involves a neutral decisionmaker, an opportunity to present a case or defense through oral or documentary evidence, a right to cross-examination and a written record that typically constitutes the basis for decision. But unlike a typical court proceeding, the agency process also may involve considerable hearsay, resolution of factual disputes through the use of "official notice," and final decisionmaking by a Commission that remains free to disregard the initial decision and decide the matter on its own—indeed through the application of substantive as well as procedural rules, that it, the Commission, itself has created. . . .

The outcome of this process is often a Commission order, say an order that tells a party to cease and desist from certain activity or that tells one party to pay money damages (called "reparations") to another. The Commission cannot itself enforce such an order. Rather, the Shipping Act says that, to obtain enforcement of an order providing for money damages, the private party beneficiary of the order must obtain a court order. It adds that, to obtain enforcement of other commission orders, either the private party or the Attorney General must go to court. It also permits the Commission to seek a court injunction prohibiting any person from violating the Shipping Act. And it authorizes the Commission to assess civil penalties (payable to the United States) against a person who fails to obey a Commission order; but to collect the penalties, the Commission, again, must go to court.

The upshot is that this case involves a typical Executive Branch agency exercising typical Executive Branch powers seeking to determine whether a particular person has violated federal law. . . . The particular person in this instance is a state entity, the South Carolina State Ports Authority, and the agency is acting in response to the request of a private individual. But at first blush it is difficult to see why these special circumstances matter. After all, the Constitution created a Federal Government empowered to enact laws that would bind the States and it empowered that Federal Government to enforce those laws against the States. See Knickerbocker Ice Co. v. Stewart, 253 U.S. 149, 160 (1920). It also left private individuals perfectly free to complain to the Federal Government about unlawful state activity, and it left the Federal Government free to take subsequent legal action. Where then can the Court find its constitutional principle—the principle that the Constitution forbids an Executive Branch agency to determine through ordinary adjudicative processes whether such a private complaint is justified? As I have said, I cannot find that principle anywhere in the Constitution.

II

The Court's principle lacks any firm anchor in the Constitution's text. The Eleventh Amendment cannot help. It says:

> "The *Judicial* power of the United States shall not . . . extend to any suit . . . commenced or prosecuted against one of the . . . States by Citizens of another State." (Emphasis added.)

Federal administrative agencies do not exercise the "[j]udicial power of the United States." . . . Of course, this Court has read the words "Citizens of another State" as if they also said "citizen of the same State." Hans v. Louisiana, 134 U.S. 1 (1890). But it has never said that the words "[j]udicial power of the United States" mean "the executive power of the United States." Nor should it.

The Tenth Amendment cannot help. It says:

"The powers not delegated to the United States by the Constitution, nor prohibited by it to the States, are reserved to the States respectively, or to the people."

The Constitution has "delegated to the United States" the power here in question, the power "[t]o regulate Commerce with foreign Nations, and among the several States." U.S. Const., Art. I, § 8, cl. 3; see California v. United States, 320 U.S. 577, 586 (1944). The Court finds within this delegation a hidden reservation, a reservation that, due to sovereign immunity, embodies the legal principle the Court enunciates. But the text of the Tenth Amendment says nothing about any such hidden reservation, one way or the other.

Indeed, the Court refers for textual support only to an earlier case, namely Alden v. Maine, 527 U.S. 706 (1999) (holding that sovereign immunity prohibits a private citizen from suing a State in state court), and, through *Alden,* to the texts that *Alden* mentioned. These textual references include: (1) what Alexander Hamilton described as a constitutional "postulate," namely that the States retain their immunity from "suits, without their consent," unless there has been a "surrender" of that immunity "in the plan of the convention," id., at 730 (internal quotation marks omitted); (2) what the *Alden* majority called "the system of federalism established by the Constitution," ibid.; and (3) what the *Alden* majority called "the constitutional design," id., at 731. See also id., at 760–762 (Souter, J., dissenting) (noting that the Court's opinion nowhere relied on constitutional text).

Considered purely as constitutional text, these words—"constitutional design," "system of federalism," and "plan of the convention" —suffer several defects. Their language is highly abstract, making them difficult to apply. They invite differing interpretations at least as much as do the Constitution's own broad liberty-protecting phrases, such as "due process of law" or the word "liberty" itself. And compared to these latter phrases, they suffer the additional disadvantage that they do not actually appear anywhere in the Constitution.... Regardless, unless supported by considerations of history, of constitutional purpose, or of related consequence, those abstract phrases cannot support today's result.

III

Conceding that its conception of sovereign immunity is ungrounded in the Constitution's text, the Court attempts to support its holding with history. But this effort is similarly destined to fail, because the very history to which the majority turned in *Alden* here argues against the Court's basic analogy—between a federal administrative proceeding triggered by a private citizen and a private citizen's lawsuit against a State.

In *Alden* the Court said that feudal law had created an 18th-century legal norm to the effect that " 'no lord could be sued by a vassal in his own court, but each petty lord was subject to suit in the courts of a higher lord.' " 527 U.S., at 741. It added that the Framers' silence about the matter had woven that feudal "norm" into the "constitutional design," i.e., had made it part of our "system of federalism" unchanged by the " 'plan of the convention.' " Id., at 714–717, 730, 740–743. And that norm, said the *Alden* Court, by analogy forbids a citizen ("vassal") to sue a State ("lord") in the "lord's" own courts. Here that same norm argues against immunity, for the forum at issue is federal—belonging by analogy to the "higher lord." And total 18th-century silence about state immunity in Article I proceedings would argue against, not in favor of, immunity.

In any event, the 18th century was not totally silent. The Framers enunciated in the "plan of the convention," the principle that the Federal Government may sue a State without its consent. See, e.g., West Virginia v. United States, 479 U.S. 305, 311 (1987). They also described in the First Amendment the right of a citizen to petition the Federal Government for a redress of grievances. See also United States v. Cruikshank, 92 U.S. 542, 552–553; cf. generally Mark, The Vestigial Constitution: The History and Significance of the Right to Petition, 66 Ford. L.Rev. 2153, 2227 (1998). The first principle applies here because only the Federal Government, not the private party, can—in light of this Court's recent sovereign immunity jurisprudence, see Seminole Tribe of Fla. v. Florida, 517 U.S. 44 (1996)— bring the ultimate court action necessary legally to force a State to comply with the relevant federal law. The second principle applies here because a private citizen has asked the Federal Government to determine whether the State has complied with federal law and, if not, to take appropriate legal action in court.

Of course these two principles apply only through analogy. (The Court's decision also relies on analogy—one that jumps the separation-of-powers boundary that the Constitution establishes.) Yet the analogy seems apt. A private citizen, believing that a State has violated federal law, seeks a determination by an Executive Branch agency that he is right; the agency will make that determination through use of its own adjudicatory agency processes; and, if the State fails to comply, the Federal Government may bring an action against the State in federal court to enforce the federal law.

Twentieth-century legal history reinforces the appropriateness of this description. The growth of the administrative state has led this Court to determine that administrative agencies are not Article III courts, ... that they have broad discretion to proceed either through agency adjudication or through rulemaking, ... and that they may bring administrative enforcement proceedings against States. At a minimum these historically established legal principles argue strongly against any effort to analogize the present proceedings to a lawsuit brought by a private individual against a State in a state court or to an Eleventh Amendment type lawsuit brought by a private individual against a State in a federal court.

This is not to say that the analogy (with a citizen petitioning for federal intervention) is, historically speaking, a perfect one. As the Court points out, the Framers may not have "anticipated the vast growth of the administrative state," and the history of their debates "does not provide direct guidance." But the Court is wrong to ignore the relevance and importance of what the Framers did say. And it is doubly wrong to attach "great" legal "significance" to the absence of 18th-and 19th-century administrative agency experience. Even if those alive in the 18th century did not "anticipat[e] the vast growth of the administrative state," they did write a Constitution designed to provide a framework for Government across the centuries, a framework that is flexible enough to meet modern needs. And we cannot read their silence about particular means as if it were an instruction to forbid their use.

IV

The Court argues that the basic purpose of "sovereign immunity" doctrine—namely preservation of a State's "dignity" —requires application of that doctrine here. It rests this argument upon (1) its efforts to analogize agency proceedings to court proceedings, and (2) its claim that the agency proceedings constitute a form of "compulsion" exercised by a private individual against the State. As I have just explained, I believe its efforts to analogize agencies to courts are, constitutionally speaking, too frail to support its conclusion. Neither can its claim of "compulsion" provide the necessary support.

Viewed from a purely legal perspective, the "compulsion" claim is far too weak. That is because the private individual lacks the legal authority to compel the State to comply with the law. For as I have noted, in light of the Court's recent sovereign immunity decisions, if an individual does bring suit to enforce the Commission's order, see 46 U.S.C.App. § 1713, the State would arguably be free to claim sovereign immunity. See *Seminole Tribe of Fla.*, supra. Only the Federal Government, acting through the Commission or the Attorney General, has the authority to compel the State to act.

In a typical instance, the private individual will file a complaint, the agency will adjudicate the complaint, and the agency will reach a decision. The State subsequently may take the matter to court in order to obtain judicial review of any adverse agency ruling, but, if it does so, its opponent in that court proceeding is *not* a private party, but the agency itself. 28 U.S.C. § 2344. (And unlike some other administrative schemes, see, e.g., Verizon Md., Inc. v. Public Serv. Comm'n of Md., 535 U.S. 635, 651–652 (2002) (SOUTER, J., concurring), the Commission would not be a party in name only.) Alternatively, the State may do nothing, in which case either the Commission or the Attorney General must seek a court order compelling the State to obey. 46 U.S.C.App. §§ 1710, 1713. The Commission, but not a private party, may assess a penalty against the State for noncompliance, § 1712; and only a court acting at the Commission's request can compel compliance with a penalty order. In sum, no one can legally compel the State's obedience to the Shipping Act's requirements without a court order, and in no case would a court issue such an order (absent a State's voluntary waiver of sovereign immunity, see Atascadero State Hospital v. Scanlon, 473 U.S. 234, 238 (1985)) absent the request of a federal agency or other federal instrumentality.

In *Alden* this Court distinguished for sovereign immunity purposes between (a) a lawsuit brought by the Federal Government and (b) a lawsuit brought by a private person. It held that principles of "sovereign immunity" barred suit in the latter instance but not the former, because the former—a suit by the Federal Government—"require[s] the exercise of political responsibility for each suit prosecuted against a State." 527 U.S., at 756. That same "exercise of political responsibility" must take place here in every instance prior to the issuance of an order that, from a legal perspective, will compel the State to obey. To repeat: Without a court proceeding the private individual cannot legally force the State to act, to pay, or to desist; only the Federal Government may institute a court proceeding; and, in deciding whether to do so, the Federal Government will exercise appropriate political responsibility. Cf. ibid.

Viewed from a practical perspective, the Court's "compulsion" claim proves far too much. Certainly, a private citizen's decision to file a complaint with the Commission can produce practical pressures upon the State to respond and eventually to comply with a Commission decision. By appearing before the Commission, the State will be able to obtain full judicial review of an adverse agency decision in a court of appeals (where it will face in opposition the Commission itself, not the private party). By appearing, the State will avoid any potential Commission-assessed monetary penalty. And by complying, it will avoid the adverse political, practical, and symbolic implications of being labeled a federal "lawbreaker."

Practical pressures such as these, however, cannot sufficiently "affront" a State's "dignity" as to warrant constitutional "sovereign immunity" protections, for it is easy to imagine comparable instances of clearly lawful private citizen complaints to Government that place a State under far greater practical pressures to comply. No one doubts, for example, that a private citizen can complain to Congress, which may threaten (should the State fail to respond) to enact a new law that the State opposes. Nor does anyone deny that a private citizen, in complaining to a federal agency, may seek a rulemaking proceeding, which may lead the agency (should the State fail to respond) to enact a new agency rule that the State opposes. A private citizen may ask an agency formally to declare that a State is not in compliance with a statute or federal rule, even though from that formal declaration may flow a host of legal consequences adverse to a State's interests. . . . And one can easily imagine a legal scheme in which a private individual files a complaint like the one before us, but asks an agency staff member to investigate the matter, which investigation would lead to an order similar to the order at issue here with similar legal and practical consequences.

Viewed solely in terms of practical pressures, the pressures upon a State to respond before Congress or the agency, to answer the private citizen's accusations, to oppose his requests for legally adverse agency or congressional action, would seem no less powerful than those at issue here. Once one avoids the temptation to think (mistakenly) of an agency as a court, it is difficult to see why the practical pressures at issue here would "affront" a State's "dignity" any more than those just mentioned. And if the latter create no constitutional "dignity" problem, why should the former? The Court's answer—that "[s]overeign immunity concerns are not implicated" unless the "Federal Government attempts to coerce States into answering the complaints of private parties in an adjudicative proceeding" —simply begs the question of *when* and *why* States should be entitled to special constitutional protection.

The Court's more direct response lies in its claim that the practical pressures here are special, arising from a set of statutes that deprive a nonresponding State of any meaningful judicial review of the agency's determinations. The Court does not explain just what makes this kind of pressure constitutionally special. But in any event, the Court's response is inadequate. The statutes clearly provide the State with full judicial review of the initial agency decision should the State choose to seek that review. 28 U.S.C. § 2342(3)(B)(iv). That review cannot "affront" the State's "dignity, for it takes place in a court proceeding in which the Commission, not the private party, will oppose the State." § 2344.

Even were that not so, Congress could easily resolve the resulting problem by making clear that the relevant statutes authorize full judicial review in an enforcement action brought against a State. For that matter, one might interpret existing statutes as permitting in such actions whatever form of judicial review the Constitution demands. Cf. Crowell v. Benson, [285 U.S. 22, 45–47 (1932)]. Statutory language that authorizes review of whether an order was "properly made and duly issued," 46 U.S.C.App. § 1713(c), does not *forbid* review that the Constitution *requires*. But even were I to make the heroic assumption (which I do not believe) that this case implicates a reviewing court's statutory inability to apply constitutionally requisite standards of judicial review, I should still conclude that the Constitution permits the agency to consider the complaint here before us. The "review standards" problem concerns the later enforceability of the agency decision, and the Court must consider any such problem later in the context of a court order granting or denying review. Ashwander v. TVA, 297 U.S. 288, 347 (1936) (Brandeis, J., concurring) (" 'It is not the habit of the Court to decide questions of a constitutional nature unless absolutely necessary to a decision of the case' ").

V

The Court cannot justify today's decision in terms of its practical consequences. The decision, while permitting an agency to bring enforcement actions against States, forbids it to use agency adjudication in order to help decide whether to do so. Consequently the agency must rely more heavily upon its own informal staff investigations in order to decide whether a citizen's complaint has merit. The natural result is less agency flexibility, a larger federal bureaucracy, less fair procedure, and potentially less effective law enforcement. . . . And at least one of these consequences, the forced growth of unnecessary federal bureaucracy, undermines the very constitutional objectives the Court's decision claims to serve. . . .

These consequences are not purely theoretical. The Court's decision may undermine enforcement against state employers of many laws designed to protect worker health and safety.... And it may inhibit the development of federal fair, rapid, and efficient, informal non-judicial responses to complaints, for example, of improper medical care (involving state hospitals). Cf. generally Macchiaroli, Medical Malpractice Screening Panels: Proposed Model Legislation to Cure Judicial Ills, 58 Geo. Wash.L.Rev. 181 (1990).

* * *

The Court's decision threatens to deny the Executive and Legislative Branches of Government the structural flexibility that the Constitution permits and which modern government demands. The Court derives from the abstract notion of state "dignity" a structural principle that limits the powers of both Congress and the President. Its reasoning rests almost exclusively upon the use of a formal analogy, which, as I have said, jumps ordinary separation-of-powers bounds. It places "great significance" upon the 18th-century absence of 20th-century administrative proceedings. And its conclusion draws little support from considerations of constitutional purpose or related consequence. In its readiness to rest a structural limitation on so little evidence and in its willingness to interpret that limitation so broadly, the majority ignores a historical lesson, reflected in a constitutional understanding that the Court adopted long ago: An overly restrictive judicial interpretation of the Constitution's structural constraints (unlike its protections of certain basic liberties) will undermine the Constitution's own efforts to achieve its far more basic structural aim, the creation of a representative form of government capable of translating the people's will into effective public action.

This understanding, underlying constitutional interpretation since the New Deal, reflects the Constitution's demands for structural flexibility sufficient to adapt substantive laws and institutions to rapidly changing social, economic, and technological conditions. It reflects the comparative inability of the Judiciary to understand either those conditions or the need for new laws and new administrative forms they may create. It reflects the Framers' own aspiration to write a document that would "constitute" a democratic, liberty-protecting form of government that would endure through centuries of change. This understanding led the New Deal Court to reject overly restrictive formalistic interpretations of the Constitution's structural provisions, thereby permitting Congress to enact social and economic legislation that circumstances had led the public to demand. And it led that Court to find in the Constitution authorization for new forms of administration, including independent administrative agencies, with the legal authority flexibly to implement, *i.e.*, to "execute," through adjudication, through rulemaking, and in other ways, the legislation that Congress subsequently enacted....

Where I believe the Court has departed from this basic understanding I have consistently dissented.... These decisions set loose an interpretive principle that restricts far too severely the authority of the Federal Government to regulate innumerable relationships between State and citizen. Just as this principle has no logical starting place, I fear that neither does it have any logical stopping point.

Today's decision reaffirms the need for continued dissent—unless the consequences of the Court's approach prove anodyne, as I hope, rather than randomly destructive, as I fear.[55]

Tennessee v. Lane

Supreme Court of the United States, 2004.
541 U.S. 509, 124 S.Ct. 1978, 158 L.Ed.2d 820.

■ JUSTICE STEVENS delivered the opinion of the Court.

Title II of the Americans with Disabilities Act of 1990 (ADA or Act), 104 Stat. 337, 42 U.S.C. §§ 12131–12165, provides that "no qualified individual with a disability shall, by reason of such disability, be excluded from participation in or be denied the benefits of the services, programs or activities of a public entity, or be subjected to discrimination by any such entity." § 12132. The question presented in this case is whether Title II exceeds Congress' power under § 5 of the Fourteenth Amendment.

I

In August 1998, respondents George Lane and Beverly Jones filed this action against the State of Tennessee and a number of Tennessee counties, alleging past and ongoing violations of Title II. Respondents, both of whom are paraplegics who use wheelchairs for mobility, claimed that they were denied access to, and the services of, the state court system by reason of their disabilities. Lane alleged that he was compelled to appear to answer a set of criminal charges on the second floor of a county courthouse that had no elevator. At his first appearance, Lane crawled up two flights of stairs to get to the courtroom. When Lane returned to the courthouse for a hearing, he refused to crawl again or to be carried by officers to the courtroom; he consequently was arrested and jailed for failure to appear. Jones, a certified court reporter, alleged that she has not been able to gain access to a

---

[**55.** See Comment, *Federal Maritime Commission v. South Carolina Ports Authority*: Judicial Incursions into Executive Power, 69 Brook.L.Rev. 1555 (2004).

In Tennessee Student Assistance Corp. v. Hood, 541 U.S. 440 (2004), the Court held that "a proceeding initiated by a debtor to determine the dischargeability of a student loan debt is not a suit against the State for purposes of the Eleventh Amendment...." The Court's holding turned on its determination that the bankruptcy court exercises in rem jurisdiction over the estate of the debtor, rather than in personam jurisdiction over creditors with claims against that estate. In light of this determination, the Court left unreviewed the holding below that Congress is empowered to abrogate state sovereign immunity in the exercise of its plenary Article I power "[t]o establish ... uniform Laws on the subject of Bankruptcies throughout the United States." Justice Thomas, joined by Justice Scalia, dissented on the ground that the Article I argument was flatly contradicted by the *Federal Maritime Commission* case, and that the alternate in rem argument adopted by the Court was not properly presented in this case.]

number of county courthouses, and, as a result, has lost both work and an opportunity to participate in the judicial process. Respondents sought damages and equitable relief.

The State moved to dismiss the suit on the ground that it was barred by the Eleventh Amendment. The District Court denied the motion without opinion, and the State appealed.[56] The United States intervened to defend Title II's abrogation of the States' Eleventh Amendment immunity. On April 28, 2000, after the appeal had been briefed and argued, the Court of Appeals for the Sixth Circuit entered an order holding the case in abeyance pending our decision in Board of Trustees of Univ. of Ala. v. Garrett, 531 U.S. 356 (2001).

In *Garrett,* we concluded that the Eleventh Amendment bars private suits seeking money damages for state violations of Title I of the ADA. We left open, however, the question whether the Eleventh Amendment permits suits for money damages under Title II. Id., at 360, n. 1. Following the *Garrett* decision, the Court of Appeals, sitting en banc, heard argument in a Title II suit brought by a hearing-impaired litigant who sought money damages for the State's failure to accommodate his disability in a child custody proceeding. Popovich v. Cuyahoga County Court, 276 F.3d 808 (CA6 2002). A divided court permitted the suit to proceed despite the State's assertion of Eleventh Amendment immunity. The majority interpreted *Garrett* to bar private ADA suits against States based on equal protection principles, but not those that rely on due process principles. 276 F.3d, at 811–816. The minority concluded that Congress had not validly abrogated the States' Eleventh Amendment immunity for any Title II claims, id., at 821, while the concurring opinion concluded that Title II validly abrogated state sovereign immunity with respect to both equal protection and due process claims, id., at 818.

Following the en banc decision in *Popovich,* a panel of the Court of Appeals entered an order affirming the District Court's denial of the State's motion to dismiss in this case. Judgt. order reported at 40 Fed. Appx. 911 (CA6 2002). The order explained that respondents' claims were not barred because they were based on due process principles. In response to a petition for rehearing arguing that *Popovich* was not controlling because the complaint did not allege due process violations, the panel filed an amended opinion. It explained that the Due Process Clause protects the right of access to the courts, and that the evidence before Congress when it enacted Title II "established that physical barriers in government buildings, including courthouses and in the courtrooms themselves, have had the effect of denying disabled people the opportunity to access vital services and to exercise fundamental rights guaranteed by the Due Process Clause." 315 F.3d 680, 682 (CA6 2003). Moreover, that "record demonstrated that public entities' failure to accommodate the needs of qualified persons with disabil-

---

56. In Puerto Rico Aqueduct and Sewer Authority v. Metcalf & Eddy, Inc., 506 U.S. 139 (1993), we held that "States and state entities that claim to be 'arms of the State' may take advantage of the collateral order doctrine to appeal a district court order denying a claim of Eleventh Amendment immunity." Id., at 147.

ities may result directly from unconstitutional animus and impermissible stereotypes." Id., at 683. The panel did not, however, categorically reject the State's submission. It instead noted that the case presented difficult questions that "cannot be clarified absent a factual record," and remanded for further proceedings. Ibid. We granted certiorari, 539 U.S. 941 (2003), and now affirm.

II

The ADA was passed by large majorities in both Houses of Congress after decades of deliberation and investigation into the need for comprehensive legislation to address discrimination against persons with disabilities. In the years immediately preceding the ADA's enactment, Congress held 13 hearings and created a special task force that gathered evidence from every State in the Union. The conclusions Congress drew from this evidence are set forth in the task force and Committee Reports, described in lengthy legislative hearings, and summarized in the preamble to the statute. Central among these conclusions was Congress' finding that

> "individuals with disabilities are a discrete and insular minority who have been faced with restrictions and limitations, subjected to a history of purposeful unequal treatment, and relegated to a position of political powerlessness in our society, based on characteristics that are beyond the control of such individuals and resulting from stereotypic assumptions not truly indicative of the individual ability of such individuals to participate in, and contribute to, society." 42 U.S.C. § 12101(a)(7).

Invoking "the sweep of congressional authority, including the power to enforce the fourteenth amendment and to regulate commerce," the ADA is designed "to provide a clear and comprehensive national mandate for the elimination of discrimination against individuals with disabilities." §§ 12101(b)(1), (b)(4). It forbids discrimination against persons with disabilities in three major areas of public life: employment, which is covered by Title I of the statute; public services, programs, and activities, which are the subject of Title II; and public accommodations, which are covered by Title III.

Title II, §§ 12131–12134, prohibits any public entity from discriminating against "qualified" persons with disabilities in the provision or operation of public services, programs, or activities. The Act defines the term "public entity" to include state and local governments, as well as their agencies and instrumentalities. § 12131(1). Persons with disabilities are "qualified" if they, "with or without reasonable modifications to rules, policies, or practices, the removal of architectural, communication, or transportation barriers, or the provision of auxiliary aids and services, mee[t] the essential eligibility requirements for the receipt of services or the participation in programs or activities provided by a public entity." § 12131(2). Title II's enforcement provision incorporates by reference § 505 of the Rehabilitation Act of 1973, 92 Stat. 2982, as added, 29 U.S.C. § 794a, which authorizes private citizens to bring suits for money damages. 42 U.S.C. § 12133.

III

The Eleventh Amendment renders the States immune from "any suit in law or equity, commenced or prosecuted . . . by Citizens of another State, or by Citizens or Subjects of any Foreign State." Even though the Amendment "by its terms . . . applies only to suits against a State by citizens of another State," our cases have repeatedly held that this immunity also applies to unconsented suits brought by a State's own citizens. *Garrett*, 531 U.S., at 363; Kimel v. Florida Bd. of Regents, 528 U.S. 62, 72–73 (2000). Our cases have also held that Congress may abrogate the State's Eleventh Amendment immunity. To determine whether it has done so in any given case, we "must resolve two predicate questions: first, whether Congress unequivocally expressed its intent to abrogate that immunity; and second, if it did, whether Congress acted pursuant to a valid grant of constitutional authority." Id., at 73.

The first question is easily answered in this case. The Act specifically provides: "A State shall not be immune under the eleventh amendment to the Constitution of the United States from an action in Federal or State court of competent jurisdiction for a violation of this chapter." 42 U.S.C. § 12202. As in *Garrett*, see 531 U.S., at 363–364, no party disputes the adequacy of that expression of Congress' intent to abrogate the States' Eleventh Amendment immunity. The question, then, is whether Congress had the power to give effect to its intent.

In Fitzpatrick v. Bitzer, 427 U.S. 445 (1976), we held that Congress can abrogate a State's sovereign immunity when it does so pursuant to a valid exercise of its power under § 5 of the Fourteenth Amendment to enforce the substantive guarantees of that Amendment. Id., at 456. This enforcement power, as we have often acknowledged, is a "broad power indeed." Mississippi Univ. for Women v. Hogan, 458 U.S. 718, 732 (1982), citing Ex parte Virginia, 100 U.S. 339, 346 (1880). It includes "the authority both to remedy and to deter violation of rights guaranteed [by the Fourteenth Amendment] by prohibiting a somewhat broader swath of conduct, including that which is not itself forbidden by the Amendment's text." *Kimel*, 528 U.S., at 81. We have thus repeatedly affirmed that "Congress may enact so-called prophylactic legislation that proscribes facially constitutional conduct, in order to prevent and deter unconstitutional conduct." Nevada Dept. of Human Resources v. Hibbs, 538 U.S. 721, 727–728 (2003). See also City of Boerne v. Flores, 521 U.S. 507, 518 (1997). The most recent affirmation of the breadth of Congress' § 5 power came in *Hibbs*, in which we considered whether a male state employee could recover money damages against the State for its failure to comply with the family-care leave provision of the Family and Medical Leave Act of 1993 (FMLA), 107 Stat. 6, 29 U.S.C. § 2601 *et seq.* We upheld the FMLA as a valid exercise of Congress' § 5 power to combat unconstitutional sex discrimination, even though there was no suggestion that the State's leave policy was adopted or applied with a discriminatory purpose that would render it unconstitutional under the rule of Personnel Administrator of Mass. v. Feeney, 442 U.S. 256 (1979). When Congress seeks to remedy or prevent unconstitutional discrimination, § 5 authorizes it to enact prophylactic legislation proscribing practices that are discriminatory in effect, if not in intent, to carry out the basic objectives of the Equal Protection Clause.

Congress' § 5 power is not, however, unlimited. While Congress must have a wide berth in devising appropriate remedial and preventative measures for unconstitutional actions, those measures may not work a "substantive change in the governing law." *Boerne,* 521 U.S., at 519. In *Boerne,* we recognized that the line between remedial legislation and substantive redefinition is "not easy to discern," and that "Congress must have wide latitude in determining where it lies." Id., at 519–520. But we also confirmed that "the distinction exists and must be observed," and set forth a test for so observing it: Section 5 legislation is valid if it exhibits "a congruence and proportionality between the injury to be prevented or remedied and the means adopted to that end." Id., at 520.

In *Boerne,* we held that Congress had exceeded its § 5 authority when it enacted the Religious Freedom Restoration Act of 1993 (RFRA). We began by noting that Congress enacted RFRA "in direct response" to our decision in Employment Div., Dept. of Human Resources of Ore. v. Smith, 494 U.S. 872 (1990), for the stated purpose of "restor[ing]" a constitutional rule that *Smith* had rejected. 521 U.S., at 512, 515 (internal quotation marks omitted). Though the respondent attempted to defend the statute as a reasonable means of enforcing the Free Exercise Clause as interpreted in *Smith,* we concluded that RFRA was "so out of proportion" to that objective that it could be understood only as an attempt to work a "substantive change in constitutional protections." Id., at 529, 532. Indeed, that was the very purpose of the law.

This Court further defined the contours of *Boerne*'s "congruence and proportionality" test in Florida Prepaid Postsecondary Ed. Expense Bd. v. College Savings Bank, 527 U.S. 627 (1999). At issue in that case was the validity of the Patent and Plant Variety Protection Remedy Clarification Act (hereinafter Patent Remedy Act), a statutory amendment Congress enacted in the wake of our decision in Atascadero State Hospital v. Scanlon, 473 U.S. 234 (1985), to clarify its intent to abrogate state sovereign immunity from patent infringement suits. *Florida Prepaid,* 527 U.S., at 631–632. Noting the virtually complete absence of a history of unconstitutional patent infringement on the part of the States, as well as the Act's expansive coverage, the Court concluded that the Patent Remedy Act's apparent aim was to serve the Article I concerns of "provid[ing] a uniform remedy for patent infringement and . . . plac[ing] States on the same footing as private parties under that regime," and not to enforce the guarantees of the Fourteenth Amendment. Id., at 647–648. See also *Kimel,* 528 U.S. 62 (finding that the Age Discrimination in Employment Act exceeded Congress' § 5 powers under *Boerne*); United States v. Morrison, 529 U.S. 598 (2000) (Violence Against Women Act).

Applying the *Boerne* test in *Garrett,* we concluded that Title I of the ADA was not a valid exercise of Congress' § 5 power to enforce the Fourteenth Amendment's prohibition on unconstitutional disability discrimination in public employment. As in *Florida Prepaid,* we concluded Congress' exercise of its prophylactic § 5 power was unsupported by a relevant history and pattern of constitutional violations. 531 U.S., at 368. Although the dissent pointed out that Congress had before it a great deal of evidence of discrimination by the States against persons with disabilities, id., at 379 (BREYER, J., dissenting), the Court's opinion noted that the "overwhelming majority" of that evidence related to "the provision of public services and public accommodations, which areas are addressed in Titles II and III," rather than Title I, id., at 371, n. 7. We also noted that neither the ADA's legislative findings nor its legislative history reflected a concern that the States had been engaging in a pattern of unconstitutional employment discrimination. We emphasized that the House and Senate Committee Reports on the ADA focused on " 'discrimination [in] ... *employment in the private sector,*' " and made no mention of discrimination in public employment. Id., at 371–372 (quoting S.Rep. No. 101–116, p. 6 (1989), and H.R.Rep. No. 101–485, pt. 2, p. 28 (1990), U.S.Code Cong. & Admin.News 1990, pp. 303, 310) (emphasis in *Garrett*). Finally, we concluded that Title I's broad remedial scheme was insufficiently targeted to remedy or prevent unconstitutional discrimination in public employment. Taken together, the historical record and the broad sweep of the statute suggested that Title I's true aim was not so much to enforce the Fourteenth Amendment's prohibitions against disability discrimination in public employment as it was to "rewrite" this Court's Fourteenth Amendment jurisprudence. 531 U.S., at 372–374.

In view of the significant differences between Titles I and II, however, *Garrett* left open the question whether Title II is a valid exercise of Congress' § 5 enforcement power. It is to that question that we now turn.

IV

The first step of the *Boerne* inquiry requires us to identify the constitutional right or rights that Congress sought to enforce when it enacted Title II. *Garrett,* 531 U.S., at 365. In *Garrett* we identified Title I's purpose as enforcement of the Fourteenth Amendment's command that "all persons similarly situated should be treated alike." Cleburne v. Cleburne Living Center, Inc., 473 U.S. 432, 439 (1985). As we observed, classifications based on disability violate that constitutional command if they lack a rational relationship to a legitimate governmental purpose. *Garrett,* 531 U.S., at 366 (citing *Cleburne,* 473 U.S., at 446).

Title II, like Title I, seeks to enforce this prohibition on irrational disability discrimination. But it also seeks to enforce a variety of other basic constitutional guarantees, infringements of which are subject to more searching judicial review.... These rights include some, like the right of access to the courts at issue in this case, that are protected by the Due Process Clause of the Fourteenth Amendment. The Due Process Clause and the Confrontation Clause of the Sixth Amendment, as applied to the States via the Fourteenth Amendment, both guarantee to a criminal defendant such as respondent Lane the "right to be present at all stages of the trial where his absence might frustrate the fairness of the proceedings." Faretta v. California, 422 U.S. 806, 819, n.15 (1975). The Due Process Clause also requires the States to afford certain civil litigants a "meaningful opportunity to be heard" by removing obstacles to their full participation in judicial proceedings. Boddie v. Connecticut, 401 U.S. 371, 379 (1971); M.L.B. v. S.L. J., 519 U.S. 102 (1996). We have held that the Sixth Amendment guarantees to criminal defendants the right to trial by a jury composed of a fair cross section of the community, noting that the exclusion of "identifiable segments playing major roles in the community cannot be squared with the constitutional concept of jury trial." Taylor v. Louisiana, 419 U.S. 522, 530 (1975). And, finally, we have recognized that members of the public have a right of access to criminal proceedings secured by the First Amendment. Press–Enterprise Co. v. Superior Court of Cal., County of Riverside, 478 U.S. 1, 8–15 (1986).

Whether Title II validly enforces these constitutional rights is a question that "must be judged with reference to the historical experience which it reflects." South Carolina v. Katzenbach, 383 U.S. 301, 308 (1966). See also *Florida Prepaid,* 527 U.S., at 639–640; *Boerne,* 521 U.S., at 530. While § 5 authorizes Congress to enact reasonably prophylactic remedial legislation, the appropriateness of the remedy depends on the gravity of the harm it seeks to prevent. "Difficult and intractable problems often require powerful remedies," *Kimel,* 528 U.S., at 88, but it is also true that "[s]trong measures appropriate to address one harm may be an unwarranted response to another, lesser one," *Boerne,* 521 U.S., at 530.

It is not difficult to perceive the harm that Title II is designed to address. Congress enacted Title II against a backdrop of pervasive unequal treatment in the administration of state services and programs, including systematic deprivations of fundamental rights. For example, "[a]s of 1979, most States ... categorically disqualified 'idiots' from voting, without regard to individual capacity." [57] The majority of these laws remain on the books, and have been the subject of legal challenge as recently as 2001. Similarly, a number of States have prohibited and continue to prohibit persons with disabilities from engaging in activities such as marrying and serving as jurors. The historical experience that Title II reflects is also documented in this Court's cases, which have identified unconstitutional treatment of disabled persons by state agencies in a variety of settings, including unjustified commitment, e.g., Jackson v. Indiana, 406 U.S. 715 (1972); the abuse and neglect of persons committed to state mental health hospitals, Youngberg v. Romeo, 457 U.S. 307 (1982); and irrational discrimination in zoning decisions, Cleburne v. Cleburne Living Center, Inc., 473 U.S. 432 (1985). The decisions of other courts, too, document a pattern of unequal treatment in the administration of a wide range of public services, programs, and activities, including the penal system, public education, and

---

57. Cleburne v. Cleburne Living Center, Inc., 473 U.S. 432, 464, and n. 14 (1985) (Marshall, J., concurring in judgment in part and dissenting in part) (citing Note, Mental Disability and the Right to Vote, 88 Yale L.J. 1644 (1979)).

voting. Notably, these decisions also demonstrate a pattern of unconstitutional treatment in the administration of justice.

This pattern of disability discrimination persisted despite several federal and state legislative efforts to address it. In the deliberations that led up to the enactment of the ADA, Congress identified important shortcomings in existing laws.... It also uncovered further evidence of those shortcomings, in the form of hundreds of examples of unequal treatment of persons with disabilities by States and their political subdivisions.... As the Court's opinion in *Garrett* observed, the "overwhelming majority" of these examples concerned discrimination in the administration of public programs and services. Id., at 371, n. 7 ....

With respect to the particular services at issue in this case, Congress learned that many individuals, in many States across the country, were being excluded from courthouses and court proceedings by reason of their disabilities....

Given the sheer volume of evidence demonstrating the nature and extent of unconstitutional discrimination against persons with disabilities in the provision of public services, the dissent's contention that the record is insufficient to justify Congress' exercise of its prophylactic power is puzzling, to say the least. Just last Term in *Hibbs,* we approved the family-care leave provision of the FMLA as valid § 5 legislation based primarily on evidence of disparate provision of parenting leave, little of which concerned unconstitutional state conduct. 538 U.S., at 728–733. We explained that because the FMLA was targeted at sex-based classifications, which are subject to a heightened standard of judicial scrutiny, "it was easier for Congress to show a pattern of state constitutional violations" than in *Garrett* or *Kimel,* both of which concerned legislation that targeted classifications subject to rational-basis review. 538 U.S., at 735–737. Title II is aimed at the enforcement of a variety of basic rights, including the right of access to the courts at issue in this case, that call for a standard of judicial review at least as searching, and in some cases more searching, than the standard that applies to sex-based classifications. And in any event, the record of constitutional violations in this case—including judicial findings of unconstitutional state action, and statistical, legislative, and anecdotal evidence of the widespread exclusion of persons with disabilities from the enjoyment of public services—far exceeds the record in *Hibbs.*

The conclusion that Congress drew from this body of evidence is set forth in the text of the ADA itself: "[D]iscrimination against individuals with disabilities persists in such critical areas as ... education, transportation, communication, recreation, institutionalization, health services, voting, and *access to public services.*" 42 U.S.C. § 12101(a)(3) (emphasis added). This finding, together with the extensive record of disability discrimination that underlies it, makes clear beyond peradventure that inadequate provision of public services and access to public facilities was an appropriate subject for prophylactic legislation.

V

The only question that remains is whether Title II is an appropriate response to this history and pattern of unequal treatment. At the outset, we must determine the scope of that inquiry. Title II—unlike RFRA, the Patent Remedy Act, and the other statutes we have reviewed for validity under § 5—reaches a wide array of official conduct in an effort to enforce an equally wide array of constitutional guarantees. Petitioner urges us both to examine the broad range of Title II's applications all at once, and to treat that breadth as a mark of the law's invalidity. According to petitioner, the fact that Title II applies not only to public education and voting-booth access but also to seating at state-owned hockey rinks indicates that Title II is not appropriately tailored to serve its objectives. But nothing in our case law requires us to consider Title II, with its wide variety of applications, as an undifferentiated whole. Whatever might be said about Title II's other applications, the question presented in this case is not whether Congress can validly subject the States to private suits for money damages for failing to provide reasonable access to hockey rinks, or even to voting booths, but whether Congress had the power under § 5 to enforce the constitutional right of access to the courts. Because we find that Title II unquestionably is valid § 5 legislation as it applies to the class of cases implicating the accessibility of judicial services, we need go no further. See United States v. Raines, 362 U.S. 17, 26 (1960).[58]

Congress' chosen remedy for the pattern of exclusion and discrimination described above, Title II's requirement of program accessibility, is congruent and proportional to its object of enforcing the right of access to the courts. The unequal treatment of disabled persons in the administration of judicial services has a long history, and has persisted despite several legislative efforts to remedy the problem of disability discrimination. Faced with considerable evidence of the shortcomings of previous legislative responses, Congress was justified in concluding that this "difficult and intractable proble[m]" warranted "added prophylactic measures in response." *Hibbs,* 538 U.S., at 737 (internal quotation marks omitted).

The remedy Congress chose is nevertheless a limited one. Recognizing that failure to accommodate persons with disabilities will often have the same practical effect as outright exclusion, Congress required the States to take reasonable measures to remove architectural and other barriers to accessibility. 42 U.S.C. § 12131(2). But Title II does not require States to employ any and all means to make judicial services accessible to persons with disabilities, and it does not require States to compromise their essential eligibility criteria for public programs. It requires only "reasonable modifications" that would not fundamentally alter the nature of the

---

58. In *Raines,* a State subject to suit under the Civil Rights Act of 1957 contended that the law exceeded Congress' power to enforce the Fifteenth Amendment because it prohibited "any person," and not just state actors, from interfering with voting rights. We rejected that argument, concluding that "if the complaint here called for an application of the statute clearly constitutional under the Fifteenth Amendment, that should have been an end to the question of constitutionality." 362 U.S., at 24–25.

service provided, and only when the individual seeking modification is otherwise eligible for the service. Ibid. As Title II's implementing regulations make clear, the reasonable modification requirement can be satisfied in a number of ways. In the case of facilities built or altered after 1992, the regulations require compliance with specific architectural accessibility standards. 28 CFR § 35.151 (2003). But in the case of older facilities, for which structural change is likely to be more difficult, a public entity may comply with Title II by adopting a variety of less costly measures, including relocating services to alternative, accessible sites and assigning aides to assist persons with disabilities in accessing services. § 35.150(b)(1). Only if these measures are ineffective in achieving accessibility is the public entity required to make reasonable structural changes. Ibid. And in no event is the entity required to undertake measures that would impose an undue financial or administrative burden, threaten historic preservation interests, or effect a fundamental alteration in the nature of the service. §§ 35.150(a)(2), (a)(3).

This duty to accommodate is perfectly consistent with the well-established due process principle that, "within the limits of practicability, a State must afford to all individuals a meaningful opportunity to be heard" in its courts. *Boddie,* 401 U.S., at 379 (internal quotation marks and citation omitted).[59] Our cases have recognized a number of affirmative obligations that flow from this principle: the duty to waive filing fees in certain family-law and criminal cases, the duty to provide transcripts to criminal defendants seeking review of their convictions, and the duty to provide counsel to certain criminal defendants. Each of these cases makes clear that ordinary considerations of cost and convenience alone cannot justify a State's failure to provide individuals with a meaningful right of access to the courts. Judged against this backdrop, Title II's affirmative obligation to accommodate persons with disabilities in the administration of justice cannot be said to be "so out of proportion to a supposed remedial or preventive object that it cannot be understood as responsive to, or designed to prevent, unconstitutional behavior." *Boerne,* 521 U.S., at 532; *Kimel,* 528 U.S., at 86.[60] It is, rather, a reasonable prophylactic measure, reasonably targeted to a legitimate end.

---

59. Because this case implicates the right of access to the courts, we need not consider whether Title II's duty to accommodate exceeds what the Constitution requires in the class of cases that implicate only *Cleburne*'s prohibition on irrational discrimination. See *Garrett,* 531 U.S., at 372.

60. THE CHIEF JUSTICE contends that Title II cannot be understood as remedial legislation because it "subjects a State to liability for failing to make a vast array of special accommodations, *without regard for whether the failure to accommodate results in a constitutional wrong.*" ([E]mphasis in original.) But as we have often acknowledged, Congress "is not confined to the enactment of legislation that merely parrots the precise wording of the Fourteenth Amendment," and may prohibit "a somewhat broader swath of conduct, including that which is not itself forbidden by the Amendment's text." *Kimel,* 528 U.S., at 81. Cf. *Hibbs,* 538 U.S. 721 (upholding the FMLA as valid remedial legislation without regard to whether failure to provide the statutorily mandated 12 weeks' leave results in a violation of the Fourteenth Amendment).

For these reasons, we conclude that Title II, as it applies to the class of cases implicating the fundamental right of access to the courts, constitutes a valid exercise of Congress' § 5 authority to enforce the guarantees of the Fourteenth Amendment. The judgment of the Court of Appeals is therefore affirmed.

It is so ordered.

[Concurring opinions of Justice Souter (joined by Justice Ginsburg) and Justice Ginsburg (joined by Justice Souter and Justice Breyer) are omitted.]

■ Chief Justice Rehnquist, with whom Justice Kennedy and Justice Thomas join, dissenting.

In Board of Trustees of Univ. of Ala. v. Garrett, 531 U.S. 356 (2001), we held that Congress did not validly abrogate States' Eleventh Amendment immunity when it enacted Title I of the Americans with Disabilities Act of 1990 (ADA), 42 U.S.C. §§ 12111–12117. Today, the Court concludes that Title II of that Act, §§ 12131–12165, does validly abrogate that immunity, at least insofar "as it applies to the class of cases implicating the fundamental right of access to the courts." Because today's decision is irreconcilable with *Garrett* and the well-established principles it embodies, I dissent.

The Eleventh Amendment bars private lawsuits in federal court against an unconsenting State. E.g., Nevada Dept. of Human Resources v. Hibbs, 538 U.S. 721, 726 (2003); *Garrett*, supra, at 363; Kimel v. Florida Bd. of Regents, 528 U.S. 62, 73 (2000). Congress may overcome States' sovereign immunity and authorize such suits only if it unmistakably expresses its intent to do so, and only if it "acts pursuant to a valid exercise of its power under § 5 of the Fourteenth Amendment." *Hibbs*, supra, at 726. While the Court correctly holds that Congress satisfied the first prerequisite, I disagree with its conclusion that Title II is valid § 5 enforcement legislation.

Section 5 of the Fourteenth Amendment grants Congress the authority "to enforce, by appropriate legislation," the familiar substantive guarantees contained in § 1 of that Amendment. U.S. Const., Amdt. 14, § 1 ("No State shall ... deprive any person of life, liberty, or property, without due process of law; nor deny to any person within its jurisdiction the equal protection of the laws"). Congress' power to enact "appropriate" enforcement legislation is not limited to "mere legislative repetition" of this Court's Fourteenth Amendment jurisprudence. *Garrett*, supra, at 365. Congress may "remedy" and "deter" state violations of constitutional rights by "prohibiting a somewhat broader swath of conduct, including that which is not itself forbidden by the Amendment's text." *Hibbs,* 538 U.S., at 727 (internal quotation marks omitted). Such "prophylactic" legislation, however, "must be an appropriate remedy for identified constitutional violations, not 'an attempt to substantively redefine the States' legal obligations.' " Id., at 727–728 (quoting *Kimel,* supra, at 88); City of Boerne v. Flores, 521 U.S. 507, 525 (1997) (enforcement power is "corrective or preventive, not definitional"). To ensure that Congress does not usurp this Court's responsibility to define the meaning of the Fourteenth Amendment, valid § 5 legislation must exhibit " 'congruence and proportionality between the injury to be prevented or remedied and the means adopted to that end.' " *Hibbs*, supra, at 728 (quoting *City of Boerne*, supra, at 520). While the Court today pays lipservice to the "congruence and proportionality" test, it applies it in a manner inconsistent with our recent precedents.

In *Garrett,* we conducted the three-step inquiry first enunciated in *City of Boerne* to determine whether Title I of the ADA satisfied the congruence-and-proportionality test. A faithful application of that test to Title II reveals that it too " 'substantively redefine[s],' " rather than permissibly enforces, the rights protected by the Fourteenth Amendment. *Hibbs*, supra, at 728.

. . . . .

■ JUSTICE SCALIA, dissenting.

Section 5 of the Fourteenth Amendment provides that Congress "shall have power to enforce, by appropriate legislation, the provisions" of that Amendment—including, of course, the Amendment's Equal Protection and Due Process Clauses. In Katzenbach v. Morgan, 384 U.S. 641 (1966), we decided that Congress could, under this provision, forbid English literacy tests for Puerto Rican voters in New York State who met certain educational criteria. Though those tests were not themselves in violation of the Fourteenth Amendment, we held that § 5 authorizes prophylactic legislation—that is, "legislation that proscribes facially constitutional conduct," Nevada Dept. of Human Resources v. Hibbs, 538 U.S. 721, 728 (2003), when Congress determines such proscription is desirable " 'to make the amendments fully effective,' " *Morgan*, supra, at 648 (quoting Ex parte Virginia, 100 U.S. 339, 345 (1880)). We said that "the measure of what constitutes 'appropriate legislation' under § 5 of the Fourteenth Amendment" is the flexible "necessary and proper" standard of McCulloch v. Maryland, 4 Wheat. [17 U.S.] 316, 342, 421 (1819). *Morgan,* 384 U.S., at 651. We described § 5 as "a positive grant of legislative power authorizing Congress to exercise its discretion in determining whether and what legislation is needed to secure the guarantees of the Fourteenth Amendment." Ibid.

The *Morgan* opinion followed close upon our decision in South Carolina v. Katzenbach, 383 U.S. 301 (1966), which had upheld prophylactic application of the similarly worded "enforce" provision of the Fifteenth Amendment (§ 2) to challenged provisions of the Voting Rights Act of 1965. But the Fourteenth Amendment, unlike the Fifteenth, is not limited to denial of the franchise and not limited to the denial of other rights on the basis of race. In City of Boerne v. Flores, 521 U.S. 507 (1997), we confronted Congress's inevitable expansion of the Fourteenth Amendment, as interpreted in *Morgan,* beyond the field of racial discrimination.[61] There

---

61. Congress had previously attempted such an extension in the Voting Rights Act Amendments of 1970, 84 Stat. 318, which sought to lower the voting age in state elections from 21

Congress had sought, in the Religious Freedom Restoration Act of 1993, 107 Stat. 1488, 42 U.S.C. § 2000bb *et seq.,* to impose upon the States an interpretation of the First Amendment's Free Exercise Clause that this Court had explicitly rejected. To avoid placing in congressional hands effective power to rewrite the Bill of Rights through the medium of § 5, we formulated the "congruence and proportionality" test for determining what legislation is "appropriate." When Congress enacts prophylactic legislation, we said, there must be "proportionality or congruence between the means adopted and the legitimate end to be achieved." 521 U.S., at 533.

I joined the Court's opinion in *Boerne* with some misgiving. I have generally rejected tests based on such malleable standards as "proportionality," because they have a way of turning into vehicles for the implementation of individual judges' policy preferences. . . . Even so, I signed on to the "congruence and proportionality" test in *Boerne,* and adhered to it in later cases: Florida Prepaid Postsecondary Ed. Expense Bd. v. College Savings Bank, 527 U.S. 627 (1999), where we held that the provisions of the Patent and Plant Variety Protection Remedy Clarification Act, 35 U.S.C. §§ 271(h), 296(a), were " 'so out of proportion to a supposed remedial or preventive object that [they] cannot be understood as responsive to, or designed to prevent, unconstitutional behavior,' " 527 U.S., at 646 (quoting *Boerne,* supra, at 532); Kimel v. Florida Bd. of Regents, 528 U.S. 62 (2000), where we held that the Age Discrimination in Employment Act of 1967, 81 Stat. 602, as amended, 29 U.S.C. § 621 *et seq.* (1994 ed. and Supp. III), imposed on state and local governments requirements "disproportionate to any unconstitutional conduct that conceivably could be targeted by the Act," 528 U.S., at 83; United States v. Morrison, 529 U.S. 598 (2000), where we held that a provision of the Violence Against Women Act, 42 U.S.C. § 13981, lacked congruence and proportionality because it was "not aimed at proscribing discrimination by officials which the Fourteenth Amendment might not itself proscribe," 529 U.S., at 626; and Board of Trustees of Univ. of Ala. v. Garrett, 531 U.S. 356 (2001), where we said that Title I of the Americans with Disabilities Act of 1990 (ADA), 104 Stat. 330, 42 U.S.C. §§ 12111–12117, raised "the same sort of concerns as to congruence and proportionality as were found in *City of Boerne,*" 531 U.S., at 372.

But these cases were soon followed by *Nevada Dept. of Human Resources v. Hibbs,* in which the Court held that the Family and Medical Leave Act of 1993, 107 Stat. 9, 29 U.S.C. § 2612 *et seq.,* which required States to provide their employees up to 12 work weeks of unpaid leave (for various purposes) annually, was "congruent and proportional to its remedial object [of preventing sex discrimination], and can be understood as responsive to, or designed to prevent, unconstitutional behavior." 538 U.S., at 740 (internal quotation marks omitted). I joined Justice Kennedy's dissent, which established (conclusively, I thought) that Congress had identified no unconstitutional state action to which the statute could

---

to 18. This extension was rejected, but in three separate opinions, none of which commanded a majority of the Court.

conceivably be a proportional response. And now we have today's decision, holding that Title II of the ADA is congruent and proportional to the remediation of constitutional violations, in the face of what seems to me a compelling demonstration of the opposite by THE CHIEF JUSTICE's dissent.

I yield to the lessons of experience. The "congruence and proportionality" standard, like all such flabby tests, is a standing invitation to judicial arbitrariness and policy-driven decisionmaking. Worse still, it casts this Court in the role of Congress's taskmaster. Under it, the courts (and ultimately this Court) must regularly check Congress's homework to make sure that it has identified sufficient constitutional violations to make its remedy congruent and proportional. As a general matter, we are ill advised to adopt or adhere to constitutional rules that bring us into constant conflict with a coequal branch of Government. And when conflict is unavoidable, we should not come to do battle with the United States Congress armed only with a test ("congruence and proportionality") that has no demonstrable basis in the text of the Constitution and cannot objectively be shown to have been met or failed. As I wrote for the Court in an earlier case, "low walls and vague distinctions will not be judicially defensible in the heat of interbranch conflict." Plaut v. Spendthrift Farm, Inc., 514 U.S. 211, 239 (1995).

I would replace "congruence and proportionality" with another test—one that provides a clear, enforceable limitation supported by the text of § 5. Section 5 grants Congress the power "to *enforce,* by appropriate legislation," the other provisions of the Fourteenth Amendment. U.S. Const., Amdt. 14 (emphasis added). *Morgan* notwithstanding, one does not, within any normal meaning of the term, "enforce" a prohibition by issuing a still broader prohibition directed to the same end. One does not, for example, "enforce" a 55–mile-per-hour speed limit by imposing a 45–mile-per-hour speed limit—even though that is indeed directed to the same end of automotive safety and will undoubtedly result in many fewer violations of the 55–mile-per-hour limit. And one does not "enforce" the right of access to the courts at issue in this case by requiring that disabled persons be provided access to *all* of the "services, programs, or activities" furnished or conducted by the State, 42 U.S.C. § 12132. That is simply not what the power to enforce means—or ever meant. The 1860 edition of Noah Webster's American Dictionary of the English Language, current when the Fourteenth Amendment was adopted, defined "enforce" as: "To put in execution; to cause to take effect; as, to *enforce* the laws." Id., at 396. See also J. Worcester, Dictionary of the English Language 484 (1860) ("To put in force; to cause to be applied or executed; as, 'To *enforce* a law' "). Nothing in § 5 allows Congress to go *beyond* the provisions of the Fourteenth Amendment to proscribe, prevent, or "remedy" conduct that does not *itself* violate any provision of the Fourteenth Amendment. So-called "prophylactic legislation" is reinforcement rather than enforcement.

Morgan asserted that this commonsense interpretation "would confine the legislative power ... to the insignificant role of abrogating only those state laws that the judicial branch was prepared to adjudge unconstitutional, or of merely informing the judgment of the judiciary by particularizing the 'majestic generalities' of § 1 of the Amendment." 384 U.S., at 648–649. That is not so. One must remember "that in 1866 the lower federal courts had no general jurisdiction of cases alleging a deprivation of rights secured by the Constitution." R. Berger, Government By Judiciary 147 (2d ed.1997). If, just after the Fourteenth Amendment was ratified, a State had enacted a law imposing racially discriminatory literacy tests (different questions for different races) a citizen prejudiced by such a test would have had no means of asserting his constitutional right to be free of it. Section 5 authorizes Congress to create a cause of action through which the citizen may vindicate his Fourteenth Amendment rights. One of the first pieces of legislation passed under Congress's § 5 power was the Ku Klux Klan Act of April 20, 1871, 17 Stat. 13, entitled *"An Act to enforce the Provisions of the Fourteenth Amendment to the Constitution of the United States, and for other Purposes."* Section 1 of that Act, later codified as Rev. Stat. § 1979, 42 U.S.C. § 1983, authorized a cause of action against "any person who, under color of any law, statute, ordinance, regulation, custom, or usage of any State, shall subject, or cause to be subjected, any person within the jurisdiction of the United States to the deprivation of any rights, privileges, or immunities secured by the Constitution of the United States." 17 Stat. 13. Section 5 would also authorize measures that do not restrict the States' substantive scope of action but impose requirements directly related to the *facilitation* of "enforcement" —for example, reporting requirements that would enable violations of the Fourteenth Amendment to be identified.[62] But what § 5 does *not* authorize is so-called "prophylactic" measures, prohibiting primary conduct that is itself not forbidden by the Fourteenth Amendment.

The major impediment to the approach I have suggested is *stare decisis.* A lot of water has gone under the bridge since *Morgan,* and many important and well-accepted measures, such as the Voting Rights Act, assume the validity of *Morgan* and *South Carolina.* As Prof. Archibald Cox put it in his Supreme Court Foreword: "The etymological meaning of section 5 may favor the narrower reading. Literally, 'to enforce' means to compel performance of the obligations imposed; but the linguistic argument lost much of its force once the *South Carolina* and *Morgan* cases decided that the power to enforce embraces any measure appropriate to effectuating the performance of the state's constitutional duty." Foreword: Constitutional Adjudication and the Promotion of Human Rights, 80 Harv.L.Rev. 91, 110–111 (1966).

---

62. Professor Tribe's treatise gives some examples of such measures that facilitate enforcement in the context of the Fifteenth Amendment:

"The Civil Rights Act of 1957, 71 Stat. 634, authorized the Attorney General to seek injunctions against interference with the right to vote on racial grounds. The Civil Rights Act of 1960, 74 Stat. 86, permitted joinder of states as parties defendant, gave the Attorney General access to local voting records, and authorized courts to register voters in areas of systemic discrimination. The Civil Rights Act of 1964, 78 Stat. 241, expedited the hearing of voting cases before three-judge courts...." L. Tribe, American Constitutional Law 931, n.5 (3d ed.2000).

However, *South Carolina* and *Morgan,* all of our later cases except *Hibbs* that give an expansive meaning to "enforce" in § 5 of the Fourteenth Amendment, and all of our earlier cases that even suggest such an expansive meaning in dicta, involved congressional measures that were directed exclusively against, or were used in the particular case to remedy, *racial discrimination.* . . .

Giving § 5 more expansive scope with regard to measures directed against racial discrimination by the States accords to practices that are distinctively violative of the principal purpose of the Fourteenth Amendment a priority of attention that this Court envisioned from the beginning, and that has repeatedly been reflected in our opinions. . . .

. . . . .

Thus, principally for reasons of *stare decisis,* I shall henceforth apply the permissive *McCulloch* standard to congressional measures designed to remedy racial discrimination by the States. I would not, however, abandon the requirement that Congress may impose prophylactic § 5 legislation only upon those particular States in which there has been an identified history of relevant constitutional violations. . . . I would also adhere to the requirement that the prophylactic remedy predicated upon such state violations must be directed against the States or state actors rather than the public at large. See *Morrison*, supra, at 625–626. And I would not, of course, permit any congressional measures that violate other provisions of the Constitution. When those requirements have been met, however, I shall leave it to Congress, under constraints no tighter than those of the Necessary and Proper Clause, to decide what measures are appropriate under § 5 to prevent or remedy racial discrimination by the States.

I shall also not subject to "congruence and proportionality" analysis congressional action under § 5 that is *not* directed to racial discrimination. Rather, I shall give full effect to that action when it consists of "enforcement" of the provisions of the Fourteenth Amendment, within the broad but not unlimited meaning of that term I have described above. When it goes beyond enforcement to prophylaxis, however, I shall consider it ultra vires. The present legislation is plainly of the latter sort.

* * *

Requiring access for disabled persons to all public buildings cannot remotely be considered a means of "enforcing" the Fourteenth Amendment. The considerations of long accepted practice and of policy that sanctioned such distortion of language where state racial discrimination is at issue do not apply in this field of social policy far removed from the principal object of the Civil War Amendments. "The seductive plausibility of single steps in a chain of evolutionary development of a legal rule is often not perceived until a third, fourth, or fifth 'logical' extension occurs. Each step, when taken, appeared a reasonable step in relation to that which preceded it, although the aggregate or end result is one that would never have been seriously considered in the first instance. This kind of gestative propensity calls for the 'line drawing' familiar in the judicial, as in the legislative process: 'thus far but not beyond.' " United States v. 12 200–ft. Reels of Super 8MM. Film, 413 U.S. 123, 127 (1973) (Burger, C. J., for the Court) (footnote omitted). It is past time to draw a line limiting the uncontrolled spread of a well-intentioned textual distortion. For these reasons, I respectfully dissent from the judgment of the Court.

■ JUSTICE THOMAS, dissenting.

I join THE CHIEF JUSTICE's dissent. I agree that Title II of the Americans with Disabilities Act of 1990 cannot be a congruent and proportional remedy to the States' alleged practice of denying disabled persons access to the courts.... Because I joined the dissent in Nevada Dept. of Human Resources v. Hibbs, 538 U.S. 721 (2003), and continue to believe that *Hibbs* was wrongly decided, I write separately only to disavow any reliance on *Hibbs* in reaching this conclusion.[63]

SECTION 5. THE THREE–JUDGE COURT STATUTES

---

§ 2284. Three-judge court; when required; composition; procedure

(a) A district court of three judges shall be convened when otherwise required by Act of Congress,[64] or when an action is filed challenging the constitutionality of the apportionment of congressional districts or the apportionment of any statewide legislative body.

(b) In any action required to be heard and determined by a district court of three judges under subsection (a) of this section, the composition and procedure of the court shall be as follows:

(1) Upon the filing of a request for three judges, the judge to whom the request is presented shall, unless he determines that three judges are not

---

[63. The Supreme Court again addressed Title II of the Americans with Disabilities Act in United States v. Georgia, 546 U.S. 151 (2006), holding unanimously that Title II validly abrogates states' sovereign immunity insofar as it creates a private cause of action for damages against states for conduct that actually violates the Fourteenth Amendment.]

[64. This refers to certain provisions of the Civil Rights Act of 1964 and the Voting Rights Act of 1965 that require or permit a three-judge court. A three-judge court is mandatory in suits under various provisions of the 1965 statute, 42 U.S.C. §§ 1973b(a), 1973c, 1973h(c), 1973aa–2, 1973bb–2(a)(2). The Attorney General may request a three-judge court in actions under the public accommodations and equal employment provisions of the 1964 statute, 42 U.S.C. §§ 2000a–5(b), 2000e–6(b). Either the Attorney General or the defendant may request a three-judge court in actions under the voting provisions of the 1964 statute, 42 U.S.C. § 1971g. A three-judge court is also required in suits to implement the Presidential Election Campaign Fund Act, 26 U.S.C. § 9011(b)(2).

When enacting high-profile, constitutionally controversial legislation, Congress is apt to expedite judicial review by specifying that attacks on the legislation are to be heard by a special three-judge court, with direct review of its judgment by the Supreme Court. A recent example is § 403 of the Bipartisan Campaign Reform Act of 2002. See McConnell v. Federal Election Commission, 540 U.S. 93, 132–133 (2003).]

required, immediately notify the chief judge of the circuit, who shall designate two other judges, at least one of whom shall be a circuit judge. The judges so designated, and the judge to whom the request was presented, shall serve as members of the court to hear and determine the action or proceeding.

(2) If the action is against a State, or officer or agency thereof, at least five days' notice of hearing of the action shall be given by registered or certified mail to the Governor and attorney general of the State.

(3) A single judge may conduct all proceedings except the trial, and enter all orders permitted by the rules of civil procedure except as provided in this subsection. He may grant a temporary restraining order on a specific finding, based on evidence submitted, that specified irreparable damage will result if the order is not granted, which order, unless previously revoked by the district judge, shall remain in force only until the hearing and determination by the district court of three judges of an application for a preliminary injunction. A single judge shall not appoint a master, or order a reference, or hear and determine any application for a preliminary or permanent injunction or motion to vacate such an injunction, or enter judgment on the merits. Any action of a single judge may be reviewed by the full court at any time before final judgment.[65]

SECTION 6. STATUTORY RESTRICTIONS ON ENJOINING STATE OFFICERS[66]

THE JOHNSON ACT OF 1934 (AS RECODIFIED)
28 U.S.C. § 1342. Rate orders of State agencies

The district courts shall not enjoin, suspend or restrain the operation of, or compliance with, any order affecting rates chargeable by a public

---

[65. This is the statute as substantially amended in 1976. Prior to that year a three-judge court had been required whenever an injunction was sought against a state or federal statute or a state administrative order on the ground of unconstitutionality.

See Wright & Kane, Federal Courts § 50 (6th ed.2002); 22 Moore's Federal Practice ch. 404 (3d ed.1998); 17 Wright, Miller & Cooper, Federal Practice and Procedure: Jurisdiction 2d §§ 4234–4235 (1988); Solimine, Congress, *Ex Parte Young*, and the Fate of the Three–Judge District Court, 70 U.Pitt.L.Rev. 101 (2008); Solimine, The Three–Judge District Court in Voting Rights Litigation, 30 U.Mich.J.L.Ref. 79 (1996); Williams, The New Three–Judge Courts of Reapportionment and Continuing Problems of Three–Judge Court Procedure, 65 Geo.L.J. 971 (1977).]

[66. See Wright & Kane, Federal Courts § 51 (6th ed.2002); 17 Moore's Federal Practice ch 121 (3d ed.1998); 17 Wright, Miller & Cooper, Federal Practice and Procedure: Jurisdiction 2d §§ 4236–4237 (1988).

The Civil Rights of Institutionalized Persons Act of 1980, 42 U.S.C. § 1997e, granted federal district judges discretionary powers to require a state prisoner to exhaust state administrative remedies before bringing a federal civil rights suit under 42 U.S.C. § 1983. This exhaustion requirement was stiffened and made mandatory to all suits by either state or federal prisoners "with respect to prison conditions" by the Prison Litigation Reform Act of 1995 (PLRA), 42 U.S.C. § 1997e(a). A unanimous Supreme Court adopted a very broad construction of "prison conditions" in Porter v. Nussle, 534 U.S. 516, 532 (2002): "[T]he

utility and made by a State administrative agency or a rate-making body of a State political subdivision, where:

(1) Jurisdiction is based solely on diversity of citizenship or repugnance of the order to the Federal Constitution; and,

(2) The order does not interfere with interstate commerce; and,

(3) The order has been made after reasonable notice and hearing; and,

(4) A plain, speedy and efficient remedy may be had in the courts of such State. [Act of May 14, 1934, 48 Stat. 775.][67]

THE TAX INJUNCTION ACT OF 1937 (AS RECODIFIED)

28 U.S.C. § 1341. Taxes by States

The district courts shall not enjoin, suspend or restrain the assessment, levy or collection of any tax under State law where a plain, speedy and efficient remedy may be had in the courts of such State. [Act of Aug. 21, 1937, 50 Stat. 738.][68]

PLRA's exhaustion requirement applies to all inmate suits about prison life, whether they involve general circumstances or particular episodes, and whether they allege excessive force or some other wrong."

However, in Jones v. Bock, 549 U.S. 199 (2007), the Supreme Court found that the Sixth Circuit went too far in requiring prisoners, pursuant to the Sixth Circuit's procedural rules, to allege and demonstrate exhaustion in the complaint. The Court held that although exhaustion is mandatory under the PLRA, Federal Rule of Civil Procedure 8(a) requires only a "short and plain statement of the claim" and the PLRA does not itself require plaintiffs to plead exhaustion. Accordingly, the failure to exhaust is an affirmative defense, and prisoners are not required to plead or demonstrate exhaustion in their complaint.]

[67. What is the significance of clause (2)? See Public Utilities Comm. of Ohio v. United Fuel Gas Co., 317 U.S. 456 (1943); Kansas–Nebraska Natural Gas Co. v. City of St. Edward, Neb., 234 F.2d 436 (8th Cir.1956). Compare ALI Study § 1371(b).

Is the state remedy plain, speedy, and efficient if state law does not permit a stay of the rate order pending judicial review? Mountain States Power Co. v. Public Service Comm. of Montana, 299 U.S. 167 (1936). Compare ALI Study § 1371(d) and Commentary at 291.]

[68. See also 28 U.S.C. § 7421(a) for a similar provision restricting injunctions against collection of federal taxes. See California v. Grace Brethren Church, 457 U.S. 393 (1982).

The Declaratory Judgment Act, 28 U.S.C. § 2201, reprinted supra p. 64, expressly excludes actions "with respect to Federal taxes." May a federal court give a declaratory judgment with respect to state taxes? The Supreme Court's answer was "no" in Great Lakes Dredge & Dock Co. v. Huffman, 319 U.S. 293 (1943).

A "plain, speedy and efficient remedy," within the meaning of the Tax Injunction Act, is merely one that meets minimal procedural criteria. The state remedy satisfied these criteria even though it took two years to get a refund of taxes paid on an excessive assessment and the state did not pay interest on the refund. Rosewell v. LaSalle Nat. Bank, 450 U.S. 503

SECTION 7. THE ABSTENTION DOCTRINES[69]

Railroad Commission of Texas v. Pullman Co.

Supreme Court of the United States, 1941.
312 U.S. 496, 61 S.Ct. 643, 85 L.Ed. 971.

Appeal from a decree of the District Court of three judges which enjoined the enforcement of an order of the above-named Railroad Commission.

■ MR. JUSTICE FRANKFURTER delivered the opinion of the Court.

In those sections of Texas where the local passenger traffic is slight, trains carry but one sleeping car. These trains, unlike trains having two or more sleepers, are without a Pullman conductor; the sleeper is in charge of a porter who is subject to the train conductor's control. As is well known, porters on Pullmans are colored and conductors are white. Addressing itself to this situation, the Texas Railroad Commission after due hearing ordered that "no sleeping car shall be operated on any line or railroad in the State

---

(1981). The Tax Injunction Act cannot be held inapplicable on mere speculation that there is no plain, speedy, and efficient remedy in the state courts. Franchise Tax Board of California v. Alcan Aluminum Ltd., 493 U.S. 331 (1990).

When a litigant seeks declaratory or injunctive relief against a state tax pursuant to 42 U.S.C. § 1983, state courts, like their federal counterparts, must refrain from granting relief under § 1983 if there is an adequate legal remedy. National Private Truck Council v. Oklahoma Tax Commission, 515 U.S. 582 (1995).

The Tax Injunction Act is subject to a judicial exception where the United States sues to protect itself or its instrumentalities from state taxation. But the mere formal status of an entity—here a Production Credit Association—as an instrumentality of the federal government is not sufficient to invoke the exception where the United States is not a coplaintiff, opposes the exercise of federal jurisdiction, and the entity in question does not exercise substantial regulatory authority. Arkansas v. Farm Credit Services of Central Arkansas, 520 U.S. 821 (1997).

A narrowly divided Court held that the Tax Injunction Act is inapplicable to a suit seeking to enjoin a state tax *credit* on Establishment Clause grounds in Hibbs v. Winn, 542 U.S. 88 (2004).]

[69.   Wright & Kane, Federal Courts § 52 (6th ed.2002); 17 Moore's Federal Practice ch. 122 (3d ed.1998); 17A Wright, Miller & Cooper, Federal Practice and Procedure: Jurisdiction 2d §§ 4241–4248 (1988); ALI Study § 1371 and Commentary at 282–298; Report on the Abstention Doctrine: The Consequence of Federal Court Deference to State Court Proceedings, by the Committee on Federal Courts of the New York State Bar Association, 122 F.R.D. 89 (1988); Staver, The Abstention Doctrines: Balancing Comity with Federal Court Intervention, 28 Seton Hall L.Rev. 1102 (1998); Lee & Wilkins, An Analysis of Supplemental Jurisdiction and Abstention with Recommendations for Legislative Action, 1990 B.Y.U.L.Rev. 321; Friedman, A Revisionist Theory of Abstention, 88 Mich.L.Rev. 530 (1989); Redish, Abstention, Separation of Powers, and the Limits of the Judicial Function, 94 Yale L.J. 71 (1984); Wells, Why Professor Redish is Wrong About Abstention, 19 Ga.L.Rev. 1097 (1985); Shapiro, Jurisdiction and Discretion, 60 N.Y.U.L.Rev. 543 (1985).]

of Texas unless such cars are continuously in the charge of an employee ... having the rank and position of Pullman conductor." Thereupon, the Pullman Company and the railroads affected brought this action in a federal district court to enjoin the Commission's order. Pullman porters were permitted to intervene as complainants, and Pullman conductors entered the litigation in support of the order. Three judges having been convened, Judicial Code, § 266, as amended, 28 U.S.C. § 380, the court enjoined enforcement of the order. From this decree, the case came here directly. Judicial Code, § 238, as amended, 28 U.S.C. § 345.

The Pullman Company and the railroads assailed the order as unauthorized by Texas law as well as violative of the Equal Protection, the Due Process and the Commerce Clauses of the Constitution. The intervening porters adopted these objections but mainly objected to the order as a discrimination against Negroes in violation of the Fourteenth Amendment.

The complaint of the Pullman porters undoubtedly tendered a substantial constitutional issue. It is more than substantial. It touches a sensitive area of social policy upon which the federal courts ought not to enter unless no alternative to its adjudication is open. Such constitutional adjudication plainly can be avoided if a definitive ruling on the state issue would terminate the controversy. It is therefore our duty to turn to a consideration of questions under Texas law.

The Commission found justification for its order in a Texas statute which we quote in the margin.[70] It is common ground that if the order is within the Commission's authority its subject matter must be included in the Commission's power to prevent "unjust discrimination ... and to prevent any and all other abuses" in the conduct of railroads. Whether arrangements pertaining to the staffs of Pullman cars are covered by the Texas concept of "discrimination" is far from clear. What practices of the railroads may be deemed to be "abuses" subject to the Commission's correction is equally doubtful. Reading the Texas statutes and the Texas decisions as outsiders without special competence in Texas law, we would have little confidence in our independent judgment regarding the application of that law to the present situation. The lower court did deny that the Texas statutes sustained the Commission's assertion of power. And this

---

70. Vernon's Anno. Texas Civil Statutes, Article 6445:

"Power and authority are hereby conferred upon the Railroad Commission of Texas over all railroads, and suburban, belt and terminal railroads, and over all public wharves, docks, piers, elevators, warehouses, sheds, tracks and other property used in connection therewith in this State, and over all persons, associations and corporations, private or municipal, owning or operating such railroad, wharf, dock, pier, elevator, warehouse, shed, track or other property to fix, and it is hereby made the duty of the said Commission to adopt all necessary rates, charges and regulations, to govern and regulate such railroads, persons, associations and corporations, and to correct abuses and prevent unjust discrimination in the rates, charges and tolls of such railroads, persons, associations and corporations, and to fix division of rates, charges and regulations between railroads and other utilities and common carriers where a division is proper and correct, and to prevent any and all other abuses in the conduct of their business and to do and perform such other duties and details in connection therewith as may be provided by law."

represents the view of an able and experienced circuit judge of the circuit which includes Texas and of two capable district judges trained in Texas law. Had we or they no choice in the matter but to decide what is the law of the state, we should hesitate long before rejecting their forecast of Texas law. But no matter how seasoned the judgment of the district court may be, it cannot escape being a forecast rather than a determination. The last word on the meaning of Article 6445 of the Texas Civil Statutes, and therefore the last word on the statutory authority of the Railroad Commission in this case, belongs neither to us nor to the district court but to the supreme court of Texas. In this situation a federal court of equity is asked to decide an issue by making a tentative answer which may be displaced tomorrow by a state adjudication. Glenn v. Field Packing Co., 290 U.S. 177; Lee v. Bickell, 292 U.S. 415. The reign of law is hardly promoted if an unnecessary ruling of a federal court is thus supplanted by a controlling decision of a state court. The resources of equity are equal to an adjustment that will avoid the waste of a tentative decision as well as the friction of a premature constitutional adjudication.

An appeal to the chancellor, as we had occasion to recall only the other day, is an appeal to the "exercise of the sound discretion, which guides the determination of courts of equity." Beal v. Missouri Pacific R.R., 312 U.S. 45, decided January 20, 1941. The history of equity jurisdiction is the history of regard for public consequences in employing the extraordinary remedy of the injunction. There have been as many and as variegated applications of this supple principle as the situations that have brought it into play. See, for modern instances, Beasley v. Texas & Pacific Ry., 191 U.S. 492; Harrisonville v. Dickey Clay Co., 289 U.S. 334; United States v. Dern, 289 U.S. 352. Few public interests have a higher claim upon the discretion of a federal chancellor than the avoidance of needless friction with state policies, whether the policy relates to the enforcement of the criminal law, Fenner v. Boykin, 271 U.S. 240; Spielman Motor Sales Co. v. Dodge, 295 U.S. 89; or the administration of a specialized scheme for liquidating embarrassed business enterprises, Pennsylvania v. Williams, 294 U.S. 176; or the final authority of a state court to interpret doubtful regulatory laws of the state, Gilchrist v. Interborough Co., 279 U.S. 159; cf. Hawks v. Hamill, 288 U.S. 52, 61. These cases reflect a doctrine of abstention appropriate to our federal system whereby the federal courts, "exercising a wise discretion" , restrain their authority because of "scrupulous regard for the rightful independence of the state governments" and for the smooth working of the federal judiciary. See Cavanaugh v. Looney, 248 U.S. 453, 457; Di Giovanni v. Camden Fire Ins. Ass'n, 296 U.S. 64, 73. This use of equitable powers is a contribution of the courts in furthering the harmonious relation between state and federal authority without the need of rigorous congressional restriction of those powers. Compare 37 Stat. 1013; Judicial Code, § 24(1), as amended, 28 U.S.C. § 41(1); 47 Stat. 70, 29 U.S.C. §§ 101–115.

Regard for these important considerations of policy in the administration of federal equity jurisdiction is decisive here. If there was no warrant in state law for the Commission's assumption of authority there is an end of the litigation; the constitutional issue does not arise. The law of Texas appears to furnish easy and ample means for determining the Commission's authority. Article 6453 of the Texas Civil Statutes gives a review of such an order in the state courts. Or, if there are difficulties in the way of this procedure of which we have not been apprised, the issue of state law may be settled by appropriate action on the part of the State to enforce obedience to the order. *Beal v. Missouri Pacific R.R.*, supra; Article 6476, Texas Civil Statutes. In the absence of any showing that these obvious methods for securing a definitive ruling in the state courts cannot be pursued with full protection of the constitutional claims, the district court should exercise its wise discretion by staying its hands. Compare Thompson v. Magnolia Co., 309 U.S. 478.

We therefore remand the cause to the district court, with directions to retain the bill pending a determination of proceedings, to be brought with reasonable promptness, in the state court in conformity with this opinion. Compare Atlas Ins. Co. v. W.I. Southern Inc., 306 U.S. 563, 573, and cases cited.

Reversed and remanded.

■ MR. JUSTICE ROBERTS took no part in the consideration or decision of this case.[71]

Burford v. Sun Oil Co.

Supreme Court of the United States, 1943.
319 U.S. 315, 63 S.Ct. 1098, 87 L.Ed. 1424.

Certiorari, 317 U.S. 621, to review a judgment reversing a judgment of the District Court which dismissed the complaint of the Sun Oil Company in a suit against the Railroad Commission of Texas et al., to enjoin the execution of an order of the Commission permitting the drilling and operation of certain oil wells in the East Texas Oil Field, and also dismissing the complaint of the Magnolia Petroleum Company, Intervener. The judgment of the District Court had at first been affirmed, 124 F.2d 467.

[71. The abstention doctrine has often been held appropriate, to avoid possibly unnecessary decision on a constitutional issue, even where the federal suit is brought under 42 U.S.C. § 1983 and its jurisdictional counterpart, 28 U.S.C. § 1343, to challenge a deprivation of civil rights. Harrison v. National Assn. for the Advancement of Colored People, 360 U.S. 167 (1959). Compare the view of a distinguished commentator that there should be a statutory denial of jurisdiction in most cases in which state legislative or administrative action is challenged on federal grounds, and an adequate remedy is available in the state courts, but that there should be no abstention when a litigant is seeking to enforce the rights of action specifically conferred by Congress in the civil rights laws. Wechsler, Federal Jurisdiction and the Revision of the Judicial Code, 13 Law & Contemp.Prob. 216, 230 (1948). ALI Study § 1371(g) takes essentially this position and would bar abstention in actions claiming denial of the right to vote or the equal protection of the laws, if the denial is alleged to be on the basis of race, creed, color, or national origin.]

■ MR. JUSTICE BLACK delivered the opinion of the Court.

In this proceeding brought in a federal district court, the Sun Oil Co. attacked the validity of an order of the Texas Railroad Commission granting the petitioner Burford a permit to drill four wells on a small plot of land in the East Texas oil field. Jurisdiction of the federal court was invoked because of the diversity of citizenship of the parties, and because of the Companies' contention that the order denied them due process of law. There is some argument that the action is an "appeal" from the State Commission to the federal court since an appeal to a State court can be taken under relevant Texas statutes; but of course the Texas legislature may not make a federal district court, a court of original jurisdiction, into an appellate tribunal or otherwise expand its jurisdiction, and the Circuit Court of Appeals in its decision correctly viewed this as a simple proceeding in equity to enjoin the enforcement of the Commission's order.

Although a federal equity court does have jurisdiction of a particular proceeding, it may, in its sound discretion, whether its jurisdiction is invoked on the ground of diversity of citizenship or otherwise, "refuse to enforce or protect legal rights, the exercise of which may be prejudicial to the public interest" ;[72] for it "is in the public interest that federal courts of equity should exercise their discretionary power with proper regard for the rightful independence of state governments in carrying out their domestic policy." [73] While many other questions are argued, we find it necessary to decide only one: Assuming that the federal district court had jurisdiction, should it, as a matter of sound equitable discretion, have declined to exercise that jurisdiction here?

The order under consideration is part of the general regulatory system devised for the conservation of oil and gas in Texas, an aspect of "as thorny a problem as has challenged the ingenuity and wisdom of legislatures." Railroad Commission v. Rowan & Nichols Oil Co., 310 U.S. 573, 579. The East Texas field, in which the Burford tract is located, is one of the largest in the United States. It is approximately forty miles long and between five and nine miles wide, and over 26,000 wells have been drilled in it. Oil exists in the pores and crevices of rocks and sand and moves through these channels. A large area of this sort is called a pool or reservoir and the East Texas field is a giant pool. The chief forces causing oil to move are gas and water, and it is essential that the pressures be maintained at a level which will force the oil through wells to the surface. As the gas pressure is dissipated, it becomes necessary to put the well "on the pump" at great expense; and the sooner the gas from a field is exhausted, the more oil is irretrievably lost. Since the oil moves through the entire field, one operator can not only draw the oil from under his own surface area, but can also, if

---

72. United States v. Dern, 289 U.S. 352, 360.

73. Pennsylvania v. Williams, 294 U.S. 176, 185. "Reluctance there has been to use the process of federal courts in restraint of state officials though the rights asserted by the complainants are strictly federal in origin. . . . There must be reluctance even greater when the rights are strictly local; jurisdiction having no other basis than the accidents of residence." Hawks v. Hamill, 288 U.S. 52, 61.

he is advantageously located, drain oil from the most distant parts of the reservoir. The practice of attempting to drain oil from under the surface holdings of others leads to offset wells and other wasteful practices; and this problem is increased by the fact that the surface rights are split up into many small tracts. There are approximately nine hundred operators in the East Texas field alone.

For these, and many other reasons based on geologic realities, each oil and gas field must be regulated as a unit for conservation purposes. Compare Railroad Commission v. Rowan & Nichols Oil Co., 311 U.S. 570, 574. The federal government, for the present at least, has chosen to leave the principal regulatory responsibility with the states, but does supplement state control. While there is no question of the constitutional power of the State to take appropriate action to protect the industry and protect the public interest, Ohio Oil Co. v. Indiana, 177 U.S. 190; Champlin Refining Co. v. Corporation Commission, 286 U.S. 210, the State's attempts to control the flow of oil and at the same time protect the interest of the many operators have from time to time been entangled in geological-legal problems of novel nature.

Texas' interests in this matter are more than that very large one of conserving gas and oil, two of our most important natural resources. It must also weigh the impact of the industry on the whole economy of the state and must consider its revenue, much of which is drawn from taxes on the industry and from mineral lands preserved for the benefit of its educational and eleemosynary institutions. To prevent "past, present, and imminent evils" in the production of natural gas, a statute was enacted "for the protection of public and private interests against such evils by prohibiting waste and compelling ratable production." The primary task of attempting adjustment of these diverse interests is delegated to the Railroad Commission which Texas has vested with "broad discretion" in administering the law.

The Commission, in cooperation with other oil producing states, has accepted State oil production quotas and has undertaken to translate the amount to be produced for the State as a whole into a specific amount for each field and for each well. These judgments are made with due regard for the factors of full utilization of the oil supply, market demand, and protection of the individual operators, as well as protection of the public interest. As an essential aspect of the control program, the State also regulates the spacing of wells. The legislature has disavowed a purpose of requiring that "the separately owned properties in any pool [should] be unitized under one management, control or ownership" and the Commission must thus work out the difficult spacing problem with due regard for whatever rights Texas recognizes in the separate owners to a share of the common reservoir. At the same time it must restrain waste, whether by excessive production or by the unwise dissipation of the gas and other geologic factors that cause the oil to flow.

Since 1919 the Commission has attempted to solve this problem by its Rule 37. The rule provides for certain minimum spacing between wells, but also allows exceptions where necessary "to prevent waste or to prevent the confiscation of property." The prevention of confiscation is based on the premises that, insofar as these privileges are compatible with the prevention of waste and the achievement of conservation, each surface owner should be permitted to withdraw the oil under his surface area, and that no one else can fairly be permitted to drain his oil away. Hence the Commission may protect his interest either by adjusting his amount of production upward, or by permitting him to drill additional wells. "By this method each person will be entitled to recover a quantity of oil and gas substantially equivalent in amount to the recoverable oil and gas under his land."

Additional wells may be required to prevent waste as has been noticed, where geologic circumstances require immediate drilling: "The term 'waste,' as used in oil and gas Rule 37, undoubtedly means the ultimate loss of oil. If a substantial amount of oil will be saved by the drilling of a well that otherwise would ultimately be lost, the permit to drill such well may be justified under one of the exceptions provided in Rule 37 to prevent waste." Gulf Land Co. v. Atlantic Refining Co., 134 Tex. 59, 70, 131 S.W.2d 73, 80.

The delusive simplicity with which these principles of exception to Rule 37 can be stated should not obscure the actual non-legal complexities involved in their application. While the surface holder may, subject to qualifications noted, be entitled under current Texas law to the oil under his land, there can be no absolute certainty as to how much oil actually is present, Railroad Comm. v. Rowan & Nichols Oil Co., 311 U.S. 570, 576 and since the waste and confiscation problems are as a matter of physical necessity so closely interrelated, decision of one of the questions necessarily involves recognition of the other. The sheer quantity of exception cases makes their disposition of great public importance. It is estimated that over two-thirds of the wells in the East Texas field exist as exceptions to the rule, and since each exception may provoke a conflict among the interested parties, the volume of litigation arising from the administration of the rule is considerable. The instant case arises from just such an exception. It is not peculiar that the state should be represented here by its Attorney General, for cases like this, involving "confiscation" , are not mere isolated disputes between private parties. Aside from the general principles which may evolve from these proceedings, the physical facts are such that an additional permit may affect pressure on a well miles away. The standards applied by the Commission in a given case necessarily affect the entire state conservation system. Of far more importance than any other private interest is the fact that the over-all plan of regulation, as well as each of its case by case manifestations, is of vital interest to the general public which must be assured that the speculative interests of individual tract owners will be put aside when necessary to prevent the irretrievable loss of oil in other parts of the field. The Commission in applying the statutory standards of course considers the Rule 37 cases as a part of the entire conservation program with implications to the whole economy of the state.

With full knowledge of the importance of the decisions of the Railroad Commission both to the State and to the oil operators, the Texas legislature has established a system of thorough judicial review by its own State courts. The Commission orders may be appealed to a State district court in Travis County, and are reviewed by a branch of the Court of Civil Appeals and by the State Supreme Court. While the constitutional power of the Commission to enforce Rule 37 or to make exceptions to it is seldom seriously challenged, Brown v. Humble Oil & Ref. Co., 126 Tex. 296, 307, 83 S.W.2d 935, 87 S.W.2d 1069, the validity of particular orders from the standpoint of statutory interpretation may present a serious problem, and a substantial number of such cases have been disposed of by the Texas courts which alone have the power to give definite answers to the questions of State law posed in these proceedings.

In describing the relation of the Texas court to the Commission no useful purpose will be served by attempting to label the court's position as legislative, Prentis v. Atlantic Coast Line Co., 211 U.S. 210; Keller v. Potomac Elec. Co., 261 U.S. 428, or judicial, Bacon v. Rutland Railroad Co., 232 U.S. 134—suffice it to say that the Texas courts are working partners with the Railroad Commission in the business of creating a regulatory system for the oil industry.... The court has fully as much power as the Commission to determine particular cases, since after trial de novo it can either restrain the leaseholder from proceeding to drill, or if the case is appropriate, can restrain the Commission from interfering with the lease-holder. The court may even formulate new standards for the Commission's administrative practice and suggest that the Commission adopt them. Thus, in [Railroad Comm'n v. Shell Oil Co., 139 Tex. 66, 73, 161 S.W. 2d 1022], the Court took the responsibility of "laying down some standard to guide the Commission in the exercise of its discretion" in Rule 37 cases; and in *Brown v. Humble Oil Co.*, supra, 312, the Court explicitly suggested a revision in Rule 37.

To prevent the confusion of multiple review of the same general issues, the legislature provided for concentration of all direct review of the Commission's orders in the State district courts of Travis County. The Texas courts have authoritatively declared the purpose of this restriction: "If an order of the commission, lawful on its face, can be collaterally attacked in the various courts and counties of the state on grounds such as those urged in the instant case, interminable confusion would result." Texas Steel Co. v. Fort Worth and D.C. Ry. Co., 120 Tex. 597, 604, 40 S.W.2d 78.... Concentration of judicial supervision of Railroad Commission orders permits the state courts, like the Railroad Commission itself, to acquire a specialized knowledge which is useful in shaping the policy of regulation of the ever-changing demands in this field. At the present time, less than ten per cent of these cases come before the federal district court.

The very "confusion" which the Texas legislature and Supreme Court feared might result from review by many state courts of the Railroad Commission's orders has resulted from the exercise of federal equity jurisdiction. As a practical matter, the federal courts can make small contribution to the well organized system of regulation and review which the Texas statutes provide. Texas courts can give fully as great relief, including temporary restraining orders, as the federal courts. Delay, misunderstanding of local law, and needless federal conflict with the State policy, are the inevitable product of this double system of review. . . .

These federal court decisions on state law have created a constant task for the Texas Governor, the Texas legislature, and the Railroad Commission. The Governor of Texas, as has been noted above, felt called upon to forge his oil program in the light of the remotest inferences of federal court opinions. In one instance he thought it necessary to declare martial law. Special sessions of the legislature have been occupied with consideration of federal court decisions. Legislation passed under the circumstances of the strain and doubt created by these decisions was necessarily unsatisfactory. The Railroad Commission has had to adjust itself to the permutations of the law as seen by the federal courts. The most recent example was in connection with the *Rowan & Nichols* case in which the Commission felt compelled to adopt a new proration scheme to comply with the demands of a federal court decision which was reversed when it came to this Court. 311 U.S. 570, 572.

As has been noted, the federal court cases have dealt primarily with the interpretation of state law, some of it state law fairly remote from oil and gas problems. The instant case raised a number of problems of no general significance on which a federal court can only try to ascertain state law. For example, we are asked to determine whether a previous Travis county district court decision makes this case res adjudicata and whether another case pending in Travis county deprived the Commission of jurisdiction to consider Burford's application. The existence of these problems throughout the oil regulatory field creates a further possibility of serious delay which can injure the conservation program, for under our decision in Railroad Commission v. Pullman Co., 312 U.S. 496, it may be necessary to stay federal action pending authoritative determination of the difficult state questions.

The conflict between federal courts and Texas has lessened appreciably in recent years primarily as a result of the decisions in the *Rowan & Nichols* case. 310 U.S. 573; 311 U.S. 614; 311 U.S. 570. In those cases we assumed that the principal issue in the review of Railroad Commission orders was whether the Commission had confined itself within the boundaries of due process of law, and held that any special relief provided by state statutes must be pursued in a state court. It is now argued that under the decision of the Texas Supreme Court in Railroad Commission v. Shell Oil Co., 139 Tex. 66, 161 S.W.2d 1022, the courts, whether federal or state, are required to review the Commission's order not for constitutional validity, but for compliance with a standard of "reasonableness" under the state statute which, it is said, is different from the constitutional standard of due process.

The whole cycle of federal-state conflict cannot be permitted to begin again by acceptance of this view. Insofar as we have discretion to do so, we should leave these problems of Texas law to the State court where each may be handled as "one more item in a continuous series of adjustments." *Rowan & Nichols*, supra, 310 U.S., at page 584.

These questions of regulation of the industry by the State administrative agency, whether involving gas or oil prorationing programs or Rule 37 cases, so clearly involves basic problems of Texas policy that equitable discretion should be exercised to give the Texas courts the first opportunity to consider them. "Few public interests have a higher claim upon the discretion of a federal chancellor than the avoidance of needless friction with state policies, ... These cases reflect a doctrine of abstention appropriate to our federal system whereby the federal courts, 'exercising a wise discretion,' restrain their authority because of 'scrupulous regard for the rightful independence of the state governments' and for the smooth working of the federal judiciary ... This use of equitable powers is a contribution of the courts in furthering the harmonious relation between state and federal authority without the need of rigorous congressional restriction of those powers." *Railroad Commission v. Pullman Co.*, supra, 312 U.S., [at] 500, 501.

The State provides a unified method for the formation of policy and determination of cases by the Commission and by the state courts. The judicial review of the Commission's decisions in the state courts is expeditious and adequate. Conflicts in the interpretation of state law, dangerous to the success of state policies, are almost certain to result from the intervention of the lower federal courts. On the other hand, if the state procedure is followed from the Commission to the State Supreme Court, ultimate review of the federal questions is fully preserved here. Cf. Matthews v. Rodgers, 284 U.S. 521. Under such circumstances, a sound respect for the independence of state action requires the federal equity court to stay its hand.

The decision of the Circuit Court of Appeals is reversed and the judgment of the District Court dismissing the complaint is affirmed for the reasons here stated.

Reversed.

■ MR. JUSTICE DOUGLAS, concurring:

I agree with the opinion of the Court and join in it. But there are observations in the dissenting opinion which impel me to add a few words. If the issues in this case were framed as the dissenting opinion frames them, I would agree that we should reach the merits and not direct a dismissal of the complaint. But the opinion of the Court as I read it does not hold or even fairly imply that "the enforcement of state rights created by state legislation and affecting state policies is limited to the state courts." Any such holding would result in a drastic inroad on diversity jurisdiction—a limitation which I agree might be desirable but which Congress, not this Court, should make. The holding in these cases, however, goes to no such length.

This decision is but an application of the principle expressed in Pennsylvania v. Williams, 294 U.S. 176, 185, that "federal courts of equity should exercise their discretionary power with proper regard for the rightful independence of state governments in carrying out their domestic policy." That case, like the present one, was in the federal court by the diversity of citizenship route. It involved a receivership of an insolvent Pennsylvania corporation. Though the federal proceeding was first in time, this Court held that the federal court should stay its hand and turn over the assets of the corporation to the state administrative agency charged by state law with the responsibility of supervision and liquidation. In that case federal action would have pre-empted the field and excluded the assertion of state authority. In these cases the result of federal action would be potentially much more serious in terms of federal-state relations, as the opinion of the Court makes plain.

The Texas statute which governs suits to set aside these orders of the Railroad Commission has been construed by the Texas courts to give to the supervising courts a large measure of control over the administrative process. That control is much greater, for example, than the control exercised by federal Circuit Courts of Appeal over the orders of such agencies as the National Labor Relations Board. The opinion of the Court calls the Railroad Commission and the Texas courts "working partners." But as its review of Texas decisions shows the courts may at times be the senior and dominant member of that partnership if they perform the functions which Texas law places on them. The courts do not sit merely to enforce rights based on orders of the state administrative agency. They sit in judgment on that agency. That to me is the crux of the matter. If the federal courts undertook to sit in review, so to speak, of this state administrative agency, they would in effect actively participate in the fashioning of the state's domestic policy. That interference would be a continuing one, as the opinion of the Court points out. Moreover, divided authority would result. Divided authority breeds friction—friction potentially more serious than would have obtained in *Pennsylvania v. Williams*, if the administration of the affairs of that insolvent corporation had been left in the federal court to the exclusion of the state administrative agency.

■ Mr. Justice Murphy joins in this opinion.

■ Mr. Justice Frankfurter, dissenting:

To deny a suitor access to a federal district court under the circumstances of this case is to disregard a duty enjoined by Congress and made manifest by the whole history of the jurisdiction of the United States courts based upon diversity of citizenship between parties. For I am assuming that law declared by this Court, in contradistinction to law declared by Congress, is something other than the manipulation of words to formulate a predetermined result. Judicial law to me implies at least some continuity of intellectual criteria and procedures in dealing with recurring problems.

I believe it to be wholly accurate to say that throughout our history it has never been questioned that a right created by state law and enforceable in the state courts can also be enforced in the federal courts where the parties to the controversy are citizens of different states. The reasons which led Congress to grant such jurisdiction to the federal courts are familiar. It was believed that, consciously or otherwise, the courts of a state may favor their own citizens. Bias against outsiders may become embedded in a judgment of a state court and yet not be sufficiently apparent to be made the basis of a federal claim. To avoid possible discriminations of this sort, so the theory goes, a citizen of a state other than that in which he is suing or being sued ought to be able to go into a wholly impartial tribunal, namely, the federal court sitting in that state. Thus, the basic premise of federal jurisdiction based upon diversity of the parties' citizenship is that the federal courts should afford remedies which are coextensive with rights created by state law and enforceable in state courts.

That is the theory of diversity jurisdiction. Whether it is a sound theory, whether diversity jurisdiction is necessary or desirable in order to avoid possible unfairness by state courts, state judges and juries, against outsiders, whether the federal courts ought to be relieved of the burden of diversity litigation,—these are matters which are not my concern as a judge. They are the concern of those whose business it is to legislate, not mine. I speak as one who has long favored the entire abolition of diversity jurisdiction. See 13 Cornell L.Q. 499, 520 et seq. But I must decide this case as a judge and not as a legislative reformer.

Aside from the Johnson Act of May 14, 1934, 48 Stat. 775, the many powerful and persistent legislative efforts to abolish or restrict diversity jurisdiction have ever since the Civil War been rejected by Congress. Again and again legislation designed to make inroads upon diversity jurisdiction has been proposed to Congress, and on each occasion Congress has deliberately refused to act. See, for example, the recent efforts to restrict diversity jurisdiction which were provoked by [Black & White Taxicab & Transfer Co. v. Brown & Yellow Taxicab & Transfer Co., 276 U.S. 518 (1928)]; Sen.Rep. No. 626, 70th Cong., 1st Sess.; Sen.Rep. No. 691, 71st Cong., 2d Sess.; Sen.Rep. No. 530 and Sen.Rep. No. 701, 72d Cong., 1st Sess. We are dealing, then, not with a jurisdiction evolved and shaped by the courts but rather with one explicitly conferred and undeviatingly maintained by Congress.

. . . . .

If, in a case of this sort, the state right sought to be enforced in the federal courts depended upon a "forecast rather than a determination" of state law, if the federal court was practically impotent to enforce state law because of its inability to fathom the complexities, legal or factual, of local law, the rule of [Railroad Comm'n v. Rowan & Nichols Oil Co., 310 U.S. 573 (1940),] would be applicable. In such a situation the line of demarcation between what belongs to the state administrative body and what to its courts should not be drawn by the federal courts. If it could be shown that the circumstances of this case warranted the application of such a doctrine of abstention, I would gladly join in the decision of the Court. But such a showing has not been attempted, nor, I believe, could it be made.

. . . . .

It is true that Texas law governing review of Commission orders under Rule 37 has not always been clear and certain, and that there may be parts of the statute and some of the Railroad Commission's Rules, with which we are not now concerned, which, like other legal materials, are not as clear as they might be. But, in a series of recent decisions, the Supreme Court of Texas has not only given precision to the concepts of "waste" and "confiscation of property" employed in Rule 37, it has also defined with clarity the scope of judicial review of Commission action. . . .

. . . . .

The opinion of the Court cuts deep into our judicial fabric. The duty of the judiciary is to exercise the jurisdiction which Congress has conferred. What the Court is doing today I might wholeheartedly approve if it were done by Congress. But I cannot justify translation of the circumstance of my membership on this Court into an opportunity of writing my private view of legislative policy into law and thereby effacing a far greater area of diversity jurisdiction than Senator Norris, as chairman of the Senate Judiciary Committee, was ever able to persuade Congress itself to do.

■ MR. JUSTICE ROBERTS and MR. JUSTICE REED join in this dissent.

■ THE CHIEF JUSTICE expresses no views as to the desirability, as a matter of legislative policy, of retaining the diversity jurisdiction. In all other respects he concurs in the opinion of MR. JUSTICE FRANKFURTER.[74]

[74. See also Kaiser Steel Corp. v. W.S. Ranch Co., 391 U.S. 593 (1968).

The *Burford* case produced strong feelings within the Court. See Lash, From the Diaries of Felix Frankfurter 226–228 (1975).

In New Orleans Public Service, Inc. v. Council of City of New Orleans, 491 U.S. 350 (1989), the Supreme Court held that *Burford* abstention was not applicable to a claim that a state governmental body setting electrical rates was prohibited by federal law from refusing to provide reimbursement for costs allocated to the claimant by the Federal Energy Regulatory Commission. "Unlike a claim that a state agency has misapplied its lawful authority or has failed to take into consideration or properly weigh relevant state-law factors, federal adjudication of this sort of preemption claim would not disrupt the State's attempt to ensure uniformity in the treatment of an 'essentially local problem.'" 491 U.S., at 361. In Chiropractic America v. Lavecchia, 180 F.3d 99 (3d Cir.1999), a divided panel of the Third Circuit upheld *Burford* abstention with respect to New Jersey's complex scheme of no-fault automobile insurance.

In Quackenbush v. Allstate Insurance Co., 517 U.S. 706 (1996), the Court held that remand or dismissal of a case on *Burford* grounds, resulting in a complete relinquishment of jurisdiction, is inappropriate where damages are sought rather than some form of equitable or otherwise discretionary relief. The Court left open whether a stay rather than a remand or dismissal could be ordered if *Burford* abstention were warranted in an action for damages.

In Johnson v. Collins Entertainment Co., Inc., 199 F.3d 710 (4th Cir.1999), the Fourth Circuit held that *Burford* abstention was required in a suit brought by habitual gamblers against the heavily regulated video-poker industry of South Carolina. The court was not deterred by two features of the suit generally deemed incompatible with *Burford* abstention: it involved federal-question rather than diversity jurisdiction, and sought damages as well as injunctive relief. In the latter respect the court bowed to *Quackenbush* by ordering a stay rather than dismissal of the damages claims, but also made it clear that the district court was to do

Reetz v. Bozanich

Supreme Court of the United States, 1970.
397 U.S. 82, 90 S.Ct. 788, 25 L.Ed.2d 68.

■ MR. JUSTICE DOUGLAS delivered the opinion of the Court.

This is an appeal from the judgment of a three-judge District Court convened under 28 U.S.C. §§ 2281, 2284, declaring certain fishing laws of Alaska and regulations under them unconstitutional and enjoining their enforcement....

The laws in question, passed in 1968, concern salmon net gear licenses for commercial fishing, not licenses for other types of salmon fishing. They are challenged because they limit licensees to a defined group of persons. The Act in material part provides:

"Persons eligible for gear licenses. (a) Except in cases of extreme hardship as defined by the Board of Fish and Game, a salmon net gear license for a specific salmon registration area may be issued only to a person who

"(1) has previously held a salmon net gear license for that specific salmon registration area; or

"(2) has, for any three years, held a commercial fishing license and while so licensed actively engaged in commercial fishing in that specific area."

The regulations provide that except in cases of "extreme hardship ... a salmon net gear license for a specific salmon registration area may be issued only to a person who:

"(A) has held in 1965 or subsequent years a salmon net gear license for that specific salmon registration area; or

"(B) has, for any three years since January 1, 1960, held a commercial fishing license and while so licensed actively engaged in commercial fishing in that specific area."

Appellees are nonresidents who applied for commercial salmon net gear licenses. They apparently are experienced net gear salmon fishermen but they cannot qualify for a salmon net gear license to fish in any of the 12 regions or areas described in the Act and the regulations.

Appellees filed a motion for summary judgment on the grounds that the Act and regulations deprived them of their rights under the Equal Protection Clause of the Fourteenth Amendment and also their rights under the Alaska Constitution. That constitution provides in Art. VIII, § 3:

"Wherever occurring in their natural state, fish, wildlife, and waters are reserved to the people for common use."

---

nothing until the damages claims had been mooted by the parallel state proceedings necessitated by its dismissal of all claims for injunctive relief. In Caudill v. Eubanks Farms, Inc., 301 F.3d 658 (6th Cir.2002), the Sixth Circuit upheld *Burford* abstention in a shareholder suit to dissolve a closely-held Kentucky corporation.]

And it provides in Art. VIII, § 15:

"No exclusive right or special privilege of fishery shall be created or authorized in the natural waters of the State."

Appellants filed a motion to dismiss or alternatively to stay the proceedings in the District Court pending the determination of the Alaska constitutional question by an Alaska court.

Appellants' motion to dismiss or to stay was denied. Appellees' motion for summary judgment was granted, the three-judge District Court holding that the Act and regulations in question were unconstitutional both under the Equal Protection Clause of the Fourteenth Amendment and under the Constitution of Alaska. 297 F.Supp., at 304–307.

This case is virtually on all fours with City of Meridian v. Southern Bell Tel. & Tel. Co., 358 U.S. 639, where a single district judge in construing a Mississippi statute held that it violated both the Federal and the State Constitutions. The Court of Appeals affirmed and we vacated its judgment and remanded to the District Court with directions to hold the case while the parties repaired to a state tribunal "for an authoritative declaration of applicable state law." Id., at 640.

We said:

"Proper exercise of federal jurisdiction requires that controversies involving unsettled questions of state law be decided in the state tribunals preliminary to a federal court's consideration of the underlying federal constitutional questions.... That is especially desirable where the questions of state law are enmeshed with federal questions.... Here, the state law problems are delicate ones, the resolution of which is not without substantial difficulty—certainly for a federal court.... In such a case, when the state court's interpretation of the statute or evaluation of its validity under the state constitution may obviate any need to consider its validity under the Federal Constitution, the federal court should hold its hand, lest it render a constitutional decision unnecessarily." Id., at 640–641.

We are advised that the provisions of the Alaska Constitution at issue have never been interpreted by an Alaska court. The District Court, feeling sure of its grounds on the merits, held, however, that this was not a proper case for abstention, saying that "if the question had been presented to an Alaska court, it would have shared our conviction that the challenged gear licensing scheme is not supportable." 297 F.Supp., at 304. The three-judge panel was a distinguished one, two being former Alaska lawyers. And they felt that prompt decision was necessary to avoid the "grave and irreparable" injury to the "economic livelihood" of the appellees which would result, if they could not engage in their occupation "during this year's forthcoming fishing season." Ibid.

It is, of course, true that abstention is not necessary whenever a federal court is faced with a question of local law, the classic case being Meredith v. City of Winter Haven, 320 U.S. 228, where federal jurisdiction was based on diversity only. Abstention certainly involves duplication of effort and expense and an attendant delay. See England v. Louisiana State Board, 375 U.S. 411. That is why we have said that this judicially created rule which stems from Railroad Comm'n v. Pullman Co., 312 U.S. 496, should be applied only where "the issue of state law is uncertain." Harman v. Forssenius, 380 U.S. 528, 534. Moreover, we said in Zwickler v. Koota, 389 U.S. 241, 248, that abstention was applicable "only in narrowly limited 'special circumstances,' " citing Propper v. Clark, 337 U.S. 472, 492. In *Zwickler,* a state statute was attacked on the ground that on its face it was repugnant to the First Amendment; and it was conceded that state court construction could not render unnecessary a decision of the First Amendment question. 389 U.S., at 250. A state court decision here, however, could conceivably avoid any decision under the Fourteenth Amendment and would avoid any possible irritant in the federal-state relationship.

The *Pullman* doctrine was based on "the avoidance of needless friction" between federal pronouncements and state policies. 312 U.S., at 500. The instant case is the classic case in that tradition, for here the nub of the whole controversy may be the state constitution. The constitutional provisions relate to fish resources, an asset unique in its abundance in Alaska. The statute and regulations relate to that same unique resource, the management of which is a matter of great state concern. We appreciate why the District Court felt concern over the effect of further delay on these plaintiffs, the appellees here; but we have concluded that the first judicial application of these constitutional provisions should properly be by an Alaska court.

We think the federal court should have stayed its hand while the parties repaired to the state courts for a resolution of their state constitutional questions. We accordingly vacate the judgment of the District Court and remand the case for proceedings consistent with this opinion.

It is so ordered.[75]

[75. "Appellants' second argument is that the commonwealth courts should be permitted to adjudicate the validity of the citizenship requirement in the light of §§ 1 and 7 of Art. II of the Puerto Rico Constitution.... Section 1 provides: 'No discrimination shall be made on account of race, color, sex, birth, social origin or condition, or political or religious ideas.' Section 7 provides: 'No person in Puerto Rico shall be denied the equal protection of the laws.' These constitutional provisions are not so interrelated with § 689 that it may be said, as in *Harris County,* that the law of the Commonwealth is ambiguous. Rather the abstention issue seems clearly controlled by Wisconsin v. Constantineau, 400 U.S. 433 (1971), where, as it was said in *Harris County,* 420 U.S., at 84–85 n. 8 'we declined to order abstention where the federal due process claim was not complicated by an unresolved state-law question, even though the plaintiffs might have sought relief under a similar provision of the state constitution.' Indeed, to hold that abstention is required because § 689 might conflict with the cited broad and sweeping constitutional provisions, would convert abstention from an exception into a general rule." Examining Board of Engineers, Architects & Surveyors v. Flores de Otero, 426 U.S. 572, 598 (1976). To the same effect, see Hawaii Housing Authority v. Midkiff, 467 U.S. 229, 236 n. 4 (1984). See also Guiney v. Roache, 833 F.2d 1079 (1st Cir.1987).]

Wilton v. Seven Falls Co.

Supreme Court of the United States, 1995.
515 U.S. 277, 115 S.Ct. 2137, 132 L.Ed.2d 214.

■ JUSTICE O'CONNOR delivered the opinion of the Court.

This case asks whether the discretionary standard set forth in Brillhart v. Excess Ins. Co. of America, 316 U.S. 491 (1942), or the "exceptional circumstances" test developed in Colorado River Water Conservation Dist. v. United States, 424 U.S. 800 (1976), and Moses H. Cone Memorial Hospital v. Mercury Constr. Corp., 460 U.S. 1 (1983), governs a district court's decision to stay a declaratory judgment action during the pendency of parallel state court proceedings, and under what standard of review a court of appeals should evaluate the district court's decision to do so.

I

In early 1992, a dispute between respondents (the Hill Group) and other parties over the ownership and operation of oil and gas properties in Winkler County, Texas, appeared likely to culminate in litigation.

The Hill Group asked petitioners (London Underwriters) to provide them with coverage under several commercial liability insurance policies. London Underwriters refused to defend or indemnify the Hill Group in a letter dated July 31, 1992. In September 1992, after a 3-week trial, a Winkler County jury entered a verdict in excess of $100 million against the Hill Group on various state law claims. The Hill Group gave London Underwriters notice of the verdict in late November 1992. On December 9, 1992, London Underwriters filed suit in the United States District Court for the Southern District of Texas, basing jurisdiction upon diversity of citizenship under 28 U.S.C. § 1332. London Underwriters sought a declaration under the Declaratory Judgment Act, 28 U.S.C. § 2201(a) (1988 ed., Supp. V), that their policies did not cover the Hill Group's liability for the Winkler County judgment. After negotiations with the Hill Group's counsel, London Underwriters voluntarily dismissed the action on January 22, 1993. London Underwriters did so, however, upon the express condition that the Hill Group give London Underwriters two weeks' notice if they decided to bring suit on the policy.

On February 23, 1993, the Hill Group notified London Underwriters of their intention to file such a suit in Travis County, Texas. London Underwriters refiled their declaratory judgment action in the Southern District of Texas on February 24, 1993. As promised, the Hill Group initiated an action against London Underwriters on March 26, 1993 in state court in Travis County. The Hill Group's codefendants in the Winkler County litigation joined in this suit and asserted claims against certain Texas insurers, thus rendering the parties nondiverse and the suit nonremovable.

On the same day that the Hill Group filed their Travis County action, they moved to dismiss or, in the alternative, to stay London Underwriters' federal declaratory judgment action. After receiving submissions from the parties on the issue, the District Court entered a stay on June 30, 1993.

The District Court observed that the state lawsuit pending in Travis County encompassed the same coverage issues raised in the declaratory judgment action and determined that a stay was warranted in order to avoid piecemeal litigation and to bar London Underwriters' attempts at forum shopping. London Underwriters filed a timely appeal. See *Moses H. Cone Memorial Hospital,* supra, at 10 (a district court's order staying federal proceedings in favor of pending state litigation is a "final decisio[n]" appealable under 28 U.S.C. § 1291).

The United States Court of Appeals for the Fifth Circuit affirmed. 41 F.3d 934 (1994). Noting that under Circuit precedent, "[a] district court has broad discretion to grant (or decline to grant) declaratory judgment," citing Torch, Inc. v. LeBlanc, 947 F.2d 193, 194 (CA5 1991), the Court of Appeals did not require application of the test articulated in *Colorado River,* supra, and *Moses H. Cone,* supra, under which district courts must point to "exceptional circumstances" to justify staying or dismissing federal proceedings. Citing the interests in avoiding duplicative proceedings and forum shopping, the Court of Appeals reviewed the District Court's decision for abuse of discretion, and found none. 41 F.3d, at 935.

We granted certiorari, 513 U.S. 1013 (1994), to resolve circuit conflicts concerning the standard governing a district court's decision to stay a declaratory judgment action in favor of parallel state litigation .... We now affirm.

II

Over 50 years ago, in Brillhart v. Excess Ins. Co., 316 U.S. 491 (1942), this Court addressed circumstances virtually identical to those present in the case before us today. An insurer, anticipating a coercive suit, sought a declaration in federal court of nonliability on an insurance policy. The District Court dismissed the action in favor of pending state garnishment proceedings, to which the insurer had been added as a defendant. The Court of Appeals reversed, finding an abuse of discretion, and ordered the District Court to proceed to the merits. Reversing the Court of Appeals and remanding to the District Court, this Court held that, "[a]lthough the District Court had jurisdiction of the suit under the Federal Declaratory Judgments Act, it was under no compulsion to exercise that jurisdiction." Id., at 494. The Court explained that "[o]rdinarily it would be uneconomical as well as vexatious for a federal court to proceed in a declaratory judgment suit where another suit is pending in a state court presenting the same issues, not governed by federal law, between the same parties." Id., at 495. The question for a district court presented with a suit under the Declaratory Judgment Act, the Court found, is "whether the questions in controversy between the parties to the federal suit, and which are not foreclosed under the applicable substantive law, can better be settled in the proceeding pending in the state court." Ibid.

Brillhart makes clear that district courts possess discretion in determining whether and when to entertain an action under the Declaratory Judgment Act, even when the suit otherwise satisfies subject matter jurisdictional prerequisites. Although *Brillhart* did not set out an exclusive list of factors governing the district court's exercise of this discretion, it did provide some useful guidance in that regard. The Court indicated, for example, that in deciding whether to enter a stay, a district court should examine "the scope of the pending state court proceeding and the nature of defenses open there." Ibid. This inquiry, in turn, entails consideration of "whether the claims of all parties in interest can satisfactorily be adjudicated in that proceeding, whether necessary parties have been joined, whether such parties are amenable to process in that proceeding, etc." Ibid. Other cases, the Court noted, might shed light on additional factors governing a district court's decision to stay or to dismiss a declaratory judgment action at the outset. See ibid. But *Brillhart* indicated that, at least where another suit involving the same parties and presenting opportunity for ventilation of the same state law issues is pending in state court, a district court might be indulging in "[g]ratuitous interference," ibid., if it permitted the federal declaratory action to proceed.

Brillhart, without more, clearly supports the District Court's decision in this case. (That the court here stayed, rather than dismissed, the action is of little moment in this regard, because the state court's decision will bind the parties under principles of res judicata.) Nonetheless, London Underwriters argue, and several Courts of Appeals have agreed, that intervening case law has supplanted *Brillhart*'s notions of broad discretion with a test under which district courts may stay or dismiss actions properly within their jurisdiction only in "exceptional circumstances." In London Underwriters' view, recent cases have established that a district court must point to a compelling reason—which, they say, is lacking here—in order to stay a declaratory judgment action in favor of pending state proceedings. To evaluate this argument, it is necessary to examine three cases handed down several decades after *Brillhart.*

In Colorado River Water Conservation Dist. v. United States, 424 U.S. 800 (1976), the Government brought an action in Federal District Court under 28 U.S.C. § 1345 seeking a declaration of its water rights, the appointment of a water master, and an order enjoining all uses and diversions of water by other parties. See Pet. for Cert. in Colorado River Water Conservation Dist. v. United States, O.T. 1976, No. 74–940, pp. 39a–40a. The District Court dismissed the action in deference to ongoing state proceedings. The Court of Appeals reversed, 504 F.2d 115 (CA10 1974), on the ground that the District Court had jurisdiction over the Government's suit and that abstention was inappropriate. This Court reversed again. Without discussing *Brillhart,* the Court began with the premise that federal courts have a "virtually unflagging obligation" to exercise the jurisdiction conferred on them by Congress. *Colorado River,* supra, at 813, 817–818, citing Cohens v. Virginia, 6 Wheat. [19 U.S.] 264, 404 (1821). The Court determined, however, that a district court could nonetheless abstain from the assumption of jurisdiction over a suit in "exceptional" circumstances, and it found such exceptional circumstances on the facts of the case. 424 U.S., at 818–820. Specifically, the Court deemed dispositive a clear federal policy against piecemeal adjudication of water rights; the existence of an elaborate state scheme for resolution of such claims; the absence of any proceedings in the District Court, other than the filing of the complaint, prior to the motion to dismiss; the extensive nature of the suit; the 300–mile distance between the District Court and the situs of the water district at issue; and the prior participation of the Federal Government in related state proceedings.

Two years after *Colorado River* we decided Will v. Calvert Fire Ins. Co., 437 U.S. 655 (1978), in which a plurality of the Court stated that, while " 'the pendency of an action in the state court is no bar to proceedings concerning the same matter in the Federal court having jurisdiction,' " id., at 662, quoting McClellan v. Carland, 217 U.S. 268, 282 (1910), a district court is " 'under no compulsion to exercise that jurisdiction,' " 437 U.S., at 662, quoting *Brillhart,* 316 U.S., at 494. *Will* concerned an action seeking damages for an alleged violation of federal securities laws brought in federal court during the pendency of related state proceedings. Although the case arose outside the declaratory judgment context, the plurality invoked *Brillhart* as the appropriate authority. *Colorado River,* according to the plurality, "in no way undermine[d] the conclusion of *Brillhart* that the decision whether to defer to the concurrent jurisdiction of a state court is, in the last analysis, a matter committed to the district court's discretion." *Will,* supra, at 664. Justice Blackmun, concurring in the judgment, criticized the plurality for not recognizing that *Colorado River* had undercut the "sweeping language" of *Brillhart.* 437 U.S., at 667. Four Justices in dissent urged that the *Colorado River* "exceptional circumstances" test supplied the governing standard.

The plurality's suggestion in *Will* that *Brillhart* might have application beyond the context of declaratory judgments was rejected by the Court in Moses H. Cone Memorial Hospital v. Mercury Constr. Corp., 460 U.S. 1 (1983). In *Moses H. Cone,* the Court established that the *Colorado River* "exceptional circumstances" test, rather than the more permissive *Brillhart* analysis, governs a district court's decision to stay a suit to compel arbitration under § 4 of the Arbitration Act in favor of pending state litigation. Noting that the combination of Justice Blackmun and the four dissenting Justices in *Will* had made five to require application of *Colorado River,* the Court rejected the argument that *Will* had worked any substantive changes in the law. " 'Abdication of the obligation to decide cases,' " the Court reasoned, " 'can be justified . . . only in the exceptional circumstance where the order to the parties to repair to the State court would clearly serve an important countervailing interest.' " 460 U.S., at 14, quoting *Colorado River,* supra, at 813. As it had in *Colorado River,* the Court articulated non-exclusive factors relevant to the existence of such exceptional circumstances, including the assumption by either court of jurisdiction over a res, the relative convenience of the fora, avoidance of piecemeal litigation, the order in which jurisdiction was obtained by the concurrent fora, whether and to what extent federal law provides the rules of decision on the merits, and the adequacy of state proceedings. Evaluating each of these factors, the Court concluded that the District Court's stay of federal proceedings was, under the circumstances, inappropriate.

Relying on these post-*Brillhart* developments, London Underwriters contend that the *Brillhart* regime, under which district courts have substantial latitude in deciding whether to stay or to dismiss a declaratory judgment suit in light of pending state proceedings (and need not point to "exceptional circumstances" to justify their actions), is an outmoded relic of another era. We disagree. Neither *Colorado River,* which upheld the dismissal of federal proceedings, nor *Moses H. Cone,* which did not, dealt with actions brought under the Declaratory Judgment Act, 28 U.S.C. § 2201(a) (1988 ed., Supp. V). Distinct features of the Declaratory Judgment Act, we believe, justify a standard vesting district courts with greater discretion in declaratory judgment actions than that permitted under the "exceptional circumstances" test of *Colorado River* and *Moses H. Cone.* No subsequent case, in our view, has called into question the application of the *Brillhart* standard to the *Brillhart* facts.

Since its inception, the Declaratory Judgment Act has been understood to confer on federal courts unique and substantial discretion in deciding whether to declare the rights of litigants. On its face, the statute provides that a court "*may* declare the rights and other legal relations of any interested party seeking such declaration," 28 U.S.C. § 2201(a) (1988 ed., Supp. V) (emphasis added). See generally E. Borchard, Declaratory Judgments 312–314 (2d ed.1941); Borchard, Discretion to Refuse Jurisdiction of Actions for Declaratory Judgments, 26 Minn.L.Rev. 677 (1942). The statute's textual commitment to discretion, and the breadth of leeway we have always understood it to suggest, distinguish the declaratory judgment context from other areas of the law in which concepts of discretion surface. See generally D. Shapiro, Jurisdiction and Discretion, 60 N.Y.U.L.Rev. 543 (1985); cf. O. Fiss & D. Rendleman, Injunctions 106–108 (2d ed.1984) (describing courts' nonstatutory discretion, through application of open-ended substantive standards like "irreparable injury," in the injunction context). We have repeatedly characterized the Declaratory Judgment Act as "an enabling Act, which confers a discretion on the courts rather than an absolute right upon the litigant." Public Serv. Comm'n v. Wycoff Co., 344 U.S. 237, 241 (1952); see also Green v. Mansour, 474 U.S. 64, 72 (1985); Cardinal Chemical Co. v. Morton International, Inc., 508 U.S. 83, 95, n. 17 (1993). When all is said and done, we have concluded, "the propriety of declaratory relief in a particular case will depend upon a circumspect sense of its fitness informed by the teachings and experience concerning the functions and extent of federal judicial power." *Wycoff,* supra, at 243.

Acknowledging, as they must, the unique breadth of this discretion to decline to enter a declaratory judgment, London Underwriters nonetheless contend that, after *Colorado River* and *Moses H. Cone,* district courts lack discretion to decline to hear a declaratory judgment suit at the outset. See Brief for Petitioners 22 ("District courts must hear declaratory judgment cases absent exceptional circumstances; district courts may decline to enter the requested relief following a full trial on the merits, if no beneficial purpose is thereby served or if equity otherwise counsels"). We are not persuaded by this distinction. London Underwriters' argument depends on the untenable proposition that a district court, knowing at the commence-ment of litigation that it will exercise its broad statutory discretion to decline declaratory relief, must nonetheless go through the futile exercise of hearing a case on the merits first. Nothing in the language of the Declara-tory Judgment Act recommends London Underwriters' reading, and we are unwilling to impute to Congress an intention to require such a wasteful expenditure of judicial resources. If a district court, in the sound exercise of its judgment, determines after a complaint is filed that a declaratory judgment will serve no useful purpose, it cannot be incumbent upon that court to proceed to the merits before staying or dismissing the action.

We agree, for all practical purposes, with Professor Borchard, who observed half a century ago that "[t]here is ... nothing automatic or obligatory about the assumption of 'jurisdiction' by a federal court" to hear a declaratory judgment action. Borchard, Declaratory Judgments, at 313. By the Declaratory Judgment Act, Congress sought to place a remedial arrow in the district court's quiver; it created an opportunity, rather than a duty, to grant a new form of relief to qualifying litigants. Consistent with the nonobligatory nature of the remedy, a district court is authorized, in the sound exercise of its discretion, to stay or to dismiss an action seeking a declaratory judgment before trial or after all arguments have drawn to a close.[76] In the declaratory judgment context, the normal principle that federal courts should adjudicate claims within their jurisdiction yields to considerations of practicality and wise judicial administration.

III

As Judge Friendly observed, the Declaratory Judgment Act "does not speak," on its face, to the question whether discretion to entertain declara-tory judgment actions is vested in district courts alone or in the entire judicial system. Friendly, Indiscretion about Discretion, 31 Emory L.J. 747, 778 (1982). The Court of Appeals reviewed the District Court's decision to stay London Underwriters' action for abuse of discretion, and found none. London Underwriters urge us to follow those other Courts of Appeals that review decisions to grant (or to refrain from granting) declaratory relief de novo. See, e.g., Genentech, Inc. v. Eli Lilly & Co., 998 F.2d [931, 936 (CA Fed. 1993)]; Cincinnati Ins. Co. v. Holbrook, [1330, 1333 (CA11 1989)]. We decline this invitation. We believe it more consistent with the statute to vest district courts with discretion in the first instance, because facts bearing on the usefulness of the declaratory judgment remedy, and the fitness of the case for resolution, are peculiarly within their grasp. Cf. First Options of Chicago, Inc. v. Kaplan, 514 U.S. 938, 948 (1995) ("[T]he reviewing attitude that a court of appeals takes toward a district court decision should depend upon 'the respective institutional advantages of trial and appellate courts' ") (citation omitted); Miller v. Fenton, 474 U.S.

---

76. We note that where the basis for declining to proceed is the pendency of a state proceeding, a stay will often be the preferable course, insofar as it assures that the federal action can proceed without risk of a time bar if the state case, for any reason, fails to resolve the matter in controversy. See, e.g., P. Bator, D. Meltzer, P. Mishkin, & D. Shapiro, Hart and Wechsler's The Federal Courts and the Federal System 1451, n. 9 (3d ed.1988).

104, 114 (1985) ("[T]he fact/law distinction at times has turned on a determination that, as a matter of the sound administration of justice, one judicial actor is better positioned than another to decide the issue in question"). While it may be true that sound administration of the Declaratory Judgment Act calls for the exercise of "judicial discretion, hardened by experience into rule," Borchard, Declaratory Judgments, at 293, proper application of the abuse of discretion standard on appellate review can, we think, provide appropriate guidance to district courts. In this regard, we reject London Underwriters' suggestion, Brief for Petitioners 14, that review for abuse of discretion "is tantamount to no review" at all.

IV

In sum, we conclude that Brillhart v. Excess Ins. Co., 316 U.S. 491 (1942), governs this declaratory judgment action and that district courts' decisions about the propriety of hearing declaratory judgment actions, which are necessarily bound up with their decisions about the propriety of granting declaratory relief, should be reviewed for abuse of discretion. We do not attempt at this time to delineate the outer boundaries of that discretion in other cases, for example, cases raising issues of federal law or cases in which there are no parallel state proceedings. Like the Court of Appeals, we conclude only that the District Court acted within its bounds in staying this action for declaratory relief where parallel proceedings, presenting opportunity for ventilation of the same state law issues, were underway in state court. The judgment of the Court of Appeals for the Fifth Circuit is Affirmed.

■ JUSTICE BREYER took no part in the consideration or decision of this case.[77]

[77. See 17 Moore's Federal Practice ¶ 122.06 (3d ed.1998); Giesel, The Expanded Discretion of Lower Courts to Regulate Access to the Federal Courts after *Wilton v. Seven Falls Co.*: Declaratory Judgment Actions and Implication Far Beyond, 33 Hous.L.Rev. 393 (1996).

The broad discretionary standard of *Brillhart* rather than the "exceptional circumstances" test of *Colorado River* applies in deciding whether to dismiss a federal statutory-interpleader action. NYLife Distributors, Inc. v. Adherence Group, Inc., 72 F.3d 371 (3d Cir.1995), cert. denied, 517 U.S. 1209 (1996). The Fourth Circuit, answering a question left open in the principal case, has held that a district court has discretion whether to entertain or dismiss a declaratory-judgment action even though no parallel state action is pending. Aetna Casualty & Surety Co. v. Ind–Com Electric Co., 139 F.3d 419 (4th Cir.1998).

The district court has no duty sua sponte to consider declining jurisdiction in the exercise of its discretion under the Declaratory Judgment Act, and only in extraordinary circumstances should the court of appeals consider sua sponte whether the district court abused its discretion in granting declaratory relief when neither party raised an objection in the district court. If, however, a party does timely object in the district court to the exercise of discretionary jurisdiction to grant declaratory relief, sound appellate procedure requires that the district court provide written reasons for its ruling, providing an adequate record for appeal of this exercise of discretion. See Government Employees Ins. Co. v. Dizol, 133 F.3d 1220 (9th Cir.1998) (en banc). In *Dizol* the Ninth Circuit expressly conformed the standards for exercising discretionary jurisdiction under the Declaratory Judgment Act to those it had

Lehman Brothers v. Schein

Supreme Court of the United States, 1974.
416 U.S. 386, 94 S.Ct. 1741, 40 L.Ed.2d 215.

■ MR. JUSTICE DOUGLAS delivered the opinion of the Court.

These cases are here on petitions for certiorari and raise one identical question.

These are suits brought in the District Court for the Southern District of New York. Lum's, one of the respondents in the *Lehman Bros.* petition, is a Florida corporation with headquarters in Miami. Each of the three petitions which we consolidated for oral argument involve shareholder's derivative suits naming Lum's and others as defendants; and the basis of federal jurisdiction is diversity of citizenship, 28 U.S.C. § 1332(a)(1), about which there is no dispute.

The complaints allege that Chasen, president of Lum's, called Simon, a representative of Lehman Bros., and told him about disappointing projections of Lum's earnings, estimates that were confidential, not public. Simon is said to have told an employee of IDS about them. On the next day, it is alleged that the IDS defendants sold 83,000 shares of Lum's on the New York Stock Exchange for about $17.50. Later that day the exchanges halted trading in Lum's stock and on the next trading day it opened at $14.00 per share, the public being told that the projected earnings would be "substantially lower" than anticipated. The theory of the complaints was that Chasen was a fiduciary but used the inside information along with others for profit and that Chasen and his group are liable to Lum's for their unlawful profits.

Lehman and Simon defended on the ground that the IDS sale was not made through them and that neither one benefitted from the sales. Nonetheless plaintiffs claimed that Chasen and the other defendants were liable under Diamond v. Oreamuno, 24 N.Y.2d 494 (1969). *Diamond* proceeds on the theory that "inside" information of an officer or director of a corporation is an asset of the corporation which had been acquired by the insiders as fiduciaries of the company and misappropriated in violation of trust.

The District Court looked to the choice of law rules of the State of New York, Klaxon Co. v. Stentor Electric Mfg. Co., 313 U.S. 487 (1941), and held that the law of the State of incorporation governs the existence and extent of corporate fiduciary obligations, as well as the liability for violation of them. *Diamond* did indeed so indicate. 24 N.Y.2d, at 503–504.

The District Court in examining Florida law concluded that, although the highest court in Florida has not considered the question, several district courts of appeal indicate that a complaint which fails to allege both wrongful acts and damage to the corporation must be dismissed. The

---

previously prescribed for the discretionary exercise of supplemental jurisdiction. See 133 F.3d, at 1224–1225, citing Acri v. Varian Associates, 114 F.3d 999 (9th Cir.1997) (en banc), and Executive Software North America, Inc. v. United States District Court, 24 F.3d 1545 (9th Cir.1994), both discussed supra p. 313.]

District Court went on to consider whether if Florida followed the *Diamond* rationale, defendants would be liable. It concluded that the present complaints go beyond *Diamond,* as Chasen, the only fiduciary of Lum's involved in the suits, never sold any of his holdings on the basis of inside information. The other defendants were not fiduciaries of Lum's. The District Court accordingly dismissed the complaints, 335 F.Supp. 329 (1971).

The Court of Appeals by a divided vote reversed the District Court. Schein v. Chasen, 478 F.2d 817 (CA2 1973). While the Court of Appeals held that Florida law was controlling, it found none that was decisive. So it then turned to the law of other jurisdictions, particularly that of New York, to see if Florida "would probably" interpret *Diamond* to make it applicable here. The Court of Appeals concluded that the defendants had engaged with Chasen "to misuse corporate property," *Id.,* and that the theory of *Diamond* reaches that situation, "viewing the case as the Florida court would probably view it." Ibid. There were emanations from other Florida decisions that made the majority of the Court of Appeals feel that Florida would follow that reading of *Diamond.* Such a construction of *Diamond,* the Court of Appeals said, would have "the prophylactic effect of providing a disincentive to insider trading." Id., at 823. And so it would. Yet under the regime of Erie R. Co. v. Tompkins, 304 U.S. 64 (1938), a State can make just the opposite her law, providing there is no overriding federal rule which pre-empts state law by reason of federal curbs on trading in the stream of commerce.

The dissenter on the Court of Appeals urged that that court certify the state law question to the Florida Supreme Court as is provided in Fla.Stat. Ann. § 25.031 and its Rule 4.61. 478 F.2d, at 828. That path is open to this Court and to any Court of Appeals of the United States. Ibid. We have indeed used it before[78] as have Courts of Appeal.[79]

When state law does not make the certification procedure available, a federal court not infrequently will stay its hand, remitting the parties to the state court to resolve the controlling state law on which the federal rule may turn. Kaiser Steel Corp. v. W.S. Ranch Co., 391 U.S. 593 (1968). Numerous applications of that practice are reviewed in Meredith v. Winter Haven, 320 U.S. 228 (1943), which teaches that the mere difficulty in

---

78. Aldrich v. Aldrich, 375 U.S. 249 (1963); Dresner v. City of Tallahassee, 375 U.S. 136 (1963). [The Supreme Court certified to the Virginia Supreme Court two questions concerning the construction of a state statute in Virginia v. American Booksellers Assn., Inc., 484 U.S. 383 (1988).]

79. Trail Builders Supply Co. v. Reagan, 430 F.2d 828 (CA5 1970); Gaston v. Pittman, 413 F.2d 1031 (CA5 1969); Martinez v. Rodriquez, 410 F.2d 729 (CA5 1969); Moragne v. States Marine Lines, Inc., 409 F.2d 32 (CA5 1969), rev'd on other grounds, 398 U.S. 375 (1970); Hopkins v. Lockheed Aircraft Corp., 394 F.2d 656 (CA5 1968); Life Ins. Co. of Virginia v. Shifflet, 380 F.2d 375 (CA5 1967); Green v. American Tobacco Co., 325 F.2d 673 (CA5 1963); Clay v. Sun Ins. Off. Ltd., 319 F.2d 505 (CA5 1963). The Fifth Circuit's willingness to certify is in part a product of frequent state court repudiation of its interpretations of state law. See the cases summarized in United Services Life Ins. Co. v. Delaney, 328 F.2d 483, 486–487 (CA5 1964) (Brown, C.J., concurring).

ascertaining local law is no excuse for remitting the parties to a state tribunal for the start of another lawsuit. We do not suggest that where there is doubt as to local law and where the certification procedure is available, resort to it is obligatory. It does of course in the long run save time, energy, and resources and helps build a cooperative judicial federalism.[80] Its use in a given case rests in the sound discretion of the federal court.

Here resort to it would seem particularly appropriate in view of the novelty of the question and the great unsettlement of Florida law, Florida being a distant State. When federal judges in New York attempt to predict uncertain Florida law, they act, as we have referred to ourselves on this Court in matters of state law, as "outsiders" lacking the common exposure to local law which comes from sitting in the jurisdiction.

> "Reading the Texas statutes and the Texas decisions as outsiders without special competence in Texas law, we would have little confidence in our independent judgment regarding the application of that law to the present situation. The lower court did deny that the Texas statutes sustained the Commissioner's assertion of power. And this represents the view of an able and experienced circuit judge of the circuit which includes Texas and of two capable district judges trained in Texas law." Railroad Comm'n v. Pullman Co., 312 U.S. 496, 499 (1941).

See also MacGregor v. State Mut. Life Assur. Co., 315 U.S. 280, 281 (1942); Reitz v. Mealey, 314 U.S. 33, 39 (1941).

The judgment of the Court of Appeals is vacated and the cases are remanded so that Court of Appeals may reconsider whether the controlling issue of Florida law should be certified to the Florida Supreme Court pursuant to Rule 4.61 of the Florida Appellate Rules.

So ordered.

■ MR. JUSTICE REHNQUIST, concurring.

The Court says that use of state court certification procedures by federal courts "does of course in the long run save time, energy, and resources and helps build a cooperative judicial federalism." . . . It also observes that "[w]e do not suggest that where there is doubt as to local law and where the certification procedure is available, resort to it is obligatory," and further states that "[i]ts use in a given case rests in the sound discretion of the federal court." . . . I agree with each of these propositions, but think it appropriate to emphasize the scope of the discretion of federal judges in deciding whether to use such certification procedures.

.   .   .   .   .

---

80. See Wright, The Federal Courts and the Nature and Quality of State Law, 13 Wayne L.Rev. 317 (1967); Kurland, Toward a Cooperative Judicial Federalism: The Federal Court Abstention Doctrine, 24 F.R.D. 481 (1966): Note, Inter–Jurisdictional Certification: Beyond Abstention Toward Cooperative Judicial Federalism, 111 U.Pa.L.Rev. 344 (1963); Note, Florida's Interjurisdictional Certification: A Reexamination To Promote Expanded National Use, 22 U.Fla.L.Rev. 21 (1969).

The authority which Congress has granted this Court to review judgments of the courts of appeals undoubtedly vests us not only with the authority to correct errors of substantive law, but to prescribe the method by which those courts go about deciding the cases before them. Western Pacific R. Corp. v. Western Pacific R. Co., 345 U.S. 247 (1953). But a sensible respect for the experience and competence of the various integral parts of the federal judicial system suggests that we go slowly in telling the courts of appeals or the district courts how to go about deciding cases where federal jurisdiction is based on diversity of citizenship, cases which they see and decide far more often than we do.

This Court has held that a federal court may not remit a diversity plaintiff to state courts merely because of the difficulty in ascertaining local law, Meredith v. Winter Haven, 320 U.S. 228 (1943); it has also held that unusual circumstances may require a federal court having jurisdiction of an action to nonetheless abstain from deciding doubtful questions of state law, e.g., Louisiana Power & Light Co. v. City of Thibodaux, 360 U.S. 25 (1959); Kaiser Steel Corp. v. W.S. Ranch Co., 391 U.S. 593 (1968) (per curiam). In each of these situations, our decisions have dealt with the issue of how to reconcile the exercise of the jurisdiction which Congress has conferred upon the federal courts with the important considerations of comity and cooperative federalism which are inherent in a federal system, both of which must be subject to a single national policy within the federal judiciary.

At the other end of the spectrum, however, I assume it would be unthinkable to any of the Members of this Court to prescribe the process by which a district court or a court of appeals should go about researching a point of state law which arises in a diversity case. Presumably the judges of the district courts and of the courts of appeals are at least as capable as we are in determining what the Florida courts have said about a particular question of Florida law.

State certification procedures are a very desirable means by which a federal court may ascertain an undecided point of state law, especially where, as is the case in Florida, the question can be certified directly to the court of last resort within the State. But in a purely diversity case such as this one, the use of such a procedure is more a question of the considerable discretion of the federal court in going about the decision-making process than it is a question of a choice trenching upon the fundamentals of our federal-state jurisprudence.

The other side of the certification coin is that it does in fact engender delay and create additional expense for litigants. See Clay v. Sun Insurance Office, Ltd., 363 U.S. 207, 226–227 (dissenting opinion). The Supreme Court of Florida has promulgated an appellate rule, Fla.App.Rule 4.61 (1967), which provides that upon certification by a federal court to that court, the parties shall file briefs there according to a specified briefing schedule, that oral argument may be granted upon application, and that the parties shall pay the costs of the certification. Thus while the certification procedure is more likely to produce the correct determination of state law, additional time and money are required to achieve such a determination.

If a district court or court of appeals believes that it can resolve an issue of state law with available research materials already at hand, and makes the effort to do so, its determination should not be disturbed simply because the certification procedure existed but was not used. The question of whether certification on the facts of this case, particularly in view of the lateness of its suggestion by petitioner, would have advanced the goal of correctly disposing of this litigation on the state law issue is one which I would leave, and I understand that the Court would leave, to the sound judgment of the court making the initial choice. But since the Court has today for the first time expressed its view as to the use of certification procedures by the federal courts, I agree that it is appropriate to vacate the judgment of the Court of Appeals and remand the cases in order that the Court of Appeals may reconsider certification in light of the Court's opinion.[81]

———

[81. See also Bellotti v. Baird, 428 U.S. 132 (1976) where the Court repeats its praise of certification and hints that certification may be appropriate where the more cumbersome process of ordinary abstention would not.

"[E]ven where we have recognized the importance of certification in deciding whether to abstain, we have been careful to note that the availability of certification is not in itself sufficient to render abstention appropriate.... It would be manifestly inappropriate to certify a question in a case where, as here, there is no uncertain question of state law whose resolution might affect the pending federal claim.... A federal court may not properly ask a state court if it would care in effect to rewrite a statute." City of Houston v. Hill, 482 U.S. 451, 470–474 (1987).

A Uniform Certification of Questions of Law Act was approved by the Commissioners on Uniform State Laws in 1967. In 1995 the National Conference of Commissioners on Uniform State Laws approved a new "Uniform Certification of Laws [Act] [Rule]." This replaces the 1967 Uniform Act. See also ALI Study § 1371(e). Recommendation 8 of the 1995 Long Range Plan, p. 32, urges those states that have not done so to adopt certification procedures.

In Arizonans for Official English v. Arizona, 520 U.S. 43, 75–79 (1997), the Court set forth a virtually mandatory rule that in federal litigation calling for the construction of novel state legislation not yet considered in state court, the lower federal courts must certify questions of construction to state court if an effective certification mechanism is available. The Court appeared to express disfavor with *Pullman* abstention, which it termed "protracted and expensive in practice," when the alternative of certification is available.

But see In re Katrina Canal Breaches Litig., 495 F.3d 191, 207 (5th Cir. 2007), in which the Fifth Circuit acknowledged that the Louisiana Supreme Court had not interpreted the flood exclusion at issue in the case in the context presented (insurance litigation involving breached levees), but nevertheless denied the plaintiffs' motions to certify the question to the Louisiana Supreme Court, stating it could rely on Louisiana's rules of contract interpretation to resolve the dispute.]

SECTION 8. "OUR FEDERALISM"

Younger v. Harris

Supreme Court of the United States, 1971.
401 U.S. 37, 91 S.Ct. 746, 27 L.Ed.2d 669.

■ MR. JUSTICE BLACK delivered the opinion of the Court.

Appellee, John Harris, Jr., was indicted in a California state court, charged with violation of the California Penal Code §§ 11400 and 11401, known as the California Criminal Syndicalism Act .... He then filed a complaint in the Federal District Court, asking that court to enjoin the appellant, Younger, the District Attorney of Los Angeles County, from prosecuting him, and alleging that the prosecution and even the presence of the Act inhibited him in the exercise of his rights of free speech and press, rights guaranteed him by the First and Fourteenth Amendments. Appellees Jim Dan and Diane Hirsch intervened as plaintiffs in the suit, claiming that the prosecution of Harris would inhibit them as members of the Progressive Labor Party from peacefully advocating the program of their party, which was to replace capitalism with socialism and to abolish the profit system of production in this country. Appellee Farrell Broslawsky, an instructor in history at Los Angeles Valley College, also intervened claiming that the prosecution of Harris made him uncertain as to whether he could teach about the doctrines of Karl Marx or read from the Communist Manifesto as part of his classwork. All claimed that unless the United States court restrained the state prosecution of Harris each would suffer immediate and irreparable injury. A three-judge Federal District Court, convened pursuant to 28 U.S.C. § 2284, held that it had jurisdiction and power to restrain the District Attorney from prosecuting, held that the State's Criminal Syndicalism Act was void for vagueness and overbreadth in violation of the First and Fourteenth Amendments, and accordingly restrained the District Attorney from "further prosecution of the currently pending action against plaintiff Harris for alleged violation of the Act." 281 F.Supp. 507, 517 (1968).

The case is before us on appeal by the State's District Attorney Younger, pursuant to 28 U.S.C. § 1253. In his notice of appeal and his jurisdictional statement appellant presented two questions: (1) whether the decision of this Court in Whitney v. California, 274 U.S. 357, holding California's law constitutional in 1927 was binding on the District Court and (2) whether the State's law is constitutional on its face. In this Court the brief for the State of California, filed at our request, also argues that only Harris, who was indicted, has standing to challenge the State's law, and that issuance of the injunction was a violation of a long-standing judicial policy and of 28 U.S.C. § 2283, which provides:

> "A court of the United States may not grant an injunction to stay proceedings in a State court except as expressly authorized by Act of Congress, or where necessary in aid of its jurisdiction, or to protect or effectuate its judgments."

See, e.g., Atlantic Coast Line R. Co. v. Engineers, 398 U.S. 281, 285–286 (1970). Without regard to the questions raised about Whitney v. California, supra, since overruled by Brandenburg v. Ohio, 395 U.S. 444 (1969), or the constitutionality of the state law, we have concluded that the judgment of the District Court, enjoining appellant Younger from prosecuting under these California statutes, must be reversed as a violation of the national policy forbidding federal courts to stay or enjoin pending state court proceedings except under special circumstances. We express no view about the circumstances under which federal courts may act when there is no prosecution pending in state courts at the time the federal proceeding is begun.

I

Appellee Harris has been indicted, and was actually being prosecuted by California for a violation of its Criminal Syndicalism Act at the time this suit was filed. He thus has an acute, live controversy with the State and its prosecutor. But none of the other parties plaintiff in the District Court, Dan, Hirsch, or Broslawsky, has such a controversy. None has been indicted, arrested, or even threatened by the prosecutor. About these three the three-judge court said:

> "Plaintiffs Dan and Hirsch allege that they are members of the Progressive Labor Party, which advocates change in industrial owner-ship and political change, and that they feel inhibited in advocating the program of their political party through peaceful, nonviolent means, because of the presence of the Act 'on the books,' and because of the pending criminal prosecution against Harris. Plaintiff Broslawsky is a history instructor, and he alleges that he is uncertain as to whether his normal practice of teaching his students about the doctrines of Karl Marx and reading from the Communist Manifesto and other revolu-tionary works may subject him to prosecution for violation of the Act." 281 F.Supp., at 509.

Whatever right Harris, who is being prosecuted under the State Syndical-ism law may have, Dan, Hirsch, and Broslawsky cannot share it with him. If these three had alleged that they would be prosecuted for the conduct they planned to engage in, and if the District Court had found this allegation to be true—either on the admission of the State's district attorney or on any other evidence—then a genuine controversy might be said to exist. But here appellees Dan, Hirsch, and Broslawsky do not claim that they have ever been threatened with prosecution, that a prosecution is likely, or even that a prosecution is remotely possible. They claim the right to bring this suit solely because, in the language of their complaint, they "feel inhibited." We do not think this allegation even if true, is sufficient to bring the equitable jurisdiction of the federal courts into play to enjoin a pending state prosecution. A federal lawsuit to stop a prosecution in a state court is a serious matter. And persons having no fears of state prosecution except those that are imaginary or speculative, are not to be accepted as appropriate plaintiffs in such cases. See Golden v. Zwickler, 394 U.S. 103 (1969). Since Harris is actually being prosecuted under the challenged laws, however, we proceed with him as a proper party.

II

Since the beginning of this Country's history Congress has, subject to few exceptions, manifested a desire to permit state courts to try state cases free from interference by federal courts. In 1793 an Act unconditionally provided: "[N]or shall a writ of injunction be granted to stay proceedings in any court of any state . . . ." 1 Stat. 335, c. 22, § 5. A comparison of the 1793 Act with 28 U.S.C. § 2283, its present-day successor, graphically illustrates how few and minor have been the exceptions granted from the flat, prohibitory language of the old Act. During all this lapse of years from 1793 to 1970 the statutory exceptions to the 1793 congressional enactment have been only three: (1) "except as expressly authorized by Act of Congress" ; (2) "where necessary in aid of its jurisdiction" ; and (3) "to protect or effectuate its judgments." In addition, a judicial exception to the longstanding policy evidenced by the statute has been made where a person about to be prosecuted in a state court can show that he will, if the proceeding in the state court is not enjoined, suffer irreparable damages. See Ex parte Young, 209 U.S. 123 (1908).

The precise reasons for this long-standing public policy against federal court interference with state court proceedings have never been specifically identified but the primary sources of the policy are plain. One is the basic doctrine of equity jurisprudence that courts of equity should not act, and particularly should not act to restrain a criminal prosecution, when the moving party has an adequate remedy at law and will not suffer irreparable injury if denied equitable relief. The doctrine may originally have grown out of circumstances peculiar to the English judicial system and not applicable in this country, but its fundamental purpose of restraining equity jurisdiction within narrow limits is equally important under our Constitution, in order to prevent erosion of the role of the jury and avoid a duplication of legal proceedings and legal sanctions where a single suit would be adequate to protect the rights asserted. This underlying reason for restraining courts of equity from interfering with criminal prosecutions is reinforced by an even more vital consideration, the notion of "comity," that is a proper respect for state functions, a recognition of the fact that the entire country is made up of a Union of separate state governments, and a continuance of the belief that the National Government will fare best if the States and their institutions are left free to perform their separate functions in their separate ways. This, perhaps for lack of a better and clearer way to describe it, is referred to by many as "Our Federalism," and one familiar with the profound debates that ushered our Federal Constitution into existence is bound to respect those who remain loyal to the ideals and dreams of "Our Federalism." The concept does not mean blind deference to "States' Rights" any more than it means centralization of control over every important issue in our National Government and its courts. The Framers rejected both these courses. What the concept does represent is a system in which there is sensitivity to the legitimate interests of both State and National Governments, and in which the National Government, anxious though it may be to vindicate and protect federal rights and federal interests, always endeavors to do so in ways that will not unduly interfere with the legitimate activities of the States. It should never be forgotten that this slogan, "Our Federalism," born in the early struggling days of our Union of States, occupies a highly important place in our Nation's history and its future.

This brief discussion should be enough to suggest some of the reasons why it has been perfectly natural for our cases to repeat time and time again that the normal thing to do when federal courts are asked to enjoin pending proceedings in state courts is not to issue such injunctions. In Fenner v. Boykin, 271 U.S. 240 (1926), suit had been brought in the Federal District Court seeking to enjoin state prosecutions under a recently enacted state law that allegedly interfered with the free flow of interstate commerce. The Court, in a unanimous opinion made clear that such a suit, even with respect to state criminal proceedings not yet formally instituted, could be proper only under very special circumstances:

"Ex parte Young, 209 U.S. 123, and following cases have established the doctrine that, when absolutely necessary for the protection of constitutional rights, courts of the United States have power to enjoin state officers from instituting criminal actions. But this may not be done, except under extraordinary circumstances, where the danger of irreparable loss is both great and immediate. Ordinarily, there should be no interference with such officers; primarily, they are charged with the duty of prosecuting offenders against the laws of the state, and must decide when and how this is to be done. The accused should first set up and rely on his defense in the state courts, even though this involves a challenge to the validity of some statute, unless it plainly appears that this course would not afford adequate protection." Id., at 243–244.

These principles made clear in the *Fenner* case have been repeatedly followed and reaffirmed in other cases involving threatened prosecutions. See, e.g., Spielman Motor Sales Co. v. Dodge, 295 U.S. 89 (1935); Beal v. Missouri Pac. R. Co., 312 U.S. 45 (1941); Watson v. Buck, 313 U.S. 387 (1941); Williams v. Miller, 317 U.S. 599 (1942); Douglas v. City of Jeannette, 319 U.S. 157 (1943).

In all of these cases the Court stressed the importance of showing irreparable injury, the traditional prerequisite to obtaining an injunction. In addition, however, the Court also made clear that in view of the fundamental policy against federal interference with state criminal prosecutions, even irreparable injury is insufficient unless it is "both great and immediate." *Fenner,* supra. Certain types of injury, in particular, the cost, anxiety, and inconvenience of having to defend against a single criminal prosecution, could not by themselves be considered "irreparable" in the special legal sense of that term. Instead, the threat to the plaintiff's federally protected rights must be one that cannot be eliminated by his defense against a single criminal prosecution. See, e.g., *Ex parte Young*, supra, 209 U.S., at 145–147 . . . .

This is where the law stood when the Court decided Dombrowski v. Pfister, 380 U.S. 479 (1965), and held that an injunction against the enforcement of certain state criminal statutes could properly issue under the circumstances presented in that case. In *Dombrowski*, unlike many of the earlier cases denying injunctions, the complaint made substantial allegations that:

> "the threats to enforce the statutes against appellants are not made with any expectation of securing valid convictions, but rather are part of a plan to employ arrests, seizures, and threats of prosecution under color of the statutes to harass appellants and discourage them and their supporters from asserting and attempting to vindicate the constitutional rights of Negro citizens of Louisiana." 380 U.S., at 482.

The appellants in *Dombrowski* had offered to prove that their offices had been raided and all their files and records seized pursuant to search and arrest warrants that were later summarily vacated by a state judge for lack of probable cause. They also offered to prove that despite the state court order quashing the warrants and suppressing the evidence seized, the prosecutor was continuing to threaten to initiate new prosecutions of appellants under the same statutes, was holding public hearings at which photostatic copies of the illegally seized documents were being used, and was threatening to use other copies of the illegally seized documents to obtain grand jury indictments against the appellants on charges of violating the same statutes. These circumstances, as viewed by the Court sufficiently establish the kind of irreparable injury, above and beyond that associated with the defense of a single prosecution brought in good faith, that had always been considered sufficient to justify federal intervention. See, e.g., *Beal,* supra, 312 U.S., at 50. Indeed, after quoting the Court's statement in *Douglas* concerning the very restricted circumstances under which an injunction could be justified, the Court in *Dombrowski* went on to say:

> "But the allegations in this complaint depict a situation in which defense of the State's criminal prosecution will not assure adequate vindication of constitutional rights. They suggest that a substantial loss of or impairment of freedoms of expression will occur if appellants must await the state court's disposition and ultimate review in this Court of any adverse determination. These allegations, if true, clearly show irreparable injury." 380 U.S., at 485–486.

And the Court made clear that even under these circumstances the District Court issuing the injunction would have continuing power to lift it at any time and remit the plaintiffs to the state courts if circumstances warranted. 380 U.S., at 491, 492. Similarly, in Cameron v. Johnson, 390 U.S. 611 (1968), a divided Court denied an injunction after finding that the record did not establish the necessary bad faith and harassment; the dissenting Justices themselves stressed the very limited role to be allowed for federal injunctions against state criminal prosecutions and differed with the Court only on the question whether the particular facts of that case were sufficient to show that the prosecution was brought in bad faith.

It is against the background of these principles that we must judge the propriety of an injunction under the circumstances of the present case. Here a proceeding was already pending in the state court, affording Harris an opportunity to raise his constitutional claims. There is no suggestion that this single prosecution against Harris is brought in bad faith or is only one of a series of repeated prosecutions to which he will be subjected. In other words, the injury that Harris faces is solely "that incidental to every criminal proceeding brought lawfully and in good faith," *Douglas,* supra, and therefore under the settled doctrine we have already described he is not entitled to equitable relief "even if such statutes are unconstitutional," *Buck,* supra.

The District Court, however, thought that the *Dombrowski* decision substantially broadened the availability of injunctions against state criminal prosecutions and that under that decision the federal courts may give equitable relief, without regard to any showing of bad faith or harassment, whenever a state statute is found "on its face" to be vague or overly broad, in violation of the First Amendment. We recognize that there are some statements in the *Dombrowski* opinion that would seem to support this argument. But as we have already seen, such statements were unnecessary to the decision of that case, because the Court found that the plaintiffs had alleged a basis for equitable relief under the long-established standards. In addition, we do not regard the reasons adduced to support this position as sufficient to justify such a substantial departure from the established doctrines regarding the availability of injunctive relief. It is undoubtedly true, as the Court stated in *Dombrowski,* that "A criminal prosecution under a statute regulating expression usually involves imponderables and contingencies that themselves may inhibit the full exercise of First Amendment freedoms." 380 U.S., at 486. But this sort of "chilling effect," as the Court called it, should not by itself justify federal intervention. In the first place, the chilling effect cannot be satisfactorily eliminated by federal injunctive relief. In *Dombrowski* itself the Court stated that the injunction to be issued there could be lifted if the State obtained an "acceptable limiting construction" from the state courts. The Court then made clear that once this was done, prosecutions could then be brought for conduct occurring before the narrowing construction was made, and proper convictions could stand so long as the defendants were not deprived of fair warning. 380 U.S., at 491, n. 7. The kind of relief granted in *Dombrowski* thus does not effectively eliminate uncertainty as to the coverage of the state statute and leaves most citizens with virtually the same doubts as before regarding the danger that their conduct might eventually be subjected to criminal sanctions. The chilling effect can, of course, be eliminated by an injunction that would prohibit any prosecution whatever for conduct occurring prior to a satisfactory rewriting of the statute. But the States would then be stripped of all power to prosecute even the socially dangerous and constitutionally unprotected conduct that had been covered by the statute, until a new statute could be passed by the state legislature and approved by the federal courts in potentially lengthy trial and appellate proceedings. Thus, in *Dombrowski* itself the Court carefully reaffirmed the principle that even in the direct prosecution in the State's own courts, a valid narrowing construction can be applied to conduct occurring prior to the date when the narrowing construction was made, in the absence of fair warning problems.

Moreover, the existence of a "chilling effect," even in the area of First Amendment rights, has never been considered a sufficient basis, in and of itself, for prohibiting state action. Where a statute does not directly abridge free speech, but—while regulating a subject within the State's power—tends to have the incidental effect of inhibiting First Amendment rights, it is well settled that the statute can be upheld if the effect on speech is minor in relation to the need for control of the conduct and the lack of alternative means for doing so. Schneider v. State, 308 U.S. 147 (1939); Cantwell v. Connecticut, 310 U.S. 296 (1940); United Mine Workers of America, Dist. 12 v. Illinois Bar Assn., 389 U.S. 217 (1967). Just as the incidental "chilling effect" of such statutes does not automatically render them unconstitutional, so the chilling effect that admittedly can result from the very existence of certain laws on the statute books does not in itself justify prohibiting the State from carrying out the important and necessary task of enforcing these laws against socially harmful conduct that the State believes in good faith to be punishable under its laws and the Constitution.

Beyond all this is another, more basic consideration. Procedures for testing the constitutionality of a statute "on its face" in the manner apparently contemplated by *Dombrowski,* and for then enjoining all action to enforce the statute until the State can obtain court approval for a modified version, are fundamentally at odds with the function of the federal courts in our constitutional plan. The power and duty of the judiciary to declare laws unconstitutional is in the final analysis derived from its responsibility for resolving concrete disputes brought before the courts for decision; a statute apparently governing a dispute cannot be applied by judges, consistently with their obligations under the Supremacy Clause, when such an application of the statute would conflict with the Constitution. Marbury v. Madison, 1 Cranch [5 U.S.] 137 (1803). But this vital responsibility, broad as it is, does not amount to an unlimited power to survey the statute books and pass judgment on laws before the courts are called upon to enforce them. Ever since the Constitutional Convention rejected a proposal for having members of the Supreme Court render advice concerning pending legislation it has been clear that, even when suits of this kind involve a "case or controversy" sufficient to satisfy the requirements of Article III of the Constitution, the task of analyzing a proposed statute, pinpointing its deficiencies, and requiring correction of these deficiencies before the statute is put into effect, is rarely if ever an appropriate task for the judiciary. The combination of the relative remoteness of the controversy, the impact on the legislative process of the relief sought, and above all the speculative and amorphous nature of the required line-by-line analysis of detailed statutes, see, e.g., Landry v. Daley, 280 F.Supp. 938 (N.D.Ill.1968), reversed sub nom. Boyle v. Landry, 401 U.S. 77, ordinarily results in a kind of case that is wholly unsatisfactory for deciding constitutional questions, whichever way they might be decided. In light of this fundamental conception of the Framers as to the proper place of the federal courts in the governmental processes of passing and enforcing laws, it can seldom be appropriate for these courts to exercise any such power of prior approval or veto over the legislative process.

For these reasons, fundamental not only to our federal system but also to the basic functions of the Judicial Branch of the National Government under our Constitution, we hold that the *Dombrowski* decision should not be regarded as having upset the settled doctrines that have always confined very narrowly the availability of injunctive relief against state criminal prosecutions. We do not think that opinion stands for the proposition that a federal court can properly enjoin enforcement of a statute solely on the basis of a showing that the statute "on its face" abridges First Amendment rights. There may, of course, be extraordinary circumstances in which the necessary irreparable injury can be shown even in the absence of the usual prerequisites of bad faith and harassment. For example, as long ago as the *Buck* case, supra, we indicated:

> "It is of course conceivable that a statute might be flagrantly and patently violative of express constitutional prohibitions in every clause, sentence and paragraph, and in whatever manner and against whomever an effort might be made to apply it." 313 U.S., at 402.

Other unusual situations calling for federal intervention might also arise, but there is no point in our attempting now to specify what they might be. It is sufficient for purposes of the present case to hold, as we do, that the possible unconstitutionality of a statute "on its face" does not in itself justify an injunction against good faith attempts to enforce it, and that appellee Harris has failed to make any showing of bad faith, harassment, or any other unusual circumstance that would call for equitable relief. Because our holding rests on the absence of the factors necessary under equitable principles to justify federal intervention, we have no occasion to consider whether 28 U.S.C. § 2283, which prohibits an injunction against state court proceedings "except as expressly authorized by Act of Congress" would in and of itself be controlling under the circumstances of this case.[82]

The judgment of the District Court is reversed, and the case is remanded for further proceedings not inconsistent with this opinion.

Reversed.

■ MR. JUSTICE STEWART, with whom MR. JUSTICE HARLAN joins, concurring.

The questions the Court decides today are important ones. Perhaps as important, however, is a recognition of the areas into which today's holdings do not necessarily extend. In all of these cases, the Court deals only with the proper policy to be followed by a federal court when asked to intervene by injunction or declaratory judgment in a criminal prosecution which is contemporaneously pending in a state court.

[82. The following year the Court held in Mitchum v. Foster, 407 U.S. 225 (1972), that injunctions against state proceedings are "expressly authorized" by the civil rights statute, 42 U.S.C. § 1983, and thus are not barred by the Anti–Injunction Act, 28 U.S.C. § 2283.]

In basing its decisions on policy grounds, the Court does not reach any questions concerning the independent force of the federal anti-injunction statute, 28 U.S.C. § 2283. Thus we do not decide whether the word "injunction" in § 2283 should be interpreted to include a declaratory judgment, or whether an injunction to stay proceedings in a state court is "expressly authorized" by § 1 of the Civil Rights Act of 1871, now 42 U.S.C. § 1983. And since all these cases involve state criminal prosecutions, we do not deal with the considerations which should govern a federal court when it is asked to intervene in state civil proceedings, where, for various reasons, the balance might be struck differently.[83] Finally, the Court today does not resolve the problems involved when a federal court is asked to give injunctive or declaratory relief from *future* state criminal prosecutions.

. . . . .

The Court confines itself to deciding the policy considerations that in our federal system must prevail when federal courts are asked to interfere with pending state prosecutions. Within this area, we hold that a federal court must not, save in exceptional and extremely limited circumstances, intervene by way of either injunction or declaration in an existing state criminal prosecution. Such circumstances exist only when there is a threat of irreparable injury "both great and immediate." A threat of this nature might be shown if the state criminal statute in question were patently and flagrantly unconstitutional on its face; cf. Evers v. Dwyer, 358 U.S. 202, or if there has been bad faith and harassment—official lawlessness—in a statute's enforcement. In such circumstances the reasons of policy for deferring to state adjudication are outweighed by the injury flowing from the very bringing of the state proceedings, by the perversion of the very process which is supposed to provide vindication, and by the need for speedy and effective action to protect federal rights. Cf. Georgia v. Rachel, 384 U.S. 780.

■ MR. JUSTICE BRENNAN with whom MR. JUSTICE WHITE and MR. JUSTICE MARSHALL join, concurring in the result.

[These Justices agreed that the appellees other than Harris presented no justiciable controversy, and that Harris had failed to make an adequate showing of his need for federal interference in his state prosecution. He did not allege that the prosecution was in bad faith, and he would have an adequate opportunity in state court to assert his constitutional defenses.]

■ MR. JUSTICE DOUGLAS, dissenting.

The fact that we are in a period of history when enormous extrajudicial sanctions are imposed on those who assert their First Amendment rights in unpopular causes emphasizes the wisdom of Dombrowski v. Pfister, 380

---

83. Courts of equity have traditionally shown greater reluctance to intervene in criminal prosecutions than in civil cases. See *Younger v. Harris*, 401 U.S., at 43–44; Douglas v. City of Jeannette, 319 U.S. 157, 163–164. The offense to state interests is likely to be less in a civil proceeding. A State's decision to classify conduct as criminal provides some indication of the importance it has ascribed to prompt and unencumbered enforcement of its law. By contrast, the State might not even be a party in a proceeding under a civil statute.

U.S. 479. There we recognized that in times of repression, when interests with powerful spokesmen generate symbolic pogroms against nonconformists, the federal judiciary, charged by Congress with special vigilance for protection of civil rights, has special responsibilities to prevent an erosion of the individual's constitutional rights.

Dombrowski represents an exception to the general rule that federal courts should not interfere with state criminal prosecutions. The exception does not arise merely because prosecutions are threatened to which the First Amendment will be the proffered defense. *Dombrowski* governs statutes which are a blunderbuss by themselves or when used *en masse*—those that have an "overbroad" sweep. "If the rule were otherwise, the contours of regulation would have to be hammered out case by case—and tested only by those hardy enough to risk criminal prosecution to determine the proper scope of regulation." Id., at 487. It was in the context of overbroad state statutes that we spoke of the "chilling effect upon the exercise of First Amendment rights" caused by state prosecutions. Ibid.

As respects overbroad statutes we said at least as early as 1940 that when dealing with First Amendment rights we would insist on statutes "narrowly drawn to prevent the supposed evil." Cantwell v. Connecticut, 310 U.S. 296, 307.

The special circumstances when federal intervention in a state criminal proceeding is permissible are not restricted to bad faith on the part of state officials or the threat of multiple prosecutions. They also exist where for any reason the state statute being enforced is unconstitutional on its face. As Mr. Justice Butler, writing for the Court, said in Terrace v. Thompson, 263 U.S. 197, 214:

> "Equity jurisdiction will be exercised to enjoin the threatened enforcement of a state law which contravenes the federal Constitution wherever it is essential in order effectually to protect property rights and the rights of persons against injuries otherwise irremediable; and in such a case a person, who as an officer of the state is clothed with the duty of enforcing its laws and who threatens and is about to commence proceedings, either civil or criminal, to enforce such a law against parties affected, may be enjoined from such action by a Federal court of equity."

Our *Dombrowski* decision was only another facet of the same problem.

In *Younger,* "criminal syndicalism" is defined so broadly as to jeopardize "teaching" that socialism is preferable to free enterprise.

Harris' "crime" was distributing leaflets advocating change in industrial ownership through political action. The statute under which he was indicted was the one involved in Whitney v. California, 274 U.S. 357, a decision we overruled in Brandenburg v. Ohio, 395 U.S. 444, 449.

If the "advocacy" which Harris used was an attempt at persuasion through the use of bullets, bombs, and arson, we would have a different case. But Harris is charged only with distributing leaflets advocating political action toward his objective. He tried unsuccessfully to have the state court dismiss the indictment on constitutional grounds. He resorted to the state appellate court for writs of prohibition to prevent the trial, but to no avail. He went to the federal court as a matter of last resort in an effort to keep this unconstitutional trial from being saddled on him.

The "anti-injunction" statute, 28 U.S.C. § 2283, is not a bar to a federal injunction under these circumstances. That statute was adopted in 1793, 1 Stat. 335, and reflected the early view of the proper role of the federal courts within American federalism.

Whatever the balance of the pressures of localism and nationalism prior to the Civil War, they were fundamentally altered by the war. The Civil War Amendments made civil rights a national concern. Those Amendments, especially § 5 of the Fourteenth Amendment, cemented the change in American federalism brought on by the war. Congress immediately commenced to use its new powers to pass legislation. Just as the first Judiciary Act, 1 Stat. 73, and the "anti-injunction" statute represented the early views of American federalism, the Reconstruction statutes, including the enlargement of federal jurisdiction, represent a later view of American federalism.

One of the jurisdiction-enlarging statutes passed during Reconstruction was the Act of April 20, 1871. 17 Stat. 13. Beyond its jurisdictional provision that statute, now codified as 42 U.S.C. § 1983 provides:

"Every person, who under color of any statute, ordinance, regulation, custom, or usage, of any State or Territory, subjects or causes to be subjected, any citizen of the United States or other person within the jurisdiction thereof *to the deprivation of any rights, privileges, or immunities secured by the Constitution* and laws, shall be liable to the party injured in an action at law, *suit in equity,* or other proper proceeding for redress." (Emphasis added.)

A state law enforcement officer is someone acting under "color of law" even though he may be misusing his authority. Monroe v. Pape, 365 U.S. 167. And prosecution under a patently unconstitutional statute is a "deprivation of . . . rights, privileges, or immunities secured by the Constitution." "Suit[s] in equity" obviously includes injunctions.

. . . . .

In *Younger* there is a prosecution under an unconstitutional statute and relief is denied. In [Boyle v. Landry, 401 U.S. 77,][84] there is harassment

---

[84. *Boyle* was another of the six cases decided February 23, 1971, and often known as "the *Younger* sextet." In *Boyle* the Court held, on the authority of *Younger,* that it was error for a three-judge court to declare unconstitutional and to enjoin enforcement of an Illinois intimidation statute, when "[N]ot a single one of the citizens who brought this action had ever been prosecuted, charged, or even arrested under the particular intimidation statute which the court below held unconstitutional. . . . In fact, the complaint contains no mention of any specific threat by any officer or official of Chicago, Cook County, or the State of Illinois to arrest or prosecute any one or more of the plaintiffs under that statute either one time or many times. Rather, it appears from the allegations that those who originally brought this suit made a search of state statutes and city ordinances with a view to picking

but as yet no prosecution. Allegations of a prosecution or harassment under facially unconstitutional statutes should be sufficient for the exercise of federal equity powers.

Dombrowski and 42 U.S.C. § 1983 indicate why in *Boyle* federal intervention against enforcement of the state laws is appropriate. The case of *Younger* is even stronger. There the state statute challenged is the prototype of the one we held unconstitutional in *Brandenburg v. Ohio*, supra.

The eternal temptation, of course, has been to arrest the speaker rather than to correct the conditions about which he complains. I see no reason why these petitioners should be made to walk the treacherous ground of these statutes. They, like other citizens, need the umbrella of the First Amendment as they study, analyze, discuss, and debate the troubles of these days. When criminal prosecutions can be leveled against them because they express unpopular views, the society of the dialogue is in danger.

Samuels v. Mackell

Supreme Court of the United States, 1971.
401 U.S. 66, 91 S.Ct. 764, 27 L.Ed.2d 688.

■ MR. JUSTICE BLACK delivered the opinion of the Court.

[Appellants, who had been indicted in a New York state court on charges of criminal anarchy, brought an action before a three-judge federal court asking that the state courts be enjoined from further proceedings or, in the alternative, that the state law be declared unconstitutional. The three-judge court held that the state law was constitutional and dismissed the complaint. The Supreme Court held, on the authority of *Younger v. Harris*, that an injunction could not have issued and then considered the declaratory judgment aspect of the case.]

In our opinion in the *Younger* case, we set out in detail the historical and practical basis for the settled doctrine of equity that a federal court should not enjoin a state criminal prosecution begun prior to the institution of the federal suit except in very unusual situations, where necessary to prevent immediate irreparable injury. The question presented here is whether under ordinary circumstances the same considerations that require the withholding of injunctive relief will make declaratory relief equally inappropriate. The question is not, however, a novel one. It was presented and fully considered by this Court in Great Lakes Co. v. Huffman, 319 U.S. 293 (1943). We find the reasoning of this Court in the *Great Lakes* case fully persuasive and think that its holding is controlling here.

---

out certain ones that they thought might possibly be used by the authorities as devices for bad-faith prosecutions against them." 401 U.S., at 80–81.]

In the *Great Lakes* case several employers had brought suit against a Louisiana state official, seeking a declaratory judgment that the State's unemployment compensation law, which required the employers to make contributions to a state compensation fund, was unconstitutional. The lower courts had dismissed the complaint on the ground that the challenged law was constitutional. This Court affirmed the dismissal, "but solely on the ground that, in the appropriate exercise of the court's discretion, relief by way of a declaratory judgment should have been denied without consideration of the merits." Id., at 301–302. The Court, in a unanimous opinion written by Mr. Chief Justice Stone, noted first that under long-settled principles of equity, the federal courts could not have enjoined the Louisiana official from collecting the state tax at issue there unless, as was not true in that case, there was no adequate remedy available in the courts of the State. This judicial doctrine had been approved by Congress in the then recent Tax Injunction Act of 1937, 50 Stat. 738, now 28 U.S.C. § 1341. Although the declaratory judgment sought by the plaintiffs was a statutory remedy rather than a traditional form of equitable relief, the Court made clear that a suit for declaratory judgment was nevertheless "essentially an equitable cause of action," and was "analogous to the equity jurisdiction in suits *quia timet* or for a decree quieting title." 319 U.S., at 300. In addition, the legislative history of the Federal Declaratory Judgment Act of 1934, 48 Stat. 955, as amended, 28 U.S.C. § 2201, showed that Congress had explicitly contemplated that the courts would decide to grant or withhold declaratory relief on the basis of traditional equitable principles. Accordingly the Court held that in an action for a declaratory judgment, "the district court was as free as in any other suit in equity to grant or withhold the relief prayed, upon equitable grounds." 319 U.S., at 300. . . .

The continuing validity of the Court's holding in the *Great Lakes* case has been repeatedly recognized and reaffirmed by this Court. . . . Although we have found no case in this Court dealing with the application of this doctrine to cases in which the relief sought affects state criminal prosecutions rather than state tax collections, we can perceive no relevant difference between the two situations with respect to the limited question whether, in cases where the criminal proceeding was begun prior to the federal civil suit, the propriety of declaratory and injunctive relief should be judged by essentially the same standards. In both situations deeply rooted and long-settled principles of equity have narrowly restricted the scope for federal intervention, and ordinarily a declaratory judgment will result in precisely the same interference with and disruption of state proceedings that the long-standing policy limiting injunctions was designed to avoid. This is true for at least two reasons. In the first place the Declaratory Judgment Act provides that after a declaratory judgment is issued the district court may enforce it by granting "further necessary or proper relief," and therefore a declaratory judgment issued while state proceedings are pending might serve as the basis for a subsequent injunction against those proceedings to "protect or effectuate" the declaratory judgment, 28 U.S.C. § 2283, and thus result in a clearly improper interference with the state proceedings. Secondly, even if the declaratory judgment is not used as a basis for actually issuing an injunction, the declaratory relief alone has virtually the same practical impact as a formal injunction would. As we said in [Public Serv. Comm'n v. Wycoff Co., 344 U.S. 237, 247 (1952)]:

> "Is the declaration contemplated here to be res judicata, so that the [state court] can not hear evidence and decide any matter for itself? If so, the federal court has virtually lifted the case out of the State [court] before it could be heard. If not, the federal judgment serves no useful purpose as a final determination of rights."

See also H.J. Heinz Co. v. Owens, 189 F.2d 505, 508–509 (CA9 1951). We therefore hold that, in cases where the state criminal prosecution was begun prior to the federal suit, the same equitable principles relevant to the propriety of an injunction must be taken into consideration by federal district courts in determining whether to issue a declaratory judgment, and that where an injunction would be impermissible under these principles, declaratory relief should ordinarily be denied as well.

We do not mean to suggest that a declaratory judgment should never be issued in cases of this type if it has been concluded that injunctive relief would be improper. There may be unusual circumstances in which an injunction might be withheld because, despite a plaintiff's strong claim for relief under the established standards, the injunctive remedy seemed particularly intrusive or offensive; in such a situation, a declaratory judgment might be appropriate and might not be contrary to the basic equitable doctrines governing the availability of relief. Ordinarily, however, the practical effect of the two forms of relief will be virtually identical, and the basic policy against federal interference with pending state criminal prosecutions will be frustrated as much by a declaratory judgment as it would be by an injunction.

For the reasons we have stated, we hold that the court below erred in proceeding to a consideration of the merits of the New York criminal anarchy law. Here, as in the *Great Lakes* case, the judgment dismissing the complaint was based on an adjudication that the statutes challenged here are constitutional and is thus in effect a declaratory judgment. We affirm the judgment dismissing the complaint, but solely on the ground that, in the appropriate exercise of the court's discretion, relief by way of declaratory judgment should have been denied without consideration of the merits. We, of course, express no views on the propriety of declaratory relief when no state proceeding is pending at the time the federal suit is begun.

Affirmed.

■ MR. JUSTICE DOUGLAS, concurring.

. . . . .

It therefore cannot be said that the cases against Samuels and Fernandez are palpably unconstitutional. It is for the state courts to preserve such First Amendment rights as may be involved here by sifting out the chaff from the charges through motions to strike, instructions to the jury, and other procedural devices . . . .

■ [JUSTICE BRENNAN, joined by JUSTICE WHITE and JUSTICE MARSHALL, concurred in the result.]

■ [JUSTICE HARLAN and JUSTICE STEWART concurred in the result on the basis of JUSTICE STEWART's concurring opinion in *Younger*, reprinted supra p. 607, in which JUSTICE HARLAN joined.][85]

Steffel v. Thompson

Supreme Court of the United States, 1974.
415 U.S. 452, 94 S.Ct. 1209, 39 L.Ed.2d 505.

■ MR. JUSTICE BRENNAN delivered the opinion of the Court.

When a state criminal proceeding under a disputed state criminal statute is pending against a federal plaintiff at the time his federal complaint is filed, Younger v. Harris, 401 U.S. 37 (1971), and Samuels v. Mackell, 401 U.S. 66 (1971), held, respectively, that, unless bad faith enforcement or other special circumstances are demonstrated, principles of equity, comity, and federalism preclude issuance of a federal injunction restraining enforcement of the criminal statute and, in all but unusual circumstances, a declaratory judgment upon the constitutionality of the statute. This case presents the important question reserved in *Samuels v. Mackell*, id., at 73—whether declaratory relief is precluded when a state prosecution has been threatened, but is not pending, and a showing of bad faith enforcement or other special circumstances has not been made.

Petitioner, and others, filed a complaint in the District Court for the Northern District of Georgia, invoking the Civil Rights Act, 42 U.S.C. § 1983, and its jurisdictional implementation, 28 U.S.C. § 1343. The complaint requested a declaratory judgment pursuant to 28 U.S.C. §§ 2201–2202, that Ga.Code Ann. § 26–1503 was being applied in violation of petitioner's First and Fourteenth Amendment rights, and an injunction restraining respondents—the Solicitor of the Civil and Criminal Court of DeKalb County, the Chief of the DeKalb County Police, the owner of the

---

[85. In Perez v. Ledesma, 401 U.S. 82 (1971), also decided the same day as *Younger*, it was held error for a federal court to give injunctive relief suppressing evidence in a pending state criminal prosecution. Justice Douglas dissented. Justice Brennan, with whom Justices White and Marshall joined, agreed with the holding, but on an issue that the majority did not reach argued that it was proper for the lower court to give a declaratory judgment of invalidity of a local ordinance. Justice Brennan's opinion anticipated the views he later stated for the Court in *Steffel v. Thompson*, reprinted infra p. 621.

The literature on the *Younger* sextet is vast and still growing. See Wright & Kane, Federal Courts § 52A (6th ed.2002); 17A Wright, Miller & Cooper, Federal Practice and Procedure: Jurisdiction 2d §§ 4251–4255 (1988); 17 Moore's Federal Practice § 122.05 (3d ed.1998). There is fascinating history on the divisions within the Court, and the reasons why some of the cases that became the "*Younger* sextet" were argued three times, in Schwartz, Super Chief 755–757 (1983).]

North DeKalb Shopping Center, and the manager of that shopping center—from enforcing the statute so as to interfere with petitioner's constitutionally protected activities.

The parties stipulated to the relevant facts: On October 8, 1970, while petitioner and other individuals were distributing handbills protesting American involvement in Viet Nam on an exterior sidewalk of the North DeKalb Shopping Center, shopping center employees asked them to stop handbilling and leave. They declined to do so, and police officers were summoned. The officers told them that they would be arrested if they did not stop handbilling. The group then left to avoid arrest. Two days later petitioner and a companion returned to the shopping center and again began handbilling. The manager of the center called the police, and petitioner and his companion were once again told that failure to stop their handbilling would result in their arrests. Petitioner left to avoid arrest. His companion stayed, however, continued handbilling, and was arrested and subsequently arraigned on a charge of criminal trespass in violation of § 26–1503. Petitioner alleged in his complaint that, although he desired to return to the shopping center to distribute handbills, he had not done so because of his concern that he too would be arrested for violation of § 26–1503; the parties stipulated that, if petitioner returned and refused upon request to stop handbilling, a warrant would be sworn out and he might be arrested and charged with a violation of the Georgia statute.

After hearing, the District Court denied all relief and dismissed the action, finding that "no meaningful contention can be made that the state has or will in the future act in bad faith" , and therefore "the rudiments of an active controversy between the parties . . . [are] lacking." 334 F.Supp. 1386, 1389–1390 (1971). Petitioner appealed only from the denial of declaratory relief.[86] The Court of Appeals for the Fifth Circuit, one judge concurring in the result, affirmed the District Court's judgment refusing declaratory relief. 459 F.2d 919 (1972). . . . A petition for rehearing en banc was denied, three judges dissenting. 463 F.2d 1338 (1972).

. . . . .

I

At the threshold we must consider whether petitioner presents an "actual controversy," a requirement imposed by Art. III of the Constitution and the express terms of the Federal Declaratory Judgment Act, 28 U.S.C. § 2201.

Unlike three of the appellees in *Younger v. Harris*, 401 U.S., at 41, petitioner has alleged threats of prosecution that cannot be characterized as "imaginary or speculative," id., at 42. He has been twice warned to stop handbilling that he claims is constitutionally protected and has been told by the police that, if he again handbills at the shopping center and disobeys

---

86. Petitioner's notice of appeal challenged the denial of both injunctive and declaratory relief. However, in his appellate brief, he abandoned his appeal from denial of injunctive relief. Becker v. Thompson, 459 F.2d 919, 921 (CA5 1972).

a warning to stop, he will likely be prosecuted. The prosecution of petitioner's handbilling companion is ample demonstration that petitioner's concern with arrest has not been "chimerical," Poe v. Ullman, 367 U.S. 497, 508 (1961). In these circumstances, it is not necessary that petitioner first expose himself to actual arrest or prosecution to be entitled to challenge a statute that he claims deters the exercise of his constitutional rights. See, e.g., Epperson v. Arkansas, 393 U.S. 97 (1968). Moreover, petitioner's challenge is to those specific provisions of state law which have provided the basis for threats of criminal prosecution against him. Cf. Boyle v. Landry, 401 U.S. 77, 81 (1971); Watson v. Buck, 313 U.S. 387, 399–400 (1941).

Nonetheless, there remains a question as to the *continuing* existence of a live and acute controversy that must be resolved on the remand we order today.[87] In Golden v. Zwickler, 394 U.S. 103 (1969), the appellee sought a declaratory judgment that a state criminal statute prohibiting the distribution of anonymous election-campaign literature was unconstitutional. The appellee's complaint had expressed a desire to distribute handbills during the forth-coming re-election campaign of a Congressman, but it was later learned that the Congressman had retired from the House of Representatives to become a New York Supreme Court Justice. In that circumstance, we found no extant controversy, since the record revealed that appellee's sole target of distribution had been the Congressman and there was no immediate prospect of the Congressman again becoming a candidate for public office. Here, petitioner's complaint indicates that his handbilling activities were directed "against the war in Vietnam and the United States' foreign policy in Southeast Asia." Since we cannot ignore the recent developments reducing the Nation's involvement in that part of the world, it will be for the District Court on remand to determine if subsequent events have so altered petitioner's desire to engage in handbilling at the shopping center that it can no longer be said that this case presents "a substantial controversy, between parties having adverse legal interests, of sufficient immediacy and reality to warrant the issuance of a declaratory judgment." Maryland Casualty Co. v. Pacific Coal & Oil Co., 312 U.S. 270, 273 (1941); see Zwickler v. Koota, 389 U.S. 241, 244 n. 3 (1967).

II

We now turn to the question of whether the District Court and the Court of Appeals correctly found petitioner's request for declaratory relief inappropriate.

Sensitive to principles of equity, comity, and federalism, we recognized in *Younger v. Harris*, supra, that federal courts should ordinarily refrain from enjoining ongoing state criminal prosecutions. We were cognizant that a pending state proceeding, in all but unusual cases, would provide the

---

87. The rule in federal cases is that an actual controversy must be extant at all stages of review, not merely at the time the complaint is filed. See, e.g., Roe v. Wade, 410 U.S. [113, 125 (1973)]; SEC v. Medical Comm. for Human Rights, 404 U.S. 403 (1972); United States v. Munsingwear, Inc., 340 U.S. 36 (1950).

federal plaintiff with the necessary vehicle for vindicating his constitutional rights, and, in that circumstance, the restraining of an ongoing prosecution would entail an unseemly failure to give effect to the principle that state courts have the solemn responsibility, equally with the federal courts "to guard, enforce, and protect every right granted or secured by the Constitution of the United States. . . ." Robb v. Connolly, 111 U.S. 624, 637 (1884). In *Samuels v. Mackell,* supra, the Court also found that the same principles ordinarily would be flouted by issuance of a federal declaratory judgment when a state proceeding was pending, since the intrusive effect of declaratory relief "will result in precisely the same interference with and disruption of state proceedings that the longstanding policy limiting injunctions was designed to avoid." 401 U.S., at 72. We therefore held in *Samuels* that, "in cases where the state criminal prosecution was begun prior to the federal suit, the same equitable principles relevant to the propriety of an injunction must be taken into consideration by federal district courts in determining whether to issue a declaratory judgment. . . ." 401 U.S., at 73.

Neither *Younger* nor *Samuels,* however, decided the question whether federal intervention might be permissible in the absence of a pending state prosecution. . . .

These reservations anticipated the Court's recognition that the relevant principles of equity, comity, and federalism "have little force in the absence of a pending state proceeding." Lake Carriers' Ass'n v. MacMullan, 406 U.S. 498, 509 (1972). When no state criminal proceeding is pending at the time the federal complaint is filed, federal intervention does not result in duplicative legal proceedings or disruption of the state criminal justice system; nor can federal intervention, in that circumstance, be interpreted as reflecting negatively upon the state courts' ability to enforce constitutional principles. In addition, while a pending state prosecution provides the federal plaintiff with a concrete opportunity to vindicate his constitutional rights, a refusal on the part of the federal courts to intervene when no state proceeding is pending may place the hapless plaintiff between the Scylla of intentionally flouting state law and the Charybdis of foregoing what he believes to be constitutionally protected activity in order to avoid becoming enmeshed in a criminal proceeding. Cf. Dombrowski v. Pfister, 380 U.S. 479, 490 (1965).

When no state proceeding is pending and thus considerations of equity, comity, and federalism have little vitality, the propriety of granting federal declaratory relief may properly be considered independently of a request for injunctive relief. Here, the Court of Appeals held that because injunctive relief would not be appropriate since petitioner failed to demonstrate irreparable injury—a traditional prerequisite to injunctive relief, e.g., *Dombrowski v. Pfister,* supra—it followed that declaratory relief was also inappropriate. Even if the Court of Appeals correctly viewed injunctive relief as inappropriate—a question we need not reach today since petitioner has abandoned his request for that remedy—[88] the court erred in treating

---

88. We note that, in those cases where injunctive relief has been sought to restrain an imminent, but not yet pending, prosecution *for past conduct,* sufficient injury has not been

the requests for injunctive and declaratory relief as a single issue. "[W]hen no state prosecution is pending and the only question is whether declaratory relief is appropriate [,] ... the congressional scheme that makes the federal courts the primary guardians of constitutional rights, and the express congressional authorization of declaratory relief, afforded because it is a less harsh and abrasive remedy than the injunction, become the factors of primary significance." Perez v. Ledesma, 401 U.S. 82, 104 (1971) (separate opinion of BRENNAN, J.).

The subject matter jurisdiction of the lower federal courts was greatly expanded in the wake of the Civil War. A pervasive sense of nationalism led to enactment of the Civil Rights Act of 1871, 17 Stat. 13, empowering the lower federal courts to determine the constitutionality of actions, taken by persons under color of state law, allegedly depriving other individuals of rights guaranteed by the Constitution and federal law, see 42 U.S.C. § 1983, 28 U.S.C. § 1343(3). Four years later, in the Judiciary Act of March 3, 1875, 18 Stat. 470, Congress conferred upon the lower federal courts, for but the second time in their nearly century-old history, general federal question jurisdiction subject only to a jurisdictional amount requirement, see 28 U.S.C. § 1331. With this latter enactment, the lower federal courts "ceased to be restricted tribunals of fair dealing between citizens of different states and became the *primary* and powerful reliances for vindicating every right given by the Constitution, the laws, and treaties of the United States." F. Frankfurter & J. Landis, The Business of the Supreme Court 65 (1928) (emphasis added). These two statutes, together with the Court's decision in Ex parte Young, 209 U.S. 123 (1908)—holding that state officials who threaten to enforce an unconstitutional state statute may be enjoined by a federal court of equity and that a federal court may, in appropriate circumstances, enjoin future state criminal prosecutions under the unconstitutional act—have "established the modern framework for federal protection of constitutional rights from state interference." *Perez v. Ledesma*, supra, at 107 (separate opinion of BRENNAN, J.).

A "storm of controversy" raged in the wake of *Ex parte Young*, focusing principally on the power of a single federal judge to grant ex parte interlocutory injunctions against the enforcement of state statutes, Hart & Wechsler, The Federal Courts and the Federal System 967 (2d ed.1973); see

---

found to warrant injunctive relief, see Beal v. Missouri P.R. Corp., 312 U.S. 45 (1941); Spielman Motor Sales Co., Inc. v. Dodge, 295 U.S. 89 (1935); Fenner v. Boykin, 271 U.S. 240 (1926). There is some question, however, whether a showing of irreparable injury might be made in a case where, although no prosecution is pending or impending, an individual demonstrates that he will be required to *forgo* constitutionally protected activity in order to avoid arrest. Compare Dombrowski v. Pfister, 380 U.S. 479 (1965); Hygrade Provision Co., Inc. v. Sherman, 266 U.S. 497 (1925); and Terrace v. Thompson, 263 U.S. 197, 214, 216 (1923), with Douglas v. City of Jeannette, 319 U.S. 157 (1943); see generally Note, Implications of the *Younger* Cases for the Availability of Federal Equitable Relief When No State Prosecution is Pending, 72 Colum.L.Rev. 874 (1972). [It was later held in Doran v. Salem Inn, Inc., 422 U.S. 922 (1975), that in a case within the *Steffel* rule preliminary injunctive relief can be had, on a showing of irreparable injury, without regard to *Younger*'s restrictions. In Wooley v. Maynard, 430 U.S. 705 (1977), reprinted infra p. 637, a permanent injunction was upheld.]

generally Goldstein v. Cox, 396 U.S. 471 (1970); Hutcheson, A Case for Three Judges, 47 Harv.L.Rev. 795, 804–805 (1934). This uproar was only partially quelled by Congress' passage of legislation, 36 Stat. 557, requiring the convening of a three-judge District Court before a preliminary injunction against enforcement of a state statute could issue, and providing for direct appeal to this Court from a decision granting or denying such relief. See 28 U.S.C. §§ 2281, 1253. From a State's viewpoint the granting of injunctive relief—even by these courts of special dignity—"rather clumsily" crippled state enforcement of its statutes pending further review, see H.R.Rep. No. 288, 70th Cong., 1st Sess., 2 (1928); H.R.Rep. No. 94, 71st Cong., 2d Sess., 2 (1929); H.R.Rep. No. 627, 72d Cong., 1st Sess., 2 (1932). Furthermore, plaintiffs were dissatisfied with this method of testing the constitutionality of state statutes, since it placed upon them the burden of demonstrating the traditional prerequisites to equitable relief—most importantly, irreparable injury. See, e.g., Fenner v. Boykin, 271 U.S. 240, 243 (1926).

To dispel these difficulties, Congress in 1934 enacted the Declaratory Judgment Act, 28 U.S.C. §§ 2201–2202. That Congress plainly intended declaratory relief to act as an alternative to the strong medicine of the injunction and to be utilized to test the constitutionality of state criminal statutes in cases where injunctive relief would be unavailable is amply evidenced by the legislative history of the Act, traced in full detail in *Perez v. Ledesma*, supra, at 111–115 (separate opinion of BRENNAN, J.). . . .

. . . . .

The "different considerations" entering into a decision whether to grant declaratory relief have their origins in the preceding historical summary. First, as Congress recognized in 1934, a declaratory judgment will have a less intrusive effect on the administration of state criminal laws. As was observed in *Perez v. Ledesma*, 401 U.S., at 124–126 (separate opinion of BRENNAN, J.):

"Of course, a favorable declaratory judgment may nevertheless be valuable to the plaintiff though it cannot make even an unconstitutional statute disappear. A state statute may be declared unconstitutional *in toto*—that is, incapable of having constitutional applications; or it may be declared unconstitutionally vague or overbroad—that is, incapable of being constitutionally applied to the full extent of its purport. In either case, a federal declaration of unconstitutionality reflects the opinion of the federal court that the statute cannot be fully enforced. If a declaration of total unconstitutionality is affirmed by this Court, it follows that this Court stands ready to reverse any conviction under the statute. If a declaration of partial unconstitutionality is affirmed by this Court, the implication is that this Court will overturn particular applications of the statute, but that if the statute is narrowly construed by the state courts it will not be incapable of constitutional applications. Accordingly, the declaration does not necessarily bar prosecutions under the statute, as a broad injunction would. Thus, where the highest court of a State has had an opportunity to give a statute regulating expression a narrowing or clarifying construction but has failed to do so, and later a federal court declares the statute unconstitutionally vague or overbroad, it may well be open to a state prosecutor, after the federal court decision, to bring a prosecution under the statute if he reasonably believes that the defendant's conduct is not constitutionally protected and that the state courts may give the statute a construction so as to yield a constitutionally valid conviction. Even where a declaration of unconstitutionality is not reviewed by this Court, the declaration may still be able to cut down the deterrent effect of an unconstitutional state statute. The persuasive force of the court's opinion and judgment may lead state prosecutors, courts, and legislators to reconsider their respective responsibilities toward the statute. Enforcement policies or judicial construction may be changed, or the legislature may repeal the statute and start anew. Finally, the federal court judgment may have some res judicata effect, though this point is not free from difficulty and the governing rules remain to be developed with a view to the proper workings of a federal system. What is clear, however, is that even though a declaratory judgment has 'the force and effect of a final judgment,' 28 U.S.C. § 2201, it is a much milder form of relief than an injunction. Though it may be persuasive, it is not ultimately coercive; noncompliance with it may be inappropriate, but is not contempt." (Footnote omitted.)

Second, engrafting upon the Declaratory Judgment Act a requirement that all of the traditional equitable prerequisites to the issuance of an injunction be satisfied before the issuance of a declaratory judgment is considered would defy Congress' intent to make declaratory relief available in cases where an injunction would be inappropriate.... Thus, the Court of Appeals was in error when it ruled that a failure to demonstrate irreparable injury—a traditional prerequisite to injunctive relief, having no equivalent in the law of declaratory judgments, see Aetna Life Ins. Co. v. Haworth, 300 U.S. 227, 241 (1937); Nashville C. & St. L.R. Co. v. Wallace, 288 U.S. 249, 264 (1933)—precluded the granting of declaratory relief.

The only occasions where this Court has disregarded these "different considerations" and found that a preclusion of injunctive relief inevitably led to a denial of declaratory relief have been cases in which principles of federalism militated altogether against federal intervention into a class of adjudications. See Great Lakes Co. v. Huffman, 319 U.S. 293 (1943) (federal policy against interfering with the enforcement of state tax laws); Samuels v. Mackell, 401 U.S. 66 (1971). In the instant case, principles of federalism not only do not preclude federal intervention, they compel it. Requiring the federal courts totally to step aside when no state criminal prosecution is pending against the federal plaintiff would turn federalism on its head. When federal claims are premised on 42 U.S.C. § 1983 and 28 U.S.C. § 1343(3)—as they are here—we have not required exhaustion of state judicial or administrative remedies, recognizing the paramount role Congress has assigned to the federal courts to protect constitutional rights. See, e.g., McNeese v. Board of Education, 373 U.S. 668 (1963); Monroe v. Pape, 365 U.S. 167 (1961). But exhaustion of state remedies is precisely what would be required if both federal injunctive and declaratory relief were unavailable in a case where no state prosecution had been commenced.

III

Respondents, however, relying principally upon our decision in Cameron v. Johnson, 390 U.S. 611 (1968), argue that, although it may be appropriate to issue a declaratory judgment when no state criminal proceeding is pending and the attack is upon the *facial validity* of a state criminal statute, such a step would be improper where, as here, the attack is merely upon the constitutionality of the statute as applied, since the State's interest in unencumbered enforcement of its laws outweighs the minimal federal interest in protecting the constitutional rights of only a single individual. We reject the argument.

. . . . .

Indeed, the State's concern with potential interference in the administration of its criminal laws is of lesser dimension when an attack is made upon the constitutionality of a state statute as applied. A declaratory judgment of a lower federal court that a state statute is invalid *in toto*—and therefore incapable of any valid application—or is overbroad or vague—and therefore no person can properly be convicted under the statute until it is given a narrowing or clarifying construction, see, e.g., United States v. Thirty-seven Photographs, 402 U.S. 363, 369 (1971); Gooding v. Wilson, 405 U.S. 518, 520 (1972)—will likely have a more significant potential for disruption of state enforcement policies than a declaration specifying a limited number of impermissible applications of the statute. While the federal interest may be greater when a state statute is attacked on its face, since there exists the potential for eliminating any broad-ranging deterrent effect on would-be actors, see Dombrowski v. Pfister, 380 U.S. 479 (1965), we do not find this consideration controlling. The solitary individual who suffers a deprivation of his constitutional rights is no less deserving of redress than one who suffers together with others.[89]

We therefore hold that, regardless of whether injunctive relief may be appropriate, federal declaratory relief is not precluded when no state prosecution is pending and a federal plaintiff demonstrates a genuine threat of enforcement of a disputed state criminal statute, whether an attack is made on the constitutionality of the statute on its face or as applied. The judgment of the Court of Appeals is reversed, and the case is remanded for further proceedings consistent with this opinion.

It is so ordered.

---

89. Abstention, a question "entirely separate from the question of granting declaratory or injunctive relief," Lake Carriers' Ass'n v. MacMullan, 406 U.S. 498, 509 n.13 (1972), might be more appropriate when a challenge is made to the state statute as applied, rather than upon its face, since the reach of an uncertain state statute might, in that circumstance, be more susceptible to a limiting or clarifying construction that would avoid the federal constitutional question. Cf. *Zwickler v. Koota*, 389 U.S., at 249–252, 254; Baggett v. Bullitt, 377 U.S. 360, 375–378 (1964).

■ MR. JUSTICE STEWART, with whom THE CHIEF JUSTICE joins, concurring.

While joining the opinion of the Court, I add a word by way of emphasis.

Our decision today must not be understood as authorizing the invocation of federal declaratory judgment jurisdiction by a person who thinks a state criminal law is unconstitutional, even if he genuinely feels "chilled" in his freedom of action by the law's existence, and even if he honestly entertains the subjective belief that he may now or in the future be prosecuted under it.

．　．　．　．　．

The petitioner in this case has succeeded in objectively showing that the threat of imminent arrest, corroborated by the actual arrest of his companion, has created an actual concrete controversy between himself and the agents of the State. He has, therefore, demonstrated "a genuine threat of enforcement of a disputed state criminal statute. . . ." Cases where such a "genuine threat" can be demonstrated will, I think, be exceedingly rare.

■ [JUSTICE REHNQUIST, joined by the CHIEF JUSTICE, wrote a concurring opinion stating his views that (1) "any arrest prior to resolution of the federal action would constitute a pending prosecution and bar declaratory relief under the principles of *Samuels*[,]" (2) in this class of cases a declaratory judgment cannot be the basis for an injunction under the "further relief" provision of the Declaratory Judgments Act, and (3) "continued belief in the constitutionality of the statute by state prosecutorial officials would not commonly be indicative of bad faith and that such allegations, in the absence of highly unusual circumstances, would not justify a federal court's departure from the general principles of restraint discussed in *Younger*."]

■ [JUSTICE WHITE wrote a concurring opinion expressing his disagreement with the first two of JUSTICE REHNQUIST's points and stating his belief that "a final declaratory judgment entered by a federal court holding particular conduct of the federal plaintiff to be immune on federal constitutional grounds from prosecution under state law should be accorded res judicata effect in any later prosecution of that very conduct."][90]

───────

Huffman v. Pursue, Ltd.

Supreme Court of the United States, 1975.
420 U.S. 592, 95 S.Ct. 1200, 43 L.Ed.2d 482.

■ MR. JUSTICE REHNQUIST delivered the opinion of the Court.

This case requires that we decide whether our decision in Younger v. Harris, 401 U.S. 37 (1971), bars a federal district court from intervening in

---

[90. The difficult questions on the effect to be given a federal declaratory judgment in a subsequent state prosecution are ably explored in Shapiro, State Courts and Federal Declaratory Judgments, 74 Nw.U.L.Rev. 759 (1979).]

a state civil proceeding such as this, when the proceeding is based on a state statute believed by the district court to be unconstitutional....

I

[The sheriff and prosecuting attorney of an Ohio county sued a movie theatre in state court under Ohio statutes that declared a place in which lewd or obscene films are shown to be a public nuisance and provided for closing nuisances down. The state court reviewed 16 movies that had been shown at the theater, rendered a judgment that there had been a course of conduct of displaying obscene movies, and ordered the theater closed for a period of one year. Rather than appealing that judgment the theater owner sued in federal court, alleging that this use of the Ohio nuisance statute deprived it of constitutional rights under the color of state law. A three-judge district court found that the Ohio statute was not vague but did constitute an overly broad prior restraint on First Amendment rights insofar as it prevented the showing of films that had not been adjudged obscene in prior adversary hearings. It enjoined the execution of that portion of the state court's judgment that closed the theater to films that had not been adjudged obscene.]

II

Younger and its companion cases considered the propriety of federal-court intervention in pending state criminal prosecutions. The issue was not a novel one, and the Court relied heavily on Fenner v. Boykin, 271 U.S. 240 (1926), and subsequent cases which endorsed its holding that federal injunctions against the state criminal law enforcement process could be issued only "under extraordinary circumstances where the danger of irreparable loss is both great and immediate." ...

. . . . .

III

The seriousness of federal judicial interference with state civil functions has long been recognized by this Court. We have consistently required that when federal courts are confronted with requests for such relief, they should abide by standards of restraint that go well beyond those of private equity jurisprudence. For example, Massachusetts State Grange v. Benton, 272 U.S. 525 (1926), involved an effort to enjoin the operation of a state daylight savings act. Writing for the Court, Mr. Justice Holmes cited *Fenner v. Boykin*, supra, and emphasized a rule that "should be very strictly observed," 272 U.S., at 529, "that no injunction ought to issue against officers of a State clothed with authority to enforce the law in question, unless in a case reasonably free from doubt and when necessary to prevent great and irreparable injury." Id., at 527.

Although Mr. Justice Holmes was confronted with a bill seeking injunction of state executive officers, rather than of state judicial proceedings, we think that the relevant considerations of federalism are of no less weight in the latter setting. If anything, they counsel more heavily toward federal restraint, since interference with a state judicial proceeding prevents the state not only from effectuating its substantive policies, but also from continuing to perform the separate function of providing a forum competent to vindicate any constitutional objections interposed against those policies. Such interference also results in duplicative legal proceedings, and can readily be interpreted "as reflecting negatively upon the state courts' ability to enforce constitutional principles." Cf. Steffel v. Thompson, [415 U.S. 452, 462 (1974)].

The component of *Younger* which rests upon the threat to our federal system is thus applicable to a civil proceeding such as this quite as much as it is to a criminal proceeding. *Younger* however, also rests upon the traditional reluctance of courts of equity, even within a unitary system, to interfere with a criminal prosecution. Strictly speaking, this element of *Younger* is not available to mandate federal restraint in civil cases. But whatever may be the weight attached to this factor in civil litigation involving private parties, we deal here with a state proceeding which in important respects is more akin to a criminal prosecution than are most civil cases. The State is a party to the Court of Common Pleas proceeding, and the proceeding is both in aid of and closely related to criminal statutes which prohibit the dissemination of obscene materials. Thus, an offense to the State's interest in the nuisance litigation is likely to be every bit as great as it would be were this a criminal proceeding. Cf. *Younger v. Harris*, supra, 401 U.S., at 55 n. 2 (STEWART, J., concurring). Similarly, while in this case the District Court's injunction has not directly disrupted Ohio's criminal justice system, it has disrupted that State's efforts to protect the very interests which underlie its criminal laws and to obtain compliance with precisely the standards which are embodied in its criminal laws.

IV

In spite of the critical similarities between a criminal prosecution and Ohio nuisance proceedings, appellee nonetheless urges that there is also a critical difference between the two which should cause us to limit *Younger* to criminal proceedings. This difference, says appellee, is that whereas a state court criminal defendant may, after exhaustion of his state remedies, present his constitutional claims to the federal courts through habeas corpus, no analogous remedy is available to one, like appellee, whose constitutional rights may have been infringed in a state proceeding which cannot result in custodial detention or other criminal sanction.

A civil litigant may, of course, seek review in this Court of any federal claim properly asserted in and rejected by state courts. Moreover, where a final decision of a state court has sustained the validity of a state statute challenged on federal constitutional grounds, an appeal to this Court lies as a matter of right. 28 U.S.C. § 1257(2).[91] Thus, appellee in this case was

---

[91. As discussed infra p. 1009, n. 22, § 1257 was amended in 1988 to make the discretionary writ of certiorari the exclusive means by which the Supreme Court reviews state-court judgments. Appeal as of right is no longer available.]

assured of eventual consideration of its claim by this Court. But quite apart from appellee's right to appeal had it remained in state court, we conclude that it should not be permitted the luxury of federal litigation of issues presented by ongoing state proceedings, a luxury which, as we have already explained, is quite costly in terms of the interests which *Younger* seeks to protect.

Appellee's argument, that because there may be no civil counterpart to federal habeas it should have contemporaneous access to a federal forum for its federal claim, apparently depends on the unarticulated major premise that every litigant who asserts a federal claim is entitled to have it decided on the merits by a federal, rather than a state, court. We need not consider the validity of this premise in order to reject the result which appellee seeks. Even assuming, arguendo, that litigants are entitled to a federal forum for the resolution of all federal issues, that entitlement is most appropriately asserted by a state litigant when he seeks to *relitigate* a federal issue adversely determined in *completed* state court proceedings.[92] We do not understand why the federal forum must be available prior to completion of the state proceedings in which the federal issue arises, and the considerations canvassed in *Younger* militate against such a result.

The issue of whether federal courts should be able to interfere with ongoing state proceedings is quite distinct and separate from the issue of whether litigants are entitled to subsequent federal review of state court dispositions of federal questions. *Younger* turned on considerations of comity and federalism peculiar to the fact that state proceedings were pending; it did *not* turn on the fact that in any event a criminal defendant could eventually have obtained federal habeas consideration of his federal claims. The propriety of federal court interference with an Ohio nuisance proceeding must likewise be controlled by application of those same considerations of comity and federalism.

. . . . .

V

Appellee contends that even if *Younger* is applicable to civil proceedings of this sort, it nonetheless does not govern this case because at the time the District Court acted there was no longer a "pending state court proceeding" as that term is used in *Younger*. *Younger* and subsequent cases such as *Steffel* have used the term "pending proceeding" to distinguish state proceedings which have already commenced from those which are merely incipient or threatened. Here, of course, the state proceeding had begun long before appellee sought intervention by the District Court. But

---

92. We in no way intend to suggest that there is a right of access to a federal forum for the disposition of all federal issues, or that the normal rules of res judicata and judicial estoppel do not operate to bar relitigation in actions under 42 U.S.C. § 1983 of federal issues arising in state court proceedings. Cf. Preiser v. Rodriguez, 411 U.S. 475, 497 (1973). Our assumption is made solely as a means of disposing of appellee's contentions without confronting issues which have not been briefed or argued in this case. [See Allen v. McCurry, 449 U.S. 90 (1980), reprinted infra p. 709.]

appellee's point, we take it, is not that the state proceeding had not begun, but that it had ended by the time its District Court complaint was filed.[93]

Appellee apparently relies on the facts that the Allen County Court of Common Pleas had already issued its judgment and permanent injunction when this action was filed, and that no appeal from that judgment has ever been taken to Ohio's appellate courts. As a matter of state procedure, the judgment presumably became final, in the sense of being nonappealable, at some point after the District Court filing, possibly prior to entry of the District Court's own judgment, but surely after the single judge stayed the state court's judgment. We need not, however, engage in such inquiry. For regardless of when the Court of Common Pleas' judgment became final, we believe that a necessary concomitant of *Younger* is that a party in appellee's posture must exhaust his state appellate remedies before seeking relief in the District Court, unless he can bring himself within one of the exceptions specified in *Younger*.

Virtually all of the evils at which *Younger* is directed would inhere in federal intervention prior to completion of state appellate proceedings, just as surely as they would if such intervention occurred at or before trial. Intervention at the later stage is if anything more highly duplicative, since an entire trial has already taken place, and it is also a direct aspersion on the capabilities and good faith of state appellate courts. Nor, in these state-initiated nuisance proceedings, is federal intervention at the appellate stage any the less of a disruption of the State's efforts to protect interests which it deems important. Indeed, it is likely to be even more disruptive and offensive because the State has already won a *nisi prius* determination that its valid policies are being violated in a fashion which justifies judicial abatement.

Federal post-trial intervention, in a fashion designed to annul the results of a state trial, also deprives the States of a function which quite legitimately is left to them, that of overseeing trial court dispositions of constitutional issues which arise in civil litigation over which they have jurisdiction. We think this consideration to be of some importance because it is typically a judicial system's appellate courts which are by their nature a litigant's most appropriate forum for the resolution of constitutional contentions. Especially is this true when, as here, the constitutional issue involves a statute which is capable of judicial narrowing. In short, we do not believe that a State's judicial system would be fairly accorded the opportunity to resolve federal issues arising in its courts if a federal district court were permitted to substitute itself for the State's appellate courts. We therefore hold that *Younger* standards must be met to justify federal

---

93. It would ordinarily be difficult to consider this problem, that of the duration of *Younger*'s restrictions after entry of a state trial court judgment, without also considering the res judicata implications of such a judgment. However, appellants did not plead res judicata in the District Court, and it is therefore not available to them here. See Fed.Rule Civ.Proc., Rule 8(c); Sosna v. Iowa, 419 U.S. [393, 396–397 n. 3 (1975)].

intervention in a state judicial proceeding as to which a losing litigant has not exhausted his state appellate remedies.[94]

At the time appellee filed its action in the United States District Court, it had available the remedy of appeal to the Ohio appellate courts. Appellee nonetheless contends that exhaustion of state appellate remedies should not be required because an appeal would have been "futile." This claim is based on the decision of the Supreme Court of Ohio in State ex rel. Keating v. A Motion Picture Film Entitled "Vixen," 27 Ohio St.2d 278, 272 N.E.2d 137 (1971), which had been rendered at the time of the proceedings in the Court of Common Pleas. While *Keating* did uphold the use of a nuisance statute against a film which ran afoul of Ohio's statutory definition of obscenity, it had absolutely nothing to say with respect to appellee's principal contention here, that of whether the First and Fourteenth Amendments prohibit a blanket injunction against a showing of all films, including those which have not been adjudged obscene in adversary proceedings. We therefore have difficulty understanding appellee's belief that an appeal was doomed to failure.

More importantly, we are of the opinion that the considerations of comity and federalism which underlie *Younger* permit no truncation of the exhaustion requirement merely because the losing party in the state court of general jurisdiction believes that his chances of success on appeal are not auspicious. Appellee obviously believes itself possessed of a viable federal claim, else it would not so assiduously seek to litigate in the District Court. Yet, Art. VI of the United States Constitution declares that "the Judges in every State shall be bound" by the Federal Constitution, laws and treaties. Appellee is in truth urging us to base a rule on the assumption that state judges will not be faithful to their constitutional responsibilities. This we refuse to do. The District Court should not have entertained this action, seeking preappeal interference with a state judicial proceeding, unless appellee established that early intervention was justified under one of the exceptions recognized in *Younger*.[95]

---

94. By requiring exhaustion of state appellate remedies for the purposes of applying *Younger* we in no way undermine Monroe v. Pape, 365 U.S. 167 (1961). There we held that one seeking redress under 42 U.S.C. § 1983 for a deprivation of federal rights need not first initiate state proceedings based on related state causes of action. 365 U.S., at 183. *Monroe v. Pape* had nothing to do with the problem presently before us, that of the deference to be accorded state proceedings which have already been initiated and which afford a competent tribunal for the resolution of federal issues.

Our exhaustion requirement is likewise not inconsistent with such cases as City Bank Farmers' Trust Co. v. Schnader, 291 U.S. 24 (1934), and Bacon v. Rutland R. Co., 232 U.S. 134 (1914), which expressed the doctrine that a federal equity plaintiff challenging state administrative action need not have exhausted his state judicial remedies. Those cases did not deal with situations in which the state judicial process had been initiated.

95. While appellee had the option to appeal in state courts at the time it filed this action, we do not know for certain whether such remedy remained available at the time the District Court issued its permanent injunction, or whether it remains available now. In any event, appellee may not avoid the standards of *Younger* by simply failing to comply with the procedures of perfecting its appeal within the Ohio Judicial system.

VI

Younger and its civil counterpart which we apply today, do of course allow intervention in those cases where the District Court properly finds that the state proceeding is motivated by a desire to harass or is conducted in bad faith, or where the challenged statute is " 'flagrantly and patently violative of express constitutional prohibitions in every clause, sentence and paragraph, and in whatever manner and against whomever an effort might be made to apply it.' " As we have noted, the District Court in this case did not rule on the *Younger* issue, and thus apparently has not considered whether its intervention was justified by one of these narrow exceptions. Even if the District Court's opinion can be interpreted as a sub silentio determination that the case fits within the exception for statutes which are " 'flagrantly and patently violative of express constitutional prohibitions,' " such a characterization of the statute is not possible after the subsequent decision of the Supreme Court of Ohio in State ex rel. Ewing v. A Motion Picture Film Entitled "Without a Stitch," 37 Ohio St.2d 95, 307 N.E.2d 911 (1974). That case narrowly construed the Ohio nuisance statute, with a view to avoiding the constitutional difficulties which concerned the District Court.

We therefore think that this case is appropriate for remand so that the District Court may consider whether irreparable injury can be shown in light of *"Without a Stitch,"* and if so, whether that injury is of such a nature that the District Court may assume jurisdiction under an exception to the policy against federal judicial interference with state court proceedings of this kind. The judgment of the District Court is vacated and the cause is remanded for further proceedings consistent with this opinion.

It is so ordered.

■ MR. JUSTICE BRENNAN, with whom MR. JUSTICE DOUGLAS and MR. JUSTICE MARSHALL join, dissenting.

I dissent. The treatment of the state *civil* proceeding as one "in aid of and closely related to criminal statutes" is obviously only the first step toward extending to state *civil* proceedings generally the holding of Younger v. Harris, 401 U.S. 37 (1971), that federal courts should not interfere with pending state *criminal* proceedings except under extraordinary circumstances. Similarly, today's holding that the plaintiff in an action under 42 U.S.C. § 1983 may not maintain it without first exhausting state appellate procedures for review of an adverse state trial court decision is but an obvious first step toward discard of heretofore settled law that such actions may be maintained without first exhausting state judicial remedies.

. . . . .

Even if the extension of *Younger v. Harris* to pending state civil proceedings can be appropriate in any case, and I do not think it can be,[96] it

---

96. Abstention where authoritative resolution by state courts of ambiguities in a state statute is sufficiently likely to avoid or significantly modify federal questions raised by the statute is another matter. Abstention is justified in such cases primarily by the policy of

is plainly improper in the case of an action by a federal plaintiff, as in this case, grounded upon 42 U.S.C. § 1983. That statute serves a particular congressional objective long recognized and enforced by the Court. Today's extension will defeat that objective. . . .

. . . . .

Mitchum v. Foster, [407 U.S. 225 (1972)], holding that actions under § 1983 are excepted from the operation of the federal anti-injunction statute, 28 U.S.C. § 2283, is also undercut by today's extension of *Younger.* *Mitchum* canvassed the history of § 1983 and concluded that it extended "federal power in an attempt to remedy the state courts' failure to secure federal rights." 407 U.S., at 241. *Mitchum* prompted the comment that if *Younger v. Harris* were extended to civil cases, "much of the rigidity of section 2283 would be reintroduced, the significance of *Mitchum* for those seeking relief from state civil proceedings would largely be destroyed, and the recognition of section 1983 as an exception to the Anti–Injunction Statute would have been a Pyrrhic victory." [97] Today's decision fulfills that gloomy prophecy. I therefore dissent from the remand and would reach the merits.

■ Mr. Justice Douglas, while joining in the opinion of Mr. Justice Brennan, wishes to make clear that he adheres to the view he expressed in Younger v. Harris, 401 U.S. 37, 58–65 (1971) (dissenting opinion), that federal abstention from interference with state criminal prosecutions is inconsistent with demands of our federalism where important and overriding civil rights (such as those involved in the First Amendment) are about to be sacrificed.[98]

––––––

avoidance of premature constitutional adjudication. The federal plaintiff is therefore not dismissed from federal court as he is in *Younger* cases. On the contrary, he may reserve his federal questions for decision by the federal district court and not submit them to the state courts. England v. Louisiana State Board of Medical Examiners, 375 U.S. 411 (1964). Accordingly, retention by the federal court of jurisdiction of the federal complaint pending state court decision, not dismissal of the complaint, is the correct practice. Lake Carriers' Ass'n v. MacMullan, 406 U.S. 498, 512–513 (1972).

97. Note, The Supreme Court, 1971 Term, 86 Harv.L.Rev. 50, 217–218 (1972).

[98. In Hicks v. Miranda, 422 U.S. 332, 349 (1975), it is held that "where state criminal proceedings are begun against the federal plaintiffs after the federal complaint is filed but before any proceedings of substance on the merits have taken place in the federal court, the principles of *Younger v. Harris* should apply in full force."

"Whether issuance of the February temporary restraining order was a substantial federal court action or not, issuance of the June preliminary injunction certainly was. . . . A federal court action in which a preliminary injunction is granted has proceeded well beyond the 'embryonic stage,' . . . and considerations of economy, equity, and federalism counsel against *Younger*-abstention at that point." Hawaii Housing Authority v. Midkiff, 467 U.S. 229, 237 (1984).

Three bar owners sued in federal court to enjoin a local ordinance against "topless dancing." A temporary restraining order was denied. The following day one of the bars resumed "topless dancing" and state criminal charges were immediately initiated against the bar and

Wooley v. Maynard

Supreme Court of the United States, 1977.
430 U.S. 705, 97 S.Ct. 1428, 51 L.Ed.2d 752.

■ Mr. Chief Justice Burger delivered the opinion of the Court.

The issue on appeal is whether the State of New Hampshire may constitutionally enforce criminal sanctions against persons who cover the motto "Live Free or Die" on passenger vehicle license plates because that motto is repugnant to their moral and religious beliefs.

(1)

Since 1969 New Hampshire has required that noncommercial vehicles bear license plates embossed with the state motto, "Live Free or Die." N.H.Rev.Stat.Ann. § 263:1 (Supp.1975). Another New Hampshire statute makes it a misdemeanor "knowingly [to obscure] . . . the figures or letters on any number plate." N.H.Rev.Stat.Ann. § 262:27–c (Supp.1975). The term "letters" in this section has been interpreted by the State's highest court to include the state motto. State v. Hoskin, 112 N.H. 332, 295 A.2d 454 (1972).

Appellees George Maynard and his wife Maxine are followers of the Jehovah's Witnesses faith. The Maynards consider the New Hampshire State motto to be repugnant to their moral, religious, and political beliefs, and therefore assert it objectionable to disseminate this message by displaying it on their automobiles. Pursuant to these beliefs, the Maynards began early in 1974 to cover up the motto on their license plates.[99]

On November 27, 1974, Mr. Maynard was issued a citation for violating § 262:27–c. On December 6, 1974, he appeared pro se in Lebanon, N.H., District Court to answer the charge. After waiving his right to counsel, he entered a plea of not guilty and proceeded to explain his religious objections to the motto. The state trial judge expressed sympathy

---

the dancers. How do *Younger* principles apply? See Doran v. Salem Inn, Inc., 422 U.S. 922 (1975).

In Rizzo v. Goode, 423 U.S. 362 (1976), *Younger* principles were held to bar a federal court from issuing an injunction concerning the internal disciplinary affairs of the Philadelphia police department. "[T]he principles of federalism which play such an important part in governing the relationship between federal courts and state governments, though initially expounded and perhaps entitled to their greatest weight in cases where it was sought to enjoin a criminal prosecution in progress, have not been limited either to that situation or indeed to a criminal proceeding itself. We think these principles likewise have applicability where injunctive relief is sought, not against the judicial branch of the state government, but against those in charge of an executive branch of an agency of state or local governments such as petitioners here." 423 U.S., at 380. See Hansen, Use of the Federal Injunction to Protect Constitutional Rights: *Rizzo v. Goode* and the Control of Government Bureaucracies, 12 Gonz.L.Rev. 231 (1977).]

99. In May or June 1974 Mr. Maynard actually snipped the words "or Die" off the license plates, and then covered the resulting hole, as well as the words "Live Free," with tape. This was done, according to Mr. Maynard, because neighborhood children kept removing the tape. The Maynards have since been issued new license plates, and have disavowed any intention of physically mutilating them.

for Mr. Maynard's situation, but considered himself bound by the authority of *State v. Hoskin*, supra, to hold Maynard guilty. A $25 fine was imposed, but execution was suspended during "good behavior."

On December 28, 1974, Mr. Maynard was again charged with violating § 262:27–c. He appeared in court on January 31, 1975, and again chose to represent himself; he was found guilty, fined $50, and sentenced to six months in the Grafton County House of Corrections. The court suspended this jail sentence but ordered Mr. Maynard to also pay the $25 fine for the first offense. Maynard informed the court that, as a matter of conscience, he refused to pay the two fines. The court thereupon sentenced him to jail for a period of 15 days. He has served the full sentence.

Prior to trial on the second offense Mr. Maynard was charged with yet a third violation of § 262:27–c on January 3, 1975. He appeared on this complaint on the same day as for the second offense, and was, again, found guilty. This conviction was "continued for sentence" so that Maynard received no punishment in addition to the 15 days.

(2)

On March 4, 1975, appellees brought the present action pursuant to 42 U.S.C. § 1983 in the United States District Court for the District of New Hampshire. They sought injunctive and declaratory relief against enforcement of N.H.Rev.Stat.Ann. §§ 262:27–c, 263:1, insofar as these required displaying the state motto on their vehicle license plates, and made it a criminal offense to obscure the motto. On March 11, 1975, the single District Judge issued a temporary restraining order against further arrests and prosecutions of the Maynards. Because the appellees sought an injunction against a state statute on grounds of its unconstitutionality, a three-judge District Court was convened pursuant to 28 U.S.C. § 2281. Following a hearing on the merits, the District Court entered an order enjoining the State "from arresting and prosecuting [the Maynards] at any time in the future for covering over that portion of their license plates that contains the motto 'Live Free or Die.' " 406 F.Supp. 1381 (1976)....

(3)

Appellants argue that the District Court was precluded from exercising jurisdiction in this case by the principles of equitable restraint enunciated in *Younger v. Harris*, 401 U.S. 37 (1971). In *Younger* the Court recognized that principles of judicial economy, as well as proper state-federal relations, preclude federal courts from exercising equitable jurisdiction to enjoin ongoing state prosecutions. Id., at 43. However, when a genuine threat of prosecution exists, a litigant is entitled to resort to a federal forum to seek redress for an alleged deprivation of federal rights. See Steffel v. Thompson, 415 U.S. 452 (1974); Doran v. Salem Inn, Inc., 422 U.S. 922, 930–931 (1975). *Younger* principles aside, a litigant is entitled to resort to a federal forum in seeking redress under 42 U.S.C. § 1983 for an alleged deprivation of federal rights. Huffman v. Pursue, Ltd., 420 U.S. 592, 609–610, n. 21 (1975). Mr. Maynard now finds himself placed "between the Scylla of intentionally flouting state law and the Charybdis of foregoing what he believes to be constitutionally protected activity in order to avoid becoming enmeshed in [another] criminal proceeding." *Steffel v. Thompson*, supra, at 462. Mrs. Maynard, as joint owner of the family automobiles is no less likely than her husband to be subjected to state prosecution. Under these circumstances he cannot be denied consideration of a federal remedy.

Appellants, however, point out that Maynard failed to seek review of his criminal convictions and cite *Huffman v. Pursue, Ltd.*, supra, for the propositions that "a necessary concomitant of *Younger* is that a party in appellee's posture must exhaust his state appellate remedies before seeking relief in the District Court," 420 U.S., at 608, and that "*Younger* standards must be met to justify federal intervention in a state judicial proceeding as to which a losing litigant has not exhausted his state appellate remedies," id., at 609. *Huffman*, however, is inapposite. There the appellee was seeking to prevent, by means of federal intervention enforcement of a state-court judgment declaring its theater a nuisance. We held that appellee's failure to exhaust its state appeals barred federal intervention under the principles of *Younger*: "Federal post-trial intervention, in a fashion de-signed to annul the results of a state trial ... deprives the States of a function which quite legitimately is left to them, that of overseeing trial court dispositions of constitutional issues which arise in civil litigation over which they have jurisdiction." Ibid.

Here, however, the suit is in no way "designed to annul the results of a state trial" since the relief sought is wholly prospective, to preclude further prosecution under a statute alleged to violate appellees' constitutional rights. Maynard has already sustained convictions and has served a sentence of imprisonment for his prior offenses.[100] He does not seek to have his record expunged, or to annul any collateral effects those convictions may have, e.g., upon his driving privileges. The Maynards seek only to be free from prosecutions for future violations of the same statutes. *Younger* does not bar federal jurisdiction.

In their complaint, the Maynards sought both declaratory and injunctive relief against the enforcement of the New Hampshire statutes. We have recognized that although " '[o]rdinarily ... the practical effect of [injunctive and declaratory] relief will be virtually identical,' " *Doran v. Salem Inn*, supra, at 931, quoting Samuels v. Mackell, 401 U.S. 66, 73 (1971), a "district court can generally protect the interests of a federal plaintiff by entering a declaratory judgment, and therefore the stronger injunctive medicine will be unnecessary." *Doran*, supra, at 931. It is correct that generally a court will not enjoin "the enforcement of a criminal statute even though unconstitutional," Spielman Motor Co. v. Dodge, 295 U.S. 89, 95 (1935), since "[s]uch a result seriously impairs the State's interest in enforcing its criminal laws, and implicates the concerns for federalism

---

100. As to the offense which was "continued for sentence," ... the District Court found that "[n]o collateral consequences will attach as a result of it unless Mr. Maynard is arrested and prosecuted for the violation of NHRSA 262:27–c at some time in the future." 406 F.Supp., at 1384.

which lie at the heart of *Younger,"* *Doran,* supra, 422 U.S., at 931. But this is not an absolute policy and in some circumstances injunctive relief may be appropriate. "To justify such interference there must be exceptional circumstances and a clear showing that an injunction is necessary in order to afford adequate protection of constitutional rights." *Spielman Motor Co.,* supra, at 95.

We have such a situation here for, as we have noted, three successive prosecutions were undertaken against Mr. Maynard in the span of five weeks. This is quite different from a claim for federal equitable relief when a prosecution is threatened for the first time. The threat of repeated prosecutions in the future against both him and his wife, and the effect of such a continuing threat on their ability to perform the ordinary tasks of daily life which require an automobile, is sufficient to justify injunctive relief. Cf. Douglas v. City of Jeannette, 319 U.S. 157 (1943). We are therefore unwilling to say that the District Court was limited to granting declaratory relief. Having determined that the District Court was not required to stay its hand as to either appellee,[101] we turn to the merits of the Maynards' claim.

(4)

[On the merits the Court found that it was inconsistent with the freedom of intellect and spirit protected by the First Amendment for New Hampshire to require an individual to be an instrument for advocating public adherence to an ideological point of view he finds unacceptable.]

Affirmed.

■ MR. JUSTICE WHITE, with whom MR. JUSTICE BLACKMUN and MR. JUSTICE REHNQUIST join in part, dissenting in part.

Steffel v. Thompson, 415 U.S. 452 (1974), held that when state proceedings are not pending, but only threatened, a declaratory judgment may be entered with respect to the state statute at issue without regard to the strictures of Younger v. Harris, 401 U.S. 37 (1971). But *Steffel* left open whether an injunction should also issue in such circumstances. 415 U.S., at 463. Then Doran v. Salem Inn, Inc., 422 U.S. 922 (1975), approved issuance by a federal court of a preliminary injunction against a threatened state prosecution, but only pending decision on the declaratory judgment and only then subject to "stringent" standards which should cause a district court to "weigh carefully the interests on both sides," since prohibiting the enforcement of the State's criminal law against the federal plaintiff, even pending final resolution of his case, "seriously impairs the State's interest

---

101. If the totality of the appellants' arguments were accepted, a § 1983 action could never be brought to enjoin state criminal prosecutions. According to the appellants, *Younger* principles bar Mr. Maynard from seeking an injunction because he has already been subjected to prosecution. As to Mrs. Maynard, they argue, in effect, that the action is premature because no such prosecution has been instituted. Since the two spouses were similarly situated but for the fact that one has been prosecuted and one has not, we fail to see where the appellants' argument would ever leave room for federal intervention under § 1983.

in enforcing its criminal laws, and implicates the concerns for federalism which lie at the heart of *Younger*." Id., at 931. Although finding the issuance of a preliminary injunction not an abuse of discretion in that case, the Court also distinguished between a preliminary injunction pendente lite and a permanent injunction at the successful conclusion of the federal case; for "a district court can generally protect the interests of a federal plaintiff by entering a declaratory judgment, and therefore the stronger injunctive medicine will be unnecessary." Ibid.

Doran was thus true to the teachings of Douglas v. City of Jeannette, 319 U.S. 157 (1943), where the Court held that an injunction against threatened state criminal prosecutions should not issue even though the underlying state statute had already been invalidated, relying on the established rule "that courts of equity do not ordinarily restrain criminal prosecutions." Id., at 163. A threatened prosecution "even though alleged to be in violation of constitutional guaranties, is not a ground for equity relief...." Ibid. An injunction should issue only upon a showing that the danger of irreparable injury is both "great and immediate," citing the same authorities to this effect that this Court relied on in *Younger v. Harris*, supra. In each of the cited cases—and they do not exhaust the authorities to the same effect—criminal prosecutions were not pending when this Court ruled that a federal equity court should not enter the injunction. "The general rule is that equity will not interfere to prevent the enforcement of a criminal statute even though unconstitutional.... To justify such interference there must be exceptional circumstances and a clear showing that an injunction is necessary in order to afford adequate protection of constitutional rights." Spielman Motor Co. v. Dodge, 295 U.S. 89, 95 (1935).

The Court has plainly departed from the teaching of these cases. The whole point of *Douglas v. City of Jeannette*'s admonition against injunctive relief was that once a declaratory judgment had issued, further equitable relief would depend on the existence of unusual circumstances thereafter. Here the State's enforcement of its statute prior to the declaration of unconstitutionality by the federal court would appear to be no more than the performance of their duty by the State's law enforcement officers. If doing this much prior to the declaration of unconstitutionality amounts to unusual circumstances sufficient to warrant an injunction, the standard is obviously seriously eroded.

Under our cases, therefore, more is required to be shown than the Court's opinion reveals to affirm the issuance of the injunction. To that extent I dissent.

■ [Justice Rehnquist, with whom Justice Blackmun joined, also dissented separately on the merits.][102]

[102. "I am thus left with the strong impression that *Wooley* was but a subsequent gloss on the *Huffman* exhaustion requirement, a late discovery by some of the Justices of its vast

Pennzoil Co. v. Texaco, Inc.

Supreme Court of the United States, 1987.
481 U.S. 1, 107 S.Ct. 1519, 95 L.Ed.2d 1.

■ Justice Powell delivered the opinion of the Court.

The principal issue in this case is whether a federal district court lawfully may enjoin a plaintiff who has prevailed in a trial in state court from executing the judgment in its favor pending appeal of that judgment to a state appellate court.

I

Getty Oil Co. and appellant Pennzoil Co. negotiated an agreement under which Pennzoil was to purchase about three-sevenths of Getty's outstanding shares for $110 a share. Appellee Texaco, Inc. eventually purchased the shares for $128 a share. On February 8, 1984, Pennzoil filed a complaint against Texaco in the Harris County District Court, a state court located in Houston, Texas, the site of Pennzoil's corporate headquarters. The complaint alleged that Texaco tortiously had induced Getty to breach a contract to sell its shares to Pennzoil; Pennzoil sought actual damages of $7.53 billion and punitive damages in the same amount. On November 19, 1985, a jury returned a verdict in favor of Pennzoil, finding actual damages of $7.53 billion and punitive damages of $3 billion. The parties anticipated that the judgment, including prejudgment interest, would exceed $11 billion.

Although the parties disagree about the details, it was clear that the expected judgment would give Pennzoil significant rights under Texas law. By recording an abstract of a judgment in the real property records of any of the 254 counties in Texas, a judgment creditor can secure a lien on all of a judgment debtor's real property located in that county. See Tex.Prop. Code Ann. §§ 52.001–.006 (1984). If a judgment creditor wishes to have the judgment enforced by state officials so that it can take possession of any of the debtor's assets, it may secure a writ of execution from the clerk of the court that issued the judgment. See Tex.Rule Civ.Proc. 627. Rule 627 provides that such a writ usually can be obtained "after the expiration of thirty days from the time a final judgment is signed." But the judgment debtor "may suspend the execution of the judgment by filing a good and sufficient bond to be approved by the clerk." Rule 364(a). See Rule 368. For a money judgment, "the amount of the bond ... shall be at least the amount of the judgment, interest, and costs." Rule 364(b).

Even before the trial court entered judgment, the jury's verdict cast a serious cloud on Texaco's financial situation. The amount of the bond required by Rule 364(b) would have been more than $13 billion. It is clear that Texaco would not have been able to post such a bond. Accordingly, "the business and financial community concluded that Pennzoil would be

---

implications. It was an attempt to limit *Huffman*...." Fiss, *Dombrowski*, 86 Yale L.J. 1103, 1142 (1977). See also Laycock, Federal Interference with State Prosecutions: The Need for Prospective Relief, 1977 Sup.Ct.Rev. 193, 213–214.]

able, under the lien and bond provisions of Texas law, to commence enforcement of any judgment entered on the verdict before Texaco's appeals had been resolved." App. to Juris. Statement A87 (District Court's Supplemental Finding of Fact 40, Jan. 10, 1986). The effects on Texaco were substantial: the price of its stock dropped markedly; it had difficulty obtaining credit; the rating of its bonds was lowered; and its trade creditors refused to sell it crude oil on customary terms. Id., at A90–A98 (District Court's Supplemental Findings of Fact 49–70).

Texaco did not argue to the trial court that the judgment, or execution of the judgment, conflicted with federal law. Rather, on December 10, 1985—before the Texas court entered judgment[103]—Texaco filed this action in the United States District Court for the Southern District of New York . . . .

[The District Court rejected all of Pennzoil's arguments and granted injunctive relief.]

On appeal, the Court of Appeals for the Second Circuit affirmed. 784 F.2d 1133 (1986). It first addressed the *Rooker–Feldman* doctrine [Rooker v. Fidelity Trust Co., 263 U.S. 413 (1923); District of Columbia Court of Appeals v. Feldman, 460 U.S. 462 (1983)] and rejected the portion of the District Court's opinion that evaluated the merits of the state court judgment. It held, however, that the doctrine did not completely bar the District Court's jurisdiction. It concluded that the Due Process and Equal Protection claims, not presented by Texaco to the Texas courts, were within the District Court's jurisdiction because they were not " 'inextricably intertwined' " with the state court action. Id., at 1144 (quoting *District of Columbia Court of Appeals v. Feldman*, supra, at 483, n. 16).

Next, the court considered whether Texaco had stated a claim under § 1983. The question was whether Texaco's complaint sought to redress action taken "under color of" state law, 42 U.S.C. § 1983. The court noted that "Pennzoil would have to act jointly with state agents by calling on state officials to attach and seize Texaco's assets." 784 F.2d, at 1145. Relying on its reading of Lugar v. Edmondson Oil Co., 457 U.S. 922 (1982), the court concluded that the enjoined action would have been taken under

---

103. Later the same day, the Texas court entered a judgment against Texaco for $11,120,976,110.83 including prejudgment interest of approximately $600 million. During the pendency of the federal action—that now concerns only the validity of the Texas judgment enforcement procedures—the state-court action on the merits has proceeded. Texaco filed a motion for new trial, that was deemed denied by operation of law under Rule 329b(c). . . . Subsequently, Texaco appealed the judgment to the Texas Court of Appeals, challenging the judgment on a variety of state and federal grounds. The Texas Court of Appeals rendered a decision on that appeal on February 12, 1987. That decision affirmed the trial court's judgment in most respects, but remitted $2 billion of the punitive damages award, reducing the principal of the judgment to $8.53 billion.

So far as we know, Texaco has never presented to the Texas courts the challenges it makes in this case against the bond and lien provisions under federal law. Three days after it filed its federal lawsuit, Texaco did ask the Texas trial court informally for a hearing concerning possible modification of the judgment under Texas law. That request eventually was denied, because it failed to comply with Texas procedural rules.

color of state law, and thus that Texaco had stated a claim under § 1983. 784 F.2d, at 1145–1147. Because § 1983 is an exception to the Anti–Injunction Act, see Mitchum v. Foster, [407 U.S. 225 (1972)], the Court also found that the Anti–Injunction Act did not prevent the District Court from granting the relief sought by Texaco.

Finally, the court held that abstention was unnecessary. First, it addressed *Pullman* abstention, see Railroad Comm'n v. Pullman Co., 312 U.S. 496 (1941). It rejected that ground of abstention, holding that "the mere possibility that the Texas courts would find Rule 364 [concerning the supersedeas bond requirements] unconstitutional as applied does not call for *Pullman* abstention." 784 F.2d, at 1149. Next, it rejected *Younger* abstention [see Younger v. Harris, 401 U.S. 37 (1971)]. It thought that "[t]he state interests at stake in this proceeding differ in both kind and degree from those present in the six cases in which the Supreme Court held that *Younger* applied." Ibid. Moreover, it thought that Texas had failed to "provide adequate procedures for adjudication of Texaco's federal claims." Id., at 1150. Turning to the merits, it agreed with the District Court that Texaco had established a likelihood of success on its constitutional claims and that the balance of hardships favored Texaco. Accordingly, it affirmed the grant of injunctive relief.

Pennzoil filed a jurisdictional statement in this Court. We noted probable jurisdiction under 28 U.S.C. § 1254(2).... We reverse.

II

The courts below should have abstained under the principles of federalism enunciated in Younger v. Harris, 401 U.S. 37 (1971). Both the District Court and the Court of Appeals failed to recognize the significant interests harmed by their unprecedented intrusion into the Texas judicial system. Similarly, neither of those courts applied the appropriate standard in determining whether adequate relief was available in the Texas courts.

A

The first ground for the *Younger* decision was "the basic doctrine of equity jurisprudence that courts of equity should not act, and particularly should not act to restrain a criminal prosecution, when the moving party has an adequate remedy at law." Id., at 43. The Court also offered a second explanation for its decision:

> "This underlying reason ... is reinforced by an even more vital consideration, the notion of 'comity,' that is, a proper respect for state functions, a recognition of the fact that the entire country is made up of a Union of separate state governments, and a continuance of the belief that the National Government will fare best if the States and their institutions are left free to perform their separate functions in their separate ways ... The concept does not mean blind deference to 'States' Rights' any more than it means centralization of control over every important issue in our National Government and its courts. The Framers rejected both these courses. What the concept does represent

is a system in which there is sensitivity to the legitimate interests of both State and National Governments, and in which the National Government, anxious though it may be to vindicate and protect federal rights and federal interests, always endeavors to do so in ways that will not unduly interfere with the legitimate activities of the States." Id., at 44.

This concern mandates application of *Younger* abstention not only when the pending state proceedings are criminal, but also when certain civil proceedings are pending, if the State's interests in the proceeding are so important that exercise of the federal judicial power would disregard the comity between the States and the National Government. E.g., Huffman v. Pursue, Ltd., 420 U.S. 592, 603–605 (1975).

Another important reason for abstention is to avoid unwarranted determination of federal constitutional questions. When federal courts interpret state statutes in a way that raises federal constitutional questions, "a constitutional determination is predicated on a reading of the statute that is not binding on state courts and may be discredited at any time—thus essentially rendering the federal-court decision advisory and the litigation underlying it meaningless." Moore v. Sims, 442 U.S. 415, 428 (1979). See Trainor v. Hernandez, 431 U.S. 434, 445 (1977).[104] This concern has special significance in this case. Because Texaco chose not to present to the Texas courts the constitutional claims asserted in this case, it is impossible to be certain that the governing Texas statutes and procedural rules actually raise these claims. Moreover, the Texas Constitution contains an "open courts" provision, Art. I, § 13,[105] that appears to address Texaco's claims more specifically than the Due Process Clause of the Fourteenth Amendment. Thus, when this case was filed in federal court, it was entirely possible that the Texas courts would have resolved this case on state statutory or constitutional grounds, without reaching the federal constitutional questions Texaco raises in this case. As we have noted, *Younger* abstention in situations like this "offers the opportunity for narrowing constructions that might obviate the constitutional problem and intelligently mediate federal constitutional concerns and state interests." *Moore v. Sims,* supra, at 429–430.

---

104. In some cases, the probability that any federal adjudication would be effectively advisory is so great that this concern alone is sufficient to justify abstention, even if there are no pending state proceedings in which the question could be raised. See Railroad Comm'n of Texas v. Pullman Co., 312 U.S. 496 (1941). Because appellant has not argued in this Court that *Pullman* abstention is proper, we decline to address JUSTICE BLACKMUN's conclusion that *Pullman* abstention is the appropriate disposition of this case. We merely note that considerations similar to those that mandate *Pullman* abstention are relevant to a court's decision whether to abstain under *Younger.* Cf. Moore v. Sims, 442 U.S. 415, 428 (1979). The various types of abstention are not rigid pigeonholes into which federal courts must try to fit cases. Rather, they reflect a complex of considerations designed to soften the tensions inherent in a system that contemplates parallel judicial processes.

105. Article I, § 13 provides: "All courts shall be open, and every person for an injury done him, in his lands, goods, person or reputation, shall have remedy by due course of law."

Texaco's principal argument against *Younger* abstention is that exercise of the District Court's power did not implicate a "vital" or "important" state interest. Brief for Appellee 24–32. This argument reflects a misreading of our precedents. This Court repeatedly has recognized that the States have important interests in administering certain aspects of their judicial systems. E.g., *Trainor v. Hernandez*, supra, at 441; Middlesex County Ethics Comm. v. Garden State Bar Assn., 457 U.S. 423, 432 (1982). In Juidice v. Vail, 430 U.S. 327 (1977), we held that a federal court should have abstained from adjudicating a challenge to a State's contempt process. The Court's reasoning in that case informs our decision today:

> "A State's interest in the contempt process, through which it vindicates the regular operation of its judicial system, so long as that system itself affords the opportunity to pursue federal claims within it, is surely an important interest. Perhaps it is not quite as important as is the State's interest in the enforcement of its criminal laws, *Younger,* supra, or even its interest in the maintenance of a quasi-criminal proceeding such as was involved in *Huffman,* supra. But we think it is of sufficiently great import to require application of the principles of those cases." Id., at 335.

Our comments on why the contempt power was sufficiently important to justify abstention also are illuminating: "Contempt in these cases, serves, of course, to vindicate and preserve the private interests of competing litigants, . . . but its purpose is by no means spent upon purely private concerns. It stands in aid of the authority of the judicial system, so that its orders and judgments are not rendered nugatory." Id., at 336, n. 12 (citations omitted).

The reasoning of *Juidice* controls here. That case rests on the importance to the States of enforcing the orders and judgments of their courts. There is little difference between the State's interest in forcing persons to transfer property in response to a court's judgment and in forcing persons to respond to the court's process on pain of contempt. Both *Juidice* and this case involve challenges to the processes by which the State compels compliance with the judgments of its courts.[106] Not only would federal injunctions in such cases interfere with the execution of state judgments, but they would do so on grounds that challenge the very process by which those judgments were obtained. So long as those challenges relate to pending state proceedings, proper respect for the ability of state courts to resolve federal questions presented in state-court litigation mandates that the federal court stay its hand.

---

106. Thus, contrary to Justice Stevens' suggestion, the State of Texas has an interest in this proceeding "that goes beyond its interest as adjudicator of wholly private disputes." . . . Our opinion does not hold that *Younger* abstention is always appropriate whenever a civil proceeding is pending in a state court. Rather, as in *Juidice,* we rely on the State's interest in protecting "the authority of the judicial system, so that its orders and judgments are not rendered nugatory," 430 U.S., at 336, n. 12 (citations omitted).

B

Texaco also argues that *Younger* abstention was inappropriate because no Texas court could have heard Texaco's constitutional claims within the limited time available to Texaco. But the burden on this point rests on the federal plaintiff to show "that state procedural law barred presentation of [its] claims." *Moore v. Sims*, 442 U.S., at 432. See *Younger v. Harris*, 401 U.S., at 45 ("The accused should first set up and rely upon his defense in the state courts, even though this involves a challenge of the validity of some statute, unless it plainly appears that this course would not afford adequate protection") (quoting Fenner v. Boykin, 271 U.S. 240, 244 (1926)).

Moreover, denigrations of the procedural protections afforded by Texas law hardly come from Texaco with good grace, as it apparently made no effort under Texas law to secure the relief sought in this case. Cf. *Middlesex County Ethics Comm. v. Garden State Bar Assn.*, supra, at 435 (rejecting on similar grounds an assertion about the inhospitability of state procedures to federal claims). Article VI of the United States Constitution declares that "the Judges in every State shall be bound" by the Federal Constitution, laws, and treaties. We cannot assume that state judges will interpret ambiguities in state procedural law to bar presentation of federal claims. Cf. Ohio Civil Rights Comm'n v. Dayton Christian Schools, Inc., 477 U.S. 619, 629 (1986) (assuming that a state administrative commission would "construe its own statutory mandate in the light of federal constitutional principles"). Accordingly, when a litigant has not attempted to present his federal claims in related state court proceedings, a federal court should assume that state procedures will afford an adequate remedy, in the absence of unambiguous authority to the contrary.

The "open courts" provision of the Texas Constitution, Article I, § 13, see n. [105], supra, has considerable relevance here.... In light of this demonstrable and long-standing commitment of the Texas Supreme Court to provide access to the state courts, we are reluctant to conclude that Texas courts would have construed state procedural rules to deny Texaco an effective opportunity to raise its constitutional claims.

Against this background, Texaco's submission that the Texas courts were incapable of hearing its constitutional claims is plainly insufficient. Both of the courts below found that the Texas trial court had the power to consider constitutional challenges to the enforcement provisions. The Texas Attorney General filed a brief in the proceedings below, arguing that such relief was available in the Texas courts. Texaco has cited no statute or case clearly indicating that Texas courts lack such power.[107] Accordingly, Texaco has failed to meet its burden on this point.

---

107. Texaco relies on the language of Texas Rule of Civil Procedure 364, that lists no exceptions to the requirement that an appellant file a bond to suspend execution of a money judgment pending appeal. Texaco also relies on cases noting that Rule 364 requires appellants to post bond in the full amount of the judgment. E.g., Kennesaw Life and Accident Insurance Co. v. Streetman, 644 S.W.2d 915, 916–917 (Tex.App.–Austin 1983, writ refused n.r.e.). But these cases do not involve claims that the requirements of Rule 364

In sum, the lower courts should have deferred on principles of comity to the pending state proceedings. They erred in accepting Texaco's assertions as to the inadequacies of Texas procedure to provide effective relief. It is true that this case presents an unusual fact situation, never before addressed by the Texas courts, and that Texaco urgently desired prompt relief. But we cannot say that those courts, when this suit was filed, would have been any less inclined than a federal court to address and decide the federal constitutional claims. Because Texaco apparently did not give the Texas courts an opportunity to adjudicate its constitutional claims, and because Texaco cannot demonstrate that the Texas courts were not then open to adjudicate its claims, there is no basis for concluding that the Texas law and procedures were so deficient that *Younger* abstention is inappropriate. Accordingly, we conclude that the District Court should have abstained.

III

In this opinion, we have addressed the situation that existed on the morning of December 10, 1985, when this case was filed in the United States District Court for the Southern District of New York. We recognize that much has transpired in the Texas courts since then. Later that day, the Texas trial court entered judgment. On February 12 of this year, the Texas Court of Appeals substantially affirmed the judgment. We are not unmindful of the unique importance to Texaco of having its challenges to that judgment authoritatively considered and resolved. We of course express no opinion on the merits of those challenges. Similarly, we express no opinion on the claims Texaco has raised in this case against the Texas bond and lien provisions, nor on the possibility that Texaco now could raise these claims in the Texas courts .... Today we decide only that it was inappropriate for the District Court to entertain these claims. If, and when, the Texas courts render a final decision on any federal issue presented by this litigation, review may be sought in this Court in the customary manner.

IV

The judgment of the Court of Appeals is reversed. The case is remanded to the District Court with instructions to vacate its order and dismiss the complaint. The judgment of this Court shall issue forthwith.

It is so ordered.

---

violate other statutes or the Federal Constitution. Thus, they have "absolutely nothing to say with respect to" Texaco's claims that Rule 364 violates the Federal Constitution. See Huffman v. Pursue, Ltd., 420 U.S. 592, 610 (1975).

Also, the language of Rule 364 suggests that a trial court could suspend the bond requirement if it concluded that application of the bond requirement would violate the Federal Constitution. Rule 364(a) provides: "*Unless otherwise provided by law* or these rules, an appellant may suspend the execution of the judgment by a good and sufficient bond" (emphasis added). Texaco has failed to demonstrate that Texas courts would not construe the phrase "otherwise provided by law" to encompass claims made under the Federal Constitution. We cannot assume that Texas courts would refuse to construe the Rule, or to apply their inherent powers, to provide a forum to adjudicate substantial federal constitutional claims.

■ JUSTICE SCALIA, with whom JUSTICE O'CONNOR joins, concurring.

I join the opinion of the court. I write separately only to indicate that I do not believe that the so-called *Rooker–Feldman* doctrine deprives the Court of jurisdiction to decide Texaco's challenge to the constitutionality of the Texas stay and lien provisions. In resolving that challenge, the Court need not decide any issue either actually litigated in the Texas courts or inextricably intertwined with issues so litigated. Under these circumstances, I see no jurisdictional bar to the Court's decision in this case.

■ JUSTICE BRENNAN, with whom JUSTICE MARSHALL joins, concurring in the judgment.

Texaco's claim that the Texas bond and lien provisions violate the Fourteenth Amendment is without merit. While Texaco cannot, consistent with due process and equal protection, be arbitrarily denied the right to a meaningful opportunity to be heard on appeal, this right can be adequately vindicated even if Texaco were forced to file for bankruptcy.

I believe that the Court should have confronted the merits of this case. I wholeheartedly concur with JUSTICE STEVENS' conclusion that a creditor's invocation of a State's postjudgment collection procedures constitutes action under color of state law within the meaning of 42 U.S.C. § 1983.

I also agree with his conclusion that the District Court was not required to abstain under the principles enunciated in Younger v. Harris, 401 U.S. 37 (1971). I adhere to my view that *Younger* is, in general, inapplicable to civil proceedings, especially when a plaintiff brings a § 1983 action alleging violation of federal constitutional rights. . . .

The State's interest in this case is negligible. The State of Texas—not a party in this appeal—expressly represented to the Court of Appeals that it "has no interest in the outcome of the state-court litigation underlying this cause," except in its fair adjudication. . . .

. . . . .

Furthermore, I reject Pennzoil's contention that District of Columbia Court of Appeals v. Feldman, 460 U.S. 462 (1983), and Rooker v. Fidelity Trust Co., 263 U.S. 413 (1923), forbid collateral review in this instance. In *Rooker* and *Feldman,* the Court held that lower federal courts lack jurisdiction to engage in appellate review of state court determinations. In this case, however, Texaco filed the § 1983 action only to protect its federal constitutional right to a meaningful opportunity for appellate review, not to challenge the merits of the Texas suit. Texaco's federal action seeking a stay of judgment pending appeal is therefore an action " 'separable from and collateral to' " the merits of the state court judgment. National Socialist Party v. Skokie, 432 U.S. 43, 44 (1977) (quoting Cohen v. Beneficial Indus. Loan Corp., 337 U.S. 541, 546 (1949)).

. . . . .

[T]his case is different from the more troublesome situation where a particular corporate litigant has such special attributes as an organization that a trustee in bankruptcy, in its stead, could not effectively advance the organization's interests on an appeal. Moreover, the underlying issues in this case—arising out of a commercial contract dispute—do not involve fundamental constitutional rights. See, e.g., Henry v. First National Bank of Clarksdale, 595 F.2d 291, 299–300 (CA5 1979) (bankruptcy of NAACP would make state appellate review of First Amendment claims "so difficult" to obtain that federal injunction justified), cert. denied sub nom. Claiborne Hardware Co. v. Henry, 444 U.S. 1074 (1980).

Given the particular facts of this case, I would reverse the judgment of the Court of Appeals, and remand the case with instructions to dismiss the complaint.

■ JUSTICE MARSHALL, concurring in the judgment.

While I join in the Court's disposition of this case, I cannot join in its reasoning. The Court addresses the propriety of abstention under the doctrine of Younger v. Harris, 401 U.S. 37 (1971). There is no occasion to decide if abstention would have been proper unless the District Court had jurisdiction. Were I to reach the merits I would reverse for the reasons stated in the concurring opinions of JUSTICES BRENNAN and STEVENS, in which I join. But I can find no basis for the District Court's unwarranted assumption of jurisdiction over the subject matter of this lawsuit, and upon that ground alone I would reverse the decision below.

[JUSTICE MARSHALL concluded that the constitutional claims presented by Texaco to the district court were inextricably intertwined with the merits of the judgment rendered against it in state court. The district court thus lacked jurisdiction under the *Rooker-Feldman* doctrine.]

■ JUSTICE BLACKMUN, concurring in the judgment.

[JUSTICE BLACKMUN agreed that action under the color of state law was present. He thought that to apply *Younger* "would expand the *Younger* doctrine to an unprecedented extent and would effectively allow the invocation of *Younger* abstention whenever any state proceeding is ongoing, no matter how attenuated the State's interests are in that proceeding and no matter what abuses the federal plaintiff might be sustaining." He thought also that review was not barred by the *Rooker–Feldman* doctrine.]

I, however, refrain from joining the opinion of either JUSTICE BRENNAN or JUSTICE STEVENS when they would hold, as JUSTICE STEVENS does, that no due process violation in this context is possible, or, as JUSTICE BRENNAN does, that room must be left for some constitutional violations in post-judgment procedures, but only when the organization seeking the appeal has "special attributes as an organization" or when the underlying dispute involves "fundamental constitutional rights." . . . Those conclusions, I fear, suffer somewhat from contortions due to attempts to show that a due process violation *in this case* is not possible or is hardly possible.[108] Thus, I would not disturb the Court of Appeals' conclusion that Texaco's due process

---

108. In particular, the suggestion that Texaco could enter a Chapter 11 proceeding, pursue its appeal, and then reemerge from this proceeding to continue "business as usual" strikes me as somewhat at odds with the reality of the corporate reorganization that might occur in

claim raised a "fair groun[d] for litigation" because "an inflexible requirement for impressment of a lien and denial of a stay of execution unless a supersedeas bond in the full amount of the judgment is posted can in some circumstances be irrational, unnecessary, and self-defeating, amounting to a confiscation of the judgment debtor's property without due process." 784 F.2d 1133, 1154 (CA2 1986).

I conclude instead that this case presents an example of the "narrowly limited 'special circumstances,'" Zwickler v. Koota, 389 U.S. 241, 248 (1967), quoting Propper v. Clark, 337 U.S. 472, 492 (1949), where the District Court should have abstained under the principles announced in Railroad Comm'n of Texas v. Pullman Co., 312 U.S. 496 (1941). Although the *Pullman* issue was not pressed before us (but see Brief for Appellant 42–43), it was considered by the Court of Appeals and rejected. 784 F.2d, at 1148–1149. In particular, the court determined that "there [was] nothing unclear or uncertain about the Texas lien and bond provisions" and that abstention was not demanded when there was only a "mere possibility" that the Texas courts would find such provisions unconstitutional. Ibid. I disagree. If the extensive briefing by the parties on the numerous Texas statutes and constitutional provisions at issue here suggests anything, . . . it is that on the unique facts of *this* case "unsettled questions of state law must be resolved before a substantial federal constitutional question can be decided," Hawaii Housing Authority v. Midkiff, 467 U.S. 229, 236 (1984), because "the state courts may interpret [the] challenged state statute[s] so as to eliminate, or at least to alter materially, the constitutional question presented." Ohio Bureau of Employment Services v. Hodory, 431 U.S. 471, 477 (1977) . . . . The possibility of such a state-law resolution of this dispute seems to me still to exist.

■ JUSTICE STEVENS, with whom JUSTICE MARSHALL joins, concurring in the judgment.

In my opinion Texaco's claim that the Texas judgment lien and supersedeas bond provisions violate the Fourteenth Amendment is plainly without merit. The injunction against enforcement of those provisions must therefore be dissolved. I rest my analysis on this ground because I cannot agree with the grounds upon which the Court disposes of the case. In my view the District Court and the Court of Appeals were correct to hold that a creditor's invocation of a State's post-judgment collection procedures constitutes action "under color of" state law within the meaning of 42 U.S.C. § 1983, and that there is no basis for abstention in this case.

. . . . [109]

---

bankruptcy, especially on the facts of this case. Moreover, while there has been some discussion [in JUSTICE MARSHALL's opinion] about a "special law" for multi-billion-dollar corporations, I would have thought that our proper concern is with constitutional violations, not with our sympathy, or lack thereof, for a particular litigant. It might also be useful to point out an obvious, but overlooked, fact: Pennzoil, too, is not a corner grocery store.

[109. Six days after the decision in the principal case Texaco went into bankruptcy under Chapter 11.

SECTION 9. THE *ROOKER-FELDMAN* DOCTRINE[110]

Exxon Mobil Corp. v. Saudi Basic Indus. Corp.

Supreme Court of the United States, 2005.
544 U.S. 280, 125 S.Ct. 1517, 161 L.Ed.2d 454.

■ JUSTICE GINSBURG delivered the opinion of the Court.

This case concerns what has come to be known as the *Rooker-Feldman* doctrine, applied by this Court only twice, first in Rooker v. Fidelity Trust Co., 263 U.S. 413 (1923), then, 60 years later, in District of Columbia Court of Appeals v. Feldman, 460 U.S. 462 (1983). Variously interpreted in the lower courts, the doctrine has sometimes been construed to extend far beyond the contours of the *Rooker* and *Feldman* cases, overriding Congress' conferral of federal-court jurisdiction concurrent with jurisdiction exercised by state courts, and superseding the ordinary application of preclusion law pursuant to 28 U.S.C. § 1738....

Rooker was a suit commenced in Federal District Court to have a judgment of a state court, adverse to the federal court plaintiffs, "declared

---

See Stravitz, *Younger* Abstention Reaches a Civil Maturity: *Pennzoil Co. v. Texaco Inc.*, 57 Fordham L.Rev. 997 (1989); Althouse, The Misguided Search for State Interest in Abstention Cases: Observations on the Occasion of *Pennzoil v. Texas*, 63 N.Y.U.L.Rev. 1051 (1988).

The *Younger* rules apply to state administrative proceedings in which important state interests are vindicated, so long as in those proceedings the federal plaintiff will have a full and fair opportunity to litigate his constitutional claim. Ohio Civil Rights Commn. v. Dayton Christian Schools, 477 U.S. 619 (1986). But this is true only if the state administrative proceedings are judicial in nature. If they are legislative or executive in nature, the *Younger* rules do not apply. New Orleans Public Service, Inc. v. Council of City of New Orleans, 491 U.S. 350 (1989).

Various of the opinions in the *Pennzoil* case discuss the *Rooker–Feldman* doctrine. The jurisdiction-limiting effect of this murky doctrine was long a source of great difficulty for the lower federal courts. See generally 18B Wright, Miller & Cooper, Federal Practice and Procedure: Jurisdiction 2d § 4469.1 (2002). Its overuse was decisively curtailed by a unanimous Court in Exxon Mobil Corp. v. Saudi Basic Industries Corp., 544 U.S. 280 (2005), reprinted infra p. 652.]

[110. Friedman, Failed Enterprise: The Supreme Court's Habeas Reform, 83 Calif.L.Rev. 485 (1995); Yackle, The Habeas Hagioscope, 66 S.Cal.L.Rev. 2331 (1993); Tabak & Lane, Judicial Activism and Legislative "Reform" of Federal Habeas Corpus: A Critical Analysis of Recent Developments and Current Proposals, 55 Albany L.Rev. 1 (1991); Hughes, The Decline of Habeas Corpus (1990); Hoffman, The Supreme Court's New Vision of Federal Habeas Corpus for State Prisoners, 1989 Sup.Ct.Rev. 165; Wechsler, Habeas Corpus and the Supreme Court: Reconsidering the Reach of the Great Writ, 59 U.Colo.L.Rev. 167 (1988); Wright, Habeas Corpus: Its History and Its Future, 81 Mich.L.Rev. 802 (1983); Cover & Aleinikoff, Dialectical Federalism: Habeas Corpus and the Court, 86 Yale L.J. 1035 (1977); 17A Wright, Miller & Cooper, Federal Practice and Procedure: Jurisdiction 2d §§ 4261–4268.5 (1988); Wright & Kane, Federal Courts § 53 (6th ed.2002); 28 Moore's Federal Practice ch. 671 (3d ed.1998).]

null and void." 263 U.S., at 414. In *Feldman*, parties unsuccessful in the District of Columbia Court of Appeals (the District's highest court) commenced a federal-court action against the very court that had rejected their applications. Holding the federal suits impermissible, we emphasized that appellate jurisdiction to reverse or modify a state-court judgment is lodged, ... by 28 U.S.C. § 1257, exclusively in this Court. Federal district courts, we noted, are empowered to exercise original, not appellate, jurisdiction. Plaintiffs in *Rooker* and *Feldman* had litigated and lost in state court. Their federal complaints, we observed, essentially invited federal courts of first instance to review and reverse unfavorable state-court judgments. We declared such suits out of bounds, i.e., properly dismissed for want of subject-matter jurisdiction.

The *Rooker-Feldman* doctrine, we hold today, is confined to cases of the kind from which the doctrine acquired its name: cases brought by state-court losers complaining of injuries caused by state-court judgments rendered before the district court proceedings commenced and inviting district court review and rejection of those judgments. *Rooker-Feldman* does not otherwise override or supplant preclusion doctrine or augment the circumscribed doctrines that allow federal courts to stay or dismiss proceedings in deference to state-court actions.

In the case before us, the Court of Appeals for the Third Circuit misperceived the narrow ground occupied by *Rooker-Feldman*, and consequently erred in ordering the federal action dismissed for lack of subject-matter jurisdiction. We therefore reverse the Third Circuit's judgment.

I

In Rooker v. Fidelity Trust Co., 263 U.S. 413, the parties defeated in state court turned to a Federal District Court for relief. Alleging that the adverse state-court judgment was rendered in contravention of the Constitution, they asked the federal court to declare it "null and void." Id., at 414–415. This Court noted preliminarily that the state court had acted within its jurisdiction. Id., at 415. If the state-court decision was wrong, the Court explained, "that did not make the judgment void, but merely left it open to reversal or modification in an appropriate and timely appellate proceeding." Ibid. Federal district courts, the *Rooker* Court recognized, lacked the requisite appellate authority, for their jurisdiction was "strictly original." Id., at 416. Among federal courts, the *Rooker* Court clarified, Congress had empowered only this Court to exercise appellate authority "to reverse or modify" a state-court judgment. Ibid. Accordingly, the Court affirmed a decree dismissing the suit for lack of jurisdiction. Id., at 415.

Sixty years later, the Court decided District of Columbia Court of Appeals v. Feldman, 460 U.S. 462. The two plaintiffs in that case, Hickey and Feldman, neither of whom had graduated from an accredited law school, petitioned the District of Columbia Court of Appeals to waive a court Rule that required D.C. bar applicants to have graduated from a law school approved by the American Bar Association. After the D.C. court denied their waiver requests, Hickey and Feldman filed suits in the United

States District Court for the District of Columbia. Id., at 465–473. The District Court and the Court of Appeals for the District of Columbia Circuit disagreed on the question whether the federal suit could be maintained, and we granted certiorari. Id., at 474–475.

Recalling *Rooker*, this Court's opinion in *Feldman* observed first that the District Court lacked authority to review a final judicial determination of the D.C. high court. "Review of such determinations," the *Feldman* opinion reiterated, "can be obtained only in this Court." 460 U.S., at 476. The "crucial question," the Court next stated, was whether the proceedings in the D.C. court were "judicial in nature." Ibid. Addressing that question, the Court concluded that the D.C. court had acted both judicially and legislatively.

In applying the accreditation Rule to the Hickey and Feldman waiver petitions, this Court determined, the D.C. court had acted judicially. Id., at 479–482. As to that adjudication, *Feldman* held, this Court alone among federal courts had review authority. Hence, "to the extent that Hickey and Feldman sought review in the District Court of the District of Columbia Court of Appeals' denial of their petitions for waiver, the District Court lacked subject-matter jurisdiction over their complaints." Id., at 482. But that determination did not dispose of the entire case, for in promulgating the bar admission rule, this Court said, the D.C. court had acted legislatively, not judicially. Id., at 485–486. "Challenges to the constitutionality of state bar rules," the Court elaborated, "do not necessarily require a United States district court to review a final state-court judgment in a judicial proceeding." Id., at 486. Thus, the Court reasoned, 28 U.S.C. § 1257 did not bar District Court proceedings addressed to the validity of the accreditation Rule itself. *Feldman*, 460 U.S., at 486. The Rule could be contested in federal court, this Court held, so long as plaintiffs did not seek review of the Rule's application in a particular case. Ibid.

The Court endeavored to separate elements of the Hickey and Feldman complaints that failed the jurisdictional threshold from those that survived jurisdictional inspection. Plaintiffs had urged that the District of Columbia Court of Appeals acted arbitrarily in denying the waiver petitions of Hickey and Feldman, given that court's "former policy of granting waivers to graduates of unaccredited law schools." Ibid. That charge, the Court held, could not be pursued, for it was "inextricably intertwined with the District of Columbia Court of Appeals' decisions, in judicial proceedings, to deny [plaintiffs'] petitions." Id., at 486–487.[111]

On the other hand, the Court said, plaintiffs could maintain "claims that the [bar admission] rule is unconstitutional because it creates an irrebuttable presumption that only graduates of accredited law schools are fit to practice law, discriminates against those who have obtained equiva-

---

111. Earlier in the opinion the Court had used the same expression. In a footnote, the Court explained that a district court could not entertain constitutional claims attacking a state-court judgment, even if the state court had not passed directly on those claims, when the constitutional attack was "inextricably intertwined" with the state court's judgment. District of Columbia Court of Appeals v. Feldman, 460 U.S. 462, 482 n.16 (1983).

lent legal training by other means, and impermissibly delegates the District of Columbia Court of Appeals' power to regulate the bar to the American Bar Association," for those claims "do not require review of a judicial decision in a particular case." Id., at 487. The Court left open the question whether the doctrine of res judicata foreclosed litigation of the elements of the complaints spared from dismissal for want of subject-matter jurisdiction. Id., at 487–488.

Since *Feldman*, this Court has never applied *Rooker-Feldman* to dismiss an action for want of jurisdiction. The few decisions that have mentioned *Rooker* and *Feldman* have done so only in passing or to explain why those cases did not dictate dismissal. . . .

II

In 1980, two subsidiaries of petitioner Exxon Mobil Corporation (then the separate companies Exxon Corp. and Mobil Corp.) formed joint ventures with respondent Saudi Basic Industries Corp. (SABIC) to produce polyethylene in Saudi Arabia. 194 F.Supp.2d 378, 384 (D.N.J.2002). Two decades later, the parties began to dispute royalties that SABIC had charged the joint ventures for sublicenses to a polyethylene manufacturing method. 364 F.3d 102, 103 (CA3 2004).

SABIC preemptively sued the two Exxon Mobil subsidiaries in Delaware Superior Court in July 2000 seeking a declaratory judgment that the royalty charges were proper under the joint venture agreements. 194 F.Supp.2d, at 385–386. About two weeks later, Exxon Mobil and its subsidiaries countersued SABIC in the United States District Court for the District of New Jersey, alleging that SABIC overcharged the joint ventures for the sublicenses. Id., at 385. Exxon Mobil invoked subject-matter jurisdiction in the New Jersey action under 28 U.S.C. § 1330, which authorizes district courts to adjudicate actions against foreign states. 194 F.Supp.2d, at 401.[112]

In January 2002, the Exxon Mobil subsidiaries answered SABIC's state-court complaint, asserting as counterclaims the same claims Exxon Mobil had made in the federal suit in New Jersey. 364 F.3d, at 103. The state suit went to trial in March 2003, and the jury returned a verdict of over $400 million in favor of the Exxon Mobil subsidiaries. Ibid. SABIC appealed the judgment entered on the verdict to the Delaware Supreme Court.

Before the state-court trial, SABIC moved to dismiss the federal suit, alleging, inter alia, immunity under the Foreign Sovereign Immunities Act of 1976, 28 U.S.C. § 1602 *et seq.* (2000 ed.and Supp. II). The Federal District Court denied SABIC's motion to dismiss. 194 F.Supp.2d, at 401–407. SABIC took an interlocutory appeal, and the Court of Appeals heard argument in December 2003, over eight months after the state-court jury verdict. 364 F.3d, at 103–104.

---

112. SABIC is a Saudi Arabian corporation, 70% owned by the Saudi Government and 30% owned by private investors. 194 F.Supp.2d, at 384.

The Court of Appeals, on its own motion, raised the question whether "subject matter jurisdiction over this case fails under the *Rooker-Feldman* doctrine because Exxon Mobil's claims have already been litigated in state court." Id., at 104. The court did not question the District Court's possession of subject-matter jurisdiction at the outset of the suit, but held that federal jurisdiction terminated when the Delaware Superior Court entered judgment on the jury verdict. Id., at 104–105. The court rejected Exxon Mobil's argument that *Rooker-Feldman* could not apply because Exxon Mobil filed its federal complaint well before the state-court judgment. The only relevant consideration, the court stated, "is whether the state judgment precedes a federal judgment on the same claims." 364 F.3d, at 105. If *Rooker-Feldman* did not apply to federal actions filed prior to a state-court judgment, the Court of Appeals worried, "we would be encouraging parties to maintain federal actions as 'insurance policies' while their state court claims were pending." 364 F.3d, at 105. Once Exxon Mobil's claims had been litigated to a judgment in state court, the Court of Appeals held, *Rooker-Feldman* "preclude[d] [the] federal district court from proceeding." 364 F.3d, at 104. . . .

Exxon Mobil, at that point prevailing in Delaware, was not seeking to overturn the state-court judgment. Nevertheless, the Court of Appeals hypothesized that, if SABIC won on appeal in Delaware, Exxon Mobil would be endeavoring in the federal action to "invalidate" the state-court judgment, "the very situation," the court concluded, "contemplated by *Rooker-Feldman*'s 'inextricably intertwined' bar." Id., at 106.

We granted certiorari . . . to resolve conflict among the Courts of Appeals over the scope of the *Rooker-Feldman* doctrine. We now reverse the judgment of the Court of Appeals for the Third Circuit.

III

Rooker and *Feldman* exhibit the limited circumstances in which this Court's appellate jurisdiction over state-court judgments, 28 U.S.C. § 1257, precludes a United States district court from exercising subject-matter jurisdiction in an action it would otherwise be empowered to adjudicate under a congressional grant of authority, e.g., § 1330 (suits against foreign states), § 1331 (federal question), and § 1332 (diversity). In both cases, the losing party in state court filed suit in federal court after the state proceedings ended, complaining of an injury caused by the state-court judgment and seeking review and rejection of that judgment. Plaintiffs in both cases, alleging federal-question jurisdiction, called upon the District Court to overturn an injurious state-court judgment. Because § 1257, as long interpreted, vests authority to review a state court's judgment solely in this Court, . . . the District Courts in *Rooker* and *Feldman* lacked subject-matter jurisdiction. . . .[113]

---

113. Congress, if so minded, may explicitly empower district courts to oversee certain state-court judgments and has done so, most notably, in authorizing federal habeas review of state prisoners' petitions. 28 U.S.C. § 2254(a).

When there is parallel state and federal litigation, *Rooker-Feldman* is not triggered simply by the entry of judgment in state court. This Court has repeatedly held that "the pendency of an action in the state court is no bar to proceedings concerning the same matter in the Federal court having jurisdiction." ... Comity or abstention doctrines may, in various circumstances, permit or require the federal courts to stay or dismiss the federal action in favor of the state-court litigation. See, e.g., Colorado River Water Conservation Dist. v. United States, 424 U.S. 800 (1976); Younger v. Harris, 401 U.S. 37 (1971); Burford v. Sun Oil Co., 319 U.S. 315 (1943); Railroad Comm'n of Tex. v. Pullman Co., 312 U.S. 496 (1941). But neither *Rooker* nor *Feldman* supports the notion that properly invoked concurrent jurisdiction vanishes if a state court reaches judgment on the same or related question while the case remains sub judice in a federal court.

Disposition of the federal action, once the state-court adjudication is complete, would be governed by preclusion law. The Full Faith and Credit Act, 28 U.S.C. § 1738, ... requires the federal court to "give the same preclusive effect to a state-court judgment as another court of that State would give." ... Preclusion, of course, is not a jurisdictional matter. See Fed. Rule Civ. Proc. 8(c) (listing res judicata as an affirmative defense). In parallel litigation, a federal court may be bound to recognize the claim- and issue-preclusive effects of a state-court judgment, but federal jurisdiction over an action does not terminate automatically on the entry of judgment in the state court.

Nor does § 1257 stop a district court from exercising subject-matter jurisdiction simply because a party attempts to litigate in federal court a matter previously litigated in state court. If a federal plaintiff "present[s] some independent claim, albeit one that denies a legal conclusion that a state court has reached in a case to which he was a party ..., then there is jurisdiction and state law determines whether the defendant prevails under principles of preclusion." ...

This case surely is not the "paradigm situation in which *Rooker-Feldman* precludes a federal district court from proceeding." 364 F.3d, at 104 .... Exxon Mobil plainly has not repaired to federal court to undo the Delaware judgment in its favor. Rather, it appears Exxon Mobil filed suit in Federal District Court (only two weeks after SABIC filed in Delaware and well before any judgment in state court) to protect itself in the event it lost in state court on grounds (such as the state statute of limitations) that might not preclude relief in the federal venue....[114] *Rooker-Feldman* did

---

114. The Court of Appeals criticized Exxon Mobil for pursuing its federal suit as an "insurance policy" against an adverse result in state court. 364 F.3d 102, 105–106 (CA3 2004). There is nothing necessarily inappropriate, however, about filing a protective action. See, e.g., Rhines v. Weber, 544 U.S. 269 (2005) (permitting a federal district court to stay a federal habeas action and hold the petition in abeyance while a petitioner exhausts claims in state court); Union Pacific R. Co. v. Dept. of Revenue of Ore., 920 F.2d 581, 584, and n.9 (CA9 1990) (noting that the railroad company had filed protective actions in state court to prevent expiration of the state statute of limitations); Government of Virgin Islands v. Neadle, 861 F.Supp. 1054, 1055 (M.D.Fla.1994) (staying an action brought by plaintiffs "to protect themselves" in the event that personal jurisdiction over the defendants failed in the

not prevent the District Court from exercising jurisdiction when Exxon Mobil filed the federal action, and it did not emerge to vanquish jurisdiction after Exxon Mobil prevailed in the Delaware courts.

For the reasons stated, the judgment of the Court of Appeals for the Third Circuit is reversed, and the case is remanded for further proceedings consistent with this opinion.

It is so ordered.

SECTION 10. HABEAS CORPUS[115]

STATUTES

Title I of the Antiterrorism and Effective Death Penalty Act of 1996 (AEDPA), April 24, 1996, Pub.L. 104–132, 110 Stat. 1214, enacted the most drastic changes to the federal writ of habeas corpus since the Great Writ was made applicable to state judicial proceedings in 1867. See Lee, Section 2254(d) of the New Habeas Statute: An (Opinionated) User's Manual, 51 Vand.L.Rev. 104 (1998); Note, The Avoidance of Constitutional Questions and the Preservation of Judicial Review: Federal Court Treatment of the New Habeas Provisions, 111 Harv.L.Rev. 1578 (1998); Note, Rewriting the Great Writ: Standards of Review for Habeas Corpus Under the New 28 U.S.C. § 2254, 110 Harv.L.Rev. 1868 (1997); Yackle, A Primer on the New Habeas Corpus Statute, 44 Buff.L.Rev. 381 (1996); Yackle, Federal Evidentiary Hearings Under the New Habeas Corpus Statute, 6 B.U.Pub.Int.L.J. 135 (1996).

The basic statute, 28 U.S.C. § 2241, was unchanged, but major changes were made in §§ 2244 and 2254. They are shown with the language added in 1996 in italics.

United States District Court for the Virgin Islands); see also England v. Louisiana Bd. of Medical Examiners, 375 U.S. 411, 421 (1964) (permitting a party to reserve litigation of federal constitutional claims for federal court while a state court resolves questions of state law).

[115. Friedman, Failed Enterprise: The Supreme Court's Habeas Reform, 83 Cal.L.Rev. 485 (1995); Yackle, The Habeas Hagioscope, 66 S.Cal.L.Rev. 2331 (1993); Tabak & Lane, Judicial Activism and Legislative "Reform" of Federal Habeas Corpus: A Critical Analysis of Recent Developments and Current Proposals, 55 Albany L.Rev. 1 (1991); Hughes, The Decline of Habeas Corpus (1990); Hoffman, The Supreme Court's New Vision of Federal Habeas Corpus for State Prisoners, 1989 Sup.Ct.Rev. 165; Wechsler, Habeas Corpus and the Supreme Court: Reconsidering the Reach of the Great Writ, 59 U.Colo.L.Rev. 167 (1988); Wright, Habeas Corpus: Its History and Its Future, 81 Mich.L.Rev. 802 (1983); Cover & Aleinikoff, Dialectical Federalism: Habeas Corpus and the Court, 86 Yale L.J. 1035 (1977); 17A Wright, Miller & Cooper, Federal Practice and Procedure: Jurisdiction 2d §§ 4261–4268.5 (1988); Wright & Kane, Federal Courts § 53 (6th ed.2002); 28 Moore's Federal Practice ch. 671 (3d ed.1998).]

28 U.S.C. § 2241. Power to grant writ[116]

(a) Writs of habeas corpus may be granted by the Supreme Court, any justice thereof, the district courts and any circuit judge within their respective jurisdictions. The order of a circuit judge shall be entered in the records of the district court of the district wherein the restraint complained of is had.

(b) The Supreme Court, any justice thereof, and any circuit judge may decline to entertain an application for a writ of habeas corpus and may transfer the application for hearing and determination to the district court having jurisdiction to entertain it.

(c) The writ of habeas corpus shall not extend to a prisoner unless—

(1) He is in custody under or by color of the authority of the United States or is committed for trial before some court thereof; or

(2) He is in custody for an act done or omitted in pursuance of an Act of Congress, or an order,[117] process, judgment or decree of a court or judge of the United States; or

(3) He is in custody[118] in violation of the Constitution or laws or treaties of the United States; or

---

[116. Statutory authorizations of habeas corpus were passed and amplified, usually in time of crisis, in 1789, 1833, 1842, and 1867. The present statutes, largely based on the old statutes in substance but with new procedural provisions, were adopted in the Judicial Code of 1948. See Parker, Limiting the Abuse of Habeas Corpus, 8 F.R.D. 171 (1948). They were amended in 1966, and, as stated in the text, in 1996.

28 U.S.C. § 2255 provides a remedy by motion for prisoners convicted in federal court. It has spawned a large body of law. See 3 Wright, King & Klein, Federal Practice and Procedure: Criminal 3d §§ 589–602 (2004); 28 Moore's Federal Practice ¶ 671.06 (3d ed.1998).]

[117. See the historic and dramatic case of In re Neagle, 135 U.S. 1 (1890), the background of which is described in Swisher, Stephen J. Field: Craftsman of the Law 321–361 (1930). The tale is also told in a fascinating book, Kroninger, Sarah and the Senator (1964).

Notice that there is also statutory provision for removal of cases against federal officers acting under color of office. 28 U.S.C. § 1442.]

[118. Is a prisoner who is serving a sentence he does not challenge "in custody" within the meaning of this phrase under a second sentence to be served after the first is ended so that he may now bring habeas corpus to attack the second sentence? Peyton v. Rowe, 391 U.S. 54 (1968). What if the second sentence is from a different state? Braden v. 30th Judicial Court, 410 U.S. 484 (1973).

Is the requirement of "custody" satisfied by one who is free on his own recognizance after he has exhausted all state remedies? See Hensley v. Municipal Court, 411 U.S. 345 (1973).

On the circumstances in which a state prisoner challenging actions of prison authorities must proceed by habeas corpus, in which exhaustion of state remedies is required, rather than by a civil-rights action under 42 U.S.C. § 1983, in which exhaustion is not required, see Preiser v. Rodriguez, 411 U.S. 475 (1973).

In Heck v. Humphrey, 512 U.S. 477 (1994), the Supreme Court disapproved of dicta in Preiser v. Rodriguez, 411 U.S. 475, 494 (1973), suggesting that a prisoner seeking damages rather than release for allegedly unlawful police conduct leading to his conviction could bring suit under 42 U.S.C. § 1983 "without any requirement of prior exhaustion of state remedies." While his appeal of his conviction was still pending in state court, the imprisoned Heck filed a pro se suit seeking damages for unlawful arrest and other police misconduct affecting the evidence at his trial. The Supreme Court held that Heck's suit had properly been dismissed

(4) He, being a citizen of a foreign state and domiciled therein is in custody for an act done or omitted under any alleged right, title, authority, privilege, protection, or exemption claimed under the commission, order or sanction of any foreign state, or under color thereof, the validity and effect of which depend upon the law of nations; or

(5) It is necessary to bring him into court to testify or for trial.

(d) Where an application for a writ of habeas corpus is made by a person in custody under the judgment and sentence of a State court of a State which contains two or more Federal judicial districts, the application may be filed in the district court for the district wherein such person is in custody or in the district court for the district within which the State court was held which convicted and sentenced him and each of such district courts shall have concurrent jurisdiction to entertain the application. The district court for the district wherein such an application is filed in the exercise of its discretion and in furtherance of justice may transfer the application to the other district court for hearing and determination.[119]

28 U.S.C. § 2244. Finality of determination

(a) No circuit or district judge shall be required to entertain an application for a writ of habeas corpus to inquire into the detention of a person pursuant to a judgment of a court of the United States if it appears that the legality of such detention has been determined by a judge or court of the United States on a prior application for a writ of habeas corpus, *except as provided in section 2255.*

(b)[120] *(1) A claim presented in a second or successive habeas corpus application under section 2254 that was presented in a prior application*[121] *shall be dismissed.*

---

as premature, declaring that "in order to recover damages for allegedly unconstitutional conviction or imprisonment, or for other harm caused by actions whose unlawfulness would render a conviction or sentence invalid, a § 1983 plaintiff must prove that the conviction or sentence has been reversed on direct appeal, expunged by executive order, declared invalid by a state tribunal authorized to make such determination, or called into question by a federal court's issuance of a writ of habeas corpus, 28 U.S.C. § 2254." 512 U.S., at 486–487.]

[**119.** Subsection (d) was added in 1966.]

[**120.** When adding new subsection (b) to 28 U.S.C. § 2244, AEDPA redesignated former subsection (b) as subsection (c). In a case that came down only two months after the new statute became law, the Supreme Court unanimously upheld the provisions of the new § 2244(b) sharply restricting a second or successive habeas-corpus application. See Felker v. Turpin, 518 U.S. 651 (1996). The Court held, however, that nothing in those provisions limits the power of the Supreme Court to entertain original petitions for habeas corpus pursuant to 28 U.S.C. §§ 2241 and 2254.]

[**121.** The Court has adopted a strict construction of what constitutes a forbidden "second or successive" habeas petition. When a claim in a habeas petition has been dismissed as premature because state remedies remain unexhausted, or because the claim is not yet ripe, the district court is not barred by § 2244(b) from acting upon a later request for a decision on the merits of the claim. If a claim was timely raised in a first petition but was not then procedurally or factually ripe for adjudication, the claim is to be treated as having been deferred rather than dismissed. See Stewart v. Martinez–Villareal, 523 U.S. 637 (1998), holding that a state prisoner was entitled to a hearing on the merits of his previously

(2) A claim presented in a second or successive habeas corpus application under section 2254 that was not presented in a prior application shall be dismissed unless—

(A) the applicant shows that the claim relies on a new rule of constitutional law, made retroactive to cases on collateral review by the Supreme Court, that was previously unavailable;[122] *or*

(B)(i) the factual predicate for the claim could not have been discovered previously through the exercise of due diligence; and

(ii) the facts underlying the claim, if proven and viewed in light of the evidence as a whole, would be sufficient to establish by clear and convincing evidence that, but for constitutional error, no reasonable factfinder would have found the applicant guilty of the underlying offense.

(3)(A) Before a second or successive application permitted by this section is filed in the district court, the applicant shall move in the appropriate court of appeals for an order authorizing the district court to consider the application.

(B) A motion in the court of appeals for an order authorizing the district court to consider a second or successive application shall be determined by a three-judge panel of the court of appeals.

(C) The court of appeals may authorize the filing of a second or successive application only if it determines that the application makes a prima facie showing that the application satisfies the requirements of this subsection.

---

dismissed claim—which did not become ripe until his execution was actually imminent—that he was presently insane and therefore could not constitutionally be put to death. But a sharply divided Court held in Calderon v. Thompson, 523 U.S. 538 (1998), that the inherent power of a court of appeals to recall its mandate should be applied in harmony with the severe restrictions on successive applications for habeas relief imposed by § 2244(b). Although the court below had there recalled its mandate because of administrative error in the processing of an appeal of the district court's judgment with respect to a habeas petitioner's first application for the writ, and the recall thus did not directly contradict the AEDPA's near-absolute bar on successive petitions, the recall conflicted with the policy of the AEDPA and for lack of sufficiently extraordinary justification was a grave abuse of discretion. The four dissenting Justices, while critical of the lower court's process for recalling its mandate, would have applied the conventional and more deferential "abuse of discretion" standard and affirmed for lack of abuse of discretion.]

[**122.** In Tyler v. Cain, 533 U.S. 656 (2001), a narrowly divided Court adopted a very strict construction of § 2244(b)(2)(A)'s exception permitting a second or successive application for a writ of habeas corpus grounded in a "new rule" that the Supreme Court has "made retroactive" for habeas purposes. Teague v. Lane, 489 U.S. 288 (1989), continues to govern whether a "new rule" should be "made" retroactive. *Teague* generally bars retroactive habeas application of new rules, subject to one substantive and one procedural exception: when (1) the new rule constitutionally decriminalizes "certain kinds of primary, private individual conduct" by placing them "beyond the power of the criminal law-making authority to proscribe" ; or when (2) the new rule is a "watershed rule of criminal procedure" that is either closely tied either to "the likelihood of obtaining an accurate conviction" or to "bedrock procedural elements essential to the fairness of a proceeding." 489 U.S., at 311.]

(D) The court of appeals shall grant or deny the authorization to file a second or successive application not later than 30 days after the filing of the motion.

(E) The grant or denial of an authorization by a court of appeals to file a second or successive application shall not be appealable and shall not be the subject of a petition for rehearing or for a writ of certiorari.

(4) A district court shall dismiss any claim presented in a second or successive application that the court of appeals has authorized to be filed unless the applicant shows that the claim satisfies the requirements of this section.

(c) In a habeas corpus proceeding brought in behalf of a person in custody pursuant to the judgment of a State court, a prior judgment of the Supreme Court of the United States on an appeal or review by a writ of certiorari at the instance of the prisoner of the decision of such State court, shall be conclusive as to all issues of fact or law with respect to an asserted denial of a Federal right which constitutes ground for discharge in a habeas corpus proceeding, actually adjudicated by the Supreme Court therein, unless the applicant for the writ of habeas corpus shall plead and the court shall find the existence of a material and controlling fact which did not appear in the record of the proceeding in the Supreme Court and the court shall further find that the applicant for the writ of habeas corpus could not have caused such fact to appear in such record by the exercise of reasonable diligence.

(d)(1) A 1–year period of limitation shall apply to an application for a writ of habeas corpus by a person in custody pursuant to the judgment of a State court. The limitation period shall run from the latest of—

(A) the date on which the judgment became final by the conclusion of direct review or the expiration of the time for seeking such review;

(B) the date on which the impediment to filing an application created by State action in violation of the Constitution or laws of the United States is removed, if the applicant was prevented from filing by such State action;

(C) the date on which the constitutional right asserted was initially recognized by the Supreme Court, if the right has been newly recognized by the Supreme Court and made retroactively applicable to cases on collateral review; or

(D) the date on which the factual predicate of the claim or claims presented could have been discovered through the exercise of due diligence.

(2) The time during which a properly filed application for State post-conviction or other collateral review with respect to the pertinent

judgment or claim is pending shall not be counted toward any period of limitation under this subsection.[123]

28 U.S.C. § 2254. State custody; remedies in Federal courts

(a) The Supreme Court, a Justice thereof, a circuit judge, or a district court shall entertain an application for a writ of habeas corpus in behalf of a person in custody pursuant to the judgment of a State court only on the ground that he is in custody in violation of the Constitution or laws or treaties of the United States.

(b)(1) An application for a writ of habeas corpus on behalf of a person in custody pursuant to the judgment of a State court shall not be granted unless it appears that—

(A) the applicant has exhausted the remedies available in the courts of the State; or

---

[123.   If a "properly filed application for State post-conviction or other collateral review" is denied by an inferior state court, is the application "pending" —and the federal one-year limitations period accordingly tolled—during the period in which the denial of state habeas relief is subject to state appellate review? All members of the Court agreed that the federal period is tolled during throughout the appellate process, including the normally brief period between the denial of relief by a lower court and the prisoner's filing of a notice of appeal of that adverse ruling. But the Court fractured in applying this rule to California's unusual system of post-conviction appellate review, which permits a prisoner who has unsuccessfully sought habeas relief from a lower court to seek review of that adverse ruling either by appeal or by filing an independent but essentially identical petition for a writ of habeas corpus in a higher court. California prisoners typically choose the second option, and although the independent habeas petition must be filed in the appellate court within a "reasonable" time, unlike a notice of appeal it is not required to be filed within a determinate period. A narrow majority generously construed § 2244(d)(2) to toll the federal one-year limitations period throughout a gap of even several months between the denial of Saffold's habeas petition by a lower state court and the filing of an independent petition for habeas relief in the reviewing court, provided that on remand it was determined that this delay (which apparently resulted from the failure of the lower court to notify Saffold of its denial of his petition) was not "unreasonable" as a matter of state law. Carey v. Saffold, 536 U.S. 214 (2002).

The Supreme Court reiterated the necessity of complying with the procedural requirements of section 2244(b) where a state prisoner filed a habeas petition challenging his conviction while the state courts were still reviewing the sentence imposed, and then the prisoner subsequently filed a second habeas petition challenging his sentence. Burton v. Stewart, 549 U.S. 147, 127 S.Ct. 793 (2007).

The one-year filing deadline in § 2244(d) may, according to the Supreme Court, be equitably tolled in appropriate cases. The Court noted that AEDPA's limitations period is not jurisdictional, and that "a nonjurisdictional federal statute of limitations is normally subject to a rebuttable presumption in favor of equitable tolling." Holland v. Florida, 560 U.S. ___, 130 S.Ct. 2549 (2010).

Emphasizing that the tolling provision of § 2244(d)(2) is intended to "provide[] a powerful incentive for litigants to exhaust *all* available state remedies before proceeding in the lower federal courts," the Supreme Court held that the section's reference to "collateral review" means "judicial review of a judgment in a proceeding that is not part of direct review," and thus includes review of a prisoner's motion for a reduction in his sentence even when such a motion amounts merely to a plea for leniency. Wall v. Kholi, 562 U.S. ___, 131 S.Ct. 1278 (2011).]

(B)(i) there is an absence of available State corrective process;
or

> *(ii) circumstances exist that render such process ineffective to protect the rights of the applicant.*

(2) An application for a writ of habeas corpus may be denied on the merits, notwithstanding the failure of the applicant to exhaust the remedies available in the courts of the State.

(3) A State shall not be deemed to have waived the exhaustion requirement or be estopped from reliance upon the requirement unless the State, through counsel, expressly waives the requirement.

(c) An applicant shall not be deemed to have exhausted the remedies available in the courts of the State, within the meaning of this section, if he has the right under the law of the State to raise, by any available procedure, the question presented.[124]

(d) An application for a writ of habeas corpus on behalf of a person in custody pursuant to the judgment of a State court shall not be granted with respect to any claim that was adjudicated on the merits in State court proceedings unless the adjudication of the claim—[125]

> *(1) resulted in a decision that was contrary to, or involved an unreasonable application of, clearly established Federal law, as determined by the Supreme Court of the United States; or*[126]

[124. Has the prisoner exhausted his state remedies if he has raised the question in the state court, and it has been decided adversely to him, but there are other state procedures by which he can continue to raise the question again? The draftsman of the statute thought not, Parker, Limiting the Abuse of Habeas Corpus, 8 F.R.D. 171, 176 (1948), but the Supreme Court held to the contrary. Brown v. Allen, 344 U.S. 443, 447–450 (1953).]

[125. In a non-capital case, the Supreme Court held that § 2254(d)'s reference to claims "adjudicated on the merits in State court" does not require a state court to have provided reasons for its decision to deny post-conviction relief, and thus federal constitutional claims summarily denied by a state court qualify as claims adjudicated on the merits. The Court explained that a federal habeas court must presume that the state court's decision was on the merits absent any indication or state law procedural principles to the contrary. Harrington v. Richter, 562 U.S. ___, 131 S.Ct. 770 (2011).]

[126. A state court's refusal to apply a specific rule of decision that had not been "squarely established" by the U.S. Supreme Court cannot be "unreasonable" under "clearly established Federal law" within the meaning of § 2254(d)(1). Knowles v. Mirzayance, 556 U.S. 111 (2009).

When jury instructions did not require the jury to determine the existence of each individual mitigating factor unanimously, nor required individual determinations that each mitigating circumstance existed, the instructions did not violate Mills v. Maryland, 486 U.S. 367 (1988), and thus the state court's decision to uphold the mitigation instructions was not "contrary to, or . . . an unreasonable application of, clearly established Federal law, as determined by [the Supreme] Court," and accordingly, § 2254(d)(1) could not serve as a basis for habeas relief. Smith v. Spisak, 558 U.S. ___, 130 S.Ct. 676 (2010).

In reviewing whether the state court's denial of the prisoner's constitutional claim was "contrary to, or an unreasonable application of, clearly established Federal law" under § 2254(d)(1), a federal court may not consider new mitigating evidence, but instead is restricted to the evidence that was before the state court, despite the absence of such

(2) resulted in a decision that was based on an unreasonable determination of the facts in light of the evidence presented in the State court proceeding.[127]

(e)(1) In a proceeding instituted by an application for a writ of habeas corpus by a person in custody pursuant to the judgment of a State court, a determination of a factual issue made by a State court shall be presumed to be correct. The applicant shall have the burden of rebutting the presumption of correctness by clear and convincing evidence.[128]

(2) If the applicant has failed to develop the factual basis of a claim in State court proceedings, the court shall not hold an evidentiary hearing on the claim unless the applicant shows that—

(A) the claim relies on—

(i) a new rule of constitutional law, made retroactive to cases on collateral review by the Supreme Court, that was previously unavailable; or

(ii) a factual predicate that could not have been previously discovered through the exercise of due diligence; and

(B) the facts underlying the claim would be sufficient to establish by clear and convincing evidence that but for constitutional error, no reasonable factfinder would have found the applicant guilty of the underlying offense.

(f)[129] If the applicant challenges the sufficiency of the evidence adduced in such State court proceeding to support the State court's determination of a factual issue made therein, the applicant, if able, shall produce that part of the record pertinent to a determination of the sufficiency of the evidence to support such determination. If the applicant, because of indigency or other reason is unable to produce such part of the record, then the State shall produce such part of the record and the Federal court shall direct the State to do so by order directed to an appropriate State official. If the State cannot provide such pertinent part of the record, then the court

---

limiting language in (d)(1) (as contrasted with (d)(2) and (e)(2)). Cullen v. Pinholster, 563 U.S. ___, 131 S.Ct. 1388 (2011).]

[**127.** A state court's factual finding that defense counsel acted as a matter of strategy rather than negligence in failing to present mitigating evidence of the defendant's mental deficiencies during the penalty phase of a capital trial did not constitute "an unreasonable determination of the facts in light of the evidence presented in the State court proceeding" under § 2254(d)(2). Wood v. Allen, 558 U.S. ___, 130 S.Ct. 841 (2010).]

[**128.** "In the § 2254(d) context, as elsewhere, the appropriate methodology for distinguishing questions of fact from questions of law has been, to say the least, elusive." Miller v. Fenton, 474 U.S. 104, 113 (1985). In that case the Court, after discussing such general principles as it could find, held that the voluntariness of a confession is a legal inquiry requiring plenary federal review rather than a fact to which the presumption of correctness of § 2254(d) applies.]

[**129.** Subsections (f) and (g) of § 2254 as amended in 1996 were redesignated but otherwise unchanged. They had been designated subsections (e) and (f) in former § 2254 as enacted in 1948 and amended in 1966.]

shall determine under the existing facts and circumstances what weight shall be given to the State court's factual determination.

(g) A copy of the official records of the State court, duly certified by the clerk of such court to be a true and correct copy of a finding, judicial opinion, or other reliable written indicia showing such a factual determination by the State court shall be admissible in the Federal court proceeding.

(h) Except as provided in section 408 of the Controlled Substances Act, in all proceedings brought under this section, and any subsequent proceedings on review, the court may appoint counsel for an applicant who is or becomes financially unable to afford counsel, except as provided by a rule promulgated by the Supreme Court pursuant to statutory authority. Appointment of counsel under this section shall be governed by section 3006A of title 18.

(i) The ineffectiveness or incompetence of counsel during Federal or State collateral post-conviction proceedings shall not be a ground for relief in a proceeding arising under section 2254.

In addition to making the drastic changes just seen in 28 U.S.C. §§ 2244 and 2254 and also making similar changes in the procedure for postconviction review of federal criminal judgments under 28 U.S.C. § 2255, the 1996 Act substantially narrowed the opportunity for a state prisoner to appeal the denial of federal habeas relief under § 2253, and enacted (as 28 U.S.C. §§ 2261–2266) a special set of habeas procedures applicable only to death-penalty cases in states adopting a statewide mechanism for appointing postconviction counsel for all condemned prisoners. It is questionable whether many states will incur the expense of setting up qualifying procedures for providing postconviction counsel in death-penalty cases, since absent such procedures the stringent new time limitations for general habeas petitions under § 2254 will apply equally to death-penalty cases, and the new preclusion rules of § 2254 will function to bar federal habeas relief for most condemned prisoners because of defects in the pleading and prosecution of state-court habeas petitions that were filed either without the benefit of counsel, or with the hurried assistance of volunteer counsel whose ineffective assistance cannot be remedied by terms of new § 2254(i). See generally Wright, Miller & Cooper, 17A Federal Practice & Procedure; Jurisdiction 2d § 4261.1 (1988 & Supp.2005).

AEDPA permits the appeal of a final order in proceedings for habeas relief from state detention, or for the analogous relief from federal detention authorized by 28 U.S.C. § 2255, only if the appellant has first obtained from a circuit justice or judge a certificate of appealability to be issued "only if the applicant has made a substantial showing of the denial of a constitutional right." 28 U.S.C. § 2253(c). A sharply divided Supreme Court has held that the decision of a court of appeals to deny such a certificate is reviewable by certiorari as a "judgment or decree" in a "case" within the meaning of 28 U.S.C. § 1254(1). Hohn v. United States, 524 U.S. 236 (1998), also discussed below at page 1010, n. 25.

Congress expressly declared the special habeas provisions applicable to capital cases under new 28 U.S.C. §§ 2261–2266 to be retroactively applicable to pending cases. A narrowly divided Court has reasoned by implication that Congress must not have intended the new federal habeas procedures applicable to noncapital cases to be similarly retroactive. Lindh v. Murphy, 521 U.S. 320 (1997).

Wainwright v. Sykes

Supreme Court of the United States, 1977.
433 U.S. 72, 97 S.Ct. 2497, 53 L.Ed.2d 594.

■ MR. JUSTICE REHNQUIST delivered the opinion of the Court.

We granted certiorari to consider the availability of federal habeas to review a state convict's claim that testimony was admitted at his trial in violation of his *Miranda* rights [see Miranda v. Arizona, 384 U.S. 436 (1966)], a claim which the Florida courts have previously refused to consider on the merits because of noncompliance with a state contemporaneous objection rule. Petitioner Wainwright, on behalf of the State of Florida, here challenges a decision of the Court of Appeals for the Fifth Circuit ordering a hearing in state court on the merits of respondent's contention.

Respondent Sykes was convicted of third-degree murder after a jury trial in the Circuit Court of DeSoto County. He testified at trial that on the evening of January 8, 1972, he commanded his wife to summon the police because he had just shot Willie Gilbert. Other evidence indicated that when the police arrived at respondent's trailer home, they found Gilbert dead of a shotgun wound, lying a few feet from the front porch. Shortly after their arrival, respondent came from across the road and volunteered that he had shot Gilbert, and a few minutes later respondent's wife approached the police and told them the same thing. Sykes was immediately arrested and taken to the police station.

Once there, it is conceded that he was read his *Miranda* rights, and that he declined to seek the aid of counsel and indicated a desire to talk. He then made a statement, which was admitted into evidence at trial through the testimony of the two officers who heard it, to the effect that he had shot Gilbert from the front porch of his trailer home. There were several references during the trial to respondent's consumption of alcohol during the preceding day and to his apparent state of intoxication, facts which were acknowledged by the officers who arrived at the scene. At no time during the trial, however, was the admissibility of any of respondent's statements challenged by his counsel on the ground that respondent had not understood the *Miranda* warnings. Nor did the trial judge question their admissibility on his own motion or hold a fact-finding hearing bearing on that issue.

Respondent appealed his conviction, but apparently did not challenge the admissibility of the inculpatory statements. He later filed in the trial court a motion to vacate the conviction and, in the State District Court of Appeals and Supreme Court, petitions for habeas corpus. These filings, apparently for the first time, challenged the statements made to police on grounds of involuntariness. In all of these efforts respondent was unsuccessful.

Having failed in the Florida courts, respondent initiated the present action under 28 U.S.C. § 2254, asserting the inadmissibility of his statements by reason of his lack of understanding of the *Miranda* warnings. The United States District Court for the Middle District of Florida ruled that Jackson v. Denno, 378 U.S. 368 (1964), requires a hearing in a state criminal trial prior to the admission of an inculpatory out-of-court statement by the defendant. It held further that respondent had not lost his right to assert such a claim by failing to object at trial or on direct appeal, since only "exceptional circumstances" of "strategic decisions at trial" can create such a bar to raising federal constitutional claims in a federal habeas action. The court stayed issuance of the writ to allow the state court to hold a hearing on the "voluntariness" of the statements.

Petitioner warden appealed this decision to the United States Court of Appeals for the Fifth Circuit. That court first considered the nature of the right to exclusion of statements made without a knowing waiver of the right to counsel and the right not to incriminate oneself. It noted that *Jackson v. Denno*, supra, guarantees a right to a hearing on whether a defendant has knowingly waived his rights as described to him in the *Miranda* warning, and stated that under Florida law "the burden is on the State to secure [a] prima facie determination of voluntariness, not upon the defendant to demand it." Wainwright v. Sykes, 528 F.2d 522, 525 (CA5 1976).

The court then directed its attention to the effect on respondent's right of Florida Rule of Criminal Procedure 3.190(i), which it described as "a contemporaneous objection rule" applying to motions to suppress a defendant's inculpatory statements. It focused on this Court's decisions in Henry v. Mississippi, 379 U.S. 443 (1965); Davis v. United States, 411 U.S. 233 (1973), and Fay v. Noia, 372 U.S. 391 (1963), and concluded that the failure to comply with the rule requiring objection at the trial would only bar review of the suppression claim where the right to object was deliberately by-passed for reasons relating to trial tactics. The Court of Appeals distinguished our decision in *Davis,* supra (where failure to comply with a rule requiring pretrial objection to the indictment was found to bar habeas review of the underlying constitutional claim absent showing of cause for the failure and prejudice resulting), for the reason that "[a] major tenet of the *Davis* decision was that no prejudice was shown" to have resulted from the failure to object. It found that prejudice is "inherent" in any situation, like the present one, where the admissibility of an incriminating statement is concerned. Concluding that "[t]he failure to object in this case cannot be dismissed as a trial tactic, and thus a deliberate by-pass," the court affirmed the District Court order that the State hold a hearing on whether respondent knowingly waived his *Miranda* rights at the time he made the statements.

The simple legal question before the Court calls for a construction of the language of 28 U.S.C. § 2254(a), which provides that the federal courts shall entertain an application for a writ of habeas corpus "in behalf of a person in custody pursuant to the judgment of the state court only on the ground that he is in custody in violation of the Constitution or laws or treaties of the United States." But, to put it mildly, we do not write on a clean slate in construing this statutory provision.[130] Its earliest counterpart, applicable only to prisoners detained by federal authority, is found in the Judiciary Act of 1789. Construing that statute for the Court in Ex parte Watkins, 3 Pet. [28 U.S.] 193, 202 (1830), Chief Justice Marshall said:

> "An imprisonment under a judgment cannot be unlawful, unless that judgment be an absolute nullity; and it is not a nullity if the Court has general jurisdiction of the subject, although it should be erroneous."

See Ex parte Kearney, 7 Wheat. [20 U.S.] 38 (1822).

In 1867, Congress expanded the statutory language so as to make the writ available to one held in state as well as federal custody. For more than a century since the 1867 Amendment, this Court has grappled with the relationship between the classical common law writ of habeas corpus and the remedy provided in 28 U.S.C. § 2254. Sharp division within the Court has been manifested on more than one aspect of the perplexing problems which have been litigated in this connection. Where the habeas petitioner challenges a final judgment of conviction rendered by a state court, this Court has been called upon to decide no fewer than four different questions, all to a degree interrelated with one another: (1) What types of federal claims may a federal habeas court properly consider; (2) Where a federal claim is cognizable by a federal habeas court, to what extent must that court defer to a resolution of the claim in prior state proceedings; (3) To what extent must the petitioner who seeks federal habeas exhaust state remedies before resorting to the federal court; (4) In what instances will an adequate and independent state ground bar consideration of otherwise cognizable federal issues on federal habeas review?

Each of these four issues has spawned its share of litigation. With respect to the first, the rule laid down in *Ex parte Watkins*, supra, was gradually changed by judicial decisions expanding the availability of habeas relief beyond attacks focused narrowly on the jurisdiction of the sentencing

---

130. For divergent discussions of the historic role of federal habeas corpus, compare: Hart, Foreword: The Time Chart of the Justices, 73 Harv.L.Rev. 84 (1959); Reitz, Federal Habeas Corpus: Impact of an Abortive State Proceeding, 74 Harv.L.Rev. 1315 (1961); Brennan, Federal Habeas Corpus and State Prisoners: An Exercise in Federalism, 7 Utah L.Rev. 423 (1961); Bator, Finality in Criminal Law and Federal Habeas Corpus for State Prisoners, 76 Harv.L.Rev. 441, 468 (1963); Oaks, Legal History in the High Court—Habeas Corpus, 64 Mich.L.Rev. 451 (1966); Friendly, Is Innocence Irrelevant? Collateral Attack on Criminal Judgments, 38 U.Chi.L.Rev. 142, 170–171 (1970); and Developments in the Law—Federal Habeas Corpus, 83 Harv.L.Rev. 1038 (1970).

court. See Ex parte Wells, 18 How. [59 U.S.] 307 (1855); Ex parte Lange, 18 Wall. [85 U.S.] 163 (1873). Ex parte Siebold, 100 U.S. 371 (1879), authorized use of the writ to challenge a conviction under a federal statute where the statute was claimed to violate the United States Constitution. Frank v. Mangum, 237 U.S. 309 (1915) and Moore v. Dempsey, 261 U.S. 86 (1923), though in large part inconsistent with one another, together broadened the concept of jurisdiction to allow review of a claim of "mob domination" of what was in all other respects a trial in a court of competent jurisdiction.

In Johnson v. Zerbst, 304 U.S. 458 (1938), an indigent federal prisoner's claim that he was denied the right to counsel at his trial was held to state a contention going to the "power and authority" of the trial court, which might be reviewed on habeas. Finally, in Waley v. Johnston, 316 U.S. 101 (1942), the Court openly discarded the concept of jurisdiction—by then more a fiction than anything else—as a touchstone of the availability of federal habeas review, and acknowledged that such review is available for claims of "disregard of the constitutional rights of the accused, and where the writ is the only effective means of preserving his rights." Id., at 104–105. In Brown v. Allen, 344 U.S. 443 (1953), it was made explicit that a state prisoner's challenge to the trial court's resolution of dispositive federal issues is always fair game on federal habeas. Only last Term in Stone v. Powell, 428 U.S. 465 (1976), the Court removed from the purview of a federal habeas court challenges resting on the Fourth Amendment, where there has been a full and fair opportunity to raise them in the state court. See Schneckloth v. Bustamonte, 412 U.S. 218, 250 (1973) (Powell, J., concurring).

The degree of deference to be given to a state court's resolution of a federal law issue was elaborately canvassed in the Court's opinions in *Brown v. Allen*, supra. Speaking for the Court, Mr. Justice Reed stated that such "state adjudication carries the weight that federal practice gives to the conclusion of a court of last resort of another jurisdiction on federal constitutional issues. It is not res judicata." 344 U.S., at 458. The duty of the federal habeas court to hold a factfinding hearing in specific situations, notwithstanding the prior resolution of the issues in state court, was thoroughly explored in this Court's later decision in Townsend v. Sain, 372 U.S. 293 (1963). Congress addressed this aspect of federal habeas in 1966 when it amended § 2254 to deal with the problem treated in *Townsend*. 80 Stat. 1105. See LaVallee v. Delle Rose, 410 U.S. 690 (1973).

The exhaustion-of-state-remedies requirement was first articulated by this Court in the case of Ex parte Royall, 117 U.S. 241 (1886). There, a state defendant sought habeas in advance of trial on a claim that he had been indicted under an unconstitutional statute. The writ was dismissed by the District Court, and this Court affirmed, stating that while there was power in the federal courts to entertain such petitions, as a matter of comity they should usually stay their hand pending consideration of the issue in the normal course of the state trial. This rule has been followed in subsequent cases, e.g., Cook v. Hart, 146 U.S. 183 (1892); Whitten v. Tomlinson, 160 U.S. 231 (1895); Baker v. Grice, 169 U.S. 284 (1898);

Mooney v. Holohan, 294 U.S. 103 (1935), and has been incorporated into the language of § 2254. Like other issues surrounding the availability of federal habeas corpus relief, though, this line of authority has not been without historical uncertainties and changes in direction on the part of the Court. See Ex parte Hawk, 321 U.S. 114, 116–117 (1944); Darr v. Burford, 339 U.S. 200 (1950); Irvin v. Dowd, 359 U.S. 394, 405–406 (1959); Fay v. Noia, 372 U.S. 391, 435 (1963).

There is no need to consider here in greater detail these first three areas of controversy attendant to federal habeas review of state convictions. Only the fourth area—the adequacy of state grounds to bar federal habeas review—is presented in this case. The foregoing discussion of the other three is pertinent here only as it illustrates this Court's historic willingness to overturn or modify its earlier views of the scope of the writ, even where the statutory language authorizing judicial action has remained unchanged.

As to the role of adequate and independent state grounds, it is a well-established principle of federalism that a state decision resting on an adequate foundation of state substantive law is immune from review in the federal courts. Fox Film Corp. v. Muller, 296 U.S. 207 (1935); Murdock v. Memphis, 20 Wall. [87 U.S.] 590 (1875). The application of this principle in the context of a federal habeas proceeding has therefore excluded from consideration any questions of state *substantive* law, and thus effectively barred federal habeas review where questions of that sort are either the only ones raised by a petitioner or are in themselves dispositive of his case. The area of controversy which has developed has concerned the reviewability of federal claims which the state court has declined to pass on because not presented in the manner prescribed by its *procedural* rules. The adequacy of such an independent state procedural ground to prevent federal habeas review of the underlying federal issue has been treated very differently than where the state law ground is substantive. The pertinent decisions marking the Court's somewhat tortuous efforts to deal with this problem are: Ex parte Spencer, 228 U.S. 652 (1913); Daniels v. Allen, 344 U.S. 443 (1953); *Fay v. Noia*, supra; Davis v. United States, 411 U.S. 233 (1973); and Francis v. Henderson, 425 U.S. 536 (1976).

In *Daniels*, supra, petitioners' lawyer had failed to mail the appeal papers to the state supreme court on the last day provided by law for filing, and hand delivered them one day after that date. Citing the state rule requiring timely filing, the Supreme Court of North Carolina refused to hear the appeal. This Court, relying in part on its earlier decision in *Ex parte Spencer*, supra, held that federal habeas was not available to review a constitutional claim which could not have been reviewed on direct appeal here because it rested on an independent and adequate state procedural ground. 344 U.S., at 486–487.

In *Fay v. Noia*, supra, respondent Noia sought federal habeas to review a claim that his state court conviction had resulted from the introduction of a coerced confession in violation of the Fifth Amendment to the United States Constitution. While the convictions of his two codefendants were reversed on that ground in collateral proceedings following their appeals,

Noia did not appeal and the New York courts ruled that his subsequent coram nobis action was barred on account of that failure. This Court held that petitioner was nonetheless entitled to raise the claim in federal habeas, and thereby overruled its decision 10 years earlier in *Daniels v. Allen*, supra:

> "[T]he doctrine under which state procedural defaults are held to constitute an adequate and independent state law ground barring direct Supreme Court review is not to be extended to limit the power granted the federal courts under the federal habeas statute." 372 U.S., at 399.

As a matter of comity but not of federal power, the Court acknowledged "a limited discretion in the federal judge to deny relief ... to an applicant who had deliberately by-passed the orderly procedure of the state courts and in so doing has forfeited his state remedies." Id., at 438. In so stating, the Court made clear that the waiver must be knowing and actual—"an intentional relinquishment or abandonment of a known right or privilege." Id., at 439, quoting *Johnson v. Zerbst*, supra, at 464. Noting petitioner's "grisly choice" between acceptance of his life sentence and pursuit of an appeal which might culminate in a sentence of death, the Court concluded that there had been no deliberate bypass of the right to have the federal issues reviewed through a state appeal.[131]

A decade later we decided Davis v. United States, 411 U.S. 233 (1973), in which a federal prisoner's application under § 2255 sought for the first time to challenge the makeup of the grand jury which indicted him. The Government contended that he was barred by the requirement of Fed.Rule Crim.Proc. 12(b)(2) providing that such challenges must be raised "by motion before trial." The rule further provides that failure to so object constitutes a waiver of the objection, but that "the Court for cause shown may grant relief from the waiver." We noted that the rule "promulgated by this Court and, pursuant to 18 U.S.C. § 3771, 'adopted' by Congress, governs by its terms the manner in which the claims of defects in the institution of criminal proceedings may be waived," id., at 241, and held

---

131. Not long after *Fay*, the Court in Henry v. Mississippi, 379 U.S. 443 (1965), considered the question of the adequacy of a state procedural ground to bar Supreme Court review on direct review, and concluded that failure to comply with a state contemporaneous objection rule applying to the admission of evidence did not necessarily foreclose consideration of the underlying Fourth Amendment claim. The state procedural ground would be "adequate," and thus dispositive of the case on direct appeal to the United States Supreme Court, only where "the State's insistence on compliance with its procedural rule serves a legitimate state interest." Id., at 447. Because, the Court reasoned, the purposes of the contemporaneous objection rule were largely served by the motion for a directed verdict at the close of the State's case, enforcement of the contemporaneous objection rule was less than essential and therefore lacking in the necessary "legitimacy" to make it an adequate state ground.

Rather than searching the merits of the constitutional claim, though, the Court remanded for determination whether a separate adequate state ground might exist—that is, whether petitioner had knowingly and deliberately waived his right to object at trial for tactical or other reasons. This was the same type of waiver which the Court in *Fay* had said must be demonstrated in order to bar review on state procedural grounds in a federal habeas proceeding.

that this standard contained in the rule, rather than the *Fay v. Noia* concept of waiver, should pertain in federal habeas as on direct review. Referring to previous constructions of Rule 12(b)(2), we concluded that review of the claim should be barred on habeas, as on direct appeal, absent a showing of cause for the noncompliance and some showing of actual prejudice resulting from the alleged constitutional violation.

Last Term, in Francis v. Henderson, 425 U.S. 536 (1976), the rule of *Davis* was applied to the parallel case of a state procedural requirement that challenges to grand jury composition be raised before trial. The Court noted that there was power in the federal courts to entertain an application in such a case, but rested its holding on "considerations of comity and concerns for the orderly administration of criminal justice ...." Id., at 538–539. While there was no counterpart provision of the state rule which allowed an exception upon some showing of cause, the Court concluded that the standard derived from the federal rule should nonetheless be applied in that context since "[t]here is no reason to ... give greater preclusive effect to procedural defaults by federal defendants than to similar defaults by state defendants." Id., at 542, quoting Kaufman v. United States, 394 U.S. 217, 218 (1969). As applied to the federal petitions of state convicts, the *Davis* cause-and-prejudice standard was thus incorporated directly into the body of law governing the availability of federal habeas corpus review.

To the extent that the dicta of *Fay v. Noia* may be thought to have laid down an all-inclusive rule rendering state timely objection rules ineffective to bar review of underlying federal claims in federal habeas proceedings— absent a "knowing waiver" or a "deliberate by-pass" of the right to so object—its effect was limited by *Francis,* which applied a different rule and barred a habeas challenge to the makeup of a grand jury. Petitioner Wainwright in this case urges that we further confine its effect by applying the principle enunciated in *Francis* to a claimed error in the admission of a defendant's confession.

Respondent first contends that any discussion as to the effect that noncompliance with a state procedural rule should have on the availability of federal habeas is quite unnecessary because in his view Florida did not actually have a contemporaneous objection rule. He would have us inter-pret Florida Rule of Criminal Procedure 3.190(i), which petitioner asserts is a traditional "contemporaneous objection rule," to place the burden on the trial judge to raise on his own motion the question of the admissibility of any inculpatory statement. Respondent's approach is, to say the least, difficult to square with the language of the rule, which in unmistakable terms and with specified exceptions requires that the motion to suppress be raised before trial. Since all of the Florida appellate courts refused to review petitioner's federal claim on the merits after his trial, and since their action in so doing is quite consistent with a line of Florida authorities interpreting the rule in question as requiring a contemporaneous objection, we accept the State's position on this point. See Blatch v. State, 216 So.2d 261, 264 (3d Fla.D.C.App.1968); Dodd v. State, 232 So.2d 235, 238 (4th

Fla.D.C.App.1970); Thomas v. State, 249 So.2d 510, 512 (3d Fla.D.C.App. 1971).

Respondent also urges that a defendant has a right under Jackson v. Denno, 378 U.S. 368 (1964), to a hearing as to the voluntariness of a confession, even though the defendant does not object to its admission. But we do not read *Jackson* as creating any such requirement. In that case the defendant's objection to the use of his confession was brought to the attention of the trial court, id., at 374, and n. 4, and nothing in the Court's opinion suggests that a hearing would have been required even if it had not been. To the contrary, the Court prefaced its entire discussion of the merits of the case with a statement of the constitutional rule that was to prove dispositive—that a defendant has a "right at some stage in the proceedings *to object* to the use of the confession and to have a fair hearing and a reliable determination on the issue of voluntariness . . . ." Id., at 376—377 (emphasis added). Language in subsequent decisions of this Court has reaffirmed the view that the Constitution does not require a voluntariness hearing absent some contemporaneous challenge to the use of the confession.

We therefore conclude that Florida procedure did, consistently with the United States Constitution, require that petitioner's confession be challenged at trial or not at all, and thus his failure to timely object to its admission amounted to an independent and adequate state procedural ground which would have prevented direct review here. See Henry v. Mississippi, 379 U.S. 443 (1965). We thus come to the crux of this case. Shall the rule of *Francis v. Henderson*, supra, barring federal habeas review absent a showing of "cause" and "prejudice" attendant to a state procedural waiver, be applied to a waived objection to the admission of a confession at trial?[132] We answer that question in the affirmative.

As earlier noted in the opinion, since *Brown v. Allen*, supra, it has been the rule that the federal habeas petitioner who claims he is detained pursuant to a final judgment of a state court in violation of the U.S. Constitution is entitled to have the federal habeas court make its own independent determination of his federal claim, without being bound by the

---

132. Petitioner does not argue, and we do not pause to consider whether a bare allegation of a *Miranda* violation, without accompanying assertions going to the actual voluntariness or reliability of the confession, is a proper subject for consideration on federal habeas review, where there has been a full and fair opportunity to raise the argument in the state proceeding. See Stone v. Powell, 428 U.S. 465 (1976). We do not address the merits of that question because of our resolution of the case on alternative grounds.

[In Withrow v. Williams, 507 U.S. 680 (1993), a narrowly divided Court held that the rule of *Stone v. Powell*, excluding Fourth Amendment search-and-seizure claims from the scope of federal habeas corpus where the petitioner had a full and fair opportunity to litigate the claim in state court, should not be extended to also bar from federal habeas review Fifth Amendment self-incrimination claims predicated on violation of *Miranda*'s prophylactic constraints on custodial interrogation. Thus, *Miranda* claims remain cognizable on federal habeas corpus notwithstanding their prior adverse resolution after a "full and fair" suppression hearing in state court. Justice Souter wrote for the Court. There are dissents by Justice O'Connor, joined by Chief Justice Rehnquist, and by Justice Scalia, joined by Justice Thomas.]

determination on the merits of that claim reached in the state proceedings. This rule of *Brown v. Allen* is in no way changed by our holding today. Rather, we deal only with contentions of federal law which were *not* resolved on the merits in the state proceeding due to the petitioner's failure to raise them there as required by state procedure. We leave open for resolution in future decisions the precise definition of the "cause" and "prejudice" standard, and note here only that it is narrower than the standard set forth in dicta in *Fay v. Noia*, supra, which would make federal habeas review generally available to state convicts absent a knowing and deliberate waiver of the federal constitutional contention. It is the sweeping language of *Fay v. Noia*, supra, going far beyond the facts of the case eliciting it, which we today reject.[133]

The reasons for our rejection of it are several. The contemporaneous objection rule itself is by no means peculiar to Florida, and deserves greater respect than *Fay* gives it, both for the fact that it is employed by a coordinate jurisdiction within the federal system and for the many interests which it serves in its own right. A contemporaneous objection enables the record to be made with respect to the constitutional claim when the recollections of witnesses are freshest, not years later in a federal habeas proceeding. It enables the judge who observed the demeanor of those witnesses to make the factual determinations necessary for properly deciding the federal constitutional question. While the 1966 amendment to § 2254 requires deference to be given to such determinations made by state courts, the determinations themselves are less apt to be made in the first instance if there is no contemporaneous objection to the admission of the evidence on federal constitutional grounds.

A contemporaneous objection rule may lead to the exclusion of the evidence objected to, thereby making a major contribution to finality in criminal litigation. Without the evidence claimed to be vulnerable on federal constitutional grounds, the jury may acquit the defendant, and that will be the end of the case; or it may nonetheless convict the defendant, and he will have one less federal constitutional claim to assert in his federal habeas petition.[134] If the state trial judge admits the evidence in question

---

133.   We have no occasion today to consider the *Fay* rule as applied to the facts there confronting the Court. Whether the *Francis* rule should preclude federal habeas review of claims not made in accordance with state procedure where the criminal defendant has surrendered, other than for reasons of tactical advantage, the right to have all of his claims of trial error considered by a state appellate court, we leave for another day.

The Court in *Fay* stated its knowing and deliberate waiver rule in language which applied not only to the waiver of the right to appeal, but to failures to raise individual substantive objections in the state trial. Then, with a single sentence in footnote, the Court swept aside all decisions of this Court "to the extent that [they] may be read to suggest a standard of discretion in federal habeas corpus proceedings different from what we lay down today...." 372 U.S., at 439 n. 44. We do not choose to paint with a similarly broad brush here.

134.   Responding to concerns such as these, Mr. Justice Powell's concurring opinion last Term in Estelle v. Williams, 425 U.S. 501, 513 (1976), proposed an "inexcusable procedural default" test to bar the availability of federal habeas review where the substantive right claimed could have been safeguarded if the objection had been raised in a timely manner at trial.

after a full hearing, the federal habeas court pursuant to the 1966 amendment to § 2254 will gain significant guidance from the state ruling in this regard. Subtler considerations as well militate in favor of honoring a state contemporaneous objection rule. An objection on the spot may force the prosecution to take a hard look at its hole card, and even if the prosecutor thinks that the state trial judge will admit the evidence he must contemplate the possibility of reversal by the state appellate courts or the ultimate issuance of a writ of federal habeas corpus based on the impropriety of the state court's rejection of the federal constitutional claim.

We think that the rule of *Fay v. Noia*, broadly stated, may encourage "sand bagging" on the part of defense lawyers, who may take their chances on a verdict of not guilty in a state trial court and intend to raise their constitutional claims in a federal habeas court if their initial gamble does not pay off. The refusal of federal habeas courts to honor contemporaneous objection rules may also make state courts themselves less stringent in their enforcement. Under the rule of *Fay v. Noia*, supra, state appellate courts know that a federal constitutional issue raised for the first time in the proceeding before them may well be decided in any event by a federal *habeas* tribunal. Thus their choice is between addressing the issue notwithstanding the petitioner's failure to timely object, or else face the prospect that the federal habeas court will decide the question without the benefit of their views.

The failure of the federal habeas courts generally to require compliance with a contemporaneous objection rule tends to detract from the perception of the trial of a criminal case in state court as a decisive and portentous event. A defendant has been accused of a serious crime, and this is the time and place set for him to be tried by a jury of his peers and found either guilty or not guilty by that jury. To the greatest extent possible all issues which bear on this charge should be determined in this proceeding: the accused is in the court room, the jury is in the box, the judge is on the bench, and the witnesses, having been subpoenaed and duly sworn, await their turns to testify. Society's resources have been concentrated at that time and place in order to decide, within the limits of human fallibility, the question of guilt or innocence of one of its citizens. Any procedural rule which encourages the result that those proceedings be as free of error as possible is thoroughly desirable, and the contemporaneous objection rule surely falls within this classification.

We believe the adoption of the *Francis* rule in this situation will have the salutary effect of making the state trial on the merits the "main event," so to speak, rather than a tryout on the road for what will later be the determinative federal habeas hearing. There is nothing in the Constitution or in the language of § 2254 which requires that the state trial on the issue of guilt or innocence be devoted largely to the testimony of fact witnesses directed to the elements of the state crime, while only later will there occur in a federal habeas hearing a full airing of the federal constitutional claims which were not raised in the state proceedings. If a criminal defendant thinks that an action of the state trial court is about to deprive him of a federal constitutional right there is every reason for his following state procedure in making known his objection.

The "cause" and "prejudice" exception of the *Francis* rule will afford an adequate guarantee, we think, that the rule will not prevent a federal habeas court from adjudicating for the first time the federal constitutional claim of a defendant who in the absence of such an adjudication will be the victim of a miscarriage of justice. Whatever precise content may be given those terms by later cases, we feel confident in holding without further elaboration that they do not exist here. Respondent has advanced no explanation whatever for his failure to object at trial,[135] and, as the proceeding unfolded, the trial judge is certainly not to be faulted for failing to question the admission of the confession himself. The other evidence of guilt presented at trial, moreover, was substantial to a degree that would negate any possibility of actual prejudice resulting to the respondent from the admission of his inculpatory statement.

We accordingly conclude that the judgment of the Court of Appeals for the Fifth Circuit must be reversed, and the cause remanded to the United States District Court for the Middle District of Florida with instructions to dismiss respondent's petition for a writ of habeas corpus.

It is so ordered.

■ MR. CHIEF JUSTICE BURGER, concurring.

I concur fully in the judgment and in the Court's opinion. I write separately to emphasize one point which, to me, seems of critical importance to this case. In my view, the "deliberate bypass" standard enunciated in Fay v. Noia, 372 U.S. 391 (1963), was never designed for, and is inapplicable to, errors—even of constitutional dimension—alleged to have been committed during trial.

.   .   .   .   .

■ MR. JUSTICE STEVENS, concurring.

.   .   .   .   .

■ MR. JUSTICE WHITE, concurring in the judgment.

.   .   .   .   .

■ MR. JUSTICE BRENNAN, with whom MR. JUSTICE MARSHALL joins, dissenting.

---

135. In *Henry v. Mississippi*, supra, the Court noted that decisions of counsel relating to trial strategy, even when made without the consultation of the defendant, would bar direct federal review of claims thereby foregone, except where "the circumstances are exceptional." 379 U.S., at 451.

Last Term in Estelle v. Williams, 425 U.S. 501 (1976), the Court reiterated the burden on a defendant to be bound by the trial judgments of his lawyer.

"Under our adversary system, once a defendant has the assistance of counsel the vast array of trial decisions, strategic and tactical, which must be made before and during trial rests with the accused and his attorney." Id., at 512.

Over the course of the last decade, the deliberate bypass standard announced in Fay v. Noia, 372 U.S. 391, 438–439 (1963), has played a central role in efforts by the federal judiciary to accommodate the constitutional rights of the individual with the States' interests in the integrity of their judicial procedural regimes. The Court today decides that this standard should no longer apply with respect to procedural defaults occurring during the trial of a criminal defendant. In its place, the Court adopts the two-part "cause" and "prejudice" test originally developed in Davis v. United States, 411 U.S. 233 (1973), and Francis v. Henderson, 425 U.S. 536 (1976). As was true with these earlier cases,[136] however, today's decision makes no effort to provide concrete guidance as to the content of those terms. More particularly, left unanswered is the thorny question that must be recognized to be central to a realistic rationalization of this area of law: How should the federal habeas court treat a state procedural default that is attributable purely and simply to the error or negligence of a defendant's trial counsel? Because this key issue remains unresolved, I shall attempt in this opinion a re-examination of the policies that should inform—and in *Fay* did inform—the selection of the standard governing the availability of federal habeas corpus jurisdiction in the face of an intervening state procedural default.

. . . . .[137]

---

136. The Court began its retreat from the deliberate bypass standard of *Fay* in *Davis v. United States*, supra, where a congressional intent to restrict the bypass formulation with respect to collateral review under 28 U.S.C. § 2255 was found to inhere in Rule 12(b)(2) of the Federal Rules of Criminal Procedure. By relying upon Congress' purported intent, *Davis* managed to evade any consideration of the justifications and any shortcomings of the bypass test. Subsequently, in *Francis v. Henderson*, supra, a controlling congressional expression of intent no longer was available, and the Court therefore employed the shibboleth of "considerations of comity and federalism" to justify application of *Davis* to a § 2254 proceeding. 425 U.S., at 541. Again, any coherent analysis of the bypass standard or the waivability of constitutional rights was avoided—as it was that same day in Estelle v. Williams, 425 U.S. 501 (1976), which proceeded to find a surrender of a constitutional right in an opinion that was simply oblivious to some 40 years of existing case law.... Thus, while today's opinion follows from *Davis, Francis,* and *Estelle,* the entire edifice is a mere house of cards whose foundation has escaped any systematic inspection.

[**137.** There was "cause" for failure of defendant's counsel to raise a claim in accordance with state procedure where the claim was so novel that its legal basis was not reasonably available to counsel, and thus the claim could be raised on habeas corpus. Reed v. Ross, 468 U.S. 1 (1984). But an inadvertent failure by counsel to raise a point on appeal is not "cause" within the rule of *Wainwright v. Sykes*. See Murray v. Carrier, 477 U.S. 478 (1986).

It was held in Edwards v. Carpenter, 529 U.S. 446 (2000), that ineffective assistance of counsel (IAC) is not "cause" excusing ineffective counsel's procedural default of an independent constitutional claim for federal habeas relief. Although counsel's procedural default forfeits the independent constitutional basis for relief from the underlying state-court conviction, the defendant may still seek federal habeas relief on IAC grounds.

The Supreme Court has held that the "plain statement" rule of Michigan v. Long, 463 U.S. 1032 (1983), applies also to federal habeas-corpus proceedings so that a procedural default will not bar consideration of a federal claim on habeas review unless the state court rendering judgment in the case has clearly and expressly stated that the judgment rested on a state procedural bar. Harris v. Reed, 489 U.S. 255 (1989). But in Coleman v. Thompson, 501 U.S. 722 (1991), it was held that the "plain statement" rule applies only if the decision appears to rest primarily on, or to be interwoven with, federal law. The *Coleman* case also held that the "cause" and "prejudice" rule applies to failure to take a direct appeal.

The constitutionality of *Coleman v. Thompson* and other pre-AEDPA cases curtailing the scope of federal habeas-corpus jurisdiction was questioned in Steiker, Incorporating the Suspension Clause: Is There a Constitutional Right to Federal Habeas Corpus for State Prisoners?, 92 Mich.L.Rev. 862 (1994). See also Woolhandler, Demodeling Habeas, 45 Stan.L.Rev. 575 (1993).

Is it unconstitutional, and hence subject to prohibition by federal writ of habeas corpus, to execute an innocent person if the judgment of conviction and sentence of death resulted from state-court proceedings that suffered from no federal constitutional defect, and it is only because of newly discovered evidence that the innocence of the condemned has become apparent? In Herrera v. Collins, 506 U.S. 390 (1993), the Court assumed arguendo "that in a capital case a truly persuasive demonstration of 'actual innocence' made after trial would render the execution of a defendant unconstitutional, and warrant federal habeas relief if there were no state avenue open to process such a claim." In separate opinions a total of five Justices indicated that in an appropriate case they would turn the assumption into a holding, and only Justices Scalia and Thomas indicated that actual innocence, unconnected to any federal constitutional error in the underlying state proceedings, was irrelevant to the constitutionality of carrying out an execution. But Herrera's claim of "actual innocence" was held too weak by the majority to warrant even a hearing, and the denial of habeas relief was affirmed. See Steiker, Innocence and Federal Habeas, 41 UCLA L.Rev. 303 (1993).

In Schlup v. Delo, 513 U.S. 298 (1995), the Court held that when a prisoner who has been sentenced to death raises a claim of actual innocence to avoid a procedural bar that otherwise would prevent the consideration of the merits of his constitutional claim, the test is whether the constitutional violation has *probably* resulted in the conviction of one who is actually innocent. The prisoner was not required to show "by clear and convincing evidence" that but for a constitutional error, no reasonable juror would have found him guilty. Congress apparently substituted the "clear and convincing evidence" standard in 28 U.S.C. § 2244(b)(2) as amended by AEDPA, but without explicitly overruling *Schlup*. The wisdom and constitutionality of this statutory change are questioned in Note, The Gateway for Successive Habeas Petitions: An Argument for *Schlup v. Delo*'s Probability Standard for Actual Innocence Claims, 19 Cardozo L.Rev. 2341 (1998).

The Anti–Drug Abuse Act of 1988 not only established a federal death penalty for certain drug offenses but also created a statutory right to free counsel and investigatory services for any indigent capital defendant seeking federal habeas relief from a death sentence, 21 U.S.C. § 848(q)(4)(B). Under 28 U.S.C. § 2251, a federal court can stay a death sentence pending resolution of a petition for habeas relief. But under the strict "abuse of the writ" doctrine of McCleskey v. Zant, 499 U.S. 467, 494 (1991), since codified by 28 U.S.C. § 2254(b) as amended by AEDPA, virtually any claims for relief not included in the first habeas petition to be litigated to judgment in federal court will be deemed waived. For indigent capital defendants lacking habeas counsel and facing imminent execution, *McCleskey* appeared to create a classic "Catch 22" situation. If they filed an uncounseled, pro forma federal habeas petition as the predicate both for a formal request for counsel and for a stay of execution pending recruitment of counsel, they were at severe risk that the petition would be summarily dismissed on the merits for failing to state a substantial federal claim under the heightened-pleading requirements applicable to habeas petitions. See Rule 4, Rules Governing 2254 Cases in the United States District Courts. Should this occur, the stay might still remain in effect, but to no purpose other than postponing a now inevitable doom, since even the most meritorious of claims to habeas relief that duly appointed § 848 counsel might later discover and present would then be summarily dismissed as a "successive petition" and hence an "abuse of the writ." The Supreme Court resolved this problem in McFarland v. Scott, 512 U.S. 849 (1994), holding that a pro se request for § 848 counsel, unaccompanied by any attempt to plead a basis for habeas relief, was sufficient to permit a federal district court both to appoint counsel and to stay the execution of the prisoner pending the preparation by counsel of what will be regarded as an initial petition for habeas relief.]

Lee v. Kemna

Supreme Court of the United States, 2002.
534 U.S. 362, 122 S.Ct. 877, 151 L.Ed.2d 820.

■ JUSTICE GINSBURG delivered the opinion of the Court.

Petitioner Remon Lee asserts that a Missouri trial court deprived him of due process when the court refused to grant an overnight continuance of his trial. Lee sought the continuance to locate subpoenaed, previously present, but suddenly missing witnesses key to his defense against felony charges. On direct review, the Missouri Court of Appeals disposed of the case on a state procedural ground. That court found the continuance motion defective under the State's rules. It therefore declined to consider the merits of Lee's plea that the trial court had denied him a fair opportunity to present a defense. Whether the state ground dispositive in the Missouri Court of Appeals is adequate to preclude federal habeas corpus review is the question we here consider and decide.

On the third day of his trial, Lee was convicted of first-degree murder and armed criminal action. His sole affirmative defense was an alibi; Lee maintained he was in California, staying with his family, when the Kansas City crimes for which he was indicted occurred. Lee's mother, stepfather, and sister voluntarily came to Missouri to testify on his behalf. They were sequestered in the courthouse at the start of the trial's third day. For reasons then unknown, they were not in the courthouse later in the day when defense counsel sought to present their testimony. Discovering their absence, defense counsel moved for a continuance until the next morning so that he could endeavor to locate the three witnesses and bring them back to court.

The trial judge denied the motion, stating that it looked to him as though the witnesses had "in effect abandoned the defendant" and that, for personal reasons, he would "not be able to be [in court the next day] to try the case." Furthermore, he had "another case set for trial" the next weekday. The trial resumed without pause, no alibi witnesses testified, and the jury found Lee guilty as charged.

Neither the trial judge nor the prosecutor identified any procedural flaw in the presentation or content of Lee's motion for a continuance. The Missouri Court of Appeals, however, held the denial of the motion proper because Lee's counsel had failed to comply with Missouri Supreme Court Rules not relied upon or even mentioned in the trial court: Rule 24.09, which requires that continuance motions be in written form, accompanied by an affidavit; and Rule 24.10, which sets out the showings a movant must make to gain a continuance grounded on the absence of witnesses.

We hold that the Missouri Rules, as injected into this case by the state appellate court, did not constitute a state ground adequate to bar federal habeas review. Caught in the midst of a murder trial and unalerted to any procedural defect in his presentation, defense counsel could hardly be expected to divert his attention from the proceedings rapidly unfolding in the courtroom and train, instead, on preparation of a written motion and affidavit. Furthermore, the trial court, at the time Lee moved for a continuance, had in clear view the information needed to rule intelligently on the merits of the motion. Beyond doubt, Rule 24.10 serves the State's important interest in regulating motions for a continuance—motions readily susceptible to use as a delaying tactic. But under the circumstances of this case, we hold that petitioner Lee, having substantially, if imperfectly, made the basic showings Rule 24.10 prescribes, qualifies for adjudication of his federal, due process claim. His asserted right to defend should not depend on a formal "ritual ... [that] would further no perceivable state interest." Osborne v. Ohio, 495 U.S. 103, 124 (1990) (quoting James v. Kentucky, 466 U.S. 341, 349 (1984) (in turn quoting Staub v. City of Baxley, 355 U.S. 313, 320 (1958))) (internal quotation marks omitted).

I

On August 27, 1992, Reginald Rhodes shot and killed Steven Shelby on a public street in Kansas City, Missouri. He then jumped into the passenger side of a waiting truck, which sped away. Rhodes pleaded guilty, and Remon Lee, the alleged getaway driver, was tried for first-degree murder and armed criminal action.

Lee's trial took place within the span of three days in February 1994. His planned alibi defense—that he was in California with his family at the time of the murder—surfaced at each stage of the proceedings....

The planned alibi defense figured prominently in counsels' opening statements on day two of Lee's trial. The prosecutor, at the close of her statement, said she expected an alibi defense from Lee and would present testimony to disprove it. Defense counsel, in his opening statement, described the alibi defense in detail, telling the jury that the evidence would show Lee was not in Kansas City, and therefore could not have engaged in crime there, in August 1992. Specifically, defense counsel said three close family members would testify that Lee came to visit them in Ventura, California, in July 1992 and stayed through the end of October. Lee's mother and stepfather would say they picked him up from the airport at the start of his visit and returned him there at the end. Lee's sister would testify that Lee resided with her and her four children during this time. All three would affirm that they saw Lee regularly throughout his unbroken sojourn.

During the prosecution case, two eyewitnesses to the shooting identified Lee as the driver. The first, Reginald Williams, admitted during cross-examination that he had told Lee's first defense counsel in a taped interview that Rhodes, not Lee, was the driver.... The second eyewitness, William Sanders, was unable to pick Lee out of a photographic array on the day of the shooting ....

Two other witnesses, Rhonda Shelby and Lynne Bryant, were called by the prosecutor. Each testified that she knew Lee and had seen him in Kansas City the night before the murder. Both said Lee was with Rhodes, who had asked where Steven Shelby (the murder victim) was. The State offered no physical evidence connecting Lee to the murder and did not suggest a motive.

The defense case began at 10:25 a.m. on the third and final day of trial. Two impeachment witnesses testified that morning. Just after noon, counsel met with the trial judge in chambers for a charge conference. At that meeting, the judge apparently agreed to give an alibi instruction submitted by Lee.[138]

At some point in the late morning or early afternoon, the alibi witnesses left the courthouse. Just after one o'clock, Lee took the stand outside the presence of the jury and, for the record, responded to his counsel's questions concerning his knowledge of the witnesses' unanticipated absence. Lee, under oath, stated that Gladys and James Edwards and Laura Lee had voluntarily traveled from California to testify on his behalf. He affirmed his counsel's representations that the three witnesses, then staying with Lee's uncle in Kansas City, had met with Lee's counsel and received subpoenas from him; he similarly affirmed that the witnesses had met with a Kansas City police officer, who interviewed them on behalf of the prosecutor. Lee said he had seen his sister, mother, and stepfather in the courthouse that morning at 8:30 and later during a recess.

On discovering the witnesses' absence, Lee could not call them at his uncle's house because there was no phone on the premises. He asked his girlfriend to try to find the witnesses, but she was unable to do so. Although Lee did not know the witnesses' whereabouts at that moment, he said he knew "in fact they didn't go back to California" because "they had some ministering ... to do" in Kansas City both Thursday and Friday evenings. He asked for "a couple hours' continuance [to] try to locate them, because it's very valuable to my case." Defense counsel subsequently moved for a continuance until the next morning, to gain time to enforce the subpoenas he had served on the witnesses. The trial judge responded that he could not hold court the next day because "my daughter is going to be in the hospital all day ... [s]o I've got to stay with her."

After a brief further exchange between court and counsel, the judge denied the continuance request....

. . . . .

When the jurors returned, defense counsel informed them that the three witnesses from California he had planned to call "were here and have gone" ; further, counsel did not "know why they've gone." The defense then rested....

After deliberating for three hours, the jury convicted Lee on both counts. He was subsequently sentenced to prison for life without possibility of parole.

. . . . .

---

138. That Lee had submitted an alibi instruction during the charge conference became apparent when the trial judge, delivering the charge, began to read the proposed instruction. He was interrupted by the prosecutor and defense counsel, who reminded him that the instruction was no longer necessary.

The Missouri Court of Appeals affirmed Lee's conviction and the denial of postconviction relief. State v. Lee, 935 S.W.2d 689 (1996). The appellate court first noted that Lee's continuance motion was oral and therefore did not comply with Missouri Supreme Court Rule 24.09 (Rule 24.09), which provides that such applications shall be in written form, accompanied by an affidavit. "Thus," the Court of Appeals said, "the trial court could have properly denied the motion for a failure to comply with Rule 24.09." Even assuming the adequacy of Lee's oral motion, the court continued, the application "was made without the factual showing required by Rule 24.10." The court did not say which components of Rule 24.10 were unsatisfied. "When a denial to grant a motion for continuance is based on a deficient application," the Court of Appeals next said, "it does not constitute an abuse of discretion." Lee's subsequent motions for rehearing and transfer to the Missouri Supreme Court were denied.

In January 1998, Lee, proceeding pro se, filed an application for writ of habeas corpus in the United States District Court for the Western District of Missouri. Lee once again challenged the denial of his continuance motion. He appended affidavits from the three witnesses, each of whom swore to Lee's alibi; sister, mother, and stepfather alike stated that they had left the courthouse while the trial was underway because a court officer told them their testimony would not be needed that day. Lee maintained that the State had engineered the witnesses' departure; accordingly, he asserted that prosecutorial misconduct, not anything over which he had control, prompted the need for a continuance.

The District Court denied the writ. The witnesses' affidavits were not cognizable in federal habeas proceedings, the court held, because Lee could have offered them to the state courts but failed to do so. The Federal District Court went on to reject Lee's continuance claim, finding in the Missouri Court of Appeals' invocation of Rule 24.10 an adequate and independent state-law ground barring further review.

The Court of Appeals for the Eighth Circuit granted a certificate of appealability, limited to the question whether Lee's "due process rights were violated by the state trial court's failure to allow him a continuance," and affirmed the denial of Lee's habeas petition. 213 F.3d 1037 (2000) (per curiam).... "The Missouri Court of Appeals rejected Lee's claim because his motion for a continuance did not comply with [Rules] 24.09 and 24.10," the Eighth Circuit ... stated. Thus, that court concluded, "the claim was procedurally defaulted." 213 F.3d, at 1038.

. . . . .

We granted Lee's pro se petition for a writ of certiorari, 531 U.S. 1189 (2001), and appointed counsel, 532 U.S. 956 (2001). We now vacate the Court of Appeals judgment.

II

This Court will not take up a question of federal law presented in a case "if the decision of [the state] court rests on a state law ground that is

independent of the federal question and *adequate* to support the judgment."
Coleman v. Thompson, 501 U.S. 722, 729 (1991) (emphases added). The
rule applies with equal force whether the state-law ground is substantive or
procedural. We first developed the independent and adequate state ground
doctrine in cases on direct review from state courts, and later applied it as
well "in deciding whether federal district courts should address the claims
of state prisoners in habeas corpus actions." Ibid. "[T]he adequacy of state
procedural bars to the assertion of federal questions," we have recognized,
is not within the State's prerogative finally to decide; rather, adequacy "is
itself a federal question." Douglas v. Alabama, 380 U.S. 415, 422 (1965).

Lee does not suggest that Rules 24.09 and 24.10, as brought to bear on
this case by the Missouri Court of Appeals, depended in any way on federal
law. Nor does he question the general applicability of the two codified
Rules. He does maintain that both Rules—addressed initially to Missouri
trial courts, but in his case invoked only at the appellate stage—are
inadequate, under the extraordinary circumstances of this case, to close out
his federal, fair-opportunity-to-defend claim. We now turn to that dispositive issue.

Ordinarily, violation of "firmly established and regularly followed"
state rules—for example, those involved in this case—will be adequate to
foreclose review of a federal claim. James v. Kentucky, 466 U.S. 341, 348
(1984); see Ford v. Georgia, 498 U.S. 411, 422–424 (1991). There are,
however, exceptional cases in which exorbitant application of a generally
sound rule renders the state ground inadequate to stop consideration of a
federal question. See Davis v. Wechsler, 263 U.S. 22, 24 (1923) (Holmes, J.)
("Whatever springes the State may set for those who are endeavoring to
assert rights that the State confers, the assertion of federal rights, when
plainly and reasonably made, is not to be defeated under the name of local
practice."). This case fits within that limited category.

Our analysis and conclusion are informed and controlled by Osborne v.
Ohio, 495 U.S. 103 (1990). There, the Court considered Osborne's objections that his child pornography conviction violated due process because
the trial judge had not required the government to prove two elements of
the alleged crime: lewd exhibition and scienter. Id., at 107, 122–125. The
Ohio Supreme Court held the constitutional objections procedurally barred
because Osborne had failed to object contemporaneously to the judge's
charge, which did not instruct the jury that it could convict only for
conduct that satisfied both the scienter and the lewdness elements. . . .

We agreed with the State that Osborne's failure to urge the trial court
to instruct the jury on scienter qualified as an "adequate state-law ground
[to] preven[t] us from reaching Osborne's due process contention on that
point." 495 U.S., at 123. Ohio law, which was not in doubt, required proof
of scienter unless the applicable statute specified otherwise. The State's
contemporaneous objection rule, we observed, "serves the State's important interest in ensuring that counsel do their part in preventing trial
courts from providing juries with erroneous instructions." Id., at 123.

"With respect to the trial court's failure to instruct on lewdness, however, we reach[ed] a different conclusion." Ibid. Counsel for Osborne had made his position on that essential element clear in a motion to dismiss overruled just before trial, and the trial judge, "in no uncertain terms," id., at 124, had rejected counsel's argument. After a brief trial, the judge charged the jury in line with his ruling against Osborne on the pretrial motion to dismiss. Counsel's failure to object to the charge by reasserting the argument he had made unsuccessfully on the motion to dismiss, we held, did not deter our disposition of the constitutional question. "Given this sequence of events," we explained, it was proper to "reach Osborne's [second] due process claim," for Osborne's attorney had "pressed the issue of the State's failure of proof on lewdness before the trial court and ... nothing would be gained by requiring Osborne's lawyer to object a second time, specifically to the jury instructions." Ibid. In other words, although we did not doubt the general applicability of the Ohio Rule of Criminal Procedure requiring contemporaneous objection to jury charges, we nevertheless concluded that, in this atypical instance, the Rule would serve "no perceivable state interest." Ibid. (internal quotation marks omitted).

Our decision, we added in *Osborne,* followed from "the general principle that an objection which is ample and timely to bring the alleged federal error to the attention of the trial court and enable it to take appropriate corrective action is sufficient to serve legitimate state interests, and therefore sufficient to preserve the claim for review here." Id., at 125 (quoting *Douglas,* 380 U.S., at 422 (internal quotation marks omitted)). This general principle, and the unusual "sequence of events" before us—rapidly unfolding events that Lee and his counsel could not have foreseen, and for which they were not at all responsible—similarly guide our judgment in this case.

The dissent strives mightily to distinguish *Osborne,* an opinion JUSTICES KENNEDY and SCALIA joined, but cannot do so convincingly. . . .

. . . . .

Three considerations, in combination, lead us to conclude that this case falls within the small category of cases in which asserted state grounds are inadequate to block adjudication of a federal claim. First, when the trial judge denied Lee's motion, he stated a reason that could not have been countered by a perfect motion for continuance. The judge said he could not carry the trial over until the next day because he had to be with his daughter in the hospital; the judge further informed counsel that another scheduled trial prevented him from concluding Lee's case on the following business day. Although the judge hypothesized that the witnesses had "abandoned" Lee, he had not "a scintilla of evidence or a shred of information" on which to base this supposition, 213 F.3d, at 1040 (Bennett, C. J., dissenting).

Second, no published Missouri decision directs flawless compliance with Rules 24.09 and 24.10 in the unique circumstances this case presents—the sudden, unanticipated, and at the time unexplained disappearance of critical, subpoenaed witnesses on what became the trial's last day.

Lee's predicament, from all that appears, was one Missouri courts had not confronted before. "[A]lthough [the rules themselves] may not [have been] novel, ... [their] application to the facts here was." Sullivan v. Little Hunting Park, Inc., 396 U.S. 229, 245 (1969) (Harlan, J., dissenting).

Third and most important ... Lee substantially complied with Missouri's key Rule.... In sum, we are drawn to the conclusion reached by the Eighth Circuit dissenter: "[A]ny seasoned trial lawyer would agree" that insistence on a written continuance application, supported by an affidavit, "in the midst of trial upon the discovery that subpoenaed witnesses are suddenly absent, would be so bizarre as to inject an Alice-in-Wonderland quality into the proceedings." 213 F.3d, at 1047.

．　．　．　．　．

Rule 24.10, like other state and federal rules of its genre, serves a governmental interest of undoubted legitimacy. It is designed to arm trial judges with the information needed to rule reliably on a motion to delay a scheduled criminal trial. The Rule's essential requirements, however, were substantially met in this case. Few transcript pages need be read to reveal the information called for by Rule 24.10. "[N]othing would [have] be[en] gained by requiring" Lee's counsel to recapitulate in (a), (b), (c), (d) order the showings the Rule requires.... "Where it is inescapable that the defendant sought to invoke the substance of his federal right, the asserted state-law defect in form must be more evident than it is here." *James v. Kentucky*, 466 U.S., at 351.[139]

The dissent critiques at great length Henry v. Mississippi, 379 U.S. 443 (1965), a case on which we do not rely in reaching our decision.[140] This protracted exercise is a prime example of the dissent's vigorous attack on an imaginary opinion that bears scant, if any, resemblance to the actual decision rendered today. We chart no new course. We merely apply *Osborne*'s sound reasoning and limited holding to the circumstances of this case. If the dissent's shrill prediction that today's decision will disrupt our federal system were accurate, we would have seen clear signals of such

---

139. The dissent, indulging in hyperbole, describes our narrow opinion as a "comb" and "searc[h]" order to lower courts. We hold, simply and only, that Lee satisfied Rule 24.10's essential elements. [W]e place no burden *on courts* to rummage through a ponderous trial transcript in search of an excuse for a defense counsel's lapse. The dissent, in this and much else, tilts at a windmill of its own invention.

140. *Henry* has been called "radical," ... R. Fallon, D. Meltzer, & D. Shapiro, Hart and Wechsler's The Federal Courts and the Federal System 584 (4th ed.1996) ..., not for pursuing an "as applied" approach, as the dissent states, but for suggesting that the failure to comply with an anterior procedure was cured by compliance with some subsequent procedure. See id., at 584–585. In *Henry*, the Court indicated that although there was no contemporaneous objection at trial to the admission of evidence alleged to have been derived from an unconstitutional search, a directed verdict motion made at the end of the prosecution's case was an adequate substitute. 379 U.S., at 448–449. Nothing of the sort is involved in this case. Lee is not endeavoring to designate some later motion, e.g., one for a new trial, as an adequate substitute for a continuance motion. The question here is whether the movant must enunciate again, when making the right motion at the right time, supporting statements plainly and repeatedly made the days before....

disruption in the eleven years since *Osborne.* The absence of even dim distress signals demonstrates both the tight contours of *Osborne* and the groundlessness of the dissent's frantic forecast of doom. See United States v. Travers, 514 F.2d 1171, 1174 (CA2 1974) (Friendly, J.) ("Cassandra-like predictions in dissent are not a sure guide to the breadth of the majority's ruling").

. . . . .

To summarize, there was in this case no reference whatever in the trial court to Rules 24.09 and 24.10, the purported procedural impediments the Missouri Court of Appeals later pressed. Nor is there any indication that formally perfect compliance with the Rules would have changed the trial court's decision. Furthermore, no published Missouri decision demands unmodified application of the Rules in the urgent situation Lee's case presented. Finally, the purpose of the Rules was served by Lee's submissions both immediately before and at the short trial. Under the special circumstances so combined, we conclude that no adequate state-law ground hinders consideration of Lee's federal claim.[141]

Because both the District Court and the Court of Appeals held Lee's due process claim procedurally barred, neither court addressed it on the merits. We remand the case for that purpose. See National Collegiate Athletic Assn. v. Smith, 525 U.S. 459, 470 (1999) (We ordinarily "do not decide in the first instance issues not decided below.").

* * *

For the reasons stated, the judgment of the United States Court of Appeals for the Eighth Circuit is vacated, and the case is remanded for further proceedings consistent with this opinion.

It is so ordered.

■ JUSTICE KENNEDY, with whom JUSTICE SCALIA and JUSTICE THOMAS join, dissenting.

The Court's decision commits us to a new and, in my view, unwise course. Its contextual approach places unnecessary and unwarranted new responsibilities on state trial judges, injects troubling instability into the criminal justice system, and reaches the wrong result even under its own premises. These considerations prompt my respectful dissent.

I

The rule that an adequate state procedural ground can bar federal review of a constitutional claim has always been "about federalism," Coleman v. Thompson, 501 U.S. 722, 726 (1991), for it respects state rules of procedure while ensuring that they do not discriminate against federal

---

141. In view of this disposition, we do not reach further questions raised by Lee, i.e., whether he has shown "cause" and "prejudice" to excuse any default, Wainwright v. Sykes, 433 U.S. 72, 90–91 (1977), or has made sufficient showing of "actual innocence" under Schlup v. Delo, 513 U.S. 298, 315 (1995), to warrant a hearing of the kind ordered in that case.

rights. The doctrine originated in cases on direct review, where the existence of an independent and adequate state ground deprives this Court of jurisdiction. The rule applies with equal force, albeit for somewhat different reasons, when federal courts review the claims of state prisoners in habeas corpus proceedings, where ignoring procedural defaults would circumvent the jurisdictional limits of direct review and "undermine the State's interest in enforcing its laws." Id., at 731.

Given these considerations of comity and federalism, a procedural ground will be deemed inadequate only when the state rule "force[s] resort to an arid ritual of meaningless form." Staub v. City of Baxley, 355 U.S. 313, 320 (1958). *Staub*'s formulation was imprecise, but the cases that followed clarified the two essential components of the adequate state ground inquiry: first, the defendant must have notice of the rule; and second, the State must have a legitimate interest in its enforcement.

The Court need not determine whether the requirement of Missouri Supreme Court Rule 24.09 that all continuance motions be made in writing would withstand scrutiny under the second part of this test . . . . Even if it could be assumed, for the sake of argument, that Rule 24.09 would not afford defendants a fair opportunity to raise a federal claim, the same cannot be said of Rule 24.10. The latter Rule simply requires a party requesting a continuance on account of missing witnesses to explain why it is needed, and the Rule serves an undoubted and important state interest in facilitating the orderly management of trials. Other States have similar requirements. . . . The Court's explicit depreciation of Rule 24.10—and implicit depreciation of its many counterparts—is inconsistent with the respect due to state courts and state proceedings.

A

The initial step of the adequacy inquiry considers whether the State has put litigants on notice of the rule. The Court will disregard state procedures not firmly established and regularly followed. . . .

. . . . .

Lee was on notice of the applicability of Rule 24.10, and the Court appears to recognize as much. The consideration most important to the Court's analysis . . . relates not to this initial question, but rather to the second part of the adequacy inquiry, which asks whether the rule serves a legitimate state interest. Here, too, in my respectful view, the Court errs.

B

A defendant's failure to comply with a firmly established and regularly followed rule has been deemed an inadequate state ground only when the State had no legitimate interest in the rule's enforcement. . . . Most state procedures are supported by various legitimate interests, so established rules have been set aside only when they appeared to be calculated to discriminate against federal law, or, as one treatise puts it, they did not afford the defendant "a reasonable opportunity to assert federal rights."

16B Charles Alan Wright, Arthur R. Miller, & Edward H. Cooper, Federal Practice and Procedure, § 4027, p. 392 (2d ed.1996) . . . .

In light of this standard, the adequacy of Rule 24.10 has been demonstrated. Delays in criminal trials can be "a distinct reproach to the administration of justice," Powell v. Alabama, 287 U.S. 45, 59 (1932), and States have a strong interest in ensuring that continuances are granted only when necessary. Rule 24.10 anticipates that at certain points during a trial, important witnesses may not be available. In these circumstances, a continuance may be appropriate if the movant makes certain required representations demonstrating good cause to believe the continuance would make a real difference to the case.

Yet the Court deems Lee's default inadequate because, it says, to the extent feasible under the circumstances, he substantially complied with the Rule's essential requirements. These precise terms have not been used in the Court's adequacy jurisprudence before, and it is necessary to explore their implications. The argument is not that Missouri has no interest in enforcing compliance with the Rule in general, but rather that it had no interest in enforcing full compliance in this particular case. This is so, the Court holds, because the Rule's essential purposes were substantially served by other procedural devices, such as opening statement, voir dire, and Lee's testimony on the stand. . . . So viewed, the Court's substantial-compliance terminology begins to look more familiar: It simply paraphrases the flawed analytical approach first proposed by the Court in Henry v. Mississippi, 379 U.S. 443 (1965), but not further ratified or in fact used to set aside a procedural rule until today.

Before *Henry,* the adequacy inquiry focused on the general legitimacy of the established procedural rule, overlooking its violation only when the rule itself served no legitimate interest. . . . *Henry* was troubling, and much criticized, because it injected an as-applied factor into the equation. . . . The petitioner in *Henry* had defaulted his Fourth Amendment claim in state court by failing to lodge a contemporaneous objection to the admission of the contested evidence. Despite conceding the legitimate state interest in enforcing this common rule, the Court vacated the state-court judgment, proposing that the default may have been inadequate because the rule's "purpose . . . may have been substantially served by petitioner's motion at the close of the State's evidence asking for a directed verdict." *Henry v. Mississippi,* supra, at 448. The suggestion, then, was that a violation of a rule serving a legitimate state interest may be ignored when, in the peculiar circumstances of a given case, the defendant utilized some other procedure serving the same interest.

For all *Henry* possessed in mischievous potential, however, it lacked significant precedential effect. *Henry* itself did not hold the asserted state ground inadequate; instead it remanded for the state court to determine whether "petitioner's counsel deliberately bypassed the opportunity to make timely objection in the state court." 379 U.S., at 449–453. The cornerstone of that analysis, the deliberate-bypass standard of Fay v. Noia, 372 U.S. 391, 426–434 (1963), later was limited to its facts in Wainwright v.

Sykes, 433 U.S. 72, 87–88 (1977), and then put to rest in *Coleman v. Thompson*, 501 U.S., at 750. Subsequent cases maintained the pre-*Henry* focus on the general validity of the challenged state practice, either declining to cite *Henry* or framing its holding in innocuous terms. . . .

There is no meaningful distinction between the *Henry* Court's analysis and the standard the Court applies today, and this surprising reinvigoration of the case-by-case approach is contrary to the principles of federalism underlying our habeas corpus jurisprudence. Procedural rules, like the substantive laws they implement, are the products of sovereignty and democratic processes. The States have weighty interests in enforcing rules that protect the integrity and uniformity of trials, even when "the reason for the rule does not clearly apply." *Staub v. City of Baxley*, 355 U.S., at 333 (Frankfurter, J., dissenting). Regardless of the particular facts in extraordinary cases, then, Missouri has a freestanding interest in Rule 24.10 as a rule.

By ignoring that interest, the majority's approach invites much mischief at criminal trials, and the burden imposed upon States and their courts will be heavy. All requirements of a rule are, in the rulemaker's view, essential to fulfill its purposes; imperfect compliance is thus, by definition, not compliance at all. Yet the State's sound judgment on these matters can now be overridden by a federal court, which may determine for itself, given its own understanding of the rule's purposes, whether a requirement was essential or compliance was substantial in the unique circumstances of any given case. Henceforth, each time a litigant does not comply with an established state procedure, the judge must inquire, even "in the midst of trial, . . . whether noncompliance should be excused because some alternative procedure might be deemed adequate in the particular situation." [R. Fallon, D. Meltzer, & D. Shapiro, Hart and Wechsler's The Federal Courts and the Federal System] 585 [(4th ed.1996)]. The trial courts, then the state appellate courts, and, in the end, the federal habeas courts in numerous instances must comb through the full transcript and trial record, searching for ways in which the defendant might have substantially complied with the essential requirements of an otherwise broken rule.

The Court seeks to ground its renewal of *Henry*'s long-quiescent dictum in our more recent decision in *Osborne v. Ohio*, 495 U.S., at 122–125. Though isolated statements in *Osborne* might appear to support the majority's approach—or, for that matter, *Henry*'s approach—*Osborne*'s holding does not.

．　．　．　．　．

In sum, Rule 24.10 served legitimate state interests, both as a general matter and as applied to the facts of this case. Lee's failure to comply was an adequate state ground, and the Court's contrary determination does not bode well for the adequacy doctrine or federalism.

II

A federal court could consider the merits of Lee's defaulted federal claim if he had shown cause for the default and prejudice therefrom, see *Wainwright v. Sykes*, 433 U.S., at 90–91, or made out a compelling case of actual innocence, see Schlup v. Delo, 513 U.S. 298, 314–315 (1995). He has done neither.

As to the first question, Lee says the sudden disappearance of his witnesses caused him to neglect Rule 24.10. In one sense, of course, he is right, for he would not have requested the continuance, much less failed to comply with Rule 24.10, if his witnesses had not left the courthouse. The argument, though, is unavailing. The cause component of the cause-and-prejudice analysis requires more than a but-for causal relationship between the cause and the default. Lee must also show, given the state of the trial when the motion was made, that an external factor "impeded counsel's efforts to comply with the State's procedural rule." Murray v. Carrier, 477 U.S. 478, 488 (1986). While the departure of his key witnesses may have taken him by surprise (and caused him not to comply with Rule 24.09's writing requirement), nothing about their quick exit stopped him from making a complete oral motion and explaining their absence, the substance of their anticipated testimony, and its materiality.

Nor has Lee shown that an evidentiary hearing is needed to determine whether "a constitutional violation has probably resulted in the conviction of one who is actually innocent." Id., at 496. To fall within this "narrow class of cases," McCleskey v. Zant, 499 U.S. 467, 494 (1991), Lee must demonstrate "that it is more likely than not that no reasonable juror would have convicted him in light of the new evidence." *Schlup v. Delo*, supra, at 332. Lee would offer the testimony of his mother, stepfather, and sister; but to this day, almost eight years after the trial, Lee has not produced a shred of tangible evidence corroborating their story that he had flown to California to attend a 4–month long birthday party at the time of the murder. To acquit, the jury would have to overlook this problem, ignore the relatives' motive to concoct an alibi for their kin, and discount the prosecution's four eyewitnesses. Even with the relatives' testimony, a reasonable juror could vote to convict.

* * *

"Flying banners of federalism, the Court's opinion actually raises storm signals of a most disquieting nature." So wrote Justice Harlan, dissenting in *Henry v. Mississippi*, 379 U.S., at 457. The disruption he predicted failed to spread, not because *Henry*'s approach was sound but because in later cases the Court, heeding his admonition, refrained from following the course *Henry* prescribed. Though the Court disclaims reliance upon *Henry,* it has in fact revived that case's discredited rationale. Serious doubt is now cast upon many state procedural rules and the convictions sustained under them.

Sound principles of federalism counsel against this result. I would affirm the judgment of the Court of Appeals.[142]

Brown v. Payton

Supreme Court of the United States, 2005.
544 U.S. 133, 125 S.Ct. 1432, 161 L.Ed.2d 334.

■ JUSTICE KENNEDY delivered the opinion of the Court.

The United States Court of Appeals for the Ninth Circuit, convening en banc, granted habeas relief to respondent William Payton. It held that the jury instructions in the penalty phase of his trial for capital murder did not permit consideration of all the mitigation evidence Payton presented. The error, the court determined, was that the general mitigation instruction did not make it clear to the jury that it could consider evidence concerning Payton's postcrime religious conversion and the prosecutor was allowed to urge this erroneous interpretation. We granted the petition for certiorari, 541 U.S. 1062 (2004), to decide whether the Ninth Circuit's decision was contrary to the limits on federal habeas review imposed by 28 U.S.C. § 2254(d). We now reverse.

I

In 1980, while spending the night at a boarding house, Payton raped another boarder, Pamela Montgomery, and then used a butcher knife to stab her to death. Payton proceeded to enter the bedroom of the house's patron, Patricia Pensinger and to stab her as she slept aside her 10-year-old son, Blaine. When Blaine resisted, Payton started to stab him as well. Payton's knife blade bent, and he went to the kitchen to retrieve another. Upon the intervention of other boarders, Payton dropped the second knife and fled.

Payton was arrested and tried for the first-degree murder and rape of Pamela Montgomery and for the attempted murders of Patricia and Blaine Pensinger. Payton presented no evidence in the guilt phase of the trial and was convicted on all counts. The trial proceeded to the penalty phase, where the prosecutor introduced evidence of a prior incident when Payton stabbed a girlfriend; a prior conviction for rape; a prior drug-related felony conviction; and evidence of jailhouse conversations in which Payton admitted he had an "urge to kill" and a "severe problem with sex and women" that caused him to view all women as potential victims to "stab . . . and rape." People v. Payton, 3 Cal.4th 1050, 1058, 839 P.2d 1035, 1040 (1992) (internal quotation marks omitted).

[142. A state procedural rule is not automatically "inadequate" under the "adequate state grounds" doctrine merely because the state rule is discretionary rather than mandatory. Beard v. Kindler, 558 U.S. ___, 130 S.Ct. 612 (2009). See generally Struve, Direct and Collateral Federal Court Review of the Adequacy of State Procedural Rules, 103 Colum.L.Rev. 243 (2003).]

Defense counsel concentrated on Payton's postcrime behavior and presented evidence from eight witnesses. They testified that in the year and nine months Payton spent in prison since his arrest, he had made a sincere commitment to God, participated in prison Bible study classes and a prison ministry, and had a calming effect on other prisoners.

Before the penalty phase closing arguments, the judge held an in-chambers conference with counsel to discuss jury instructions. He proposed to give—and later did give—an instruction which followed verbatim the text of a California statute. Cal.Penal Code Ann. § 190.3 (West 1988). The instruction set forth 11 different factors, labeled (a) through (k), for the jury to "consider, take into account and be guided by" in determining whether to impose a sentence of life imprisonment or death. 1 Cal. Jury Instr., Crim., No. 8.84.1 (4th rev. ed.1979).

The in-chambers conference considered in particular the last instruction in the series, the so-called factor (k) instruction. Factor (k) was a catchall instruction, in contrast to the greater specificity of the instructions that preceded it. As set forth in the statute, and as explained to the jury, it directed jurors to consider "[a]ny other circumstance which extenuates the gravity of the crime even though it is not a legal excuse for the crime." Cal.Penal Code Ann. § 190.3 (West 1988). (The statute has since been amended).

Defense counsel objected to the instruction and asked that it be modified to direct the jury, in more specific terms, to consider evidence of the defendant's character and background. The prosecution, on the other hand, indicated that in its view factor (k) was not intended to encompass evidence concerning a defendant's background or character. The court agreed with defense counsel that factor (k) was a general instruction covering all mitigating evidence. It declined, however, to modify the wording, in part because the instruction repeated the text of the statute. In addition, the court stated "I assume you gentlemen, as I said, in your argument can certainly relate—relate back to those factors and certainly can argue the defendant's character, background, history, mental condition, physical condition; certainly fall into category 'k' and certainly make a clear argument to the jury."

The judge prefaced closing arguments by instructing the jury that what it would hear from counsel was "not evidence but argument" and "[you] should rely on your own recollection of the evidence." In his closing, the prosecutor offered jurors his opinion that factor (k) did not allow them to consider anything that happened "after the [crime] or later." The parties do not now dispute that this was a misstatement of law. The defense objected to the comment and moved for a mistrial, which the trial court denied. The court admonished the jury that the prosecutor's comments were merely argument, but it did not explicitly instruct the jury that the prosecutor's interpretation was incorrect.

Although the prosecutor again told the jury several times that, in his view, the jury had not heard any evidence of mitigation, he proceeded to argue that the circumstances and facts of the case, coupled with Payton's prior violent acts, outweighed the mitigating effect of Payton's newfound Christianity. He discussed the mitigation evidence in considerable detail and concluded by urging that the circumstances of the case and Payton's prior violent acts outweighed his religious conversion. In his closing, defense counsel argued to the jury that, although it might be awkwardly worded, factor (k) was a catchall instruction designed to cover precisely the kind of evidence Payton had presented.

The trial court's final instructions to the jury included the factor (k) instruction, as well as an instruction directing the jury to consider all evidence presented during the trial. The jury found the special circumstance of murder in the course of committing rape and returned a verdict recommending a death sentence. The judge sentenced Payton to death for murder and to 21 years and 8 months for rape and attempted murder.

On direct appeal to the California Supreme Court, Payton argued that his penalty phase jury incorrectly was led to believe it could not consider the mitigating evidence of his postconviction conduct in determining whether he should receive a sentence of life imprisonment or death, in violation of the Eighth Amendment of the U.S. Constitution. Lockett v. Ohio, 438 U.S. 586, 602–609 (1978) (plurality opinion). The text of the factor (k) instruction, he maintained, was misleading, and rendered more so in light of the prosecutor's argument.

In a 5-to-2 decision, the California Supreme Court rejected Payton's claims and affirmed his convictions and sentence. People v. Payton, 3 Cal.4th 1050, 839 P.2d 1035 (1992). Applying Boyde v. California, 494 U.S. 370 (1990), which had considered the constitutionality of the same factor (k) instruction, the state court held that in the context of the proceedings there was no reasonable likelihood that Payton's jury believed it was required to disregard his mitigating evidence. 3 Cal.4th, at 1070–1071 839 P.2d, at 1048. Payton sought review of the California Supreme Court's decision here. We declined to grant certiorari. Payton v. California, 510 U.S. 1040 (1994).

Payton filed a petition for a writ of habeas corpus in the United States District Court for the Central District of California, reiterating that the jury was prevented from considering his mitigation evidence. The District Court held that the Antiterrorism and Effective Death Penalty Act of 1996 (AEDPA), 110 Stat. 1214, did not apply to Payton's petition because he had filed a motion for appointment of counsel before AEDPA's effective date, even though he did not file the petition until after that date. The District Court considered his claims de novo and granted the petition.

On appeal to the Court of Appeals for the Ninth Circuit, a divided panel reversed. Payton v. Woodford, 258 F.3d 905 (2001). The Court of Appeals granted Payton's petition for rehearing en banc and, by a 6-to-5 vote, affirmed the District Court's order granting habeas relief. Payton v. Woodford, 299 F.3d 815 (2002). The en banc panel, like the District Court, held that AEDPA did not govern Payton's petition. It, too, conducted a de novo review of his claims, and concluded that postcrime mitigation evidence was not encompassed by the factor (k) instruction, a view it found to have been reinforced by the prosecutor's arguments.

The State petitioned for certiorari. Pursuant to Woodford v. Garceau, 538 U.S. 202 (2003), which held that a request for appointment of counsel did not suffice to make "pending" a habeas petition filed after AEDPA's effective date, we granted the State's petition, Woodford v. Payton, 538 U.S. 975 (2003), and remanded to the Court of Appeals for reconsideration of its decision under AEDPA's deferential standards. See Williams v. Taylor, 529 U.S. 362 (2000).

On remand, the en banc panel affirmed the District Court's previous grant of habeas relief by the same 6–to–5 vote. Payton v. Woodford, 346 F.3d 1204 (CA9 2003). In light of *Garceau,* the Court of Appeals purported to decide the case under the deferential standard AEDPA mandates. It concluded, however, that the California Supreme Court had unreasonably applied this Court's precedents in holding the factor (k) instruction was not unconstitutionally ambiguous in Payton's case.

The Court of Appeals relied, as it had in its initial decision, on the proposition that *Boyde* concerned precrime, not postcrime, mitigation evidence. *Boyde,* in its view, reasoned that a jury would be unlikely to disregard mitigating evidence as to character because of the long-held social belief that defendants who commit criminal acts attributable to a disadvantaged background may be less culpable than defendants who have no such excuse. As to postcrime mitigating evidence, however, the Court of Appeals concluded that "there is reason to doubt that a jury would similarly consider post-crime evidence of a defendant's religious conversion and good behavior in prison." 346 F.3d, at 1212. It cited no precedent of this Court to support that supposition.

In addition, it reasoned that unlike in *Boyde* the prosecutor in Payton's case misstated the law and the trial court did not give a specific instruction rejecting that misstatement, relying instead on a general admonition that counsel's arguments were not evidence. These two differences, the Court of Appeals concluded, made Payton's case unlike *Boyde*, 346 F.3d, at 1216. In its view, the factor (k) instruction was likely to have misled the jury and it was an unreasonable application of this Court's cases for the California Supreme Court to have concluded otherwise.

II

AEDPA provides that, when a habeas petitioner's claim has been adjudicated on the merits in state-court proceedings, a federal court may not grant relief unless the state court's adjudication of the claim "resulted in a decision that was contrary to, or involved an unreasonable application of, clearly established Federal law, as determined by the Supreme Court of the United States." 28 U.S.C. § 2254(d)(1). A state-court decision is contrary to this Court's clearly established precedents if it applies a rule that contradicts the governing law set forth in our cases, or if it confronts a set of facts that is materially indistinguishable from a decision of this Court but reaches a different result. *Williams v. Taylor*, supra, at 405; Early v.

Packer, 537 U.S. 3, 8 (2002) (per curiam). A state-court decision involves an unreasonable application of this Court's clearly established precedents if the state court applies this Court's precedents to the facts in an objectively unreasonable manner. *Williams v. Taylor,* supra, at 405; Woodford v. Visciotti, 537 U.S. 19, 24–25 (2002) (per curiam). These conditions for the grant of federal habeas relief have not been established.

A

The California Supreme Court was correct to identify *Boyde* as the starting point for its analysis. *Boyde* involved a challenge to the same instruction at issue here, factor (k). As to the text of factor (k), *Boyde* established that it does not limit the jury's consideration of extenuating circumstances solely to circumstances of the crime. See 494 U.S., at 382. In so holding, we expressly rejected the suggestion that factor (k) precluded the jury from considering evidence pertaining to a defendant's background and character because those circumstances did not concern the crime itself. *Boyde* instead found that factor (k), by its terms, directed the jury to consider any other circumstance that might excuse the crime, including factors related to a defendant's background and character. We held:

> "The [factor (k)] instruction did not, as petitioner seems to suggest, limit the jury's consideration to 'any other circumstance *of the crime* which extenuates the gravity of the crime.' The jury was directed to consider *any other circumstance* that might excuse the crime, which certainly includes a defendant's background and character." Ibid. (emphasis in original).

The California Supreme Court read *Boyde* as establishing that the text of factor (k) was broad enough to accommodate the postcrime mitigating evidence Payton presented. *People v. Payton,* 3 Cal.4th, at 1070, 839 P.2d, at 1048. The Court of Appeals held *Boyde*'s reasoning did not control Payton's case because *Boyde* concerned precrime, not postcrime, mitigation evidence. 346 F.3d, at 1211–1212.

We do not think that, in light of *Boyde,* the California Supreme Court acted unreasonably in declining to distinguish between precrime and postcrime mitigating evidence. After all, *Boyde* held that factor (k) directed consideration of any circumstance that might excuse the crime, and it is not unreasonable to believe that a postcrime character transformation could do so. Indeed, to accept the view that such evidence could not because it occurred after the crime, one would have to reach the surprising conclusion that remorse could never serve to lessen or excuse a crime. But remorse, which by definition can only be experienced after a crime's commission, is something commonly thought to lessen or excuse a defendant's culpability.

B

That leaves respondent to defend the decision of the Court of Appeals on grounds that, even if it was at least reasonable for the California Supreme Court to conclude that the text of factor (k) allowed the jury to consider the postcrime evidence, it was unreasonable to conclude that the prosecutor's argument and remarks did not mislead the jury into believing it could not consider Payton's mitigation evidence. As we shall explain, however, the California Supreme Court's conclusion that the jury was not reasonably likely to have accepted the prosecutor's narrow view of factor (k) was an application of *Boyde* to similar but not identical facts. Even on the assumption that its conclusion was incorrect, it was not unreasonable, and is therefore just the type of decision that AEDPA shields on habeas review.

The following language from *Boyde* should be noted at the outset:

"We think the proper inquiry in such a case is whether there is a reasonable likelihood that the jury has applied the challenged instruction in a way that prevents the consideration of constitutionally relevant evidence.... [J]urors do not sit in solitary isolation booths parsing instructions for subtle shades of meaning in the same way that lawyers might. Differences among them in interpretation of instructions may be thrashed out in the deliberative process, with common-sense understanding of the instructions in the light of all that has taken place at the trial likely to prevail over technical hairsplitting." 494 U.S., at 380–381 (footnote omitted).

Unlike in *Boyde,* the prosecutor here argued to jurors during his closing that they should not consider Payton's mitigation evidence, evidence which concerned postcrime as opposed to precrime conduct. Because *Boyde* sets forth a general framework for determining whether a challenged instruction precluded jurors from considering a defendant's mitigation evidence, however, the California Supreme Court was correct to structure its own analysis on the premises that controlled *Boyde.* The *Boyde* analysis applies here, and, even if it did not dictate a particular outcome in Payton's case, it refutes the conclusion of the Court of Appeals that the California Supreme Court was unreasonable.

The prosecutor's mistaken approach appears most prominently at three different points in the penalty phase. First, in chambers and outside the presence of the jury he argued to the judge that background and character (whether of precrime or postcrime) was simply beyond the ambit of the instruction. Second, he told the jurors in his closing statement that factor (k) did not allow them to consider what happened "after the [crime] or later." Third, after defense counsel objected to his narrow view, he argued to the jury that it had not heard any evidence of mitigation. Id., at 70. *Boyde,* however, mandates that the whole context of the trial be considered. And considering the whole context of the trial, it was not unreasonable for the state court to have concluded that this line of prosecutorial argument did not put Payton's mitigating evidence beyond the jury's reach.

The prosecutor's argument came after the defense presented eight witnesses, spanning two days of testimony without a single objection from the prosecution as to its relevance. As the California Supreme Court recognized, like in *Boyde,* for the jury to have believed it could not consider

Payton's mitigating evidence, it would have had to believe that the penalty phase served virtually no purpose at all. Payton's counsel recognized as much, arguing to the jury that "[t]he whole purpose for the second phase [of the] trial is to decide the proper punishment to be imposed. Everything that was presented by the defense relates directly to that." He told the jury that if the evidence Payton presented was not entitled to consideration, and therefore "all the evidence we presented [would not be] applicable, why didn't we hear any objections to its relevance?" Ibid. The prosecutor was not given an opportunity to rebut defense counsel's argument that factor (k) required the jury to consider Payton's mitigating evidence.

For his part, the prosecutor devoted specific attention to disputing the sincerity of Payton's evidence, stating that "everybody seems to get religion in jail when facing the death penalty" and that "[s]tate prison is full of people who get religion when they are in jail." Later, he intimated the timing of Payton's religious conversion was suspect, stating "he becomes a newborn Christian, after he's in custody" after "he gets caught." As the California Supreme Court reasonably surmised, this exercise would have been pointless if the jury believed it could not consider the evidence.

Along similar lines, although the prosecutor characterized Payton's evidence as not being evidence of mitigation, he devoted substantial attention to discounting its importance as compared to the aggravating factors. He said:

> "The law in its simplicity is that the aggravating—if the aggravating factors outweigh the mitigating, the sentence the jury should vote for should be the death penalty. How do the factors line up? The circumstances and facts of the case, the defendant's other acts showing violence ..., the defendant's two prior convictions line up against really nothing except [the] defendant's newborn Christianity and the fact that he's 28 years old. This is not close. You haven't heard anything to mitigate what he's done. If you wanted to distribute a thousand points over the factors, 900 would have to go to what he did to [the victim], and I really doubt if [defense counsel] would dispute that breakdown of the facts."

Indeed, the prosecutor characterized testimony concerning Payton's religious conversion as "evidence" on at least four separate occasions. In context, it was not unreasonable for the state court to conclude that the jury believed Payton's evidence was neither credible nor sufficient to outweigh the aggravating factors, not that it was not evidence at all.

To be sure, the prosecutor advocated a narrow interpretation of factor (k), an interpretation that neither party accepts as correct. There is, however, no indication that the prosecutor's argument was made in bad faith, nor does Payton suggest otherwise. In addition, the first time the jury was exposed to the prosecutor's narrow and incorrect view of factor (k), it had already heard the entirety of Payton's mitigating evidence. Defense counsel immediately objected to the prosecutor's narrow characterization, and the trial court, noting at a side bar that one could "argue it either way," admonished the jury that "the comments by both the prosecution and the defense are not evidence. You've heard the evidence and, as I said, this is argument. And it's to be placed in its proper perspective."

The trial judge, of course, should have advised the jury that it could consider Payton's evidence under factor (k), and allowed counsel simply to argue the evidence's persuasive force instead of the meaning of the instruction itself. The judge is, after all, the one responsible for instructing the jury on the law, a responsibility that may not be abdicated to counsel. Even in the face of the trial court's failure to give an instant curative instruction, however, it was not unreasonable to find that the jurors did not likely believe Payton's mitigation evidence beyond their reach. The jury was not left without any judicial direction. Before it began deliberations as to what penalty was appropriate, the court instructed it to consider all evidence received "during any part of the trial in this case, except as you may be hereafter instructed," and it was not thereafter instructed to disregard anything. It was also instructed as to factor (k) which, as we held in *Boyde,* by its terms directs jurors to consider any other circumstance that might lessen a defendant's culpability.

Testimony about a religious conversion spanning one year and nine months may well have been considered altogether insignificant in light of the brutality of the crimes, the prior offenses, and a proclivity for committing violent acts against women. It was not unreasonable for the state court to determine that the jury most likely believed that the evidence in mitigation, while within the reach of the factor (k) instruction, was simply too insubstantial to overcome the arguments for imposing the death penalty; nor was it unreasonable for the state court to rely upon *Boyde* to support its analysis. Even were we to assume the " 'relevant state-court decision applied clearly established federal law erroneously or incorrectly,' " Lockyer v. Andrade, 538 U.S. 63 (2003) (quoting *Williams v. Taylor,* 529 U.S., at 411), there is no basis for further concluding that the application of our precedents was "objectively unreasonable." *Lockyer,* supra, at 76. The Court of Appeals made this last mentioned assumption, and it was in error to do so. The judgment of the Ninth Circuit is reversed.

It is so ordered.

■ THE CHIEF JUSTICE took no part in the decision of this case.

■ JUSTICE SCALIA, with whom JUSTICE THOMAS joins, concurring.

I join the Court's opinion, which correctly holds that the California Supreme Court's decision was not "contrary to" or "an unreasonable application of" our cases. 28 U.S.C. § 2254(d)(1). Even if our review were not circumscribed by statute, I would adhere to my view that limiting a jury's discretion to consider all mitigating evidence does not violate the Eighth Amendment. See Walton v. Arizona, 497 U.S. 639, 673 (1990) (SCALIA, J., concurring in part and concurring in judgment).

■ JUSTICE BREYER, concurring.

In my view, this is a case in which Congress' instruction to defer to the reasonable conclusions of state-court judges makes a critical difference. See

28 U.S.C. § 2254(d)(1). Were I a California state judge, I would likely hold that Payton's penalty-phase proceedings violated the Eighth Amendment.

Unlike Boyde [v. California, 494 U.S. 370 (1990)], the prosecutor here told the jury repeatedly—and incorrectly—that factor (k) did not permit it to take account of Payton's postcrime religious conversion. Moreover, the trial judge—also incorrectly—did nothing to correct the record, likely leaving the jury with the impression that it could not do that which the Constitution says it *must*. Finally, factor (k) is ambiguous as to whether it encompassed Payton's mitigation case. Factor (k)'s text focuses on evidence that reduces a defendant's moral culpability for committing the offense. And evidence of postcrime conversion is less obviously related to moral culpability than is evidence of precrime background and character. See *Boyde,* supra, at 382, n.5 (suggesting a distinction between precrime and postcrime evidence). For all these reasons, one could conclude that the jury here might have thought factor (k) barred its consideration of mitigating evidence, even if the jury in *Boyde* would not there have reached a similar conclusion.

Nonetheless, in circumstances like the present, a federal judge must leave in place a state-court decision unless the federal judge believes that it is "contrary to, or involved an unreasonable application of, clearly established Federal law, as determined by the Supreme Court of the United States." § 2254(d)(1). For the reasons that the Court discusses, I cannot say that the California Supreme Court decision fails this deferential test. I therefore join the Court's opinion.

■ JUSTICE SOUTER, with whom JUSTICE STEVENS and JUSTICE GINSBURG join, dissenting.

From a time long before William Payton's trial, it has been clear law under the Eighth and Fourteenth Amendments that a sentencing jury in a capital case must be able to consider and give effect to all relevant mitigating evidence a defendant offers for a sentence less than death. The prosecutor in Payton's case effectively negated this principle in arguing repeatedly to the jury that the law required it to disregard Payton's mitigating evidence of postcrime religious conversion and rehabilitation. The trial judge utterly failed to correct these repeated misstatements or in any other way to honor his duty to give the jury an accurate definition of legitimate mitigation. It was reasonably likely in these circumstances that the jury failed to consider Payton's mitigating evidence, and in concluding otherwise, the Supreme Court of California unreasonably applied settled law, with substantially injurious effect. The Court of Appeals was correct, and I respectfully dissent.

. . . . .

IV

By the State's admission in this case, the prosecutor's argument was a "misstatement" of constitutional law. By the State's admission in Boyde [v. California, 494 U.S. 370 (1990)], the prosecutor here "misled" the jury.

Despite objection by defense counsel, the trial judge refused to correct the misstatement, which the prosecutor proceeded to repeat. The judge's subsequent charge to consider all evidence was subject to a qualification that the jury could reasonably have understood only as referring to the mitigation evidence the prosecutor had branded as irrelevant under a straightforward reading of the pattern instructions.

If a prosecutor had stood before a jury and denied that a defendant was entitled to a presumption of innocence; if the judge refused to correct him and failed to give any instruction on the presumption of innocence; if the judge's instructions affirmatively suggested there might not be a presumption of innocence; would anyone doubt that there was a reasonable possibility that the jury had been misled? There is no more room here to doubt the reasonable possibility that Payton's jurors failed to consider the postoffense mitigation evidence that the Constitution required them to consider. In a case that contrasts with *Boyde* at every significant step, the State Supreme Court's affirmance of Payton's conviction can only be seen as an unreasonable misapplication of the governing federal standard, not mere error. And since Payton's death sentence is subject to this reasonable possibility of constitutional error, since he may die as a consequence, the effect of the instruction failure is surely substantial and injurious, Brecht v. Abrahamson, 507 U.S. 619, 638 (1993), beyond any possible excuse as harmless error.[143]

COMMENT ON RECENT DEVELOPMENTS
IN FEDERAL HABEAS LAW

A. Military Detention

The Supreme Court's most significant recent decision dealing with the habeas status of persons detained by the military as alleged enemy combatants is *Boumediene v. Bush*, which appears as a principal case at the end of Chapter I. See supra p. 85.

In Qassim v. Bush, 407 F.Supp.2d 198 (D.D.C. 2005), the United States District Court for the District of Columbia found itself in an unusual position in addressing the habeas petitions of two aliens who were found by a military tribunal not to be enemy combatants, but who had not been accepted by another country. Acknowledging that the aliens' detention had become indefinite and that their continued detention was unlawful, the court nevertheless denied habeas relief, stating that the separation of powers doctrine barred the court from ordering that the aliens be released either into the general population at Guantanamo Bay or into the United States. Thus, the court concluded, it "ha[d] no relief to offer."

At the end of the 2005 Term, the Supreme Court decided Hamdan v. Rumsfeld, 548 U.S. 557 (2006), which questioned the legality of the

---

143. See generally 17A Wright, Miller & Cooper, Federal Practice and Procedure: Jurisdiction 2d § 4263 (1988 & Supp.2005).

military commissions at Guantanamo Bay. The federal district court stated that a military commission could not be held unless it was first shown, pursuant to the Geneva Conventions, that Hamdan was not a prisoner of war. The U.S. Court of Appeals for the District of Columbia Circuit reversed, holding that military commissions are legitimate forums in which to try enemy combatants because Congress has approved the commissions, and also holding that the Geneva Conventions do not confer individual rights and remedies. The Supreme Court concluded that the military commission convened to try Hamdan lacked the power to proceed because its structure and procedures violated both the Uniform Code of Military Justice and the Geneva Conventions.

B.   Construction and Application of AEDPA

§ 2254

As amended by the Antiterrorism and Effective Death Penalty Act of 1996 (AEDPA) § 2254(b)(1) requires a state prisoner to "exhaust" state remedies by first presenting any federal grounds for relief from a conviction to the courts of the state that rendered the judgment in question. In Baldwin v. Reese, 541 U.S. 27 (2004), the Court held that this requires that the federal grounds be specifically presented at all stages of post-conviction proceedings in state court, including an application for discretionary review by the state supreme court. The failure to inform the state supreme court that a claim of ineffective assistance of appellate counsel was predicated on federal as well as state-law grounds was thus fatal to later federal habeas proceedings, even though the lower-court ruling that the state supreme court was asked to review had specifically rejected the IAC claim as a matter of federal as well as state law. The Court declared that the federal ground was not "fairly presented" to a state appellate court on the assumption that the appellate justices would read the discussion of the federal ground in the opinion of the trial court. Only Justice Stevens dissented from Justice Breyer's opinion for the Court.

If the state courts adjudicate "fairly presented" federal claims on the merits, § 2254(d)(1) forbids a federal court from granting habeas relief even if the state court erred in its construction and application of federal law. Mere error is not enough. The state court's error must have "resulted in a decision that was contrary to, or involved an unreasonable application of, clearly established Federal law, as determined by the Supreme Court of the United States." This deferential standard—like horseshoes and hand grenades, getting close is good enough—has troubled the federal courts of appeals. The Court's fractured opinion in Williams v. Taylor, 529 U.S. 362 (2000), may have sent too permissive a signal. In a recent series of brusque per curiam reversals the Court has made clear that Congress's limitation of the scope of habeas corpus is to be taken seriously. See Yarborough v. Gentry, 540 U.S. 1 (2003); Mitchell v. Esparza, 540 U.S. 12 (2003); Middleton v. McNeil, 541 U.S. 433 (2004); Holland v. Jackson, 542 U.S. 649 (2004); Bell v. Cone, 543 U.S. 447 (2005). The Court had given warning of its stern approach when the lattermost case was first before it, in an opinion by Chief Justice Rehnquist from which only Justice Stevens dissented. See Bell v. Cone, 535 U.S. 685 (2002).[144]

In Yarborough v. Alvarado, 541 U.S. 652 (2004), the Court split 5–4 in reversing on § 2254(d)(1) grounds the Ninth Circuit's grant of habeas relief in a case in which the key issue was whether the California Court of Appeal had unreasonably determined that a youth suspected of murder and taken to a police station by his parents was not in custody when he confessed during police interrogation. The future strict construction of § 2254(d)(1) seems assured by Justice Breyer's joining of the majority in *Brown v. Payton*, reprinted supra p. 692.

§ 2253

If the district court denies habeas relief under § 2254 to a state prisoners, or analogous federal postconviction relief under § 2255 to a federal prisoners, AEDPA's amendment of § 2253(c) forecloses an appeal unless "a circuit justice or judge" of the relevant regional court of appeals issues a "certificate of appealability" (COA) upon a finding that the applicant has "made a substantial showing" of the denial of some specifically identified constitutional right. In Slack v. McDaniel, 529 U.S. 473 (2000), the Court held that the COA requirement applies to any attempted appellate review of the denial of postconviction relief initiated after AEDPA's effective date—April 24, 1996—even if the habeas petition in question was initiated before AEDPA took effect. But at virtually every other turn, the Court has interpreted § 2253 so as to minimize its jurisdiction-stripping effect, and hence to protect its own institutional role in shaping federal habeas policy as a matter of constitutional, statutory, and decisional law.[145]

First, in Hohn v. United States, 524 U.S. 236 (1998), the Court held that the denial of a COA was reviewable by certiorari under 28 U.S.C. § 1254 as a "judgment or decree" in a "case in" the court of appeals. Then, in *Slack*, the Court held that a COA should issue when the district court dismisses a petition on procedural grounds without reaching the merits of a constitutional claim, provided that "jurists of reason" would find debatable both the merits of the constitutional claim and the procedural grounds for dismissal. This lenient treatment of § 2253(c) continued in Miller–El v. Cockrell, 537 U.S. 322 (2003).

In two recent cases the Court chastised the Fifth Circuit for failing to follow the Court's expansive COA standards, thereby foreclosing review of a debatable denial of habeas relief. In Banks v. Dretke, 540 U.S. 668 (2004), the Fifth Circuit ignored the Court's own precedent in treating Federal

---

144. See generally Berry, Seeking Clarity in the Federal Habeas Fog: Determining What Constitutes "Clearly Established" Law Under the Antiterrorism and Effective Death Penalty Act, 54 Catholic U.L.Rev. 747 (2005).

[**145.** In Harbison v. Bell, 556 U.S. 180 (2009), the Supreme Court held that the certificate of appealability required by § 2253 does not apply to orders denying requests for federally appointed counsel pursuant to 18 U.S.C. § 3599, because § 2253(c)(1)(A) governs only final orders that dispose of a habeas proceeding on the merits.]

Rule of Civil Procedure 15(b) as not even debatably applicable to avoid the procedural default of an unpleaded constitutional claim that had arisen and been argued on the basis of evidence presented to and considered by the district court. In Tennard v. Dretke, 542 U.S. 274 (2004), the Fifth Circuit denied a COA with respect to a claim that the jury had been improperly instructed with respect to a capital defendant's claim of mental retardation. Notwithstanding the Court's previous grant of certiorari and remand to the Fifth Circuit to consider the petitioner's claim in light of Atkins v. Virginia, 536 U.S. 304 (2002) (holding that the Eighth Amendment prohibits the execution of a mentally retarded criminal), the Fifth Circuit reinstated its prior panel opinion denying a COA on grounds that the Court later declared in *Tennard* to have "no foundation in the decisions of this Court." 542 U.S., at 284.

§§ 2244 and 2255

As amended by AEDPA, § 2244(b) requires dismissal of a "second or successive" (SOS) application for habeas relief by a state prisoner except in very narrow circumstances. Section 2244(d), added by AEDPA, imposes a one-year time limit on a state prisoner's application for habeas relief, which generally runs from the date the underlying state-court conviction became final after direct review. Section 2255 was amended by AEDPA to add a similar one-year time limit, and a similar foreclosure of consideration of SOS applications, when federal prisoners seek collateral review of their convictions.[146]

In Johnson v. United States, 544 U.S. 295 (2005), construing § 2255's counterpart to § 2254(d)(1), the Court held that the vacatur of a prior conviction used as a sentencing enhancement can in some circumstances

---

146. AEDPA's one-year time limit has been the source of much litigation, including Day v. McDonough, 547 U.S. 198 (2006) (holding that federal district courts "are permitted, but not obliged, to consider, *sua sponte*, the timeliness of a state prisoner's habeas petition"); Evans v. Chavis, 546 U.S. 189 (2006) (federal courts may not treat California Supreme Court order denying a state habeas petition "on the merits" as automatically indicating that the petition was timely filed; federal courts must make determination whether petition was filed within a "reasonable time"); Mayle v. Felix, 545 U.S. 644 (2005) (addressing the application of Fed. Rule Civ. Proc. 15's "relation back" doctrine with the one-year time limit under § 2244, and holding that the application of the "relation back" doctrine, which permits the addition of a new claim to a timely filed federal habeas petition after the filing deadline has passed, requires that the new claim be based on the same "core of operative facts," and not merely on the same trial or conviction); Pace v. DiGuglielmo, 544 U.S. 408 (2005) (addressing one-year time limit under § 2244, and holding that an application ultimately dismissed as untimely does not qualify as a "properly filed" application for purposes of tolling the running of the limitations period for filing federal habeas petitions); Dodd v. United States, 545 U.S. 353 (2005) (addressing one-year time limit under § 2255, and holding that when a federal prisoner seeks collateral relief from a conviction or sentence on the basis of a constitutional right newly recognized by the Supreme Court, the one-year limitations period is counted from the date that the Supreme Court initially recognized that new right, rather than from the date on which the right was declared retroactive). See also Jimenez v. Quarterman, 555 U.S. 113 (2009) (holding that where a defendant is granted the right to file an out-of-time appeal, the one-year period for filing a habeas petition does not begin to run until the date that the conviction becomes final following the out-of-time direct appeal).

qualify as a newly discovered "factual predicate" for a habeas claim, renewing the one-year period for seeking habeas relief.

In Castro v. United States, 540 U.S. 375 (2003), the Court dealt with the consequences of a federal prisoner's unsuccessful *pro se* motion for a new trial under Federal Rule of Criminal Procedure 33, which the district court recharacterized as an application for habeas relief from his conviction under § 2255. When the prisoner later filed a motion expressly seeking relief under § 2255 on grounds not asserted in the earlier Rule 33 motion, including ineffective assistance of counsel, this application was dismissed on SOS grounds. The Court held that "when a court recharacterizes a *pro se* litigant's motion as a first § 2255 motion … the district court must notify the *pro se* litigant that it intends to recharacterize the pleading, warn the litigant that this recharacterization means that any subsequent § 2255 motion will be subject to the restrictions on 'second or successive' motions, and provide the litigant an opportunity to withdraw the motion or to amend it so that it contains all the § 2255 claims that he believes he has." 540 U.S., at 383. Absent such a warning, the Court held that the SOS restriction did not apply to the later motion.

In Pliler v. Ford, 542 U.S. 225 (2004), the Court was less generous in dealing with the procedural puzzle created by the intersection of § 2244(d)'s one-year time limit and the requirement of Rose v. Lundy, 455 U.S. 509 (1982), that federal district courts dismiss "mixed" habeas petitions under § 2254 that present both "exhausted" claims previously presented to a state court and "unexhausted" claims not yet submitted for state-court consideration. The outright dismissal of a mixed petition that has been filed near the end of § 2244(d)'s one-year period, so that nothing remains pending in federal court while the unexhausted claims are presented to a state court, will almost certainly result in the federal habeas petition being barred as untimely under § 2244(d) once it is refiled after exhaustion of the previously unexhausted state claims. The *Pliler* Court deferred ruling on whether this harsh outcome can be avoided by a "stay-and-abeyance" procedure, whereby the district court dismisses only the unexhausted claims and stays adjudication of the remaining, exhausted claims until the dismissed, unexhausted claims have been considered by a state court, whereupon the petitioner may amend the stayed habeas petition to restore the previously unexhausted claims—such that they relate back to its original date of filing within the one-year period. But *Pliler* held that a district court confronting this scenario is under no obligation to advise a pro se litigant either that the stay-and-abeyance procedure offers the best hope of avoiding the limitations bar of § 2244(d), or that the dismissal of the entire petition on *Rose v. Lundy* grounds will almost surely leave the petitioner foreclosed from any federal habeas relief on timeliness grounds. In the case before it, however, the district court had informed the petitioner that a *Rose v. Lundy* dismissal would be "without prejudice," and the Supreme Court remanded the case for a determination whether relief from § 2244(d) was thus justified because the petitioner had been "affirmatively misled."

One year later, in Rhines v. Weber, 544 U.S. 269, 277 (2005), the Court ruled on the underlying issue not reached in *Pliler*. It held that district courts have discretion to employ the stay-and-abeyance procedure "in limited circumstances ... when the district court determines there was good cause for the petitioner's failure to exhaust his claims first in state court." If the unexhausted claims are "plainly meritless," however, the district court should dismiss them outright while proceeding to adjudicate without delay the exhausted claims.

Another "recharacterization" issue was presented in Nelson v. Campbell, 541 U.S. 637 (2004). An Alabama prisoner faced execution by lethal injection. Years of drug abuse had compromised his veins, leading the state to believe that they would be inaccessible for intravenous administration of the lethal injection by needle. The warden ordered prison personnel to make a two-inch incision in the prisoner's arm or leg, under local anesthetic and without requiring the use or presence of a physician, one hour before the scheduled execution. Three days before that date the prisoner brought an action under 42 U.S.C. § 1983, seeking to enjoin the state from using this "cut-down" procedure on the ground that it would violate the Eighth Amendment's prohibitions of cruel and unusual punishment, and deliberate indifference to his serious medical needs. Because the prisoner had previously sought federal habeas relief under § 2254, the defendant prison officials successfully argued in the district court and the Eleventh Circuit that the § 1983 suit should be recharacterized as a habeas petition and dismissed on SOS grounds under § 2244(b).

The Supreme Court reversed. The Court acknowledged that there is a sometimes-hazy line between claims for injunctive relief "challenging the fact of [an inmate's] conviction or the duration of his sentence," which "fall within the 'core' of habeas corpus and thus are not cognizable when brought pursuant to § 1983," and "constitutional claims that merely challenge the conditions of a prisoner's confinement, whether the inmate seeks injunctive or monetary relief" which "may be brought pursuant to § 1983 in the first instance." 541 U.S., at 643. Because the prisoner had carefully asserted that constitutionally unproblematic alternative procedures existed for proceeding with the execution, and thus sought relief that would not in effect prohibit the carrying out of his death sentence, the Court held that the district court should hold an evidentiary hearing to explore these alternative procedures for administering a lethal injection. In the case before it, the execution warrant had expired and no stay was presently required during the pendency of proceedings on remand. Should the prisoner's execution be rescheduled before those proceedings were concluded, the Court left open for the district court's initial determination the difficult question whether a stay of execution could be issued in connection with a suit for a method-of-execution injunction without converting that suit into a habeas proceeding.

C.   Elaboration of pre-AEDPA Standards

In Lindh v. Murphy, 521 U.S. 320 (1997), the Court held that AEDPA's new procedures for the adjudication of habeas claims in the district court, such as prescribed by amended § 2254, do not apply to petitions filed before AEDPA's effective date. Banks v. Dretke, 540 U.S. 668 (2004), discussed above in connection with COA standards, was such a case. It involved a complicated question of whether the petitioner was entitled to present new evidence, not adduced in prior proceedings in state court, in support of a constitutional claim of the prosecution's failure to turn over exculpatory evidence in violation of Brady v. Maryland, 373 U.S. 83 (1963). In holding that the petitioner was entitled to present the evidence, the Court discussed at length the proper application of the "cause and prejudice" standard for relief from a procedural default—the standard introduced into pre-AEDPA habeas law by Wainwright v. Sykes, 433 U.S. 72 (1977), reprinted supra p. 667. See 540 U.S., at 692–703.

The pre-AEDPA "cause and prejudice" standard also governs post-AEDPA habeas cases in the following circumstance. As required by amended § 2254(b)(1), the petitioner exhausts his state remedies by seeking state post-conviction relief on federal constitutional grounds. If the state court denies relief by ruling against the petitioner on the merits of the federal claim, amended § 2254(d) requires deference—right or wrong—to the state court's merits determination, unless it was so far off the mark as to be "contrary to, or . . . an unreasonable application of, clearly established Federal law, as determined by the Supreme Court of the United States," § 2254(d)(1), or was based on "an unreasonable determination of the facts in light of the evidence presented in the State court proceeding," § 2254(d)(2). But if the state court refuses to reach the merits of a federal claim because, in its view, the claim has been procedurally defaulted, then "the general principle that federal courts will not disturb state court judgments based on adequate and independent state law procedural grounds" acts as a "corollary to the habeas statute's exhaustion requirement." Dretke v. Haley, 541 U.S. 386, 392 (2004).

> But, while an adequate and independent state procedural disposition strips this Court of certiorari jurisdiction to review a state court's judgment, it provides only a strong prudential reason, grounded in "considerations of comity and concerns for the orderly administration of justice," not to pass upon a defaulted constitutional claim presented for federal habeas review. . . . That being the case, we have recognized an equitable exception to the bar when a habeas applicant can demonstrate cause and prejudice for the procedural default.

Id., at 392–393 (quoting Francis v. Henderson, 425 U.S. 536, 538–539 (1976), and citing *Wainwright v. Sykes*, 433 U.S., at 87). The *Haley* Court went on to note that actual innocence of a substantive offense or sentencing criterion may in some instances excuse a procedural default, but held that the "actual innocence" exception should be invoked only after a federal habeas court has first determined that conventional "cause and prejudice" analysis is insufficient to excuse a procedural default.

"Cause and prejudice" analysis may also be avoided if the procedural default, although independently based on state law, is not deemed an "adequate" ground for defaulting federal claims. *Lee v. Kemna*, reprinted supra p. 680, demonstrates that an "adequacy" attack on a procedurally defaulted state rule, while difficult, can still succeed in opening the door to federal habeas relief.

Another knotty pre-AEDPA doctrine that retains force in post-AEDPA cases is the non-retroactivity principle of Teague v. Lane, 489 U.S. 288 (1989). "Under our retroactivity analysis as set forth in *Teague* . . ., federal habeas corpus petitioners may not avail themselves of new rules of criminal procedure outside two narrow exceptions." Beard v. Banks, 542 U.S. 406, 408 (2004). *Beard* held that even if a state court itself applies and rejects on the merits a putatively new federal rule of criminal procedure in denying state post-conviction relief, a federal habeas court should not apply the standards of § 2254(d) to determine whether the state court unreasonably applied that rule without first answering *Teague*'s two antecedent questions: first, whether the rule in question is indeed a "new rule" established only after the underlying state conviction became final, and second, whether such a new rule falls within one of the two exceptions to *Teague*'s foreclosure of federal habeas relief predicated on a new rule. *Beard* further held that Mills v. Maryland, 486 U.S. 367 (1988), had indeed announced a *Teague*-barred "new rule" pertaining to jury consideration of mitigating factors in a capital case, and hence could not be invoked as a basis for federal habeas relief from a death sentence that became final in 1987. In Schriro v. Summerlin, 542 U.S. 348 (2004), decided the same day as *Beard*, the Court also held that *Teague* barred retroactive habeas relief based on the new rule of Ring v. Arizona, 536 U.S. 584 (2002), which held that the presence of aggravating circumstances in a capital case must be determined by the jury rather than the judge. But while the post-AEDPA applicability of *Teague* is clear, *how* it is to be applied remains controversial: Justices Stevens, Souter, Ginsburg, and Breyer dissented from the *Teague*-based denial of habeas relief in both *Beard* and *Schriro*.

At the end of the 2005 Term, the Supreme Court addressed the "actual innocence" exception to procedural default in a federal habeas action in House v. Bell, 547 U.S. 518 (2006). In *House*, the defendant was convicted and sentenced to death for the first-degree murder of Carolyn Muncey. In his habeas proceedings, the defendant presented new evidence, including DNA evidence that it was not his semen on Muncey's clothes, that the blood on his clothing was spilled onto his clothing after Muncey's autopsy, and that Muncey's husband had confessed to the murder. The Court ruled that the standard under the "actual innocence" exception to procedural default requires a showing that "it is more likely than not that no reasonable juror would have found petitioner guilty beyond a reasonable doubt," quoting Schlup v. Delo, 513 U.S. 298, 327 (1995). The Court found that the defendant had satisfied the *Schlup* standard, concluding: "This is not a case of conclusive exoneration. Some aspects of the State's evidence . . . still support an inference of guilt. Yet the central forensic proof connecting House to the crime—the blood and the semen—has been called into question, and House has put forward substantial evidence pointing to a different suspect. Accordingly, and although the issue is close, we conclude that this is the rare case where—had the jury heard all the conflicting testimony—it is more likely than not that no reasonable juror viewing the record as a whole would lack reasonable doubt."

SECTION 11. EFFECT OF A PRIOR STATE JUDGMENT

Allen v. McCurry

Supreme Court of the United States, 1980.
449 U.S. 90, 101 S.Ct. 411, 66 L.Ed.2d 308.

■ JUSTICE STEWART delivered the opinion of the Court.

At a hearing before his criminal trial in a Missouri court, the respondent, Willie McCurry, invoked the Fourth and Fourteenth Amendments to suppress evidence that had been seized by the police. The trial court denied the suppression motion in part, and McCurry was subsequently convicted after a jury trial. The conviction was later affirmed on appeal. State v. McCurry, 587 S.W.2d 337 (Mo.Ct.App.). Because he did not assert that the state courts had denied him a "full and fair opportunity" to litigate his search and seizure claim, McCurry was barred by this Court's decision in Stone v. Powell, 428 U.S. 465, from seeking a writ of habeas corpus in a federal district court. Nevertheless, he sought federal court redress for the alleged constitutional violation by bringing a damage suit under 42 U.S.C. § 1983 against the officers who had entered his home and seized the evidence in question. We granted certiorari to consider whether the unavailability of federal habeas corpus prevented the police officers from raising the state courts' partial rejection of McCurry's constitutional claim as a collateral estoppel defense to the § 1983 suit against them for damages. 444 U.S. 1070.

I

In April 1977, several undercover police officers, following an informant's tip that McCurry was dealing in heroin, went to his house in St. Louis, Mo., to attempt a purchase. Two officers, petitioners Allen and Jacobsmeyer, knocked on the front door, while the other officers hid nearby. When McCurry opened the door, the two officers asked to buy some heroin "caps." McCurry went back into the house and returned soon thereafter, firing a pistol at and seriously wounding Allen and Jacobsmeyer. After a gun battle with the other officers and their reinforcements, McCurry retreated into the house; he emerged again when the police demanded that he surrender. Several officers then entered the house without a warrant, purportedly to search for other persons inside. One of the officers seized drugs and other contraband that lay in plain view, as well as additional contraband he found in dresser drawers and in auto tires on the porch.

McCurry was charged with possession of heroin and assault with intent to kill. At the pretrial suppression hearing, the trial judge excluded the evidence seized from the dresser drawers and tires, but denied suppression of the evidence found in plain view. McCurry was convicted of both the heroin and assault offenses.

McCurry subsequently filed the present § 1983 action for $1 million in damages against petitioners Allen and Jacobsmeyer, other unnamed individual police officers, and the city of St. Louis and its police department. The complaint alleged a conspiracy to violate McCurry's Fourth Amendment rights, an unconstitutional search and seizure of his house, and an assault on him by unknown police officers after he had been arrested and handcuffed. The petitioners moved for summary judgment. The District Court apparently understood the gist of the complaint to be the allegedly unconstitutional search and seizure and granted summary judgment, holding that collateral estoppel prevented McCurry from relitigating the search and seizure question already decided against him in the state courts. McCurry v. Allen, 466 F.Supp. 514 (E.D.Mo.1978).[147]

The Court of Appeals reversed the judgment and remanded the case for trial. McCurry v. Allen, 606 F.2d 795 (CA8). The appellate court said it was not holding that collateral estoppel was generally inapplicable in a § 1983 suit raising issues determined against the federal plaintiff in a state criminal trial. Id., at 798. But noting that *Stone v. Powell*, supra, barred McCurry from federal habeas corpus relief, and invoking "the special role of the federal courts in protecting civil rights," id., at 799, the court concluded that the § 1983 suit was McCurry's only route to a federal forum for his constitutional claim and directed the trial court to allow him to proceed to trial unencumbered by collateral estoppel.[148]

---

147. The merits of the Fourth Amendment claim are discussed in the opinion of the Missouri Court of Appeals. State v. McCurry, 587 S.W.2d 337. The state courts upheld the entry of the house as a reasonable response to emergency circumstances, but held illegal the seizure of any evidence discovered as a result of that entry except what was in plain view. Id., at 340. McCurry therefore argues here that even if the doctrine of collateral estoppel generally applies to this case, he should be able to proceed to trial to obtain damages for the part of the seizure declared illegal by the state courts. The petitioners contend, on the other hand, that the complaint alleged essentially an illegal entry, adding that only the entry could possibly justify the $1 million prayer. Since the state courts upheld the entry, the petitioners argue that if collateral estoppel applies here at all, it removes from trial all issues except the alleged assault. The Court of Appeals, however, addressed only the broad question of the applicability of collateral estoppel to § 1983 suits brought by plaintiffs in McCurry's circumstances, and questions as to the scope of collateral estoppel with respect to the particular issues in this case are not now before us.

148. Nevertheless, relying on the doctrine of Younger v. Harris, 401 U.S. 37, the Court of Appeals directed the District Court to abstain from conducting the trial until McCurry had exhausted his opportunities for review of his claim in the state appellate courts. 606 F.2d, at 799.

[In Deakins v. Monaghan, 484 U.S. 193 (1988), the Supreme Court held that if the *Younger* doctrine requires abstention on claims for equitable relief, the court should not dismiss a

II

The federal courts have traditionally adhered to the related doctrines of res judicata and collateral estoppel. Under res judicata, a final judgment on the merits of an action precludes the parties or their privies from relitigating issues that were or could have been raised in that action. Cromwell v. County of Sac., 94 U.S. 351, 352. Under collateral estoppel, once a court has decided an issue of fact or law necessary to its judgment, that decision may preclude relitigation of the issue in a suit on a different cause of action involving a party to the first case. Montana v. United States, 440 U.S. 147, 153.[149] As this Court and other courts have often recognized, res judicata and collateral estoppel relieve parties of the cost and vexation of multiple lawsuits, conserve judicial resources, and, by preventing inconsistent decisions, encourage reliance on adjudication. Id., at 153–154.

In recent years, this Court has reaffirmed the benefits of collateral estoppel in particular, finding the policies underlying it to apply in contexts not formerly recognized at common law. Thus, the Court has eliminated the requirement of mutuality in applying collateral estoppel to bar relitigation of issues decided earlier in federal court suits, Blonder–Tongue Laboratories, Inc. v. University of Illinois, 402 U.S. 313, and has allowed a litigant who was not a party to a federal case to use collateral estoppel "offensively" in a new federal suit against the party who lost on the decided issue in the first case, Parklane Hosiery Co. v. Shore, 439 U.S. 322. But one general limitation the Court has repeatedly recognized is that the concept of collateral estoppel cannot apply when the party against whom the earlier decision is asserted did not have a "full and fair opportunity" to litigate that issue in the earlier case. *Montana v. United States*, supra, 440 U.S., at 153; *Blonder–Tongue Laboratories, Inc. v. University of Illinois Foundation*, supra, 402 U.S., at 328–329.[150]

---

plaintiff's claims for monetary relief that cannot be redressed in the state proceeding, but should stay those claims until the state proceeding is ended.]

149. The Restatement of Judgments now speaks of res judicata as "claim preclusion" and collateral estoppel as "issue preclusion." Restatement of Judgments (Second) § 74 (Tent. Draft No. 3, 1976). [The section referred to became § 31 in Restatement Second of Judgments (1982).] Some courts and commentators use "res judicata" as generally meaning both forms of preclusion.

Contrary to a suggestion in the dissenting opinion, this case does not involve the question whether a § 1983 claimant can litigate in federal court an issue he might have raised but did not raise in previous litigation.

150. Other factors, of course, may require an exception to the normal rules of collateral estoppel in particular cases. E.g., Montana v. United States, 440 U.S. 147, 162 (unmixed questions of law in successive actions between the same parties on unrelated claims).

Contrary to the suggestion of the dissent, ... our decision today does not "fashion" any new more stringent doctrine of collateral estoppel, nor does it hold that the collateral estoppel effect of a state court decision turns on the single factor of whether the State gave the federal claimant a full and fair opportunity to litigate a federal question. Our decision does not "fashion" any doctrine of collateral estoppel at all. Rather, it construes § 1983 to determine whether the conventional doctrine of collateral estoppel applies to the case at hand. It must be emphasized that the question whether any exceptions or qualifications

The federal courts generally have also consistently accorded preclusive effect to issues decided by state courts. E.g., *Montana v. United States*, supra; Angel v. Bullington, 330 U.S. 183. Thus, res judicata and collateral estoppel not only reduce unnecessary litigation and foster reliance on adjudication, but also promote the comity between state and federal courts that has been recognized as a bulwark of the federal system. See Younger v. Harris, 401 U.S. 37, 43–45.

Indeed, though the federal courts may look to the common law or to the policies supporting res judicata and collateral estoppel in assessing the preclusive effect of decisions of other federal courts, Congress has specifically required all federal courts to give preclusive effect to state-court judgments whenever the courts of the State from which the judgments emerged would do so:

> "[J]udicial proceedings [of any court of any State] shall have the same full faith and credit in every court within the United States and its Territories and Possessions as they have by law or usage in the courts of such State...." 28 U.S.C. § 1738 (1976).[151]

Huron Holding Corp. v. Lincoln Mine Operations, 312 U.S. 183, 193; Davis v. Davis, 305 U.S. 32, 40. It is against this background that we examine the relationship of § 1983 and collateral estoppel, and the decision of the Court of Appeals in this case.

III

This Court has never directly decided whether the rules of res judicata and collateral estoppel are generally applicable to § 1983 actions. But in Preiser v. Rodriguez, 411 U.S. 475, 497, the Court noted with implicit approval the view of other federal courts that res judicata principles fully apply to civil rights suits brought under that statute. See also Huffman v. Pursue, 420 U.S. 592, 606, n. 18; Wolff v. McDonnell, 418 U.S. 539, 554, n. 12.[152] And the virtually unanimous view of the Courts of Appeals since *Preiser* has been that § 1983 presents no categorical bar to the application of res judicata and collateral estoppel concepts.[153] These federal appellate

---

within the bounds of that doctrine might ultimately defeat a collateral estoppel defense in this case is not before us.

151. This statute has existed in essentially unchanged form since its enactment just after the ratification of the Constitution, Act of May 26, 1790, ch. 11, 1 Stat. 122, and its reenactment soon thereafter, Act of Mar. 27, 1804, ch. 56, 2 Stat. 298–299. Congress has also provided means for authenticating the records of the state proceedings to which the federal courts are to give full faith and credit. 28 U.S.C. § 1738.

152. The cases noted in *Preiser* applied res judicata to issues decided both in state civil proceedings, e.g., Coogan v. Cincinnati Bar Assn., 431 F.2d 1209, 1211 (CA6 1970), and state criminal proceedings, e.g., Goss v. Illinois, 312 F.2d 257, 259 (CA7 1963).

153. E.g., Robbins v. District Court, 592 F.2d 1015 (CA8 1979); Jennings v. Caddo Parish School Bd., 531 F.2d 1331 (CA5 1976); Lovely v. Laliberte, 498 F.2d 1261 (CA1 1974); Brown v. Georgia Power Co., 491 F.2d 117 (CA5 1974); Tang v. Appellate Div., 487 F.2d 138 (CA2 1973).

A very few courts have suggested that the normal rules of claim preclusion should not apply in § 1983 suits in one peculiar circumstance: Where a § 1983 plaintiff seeks to litigate in

court decisions have spoken with little explanation or citation in assuming the compatibility of § 1983 and rules of preclusion, but the statute and its legislative history clearly support the courts' decisions.

Because the requirement of mutuality of estoppel was still alive in the federal courts until well into this century, see *Blonder–Tongue Laboratories, Inc. v. University of Illinois Foundation*, supra, 402 U.S., at 322–323, the drafters of the 1871 Civil Rights Act, of which § 1983 is a part, may have had less reason to concern themselves with rules of preclusion than a modern Congress would. Nevertheless, in 1871 res judicata and collateral estoppel could certainly have applied in federal suits following state-court litigation between the same parties or their privies, and nothing in the language of § 1983 remotely expresses any congressional intent to contravene the common-law rules of preclusion or to repeal the express statutory requirements of the predecessor of 28 U.S.C. § 1738. Section 1983 creates a new federal cause of action.[154] It says nothing about the preclusive effect of state-court judgments.[155]

Moreover, the legislative history of § 1983 does not in any clear way suggest that Congress intended to repeal or restrict the traditional doctrines of preclusion. The main goal of the Act was to override the corrupting influence of the Ku Klux Klan and its sympathizers on the governments and law enforcement agencies of the Southern States, see Monroe v. Pape, 365 U.S. 167, 174, and of course the debates show that one strong motive behind its enactment was grave congressional concern that the state courts had been deficient in protecting federal rights, Mitchum v. Foster, 407 U.S. 225, 241–242; *Monroe v. Pape*, supra, 365 U.S., at 180. But in the context of the legislative history as a whole, this congressional concern lends only the most equivocal support to any argument that, in cases where the state courts have recognized the constitutional claims asserted and provided fair

---

federal court a federal issue which he could have raised but did not raise in an earlier state court suit against the same adverse party. Graves v. Olgiati, 550 F.2d 1327 (CA2 1977); Lombard v. Bd. of Educ., 502 F.2d 631 (CA2 1974); Mack v. Florida Bd. of Dentistry, 430 F.2d 862 (CA5 1970). These cases present a narrow question not now before us, and we intimate no view as to whether they were correctly decided.

154. [The Court first quoted in full 42 U.S.C. § 1983, reprinted supra p. 469, n. 1.]

It has been argued that, since there remains little federal common law after Erie R.R. Co. v. Tompkins, 304 U.S. 64 to hold that the creation of a federal cause of action by itself does away with the rules of preclusion would take away almost all meaning from § 1738. Currie, Res Judicata: The Neglected Defense, 45 U.Chi.L.Rev. 317, 328 (1978).

155. By contrast, the roughly contemporaneous statute extending the federal writ of habeas corpus to state prisoners expressly rendered "null and void" any state-court proceeding inconsistent with the decision of a federal habeas court, Act of Feb. 5, 1867, ch. 28, § 1, 14 Stat. 385, 386 (1867) (current version, at 28 U.S.C. § 2254), and the modern habeas statute also expressly adverts to the effect of state-court criminal judgments by requiring the applicant for the writ to exhaust his state-court remedies, 28 U.S.C. § 2254(b), and by presuming a state court resolution of a factual issue to be correct except in eight specific circumstances, id., § 2254(d). In any event, the traditional exception to res judicata for habeas corpus review, see *Preiser v. Rodriguez*, supra, 411 U.S., at 497, provides no analogy to § 1983 cases, since that exception finds its source in the unique purpose of habeas corpus—to release the applicant for the writ from unlawful confinement. Sanders v. United States, 373 U.S. 1, 8.

procedures for determining them, Congress intended to override § 1738 or the common-law rules of collateral estoppel and res judicata. Since repeals by implication are disfavored, Radzanower v. Touche Ross & Co., 426 U.S. 148, 154, much clearer support than this would be required to hold that § 1738 and the traditional rules of preclusion are not applicable to § 1983 suits.

As the Court has understood the history of the legislation, Congress realized that in enacting § 1983 it was altering the balance of judicial power between the state and federal courts. See *Mitchum v. Foster*, supra, 407 U.S., at 241. But in doing so, Congress was adding to the jurisdiction of the federal courts, not subtracting from that of the state courts. See *Monroe v. Pape*, supra, 365 U.S., at 183 ("The federal remedy is supplementary to the state remedy . . . .").[156] The debates contain several references to the concurrent jurisdiction of the state courts over federal questions,[157] and numerous suggestions that the state courts would retain their established jurisdiction so that they could, when the then current political passions abated, demonstrate a new sensitivity to federal rights.

To the extent that it did intend to change the balance of power over federal questions between the state and federal courts, the 42d Congress was acting in a way thoroughly consistent with the doctrines of preclusion. In reviewing the legislative history of § 1983 in *Monroe v. Pape*, supra, the Court inferred that Congress had intended a federal remedy in three circumstances: where state substantive law was facially unconstitutional, where state procedural law was inadequate to allow full litigation of a constitutional claim, and where state procedural law, though adequate in theory, was inadequate in practice. 365 U.S., at 173–174. In short, the federal courts could step in where the state courts were unable or unwilling to protect federal rights. Id., at 176. This understanding of § 1983 might well support an exception to res judicata and collateral estoppel where state law did not provide fair procedures for the litigation of constitutional claims, or where a state court failed to even acknowledge the existence of the constitutional principle on which a litigant based his claim. Such an exception, however, would be essentially the same as the important general limit on rules of preclusion that already exists: Collateral estoppel does not apply where the party against whom an earlier court decision is asserted did not have a full and fair opportunity to litigate the claim or issue decided by the first court. But the Court's view of § 1983 in *Monroe* lends no strength to any argument that Congress intended to allow relitigation of

---

156. To the extent that Congress in the post-Civil War period did intend to deny full faith and credit to state court decisions on constitutional issues, it expressly chose the very different means of post-judgment removal for state court defendants whose civil rights were threatened by biased state courts and who therefore "are denied or cannot enforce [their civil rights] in the courts or tribunals of the State." Act of Apr. 9, 1866, ch. 31, § 3, 14 Stat. 27.

157. E.g., Cong. Globe, 42d Cong., 1st Sess., 514 (Rep. Poland); id., at 695 (Sen. Edmunds); see Martinez v. California, 444 U.S. 277, 283 (noting that the state courts may entertain § 1983 claims, while reserving the question whether the state courts must do so).

federal issues decided after a full and fair hearing in a state court simply because the state court's decision may have been erroneous.[158]

The Court of Appeals in this case acknowledged that every Court of Appeals that has squarely decided the question has held that collateral estoppel applies when § 1983 plaintiffs attempt to relitigate in federal court issues decided against them in state criminal proceedings. But the court noted that the only two federal appellate decisions invoking collateral estoppel to bar relitigation of Fourth Amendment claims decided adversely to the § 1983 plaintiffs in state courts came before this Court's decision in *Stone v. Powell.* It also noted that some of the decisions holding collateral estoppel applicable to § 1983 actions were based at least in part on the estopped party's access to another federal forum through habeas corpus. The Court of Appeals thus concluded that since *Stone v. Powell* had removed McCurry's right to a hearing of his Fourth Amendment claim in federal habeas corpus, collateral estoppel should not deprive him of a federal judicial hearing of that claim in a § 1983 suit.

Stone v. Powell does not provide a logical doctrinal source for the court's ruling. This Court in *Stone* assessed the costs and benefits of the judge-made exclusionary rule within the boundaries of the federal courts' statutory power to issue writs of habeas corpus, and decided that the incremental deterrent effect that the issuance of the writ in Fourth Amendment cases might have on police conduct did not justify the cost the writ imposed upon the fair administration of criminal justice. 428 U.S., at 489–496. The *Stone* decision concerns only the prudent exercise of federal court jurisdiction under 28 U.S.C. § 2254. It has no bearing on § 1983 suits or on the question of the preclusive effect of state court judgments.

The actual basis of the Court of Appeals' holding appears to be a generally framed principle that every person asserting a federal right is entitled to one unencumbered opportunity to litigate that right in a federal district court, regardless of the legal posture in which the federal claim arises. But the authority for this principle is difficult to discern. It cannot

---

158. The dissent suggests ... that the Court's decision in England v. Medical Examiners, 375 U.S. 411, demonstrates the impropriety of affording preclusive effect to the state court decision in this case. The *England* decision is inapposite to the question before us. In the *England* case, a party first submitted to a federal court his claim that a state statute violated his constitutional rights. The federal court abstained and remitted the plaintiff to the state courts, holding that a state court decision that the statute did not apply to the plaintiff would moot the federal question. Id., at 413. The plaintiff submitted both the state and federal law questions to the state courts, which decided both questions adversely to him. Id., at 414. This Court held that in such a circumstance, a plaintiff who properly reserved the federal issue by informing the state courts of his intention to return to federal court, if necessary, was not precluded from litigating the federal question in federal court. The holding in *England* depended entirely on this Court's view of the purpose of abstention in such a case: Where a plaintiff properly invokes federal court jurisdiction in the first instance on a federal claim, the federal court has a duty to accept that jurisdiction. Id., at 415. Abstention may serve only to postpone rather than to abdicate, jurisdiction, since its purpose is to determine whether resolution of the federal question is even necessary, or to obviate the risk of a federal court's erroneous construction of state law. Id., at 416, and n. 7. These concerns have no bearing whatsoever on the present case.

lie in the Constitution, which makes no such guarantee, but leaves the scope of the jurisdiction of the federal district courts to the wisdom of Congress. And no such authority is to be found in § 1983 itself. For reasons already discussed at length, nothing in the language or legislative history of § 1983 proves any congressional intent to deny binding effect to a state court judgment or decision when the state court, acting within its proper jurisdiction, has given the parties a full and fair opportunity to litigate federal claims, and thereby has shown itself willing and able to protect federal rights. And nothing in the legislative history of § 1983 reveals any purpose to afford less deference to judgments in state criminal proceedings than to those in state civil proceedings. There is, in short, no reason to believe that Congress intended to provide a person claiming a federal right an unrestricted opportunity to relitigate an issue already decided in state court simply because the issue arose in a state proceeding in which he would rather not have been engaged at all.[159]

Through § 1983, the 42d Congress intended to afford an opportunity for legal and equitable relief in a federal court for certain types of injuries. It is difficult to believe that the drafters of that Act considered it a substitute for a federal writ of habeas corpus, the purpose of which is not to redress civil injury, but to release the applicant from unlawful physical confinement, *Preiser v. Rodriguez*, supra, 411 U.S., at 484; Fay v. Noia, 372 U.S. 391, 399, n.5,[160] particularly in light of the extremely narrow scope of federal habeas relief for state prisoners in 1871.

The only other conceivable basis for finding a universal right to litigate a federal claim in a federal district court is hardly a legal basis at all, but rather a general distrust of the capacity of the state courts to render correct decisions on constitutional issues. It is ironic that *Stone v. Powell* provided the occasion for the expression of such an attitude in the present litigation, in view of this Court's emphatic reaffirmation in that case of the constitutional obligation of the state courts to uphold federal law, and its expression of confidence in their ability to do so. 428 U.S., at 493–494, n. 35; see Robb v. Connolly, 111 U.S. 624, 637 (Harlan, J.).

The Court of Appeals erred in holding that McCurry's inability to obtain federal habeas corpus relief upon his Fourth Amendment claim renders the doctrine of collateral estoppel inapplicable to his § 1983 suit.[161] Accordingly, the judgment is reversed, and the case is remanded to the Court of Appeals for proceedings consistent with this opinion.

---

159. The Court of Appeals did not suggest that the prospect of collateral estoppel in a § 1983 suit would deter a defendant in a state criminal case from raising Fourth Amendment claims, and it is difficult to imagine a defendant risking conviction and imprisonment because he hoped to win a later civil judgment based upon an allegedly illegal search and seizure.

160. Under the modern statute, federal habeas corpus is bounded by a requirement of exhaustion of state remedies and by special procedural rules, 28 U.S.C. § 2254 (1976), which have no counterparts in § 1983, and which therefore demonstrate the continuing illogic of treating federal habeas and § 1983 suits as fungible remedies for constitutional violations.

161. We do not decide *how* the body of collateral estoppel doctrine or 28 U.S.C. § 1738 should apply in this case.

It is so ordered.

■ JUSTICE BLACKMUN, with whom JUSTICE BRENNAN and JUSTICE MARSHALL join, dissenting.

The legal principles with which the Court is concerned in this civil case obviously far transcend the ugly facts of respondent's criminal convictions in the courts of Missouri for heroin possession and assault.

The Court today holds that notions of collateral estoppel apply with full force to this suit brought under 42 U.S.C. § 1983. In my view, the Court, in so ruling, ignores the clear import of the legislative history of that statute and disregards the important federal policies that underlie its enforcement. It also shows itself insensitive both to the significant differences between the § 1983 remedy and the exclusionary rule, and to the pressures upon a criminal defendant that make a free choice of forum illusory. I do not doubt that principles of preclusion are to be given such effect as is appropriate in a § 1983 action. In many cases, the denial of res judicata or collateral estoppel effect would serve no purpose and would harm relations between federal and state tribunals. Nonetheless, the Court's analysis in this particular case is unacceptable to me. It works injustice on this § 1983 plaintiff, and it makes more difficult the consistent protection of constitutional rights, a consideration that was at the core of the enacters' intent. Accordingly, I dissent.

. . . . .

One should note also that in England v. Medical Examiners, 375 U.S. 411 (1964), the Court had affirmed the federal courts' special role in protecting constitutional rights under § 1983. In that case it held that a plaintiff required by the abstention doctrine to submit his constitutional claim first to a state court could not be precluded entirely from having the federal court, in which he initially had sought relief, pass on his constitutional claim. The Court relied on "the unqualified terms in which Congress, pursuant to constitutional authorization, has conferred specific categories of jurisdiction upon the federal courts," and on its "fundamental objections to any conclusion that a litigant who has properly invoked the jurisdiction of a federal district court to consider federal constitutional claims can be compelled, without his consent and through no fault of his own, to accept instead a state court's determination of those claims." Id., at 415. The Court set out its understanding as to when a litigant in a § 1983 case might be precluded by prior litigation, holding that "if a party freely and without reservation submits his federal claims for decision by the state courts, litigates them there, and has them decided there, then—whether or not he seeks direct review of the state decision in this Court—he has elected to forgo his right to return to the District Court." Id., at 419. I do not understand why the Court today should abandon this approach.

The Court now fashions a new doctrine of preclusion, applicable only to actions brought under § 1983, that is more strict and more confining than the federal rules of preclusion applied in other cases. In Montana v. United States, 440 U.S. 147 (1979), the Court pronounced three major factors to be considered in determining whether collateral estoppel serves as a barrier in the federal court:

> "[W]hether the issues presented ... are in substance the same ... ; whether controlling facts or legal principles have changed significantly since the state-court judgment; and finally, whether other special circumstances warrant an exception to the normal rules of preclusion." Id., at 155.

But now the Court states that the collateral estoppel effect of prior state adjudication should turn on only one factor, namely, what it considers the "one general limitation" inherent in the doctrine of preclusion: "that the concept of collateral estoppel cannot apply when the party against whom the earlier decision is asserted did not have a 'full and fair opportunity' to litigate that issue in the earlier case." ... If that one factor is present, the Court asserts, the litigant properly should be barred from relitigating the issue in federal court.[162] One cannot deny that this factor is an important one. I do not believe, however, that the doctrine of preclusion requires the inquiry to be so narrow,[163] and my understanding of the policies underlying § 1983 would lead me to consider all relevant factors in each case before concluding that preclusion was warranted.

In this case, the police officers seek to prevent a criminal defendant from relitigating the constitutionality of their conduct in searching his house, after the state trial court had found that conduct in part violative of the defendant's Fourth Amendment rights and in part justified by the circumstances. I doubt that the police officers, now defendants in this § 1983 action, can be considered to have been in privity with the State in its role as prosecutor. Therefore, only "issue preclusion" is at stake.

The following factors persuade me to conclude that this respondent should not be precluded from asserting his claim in federal court. First, at the time § 1983 was passed, a nonparty's ability, as a practical matter, to invoke collateral estoppel was nonexistent. One could not preclude an opponent from relitigating an issue in a new cause of action, though that issue had been determined conclusively in a prior proceeding, unless there was "mutuality." Additionally, the definitions of "cause of action" and "issue" were narrow.[164] As a result, and obviously, no preclusive effect

---

162. This articulation of the preclusion doctrine of course would bar a § 1983 litigant from relitigating any issue he *might* have raised, as well as any issue he actually litigated in his criminal trial.

163. See Restatement (Second) of Judgments § 68.1 (Tent.Draft No. 4, April 15, 1977) [referring to what became § 28 in Restatement Second of Judgments (1982)]; F. James & G. Hazard, Civil Procedure §§ 11.16–11.22 (2d ed.1977).

164. Compare McCaskill, Actions and Causes of Action, 34 Yale L.J. 614, 638 (1925) (defining "cause of action" as "that group of operative facts which, standing alone, would show a single right in the plaintiff and a single delict to that right giving cause for the state, through its courts, to afford relief to the party or parties whose right was invaded"), with C. Clark, Handbook on the Law of Code Pleading 84 (1928) (adopting "modern" rule expanding "cause of action" to include more than one "right"). See also 1 H. Herman, Law of Estoppel and Res Judicata §§ 92, 96 ("cause of action"), 98, 103, 111 ("issue") (1886); Developments in the Law—Res Judicata, 65 Harv.L.Rev. 818, 826, 841–843 (1952).

could arise out of a criminal proceeding that would affect subsequent *civil* litigation. Thus, the 42d Congress could not have anticipated or approved that a criminal defendant, tried and convicted in state court, would be precluded from raising against police officers a constitutional claim arising out of his arrest.

Also, the process of deciding in a state criminal trial whether to exclude or admit evidence is not at all the equivalent of a § 1983 proceeding. The remedy sought in the latter is utterly different. In bringing the civil suit the criminal defendant does not seek to challenge his conviction collaterally. At most, he wins damages. In contrast, the exclusion of evidence may prevent a criminal conviction. A trial court, faced with the decision whether to exclude relevant evidence, confronts institutional pressures that may cause it to give a different shape to the Fourth Amendment right from what would result in civil litigation of a damages claim. Also, the issue whether to exclude evidence is subsidiary to the purpose of a criminal trial, which is to determine the guilt or innocence of the defendant, and a trial court, at least subconsciously, must weigh the potential damage to the truth-seeking process caused by excluding relevant evidence. See Stone v. Powell, 428 U.S. 465, 489–495 (1976). Cf. Bivens v. Six Unknown Federal Narcotics Agents, 403 U.S. 388, 411–424 (dissenting opinion).

A state criminal defendant cannot be held to have chosen "voluntarily" to litigate his Fourth Amendment claim in the state court. The risk of conviction puts pressure upon him to raise all possible defenses. He also faces uncertainty about the wisdom of forgoing litigation on *any* issue, for there is the possibility that he will be held to have waived his right to appeal on that issue. The "deliberate bypass" of state procedures, which the imposition of collateral estoppel under these circumstances encourages, surely is not a preferred goal. To hold that a criminal defendant who raises a Fourth Amendment claim at his criminal trial "freely and without reservation submits his federal claims for decision by the state courts," see *England v. Medical Examiners*, 375 U.S., at 419, is to deny reality. The criminal defendant is an involuntary litigant in the state tribunal, and against him all the forces of the State are arrayed. To force him to a choice between forgoing either a potential defense or a federal forum for hearing his constitutional civil claim is fundamentally unfair.

I would affirm the judgment of the Court of Appeals.[165]

[165. See Restatement Second of Judgments § 86 (1982). 18 Wright, Miller & Cooper, Federal Practice and Procedure: Jurisdiction 2d § 4471 (1981); 28 Moore's Federal Practice ¶ 132.02[4][d] (3d ed.1998); Casad, Two Important Books on Res Judicata, 80 Mich.L.Rev. 664 (1982). See also Wright, Federal Courts § 100A (5th ed.1994); Symposium, Preclusion in a Federal System, 70 Cornell L.Rev. 599 (1985).

In a federal civil-rights action under 42 U.S.C. § 1983, a state-court judgment has the same claim-preclusive effect that it would have in state court. Migra v. Warren City School District, 465 U.S. 75 (1984).

Matsushita Electric Industrial Co. v. Epstein

Supreme Court of the United States, 1996.
516 U.S. 367, 116 S.Ct. 873, 134 L.Ed.2d 6.

■ JUSTICE THOMAS delivered the opinion of the Court.

This case presents the question whether a federal court may withhold full faith and credit from a state-court judgment approving a class-action settlement simply because the settlement releases claims within the exclusive jurisdiction of the federal courts. The answer is no. Absent a partial repeal of the Full Faith and Credit Act, 28 U.S.C. § 1738, by another federal statute, a federal court must give the judgment the same effect that it would have in the courts of the State in which it was rendered.

I

In 1990, petitioner Matsushita Electric Industrial Co. made a tender offer for the common stock of MCA, Inc., a Delaware corporation. The tender offer not only resulted in Matsushita's acquisition of MCA, but also precipitated two lawsuits on behalf of the holders of MCA's common stock. First, a class action was filed in the Delaware Court of Chancery against MCA and its directors for breach of fiduciary duty in failing to maximize shareholder value. The complaint was later amended to state additional claims against MCA's directors for, inter alia, waste of corporate assets by exposing MCA to liability under the federal securities laws. In addition, Matsushita was added as a defendant and was accused of conspiring with MCA's directors to violate Delaware law. The Delaware suit was based purely on state-law claims.

While the state class action was pending, the instant suit was filed in Federal District Court in California. The complaint named Matsushita as a defendant and alleged that Matsushita's tender offer violated Securities Exchange Commission (SEC) Rules 10b–3 and 14d–10. These Rules were created by the SEC pursuant to the 1968 Williams Act Amendments to the Securities Exchange Act of 1934 (Exchange Act), 48 Stat. 881, as amended, 15 U.S.C. § 78a et seq. Section 27 of the Exchange Act confers exclusive jurisdiction upon the federal courts for suits brought to enforce the Act or rules and regulations promulgated thereunder. See 15 U.S.C. § 78aa. The District Court declined to certify the class, entered summary judgment for Matsushita, and dismissed the case. The plaintiffs appealed to the Court of Appeals for the Ninth Circuit.

After the federal plaintiffs filed their notice of appeal but before the Ninth Circuit handed down a decision, the parties to the Delaware suit negotiated a settlement. In exchange for a global release of all claims arising out of the Matsushita–MCA acquisition, the defendants would deposit $2 million into a settlement fund to be distributed pro rata to the members of the class. As required by Delaware Chancery Rule 23, which is

---

A defendant who has pleaded guilty in state court is not precluded from bringing a § 1983 action in federal court claiming damages for an illegal search. Haring v. Prosise, 462 U.S. 306 (1983).]

modeled on Federal Rule of Civil Procedure 23, the Chancery Court certified the class for purposes of settlement and approved a notice of the proposed settlement. The notice informed the class members of their right to request exclusion from the settlement class and to appear and present argument at a scheduled hearing to determine the fairness of the settlement. In particular, the notice stated that "[b]y filing a valid Request for Exclusion, a member of the Settlement Class will not be precluded by the Settlement from individually seeking to pursue the claims alleged in the . . . California Federal Actions, . . . or any other claim relating to the events at issue in the Delaware Actions." . . . Two such notices were mailed to the class members and the notice was also published in the national edition of the Wall Street Journal. The Chancery Court then held a hearing. After argument from several objectors, the Court found the class representation adequate and the settlement fair. The order and final judgment of the Chancery Court incorporated the terms of the settlement agreement, providing:

> "All claims, rights and causes of action (state or federal, including but not limited to claims arising under the federal securities law, any rules or regulations promulgated thereunder, or otherwise), whether known or unknown that are, could have been or might in the future be asserted by any of the plaintiffs or any member of the Settlement Class *(other than those who have validly requested exclusion therefrom),* . . . in connection with or that arise now or hereafter out of the Merger Agreement, the Tender Offer, the Distribution Agreement, the Capital Contribution Agreement, the employee compensation arrangements, the Tender Agreements, the Initial Proposed Settlement, this Settlement . . . *and including without limitation the claims asserted in the California Federal Actions* . . . are hereby compromised, settled, released and discharged with prejudice by virtue of the proceedings herein and this Order and Final Judgment." In re MCA, Inc. Shareholders Litigation, C.A. No. 11740 (Feb. 22, 1993) . . . (emphasis added).

The judgment also stated that the notice met all the requirements of due process. The Delaware Supreme Court affirmed. In re MCA, Inc., Shareholders Litigation, 633 A.2d 370 (1993) (judgt. order).

Respondents were members of both the state and federal plaintiff classes. Following issuance of the notice of proposed settlement of the Delaware litigation, respondents neither opted out of the settlement class nor appeared at the hearing to contest the settlement or the representation of the class. On appeal in the Ninth Circuit, petitioner Matsushita invoked the Delaware judgment as a bar to further prosecution of that action under the Full Faith and Credit Act, 28 U.S.C. § 1738.

The Ninth Circuit rejected petitioner's argument, ruling that § 1738 did not apply. Epstein v. MCA, Inc., 50 F.3d 644, 661–666 (1995). Instead, the Court of Appeals fashioned a test under which the preclusive force of a state court settlement judgment is limited to those claims that "could . . . have been extinguished by the issue preclusive effect of an adjudication of the state claims." Id., at 665. The lower courts have taken varying approaches to determining the preclusive effect of a state court judgment, entered in a class or derivative action, that provides for the release of exclusively federal claims. We granted certiorari to clarify this important area of federal law. 515 U.S. 1187 (1995).

II

The Full Faith and Credit Act mandates that the "judicial proceedings" of any State "shall have the same full faith and credit in every court within the United States ... as they have by law or usage in the courts of such State ... from which they are taken." 28 U.S.C. § 1738. The Act thus directs all courts to treat a state court judgment with the same respect that it would receive in the courts of the rendering state. Federal courts may not "employ their own rules ... in determining the effect of state judgments," but must "accept the rules chosen by the State from which the judgment is taken." Kremer v. Chemical Constr. Corp., 456 U.S. 461, 481–482 (1982). Because the Court of Appeals failed to follow the dictates of the Act, we reverse.

A

The state court judgment in this case differs in two respects from the judgments that we have previously considered in our cases under the Full Faith and Credit Act. As respondents and the Court of Appeals stressed, the judgment was the product of a class action and incorporated a settlement agreement releasing claims within the exclusive jurisdiction of the federal courts. Though respondents urge "the irrelevance of section 1738 to this litigation," Brief for Respondents 25, we do not think that either of these features exempts the judgment from the operation of § 1738.

That the judgment at issue is the result of a class action, rather than a suit brought by an individual, does not undermine the initial applicability of § 1738. The judgment of a state court in a class action is plainly the product of a "judicial proceeding" within the meaning of § 1738. Cf. McDonald v. West Branch, 466 U.S. 284, 287–288 (1984) (holding that § 1738 does not apply to arbitration awards because arbitration is not a "judicial proceeding"). Therefore, a judgment entered in a class action, like any other judgment entered in a state judicial proceeding, is presumptively entitled to full faith and credit under the express terms of the Act.

Further, § 1738 is not irrelevant simply because the judgment in question might work to bar the litigation of exclusively federal claims. Our decision in Marrese v. American Academy of Orthopaedic Surgeons, 470 U.S. 373 (1985), made clear that where § 1738 is raised as a defense in a subsequent suit, the fact that an allegedly precluded "claim is within the exclusive jurisdiction of the federal courts *does not necessarily make § 1738 inapplicable*." Id., at 380 (emphasis added). In so holding, we relied primarily on *Kremer v. Chemical Constr. Corp.*, supra, which held, without deciding whether Title VII claims are exclusively federal, that state court proceedings may be issue preclusive in Title VII suits in federal court.

Kremer, we said, "implies that absent an exception to § 1738, state law determines at least the ... preclusive effect of a prior state judgment in a subsequent action involving a claim within the exclusive jurisdiction of the federal courts." *Marrese*, 470 U.S., at 381. Accordingly, we decided that "a state court judgment may in some circumstances have preclusive effect in a subsequent action within the exclusive jurisdiction of the federal courts." Id., at 380.

In *Marrese*, we discussed Nash County Board of Education v. Biltmore Co., 640 F.2d 484 (CA4), cert. denied, 454 U.S. 878 (1981), a case that concerned a state court settlement judgment. In *Nash*, the question was whether the judgment, which approved the settlement of state antitrust claims, prevented the litigation of exclusively federal antitrust claims. See 470 U.S., at 382, n. 2. We suggested that the approach outlined in *Marrese* would also apply in cases like *Nash* that involve judgments upon settlement: that is, § 1738 would control at the outset. See ibid. In accord with these precedents, we conclude that § 1738 is generally applicable in cases in which the state court judgment at issue incorporates a class action settlement releasing claims solely within the jurisdiction of the federal courts.

B

Marrese provides the analytical framework for deciding whether the Delaware court's judgment precludes this exclusively federal action. When faced with a state court judgment relating to an exclusively federal claim, a federal court must first look to the law of the rendering State to ascertain the effect of the judgment. See id., at 381–382. If state law indicates that the particular claim or issue would be barred from litigation in a court of that state, then the federal court must next decide whether, "as an exception to § 1738," it "should refuse to give preclusive effect to [the] state court judgment." Id., at 383. See also Migra v. Warren City School Dist. Bd. of Ed., 465 U.S. 75, 80 (1984) ("[I]n the absence of federal law modifying the operation of § 1738, the preclusive effect in federal court of [a] state-court judgment is determined by [state] law").

1

We observed in *Marrese* that the inquiry into state law would not always yield a direct answer. Usually, "a state court will not have occasion to address the specific question whether a state judgment has issue or claim preclusive effect in a later action that can be brought only in federal court." 470 U.S., at 381–382. Where a judicially approved settlement is under consideration, a federal court may consequently find guidance from general state law on the preclusive force of settlement judgments. See, e.g., id., at 382–383, n. 2 (observing in connection with *Nash* that "[North Carolina] law gives preclusive effect to consent judgment[s]"). Here, in addition to providing rules regarding the preclusive force of class-action settlement judgments in subsequent suits in state court, the Delaware courts have also spoken to the particular effect of such judgments in federal court.

Delaware has traditionally treated the impact of settlement judgments on subsequent litigation in state court as a question of claim preclusion. . . .

. . . These cases indicate that even if, as here, a claim could not have been raised in the court that rendered the settlement judgment in a class action, a Delaware court would still find that the judgment bars subsequent pursuit of the claim.

The Delaware Supreme Court has further manifested its understanding that when the Court of Chancery approves a global release of claims, its settlement judgment should preclude on-going or future federal court litigation of any released claims. . . . Perhaps the clearest statement of the Delaware Chancery Court's view on this matter was articulated in the suit preceding this one: "When a state court settlement of a class action releases all claims which arise out of the challenged transaction and is determined to be fair and to have met all due process requirements, the class members are bound by the release or the doctrine of issue preclusion. Class members cannot subsequently relitigate the claims barred by the settlement in a federal court." In re MCA, Inc. Shareholders Litigation, 598 A.2d 687, 691 (1991).[166] We are aware of no Delaware case that suggests otherwise.

Given these statements of Delaware law, we think that a Delaware court would afford preclusive effect to the settlement judgment in this case, notwithstanding the fact that respondents could not have pressed their Exchange Act claims in the Court of Chancery. The claims are clearly within the scope of the release in the judgment, since the judgment specifically refers to this lawsuit. As required by Delaware Court of Chancery Rule 23, see Prezant v. De Angelis, 636 A.2d 915, 920 (1994), the Court of Chancery found, and the Delaware Supreme Court affirmed, that the settlement was "fair, reasonable and adequate and in the best interests of the . . . Settlement class" and that notice to the class was "in full compliance with . . . the requirements of due process." In re MCA, Inc. Shareholders Litigation, C.A. No. 11740 (Feb. 22, 1993), reprinted in App. to Pet. for Cert. 73a, 74a. Cf. Phillips Petroleum Co. v. Shutts, 472 U.S. 797, 812 (1985) (due process for class action plaintiffs requires "notice plus an opportunity to be heard and participate in the litigation"). The Court of Chancery "further determined that the plaintiffs[,] . . . as representatives of the Settlement Class, have fairly and adequately protected the interests of the Settlement Class." In re MCA, Inc. Shareholders Litigation, supra . . . . Cf. Phillips Petroleum Co., supra, at 812 (due process requires "that the named plaintiff at all times adequately represent the interests of the absent class members").[167] Under Delaware Rule 23, as under Federal

---

166. In fact, the Chancery Court rejected the first settlement, which contained no opt-out provision, as unfair to the class precisely because it believed that the settlement would preclude the class from pursuing their exclusively federal claims in federal court. See In re MCA Inc. Shareholders Litigation, 598 A.2d 687, 692 (1991) ("[I]f this Court provides for the release of all the claims arising out of the challenged transaction, the claims which the Objectors have asserted in the federal suit will likely be forever barred").

167. Apart from any discussion of Delaware law, respondents contend that the settlement proceedings did not satisfy due process because the class was inadequately represented. See

Rule of Civil Procedure 23, "[a]ll members of the class, whether of a plaintiff or a defendant class, are bound by the judgment entered in the action unless, in a Rule 23(b)(3) action, they make a timely election for exclusion." 2 H. Newberg, Class Actions § 2755, p. 1224 (1977). See also Cooper v. Federal Reserve Bank of Richmond, 467 U.S. 867, 874 (1984) ("There is of course no dispute that under elementary principles of prior adjudication a judgment in a properly entertained class action is binding on class members in any subsequent litigation"). Respondents do not deny that, as shareholders of MCA's common stock, they were part of the plaintiff class and that they never opted out; they are bound, then, by the judgment.[168]

2

Because it appears that the settlement judgment would be res judicata under Delaware law, we proceed to the second step of the *Marrese* analysis and ask whether § 27 of the Exchange Act, which confers exclusive jurisdiction upon the federal courts for suits arising under the Act, partially repealed § 1738. Section 27 contains no express language regarding its relationship with § 1738 or the preclusive effect of related state court proceedings. Thus, any modification of § 1738 by § 27 must be implied. In deciding whether § 27 impliedly created an exception to § 1738, the "general question is whether the concerns underlying a particular grant of exclusive jurisdiction justify a finding of an implied partial repeal of § 1738." *Marrese*, 470 U.S., at 386. "Resolution of this question will depend on the particular federal statute as well as the nature of the claim or issue involved in the subsequent federal action.... [T]he primary consideration must be the intent of Congress." Ibid.

. . . . .

Section 27 provides that "[t]he district courts of the United States ... shall have exclusive jurisdiction ... of all suits in equity and actions at law brought to enforce any liability or duty created by this chapter or the rules

---

Brief for Respondents 34–45. Respondents make this claim in spite of the Chancery Court's express ruling, following argument on the issue, that the class representatives fairly and adequately protected the interests of the class. Cf. Prezant v. De Angelis, 636 A.2d 915, 923 (Del.1994) ("[The] constitutional requirement [of adequacy of representation] is embodied in [Delaware] Rule 23(a)(4), which requires that the named plaintiff 'fairly and adequately protect the interests of the class' "). We need not address the due process claim, however, because it is outside the scope of the question presented in this Court. See Yee v. Escondido, 503 U.S. 519, 533 (1992). While it is true that a respondent may defend a judgment on alternative grounds, we generally do not address arguments that were not the basis for the decision below. See Peralta v. Heights Medical Center, Inc., 485 U.S. 80, 86 (1988).

168. Respondents argue that their failure to opt out of the settlement class does not constitute consent to the terms of the settlement under traditional contract principles. Again, the issue raised by respondent—whether the settlement could bar this suit as a matter of contract law, as distinguished from § 1738 law—is outside the scope of the question on which we granted certiorari. We note, however, that if a State chooses to approach the preclusive effect of a judgment embodying the terms of a settlement agreement as a question of pure contract law, a federal court must adhere to that approach under § 1738. Kremer v. Chemical Constr. Corp., 456 U.S. 461, 481–482 (1982).

and regulations thereunder." 15 U.S.C. § 78aa. There is no suggestion in § 27 that Congress meant for plaintiffs with Exchange Act claims to have more than one day in court to challenge the legality of a securities transaction. Though the statute plainly mandates that suits alleging violations of the Exchange Act may be maintained only in federal court, nothing in the language of § 27 "remotely expresses any congressional intent to contravene the common-law rules of preclusion or to repeal the express statutory requirements of ... 28 U.S.C. § 1738." Allen v. McCurry [449 U.S. 90 (1980)], at 97–98.

Nor does § 27 evince any intent to prevent litigants in state court—whether suing as individuals or as part of a class—from voluntarily releasing Exchange Act claims in judicially approved settlements. While § 27 prohibits state courts from adjudicating claims arising under the Exchange Act, it does not prohibit state courts from approving the release of Exchange Act claims in the settlement of suits over which they have properly exercised jurisdiction, i.e., suits arising under state law or under federal law for which there is concurrent jurisdiction. In this case, for example, the Delaware action was not "brought to enforce" any rights or obligations under the Act. The Delaware court asserted judicial power over a complaint asserting purely state law causes of action[169] and, after the parties agreed to settle, certified the class and approved the settlement pursuant to the requirements of Delaware Rule of Chancery 23 and the Due Process Clause. Thus, the Delaware court never trespassed upon the exclusive territory of the federal courts, but merely approved the settlement of a common-law suit pursuant to state and nonexclusive federal law. . . .

. . . . .

Finally, precedent supports the conclusion that the concerns underlying the grant of exclusive jurisdiction in § 27 are not undermined by state-court approval of settlements releasing Exchange Act claims. We have held that state court proceedings may, in various ways, subsequently affect the litigation of exclusively federal claims without running afoul of the federal jurisdictional grant in question. In Becher v. Contoure Laboratories, Inc., 279 U.S. 388 (1929) (cited in *Marrese*, 470 U.S., at 381), we held that state court findings of fact were issue preclusive in federal patent suits. We did so with full recognition that "the logical conclusion from the establishing of [the state law] claim is that Becher's patent is void." 279 U.S., at 391. . . .

We have also held that Exchange Act claims may be resolved by arbitration rather than litigation in federal court. In Shearson/American Express Inc. v. McMahon, 482 U.S. 220 (1987), we found that parties to an arbitration agreement could waive the right to have their Exchange Act claims tried in federal court and agree to arbitrate the claims. Id., at 227–

---

169. Though the plaintiff class premised one of its claims of fiduciary breach on the allegation that MCA wasted corporate assets by exposing the corporation to liability under the federal securities laws, the cause pleaded was nonetheless a state common-law action for breach of fiduciary duty.

228. It follows that state court litigants ought also to be able to waive, or "release," the right to litigate Exchange Act claims in a federal forum as part of a settlement agreement. As *Shearson/American Express Inc.* demonstrates, a statute conferring exclusive federal jurisdiction for a certain class of claims does not necessarily require resolution of those claims in a federal court. Taken together, these cases stand for the general proposition that even when exclusively federal claims are at stake, there is no "universal right to litigate a federal claim in a federal district court." *Allen v. McCurry*, 449 U.S., at 105. If class action plaintiffs wish to preserve absolutely their right to litigate exclusively federal claims in federal court, they should either opt out of the settlement class or object to the release of any exclusively federal claims. In fact, some of the plaintiffs in the Delaware class action requested exclusion from the settlement class. They are now proceeding in federal court with their federal claims, unimpeded by the Delaware judgment.

In the end, §§ 27 and 1738 "do not pose an either-or proposition." Connecticut Nat. Bank v. Germain, 503 U.S. 249, 253 (1992). They can be reconciled by reading § 1738 to mandate full faith and credit of state court judgments incorporating global settlements, provided the rendering court had jurisdiction over the underlying suit itself, and by reading § 27 to prohibit state courts from exercising jurisdiction over suits arising under the Exchange Act. Cf. C. Wright, A. Miller, & E. Cooper, Federal Practice and Procedure § 4470 pp. 688–689 (1981) ("[S]ettlement of state court litigation has been held to defeat a subsequent federal action if the settlement was intended to apply to claims in exclusive federal jurisdiction as well as other claims.... These rulings are surely correct"). Congress' intent to provide an exclusive federal forum for adjudication of suits to enforce the Exchange Act is clear enough. But we can find no suggestion in § 27 that Congress meant to override the "principles of comity and repose embodied in § 1738," *Kremer v. Chemical Constr. Corp.*, 456 U.S., at 463, by allowing plaintiffs with Exchange Act claims to release those claims in state court and then litigate them in federal court. We conclude that the Delaware courts would give the settlement judgment preclusive effect in a subsequent proceeding and, further, that § 27 did not effect a partial repeal of § 1738.

C

The Court of Appeals did not engage in any analysis of Delaware law pursuant to § 1738. Rather, the Court of Appeals declined to apply § 1738 on the ground that where the rendering forum lacked jurisdiction over the subject matter or the parties, full faith and credit is not required. 50 F.3d, at 661, 666.... The Court of Appeals decided that the subject-matter jurisdiction exception to full faith and credit applies to this case because the Delaware court acted outside the bounds of its own jurisdiction in approving the settlement, since the settlement released exclusively federal claims. See 50 F.3d, at 661–662, and n. 25.

As explained above, the state court in this case clearly possessed jurisdiction over the subject matter of the underlying suit and over the defendants. Only if this were not so—for instance, if the complaint alleged violations of the Exchange Act and the Delaware court rendered a judgment on the merits of those claims—would the exception to § 1738 for lack of subject-matter jurisdiction apply. Where, as here, the rendering court in fact had subject-matter jurisdiction, the subject-matter-jurisdiction exception to full faith and credit is simply inapposite. In such a case, the relevance of a federal statute that provides for exclusive federal jurisdiction is not to the state court's possession of jurisdiction per se, but to the existence of a partial repeal of § 1738.[170]

* * *

The judgment of the Court of Appeals is reversed and remanded for proceedings consistent with this opinion.

It is so ordered.

■ JUSTICE STEVENS, concurring in part and dissenting in part.

While I join Parts I, II–A, and II–C of the Court's opinion, and while I also agree with the Court's reasons for concluding that § 27 of the Exchange Act does not create an implied partial repeal of the Full Faith and Credit Act, I join neither Part II–B nor the Court's judgment because I agree with JUSTICE GINSBURG that the question of Delaware law should be addressed by the Court of Appeals in the first instance, and that the Ninth Circuit remains free to consider whether Delaware courts fully and fairly litigated the adequacy of class representation.

■ JUSTICE GINSBURG, with whom JUSTICE STEVENS joins, and with whom JUSTICE SOUTER joins as to Part II–B, concurring in part and dissenting in part.

I join the Court's judgment to the extent that it remands the case to the Ninth Circuit. I agree that a remand is in order because the Court of Appeals did not attend to this Court's reading of 28 U.S.C. § 1738 in a controlling decision, Kremer v. Chemical Constr. Corp., 456 U.S. 461 (1982). But I would not endeavor, as the Court does, to speak the first word on the content of Delaware preclusion law. Instead, I would follow our standard practice of remitting that issue for decision, in the first instance, by the lower federal courts. See, e.g., Marrese v. American Academy of Orthopaedic Surgeons, 470 U.S. 373, 387 (1985).

I write separately to emphasize a point key to the application of § 1738: A state-court judgment generally is not entitled to full faith and credit unless it satisfies the requirements of the Fourteenth Amendment's

---

170. Kalb v. Feuerstein, 308 U.S. 433 (1940), is not to the contrary. In that case, the federal statute at issue expressly prohibited certain common-law actions from being either instituted or maintained in state court. Id., at 440–441. Thus, by merely entertaining a common-law foreclosure suit, over which it otherwise would have had jurisdiction, the state court violated the terms of the Act. That is not the situation here, where there is no contention that just by entertaining the class action the Delaware court acted in violation of federal law.

Due Process Clause. See *Kremer*, 456 U.S., at 482–483. In the class action setting, adequate representation is among the due process ingredients that must be supplied if the judgment is to bind absent class members. See Phillips Petroleum Co. v. Shutts, 472 U.S. 797, 808, 812 (1985); Prezant v. De Angelis, 636 A.2d 915, 923–924 (Del.1994).

Suitors in this action (called the "Epstein plaintiffs" in this opinion), respondents here, argued before the Ninth Circuit, and again before this Court, that they cannot be bound by the Delaware settlement because they were not adequately represented by the Delaware class representatives. They contend that the Delaware representatives' willingness to release federal securities claims within the exclusive jurisdiction of the federal courts for a meager return to the class members, but a solid fee to the Delaware class attorneys, disserved the interests of the class, particularly, the absentees. The inadequacy of representation was apparent, the Epstein plaintiffs maintained, for at the time of the settlement, the federal claims were *sub judice* in the proper forum for those claims—the federal judiciary. Although the Ninth Circuit decided the case without reaching the due process check on the full faith and credit obligation, that inquiry remains open for consideration on remand. . . .

. . . . .

II

A

Section 1738's full faith and credit instruction, as the Court indicates, requires the forum asked to recognize a judgment first to determine the preclusive effect the judgment would have in the rendering court. See *Kremer*, 456 U.S., at 466; *Marrese*, 470 U.S., at 381. Because the Ninth Circuit did not evaluate the preclusive effect of the Delaware judgment through the lens of that State's preclusion law, I would remand for that determination. See id., at 386–387; Migra v. Warren City School Dist. Bd. of Ed., 465 U.S. 75, 87 (1984) ("Prudence . . . dictates that it is the District Court, in the first instance, not this Court, that should interpret Ohio preclusion law and apply it.").

B

Every State's law on the preclusiveness of judgments is pervasively affected by the supreme law of the land. To be valid in the rendition forum, and entitled to recognition nationally, a state court's judgment must measure up to the requirements of the Fourteenth Amendment's Due Process Clause. *Kremer*, 456 U.S., at 482–483. "A State may not grant preclusive effect in its own courts to a constitutionally infirm judgment, and other state and federal courts are not required to accord full faith and credit to such a judgment." Id., at 482 (footnote omitted).

In *Phillips Petroleum Co. v. Shutts*, this Court listed minimal procedural due process requirements a class action money judgment must meet if it is to bind absentees; those requirements include notice, an opportunity to be heard, a right to opt out, and adequate representation. 472 U.S., at 812.

"[T]he Due Process Clause of course requires that the named plaintiff at all times adequately represent the interests of the absent class members." Ibid. (citing Hansberry v. Lee, 311 U.S. 32, 42–43, 45 (1940)). As the *Shutts* Court's phrase "at all times" indicates, the class representative's duty to represent absent class members adequately is a continuing one. 472 U.S., at 812; see also Gonzales v. Cassidy, 474 F.2d 67, 75 (CA5 1973) (representative's failure to pursue an appeal rendered initially adequate class representation inadequate, so that judgment did not bind the class).

. . . . .

In the instant case, the Epstein plaintiffs challenge the preclusive effect of the Delaware settlement, arguing that the Vice Chancellor never in fact made the constitutionally required determination of adequate representation.... They contend that the state court left unresolved key questions: notably, did the class representatives share substantial common interests with the absent class members, and did counsel in Delaware vigorously press the interests of the class in negotiating the settlement.[171] In particular, the Epstein plaintiffs question whether the Delaware class representatives—who filed the state lawsuit on September 26, 1990, two months before the November 26 tender offer announcement—actually tendered shares in December, thereby enabling them to litigate a Rule 14d–10 claim in federal court. They also suggest that the Delaware representatives undervalued the federal claims—claims they could only settle, but never litigate, in a Delaware court. Finally, the Epstein plaintiffs contend that the Vice Chancellor improperly shifted the burden of proof;[172] he rejected the Delaware objectors' charges of "collusion" for want of evidence while acknowledging that "suspicions [of collusion] abound." In re MCA, Inc. Shareholders Litigation, 1993 WL 43024, at *5.

Mindful that this is a court of final review and not first view, I do not address the merits of the Epstein plaintiffs' contentions, or Matsushita's counterargument that the issue of adequate representation was resolved by full and fair litigation in the Delaware Court of Chancery. These arguments remain open for airing on remand. I stress, however, the centrality of the procedural due process protection of adequate representation in class action lawsuits, emphatically including those resolved by settlement. See generally

---

171. The order approving the class for settlement purposes, the Epstein plaintiffs urge, contains no discussion of the adequacy of the representatives, see App. 198, and the order and final judgment approving the settlement contains only boilerplate language referring to the adequacy of representation, see id., at 204–205. The Delaware Supreme Court approved the Court of Chancery's judgment in a one paragraph order. See In re MCA, Inc. Shareholders Litigation, 633 A.2d 370 (1993) (judgment order).

172. Delaware law appears to place the burden of proof on the class representatives. See 2 Balotti & Finkelstein, [Delaware Law of Corporations and Business Organizations] § 13–17, p. 13–121 (class representative must prove satisfaction of Del.Ch. Rule 23(a) requirements, including adequacy of representation); see also 7A C. Wright, A. Miller, & M. Kane, Federal Practice and Procedure § 1765, pp. 273–274, and n. 29 (2d ed.1986); 3B J. Moore, Moore's Federal Practice ¶ 3.02–2 (2d ed.1995).

J. Coffee, Suspect Settlements in Securities Litigation, N.Y.L.J., March 28, 1991, p. 5, col. 1.[173]

[**173.** See Kahan & Silberman, Matsushita and Beyond: The Role of State Courts in Class Actions Involving Exclusive Federal Claims, 1996 Sup.Ct.Rev. 219.

It took three years for the Ninth Circuit to decide, on remand, that the preclusive effect of the Delaware judgment at issue in the principal case was binding on the Epstein plaintiffs. In an opinion reported in 1997 at 126 F.3d 1235 but withdrawn in 1999, a divided panel of the Ninth Circuit initially held that the Supreme Court had left it open for the Epstein plaintiffs to challenge the adequacy of the representation of their interests. In 1998 the panel voted to rehear the case. Upon rehearing, one judge having retired and another changing his vote, a divided panel ultimately held that the Supreme Court's decision in the principal case had foreclosed further inquiry into the adequacy of representation of absent class members in the Delaware class action. Epstein v. MCA, Inc., 179 F.3d 641 (9th Cir.1999), cert. denied sub nom. Epstein v. Matsushita Electric Industrial Co., Ltd., 528 U.S. 1004 (1999).

The Ninth Circuit's analysis conflicts with that of the Second Circuit, which has permitted class members to raise the issue of the adequacy of their representation by collateral attack on a putatively binding class judgment. See Stephenson v. Dow Chemical Co., 273 F.3d 249 (2d Cir.2001), aff'd in part by an equally divided Court and vacated in part, 539 U.S. 111 (2003). Justice Stevens's non-participation deprived the Court of a deciding vote.

In Parsons Steel, Inc. v. First Alabama Bank, 474 U.S. 518 (1986), the Supreme Court dealt with the Anti–Injunction Act, 28 U.S.C. § 2283, reprinted supra p. 478. The *Parsons* Court held that the third exception to the Anti–Injunction Act—"to protect or effectuate its judgment" —is not an implied repeal of the full Faith and Credit Act. "We believe that the Anti–Injunction Act and the Full Faith and Credit Act can be construed consistently, simply by limiting the relitigation exception of the Anti–Injunction Act to those situations in which the state court has not yet ruled on the merits of the res judicata issue. Once the state court has finally rejected a claim of res judicata, then the Full Faith and Credit Act becomes applicable and federal courts must turn to state law to determine the preclusive effect of the state court's action." 474 U.S., at 524.

In Richards v. Jefferson County, 517 U.S. 793 (1996), the Court reaffirmed that while "[s]tate courts are generally free to develop their own rules for protecting against the relitigation of common issues or the piecemeal resolution of disputes," state power to enforce "extreme applications of the doctrine of res judicata" is limited by the federal constitutional right to due process of law. Although modern conceptions of "privity" permit persons to be precluded by prior litigation to which they were not party in any formal sense, due process demands that their interests have been adequately represented. In holding that the present plaintiffs' due-process rights were violated for lack of adequate representation of their interests in a previous, putatively preclusive lawsuit, the Court appeared to give particular weight to the fact that the prior judgment had not addressed the federal constitutional claims that the present plaintiffs sought to litigate.

See also Taylor v. Sturgell, 553 U.S. 880 (2008) (disapproving attempts by some circuit courts to expand the reach of nonparty preclusion through the concept of "virtual representation," in which a nonparty could be bound by a judgment if she had been "virtually represented" by a party based on a variety of factors).]

CHAPTER X

THE LAW APPLIED IN THE FEDERAL COURTS

SECTION 1. THE ERIE DOCTRINE

STATUTES

28 U.S.C. § 1652. State laws as rules of decision (Rules of Decision Act)

The laws of the several states, except where the Constitution or treaties of the United States or Acts of Congress otherwise require or provide, shall be regarded as rules of decision in civil actions in the courts of the United States, in cases where they apply.[1]

28 U.S.C. § 2072. Rules of Procedure and Evidence; Power to Prescribe. (Rules Enabling Act)

(a) The Supreme Court shall have the power to prescribe general rules of practice and procedure and rules of evidence for cases in the United States district courts (including proceedings before magistrates thereof) and courts of appeals.

(b) Such rules shall not abridge, enlarge or modify any substantive right. All laws in conflict with such rules shall be of no further force or effect after such rules have taken effect.

(c) Such rules may define when a ruling of a district court is final for the purposes of appeal under section 1291 of this title.

[1. The section is derived from the Judiciary Act of 1789 (Act of September 24, 1789, Ch. 20, § 34, 1 Stat. 92). Charles Warren gives an illuminating account of the legislative history of the Act, in his article, New Light on the History of the Federal Judiciary Act of 1789, 37 Harv.L.Rev. 49 (1923). He deals with this section at pp. 81–88, and see especially p. 87. His view, which is summarized infra n. 6, is sharply challenged in Ritz, Rewriting the History of the Judiciary Act of 1789 (1990).

The issues of this chapter, and other problems, are dealt with in two wideranging and suggestive discussions, Hart, The Relations between State and Federal Law, 54 Colum.L.Rev. 489 (1954), and Friendly, In Praise of Erie—And of the New Federal Common Law, 39 N.Y.U.L.Rev. 383 (1964).]

Erie Railroad Co. v. Tompkins

Supreme Court of the United States, 1938.
304 U.S. 64, 58 S.Ct. 817, 82 L.Ed. 1188.

Certiorari, 302 U.S. 671, to review the affirmance of a judgment recovered against the railroad company in an action for personal injuries. The accident was in Pennsylvania. The action was in New York, jurisdiction being based on diversity of citizenship.

Mr. Theodore Kiendl, with whom Messrs. William C. Cannon and Harold W. Bissell were on the brief, for petitioner.

. . . . .

We do not question the finality of the holding of this Court in Swift v. Tyson, 16 Pet. [41 U.S.] 1, that the "laws of the several States" referred to in the Rules of Decision Act do not include state court decisions as such. But whether by virtue of the Act or of comity, it is well settled that such decisions are pertinent, and, under certain circumstances, controlling in ascertaining or determining the law of the State.

. . . . .

The implication from the *Swift* case would seem to be that the federal courts would follow the state rule if established with such definiteness and finality that the state courts would no longer resort to the general sources of the common law or to general reasoning and legal analogies, but would regard the question as foreclosed in the State.

. . . . .

The Pennsylvania decisions denying permissive rights on longitudinal pathways, as distinguished from crossing, declare a Pennsylvania rule sufficiently local in nature to be controlling, even though more definiteness and finality might be required in a rule of a more general nature. It rests expressly on a local policy relating to the efficient operation of railroads, a policy which presumably was dictated by local conditions.

Mr. Fred H. Rees, with whom Messrs. Alexander L. Strouse and William Walsh were on the brief, for respondent.

In cases involving questions of general law, federal courts will exercise their independent judgment.

This doctrine, which is now elementary, found its inception in Swift v. Tyson, 16 Pet. [41 U.S.] 1; has constantly been reaffirmed by this Court and was most recently applied in the case of Black & White Taxicab Co. v. Brown & Yellow Taxicab Co., 276 U.S. 518.

Decisions of this Court, as well as logic and reason, have established that questions of the type presented here, involving railroad accidents, are questions of general law, upon which independent judgment may be exercised by federal courts. . . .

. . . . .

■ MR. JUSTICE BRANDEIS delivered the opinion of the Court.

The question for decision is whether the oft-challenged doctrine of *Swift v. Tyson*[2] shall now be disapproved.

Tompkins, a citizen of Pennsylvania, was injured on a dark night by a passing freight train of the Erie Railroad Company while walking along its right of way at Hughestown in that State. He claimed that the accident occurred through negligence in the operation, or maintenance, of the train; that he was rightfully on the premises as licensee because on a commonly used beaten footpath which ran for a short distance alongside the tracks; and that he was struck by something which looked like a door projecting from one of the moving cars. To enforce that claim he brought an action in the federal court for southern New York, which had jurisdiction because the company is a corporation of that State. It denied liability; and the case was tried by a jury.

The Erie insisted that its duty to Tompkins was no greater than that owed to a trespasser. It contended, among other things, that its duty to Tompkins, and hence its liability, should be determined in accordance with the Pennsylvania law; that under the law of Pennsylvania, as declared by its highest court, persons who use pathways along the railroad right of way—that is a longitudinal pathway as distinguished from a crossing—are to be deemed trespassers; and that the railroad is not liable for injuries to undiscovered trespassers resulting from its negligence, unless it be wanton or wilful. Tompkins denied that any such rule had been established by the decisions of the Pennsylvania courts; and contended that, since there was no statute of the State on the subject, the railroad's duty and liability is to be determined in federal courts as a matter of general law.

The trial judge refused to rule that the applicable law precluded recovery. The jury brought in a verdict of $30,000; and the judgment entered thereon was affirmed by the Circuit Court of Appeals, which held, 90 F.2d 603, 604, that it was unnecessary to consider whether the law of Pennsylvania was as contended, because the question was one not of local, but of general, law and that "upon questions of general law the federal courts are free, in the absence of a local statute, to exercise their independent judgment as to what the law is; and it is well settled that the question of the responsibility of a railroad for injuries caused by its servants is one of general law.... Where the public has made open and notorious use of a

---

2. 16 Pet. [41 U.S.] 1 (1842). Leading cases applying the doctrine are collected in Black & White Taxicab Co. v. Brown & Yellow Taxicab Co., 276 U.S. 518, 530, 531. Dissent from its application or extension was expressed as early as 1845 by Mr. Justice McKinley (and Mr. Chief Justice Taney) in Lane v. Vick, 3 How. [44 U.S.] 464, 477. Dissenting opinions were also written by Mr. Justice Daniel in Rowan v. Runnels, 5 How. [46 U.S.] 134, 140; by Mr. Justice Nelson in Williamson v. Berry, 8 How. [49 U.S.] 495, 550, 558; by Mr. Justice Campbell in Pease v. Peck, 18 How. [59 U.S.] 595, 599, 600; and by Mr. Justice Miller in Gelpcke v. City of Dubuque, 1 Wall. [68 U.S.] 175, 207, and Butz v. City of Muscatine, 8 Wall. [75 U.S.] 575, 585. Vigorous attack upon the entire doctrine was made by Mr. Justice Field in Baltimore & Ohio R. Co. v. Baugh, 149 U.S. 368, 390, and by Mr. Justice Holmes in Kuhn v. Fairmont Coal Co., 215 U.S. 349, 370, and in the *Taxicab* case, 276 U.S., at page 532.

railroad right of way for a long period of time and without objection, the company owes to persons on such permissive pathway a duty of care in the operation of its trains.... It is likewise generally recognized law that a jury may find that negligence exists toward a pedestrian using a permissive path on the railroad right of way if he is hit by some object projecting from the side of the train."

The Erie had contended that application of the Pennsylvania rule was required, among other things, by § 34 of the Federal Judiciary Act of September 24, 1789, c. 20, 28 U.S.C. § 725, which provides:

> "The laws of the several States, except where the Constitution, treaties, or statutes of the United States otherwise require or provide, shall be regarded as rules of decision in trials at common law, in the courts of the United States, in cases where they apply."

Because of the importance of the question whether the federal court was free to disregard the alleged rule of the Pennsylvania common law, we granted certiorari.

First. Swift v. Tyson, 16 Pet. [41 U.S.] 1, 18, held that federal courts exercising jurisdiction on the ground of diversity of citizenship need not, in matters of general jurisprudence, apply the unwritten law of the State as declared by its highest court; that they are free to exercise an independent judgment as to what the common law of the State is—or should be ....[3]

. . . . .

The Court in applying the rule of § 34 to equity cases, in Mason v. United States, 260 U.S. 545, 559, said: "The statute, however, is merely declarative of the rule which would exist in the absence of the statute." The federal courts assumed, in the broad field of "general law," the power to declare rules of decision which Congress was confessedly without power to enact as statutes. Doubt was repeatedly expressed as to the correctness of the construction given § 34,[4] and as to the soundness of the rule which it

---

[3. In *Swift v. Tyson*, Justice Story, writing for the Court, had said: "In the ordinary use of language it will hardly be contended that the decisions of courts constitute laws. They are, at most, only evidence of what the laws are, and are not of themselves laws." He interpreted the Rules of Decision Act as limited "to state laws strictly local, that is to say, to the positive statutes of the state, and the construction thereof adopted by local tribunals, and to rights and titles to things having a permanent locality, such as the rights and titles to real estate, and to other matters immovable and intraterritorial in their nature and character." The Act did not apply to questions of general commercial law, dependent not on "the decisions of the local tribunals, but in the general principles and doctrines of commercial jurisprudence." See generally Wright & Kane, Federal Courts § 54 (6th ed.2002); 17 Moore's Federal Practice ¶¶ 124App.0102 (3d ed.1998); LaPiana, *Swift v. Tyson* and the Brooding Omnipresence in the Sky: An Investigation of the Idea of Law in Antebellum America, 20 Suffolk U.L.Rev. 771 (1986); Comment, *Swift v. Tyson* Exhumed, 79 Yale L.J. 284 (1969); Fletcher, The General Common Law and Section 34 of the Judiciary Act of 1789: The Example of Marine Insurance, 97 Harv.L.Rev. 1513 (1984).]

4. Pepper, The Border Land of Federal and State Decisions (1889) 57; Gray, The Nature and Sources of Law (1909 ed.) §§ 533–34; Trickett, Non–Federal Law Administered in Federal Courts (1906) 40 Am.L.Rev. 819, 821–24.

introduced.[5] But it was the more recent research of a competent scholar, who examined the original document, which established that the construction given to it by the Court was erroneous; and that the purpose of the section was merely to make certain that, in all matters except those in which some federal law is controlling, the federal courts exercising jurisdiction in diversity of citizenship cases would apply as their rules of decision the law of the State, unwritten as well as written.[6]

Criticism of the doctrine became widespread after the decision of Black & White Taxicab Co. v. Brown & Yellow Taxicab Co., 276 U.S. 518.[7] There Brown and Yellow, a Kentucky corporation owned by Kentuckians, and the Louisville and Nashville Railroad, also a Kentucky corporation, wished that the former should have the exclusive privilege of soliciting passenger and baggage transportation at the Bowling Green, Kentucky, railroad station; and that the Black and White, a competing Kentucky corporation, should be prevented from interfering with that privilege. Knowing that such a contract would be void under the common law of Kentucky, it was arranged that the Brown and Yellow reincorporate under the law of Tennessee, and that the contract with the railroad should be executed there. The suit was then brought by the Tennessee corporation in the federal court for western Kentucky to enjoin competition by the Black and White; an injunction issued by the District Court was sustained by the Court of Appeals; and

---

5.   Street, Is There a General Commercial Law of the United States (1873) 21 Am.L.Reg. 473; Hornblower, Conflict between State and Federal Decisions (1880) 14 Am.L.Rev. 211; Meigs, Decisions of the Federal Courts on Questions of State Law (1882) 8 So.L.Rev. (n.s.) 452, (1911) 45 Am.L.Rev. 47; Heiskell, Conflict between Federal and State Decisions (1882) 16 Am.L.Rev. 743; Rand, *Swift v. Tyson* versus *Gelpcke v. Dubuque* (1895) 8 Harv.L.Rev. 328, 341–43; Mills, Should Federal Courts Ignore State Laws? (1900) 34 Am.L.Rev. 51; Carpenter, Court Decisions and the Common Law (1917) 17 Col.L.Rev. 593, 602–03.

6.   Charles Warren, New Light on the History of the Federal Judiciary Act of 1789 (1923) 37 Harv.L.Rev. 49, 51–52, 81–88, 108. [Mr. Warren uncovered an earlier draft of the Rules of Decision Act in which the language used was "the Statute law of the several States in force for the time being and their unwritten or common law now in use, whether by adoption from the common law of England, the ancient statutes of the same or otherwise." As finally adopted, the Act spoke only of "laws of the several states." Mr. Warren thought that the latter phrase was a shorthand expression of the longer phrase in the earlier draft and that it included decisions of state courts. Mr. Warren's scholarship is criticized, and his thesis sharply attacked, in Ritz, Rewriting the History of the Judiciary Act of 1789, 8–12, 126–148 (Holt & LaRue eds. 1990). Ritz argues that: (1) the earlier draft Warren found was not used by the Senate in its work on § 34; (2) "the laws of the several states" was meant to refer to American law, as distinguished from British law; and (3) the purpose of § 34 may have been to allow development of a federal common law of crimes, pending the time when Congress might develop criminal statutes.]

7.   Shelton, Concurrent Jurisdiction—Its Necessity and Its Dangers (1928) 15 Va.L.Rev. 137; Frankfurter, Distribution of Judicial Power Between Federal and State Courts (1928) 13 Corn.L.Q. 499, 524–530; Johnson, State Law and the Federal Courts (1929) 17 Ky.L.J. 355; Fordham, The Federal Courts and the Construction of Uniform State Laws (1929) 7 N.C.L.Rev. 423; Dobie, Seven Implications of *Swift v. Tyson* (1930) 16 Va.L.Rev. 225; Dawson, Conflict of Decisions between State and Federal Courts in Kentucky, and the Remedy (1931) 20 Ky.L.J. 1; Campbell, Is *Swift v. Tyson* an Argument for or against Abolishing Diversity of Citizenship Jurisdiction? (1932) 18 A.B.A. 809; Ball, Revision of Federal Diversity Jurisdiction (1933) 28 Ill.L.Rev. 356, 362–64; Fordham, *Swift v. Tyson* and the Construction of State Statutes (1935) 41 W.Va.L.Q. 131.

this Court, citing many decisions in which the doctrine of *Swift v. Tyson* had been applied, affirmed the decree.

Second. Experience in applying the doctrine of *Swift v. Tyson*, had revealed its defects, political and social; and the benefits expected to flow from the rule did not accrue. Persistence of state courts in their own opinions on questions of common law prevented uniformity;[8] and the impossibility of discovering a satisfactory line of demarcation between the province of general law and that of local law developed a new well of uncertainties.[9]

On the other hand, the mischievous results of the doctrine had become apparent. Diversity of citizenship jurisdiction was conferred in order to prevent apprehended discrimination in state courts against those not citizens of the State. *Swift v. Tyson* introduced grave discrimination by non-citizens against citizens. It made rights enjoyed under the unwritten "general law" vary according to whether enforcement was sought in the state or in the federal court; and the privilege of selecting the court in which the right should be determined was conferred upon the non-citizen.[10] Thus, the doctrine rendered impossible equal protection of the law. In attempting to promote uniformity of law throughout the United States, the doctrine had prevented uniformity in the administration of the law of the State.

The discrimination resulting became in practice far-reaching. This resulted in part from the broad province accorded to the so-called "general law" as to which federal courts exercised an independent judgment.[11] In addition to questions of purely commercial law, "general law" was held to include the obligations under contracts entered into and to be performed within the State, the extent to which a carrier operating within a State may

---

8. Compare Mr. Justice Miller in Gelpcke v. City of Dubuque, 1 Wall. [68 U.S.] 175, 209. The conflicts listed in Holt, The Concurrent Jurisdiction of the Federal and State Courts (1888) 160 et seq. cover twenty-eight pages. See also Frankfurter, supra note [7], at 524–30; Dawson, supra note [7]; Note, Aftermath of the Supreme Court's Stop, Look and Listen Rule (1930) 43 Harv.L.Rev. 926; cf. Yntema and Jaffin, Preliminary Analysis of Concurrent Jurisdiction (1931) 79 U. of Pa.L.Rev. 869, 881–86. Moreover, as pointed out by Judge Augustus N. Hand in Cole v. Pennsylvania R. Co., 43 F.2d 953, 956–57, decisions of this Court on common law questions are less likely than formerly to promote uniformity.

9. Compare 2 Warren, The Supreme Court in United States History (rev. ed.1935) 89: "Probably no decision of the Court has ever given rise to more uncertainty as to legal rights; and though doubtless intended to promote uniformity in the operation of business transactions, its chief effect has been to render it difficult for business men to know in advance to what particular topic the Court would apply the doctrine. . . ." The Federal Digest, through the 1937 volume lists nearly 1000 decisions involving the distinction between questions of general and of local law.

10. It was even possible for a nonresident plaintiff defeated on a point of law in the highest court of a State nevertheless to win out by taking a nonsuit and reviewing the controversy in the federal court. Compare Gardner v. Michigan Cent. R. Co., 150 U.S. 349; Harrison v. Foley, 206 F. 57 (C.C.A. 8 [1913]); Interstate Realty & Inv. Co. v. Bibb County, 293 F. 721 (C.C.A. 5 [1923]); see Mills, supra note [5], at p. 54.

11. For a recent survey of the scope of the doctrine, see Sharp & Brennan, The Application of the Doctrine of *Swift v. Tyson* since 1900 (1929) 4 Ind.L.J. 367.

stipulate for exemption from liability for his own negligence or that of his employee; the liability for torts committed within the State upon persons resident or property located there, even where the question of liability depended upon the scope of a property right conferred by the State; and the right to exemplary or punitive damages. Furthermore, state decisions construing local deeds, mineral conveyances, and even devises of real estate were disregarded.

In part the discrimination resulted from the wide range of persons held entitled to avail themselves of the federal rule by resort to the diversity of citizenship jurisdiction. Through this jurisdiction individual citizens willing to remove from their own State and become citizens of another might avail themselves of the federal rule.[12] And, without even change of residence, a corporate citizen of the State could avail itself of the federal rule by re-incorporating under the laws of another State, as was done in the *Taxicab* case.

The injustice and confusion incident to the doctrine of *Swift v. Tyson* have been repeatedly urged as reasons for abolishing or limiting diversity of citizenship jurisdiction.[13] Other legislative relief has been proposed. If only a question of statutory construction were involved, we should not be prepared to abandon a doctrine so widely applied throughout nearly a century.[14] But the unconstitutionality of the course pursued has now been made clear and compels us to do so.

Third. Except in matters governed by the Federal Constitution or by Acts of Congress, the law to be applied in any case is the law of the State. And whether the law of the State shall be declared by its Legislature in a statute or by its highest court in a decision is not a matter of federal concern. There is no federal general common law. Congress has no power to declare substantive rules of common law applicable in a State whether they be local in their nature or "general," be they commercial law or a part of the law of torts. And no clause in the Constitution purports to confer such

---

12. See Cheever v. Wilson, 9 Wall. [76 U.S.] 108, 123; Robertson v. Carson, 19 Wall. [86 U.S.] 94, 106, 107; Morris v. Gilmer, 129 U.S. 315, 328; Dickerman v. Northern Trust Co., 176 U.S. 181, 192; Williamson v. Osenton, 232 U.S. 619, 625.

13. See, e.g., Hearings Before a Subcommittee of the Senate Committee on the Judiciary on S. 937, S. 939, and S. 3243, 72d Cong., 1st Sess. (1932) 6–8; Hearing before the House Committee on the Judiciary on H.R. 10594, H.R. 4526, and H.R. 11508, 72d Cong., 1st Sess. ser. 12 (1932) 97–104; Sen.Rep. No. 530, 72 Cong., 1st Sess. (1932) 4–6; Collier, A Plea Against Jurisdiction Because of Diversity (1913) 76 Cent.L.J. 263, 264, 266; Frankfurter, supra note [7]; Ball, supra note [7]; Warren, Corporations and Diversity of Citizenship (1933) 19 Va.L.Rev. 661, 686.

14. The doctrine has not been without defenders. See Eliot, The Common Law of the Federal Courts (1902) 36 Am.L.Rev. 498, 523–25; A.B. Parker, The Common Law Jurisdiction of the United States Courts (1907) 17 Yale L.J. 1; Schofield, *Swift v. Tyson*: Uniformity of Judge–Made State Law in State and Federal Courts (1910) 4 Ill.L.Rev. 533; Brown, The Jurisdiction of the Federal Courts Based on Diversity of Citizenship (1929) 78 U.Pa.L.Rev. 179, 189–91; J.J. Parker, The Federal Jurisdiction and Recent Attacks Upon It, 18 A.B.A.J. 433, 438 (1932); Yntema, The Jurisdiction of the Federal Courts in Controversies Between Citizens of Different States (1933) 19 A.B.A.J. 71, 74–75; Beutel, Common Law Judicial Technique and the Law of Negotiable Instruments—Two Unfortunate Decisions (1934) 9 Tulane L.Rev. 64.

a power upon the federal courts. As stated by Mr. Justice Field when protesting in Baltimore & Ohio R. Co. v. Baugh, 149 U.S. 368, 401, against ignoring the Ohio common law of fellow servant liability:

> "I am aware that what has been termed the general law of the country—which is often little less than what the judge advancing the doctrine thinks at the time should be the general law on a particular subject—has been often advanced in judicial opinions of this court to control a conflicting law of a State. I admit that learned judges have fallen into the habit of repeating this doctrine as a convenient mode of brushing aside the law of a State in conflict with their views. And I confess that, moved and governed by the authority of the great names of those judges, I have, myself, in many instances, unhesitatingly and confidently, but I think now erroneously, repeated the same doctrine. But, notwithstanding the great names which may be cited in favor of the doctrine, and notwithstanding the frequency with which the doctrine has been reiterated, there stands, as a perpetual protest against its repetition, the Constitution of the United States, which recognizes and preserves the autonomy and independence of the States—independence in their legislative and independence in their judicial departments. Supervision over either the legislative or the judicial action of the States is in no case permissible except as to matters by the Constitution specifically authorized or delegated to the United States. Any interference with either, except as thus permitted, is an invasion of the authority of the State and, to that extent, a denial of its independence."

The fallacy underlying the rule declared in *Swift v. Tyson* is made clear by Mr. Justice Holmes.[15] The doctrine rests upon the assumption that there is a "transcendental body of law outside of any particular State but obligatory within it unless and until changed by statute," that federal courts have the power to use their judgment as to what the rules of common law are; and that in the federal courts "the parties are entitled to an independent judgment on matters of general law":

> "but law in the sense in which courts speak of it today does not exist without some definite authority behind it. The common law so far as it is enforced in a State, whether called common law or not, is not the common law generally but the law of that State existing by the authority of that State without regard to what it may have been in England or anywhere else. . . .

> "the authority and only authority is the State, and if that be so, the voice adopted by the State as its own [whether it be of its Legislature or of its Supreme Court] should utter the last word."

Thus the doctrine of *Swift v. Tyson* is, as Mr. Justice Holmes said, "an unconstitutional assumption of powers by courts of the United States which no lapse of time or respectable array of opinion should make us

---

15. Kuhn v. Fairmont Coal Co., 215 U.S. 349, 370–372; Black & White Taxicab Co. v. Brown & Yellow Taxicab Co., 276 U.S. 518, 532–536.

hesitate to correct." In disapproving that doctrine we do not hold unconstitutional § 34 of the Federal Judiciary Act of 1789 or any other Act of Congress. We merely declare that in applying the doctrine this Court and the lower courts have invaded rights which in our opinion are reserved by the Constitution to the several States.

Fourth. The defendant contended that by the common law of Pennsylvania as declared by its highest court in Falchetti v. Pennsylvania R. Co., 307 Pa. 203, 160 A. 859, the only duty owed to the plaintiff was to refrain from wilful or wanton injury. The plaintiff denied that such is the Pennsylvania law.[16] In support of their respective contentions the parties discussed and cited many decisions of the Supreme Court of the State. The Circuit Court of Appeals ruled that the question of liability is one of general law; and on that ground declined to decide the issue of state law. As we hold this was error, the judgment is reversed and the case remanded to it for further proceedings in conformity with our opinion.

Reversed.

■ MR. JUSTICE CARDOZO took no part in the consideration or decision of this case.

■ MR. JUSTICE BUTLER.

. . . . .

So far as appears, no litigant has ever challenged the power of Congress to establish the rule as construed. It has so long endured that its destruction now without appropriate deliberation cannot be justified. There is nothing in the opinion to suggest that consideration of any constitutional question is necessary to a decision of the case. By way of reasoning, it contains nothing that requires the conclusion reached. Admittedly, there is no authority to support that conclusion. Against the protest of those joining in this opinion, the Court declines to assign the case for reargument. It may not justly be assumed that the labor and argument of counsel for the parties would not disclose the right conclusion and aid the Court in the statement of reasons to support it. Indeed, it would have been appropriate to give Congress opportunity to be heard before divesting it of power to prescribe rules of decision to be followed in the courts of the United States. See Myers v. United States, 272 U.S. 52, 176.

The course pursued by the Court in this case is repugnant to the Act of Congress of August 24, 1937, 50 Stat. 751. It declares: "That whenever the constitutionality of any Act of Congress affecting the public interest is drawn in question in any court of the United States in any suit or proceeding to which the United States, or any agency thereof, or any officer or employee thereof, as such officer or employee, is not a party, the court having jurisdiction of the suit or proceeding shall certify such fact to the

---

16. Tompkins also contended that the alleged rule of the *Falchetti* case is not in any event applicable here because he was struck at the intersection of the longitudinal pathway and a transverse crossing. The court below found it unnecessary to consider this contention, and we leave the question open.

Attorney General. In any such case the court shall permit the United States to intervene and become a party for presentation of evidence (if evidence is otherwise receivable in such suit or proceeding) and argument upon the question of the constitutionality of such Act. In any such suit or proceeding the United States shall, subject to the applicable provisions of law, have all the rights of a party and the liabilities of a party as to court costs to the extent necessary for a proper presentation of the facts and law relating to the constitutionality of such Act." That provision extends to this Court. § 5. If defendant had applied for and obtained the writ of certiorari upon the claim that, as now held, Congress has no power to prescribe the rule of decision, [by] § 34 as construed, it would have been the duty of this Court to issue the prescribed certificate to the Attorney General in order that the United States might intervene and be heard on the constitutional question. Within the purpose of the statute and its true intent and meaning, the constitutionality of that measure has been "drawn in question." Congress intended to give the United States the right to be heard in every case involving constitutionality of an Act affecting the public interest. In view of the rule that, in the absence of challenge of constitutionality, statutes will not here be invalidated on that ground, the Act of August 24, 1937 extends to cases where constitutionality is first "drawn in question" by the Court. No extraordinary or unusual action by the Court after submission of the cause should be permitted to frustrate the wholesome purpose of that Act. The duty it imposes ought here to be willingly assumed. If it were doubtful whether this case if within the scope of the Act, the Court should give the United States opportunity to intervene, and, if so advised, to present argument on the constitutional question, for undoubtedly it is one of great public importance. That would be to construe the Act according to its meaning.

The Court's opinion in its first sentence defines the question to be whether the doctrine of *Swift v. Tyson* shall now be disapproved; it recites that Congress is without power to prescribe rules of decision that have been followed by federal courts as a result of the construction of § 34 in *Swift v. Tyson* and since; after discussion, it declares [p. 738] that "the unconstitutionality of the course pursued [meaning the rule of decision resulting from that construction] compels" abandonment of the doctrine so long applied; and then near the end of the last page the Court states that it does not hold § 34 unconstitutional, but merely that, in applying the doctrine of *Swift v. Tyson* construing it, this Court and the lower courts have invaded rights which are reserved by the Constitution to the several States. But plainly through the form of words employed the substance of the decision appears; it strikes down as unconstitutional § 34 as construed by our decisions; it divests the Congress of power to prescribe rules to be followed by federal courts when deciding questions of general law. In that broad field it compels this and the lower federal courts to follow decisions of the courts of a particular State.

I am of opinion that the constitutional validity of the rule need not be considered, because under the law, as found by the courts of Pennsylvania and generally throughout the country, it is plain that the evidence required a finding that plaintiff was guilty of negligence that contributed to cause his injuries and that the judgment below should be reversed upon that ground.

■ MR. JUSTICE MCREYNOLDS concurs in this opinion.

■ MR. JUSTICE REED.

I concur in the conclusion reached in this case, in the disapproval of the doctrine of *Swift v. Tyson*, and in the reasoning of the majority opinion except in so far as it relies upon the unconstitutionality of the "course pursued" by the federal courts.

The "doctrine of *Swift v. Tyson*," as I understand it, is that the words "the laws," as used in § 34, line one, of the Federal Judiciary Act of September 24, 1789, do not include in their meaning "the decisions of the local tribunals." Mr. Justice Story, in deciding that point, said (16 Pet. 19):

> "Undoubtedly, the decisions of the local tribunals upon such subjects are entitled to, and will receive, the most deliberate attention and respect of this Court; but they cannot furnish positive rules, or conclusive authority, by which our own judgments are to be bound up and governed."

To decide the case now before us and to "disapprove" the doctrine of *Swift v. Tyson* requires only that we say that the words "the laws" include in their meaning the decisions of the local tribunals. As the majority opinion shows, by its reference to Mr. Warren's researches and the first quotation from Mr. Justice Holmes, that this Court is now of the view that "laws" includes "decisions," it is unnecessary to go further and declare that the "course pursued" was "unconstitutional," instead of merely erroneous.

The "unconstitutional" course referred to in the majority opinion is apparently the ruling in *Swift v. Tyson* that the supposed omission of Congress to legislate as to the effect of decisions leaves federal courts free to interpret general law for themselves. I am not at all sure whether, in the absence of federal statutory direction, federal courts would be compelled to follow state decisions. There was sufficient doubt about the matter in 1789 to induce the first Congress to legislate. No former opinions of this Court have passed upon it. Mr. Justice Holmes evidently saw nothing "unconstitutional" which required the overruling of *Swift v. Tyson*, for he said in the very opinion quoted by the majority, "I should leave *Swift v. Tyson* undisturbed, as I indicated in Kuhn v. Fairmont Coal Co., [215 U.S. 349,] but I would not allow it to spread the assumed dominion into new fields." Black & White Taxicab Co. v. Brown & Yellow Taxicab Co., 276 U.S. 518, 535. If the opinion commits this Court to the position that the Congress is without power to declare what rules of substantive law shall govern the federal courts, that conclusion also seems questionable. The line between procedural and substantive law is hazy but no one doubts federal power over procedure. Wayman v. Southard, 10 Wheat. [23 U.S.] 1. The Judiciary Article and the "necessary and proper" clause of Article One may fully authorize legislation, such as this section of the Judiciary Act.

In this Court, *stare decisis*, in statutory construction, is a useful rule, not an inexorable command. Burnet v. Coronado Oil & Gas Co., 285 U.S. 393, dissent, [285 U.S., at] p. 406, note 1. Compare Read v. Bishop of Lincoln, [1892] A.C. 644, 655; London Street Tramways Co. v. London County Council, [1898] A.C. 375, 379. It seems preferable to overturn an established construction of an Act of Congress, rather than, in the circumstances of this case, to interpret the Constitution. Cf. United States v. Delaware & Hudson Co., 213 U.S. 366.

There is no occasion to discuss further the range or soundness of these few phrases of the opinion. It is sufficient now to call attention to them and express my own non-acquiescence.[17]

Guaranty Trust Co. of New York v. York

Supreme Court of the United States, 1945.
326 U.S. 99, 65 S.Ct. 1464, 89 L.Ed. 2079.

Certiorari, 323 U.S. 693, to review the reversal of a summary judgment for the defendant (petitioner here) in a suit of which the federal court had jurisdiction solely because of diversity of citizenship of the parties.

■ MR. JUSTICE FRANKFURTER delivered the opinion of the Court.

In Russell v. Todd, 309 U.S. 280, 294, we had "no occasion to consider the extent to which federal courts, in the exercise of the authority conferred upon them by Congress to administer equitable remedies, are bound to follow state statutes and decisions affecting those remedies." The question thus carefully left open in *Russell v. Todd* is now before us. It arises under the following circumstances.

In May, 1930, Van Sweringen Corporation issued notes to the amount of $30,000,000. Under an indenture of the same date, petitioner, Guaranty Trust Co., was named trustee with power and obligations to enforce the rights of the noteholders in the assets of the Corporation and of the Van Sweringen brothers. In October, 1930, petitioner, with other banks, made large advances to companies affiliated with the Corporation and wholly controlled by the Van Sweringens. In October, 1931, when it was apparent that the Corporation could not meet its obligations, Guaranty cooperated in a plan for the purchase of the outstanding notes on the basis of cash for 50% of the face value of the notes and twenty shares of Van Sweringen Corporation's stock for each $1,000 note. This exchange offer remained open until December 15, 1931.

[17. See 19 Wright, Miller & Cooper, Federal Practice and Procedure: Jurisdiction 2d § 4503 (1996); 17 Moore's Federal Practice ¶¶ 124.01, 124 App.03 (3d ed.1998). There is a fascinating account of the litigation in the *Erie* case itself in Younger, What Happened in *Erie*, 56 Tex.L.Rev. 1010 (1978).

The historical, pragmatic, and philosophical justifications for the *Erie* doctrine are criticized in Borchers, The Origins of Diversity Jurisdiction, The Rise of Legal Positivism, and a Brave New World for *Erie* and *Klaxon*, 72 Tex.L.Rev. 79 (1993).]

Respondent York received $6,000 of the notes as a gift in 1934, her donor not having accepted the offer of exchange. In April, 1940, three accepting noteholders began suit against petitioner, charging fraud and misrepresentation. Respondent's application to intervene in that suit was denied, Hackner v. Guaranty Trust Co., 2 Cir., 117 F.2d 95, and summary judgment in favor of Guaranty was affirmed. Hackner v. Morgan, 2 Cir., 130 F.2d 300. After her dismissal from the *Hackner* litigation, respondent, on January 22, 1942, began the present proceedings.

The suit, instituted as a class action on behalf of non-accepting noteholders and brought in a federal court solely because of diversity of citizenship, is based on an alleged breach of trust by Guaranty in that it failed to protect the interests of the noteholders in assenting to the exchange offer and failed to disclose its self-interest when sponsoring the offer. Petitioner moved for summary judgment, which was granted, upon the authority of the *Hackner* case. On appeal, the Circuit Court of Appeals, one Judge dissenting, found that the *Hackner* decision did not foreclose this suit, and held that in a suit brought on the equity side of a federal district court that court is not required to apply the State statute of limitations that would govern like suits in the courts of a State where the federal court is sitting even though the exclusive basis of federal jurisdiction is diversity of citizenship. 143 F.2d 503. The importance of the question for the disposition of litigation in the federal courts led us to bring the case here. . . .

In view of the basis of the decision below, it is not for us to consider whether the New York statute would actually bar this suit were it brought in a State court. Our only concern is with the holding that the federal courts in a suit like this are not bound by local law.

. . . [T]he body of adjudications concerning equitable relief in diversity cases leaves no doubt that the federal courts enforced State-created substantive rights if the mode of proceeding and remedy were consonant with the traditional body of equitable remedies, practice and procedure, and in so doing they were enforcing rights created by the States and not arising under any inherent or statutory federal law.

Inevitably, therefore, the principle of Erie R. Co. v. Tompkins, [304 U.S. 64,] an action at law, was promptly applied to a suit in equity. Ruhlin v. New York Life Ins. Co., 304 U.S. 202.

And so this case reduces itself to the narrow question whether, when no recovery could be had in a State court because the action is barred by the statute of limitations, a federal court in equity can take cognizance of the suit because there is diversity of citizenship between the parties. Is the outlawry, according to State law, of a claim created by the States a matter of "substantive rights" to be respected by a federal court of equity when that court's jurisdiction is dependent on the fact that there is a State-created right, or is such statute of "a mere remedial character," Henrietta Mills v. Rutherford Co., [281 U.S. 121, 128], which a federal court may disregard?

Matters of "substance" and matters of "procedure" are much talked about in the books as though they defined a great divide cutting across the whole domain of law. But, of course, "substance" and "procedure" are the same key-words to very different problems. Neither "substance" nor "procedure" represents the same invariants. Each implies different variables depending upon the particular problem for which it is used. See Home Ins. Co. v. Dick, 281 U.S. 397, 409. And the different problems are only distantly related at best, for the terms are in common use in connection with situations turning on such different considerations as those that are relevant to questions pertaining to ex post facto legislation, the impairment of the obligations of contract, the enforcement of federal rights in the State courts and the multitudinous phases of the conflict of laws. See, e.g., American Ry. Exp. Co. v. Levee, 263 U.S. 19, 21; Davis v. Wechsler, 263 U.S. 22, 24, 25; Worthen Co. v. Kavanaugh, 295 U.S. 56, 60; Garrett v. Moore–McCormack Co., 317 U.S. 239, 248, 249; and see Tunks, Categorization and Federalism: "Substance" and "Procedure" After *Erie Railroad v. Tompkins* (1939) 34 Ill.L.Rev. 271, 274–276; Cook, Logical and Legal Bases of Conflict of Laws (1942) 163–165.

Here we are dealing with a right to recover derived not from the United States but from one of the States. When, because the plaintiff happens to be a nonresident, such a right is enforceable in a federal as well as in a State court, the forms and mode of enforcing the right may at times, naturally enough, vary because the two judicial systems are not identic. But since a federal court adjudicating a state-created right solely because of the diversity of citizenship of the parties is for that purpose, in effect, only another court of the State, it cannot afford recovery if the right to recover is made unavailable by the State nor can it substantially affect the enforcement of the right as given by the State.

And so the question is not whether a statute of limitations is deemed a matter of "procedure" in some sense. The question is whether such a statute concerns merely the manner and the means by which a right to recover, as recognized by the State, is enforced, or whether such statutory limitation is a matter of substance in the aspect that alone is relevant to our problem, namely does it significantly affect the result of a litigation for a federal court to disregard a law of a State that would be controlling in an action upon the same claim by the same parties in a State court?

It is therefore immaterial whether statutes of limitation are characterized either as "substantive" or "procedural" in State court opinions in any use of those terms unrelated to the specific issue before us. *Erie R. Co. v. Tompkins* was not an endeavor to formulate scientific legal terminology. It expressed a policy that touches vitally the proper distribution of judicial power between State and federal courts. In essence, the intent of that decision was to insure that, in all cases where a federal court is exercising jurisdiction solely because of the diversity of citizenship of the parties, the outcome of the litigation in the federal court should be substantially the same, so far as legal rules determine the outcome of a litigation, as it would be if tried in a State court. The nub of the policy that underlies *Erie R. Co.*

v. Tompkins is that for the same transaction the accident of a suit by a nonresident litigant in a federal court instead of in a State court a block away, should not lead to a substantially different result. And so, putting to one side abstractions regarding "substance" and "procedure," we have held that in diversity cases the federal courts must follow the law of the State as to burden of proof, Cities Service Oil Co. v. Dunlap, 308 U.S. 208, as to conflict of laws, Klaxon Co. v. Stentor Co.,[18] 313 U.S. 487, [and] as to contributory negligence, Palmer v. Hoffman, 318 U.S. 109, 117. . . . *Erie R. Co. v. Tompkins* has been applied with an eye alert to essentials in avoiding disregard of State law in diversity cases in the federal courts. A policy so

---

[18. The *Klaxon* case presented an interesting conceptual puzzle, which doubtless contributed to Justice Frankfurter's determination, in *York*, that the substance/procedural dichotomy did not provide a workable standard for the scope of the *Erie* doctrine. It involved a diversity suit in federal court in Delaware to remedy the breach of a contract executed and initially performed in New York. Klaxon, the petitioner, lost the case at trial when the jury returned a verdict of $100,000 in favor of respondent Stentor. Stentor then moved successfully for the district judge to add to that sum the prejudgment interest that would have been granted by a New York state court.

Delaware conflicts law, like that of virtually every other state at that time, adopted the *lex locus contractu* principle for choice of law in contract cases—applying the law of the place where the contract was made. But this was true only as to "substantive" law. The forum could still apply its own "procedural" law. For conflicts purposes, a statute of limitations (such as the one at issue in the *York* case) was considered "procedural." By contrast, most states (and the Restatement of Conflict of Laws) deemed the right to prejudgment interest for breach of a contract to be a "substantive" right and therefore governed by the law of the state where the contract was made, pursuant to the *lex locus contractu* rule. In *Klaxon*, however, the petitioner argued that Delaware courts would follow the minority rule, treat the right to prejudgment interest as "procedural," and apply Delaware rather than New York law. It violated *Erie*, petitioner Klaxon claimed, for the federal district court in Delaware to have added interest to the judgment when a Delaware state court would not have done so.

This presented the following conundrum: (1) it was thought that *Erie* only requires federal courts to follow state "substantive" law; (2) if the right to prejudgment interest is indeed "substantive" then New York law should be applied under Delaware's *lex locus contractu* rule—which is exactly what the district court did and the court of appeals affirmed; (3) if Delaware courts indeed (and this was an open question) treated the right to prejudgment interest as "procedural" for conflicts purposes and hence governed by forum law rather than the *lex locus contractu* rule, this would not be the sort of state law that is binding on federal courts under *Erie* because by Delaware's own determination it would make the right to prejudgment interest a matter of "procedural" rather than "substantive" law.

The Supreme Court held in *Klaxon* that *Erie* required a federal district court trying a diversity case in Delaware to follow all of Delaware's conflict-of-laws rules, even those that turned on Delaware's idiosyncratic classification of some issue as procedural in nature, and hence subject to forum law notwithstanding Delaware's mainstream adherence to the *lex locus contractu* rule as to substantive issues. *Erie* required deference to Delaware's conflict-of-laws rules notwithstanding that the "better view" for conflicts purposes might be to deem the issue in question substantive rather than procedural.

The *Klaxon* rule mandating that federal courts strictly adhere to state choice-of-law rules in diversity cases was strongly reaffirmed in Day & Zimmermann, Inc. v. Challoner, 423 U.S. 3 (1975) (per curiam). See generally Wright & Kane, Federal Courts § 57 (6th ed.2002); Fruenwald, Choice of Law in Federal Courts: A Reevaluation, 37 Brandeis L.J. 21 (1999); Cotter, *Klaxon Company v. Stentnor Electric Manufacturing Company*: Rule or Relic?, 4 Cooley L.Rev. 101 (1986).]

important to our federalism must be kept free from entanglements with analytical or terminological niceties.

Plainly enough, a statute that would completely bar recovery in a suit if brought in a State court bears on a State-created right vitally and not merely formally or negligibly. As to consequences that so intimately affect recovery or nonrecovery a federal court in a diversity case should follow State law. See Morgan, Choice of Law, Governing Proof (1944) 58 Harv. L.Rev. 153, 155–158. . . .

Prior to *Erie R. Co. v. Tompkins* it was not necessary, as we have indicated, to make the critical analysis required by the doctrine of that case of the nature of jurisdiction of the federal courts in diversity cases. But even before *Erie R. Co. v. Tompkins*, federal courts relied on statutes of limitations of the States in which they sat. In suits at law State limitations statutes were held to be "rules of decision" within § 34 of the Judiciary Act of 1789 and as such applied in "trials at common law." McClung v. Silliman, 3 Pet. [28 U.S.] 270, 277; President and Directors of Bank of Alabama v. Dalton, 9 How. [50 U.S.] 522; Leffingwell v. Warren, 2 Black [67 U.S.] 599; Bauserman v. Blunt, 147 U.S. 647. While there was talk of freedom of equity from such State statutes of limitations, the cases generally refused recovery where suit was barred in a like situation in the State courts, even if only by way of analogy. See, e.g., Godden v. Kimmell, 99 U.S. 201; Alsop v. Riker, 155 U.S. 448; Benedict v. City of New York, 250 U.S. 321, 327, 328. However in Kirby v. Lake Shore & M.S. Co., 120 U.S. 130, the Court disregarded a State statute of limitations where the Court deemed it inequitable to apply it.

To make an exception to *Erie R. Co. v. Tompkins* on the equity side of a federal court is to reject the considerations of policy which, after long travail, led to that decision. Judge Augustus N. Hand thus summarized below the fatal objection to such inroad upon *Erie R. Co. v. Tompkins*: "In my opinion it would be a mischievous practice to disregard state statutes of limitation whenever federal courts think that the result of adopting them may be inequitable. Such procedure would promote the choice of United States rather than of state courts in order to gain the advantage of different laws. The main foundation for the criticism of *Swift v. Tyson* was that a litigant in cases where federal jurisdiction is based only on diverse citizenship may obtain a more favorable decision by suing in the United States courts." 143 F.2d 503, 529, 531.

Diversity jurisdiction is founded on assurance to non-resident litigants of courts free from susceptibility to potential local bias. The Framers of the Constitution, according to Marshall, entertained "apprehensions" less distant suitors be subjected to local bias in State courts, or, at least, viewed with "indulgence the possible fears and apprehensions" of such suitors. Bank of the United States v. Deveaux, 5 Cranch [9 U.S.] 61, 87. And so Congress afforded out-of-State litigants another tribunal, not another body of law. The operation of a double system of conflicting laws in the same State is plainly hostile to the reign of law. Certainly, the fortuitous circumstance of residence out of a State of one of the parties to a litigation ought not to give rise to a discrimination against others equally concerned but locally resident. The source of substantive rights enforced by a federal court under diversity jurisdiction, it cannot be said too often, is the law of the States. Whenever that law is authoritatively declared by a State, whether its voice be the legislature or its highest court, such law ought to govern in litigation founded on that law, whether the forum of application is a State or a federal court and whether the remedies be sought at law or may be had in equity.

. . . . .

The judgment is reversed and the case is remanded for proceedings not inconsistent with this opinion.

So ordered.

■ MR. JUSTICE ROBERTS and MR. JUSTICE DOUGLAS took no part in the consideration or decision of this case.

■ MR. JUSTICE RUTLEDGE.

I dissent. . . .

. . . . .

If any characteristic of equity jurisprudence has descended unbrokenly from and within "the traditional scope of equity as historically evolved in the English Court of Chancery," it is that statutes of limitations, often in terms applying only to actions at law, have never been deemed to be rigidly applicable as absolute barriers to suits in equity as they are to actions at law. That tradition, it would seem, should be regarded as having been incorporated in the various Acts of Congress which have conferred equity jurisdiction upon the federal courts. So incorporated, it has been reaffirmed repeatedly by the decisions of this and other courts. It is now excised from those Acts. If there is to be excision, Congress, not this Court, should make it.

. . . . .

■ MR. JUSTICE MURPHY joins in this opinion.

———

Byrd v. Blue Ridge Rural Electric Cooperative, Inc.

Supreme Court of the United States, 1958.
356 U.S. 525, 78 S.Ct. 893, 2 L.Ed.2d 953.

■ MR. JUSTICE BRENNAN delivered the opinion of the Court.

[A lineman in the construction crew of a contractor was injured in the course of building new power lines, and sued the defendant, for whom the lines were built, for personal injuries. Jurisdiction was based on diversity. Defendant raised the affirmative defense that under South Carolina law plaintiff had the status of a statutory employee and was required to accept workmen's compensation benefits as his exclusive remedy, rather than suing for personal injuries. The district court erroneously struck the affirmative defense as a matter of law, and the jury returned a verdict in plaintiff's favor. The Fourth Circuit ordered judgment notwithstanding the verdict for defendant on the basis of this "statutory employer" defense, but the Supreme Court held that plaintiff should have had a new trial at which he might introduce evidence to show that he was not a statutory employee, evidence that, because of its misconstruction of the governing law, the trial court had not allowed to be introduced. The Court also considered the form of trial of this issue on remand.]

II.

A question is also presented as to whether on remand the factual issue is to be decided by the judge or by the jury. The respondent argues on the basis of the decision of the Supreme Court of South Carolina in Adams v. Davison–Paxon Co., 230 S.C. 532, 96 S.E.2d 566, that the issue of immunity should be decided by the judge and not by the jury. That was a negligence action brought in the state trial court against a store owner by an employee of an independent contractor who operated the store's millinery department. The trial judge denied the store owner's motion for a directed verdict made upon the ground that § 72–111 barred the plaintiff's action. The jury returned a verdict for the plaintiff. The South Carolina Supreme Court reversed, holding that it was for the judge and not the jury to decide on the evidence whether the owner was a statutory employer, and that the store owner had sustained his defense. The court rested its holding on decisions . . . involving judicial review of the Industrial Commission and said:

> "Thus the trial court should have in this case resolved the conflicts in the evidence and determined the fact of whether . . . [the independent contractor] was performing a part of the 'trade, business or occupation' of the department store-appellant and, therefore, whether . . . [the employee's] remedy is exclusively under the Workmen's Compensation Law." 230 S.C., at 543, 96 S.E.2d, at 572.

The respondent argues that this state-court decision governs the present diversity case and "divests the jury of its normal function" to decide the disputed fact question of the respondent's immunity under § 72–111. This is to contend that the federal court is bound under Erie R. Co. v. Tompkins, 304 U.S. 64, to follow the state court's holding to secure uniform enforcement of the immunity created by the State.

First. It was decided in *Erie R. Co. v. Tompkins* that the federal courts in diversity cases must respect the definition of state-created rights and obligations by the state courts. We must, therefore, first examine the rule in *Adams v. Davison–Paxon Co.* to determine whether it is bound up with these rights and obligations in such a way that its application in the federal court is required. Cities Service Oil Co. v. Dunlap, 308 U.S. 208.

The Workmen's Compensation Act is administered in South Carolina by its Industrial Commission. The South Carolina courts hold that, on judicial review of actions of the Commission under § 72–111, the question whether the claim of an injured workman is within the Commission's jurisdiction is a matter of law for decision by the court, which makes its own findings of fact relating to that jurisdiction. The South Carolina Supreme Court states no reasons in *Adams v. Davison–Paxon Co.* why, although the jury decides all other factual issues raised by the cause of action and defenses, the jury is displaced as to the factual issue raised by the affirmative defense under § 72–111. The decisions cited to support the holding are … concerned solely with defining the scope and method of judicial review of the Industrial Commission. A State may, of course, distribute the functions of its judicial machinery as it sees fit. The decisions relied upon, however, furnish no reason for selecting the judge rather than the jury to decide this single affirmative defense in the negligence action. They simply reflect a policy, cf. Crowell v. Benson, 285 U.S. 22, that administrative determination of "jurisdictional facts" should not be final but subject to judicial review. The conclusion is inescapable that the *Adams* holding is grounded in the practical consideration that the question had theretofore come before the South Carolina courts from the Industrial Commission and the courts had become accustomed to deciding the factual issue of immunity without the aid of juries. We find nothing to suggest that this rule was announced as an integral part of the special relationship created by the statute. Thus the requirement appears to be merely a form and mode of enforcing the immunity, Guaranty Trust Co. v. York, 326 U.S. 99, 108, and not a rule intended to be bound up with the definition of the rights and obligations of the parties. The situation is therefore not analogous to that in Dice v. Akron, C. & Y. R. Co., 342 U.S. 359, where this Court held that the right to trial by jury is so substantial a part of the cause of action created by the Federal Employers' Liability Act, 45 U.S.C. § 51 et seq. that the Ohio courts could not apply, in an action under that statute, the Ohio rule that the question of fraudulent release was for determination by a judge rather than by a jury.

Second. But cases following *Erie* have evinced a broader policy to the effect that the federal courts should conform as near as may be—in the absence of other considerations—to state rules even of form and mode where the state rules may bear substantially on the question whether the litigation would come out one way in the federal court and another way in the state court if the federal court failed to apply a particular local rule. E.g., *Guaranty Trust Co. v. York*, supra; Bernhardt v. Polygraphic Co., 350 U.S. 198. Concededly the nature of the tribunal which tries issues may be important in the enforcement of the parcel of rights making up a cause of action or defense, and bear significantly upon achievement of uniform enforcement of the right. It may well be that in the instant personal-injury case the outcome would be substantially affected by whether the issue of immunity is decided by a judge or a jury. Therefore, were "outcome" the only consideration, a strong case might appear for saying that the federal court should follow the state practice.

But there are affirmative countervailing considerations at work here. The federal system is an independent system for administering justice to litigants who properly invoke its jurisdiction. An essential characteristic of that system is the manner in which, in civil common-law actions, it distributes trial functions between judge and jury and, under the influence—if not the command[19]—of the Seventh Amendment, assigns the decisions of disputed questions of fact to the jury. Jacob v. City of New York, 315 U.S. 752. The policy of uniform enforcement of state-created rights and obligations, see, e.g., *Guaranty Trust Co. v. York*, supra, cannot in every case exact compliance with a state rule—not bound up with rights and obligations—which disrupts the federal system of allocating functions between judge and jury. Herron v. Southern Pacific Co., 283 U.S. 91. Thus the inquiry here is whether the federal policy favoring jury decisions of disputed fact questions should yield to the state rule in the interest of furthering the objective that the litigation should not come out one way in the federal court and another way in the state court.

We think that in the circumstances of this case the federal court should not follow the state rule. It cannot be gainsaid that there is a strong federal policy against allowing state rules to disrupt the judge-jury relationship in the federal courts. In *Herron v. Southern Pacific Co.*, supra, the trial judge in a personal-injury negligence action brought in the District Court for Arizona on diversity grounds directed a verdict for the defendant when it appeared as a matter of law that the plaintiff was guilty of contributory negligence. The federal judge refused to be bound by a provision of the Arizona Constitution which made the jury the sole arbiter of the question of contributory negligence. This Court sustained the action of the trial judge, holding that "state laws cannot alter the essential character or function of a federal court" because that function "is not in any sense a local matter, and state statutes which would interfere with the appropriate performance of that function are not binding upon the federal court under either the Conformity Act or the 'Rules of Decision' Act." Id., at 94. Perhaps even more clearly in light of the influence of the Seventh Amendment, the function assigned to the jury "is an essential factor in the process for which the Federal Constitution provides." Id., at 95. Concededly the *Herron* case was decided before *Erie R. Co. v. Tompkins*, but even when Swift v. Tyson, 16 Pet. [41 U.S.] 1, was governing law and allowed federal courts sitting in diversity cases to disregard state decisional law, it was never thought that state statutes or constitutions were similarly to be disregarded. Green v. Neal's Lessee, 6 Pet. [31 U.S.] 291. Yet *Herron* held that state statutes and constitutional provisions could not disrupt or alter the essential character or function of a federal court.[20]

Third. We have discussed the problem upon the assumption that the outcome of the litigation may be substantially affected by whether the issue of immunity is decided by a judge or a jury. But clearly there is not present here the certainty that a different result would follow, cf. *Guaranty Trust*

---

19.   Our conclusion makes unnecessary the consideration of—and we intimate no view upon—the constitutional question whether the right of jury trial protected in federal courts by the Seventh Amendment embraces the factual issue of statutory immunity when asserted, as here, as an affirmative defense in a common-law negligence action.

20.   Diederich v. American News Co., 128 F.2d 144, decided after *Erie R. Co. v. Tompkins*, held that an almost identical provision of the Oklahoma Constitution, art. 23, § 6, O.S.1951, was not binding on a federal judge in a diversity case.

Co. v. York, supra, or even the strong possibility that this would be the case, cf. *Bernhardt v. Polygraphic Co.*, supra. There are factors present here which might reduce that possibility. The trial judge in the federal system has powers denied the judges of many States to comment on the weight of evidence and credibility of witnesses, and discretion to grant a new trial if the verdict appears to him to be against the weight of the evidence. We do not think the likelihood of a different result is so strong as to require the federal practice of jury determination of disputed factual issues to yield to the state rule in the interest of uniformity of outcome.[21]

. . . . .

Reversed and remanded.

■ MR. JUSTICE WHITTAKER concurring in part and dissenting in part.

. . . . .

Inasmuch as the law of South Carolina, as construed by its highest court, requires its courts—not juries—to determine whether jurisdiction over the subject matter of cases like this is vested in its Industrial Commission, and inasmuch as the Court's opinion concedes "that in the instant personal-injury case the outcome would be substantially affected by whether the issue of immunity is decided by a judge or a jury," it follows that in this diversity case the jurisdictional issue must be determined by the judge—not by the jury. Insofar as the Court holds that the question of jurisdiction should be determined by the jury, I think the Court departs from its past decisions. I therefore respectfully dissent from part II of the opinion of the Court.

■ MR. JUSTICE FRANKFURTER, whom MR. JUSTICE HARLAN joins, dissenting.

[Justice Frankfurter agreed with the Fourth Circuit that the evidence of record established as a matter of law that defendant had been plaintiff's "statutory employer" and hence was entitled to judgment n.o.v. Seeing no need for further trial of the statutory-employer issue, Justice Frankfurter did not discuss Part II of the Court's opinion.]

Hanna v. Plumer

Supreme Court of the United States, 1965.
380 U.S. 460, 85 S.Ct. 1136, 14 L.Ed.2d 8.

■ MR. CHIEF JUSTICE WARREN delivered the opinion of the Court.

The question to be decided is whether, in a civil action where the jurisdiction of the United States district court is based upon diversity of

---

21.   Stoner v. New York Life Ins. Co., 311 U.S. 464, is not contrary. It was there held that the federal court should follow the state rule defining the evidence sufficient to raise a jury question whether the state-created right was established. But the state rule did not have the effect of nullifying the function of the federal judge to control a jury submission as did the Arizona constitutional provision which was denied effect in *Herron*. The South Carolina rule here involved affects the jury function as the Arizona provision affected the function of the judge: The rule entirely displaces the jury without regard to the sufficiency of the evidence to support a jury finding of immunity.

citizenship between the parties, service of process shall be made in the manner prescribed by state law or that set forth in Rule 4(d)(1) of the Federal Rules of Civil Procedure.

On February 6, 1963, petitioner, a citizen of Ohio, filed her complaint in the District Court for the District of Massachusetts, claiming damages in excess of $10,000 for personal injuries resulting from an automobile accident in South Carolina, allegedly caused by the negligence of one Louise Plumer Osgood, a Massachusetts citizen deceased at the time of the filing of the complaint. Respondent, Mrs. Osgood's executor and also a Massachusetts citizen, was named as defendant. On February 8, service was made by leaving copies of the summons and the complaint with respondent's wife at his residence, concededly in compliance with Rule 4(d)(1), which provides:

> "The summons and complaint shall be served together. The plaintiff shall furnish the person making service with such copies as are necessary. Service shall be made as follows:

> "(1) Upon an individual other than an infant or an incompetent person, by delivering a copy of the summons and of the complaint to him personally or by leaving copies thereof at his dwelling house or usual place of abode with some person of suitable age and discretion then residing therein...."

Respondent filed his answer on February 26, alleging, *inter alia*, that the action could not be maintained because it had been brought "contrary to and in violation of the provisions of Massachusetts General Laws (Ter.Ed.) Chapter 197, Section 9." That section provides:

> "Except as provided in this chapter, an executor or administrator shall not be held to answer to an action by a creditor of the deceased which is not commenced within one year from the time of his giving bond for the performance of his trust, or to such an action which is commenced within said year unless before the expiration thereof the writ in such action has been served by delivery in hand upon such executor or administrator or service thereof accepted by him or a notice stating the name of the estate, the name and address of the creditor, the amount of the claim and the court in which the action has been brought has been filed in the proper registry of probate...." Mass.Gen. Laws Ann., c. 197, § 9 (1958).

On October 17, 1963, the District Court granted respondent's motion for summary judgment, citing Ragan v. Merchants Transfer Co., 337 U.S. 530, and Guaranty Trust Co. v. York, [326 U.S. 99,] in support of its conclusion that the adequacy of the service was to be measured by § 9, with which, the court held, petitioner had not complied. On appeal, petitioner admitted noncompliance with § 9, but argued that Rule 4(d)(1) defines the method by which service of process is to be effected in diversity actions. The Court of Appeals for the First Circuit, finding that "[r]elatively recent amendments [to § 9] evince a clear legislative purpose to require personal notification within the year,"[22] concluded that the conflict of state and federal rules was over "a substantive rather than a procedural matter," and unanimously affirmed. 331 F.2d 157. Because of the threat to the goal of uniformity of federal procedure posed by the decision below, we granted certiorari, 379 U.S. 813.

We conclude that the adoption of Rule 4(d)(1), designed to control service of process in diversity actions, neither exceeded the congressional mandate embodied in the Rules Enabling Act nor transgressed constitutional bounds, and that the Rule is therefore the standard against which the District Court should have measured the adequacy of the service. Accordingly, we reverse the decision of the Court of Appeals.

... Under the cases construing the scope of the Enabling Act, Rule 4(d)(1) clearly passes muster. Prescribing the manner in which a defendant is to be notified that a suit has been instituted against him, it relates to the "practice and procedure of the district courts." ...

Thus were there no conflicting state procedure, Rule 4(d)(1) would clearly control. National Equipment Rental, Limited v. Szukhent, 375 U.S. 311, 316. However, respondent, focusing on the contrary Massachusetts rule, calls to the Court's attention another line of cases, a line which—like the Federal Rules—had its birth in 1938. Erie R. Co. v. Tompkins, 304 U.S. 64, overruling Swift v. Tyson, 16 Pet. [41 U.S.] 1, held that federal courts sitting in diversity cases, when deciding questions of "substantive" law, are bound by state court decisions as well as state statutes. The broad command of *Erie* was therefore identical to that of the Enabling Act: federal courts are to apply state substantive law and federal procedural law. However, as subsequent cases sharpened the distinction between substance and procedure, the line of cases following *Erie* diverged markedly from the line construing the Enabling Act. Guaranty Trust Co. v. York, 326 U.S. 99,

---

22.   Section 9 is in part a statute of limitations, providing that an executor need not "answer to an action ... which is not commenced within one year from the time of his giving bond...." This part of the statute, the purpose of which is to speed the settlement of estates, Spaulding v. McConnell, 307 Mass. 144, 146, 29 N.E.2d 713, 715 (1940); Doyle v. Moylan, 141 F.Supp. 95 (D.C.D.Mass.1956), is not involved in this case, since the action clearly was timely commenced. (Respondent filed bond on March 1, 1962; the complaint was filed February 6, 1963; and the service—the propriety of which is in dispute—was made on February 8, 1963.) 331 F.2d, at 159. Cf. *Guaranty Trust Co. v. York*, supra; *Ragan v. Merchants Transfer & Warehouse Co.*, supra.

Section 9 also provides for the manner of service. Generally, service of process must be made by "delivery in hand," although there are two alternatives: acceptance of service by the executor, or filing of a notice of claim, the components of which are set out in the statute, in the appropriate probate court. The purpose of this part of the statute, which *is* involved here, is, as the court below noted, to insure that executors will receive actual notice of claims. Parker v. Rich, 297 Mass. 111, 113–114, 8 N.E.2d 345, 347 (1937). Actual notice is of course also the goal of Rule 4(d)(1); however, the Federal Rule reflects a determination that this goal can be achieved by a method less cumbersome than that prescribed in § 9. In this case the goal seems to have been achieved; although the affidavit filed by respondent in the District Court asserts that he had not been served in hand nor had he accepted service, it does not allege lack of actual notice.

made it clear that *Erie*-type problems were not to be solved by reference to any traditional or common-sense substance-procedure distinction:

> "And so the question is not whether a statute of limitations is deemed a matter of 'procedure' in some sense. The question is ... does it significantly affect the result of a litigation for a federal court to disregard a law of a State that would be controlling in an action upon the same claim by the same parties in a State court?" 326 U.S., at 109.

Respondent, by placing primary reliance on *York* and *Ragan*, suggests that the *Erie* doctrine acts as a check on the Federal Rules of Civil Procedure, that despite the clear command of Rule 4(d)(1), *Erie* and its progeny demand the application of the Massachusetts rule. Reduced to essentials, the argument is: (1) *Erie*, as refined in *York*, demands that federal courts apply state law whenever application of federal law in its stead will alter the outcome of the case. (2) In this case, a determination that the Massachusetts service requirements obtain will result in immediate victory for respondent. If, on the other hand, it should be held that Rule 4(d)(1) is applicable, the litigation will continue, with possible victory for petitioner. (3) Therefore, *Erie* demands application of the Massachusetts rule. The syllogism possesses an appealing simplicity, but is for several reasons invalid.

In the first place, it is doubtful that, even if there were no Federal Rule making it clear that in-hand service is not required in diversity actions, the *Erie* rule would have obligated the District Court to follow the Massachusetts procedure. "Outcome-determination" analysis was never intended to serve as a talisman. Byrd v. Blue Ridge Rural Elec. Cooperative, 356 U.S. 525, 537. Indeed, the message of *York* itself is that choices between state and federal law are to be made not by application of any automatic, "litmus paper" criterion, but rather by reference to the policies underlying the *Erie* rule. *Guaranty Trust Co. v. York*, supra, at 108–112.

The *Erie* rule is rooted in part in a realization that it would be unfair for the character or result of a litigation materially to differ because the suit had been brought in a federal court.... The decision was also in part a reaction to the practice of "forum-shopping" which had grown up in response to the rule of *Swift v. Tyson*. 304 U.S., at 73–74. That the *York* test was an attempt to effectuate these policies is demonstrated by the fact that the opinion framed the inquiry in terms of "substantial" variations between state and federal litigation. 326 U.S., at 109. Not only are nonsubstantial, or trivial, variations not likely to raise the sort of equal protection problems which troubled the Court in *Erie*; they are also unlikely to influence the choice of a forum. The "outcome-determination" test therefore cannot be read without reference to the twin aims of the *Erie* rule: discouragement of forum-shopping and avoidance of inequitable administration of the laws.[23]

---

23. The Court of Appeals seemed to frame the inquiry in terms of how "important" § 9 is to the State. In support of its suggestion that § 9 serves some interest the State regards as vital to its citizens, the court noted that something like § 9 has been on the books in

The difference between the conclusion that the Massachusetts rule is applicable, and the conclusion that it is not, is of course at this point "outcome-determinative" in the sense that if we hold the state rule to apply, respondent prevails, whereas if we hold that Rule 4(d)(1) governs, the litigation will continue. But in this sense *every* procedural variation is "outcome-determinative." For example, having brought suit in a federal court, a plaintiff cannot then insist on the right to file subsequent pleadings in accord with the time limits applicable in state courts, even though enforcement of the federal timetable will, if he continues to insist that he must meet only the state time limit, result in determination of the controversy against him. So it is here. Though choice of the federal or state rule will at this point have a marked effect upon the outcome of the litigation, the difference between the two rules would be of scant, if any, relevance to the choice of a forum. Petitioner, in choosing her forum, was not presented with a situation where application of the state rule would wholly bar recovery; rather, adherence to the state rule would have resulted only in altering the way in which process was served.[24] Moreover, it is difficult to argue that permitting service of defendant's wife to take the place of in-hand service of defendant himself alters the mode of enforcement of state-created rights in a fashion sufficiently "substantial" to raise the sort of equal protection problems to which the *Erie* opinion alluded.

There is, however, a more fundamental flaw in respondent's syllogism: the incorrect assumption that the rule of *Erie R. Co. v. Tompkins* constitutes the appropriate test of the validity and therefore the applicability of a Federal Rule of Civil Procedure. The *Erie* rule has never been invoked to void a Federal Rule. It is true that there have been cases where this Court has held applicable a state rule in the face of an argument that the situation was governed by one of the Federal Rules. But the holding of each such case was not that *Erie* commanded displacement of a Federal Rule by an inconsistent state rule, but rather that the scope of the Federal Rule was not as broad as the losing party urged, and therefore, there being no Federal Rule which covered the point in dispute, *Erie* commanded the enforcement of state law.

Massachusetts a long time, that § 9 has been amended a number of times and that § 9 is designed to make sure that executors receive actual notice. The apparent lack of relation among these three observations is not surprising, because it is not clear to what sort of question the Court of Appeals was addressing itself. One cannot meaningfully ask how important something is without first asking "important for what purpose?" *Erie* and its progeny make clear that when a federal court sitting in a diversity case is faced with a question of whether or not to apply state law, the importance of a state rule is indeed relevant, but only in the context of asking whether application of the rule would make so important a difference to the character or result of the litigation that failure to enforce it would unfairly discriminate against citizens of the forum State, or whether application of the rule would have so important an effect upon the fortunes of one or both of the litigants that failure to enforce it would be likely to cause a plaintiff to choose the federal court.

24. Cf. Monarch Insurance Co. of Ohio v. Spach, 281 F.2d 401, 412 (C.A.5th Cir.1960). We cannot seriously entertain the thought that one suing an estate would be led to choose the federal court because of a belief that adherence to Rule 4(d)(1) is less likely to give the executor actual notice than § 9, and therefore more likely to produce a default judgment. Rule 4(d)(1) is well designed to give actual notice, as it did in this case.

"Respondent contends in the first place that the charge was correct because of the fact that Rule 8(c) of the Rules of Civil Procedure makes contributory negligence an affirmative defense. We do not agree. Rule 8(c) covers only the manner of pleading. The question of the burden of establishing contributory negligence is a question of local law which federal courts in diversity of citizenship cases (Erie R. Co. v. Tompkins, 304 U.S. 64) must apply." Palmer v. Hoffman, 318 U.S. 109, 117.[25]

(Here, of course, the clash is unavoidable; Rule 4(d)(1) says—implicitly, but with unmistakable clarity—that in-hand service is not required in federal courts.) At the same time, in cases adjudicating the validity of Federal Rules, we have not applied the *York* rule or other refinements of *Erie*, but have to this day continued to decide questions concerning the scope of the Enabling Act and the constitutionality of specific Federal Rules in light of the distinction set forth in Sibbach [v. Wilson & Co., 312 U.S. 1]. E.g., Schlagenhauf v. Holder, 379 U.S. 104.

Nor has the development of two separate lines of cases been inadvertent. The line between "substance" and "procedure" shifts as the legal context changes. "Each implies different variables depending upon the particular problem for which it is used." *Guaranty Trust Co. v. York*, supra, at 108; Cook, The Logical and Legal Bases of the Conflict of Laws, pp. 154–183 (1942). It is true that both the Enabling Act and the *Erie* rule say, roughly, that federal courts are to apply state "substantive" law and federal "procedural" law, but from that it need not follow that the tests are identical. For they were designed to control very different sorts of decisions. When a situation is covered by one of the Federal Rules, the question facing the court is a far cry from the typical, relatively unguided *Erie* choice: the court has been instructed to apply the Federal Rule, and can refuse to do so only if the Advisory Committee, this Court, and Congress erred in their prima facie judgment that the Rule in question transgresses neither the terms of the Enabling Act nor constitutional restrictions.

We are reminded by the *Erie* opinion that neither Congress nor the federal courts can, under the guise of formulating rules of decision for federal courts, fashion rules which are not supported by a grant of federal authority contained in Article I or some other section of the Constitution; in such areas state law must govern because there can be no other law. But the opinion in *Erie*, which involved no Federal Rule and dealt with a question which was "substantive" in every traditional sense (whether the railroad owed a duty of care to Tompkins as a trespasser or a licensee), surely neither said nor implied that measures like Rule 4(d)(1) are unconstitutional. For the constitutional provision for a federal court system (augmented by the Necessary and Proper Clause) carries with it congressional power to make rules governing the practice and pleading in those

---

25. To the same effect, see *Ragan v. Merchants Co.*, supra; Cohen v. Beneficial Loan Corp., [337 U.S. 541,] 556; id., at 557 (Douglas, J., dissenting); cf. Bernhardt v. Polygraphic Co., [350 U.S. 198,] 201–202; see generally Iovino v. Waterson [274 F.2d 41, 47–48 (C.A. 2d Cir.1959)].

courts, which in turn includes a power to regulate matters which, though falling within the uncertain area between substance and procedure, are rationally capable of classification as either. Cf. M'Culloch v. Maryland, 4 Wheat. [17 U.S.] 316, 421. Neither *York* nor the cases following it ever suggested that the rule there laid down for coping with situations where no Federal Rule applies is coextensive with the limitation on Congress to which *Erie* had adverted. Although this Court has never before been confronted with a case where the applicable Federal Rule is in direct collision with the law of the relevant State,[26] courts of appeals faced with such clashes have rightly discerned the implications of our decisions.

> "One of the shaping purposes of the Federal Rules is to bring about uniformity in the federal courts by getting away from local rules. This is especially true of matters which relate to the administration of legal proceedings, an area in which federal courts have traditionally exerted strong inherent power, completely aside from the powers Congress expressly conferred in the Rules. The purpose of the *Erie* doctrine, even as extended in *York* and *Ragan*, was never to bottle up federal courts with 'outcome-determinative' and 'integral-relations' stoppers—when there are 'affirmative countervailing (federal) considerations' and when there is a Congressional mandate (the Rules) supported by constitutional authority." Lumbermen's Mutual Casualty Co. v. Wright, 322 F.2d 759, 764 (C.A. 5th Cir. 1963).[27]

Erie and its offspring cast no doubt on the long-recognized power of Congress to prescribe housekeeping rules for federal courts even though some of those rules will inevitably differ from comparable state rules. Cf. Herron v. Southern Pacific Co., 283 U.S. 91. "When, because the plaintiff happens to be a non-resident, such a right is enforceable in a federal as well as in a State court, the forms and mode of enforcing the right may at times, naturally enough, vary because the two judicial systems are not identical." *Guaranty Trust Co. v. York*, supra, at 108; Cohen v. Beneficial Loan Corp., 337 U.S. 541, 555. Thus, though a court, in measuring a Federal Rule against the standards contained in the Enabling Act and the Constitution, need not wholly blind itself to the degree to which the Rule makes the character and result of the federal litigation stray from the course it would follow in state courts, *Sibbach v. Wilson & Co.*, supra, at 13–14, it cannot be forgotten that the *Erie* rule, and the guidelines suggested in *York*, were created to serve another purpose altogether. To hold that a Federal Rule of Civil Procedure must cease to function whenever it alters the mode of enforcing state-created rights would be to disembowel either the Constitution's grant of power over federal procedure or Congress' attempt to

---

26. In *Sibbach v. Wilson & Co.*, supra, the law of the forum State (Illinois) forbade the sort of order authorized by Rule 35. However, *Sibbach* was decided before *Klaxon Co. v. Stentor Co.*, [313 U.S. 487], and the *Sibbach* opinion makes clear that the Court was proceeding on the assumption that if the law of any State was relevant, it was the law of the State where the tort occurred (Indiana), which, like Rule 35, made provision for such orders. 312 U.S., at 6–7, 10–11.

27. To the same effect, see D'Onofrio Construction Co. v. Recon Co., 255 F.2d 904, 909–910 (C.A. 1st Cir. 1958).

exercise that power in the Enabling Act. Rule 4(d)(1) is valid and controls the instant case.

Reversed.

■ MR. JUSTICE BLACK concurs in the result.

■ MR. JUSTICE HARLAN, concurring.

It is unquestionably true that up to now *Erie* and the cases following it have not succeeded in articulating a workable doctrine governing choice of law in diversity actions. I respect the Court's effort to clarify the situation in today's opinion. However, in doing so I think it has misconceived the constitutional premises of *Erie* and has failed to deal adequately with those past decisions upon which the courts below relied.

Erie was something more than an opinion which worried about "forum-shopping and avoidance of inequitable administration of the laws," . . . although to be sure these were important elements of the decision. I have always regarded that decision as one of the modern cornerstones of our federalism, expressing policies that profoundly touch the allocation of judicial power between the state and federal systems. *Erie* recognized that there should not be two conflicting systems of law controlling the primary activity of citizens, for such alternative governing authority must necessarily give rise to a debilitating uncertainty in the planning of everyday affairs. And it recognized that the scheme of our Constitution envisions an allocation of lawmaking functions between state and federal legislative processes which is undercut if the federal judiciary can make substantive law affecting state affairs beyond the bounds of congressional legislative powers in this regard. Thus, in diversity cases *Erie* commands that it be the state law governing primary private activity which prevails.

The shorthand formulations which have appeared in some past decisions are prone to carry untoward results that frequently arise from oversimplification. The Court is quite right in stating that the "outcome-determinative" test of Guaranty Trust Co. v. York, 326 U.S. 99, if taken literally, proves too much, for any rule, no matter how clearly "procedural," can affect the outcome of litigation if it is not obeyed. In turning from the "outcome" test of *York* back to the unadorned forum-shopping rationale of *Erie*, however, the Court falls prey to like oversimplification, for a simple forum-shopping rule also proves too much; litigants often choose a federal forum merely to obtain what they consider the advantages of the Federal Rules of Civil Procedure or to try their cases before a supposedly more favorable judge. To my mind the proper line of approach in determining whether to apply a state or a federal rule, whether "substantive" or "procedural," is to stay close to basic principles by inquiring if the choice of rule would substantially affect those primary decisions respecting human conduct which our constitutional system leaves to state regulation. If so, *Erie* and the Constitution require that the state rule prevail, even in the face of a conflicting federal rule.

The Court weakens, if indeed it does not submerge, this basic principle by finding, in effect, a grant of substantive legislative power in the constitutional provision for a federal court system (compare Swift v. Tyson, 16 Pet. [41 U.S.] 1), and through it, setting up the Federal Rules as a body of law inviolate.... So long as a reasonable man could characterize any duly adopted federal rule as "procedural," the Court, unless I misapprehend what is said, would have it apply no matter how seriously it frustrated a State's substantive regulation of the primary conduct and affairs of its citizens. Since the members of the Advisory Committee, the Judicial Conference, and this Court who formulated the Federal Rules are presumably reasonable men, it follows that the integrity of the Federal Rules is absolute. Whereas the unadulterated outcome and forum-shopping tests may err too far toward honoring state rules, I submit that the Court's "arguably procedural, *ergo* constitutional" test moves too fast and far in the other direction.

The courts below relied upon this Court's decisions in Ragan v. Merchants Transfer Co., 337 U.S. 530, and Cohen v. Beneficial Indus. Loan Corp., 337 U.S. 541. Those cases deserve more attention than this Court has given them, particularly *Ragan* which, if still good law, would in my opinion call for affirmance of the result reached by the Court of Appeals. Further, a discussion of these two cases will serve to illuminate the "diversity" thesis I am advocating.

In *Ragan* a Kansas statute of limitations provided that an action was deemed commenced when service was made on the defendant. Despite Federal Rule 3 which provides that an action commences with the filing of the complaint, the Court held that for purposes of the Kansas statute of limitations a diversity tort action commenced only when service was made upon the defendant. The effect of this holding was that although the plaintiff had filed his federal complaint within the state period of limitations, his action was barred because the federal marshal did not serve a summons on the defendant until after the limitations period had run. I think that the decision was wrong. At most, application of the Federal Rule would have meant that potential Kansas tort defendants would have to defer for a few days the satisfaction of knowing that they had not been sued within the limitations period. The choice of the Federal Rule would have had no effect on the primary stages of private activity from which torts arise, and only the most minimal effect on behavior following the commission of the tort. In such circumstances the interest of the federal system in proceeding under its own rules should have prevailed.

Cohen v. Beneficial Loan Corp. held that a federal diversity court must apply a state statute requiring a small stockholder in a stockholder derivative suit to post a bond securing payment of defense costs as a condition to prosecuting an action. Such a statute is not "outcome determinative"; the plaintiff can win with or without it. The Court now rationalizes the case on the ground that the statute might affect the plaintiff's choice of forum ..., but as has been pointed out, a simple forum-shopping test proves too much. The proper view of *Cohen* is in my opinion, that the statute was meant to inhibit small stockholders from instituting "strike suits," and thus it was designed and could be expected to have a substantial impact on private primary activity. Anyone who was at the trial bar during the period when *Cohen* arose can appreciate the strong state policy reflected in the statute. I think it wholly legitimate to view Federal Rule 23 as not purporting to deal with the problem. But even had the Federal Rules purported to do so, and in so doing provided a substantially less effective deterrent to strike suits, I think the state rule should still have prevailed. That is where I believe the Court's view differs from mine; for the Court attributes such overriding force to the Federal Rules that it is hard to think of a case where a conflicting state rule would be allowed to operate, even though the state rule reflected policy considerations which, under *Erie*, would lie within the realm of state legislative authority.

It remains to apply what has been said to the present case. The Massachusetts rule provides that an executor need not answer suits unless in-hand service was made upon him or notice of the action was filed in the proper registry of probate within one year of his giving bond. The evident intent of this statute is to permit an executor to distribute the estate which he is administering without fear that further liabilities may be outstanding for which he could be held personally liable. If the Federal District Court in Massachusetts applies Rule 4(d)(1) of the Federal Rules of Civil Procedure instead of the Massachusetts service rule, what effect would that have on the speed and assurance with which estates are distributed? As I see it, the effect would not be substantial. It would mean simply that an executor would have to check at his own house or the federal courthouse as well as the registry of probate before he could distribute the estate with impunity. As this does not seem enough to give rise to any real impingement on the vitality of the state policy which the Massachusetts rule is intended to serve, I concur in the judgment of the Court.[28]

[28. See Ely, The Irrepressible Myth of *Erie*, 87 Harv.L.Rev. 693 (1974), and the commentaries on that article, Chayes, The Bead Game, 87 Harv.L.Rev. 741 (1974), Ely, The Necklace, 87 Harv.L.Rev. 753 (1974), and Mishkin, The Thread, 87 Harv.L.Rev. 1682 (1974).

See also Burbank, The Rules Enabling Act of 1934, 130 U.Pa.L.Rev. 1015 (1982); Westen & Lehman, Is There Life for *Erie* After the Death of Diversity?, 78 Mich.L.Rev. 311 (1980); Redish, Continuing the *Erie* Debate: A Response to Westen and Lehman, 78 Mich.L.Rev. 959 (1980); Westen, After "Life for *Erie*"—A Reply, 78 Mich.L.Rev. 971 (1980); Redish & Phillips, *Erie* and the Rules of Decision Act: In Search of the Appropriate Dilemma, 91 Harv.L.Rev. 356 (1977); Thomas, The Erosion of *Erie* in the Federal Courts: Is State Law Losing Ground?, 1977 B.Y.U.L.Rev. 1 (1977); Comment, The Law Applied in Diversity Cases: The Rules of Decision Act and the *Erie* Doctrine, 85 Yale L.J. 678 (1976).

The 50th anniversary in 1988 of the *Erie* decision and of the adoption of the Federal Rules of Civil Procedure stimulated much scholarly reconsideration of both events and of their relation. See Braman & Neumann, The Still Unrepressed Myth of *Erie*, 19 U.Balt.L.Rev. 403 (1989); Carrington, "Substance" and "Procedure" in the Rules Enabling Act, 1989 Duke L.J. 281; Freer, *Erie*'s Mid–Life Crisis, 63 Tul.L.Rev. 1087 (1989); Subrin, Fireworks on the 50th Anniversary of the Federal Rules of Civil Procedure, 73 Judicature 4 (1989); Gelfand & Abrams, Putting *Erie* on the Right Track, 49 U.Pitt.L.Rev. 937 (1988); Kane, The Golden Wedding Year: *Erie Railroad Company v. Tompkins* and the Federal Rules, 63 Notre Dame L.Rev. 671 (1988); Rubin, Hazards of a Civilian Venturer in a Federal Court: Travel and Travail on the *Erie* Railroad, 48 La.L.Rev. 1369 (1988); Weinstein, The Ghost of Process

Commissioner of Internal Revenue v. Estate of Bosch

Supreme Court of the United States, 1967.
387 U.S. 456, 87 S.Ct. 1776, 18 L.Ed.2d 886.

■ MR. JUSTICE CLARK delivered the opinion of the Court.

These two federal estate tax cases present a common issue for our determination: Whether a federal court or agency in a federal estate tax controversy is conclusively bound by a state trial court adjudication of property rights or characterization of property interests when the United States is not made a party to such proceeding.

[The federal estate tax liability of an estate would depend on whether decedent's widow had validly released a general power of appointment she had been given in a trust created by decedent. If the release, executed in 1951, was valid, the wife would have converted the general power of appointment into a special power of appointment and the assets covered by it would have been included in the decedent's estate. If the release was invalid, the wife would still have retained a general power of appointment when her husband died and the trust would qualify for the marital deduction from the estate tax. While proceedings were pending in the Tax Court, the estate obtained a determination from the state court with jurisdiction over the estate that the release was a nullity. The Tax Court and the Court of Appeals held that this determination was decisive of the estate tax liability of the estate. The Supreme Court disagreed and reversed. A case on federal tax liability is not covered by the *Erie* doctrine, but excerpts from the opinions are included here because of their description of the effect the Court accords to decisions of lower state courts in cases in which *Erie* is applicable.]

... We find that the report of the Senate Finance Committee recommending enactment of the marital deduction used very guarded language in referring to the very question involved here. It said that "proper regard," not finality, "should be given to interpretations of the will" by state courts and then only when entered by a court "in a bona fide adversary proceeding." S.Rep. No. 1013, Pt. 2, 80th Cong., 2d Sess., 4. We cannot say that the authors of this directive intended that the decrees of state trial courts were to be conclusive and binding on the computation of the federal estate tax as levied by the Congress. If the Congress had intended state trial court determinations to have that effect on the federal actions, it certainly would have said so—which it did not do. On the contrary, we believe it intended the marital deduction to be strictly construed and applied. Not only did it indicate that only "proper regard" was to be accorded state decrees but it placed specific limitations on the allowance of the deduction as set out in §§ 2056(b), (c), and (d). These restrictive limitations clearly indicate the great care that Congress exercised in the drawing of the Act and indicate also a definite concern with the elimination of loopholes and escape hatches that might jeopardize the federal revenue. This also is in keeping with the

Past: The Fiftieth Anniversary of the Federal Rules of Civil Procedure and *Erie*, 54 Brook. L.Rev. 1 (1988).]

long-established policy of the Congress, as expressed in the Rules of Decision Act, 28 U.S.C. § 1652. There it is provided that in the absence of federal requirements such as the Constitution or Acts of Congress, the "laws of the several states . . . shall be regarded as rules of decision in civil actions in the courts of the United States, in cases where they apply." This Court has held that judicial decisions are "laws of the . . . state" within the section. Erie R. Co. v. Tompkins, [304 U.S. 64 (1938)]; Cohen v. Beneficial Loan Corp., 337 U.S. 541 (1949); King v. Order of Travelers, 333 U.S. 153 (1948). Moreover, even in diversity cases this Court has further held that while the decrees of "lower state courts" should be "attributed some weight . . . the decision [is] not controlling . . ." where the highest court of the State has not spoken on the point. *King v. Order of Travelers*, supra, at 160–161. And in West v. A.T. & T. Co., 311 U.S. 223 (1940), this Court further held that "an intermediate appellate state court . . . is a datum for ascertaining state law which is not to be disregarded by a federal court *unless it is convinced by other persuasive data that the highest court of the state would decide otherwise.*" At 237. (Emphasis supplied.) Thus, under some conditions, federal authority may not be bound even by an intermediate state appellate court ruling. It follows here then, that when the application of a federal statute is involved, the decision of a state trial court as to an underlying issue of state law should *a fortiori* not be controlling. This is but an application of the rule of *Erie R. Co. v. Tompkins*, supra, where state law as announced by the highest court of the State is to be followed. This is not a diversity case but the same principle may be applied for the same reasons, viz., the underlying substantive rule involved is based on state law and the State's highest court is the best authority on its own law. If there be no decision by that court then federal authorities must apply what they find to be the state law after giving "proper regard" to relevant rulings of other courts of the State. In this respect, it may be said to be, in effect, sitting as a state court. Bernhardt v. Polygraphic Co., 350 U.S. 198 (1956).

. . . . .

The judgment in No. 240 therefore affirmed while that in No. 673 is reversed and remanded for proceedings not inconsistent with this opinion.

It is so ordered.

■ MR. JUSTICE DOUGLAS, dissenting.

. . . . .

Since our 1938 decision in Erie R. Co. v. Tompkins, 304 U.S. 64, an unbroken line of cases has held that the federal courts must look to state legislation, state decisions, state administrative practice, for the state law that is to be applied. See, e.g., Cities Service Oil Co. v. Dunlap, 308 U.S. 208; Bernhardt v. Polygraphic Co., 350 U.S. 198. Those were diversity cases; and in them we have never suggested that the federal court may ignore a relevant state court decision because it was not entered by the highest state court. Indeed, we have held that the federal court is obligated to follow the decision of a lower state court in the absence of decisions of the State Supreme Court showing that the state law is other than announced by the lower court. See, e.g., Fidelity Union Trust Co. v. Field, 311 U.S. 169; West v. A. T. & T. Co., 311 U.S. 223; Six Companies of California v. Joint Highway District, 311 U.S. 180; Stoner v. New York Life Ins. Co., 311 U.S. 464.

It is true that in King v. Order of Travelers, 333 U.S. 153, we held that a federal court of appeals did not have to accept the decision of a state court of common pleas on a matter of state law. But that case was unique. . . .

. . . . .

This is not to say that a federal court is bound by all state court decrees. A federal court might not be bound by a consent decree, for it does not purport to be a declaration of state law; it may be merely a judicial stamp placed upon the parties' contractual settlement. Nor need the federal court defer to a state court decree which has been obtained by fraud or collusion. But where, absent those considerations, a state court has reached a deliberate conclusion, where it has construed state law, the federal court should consider the decision to be an exposition of the controlling state law and give it effect as such.

■ Mr. Justice Harlan, whom Mr. Justice Fortas joins, dissenting.

. . . . .

It is, of course, plain that the Rules of Decision Act, 28 U.S.C. § 1652, is applicable here, as it is, by its terms, to any situation in which a federal court must ascertain and apply the law of any of the several States. Nor may it be doubted that the judgments of state courts must be accepted as a part of the state law to which the Act gives force in federal courts, Erie R. Co. v. Tompkins, 304 U.S. 64; it is not, for that purpose, material whether the jurisdiction of the federal court in a particular case is founded upon diversity of citizenship or involves a question arising under the laws of the United States. This need not mean, however, that every state judgment must be accepted by federal courts as conclusive of state law. The Court has, for example, never held, even in diversity cases, where the federal interest consists at most in affording a "neutral" forum, that the judgments of state trial courts must in all cases be taken as conclusive statements of state law; apart from a series of cases decided at the 1940 Term,[29] the Court has consistently acknowledged that the character both of the state proceeding and of the state court itself may be relevant in determining a judgment's conclusiveness as a statement of state law. This same result must surely follow *a fortiori* in cases in which the application of a federal statute is at issue.

---

29. . . . All these cases . . . have been strongly and repeatedly criticized by commentators. Judge Friendly, for example, described them as "outrages," [In Praise of *Erie*—and of the New Federal Common Law, 39 N.Y.U.L.Rev. 383], at 401. See also Corbin, The Laws of the Several States, 50 Yale L.J. 762, 766–768; Clark, State Law in the Federal Courts, 55 Yale L.J. 267, 290–292; and 2 Crosskey, Politics and the Constitution 922–927 (1953). It may also be wondered whether these cases have any vitality left after *King* and *Bernhardt*, supra.

Similarly, it is difficult to see why the formula now ordinarily employed to determine state law in diversity cases—essentially, that, absent a recent judgment of the State's highest court, state cases are only data from which the law must be derived—is necessarily applicable without modification in all situations in which federal courts must ascertain state law. The relationship between the state and federal judicial systems is simply too delicate and important to be reduced to any single standard. See Hill, The *Erie* Doctrine in Bankruptcy, 66 Harv.L.Rev. 1013; Note, The Competence of Federal Courts to Formulate Rules of Decision, 77 Harv.L.Rev. 1084. Compare, e.g., Morgan v. Commissioner, 309 U.S. 78, 80–81, 60; Cardozo, Federal Taxes and the Radiating Potencies of State Court Decisions, 51 Yale L.J. 783. The inadequacy of this formula is particularly patent here, where, unlike the cases in which it was derived, the federal court is confronted by precisely the legal and factual circumstances upon which the state court has already passed.

Accordingly, although the Rules of Decision Act and the *Erie* doctrine plainly offer relevant guidance to the appropriate result here, they can scarcely be said to demand any single conclusion.

. . . . .

I would therefore hold that in cases in which state-adjudicated property rights are contended to have federal tax consequences, federal courts must attribute conclusiveness to the judgment of a state court, of whatever level in the state procedural system, unless the litigation from which the judgment resulted does not bear the indicia of a genuinely adversary proceeding. . . .

. . . . .

■ [Justice Fortas, who joined the dissenting opinion of Justice Harlan, also filed a brief dissenting opinion of his own.][30]

[**30.** The degree of deference to be given for *Erie* purposes to the decisions of lower state courts regarding an unsettled issue of state law has long troubled the Supreme Court. In Fidelity Union Trust Co. v. Field, 311 U.S. 169 (1940), the Court held that decisions of intermediate appellate courts were normally binding on federal courts for *Erie* purposes. This holding was limited and distinguished in King v. Order of United Commercial Travelers, 333 U.S. 153 (1948), which held that a federal court was not bound to regard as a controlling precedent the unreported decision of a state trial court.

In Salve Regina College v. Russell, 499 U.S. 225 (1991), the Court held that a district court's determination of the content of state law to be applied under *Erie* is a question of law to be reviewed de novo on appeal, without the deference to the district court's judgment entailed by the "abuse of discretion" standard that is applicable to review of questions of fact and (in general) mixed questions of fact and law.

" '[A] judgment of a federal court ruled by state law and correctly applying that law as authoritatively declared by the state courts when the judgment was rendered, must be reversed on appellate review if in the meantime the state courts have disapproved of their former rulings and adopted different ones.' " Lords Landing Village Condominium Council v. Continental Ins. Co., 520 U.S. 893, 896 (1997) (per curiam) (granting certiorari, vacating

Walker v. Armco Steel Corp.

Supreme Court of the United States, 1980.
446 U.S. 740, 100 S.Ct. 1978, 64 L.Ed.2d 659.

■ MR. JUSTICE MARSHALL delivered the opinion of the Court.

This case presents the issue whether in a diversity action the federal court should follow state law or, alternatively, Rule 3 of the Federal Rules of Civil Procedure in determining when an action is commenced for the purpose of tolling the state statute of limitations.

I

According to the allegations of the complaint, petitioner, a carpenter, was injured on August 22, 1975, in Oklahoma City, Okla., while pounding a Sheffield nail into a cement wall. Respondent was the manufacturer of the nail. Petitioner claimed that the nail contained a defect which caused its head to shatter and strike him in the right eye, resulting in permanent injuries. The defect was allegedly caused by respondent's negligence in manufacture and design.

Petitioner is a resident of Oklahoma, and respondent is a foreign corporation having its principal place of business in a State other than Oklahoma. Since there was diversity of citizenship, petitioner brought suit in the United States District Court for the Western District of Oklahoma. The complaint was filed on August 19, 1977. Although summons was issued that same day, service of process was not made on respondent's authorized service agent until December 1, 1977.[31] On January 5, 1978, respondent filed a motion to dismiss the complaint on the ground that the action was barred by the applicable Oklahoma statute of limitations. Although the complaint had been filed within the 2–year statute of limitations, Okla. Stat., Tit. 12, § 95 (1971), state law does not deem the action "commenced" for purposes of the statute of limitations until service of the summons on the defendant. Okla.Stat., Tit. 12, § 97 (1971).[32] If the

---

the judgment of the court of appeals, and remanding with instructions to consider the quoted language from Huddleston v. Dwyer, 322 U.S. 232, 236 (1944)). The Fourth Circuit had denied rehearing despite an uncontroverted showing that an intervening decision of the relevant state's highest court had disapproved the cases upon which the Fourth Circuit had relied in its earlier affirmance of the district court's construction of state law in a diversity case.

See Wright & Kane, Federal Courts § 58 (6th ed.2002); 19 Wright, Miller & Cooper, Federal Practice & Procedure: Jurisdiction 2d § 4507 (1996); Yonover, Ascertaining State Law: The Continuing *Erie* Dilemma, 38 DePaul L.Rev. 1 (1988).]

31. The record does not indicate why this delay occurred. The face of the process record shows that the United States Marshal acknowledged receipt of the summons on December 1, 1977, and that service was effectuated that same day. At oral argument counsel for petitioner stated that the summons was found "in an unmarked folder in the filing cabinet" in counsel's office some 90 days after the complaint had been filed. Tr. of Oral Arg. 3. . . . Counsel conceded that the summons was not delivered to the marshal until December 1. Id., at 3–4. It is unclear why the summons was placed in the filing cabinet. See id., at 17.

32. Okla.Stat., Tit. 12, § 97 (1971) provides in pertinent part: "An action shall be deemed commenced, within the meaning of this article [the statute of limitations], as to each

complaint is filed within the limitations period, however, the action is deemed to have commenced from that date of filing if the plaintiff serves the defendant within 60 days, even though that service may occur outside the limitations period. Ibid. In this case, service was not effectuated until long after this 60–day period had expired. Petitioner in his reply brief to the motion to dismiss admitted that his case would be foreclosed in state court, but he argued that Rule 3 of the Federal Rules of Civil Procedure governs the manner in which an action is commenced in federal court for all purposes, including the tolling of the state statute of limitations.

The District Court dismissed the complaint as barred by the Oklahoma statute of limitations. 452 F.Supp. 243 (1978). The court concluded that Okla.Stat., Tit. 12, § 97 (1971) was "an integral part of the Oklahoma statute of limitations," 452 F.Supp, at 245, and therefore under Ragan v. Merchants Transfer & Warehouse Co., 337 U.S. 530 (1949), state law applied. The court rejected the argument that *Ragan* had been implicitly overruled in Hanna v. Plumer, 380 U.S. 460 (1965).

The United States Court of Appeals for the Tenth Circuit affirmed. 592 F.2d 1133 (1979). That court concluded that Okla.Stat., Tit. 12, § 97 (1971) was in "direct conflict" with Rule 3. Id., at 1135. However, the Oklahoma statute was "indistinguishable" from the statute involved in *Ragan,* and the court felt itself "constrained" to follow *Ragan.* 592 F.2d, at 1136.

We granted certiorari, 444 U.S. 823 (1979), because of a conflict among the Courts of Appeals. We now affirm.

II

The question whether state or federal law should apply on various issues arising in an action based on state law which has been brought in federal court under diversity of citizenship jurisdiction has troubled this Court for many years. In the landmark decision of Erie R. Co. v. Tompkins, 304 U.S. 64 (1938), we overturned the rule expressed in Swift v. Tyson, 16 Pet. [41 U.S.] 1 (1842), that federal courts exercising diversity jurisdiction need not, in matters of "general jurisprudence," apply the nonstatutory law of the State. The Court noted that "[d]iversity of citizenship jurisdiction was conferred in order to prevent apprehended discrimination in state courts against those not citizens of the State," *Erie R. Co. v. Tompkins,* supra, at 74. The doctrine of *Swift v. Tyson* had led to the undesirable results of discrimination in favor of noncitizens, prevention of uniformity in the administration of state law, and forum shopping. 304 U.S., at 74–75. In response, we established the rule that "[e]xcept in matters governed by the Federal Constitution or by Acts of Congress, the law to be applied in any [diversity] case is the law of the State," id., at 78.

---

defendant, at the date of the summons which is served on him, or on a codefendant, who is a joint contractor or otherwise united in interest with him . . . . An attempt to commence an action shall be deemed equivalent to the commencement thereof, within the meaning of this article, when the party faithfully, properly and diligently endeavors to procure a service; but such attempt must be followed by the first publication or service of the summons, . . . within sixty (60) days."

In Guaranty Trust Co. v. York, 326 U.S. 99 (1945), we addressed ourselves to "the narrow question whether, when no recovery could be had in a State court because the action is barred by the statute of limitations, a federal court in equity can take cognizance of the suit because there is diversity of citizenship between the parties," id., at 107. The Court held that the *Erie* doctrine applied to suits in equity as well as to actions at law. In construing *Erie* we noted that "[i]n essence, the intent of that decision was to insure that, in all cases where a federal court is exercising jurisdiction solely because of the diversity of citizenship of the parties, the outcome of the litigation in the federal court should be substantially the same, so far as legal rules determine the outcome of a litigation, as it would be if tried in a State court." 326 U.S., at 109. We concluded that the state statute of limitations should be applied. "Plainly enough, a statute that would completely bar recovery in a suit if brought in a State court bears on a State-created right vitally and not merely formally or negligibly. As to consequences that so intimately affect recovery or non-recovery a federal court in a diversity case should follow State law." Id., at 110.

The decision in *York* led logically to our holding in *Ragan v. Merchants Transfer & Warehouse Co.*, supra. In *Ragan,* the plaintiff had filed his complaint in federal court on September 4, 1945, pursuant to Rule 3 of the Federal Rules of Civil Procedure. The accident from which the claim arose had occurred on October 1, 1943. Service was made on the defendant on December 28, 1945. The applicable statute of limitations supplied by Kansas law was two years. Kansas had an additional statute which provided that "[a]n action shall be deemed commenced within the meaning of [the statute of limitations], as to each defendant, at the date of the summons which is served on him.... An attempt to commence an action shall be deemed equivalent to the commencement thereof within the meaning of this article when the party faithfully, properly and diligently endeavors to procure a service; but such attempt must be followed by the first publication or service of the summons within sixty days." Kan.Gen. Stats. § 60–308. The defendant moved for summary judgment on the ground that the Kansas statute of limitations barred the action since service had not been made within either the two-year period or the 60–day period. It was conceded that had the case been brought in Kansas state court it would have been barred. Nonetheless, the District Court held that the statute had been tolled by the filing of the complaint. The Court of Appeals reversed because "the requirement of service of summons within the statutory period was an integral part of that state's statute of limitations." *Ragan,* 337 U.S., at 532.

We affirmed, relying on *Erie* and *York*. "We cannot give [the cause of action] longer life in the federal court than it would have had in the state court without adding something to the cause of action. We may not do that consistently with *Erie R. Co. v. Tompkins.*" 337 U.S., at 533–534. We rejected the argument that Rule 3 of the Federal Rules of Civil Procedure governed the manner in which an action was commenced in federal court for purposes of tolling the state statute of limitations. Instead, we held that the service of summons statute controlled because it was an integral part of the state statute of limitations, and under *York* that statute of limitations was part of the state law cause of action.

Ragan was not our last pronouncement in this difficult area, however. In 1965 we decided Hanna v. Plumer, 380 U.S. 460, holding that in a civil action where federal jurisdiction was based upon diversity of citizenship, Rule 4(d)(1) of the Federal Rules of Civil Procedure, rather than state law, governed the manner in which process was served. Massachusetts law required in-hand service on an executor or administrator of an estate, whereas Rule 4 permits service by leaving copies of the summons and complaint at the defendant's home with some person "of suitable age and discretion." The Court noted that in the absence of a conflicting state procedure, the federal rule would plainly control, 380 U.S., at 465. We stated that the "outcome-determination" test of *Erie* and *York* had to be read with reference to the "twin aims" of *Erie:* "discouragement of forum-shopping and avoidance of inequitable administration of the laws." 380 U.S., at 468. We determined that the choice between the state in-hand service rule and the federal rule "would be of scant, if any, relevance to the choice of forum," for the plaintiff "was not presented with a situation where application of the state rule would wholly bar recovery; rather, adherence to the state rule would have resulted only in altering the way in which process was served." Id., at 469 (footnote omitted). This factor served to distinguish that case from *York* and *Ragan.* See 380 U.S., at 469, n. 10.

The Court in *Hanna,* however, pointed out "a more fundamental flaw" in the defendant's argument in that case. Id., at 469. The Court concluded that the *Erie* doctrine was simply not the appropriate test of the validity and applicability of one of the Federal Rules of Civil Procedure:

> "The *Erie* rule has never been invoked to void a Federal Rule. It is true that there have been cases where this Court had held applicable a state rule in the face of an argument that the situation was governed by one of the Federal Rules. But the holding of each such case was not that *Erie* commanded displacement of a Federal Rule by an inconsistent state rule, but rather that the scope of the Federal Rule was not as broad as the losing party urged, and therefore, there being no Federal Rule which governed the point in dispute, *Erie* commanded the enforcement of state law." 380 U.S., at 470.

The Court cited *Ragan* as one of the examples of this proposition, 380 U.S., at 470, n. 12 [supra n. 25]. The Court explained that where the federal rule was clearly applicable, as in *Hanna,* the test was whether the rule was within the scope of the Rules Enabling Act, 28 U.S.C. § 2072, and if so, within a constitutional grant of power such as the Necessary and Proper Clause of Art. I. 380 U.S., at 470–472.

III

The present case is indistinguishable from *Ragan.* The statutes in both cases require service of process to toll the statute of limitations, and in fact the predecessor to the Oklahoma statute in this case was derived from the predecessor to the Kansas statute in *Ragan*. See Dr. Koch Vegetable Tea Co. v. Davis, 48 Okl. 14, 22, 145 P. 337, 340 (1914). Here, as in *Ragan*, the complaint was filed in federal court under diversity jurisdiction within the 2-year statute of limitations, but service of process did not occur until after the two-year period and the 60-day service period had run. In both cases the suit would concededly have been barred in the applicable state court, and in both instances the state service statute was held to be an integral part of the statute of limitations by the lower court more familiar than we with state law. Accordingly, as the Court of Appeals held below, the instant action is barred by the statute of limitations unless *Ragan* is no longer good law.

Petitioner argues that the analysis and holding of *Ragan* did not survive our decision in *Hanna*.[33] Petitioner's position is that Okla.Stat., Tit. 12, § 97 (1971) is in direct conflict with the federal rule. Under *Hanna*, petitioner contends, the appropriate question is whether Rule 3 is within the scope of the Rules Enabling Act and, if so, within the constitutional power of Congress. In petitioner's view, the federal rule is to be applied unless it violates one of those two restrictions. This argument ignores both the force of stare decisis and the specific limitations that we carefully placed on the *Hanna* analysis.

We note at the outset that the doctrine of stare decisis weighs heavily against petitioner in this case. Petitioner seeks to have us overrule our decision in *Ragan*. Stare decisis does not mandate that earlier decisions be enshrined forever, of course, but it does counsel that we use caution in rejecting established law. In this case, the reasons petitioner asserts for overruling *Ragan* are the same factors which we concluded in *Hanna* did not undermine the validity of *Ragan*. A litigant who in effect asks us to reconsider not one but two prior decisions bears a heavy burden of supporting such a change in our jurisprudence. Petitioner here has not met that burden.

This Court in *Hanna* distinguished *Ragan* rather than overruled it, and for good reason. Application of the *Hanna* analysis is premised on a "direct collision" between the federal rule and the state law. 380 U.S., at 472. In *Hanna* itself the "clash" between Rule 4(d)(1) and the state in-hand service requirement was "unavoidable." 380 U.S., at 470. The first question must therefore be whether the scope of the federal rule in fact is sufficiently broad to control the issue before the Court. It is only if that question is answered affirmatively that the *Hanna* analysis applies.[34]

As has already been noted, we recognized in *Hanna* that the present case is an instance where "the scope of the Federal Rule [is] not as broad as

---

33. Justice Harlan in his concurring opinion in *Hanna* concluded that *Ragan* was no longer good law. 380 U.S., at 474–478. See also Sylvestri v. Warner & Swasey Co., 398 F.2d 598 (CA2 1968).

34. This is not to suggest that the Federal Rules of Civil Procedure are to be narrowly construed in order to avoid a "direct collision" with state law. The Federal Rules should be given their plain meaning. If a direct collision with state law arises from that plain meaning, then the analysis developed in *Hanna v. Plumer* applies.

the losing party urge[s], and therefore, there being no Federal Rule which cover[s] the point in dispute, *Erie* command[s] the enforcement of state law." Ibid. Rule 3 simply states that "[a] civil action is commenced by filing a complaint with the court." There is no indication that the Rule was intended to toll a state statute of limitations,[35] much less that it purported to displace state tolling rules for purposes of state statutes of limitations. In our view, in diversity actions[36] Rule 3 governs the date from which various timing requirements of the federal rules begin to run, but does not affect state statutes of limitations. Cf. 4 C. Wright & A. Miller, Federal Practice and Procedure, § 1057, pp. 190–191 (1969); id., § 1051, at 165–166.

In contrast to Rule 3 the Oklahoma statute is a statement of a substantive decision by that State that actual service on, and accordingly actual notice by, the defendant is an integral part of the several policies served by the statute of limitations. See C & C Tile Co. v. Independent School District No. 7 of Tulsa County, 503 P.2d 554, 559 (Okla.1972). The statute of limitations establishes a deadline after which the defendant may legitimately have peace of mind; it also recognizes that after a certain period of time it is unfair to require the defendant to attempt to piece together his defense to an old claim. A requirement of actual service promotes both of those functions of the statute. See generally ibid.; Seitz v. Jones, 370 P.2d 300, 302 (Okla.1961). See also Ely, The Irrepressible Myth of *Erie*, 87 Harv.L.Rev. 693, 730–731 (1974). It is these policy aspects which make the service requirement an "integral" part of the statute of limita-

---

35. "Rule 3 simply provides that an action is commenced by filing the complaint and has as its primary purpose the measuring of time periods that begin running from the date of commencement; the rule does not state that filing tolls the statute of limitations." 4 C. Wright & A. Miller, Federal Practice and Procedure, § 1057, p. 191 (1969) (footnote omitted).

The Note of the Advisory Committee on the Rules states:

"When a Federal or State statute of limitations is pleaded as a defense, a question may arise under this rule whether the mere filing of the complaint stops the running of the statute, or whether any further step is required, such as, service of the summons and complaint or their delivery to the marshal for service. The answer to this question may depend on whether it is competent for the Supreme Court, exercising the power to make rules of procedure without affecting substantive rights, to vary the operation of statutes of limitations. The requirement of Rule 4(a) that the clerk shall forthwith issue the summons and deliver it to the marshal for service will reduce the chances of such a question arising." 28 U.S.C.App., pp. 394–395.

This Note establishes that the Advisory Committee predicted the problem which arose in *Ragan* and arises again in the instant case. It does not indicate, however, that Rule 3 was *intended* to serve as a tolling provision for statute of limitations purposes; it only suggests that the Advisory Committee thought the Rule *might* have that effect.

36. The Court suggested in *Ragan* that in suits to enforce rights under a federal statute Rule 3 means that filing of the complaint tolls the applicable statute of limitations. 337 U.S., at 533, distinguishing Bomar v. Keyes, 162 F.2d 136, 140–141 (CA2), cert. denied, 332 U.S. 825 (1947). See Ely, The Irrepressible Myth of *Erie*, 87 Harv.L.Rev. 693, 729 (1974). See also Walko Corp. v. Burger Chef Systems, Inc., 180 U.S.App.D.C. [306], at 308, n. 19, 554 F.2d [1165], 1167, n. 19 [(1977)]; 4 C. Wright & A. Miller, supra, § 1056, and authorities collected therein. We do not here address the role of Rule 3 as a tolling provision for a statute of limitations, whether set by federal law or borrowed from state law, if the cause of action is based on federal law.

tions both in this case and in *Ragan*. As such, the service rule must be considered part and parcel of the statute of limitations.[37] Rule 3 does not replace such policy determinations found in state law. Rule 3 and Okla. Stat., Tit. 12, § 97 (1971) can exist side-by-side, therefore, each controlling its own intended sphere of coverage without conflict.

Since there is no direct conflict between the federal rule and the state law, the *Hanna* analysis does not apply.[38] Instead, the policies behind *Erie* and *Ragan* control the issue whether, in the absence of a federal rule directly on point, state service requirements which are an integral part of the state statute of limitations should control in an action based on state law which is filed in federal court under diversity jurisdiction. The reasons for the application of such a state service requirement in a diversity action in the absence of a conflicting federal rule are well explained in *Erie* and *Ragan*, ... and need not be repeated here. It is sufficient to note that although in this case failure to apply the state service law might not create any problem of forum shopping,[39] the result would be an "inequitable administration" of the law. *Hanna v. Plumer*, 380 U.S., at 468. There is simply no reason why, in the absence of a controlling federal rule, an action based on state law which concededly would be barred in the state courts by the state statute of limitations should proceed through litigation to judgment in federal court solely because of the fortuity that there is diversity of citizenship between the litigants. The policies underlying diversity jurisdiction do not support such a distinction between state and federal plaintiffs, and *Erie* and its progeny do not permit it.

The judgment of the Court of Appeals is

Affirmed.[40]

------

37. The substantive link of § 97 to the statute of limitations is made clear as well by another provision of Oklahoma law. Under Okla.Stat., Tit. 12, § 151 (1971), "[a] civil action is deemed commenced by filing in the office of the court clerk of the proper court a petition and by the clerk's issuance of summons thereon." This is the state law corollary to Rule 3. However, § 97, not § 151, controls the commencement of the lawsuit for statute of limitations purposes. See Tyler v. Taylor, 578 P.2d 1214 (Okla.App.1977). Just as § 97 and § 151 can both apply in state court for their separate purposes, so too § 97 and Rule 3 may both apply in federal court in a diversity action.

38. Since we hold that Rule 3 does not apply, it is unnecessary for us to address the second question posed by the *Hanna* analysis: whether Rule 3, if it applied, would be outside the scope of the Rules Enabling Act or beyond the power of Congress under the Constitution.

39. There is no indication that when petitioner filed his suit in federal court he had any reason to believe that he would be unable to comply with the service requirements of Oklahoma law or that he chose to sue in federal court in an attempt to avoid those service requirements.

[40. It is clear that an amendment of the pleadings relates back, for purposes of the statute of limitations, if the conditions described in Civil Rule 15(c) are met, even though the statute of limitations would bar the amendment in state court. But what of the converse situation, in which a state would hold that an amendment changing the parties relates back even though Rule 15(c) is not satisfied? In Schiavone v. Fortune, 477 U.S. 21 (1986), the Supreme Court held that an amendment changing parties relates back only if the party to

Burlington Northern Railroad Co. v. Woods

Supreme Court of the United States, 1987.
480 U.S. 1, 107 S.Ct. 967, 94 L.Ed.2d 1.

■ JUSTICE MARSHALL delivered the opinion of the Court.

This case presents the issue whether, in diversity actions, federal court must apply a state statute that imposes a fixed penalty on appellants who obtain stays of judgment pending unsuccessful appeals.

I

Respondents brought this tort action in Alabama state court to recover damages for injuries sustained in a motorcycle accident. Petitioner removed the case to a Federal District Court having diversity jurisdiction. A jury trial resulted in a judgment of $300,000 for respondent Alan Woods and $5,000 for respondent Cara Woods. Petitioner posted bond to stay the judgment pending appeal, and the Court of Appeals affirmed without modification. 768 F.2d 1287 (CA11 1985).

Respondents then moved in the Court of Appeals, pursuant to Ala.Code § 12–22–72 (1986), for imposition of that State's mandatory affirmance penalty of 10% of the amount of judgment. Petitioner challenged the application of this statute as violative of the equal protection and due process guarantees of the Fourteenth Amendment and as "a procedural rule . . . inapplicable in federal court under the doctrine of Erie Railroad Company v. Tompkins, 304 U.S. 64 (1938) and its progeny." App. to Pet. for Cert. A–5. The Court of Appeals summarily granted respondents' motion to assess the penalty and subsequently denied a petition for rehearing. The parties have stipulated that the final judgment has been

---

be named had notice of the pendency of the suit before the statute of limitations has run. Notice within a reasonable additional time for serving process is not sufficient. The Court reached this result wholly as a construction of Rule 15(c) and did not discuss what a state court might have done in this diversity case. See Lewis, The Excessive History of Federal Rule 15(c) and Its Lessons for Civil Rule Revision, 85 Mich.L.Rev. 1507 (1987); Brussack, Outrageous *Fortune*: The Case for Amending Rule 15(c) Again, 61 S.Cal.L.Rev. 671 (1988). The rule was amended in 1991 as the commentators had urged. What is now Rule 15(c)(1) provides that an amendment relates back whenever "relation back is permitted by the law that provides the statute of limitations applicable to the action."

Rule 11 of the Texas Rules of Civil Procedure, providing that no agreement between attorneys or parties "touching any suit pending" is to be enforced unless it is in writing, signed and filed with the papers as part of the record, or made in open court and entered in the record, is a rule of substance that must be applied in a federal diversity proceeding. Condit Chemical & Grain Co. v. Helena Chemical Corp., 789 F.2d 1101 (5th Cir.1986).

Rule 42(b), of the Federal Rules of Civil Procedure allowing a court to order separate trials on issues of liability and damages, applies in a diversity case even in a state that does not allow the issues of liability and damages to be separated. Rosales v. Honda Motor Co., Ltd., 726 F.2d 259 (5th Cir.1984).

Although Rule 238 of the Pennsylvania Rules of Civil Procedure, requiring prejudgment interest in certain cases, was upheld by the Pennsylvania Supreme Court as a valid exercise of its power to make rules of "procedure," it nevertheless must be applied by a federal court in a diversity case. Jarvis v. Johnson, 668 F.2d 740 (3d Cir.1982).]

paid, except for the $30,500 statutory affirmance penalty, which petitioner has withheld pending proceedings in this Court.

We granted certiorari to consider the equal protection and due process challenges as well as the *Erie* claim. 475 U.S. 1080 (1986). Because we conclude that the Alabama statute imposing a mandatory affirmance penalty has no application in federal diversity actions, we decline to reach the Fourteenth Amendment issues.

II

The Alabama statute provides in relevant part:

> "When a judgment or decree is entered or rendered for money, whether debt or damages, and the same has been stayed on appeal by the execution of bond, with surety, if the appellate court affirms the judgment of the court below, it must also enter judgment against all or any of the obligors on the bond for the amount of the affirmed judgment, 10 percent damages thereon and the costs of the appellate court...." Ala.Code § 12–22–72 (1986).[41]

As set forth in the statute, then, a combination of three conditions will automatically trigger the 10% penalty: (1) the trial court must enter a money judgment or decree, (2) the judgment or decree must be stayed by the requisite bond,[42] and (3) the judgment or decree must be affirmed without substantial modification. E.g., Chapman v. Rivers Construction Co., 284 Ala. 633, 644–645, 227 So.2d 403, 414–415 (1969). The purposes of the mandatory affirmance penalty are to penalize frivolous appeals and appeals interposed for delay, Montgomery Light & Water Power Co. v. Thombs, 204 Ala. 678, 684, 87 So. 205, 211 (1920), and to provide "additional damages" as compensation to the appellees for having to suffer the ordeal of defending the judgments on appeal. Birmingham v. Bowen, 254 Ala. 41, 46–47, 47 So.2d 174, 179–180 (1950).

Petitioner contends that the statute's underlying purposes and mandatory mode of operation conflict with the purposes and operation of Rule 38 of the Federal Rules of Appellate Procedure, and therefore that the statute should not be applied by federal courts sitting in diversity. Entitled "Damages for delay," Rule 38 provides: "If the court of appeals shall determine that an appeal is frivolous, it may award just damages and single or double costs to the appellee." See also 28 U.S.C. § 1912. Under this Rule, "damages are awarded by the court in its discretion in the case of a frivolous appeal as a matter of justice to the appellee and as a penalty against the appellant." Advisory Committee's Notes on Fed.Rule App.Proc. 38, 28 U.S.C.App., p. 492.

---

41. Compare Ky.Rev.Stat. § 26A.300 (1985) (mandatory 10% penalty for second appeal); Miss.Code Ann. § 11–3–23 (Supp.1986) (15% mandatory penalty regardless of stay); Va.Code § 16.1–113 (Supp.1986) (10% mandatory penalty regardless of stay).

42. Under Alabama law, an appellant may obtain a stay of judgment pending appeal by providing an acceptable surety bond of a set amount, which in this case would have been 125% of the trial court's judgment had the case been tried in state court. Ala.Rule App.Proc. 8(a)(1).

In Hanna v. Plumer, 380 U.S. 460 (1965), we set forth the appropriate test for resolving conflicts between state law and the Federal Rules. The initial step is to determine whether, when fairly construed, the scope of Federal Rule 38 is "sufficiently broad" to cause a "direct collision" with the state law or, implicitly, to "control the issue" before the court, thereby leaving no room for the operation of that law. Walker v. Armco Steel Corp., 446 U.S. 740, 749–750, and n. 9 (1980); *Hanna,* supra, 380 U.S., at 471–472. The Rule must then be applied if it represents a valid exercise of Congress' rulemaking authority, which originates in the Constitution and has been bestowed on this Court by the Rules Enabling Act, 28 U.S.C. § 2072. *Hanna*, 380 U.S., at 471–474.

The constitutional constraints on the exercise of this rulemaking authority define a test of reasonableness. Rules regulating matters indisputably procedural are *a priori* constitutional. Rules regulating matters "which, though falling within the uncertain area between substance and procedure, are rationally capable of classification as either," also satisfy this constitutional standard. Id., at 472. The Rules Enabling Act, however, contains an additional requirement. The Federal Rule must not "abridge, enlarge or modify any substantive right...." 28 U.S.C. § 2072. The cardinal purpose of Congress in authorizing the development of a uniform and consistent system of rules governing federal practice and procedure suggests that Rules which incidentally affect litigants' substantive rights do not violate this provision if reasonably necessary to maintain the integrity of that system of rules. See *Hanna,* supra, at 464–465; Mississippi Publishing Corp. v. Murphree, 326 U.S. 438, 445–446 (1946); 19 C. Wright, A. Miller, & E. Cooper, Federal Practice and Procedure § 4509, pp. 145–146 (1982). Moreover, the study and approval given each proposed Rule by the Advisory Committee, the Judicial Conference, and this Court, and the statutory requirement that the Rule be reported to Congress for a period of review before taking effect, see 28 U.S.C. § 2072, give the Rules presumptive validity under both the constitutional and statutory constraints. See *Hanna,* supra, at 471.

Applying the *Hanna* analysis to an analogous Mississippi statute which provides for a mandatory affirmance penalty, the United States Court of Appeals for the Fifth Circuit concluded in Affholder, Inc. v. Southern Rock, Inc., 746 F.2d 305 (1984), that the statute conflicted with Rule 38 and thus was not applicable in federal diversity actions. The Fifth Circuit discussed two aspects of the conflict: (1) the discretionary mode of operation of the Federal Rule, compared to the mandatory operation of the Mississippi statute, and (2) the limited effect of the Rule in penalizing only frivolous appeals or appeals interposed for purposes of delay, compared to the effect of the Mississippi statute in penalizing every unsuccessful appeal regardless of merit. Id., at 308–309.

We find the Fifth Circuit's analysis persuasive. Rule 38 affords a court of appeals plenary discretion to assess "just damages" in order to penalize an appellant who takes a frivolous appeal and to compensate the injured appellee for the delay and added expense of defending the district court's judgment. Thus, the Rule's discretionary mode of operation unmistakably conflicts with the mandatory provision of Alabama's affirmance penalty statute. Moreover, the purposes underlying the Rule are sufficiently coextensive with the asserted purposes of the Alabama statute to indicate that the Rule occupies the statute's field of operation so as to preclude its application in federal diversity actions.[43]

Respondents argue that, because Alabama has a similar Appellate Rule which may be applied in state court alongside the affirmance penalty statute, see Ala.Rule App.Proc. 38; McAnnally v. Levco, Inc., 456 So.2d 66, 67 (Ala.1984), a federal court sitting in diversity could impose the mandatory penalty and likewise remain free to exercise its discretionary authority under Federal Rule 38. This argument, however, ignores the significant possibility that a court of appeals may, in any given case, find a limited justification for imposing penalties in an amount *less than* 10% of the lower court's judgment. Federal Rule 38 adopts a case-by-case approach to identifying and deterring frivolous appeals; the Alabama statute precludes any exercise of discretion within its scope of operation. Whatever circumscriptive effect the mandatory affirmance penalty statute may have on the state court's exercise of discretion under Alabama's Rule 38, that Rule provides no authority for defining the scope of discretion allowed under Federal Rule 38.

Federal Rule 38 regulates matters which can reasonably be classified as procedural, thereby satisfying the constitutional standard for validity. Its displacement of the Alabama statute also satisfies the statutory constraints of the Rules Enabling Act. The choice made by the drafters of the Federal Rules in favor of a discretionary procedure affects only the process of enforcing litigants' rights and not the rights themselves.

III

We therefore hold that the Alabama mandatory affirmance penalty statute has no application to judgments entered by federal courts sitting in diversity.

Reversed.[44]

---

43. Rule 37 of the Federal Rules of Appellate Procedure provides further indication that the Rules occupy the Alabama statute's field of operation so as to preclude its application in diversity actions. Since the affirmance penalty only applies if a trial court's judgment is stayed pending appeal, see Ala.Code § 12–22–72 (1986), it operates to compensate a victorious appellee for the lost use of the judgment proceeds during the period of appeal. Federal Rule 37, however, already serves this purpose by providing for an award of postjudgment interest following an unsuccessful appeal. See also 28 U.S.C. § 1961.

In addition, we note that federal provisions governing the availability of a stay of judgment pending appeal do not condition the procurement of a stay on exposure to payment of any additional damages in the event the appeal is unsuccessful and, unlike the state provision in this case, allow the federal courts to set the amount of security in their discretion. Compare Fed.Rules Civ.Proc. 62(d) and 62(g) and Fed.Rule App.Proc. 8(b) with Ala.Rule App.Proc. 8(b). See also 28 U.S.C. § 1651.

[**44.** See Whitten, *Erie* and the Federal Rules: A Review and Reappraisal After *Burlington Northern Railroad v. Woods*, 21 Creighton L.Rev. 1 (1988).

Shady Grove Orthopedic Associates v. Allstate Insurance Co.

Supreme Court of the United States, 2010.
559 U.S. ___, 130 S.Ct. 1431, 176 L.Ed.2d 311.

■ JUSTICE SCALIA announced the judgment of the Court and delivered the opinion of the Court with respect to Parts I and II–A, an opinion with respect to Parts II–B and II–D, in which THE CHIEF JUSTICE, JUSTICE THOMAS, and JUSTICE SOTOMAYOR join, and an opinion with respect to Part II–C, in which THE CHIEF JUSTICE and JUSTICE THOMAS join.

New York law prohibits class actions in suits seeking penalties or statutory minimum damages.[45] We consider whether this precludes a feder-

---

Stewart Organization, Inc. v. Ricoh Corp., 487 U.S. 22 (1988), arose out of a contract that contained a clause providing that any disputes could be brought only in a court in New York. A diversity action was brought in federal court in Alabama. Alabama was a proper venue but defendant, relying on the forum-selection clause, moved to transfer the suit to the Southern District of New York. The Eleventh Circuit divided sharply on whether, in a diversity case, a federal court should look to Alabama law, which regards forum-selection clauses as unenforceable, or to federal law, which was thought to enforce such clauses if they are not unreasonable. The Supreme Court concluded that this was not the right question. It held that 28 U.S.C. § 1404(a) governs whether to transfer a case, so that state law is not controlling, and that the forum-selection clause is only one of the factors the federal court should take into account in exercising its discretion under the statute.

In a diversity case, a federal court is to apply federal notions of whether to dismiss on the ground of *forum non conveniens* and is not to look to state law on this point. In re Air Crash Disaster Near New Orleans, 821 F.2d 1147, 1154–1159 (5th Cir.1987), noted 62 Tul.L.Rev. 813 (1988); Sibaja v. Dow Chemical Co., 757 F.2d 1215 (11th Cir.1985). But see Stein, *Erie* and Court Access, 100 Yale L.J. 1935 (1991).

On the other hand, when an admiralty action is tried in a state court, the state court may apply state notions of whether to dismiss on *forum non conveniens* grounds, and is not bound by federal law on this point. American Dredging Co. v. Miller, 510 U.S. 443, 452 (1994).

A New Hampshire statute precludes a defendant, without plaintiff's consent, from maintaining an action for contribution prior to resolution of the plaintiff's principal action. If plaintiff sues in federal court, can defendant use Rule 14 to implead a third party seeking contribution from that party? Compare Connors v. Suburban Propane Co., 916 F.Supp. 73 (D.N.H.1996) ("Because its use to implead third-party contribution defendants would violate the Rules Enabling Act (by limiting plaintiffs' and enlarging defendant's substantive rights under applicable state law), Fed.R.Civ.P. 14 cannot be invoked, without plaintiffs' consent....") with Chapman v. Therriault, 1998 WL 1110691 (D.N.H.1998) (contra). See also Riccitelli v. Water Pik Technologies, Inc., 203 F.R.D. 62 (D.N.H.2001).]

45. N.Y. Civ. Prac. Law Ann. § 901 (West 2006) provides:

"(a) One or more members of a class may sue or be sued as representative parties on behalf of all if:"

"1. the class is so numerous that joinder of all members, whether otherwise required or permitted, is impracticable;"

"2. there are questions of law or fact common to the class which predominate over any questions affecting only individual members;"

"3. the claims or defenses of the representative parties are typical of the claims or defenses of the class;"

"4. the representative parties will fairly and adequately protect the interests of the class; and"

al district court sitting in diversity from entertaining a class action under Federal Rule of Civil Procedure 23.[46]

I

The petitioner's complaint alleged the following: Shady Grove Orthopedic Associates, P. A., provided medical care to Sonia E. Galvez for injuries she suffered in an automobile accident. As partial payment for that care, Galvez assigned to Shady Grove her rights to insurance benefits under a policy issued in New York by Allstate Insurance Co. Shady Grove tendered a claim for the assigned benefits to Allstate, which under New York law had 30 days to pay the claim or deny it. See N.Y. Ins. Law Ann. § 5106(a) (West 2009). Allstate apparently paid, but not on time, and it refused to pay the statutory interest that accrued on the overdue benefits (at two percent per month), see ibid.

Shady Grove filed this diversity suit in the Eastern District of New York to recover the unpaid statutory interest. Alleging that Allstate routinely refuses to pay interest on overdue benefits, Shady Grove sought relief on behalf of itself and a class of all others to whom Allstate owes interest. The District Court dismissed the suit for lack of jurisdiction. 466 F.Supp.2d 467 (2006). It reasoned that N.Y. Civ. Prac. Law Ann. § 901(b), which precludes a suit to recover a "penalty" from proceeding as a class action, applies in diversity suits in federal court, despite Federal Rule of Civil Procedure 23. Concluding that statutory interest is a "penalty" under New York law, it held that § 901(b) prohibited the proposed class action. And, since Shady Grove conceded that its individual claim (worth roughly $500) fell far short of the amount-in-controversy requirement for individual suits under 28 U.S.C. § 1332(a), the suit did not belong in federal court.[47]

"5. a class action is superior to other available methods for the fair and efficient adjudication of the controversy."

"(b) Unless a statute creating or imposing a penalty, or a minimum measure of recovery specifically authorizes the recovery thereof in a class action, an action to recover a penalty, or minimum measure of recovery created or imposed by statute may not be maintained as a class action."

46. Rule 23(a) provides:

"(a) Prerequisites. One or more members of a class may sue or be sued as representative parties on behalf of all members only if:"

"(1) the class is so numerous that joinder of all members is impracticable;"

"(2) there are questions of law or fact common to the class;"

"(3) the claims or defenses of the representative parties are typical of the claims or defenses of the class; and"

"(4) the representative parties will fairly and adequately protect the interests of the class."

Subsection (b) says that "[a] class action may be maintained if Rule 23(a) is satisfied and if" the suit falls into one of three described categories (irrelevant for present purposes).

47. Shady Grove had asserted jurisdiction under 28 U.S.C. § 1332(d)(2), which relaxes, for class actions seeking at least $5 million, the rule against aggregating separate claims for calculation of the amount in controversy. See Exxon Mobil Corp. v. Allapattah Services, Inc., 545 U.S. 546, 571 (2005).

The Second Circuit affirmed. 549 F.3d 137 (2008). The court did not dispute that a federal rule adopted in compliance with the Rules Enabling Act, 28 U.S.C. § 2072, would control if it conflicted with § 901(b). But there was no conflict because (as we will describe in more detail below) the Second Circuit concluded that Rule 23 and § 901(b) address different issues. Finding no federal rule on point, the Court of Appeals held that § 901(b) is "substantive" within the meaning of Erie R. Co. v. Tompkins, 304 U.S. 64 (1938), and thus must be applied by federal courts sitting in diversity.

We granted certiorari.

II

The framework for our decision is familiar. We must first determine whether Rule 23 answers the question in dispute. Burlington Northern R. Co. v. Woods, 480 U.S. 1, 4–5 (1987). If it does, it governs—New York's law notwithstanding—unless it exceeds statutory authorization or Congress's rulemaking power. Id., at 5; see Hanna v. Plumer, 380 U.S. 460, 463–464 (1965). We do not wade into *Erie*'s murky waters unless the federal rule is inapplicable or invalid. See 380 U.S., at 469–471.

A

The question in dispute is whether Shady Grove's suit may proceed as a class action. Rule 23 provides an answer. It states that "[a] class action may be maintained" if two conditions are met: The suit must satisfy the criteria set forth in subdivision (a) (i.e., numerosity, commonality, typicality, and adequacy of representation), and it also must fit into one of the three categories described in subdivision (b). Fed. Rule Civ. Proc. 23(b). By its terms this creates a categorical rule entitling a plaintiff whose suit meets the specified criteria to pursue his claim as a class action. (The Federal Rules regularly use "may" to confer categorical permission, see, e.g., Fed. Rules Civ. Proc. 8(d)(2)-(3), 14(a)(1), 18(a)-(b), 20(a)(1)-(2), 27(a)(1), 30(a)(1), as do federal statutes that establish procedural entitlements, see, e.g., 29 U.S.C. § 626(c)(1); 42 U.S.C. § 2000e–5(f)(1).) Thus, Rule 23 provides a one-size-fits-all formula for deciding the class-action question. Because § 901(b) attempts to answer the same question—i.e., it states that Shady Grove's suit "may not be maintained as a class action" (emphasis added) because of the relief it seeks—it cannot apply in diversity suits unless Rule 23 is ultra vires.

The Second Circuit believed that § 901(b) and Rule 23 do not conflict because they address different issues. Rule 23, it said, concerns only the criteria for determining whether a given class can and should be certified; section 901(b), on the other hand, addresses an antecedent question: whether the particular type of claim is eligible for class treatment in the first place—a question on which Rule 23 is silent. See 549 F.3d, at 143–144. Allstate embraces this analysis.

We disagree. To begin with, the line between eligibility and certifiability is entirely artificial. Both are preconditions for maintaining a class action. Allstate suggests that eligibility must depend on the "particular cause of action" asserted, instead of some other attribute of the suit. But that is not so. Congress could, for example, provide that only claims involving more than a certain number of plaintiffs are "eligible" for class treatment in federal court. In other words, relabeling Rule 23(a)'s prerequisites "eligibility criteria" would obviate Allstate's objection—a sure sign that its eligibility-certifiability distinction is made-to-order.

There is no reason, in any event, to read Rule 23 as addressing only whether claims made eligible for class treatment by some other law should be certified as class actions. Allstate asserts that Rule 23 neither explicitly nor implicitly empowers a federal court "to certify a class in each and every case" where the Rule's criteria are met. Id., at 13–14. But that is exactly what Rule 23 does: It says that if the prescribed preconditions are satisfied "[a] class action may be maintained" (emphasis added)—not "a class action may be permitted." Courts do not maintain actions; litigants do. The discretion suggested by Rule 23's "may" is discretion residing in the plaintiff: He may bring his claim in a class action if he wishes. And like the rest of the Federal Rules of Civil Procedure, Rule 23 automatically applies "in all civil actions and proceedings in the United States district courts," Fed. Rule Civ. Proc. 1. See Califano v. Yamasaki, 442 U.S. 682, 699–700 (1979).

Allstate points out that Congress has carved out some federal claims from Rule 23's reach, see, e.g., 8 U.S.C. § 1252(e)(1)(B)—which shows, Allstate contends, that Rule 23 does not authorize class actions for all claims, but rather leaves room for laws like § 901(b). But Congress, unlike New York, has ultimate authority over the Federal Rules of Civil Procedure; it can create exceptions to an individual rule as it sees fit—either by directly amending the rule or by enacting a separate statute overriding it in certain instances. Cf. Henderson v. United States, 517 U.S. 654, 668 (1996). The fact that Congress has created specific exceptions to Rule 23 hardly proves that the Rule does not apply generally. In fact, it proves the opposite. If Rule 23 did not authorize class actions across the board, the statutory exceptions would be unnecessary.

Allstate next suggests that the structure of § 901 shows that Rule 23 addresses only certifiability. Section 901(a), it notes, establishes class-certification criteria roughly analogous to those in Rule 23 (wherefore it agrees that subsection is pre-empted). But § 901(b)'s rule barring class actions for certain claims is set off as its own subsection, and where it applies § 901(a) does not. This shows, according to Allstate, that § 901(b) concerns a separate subject. Perhaps it does concern a subject separate from the subject of § 901(a). But the question before us is whether it concerns a subject separate from the subject of Rule 23—and for purposes of answering that question the way New York has structured its statute is immaterial. Rule 23 permits all class actions that meet its requirements, and a State cannot limit that permission by structuring one part of its statute to track Rule 23 and enacting another part that imposes additional requirements. Both of § 901's subsections undeniably answer the same question as Rule 23: whether a class action may proceed for a given suit. Cf. *Burlington*, 480 U.S., at 7–8.

The dissent argues that § 901(b) has nothing to do with whether Shady Grove may maintain its suit as a class action, but affects only the remedy it may obtain if it wins. See post (opinion of Ginsburg, J.). Whereas "Rule 23 governs procedural aspects of class litigation" by "prescrib[ing] the considerations relevant to class certification and postcertification proceedings," § 901(b) addresses only "the size of a monetary award a class plaintiff may pursue." Accordingly, the dissent says, Rule 23 and New York's law may coexist in peace.

We need not decide whether a state law that limits the remedies available in an existing class action would conflict with Rule 23; that is not what § 901(b) does. By its terms, the provision precludes a plaintiff from "maintain[ing]" a class action seeking statutory penalties. Unlike a law that sets a ceiling on damages (or puts other remedies out of reach) in properly filed class actions, § 901(b) says nothing about what remedies a court may award; it prevents the class actions it covers from coming into existence at all.[48] Consequently, a court bound by § 901(b) could not certify a class action seeking both statutory penalties and other remedies even if it announces in advance that it will refuse to award the penalties in the event the plaintiffs prevail; to do so would violate the statute's clear prohibition on "maintain[ing]" such suits as class actions.

The dissent asserts that a plaintiff can avoid § 901(b)'s barrier by omitting from his complaint (or removing) a request for statutory penalties. See post. Even assuming all statutory penalties are waivable, the fact that a complaint omitting them could be brought as a class action would not at all prove that § 901(b) is addressed only to remedies. If the state law instead banned class actions for fraud claims, a would-be class-action plaintiff could drop the fraud counts from his complaint and proceed with the remainder in a class action. Yet that would not mean the law provides no remedy for fraud; the ban would affect only the procedural means by which the remedy may be pursued. In short, although the dissent correctly abandons Allstate's eligibility-certifiability distinction, the alternative it offers fares no better.

The dissent all but admits that the literal terms of § 901(b) address the same subject as Rule 23—i.e., whether a class action may be maintained—but insists the provision's purpose is to restrict only remedies. See post ("[W]hile phrased as responsive to the question whether certain class actions may begin, § 901(b) is unmistakably aimed at controlling how those

---

48. Contrary to the dissent's implication, post, we express no view as to whether state laws that set a ceiling on damages recoverable in a single suit, see App. A to Brief for Respondent, are pre-empted. Whether or not those laws conflict with Rule 23, § 901(b) does conflict because it addresses not the remedy, but the procedural right to maintain a class action. As Allstate and the dissent note, several federal statutes also limit the recovery available in class actions. See, e.g., 12 U.S.C. § 2605(f)(2)(B); 15 U.S.C. § 1640(a)(2)(B); 29 U.S.C. § 1854(c)(1). But Congress has plenary power to override the Federal Rules, so its enactments, unlike those of the States, prevail even in case of a conflict.

actions must end"). Unlike Rule 23, designed to further procedural fairness and efficiency, § 901(b) (we are told) "responds to an entirely different concern": the fear that allowing statutory damages to be awarded on a class-wide basis would "produce overkill." Post (internal quotation marks omitted). The dissent reaches this conclusion on the basis of (1) constituent concern recorded in the law's bill jacket; (2) a commentary suggesting that the Legislature "apparently fear[ed]" that combining class actions and statutory penalties "could result in annihilating punishment of the defendant," V. Alexander, Practice Commentaries, C901:11, reprinted in 7B McKinney's Consolidated Laws of New York Ann., p. 104 (2006) (internal quotation marks omitted); (3) a remark by the Governor in his signing statement that § 901(b) " 'provides a controlled remedy,' " post (quoting Memorandum on Approving L. 1975, Ch. 207, reprinted in 1975 N.Y. Laws, at 1748; emphasis deleted), and (4) a state court's statement that the final text of § 901(b) " 'was the result of a compromise among competing interests,' "post (quoting Sperry v. Crompton Corp., 863 N.E.2d 1012, 1015 (2007)).

This evidence of the New York Legislature's purpose is pretty sparse. But even accepting the dissent's account of the Legislature's objective at face value, it cannot override the statute's clear text. Even if its aim is to restrict the remedy a plaintiff can obtain, § 901(b) achieves that end by limiting a plaintiff's power to maintain a class action. The manner in which the law "could have been written," post, has no bearing; what matters is the law the Legislature did enact. We cannot rewrite that to reflect our perception of legislative purpose, see Oncale v. Sundowner Offshore Services, Inc., 523 U.S. 75, 79–80 (1998).[49] The dissent's concern for state prerogatives is frustrated rather than furthered by revising state laws when a potential conflict with a Federal Rule arises; the state-friendly approach would be to accept the law as written and test the validity of the Federal Rule.

The dissent's approach of determining whether state and federal rules conflict based on the subjective intentions of the state legislature is an enterprise destined to produce "confusion worse confounded," Sibbach v. Wilson & Co., 312 U.S. 1, 14 (1941). It would mean, to begin with, that one State's statute could survive pre-emption (and accordingly affect the proce-

---

49. Our decision in Walker v. Armco Steel Corp., 446 U.S. 740 (1980), discussed by the dissent, post, is not to the contrary. There we held that Rule 3 (which provides that a federal civil action is " 'commenced' "by filing a complaint in federal court) did not displace a state law providing that " '[a]n action shall be deemed commenced, within the meaning of this article [the statute of limitations], as to each defendant, at the date of the summons which is served on him. . . . ' "446 U.S., at 743, n.4 (quoting Okla. Stat., Tit. 12, § 97 (1971); alteration in original, emphasis added). Rule 3, we explained, "governs the date from which various timing requirements of the Federal Rules begin to run, but does not affect state statutes of limitations" or tolling rules, which it did not "purpor[t] to displace." 446 U.S., at 751. The texts were therefore not in conflict. While our opinion observed that the State's actual-service rule was (in the State's judgment) an "integral part of the several policies served by the statute of limitations," id., at 751, nothing in our decision suggested that a federal court may resolve an obvious conflict between the texts of state and federal rules by resorting to the state law's ostensible objectives.

dures in federal court) while another State's identical law would not, merely because its authors had different aspirations. It would also mean that district courts would have to discern, in every diversity case, the purpose behind any putatively pre-empted state procedural rule, even if its text squarely conflicts with federal law. That task will often prove arduous. Many laws further more than one aim, and the aim of others may be impossible to discern. Moreover, to the extent the dissent's purpose-driven approach depends on its characterization of § 901(b)'s aims as substantive, it would apply to many state rules ostensibly addressed to procedure. Pleading standards, for example, often embody policy preferences about the types of claims that should succeed—as do rules governing summary judgment, pretrial discovery, and the admissibility of certain evidence. Hard cases will abound. It is not even clear that a state supreme court's pronouncement of the law's purpose would settle the issue, since existence of the factual predicate for avoiding federal pre-emption is ultimately a federal question. Predictably, federal judges would be condemned to poring through state legislative history—which may be less easily obtained, less thorough, and less familiar than its federal counterpart, see R. Mersky & D. Dunn, Fundamentals of Legal Research 233 (8th ed.2002); Torres & Windsor, State Legislative Histories: A Select, Annotated Bibliography, 85 L. Lib. J. 545, 547 (1993).

But while the dissent does indeed artificially narrow the scope of § 901(b) by finding that it pursues only substantive policies, that is not the central difficulty of the dissent's position. The central difficulty is that even artificial narrowing cannot render § 901(b) compatible with Rule 23. Whatever the policies they pursue, they flatly contradict each other. Allstate asserts (and the dissent implies) that we can (and must) interpret Rule 23 in a manner that avoids overstepping its authorizing statute.[50] If the Rule were susceptible of two meanings—one that would violate § 2072(b) and another that would not—we would agree. See Ortiz v. Fibreboard Corp., 527 U.S. 815, 842, 845 (1999); cf. Semtek Int'l Inc. v. Lockheed Martin Corp., 531 U.S. 497, 503–504 (2001). But it is not. Rule 23 unambiguously authorizes any plaintiff, in any federal civil proceeding, to maintain a class

---

50. The dissent also suggests that we should read the Federal Rules " 'with sensitivity to important state interests' " and " 'to avoid conflict with important state regulatory policies.' "Post (quoting Gasperini v. Center for Humanities, Inc., 518 U.S. 415, 427, n. 7, 438, n. 22 (1996)). The search for state interests and policies that are "important" is just as standardless as the "important or substantial" criterion we rejected in Sibbach v. Wilson & Co., 312 U.S. 1, 13–14 (1941), to define the state-created rights a Federal Rule may not abridge.

If all the dissent means is that we should read an ambiguous Federal Rule to avoid "substantial variations [in outcomes] between state and federal litigation," Semtek Int'l Inc. v. Lockheed Martin Corp., 531 U.S. 497, 504 (2001) (internal quotation marks omitted), we entirely agree. We should do so not to avoid doubt as to the Rule's validity—since a Federal Rule that fails *Erie*'s forum-shopping test is not ipso facto invalid, see Hanna v. Plumer, 380 U.S. 460, 469–472 (1965)—but because it is reasonable to assume that "Congress is just as concerned as we have been to avoid significant differences between state and federal courts in adjudicating claims," Stewart Organization, Inc. v. Ricoh Corp., 487 U.S. 22, 37–38 (1988) (SCALIA, J., dissenting). The assumption is irrelevant here, however, because there is only one reasonable reading of Rule 23.

action if the Rule's prerequisites are met. We cannot contort its text, even to avert a collision with state law that might render it invalid. See Walker v. Armco Steel Corp., 446 U.S. 740, 750, n. 9 (1980).[51] What the dissent's approach achieves is not the avoiding of a "conflict between Rule 23 and § 901(b)," post, but rather the invalidation of Rule 23 (pursuant to § 2072(b) of the Rules Enabling Act) to the extent that it conflicts with the substantive policies of § 901. There is no other way to reach the dissent's destination. We must therefore confront head-on whether Rule 23 falls within the statutory authorization.

B

Erie involved the constitutional power of federal courts to supplant state law with judge-made rules. In that context, it made no difference whether the rule was technically one of substance or procedure; the touchstone was whether it "significantly affect[s] the result of a litigation." Guaranty Trust Co. v. York, 326 U.S. 99, 109 (1945). That is not the test for either the constitutionality or the statutory validity of a Federal Rule of Procedure. Congress has undoubted power to supplant state law, and undoubted power to prescribe rules for the courts it has created, so long as those rules regulate matters "rationally capable of classification" as proce-dure. *Hanna*, 380 U.S., at 472. In the Rules Enabling Act, Congress authorized this Court to promulgate rules of procedure subject to its review, 28 U.S.C. § 2072(a), but with the limitation that those rules "shall not abridge, enlarge or modify any substantive right," § 2072(b).

We have long held that this limitation means that the Rule must "really regulat[e] procedure,—the judicial process for enforcing rights and duties recognized by substantive law and for justly administering remedy and redress for disregard or infraction of them," *Sibbach*, 312 U.S., at 14; see *Hanna*, at 464; *Burlington*, 480 U.S., at 8. The test is not whether the rule affects a litigant's substantive rights; most procedural rules do. Missis-sippi Publishing Corp. v. Murphree, 326 U.S. 438, 445 (1946). What matters is what the rule itself regulates: If it governs only "the manner and the means" by which the litigants' rights are "enforced," it is valid; if it alters "the rules of decision by which [the] court will adjudicate [those] rights," it is not. Id., at 446 (internal quotation marks omitted).

Applying that test, we have rejected every statutory challenge to a Federal Rule that has come before us. We have found to be in compliance with § 2072(b) rules prescribing methods for serving process, see id., at 445–446 (Fed. Rule Civ. Proc. 4(f)); *Hanna*, supra, at 463–465 (Fed. Rule Civ. Proc. 4(d)(1)), and requiring litigants whose mental or physical condi-tion is in dispute to submit to examinations, see *Sibbach*, supra, at 14–16 (Fed. Rule Civ. Proc. 35); Schlagenhauf v. Holder, 379 U.S. 104, 113–114

---

51. The cases chronicled by the dissent, see post, each involved a Federal Rule that we concluded could fairly be read not to "control the issue" addressed by the pertinent state law, thus avoiding a "direct collision" between federal and state law, *Walker*, 446 U.S., at 749 (internal quotation marks omitted). But here, as in *Hanna*, supra, at 470, a collision is "unavoidable."

(1964) (same). Likewise, we have upheld rules authorizing imposition of sanctions upon those who file frivolous appeals, see *Burlington*, supra, at 8 (Fed. Rule App. Proc. 38), or who sign court papers without a reasonable inquiry into the facts asserted, see Business Guides, Inc. v. Chromatic Communications Enterprises, Inc., 498 U.S. 533, 551–554 (1991) (Fed. Rule Civ. Proc. 11). Each of these rules had some practical effect on the parties' rights, but each undeniably regulated only the process for enforcing those rights; none altered the rights themselves, the available remedies, or the rules of decision by which the court adjudicated either.

Applying that criterion, we think it obvious that rules allowing multiple claims (and claims by or against multiple parties) to be litigated together are also valid. See, e.g., Fed. Rules Civ. Proc. 18 (joinder of claims), 20 (joinder of parties), 42(a) (consolidation of actions). Such rules neither change plaintiffs' separate entitlements to relief nor abridge defendants' rights; they alter only how the claims are processed. For the same reason, Rule 23—at least insofar as it allows willing plaintiffs to join their separate claims against the same defendants in a class action-falls within § 2072(b)'s authorization. A class action, no less than traditional joinder (of which it is a species), merely enables a federal court to adjudicate claims of multiple parties at once, instead of in separate suits. And like traditional joinder, it leaves the parties' legal rights and duties intact and the rules of decision unchanged.

Allstate contends that the authorization of class actions is not substantively neutral: Allowing Shady Grove to sue on behalf of a class "transform[s][the] dispute over a five hundred dollar penalty into a dispute over a five million dollar penalty." Brief for Respondent 1. Allstate's aggregate liability, however, does not depend on whether the suit proceeds as a class action. Each of the 1,000–plus members of the putative class could (as Allstate acknowledges) bring a freestanding suit asserting his individual claim. It is undoubtedly true that some plaintiffs who would not bring individual suits for the relatively small sums involved will choose to join a class action. That has no bearing, however, on Allstate's or the plaintiffs' legal rights. The likelihood that some (even many) plaintiffs will be induced to sue by the availability of a class action is just the sort of "incidental effec[t]" we have long held does not violate § 2072(b), *Mississippi Publishing*, supra, at 445.

Allstate argues that Rule 23 violates § 2072(b) because the state law it displaces, § 901(b), creates a right that the Federal Rule abridges—namely, a "substantive right ... not to be subjected to aggregated class-action liability" in a single suit. To begin with, we doubt that that is so. Nothing in the text of § 901(b) (which is to be found in New York's procedural code) confines it to claims under New York law; and of course New York has no power to alter substantive rights and duties created by other sovereigns. As we have said, the consequence of excluding certain class actions may be to cap the damages a defendant can face in a single suit, but the law itself alters only procedure. In that respect, § 901(b) is no different from a state law forbidding simple joinder. As a fallback argument, Allstate argues that even if § 901(b) is a procedural provision, it was enacted "for substantive reasons," id., at 24 (emphasis added). Its end was not to improve "the conduct of the litigation process itself" but to alter "the outcome of that process." Id., at 26.

The fundamental difficulty with both these arguments is that the substantive nature of New York's law, or its substantive purpose, makes no difference. A Federal Rule of Procedure is not valid in some jurisdictions and invalid in others—or valid in some cases and invalid in others—depending upon whether its effect is to frustrate a state substantive law (or a state procedural law enacted for substantive purposes). That could not be clearer in *Sibbach*:

> "The petitioner says the phrase ['substantive rights' in the Rules Enabling Act] connotes more; that by its use Congress intended that in regulating procedure this Court should not deal with important and substantial rights theretofore recognized. Recognized where and by whom? The state courts are divided as to the power in the absence of statute to order a physical examination. In a number such an order is authorized by statute or rule. . . . ""

> "The asserted right, moreover, is no more important than many others enjoyed by litigants in District Courts sitting in the several states before the Federal Rules of Civil Procedure altered and abolished old rights or privileges and created new ones in connection with the conduct of litigation. . . . If we were to adopt the suggested criterion of the importance of the alleged right we should invite endless litigation and confusion worse confounded. The test must be whether a rule really regulates procedure. . . . " 312 U.S., at 13–14 (footnotes omitted).

Hanna unmistakably expressed the same understanding that compliance of a Federal Rule with the Enabling Act is to be assessed by consulting the Rule itself, and not its effects in individual applications:

> "[T]he court has been instructed to apply the Federal Rule, and can refuse to do so only if the Advisory Committee, this Court, and Congress erred in their prima facie judgment that the Rule in question transgresses neither the terms of the Enabling Act nor constitutional restrictions." 380 U.S., at 471.

In sum, it is not the substantive or procedural nature or purpose of the affected state law that matters, but the substantive or procedural nature of the Federal Rule. We have held since *Sibbach*, and reaffirmed repeatedly, that the validity of a Federal Rule depends entirely upon whether it regulates procedure. See *Sibbach*, supra, at 14; *Hanna*, supra, at 464; *Burlington*, 480 U.S., at 8. If it does, it is authorized by § 2072 and is valid in all jurisdictions, with respect to all claims, regardless of its incidental effect upon state-created rights.

C

A few words in response to the concurrence. We understand it to accept the framework we apply—which requires first, determining whether the federal and state rules can be reconciled (because they answer different questions), and second, if they cannot, determining whether the Federal Rule runs afoul of § 2072(b). Post (STEVENS, J., concurring in part and concurring in judgment). The concurrence agrees with us that Rule 23 and § 901(b) conflict, and departs from us only with respect to the second part of the test, i.e., whether application of the Federal Rule violates § 2072(b). Like us, it answers no, but for a reason different from ours.

The concurrence would decide this case on the basis, not that Rule 23 is procedural, but that the state law it displaces is procedural, in the sense that it does not "function as a part of the State's definition of substantive rights and remedies." A state procedural rule is not preempted, according to the concurrence, so long as it is "so bound up with," or "sufficiently intertwined with," a substantive state-law right or remedy "that it defines the scope of that substantive right or remedy."

This analysis squarely conflicts with *Sibbach*, which established the rule we apply. The concurrence contends that *Sibbach* did not rule out its approach, but that is not so. Recognizing the impracticability of a test that turns on the idiosyncrasies of state law, *Sibbach* adopted and applied a rule with a single criterion: whether the Federal Rule "really regulates procedure." 312 U.S., at 14.[52] That the concurrence's approach would have yielded the same result in *Sibbach* proves nothing; what matters is the rule we did apply, and that rule leaves no room for special exemptions based on the function or purpose of a particular state rule.[53] We have rejected an attempt to read into *Sibbach* an exception with no basis in the opinion, see *Schlagenhauf*, 379 U.S., at 113–114, and we see no reason to find such an implied limitation today.

---

52. The concurrence claims that in *Sibbach* "[t]he Court ... had no occasion to consider whether the particular application of the Federal Rules in question would offend the Enabling Act." Had *Sibbach* been applying the concurrence's theory, that is quite true— which demonstrates how inconsistent that theory is with *Sibbach*. For conformity with the Rules Enabling Act was the very issue *Sibbach* decided: The petitioner's position was that Rules 35 and 37 exceeded the Enabling Act's authorization, 312 U.S., at 9, 13; the Court faced and rejected that argument, id., at 13–16, and proceeded to reverse the lower court for failing to apply Rule 37 correctly, id., at 16. There could not be a clearer rejection of the theory that the concurrence now advocates. The concurrence responds that "the specific question of ''the obligation of federal courts to apply the substantive law of a state'' was not before the Court, post (quoting *Sibbach*, supra, at 9). It is clear from the context, however, that this passage referred to the *Erie* prohibition of court-created rules that displace state law. The opinion unquestionably dealt with the Federal Rules' compliance with § 2072(b), and it adopted the standard we apply here to resolve the question, which does not depend on whether individual applications of the Rule abridge or modify state-law rights. See 312 U.S., at 13–14. To the extent *Sibbach* did not address the Federal Rules' validity vis-à-vis contrary state law, *Hanna* surely did, see 380 U.S., at 472, and it made clear that *Sibbach*'s test still controls, see 380 U.S., at 464–465, 470–471.

53. The concurrence insists that we have misread *Sibbach*, since surely a Federal Rule that "in most cases" regulates procedure does not do so when it displaces one of those "rare" state substantive laws that are disguised as rules of procedure. This mistakes what the Federal Rule regulates for its incidental effects. As we have explained, supra, most Rules have some effect on litigants' substantive rights or their ability to obtain a remedy, but that does not mean the Rule itself regulates those rights or remedies.

In reality, the concurrence seeks not to apply *Sibbach*, but to overrule it (or, what is the same, to rewrite it). Its approach, the concurrence insists, gives short shrift to the statutory text forbidding the Federal Rules from "abridg[ing], enlarg[ing], or modify[ing] any substantive right," § 2072(b). There is something to that. It is possible to understand how it can be determined whether a Federal Rule "enlarges" substantive rights without consulting State law: If the Rule creates a substantive right, even one that duplicates some state-created rights, it establishes a new federal right. But it is hard to understand how it can be determined whether a Federal Rule "abridges" or "modifies" substantive rights without knowing what state-created rights would obtain if the Federal Rule did not exist. *Sibbach*'s exclusive focus on the challenged Federal Rule—driven by the very real concern that Federal Rules which vary from State to State would be chaos, see 312 U.S., at 13–14—is hard to square with § 2072(b)'s terms.[54]

Sibbach has been settled law, however, for nearly seven decades.[55] Setting aside any precedent requires a "special justification" beyond a bare belief that it was wrong. Patterson v. McLean Credit Union, 491 U.S. 164, 172 (1989) (internal quotation marks omitted). And a party seeking to overturn a statutory precedent bears an even greater burden, since Congress remains free to correct us, ibid., and adhering to our precedent enables it do so, see, e.g., Finley v. United States, 490 U.S. 545, 556 (1989); 28 U.S.C. § 1367; Exxon Mobil Corp. v. Allapattah Services, Inc., 545 U.S. 546, 558 (2005). We do Congress no service by presenting it a moving target. In all events, Allstate has not even asked us to overrule *Sibbach*, let alone carried its burden of persuading us to do so. Cf. IBP, Inc. v. Alvarez,

---

54. The concurrence's approach, however, is itself unfaithful to the statute's terms. Section 2072(b) bans abridgement or modification only of "substantive rights," but the concurrence would prohibit pre-emption of "procedural rules that are intimately bound up in the scope of a substantive right or remedy," post. This would allow States to force a wide array of parochial procedures on federal courts so long as they are "sufficiently intertwined with a state right or remedy."

55. The concurrence implies that *Sibbach* has slipped into desuetude, apparently for lack of sufficient citations. See post. We are unaware of any rule to the effect that a holding of ours expires if the case setting it forth is not periodically revalidated. In any event, the concurrence's account of our shunning of *Sibbach* is greatly exaggerated. *Hanna* did not merely cite the case, but recognized it as establishing the governing rule. 380 U.S., at 464–465, 470–471. Mississippi Publishing Corp. v. Murphree, 326 U.S. 438, 445–446 (1946), likewise cited *Sibbach* and applied the same test, examining the Federal Rule, not the state law it displaced. True, Burlington Northern R. Co. v. Woods, 480 U.S. 1 (1987), and for that matter Business Guides, Inc. v. Chromatic Communications Enterprises, Inc., 498 U.S. 533 (1991), did not cite *Sibbach*. But both cited and followed *Hanna*—which as noted held out *Sibbach* as setting forth the governing rule. See *Burlington Northern*, supra, at 5–6, 8; *Business Guides*, supra, at 552–554. Thus, while *Sibbach* itself may appear infrequently in the U.S. Reports, its rule—and in particular its focus on the Federal Rule as the proper unit of analysis—is alive and well. In contrast, *Hanna*'s obscure obiter dictum that a court "need not wholly blind itself" to a Federal Rule's effect on a case's outcome, 380 U.S., at 473—which the concurrence invokes twice—has never resurfaced in our opinions in the 45 years since its first unfortunate utterance. Nor does it cast doubt on *Sibbach*'s straightforward test: As the concurrence notes, *Hanna* cited *Sibbach* for that statement, 380 U.S., at 473, showing it saw no inconsistency between the two.

546 U.S. 21, 32 (2005). Why we should cast aside our decades-old decision escapes us, especially since (as the concurrence explains) that would not affect the result.[56]

The concurrence also contends that applying *Sibbach* and assessing whether a Federal Rule regulates substance or procedure is not always easy. Undoubtedly some hard cases will arise (though we have managed to muddle through well enough in the 69 years since *Sibbach* was decided). But as the concurrence acknowledges, the basic difficulty is unavoidable: The statute itself refers to "substantive right[s]," § 2072(b), so there is no escaping the substance-procedure distinction. What is more, the concurrence's approach does nothing to diminish the difficulty, but rather magnifies it many times over. Instead of a single hard question of whether a Federal Rule regulates substance or procedure, that approach will present hundreds of hard questions, forcing federal courts to assess the substantive or procedural character of countless state rules that may conflict with a single Federal Rule.[57] And it still does not sidestep the problem it seeks to avoid. At the end of the day, one must come face to face with the decision whether or not the state policy (with which a putatively procedural state rule may be "bound up") pertains to a "substantive right or remedy," that is, whether it is substance or procedure.[58] The more one explores the alternatives to *Sibbach*'s rule, the more its wisdom becomes apparent.

---

56. The concurrence is correct, post, that under our disposition any rule that "really regulates procedure," *Sibbach*, supra, at 14, will preempt a conflicting state rule, however "bound up" the latter is with substantive law. The concurrence is wrong, however, that that result proves our interpretation of § 2072(b) implausible, post. The result is troubling only if one stretches the term "substantive rights" in § 2072(b) to mean not only state-law rights themselves, but also any state-law procedures closely connected to them. Neither the text nor our precedent supports that expansive interpretation. The examples the concurrence offers—statutes of limitations, burdens of proof, and standards for appellate review of damages awards—do not make its broad definition of substantive rights more persuasive. They merely illustrate that in rare cases it may be difficult to determine whether a rule "really regulates" procedure or substance. If one concludes the latter, there is no preemption of the state rule; the Federal Rule itself is invalid. The concurrence's concern would make more sense if many Federal Rules that effectively alter state-law rights "bound up with procedures" would survive under *Sibbach*. But as the concurrence concedes, post, very few would do so. The possible existence of a few outlier instances does not prove *Sibbach*'s interpretation is absurd. Congress may well have accepted such anomalies as the price of a uniform system of federal procedure.

57. The concurrence argues that its approach is no more "taxing" than ours because few if any Federal Rules that are "facially valid" under the Enabling Act will fail the concurrence's test. But that conclusion will be reached only after federal courts have considered hundreds of state rules applying the concurrence's inscrutable standard.

58. The concurrence insists that the task will be easier if courts can "conside[r] the nature and functions of the state law" regardless of the law's "form," post (emphasis deleted), i.e., what the law actually says. We think that amorphous inquiry into the "nature and functions" of a state law will tend to increase, rather than decrease, the difficulty of classifying Federal Rules as substantive or procedural. Walking through the concurrence's application of its test to § 901(b), post, gives little reason to hope that its approach will lighten the burden for lower courts.

D

We must acknowledge the reality that keeping the federal-court door open to class actions that cannot proceed in state court will produce forum shopping. That is unacceptable when it comes as the consequence of judge-made rules created to fill supposed "gaps" in positive federal law. See *Hanna*, 380 U.S., at 471–472. For where neither the Constitution, a treaty, nor a statute provides the rule of decision or authorizes a federal court to supply one, "state law must govern because there can be no other law." Ibid.; see Clark, *Erie*'s Constitutional Source, 95 Cal. L.Rev. 1289, 1302, 1311 (2007). But divergence from state law, with the attendant consequence of forum shopping, is the inevitable (indeed, one might say the intended) result of a uniform system of federal procedure. Congress itself has created the possibility that the same case may follow a different course if filed in federal instead of state court. Cf. *Hanna*, 380 U.S., at 472–473. The short of the matter is that a Federal Rule governing procedure is valid whether or not it alters the outcome of the case in a way that induces forum shopping. To hold otherwise would be to "disembowel either the Constitution's grant of power over federal procedure" or Congress's exercise of it. Id., at 473–474.

* * *

The judgment of the Court of Appeals is reversed, and the case is remanded for further proceedings.

It is so ordered.

[The opinion of Justice Stevens, concurring in part and concurring in the judgment, is omitted.]

■ Justice Ginsburg, with whom Justice Kennedy, Justice Breyer, and Justice Alito join, dissenting.

The Court today approves Shady Grove's attempt to transform a $500 case into a $5,000,000 award, although the State creating the right to recover has proscribed this alchemy. If Shady Grove had filed suit in New York state court, the 2% interest payment authorized by New York Ins. Law Ann. § 5106(a) (West 2009) as a penalty for overdue benefits would, by Shady Grove's own measure, amount to no more than $500. By instead filing in federal court based on the parties' diverse citizenship and requesting class certification, Shady Grove hopes to recover, for the class, statutory damages of more than $5,000,000. The New York Legislature has barred this remedy, instructing that, unless specifically permitted, "an action to recover a penalty, or minimum measure of recovery created or imposed by statute may not be maintained as a class action." N.Y. Civ. Prac. Law Ann. (CPLR) § 901(b) (West 2006). The Court nevertheless holds that Federal Rule of Civil Procedure 23, which prescribes procedures for the conduct of class actions in federal courts, preempts the application of § 901(b) in diversity suits.

The Court reads Rule 23 relentlessly to override New York's restriction on the availability of statutory damages. Our decisions, however, caution us to ask, before undermining state legislation: Is this conflict really necessary? Cf. Traynor, Is This Conflict Really Necessary? 37 Tex. L.Rev. 657 (1959). Had the Court engaged in that inquiry, it would not have read Rule 23 to collide with New York's legitimate interest in keeping certain monetary awards reasonably bounded. I would continue to interpret Federal Rules with awareness of, and sensitivity to, important state regulatory policies. Because today's judgment radically departs from that course, I dissent.

I

A

"Under the *Erie* doctrine," it is long settled, "federal courts sitting in diversity apply state substantive law and federal procedural law." Gasperini v. Center for Humanities, Inc., 518 U.S. 415, 427 (1996); see Erie R. Co. v. Tompkins, 304 U.S. 64 (1938). Justice Harlan aptly conveyed the importance of the doctrine; he described *Erie* as "one of the modern cornerstones of our federalism, expressing policies that profoundly touch the allocation of judicial power between the state and federal systems." Hanna v. Plumer, 380 U.S. 460, 474 (1965) (concurring opinion). Although we have found *Erie*'s application "sometimes [to be] a challenging endeavor," *Gasperini*, 518 U.S., at 427, two federal statutes mark our way.

The first, the Rules of Decision Act prohibits federal courts from generating substantive law in diversity actions. See *Erie*, 304 U.S., at 78. Originally enacted as part of the Judiciary Act of 1789, this restraint serves a policy of prime importance to our federal system. We have therefore applied the Act "with an eye alert to . . . avoiding disregard of State law." Guaranty Trust Co. v. York, 326 U.S. 99, 110 (1945).

The second, the Rules Enabling Act, enacted in 1934, authorizes us to "prescribe general rules of practice and procedure" for the federal courts, but with a crucial restriction: "Such rules shall not abridge, enlarge or modify any substantive right." 28 U.S.C. § 2072. Pursuant to this statute, we have adopted the Federal Rules of Civil Procedure. In interpreting the scope of the Rules, including, in particular, Rule 23, we have been mindful of the limits on our authority. See, e.g., Ortiz v. Fibreboard Corp., 527 U.S. 815, 845 (1999) (The Rules Enabling Act counsels against "adventurous application" of Rule 23; any tension with the Act "is best kept within tolerable limits."); Amchem Products, Inc. v. Windsor, 521 U.S. 591, 612–613 (1997). See also Semtek Int'l Inc. v. Lockheed Martin Corp., 531 U.S. 497, 503–504 (2001).

If a Federal Rule controls an issue and directly conflicts with state law, the Rule, so long as it is consonant with the Rules Enabling Act, applies in diversity suits. See *Hanna*, 380 U.S., at 469–474. If, however, no Federal Rule or statute governs the issue, the Rules of Decision Act, as interpreted in *Erie*, controls. That Act directs federal courts, in diversity cases, to apply state law when failure to do so would invite forum-shopping and yield markedly disparate litigation outcomes. See *Gasperini*, 518 U.S., at 428; *Hanna*, 380 U.S., at 468. Recognizing that the Rules of Decision Act and the Rules Enabling Act simultaneously frame and inform the *Erie* analysis, we have endeavored in diversity suits to remain safely within the bounds of both congressional directives.

B

In our prior decisions in point, many of them not mentioned in the Court's opinion, we have avoided immoderate interpretations of the Federal Rules that would trench on state prerogatives without serving any countervailing federal interest. "Application of the *Hanna* analysis," we have said, "is premised on a ''direct collision'' between the Federal Rule and the state law." Walker v. Armco Steel Corp., 446 U.S. 740, 749–750 (1980) (quoting *Hanna*, 380 U.S., at 472). To displace state law, a Federal Rule, "when fairly construed," must be " 'sufficiently broad' "so as "to ''control the issue' before the court, thereby leaving no room for the operation of that law." Burlington Northern R. Co. v. Woods, 480 U.S. 1, 4–5 (1987) quoting *Walker*, 446 U.S., at 749–750, and n. 9 (emphasis added); cf. Stewart Organization, Inc. v. Ricoh Corp., 487 U.S. 22, 37–38 (1988) (Scalia, J., dissenting) ("[I]n deciding whether a federal . . . Rule of Procedure encompasses a particular issue, a broad reading that would create significant disuniformity between state and federal courts should be avoided if the text permits.").

In pre-*Hanna* decisions, the Court vigilantly read the Federal Rules to avoid conflict with state laws. In Palmer v. Hoffman, 318 U.S. 109, 117 (1943), for example, the Court read Federal Rule 8(c), which lists affirmative defenses, to control only the manner of pleading the listed defenses in diversity cases; as to the burden of proof in such cases, *Palmer* held, state law controls.

Six years later, in Ragan v. Merchants Transfer & Warehouse Co., 337 U.S. 530 (1949), the Court ruled that state law determines when a diversity suit commences for purposes of tolling the state limitations period. Although Federal Rule 3 specified that "[a] civil action is commenced by filing a complaint with the court," we held that the Rule did not displace a state law that tied an action's commencement to service of the summons. Id., at 531–533. The "cause of action [wa]s created by local law," the Court explained, therefore "the measure of it [wa]s to be found only in local law." Id., at 533.

Similarly in Cohen v. Beneficial Industrial Loan Corp., 337 U.S. 541 (1949), the Court held applicable in a diversity action a state statute requiring plaintiffs, as a prerequisite to pursuit of a stockholder's derivative action, to post a bond as security for costs. At the time of the litigation, Rule 23, now Rule 23.1, addressed a plaintiff's institution of a derivative action in federal court. Although the Federal Rule specified prerequisites to a stockholder's maintenance of a derivative action, the Court found no conflict between the Rule and the state statute in question; the requirements of both could be enforced, the Court observed. See id., at 556. Burdensome as the security-for-costs requirement may be, *Cohen* made plain, suitors could not escape the upfront outlay by resorting to the federal court's diversity jurisdiction.

In all of these cases, the Court stated in *Hanna*, "the scope of the Federal Rule was not as broad as the losing party urged, and therefore, there being no Federal Rule which covered the point in dispute, *Erie* commanded the enforcement of state law." 380 U.S., at 470. In *Hanna* itself, the Court found the clash "unavoidable," ibid.; the petitioner had effected service of process as prescribed by Federal Rule 4(d)(1), but that "how-to" method did not satisfy the special Massachusetts law applicable to service on an executor or administrator. Even as it rejected the Massachusetts prescription in favor of the federal procedure, however, "[t]he majority in *Hanna* recognized ... that federal rules ... must be interpreted by the courts applying them, and that the process of interpretation can and should reflect an awareness of legitimate state interests." R. Fallon, J. Manning, D. Meltzer, & D. Shapiro, Hart and Wechsler's The Federal Courts and the Federal System 593 (6th ed.2009) (hereinafter Hart & Wechsler).

Following *Hanna*, we continued to "interpre[t] the federal rules to avoid conflict with important state regulatory policies." Hart & Wechsler, 593. In *Walker*, the Court took up the question whether *Ragan* should be overruled; we held, once again, that Federal Rule 3 does not directly conflict with state rules governing the time when an action commences for purposes of tolling a limitations period. 446 U.S., at 749–752. Rule 3, we said, addresses only "the date from which various timing requirements of the Federal Rules begin to run," id., at 751, and does not "purpor[t] to displace state tolling rules," id., at 750–751. Significant state policy interests would be frustrated, we observed, were we to read Rule 3 as superseding the state rule, which required actual service on the defendant to stop the clock on the statute of limitations. Id., at 750–752.

We were similarly attentive to a State's regulatory policy in *Gasperini*. That diversity case concerned the standard for determining when the large size of a jury verdict warrants a new trial. Federal and state courts alike had generally employed a "shock the conscience" test in reviewing jury awards for excessiveness. See 518 U.S., at 422. Federal courts did so pursuant to Federal Rule 59(a) which, as worded at the time of *Gasperini*, instructed that a trial court could grant a new trial "for any of the reasons for which new trials have heretofore been granted in actions at law in the courts of the United States." Fed. Rule Civ. Proc. 59(a) (West 1995). In an effort to provide greater control, New York prescribed procedures under which jury verdicts would be examined to determine whether they "deviate[d] materially from what would be reasonable compensation." See *Gasperini*, 518 U.S., at 423–425 (quoting CPLR § 5501(c)). This Court held that Rule 59(a) did not inhibit federal-court accommodation of New York's invigorated test.

Most recently, in *Semtek*, we addressed the claim-preclusive effect of a federal-court judgment dismissing a diversity action on the basis of a California statute of limitations. The case came to us after the same plaintiff renewed the same fray against the same defendant in a Maryland state court. (Plaintiff chose Maryland because that State's limitations period had not yet run.) We held that Federal Rule 41(b), which provided that an involuntary dismissal "operate[d] as an adjudication on the merits," did not bar maintenance of the renewed action in Maryland. To hold that Rule 41(b) precluded the Maryland courts from entertaining the case, we said, "would arguably violate the jurisdictional limitation of the Rules Enabling Act," 531 U.S., at 503, and "would in many cases violate [*Erie*'s] federalism principle," id., at 504.

In sum, both before and after *Hanna*, the above-described decisions show, federal courts have been cautioned by this Court to "interpre[t] the Federal Rules ... with sensitivity to important state interests," *Gasperini*, 518 U.S., at 427, n. 7, and a will "to avoid conflict with important state regulatory policies," id., at 438, n.22 (internal quotation marks omitted). The Court veers away from that approach—and conspicuously, its most recent reiteration in *Gasperini*—in favor of a mechanical reading of Federal Rules, insensitive to state interests and productive of discord.

C

Our decisions instruct over and over again that, in the adjudication of diversity cases, state interests—whether advanced in a statute, e.g., *Cohen*, or a procedural rule, e.g., *Gasperini*—warrant our respectful consideration. Yet today, the Court gives no quarter to New York's limitation on statutory damages and requires the lower courts to thwart the regulatory policy at stake: To prevent excessive damages, New York's law controls the penalty to which a defendant may be exposed in a single suit. The story behind § 901(b)'s enactment deserves telling.

In 1975, the Judicial Conference of the State of New York proposed a new class-action statute designed "to set up a flexible, functional scheme" that would provide "an effective, but controlled group remedy." Judicial Conference Report on CPLR, reprinted in 1975 N.Y. Laws pp. 1477, 1493 (McKinney). As originally drafted, the legislation addressed only the procedural aspects of class actions; it specified, for example, five prerequisites for certification, eventually codified at § 901(a), that closely tracked those listed in Rule 23. See CPLR § 901(a) (requiring, for class certification, numerosity, predominance, typicality, adequacy of representation, and superiority).

While the Judicial Conference proposal was in the New York Legislature's hopper, "various groups advocated for the addition of a provision that would prohibit class action plaintiffs from being awarded a statutorily-created penalty ... except when expressly authorized in the pertinent statute." Sperry v. Crompton Corp., 863 N.E.2d 1012, 1015 (NY 2007). These constituents "feared that recoveries beyond actual damages could lead to excessively harsh results." Ibid. "They also argued that there was no need to permit class actions ... [because] statutory penalties ... provided an aggrieved party with a sufficient economic incentive to pursue a claim." Ibid. Such penalties, constituents observed, often far exceed a plaintiff's actual damages. "When lumped together," they argued, "penalties and class actions produce overkill." Attachment to Letter from G. Perkinson, New York State Council of Retail Merchants, Inc., to J. Gribetz, Executive Chamber (June 4, 1975) (Legislative Report), Bill Jacket, L. 1975, Ch. 207.

Aiming to avoid "annihilating punishment of the defendant," the New York Legislature amended the proposed statute to bar the recovery of statutory damages in class actions. V. Alexander, Practice Commentaries, C901:11, reprinted in 7B McKinney's Consolidated Laws of New York Ann., p. 104 (2006) (internal quotation marks omitted). In his signing statement, Governor Hugh Carey stated that the new statute "empowers the court to prevent abuse of the class action device and provides a controlled remedy." Memorandum on Approving L. 1975, Ch. 207, reprinted in 1975 N.Y. Laws, at 1748 (emphasis added).

"[T]he final bill ... was the result of a compromise among competing interests." *Sperry*, 863 N.E.2d at 1015. Section 901(a) allows courts leeway in deciding whether to certify a class, but § 901(b) rejects the use of the class mechanism to pursue the particular remedy of statutory damages. The limitation was not designed with the fair conduct or efficiency of litigation in mind. Indeed, suits seeking statutory damages are arguably best suited to the class device because individual proof of actual damages is unnecessary. New York's decision instead to block class-action proceedings for statutory damages therefore makes scant sense, except as a means to a manifestly substantive end: Limiting a defendant's liability in a single lawsuit in order to prevent the exorbitant inflation of penalties—remedies the New York Legislature created with individual suits in mind.

D

Shady Grove contends—and the Court today agrees—that Rule 23 unavoidably preempts New York's prohibition on the recovery of statutory damages in class actions. The Federal Rule, the Court emphasizes, states that Shady Grove's suit "may be" maintained as a class action, which conflicts with § 901(b)'s instruction that it "may not" so proceed. Accordingly, the Court insists, § 901(b) "cannot apply in diversity suits unless Rule 23 is ultra vires." Concluding that Rule 23 does not violate the Rules Enabling Act, the Court holds that the federal provision controls Shady Grove's ability to seek, on behalf of a class, a statutory penalty of over $5,000,000.

The Court, I am convinced, finds conflict where none is necessary. Mindful of the history behind § 901(b)'s enactment, the thrust of our precedent, and the substantive-rights limitation in the Rules Enabling Act, I conclude, as did the Second Circuit and every District Court to have considered the question in any detail, that Rule 23 does not collide with § 901(b). As the Second Circuit well understood, Rule 23 prescribes the considerations relevant to class certification and postcertification proceedings—but it does not command that a particular remedy be available when a party sues in a representative capacity. See 549 F.3d 137, 143 (2008).

Section 901(b), in contrast, trains on that latter issue. Sensibly read, Rule 23 governs procedural aspects of class litigation, but allows state law to control the size of a monetary award a class plaintiff may pursue.

In other words, Rule 23 describes a method of enforcing a claim for relief, while § 901(b) defines the dimensions of the claim itself. In this regard, it is immaterial that § 901(b) bars statutory penalties in wholesale, rather than retail, fashion. The New York Legislature could have embedded the limitation in every provision creating a cause of action for which a penalty is authorized; § 901(b) operates as shorthand to the same effect. It is as much a part of the delineation of the claim for relief as it would be were it included claim by claim in the New York Code.

The Court single-mindedly focuses on whether a suit "may" or "may not" be maintained as a class action. See ante. Putting the question that way, the Court does not home in on the reason why. Rule 23 authorizes class treatment for suits satisfying its prerequisites because the class mechanism generally affords a fair and efficient way to aggregate claims for adjudication. Section 901(b) responds to an entirely different concern; it does not allow class members to recover statutory damages because the New York Legislature considered the result of adjudicating such claims en masse to be exorbitant. The fair and efficient conduct of class litigation is the legitimate concern of Rule 23; the remedy for an infraction of state law, however, is the legitimate concern of the State's lawmakers and not of the federal rulemakers. Cf. Ely, The Irrepressible Myth of *Erie*, 87 Harv. L.Rev. 693, 722 (1974) (It is relevant "whether the state provision embodies a substantive policy or represents only a procedural disagreement with the federal rulemakers respecting the fairest and most efficient way of conducting litigation.").

Suppose, for example, that a State, wishing to cap damages in class actions at $1,000,000, enacted a statute providing that "a suit to recover more than $1,000,000 may not be maintained as a class action." Under the Court's reasoning—which attributes dispositive significance to the words "may not be maintained"—Rule 23 would preempt this provision, nevermind that Congress, by authorizing the promulgation of rules of procedure for federal courts, surely did not intend to displace state-created ceilings on damages. The Court suggests that the analysis might differ if the statute "limit[ed] the remedies available in an existing class action," ante, such that Rule 23 might not conflict with a state statute prescribing that "no more than $1,000,000 may be recovered in a class action." There is no real difference in the purpose and intended effect of these two hypothetical statutes. The notion that one directly impinges on Rule 23's domain, while the other does not, fundamentally misperceives the office of Rule 23.

The absence of an inevitable collision between Rule 23 and § 901(b) becomes evident once it is comprehended that a federal court sitting in diversity can accord due respect to both state and federal prescriptions. Plaintiffs seeking to vindicate claims for which the State has provided a statutory penalty may pursue relief through a class action if they forgo statutory damages and instead seek actual damages or injunctive or declaratory relief; any putative class member who objects can opt out and pursue actual damages, if available, and the statutory penalty in an individual action. See, e.g., Mendez v. The Radec Corp., 260 F.R.D. 38, 55 (W.D.N.Y. 2009); Brzychnalski v. Unesco, Inc., 35 F.Supp.2d 351, 353 (S.D.N.Y.1999). See also Alexander, Practice Commentaries, at 105 ("Even if a statutory penalty or minimum recovery is involved, most courts hold that it can be waived, thus confining the class recovery to actual damages and eliminating the bar of CPLR 901(b)."). In this manner, the Second Circuit explained, "Rule 23's procedural requirements for class actions can be applied along with the substantive requirement of CPLR 901(b)." 549 F.3d, at 144. In sum, while phrased as responsive to the question whether certain class actions may begin, § 901(b) is unmistakably aimed at controlling how those actions must end. On that remedial issue, Rule 23 is silent.

Any doubt whether Rule 23 leaves § 901(b) in control of the remedial issue at the core of this case should be dispelled by our *Erie* jurisprudence, including *Hanna*, which counsels us to read Federal Rules moderately and cautions against stretching a rule to cover every situation it could conceivably reach. The Court states that "[t]here is no reason ... to read Rule 23 as addressing only whether claims made eligible for class treatment by some other law should be certified as class actions." To the contrary, *Palmer*, *Ragan*, *Cohen*, *Walker*, *Gasperini*, and *Semtek* provide good reason to look to the law that creates the right to recover. That is plainly so on a more accurate statement of what is at stake: Is there any reason to read Rule 23 as authorizing a claim for relief when the State that created the remedy disallows its pursuit on behalf of a class? None at all is the answer our federal system should give.

Notably, New York is not alone in its effort to contain penalties and minimum recoveries by disallowing class relief; Congress, too, has precluded class treatment for certain claims seeking a statutorily designated minimum recovery. See, e.g., 15 U.S.C. § 1640(a)(2)(B) (Truth in Lending Act) ("[I]n the case of a class action ... no minimum recovery shall be applicable."); § 1693m(a)(2)(B) (Electronic Fund Transfer Act) (same); 12 U.S.C. § 4010(a)(2)(B)(i) (Expedited Fund Availability Act) (same). Today's judgment denies to the States the full power Congress has to keep certain monetary awards within reasonable bounds. Cf. Beard v. Kindler, 558 U.S. ___, ___, 130 S.Ct. 612, 618–19 (2009) ("In light of ... federalism and comity concerns ... it would seem particularly strange to disregard state ... rules that are substantially similar to those to which we give full force in our own courts."). States may hesitate to create determinate statutory penalties in the future if they are impotent to prevent federal-court distortion of the remedy they have shaped.

By finding a conflict without considering whether Rule 23 rationally should be read to avoid any collision, the Court unwisely and unnecessarily retreats from the federalism principles undergirding *Erie*. Had the Court reflected on the respect for state regulatory interests endorsed in our decisions, it would have found no cause to interpret Rule 23 so woodenly— and every reason not to do so. Cf. Traynor, 37 Tex. L.Rev., at 669 ("It is bad enough for courts to prattle unintelligibly about choice of law, but unforgiveable when inquiry might have revealed that there was no real conflict.'').

II

Because I perceive no unavoidable conflict between Rule 23 and § 901(b), I would decide this case by inquiring ''whether application of the [state] rule would have so important an effect upon the fortunes of one or both of the litigants that failure to [apply] it would be likely to cause a plaintiff to choose the federal court.'' *Hanna*, 380 U.S., at 468, n. 9, 85 S.Ct. 1136. See *Gasperini*, 518 U.S., at 428.

Seeking to pretermit that inquiry, Shady Grove urges that the class-action bar in § 901(b) must be regarded as ''procedural'' because it is contained in the CPLR, which ''govern[s] the procedure in civil judicial proceedings in all courts of the state.'' Brief for Petitioner 34 (quoting CPLR § 101; emphasis in original). Placement in the CPLR is hardly dispositive. The provision held ''substantive'' for *Erie* purposes in *Gasperini* is also contained in the CPLR (§ 5501(c)), as are limitations periods, § 201 et seq., prescriptions plainly ''substantive'' for *Erie* purposes however they may be characterized for other purposes, see *York*, 326 U.S., at 109–112. See also, e.g., 1 Restatement (Second) of Conflict of Laws § 133, Reporter's Note, p. 369 (1969) (hereinafter Restatement) (''Under the rule of *Erie* . . . the federal courts have classified the burden of persuasion as to contributory negligence as a matter of substantive law that is governed by the rule of the State in which they sit even though the courts of that State have characterized their rule as procedural for choice-of-law purposes.''); Cook, ''Substance'' and ''Procedure'' in the Conflict of Laws, 42 Yale L.J. 333 (1933).

Shady Grove also ranks § 901(b) as ''procedural'' because ''nothing in [the statute] suggests that it is limited to rights of action based on New York state law, as opposed to federal law or the law of other states''; instead it ''applies to actions seeking penalties under any statute.'' Brief for Petitioner 35–36. . . . It is true that § 901(b) is not specifically limited to claims arising under New York law. But neither is it expressly extended to claims arising under foreign law. The rule prescribes, without elaboration either way, that ''an action to recover a penalty . . . may not be maintained as a class action.'' We have often recognized that ''general words'' appearing in a statute may, in fact, have limited application; ''[t]he words 'any person or persons,' '' for example, ''are broad enough to comprehend every human being. But general words must not only be limited to cases within the jurisdiction of the state, but also to those objects to which the legislature intended to apply them.'' United States v. Palmer, 3 Wheat. [16 U.S.] 610, 631 (1818) (opinion for the Court by Marshall, C. J.). See also Small v. United States, 544 U.S. 385, 388 (2005) (''In law, a legislature that uses the statutory phrase 'any person' may or may not mean to include 'persons' outside the jurisdiction of the state.'' (some internal quotation marks omitted)); Flora v. United States, 362 U.S. 145, 149 (1960) (The term " 'any sum' is a catchall [phrase,] . . . but to say this is not to define what it catches.").

Moreover, Shady Grove overlooks the most likely explanation for the absence of limiting language: New York legislators make law with New York plaintiffs and defendants in mind, i.e., as if New York were the universe. See Baxter, Choice of Law and the Federal System, 16 Stan. L.Rev. 1, 11 (1963) ("[L]awmakers often speak in universal terms but must be understood to speak with reference to their constituents."); cf. Smith v. United States, 507 U.S. 197, 204, n. 5 (1993) (presumption against extraterritoriality rooted in part in "the commonsense notion that Congress generally legislates with domestic concerns in mind").

The point was well put by Brainerd Currie in his seminal article on governmental interest analysis in conflict-of-laws cases. The article centers on a now-archaic Massachusetts law that prevented married women from binding themselves by contract as sureties for their husbands. Discussing whether the Massachusetts prescription applied to transactions involving foreign factors (a foreign forum, foreign place of contracting, or foreign parties), Currie observed:

> "When the Massachusetts legislature addresses itself to the problem of married women as sureties, the undeveloped image in its mind is that of Massachusetts married women, husbands, creditors, transactions, courts, and judgments. In the history of Anglo–American law the domestic case has been normal, the conflict-of-laws case marginal." Married Women''s Contracts: A Study in Conflict-of-Laws Method, 25 U. Chi. L.Rev. 227, 231 (1958) (emphasis added).

Shady Grove's suggestion that States must specifically limit their laws to domestic rights of action if they wish their enactments to apply in federal diversity litigation misses the obvious point: State legislators generally do not focus on an interstate setting when drafting statutes. . . .

Moreover, statutes qualify as "substantive" for *Erie* purposes even when they have "procedural" thrusts as well. See, e.g., *Cohen*, 337 U.S., at 555; cf. Woods v. Interstate Realty Co., 337 U.S. 535, 536–538, and n. 1 (1949) (holding diversity case must be dismissed based on state statute that, by its terms, governed only proceedings in state court). Statutes of limitations are, again, exemplary. They supply "substantive" law in diversity suits, see *York*, 326 U.S., at 109–112, even though, as Shady Grove acknowledges, state courts often apply the forum's limitations period as a "procedural" bar to claims arising under the law of another State. See Restatement §§ 142–143 (when adjudicating a foreign cause of action, State may use either its own or the foreign jurisdiction's statute of limitations, whichever is shorter). Similarly, federal courts sitting in diversity give effect to state laws governing the burden of proving contributory negligence, see Palmer v. Hoffman, 318 U.S. 109, 117 (1943), yet state courts adjudicating foreign causes of action often apply their own local law to this issue. See Restatement § 133 and Reporter's Note.

In short, Shady Grove's effort to characterize § 901(b) as simply "procedural" cannot successfully elide this fundamental norm: When no federal law or rule is dispositive of an issue, and a state statute is outcome affective in the sense our cases on *Erie* (pre-and post-*Hanna*) develop, the Rules of Decision Act commands application of the State's law in diversity suits. *Gasperini*, 518 U.S., at 428; *Hanna*, 380 U.S., at 468, n. 9; *York*, 326 U.S., at 109. As this case starkly demonstrates, if federal courts exercising diversity jurisdiction are compelled by Rule 23 to award statutory penalties in class actions while New York courts are bound by § 901(b)'s proscription, "substantial variations between state and federal [money judgments] may be expected." *Gasperini*, 518 U.S., at 430 (quoting *Hanna*, 380 U.S., at 467–468 (internal quotation marks omitted)). The "variation" here is indeed "substantial." Shady Grove seeks class relief that is ten thousand times greater than the individual remedy available to it in state court. As the plurality acknowledges, forum shopping will undoubtedly result if a plaintiff need only file in federal instead of state court to seek a massive monetary award explicitly barred by state law. See *Gasperini*, 518 U.S., at 431 ("*Erie* precludes a recovery in federal court significantly larger than the recovery that would have been tolerated in state court.").[59] The "accident of diversity of citizenship," Klaxon Co. v. Stentor Elec. Mfg. Co., 313 U.S. 487, 496 (1941), should not subject a defendant to such augmented liability. See *Hanna*, 380 U.S., at 467 ("The *Erie* rule is rooted in part in a realization that it would be unfair for the character or result of a litigation materially to differ because the suit had been brought in a federal court.").

It is beyond debate that "a statutory cap on damages would supply substantive law for *Erie* purposes." *Gasperini*, 518 U.S., at 428. See also id., at 439–440 (STEVENS, J., dissenting) ("A state-law ceiling on allowable damages . . . is a substantive rule of decision that federal courts must apply in diversity cases governed by New York law."); id., at 464 (SCALIA, J., dissenting) ("State substantive law controls what injuries are compensable and in what amount."). In *Gasperini*, we determined that New York's standard for measuring the alleged excessiveness of a jury verdict was designed to provide a control analogous to a damages cap. Id., at 429. The statute was framed as "a procedural instruction," we noted, "but the State's objective [wa]s manifestly substantive." Ibid.

Gasperini's observations apply with full force in this case. By barring the recovery of statutory damages in a class action, § 901(b) controls a defendant's maximum liability in a suit seeking such a remedy. The remedial provision could have been written as an explicit cap: "In any class action seeking statutory damages, relief is limited to the amount the named plaintiff would have recovered in an individual suit." That New York's

---

59. In contrast, many "state rules ostensibly addressed to procedure," ante (majority opinion)—including pleading standards and rules governing summary judgment, pretrial discovery, and the admissibility of certain evidence—would not so hugely impact forum choices. It is difficult to imagine a scenario that would promote more forum shopping than one in which the difference between filing in state and federal court is the difference between a potential award of $500 and one of $5,000,000.

Legislature used other words to express the very same meaning should be inconsequential.

We have long recognized the impropriety of displacing, in a diversity action, state-law limitations on state-created remedies. See *Woods*, 337 U.S., at 538 (in a diversity case, a plaintiff "barred from recovery in the state court ... should likewise be barred in the federal court"); *York*, 326 U.S. at 108–109 (federal court sitting in diversity "cannot afford recovery if the right to recover is made unavailable by the State nor can it substantively affect the enforcement of the right as given by the State"). Just as *Erie* precludes a federal court from entering a deficiency judgment when a State has "authoritatively announced that [such] judgments cannot be secured within its borders," Angel v. Bullington, 330 U.S. 183, 191 (1947), so too *Erie* should prevent a federal court from awarding statutory penalties aggregated through a class action when New York prohibits this recovery. See also *Ragan*, 337 U.S., at 533 ("Where local law qualifies or abridges [a claim], the federal court must follow suit. Otherwise there is a different measure of the cause of action in one court than in the other, and the principle of *Erie* ... is transgressed."). In sum, because "New York substantive law governs [this] claim for relief, New York law ... guide[s] the allowable damages." *Gasperini*, 518 U.S., at 437 ...

III

The Court's erosion of *Erie*'s federalism grounding impels me to point out the large irony in today's judgment. Shady Grove is able to pursue its claim in federal court only by virtue of the recent enactment of the Class Action Fairness Act of 2005 (CAFA), 28 U.S.C. § 1332(d). In CAFA, Congress opened federal-court doors to state-law-based class actions so long as there is minimal diversity, at least 100 class members, and at least $5,000,000 in controversy. Ibid. By providing a federal forum, Congress sought to check what it considered to be the overreadiness of some state courts to certify class actions. See, e.g., S.Rep.No. 109–14, p. 4 (2005) (CAFA prevents lawyers from "gam[ing] the procedural rules [to] keep nationwide or multi-state class actions in state courts whose judges have reputations for readily certifying classes." (internal quotation marks omitted)); id., at 22 (disapproving "the 'I never met a class action I didn't like' approach to class certification" that "is prevalent in state courts in some localities"). In other words, Congress envisioned fewer—not more—class actions overall. Congress surely never anticipated that CAFA would make federal courts a mecca for suits of the kind Shady Grove has launched: class actions seeking state-created penalties for claims arising under state law—claims that would be barred from class treatment in the State's own courts. Cf. *Woods*, 337 U.S., at 537 ("[T]he policy of *Erie* ... preclude[s] maintenance in ... federal court ... of suits to which the State ha[s] closed its courts.").[60]

---

60. It remains open to Congress, of course, to exclude from federal-court jurisdiction under the Class Action Fairness Act of 2005, 28 U. S. C. § 1332(d), claims that could not be maintained as a class action in state court.

* * *

I would continue to approach *Erie* questions in a manner mindful of the purposes underlying the Rules of Decision Act and the Rules Enabling Act, faithful to precedent, and respectful of important state interests. I would therefore hold that the New York Legislature's limitation on the recovery of statutory damages applies in this case, and would affirm the Second Circuit's judgment .. [61]

Semtek Int'l Inc. v. Lockheed Martin Corp.

Supreme Court of the United States, 2001.
531 U.S. 497, 121 S.Ct. 1021, 149 L.Ed.2d 32.

■ JUSTICE SCALIA delivered the opinion of the Court.

This case presents the question whether the claim-preclusive effect of a federal judgment dismissing a diversity action on statute-of-limitations grounds is determined by the law of the State in which the federal court sits.

I

Petitioner filed a complaint against respondent in California state court, alleging breach of contract and various business torts. Respondent removed the case to the United States District Court for the Central District of California on the basis of diversity of citizenship, see 28 U.S.C. §§ 1332, 1441, and successfully moved to dismiss petitioner's claims as barred by California's 2–year statute of limitations. In its order of dismissal, the District Court, adopting language suggested by respondent, dismissed petitioner's claims "in [their] entirety on the merits and with prejudice." Without contesting the District Court's designation of its dismissal as "on the merits," petitioner appealed to the Court of Appeals for the Ninth Circuit, which affirmed the District Court's order. 168 F.3d 501 (1999) (table). Petitioner also brought suit against respondent in the State Circuit Court for Baltimore City, Maryland, alleging the same causes of action, which were not time barred under Maryland's 3–year statute of limitations. Respondent sought injunctive relief against this action from the California federal court under the All Writs Act, 28 U.S.C. § 1651, and removed the action to the United States District Court for the District of Maryland on federal-question grounds (diversity grounds were not available because Lockheed "is a Maryland citizen," Semtek Int'l Inc. v. Lockheed Martin Corp., 988 F.Supp. 913, 914 (1997)). The California federal court denied the relief requested, and the Maryland federal court remanded the case to state court because the federal question arose only by way of defense. Following a hearing, the Maryland state court granted respon-

---

[**61.** See generally Bassett, Enabling the Federal Rules, 44 Creighton L. Rev. 7 (2010) (Symposium); Oakley, Illuminating *Shady Grove*: A General Approach to Resolving *Erie* Problems, 44 Creighton L. Rev. 79 (2010) (Symposium).]

dent's motion to dismiss on the ground of res judicata. Petitioner then returned to the California federal court and the Ninth Circuit, unsuccessfully moving both courts to amend the former's earlier order so as to indicate that the dismissal was not "on the merits." Petitioner also appealed the Maryland trial court's order of dismissal to the Maryland Court of Special Appeals. The Court of Special Appeals affirmed, holding that, regardless of whether California would have accorded claim-preclusive effect to a statute-of-limitations dismissal by one of its own courts, the dismissal by the California federal court barred the complaint filed in Maryland, since the res judicata effect of federal diversity judgments is prescribed by federal law, under which the earlier dismissal was on the merits and claim preclusive. 128 Md.App. 39, 736 A.2d 1104 (1999). After the Maryland Court of Appeals declined to review the case, we granted certiorari.

II

Petitioner contends that the outcome of this case is controlled by Dupasseur v. Rochereau, 21 Wall. [88 U.S.] 130, 135 (1875), which held that the res judicata effect of a federal diversity judgment "is such as would belong to judgments of the State courts rendered under similar circumstances," and may not be accorded any "higher sanctity or effect." Since, petitioner argues, the dismissal of an action on statute-of-limitations grounds by a California state court would not be claim preclusive, it follows that the similar dismissal of this diversity action by the California federal court cannot be claim preclusive. While we agree that this would be the result demanded by *Dupasseur,* the case is not dispositive because it was decided under the Conformity Act of 1872, 17 Stat. 196, which required federal courts to apply the procedural law of the forum State in nonequity cases. That arguably affected the outcome of the case. See *Dupasseur,* supra, at 135. See also Restatement (Second) of Judgments § 87, Comment a, p. 315 (1980) (hereinafter Restatement) ("Since procedural law largely determines the matters that may be adjudicated in an action, state law had to be considered in ascertaining the effect of a federal judgment").

Respondent, for its part, contends that the outcome of this case is controlled by Federal Rule of Civil Procedure 41(b), which provides as follows:

> "Involuntary Dismissal: Effect Thereof. For failure of the plaintiff to prosecute or to comply with these rules or any order of court, a defendant may move for dismissal of an action or of any claim against the defendant. Unless the court in its order for dismissal otherwise specifies, a dismissal under this subdivision and any dismissal not provided for in this rule, other than a dismissal for lack of jurisdiction, for improper venue, or for failure to join a party under Rule 19, operates as an adjudication upon the merits."

Since the dismissal here did not "otherwise specif[y]" (indeed, it specifically stated that it *was* "on the merits"), and did not pertain to the excepted subjects of jurisdiction, venue, or joinder, it follows, respondent contends, that the dismissal "is entitled to claim preclusive effect." Brief for Respondent 3–4.

Implicit in this reasoning is the unstated minor premise that all judgments denominated "on the merits" are entitled to claim-preclusive effect. That premise is not necessarily valid. The original connotation of an "on the merits" adjudication is one that actually "pass[es] directly on the substance of [a particular] claim" before the court. Restatement § 19, Comment a, at 161. That connotation remains common to every jurisdiction of which we are aware. See ibid. ("The prototyp[ical] [judgment on the merits is] one in which the merits of [a party's] claim are in fact adjudicated [for or] against the [party] after trial of the substantive issues"). And it is, we think, the meaning intended in those many statements to the effect that a judgment "on the merits" triggers the doctrine of res judicata or claim preclusion. See, e.g., Parklane Hosiery Co. v. Shore, 439 U.S. 322, 326, n. 5 (1979) ("Under the doctrine of res judicata, a judgment on the merits in a prior suit bars a second suit involving the same parties or their privies based on the same cause of action"); Goddard v. Security Title Ins. & Guarantee Co., 14 Cal.2d 47, 51, 92 P.2d 804, 806 (1939) ("[A] final judgment, rendered upon the merits by a court having jurisdiction of the cause ... is a complete bar to a new suit between [the parties or their privies] on the same cause of action" (internal quotation marks and citations omitted)).

But over the years the meaning of the term "judgment on the merits" "has gradually undergone change," R. Marcus, M. Redish, & E. Sherman, Civil Procedure: A Modern Approach 1140–1141 (3d ed.2000), and it has come to be applied to some judgments (such as the one involved here) that do *not* pass upon the substantive merits of a claim and hence do *not* (in many jurisdictions) entail claim-preclusive effect. Compare, e.g., Western Coal & Mining Co. v. Jones, 27 Cal.2d 819, 826, 167 P.2d 719, 724 (1946), and Koch v. Rodlin Enterprises, Inc., 223 Cal.App.3d 1591, 1596, 273 Cal.Rptr. 438, 441 (1990), with Plaut v. Spendthrift Farm, Inc., 514 U.S. 211, 228 (1995) (statute of limitations); *Goddard*, supra, at 50–51, 92 P.2d, at 806–807, and Allston v. Incorporated Village of Rockville Centre, 25 App.Div.2d 545, 546, 267 N.Y.S.2d 564, 565–566 (1966), with Federated Department Stores, Inc. v. Moitie, 452 U.S. 394, 399, n. 3 (1981) (demurrer or failure to state a claim). See also Restatement § 19, Comment *a* and Reporter's Note; 18 C. Wright, A. Miller, & E. Cooper, Federal Practice and Procedure § 4439, pp. 355–358 (1981) (hereinafter Wright & Miller). That is why the Restatement of Judgments has abandoned the use of the term— "because of its possibly misleading connotations," Restatement § 19, Comment a, at 161.

In short, it is no longer true that a judgment "on the merits" is necessarily a judgment entitled to claim-preclusive effect; and there are a number of reasons for believing that the phrase "adjudication upon the merits" does not bear that meaning in Rule 41(b). To begin with, Rule 41(b) sets forth nothing more than a default rule for determining the import of a dismissal (a dismissal is "upon the merits," with the three stated exceptions, unless the court "otherwise specifies"). This would be a highly peculiar context in which to announce a federally prescribed rule on the complex question of claim preclusion, saying in effect, "All federal dismissals (with three specified exceptions) preclude suit elsewhere, unless the court otherwise specifies."

And even apart from the purely default character of Rule 41(b), it would be peculiar to find a rule governing the effect that must be accorded federal judgments by other courts ensconced in rules governing the internal procedures of the rendering court itself. Indeed, such a rule would arguably violate the jurisdictional limitation of the Rules Enabling Act: that the Rules "shall not abridge, enlarge or modify any substantive right," 28 U.S.C. § 2072(b). Cf. Ortiz v. Fibreboard Corp., 527 U.S. 815, 842 (1999) (adopting a "limiting construction" of Federal Rule of Civil Procedure 23(b)(1)(B) in order to "minimiz[e] potential conflict with the Rules Enabling Act, and [to] avoi[d] serious constitutional concerns"). In the present case, for example, if California law left petitioner free to sue on this claim in Maryland even after the California statute of limitations had expired, the federal court's extinguishment of that right (through Rule 41(b)'s mandated claim-preclusive effect of its judgment) would seem to violate this limitation.

Moreover, as so interpreted, the Rule would in many cases violate the federalism principle of Erie R. Co. v. Tompkins, 304 U.S. 64, 78–80 (1938), by engendering " 'substantial' variations [in outcomes] between state and federal litigation" which would "[l]ikely . . . influence the choice of a forum," Hanna v. Plumer, 380 U.S. 460, 467–468 (1965). See also Guaranty Trust Co. v. York, 326 U.S. 99, 108–110 (1945). Cf. Walker v. Armco Steel Corp., 446 U.S. 740, 748–753 (1980). With regard to the claim-preclusion issue involved in the present case, for example, the traditional rule is that expiration of the applicable statute of limitations merely bars the remedy and does not extinguish the substantive right, so that dismissal on that ground does not have claim-preclusive effect in other jurisdictions with longer, unexpired limitation periods. See Restatement (Second) of Conflict of Laws §§ 142(2), 143 (1969); Restatement of Judgments § 49, Comment a (1942). Out-of-state defendants sued on stale claims in California and in other States adhering to this traditional rule would systematically remove state-law suits brought against them to federal court—where, unless otherwise specified, a statute-of-limitations dismissal would bar suit everywhere.

Finally, if Rule 41(b) did mean what respondent suggests, we would surely have relied upon it in our cases recognizing the claim-preclusive effect of federal judgments in federal-question cases. Yet for over half a century since the promulgation of Rule 41(b), we have not once done so. See, e.g., Heck v. Humphrey, 512 U.S. 477, 488–489, n. 9 (1994); *Federated Department Stores, Inc. v. Moitie*, supra, at 398; Blonder–Tongue Laboratories, Inc. v. University of Ill. Foundation, 402 U.S. 313, 324, n. 12 (1971).

We think the key to a more reasonable interpretation of the meaning of "operates as an adjudication upon the merits" in Rule 41(b) is to be found in Rule 41(a), which, in discussing the effect of voluntary dismissal by the plaintiff, makes clear that an "adjudication upon the merits" is the opposite of a "dismissal without prejudice":

> "Unless otherwise stated in the notice of dismissal or stipulation, the dismissal is without prejudice, except that a notice of dismissal operates as an adjudication upon the merits when filed by a plaintiff who has once dismissed in any court of the United States or of any state an action based on or including the same claim."

See also 18 Wright & Miller, § 4435, at 329, n. 4 ("Both parts of Rule 41 . . . use the phrase 'without prejudice' as a contrast to adjudication on the merits"); 9 id., § 2373, at 396, n. 4 (" '[W]ith prejudice' is an acceptable form of shorthand for 'an adjudication upon the merits' "). See also *Goddard*, 14 Cal.2d, at 54, 92 P.2d, at 808 (stating that a dismissal "with prejudice" evinces "[t]he intention of the court to make [the dismissal] on the merits"). The primary meaning of "dismissal without prejudice," we think, is dismissal without barring the defendant from returning later, to the same court, with the same underlying claim. That will also ordinarily (though not always) have the consequence of not barring the claim from *other* courts, but its primary meaning relates to the dismissing court itself. Thus, Black's Law Dictionary (7th ed.1999) defines "dismissed without prejudice" as "removed from the court's docket in such a way that the plaintiff may refile the same suit on the same claim," id., at 482, 92 P.2d 804, and defines "dismissal without prejudice" as "[a] dismissal that does not bar the plaintiff from refiling the lawsuit within the applicable limitations period," ibid.

We think, then, that the effect of the "adjudication upon the merits" default provision of Rule 41(b)—and, presumably, of the explicit order in the present case that used the language of that default provision—is simply that, unlike a dismissal "without prejudice," the dismissal in the present case barred refiling of the same claim in the United States District Court for the Central District of California. That is undoubtedly a necessary condition, but it is not a sufficient one, for claim-preclusive effect in other courts.[62]

III

Having concluded that the claim-preclusive effect, in Maryland, of this California federal diversity judgment is dictated neither by *Dupasseur v. Rochereau*, as petitioner contends, nor by Rule 41(b), as respondent contends, we turn to consideration of what determines the issue. Neither the Full Faith and Credit Clause, U.S. Const., Art. IV, § 1,[63] nor the full faith

---

62. We do not decide whether, in a diversity case, a federal court's "dismissal upon the merits" (in the sense we have described), under circumstances where a state court would decree only a "dismissal without prejudice," abridges a "substantive right" and thus exceeds the authorization of the Rules Enabling Act. We think the situation will present itself more rarely than would the arguable violation of the Act that would ensue from interpreting Rule 41(b) as a rule of claim preclusion; and if it is a violation, can be more easily dealt with on direct appeal.

63. Article IV, § 1 provides as follows:

and credit statute, 28 U.S.C. § 1738,[64] addresses the question. By their terms they govern the effects to be given only to state-court judgments (and, in the case of the statute, to judgments by courts of territories and possessions). And no other federal textual provision, neither of the Constitution nor of any statute, addresses the claim-preclusive effect of a judgment in a federal diversity action.

It is also true, however, that no federal textual provision addresses the claim-preclusive effect of a federal-court judgment in a federal-question case, yet we have long held that States cannot give those judgments merely whatever effect they would give their own judgments, but must accord them the effect that this Court prescribes. See Stoll v. Gottlieb, 305 U.S. 165, 171–172 (1938); Gunter v. Atlantic Coast Line R. Co., 200 U.S. 273, 290–291 (1906); Deposit Bank v. Frankfort, 191 U.S. 499, 514–515 (1903). The reasoning of that line of cases suggests, moreover, that even when States are allowed to give federal judgments (notably, judgments in diversity cases) no more than the effect accorded to state judgments, that disposition is by direction of *this* Court, which has the last word on the claim-preclusive effect of *all* federal judgments:

> "It is true that for some purposes and within certain limits it is only required that the judgments of the courts of the United States shall be given the same force and effect as are given the judgments of the courts of the States wherein they are rendered; but it is equally true that whether a Federal judgment has been given due force and effect in the state court is a Federal question reviewable by this court, which will determine for itself whether such judgment has been given due weight or otherwise....
>
> "When is the state court obliged to give to Federal judgments only the force and effect it gives to state court judgments within its own jurisdiction? Such cases are distinctly pointed out in the opinion of Mr. Justice Bradley in *Dupasseur v. Rochereau* [which stated that the case was a diversity case, applying state law under state procedure]." Ibid.

In other words, in *Dupasseur* the State was allowed (indeed, required) to give a federal diversity judgment no more effect than it would accord one of its own judgments only because reference to state law was *the federal rule that this Court deemed appropriate*. In short, federal common law governs the claim-preclusive effect of a dismissal by a federal court sitting in diversity. See generally R. Fallon, D. Meltzer, & D. Shapiro, Hart and

---

"Full Faith and Credit shall be given in each State to the public Acts, Records, and judicial Proceedings of every other State. And the Congress may by general Laws prescribe the Manner in which such Acts, Records and Proceedings shall be proved, and the Effect thereof."

64. Title 28 U.S.C. § 1738 provides in relevant part as follows:

"The records and judicial proceedings of any court of any ... State, Territory or Possession ... shall have the same full faith and credit in every court within the United States and its Territories and Possessions as they have by law or usage in the courts of such State, Territory or Possession from which they are taken."

Wechsler's The Federal Courts and the Federal System 1473 (4th ed.1996); Degnan, Federalized Res Judicata, 85 Yale L.J. 741 (1976).

It is left to us, then, to determine the appropriate federal rule. And despite the sea change that has occurred in the background law since *Dupasseur* was decided—not only repeal of the Conformity Act but also the watershed decision of this Court in *Erie*—we think the result decreed by *Dupasseur* continues to be correct for diversity cases. Since state, rather than federal, substantive law is at issue there is no need for a uniform federal rule. And indeed, nationwide uniformity in the substance of the matter is better served by having the same claim-preclusive rule (the state rule) apply whether the dismissal has been ordered by a state or a federal court. This is, it seems to us, a classic case for adopting, as the federally prescribed rule of decision, the law that would be applied by state courts in the State in which the federal diversity court sits. See Gasperini v. Center for Humanities, Inc., 518 U.S. 415, 429–431 (1996); *Walker v. Armco Steel Corp.*, 446 U.S., at 752–753; Bernhardt v. Polygraphic Co. of America, 350 U.S. 198, 202–205 (1956); Palmer v. Hoffman, 318 U.S. 109, 117 (1943); Klaxon Co. v. Stentor Elec. Mfg. Co., 313 U.S. 487, 496 (1941); Cities Service Oil Co. v. Dunlap, 308 U.S. 208, 212 (1939). As we have alluded to above, any other rule would produce the sort of "forum-shopping . . . and . . . inequitable administration of the laws" that *Erie* seeks to avoid, *Hanna,* 380 U.S., at 468, since filing in, or removing to, federal court would be encouraged by the divergent effects that the litigants would anticipate from likely grounds of dismissal. See *Guaranty Trust Co. v. York*, 326 U.S., at 109–110.

This federal reference to state law will not obtain, of course, in situations in which the state law is incompatible with federal interests. If, for example, state law did not accord claim-preclusive effect to dismissals for willful violation of discovery orders, federal courts' interest in the integrity of their own processes might justify a contrary federal rule. No such conflict with potential federal interests exists in the present case. Dismissal of this state cause of action was decreed by the California federal court only because the California statute of limitations so required; and there is no conceivable federal interest in giving that time bar more effect in other courts than the California courts themselves would impose.

* * *

Because the claim-preclusive effect of the California federal court's dismissal "upon the merits" of petitioner's action on statute-of-limitations grounds is governed by a federal rule that in turn incorporates California's law of claim preclusion (the content of which we do not pass upon today), the Maryland Court of Special Appeals erred in holding that the dismissal necessarily precluded the bringing of this action in the Maryland courts. The judgment is reversed, and the case remanded for further proceedings not inconsistent with this opinion.

It is so ordered.

———

SECTION 2. FEDERAL COMMON LAW AND IMPLIED RIGHTS OF ACTION

Clearfield Trust Co. v. United States

Supreme Court of the United States, 1943.
318 U.S. 363, 63 S.Ct. 573, 87 L.Ed. 838.

■ MR. JUSTICE DOUGLAS delivered the opinion of the Court.

On April 28, 1936, a check was drawn on the Treasurer of the United States through the Federal Reserve Bank of Philadelphia to the order of Clair A. Barner in the amount of $24.20. It was dated at Harrisburg, Pennsylvania and was drawn for services rendered by Barner to the Works Progress Administration. The check was placed in the mail addressed to Barner at his address in Mackeyville, Pa. Barner never received the check. Some unknown person obtained it in a mysterious manner and presented it to the J.C. Penney Co. store in Clearfield, Pa., representing that he was the payee and identifying himself to the satisfaction of the employees of J.C. Penney Co. He endorsed the check in the name of Barner and transferred it to J.C. Penney Co. in exchange for cash and merchandise. Barner never authorized the endorsement nor participated in the proceeds of the check. J.C. Penney Co. endorsed the check over to the Clearfield Trust Co. which accepted it as agent for the purpose of collection and endorsed it as follows: "Pay to the order of Federal Reserve Bank of Philadelphia, Prior Endorsements Guaranteed." Clearfield Trust Co. collected the check from the United States through the Federal Reserve Bank of Philadelphia and paid the full amount thereof to J.C. Penney Co. Neither the Clearfield Trust Co. nor J.C. Penney Co. had any knowledge or suspicion of the forgery. Each acted in good faith. On or before May 10, 1936, Barner advised the timekeeper and the foreman of the W.P.A. project on which he was employed that he had not received the check in question. This information was duly communicated to other agents of the United States and on November 30, 1936, Barner executed an affidavit alleging that the endorsement of his name on the check was a forgery. No notice was given the Clearfield Trust Co. or J.C. Penney Co. of the forgery until January 12, 1937, at which time the Clearfield Trust Co. was notified. The first notice received by Clearfield Trust Co. that the United States was asking reimbursement was on August 31, 1937.

This suit was instituted in 1939 by the United States against the Clearfield Trust Co., the jurisdiction of the federal District Court being invoked pursuant to the provisions of § 24(1) of the Judicial Code, 28 U.S.C. § 41(1). The cause of action was based on the express guaranty of prior endorsements made by Clearfield Trust Co. J.C. Penney Co. intervened as a defendant. The case was heard on complaint, answer and stipulation of facts. The District Court held that the rights of the parties were to be determined by the law of Pennsylvania and that since the United States unreasonably delayed in giving notice of the forgery to the Clearfield Trust Co., it was barred from recovery under the rule of Market Street Title & Trust Co. v. Chelten T. Co., 296 Pa. 230, 145 A. 848. It accordingly dismissed the complaint. On appeal the [Third] Circuit Court of Appeals reversed. 130 F.2d 93. The case is here on a petition for a writ of certiorari which we granted, because of the importance of the problems raised and the conflict between the decision below and Security–First Nat. Bank v. United States, 103 F.2d 188, from the Ninth Circuit.

We agree with the Circuit Court of Appeals that the rule of Erie R. Co. v. Tompkins, 304 U.S. 64, does not apply to this action. The rights and duties of the United States on commercial paper which it issues are governed by Federal rather than local law. When the United States disburses its funds or pays its debts, it is exercising a constitutional function or power. This check was issued for services performed under the Federal Emergency Relief Act of 1935, 49 Stat. 115, 15 U.S.C. §§ 721–728. The authority to issue the check had its origin in the Constitution and the statutes of the United States and was in no way dependent on the laws of Pennsylvania or of any other state. Cf. Board of Commissioners v. United States, 308 U.S. 343; Royal Indemnity Co. v. United States, 313 U.S. 289. The duties imposed upon the United States and the rights acquired by it as a result of the issuance find their roots in the same federal sources.[65] Cf. Deitrick v. Greaney, 309 U.S. 190; D'Oench, Duhme & Co. v. Federal Deposit Ins. Corp., 315 U.S. 447. In absence of an applicable Act of Congress it is for the federal courts to fashion the governing rule of law according to their own standards. United States v. Guaranty Trust Co., 293 U.S. 340, is not opposed to this result. That case was concerned with a conflict of laws rule as to the title acquired by a transferee in Yugoslavia under a forged endorsement. Since the payee's address was Yugoslavia, the check had "something of the quality of a foreign bill" and the law of Yugoslavia was applied to determine what title the transferee acquired.

In our choice of the applicable federal rule we have occasionally selected state law. See *Royal Indemnity Co. v. United States*, supra. But reasons which may make state law at times the appropriate federal rule are singularly inappropriate here. The issuance of commercial paper by the United States is on a vast scale and transactions in that paper from issuance to payment will commonly occur in several states. The application of state law, even without the conflict of laws rules of the forum, would subject the rights and duties of the United States to exceptional uncertainty. It would lead to great diversity in results by making identical transactions subject to the vagaries of the laws of the several states. The desirabili-

---

65. Various Treasury Regulations govern the payment and endorsement of government checks and warrants and the reimbursement of the Treasurer of the United States by Federal Reserve banks and member bank depositories on payment of checks or warrants bearing a forged endorsement. See 31 Code of Federal Regulations §§ 202.0, 202.32–202.34. Forgery of the check was an offense against the United States. Criminal Code § 148, 18 U.S.C. § 262, 18 U.S.C. § 262.

ty of a uniform rule is plain. And while the federal law merchant developed for about a century under the regime of Swift v. Tyson, 16 Pet. [41 U.S.] 1, represented general commercial law rather than a choice of a federal rule designed to protect a federal right, it nevertheless stands as a convenient source of reference for fashioning federal rules applicable to these federal questions.

United States v. National Exchange Bank, 214 U.S. 302, falls in that category. Its facts are practically on all fours with those of the present case. The Court held that the United States could recover as drawee from one who presented for payment a pension check on which the name of the payee had been forged, in spite of a protracted delay on the part of the United States in giving notice of the forgery. The Court followed Leather Mfrs.' Bank v. Merchants Bank, 128 U.S. 26, which held that the right of the drawee against one who presented a check with a forged endorsement of the payee's name accrued at the date of payment and was not dependent on notice or demand. The theory of the *National Exchange Bank* case is that he who presents a check for payment warrants that he has title to it and the right to receive payment.[66] If he has acquired the check through a forged endorsement, the warranty is breached at the time the check is cashed. See Manufacturers' Trust Co. v. Harriman Nat. Bank Trust Co., 146 Misc. 551, 262 N.Y.S. 482; Bergman v. Avenue State Bank, 284 Ill.App. 516, 1 N.E.2d 432. The theory of the warranty has been challenged. Ames, The Doctrine of *Price v. Neal*, 4 Harv.L.Rev. 297, 301–302. It has been urged that "the right to recover is a quasi contractual right, resting upon the doctrine that one who confers a benefit in misreliance upon a right or duty is entitled to restitution." Woodward, Quasi Contracts (1913) § 80; First Nat. Bank v. City Nat. Bank, 182 Mass. 130, 134, 65 N.E. 24. But whatever theory is taken, we adhere to the conclusion of the *National Exchange Bank* case that the drawee's right to recover accrues when the payment is made. There is no other barrier to the maintenance of the cause of action. The theory of the drawee's responsibility where the drawer's signature is forged (Price v. Neal, 3 Burr. 1354 [97 Eng. Rep. 871 (1762)]; United States v. Chase Nat. Bank, 252 U.S. 485) is inapplicable here. The drawee, whether it be the United States or another, is not chargeable with the knowledge of the signature of the payee. *United States v. National Exchange Bank*, supra, p. 317; State v. Broadway Nat. Bank, 153 Tenn. 113, 282 S.W. 194.

The *National Exchange Bank* case went no further than to hold that prompt notice of the discovery of the forgery was not a condition precedent to suit. It did not reach the question whether lack of prompt notice might be a defense. We think it may. If it is shown that the drawee on learning of

---

66. We need not determine whether the guarantee of prior endorsements adds to the drawee's rights. See Brannan's Negotiable Instruments Law (6th ed.) pp. 330–331, 816–817; First Nat. Bank v. City Nat. Bank, 182 Mass. 130, 134, 65 N.E. 24. Cf. Home Ins. Co. v. Mercantile Trust Co., 219 Mo.App. 645, 284 S.W. 834. Under the theory of the *National Exchange Bank* case, the warranty of the title of him who presents the check for payment would be implied in any event. See Philadelphia Nat. Bank v. Fulton Nat. Bank, 25 F.2d 995, 997.

the forgery did not give prompt notice of it and that damage resulted, recovery by the drawee is barred. See Ladd & Tilton Bank v. United States, 30 F.2d 334; United States v. National Rockland Bank, 35 F.Supp. 912; United States v. National City Bank, 28 F.Supp. 144. The fact that the drawee is the United States and the laches those of its employees are not material. Cooke v. United States, 91 U.S. 389, 398. The United States as drawee of commercial paper stands in no different light than any other drawee. As stated in United States v. National Exchange Bank, 270 U.S. 527, 534. "The United States does business on business terms." It is not excepted from the general rules governing the rights and duties of drawees "by the largeness of its dealings and its having to employ agents to do what if done by a principal in person would leave no room for doubt." Id., p. 535. But the damage occasioned by the delay must be established and not left to conjecture. Cases such as *Market St. Title & Trust Co. v. Chelten Trust Co.,* supra, place the burden on the drawee of giving prompt notice of the forgery—injury to the defendant being presumed by the mere fact of delay. See London & River Plate Bk. v. Bank of Liverpool, [1896] 1 Q.B. 7. But we do not think that he who accepts a forged signature of a payee deserves that preferred treatment. It is his neglect or error in accepting the forger's signature which occasions the loss. See Bank of Commerce v. Union Bank, 3 N.Y. 230, 236. He should be allowed to shift that loss to the drawee only on a clear showing that the drawee's delay in notifying him of the forgery caused him damage. See Woodward, Quasi Contracts (1913) § 25. No such damage has been shown by Clearfield Trust Co. who so far as appears can still recover from J.C. Penney Co. The only showing on the part of the latter is contained in the stipulation to the effect that if a check cashed for a customer is returned unpaid or for reclamation a short time after the date on which it is cashed, the employees can often locate the person who cashed it. It is further stipulated that when J.C. Penney Co. was notified of the forgery in the present case none of its employees was able to remember anything about the transaction or check in question. The inference is that the more prompt the notice the more likely the detection of the forger. But that falls short of a showing that the delay caused a manifest loss. Third Nat. Bank v. Merchants' Nat. Bank, 76 Hun 475, 27 N.Y.S. 1070. It is but another way of saying that mere delay is enough.

Affirmed.[67]

[67. "A federal court sitting in a nondiversity case such as this does not sit as a local tribunal. In some cases it may see fit for special reasons to give the law of a particular state highly persuasive or even controlling effect, but in the last analysis its decision turns upon the law of the United States, not that of any state. Federal law is no juridical chameleon changing complexion to match that of each state wherein lawsuits happen to be commenced because of the accidents of service of process and of the application of the venue statutes. It is found in the federal Constitution, statutes, or common law. Federal common law implements the federal Constitution and statutes, and is conditioned by them. Within these limits, federal courts are free to apply the traditional common-law technique of decision and to draw upon sources of the common law in cases such as the present." D'Oench, Duhme & Co. v. Federal Deposit Insurance Corp., 315 U.S. 447, 471–472 (1942) (Jackson, J., concurring).

Bank of America Nat. Trust & Sav. Assn. v. Parnell, 352 U.S. 29 (1956), was a diversity action between private parties involving United States bonds. The bank was suing Parnell to

De Sylva v. Ballentine

Supreme Court of the United States, 1956.
351 U.S. 570, 76 S.Ct. 974, 100 L.Ed. 1415.

■ Opinion of the Court by MR. JUSTICE HARLAN, announced by MR. JUSTICE BURTON.

The present Copyright Act provides for a second 28–year copyright after the expiration of the original 28–year term, if application for renewal

---

recover money he had obtained by cashing bonds that had been stolen from the bank. One issue was whether the bonds, which were not yet to mature but which had been called by the government, were "overdue." The other issue was whether Parnell had acted in good faith in redeeming the bonds, and whether he had the burden of proving good faith or the bank had the burden of proving lack of it. It was held that whether the bonds were "overdue" concerned the interpretation of the nature of the rights and obligations created by the government bonds themselves, and was controlled by federal law, but that the burden of proof of good faith represented essentially a private transaction to be dealt with by the local law of the state where the transactions took place. In a later case the Court reaffirmed *Parnell*, which it cited as having established the general rule that "decision under federal common law" is not required where "the litigation is among private parties and no substantial rights and duties of the United States hinge on its outcome." Miree v. DeKalb County, 433 U.S. 25, 31 (1977).

Federal common law, when it exists, controls not only in diversity cases, but also in state-court litigation. Free v. Bland, 369 U.S. 663 (1962).

See 19 Wright, Miller & Cooper, Federal Practice and Procedure: Jurisdiction 2d 4514, 4515 (1996); 17 Moore's Federal Practice ¶¶ 124.40–47 (3d ed.1998); Mishkin, The Variousness of "Federal Law": Competence and Discretion in the Choice of National and State Rules for Decision, 105 U.Pa.L.Rev. 797 (1957); Friendly, In Praise of *Erie* and of the New Federal Common Law, 39 N.Y.U.L.Rev. 383 (1964); Field, Sources of Law: The Scope of Federal Common Law, 99 Harv.L.Rev. 881 (1986).

There is a fascinating exchange between Professors Martin Redish and Louise Weinberg in 83 Nw.U.L.Rev. 761 (1989); Redish, Federal Common Law, Political Legitimacy, and the Interpretative Process: An Institutional Perspective, 83 Nw.U.L.Rev. 761; Weinberg, Federal Common Law, 83 Nw.U.L.Rev. 805; Redish, Federal Common Law and American Political Theory: A Response to Professor Weinberg, 83 Nw.U.L.Rev. 853; Weinberg, The Curious Notion That the Rules of Decision Act Blocks Supreme Court Federal Common Law, 83 Nw.U.L.Rev. 860.

Fifty years after its decision in *Clearfield Trust*, the Supreme Court articulated a much more limited view of its power to fashion federal common law where state law might inconvenience the federal government. In United States v. California, 507 U.S. 746 (1993), the United States asserted a federal common-law right to recover taxes, illegally collected by a state from a federal contractor, which the United States had paid under an indemnity provision in the federal contract. The Supreme Court held that no such right existed, and refused to rescue the United States from a loss that it could have avoided by timely assertion of its rights as an intervenor in the state tax-collection proceedings. In a significant departure from the philosophy of *Clearfield Trust*, a unanimous Court told the government to look elsewhere for relief when state law pinches the federal foot. "If our decision today results in an intolerable drain on the public fisc, Congress, which can take into account the concerns of the States as well as the Federal Government, is free to address the situation." The Court took a similarly conservative stance toward expansion of the federal common law the following year, again acting unanimously. The Court dealt with a case in which state agency law would shield a law firm from liability to the federal receiver of a failed, federally insured savings bank despite allegedly negligent acts of the law firm as counsel to the bank, undertaken with the knowledge of the bank's officers. The Court declared that "displacement of California law" would be inappropriate absent significant conflict with an identifiable federal policy or interest. "We conclude that this is not one of those extraordinary cases in which the judicial creation of a federal rule of decision is warranted." O'Melveny & Myers v. F.D.I.C., 512 U.S. 79, 85 (1994).]

is made within one year before the expiration of the original term. This right to renew the copyright appears in § 24 of the Act:

> "*And provided further,* That in the case of any other copyrighted work, ... the author of such work, if still living, or the widow, widower, or children of the author, if the author be not living, or if such author, widow, widower, or children be not living, then the author's executors, or in the absence of a will, his next of kin shall be entitled to a renewal and extension of the copyright in such work for a further term of twenty-eight years when application for such renewal and extension shall have been made to the copyright office and duly registered therein within one year prior to the expiration of the original term of copyright ...."

In this case, an author who secured original copyrights on numerous musical compositions died before the time to apply for renewals arose. He was survived by his widow and one illegitimate child, who are both still living. The question this case presents is whether that child is entitled to share in the copyrights which come up for renewal during the widow's lifetime.

Respondent, the child's mother, brought this action on the child's behalf against the widow, who is the petitioner here, seeking a declaratory judgment that the child has an interest in the copyrights already renewed by the widow and those that will become renewable during her lifetime, and for an accounting of profits from such copyrights as have been already renewed. The District Court, holding that the child was within the meaning of the term "children" as used in the statute but that the renewal rights belonged *exclusively* to the widow, gave judgment for the widow. Agreeing with the District Court on the first point, the Court of Appeals reversed holding that on the author's death *both* widow and child shared in the renewal copyrights. 226 F.2d 623. Because of the great importance of these questions in the administration of the Copyright Act, we granted certiorari, 350 U.S. 931.

The controversy centers around the words "or the widow, widower or children of the author, if the author be not living." Two questions are involved: (1) do the widow and children take as a class, or in order of enumeration, and (2) if they take as a class, does "children" include an illegitimate child. Strangely enough, these questions have never before been decided, although the statutory provisions involved have been part of the Act in their present form since 1870.

I.

The widow first contends that, after the death of the author, she alone is entitled to renew copyrights during her lifetime, exclusive of any interest in "children" of the author. That is, she interprets the clause as providing for the passing of the renewal rights, on the death of the author, first to the widow, and then only after her death to the "children" of the author....

. . . . .

While the matter is far from clear, we think, on balance, the more likely meaning of the statute to be that adopted by the Court of Appeals, and we hold that, on the death of the author, the widow and children of the author succeed to the right of renewal as a class, and are each entitled to share in the renewal term of the copyright.

II.

We come, then, to the question of whether an illegitimate child is included within the term "children" as used in § 24. The scope of a federal right is, of course, a federal question, but that does not mean that its content is not to be determined by state, rather than federal law. Cf. Reconstruction Finance Corp. v. Beaver County, 328 U.S. 204; Board of County Commissioners v. United States, 308 U.S. 343, 351–352. This is especially true where a statute deals with a familial relationship; there is no federal law of domestic relations, which is primarily a matter of state concern.

If we look at the other persons who, under this section of the Copyright Act, are entitled to renew the copyright after the author's death, it is apparent that this is the general scheme of the statute. To decide who is the widow or widower of a deceased author, or who are his executors or next of kin, requires a reference to the law of the State which created those legal relationships. The word "children," although it to some extent describes a purely physical relationship, also describes a legal status not unlike the others. To determine whether a child has been legally adopted, for example, requires a reference to state law. We think it proper, therefore, to draw on the ready-made body of state law to define the word "children" in § 24. This does not mean that a State would be entitled to use the word "children" in a way entirely strange to those familiar with its ordinary usage, but at least to the extent that there are permissible variations in the ordinary concept of "children" we deem state law controlling. Cf. Seaboard Air Line Railway v. Kenney, 240 U.S. 489.

This raises two questions: first, to what State do we look, and second, given a particular State, what part of that State's law defines the relationship. The answer to the first question, in this case, is not difficult, since it appears from the record that the only State concerned is California, and both parties have argued the case on that assumption. The second question, however, is less clear. An illegitimate child who is acknowledged by his father, by a writing signed in the presence of a witness, is entitled under § 255 of the California Probate Code[68] to inherit his father's estate as well

---

68.   "Every illegitimate child is an heir of his mother, and also of the person who, in writing, signed in the presence of a competent witness, acknowledges himself to be the father, and inherits his or her estate, in whole or in part, as the case may be, in the same manner as if

as his mother's. The District Court found that the child here was within the terms of that section. Under California law the child is not legitimate for all purposes, however; compliance with § 230 of the Civil Code[69] is necessary for full legitimation, and there are no allegations in the complaint sufficient to bring the child within that section. Hence, we may take it that the child is not "adopted" in the sense that he is to be regarded as a legitimate child of the author.

Considering the purposes of § 24 of the Copyright Act, we think it sufficient that the status of the child is that described by § 255 of the California Probate Code. The evident purpose of § 24 is to provide for the family of the author after his death. Since the author cannot assign his family's renewal rights, § 24 takes the form of a compulsory bequest of the copyright to the designated persons. This is really a question of the descent of property, and we think the controlling question under state law should be whether the child would be an heir of the author. It is clear that under § 255 the child is, at least to that extent, included within the term "children."

Finally, there remains the question of what are the respective rights of the widow and child in the copyright renewals, once it is accepted that they both succeed to the renewals as members of the same class. Since the parties have not argued this point, and neither court below has passed on it, we think it should not be decided at this time.

For the foregoing reasons, the judgment of the Court of Appeals is affirmed.

Affirmed.

■ MR. JUSTICE DOUGLAS, with whom MR. JUSTICE BLACK joins, concurring.

The meaning of the word "children" as used in § 24 of the Copyright Act is a federal question. Congress could of course give the word the meaning it has under the laws of the several States. See Hutchinson Investment Co. v. Caldwell, 152 U.S. 65, 68–69; Poff v. Pennsylvania R. Co., 327 U.S. 399, 401. But I would think the statutory policy of protecting dependents would be better served by uniformity, rather than by the diversity which would flow from incorporating into the Act the laws of forty-eight States. Cf. Clearfield Trust Co. v. United States, 318 U.S. 363, 367; National Metropolitan Bank v. United States, 323 U.S. 454, 456;

---

he had been born in lawful wedlock; but he does not represent his father by inheriting any part of the estate of the father's kindred, either lineal or collateral, unless, before his death, his parents shall have intermarried, and his father, after such marriage, acknowledges him as his child, or adopts him into his family; in which case such child is deemed legitimate for all purposes of succession. An illegitimate child may represent his mother and may inherit any part of the state of the mother's kindred, either lineal or collateral."

69. "The father of an illegitimate child, by publicly acknowledging it as his own, receiving it as such, with the consent of his wife, if he is married, into his family, and otherwise treating it as if it were a legitimate child, thereby adopts it as such; and such child is thereupon deemed for all purposes legitimate from the time of its birth. The foregoing provisions of this Chapter do not apply to such an adoption."

Heiser v. Woodruff, 327 U.S. 726, 732; United States v. Standard Oil Co., 332 U.S. 301, 307.

An illegitimate child was given the benefits of the Federal Death Act, 46 U.S.C. § 761 et seq., by Middleton v. Luckenbach S.S. Co., 70 F.2d 326, 329–330 . . . .

I would take the same approach here and, regardless of state law, hold that illegitimate children were "children" within the meaning of § 24 of the Copyright Act, whether or not state law would allow them dependency benefits.

With this exception, I join in the opinion of the Court.[70]

Carlson v. Green

Supreme Court of the United States, 1980.
446 U.S. 14, 100 S.Ct. 1468, 64 L.Ed.2d 15.

■ MR. JUSTICE BRENNAN delivered the opinion of the Court.

Respondent brought this suit in the District Court for the Southern District of Indiana on behalf of the estate of her deceased son, Joseph Jones, Jr., alleging that he suffered personal injuries from which he died because the petitioners, federal prison officials, violated his due process, equal protection, and Eighth Amendment rights. Asserting jurisdiction

---

[70. The issue in Kamen v. Kemper Financial Services, Inc., 500 U.S. 90 (1991), was whether a stockholder's failure to demand action by the board of directors before bringing suit under the Investment Company Act against the financial adviser of a mutual fund was excused by the fact that demand would have been futile. A unanimous Court first found that neither the Act nor Civil Rule 23.1 speaks to the point. It held that the contours of the demand requirement in a derivative action under the Act are necessarily federal in character. "It does not follow, however, that the content of such a rule must be wholly the product of a federal court's own devising. Our cases indicate that a court should endeavor to fill the interstices of federal remedial schemes with uniform federal rules only when the scheme in question evidences a distinct need for nationwide legal standards . . . or when express provisions in analogous statutory schemes embody congressional policy choices readily applicable to the matter at hand. . . . Otherwise, we have indicated that federal courts should 'incorporat[e] [state law] as the federal rule of decision,' unless 'application of [the particular] state law [in question] would frustrate specific objectives of the federal programs.' United States v. Kimbell Foods, Inc., 440 U.S. 715, 728 (1979). The presumption that state law should be incorporated into federal common law is particularly strong in areas in which private parties have entered legal relationships with the expectation that their rights and obligations would be governed by state-law standards." 500 U.S., at 98. The Court found that corporation law is one such area, that the demand requirement relates to the allocation of governing powers within a corporation, and that the demand-futility exception should be applied as it is by the law of the state of incorporation.

In Gebser v. Lago Vista Indep. School Dist., 524 U.S. 274, 284 (1998), the Court reasoned that the judicially implied nature of the private right of action for damages under Title IX of the Education Amendments of 1972 gave it "a measure of latitude to shape a sensible remedial scheme" and exercised that latitude to decide that the scope of an employer's vicarious liability under Title IX should be less extensive than the virtually unrestricted respondeat-superior liability enforced under the express statutory right of action created by Title VII of the Civil Rights Act of 1964.]

under 28 U.S.C. § 1331(a), she claimed compensatory and punitive damages for the constitutional violations. Two questions are presented for decision: (1) Is a remedy available directly under the Constitution given that respondent's allegations could also support a suit against the United States under the Federal Tort Claims Act? and (2) If so, is survival of the cause of action governed by federal common law or by state statutes?

I

The District Court held that under Estelle v. Gamble, 429 U.S. 97 (1976), the allegations ... pleaded a violation of the Eighth Amendment's proscription against infliction of cruel and unusual punishment giving rise to a cause of action for damages under Bivens v. Six Unknown Named Agents of Federal Bureau of Narcotics, 403 U.S. 388 (1971). The court recognized that the decedent could have maintained this action if he had survived, but dismissed the complaint because in its view the damages remedy as a matter of federal law was limited to that provided by Indiana's survivorship and wrongful death laws and, as the court construed those laws, the damages available to Jones' estate failed to meet § 1331(a)'s $10,000 jurisdictional amount requirement. The Court of Appeals for the Seventh Circuit agreed that an Eighth Amendment violation was pleaded under *Estelle* and that a cause of action was stated under *Bivens,* but reversed the holding that § 1331(a)'s jurisdictional amount requirement was not met. Rather, the Court of Appeals held that § 1331(a) was satisfied because "whenever the relevant state survival statute would abate a *Bivens*-type action brought against defendants whose conduct results in death, the federal common law allows survival of the action." 581 F.2d 669, 675 (1978). The court reasoned that the Indiana law, if applied, would "subvert" "the policy of allowing complete vindication of constitutional rights" by making it "more advantageous for a tortfeasor to kill rather than to injure." Id., at 674.... We affirm.

II

Bivens established that the victims of a constitutional violation by a federal agent have a right to recover damages against the official in federal court despite the absence of any statute conferring such a right. Such a cause of action may be defeated in a particular case, however, in two situations. The first is when defendants demonstrate "special factors counselling hesitation in the absence of affirmative action by Congress." Id., 403 U.S., at 396; Davis v. Passman, 442 U.S. 228, 245 (1979). The second is when defendants show that Congress has provided an alternative remedy which it explicitly declared to be a *substitute* for recovery directly under the Constitution and viewed as equally effective. *Bivens,* 403 U.S., at 397; *Davis v. Passman*, 442 U.S., at 245–247.

Neither situation obtains in this case. First, the case involves no special factors counselling hesitation in the absence of affirmative action by Congress. Petitioners do not enjoy such independent status in our constitutional scheme as to suggest that judicially created remedies against them might be inappropriate. *Davis v. Passman*, 442 U.S., at 246. Moreover, even if requiring them to defend respondent's suit might inhibit their efforts to perform their official duties, the qualified immunity accorded them under Butz v. Economou, 438 U.S. 478 (1978), provides adequate protection. See *Davis v. Passman*, 442 U.S., at 246.

Second, we have here no explicit congressional declaration that persons injured by federal officers' violations of the Eighth Amendment may not recover money damages from the agents but must be remitted to another remedy, equally effective in the view of Congress. Petitioners point to nothing in the Federal Tort Claims Act (FTCA) or its legislative history to show that Congress meant to pre-empt a *Bivens* remedy or to create an equally effective remedy for constitutional violations.[71] FTCA was enacted long before *Bivens* was decided, but when Congress amended FTCA in 1974 to create a cause of action against the United States for intentional torts committed by federal law enforcement officers, 28 U.S.C. § 2680(h), the congressional comments accompanying that amendment made it crystal clear that Congress views FTCA and *Bivens* as parallel, complementary causes of action:

> "[A]fter the date of enactment of this measure, innocent individuals who are subjected to raids [like that in *Bivens*] will have a cause of action against the individual Federal agents *and* the Federal Government. Furthermore, this provision should be viewed as a *counterpart* to the *Bivens* case and its progeny [sic], in that it waives the defense of sovereign immunity so as to make the Government independently liable in damages for the same type of conduct that is alleged to have occurred in *Bivens* (and for which that case imposes liability upon the individual Government officials involved.)" S.Rep. No. 93–588, 93d Cong., 1st Sess., 3 (1973) (emphasis supplied).

In the absence of a contrary expression from Congress, § 2680(h) thus contemplates that victims of the kind of intentional wrongdoing alleged in this complaint shall have an action under FTCA against the United States as well as a *Bivens* action against the individual officials alleged to have infringed their constitutional rights.

This conclusion is buttressed by the significant fact that Congress follows the practice of explicitly stating when it means to make FTCA an exclusive remedy. . . .

Four additional factors, each suggesting that the *Bivens* remedy is more effective than the FTCA remedy, also support our conclusion that Congress did not intend to limit respondent to an FTCA action. First, the *Bivens* remedy, in addition to compensating victims, serves a deterrent purpose. See Butz v. Economou, 438 U.S. 478, 505 (1978).[72] Because the

---

71. To satisfy this test, petitioners need not show that Congress recited any specific "magic words." . . . Instead, our inquiry at this step in the analysis is whether Congress has indicated that it intends the statutory remedy to replace, rather than to complement, the *Bivens* remedy. Where Congress decides to enact a statutory remedy which it views as fully adequate only in combination with the *Bivens* remedy, e.g., 28 U.S.C. § 2680(h), that congressional decision should be given effect by the courts.

72. 42 U.S.C. § 1983 serves similar purposes. See, e.g., Robertson v. Wegmann, 436 U.S. 584, 590–591 (1978); Carey v. Piphus, 435 U.S. 247, 256 (1978); Mitchum v. Foster, 407 U.S. 225, 242 (1972); Monroe v. Pape, 365 U.S. 167, 172–187 (1961).

Bivens remedy is recoverable against individuals, it is a more effective deterrent than the FTCA remedy against the United States. It is almost axiomatic that the threat of damages has a deterrent effect,[73] Imbler v. Pachtman, 424 U.S. 409, 442 (1976) (White, J., concurring in the judgment), surely particularly so when the individual official faces personal financial liability.

Petitioners argue that FTCA liability is a more effective deterrent because the individual employees responsible for the Government's liability would risk loss of employment and because the Government would be forced to promulgate corrective policies. That argument suggests, however, that the superiors would not take the same actions when an employee is found personally liable for violation of a citizen's constitutional rights. The more reasonable assumption is that responsible superiors are motivated not only by concern for the public fisc but also by concern for the Government's integrity.

Second, our decisions, although not expressly addressing and deciding the question, indicate that punitive damages may be awarded in a *Bivens* suit. Punitive damages are "a particular remedial mechanism normally available in the federal courts," *Bivens,* 403 U.S., at 397, and are especially appropriate to redress the violation by a government official of a citizen's constitutional rights. Moreover, punitive damages are available in "a proper" § 1983 action, Carey v. Piphus, 435 U.S. 247, 257, n. 11 (1978) (punitive damages not awarded because District Court found defendants "did not act with a malicious intention to deprive respondents of their rights or to do them [some] other injury"),[74] and *Butz v. Economou,* supra, suggests that the "constitutional design" would be stood on its head if federal officials did not face at least the same liability as state officials guilty of the same constitutional transgression. 438 U.S., at 504. But punitive damages in an FTCA suit are statutorily prohibited. 28 U.S.C. § 2674. Thus FTCA is that much less effective than a *Bivens* action as a deterrent to unconstitutional acts.

Third, a plaintiff cannot opt for a jury in an FTCA action, 28 U.S.C. § 2402, as he may in a *Bivens* suit.[75] Petitioners argue that this is an irrelevant difference because juries have been biased against *Bivens* claim-

---

73. Indeed, underlying the qualified immunity which public officials enjoy for actions taken in good faith is the fear that exposure to personal liability would otherwise deter them from acting at all. See Butz v. Economou, 438 U.S. 478, 497 (1978); Scheuer v. Rhodes, 416 U.S. 232, 240 (1974).

74. Moreover, after *Carey* punitive damages may be the only significant remedy available in some § 1983 actions where constitutional rights are maliciously violated but the victim cannot prove compensable injury.

75. Petitioners argue that the availability of punitive damages or a jury trial under *Bivens* is irrelevant because neither is a *necessary* element of a remedial scheme. But that argument completely misses the mark. The issue is not whether a *Bivens* cause of action or any one of its particular features is essential. Rather the inquiry is whether Congress has created what it views as an *equally* effective remedial scheme. Otherwise the two can exist side by side. Moreover, no one difference need independently render FTCA inadequate. It can fail to be equally effective on the cumulative basis of more than one difference.

ants. Reply Brief at 7, Brief at 30–31, n. 30. Significantly, however, they do not assert that judges trying the claims as FTCA actions would have been more receptive, and they cannot explain why the plaintiff should not retain the choice.

Fourth, an action under FTCA exists only if the State in which the alleged misconduct occurred would permit a cause of action for that misconduct to go forward. 28 U.S.C. § 1346(b) (United States liable "in accordance with the law of the place where the act or omission occurred."). Yet it is obvious that the liability of federal officials for violations of citizens' constitutional rights should be governed by uniform rules. See Part III, infra. The question whether respondent's action for violations by federal officials of federal constitutional rights should be left to the vagaries of the laws of the several States admits of only a negative answer in the absence of a contrary congressional resolution.

Plainly FTCA is not a sufficient protector of the citizens' constitutional rights, and without a clear congressional mandate we cannot hold that Congress relegated respondent exclusively to the FTCA remedy.

III

Bivens actions are a creation of federal law and, therefore, the question whether respondent's action survived Jones' death is a question of federal law. See Burks v. Lasker, 441 U.S. 471, 476 (1979). Petitioners, however, would have us fashion a federal rule of survivorship that incorporates the survivorship laws of the forum State, at least where the state law is not inconsistent with federal law. Respondent argues, on the other hand, that only a uniform federal rule of survivorship is compatible with the goal of deterring federal officials from infringing federal constitutional rights in the manner alleged in respondent's complaint. We agree with respondent. Whatever difficulty we might have resolving the question were the federal involvement less clear, we hold that only a uniform federal rule of survivorship will suffice to redress the constitutional deprivation here alleged and to protect against repetition of such conduct.

. . . . .

Robertson v. Wegmann, 436 U.S. 584 (1978), holding that a § 1983 action would abate in accordance with Louisiana survivorship law is not to the contrary. There the plaintiff's death was not caused by the acts of the defendants upon which the suit was based.[76] Moreover, *Robertson* expressly

---

76. *Robertson* fashioned its holding by reference to 42 U.S.C. § 1988 which requires that § 1983 actions be governed by

> "the common law, as modified and changed by the constitution and statutes of the State wherein the court having jurisdiction of [the] civil . . . cause is held, so far as the same is not inconsistent with the Constitution and laws of the United States."

Section 1988 does not in terms apply to *Bivens* actions, and there are cogent reasons not to apply it to such actions even by analogy. *Bivens* defendants are federal officials brought into federal court for violating the Federal Constitution. No state interests are implicated by applying purely federal law to them . . . .

recognized that to prevent frustration of the deterrence goals of § 1983 (which in part also underlie *Bivens* actions, see Part II, supra) "[a] state official contemplating illegal activity must always be prepared to face the prospect of a § 1983 action being filed against him." 436 U.S., at 592. A federal official contemplating unconstitutional conduct similarly must be prepared to face the prospect of a *Bivens* action. A uniform rule that claims such as respondent's survive the decedent's death is essential if we are not to "frustrate in [an] important way the achievement" of the goals of *Bivens* actions. Auto Workers v. Hoosier Cardinal Corp., 383 U.S. 696, 702 (1966).

Affirmed.

■ MR. JUSTICE POWELL, with whom MR. JUSTICE STEWART joins, concurring in the judgment.

Although I join the judgment, I do not agree with much of the language in the Court's opinion. The Court states the principles governing *Bivens* actions as follows:

> "*Bivens* established that the victims of a constitutional violation . . . have a right to recover damages. . . . Such a cause of action may be defeated . . . in two situations. The first is when defendants demonstrate 'special factors counselling hesitation in the absence of affirmative action by Congress.' . . . The second is when defendants show that Congress has provided an alternative remedy which it explicitly declared to be a *substitute* for recovery directly under the Constitution and viewed as equally effective. . . ."

The foregoing statement contains dicta that go well beyond the prior holdings of this Court.

. . . . .

The Court's absolute language is all the more puzzling because it comes in a case where the implied remedy is plainly appropriate under any measure of discretion. The Federal Tort Claims Act, on which petitions rely, simply is not an adequate remedy. And there are reasonably clear indications that Congress did not intend that statute to displace *Bivens* claims. No substantial contrary policy has been identified, and I am aware of none. I therefore agree that a private damages remedy properly is inferred from the Constitution in this case. But I do not agree that *Bivens* plaintiffs have a "right" to such a remedy whenever the defendants fails to show that Congress has "provided an [equally effective] alternative remedy which it explicitly declared to be a *substitute* . . . ." In my view, the Court's willingness to infer federal causes of action that cannot be found in the Constitution or in a statute denigrates the doctrine of separation of powers and hardly comports with a rational system of justice. Cf. Cannon v. University of Chicago, 441 U.S. 677, 730–749 (1979) (POWELL, J., dissenting).[77]

. . . . .

---

77. I do not suggest that courts enjoy the same degree of freedom to infer causes of action from statutes as from the Constitution. See Davis v. Passman, 442 U.S. 228, 241–242 (1979).

■ MR. CHIEF JUSTICE BURGER, dissenting.

Although I would be prepared to join an opinion giving effect to Bivens v. Six Unknown Federal Narcotics Agents, 403 U.S. 388 (1971)—which I thought wrongly decided—I cannot join today's unwarranted expansion of that decision. The Federal Tort Claims Act provides an adequate remedy for prisoner's claims of medical mistreatment. For me, that is the end of the matter.

. . . . .

■ MR. JUSTICE REHNQUIST, dissenting.

The Court today adopts a formalistic procedural approach for inferring private damage remedies from constitutional provisions that in my view still further highlights the wrong turn this Court took in Bivens v. Six Unknown Federal Narcotics Agents, 403 U.S. 388 (1971). Although ordinarily this Court should exercise judicial restraint in attempting to attain a wise accommodation between liberty and order under the Constitution, to dispose of this case as if *Bivens* were rightly decided would in the words of Mr. Justice Frankfurter be to start with an "unreality." Kovacs v. Cooper, 336 U.S. 77, 89 (1949) (Frankfurter, J., concurring). *Bivens* is a decision "by a closely divided court, unsupported by the confirmation of time," and, as a result of its weak precedential and doctrinal foundation, it cannot be viewed as a check on "the living process of striking a wise balance between liberty and order as new cases come here for adjudication." Cf. id.; B. & W. Taxi Co. v. B. & Y. Taxi Co., 276 U.S. 518, 532–533 (1928) (Holmes, J., dissenting); Hudgens v. National Labor Relations Board, 424 U.S. 507 (1976), overruling Amalgamated Food Employees Union v. Logan Valley Plaza, 391 U.S. 308 (1968).

. . . . .

In my view, it is "an exercise of power that the Constitution does not give us" for this Court to infer a private civil damage remedy from the Eighth Amendment or any other constitutional provision. *Bivens*, 403 U.S., at 428 (Black, J., dissenting). The creation of such remedies is a task that is more appropriately viewed as falling within the legislative sphere of authority. Ibid.

. . . . .

For the foregoing reasons I dissent, and would reverse the judgment.[78]

I do believe, however, that the Court today has overstepped the bounds of rational judicial decisionmaking in both contexts.

[78. In Bush v. Lucas, 462 U.S. 367 (1983), the Court refused to create an implied constitutional cause of action for damages for a federal employee who claimed that he was demoted in violation of the First Amendment, since Congress has provided comprehensive procedural and substantive provisions giving meaningful remedies against the United States

Thompson v. Thompson

Supreme Court of the United States, 1988.
484 U.S. 174, 108 S.Ct. 513, 98 L.Ed.2d 512.

■ JUSTICE MARSHALL delivered the opinion of the Court.

We granted certiorari in this case to determine whether the Parental Kidnaping Prevention Act of 1980, 28 U.S.C. § 1738A, furnishes an implied cause of action in federal court to determine which of two conflicting state custody decisions is valid.

I

The Parental Kidnaping Prevention Act (PKPA or Act) imposes a duty on the States to enforce a child custody determination entered by a court of a sister State if the determination is consistent with the provisions of the Act.[79] In order for a state court's custody decree to be consistent with the

---

and the employee had been reinstated and awarded full back pay through pursuit of those statutory remedies.

In F.D.I.C. v. Meyer, 510 U.S. 471 (1994), the Court held that a *Bivens* suit cannot be brought against a federal agency in its own right.

Jeffries, The Right–Remedy Gap in Constitutional Law, 109 Yale L.J. 87 (1999), discusses the legal status of implied remedies. The complicated prerequisites for a *Bivens* claim asserting a denial of access to courts are discussed in Christopher v. Harbury, 536 U.S. 403 (2002). In Gonzaga University v. Doe, 536 U.S. 273 (2002), the Court substantially elided issues of implied rights and implied remedies, holding that the question whether a particular federal statute creates a private federal right enforceable against public entities under 42 U.S.C. § 1983 requires essentially the same analysis as the more general question whether the statute was intended to create a private right of action against parties not acting under color of state law. In Barnes v. Gorman, 536 U.S. 181 (2002), the Court held that the implied right of action created by Title VI of the Civil Rights Act of 1964 does not extend to punitive damages because such damages are incompatible with the essentially contractual duties imposed by Congress when it attaches conditions to the receipt of federal funds under statutes enacted under its Spending Clause power.]

79. Section 1738A reads in relevant part:

"(a) The appropriate authorities of every State shall enforce according to its terms, and shall not modify except as provided in subsection (f) of this section, any child custody determination made consistently with the provisions of this section by a court of another State.

. . . . .

"(c) A child custody determination made by a court of a State is consistent with the provisions of this section only if—

"(1) such court has jurisdiction under the law of such state; and

"(2) one of the following conditions is met:

"(A) such State (i) is the home State of the child on the date of the commencement of the proceeding, or (ii) had been the child's home State within six months before the date of the commencement of the proceeding and the child is absent from such State because of his removal or retention by a contestant or for other reasons, and a contestant continues to live in such State;

"(B)(i) it appears that no other State would have jurisdiction under subparagraph (A), and (ii) it is in the best interest of the child that a court of such State assume jurisdiction because (I) the child and his parents, or the child and at least one

provisions of the Act, the State must have jurisdiction under its own local law and one of five conditions set out in § 1738A(c)(2) must be met. Briefly put, these conditions authorize the state court to enter a custody decree if the child's home is or recently has been in the State, if the child has no home State and it would be in the child's best interest for the State to assume jurisdiction, or if the child is present in the State and has been abandoned or abused. Once a State exercises jurisdiction consistently with the provisions of the Act, no other State may exercise concurrent jurisdiction over the custody dispute, § 1738A(g), even if it would have been empowered to take jurisdiction in the first instance,[80] and all States must accord full faith and credit to the first State's ensuing custody decree.

As the legislative scheme suggests, and as Congress explicitly specified, one of the chief purposes of the PKPA is to "avoid jurisdictional competition and conflict between State courts." Pub.L. 96–611, 94 Stat. 3569, § 7(c)(5), note following 28 U.S.C. § 1738A. This case arises out of a jurisdictional stalemate that came to pass notwithstanding the strictures of the Act. In July 1978, respondent Susan Clay (then Susan Thompson) filed a petition in Los Angeles Superior Court asking the court to dissolve her marriage to petitioner David Thompson and seeking custody of the couple's

---

contestant, have a significant connection with such State other than mere physical presence in such State, and (II) there is available in such State substantial evidence concerning the child's present or future care, protection, training, and personal relationships;

"(C) the child is physically present in such State and (i) the child has been abandoned, or (ii) it is necessary in an emergency to protect the child because he has been subjected to or threatened with mistreatment or abuse;

"(D)(i) it appears that no other State would have jurisdiction under subparagraph (A), (B), (C), or (E), or another State has declined to exercise jurisdiction on the ground that the State whose jurisdiction is in issue is the more appropriate forum to determine the custody of the child, and (ii) it is in the best interest of the child that such court assume jurisdiction; or

"(E) the court has continuing jurisdiction pursuant to subsection (d) of this section.

"(d) The jurisdiction of a court of a State which has made a child custody determination consistently with the provisions of this section continues as long as the requirement of subsection (c)(1) of this section continues to be met and such State remains the residence of the child or of any contestant.

. . . . .

"(f) A court of a State may modify a determination of the custody of the same child made by a court of another State, if—

"(1) it has jurisdiction to make such a child custody determination; and

"(2) the court of the other State no longer has jurisdiction, or it has declined to exercise such jurisdiction to modify such determination.

"(g) A court of a State shall not exercise jurisdiction in any proceeding for a custody determination commenced during the pendency of a proceeding in a court of another State where such court of that other State is exercising jurisdiction consistently with the provisions of this section to make a custody determination."

80. The sole exception to this constraint occurs where the first State either has lost jurisdiction or has declined to exercise continuing jurisdiction. See § 1738A(f).

infant son, Matthew. The court initially awarded the parents joint custody of Matthew, but that arrangement became infeasible when respondent decided to move from California to Louisiana to take a job. The court then entered an order providing that respondent would have sole custody of Matthew once she left for Louisiana. This state of affairs was to remain in effect until the court investigator submitted a report on custody, after which the court intended to make a more studied custody determination. See App. 6.

Respondent and Matthew moved to Louisiana in December of 1980. Three months later, respondent filed a petition in Louisiana state court for enforcement of the California custody decree, judgment of custody, and modification of petitioner's visitation privileges. By order dated April 7, 1981, the Louisiana court granted the petition and awarded sole custody of Matthew to respondent. Two months later, however, the California court, having received and reviewed its investigator's report, entered an order awarding sole custody of Matthew to petitioner. Thus arose the current impasse.

In August 1983, petitioner brought this action in the District Court for the Central District of California. Petitioner requested an order declaring the Louisiana decree invalid and the California decree valid, and enjoining the enforcement of the Louisiana decree. Petitioner did not attempt to enforce the California decree in a Louisiana state court before he filed suit in federal court. The District Court granted respondent's motion to dismiss the complaint for lack of subject matter and personal jurisdiction. Civ. Action No. 83–5221 (CD Cal. April 10, 1984). The Court of Appeals for the Ninth Circuit affirmed. Although it disagreed with the District Court's jurisdictional analyses, the Court of Appeals affirmed the dismissal of the complaint on the ground that petitioner had failed to state a claim upon which relief could be granted. 798 F.2d 1547 (1986). Canvassing the background, language, and legislative history of the PKPA, the Court of Appeals held that the Act does not create a private right of action in federal court to determine the validity of two conflicting custody decrees. Id., at 1552–1559. We granted certiorari, 479 U.S. 1063 (1987), and we now affirm.

II

In determining whether to infer a private cause of action from a federal statute, our focal point is Congress' intent in enacting the statute. As guides to discerning that intent, we have relied on the four factors set out in Cort v. Ash, 422 U.S. 66, 78 (1975), along with other tools of statutory construction. See Daily Income Fund, Inc. v. Fox, 464 U.S. 523, 535–536 (1984); California v. Sierra Club, 451 U.S. 287, 293 (1981); Touche Ross & Co. v. Redington, 442 U.S. 560, 575–576 (1979). Our focus on congressional intent does not mean that we require evidence that Members of Congress, in enacting the statute, actually had in mind the creation of a private cause of action. The implied cause of action doctrine would be a virtual dead letter were it limited to correcting drafting errors when

Congress simply forgot to codify its evident intention to provide a cause of action. Rather, as an *implied* cause of action doctrine suggests, "the legislative history of a statute that does not expressly create or deny a private remedy will typically be equally silent or ambiguous on the question." Cannon v. University of Chicago, 441 U.S. 677, 694 (1979). We therefore have recognized that Congress' "intent may appear implicitly in the language or structure of the statute, or in the circumstances of its enactment." Transamerica Mortgage Advisors, Inc. v. Lewis, 444 U.S. 11, 18 (1979). The intent of Congress remains the ultimate issue, however, and "unless this congressional intent can be inferred from the language of the statute, the statutory structure, or some other source, the essential predicate for implication of a private remedy simply does not exist." Northwest Airlines, Inc. v. Transport Workers Union, 451 U.S. 77, 94 (1981). In this case, the essential predicate for implication of a private remedy plainly does not exist. None of the factors that have guided our inquiry in this difficult area points in favor of inferring a private cause of action. Indeed, the context, language, and legislative history of the PKPA all point sharply away from the remedy petitioner urges us to infer.

We examine initially the context of the PKPA with an eye toward determining Congress' perception of the law that it was shaping or reshaping. See Merrill Lynch, Pierce, Fenner & Smith v. Curran, 456 U.S. 353, 378 (1982); *Cort v. Ash*, supra, 422 U.S., at 69. At the time Congress passed the PKPA, custody orders held a peculiar status under the full faith and credit doctrine, which requires each State to give effect to the judicial proceedings of other States, see U.S. Const., Art. IV, § 1; 28 U.S.C. § 1738. The anomaly traces to the fact that custody orders characteristically are subject to modification as required by the best interests of the child. As a consequence, some courts doubted whether custody orders were sufficiently "final" to trigger full faith and credit requirements, see e.g., Hooks v. Hooks, 771 F.2d 935, 948 (CA6 1985); McDougald v. Jenson, 596 F.Supp. 680, 684–685 (N.D.Fla.1984), aff'd 786 F.2d 1465 (CA11), cert. denied, 479 U.S. 860 (1986), and this Court had declined expressly to settle the question. See Ford v. Ford, 371 U.S. 187, 192 (1962). Even if custody orders were subject to full faith and credit requirements, the Full Faith and Credit Clause obliges States only to accord the same force to judgments as would be accorded by the courts of the State in which the judgment was entered. Because courts entering custody orders generally retain the power to modify them, courts in other States were no less entitled to change the terms of custody according to their own views of the child's best interest. See New York ex rel. Halvey v. Halvey, 330 U.S. 610, 614–615 (1947). For these reasons, a parent who lost a custody battle in one State had an incentive to kidnap the child and move to another State to relitigate the issue. This circumstance contributed to widespread jurisdictional deadlocks like this one, and more importantly, to a national epidemic of parental kidnaping. At the time the PKPA was enacted, sponsors of the Act estimated that between 25,000 and 100,000 children were kidnaped by parents who had been unable to obtain custody in a legal forum....

A number of States joined in an effort to avoid these jurisdictional conflicts by adopting the Uniform Child Custody Jurisdiction Act (UCCJA), 9 U.L.A. §§ 1–28 (1979). The UCCJA prescribed uniform standards for deciding which State could make a custody determination and obligated enacting States to enforce the determination made by the State with proper jurisdiction. The project foundered, however, because a number of States refused to enact the UCCJA while others enacted it with modifications. In the absence of uniform national standards for allocating and enforcing custody determinations, noncustodial parents still had reason to snatch their children and petition the courts of any of a number of haven States for sole custody.

The context of the PKPA therefore suggests that the principal problem Congress was seeking to remedy was the inapplicability of full faith and credit requirements to custody determinations. Statements made when the Act was introduced in Congress forcefully confirm that suggestion. The sponsors and supporters of the Act continually indicated that the purpose of the PKPA was to provide for nationwide enforcement of custody orders made in accordance with the terms of the UCCJA. . . .

The significance of Congress' full faith and credit approach to the problem of child snatching is that the Full Faith and Credit Clause, in either its constitutional or statutory incarnations, does not give rise to an implied federal cause of action. Minnesota v. Northern Securities Co., 194 U.S. 48, 72 (1904); see 13B C. Wright, A. Miller & E. Cooper, Federal Practice and Procedure § 3563, p. 50 (1984). Rather, the clause "only prescribes a rule by which courts, Federal and state, are to be guided when a question arises in the progress of a pending suit as to the faith and credit to be given by the court to the public acts, records, and judicial proceedings of a State other than that in which the court is sitting." *Northern Securities*, supra, at 72. Because Congress' chief aim in enacting the PKPA was to extend the requirements of the Full Faith and Credit Clause to custody determinations, the Act is most naturally construed to furnish a rule of decision for courts to use in adjudicating custody disputes and not to create an entirely new cause of action. It thus is not compatible with the purpose and context of the legislative scheme to infer a private cause of action. See *Cort v. Ash*, 422 U.S., at 78.

The language and placement of the statute reinforce this conclusion. The PKPA, 28 U.S.C. § 1738A, is an addendum to the full faith and credit statute, 28 U.S.C. § 1738. This fact alone is strong proof that the Act is intended to have the same operative effect as the full faith and credit statute. Similarly instructive is the heading to the PKPA: "Full faith and credit given to child custody determinations." As for the language of the Act, it is addressed entirely to States and state courts. Unlike statutes that explicitly confer a right on a specified class of persons, the PKPA is a mandate directed to state courts to respect the custody decrees of sister States. See *Cannon v. University of Chicago*, 441 U.S., at 690, n. 13; *Cort v. Ash*, supra, 422 U.S., at 81–82. We agree with the Court of Appeals that "[i]t seems highly unlikely Congress would follow the pattern of the Full

Faith and Credit Clause and section 1738 by structuring section 1738A as a command to state courts to give full faith and credit to the child custody decrees of other states, and yet, without comment, depart from the enforcement practice followed under the Clause and section 1738." 798 F.2d, at 1556.

Finally, the legislative history of the PKPA provides unusually clear indication that Congress did not intend the federal courts to play the enforcement role that petitioner urges. Two passages are particularly revealing. The first of these is a colloquy between Congressmen Conyers and Fish. Congressman Fish had been the sponsor of a competing legislative proposal—ultimately rejected by Congress—that would have extended the District Courts' diversity jurisdiction to encompass actions for enforcement of state custody orders. In the following exchange, Congressman Conyers questioned Congressman Fish about the differences between his proposal and "the Bennett proposal," which was a precursor to the PKPA.

"Mr. Conyers: Could I just interject, the difference between the Bennett proposal and yours: You would have, enforcing the full faith and credit provision, the parties removed to a Federal court. Under the Bennett provision, his bill would impose the full faith and credit enforcement on the State court.

"It seems to me that that is a very important difference. The Federal jurisdiction, could it not, Mr. Fish, result in the Federal court litigating between two State court decrees; whereas, in an alternate method previously suggested, we would be imposing the responsibility of the enforcement upon the State court, and thereby reducing, it seems to me, the amount of litigation.

"Do you see any possible merit in leaving the enforcement at the State level, rather than introducing the Federal judiciary?

"Mr. Fish: Well, I really think that it is easier on the parent that has custody of the child to go to the nearest Federal district court. . . .

"Mr. Conyers: Of course you know that the Federal courts have no experience in these kinds of matters, and they would be moving into this other area. I am just thinking of the fact that they have [many areas of federal concern and] on the average of a 21–month docket, you would now be imposing custody matters which it seems might be handled in the courts that normally handle that. . . ." Parental Kidnaping: Hearing on H.R. 1290 Before the Subcommittee on Crime of the House Committee on the Judiciary, 96th Cong., 2d Sess., 14 (1980).

This exchange suggests that Congress considered and rejected an approach to the problem that would have resulted in a "[f]ederal court litigating between two State court decrees." Ibid.

The second noteworthy entry in the legislative history is a letter from then Assistant Attorney General Patricia Wald to the Chairman of the House Judiciary Committee, which was referred to extensively during the debate on the PKPA. The letter outlined a variety of solutions to the child-snatching problem. It specifically compared proposals that would "grant jurisdiction to the federal courts to enforce state custody decrees" with an approach, such as was proposed in the PKPA, that would "impose on states a federal duty, under enumerated standards derived generally from the UCCJA, to give full faith and credit to the custody decrees of other states." Addendum to Joint Hearing 103. The letter endorsed the full faith and credit approach that eventually was codified in the PKPA. More important-ly, it "strongly oppose[d] . . . the creation of a federal forum for resolving custody disputes." Id., at 108. Like Congressman Conyers, the Justice Department reasoned that federal enforcement of state custody decrees would increase the workload of the federal courts and entangle the federal judiciary in domestic relations disputes with which they have little experi-ence and which traditionally have been the province of the States. That the views of the Justice Department and Congressman Conyers prevailed, and that Congress explicitly opted for a full faith and credit approach over reliance on enforcement by the federal courts, provide strong evidence against inferring a federal cause of action. Cf. *Cort v. Ash*, 422 U.S., at 82 (congressional determination not to create a private cause of action is dispositive).

Petitioner discounts these portions of the legislative history. He argues that the cause of action that he asks us to infer arises only in cases of an actual conflict between two state custody decrees, and thus is substantially narrower than the cause of action proposed by Congressman Fish and rejected by Congress. The Fish bill would have extended federal-diversity jurisdiction to permit federal courts to enforce custody orders in the first instance, before a second State had created a conflict by refusing to do so. This cause of action admittedly is farther reaching than that which we reject today. But the considerations that prompted Congress to reject the Fish bill also militate against the more circumscribed role for the federal courts that petitioner proposes. See Rogers v. Platt, 259 U.S.App.D.C. 154, 164, 814 F.2d 683, 693 (1987). Instructing the federal courts to play Solomon where two state courts have issued conflicting custody orders would entangle them in traditional state-law questions that they have little expertise to resolve.[81] This is a cost that Congress made clear it did not

---

81. Petitioner argues that determining which of two conflicting custody decrees should be given effect under the PKPA would not require the federal courts to resolve the merits of custody disputes and thus would not offend the longstanding tradition of reserving domes-tic-relations matters to the States. Petitioner contends that the cause of action he champi-ons would require federal courts only to analyze which of two States is given exclusive jurisdiction under a federal statute, a task for which the federal courts are well-qualified. We cannot agree with petitioner that making a jurisdictional determination under the PKPA would not involve the federal courts in substantive domestic-relations determinations. Under the Act, jurisdiction can turn on the child's "best interest" or on proof that the child has been abandoned or abused. See §§ 1738A(c)(2)(B), (C), and (D). In fact, it would seem that the jurisdictional disputes that are sufficiently complicated as to have provoked conflicting state-court holdings are the most likely to require resolution of these traditional domestic-relations inquiries. See Rogers v. Platt, 259 U.S.App.D.C. 154, 162, 814 F.2d 683, 691 (1987). Cf. Cort v. Ash, 422 U.S. 66, 84 (1975) (possibility that implied federal cause of action *may* in certain instances turn on state-law issues counsels against inferring such an action.)

want the PKPA to carry.[82]

In sum, the context, language, and history of the PKPA together make out a conclusive case against inferring a cause of action in federal court to determine which of two conflicting state custody decrees is valid. Against this impressive evidence, petitioner relies primarily on the argument that failure to infer a cause of action would render the PKPA nugatory. We note, as a preliminary response, that ultimate review remains available in this Court for truly intractable jurisdictional deadlocks. In addition, the unspoken presumption in petitioner's argument is that the States are either unable or unwilling to enforce the provisions of the Act. This is a presumption we are not prepared, and more importantly, Congress was not prepared, to indulge. State courts faithfully administer the Full Faith and Credit Clause every day; now that Congress has extended full faith and credit requirements to child custody orders, we can think of no reason why the courts' administration of federal law in custody disputes will be any less vigilant. Should state courts prove as obstinate as petitioner predicts, Congress may choose to revisit the issue. But any more radical approach to the problem will have to await further legislative action; we "will not engraft a remedy on a statute, no matter how salutary, that Congress did not intend to provide." California v. Sierra Club, 451 U.S. 287, 297 (1981). The judgment of the Court of Appeals is affirmed.

It is so ordered.

■ JUSTICE O'CONNOR, concurring in part and concurring in the judgment.

For the reasons expressed by JUSTICE SCALIA in Part I of his opinion in this case, I join all but the first full paragraph of Part II of the Court's opinion and judgment.

■ JUSTICE SCALIA, concurring in the judgment.

I write separately because in my view the Court is not being faithful to current doctrine in its dictum denying the necessity of an actual congressional intent to create a private right of action, and in referring to Cort v. Ash, 422 U.S. 66 (1975), as though its analysis had not been effectively overruled by our later opinions. I take the opportunity to suggest, at the same time, why in my view the law revision that the Court's dicta would undertake moves in precisely the wrong direction.

I

I agree that the Parental Kidnapping Prevention Act, 28 U.S.C. § 1738A (1982), does not create a private right of action in federal court to determine which of two conflicting child custody decrees is valid. I disagree,

---

82. Moreover, petitioner's argument serves to underscore the extraordinary nature of the cause of action he urges us to infer. Petitioner essentially asks that federal district courts exercise appellate review of state-court judgments. This is an unusual cause of action for Congress to grant, either expressly or by implication. Petitioner's proposal is all the more remarkable in the present case, in which he seeks to have a California District Court enjoin enforcement of a Louisiana state-court judgment before the intermediate and supreme courts of Louisiana even have had an opportunity to review that judgment.

however, with the portion of the Court's analysis that flows from the following statement:

> "Our focus on congressional intent does not mean that we require evidence that members of Congress, in enacting the statute, actually had in mind the creation of a private cause of action." ...

I am at a loss to imagine what congressional intent to create a private right of action might mean, if it does not mean that Congress had in mind the creation of a private right of action. Our precedents, moreover, give no indication of a secret meaning, but to the contrary seem to use "intent" to mean "intent." For example:

> "[T]he focus of the inquiry is on whether Congress intended to create a remedy. Universities Research Assn., Inc. v. Coutu, 450 U.S. [754, 771–772 (1984)]; Transamerica Mortgage Advisors, Inc. v. Lewis, 444 U.S. [11, 23–24 (1979)]; Touche Ross & Co. v. Redington, [442 U.S. 560, 575–576 (979)]. The federal judiciary will not engraft a remedy on a statute, no matter how salutary, that Congress did not intend to provide." California v. Sierra Club, 451 U.S. 287, 297 (1981) (WHITE, J.).

We have said, to be sure, that the existence of intent may be inferred from various indicia; but that is worlds apart from today's delphic pronouncement that intent is required but need not really exist.

I also find misleading the Court's statement that, in determining the existence of a private right of action, "we have relied on the four factors set out in *Cort v. Ash*, ... along with other tools of statutory construction." ... That is not an accurate description of what we have done. It could not be plainer that we effectively overruled the *Cort v. Ash* analysis in Touche Ross & Co. v. Redington, 442 U.S. 560, 575–76 (1979) and Transamerica Mortgage Advisors, Inc. v. Lewis, 444 U.S. 11, 18 (1979), converting one of its four factors (congressional intent) into *the determinative factor*, with the other three merely indicative of its presence or absence. Compare *Cort v. Ash*, 422 U.S., at 78, with *Transamerica*, 444 U.S., at 23–24.

Finally, the Court's opinion conveys a misleading impression of current law when it proceeds to examine the "context" of the legislation for indication of intent to create a private right of action, after having found no such indication in either text or legislative history. In my view that examination is entirely superfluous, since context alone cannot suffice. We have held context to be relevant to our determination in only two cases—both of which involved statutory language that, in the judicial interpretation of related legislation prior to the subject statute's enactment, or of the same legislation prior to its reenactment, had been held to create private rights of action. See Cannon v. University of Chicago, 441 U.S. 677 (1979); Merrill Lynch, Pierce, Fenner & Smith v. Curran, 456 U.S. 353 (1982). Since this is not a case where such textual support exists, or even where there is any support in legislative history, the "context" of the enactment is immaterial.

Contrary to what the language of today's opinion suggests, this Court has long since abandoned its hospitable attitude towards implied rights of action. In the 23 years since Justice Clark's opinion for the court in J.I. Case Co. v. Borak, 377 U.S. 426 (1964), we have *twice* narrowed the test for implying a private right, first in *Cort v. Ash*, supra, itself, and then again in *Touche Ross & Co. v. Redington*, supra, and *Transamerica Mortgage Advisors, Inc. v. Lewis*, supra. See also Cannon v. University of Chicago, 441 U.S. 677, 730 (1979) (POWELL, J. dissenting) and California v. Sierra Club, 451 U.S. 287, 301 (1981) (REHNQUIST, J., joined by BURGER, C.J., and STEWART and POWELL, JJ., concurring). The recent history of our holdings is one of repeated rejection of claims of an implied right. This has been true in 9 of 11 recent private right of action cases heard by this Court, including the instant case.... The Court's opinion exaggerates the difficulty of establishing an implied right when it surmises that "[t]he implied cause of action doctrine would be a virtual dead letter were it limited to correcting drafting errors when Congress simply forgot to codify its evident intention to provide a cause of action."... That statement rests upon the erroneous premise that one never implies anything except when he forgets to say it expressly. It is true, however, that the congressional intent test for implying private rights of action as it has evolved since the repudiation of *Cort v. Ash* is much more stringent than the Court's dicta in the present case suggest.

II

I have found the Court's dicta in the present case particularly provocative of response because it is my view that, if the current state of the law were to be changed, it should be moved in precisely the opposite direction—away from our current congressional intent test to the categorical position that federal private rights of action will not be implied.

... It is, to be sure, not beyond imagination that in a particular case Congress may intend to create a private right of action, but choose to do so by implication. One must wonder, however, whether the good produced by a judicial rule that accommodates this remote possibility is outweighed by its adverse effects. An enactment by implication cannot realistically be regarded as the product of the difficult lawmaking process our Constitution has prescribed. Committee reports, floor speeches, and even colloquies between congressmen, are frail substitute for bicameral vote upon the text of a law and its presentment to the President. See generally INS v. Chadha, 462 U.S. 919 (1983). It is at best dangerous to assume that all the necessary participants in the law-enactment process are acting upon the same unexpressed assumptions. And likewise dangerous to assume that, even with the utmost self-discipline, judges can prevent the implications they see from mirroring the policies they favor.

I suppose all this could be said, to a greater or lesser degree, of *all* implications that courts derive from statutory language, which are assuredly numerous as the stars. But as the likelihood that Congress would leave the matter to implication decreases, so does the justification for bearing the risk of distorting the constitutional process. A legislative act so significant, and so separable from the remainder of the statute, as the creation of a private right of action seems to me so implausibly left to implication that the risk should not be endured.

If we were to announce a flat rule that private rights of action will not be implied in statutes hereafter enacted, the risk that that course would occasionally frustrate genuine legislative intent would decrease from its current level of minimal to virtually zero. It would then be true that the opportunity for frustration of intent "would be a virtual dead letter[,] ... limited to ... drafting errors when Congress simply forgot to codify its ... intention to provide a cause of action." ... I believe, moreover, that Congress would welcome the certainty that such a rule would produce. Surely conscientious legislators cannot relish the current situation, in which the existence or nonexistence of a private right of action depends upon which of the opposing legislative forces may have guessed right as to the implications the statute will be found to contain.

If a change is to be made, we should get out of the business of implied private rights of action altogether.[83]

[83. An earlier case had held that there is an implied right of action under Title IX, which precludes discrimination on the basis of sex. In Franklin v. Gwinnett County Public Schools, 503 U.S. 60 (1992), it was held that this allows a suit for damages by a high school student claiming sexual harassment. "The general rule ... is that absent clear direction to the contrary by Congress, the federal courts have the power to award any appropriate relief in a cognizable cause of action brought pursuant to a federal statute." 503 U.S., at 70–71.

42 U.S.C. § 1983 grants a right of action to one whose rights "secured by the Constitution and laws" have been deprived by a person acting under color of state law. The "laws" referred to in § 1983 are all federal statutes, and not merely those protecting civil rights. Maine v. Thiboutot, 448 U.S. 1 (1980). It is held, however, that if the remedial devices provided in a particular federal statute are sufficiently comprehensive, they may suffice to demonstrate that Congress intended to preclude a remedy under § 1983. Middlesex County Sewerage Authority v. National Sea Clammers Assn., 453 U.S. 1, 19–21 (1981).

In Musick, Peeler & Garrett v. Employers Insurance of Wausau, 508 U.S. 286 (1993), the Supreme Court held that affirmative statutory endorsement of judicially implied private remedies for violations of Securities and Exchange Commission Rule 10b–5 and § 10(b) of the Securities Exchange Act of 1934 gave the courts authority to imply as well a right to contribution in Rule 10b–5 actions. Justice Thomas dissented on the ground that congressional silence on the issue of contribution did not manifest the necessary affirmative intent implicitly to create such a right, and that "legislative and administrative silence" should not be construed as "tacit license to accomplish what Congress and the SEC are unable or unwilling to do." Although Justices Blackmun and O'Connor joined the dissent, Justice Scalia—often thought to be the Court's most vigorous opponent of "judicial lawmaking"—voted with the majority.

In Alexander v. Sandoval, 532 U.S. 275 (2001), the Court held that there is no private right of action to enforce disparate-impact regulations promulgated under Title VI of the Civil Rights Act of 1964, even though there is an implied private right of action to enforce intentional discrimination in violation of § 601 of Title VI.

In Gonzaga University v. Doe, 536 U.S. 273 (2002), the Court limited the scope of the private remedy conferred by 42 U.S.C. § 1983 to cases in which a predicate federal right was

Correctional Services Corporation v. Malesko

Supreme Court of the United States, 2001.
534 U.S. 61, 122 S.Ct. 515, 151 L.Ed.2d 456.

■ CHIEF JUSTICE REHNQUIST delivered the opinion of the Court.

We decide here whether the implied damages action first recognized in Bivens v. Six Unknown Fed. Narcotics Agents, 403 U.S. 388 (1971), should be extended to allow recovery against a private corporation operating a halfway house under contract with the Bureau of Prisons. We decline to so extend *Bivens*.

Petitioner Correctional Services Corporation (CSC), under contract with the federal Bureau of Prisons (BOP), operates Community Corrections Centers and other facilities that house federal prisoners and detainees.[84] Since the late 1980's, CSC has operated Le Marquis Community Correctional Center (Le Marquis), a halfway house located in New York City. Respondent John E. Malesko is a former federal inmate who, having been convicted of federal securities fraud in December 1992, was sentenced to a term of 18 months' imprisonment under the supervision of the BOP. During his imprisonment, respondent was diagnosed with a heart condition and treated with prescription medication. Respondent's condition limited his ability to engage in physical activity, such as climbing stairs.

In February 1993, the BOP transferred respondent to Le Marquis where he was to serve the remainder of his sentence. Respondent was assigned to living quarters on the fifth floor. On or about March 1, 1994, petitioner instituted a policy at Le Marquis requiring inmates residing below the sixth floor to use the staircase rather than the elevator to travel from the first-floor lobby to their rooms. There is no dispute that respondent was exempted from this policy on account of his heart condition. Respondent alleges that on March 28, 1994, however, Jorge Urena, an employee of petitioner, forbade him to use the elevator to reach his fifth-floor bedroom. Respondent protested that he was specially permitted eleva-

---

unambiguously conferred on the party seeking relief under § 1983. A § 1983 plaintiff may not rely merely on a showing that the defendant violated a federal duty that in some more general sense benefits the plaintiff or serves the interests of the plaintiff. Thus the breach of a federal duty to maintain the confidentiality of student records imposed on a private university as a condition of receiving federal funds was held not to be actionable under § 1983—notwithstanding the assumption that by making unauthorized disclosures to state officials the university was acting under color of state law—because federal law did not unambiguously confer on the plaintiff student an individualized federal right to have his personal information remain confidential.]

84. Petitioner is hardly unique in this regard. The BOP has since 1981 relied exclusively on contracts with private institutions and state and local governments for the operation of halfway house facilities to help federal prisoners reintegrate into society. The BOP contracts not only with for-profit entities like petitioner, but also with charitable organizations like Volunteers for America (which operates facilities in Indiana, Louisiana, Maryland, Minnesota, New York, and Texas), the Salvation Army (Arkansas, Florida, Illinois, North Carolina, Tennessee, and Texas), Progress House Association (Oregon), Triangle Center (Illinois), and Catholic Social Services (Pennsylvania).

tor access, but Urena was adamant. Respondent then climbed the stairs, suffered a heart attack, and fell, injuring his left ear.

Three years after this incident occurred, respondent filed a pro se action against CSC and unnamed CSC employees in the United States District Court for the Southern District of New York. Two years later, now acting with counsel, respondent filed an amended complaint which named Urena as 1 of the 10 John Doe defendants. The amended complaint alleged that CSC, Urena, and unnamed defendants were "negligent in failing to obtain requisite medication for [respondent's] condition and were further negligent by refusing [respondent] the use of the elevator." It further alleged that respondent injured his left ear and aggravated a pre-existing condition "[a]s a result of the negligence of the Defendants." Respondent demanded judgment in the sum of $1 million in compensatory damages, $3 million in anticipated future damages, and punitive damages "for such sum as the Court and/or [j]ury may determine."

The District Court treated the amended complaint as raising claims under *Bivens v. Six Unknown Fed. Narcotics Agents*, supra, and dismissed respondent's cause of action in its entirety. Relying on our decision in FDIC v. Meyer, 510 U.S. 471 (1994), the District Court reasoned that "a *Bivens* action may only be maintained against an individual," and thus was not available against petitioner, a corporate entity. With respect to Urena and the unnamed individual defendants, the complaint was dismissed on statute of limitations grounds.

The Court of Appeals for the Second Circuit affirmed in part, reversed in part, and remanded. 229 F.3d 374 (CA2 2000). That court affirmed dismissal of respondent's claims against individual defendants as barred by the statute of limitations. Respondent has not challenged that ruling, and the parties agree that the question whether a *Bivens* action might lie against a private individual is not presented here. With respect to petitioner, the Court of Appeals remarked that *Meyer* expressly declined " 'to expand the category of defendants against whom *Bivens* actions may be brought to include not only federal agents, but federal agencies as well.' " 229 F.3d, at 378 (quoting *Meyer*, supra, at 484 (emphasis deleted)). But the court reasoned that private entities like petitioner should be held liable under *Bivens* to "accomplish the ... important *Bivens* goal of providing a remedy for constitutional violations." 229 F.3d, at 380.

We granted certiorari, 532 U.S. 902 (2001), and now reverse.[85]

In Bivens v. Six Unknown Fed. Narcotics Agents, 403 U.S. 388 (1971), we recognized for the first time an implied private action for damages against federal officers alleged to have violated a citizen's constitutional

---

85. The Courts of Appeals have divided on whether FDIC v. Meyer, 510 U.S. 471 (1994), forecloses the extension of *Bivens* to private entities. Compare Hammons v. Norfolk Southern Corp., 156 F.3d 701, 705 (CA6 1998) ("Nothing in *Meyer* prohibits a *Bivens* claim against a private corporation that engages in federal action"), with Kauffman v. Anglo–American School of Sofia, 28 F.3d 1223, 1227 (C.A.D.C.1994) ("[Under] *Meyer's* conclusion that public federal agencies are not subject to *Bivens* liability, it follows that equivalent private entities should not be liable either"). We hold today that it does.

rights. Respondent now asks that we extend this limited holding to confer a right of action for damages against private entities acting under color of federal law. He contends that the Court must recognize a federal remedy at law wherever there has been an alleged constitutional deprivation, no matter that the victim of the alleged deprivation might have alternative remedies elsewhere, and that the proposed remedy would not significantly deter the principal wrongdoer, an individual private employee. We have heretofore refused to imply new substantive liabilities under such circumstances, and we decline to do so here.

Our authority to imply a new constitutional tort, not expressly authorized by statute, is anchored in our general jurisdiction to decide all cases "arising under the Constitution, laws, or treaties of the United States." 28 U.S.C. § 1331. See, e.g., Schweiker v. Chilicky, 487 U.S. 412, 420–421 (1988); Bush v. Lucas, 462 U.S. 367, 373–374 (1983). We first exercised this authority in *Bivens,* where we held that a victim of a Fourth Amendment violation by federal officers may bring suit for money damages against the officers in federal court. *Bivens* acknowledged that Congress had never provided for a private right of action against federal officers, and that "the Fourth Amendment does not in so many words provide for its enforcement by award of money damages for the consequences of its violation." 403 U.S., at 396. Nonetheless, relying largely on earlier decisions implying private damages actions into federal statutes, see id., at 397 (citing J.I. Case Co. v. Borak, 377 U.S. 426, 433 (1964)); 403 U.S., at 402–403, n. 4 (Harlan, J., concurring in judgment) ("The *Borak* case is an especially clear example of the exercise of federal judicial power to accord damages as an appropriate remedy in the absence of any express statutory authorization of a federal cause of action"), and finding "no special factors counseling hesitation in the absence of affirmative action by Congress," id., at 395–396, we found an implied damages remedy available under the Fourth Amendment.[86]

In the decade following *Bivens,* we recognized an implied damages remedy under the Due Process Clause of the Fifth Amendment, Davis v. Passman, 442 U.S. 228 (1979), and the Cruel and Unusual Punishment Clause of the Eighth Amendment, Carlson v. Green, 446 U.S. 14 (1980). In both *Davis* and *Carlson,* we applied the core holding of *Bivens,* recognizing in limited circumstances a claim for money damages against federal officers who abuse their constitutional authority. In *Davis,* we inferred a new right of action chiefly because the plaintiff lacked any other remedy for the alleged constitutional deprivation. 442 U.S., at 245 ("For Davis, as for Bivens, it is damages or nothing"). In *Carlson,* we inferred a right of action

---

86.   Since our decision in *Borak,* we have retreated from our previous willingness to imply a cause of action where Congress has not provided one. See, e.g., Central Bank of Denver, N.A. v. First Interstate Bank of Denver, N. A., 511 U.S. 164, 188 (1994); Transamerica Mortgage Advisors, Inc. v. Lewis, 444 U.S. 11, 15–16 (1979); Cannon v. University of Chicago, 441 U.S. 677, 688 (1979); id., at 717–718 (Rehnquist, J., concurring). Just last Term it was noted that we "abandoned" the view of *Borak* decades ago, and have repeatedly declined to "revert" to "the understanding of private causes of action that held sway 40 years ago." Alexander v. Sandoval, 532 U.S. 275, 287 (2001).

against individual prison officials where the plaintiff's only alternative was a Federal Tort Claims Act (FTCA) claim against the United States. 446 U.S., at 18–23. We reasoned that the threat of suit against the United States was insufficient to deter the unconstitutional acts of individuals. Id., at 21 ("Because the *Bivens* remedy is recoverable against individuals, it is a more effective deterrent than the FTCA remedy"). We also found it "crystal clear" that Congress intended the FTCA and *Bivens* to serve as "parallel" and "complementary" sources of liability. 446 U.S., at 19–20.

Since *Carlson* we have consistently refused to extend *Bivens* liability to any new context or new category of defendants. In *Bush v. Lucas,* supra, we declined to create a *Bivens* remedy against individual Government officials for a First Amendment violation arising in the context of federal employment. Although the plaintiff had no opportunity to fully remedy the constitutional violation, we held that administrative review mechanisms crafted by Congress provided meaningful redress and thereby foreclosed the need to fashion a new, judicially crafted cause of action. 462 U.S., at 378, n. 14. We further recognized Congress' institutional competence in crafting appropriate relief for aggrieved federal employees as a "special factor counseling hesitation in the creation of a new remedy." Id., at 380. See also id., at 389 (noting that "Congress is in a far better position than a court to evaluate the impact of a new species of litigation between federal employees"). We have reached a similar result in the military context, Chappell v. Wallace, 462 U.S. 296, 304 (1983), even where the defendants were alleged to have been civilian personnel, United States v. Stanley, 483 U.S. 669 (1987).

In *Schweiker v. Chilicky,* we declined to infer a damages action against individual government employees alleged to have violated due process in their handling of Social Security applications. We observed that our "decisions have responded cautiously to suggestions that *Bivens* remedies be extended into new contexts." 487 U.S., at 421. In light of these decisions, we noted that "[t]he absence of statutory relief for a constitutional violation . . . does not by any means necessarily imply that courts should award money damages against the officers responsible for the violation." Id., at 421–422. We therefore rejected the claim that a *Bivens* remedy should be implied simply for want of any other means for challenging a constitutional deprivation in federal court. It did not matter, for example, that "[t]he creation of a *Bivens* remedy would obviously offer the prospect of relief for injuries that must now go unredressed." 487 U.S., at 425. See also *Bush,* supra, at 388 (noting that "existing remedies do not provide complete relief for the plaintiff"); *Stanley,* supra, at 683. ("[I]t is irrelevant to a special factors analysis whether the laws currently on the books afford Stanley . . . an adequate federal remedy for his injuries" (internal quotation marks omitted)). So long as the plaintiff had an avenue for some redress, bedrock principles of separation of powers foreclosed judicial imposition of a new substantive liability. *Chilicky,* supra, at 425–427.

Most recently, in *FDIC v. Meyer,* we unanimously declined an invitation to extend *Bivens* to permit suit against a federal agency, even though the agency—because Congress had waived sovereign immunity—was otherwise amenable to suit. 510 U.S., at 484–486. Our opinion emphasized that "the purpose of *Bivens* is to deter *the officer*," not the agency. Id., at 485 (emphasis in original) (citing *Carlson v. Green*, supra, at 21). We reasoned that if given the choice, plaintiffs would sue a federal agency instead of an individual who could assert qualified immunity as an affirmative defense. To the extent aggrieved parties had less incentive to bring a damages claim against individuals, "the deterrent effects of the *Bivens* remedy would be lost." 510 U.S., at 485. Accordingly, to allow a *Bivens* claim against federal agencies "would mean the evisceration of the *Bivens* remedy, rather than its extension." 510 U.S., at 485. We noted further that "special factors" counseled hesitation in light of the "potentially enormous financial burden" that agency liability would entail. Id., at 486.

From this discussion, it is clear that the claim urged by respondent is fundamentally different from anything recognized in *Bivens* or subsequent cases. In 30 years of *Bivens* jurisprudence we have extended its holding only twice, to provide an otherwise nonexistent cause of action against *individual officers* alleged to have acted unconstitutionally, or to provide a cause of action for a plaintiff who lacked *any alternative remedy* for harms caused by an individual officer's unconstitutional conduct. Where such circumstances are not present, we have consistently rejected invitations to extend *Bivens*, often for reasons that foreclose its extension here.[87]

The purpose of *Bivens* is to deter individual federal officers from committing constitutional violations. *Meyer* made clear that the threat of litigation and liability will adequately deter federal officers for *Bivens* purposes no matter that they may enjoy qualified immunity, 510 U.S., at 474, 485, are indemnified by the employing agency or entity, id., at 486, or are acting pursuant to an entity's policy, id., at 473–474. *Meyer* also made clear that the threat of suit against an individual's employer was not the kind of deterrence contemplated by *Bivens*. See 510 U.S., at 485 ("If we were to imply a damages action directly against federal agencies ... there would be no reason for aggrieved parties to bring damages actions against individual officers. [T]he deterrent effects of the *Bivens* remedy would be lost"). This case is, in every meaningful sense, the same. For if a corporate defendant is available for suit, claimants will focus their collection efforts on it, and not the individual directly responsible for the alleged injury. See, e.g., TXO Production Corp. v. Alliance Resources Corp., 509 U.S. 443, 464 (1993) (plurality opinion) (recognizing that corporations fare much worse before juries than do individuals); id., at 490–492 (O'CONNOR, J., dissenting) (same) (citing authorities). On the logic of *Meyer*, inferring a constitutional tort remedy against a private entity like CSC is therefore foreclosed.

Respondent claims that even under *Meyer*'s deterrence rationale, implying a suit against private corporations acting under color of federal law

---

87. JUSTICE STEVENS' claim that this case does not implicate an "extension" of *Bivens*, might come as some surprise to the Court of Appeals which twice characterized its own holding as "extending *Bivens* liability to reach private corporations." 229 F.3d 374, 381 (CA2 2000). See also ibid. ("*Bivens* liability should extend to private corporations").

is still necessary to advance the core deterrence purpose of *Bivens*. He argues that because corporations respond to market pressures and make decisions without regard to constitutional obligations, requiring payment for the constitutional harms they commit is the best way to discourage future harms. That may be so, but it has no relevance to *Bivens*, which is concerned solely with deterring the unconstitutional acts of individual officers. If deterring the conduct of a policy-making entity was the purpose of *Bivens*, then *Meyer* would have implied a damages remedy against the Federal Deposit Insurance Corporation; it was after all an agency policy that led to *Meyer*'s constitutional deprivation. *Meyer*, supra, at 473–474. But *Bivens* from its inception has been based not on that premise, but on the deterrence of individual officers who commit unconstitutional acts.

There is no reason for us to consider extending *Bivens* beyond this core premise here.[88] To begin with, *no federal prisoners* enjoy respondent's contemplated remedy. If a federal prisoner in a BOP facility alleges a constitutional deprivation, he may bring a *Bivens* claim against the offending individual officer, subject to the defense of qualified immunity. The prisoner may not bring a *Bivens* claim against the officer's employer, the United States or the BOP. With respect to the alleged constitutional deprivation, his only remedy lies against the individual; a remedy *Meyer* found sufficient, and which respondent did not timely pursue. Whether it makes sense to impose asymmetrical liability costs on private prison facilities alone is a question for Congress, not us, to decide.

Nor are we confronted with a situation in which claimants in respondent's shoes lack effective remedies. Cf. *Bivens*, 403 U.S., at 410 (Harlan, J., concurring in judgment) ("For people in Bivens' shoes, it is damages or nothing"); *Davis*, 442 U.S., at 245 ("For Davis, as for Bivens, it is damages or nothing" (internal quotation marks omitted)). It was conceded at oral argument that alternative remedies are at least as great, and in many respects greater, than anything that could be had under *Bivens*. For example, federal prisoners in private facilities enjoy a parallel tort remedy that is unavailable to prisoners housed in government facilities. This case demonstrates as much, since respondent's complaint in the District Court arguably alleged no more than a quintessential claim of negligence. It

---

88. JUSTICE STEVENS claims that our holding in favor of petitioner portends "tragic consequence[s]," and "jeopardize[s] the constitutional rights of . . . tens of thousands of inmates." He refers to examples of cases suggesting that private correctional providers routinely abuse and take advantage of inmates under their control (citing Brief for Legal Aid Society of New York as Amicus Curiae 8–25). See also Brief for American Civil Liberties Union as Amicus Curiae 14–16, and n. 6 (citing and discussing "abundant" examples of such abuse). In all but one of these examples, however, the private facility in question housed *state* prisoners—prisoners who already enjoy a right of action against private correctional providers under 42 U.S.C. § 1983. If it is true that the imperatives for deterring the unconstitutional conduct of private correctional providers are so strong as to demand that we imply a new right of action directly from the Constitution, then abuses of authority should be *less* prevalent in state facilities, where Congress already provides for such liability. That the trend appears to be just the opposite is not surprising given the BOP's oversight and monitoring of its private contract facilities, see Brief for United States as Amicus Curiae 4–5, 24–26, which JUSTICE STEVENS does not mention.

maintained that named and unnamed defendants were *"negligent* in failing to obtain requisite medication ... and were further *negligent* by refusing ... use of the elevator." App. 12 (emphasis added). It further maintained that respondent suffered injuries "[a]s a result of the *negligence* of the Defendants." Ibid. (emphasis added). The District Court, however, construed the complaint as raising a *Bivens* claim, presumably under the Cruel and Unusual Punishment Clause of the Eighth Amendment. Respondent accepted this theory of liability, and he has never sought relief on any other ground. This is somewhat ironic, because the heightened "deliberate indifference" standard of Eighth Amendment liability, Estelle v. Gamble, 429 U.S. 97, 104 (1976), would make it considerably more difficult for respondent to prevail than on a theory of ordinary negligence, see, e.g., Farmer v. Brennan, 511 U.S. 825, 835 (1994) ("[D]eliberate indifference describes a state of mind more blameworthy than negligence").

This also makes respondent's situation altogether different from *Bivens,* in which we found alternative state tort remedies to be "inconsistent or even hostile" to a remedy inferred from the Fourth Amendment. 403 U.S., at 393–394. When a federal officer appears at the door and requests entry, one cannot always be expected to resist. See id., at 394 ("[A] claim of authority to enter is likely to unlock the door"). Yet lack of resistance alone might foreclose a cause of action in trespass or privacy. Ibid. Therefore, we reasoned in *Bivens* that other than an implied constitutional tort remedy, "there remain[ed] ... but the alternative of resistance, which may amount to a crime." Id., at 395 (internal quotation marks and citation omitted). Such logic does not apply to respondent, whose claim of negligence or deliberate indifference requires no resistance to official action, and whose lack of alternative tort remedies was due solely to strategic choice.[89]

Inmates in respondent's position also have full access to remedial mechanisms established by the BOP, including suits in federal court for injunctive relief and grievances filed through the BOP's Administrative Remedy Program (ARP). See 28 CFR § 542.10 (2001) (explaining ARP as providing "a process through which inmates may seek formal review of an issue which relates to any aspect of their confinement"). This program provides yet another means through which allegedly unconstitutional actions and policies can be brought to the attention of the BOP and prevented from recurring. And unlike the *Bivens* remedy, which we have never considered a proper vehicle for altering an entity's policy, injunctive relief has long been recognized as the proper means for preventing entities from acting unconstitutionally.

In sum, respondent is not a plaintiff in search of a remedy as in *Bivens* and *Davis.* Nor does he seek a cause of action against an individual officer, otherwise lacking, as in *Carlson.* Respondent instead seeks a marked extension of *Bivens,* to contexts that would not advance *Bivens'* core

---

89. Where the government has directed a contractor to do the very thing that is the subject of the claim, we have recognized this as a special circumstance where the contractor may assert a defense. Boyle v. United Technologies Corp., 487 U.S. 500 (1988). The record here would provide no basis for such a defense.

purpose of deterring individual officers from engaging in unconstitutional wrongdoing. The caution toward extending *Bivens* remedies into any new context, a caution consistently and repeatedly recognized for three decades, forecloses such an extension here.

The judgment of the Court of Appeals is reversed.

It is so ordered.

■ JUSTICE SCALIA, with whom JUSTICE THOMAS joins, concurring.

I join the opinion of the Court because I agree that a narrow interpretation of the rationale of Bivens v. Six Unknown Fed. Narcotics Agents, 403 U.S. 388 (1971), would not logically produce its application to the circumstances of this case. The dissent is doubtless correct that a broad interpretation of its rationale *would* logically produce such application, but I am not inclined (and the Court has not been inclined) to construe *Bivens* broadly.

In joining the Court's opinion, however, I do not mean to imply that, *if* the narrowest rationale of *Bivens did* apply to a new context, I *would* extend its holding. I would not. *Bivens* is a relic of the heady days in which this Court assumed common-law powers to create causes of action—decreeing them to be "implied" by the mere existence of a statutory or constitutional prohibition. As the Court points out, ante, we have abandoned that power to invent "implications" in the statutory field, see Alexander v. Sandoval, 532 U.S. 275, 287 (2001). There is even greater reason to abandon it in the constitutional field, since an "implication" imagined in the Constitution can presumably not even be repudiated by Congress. I would limit *Bivens* and its two follow-on cases (Davis v. Passman, 442 U.S. 228 (1979), and Carlson v. Green, 446 U.S. 14 (1980)) to the precise circumstances that they involved.

■ JUSTICE STEVENS, with whom JUSTICE SOUTER, JUSTICE GINSBURG, and JUSTICE BREYER join, dissenting.

In Bivens v. Six Unknown Fed. Narcotics Agents, 403 U.S. 388 (1971), the Court affirmatively answered the question that it had reserved in Bell v. Hood, 327 U.S. 678 (1946): whether a violation of the Fourth Amendment "by *a federal agent* acting under color of his authority gives rise to a cause of action for damages consequent upon his unconstitutional conduct." 403 U.S., at 389 (emphasis added). Nearly a decade later, in Carlson v. Green, 446 U.S. 14 (1980), we held that a violation of the Eighth Amendment by federal prison officials gave rise to a *Bivens* remedy despite the fact that the plaintiffs also had a remedy against the United States under the Federal Tort Claims Act (FTCA). We stated: "*Bivens* established that the victims of a constitutional violation by *a federal agent* have a right to recover damages against the official in federal court despite the absence of any statute conferring such a right." 446 U.S., at 18 (emphasis added).

In subsequent cases, we have decided that a *Bivens* remedy is not available for every conceivable constitutional violation. We have never, however, qualified our holding that Eighth Amendment violations are actionable under *Bivens*.... Nor have we ever suggested that a category of federal agents can commit Eighth Amendment violations with impunity.

The parties before us have assumed that respondent's complaint has alleged a violation of the Eighth Amendment. The violation was committed by a federal agent—a private corporation employed by the Bureau of Prisons to perform functions that would otherwise be performed by individual employees of the Federal Government. Thus, the question presented by this case is whether the Court should create an exception to the straightforward application of *Bivens* and *Carlson,* not whether it should extend our cases beyond their "core premise." This point is evident from the fact that prior to our recent decision in FDIC v. Meyer, 510 U.S. 471 (1994), the Courts of Appeals had consistently and correctly held that corporate agents performing federal functions, like human agents doing so, were proper defendants in *Bivens* actions.

Meyer, which concluded that federal agencies are not suable under *Bivens,* does not lead to the outcome reached by the Court today. In that case, we did not discuss private corporate agents, nor suggest that such agents should be viewed differently from human ones. Rather, in *Meyer,* we drew a distinction between "federal agents" and "an agency of the Federal Government," 510 U.S., at 473. Indeed, our repeated references to the Federal Deposit Insurance Corporation's (FDIC) status as a "federal agency" emphasized the FDIC's affinity to the federal sovereign. We expressed concern that damages sought directly from federal agencies, such as the FDIC, would "creat[e] a potentially enormous financial burden for the Federal Government." Id., at 486. And it must be kept in mind that *Meyer* involved the FDIC's waiver of sovereign immunity, which, had the Court in *Meyer* recognized a cause of action, would have permitted the very sort of lawsuit that *Bivens* presumed impossible: "a direct action against the Government." 510 U.S., at 485.

Moreover, in *Meyer,* as in Bush v. Lucas, 462 U.S. 367 (1983), and Schweiker v. Chilicky, 487 U.S. 412 (1988), we were not dealing with a well-recognized cause of action. The cause of action alleged in *Meyer* was a violation of procedural due process, and as the *Meyer* Court noted, "a *Bivens* action alleging a violation of the Due Process Clause of the Fifth Amendment may be appropriate in some contexts, but not in others." 510 U.S., at 484, n. 9. Not only is substantive liability assumed in the present case, but respondent's Eighth Amendment claim falls in the heartland of substantive *Bivens* claims.[90]

Because *Meyer* does not dispose of this case, the Court claims that the rationales underlying *Bivens*—namely, lack of alternative remedies and deterrence—are not present in cases in which suit is brought against a private corporation serving as a federal agent. However, common sense, buttressed by all of the reasons that supported the holding in *Bivens,* leads

---

90. The Court incorrectly assumes that we are being asked "to imply a new constitutional tort." The tort here is, however, well established; the only question is whether a remedy in damages is available against a limited class of tortfeasors.

to the conclusion that corporate agents should not be treated more favorably than human agents.

First, the Court argues that respondent enjoys alternative remedies against the corporate agent that distinguish this case from *Bivens.* In doing so, the Court characterizes *Bivens* and its progeny as cases in which plaintiffs lacked "*any alternative remedy.*" In *Bivens,* however, even though the plaintiff's suit against the Federal Government under state tort law may have been barred by sovereign immunity, a suit against the officer himself under state tort law was theoretically possible. Moreover, as the Court recognized in *Carlson, Bivens* plaintiffs also have remedies available under the FTCA. Thus, the Court is incorrect to portray *Bivens* plaintiffs as lacking any other avenue of relief, and to imply as a result that respondent in this case had a substantially wider array of non-*Bivens* remedies at his disposal than do other *Bivens* plaintiffs.[91] If alternative remedies provide a sufficient justification for closing the federal forum here, where the defendant is a private corporation, the claims against the individual defendants in *Carlson,* in light of the FTCA alternative, should have been rejected as well.

It is ironic that the Court relies so heavily for its holding on this assumption that alternative effective remedies—primarily negligence actions in state court—are available to respondent. Like Justice Harlan, I think it "entirely proper that these injuries be compensable according to uniform rules of federal law, especially in light of the very large element of federal law which must in any event control the scope of official defenses to liability." *Bivens,* 403 U.S., at 409 (opinion concurring in judgment). And aside from undermining uniformity, the Court's reliance on state tort law will jeopardize the protection of the full scope of federal constitutional rights. State law might have comparable causes of action for tort claims like the Eighth Amendment violation alleged here, but other unconstitutional actions by prison employees, such as violations of the Equal Protection or Due Process Clauses, may find no parallel causes of action in state tort law. Even though respondent here may have been able to sue for some degree of relief under state law because his Eighth Amendment claim could have been pleaded as negligence, future plaintiffs with constitutional claims less like traditional torts will not necessarily be so situated.[92]

---

91. The Court recognizes that the question whether a *Bivens* action would lie against the individual employees of a private corporation like Correctional Services Corporation (CSC) is not raised in the present case. Both petitioner and respondent have assumed *Bivens* would apply to these individuals, and the United States as amicus maintains that such liability would be appropriate under *Bivens.* It does seem puzzling that *Bivens* liability would attach to the private individual employees of such corporations—*subagents* of the Federal Government—but not to the corporate agents themselves. However, the United States explicitly maintains this to be the case, and the reasoning of the Court's opinion relies, at least in part, on the availability of a remedy against employees of private prisons. Cf. ante (noting that *Meyer* "found sufficient" a remedy against the individual officer, "*which respondent did not timely pursue*"(emphasis added)).

92. The Court blames respondent, who filed his initial complaint pro se, for the lack of state remedies in this case; according to the Court, respondent's failure to bring a negligence suit in state court was "due solely to strategic choice," ante. Such strategic behavior, generally

Second, the Court claims that the deterrence goals of *Bivens* would not be served by permitting liability here. It cannot be seriously maintained, however, that tort remedies against corporate employers have less deterrent value than actions against their employees. As the Court has previously noted, the "organizational structure" of private prisons "is one subject to the ordinary competitive pressures that normally help private firms adjust their behavior in response to the incentives that tort suits provide— pressures not necessarily present in government departments." Richardson v. McKnight, 521 U.S. 399, 412 (1997). Thus, the private corporate entity at issue here is readily distinguishable from the federal agency in *Meyer*. Indeed, a tragic consequence of today's decision is the clear incentive it gives to corporate managers of privately operated custodial institutions to adopt cost-saving policies that jeopardize the constitutional rights of the tens of thousands of inmates in their custody.[93]

The Court raises a concern with imposing "asymmetrical liability costs on private prison facilities," and further claims that because federal prisoners in Government-run institutions can only sue officers, it would be unfair to permit federal prisoners in private institutions to sue an "officer's employer." Permitting liability in the present case, however, would *produce* symmetry: both private and public prisoners would be unable to sue the principal (i.e., the Government), but would be able to sue the primary federal agent (i.e., the government official or the corporation). Indeed, it is the *Court's* decision that creates asymmetry—between federal and state prisoners housed in private correctional facilities. Under 42 U.S.C. § 1983, a state prisoner may sue a private prison for deprivation of constitutional rights, see Lugar v. Edmondson Oil Co., 457 U.S. 922, 936–937 (1982) (permitting suit under § 1983 against private corporations exercising "state action"), yet the Court denies such a remedy to that prisoner's federal counterpart. It is true that we have never expressly held that the contours of *Bivens* and § 1983 are identical. The Court, however, has recognized sound jurisprudential reasons for parallelism, as different standards for claims against state and federal actors "would be incongruous and confusing." Butz v. Economou, 438 U.S. 478, 499 (1978) (internal

---

speaking, is imaginable, but there is no basis in the case before us to charge respondent with acting strategically. Cf. ibid. (discussing how proving a federal constitutional claim would be "considerably more difficult" than proving a state negligence claim). Respondent filed his complaint in federal court because he believed himself to have been severely maltreated while in federal custody, and he had no legal counsel to advise him to do otherwise. Without the aid of counsel, respondent not only failed to file for state relief, but he also failed to name the particular prison guard who was responsible for his injuries, resulting in the eventual dismissal of the claims against the individual officers as time barred. Respondent may have been an unsophisticated plaintiff, or, at worst, not entirely diligent about determining the identify of the guards, but it can hardly be said that "strategic choice" was the driving force behind respondent's litigation behavior.

93. As amici for respondent explain, private prisons are exempt from much of the oversight and public accountability faced by the Bureau of Prisons, a federal entity. See, e.g., Brief for Legal Aid Society of New York as Amicus Curiae 8–25. Indeed, because a private prison corporation's first loyalty is to its stockholders, rather than the public interest, it is no surprise that cost-cutting measures jeopardizing prisoners' rights are more likely in private facilities than in public ones.

quotation marks omitted); cf. Bolling v. Sharpe, 347 U.S. 497, 500 (1954) ("In view of our decision that the Constitution prohibits the states from maintaining racially segregated public schools, it would be unthinkable that the same Constitution would impose a lesser duty on the Federal Government"). The value of such parallelism was in fact furthered by *Meyer,* since § 1983 would not have provided the plaintiff a remedy had he pressed a similar claim against a state agency.

It is apparent from the Court's critical discussion of the thoughtful opinions of Justice Harlan and his contemporaries, and from its erroneous statement of the question presented by this case as whether *Bivens* "should be extended" to allow recovery against a private corporation employed as a federal agent, that the driving force behind the Court's decision is a disagreement with the holding in *Bivens* itself.[94] There are at least two reasons why it is improper for the Court to allow its decision in this case to be influenced by that predisposition. First, as is clear from the legislative materials cited in *Carlson,* 446 U.S., at 19–20, Congress has effectively ratified the *Bivens* remedy; surely Congress has never sought to abolish it. Second, a rule that has been such a well-recognized part of our law for over 30 years should be accorded full respect by the Members of this Court, whether or not they would have endorsed that rule when it was first announced. For our primary duty is to apply and enforce settled law, not to revise that law to accord with our own notions of sound policy.

I respectfully dissent.

———

Sosa v. Alvarez–Machain

No. 03–339.
Decided with No. 03–485, United States v. Alvarez–Machain.

Supreme Court of the United States, 2004.
542 U.S. 692, 124 S.Ct. 2739, 159 L.Ed.2d 718.

■ JUSTICE SOUTER delivered the opinion of the Court.

The two issues are whether respondent Alvarez–Machain's allegation that the Drug Enforcement Administration instigated his abduction from Mexico for criminal trial in the United States supports a claim against the Government under the Federal Tort Claims Act (FTCA or Act), 28 U.S.C. § 1346(b)(1), §§ 2671–2680, and whether he may recover under the Alien

---

94. See also ante (SCALIA, J., concurring) (arguing that *Bivens* is a "relic of . . . heady days" and should be limited, along with Carlson v. Green, 446 U.S. 14 (1980), and Davis v. Passman, 442 U.S. 228 (1979), to its facts). Such hostility to the core of *Bivens* is not new. See, e.g., *Carlson,* 446 U.S., at 32 (REHNQUIST, J., dissenting) ("[T]o dispose of this case as if *Bivens* were rightly decided would in the words of Mr. Justice Frankfurter be to start with an 'unreality'"). Nor is there anything new in the Court's disregard for precedent concerning well-established causes of action. See Alexander v. Sandoval, 532 U.S. 275, 294–297 (2001) (STEVENS, J., dissenting).

Tort Statute (ATS), 28 U.S.C. § 1350. We hold that he is not entitled to a remedy under either statute.

I

We have considered the underlying facts before, United States v. Alvarez–Machain, 504 U.S. 655 (1992). In 1985, an agent of the Drug Enforcement Administration (DEA), Enrique Camarena–Salazar, was captured on assignment in Mexico and taken to a house in Guadalajara, where he was tortured over the course of a 2–day interrogation, then murdered. Based in part on eyewitness testimony, DEA officials in the United States came to believe that respondent Humberto Alvarez–Machain (Alvarez), a Mexican physician, was present at the house and acted to prolong the agent's life in order to extend the interrogation and torture. Id., at 657.

In 1990, a federal grand jury indicted Alvarez for the torture and murder of Camarena–Salazar, and the United States District Court for the Central District of California issued a warrant for his arrest. 331 F.3d 604, 609 (CA9 2003) (en banc). The DEA asked the Mexican Government for help in getting Alvarez into the United States, but when the requests and negotiations proved fruitless, the DEA approved a plan to hire Mexican nationals to seize Alvarez and bring him to the United States for trial. As so planned, a group of Mexicans, including petitioner Jose Francisco Sosa, abducted Alvarez from his house, held him overnight in a motel, and brought him by private plane to El Paso, Texas, where he was arrested by federal officers. Ibid.

Once in American custody, Alvarez moved to dismiss the indictment on the ground that his seizure was "outrageous governmental conduct," *Alvarez-Machain,* 504 U.S., at 658, and violated the extradition treaty between the United States and Mexico. The District Court agreed, the Ninth Circuit affirmed, and we reversed, id., at 670, holding that the fact of Alvarez's forcible seizure did not affect the jurisdiction of a federal court. The case was tried in 1992, and ended at the close of the Government's case, when the District Court granted Alvarez's motion for a judgment of acquittal.

In 1993, after returning to Mexico, Alvarez began the civil action before us here. He sued Sosa, Mexican citizen and DEA operative Antonio Garate–Bustamante, five unnamed Mexican civilians, the United States, and four DEA agents. 331 F.3d, at 610. So far as it matters here, Alvarez sought damages from the United States under the FTCA, alleging false arrest, and from Sosa under the ATS, for a violation of the law of nations. The former statute authorizes suit "for ... personal injury ... caused by the negligent or wrongful act or omission of any employee of the Government while acting within the scope of his office or employment." 28 U.S.C. § 1346(b)(1). The latter provides in its entirety that "[t]he district courts shall have original jurisdiction of any civil action by an alien for a tort only, committed in violation of the law of nations or a treaty of the United States." § 1350.

The District Court granted the Government's motion to dismiss the FTCA claim, but awarded summary judgment and $25,000 in damages to Alvarez on the ATS claim. A three-judge panel of the Ninth Circuit then affirmed the ATS judgment, but reversed the dismissal of the FTCA claim. 266 F.3d 1045 (2001).

A divided en banc court came to the same conclusion. 331 F.3d, at 641. As for the ATS claim, the court called on its own precedent, "that [the ATS] not only provides federal courts with subject matter jurisdiction, but also creates a cause of action for an alleged violation of the law of nations." Id., at 612. The Circuit then relied upon what it called the "clear and universally recognized norm prohibiting arbitrary arrest and detention," id., at 620, to support the conclusion that Alvarez's arrest amounted to a tort in violation of international law. On the FTCA claim, the Ninth Circuit held that, because "the DEA had no authority to effect Alvarez's arrest and detention in Mexico," id., at 608, the United States was liable to him under California law for the tort of false arrest, id., at 640–641.

We granted certiorari in these companion cases to clarify the scope of both the FTCA and the ATS. 540 U.S. 1045 (2003). We now reverse in each.

II

The Government seeks reversal of the judgment of liability under the FTCA on two principal grounds. It argues that the arrest could not have been tortious, because it was authorized by 21 U.S.C. § 878, setting out the arrest authority of the DEA, and it says that in any event the liability asserted here falls within the FTCA exception to waiver of sovereign immunity for claims "arising in a foreign country," 28 U.S.C. § 2680(k). We think the exception applies and decide on that ground.

. . . . .

III

Alvarez has also brought an action under the ATS against petitioner, Sosa, who argues (as does the United States supporting him) that there is no relief under the ATS because the statute does no more than vest federal courts with jurisdiction, neither creating nor authorizing the courts to recognize any particular right of action without further congressional action. Although we agree the statute is in terms only jurisdictional, we think that at the time of enactment the jurisdiction enabled federal courts to hear claims in a very limited category defined by the law of nations and recognized at common law. We do not believe, however, that the limited, implicit sanction to entertain the handful of international law *cum* common law claims understood in 1789 should be taken as authority to recognize the right of action asserted by Alvarez here.

A

Judge Friendly called the ATS a "legal Lohengrin," *IIT v. Vencap, Ltd.*, 519 F.2d 1001, 1015 (CA2 1975); "no one seems to know whence it came," ibid., and for over 170 years after its enactment it provided jurisdiction in only one case. The first Congress passed it as part of the Judiciary Act of 1789, in providing that the new federal district courts "shall also have cognizance, concurrent with the courts of the several States, or the circuit courts, as the case may be, of all causes where an alien sues for a tort only in violation of the law of nations or a treaty of the United States." Act of Sept. 24, 1789, ch. 20, § 9(b), 1 Stat. 79.[95]

The parties and *amici* here advance radically different historical interpretations of this terse provision. Alvarez says that the ATS was intended not simply as a jurisdictional grant, but as authority for the creation of a new cause of action for torts in violation of international law. We think that reading is implausible. As enacted in 1789, the ATS gave the district courts "cognizance" of certain causes of action, and the term bespoke a grant of jurisdiction, not power to mold substantive law. See, e.g., The Federalist No. 81, pp. 447, 451 (J. Cooke ed.1961) (A.Hamilton) (using "jurisdiction" interchangeably with "cognizance"). The fact that the ATS was placed in § 9 of the Judiciary Act, a statute otherwise exclusively concerned with federal-court jurisdiction, is itself support for its strictly jurisdictional nature. Nor would the distinction between jurisdiction and cause of action have been elided by the drafters of the Act or those who voted on it. As Fisher Ames put it, "there is a substantial difference between the jurisdiction of courts and rules of decision." 1 Annals of Cong. 807 (Gales ed.1834). It is unsurprising, then, that an authority on the historical origins of the ATS has written that "section 1350 clearly does not create a statutory cause of action," and that the contrary suggestion is "simply frivolous." Casto, The Federal Courts' Protective Jurisdiction Over Torts Committed in Violation of the Law of Nations, 18 Conn.L.Rev. 467, 479, 480 (1986) (hereinafter Casto, Law of Nations); Cf. Dodge, The Constitutionality of the Alien Tort Statute: Some Observations on Text and Context, 42 Va. J. Int'l L. 687, 689 (2002). In sum, we think the statute was intended as jurisdictional in the sense of addressing the power of the courts to entertain cases concerned with a certain subject.

But holding the ATS jurisdictional raises a new question, this one about the interaction between the ATS at the time of its enactment and the ambient law of the era. Sosa would have it that the ATS was stillborn because there could be no claim for relief without a further statute expressly authorizing adoption of causes of action. *Amici* professors of federal jurisdiction and legal history take a different tack, that federal courts could entertain claims once the jurisdictional grant was on the books, because torts in violation of the law of nations would have been recognized within the common law of the time. Brief for Vikram Amar et

---

95. The statute has been slightly modified on a number of occasions since its original enactment. It now reads in its entirety: "The district courts shall have original jurisdiction of any civil action by an alien for a tort only, committed in violation of the law of nations or a treaty of the United States." 28 U.S.C. § 1350.

al. as Amici Curiae. We think history and practice give the edge to this latter position.

. . . . .

In sum, although the ATS is a jurisdictional statute creating no new causes of action, the reasonable inference from the historical materials is that the statute was intended to have practical effect the moment it became law. The jurisdictional grant is best read as having been enacted on the understanding that the common law would provide a cause of action for the modest number of international law violations with a potential for personal liability at the time.

IV

We think it is correct, then, to assume that the First Congress understood that the district courts would recognize private causes of action for certain torts in violation of the law of nations, though we have found no basis to suspect Congress had any examples in mind beyond those torts corresponding to Blackstone's three primary offenses: violation of safe conducts, infringement of the rights of ambassadors, and piracy. We assume, too, that no development in the two centuries from the enactment of § 1350 to the birth of the modern line of cases beginning with Filartiga v. Pena–Irala, 630 F.2d 876 (CA2 1980), has categorically precluded federal courts from recognizing a claim under the law of nations as an element of common law; Congress has not in any relevant way amended § 1350 or limited civil common law power by another statute. Still, there are good reasons for a restrained conception of the discretion a federal court should exercise in considering a new cause of action of this kind. Accordingly, we think courts should require any claim based on the present-day law of nations to rest on a norm of international character accepted by the civilized world and defined with a specificity comparable to the features of the 18th-century paradigms we have recognized. This requirement is fatal to Alvarez's claim.

. . . . .

These reasons argue for great caution in adapting the law of nations to private rights. JUSTICE SCALIA concludes that caution is too hospitable, and a word is in order to summarize where we have come so far and to focus our difference with him on whether some norms of today's law of nations may ever be recognized legitimately by federal courts in the absence of congressional action beyond § 1350. All Members of the Court agree that § 1350 is only jurisdictional. We also agree, or at least JUSTICE SCALIA does not dispute, that the jurisdiction was originally understood to be available to enforce a small number of international norms that a federal court could properly recognize as within the common law enforceable without further statutory authority. JUSTICE SCALIA concludes, however, that two subsequent developments should be understood to preclude federal courts from recognizing any further international norms as judicially enforceable today, absent further congressional action. As described before, we now tend to understand common law not as a discoverable reflection of universal reason but, in a positivistic way, as a product of human choice. And we now adhere to a conception of limited judicial power first expressed in reorienting federal diversity jurisdiction, see Erie R. Co. v. Tompkins, 304 U.S. 64 (1938), that federal courts have no authority to derive "general" common law.

Whereas JUSTICE SCALIA sees these developments as sufficient to close the door to further independent judicial recognition of actionable international norms, other considerations persuade us that the judicial power should be exercised on the understanding that the door is still ajar subject to vigilant doorkeeping, and thus open to a narrow class of international norms today. *Erie* did not in terms bar any judicial recognition of new substantive rules, no matter what the circumstances, and post-*Erie* understanding has identified limited enclaves in which federal courts may derive some substantive law in a common law way. For two centuries we have affirmed that the domestic law of the United States recognizes the law of nations. . . .

We think an attempt to justify such a position would be particularly unconvincing in light of what we know about congressional understanding bearing on this issue lying at the intersection of the judicial and legislative powers. The First Congress, which reflected the understanding of the framing generation and included some of the Framers, assumed that federal courts could properly identify some international norms as enforceable in the exercise of § 1350 jurisdiction. We think it would be unreasonable to assume that the First Congress would have expected federal courts to lose all capacity to recognize enforceable international norms simply because the common law might lose some metaphysical cachet on the road to modern realism. Later Congresses seem to have shared our view. The position we take today has been assumed by some federal courts for 24 years, ever since the Second Circuit decided Filartiga v. Pena–Irala, 630 F.2d 876 (CA2 1980), and for practical purposes the point of today's disagreement has been focused since the exchange between Judge Edwards and Judge Bork in Tel–Oren v. Libyan Arab Republic, 726 F.2d 774 (CADC 1984), Congress, however, has not only expressed no disagreement with our view of the proper exercise of the judicial power, but has responded to its most notable instance by enacting legislation [the Torture Victim Protection Act of 1991, 106 Stat. 73] supplementing the judicial determination in some detail. . . .

While we agree with JUSTICE SCALIA to the point that we would welcome any congressional guidance in exercising jurisdiction with such obvious potential to affect foreign relations, nothing Congress has done is a reason for us to shut the door to the law of nations entirely. . . .

. . . . .

We must still, however, derive a standard or set of standards for assessing the particular claim Alvarez raises, and for this case it suffices to look to the historical antecedents. Whatever the ultimate criteria for accepting a cause of action subject to jurisdiction under § 1350, we are persuaded that federal courts should not recognize private claims under federal common law for violations of any international law norm with less definite content and acceptance among civilized nations than the historical paradigms familiar when § 1350 was enacted. . . .

. . . . .

Whatever may be said for the broad principle Alvarez advances, in the present, imperfect world, it expresses an aspiration that exceeds any binding customary rule having the specificity we require. . . . It is enough to hold that a single illegal detention of less than a day, followed by the transfer of custody to lawful authorities and a prompt arraignment, violates no norm of customary international law so well defined as to support the creation of a federal remedy.

* * *

The judgment of the Court of Appeals is

Reversed.

■ JUSTICE SCALIA, with whom THE CHIEF JUSTICE and JUSTICE THOMAS join, concurring in part and concurring in the judgment.

There is not much that I would add to the Court's detailed opinion, and only one thing that I would subtract: its reservation of a discretionary power in the Federal Judiciary to create causes of action for the enforcement of international-law-based norms. Accordingly, I join Parts I, II, and III of the Court's opinion in these consolidated cases. Although I agree with much in Part IV, I cannot join it because the judicial lawmaking role it invites would commit the Federal Judiciary to a task it is neither authorized nor suited to perform.

I

The question at hand is whether the Alien Tort Statute (ATS), 28 U.S.C. § 1350, provides respondent Alvarez–Machain a cause of action to sue in federal court to recover money damages for violation of what is claimed to be a customary international law norm against arbitrary arrest and detention. The ATS provides that "[t]he district courts shall have original jurisdiction of any civil action by an alien for a tort only, committed in violation of the law of nations or a treaty of the United States." Ibid. The challenge posed by this case is to ascertain (in the Court's felicitous phrase) "the interaction between the ATS at the time of its enactment and the ambient law of the era." I begin by describing the general principles that must guide our analysis.

At the time of its enactment, the ATS provided a federal forum in which aliens could bring suit to recover for torts committed in "violation of the law of nations." The law of nations that would have been applied in this federal forum was at the time part of the so-called general common law. . . .

General common law was not federal law under the Supremacy Clause, which gave that effect only to the Constitution, the laws of the United States, and treaties. U.S. Const., Art VI, cl. 2. Federal and state courts adjudicating questions of general common law were not adjudicating questions of federal or state law, respectively—the general common law was neither. See generally Clark, Federal Common Law: A Structural Reinterpretation, 144 U. Pa. L.Rev. 1245, 1279–1285 (1996). The nonfederal nature of the law of nations explains this Court's holding that it lacked jurisdiction in New York Life Ins. Co. v. Hendren, 92 U.S. 286 (1876), where it was asked to review a state-court decision regarding "the effect, under the general public law, of a state of sectional civil war upon [a] contract of life insurance." Ibid. Although the case involved "the general laws of war, as recognized by the law of nations applicable to this case," ibid., it involved no federal question. The Court concluded: "The case, . . . having been presented to the court below for decision upon principles of general law alone, and it nowhere appearing that the constitution, laws, treaties, or executive proclamations, of the United States were necessarily involved in the decision, we have no jurisdiction." Id., 92 U.S., at 287.

This Court's decision in Erie R. Co. v. Tompkins, 304 U.S. 64 (1938), signaled the end of federal-court elaboration and application of the general common law. *Erie* repudiated the holding of Swift v. Tyson, 16 Pet. [41 U.S.] 1 (1842), that federal courts were free to "express our own opinion" upon "the principles established in the general commercial law." Id., 16 Pet., at 19, 18. After canvassing the many problems resulting from "the broad province accorded to the so-called 'general law' as to which federal courts exercised an independent judgment," 304 U.S., at 75, the *Erie* Court extirpated that law with its famous declaration that "[t]here is no federal general common law." Id., at 78. *Erie* affected the status of the law of nations in federal courts not merely by the implication of its holding but quite directly, since the question decided in *Swift* turned on the "law merchant," then a subset of the law of nations. See Clark, supra, at 1280–1281.

After the death of the old general common law in *Erie* came the birth of a new and different common law pronounced by federal courts. There developed a specifically federal common law (in the sense of judicially pronounced law) for a "few and restricted" areas in which "a federal rule of decision is necessary to protect uniquely federal interests, and those in which Congress has given the courts the power to develop substantive law." Texas Industries, Inc. v. Radcliff Materials, Inc., 451 U.S. 630, 640 (1981) (internal quotation marks and citation omitted). Unlike the general common law that preceded it, however, federal common law was self-consciously "made" rather than "discovered," by judges who sought to avoid falling under the sway of (in Holmes's hyperbolic language) "[t]he fallacy and illusion" that there exists "a transcendental body of law outside of any particular State but obligatory within it unless and until changed by statute." Black and White Taxicab & Transfer Co. v. Brown and Yellow Taxicab & Transfer Co., 276 U.S. 518, 533 (1928) (dissenting opinion).

Because post-*Erie* federal common law is made, not discovered, federal courts must possess some federal-common-law-making authority before undertaking to craft it. "Federal courts, unlike state courts, are not general common-law courts and do not possess a general power to develop and apply their own rules of decision." Milwaukee v. Illinois, 451 U.S. 304, 312 (1981).

The general rule as formulated in *Texas Industries,* 451 U.S., at 640–641, is that "[t]he vesting of jurisdiction in the federal courts does not in and of itself give rise to authority to formulate federal common law." This rule applies not only to applications of federal common law that would displace a state rule, but also to applications that simply create a private cause of action under a federal statute. Indeed, *Texas Industries* itself involved the petitioner's unsuccessful request for an application of the latter sort—creation of a right of contribution to damages assessed under the antitrust laws. See id., at 639–646. See also Northwest Airlines, Inc. v. Transport Workers, 451 U.S. 77, 99 (1981) (declining to create a federal-common-law right of contribution to damages assessed under the Equal Pay Act and Title VII).

The rule against finding a delegation of substantive lawmaking power in a grant of jurisdiction is subject to exceptions, some better established than others. The most firmly entrenched is admiralty law, derived from the grant of admiralty jurisdiction in Article III, § 2, cl. 3, of the Constitution. In the exercise of that jurisdiction federal courts develop and apply a body of general maritime law, "the well-known and well-developed venerable law of the sea which arose from the custom among seafaring men." R.M.S. Titanic, Inc. v. Haver, 171 F.3d 943, 960 (CA4 1999) (Niemeyer, J.) (internal quotation marks omitted). At the other extreme is Bivens v. Six Unknown Fed. Narcotics Agents, 403 U.S. 388 (1971), which created a private damages cause of action against federal officials for violation of the Fourth Amendment. We have said that the authority to create this cause of action was derived from "our general jurisdiction to decide all cases 'arising under the Constitution, laws, or treaties of the United States.' " Correctional Services Corp. v. Malesko, 534 U.S. 61, 66 (2001) (quoting 28 U.S.C. § 1331). While *Bivens* stands, the ground supporting it has eroded. For the past 25 years, "we have consistently refused to extend *Bivens* liability to any new context." *Correctional Services Corp.*, supra, at 68. *Bivens* is "a relic of the heady days in which this Court assumed common-law powers to create causes of action." 534 U.S., at 75 (SCALIA, J., concurring).

II

With these general principles in mind, I turn to the question presented. The Court's detailed exegesis of the ATS conclusively establishes that it is "a jurisdictional statute creating no new causes of action." The Court provides a persuasive explanation of why respondent's contrary interpretation, that "the ATS was intended not simply as a jurisdictional grant, but as authority for the creation of a new cause of action for torts in violation of international law," is wrong. Indeed, the Court properly endorses the views of one scholar that this interpretation is " 'simply frivolous.' " Ibid. (quoting Casto, The Federal Courts' Protective Jurisdiction Over Torts Committed in Violation of the Law of Nations, 18 Conn.L.Rev. 467, 479, 480 (1986)).

These conclusions are alone enough to dispose of the present case in favor of petitioner Sosa. None of the exceptions to the general rule against finding substantive lawmaking power in a jurisdictional grant apply. *Bivens* provides perhaps the closest analogy. That is shaky authority at best, but at least it can be said that *Bivens* sought to enforce a command of our *own* law—the *United States* Constitution. In modern international human rights litigation of the sort that has proliferated since Filartiga v. Pena–Irala, 630 F.2d 876 (CA2 1980), a federal court must first *create* the underlying federal command. But "the fact that a rule has been recognized as [customary international law], by itself, is not an adequate basis for viewing that rule as part of federal common law." Meltzer, Customary International Law, Foreign Affairs, and Federal Common Law, 42 Va. J. Int'l L. 513, 519 (2002). In Benthamite terms, creating a federal command (federal common law) out of "international norms," and then constructing a cause of action to enforce that command through the purely jurisdictional grant of the ATS, is nonsense upon stilts.

III

The analysis in the Court's opinion departs from my own in this respect: After concluding in Part III that "the ATS is a jurisdictional statute creating no new causes of action," the Court addresses at length in Part IV the "good reasons for a restrained conception of the *discretion* a federal court should exercise in considering a new cause of action" under the ATS (emphasis added). By framing the issue as one of "discretion," the Court skips over the antecedent question of authority. This neglects the "lesson of *Erie,*" that "grants of jurisdiction alone" (which the Court has acknowledged the ATS to be) "are not themselves grants of law-making authority." Meltzer, supra, at 541. On this point, the Court observes only that no development between the enactment of the ATS (in 1789) and the birth of modern international human rights litigation under that statute (in 1980) "has categorically *precluded* federal courts from recognizing a claim under the law of nations as an element of common law" (emphasis added). This turns our jurisprudence regarding federal common law on its head. The question is not what case or congressional action *prevents* federal courts from applying the law of nations as part of the general common law; it is what *authorizes* that peculiar exception from *Erie*'s fundamental holding that a general common law *does not exist.*

The Court would apparently find authorization in the understanding of the Congress that enacted the ATS, that "district courts would recognize private causes of action for certain torts in violation of the law of nations." But as discussed above, that understanding rested upon a notion of general common law that has been repudiated by *Erie.*

The Court recognizes that *Erie* was a "watershed" decision heralding an avulsive change, wrought by "conceptual development in understanding common law ... [and accompanied by an] equally significant rethinking of the role of the federal courts in making it." The Court's analysis, however, does not follow through on this insight, interchangeably using the unadorned phrase "common law" in Parts III and IV to refer to pre-*Erie* general common law and post-*Erie* federal common law. This lapse is crucial, because the creation of post-*Erie* federal common law is rooted in a positivist mindset utterly foreign to the American common-law tradition of the late 18th century. Post-*Erie* federal common lawmaking (all that is left to the federal courts) is so far removed from that general-common-law adjudication which applied the "law of nations" that it would be anachronistic to find authorization to do the former in a statutory grant of jurisdiction that was thought to enable the latter.[96] Yet that is precisely what the discretion-only analysis in Part IV suggests.

Because today's federal common law is not our Framers' general common law, the question presented by the suggestion of discretionary authority to enforce the law of nations is not whether to extend old-school general-common-law adjudication. Rather, it is whether to create new federal common law. The Court masks the novelty of its approach when it suggests that the difference between us is that we would "close the door to further independent judicial recognition of actionable international norms," whereas the Court would permit the exercise of judicial power "on the understanding that the door is still ajar subject to vigilant doorkeeping." The general common law was the old door. We do not close that door today, for the deed was done in *Erie*. Federal common law is a *new* door. The question is not whether that door will be left ajar, but whether this Court will open it.

. . . . .

---

96. The Court conjures the illusion of common-law-making continuity between 1789 and the present by ignoring fundamental differences. The Court's approach places the law of nations on a federal-law footing unknown to the First Congress. At the time of the ATS's enactment, the law of nations, being part of general common law, was *not* supreme federal law that could displace state law. By contrast, a judicially created federal rule based on international norms *would be* supreme federal law. Moreover, a federal-common-law cause of action of the sort the Court reserves discretion to create would "arise under" the laws of the United States, not only for purposes of Article III but also for purposes of *statutory* federal-question jurisdiction. See Illinois v. Milwaukee, 406 U.S. 91, 99–100 (1972).

The lack of genuine continuity is thus demonstrated by the fact that today's opinion renders the ATS unnecessary for federal jurisdiction over (so-called) law-of-nations claims. If the law of nations can be transformed into federal law on the basis of (1) a provision that merely grants jurisdiction, combined with (2) some residual judicial power (from whence nobody knows) to create federal causes of action in cases implicating foreign relations, then a grant of federal-question jurisdiction would give rise to a power to create international-law-based federal common law just as effectively as would the ATS. This would mean that the ATS became largely superfluous as of 1875, when Congress granted general federal-question jurisdiction subject to a $500 amount-in-controversy requirement, Act of Mar. 3, 1875, § 1, 18 Stat. 470, and entirely superfluous as of 1980, when Congress eliminated the amount-in-controversy requirement, Pub.L. 96–486, 94 Stat. 2369.

We Americans have a method for making the laws that are over us. We elect representatives to two Houses of Congress, each of which must enact the new law and present it for the approval of a President, whom we also elect. For over two decades now, unelected federal judges have been usurping this lawmaking power by converting what they regard as norms of international law into American law. Today's opinion approves that process in principle, though urging the lower courts to be more restrained.

This Court seems incapable of admitting that some matters—any matters—are none of its business. See, e.g., Rasul v. Bush, 542 U.S. 466 (2004); INS v. St. Cyr, 533 U.S. 289 (2001). In today's latest victory for its Never Say Never Jurisprudence, the Court ignores its own conclusion that the ATS provides only jurisdiction, wags a finger at the lower courts for going too far, and then—repeating the same formula the ambitious lower courts *themselves* have used—invites them to try again.

It would be bad enough if there were some assurance that future conversions of perceived international norms into American law would be approved by this Court itself. (Though we know ourselves to be eminently reasonable, self-awareness of eminent reasonableness is not really a substitute for democratic election.) But in this illegitimate lawmaking endeavor, the lower federal courts will be the principal actors; we review but a tiny fraction of their decisions. And no one thinks that all of them are eminently reasonable.

American law—the law made by the people's democratically elected representatives—does not recognize a category of activity that is so universally disapproved by other nations that it is automatically unlawful here, and automatically gives rise to a private action for money damages in federal court. That simple principle is what today's decision should have announced.

■ JUSTICE GINSBURG, with whom JUSTICE BREYER joins, concurring in part and concurring in the judgment.

I join in full the Court's disposition of Alvarez's claim pursuant to 28 U.S.C. § 1350. As to Alvarez's Federal Tort Claims Act (FTCA or Act) claim, although I agree with the Court's result and much of its reasoning, I take a different path and would adopt a different construction of 28 U.S.C. § 2680(k). . . .

. . . . .

Accordingly, I concur in the Court's judgment and concur in Parts I, III, and IV of its opinion.

■ JUSTICE BREYER, concurring in part and concurring in the judgment.

I join JUSTICE GINSBURG's concurrence and join the Court's opinion in respect to the Alien Tort Statute (ATS) claim. The Court says that to qualify for recognition under the ATS a norm of international law must have a content as definite as, and an acceptance as widespread as, those that characterized 18th-century international norms prohibiting piracy. The norm must extend liability to the type of perpetrator (e.g., a private actor) the plaintiff seeks to sue. And Congress can make clear that courts should not recognize any such norm, through a direct or indirect command or by occupying the field. The Court also suggests that principles of exhaustion might apply, and that courts should give "serious weight" to the Executive Branch's view of the impact on foreign policy that permitting an ATS suit will likely have in a given case or type of case. I believe all of these conditions are important.

I would add one further consideration. Since enforcement of an international norm by one nation's courts implies that other nations' courts may do the same, I would ask whether the exercise of jurisdiction under the ATS is consistent with those notions of comity that lead each nation to respect the sovereign rights of other nations by limiting the reach of its laws and their enforcement. In applying those principles, courts help assure that "the potentially conflicting laws of different nations" will "work together in harmony," a matter of increasing importance in an ever more interdependent world.... Such consideration is necessary to ensure that ATS litigation does not undermine the very harmony that it was intended to promote.

These comity concerns normally do not arise (or at least are mitigated) if the conduct in question takes place in the country that provides the cause of action or if that conduct involves that country's own national—where, say, an American assaults a foreign diplomat and the diplomat brings suit in an American court.... They do arise, however, when foreign persons injured abroad bring suit in the United States under the ATS, asking the courts to recognize a claim that a certain kind of foreign conduct violates an international norm.

Since different courts in different nations will not necessarily apply even similar substantive laws similarly, workable harmony, in practice, depends upon more than substantive uniformity among the laws of those nations. That is to say, substantive uniformity does not *automatically* mean that universal jurisdiction is appropriate. Thus, in the 18th century, nations reached consensus not only on the substantive principle that acts of piracy were universally wrong but also on the jurisdictional principle that any nation that found a pirate could prosecute him....

Today international law will sometimes similarly reflect not only substantive agreement as to certain universally condemned behavior but also procedural agreement that universal jurisdiction exists to prosecute a subset of that behavior.... That subset includes torture, genocide, crimes against humanity, and war crimes....

The fact that this procedural consensus exists suggests that recognition of universal jurisdiction in respect to a limited set of norms is consistent with principles of international comity. That is, allowing every nation's courts to adjudicate foreign conduct involving foreign parties in such cases will not significantly threaten the practical harmony that comity principles seek to protect. That consensus concerns criminal jurisdiction, but consensus as to universal criminal jurisdiction itself suggests that universal tort jurisdiction would be no more threatening.... Thus, universal criminal jurisdiction necessarily contemplates a significant degree of civil tort recovery as well.

Taking these matters into account, as I believe courts should, I can find no similar procedural consensus supporting the exercise of jurisdiction in this case. That lack of consensus provides additional support for the Court's conclusion that the ATS does not recognize the claim at issue here—where the underlying substantive claim concerns arbitrary arrest, outside the United States, of a citizen of one foreign country by another.

―――――

COMMENT ON FEDERAL ADMIRALTY LAW AND INDIAN LAW

There are two other areas of federal law, both too specialized for coverage in depth in a general casebook on federal courts, in which essentially common-law rules retain broad applicability within a dense fabric of federal statutes.

Article III extends federal judicial power "to all Cases of admiralty and maritime Jurisdiction." This has been implemented statutorily by 28 U.S.C. § 1333(1), which grants the district courts exclusive jurisdiction of "[a]ny civil case of admiralty or maritime jurisdiction, saving to suitors in all cases all other remedies to which they are otherwise entitled." The constitutional and statutory grants of admiralty jurisdiction have always been thought to vest the federal courts—speaking ultimately through the Supreme Court, of course—with the power to prescribe and apply substantive rules of maritime tort and contract law in cases not governed by statute. When a federal court exercises its exclusive jurisdiction under § 1333 to try cases under federal maritime law "in admiralty," certain specialized procedures and remedies apply, and there is no right to jury trial. The "saving to suitors" clause allows damages actions to be brought in ordinary state civil courts, or (when supported by diversity jurisdiction) "on the law side" of the federal district courts, subject to ordinary civil procedure and eligible for jury trial, but subject to the same substantive rules of federal maritime law that apply when the exclusive federal admiralty jurisdiction is invoked under § 1333. "Drawn from state and federal sources, the general maritime law is an amalgam of traditional common-law rules, modifications of those rules, and newly created rules." East River S.S. Corp. v. Transamerica Delaval Inc., 476 U.S. 858, 864–865 (1986).

The other specialized area in which a form of federal common law is at play is Federal Indian Law, made more complicated by the fact that there are tribal judicial systems. For example, Santa Clara Pueblo v. Martinez, 436 U.S. 49 (1978), barred federal courts from adjudicating claims arising under the Indian Civil Rights Act in order to avoid interference with tribal autonomy and self-government. In Iowa Mutual Insurance Co. v. LaPlante, 480 U.S. 9, 14–15 (1987), the Supreme Court provided a useful survey of this fault line of intersecting federal, state, and tribal jurisdiction:

We have repeatedly recognized the Federal Government's long-standing policy of encouraging tribal self-government. This policy reflects the fact that Indian tribes retain "attributes of sovereignty over both their members and their territory," to the extent that sovereignty has not been withdrawn by federal statute or treaty. The federal policy favoring tribal self-government operates even in areas where state control has not been affirmatively pre-empted by federal statute. "[A]bsent governing Acts of Congress, the question has always been whether the state action infringed on the right of reservation Indians to make their own laws and to be ruled by them."

Tribal courts play a vital role in tribal self-government, and the Federal Government has strongly encouraged their development. Although the criminal jurisdiction of the tribal courts is subject to substantial federal limitation, their civil jurisdiction is not similarly restricted. If state-court jurisdiction over Indians or activities on Indian lands would interfere with tribal sovereignty and self-government, the state courts are also generally divested of jurisdiction as a matter of federal law.

The Supreme Court went on in *LaPlante* to extend to diversity cases the rule of National Farmers Union Insurance Co. v. Crow Tribe, 471 U.S. 845 (1985), that comity demands exhaustion of tribal-court remedies before federal courts exercise concurrent federal-question jurisdiction, declaring that "[e]xhaustion is required as a matter of comity, not as a jurisdictional prerequisite. In this respect, the rule is analogous to principles of abstention articulated in Colorado River Water Conservation Dist. v. United States, 424 U.S. 800 (1976) . . . ." 480 U.S., at 16–17 & n. 8.

For a comprehensive review of the past four decades of Supreme Court decisions dealing with Indian law, see Frickey, A Common Law for Our Age of Colonialism: The Judicial Divestiture of Indian Tribal Authority over Nonmembers, 109 Yale L.J. 1 (1999). Nicholas, American–Style Justice in No Man's Land, 36 Ga.L.Rev. 895 (2002), discusses an array of problems encountered in applying basic constitutional and statutory doctrines of federal jurisdiction to parties and transactions connected to tribes and tribal land.

See also Koehn, Civil Jurisdiction: The Boundaries Between Federal and Tribal Courts, 29 Ariz.L.J. 705 (1997); Symposium: Indian Law into the Twenty–First Century, 72 Wash.L.Rev. 995 (1997); Symposium: Indian Tribal Courts and Justice, 79 Judicature 110 (1995).

CHAPTER XI

PROCEDURE IN THE DISTRICT COURT

SECTION 1. PROCESS

Henderson v. United States

Supreme Court of the United States, 1996.
517 U.S. 654, 116 S.Ct. 1638, 134 L.Ed.2d 880.

■ JUSTICE GINSBURG delivered the opinion of the Court.

This case concerns the period allowed for service of process in a civil action commenced by a seaman injured aboard a vessel owned by the United States. Recovery in such cases is governed by the Suits in Admiralty Act, 46 U.S.C.App. § 741 et seq., which broadly waives the Government's sovereign immunity. See § 742 (money judgments); § 743 (costs and interest). Rule 4 of the Federal Rules of Civil Procedure allows 120 days to effect service of the summons and timely filed complaint, a period extendable by the court. The Suits in Admiralty Act, however, instructs that service shall be made "forthwith." § 742. The question presented is whether the Act's "forthwith" instruction for service of process has been superseded by the Federal Rule.

In the Rules Enabling Act, 28 U.S.C. § 2071 et seq., Congress ordered that, in matters of "practice and procedure," § 2072(a), the Federal Rules shall govern, and "[a]ll laws in conflict with such rules shall be of no further force or effect," § 2072(b).[1] We hold that, in actions arising under

---

[1. For criticism of the current rulemaking process, see Oakley, An Open Letter on Reforming the Process of Revising the Federal Rules, 55 Mont.L.Rev. 435 (1994); Wright, The Malaise of Federal Rulemaking, 14 Rev.Litig. 1 (1994); Tobias, Opt–Outs at the Outlaw Inn: A Report from Montana, 14 Rev.Litig. 207 (1994); Walker, A Comprehensive Reform for Federal Civil Rulemaking, 61 Geo.Wash.L.Rev. 455 (1993). The changing role of the Supreme Court in both implementing and interpreting the Federal Rules is examined in Moore, The Supreme Court's Role in Interpreting the Federal Rules of Civil Procedure, 44 Hastings L.J. 1039 (1993). See generally Symposium, Reinventing Civil Litigation: Evaluating Proposals for Change, 59 Brook.L.Rev. 654 (1993).

Modern federal civil practice suffered for more than a decade from the increasing significance and autonomous effect (even when in conflict with the nationally applicable Federal Rules)

---

federal law, commenced in compliance with the governing statute of limitations, the manner and timing of serving process are generally nonjurisdictional matters of "procedure" controlled by the Federal Rules.

I

On August 27, 1991, petitioner Lloyd Henderson, a merchant mariner, was injured while working aboard a vessel owned and operated by the United States. On April 8, 1993, after exhausting administrative remedies, Henderson filed a seaman's personal injury action against the United States, pursuant to the Suits in Admiralty Act, 41 Stat. 525, as amended, 46 U.S.C.App. § 741 et seq. Under that Act, suits of the kind Henderson commenced "may be brought . . . within two years after the cause of action arises." § 745. Henderson brought his action well within that time period. He commenced suit, as Federal Rule of Civil Procedure 3 instructs, simply "by filing a complaint with the court." [2]

Having timely filed his complaint, Henderson attempted to follow the Federal Rules on service. It is undisputed that the following Rules, and nothing in the Suits in Admiralty Act, furnished the immediately relevant instructions. Federal Rule of Civil Procedure 4(a) (1988) provided: "Upon the filing of the complaint the clerk shall forthwith issue a summons and deliver the summons to the plaintiff or the plaintiff's attorney, who shall be responsible for prompt service of the summons and a copy of the complaint." Rule 4(b) provided: "The summons shall be signed by the clerk, [and] be under the seal of the court." Rule 4(d) stated: "The summons and

---

of local rules of procedure adopted pursuant to the Civil Justice Reform Act of 1990. See Wright & Kane, Federal Courts § 63A (6th ed.2002); Johnston, Civil Justice Reform: Struggling Between Politics and Perfection, 62 Fordham L.Rev. 833 (1994); Robel, Mandatory Disclosure and Local Abrogation: In Search of a Theory for Optional Rules, 14 Rev.Litig. 49 (1994); Cavanagh, The Civil Justice Reform Act of 1990 and the 1993 Amendments to the Federal Rules of Civil Procedure: Can Systemic Ills Afflicting the Federal Courts Be Remedied by Local Rules?, 67 St. John's L.Rev. 721 (1993); Mullenix, Unconstitutional Rulemaking: The Civil Justice Reform Act and Separation of Powers, 77 Minn.L.Rev. 1283 (1993); Tobias, Civil Justice Reform and the Balkanization of Federal Civil Procedure, 24 Ariz.St.L.J. 1393 (1992); Mullenix, The Counter–Reformation in Procedural Justice, 77 Minn.L.Rev. 375 (1992). The unhappy experiment has now ended. See Tobias, The Expiration of the Civil Justice Reform Act of 1990, 59 Wash. & Lee L.Rev. 541 (2002).

The 1995 Long Range Plan said, at 55, that while some "local procedural variations are appropriate to account for differing local conditions and to allow experimentation with new and innovative procedures[,] [n]evertheless the long-term emphasis of the courts . . . should be on promoting nationally uniform rules of practice and procedure. . . . The Judicial Conference and the judicial councils of the circuits should discourage further 'balkanization' of federal practice by exercising their statutory authority to review local court rules."]

2.   In a suit on a right created by federal law, filing a complaint suffices to satisfy the statute of limitations. See West v. Conrail, 481 U.S. 35, 39 (1987). In a federal-court suit on a state-created right, however, a plaintiff must serve process before the statute of limitations has run, if state law so requires for a similar state-court suit. See Walker v. Armco Steel Corp., 446 U.S. 740, 752–753 (1980) (reaffirming Ragan v. Merchants Transfer & Warehouse Co., 337 U.S. 530 (1949)). But cf. Hanna v. Plumer, 380 U.S. 460 (1965) (method of service, as distinguished from time period for commencement of civil action, is governed by Federal Rules in all actions, including suits based on state-created rights).

complaint shall be served together." [3]

A series of slips occurred in obtaining the summons required by Rule 4. Henderson's counsel requested the appropriate summons forms and file-stamped copies of the complaint on April 8, 1993, the day he filed Henderson's complaint. But the court clerk did not respond immediately. Counsel eventually obtained the forms on April 21, 1993, and completed and returned them to the clerk. On May 4, counsel received the summons mailed to him from the clerk's office, and on May 19, counsel sent the summons and complaint, by certified mail, to the Attorney General, who received them on May 25.

Service on the local United States Attorney took longer. On May 25, Henderson's counsel forwarded the summons and complaint, as received from the clerk, to a "constable" with a request to effect service. On June 1, the constable's office returned the documents, informing Henderson's counsel that the summons was not in proper form, because it lacked the court's seal. Counsel thereupon wrote to the court clerk requesting new summons forms with the appropriate court seal. Counsel repeated this request on August 19; ultimately, on August 25, Henderson's counsel received the properly sealed summons.

Once again, Henderson's counsel requested the constable's service and, on August 30, moved for an extension of time to serve the United States Attorney.[4] The court granted the motion, extending the time for service until September 15. The United States Attorney received personal service of the summons and complaint, in proper form, on September 3, 1993.

Thus, the Attorney General received the complaint 47 days after Henderson filed suit, and the United States Attorney was personally served 148 days after Henderson commenced the action by filing his complaint with the court. On November 17, 1993, the United States moved to dismiss the action. The grounds for, and disposition of, that motion led to Henderson's petition for certiorari.

The United States has never maintained that it lacked notice of Henderson's complaint within the 2–year limitation period prescribed for Suits in Admiralty Act claims. See 46 U.S.C.App. § 745; Tr. of Oral Arg. 38–39 (counsel for United States acknowledged that service on Attorney General gave Government actual notice three months before 2–year limitation period ended). Nor has the Government asserted any prejudice to the presentation of its defense stemming from the delayed service of the summons and complaint. And the manner and timing of service, it appears beyond debate, satisfied the requirements of Federal Rule of Civil Proce-

---

3. The substance of these provisions is retained in current Rules 4(a), (b), and (c)(1).

4. Federal Rule of Civil Procedure 4(j), then in force, provided for service of the summons and complaint within 120 days after the filing of the complaint, a time limit subject to extension for good cause. The substance of this provision is retained in current Rule 4(m), which permits a district court to enlarge the time for service "even if there is no good cause shown." Advisory Committee's Notes on 1993 Amendments to Fed. Rule Civ. Proc. 4, 28 U.S.C.App., p. 654.

dure 4 (titled "Summons" and detailing prescriptions on service of process).

In support of its motion to dismiss, the United States relied exclusively on § 2 of the Suits in Admiralty Act, 46 U.S.C.App. § 742, which provides in part:

> "The libelant [plaintiff] shall forthwith serve a copy of his libel [complaint] on the United States attorney for [the] district [where suit is brought] and mail a copy thereof by registered mail to the Attorney General of the United States."

This provision has remained unchanged since its enactment in 1920, 18 years before the Federal Rules of Civil Procedure became effective, and 46 years before admiralty cases were brought within the realm of the Civil Rules. The Government argued that Henderson's failure to serve process "forthwith," as required by § 742, deprived the District Court of subject-matter jurisdiction because § 742 describes the conditions of the United States' waiver of sovereign immunity.

. . . . .

[T]he District Court dismissed Henderson's complaint for lack of subject-matter jurisdiction, and the Court of Appeals ... affirmed. 51 F.3d 574 (CA5 1995). We granted certiorari to resolve disagreement among lower courts on the question whether Federal Rule 4, which authorizes an extendable 120–day period for service of process, supersedes the Suits in Admiralty Act provision that service on the United States be made "forthwith."

II

The United States first suggests that Rule 4's extendable 120–day time prescription, and the Suits in Admiralty Act's service "forthwith" instruction, can and should be read harmoniously. The Rule 4 time limit for service, Rule 4(j) at the time Henderson's action commenced,[5] provided:

> "(j) Summons: Time Limit for Service. If a service of the summons and complaint is not made upon a defendant within 120 days after the filing of the complaint and the party on whose behalf such service was required cannot show good cause why such service was not made within that period, the action shall be dismissed as to that defendant...." Fed. Rule Civ. Proc. 4(j) (1988).

Section 2 of the Suits in Admiralty Act, 46 U.S.C.App. § 742, prescribes service "forthwith," ... a word not precisely defined in the Act or in case law, but indicative of a time far shorter than 120 days. The apparent conflict dissolves, the Government urges, if one reads Rule 4 as establishing not "an affirmative right to serve [a] complaint" within 120 days, but only an outer boundary for timely service....

---

5. Currently, Rule 4(m) states the time limit for service. See supra, at ... n. [4].

We reject the Government's view of the time the Federal Rules authorize for service. Reading Rule 4 in its historical context, we conclude that the 120–day provision operates not as an outer limit subject to reduction, but as an irreducible allowance. Prior to 1983, Rule 4 contained no time limit for service. Until the changes installed that year, United States marshals attended to service. The relevant Rule 4 provisions read:

> "(a) Summons: issuance. Upon the filing of the complaint the clerk shall forthwith issue a summons and deliver it for service to the marshal or to any other person authorized by Rule 4(c) to serve it. . . .

> . . . . .

> "(c) By whom served. Service of process shall be made by a United States marshal, by his deputy, or by some person specially appointed by the court for that purpose . . . ." Fed. Rule Civ. Proc. 4(a), (c) (1980).

Marshals were expected to effect service expeditiously, and Rule 41(b), providing for dismissal "[f]or failure of the plaintiff to prosecute," could be invoked as a check against unreasonable delay. See 9 C. Wright & A. Miller, Federal Practice and Procedure § 2370, pp. 374–376 (2d ed.1995); 2 J. Moore, Moore's Federal Practice ¶ 4.18, p. 436 (2d ed.1995).

Rule 4 changes made operative in 1983 completed a shift in responsibility for service from the United States marshals to the plaintiff. See Mullenix, Hope Over Experience: Mandatory Informal Discovery and the Politics of Rulemaking, 69 N.C.L.Rev. 795, 845 (1991). With marshals no longer available as routine process servers, the Judicial Conference considered a time control necessary; the Conference proposed, and this Court approved, 120 days from the filing of the complaint as the appropriate limit. Congress relaxed the rule change by authorizing an extension of the 120–day period if the party responsible for service showed "good cause." See supra, . . .; 128 Cong. Rec. 30931–30932 (1982), reprinted in 28 U.S.C.App., p. 647.

Most recently, in 1993 amendments to the Rules, courts have been accorded discretion to enlarge the 120–day period "even if there is no good cause shown." See Advisory Committee's Notes on Fed. Rule Civ. Proc. 4, 28 U.S.C.App., p. 654.[6] And tellingly, the text of Rule 4 sets out, as "[a] specific instance of good cause," ibid., allowance of "a reasonable time" to "cur[e] the failure to serve multiple officers . . . of the United States if the plaintiff has effected service on either the United States attorney or the Attorney General" within the prescribed 120 days. Fed. Rule Civ. Proc. 4(i)(3).

---

6.   Rule 4(m), captioned "Time Limit for Service," currently provides:

"If service of the summons and complaint is not made upon a defendant within 120 days after the filing of the complaint, the court, upon motion or on its own initiative after notice to the plaintiff, shall dismiss the action without prejudice as to that defendant *or direct that service be effected within a specified time*; provided that if the plaintiff shows good cause for the failure, the court shall extend the time for service for an appropriate period. . . ." (Emphasis added.)

The Federal Rules thus convey a clear message: Complaints are not to be dismissed if served within 120 days, or within such additional time as the court may allow. Furthermore, the United States acknowledges that, § 2 of the Suits in Admiralty Act aside, Rule 4's extendable 120–day time prescription applies to the full range of civil litigation, including cases brought against the United States under the Federal Tort Claims Act, 28 U.S.C. § 2675, and the Tucker Act, ch. 359, 24 Stat. 505 (1887) (current version 28 U.S.C. §§ 1346, 1491 and other scattered sections of 28 U.S.C.). See Tr. of Oral Arg. 33. We are therefore satisfied that Rule 4's regime conflicts irreconcilably with Suits in Admiralty Act § 2's service "forthwith" instruction, and we turn to the dispositive question: Does the Rule supersede the inconsistent statutory direction?

III

The Rules Enabling Act, 28 U.S.C. § 2071 et seq., authorizes the Supreme Court "to prescribe general rules of practice and procedure ... for cases in the United States district courts ... and courts of appeals," § 2072(a), and directs:

> "Such rules shall not abridge, enlarge or modify any substantive right. All laws in conflict with such rules shall be of no further force or effect after such rules have taken effect." § 2072(b).

Correspondingly, and in confirmation of the understanding and practice under the former Federal Equity Rules, Federal Rule of Civil Procedure 82 provides: "[The Federal Rules of Civil Procedure] shall not be construed to extend or limit the jurisdiction of the United States district courts or the venue of actions therein." See 1937 Advisory Committee's Notes on Fed. Rule Civ. Proc. 82, 28 U.S.C.App., p. 821 (Rule 82 confirms that the Rules' broad allowance of claim joinder "does not extend federal jurisdiction."); see also 12 Wright & Miller, Federal Practice and Procedure § 3141, pp. 210–214.

According to the United States, Rule 4 cannot supersede § 2 of the Suits in Admiralty Act, 46 U.S.C.App. § 742, for the latter is "jurisdictional" and affects "substantive rights" by setting the terms on which the United States waives its sovereign immunity. Henderson, in contrast, characterizes the Suits in Admiralty Act's service "forthwith" instruction as a nonjurisdictional processing rule. Service "forthwith," he urges, forms no part of the immunity waiver or § 745's statute of limitations, but is simply a direction for the conduct of litigation once the case is timely launched in court—a characteristically "how to" direction in conflict with, and therefore superseded by, Rule 4.

Before examining the text of § 742 to determine the character of the service "forthwith" provision, we note that the conflict with Rule 4 is of relatively recent vintage. The Suits in Admiralty Act, which allows in personam suits against the United States for maritime torts, was enacted in 1920, 18 years before the advent of the Federal Rules. Furthermore, admiralty cases were processed, from 1845 until 1966, under discrete Admiralty Rules. Even after 1966, the year admiralty cases were brought under the governance of the Federal Rules of Civil Procedure, Rule 4 and the Suits in Admiralty Act service "forthwith" provision could co-exist. Rule 4, as just recounted, originally contained no time prescription, only the direction that, "[u]pon the filing of the complaint the clerk shall forthwith issue a summons and deliver it for service," generally to a United States marshal. . . . It was only in 1983, when plaintiffs were made responsible for service without the aid of the marshal, that the 120–day provision came into force, a provision that rendered Rule 4's time frame irreconcilable with § 742's service "forthwith" instruction.

Section 2 of the Suits in Admiralty Act, 46 U.S.C.App. § 742, captioned "Libel in personam," contains a broad waiver of sovereign immunity in its first sentence:

> "In cases where if [a vessel owned or operated by the United States] were privately owned or operated . . . a proceeding in admiralty could be maintained, any appropriate nonjury proceeding in personam may be brought against the United States . . . ."

Section 3 of the Act, 46 U.S.C.App. § 743, although captioned "Procedure in cases of libel in personam," completes the immunity waiver by providing for costs and interest on money judgments against the United States. See United States v. Bodcaw Co., 440 U.S. 202, 203–204, n. 3 (1979); Fed. Rule Civ. Proc. 54(d)(1) (absent an authorizing statute, United States is not liable for costs); Library of Congress v. Shaw, 478 U.S. 310, 314 (1986) (absent an authorizing statute, United States is not liable for interest).

The United States asserts that not just the first sentence of § 742, but that section in its entirety is "jurisdictional," spelling out the terms and conditions of the Government's waiver of sovereign immunity, in contrast to the next section of the Suits in Admiralty Act, 46 U.S.C.App. § 743, which governs "procedure," specifying in its first sentence: "Such suits shall proceed and shall be heard and determined according to the principles of law and to the rules of practice obtaining in like cases between private parties." See Brief for United States 26–27; see also [United States v.] Holmberg, 19 F.3d [1062, 1064 (CA5 1994)]; Libby v. United States, 840 F.2d 818, 820 (CA11 1988) ("The fact that the waiver of sovereign immunity is declared in section 742, while the procedures governing admiralty suits against the United States are specified in section 743, indicates that the requirements contained in section 742 are more than procedural."). The dissent adopts this argument hook, line, and sinker. . . . But just as § 743 is not "purely procedural," for it waives the Sovereign's immunity as to costs and interest, so § 742 is not pervasively "jurisdictional."

        . . . . .

. . . Rule 4, as observed at oral argument, . . . provides for dispatch of the summons and complaint to the Attorney General "by registered or certified mail." . . . The Government's sovereign-immunity waiver, counsel for the United States agreed, did not depend on registered mail service, the sole form of mailing § 742 authorizes; "in this day and age," counsel said, "certified mail would be acceptable." . . . It thus appears that several of

§ 742's provisions are not sensibly typed "substantive" or "jurisdictional." Instead, they have a distinctly facilitative, "procedural" cast. They deal with case processing, not substantive rights or consent to suit.

. . . . .

If the service "forthwith" prescription is not made "substantive" or "jurisdictional" by its inclusion—along with broad venue choices—in § 742, is it a rule of procedure superseded by Rule 4? Before we address that dispositive question, we note a preliminary issue. Rule 4(j), which contained the 120–day prescription at the time Henderson filed suit, was not simply prescribed by this Court pursuant to the Rules Enabling Act. See 28 U.S.C. § 2074 (rules transmitted by Court to Congress "not later than May 1" become effective "no earlier than December 1" of the same year unless Congress otherwise provides). Instead, the Rule was enacted into law by Congress as part of the Federal Rules of Civil Procedure Amendments Act of 1982, § 2, 96 Stat. 2527.... As the United States acknowledges, however, a Rule made law by Congress supersedes conflicting laws no less than a Rule this Court prescribes. See Brief for United States 16, n. 14 ("We agree with petitioner ... that Section 2072(b) provides the best evidence of congressional intent regarding the proper construction of Rule 4(j) and its interaction with other laws.").

Returning to the dispositive question, we need not linger over the answer. What we have so far said, and the further elaboration below, lead securely to this response: Rule 4 governs summons and service in this case in whole and not in part.

A plaintiff like Henderson, on commencement of an action under the Suits in Admiralty Act, must immediately resort to Rule 4 for instructions on service of process.... In that Rule, one finds instructions governing, inter alia, form and issuance of the summons, service of the summons together with the complaint, who may serve process, and proof of service. The Rule also describes how service shall or may be effected on various categories of defendants, including, in detail, "the United States, and Its Agencies, Corporations, or Officers." All these prescriptions, it is uncontested, apply in Suits in Admiralty Act cases, just as they apply in other federal cases. We see no reason why the prescription governing time for service is not, as is the whole of Rule 4, a nonjurisdictional rule governing "practice and procedure" in federal cases, see 28 U.S.C. § 2072(a), consistent with the Rules Enabling Act and Federal Rule 82, and rendering provisions like the Suits in Admiralty Act's service "forthwith" requirement "of no further force or effect," § 2072(b). See Jones & Laughlin Steel, Inc. v. Mon River Towing, Inc., 772 F.2d 62, 66 (CA3 1985) (just as Rule 4 "now governs the method of service of process in admiralty actions, as well as service of process on the United States in all civil cases to which it is a party," so the "congressional enactment of a uniform 120–day period for accomplishing service of process" supersedes inconsistent prior law, in particular, "the Suits in Admiralty Act's requirement of forthwith service"); Kenyon v. United States, 676 F.2d 1229, 1232 (CA9 1981) (Boochever, J., concurring) ("I can see no logical reason why there should be a different method of service in this one instance [Suits in Admiralty Act cases] in which the United States is a defendant.").

Service of process, we have come to understand, is properly regarded as a matter discrete from a court's jurisdiction to adjudicate a controversy of a particular kind,[7] or against a particular individual or entity.[8] Its essential purpose is auxiliary, a purpose distinct from the substantive matters aired in the precedent on which the dissent, wrenching cases from context, extensively relies—who may sue, on what claims, for what relief, within what limitations period. Instead, the core function of service is to supply notice of the pendency of a legal action, in a manner and at a time that affords the defendant a fair opportunity to answer the complaint and present defenses and objections.[9] Seeing service in this light, and in view of the uniform system Rule 4 of the Federal Rules of Civil Procedure provides, we are satisfied that the service "forthwith" provision of Suits in Admiralty Act, 46 U.S.C.App. § 742, has been displaced by Rule 4, and therefore has no current force or effect.

* * *

For the reasons stated, the judgment of the Court of Appeals affirming the dismissal of Henderson's complaint is reversed, and the case is remanded for proceedings consistent with this opinion.

It is so ordered.

■ JUSTICE SCALIA, with whom JUSTICE KENNEDY joins, concurring.

I join the opinion of the Court. I write separately to make clear that it is not my view, and I do not understand the Court to hold, that no procedural provision can be jurisdictional. It assuredly is within the power of Congress to condition its waiver of sovereign immunity upon strict compliance with procedural provisions attached to the waiver, with the result that failure to comply will deprive a court of jurisdiction. For the reasons stated by the Court, I do not think that the legislative scheme here makes the "forthwith" service requirement such a condition.

■ JUSTICE THOMAS, with whom THE CHIEF JUSTICE and JUSTICE O'CONNOR join, dissenting.

---

7. I.e., subject-matter jurisdiction. See 13 C. Wright, A. Miller, & E. Cooper, Federal Practice and Procedure § 3522, p. 78 (2d ed.1984); Restatement (Second) of Judgments § 11, p. 108 (1982) (defining "subject matter jurisdiction" as the "authority [of the court] to adjudicate the type of controversy involved in the action").

8. On relationships sufficient to support "jurisdiction over persons," see generally Restatement (Second) of Conflict of Laws §§ 27–32, 35–44, 47–52 (1971 and Supp.1989). See also 4 Wright & Miller, Federal Practice and Procedure § 1064.

9. See Mullane v. Central Hanover Bank & Trust Co., 339 U.S. 306, 314 (1950) (to qualify as adequate, notice generally must "apprise interested parties of the pendency of the action and afford them an opportunity to present their objections"). See also Von Mehren & Trautman, Jurisdiction to Adjudicate: A Suggested Analysis, 79 Harv.L.Rev. 1121, 1134 (1966) (recognizing notice as a matter separate from bases of adjudicatory jurisdiction); 4 Wright & Miller, Federal Practice and Procedure § 1063, p. 225 (same).

The Suits in Admiralty Act (SAA or Act) entitles the United States to be served with process "forthwith" in all admiralty proceedings brought under the Act. As a statutory condition on the Government's waiver of its immunity, this time restriction on service demands strict compliance and delimits the district court's jurisdiction to entertain suits in admiralty against the United States. The majority's conclusion that this requirement is supplanted by former Federal Rule of Civil Procedure 4(j) (now Rule 4(m)) rests on a misreading of the SAA and is irreconcilable with our sovereign immunity jurisprudence. Because I believe that Congress intended to restrict admiralty suits against the United States to those cases in which the United States receives service of process forthwith, I respectfully dissent.

. . . . .

McCurdy v. American Board of Plastic Surgery

United States Court of Appeals, Third Circuit, 1998.
157 F.3d 191.

■ Before: SLOVITER and ROTH, CIRCUIT JUDGES, and FEIKENS,[10] DISTRICT JUDGE.

■ SLOVITER, CIRCUIT JUDGE.

This appeal requires us to consider the intersection of Rules 4(m) and 12(h) of the Federal Rules of Civil Procedure, in particular whether an objection to service of process as untimely under Rule 4(m) may be waived under 12(h) if not made in compliance with Rule 12(g). Surprisingly, it is an issue we have not previously addressed.

I.

Appellant John A. McCurdy, Jr., M.D., is a licensed physician practicing cosmetic surgery in the State of Hawaii through the professional corporation of John A. McCurdy, Jr., M.D., FACS, Inc., wholly owned by McCurdy (collectively referred to as "McCurdy"). McCurdy filed for bankruptcy after a jury awarded a former patient $2 million in her malpractice suit against him. Thereafter, on June 10, 1996, McCurdy filed a complaint in the United States District Court for the District of Hawaii against the American Board of Plastic Surgery ("ABPS") (the appellee here), the Hawaii Plastic Surgery Society, the American Society of Plastic and Reconstructive Surgeons, Inc., seven individual plastic surgeons, and two professional medical corporations. McCurdy alleged unfair competition, unlawful restraint of trade and various antitrust violations in the field of cosmetic plastic surgery under the Clayton Act, 15 U.S.C. § 15 (1994), the Sherman Act, 15 U.S.C. §§ 1–2 (1994), and Haw.Rev.Stat. § 480–13(a)(1). Among the overt acts alleged was the testimony of a California plastic surgeon on behalf of the plaintiff in the malpractice suit. On October 4,

---

10.   Hon. John Feikens, Senior District Judge, United States District Court for the Eastern District of Michigan, sitting by designation.

1996, McCurdy filed an amended complaint, pursuant to Fed.R.Civ.P. 15(a), naming an additional defendant, the American Board of Medical Specialties ("ABMS").

The instant appeal involves only defendant ABPS, which was served with both the original and amended complaints on October 28, 1996, 20 days after the expiration of the original 120–day period provided for under Fed.R.Civ.P. 4(m). McCurdy claims that he failed to serve ABPS during the 120–day period because counsel had used that time to make his Rule 11 inquiry, concluding by October 4, 1996, that a factual and legal basis for suit existed. Although service had been initially mailed to ABPS on October 4, 1996, it was directed to William D. Morain, M.D., who was no longer employed by ABPS. Consequently, McCurdy re-served ABPS on October 24, 1996. This time, service was directed to Constance Hanson, an ABPS administrator, who accepted it on October 28, 1996.

On January 17, 1997, ABPS moved to dismiss McCurdy's claims under Rules 12(b)(2) and 12(b)(3) of the Federal Rules of Civil Procedure, asserting that Hawaii lacked personal jurisdiction over it and that venue was improper. ABPS did not allege a defect in the October 28 service of process pursuant to Rules 12(b)(4) or 12(b)(5).

On January 27, 1997, the Hawaii district court granted a motion to dismiss for lack of personal jurisdiction and improper venue filed by defendant ABMS. The court reasoned that under Hawaii's long-arm statute, Hawaii had no jurisdiction over ABMS and that even if it did, McCurdy's claims with respect to ABMS were barred by the statute of limitations.

McCurdy anticipated that the court would apply the same reasoning to ABPS, which like ABMS had been served under Hawaii's long-arm statute. Therefore, McCurdy sought to moot the issue of personal jurisdiction under the state long-arm statute by re-serving ABPS under the Clayton Act, which provides that process on a corporate defendant "may be served in the district of which it is an inhabitant, or wherever it may be found." 15 U.S.C. § 22 (1994). McCurdy believed that the October 4 filing of the first amended complaint initiated a new 120–day time period in which to serve ABPS, but even that period would have expired on February 3, 1997. On February 5, 1997, McCurdy filed an ex parte motion requesting the court to exercise its discretion under Fed.R.Civ.P. 4(m) to extend the 120–day period by nine days. On February 7, 1997, while the ex parte motion was pending, the amended complaint was personally served on ABPS. Although the first service was designated in counsel's cover letter as under the Hawaii long-arm statute, the February service was ostensibly under the nationwide service provision of the Clayton Act. A week later, the Hawaii magistrate judge denied without prejudice McCurdy's ex parte motion to enlarge the time in which to serve. On February 27, 1997, ABPS moved to quash the February 7, 1997 service on the ground that it was untimely under Rule 4(m). The record contains no indication of any ruling on that motion.

On April 11, 1997, the Hawaii district court, ruling on ABPS's January 17 motion to dismiss, held that it lacked personal jurisdiction over ABPS and that venue was improper. Nonetheless, the court then transferred McCurdy's suit against ABPS to the Eastern District of Pennsylvania "in the interest of justice," as it would have otherwise been time-barred as of that time. McCurdy never re-served ABPS.

On May 13, 1997, following the transfer, ABPS filed a motion to dismiss arguing that the original October 28, 1996, service was untimely. McCurdy opposed the motion and filed a cross-motion for an extension of time to effect service. McCurdy argued that ABPS had waived any challenges to the timeliness of the October service because its motion to dismiss the action in the District of Hawaii listed as grounds only lack of personal jurisdiction and venue. On November 12, 1997, the Pennsylvania district court granted ABPS's motion on the ground that McCurdy had failed to effect service within 120 days of either the original or first amended complaints. The court read the language of Rule 4(m) that requires that service of process be made within 120 days to be mandatory, and not subject to waiver. Thereafter, the court determined that McCurdy had not been diligent in attempting to serve ABPS and declined to find good cause for extending the time for service. Accordingly, the district court dismissed McCurdy's complaint against ABPS. McCurdy now appeals that dismissal.

II.

McCurdy argues on appeal that the district court erred in determining that failure to effect service in compliance with Rule 4(m) requires dismissal and is not subject to waiver by the defendant. He claims that ABPS waived any challenge to the October 28 service by not raising it in the Rule 12 motion filed in Hawaii on January 17, 1997. In that motion, ABPS moved to dismiss based on lack of personal jurisdiction and venue but not on the ground that service had been untimely. Issues concerning the propriety of service under Rule 4 are subject to plenary review. See Grand Entertainment Group, Ltd. v. Star Media Sales, Inc., 988 F.2d 476, 481 (3d Cir.1993).

Rule 12(g) provides that "[i]f a party makes a motion under this rule but omits therefrom any defense or objection then available to the party which this rule permits to be raised by motion, the party shall not thereafter make a motion based on the defense or objection so omitted." Fed.R.Civ.P. 12(g).

The Rule "contemplates the presentation of an omnibus pre-answer motion in which defendant advances every available Rule 12 defense and objection he may have that is assertable by motion." 5A Charles Alan Wright & Arthur R. Miller, Federal Practice and Procedure: Civil 2d § 1384 at 726 (1990). Thus, if a defendant seeks dismissal of the plaintiff's complaint pursuant to Rule 12(b)(5) on the ground that service of process was insufficient or ineffective, it must include that defense either in its answer or together with any other Rule 12 defenses raised in a pre-answer motion. See generally 2 James Wm. Moore et al., Moore's Federal Practice, ¶ 12.21 (3d ed.1997).

In turn, Rule 12(h) provides:

A defense of lack of jurisdiction over the person, improper venue, insufficiency of process, or *insufficiency of service of process is waived* (A) if omitted from a motion in the circumstances described in subdivision (g), or (B) if it is neither made by motion under this rule nor included in a responsive pleading or an amendment thereof permitted by Rule 15(a) to be made as a matter of course.

Fed.R.Civ.P. 12(h)(1) (emphasis added).

Thus, if a Rule 12 motion is made and the defendant omits its objection to the timeliness or effectiveness of service under Rule 12(b)(5), that objection is waived. This court has long recognized that objections to service of process are waived if not timely raised. See, e.g., Government of the Virgin Islands v. Sun Island Car Rentals, Inc., 819 F.2d 430, 433 (3d Cir.1987) (defective service waived if not challenged in first defensive pleading); Konigsberg v. Shute, 435 F.2d 551, 551–52 (3d Cir.1970) (per curiam) (finding defendant waived right to assert defenses of lack of personal jurisdiction and insufficiency of process where these objections were not raised in first responsive pleading); Zelson v. Thomforde, 412 F.2d 56, 58–59 & n. 8 (3d Cir.1969) (per curiam) (deeming defendants' objection to service of process waived where defendants initially moved to dismiss only on statute of limitations grounds).

The courts of appeals in our sister circuits have reached the same conclusion. . . .

On its face, the language of Rule 4(m) appears to be inconsistent with Rule 12's waiver scheme. It provides that where service is not effected on a defendant within 120 days of the filing of the complaint, the court "upon motion or on its own initiative . . . shall dismiss the action without prejudice as to that defendant." Fed.R.Civ.P. 4(m). The district court here concluded that an objection to the timeliness of service was governed by the "clear, mandatory time requirements set forth in the Rule," so that Rule 4(m) effectively overrides the waiver provisions of Rule 12(h). . . . Though an arguably plausible resolution, courts and commentators addressing the apparent tension between Rules 4(m) and 12(h) have unanimously concluded that Rule 4(m) does not trump Rule 12(h) and that an objection that service is untimely under Rule 4(m) is subject to waiver by the defendant if not made in compliance with Rule 12. See 4A Wright & Miller, Federal Practice and Procedure: Civil 2d § 1137 at 81 (Supp.1998) ("the mandatory-sounding language of Rule 4(m), stating that a court 'shall dismiss' an action if service is not effected within 120 days, does not affect waiver under Rule 12(h)(1)(B) if a defendant files a responsive pleading that omits insufficiency of service as a defense"); [RTC v.] Starkey, 41 F.3d [1018, 1021 (5th Cir.1995)] (objections to untimely service are waivable pursuant to Rule 12 notwithstanding Rule 4's mandatory language); Pusey v. Dallas Corp., 938 F.2d 498, 500–01 (4th Cir.1991) (failure to include defense of untimely service of process in pre-answer motion waived defense under Rule 12(h)); Pardazi v. Cullman Med. Ctr., 896 F.2d 1313, 1317–18 (11th Cir.1990) (same); Kersh v. Derozier, 851 F.2d 1509, 1511–12 (5th Cir.1988) (applying Rule 12 waiver provision to defense that service was perfected within 120 days of filing the complaint); United States v. Gluklick, 801 F.2d 834, 836–37 (6th Cir.1986) (same).

We agree that Rule 12 "purports to have universal application, and we see no reason to deviate from its plain language." *Kersh*, 851 F.2d, at 1512. One court has commented that to hold otherwise "would lead to the indefensible proposition" that a defendant, who voluntarily waives an objection to a Rule 4(j) (now Rule 4(m)) violation, can be precluded from doing so by a requirement that the court dismiss the action. *Pardazi*, 896 F.2d, at 1316–17 n. 2. Once it is recognized that the mandatory language of Rule 4(m) is applicable until occurrence of one of the circumstances covered by Rule 12(h), which governs thereafter, any facial tension between the two rules is avoided. We hold, therefore, that a defense that service of process was untimely under Rule 4(m) is subject to Rule 12's waiver provisions and may be waived if not raised in compliance with that rule. Accordingly, ABPS waived its objection to the timeliness of the October 28, 1996, service when it omitted that defense from its January 17, 1997, motion to dismiss for lack of personal jurisdiction pursuant to Rule 12(b)(2), and for improper venue pursuant to Rule 12(b)(3).

Our conclusion that ABPS waived its objection to the October 28, 1996, service as untimely does not end our inquiry. The question remains, wholly apart from McCurdy's failure to comply with Rule 4(m) with respect to the October 28 service, whether either of McCurdy's attempts at service on ABPS was effective. ABPS argues that the original service made pursuant to the Hawaii long-arm provision was ineffective because the district court in Hawaii lacked personal jurisdiction over it. We agree.

Under Hawaii law, a defendant served pursuant to the state's long-arm provision must be subject to the jurisdiction of the Hawaii courts. See Haw.Rev.Stat. § 634–35 (1996). Given the determination of the district court in Hawaii that it lacked personal jurisdiction over ABPS, it necessarily follows that the October 28, 1996, service made pursuant to Hawaii law did not effectively invoke the jurisdiction of the Hawaii court.[11] Therefore, once the case was transferred, McCurdy was required to invoke the jurisdiction of the Pennsylvania court by re-serving ABPS with service issued by that court.

In a similar situation in Buggs v. Ehrnschwender, 968 F.2d 1544 (2d Cir.1992), plaintiff, a Pennsylvania citizen who was injured in an automobile accident in New York, sued a New York citizen in a federal court in

---

[11. In a diversity case state law ordinarily determines whether a corporation is amenable to suit in the state. See Civil Rule 4(k)(1). If it is not, jurisdiction is not acquired even though the method of service satisfied what had been Rule 4(d)(3) and is now Rule 4(h). This may now be regarded as settled law, although it produced an extraordinary debate between two great judges, Henry J. Friendly and Charles E. Clark. Arrowsmith v. United Press International, 320 F.2d 219 (2d Cir.1963).]

Pennsylvania and served defendant by certified mail. The case was transferred to the federal court in New York and was dismissed for improper service. The court noted that the service of the complaint before transfer of the case was ineffective because defendant had insufficient contacts to fall within Pennsylvania's long-arm statute. Therefore, plaintiff "was obligated to effect service in the new forum" following the transfer and his failure to do so before the statute of limitations ran resulted in dismissal. Id., at 1548; see also 5A Wright & Miller, Federal Practice and Procedure: Civil 2d § 1353 at 279 (1990) ("service of process is . . . the means by which a court gives notice to defendant and asserts jurisdiction over him") (emphasis added). Accordingly, in order to invoke the jurisdiction of the Pennsylvania court, McCurdy was required to timely reserve ABPS in Pennsylvania, which he failed to do.

Finally, we note that, having objected pursuant to Rule 12(b)(2) on the ground that Hawaii lacked personal jurisdiction over it, ABPS effectively preserved the defense that the October 28, 1996, service of process was insufficient on the ground that personal jurisdiction was lacking. ABPS was not required to make the identical objection twice—once under Rule 12(b)(2) and again under Rule 12(b)(5). Where personal jurisdiction is lacking, "[c]learly, a Rule 12(b)(2) motion . . . [is] more appropriate" than one under Rule 12(b)(5). 5A Wright & Miller, § 1353 at 278–79.

We turn then to consider the possible effectiveness of McCurdy's February 7, 1997, service under the Clayton Act. McCurdy concedes that the February 1997 service was untimely by four days. In fact, he further concedes that if his first attempt at service was ineffective, then his filing of the amended complaint would not have commenced a new 120–day time period in which to perfect service. See Appellants' Br. at 17. Thus, the 120–day period, which commenced on June 10, 1996, expired on October 8, 1996, and McCurdy's second attempt at service was four months, as opposed to four days, late.

With this in mind, we examine whether the district court properly refused to grant McCurdy an extension of time in which to serve nunc pro tunc.[12] We review the district court's denial of McCurdy's cross-motion for an extension of time to serve for abuse of discretion. See Boley v. Kaymark, 123 F.3d 756, 758 (3d Cir.1997).

This court has developed a two-pronged inquiry to determine whether the grant of an extension of time in which to serve is proper under Rule 4(m). First, the court must determine whether good cause exists for the failure to have effected service in a timely manner. If so, the extension must be granted. If good cause has not been shown, however, the court still may grant the extension in the sound exercise of its discretion. See MCI

---

12. We note initially that ABPS's objection to the timeliness of the February service was not waived by its failure to include the objection in its January 17, 1997, motion to dismiss. At the time ABPS filed its motion to dismiss, the second service had not yet been attempted. Thus, the objection was not available as of the time the motion was filed. See Fed.R.Civ.P. 12(g) (requiring that a defendant's Rule 12 motion include all Rule 12 defenses "then available").

Telecomm. Corp. v. Teleconcepts, Inc., 71 F.3d 1086, 1098 (3d Cir.1995); Petrucelli v. Bohringer & Ratzinger, 46 F.3d 1298, 1305 (3d Cir.1995).

. . . . .

Our own review of the record satisfies us that the district court did not err in refusing to grant the extension that McCurdy sought. None of McCurdy's attempts at service was timely. Nor at any time did McCurdy ask any court for an extension of time *before* the time allotted under the Rules had lapsed. As the district court stated, "once the matter was transferred to [Pennsylvania], counsel did not even attempt to move to extend the deadline for service until after the defendant moved to dismiss." . . . Indeed, at the time the district court ruled, the statute of limitations on McCurdy's claims had expired almost eighteen months prior. We are well aware that the Federal Rules are meant to be applied in such a way as to promote justice. See Fed.R.Civ.P. 1. Often that will mean that courts should strive to resolve cases on their merits whenever possible. However, justice also requires that the merits of a particular dispute be placed before the court in a timely fashion so that the defendant is not forced to defend against stale claims. Here, McCurdy failed to do just that at every opportunity, and the district court was well within its authority to deny McCurdy the extension he sought.

III.

For the reasons stated above, the order of the district court dismissing McCurdy's complaint will be affirmed.[13]

────────

────────

SECTION 2. JOINDER OF PARTIES AND CLAIMS

────────

STATUTES

28 U.S.C. § 1335. Interpleader.

(a) The district courts shall have original jurisdiction of any civil action of interpleader or in the nature of interpleader filed by any person, firm, or corporation, association, or society having in his or its custody or possession money or property of the value of $500 or more, or having issued

───────────

[13. The right to object to personal jurisdiction may be "forfeited" by dilatory conduct in moving to dismiss the complaint for lack of personal jurisdiction, notwithstanding that this defense was properly asserted in the answer to the complaint and thus was not "waived" under Civil Rule 12(h)(1)(B). See Hamilton v. Atlas Turner, Inc., 197 F.3d 58, 62–63 (2d Cir.1999), where a three-year delay in moving to dismiss the complaint was deemed so egregious that the appellate court concluded "not only that Atlas forfeited its personal jurisdiction defense, but also that this is the rare case where a district judge's contrary ruling exceeds the bounds of allowable discretion."]

a note, bond, certificate, policy of insurance, or other instrument of value or amount of $500 or more, or providing for the delivery or payment or the loan of money or property of such amount or value, or being under any obligation written or unwritten to the amount of $500 or more, if

(1) Two or more adverse claimants, of diverse citizenship as defined in subsection (a) or (d) of section 1332 of this title, are claiming or may claim to be entitled to such money or property, or to any one or more of the benefits arising by virtue of any note, bond, certificate, policy or other instrument, or arising by virtue of any such obligation; and if

(2) the plaintiff has deposited such money or property or has paid the amount of or the loan or other value of such instrument or the amount due under such obligation into the registry of the court, there to abide the judgment of the court, or has given bond payable to the clerk of the court in such amount and with such surety as the court or judge may deem proper, conditioned upon the compliance by the plaintiff with the future order or judgment of the court with respect to the subject matter of the controversy.

(b) Such an action may be entertained although the titles or claims of the conflicting claimants do not have a common origin, or are not identical, but are adverse to and independent of one another.

28 U.S.C. § 1367. Supplemental jurisdiction[14]

(a) Except as provided in subsections (b) and (c) or as expressly provided otherwise by Federal statute, in any civil action of which the district courts have original jurisdiction, the district courts shall have supplemental jurisdiction over all other claims that are so related to claims in the action within such original jurisdiction that they form part of the same case or controversy under Article III of the United States Constitution. Such supplemental jurisdiction shall include claims that involve the joinder or intervention of additional parties.

(b) In any civil action of which the district courts have original jurisdiction founded solely on section 1332 of this title, the district courts shall not have supplemental jurisdiction under subsection (a) over claims by plaintiffs against persons made parties under Rule 14, 19, 20, or 24 of the Federal Rules of Civil Procedure, or over claims by persons proposed to be joined as plaintiffs under Rule 19 of such rules, or seeking to intervene as plaintiffs under Rule 24 of such rules, when exercising supplemental jurisdiction over such claims would be inconsistent with the jurisdictional requirements of section 1332.

. . . . .

[14. Although the text of the 1990 statute on supplemental jurisdiction, 28 U.S.C. § 1367, has been reproduced in full earlier, supra p. 263, subsections (a) and (b) are particularly relevant to the materials in this subchapter on joinder of parties and claims. Those subsections are set out here, along with the portion of the House Committee Report discussing subsection (b).]

28 U.S.C. § 1397. Interpleader.

Any civil action of interpleader or in the nature of interpleader under section 1335 of this title may be brought in the judicial district in which one or more of the claimants reside.

HOUSE COMMITTEE REPORT

[The following is an excerpt from H.R.Rep. No. 734, 101st Cong., 2d Sess. 1, 29 (1990), reprinted in 1990 U.S.Code Cong. & Adm.News 6860, 6875. What is here referred to as "subsection 114(b)" is 28 U.S.C. § 1367. Footnotes 14 to 16 appear in the House Report, but have been renumbered. The case cited at the end of the first paragraph is Finley v. United States, 490 U.S. 545 (1989), reprinted supra p. 278.]

Subsection 114(b) prohibits a district court in a case over which it has jurisdiction founded solely on the general diversity provision, 28 U.S.C. § 1332, from exercising supplemental jurisdiction in specified circumstances.[15] In diversity-only actions the district courts may not hear plaintiffs' supplemental claims when exercising supplemental jurisdiction would encourage plaintiffs to evade the jurisdictional requirement of 28 U.S.C. § 1332 by the simple expedient of naming initially only those defendants whose joinder satisfies section 1332's requirements and later adding claims not within original federal jurisdiction against other defendants who have intervened or been joined on a supplemental basis. In accord with case law, the subsection also prohibits the joinder or intervention of persons as plaintiffs if adding them is inconsistent with section 1332's requirements. The section is not intended to affect the jurisdictional requirements of 28 U.S.C. § 1332 in diversity-only class actions, as those requirements were interpreted prior to *Finley*.[16]

Subsection (b) makes one small change in pre-*Finley* practice. Anomalously, under current practice, the same party might intervene as of right under Federal Rule of Civil Procedure 24(a) and take advantage of supplemental jurisdiction, but not come within supplemental jurisdiction if parties already in the action sought to effect the joinder under Rule 19.[17] Subsection (b) would eliminate this anomaly, excluding Rule 24(a) plaintiff-intervenors to the same extent as those sought to be joined as plaintiffs under Rule 19.

If this exclusion threatened unavoidable prejudice to the interests of the prospective intervenor if the action proceeded in its absence, the district court should be more inclined not merely to deny the intervention

---

15. The net effect of subsection (b) is to implement the principal rationale of Owen Equipment & Erection Co. v. Kroger, 437 U.S. 365 (1978).

16. See Supreme Tribe of Ben Hur v. Cauble, 255 U.S. 356 (1921); Zahn v. International Paper Co., 414 U.S. 291 (1973).

17. See 7A C. Wright, A. Miller, & M. Kane, "Federal Practice and Procedure" § 1917, at 472–81 (2d ed.1986).

but to dismiss the whole action for refiling in state court under the criteria of Rule 19(b).

FEDERAL RULES OF CIVIL PROCEDURE[18]

Rule 13.
COUNTERCLAIM AND CROSS–CLAIM

(a) Compulsory Counterclaim.

> **(1)** *In General*. A pleading must state as a counterclaim any claim that—at the time of its service—the pleader has against an opposing party if the claim:

>> **(A)** arises out of the transaction or occurrence that is the subject matter of the opposing party's claim; and

>> **(B)** does not require adding another party over whom the court cannot acquire jurisdiction.

> **(2)** *Exceptions*. The pleader need not state the claim if:

>> **(A)** when the action was commenced, the claim was the subject of another pending action; or

>> **(B)** the opposing party sued on its claim by attachment or other process that did not establish personal jurisdiction over the pleader on that claim, and the pleader does not assert any counterclaim under this rule.

(b) Permissive Counterclaim. A pleading may state as a counterclaim against an opposing party any claim that is not compulsory.

(c) Relief Sought in a Counterclaim. A counterclaim need not diminish or defeat the recovery sought by the opposing party. It may request relief that exceeds in amount or differs in kind from the relief sought by the opposing party.

(d) Counterclaim Against the United States. These rules do not expand the right to assert a counterclaim—or to claim a credit—against the United States or a United States officer or agency.

(e) Counterclaim Maturing or Acquired After Pleading. The court may permit a party to file a supplemental pleading asserting a counterclaim that matured or was acquired by the party after serving an earlier pleading.

(f) Omitted Counterclaim. The court may permit a party to amend a pleading to add a counterclaim if it was omitted through oversight, inadvertence, or excusable neglect, or if justice so requires.

---

18. The Federal Rules of Civil Procedure were ''restyled'' effective December 1, 2007, to make the rules clearer and simpler. The complete rewriting of the rules raises the specter of unanticipated consequences—including the risk that the restyled rules might change judicial interpretations of the existing rules—despite the drafters' insistence that they did not intend to change existing procedures. For a discussion of the potential issues, see Hartnett, Against (Mere) Restyling, 82 Notre Dame L.Rev. 155 (2006).

(g) Crossclaim Against a Co–Party. A pleading may state as a crossclaim any claim by one party against a coparty if the claim arises out of the transaction or occurrence that is the subject matter of the original action or of a counterclaim, or if the claim relates to any property that is the subject matter of the original action. The crossclaim may include a claim that the coparty is or may be liable to the crossclaimant for all or part of a claim asserted in the action against the crossclaimant.

(h) Joining Additional Parties. Rules 19 and 20 govern the addition of a person as a party to a counterclaim or crossclaim.

(i) Separate Trials; Separate Judgments. If the court orders separate trials under Rule 42(b), it may enter judgment on a counterclaim or crossclaim under Rule 54(b) when it has jurisdiction so to do, even if the opposing party's claims have been dismissed or otherwise resolved.

Rule 14.

THIRD–PARTY PRACTICE

(a) When a Defending Party May Bring in a Third Party.

(1) *Timing of the Summons and Complaint*. A defending party may, as third-party plaintiff, serve a summons and complaint on a nonparty who is or may be liable to it for all or part of the claim against it. But the third-party plaintiff must, by motion, obtain the court's leave if it files the third-party complaint more than 10 days after serving its original answer.

(2) *Third-Party Defendant's Claims and Defenses*. The person served with the summons and third-party complaint—the "third-party defendant" :

    (A) must assert any defense against the third-party plaintiff's claim under Rule 12;

    (B) must assert any counterclaim against the third-party plaintiff under Rule 13(a), and may assert any counterclaim against the third-party plaintiff under Rule 13(b) or any crossclaim against another third-party defendant under Rule 13(g);

    (C) may assert against the plaintiff any defense that the third-party plaintiff has to the plaintiff's claim; and

    (D) may also assert against the plaintiff any claim arising out of the transaction or occurrence that is the subject matter of the plaintiff's claim against the third-party plaintiff.

(3) *Plaintiff's Claims Against a Third–Party Defendant*. The plaintiff may assert against the third-party defendant any claim arising out of the transaction or occurrence that is the subject matter of the plaintiff's claim against the third-party plaintiff. The third-party defendant must then assert any defense under Rule 12 and any counterclaim under Rule 13(a), and may assert any counterclaim under Rule 13(b) or any crossclaim under Rule 13(g).

(4) *Motion to Strike, Sever, or Try Separately*. Any party may move to strike the third-party claim, to sever it, or to try it separately.

(5) *Third-Party Defendant's Claim Against a Nonparty*. A third-party defendant may proceed under this rule against a nonparty who is or may be liable to the third-party defendant for all or part of any claim against it.

(6) *Third-Party Complaint In Rem*. If it is within the admiralty or maritime jurisdiction, a third-party complaint may be in rem. In that event, a reference in this rule to the "summons" includes the warrant of arrest, and a reference to the defendant or third-party plaintiff includes, when appropriate, a person who asserts a right under Supplemental Rule C(6)(a)(i) in the property arrested.

(b) When Plaintiff May Bring in a Third Party. When a counterclaim is asserted against a plaintiff, the plaintiff may bring in a third party if this rule would allow a defendant to do so.

(c) Admiralty or Maritime Claim.

(1) *Scope of Impleader*. If a plaintiff asserts an admiralty or maritime claim under Rule 9(h), the defendant or a person who asserts a right under Supplemental Rule C(6)(a)(i) may, as a third-party plaintiff, bring in a third-party defendant who may be wholly or partly liable—either to the plaintiff or to the third-party plaintiff—for remedy over, contribution, or otherwise on account of the same transaction, occurrence, or series of transactions or occurrences.

(2) *Defending Against a Demand for Judgment for the Plaintiff*. The third-party plaintiff may demand judgment in the plaintiff's favor against the third-party defendant. In that event, the third-party defendant must defend under Rule 12 against the plaintiff's claim as well as the third-party plaintiff's claim; and the action proceeds as if the plaintiff had sued both the third-party defendant and the third-party plaintiff.

Rule 19.
REQUIRED JOINDER OF PARTIES

(a) Persons Required to be Joined if Feasible.

(1) *Required Party*. A person who is subject to service of process and whose joinder will not deprive the court of subject-matter jurisdiction must be joined as a party if:

(**A**) in that person's absence, the court cannot accord complete relief among existing parties; or

(**B**) that person claims an interest relating to the subject of the action and is so situated that disposing of the action in the person's absence may:

(**i**) as a practical matter impair or impede the person's ability to protect the interest; or

(ii) leave an existing party subject to a substantial risk of incurring double, multiple, or otherwise inconsistent obligations because of the interest.

(2) *Joinder by Court Order*. If a person has not been joined as required, the court must order that the person be made a party. A person who refuses to join as a plaintiff may be made either a defendant or, in a proper case, an involuntary plaintiff.

(3) *Venue*. If a joined party objects to venue and the joinder would make venue improper, the court must dismiss that party.

(b) When Joinder Is Not Feasible. If a person who is required to be joined if feasible cannot be joined, the court must determine whether, in equity and good conscience, the action should proceed among the existing parties or should be dismissed. The factors for the court to consider include:

(1) the extent to which a judgment rendered in the person's absence might prejudice that person or the existing parties;

(2) the extent to which any prejudice could be lessened or avoided by:

(A) protective provisions in the judgment;

(B) shaping the relief; or

(C) other measures;

(3) whether a judgment rendered in the person's absence would be adequate; and

(4) whether the plaintiff would have an adequate remedy if the action were dismissed for nonjoinder.

(c) Pleading the Reasons for Nonjoinder. When asserting a claim for relief, a party must state:

(1) the name, if known, of any person who is required to be joined if feasible but is not joined; and

(2) the reasons for not joining that person.

(d) Exception for Class Actions. This rule is subject to Rule 23.

Rule 20.
PERMISSIVE JOINDER OF PARTIES

(a) Persons Who May Join or Be Joined.

(1) *Plaintiffs*. Persons may join in one action as plaintiffs if:

(A) they assert any right to relief jointly, severally, or in the alternative with respect to or arising out of the same transaction, occurrence, or series of transactions or occurrences; and

(B) any question of law or fact common to all plaintiffs will arise in the action.

(2) ***Defendants***. Persons—as well as a vessel, cargo or other property subject to admiralty process in rem—may be joined in one action as defendants if:

(A) any right to relief is asserted against them jointly, severally, or in the alternative with respect to or arising out of the same transaction, occurrence, or series of transactions or occurrences; and

(B) any question of law or fact common to all defendants will arise in the action.

(3) ***Extent of Relief***. Neither a plaintiff nor a defendant need be interested in obtaining or defending against all the relief demanded. The court may grant judgment to one or more of the plaintiffs according to their rights, and against one or more defendants according to their liabilities.

(b) Protective Measures. The court may issue orders—including an order for separate trials—to protect a party against embarrassment, delay, expense, or other prejudice that arises from including a person against whom the party asserts no claim and who asserts no claim against the party.

Rule 22.
INTERPLEADER

(a) Grounds.

(1) ***By a Plaintiff***. Persons with claims that may expose a plaintiff to double or multiple liability may be joined as defendants and required to interplead. Joinder for interpleader is proper even though:

(A) the claims of the several claimants, or the titles on which their claims depend, lack a common origin or are adverse and independent rather than identical; or

(B) the plaintiff denies liability in whole or in part to any or all of the claimants.

(2) ***By a Defendant***. A defendant exposed to similar liability may seek interpleader through a crossclaim or counterclaim.

(b) Relation to Other Rules and Statutes. This rule supplements—and does not limit—the joinder of parties allowed by Rule 20. The remedy it provides is in addition to—and does not supersede or limit—the remedy provided by 28 U.S.C. §§ 1335, 1397, and 2361. An action conducted under those statutes must be conducted under these rules.

Rule 23.[19]
CLASS ACTIONS

(a) Prerequisites. One or more members of a class may sue or be sued as representative parties on behalf of all members only if:

[19. Subsections (c) and (e) were substantially revised and new subsections (g) and (h) were added to Rule 23 by the amendments to the Civil Rules that took effect on Dec. 1, 2003.]

(1) the class is so numerous that joinder of all members is impracticable;

(2) there are questions of law or fact common to the class;

(3) the claims or defenses of the representative parties are typical of the claims or defenses of the class; and

(4) the representative parties will fairly and adequately protect the interests of the class.

(b) Types of Class Actions. A class action may be maintained if Rule 23(a) is satisfied, and if:

(1) prosecuting separate actions by or against individual class members would create a risk of:

(A) inconsistent or varying adjudications with respect to individual class members that would establish incompatible standards of conduct for the party opposing the class; or

(B) adjudications with respect to individual class members that, as a practical matter, would be dispositive of the interests of the other members not parties to the individual adjudications or would substantially impair or impede their ability to protect their interests;

(2) the party opposing the class has acted or refused to act on grounds that apply generally to the class, so that final injunctive relief or corresponding declaratory relief is appropriate respecting the class as a whole; or

(3) the court finds that the questions of law or fact common to class members predominate over any questions affecting only individual members, and that a class action is superior to other available methods for fairly and efficiently adjudicating the controversy. The matters pertinent to these findings include:

(A) the class members' interests in individually controlling the prosecution or defense of separate actions;

(B) the extent and nature of any litigation concerning the controversy already begun by or against class members;

(C) the desirability or undesirability of concentrating the litigation of the claims in the particular forum; and

(D) the likely difficulties in managing a class action.

(c) Certification Order; Notice to Class Members; Judgment; Issues Classes; Subclasses.

(1) *Certification Order*.

(A) *Time to Issue*. At an early practicable time after a person sues or is sued as a class representative, the court must determine by order whether to certify the action as a class action.

(B) *Defining the Class; Appointing Class Counsel*. An order that certifies a class action must define the class and the class claims, issues, or defenses, and must appoint class counsel under Rule 23(g).

(C) *Altering or Amending the Order*. An order that grants or denies class certification may be altered or amended before final judgment.

(2) *Notice*.

(A) *For (b)(1) or (b)(2) Classes*. For any class certified under Rule 23(b)(1) or (b)(2), the court may direct appropriate notice to the class.

(B) *For (b)(3) Classes*. For any class certified under Rule 23(b)(3), the court must direct to class members the best notice that is practicable under the circumstances, including individual notice to all members who can be identified through reasonable effort. The notice must clearly and concisely state in plain, easily understood language:

(i) the nature of the action;

(ii) the definition of the class certified;

(iii) the class claims, issues, or defenses;

(iv) that a class member may enter an appearance through an attorney if the member so desires;

(v) that the court will exclude from the class any member who requests exclusion;

(vi) the time and manner for requesting exclusion; and

(vii) the binding effect of a class judgment on members under Rule 23(c)(3).

(3) *Judgment*. Whether or not favorable to the class, the judgment in a class action must:

(A) for any class certified under Rule 23(b)(1) or (b)(2), include and describe those whom the court finds to be class members; and

(B) for any class certified under Rule 23(b)(3), include and specify or describe those to whom the Rule 23(c)(2) notice was directed, who have not requested exclusion, and whom the court finds to be class members.

(4) *Particular Issues*. When appropriate, an action may be maintained as a class action with respect to particular issues.

(5) *Subclasses*. When appropriate, a class may be divided into subclasses that are each treated as a class under this rule.

(d) **Conducting the Action.**

(1) *In General*. In conducting an action under this rule, the court may issue orders that:

(A) determine the course of proceedings or prescribe measures to prevent undue repetition or complication in presenting evidence or argument;

(B) require—to protect class members and fairly conduct the action—giving appropriate notice to some or all class members of:

(i) any step in the action;

(ii) the proposed extent of the judgment; or

(iii) the members' opportunity to signify whether they consider the representation fair and adequate, to intervene and present claims or defenses, or to otherwise come into the action;

(C) impose conditions on the representative parties or on intervenors;

(D) require that the pleadings be amended to eliminate allegations about representation of absent persons and that the action proceed accordingly; or

(E) deal with similar procedural matters.

(2) *Combining and Amending Orders*. An order under Rule 23(d)(1) may be altered or amended from time to time and may be combined with an order under Rule 16.

(e) Settlement, Voluntary Dismissal, or Compromise. The claims, issues, or defenses of a certified class may be settled, voluntarily dismissed, or compromised only with the court's approval. The following procedures apply to a proposed settlement, voluntary dismissal, or compromise:

(1) The court must direct notice in a reasonable manner to all class members who would be bound by that proposal.

(2) If the proposal would bind class members, the court may approve it only after a hearing and on finding that it is fair, reasonable, and adequate.

(3) The parties seeking approval must file a statement identifying any agreement made in connection with the proposal . .

(4) If the class action was previously certified under Rule 23(b)(3), the court may refuse to approve a settlement unless it affords a new opportunity to request exclusion to individual class members who had an earlier opportunity to request exclusion but did not do so.

(5) Any class member may object to the proposal if it requires court approval under this subdivision (e); the objection may be withdrawn only with the court's approval.

(f) Appeals. A court of appeals may permit an appeal from an order granting or denying class-action certification under this rule if a petition for permission to appeal is filed with the circuit clerk within 10 days after the order is entered. An appeal does not stay proceedings in the district court unless the district judge or the court of appeals so orders.

(g) Class Counsel.

(1) *Appointing Class Counsel.* Unless a statute provides otherwise, a court that certifies a class must appoint class counsel. In appointing class counsel, the court:

(A) must consider:

(i) the work counsel has done in identifying or investigating potential claims in the action;

(ii) counsel's experience in handling class actions, other complex litigation, and the types of claims asserted in the action;

(iii) counsel's knowledge of the applicable law; and

(iv) the resources that counsel will commit to representing the class;

(B) may consider any other matter pertinent to counsel's ability to fairly and adequately represent the interests of the class;

(C) may order potential class counsel to provide information on any subject pertinent to the appointment and to propose terms for attorney's fees and nontaxable costs;

(D) may include in the appointing order provisions about the award of attorney's fees or nontaxable costs under Rule 23(h); and

(E) may make further orders in connection with the appointment.

(2) *Standard for Appointing Class Counsel.* When one applicant seeks appointment as class counsel, the court may appoint that applicant only if the applicant is adequate under Rule 23(g)(1) and (4). If more than one adequate applicant seeks appointment, the court must appoint the applicant best able to represent the interests of the class.

(3) *Interim Counsel.* The court may designate interim counsel to act on behalf of a putative class before determining whether to certify the action as a class action.

(4) *Duty of Class Counsel.* Class counsel must fairly and adequately represent the interests of the class.

(h) Attorney's Fees and Nontaxable Costs. In a certified class action, the court may award reasonable attorney's fees and nontaxable costs that are authorized by law or by the parties' agreement. The following procedures apply:

(1) A claim for an award must be made by motion under Rule 54(d)(2), subject to the provisions of this subdivision (h), at a time the court sets. Notice of the motion must be served on all parties and, for motions by class counsel, directed to class members in a reasonable manner.

(2) A class member, or a party from whom payment is sought, may object to the motion.

(3) The court may hold a hearing and must find the facts and state its legal conclusions under Rule 52(a).

(4) The court may refer issues related to the amount of the award to a special master or a magistrate judge, as provided in Rule 54(d)(2)(D).

Rule 24.

INTERVENTION

(a) Intervention of Right. Upon timely motion, the court must permit anyone to intervene who:

(1) is given an unconditional right to intervene by a federal statute; or

(2) claims an interest relating to the property or transaction that is the subject of the action, and is so situated that disposing of the action may as a practical matter impair or impede the movant's ability to protect its interest, unless existing parties adequately represent that interest.

(b) Permissive Intervention.

(1) *In General*. On timely motion, the court may permit anyone to intervene who:

(A) is given a conditional right to intervene by a federal statute; or

(B) has a claim or defense that shares with the main action a common question of law or fact.

(2) *By a Government Officer or Agency*. On timely motion, the court may permit a federal or state governmental officer or agency to intervene if a party's claim or defense is based on:

(A) a statute or executive order administered by the officer or agency; or

(B) any regulation, order, requirement, or agreement issued or made under the statute or executive order.

(3) *Delay or Prejudice*. In exercising its discretion, the court must consider whether the intervention will unduly delay or prejudice the adjudication of the original parties' rights.

(c) Notice and Pleading Required. A motion to intervene must be served on the parties as provided in Rule 5. The motion must state the grounds for intervention and be accompanied by a pleading that sets out the claim or defense for which intervention is sought.

A. COMPULSORY JOINDER

Temple v. Synthes Corp.

Supreme Court of the United States, 1990.
498 U.S. 5, 111 S.Ct. 315, 112 L.Ed.2d 263.

■ PER CURIAM.

Petitioner Temple, a Mississippi resident, underwent surgery in October 1986 in which a "plate and screw device" was implanted in his lower spine. The device was manufactured by respondent Synthes, Ltd. (U.S.A.) (Synthes), a Pennsylvania corporation. Dr. S. Henry LaRocca performed the surgery at St. Charles General Hospital in New Orleans, Louisiana. Following surgery, the device's screws broke off inside Temple's back.

Temple filed suit against Synthes in the United States District Court for the Eastern District of Louisiana. The suit, which rested on diversity jurisdiction, alleged defective design and manufacture of the device. At the same time, Temple filed a state administrative proceeding against Dr. LaRocca and the hospital for malpractice and negligence. At the conclusion of the administrative proceeding, Temple filed suit against the doctor and the hospital in Louisiana state court.

Synthes did not attempt to bring the doctor and the hospital into the federal action by means of a third-party complaint, as provided in Federal Rule of Civil Procedure 14(a). Instead, Synthes filed a motion to dismiss Temple's federal suit for failure to join necessary parties pursuant to Federal Rule of Civil Procedure 19. Following a hearing, the District Court ordered Temple to join the doctor and the hospital as defendants within twenty days or risk dismissal of the lawsuit. According to the court, the most significant reason for requiring joinder was the interest of judicial economy. The court relied on this Court's decision in Provident Tradesmens Bank & Trust Co. v. Patterson, 390 U.S. 102 (1968), wherein we recognized that one focus of Rule 19 is "the interest of the courts and the public in complete, consistent, and efficient settlement of controversies." Id., at 111. When Temple failed to join the doctor and the hospital, the court dismissed the suit with prejudice.

Temple appealed, and the United States Court of Appeals for the Fifth Circuit affirmed. 898 F.2d 152 (1990) (judgment order). The court deemed it "obviously prejudicial to the defendants to have the separate litigations being carried on," because Synthes' defense might be that the plate was not defective but that the doctor and the hospital were negligent, while the doctor and hospital, on the other hand, might claim that they were not negligent but that the plate was defective. The Court of Appeals found that the claims overlapped and that the District Court therefore had not abused its discretion in ordering joinder under Rule 19. A petition for rehearing was denied.

In his petition for certiorari to this Court, Temple contends that it was error to label joint tortfeasors as indispensable parties under Rule 19(b) and to dismiss the lawsuit with prejudice for failure to join those parties. We agree. Synthes does not deny that it, the doctor, and the hospital are potential joint tortfeasors. It has long been the rule that it is not necessary for all joint tortfeasors to be named as defendants in a single lawsuit. See Lawlor v. National Screen Service Corp., 349 U.S. 322, 329–330 (1955); Bigelow v. Old Dominion Copper Mining & Smelting Co., 225 U.S. 111, 132 (1912). See also Nottingham v. General American Communications Corp., 811 F.2d 873, 880 (CA5) (per curiam), cert. denied, 484 U.S. 854 (1987). Nothing in the 1966 revision of Rule 19 changed that principle. See *Provident Bank,* supra, 390 U.S., at 116–117, n. 12. The Advisory Committee Notes to Rule 19(a) explicitly state that "a tortfeasor with the usual 'joint-and-several' liability is merely a permissive party to an action against another with like liability." Advisory Committee's Notes on Fed.Rule Civ.Proc. 19, 28 U.S.C.App., p. 594, at 595. There is nothing in Louisiana tort law to the contrary. See Mullin v. Skains, 252 La. 1009, 1014, 215 So.2d 643, 645 (1968); La.Civ.Code Ann., Arts. 1794, 1795 (West 1987).

The opinion in *Provident Bank,* supra, does speak of the public interest in limiting multiple litigation, but that case is not controlling here. There, the estate of a tort victim brought a declaratory judgment action against an insurance company. We assumed that the policyholder was a person "who, under § (a), should be joined if 'feasible.' " 390 U.S., at 108, and went on to discuss the appropriate analysis under Rule 19(b), because the policyholder could not be joined without destroying diversity. Id., at 109–116. After examining the factors set forth in Rule 19(b), we determined that the action could proceed without the policyholder; he therefore was not an indispensable party whose absence required dismissal of the suit. Id., at 116, 119.

Here, no inquiry under Rule 19(b) is necessary, because the threshold requirements of Rule 19(a) have not been satisfied. As potential joint tortfeasors with Synthes, Dr. LaRocca and the hospital were merely permissive parties. The Court of Appeals erred by failing to hold that the District Court abused its discretion in ordering them joined as defendants and in dismissing the action when Temple failed to comply with the court's order. For these reasons, we grant the petition for certiorari, reverse the judgment of the Court of Appeals for the Fifth Circuit, and remand for further proceedings consistent with this opinion.

It is so ordered.[20]

[20.   See Wright & Kane, Federal Courts §§ 70, 71 (6th ed.2002).]

Western Maryland Railway Co. v. Harbor Ins. Co.

United States Court of Appeals, District of Columbia Circuit, 1990.
910 F.2d 960.

■ Before EDWARDS, SENTELLE, and THOMAS, CIRCUIT JUDGES.

■ CLARENCE THOMAS, CIRCUIT JUDGE:

When a party to a federal lawsuit moves to join a nonparty resisting joinder, the district court must answer three questions: Should the absentee be joined?[21] If the absentee should be joined, can the absentee be joined?[22] If the absentee cannot be joined, should the lawsuit proceed without her nonetheless?[23] "To use the familiar [if] confusing terminology," Provident Tradesmens Bank & Trust Co. v. Patterson, 390 U.S. 102, 118 (1968): Is the absentee's presence necessary? If the absentee's presence is necessary, is her joinder feasible? If the absentee's joinder is not feasible, is she indispensable?

In each of the two cases in this consolidated appeal the district court held that the plaintiffs in the other were necessary for the just adjudication of the action in question, that joining the other plaintiffs was not feasible, and that the missing parties were indispensable. The district court accordingly dismissed both suits. Chesapeake & Ohio Ry. v. Certain Underwriters at Lloyd's, London, 716 F.Supp. 27 (D.D.C.1989); Western Md. Ry. v. Harbor Ins. Co., Civ. No. 85–3163–SSH (D.D.C. May 25, 1989) (incorporating opinion in *Chesapeake & Ohio*). We decide here that regardless of whether it was feasible, the absentees' joinder in these cases was unnecessary, and the absentees, therefore, could not have been indispensable. We accordingly reverse and remand.

We first sketch the backdrop of this appeal. Both *Chesapeake & Ohio* and *Western Maryland* arose from a spate of asbestosis claims filed by railroad employees under the Federal Employers' Liability Act (FELA), 45 U.S.C. §§ 51–60, which in turn led the railroads to sue the carriers of the

---

21. See Fed.R.Civ.P. 19(a):

A person ... shall be joined as a party in [an] action if (1) in the person's absence complete relief cannot be accorded among those already parties, or (2) the person claims an interest relating to the subject of the action and is so situated that the disposition of the action in the person's absence may (i) as a practical matter impair or impede the person's ability to protect that interest or (ii) leave any of the persons already parties subject to a substantial risk of incurring double, multiple, or otherwise inconsistent obligations by reason of the claimed interest.

[The current version of Rule 19(a) is set forth supra p. 881.]

22. See id. (requiring joinder of nonparty meeting rule 19(a) test if nonparty is a "person who is subject to service of process and whose joinder will not deprive the court of jurisdiction over the subject matter of the action").

[The current version of Rule 19(b) is set forth supra p. 882.]

23. See Fed.R.Civ.P. 19(b):

If a person as described in subdivision (a)(1)–(2) hereof cannot be made a party, the court shall determine whether in equity and good conscience the action should proceed among the parties before it, or should be dismissed, the absent person being thus regarded as indispensable.

railroads' indemnity and liability insurance. In *Chesapeake & Ohio,* three railroads sued forty insurers, seeking damages and a declaration of the railroads' rights under about six hundred policies. See 716 F.Supp., at 28 & n. 1. In *Western Maryland,* filed the same day, one railroad sued nine insurers, seeking similar relief under forty similar policies. See *Chesapeake & Ohio,* 716 F.Supp., at 29 & n. 2. All of the defendants in *Western Maryland* were also defendants in *Chesapeake & Ohio,* and the plaintiff in *Western Maryland* was a wholly owned subsidiary of one of the plaintiffs in *Chesapeake & Ohio.* See 716 F.Supp., at 29–30 (detailing railroads' corporate structure). Thirty-six of the insurance policies issued to the plaintiff in *Western Maryland* were also issued to some of the plaintiffs in *Chesapeake & Ohio.* See 716 F.Supp., at 31. All of the policies in both cases imposed "occurrence limits" for personal injury and property damage claims and all imposed "aggregate limits" for claims based on "occupational diseases." See id., at 31 & n. 8. Left for decision in each lawsuit was whether occupational disease claims included the employees' FELA claims based on asbestosis.

Western Maryland and *Chesapeake & Ohio* eventually came before the same district judge, and about seven months after the filing of the complaints, all of the defendants in both actions moved concurrently to dismiss. The defendants in *Chesapeake & Ohio* maintained that that action could not justly be adjudicated without the plaintiff in *Western Maryland,* and that because the *Western Maryland* plaintiff could not be joined in *Chesapeake & Ohio* without destroying diversity, the court should dismiss the latter case under Fed.R.Civ.P. 19. See Defendant's Motion to Dismiss at 1–2, Chesapeake & Ohio, Civ. No. 85–3162–SSH (D.D.C. Apr. 16, 1986). The defendants in *Western Maryland* repeated the arguments that they made in *Chesapeake & Ohio,* averred that the *Western Maryland* action was "duplicative, and merely a device to create diversity of citizenship," and asked the court to dismiss *Western Maryland.* Defendant's Motion to Dismiss at 2, *Western Maryland,* Civ. No. 85–3163–SSH (D.D.C. Apr. 16, 1986).

The district court granted both motions and dismissed both suits. It held that the railroads were not necessary parties within the meaning of rules 19(a)(1) or 19(a)(2)(i), but that the railroads were necessary parties under 19(a)(2)(ii). In its 19(a)(2)(ii) analysis, the court first contrasted the parties' respective positions on how to characterize the FELA claims for asbestosis: as occupational disease claims, subject to the policies' aggregate limits, or as claims for bodily injury, covered only by the limits per occurrence. The "better reading of the policies," in the district court's view, was the former one, 716 F.Supp., at 32, and that reading meant that "the four plaintiffs are claimants to a common, limited fund," id.

With the railroads' recovery for their employees' FELA claims against them capped by the aggregate limits, the plaintiff in *Western Maryland* had "an interest relating to the subject of" *Chesapeake & Ohio.* Fed.R.Civ.P. 19(a)(2). According to the district court, moreover, the failure to join all of the railroads would leave all of the insurers "subject to a substantial risk of incurring double, multiple, or otherwise inconsistent obligations." Fed.

R.Civ.P. 19(a)(2)(ii); see 716 F.Supp. at 32.[24] The district court held that joinder was not feasible because joining the railroads in the two suits would undo diversity of citizenship in both and thus deprive the court of jurisdiction. The court then decided "in equity and good conscience" that neither action should proceed without the absent parties. Fed.R.Civ.P. 19(b). It therefore dismissed both cases. See id.

As we have explained above, a district court deciding a motion under rule 19 should answer three questions in sequence.[25] The court need only decide whether an absent party is indispensable if it determines that the party's joinder is infeasible, and it need only decide whether joinder is feasible if it decides that an absentee's presence is necessary. We hold here that regardless of whether the plaintiffs absent from each of these actions could have been joined in the other, their presence was not necessary. It follows, then, that dismissal was unwarranted.

We agree with the district court's conclusion that with respect to rules 19(a)(1) and (a)(2)(i), the absent railroads were not necessary for just adjudication. Even in the absence of some of the railroads, the court could accord complete relief in each case to those already parties. Fed.R.Civ.P. 19(a)(1); see 716 F.Supp., at 31. Because *Western Maryland* and its corporate kin have chosen to litigate separately, moreover, the district court had reason to conclude that disposition of one suit in the absence of the railroads in the other would not "as a practical matter impair or impede [the railroads'] ability to protect that interest." Fed.R.Civ.P. 19(a)(2)(i); see 716 F.Supp. at 32.

We depart from the district court, however, in our analysis under rule 19(a)(2)(ii). Rule 19(a)(2)(ii) directs that an absentee be joined if disposition of the action without her might leave those present "subject to a *substantial risk* of incurring . . . inconsistent obligations." Fed.R.Civ.P. 19(a)(2)(ii) (emphasis added). A recent decision ordering the joinder of an absent insured illustrates why here, in contrast, the railroads' decision not to join one another subjected the insurers to little or no risk of the kind that rule 19 is designed to avert.

In In re Forty–Eight Insulations, Inc., 109 B.R. 315 (N.D.Ill.1989), Forty–Eight Insulations, a manufacturer of products containing asbestos, sued twenty-two insurers for a declaration of the insurers' obligations to Forty–Eight under policies issued to Forty–Eight's corporate parent, Foster Wheeler Corp. The insurers argued that Foster Wheeler was a necessary party to the suit, and they moved for an order joining Foster Wheeler

---

24. The district court explained:

> This is not a situation in which there are multiple claimants to a fund, only one of which has the right to recover. Instead, it appears that all four plaintiffs—suing over rights under the same policies issued to the samed [sic] named insured—are claimants to a limited fund. . . .

Chesapeake & Ohio, 716 F.Supp., at 32.

25. See also Freer, Rethinking Compulsory Joinder: A Proposal to Restructure Federal Rule 19, 60 N.Y.U.L.Rev. 1061, 1076 (1985) (Rule 19 "prescribes a three-step process, although this fact is obscured by its language."); id., at 1076–77 & n. 76.

under rule 19. Appraising everyone's positions, the court found that Forty–Eight and Foster Wheeler were common claimants to the defendants' limited insurance fund. Foster Wheeler, however, refused to concede that payments made to Forty–Eight would reduce the amount that it, Foster Wheeler, could recover. According to the court, Foster Wheeler's position made rule 19(a)(2)(ii) joinder appropriate:

> In this action Forty–Eight seeks a determination that the insurers owe it coverage for asbestos-related claims. If Foster Wheeler is not joined, however, the insurers could be held liable for coverage to Forty–Eight without receiving a determination as to whether payments to or on behalf of Forty–Eight reduce their liability to Foster Wheeler. Foster Wheeler could then bring suit on these same policies, and a different court could determine that the insurers owe coverage to Foster Wheeler and that payments made on behalf of Forty–Eight did not reduce the insurers' liability to Foster Wheeler.

109 B.R., at 319.

Two facts distinguish the cases on appeal from *Forty–Eight Insulations,* and each suffices to make the insurers' risk of inconsistent obligations less than substantial. First, *Western Maryland* and *Chesapeake & Ohio* are pending before the same district judge, and he has treated the cases consistently, by delimiting the scope of the occupational disease clauses the same way in both suits. Assuming, therefore, that the aggregate limits do apply to the FELA claims—a point that the plaintiffs vigorously contest, and one on which we express no opinion—the district judge can guarantee in both cases that the insurers' total obligations extend only to the aggregate limits. Under the district court's interpretation, the insurers should have to pay the railroads only the total amount provided for by the policies, no matter how many asbestosis claims have been filed. Cf. 716 F.Supp., at 33 ("[T]he Court recognizes that both actions are in front of the same court, and that the Court is thus in a position to try to fashion relief in one suit so as not to unduly prejudice the parties in the other."). Second, the plaintiffs concede that if the occupational disease clauses do apply, their own recovery will stop at the aggregate limits. See, e.g., Brief of Appellants at 16, 20–21; Appellants' Reply Brief at 2–3; Transcript of Oral Argument at 8–9, 10, 13. We take that representation to estop them from maintaining a different position on remand. See Farmland Indus. v. Grain Bd. of Iraq, 904 F.2d 732, 739 (D.C.Cir.1990).

We turn finally to the insurers' argument that the railroads improperly fabricated federal jurisdiction. The insurers argued in their motions to dismiss—and the railroads acknowledged at oral argument, see Transcript of Oral Argument at 5–6—that the railroads filed separate actions in order to preserve diversity and get into federal court. That tactic also bothered the district court: "the Court is troubled by the manner in which the claims have been divided in these actions, which appears to have been done solely for the purpose of obtaining diversity jurisdiction." *Chesapeake & Ohio,* 716 F.Supp., at 33; see also id. ("[W]hat is so troubling about the present posture of these actions [is] the extent to which the interests of the parties are intertwined."). We realize that burgeoning dockets are burdening federal courts. Yet Congress has so far proscribed only collusive joinder meant to invoke federal jurisdiction, see 28 U.S.C. § 1359; parties may still obtain a federal forum by colluding not to join. The insurers have cited no statute or precedent suggesting otherwise. On remand, however, the district court can employ the flexible procedures afforded by the Federal Rules, e.g., Fed.R.Civ.P. 42(a), to minimize any potential costs prompted by the continued existence of separate actions.

We reverse the decisions of the district court and remand these actions for proceedings consistent with this opinion.

It is so ordered.[26]

B. INTERPLEADER

State Farm Fire & Casualty Co. v. Tashire

Supreme Court of the United States, 1967.
386 U.S. 523, 87 S.Ct. 1199, 18 L.Ed.2d 270.

■ MR. JUSTICE FORTAS delivered the opinion of the Court.

Early one September morning in 1964, a Greyhound bus proceeding northward through Shasta County, California, collided with a southbound pickup truck. Two of the passengers aboard the bus were killed. Thirty-three others were injured, as were the bus driver, the driver of the truck and its lone passenger. One of the dead and 10 of the injured passengers were Canadians; the rest of the individuals involved were citizens of five American States. The ensuing litigation led to the present case, which raises important questions concerning administration of the interpleader remedy in the federal courts.

The litigation began when four of the injured passengers filed suit in California state courts, seeking damages in excess of $1,000,000. Named as

---

[26. On remand the cases were consolidated. Chesapeake & O. Ry. Co. v. Certain Underwriters at Lloyd's, London, 834 F.Supp. 456 (D.D.C.1993).

See Steinman, Postremoval Changes in the Party Structure of Diversity Cases: The Old Law, the New Law, and Rule 19, 38 U.Kan.L.Rev. 884 (1990); Lewis, Mandatory Joinder of Parties in Civil Proceedings: The Case for Analytical Pragmatism, 26 U.Fla.L.Rev. 381 (1974).

If an absent party is regarded as "indispensable" under Rule 19(b), the party cannot be joined unless its presence in the action is consistent with the statutory limitations on the subject-matter jurisdiction of the federal courts. Carlton v. Baww, Inc., 751 F.2d 781, 786 (5th Cir.1985).

If a sovereign has claims that are not frivolous and the sovereign is a required party pursuant to Rule 19, the case may not proceed if the sovereign is not amenable to suit. Republic of the Philippines v. Pimentel, 553 U.S. 851 (2008).]

defendants were Greyhound Lines, Inc., a California corporation; Theron Nauta, the bus driver; Ellis Clark, who drove the truck; and Kenneth Glasgow, the passenger in the truck who was apparently its owner as well. Each of the individual defendants was a citizen and resident of Oregon. Before these cases could come to trial and before other suits were filed in California or elsewhere, petitioner State Farm Fire & Casualty Company, an Illinois corporation, brought this action in the nature of interpleader in the United States District Court for the District of Oregon.

In its complaint State Farm asserted that at the time of the Shasta County collision it had in force an insurance policy with respect to Ellis Clark, driver of the truck, providing for bodily injury liability up to $10,000 per person and $20,000 per occurrence and for legal representation of Clark in actions covered by the policy. It asserted that actions already filed in California and others which it anticipated would be filed far exceeded in aggregate damages sought the amount of its maximum liability under the policy. Accordingly, it paid into court the sum of $20,000 and asked the court (1) to require all claimants to establish their claims against Clark and his insurer in this single proceeding and in no other, and (2) to discharge State Farm from all further obligations under its policy—including its duty to defend Clark in lawsuits arising from the accident. Alternatively, State Farm expressed its conviction that the policy issued to Clark excluded from coverage accidents resulting from his operation of a truck which belonged to another and was being used in the business of another. The complaint, therefore, requested that the court decree that the insurer owed no duty to Clark and was not liable on the policy, and it asked the court to refund the $20,000 deposit.

Joined as defendants were Clark, Glasgow, Nauta, Greyhound Lines, and each of the prospective claimants. Jurisdiction was predicated upon 28 U.S.C. § 1335, the federal interpleader statute, and upon general diversity of citizenship, there being diversity between two or more of the claimants to the fund and between State Farm and all of the named defendants.

[Personal service was made on the American defendants and service by registered mail on the Canadian defendants. The district court ultimately issued an injunction restraining the filing or prosecution of any action arising out of the accident against Clark, State Farm, Greyhound, and Nauta except in the interpleader proceeding. The Ninth Circuit reversed.]

... It held that in States like Oregon which do not permit "direct action" suits against insurance companies until judgments are obtained against the insured, the insurance companies may not invoke federal interpleader until the claims against the insured, the alleged tortfeasor, have been reduced to judgment. Until that is done, said the court, claimants with unliquidated tort claims are not "claimants" within the meaning of § 1335, nor are they "[p]ersons having claims against the plaintiff" within the meaning of Rule 22 of the Federal Rules of Civil Procedure.[27]

. . . .

---

27. We need not pass upon the Court of Appeals' conclusions with respect to the interpretation of interpleader under Rule 22, which provides that "(1) Persons having claims against

I.

Before considering the issues presented by the petition for certiorari, we find it necessary to dispose of a question neither raised by the parties nor passed upon by the courts below. Since the matter concerns our jurisdiction, we raise it on our own motion. Treinies v. Sunshine Mining Co., 308 U.S. 66 (1939). The interpleader statute, 28 U.S.C. § 1335, applies where there are "Two or more adverse claimants, of diverse citizenship ...." This provision has been uniformly construed to require only "minimal diversity," that is, diversity of citizenship between two or more claimants, without regard to the circumstance that other rival claimants may be co-citizens.[28] The language of the statute, the legislative purpose broadly to remedy the problems posed by multiple claimants to a single fund, and the consistent judicial interpretation tacitly accepted by Congress, persuade us that the statute requires no more. There remains, however, the question whether such a statutory construction is consistent with Article III of our Constitution, which extends the federal judicial power to "Controversies ... between citizens of different States ... and between a State, or the Citizens thereof, and foreign States, Citizens or Subjects." In Strawbridge v. Curtiss, 3 Cranch [7 U.S.] 267 (1806), this Court held that the diversity of citizenship statute required "complete diversity": where co-citizens appeared on both sides of a dispute, jurisdiction was lost. But Chief Justice Marshall there purported to construe only "The words of the act of congress," not the Constitution itself.[29] And in a variety of contexts this Court and the lower courts have concluded that

the plaintiff may be joined as defendants and required to interplead when their claims are such that the plaintiff is or may be exposed to double or multiple liability ..." First, as we indicate today, this action was properly brought under § 1335. Second, State Farm did not purport to invoke Rule 22. Third, State Farm could not have invoked it in light of venue and service of process limitations. Whereas statutory interpleader may be brought in the district where any claimant resides (28 U.S.C. § 1397), Rule interpleader based upon diversity of citizenship may be brought only in the district where all plaintiffs or all defendants reside (28 U.S.C. § 1391(a)). And whereas statutory interpleader enables a plaintiff to employ nationwide service of process (28 U.S.C. § 2361), service of process under Rule 22 is confined to that provided in Rule 4. See generally 3 Moore, Federal Practice ¶ 22.04.

With respect to the Court of Appeals' views on Rule 22, which seem to be shared by our Brother *Douglas*, compare Underwriters at Lloyd's v. Nichols, 363 F.2d 357 (C.A. 8th Cir.1966), and A/S Krediit Pank v. Chase Manhattan Bank, 155 F.Supp. 30 (D.C.S.D.N.Y. 1957), aff'd, 303 F.2d 648 (C.A. 2d Cir.1962), with National Casualty Co. v. Insurance Co. of North America, 230 F.Supp. 617 (D.C.N.D.Ohio 1964), and American Indemnity Co. v. Hale, 71 F.Supp. 529 (D.C.W.D.Mo.1947). See also 3 Moore, Federal Practice ¶ 22.04, at 3008 and n. 4.

28. See, e.g., Haynes v. Felder, 239 F.2d 868, 872–875 (C.A. 5th Cir.1957); Holcomb v. Aetna Life Insurance Co., 255 F.2d 577, 582 (CA10th Cir.), cert. denied sub nom. Fleming v. Aetna Life Insurance Co., 358 U.S. 879 (1958); Cramer v. Phoenix Mut. Life Ins. Co., 91 F.2d 141, 146–147 (C.A. 8th Cir.), cert. denied, 302 U.S. 739 (1937); Commercial Union Insurance Co. of New York v. Adams, 231 F.Supp. 860, 863 (D.C.S.D.Ind.1964); 3 Moore, Federal Practice ¶ 22.09, at 3033.

29. Subsequent decisions of this Court indicate that *Strawbridge* is not to be given an expansive reading. See, e.g., Louisville Railroad Co. v. Letson, 2 How. [43 U.S.] 497, 554–556 (1844), expressing the view that in 1839 Congress had in fact acted to "rid the courts of the decision in the case of Strawbridge and Curtis." Id., at 556.

Article III poses no obstacle to the legislative extension of federal jurisdiction, founded on diversity, so long as any two adverse parties are not co-citizens.[30] Accordingly, we conclude that the present case is properly in the federal courts.

II.

We do not agree with the Court of Appeals that, in the absence of a state law or contractual provision for "direct action" suits against the insurance company, the company must wait until persons asserting claims against its insured have reduced those claims to judgment before seeking to invoke the benefits of federal interpleader. That may have been a tenable position under the 1926 and 1936 interpleader statutes. These statutes did not carry forward the language in the 1917 Act authorizing interpleader where adverse claimants "may claim" benefits as well as where they "are claiming" them.[31] In 1948, however, in the revision of the Judicial Code, the "may claim" language was restored. Until the decision below, every court confronted by the question has concluded that the 1948 revision removed whatever requirement there might previously have been that the insurance company wait until at least two claimants reduced their claims to judgments. The commentators are in accord.

Considerations of judicial administration demonstrate the soundness of this view which, in any event, seems compelled by the language of the present statute, which is remedial and to be liberally construed. Were an insurance company required to await reduction of claims to judgment, the first claimant to obtain such a judgment or to negotiate a settlement might appropriate all or a disproportionate slice of the fund before his fellow claimants were able to establish their claims. The difficulties such a race to judgment pose for the insurer, and the unfairness which may result to some claimants, were among the principal evils the interpleader device was intended to remedy.

---

30. See, e.g., American Fire & Cas. Co. v. Finn, 341 U.S. 6, 10, n. 3 (1951), and Barney v. Latham, 103 U.S. 205, 213, construing the removal statute, now 28 U.S.C. § 1441(c); Supreme Tribe of Ben–Hur v. Cauble, 255 U.S. 356 (1921), concerning class actions; Wichita R.R. & Light Co. v. Public Util. Comm., 260 U.S. 48 (1922), dealing with intervention by cocitizens. Full-dress arguments for the constitutionality of "minimal diversity" in situations like interpleader, which arguments need not be rehearsed here, are set out in Judge Tuttle's opinion in Haynes v. Felder, 239 F.2d, at 875–876; in Judge Weinfeld's opinion in Twentieth Century–Fox Film Corp. v. Taylor, 239 F.Supp. 913, 918–921 (D.C.S.D.N.Y.1965); and in ALI, Study of the Division of Jurisdiction Between State and Federal Courts 180–190 (Official Draft, Pt. 1, 1965); 3 Moore, Federal Practice ¶ 22.09, at 3033–3037; Chafee, Federal Interpleader Since the Act of 1936, 49 Yale L.J. 377, 393–406 (1940); Chafee, Interpleader in the United States Courts, 41 Yale L.J. 1134, 1165–1169 (1932). We note that the American Law Institute's proposals for revision of the Judicial Code to deal with the problem of multiparty, multijurisdiction litigation are predicated upon the permissibility of "minimal diversity" as a jurisdictional basis.

31. 39 Stat. 929 (1917). See Klaber v. Maryland Casualty Co., 69 F.2d 934, 938–939, 106 A.L.R. 617 (C.A. 8th Cir.1934), which held that the omission in the 1926 Act of the earlier statute's "may claim" language required the denial of interpleader in the face of unliquidated claims (alternative holding).

III.

The fact that State Farm had properly invoked the interpleader jurisdiction under § 1335 did not, however, entitle it to an order both enjoining prosecution of suits against it outside the confines of the interpleader proceeding and also extending such protection to its insured, the alleged tortfeasor. Still less was Greyhound Lines entitled to have that order expanded so as to protect itself and its driver, also alleged to be tortfeasors, from suits brought by its passengers in various state or federal courts. Here, the scope of the litigation, in terms of parties and claims, was vastly more extensive than the confines of the "fund," the deposited proceeds of the insurance policy. In these circumstances, the mere existence of such a fund cannot, by use of interpleader, be employed to accomplish purposes that exceed the needs of orderly contest with respect to the fund.

There are situations, of a type not present here, where the effect of interpleader is to confine the total litigation to a single forum and proceeding. One such case is where a stakeholder, faced with rival claims to the fund itself, acknowledges—or denies—his liability to one or the other of the claimants. In this situation, the fund itself is the target of the claimants. It marks the outer limits of the controversy. It is, therefore, reasonable and sensible that interpleader, in discharge of its office to protect the fund, should also protect the stakeholder from vexations and multiple litigation. In this context, the suits sought to be enjoined are squarely within the language of 28 U.S.C. § 2361, which provides in part:

> "In any civil action of interpleader or in the nature of interpleader under section 1335 of this title, a district court may issue its process for all claimants and enter its order restraining them from instituting or prosecuting *any proceeding* in any State or United States court *affecting the property, instrument or obligation involved in the interpleader action* . . . ." (Emphasis added.)

But the present case is another matter. Here, an accident has happened. Thirty-five passengers or their representatives have claims which they wish to press against a variety of defendants: the bus company, its driver, the owner of the truck, and the truck driver. The circumstance that one of the prospective defendants happens to have an insurance policy is a fortuitous event which should not of itself shape the nature of the ensuing litigation. For example, a resident of California, injured in California aboard a bus owned by a California corporation should not be forced to sue that corporation anywhere but in California simply because another prospective defendant carried an insurance policy. And an insurance company whose maximum interest in the case cannot exceed $20,000 and who in fact asserts that it has no interest at all, should not be allowed to determine that dozens of tort plaintiffs must be compelled to press their claims—even those claims which are not against the insured and which in no event could be satisfied out of the meager insurance fund—in a single forum of the insurance company's choosing. There is nothing in the statutory scheme, and very little in the judicial and academic commentary upon that scheme, which requires that the tail be allowed to wag the dog in this fashion.

State Farm's interest in this case, which is the fulcrum of the interpleader procedure, is confined to its $20,000 fund. That interest receives full vindication when the court restrains claimants from seeking to enforce against the insurance company any judgment obtained against its insured, except in the interpleader proceeding itself. To the extent that the District Court sought to control claimants' lawsuits against the insured and other alleged tortfeasors, it exceeded the powers granted to it by the statutory scheme.

We recognize, of course, that our view of interpleader means that it cannot be used to solve all the vexing problems of multiparty litigation arising out of a mass tort. But interpleader was never intended to perform such a function, to be an all-purpose "bill of peace." Had it been so intended, careful provision would necessarily have been made to insure that a party with little or no interest in the outcome of a complex controversy should not strip truly interested parties of substantial rights— such as the right to choose the forum in which to establish their claims, subject to generally applicable rules of jurisdiction, venue, service of process, removal, and change of venue. None of the legislative and academic sponsors of a modern federal interpleader device viewed their accomplishment as a "bill of peace," capable of sweeping dozens of lawsuits out of the various state and federal courts in which they were brought and into a single interpleader proceeding. . . .

In light of the evidence that federal interpleader was not intended to serve the function of a "bill of peace" in the context of multiparty litigation arising out of a mass tort, of the anomalous power which such a construction of the statute would give the stakeholder, and of the thrust of the statute and the purpose it was intended to serve, we hold that the interpleader statute did not authorize the injunction entered in the present case. Upon remand, the injunction is to be modified consistently with this opinion.

IV.

The judgment of the Court of Appeals is reversed, and the case is remanded to the United States District Court for proceedings consistent with this opinion.

It is so ordered.

■ MR. JUSTICE DOUGLAS, dissenting in part.

While I agree with the Court's view as to "minimal diversity" and that the injunction, if granted, should run only against prosecution of suits against the insurer, I feel that the use which we today allow to be made of the federal interpleader statute, 28 U.S.C. § 1335, is, with all deference, unwarranted. How these litigants are "claimants" to this fund in the statutory sense is indeed a mystery. If they are not "claimants" of the fund, neither are they in the category of those who "are claiming" or who "may claim" to be entitled to it.

. . . . .

Thus under this insurance policy as enforced in California and in Oregon a "claimant" against the insured can become a "claimant" against the insurer only after final judgment against the insured or after a consensual written agreement of the insurer, a litigant, and the insured. Neither of those two events has so far happened.

This construction of the word "claimant" against the fund is borne out, as the Court of Appeals noted, by Rule 22(1) of the Federal Rules of Civil Procedure. That Rule, also based on diversity of citizenship, differs only in the district where the suit may be brought and in the reach of service of process, as the Court points out. But it illuminates the nature of federal interpleader for it provides that only "persons having claims against the plaintiff [insurer] may be joined as defendants and required to interplead."

Can it be that we have two kinds of interpleader statutes as between which an insurance company can choose: one that permits "claimants" against the insurer ("persons having claims against the plaintiff") to be joined and the other that permits "claimants" against the insured to be joined for the benefit of the insurer even though they may never be "claimants" against the insurer? I cannot believe that Congress launched such an irrational scheme.

... Absent a direct-action statute, the victims are not "claimants" against the insurer until their claims against the insured have been reduced to judgment. Understandably, the insurance company wants the best of two worlds. It does not want an action against it until judgment against its insured. But, at the same time, it wants the benefits of an interpleader statute. Congress could of course confer such a benefit. But it is not for this Court to grant dispensations from the effects of the statutory scheme which Congress has erected.

I would construe its words in the normal sense and affirm the Court of Appeals.[32]

———

[32.   See generally Ilsen & Sardell, Interpleader in the Federal Courts, 35 St. John's L.Rev. 1 (1960); 2 Moore's Manual: Federal Practice and Procedure § 14.06 (1998); Wright & Kane, Federal Courts § 74 (6th ed.2002).

The origins of interpleader are in equity. Does this preclude jury trial in such actions? See note 66 in Ross v. Bernhard, 396 U.S. 531 (1970), as reprinted infra p. 950.

In Cory v. White, 457 U.S. 85 (1982), it was held that the Eleventh Amendment protects a state from being required to interplead in a district court.

A divided panel of the Third Circuit has ruled that the federal interpleader statute does not limit the broad equitable discretion historically associated with interpleader relief. In an appropriate case a federal district court may refuse to exercise statutory interpleader jurisdiction and defer to parallel proceedings in state court. The standard for the exercise of this equitable discretion is not the "exceptional circumstances" test of Colorado River Water Conservation District v. United States, 424 U.S. 800 (1976), but rather is analogous to that exercised in declaratory-judgment actions under Wilton v. Seven Falls Co., 515 U.S. 277 (1995), reprinted supra p. 595. See NYLife Distributors, Inc. v. The Adherence Group, Inc., 72 F.3d 371 (3d Cir.1995), certiorari denied 517 U.S. 1209 (1996).

C.   COUNTERCLAIMS AND CROSS-CLAIMS

Moore v. New York Cotton Exchange

Supreme Court of the United States, 1926.
270 U.S. 593, 46 S.Ct. 367, 70 L.Ed. 750.

Appeal from a decree of the Circuit Court of Appeals which on interlocutory appeal sustained orders of the District Court (291 F. 681) refusing an interlocutory injunction to the plaintiff and granting one for a defendant on a counterclaim, and which directed a final decree dismissing the bill and making the injunction permanent. The suit was based on the Sherman Law and primarily concerned the validity of a contract between the New York Cotton Exchange and the Western Union Telegraph Company for the distribution of quotations of that exchange to such persons only as received its approval.

. . . . .

■ MR. JUSTICE SUTHERLAND delivered the opinion of the Court.

The Odd–Lot Cotton Exchange is an organization whose members make contracts for themselves and for customers for the future delivery of cotton in lots of not more than 100 nor less than 10 bales. The members of the New York Cotton Exchange, which is organized under a special act of the New York Legislature, c. 365, Laws 1871, p. 724, also make contracts for the purchase and sale of cotton for future delivery, either for themselves or for customers; such contracts being made only upon open *viva voce* bidding, between certain hours of the day and in the rooms of the exchange in New York City. Quotations of prices thus established are collected by the New York exchange, and, under the terms of a written agreement with that exchange, the Western Union company pays $27,500 annually for the privilege of receiving and distributing them throughout the United States, to such persons as the exchange approves. Applicants for such quotations must sign an application and agree not to use them in connection with a bucket shop or to give them out to other persons. The Gold & Stock Telegraph Company, a New York corporation and a subsidiary of, and controlled by, the Western Union, is engaged in disseminating quotations of cotton prices by means of ticker service, owned and operated by it, tickers being located in exchanges, brokerage houses and elsewhere in the several states. The Odd–Lot exchange made application to the two telegraph companies for this service in the form required by the contract with the New York exchange. It was refused, the New York exchange having declined to give its consent to the installation on the ground, among others, that, after investigation, it had ascertained that the Odd–Lot had succeeded another exchange which had been convicted of conducting a bucket shop

See Doernberg, What's Wrong with This Picture?: Rule Interpleader, the Anti–Injunction Act, In Personam Jurisdiction, and M.C. Escher, 67 U.Colo.L.Rev. 551 (1996), described supra p. 479, n. 9.]

and that the Odd–Lot had in its membership many members of the convicted exchange and was organized as a cover to enable its members to engage in the same unlawful business.

Federal jurisdiction is invoked under the anti-trust laws of the United States. The bill avers that the contracts between members of the Odd–Lot are chiefly for producers of cotton and others located, resident and in business in other states than New York, and are made and effectuated by communications through the Western Union by wire; that such contracts concern and include deliveries of cotton from cotton-growing states to and into the State of New York, involving actual interstate shipment and transportation; that the New York exchange has a monopoly upon the receipt and dissemination of cotton price quotations, through which quotations and prices of cotton, both spot and for future delivery are influenced, guided and fixed in the exchanges and markets throughout the United States; that the contract with the Western Union is in restraint of interstate trade and commerce in cotton and was entered into for the purpose of monopolizing and restraining that commerce. There is an attempt to allege unfair methods of competition, which may be put aside at once, since relief in such cases under the Trade Commission Act must be afforded in the first instance by the commission.

The prayer is for a decree cancelling the Western Union contract, adjudging the New York Cotton Exchange to be a monopoly, restraining appellees from refusing to install a ticker and furnish the Odd–Lot and its members, as they do others, with continuous cotton quotations, and for other relief.

The answer, in addition to denials and affirmative defensive matter, sets up a counterclaim to the effect that the Odd–Lot, though it had been refused permission to use the quotations of the New York exchange, was purloining them, or receiving them from some person who was purloining them, and giving them out to its members, who were distributing them to bucket shops, with the consequent impairment of the value of appellees' property therein. An injunction against the continuance of this practice was asked.

Both parties moved for interlocutory injunctions. The district court denied appellant's motion and granted that of appellees. 291 F. 681. Upon appeal, both orders were affirmed by the court of appeals. 296 F. 61. By stipulation of the parties authorizing such action, the court of appeals remanded the cause with directions to the district court to enter a final decree dismissing the bill and making permanent the injunction granted appellees. Since this left to the district court only the ministerial duty of complying with the mandate, the decree below, for purposes of appeal, is final. Gulf Refining Co. v. United States, 269 U.S. 125, 136.

First. We are of opinion that upon the allegations of the bill no case is made under the federal anti-trust laws. . . .

. . . . .

Second. The decree granting an injunction upon the counterclaim is challenged on the grounds, shortly stated: (1) that the court, having dismissed the bill for lack of jurisdictional facts, should have dismissed the counterclaim also, there being no independent basis of jurisdiction; (2) that the counterclaim does not arise out of any transaction which is the subject-matter of the suit; and (3) that the decree is not justified by the allegations of the counterclaim or the proof.

1. We do not understand that the dismissal was for the reason that there was an absence of jurisdiction to entertain the bill. What the court held was that the facts alleged were insufficient to establish a case under the Anti–Trust Act.

. . . . .

We think there is enough in the bill to call for the exercise of the jurisdiction of a federal court to decide, upon the merits, the issue of the legal sufficiency of the allegations to make out the claim of federal right. This was evidently the view of the court below, and we construe its mandate as a direction to dismiss the bill on the merits and not for want of jurisdiction.

2. Equity Rule 30 in part provides:

"The answer must state in short and simple form any counterclaim arising out of the transaction which is the subject matter of the suit, and may, without cross-bill, set up any set-off or counterclaim against the plaintiff which might be subject of an independent suit in equity against him, and such set-off or counterclaim, so set up, shall have the same effect as a cross-suit, so as to enable the court to pronounce a final decree in the same suit on both the original and the cross-claims."

Two classes of counterclaims thus are provided for: (a) one "arising out of the transaction which is the subject matter of the suit," which must be pleaded, and (b) another "which might be the subject of an independent suit in equity" and which may be brought forward at the option of the defendant. We are of opinion that this counterclaim comes within the first branch of the rule; and we need not consider the point that, under the second branch, federal jurisdiction independent of the original bill must appear, as was held in Cleveland Engineering Co. v. Galion D.M. Truck Co., D.C.Ohio, 243 F. 405, 407.

The bill sets forth the contract with the Western Union and the refusal of the New York exchange to allow appellant to receive the continuous cotton quotations, and asks a mandatory injunction to compel appellees to furnish them. The answer admits the refusal and justifies it. The counter-claim sets up that, nevertheless, appellant is purloining or otherwise illegally obtaining them, and asks that this practice be enjoined. "Transaction" is a word of flexible meaning. It may comprehend a series of many occurrences, depending not so much upon the immediateness of their connection as upon their logical relationship. The refusal to furnish the quotations is one of the links in the chain which constitutes the transaction upon which appellant here bases its cause of action. It is an important part of the transaction constituting the subject-matter of the counterclaim. It is the one circumstance without which neither party would have found it necessary to seek relief. Essential facts alleged by appellant enter into and constitute in part the cause of action set forth in the counterclaim. That they are not precisely identical, or that the counterclaim embraces additional allegations, as, for example, that appellant is unlawfully getting the quotations, does not matter. To hold otherwise would be to rob this branch of the rule of all serviceable meaning, since the facts relied upon by the plaintiff rarely, if ever, are, in all particulars, the same as those constituting the defendant's counterclaim. Compare The Xenia Branch Bank v. Lee, 15 N.Y.Super.Ct. 694, 7 Abb.Pr. 372, 390–394. And see generally, *Cleveland Engineering Co. v. Galion D.M. Truck Co.*, supra, p. 408; Champion Spark Plug Co. v. Champion Ignition Co., D.C.Mich., 247 F. 200, 203–205.

So close is the connection between the case sought to be stated in the bill and that set up in the counterclaim, that it only needs the failure of the former to establish a foundation for the latter; but the relief afforded by the dismissal of the bill is not complete without an injunction restraining appellant from continuing to obtain by stealthy appropriation what the court had held it could not have by judicial compulsion.

. . . . .

Decree affirmed.[33]

Scott v. Fancher

United States Court of Appeals, Fifth Circuit, 1966.
369 F.2d 842.

■ Before TUTTLE, CHIEF JUDGE, and JONES and GEWIN, CIRCUIT JUDGES.

■ GEWIN, CIRCUIT JUDGE:

This personal injury case arose out of a three truck collision involving trucks operated by William C. Fancher, a Texas resident, Ray Scott, an

---

[33.   See Comment, Narrowing the Scope of Rule 13(a), 60 U.Chi.L.Rev. 141 (1993).

The conceptual overlap of counterclaims and defenses is discussed in Reiter v. Cooper, 507 U.S. 258 (1993).

Suppose a claim could be but is not advanced as a compulsory counterclaim in a federal action. Is such claim barred in a state court? See London v. City of Philadelphia, 412 Pa. 496, 194 A.2d 901 (1963); Jocie Motor Lines, Inc. v. Johnson, 231 N.C. 367, 57 S.E.2d 388 (1950); Conrad v. West, 98 Cal.App.2d 116, 219 P.2d 477 (1950); Wright, Estoppel By Rule: The Compulsory Counterclaims Under Modern Pleading, 38 Minn.L.Rev. 423, 436 (1954); Note, 15 U.Chi.L.Rev. 446 (1948). Compare Phoenix Ins. Co. v. Haney, 235 Miss. 60, 108 So.2d 227 (1959).

It is held, however, in Chapman v. Aetna Finance Co., 615 F.2d 361 (5th Cir.1980), that full faith and credit does not require a federal court to honor the fact that a claim would be barred in state court by failure to assert it as a counterclaim in a state-court action under the state compulsory-counterclaim rule. Nevertheless the court said that as a matter of comity the federal court could refuse to hear a claim when to do so would derogate the policies of both the state and federal compulsory-counterclaim rules. Failure to raise the claim in the state action was held to bar a federal suit in Springs v. First Nat. Bank of Cut Bank, 835 F.2d 1293 (9th Cir.1988).

In a suit against a lender under the Truth-in-Lending Act for failure to make required disclosures, is the lender's claim for the underlying debt a compulsory counterclaim? Compare Plant v. Blazer Financial Services, Inc. of Georgia, 598 F.2d 1357 (5th Cir.1979), with Valencia v. Anderson Bros. Ford, 617 F.2d 1278 (7th Cir.1980), reversed on other grounds 452 U.S. 205 (1981).]

Oklahoma resident, and E.F. Short, an Oklahoma resident. The collision took place in Texas. The truck driven by Fancher was traveling north on U.S. Highway 287 and the two Oklahoma trucks were traveling south. The truck driven by Fancher was owned by American Petro–Fina Company of Texas (Petro–Fina), a corporation organized under the laws of Texas. As a result of a head-on collision between the Petro–Fina truck and the Scott truck, the Petro–Fina truck turned on its side, slid across the highway and collided with the truck driven by Short which had been traveling some distance behind and in the same direction as the Scott truck. Fancher was seriously injured and Short was killed in the accident. Scott suffered only mild injuries. The administrator of Short's estate brought suit against Fancher, Petro–Fina, and Scott in an Oklahoma state court. Service of process was not perfected on Fancher in the Oklahoma state court action. Petro–Fina and Fancher filed this suit in the United States District Court for the Northern District of Texas alleging negligence on the part of both Scott and Short. Scott counterclaimed against Petro–Fina and Fancher, and the administrator of Short's estate filed a counterclaim against Petro–Fina and Fancher and a cross-claim against Scott. Jurisdiction was based on diversity of citizenship. The jury absolved Fancher, Petro–Fina, and Short of liability and returned a verdict against Scott. Judgment was entered against Scott in accordance with the verdict. Scott appeals from that judgment alleging that the district court was without jurisdiction as to both the original action and the cross-claim by Short's administrator against Scott, because the requisite diversity of citizenship was lacking; and further, that the testimony of one of his witnesses, presented as an expert, should have been admitted.

Scott asserts that a proper alignment of the parties would cast Scott and Short as opposing parties because under no theory of the facts could Short have been found at fault. Thus, he concludes, the district court was without jurisdiction because Short and Scott are both Oklahoma residents. Re-alignment of the parties is to be accomplished on the basis of the facts available at the commencement of the action. Petro–Fina and Fancher had charged both Scott and Short with negligence and at that time it could not be said that the allegations were baseless. Accordingly, no re-alignment was required. Texas Pac. Coal & Oil Co. v. Mayfield, 152 F.2d 956 (5 Cir.1946).

We also reject Scott's contention that Short's cross-claim against Scott was not ancillary to the original suit and therefore required an independent jurisdictional base. Short's cross-claim arose out of the same transaction and involved the same parties as did the original action. In such cases jurisdiction rests with the primary suit. Childress v. Cook, 245 F.2d 798 (5 Cir.1957); Collier v. Harvey, 179 F.2d 664 (10 Cir.1949).

Scott further argues that since there was an action pending in the Oklahoma state courts, Short's action in the federal court against Fancher, Petro–Fina and Scott was a permissive counterclaim rather than a compulsory one. He bases his argument on the language of Rule 13(a) which provides that claims arising out of the same transaction or occurrence "need not be so stated if at the time the action was commenced the claim was the subject of another pending action." Fed.R.Civ.P. 13(a). This language, he asserts, converts the counterclaim into a permissive one and requires that an independent jurisdictional base exist.[34] It is argued that

---

[34. The rule that an independent jurisdictional basis is required for a permissive counterclaim is well-settled in the cases but is criticized in Green, Federal Jurisdiction over Counterclaims, 48 Nw.U.L.Rev. 271 (1953). The rule is subject to one limited exception, however: "no independent jurisdictional grounds are required for a permissive counterclaim if it is the nature of a set-off and is used to reduce a plaintiff's judgment rather than as a basis for affirmative relief." Wright & Kane, Federal Courts, § 79, at 576 (6th ed.2002).

In a concurring opinion in U.S. for Use of D'Agostino Excavators, Inc. v. Heyward–Robinson Co., Inc., 430 F.2d 1077, 1088 (2d Cir.1970), Judge Friendly said that he "would now reject the conventional learning" and would hold that a permissive counterclaim does not require independent jurisdictional grounds.

In Ambromovage v. United Mine Workers of America, 726 F.2d 972, 990 (3d Cir.1984), the court concluded that "the determination that a counterclaim is permissive within the meaning of Rule 13 is not dispositive of the constitutional question whether there is federal jurisdiction over that counterclaim." In the case before it the court held that ancillary jurisdiction extended to a permissive counterclaim. But the traditional rule that a permissive counterclaim requires an independent jurisdictional basis is reaffirmed in East–Bibb Twiggs Neighborhood Ass'n v. Macon Bibb Planning & Zoning Com'n, 888 F.2d 1576 (11th Cir.1989). Has the traditional rule been changed by the 1990 statute on supplemental jurisdiction? See 28 U.S.C. § 1367(a), (b), reprinted supra p. 877.

The traditional view, that independent jurisdictional grounds are required for a permissive counterclaim, is applied in Frumkin v. International Business Machines Corp., 801 F.Supp. 1029, 1044 (S.D.N.Y.1992), and in Shamblin v. City of Colchester, 793 F.Supp. 831 (C.D.Ill.1992).

In Channell v. Citicorp National Services, Inc., 89 F.3d 379, 384–387 (7th Cir.1996), Judge Easterbrook's opinion for the court concludes that the traditional distinction between permissive and compulsory counterclaims was developed as part of the law of preclusion, and that the jurisdictional significance of this traditional distinction was merely a side-effect of avoiding giving preclusive effect to the failure to join a counterclaim (e.g., a merely "permissive" counterclaim) over which a federal court would have lacked jurisdiction. Given the advent of express statutory authority to exercise supplemental jurisdiction under 28 U.S.C. § 1367(a), the court held that a counterclaim deemed too remote from the main action to be regarded as part of the same "transaction or occurrence," and hence classified as a permissive counterclaim for preclusion purposes, nonetheless had the requisite "loose factual connection" to the main action that suffices under Seventh Circuit precedent to make it part of the same "case or controversy" for statutory supplemental-jurisdiction purposes. Thus, it was error for the trial judge to refuse to adjudicate the permissive counterclaim for lack of supplemental jurisdiction, although it remained open on remand for the judge to decline to exercise that jurisdiction pursuant to the discretionary standards of 28 U.S.C. § 1367(c).

Plaintiff filed a diversity claim that might or might not have been held to exceed $50,000, which was then the required amount in controversy. Defendant filed an answer in which he asserted that the court lacked jurisdiction because the amount in controversy did not exceed $50,000. The answer also contained a compulsory counterclaim for more than a million dollars. In a questionable decision the Third Circuit, 2–1, ruled that jurisdiction existed. "We hold that where, as here, a defendant elects not to file a motion to dismiss for lack of jurisdiction, but answers a complaint by asserting a compulsory counterclaim, the amount of that counterclaim may be considered by the court in determining if the amount in

since Scott and Short are both Oklahoma residents the court was without jurisdiction. We need not determine, however, whether the pendency of an action in another court alters the jurisdictional requirements of counterclaims which would otherwise be compulsory counterclaims because under Rule 13(a) Short counterclaimed only against Petro–Fina and Fancher, both Texas residents.[35] The action against Scott was a cross-claim under Rule 13(g), and since we have held that action to be ancillary to the primary suit, no independent jurisdictional grounds are required. The rule is clearly stated in Wright, Federal Courts, (1963) at p. 307:

> "By definition cross-claims must be closely related to the existing action. Thus they are always treated as within the ancillary jurisdiction of the court, and independent jurisdictional grounds are not required nor can there be any venue objection."

.   .   .   .   .

The judgment is affirmed.[36]

D.   INTERVENTION

Johnson v. San Francisco Unified School District

United States Court of Appeals, Ninth Circuit, 1974.
500 F.2d 349.

■ Before MERRILL, KOELSCH and BROWNING, CIRCUIT JUDGES.

OPINION

■ PER CURIAM:

This litigation was initiated by parents of black children attending public elementary schools in the San Francisco Unified School District.

---

controversy exceeds the statutory requirement for diversity jurisdiction." Spectacor Management Group v. Brown, 131 F.3d 120, 121 (3d Cir.1997).

Defendant's joinder, pursuant to Rule 13(h), of nondiverse parties as defendants to a counterclaim did not destroy complete diversity. The limitations in the supplemental-jurisdiction statute, 28 U.S.C. § 1367(b), reprinted supra p. 877, on the joinder of nondiverse parties expressly apply only to plaintiffs. United Capitol Ins. Co. v. Kapiloff, 155 F.3d 488, 492–493 (4th Cir.1998).]

35. A counterclaim is defined by Rule 13(a) as an action against an opposing party, while a cross-claim under Rule 13(g) is an action against a co-party. Professor Wright has noted that some confusion has resulted in the use of these terms:

> "The courts have not always distinguished clearly between a cross-claim and a counterclaim, and have used one name where the other is proper under the rules, perhaps because in some states, and in the old equity practice, the term cross-complaint or cross-bill is used for what the rules regard as a counterclaim. Under Rule 13 a counterclaim is a claim against an opposing party, while a cross-claim is against a co-party."

[**36.** On cross-claims, see Wright & Kane, Federal Courts § 80 (6th ed.2002).]

They seek desegregation of those schools. The schools of the District have never been subject to a statutorily imposed "dual school system" separating blacks from whites. The plaintiffs contend that acts of de jure segregation have been committed by the School Board with the result that the responsibility fell upon the Board to desegregate the school system. The district court ruled in favor of the plaintiffs upon this issue and called upon the parties to submit plans for accomplishing desegregation. Two plans were submitted, one by the plaintiffs and one by the defendants. Both plans provided for the balancing not only of blacks and whites but of Chinese–Americans and other ethnic groups as well.

Before court hearings on the plans were scheduled to commence, parents of children of Chinese ancestry attending public elementary schools in the district sought leave to intervene. They additionally sought an order shortening time for service of the moving papers so that their application might be ruled upon in time for them to participate in those hearings. The district court refused to shorten time, and the hearings were held without their participation. Thereafter, the district court denied their application to intervene.

The court approved both plans and directed defendants forthwith to carry out desegregation of the elementary schools in the manner provided by one or the other of the two plans. Its findings and judgment are set forth in 339 F.Supp. 1315 (N.D.Cal.1971). Defendants elected to follow the plan which they themselves had submitted. They have been operating under that plan ever since.

I. *De Jure Segregation*

[The court found that the lower court had applied the wrong standard in determining that de jure segregation had existed. It remanded for further consideration of that question while leaving in effect, pending further determination, the desegregation plan the lower court had ordered and under which the schools were currently operating.]

II. *Intervention*

(No. 71–2105)

Parents of elementary school children of Chinese ancestry claim entitlement to intervene as a matter of right under Rule 24(a)(2), F.R.Civ.P. They oppose the compulsory reassignment of such students to schools outside the area in which they reside. Alleging, inter alia, that such reassignment will make it impossible for such children to attend community schools offering education in Chinese language, art, culture and history, they contend, on constitutional and equitable grounds, that they are not properly bound by the court's decree, or that, if they are so bound, they are entitled to participate in the fashioning of that decree.

Rule 24(a)(2) permits timely intervention when the applicant shows: (1) an interest relating to the property or transaction which is the subject of the action;[37] (2) that the disposition of the action may as a practical matter impair or impede his ability to protect that interest; and (3) that the interest is not adequately represented by existing parties.[38]

Appellants claim a sufficient interest in the outcome of the action to satisfy the first requirement of the rule. In Smuck v. Hobson, 408 F.2d 175, 180 (D.C.Cir.1969), the District of Columbia Court of Appeals, sitting in banc, concluded that the "concern [of parents seeking intervention in a desegregation suit] for their children's welfare" was sufficient under the circumstances to satisfy that requirement.[39] We adopted the general rationale of *Smuck* in Spangler v. Pasadena City Board of Education, 427 F.2d 1352, 1353 (9th Cir.1970), but there we reached a different result because the third requirement of the rule was not satisfied. Moreover, other courts have recognized that, for purposes of Rule 24(a)(2), all students and parents, whatever their race, have an interest in a sound educational system and in the operation of that system in accordance with the law. That interest is surely no less significant where, as here, it is entangled with the constitutional claims of a racially defined class.

The second requirement of the rule, that the applicant be "so situated that the disposition of the action may as a practical matter impair or impede his ability to protect that interest," is similarly satisfied. It is true that here the denial of intervention may leave appellants the practical alternative of asserting in a subsequent lawsuit that the new policies adopted by the school district are unconstitutional. However, appellants additionally seek to influence the manner in which the school district exercises its admitted discretion in formulating and implementing such policies. The denial of intervention may eliminate appellants' opportunity to challenge new policies which, although they may not be constitutionally required, are nevertheless constitutionally permissible. See *Smuck,* supra,

---

[37. In Donaldson v. United States, 400 U.S. 517, 531 (1971), the Court said that when the rule speaks of "an interest" that "[w]hat is obviously meant there is a significantly protectable interest."]

[38. The third element in Rule 24(a)(2) is "unless the applicant's interest is adequately represented by existing parties." Is there any significant difference between what the rule says and the court's paraphrase of it?]

39. The *Smuck* court looked to the policies underlying the rule, observing as follows at 179–180:

"The goal of 'disposing of lawsuits by involving as many apparently concerned persons as is compatible with efficiency and due process' may in certain circumstances be met by allowing parents whose only 'interest' is the education of their children to intervene. In determining whether such circumstances are present, the first requirement of Rule 24(a)(2), that of an 'interest' in the transaction, may be a less useful point of departure than the second and third requirements, that the applicant may be impeded in protecting his interest by the action and that his interest is not adequately represented by others.

"This does not imply that the need for an 'interest' in the controversy should or can be read out of the rule. But the requirement should be viewed as a prerequisite rather than relied upon as a determinative criterion for intervention. If barriers are needed to limit extension of the right to intervene, the criteria of practical harm to the applicant and the adequacy of representation by others are better suited to the task."

408 F.2d, at 180–181. Moreover, the actual outcome in the court below—the approval of plans balancing the very class appellants claim to represent—demonstrates that their interest may indeed be affected.

The third requirement for intervention of right is that the applicant's interest not be "adequately represented by existing parties." The district court found that "[t]he vague and conclusory allegations of the complaint in intervention are insufficient to overcome the presumption that government officials are adequately representing the interests of all citizens."

The factual situation before us bears a similarity to that in Trbovich v. United Mine Workers of America, 404 U.S. 528 (1972), in which the Supreme Court held that there was sufficient doubt about the adequacy of representation of a complaining union member by the Secretary of Labor in a suit to set aside an election of union officials to warrant the union member's intervention of right.[40] Here we cannot agree with the district court's conclusion that the school district, which is charged with the representation of all parents within the district and which authored the very plan which appellants claim impairs their interest, adequately represents appellants. Nor do we agree with appellee's contention that the other intervenors in the action, a group of racially mixed parents, adequately represent appellants' distinct viewpoint.

The remaining question is whether appellants' application was timely made within the meaning of Rule 24(a)(2).[41] Here, where appellants filed their application eleven days after the proposed plans were filed, but prior to entry of the court's ultimate decree, the district court ruled "that to allow intervention at this juncture would unduly delay and prejudice the

---

40. The Court observed at 538–539:

"The statute [29 U.S.C. § 482(b)] plainly imposes on the Secretary the duty to serve two distinct interests, which are related, but not identical. First, the statute gives the individual union members certain rights against their union, and 'the Secretary of Labor in Effect becomes the union member's lawyer' for purposes of enforcing those rights. [Citation omitted.] And, second, the Secretary has an obligation to protect the 'vital public interest in assuring free and democratic union elections that transcends the narrower interest of the complaining union member.' [Citation omitted.] Both functions are important, and they may not always dictate precisely the same approach to the conduct of the litigation. Even if the Secretary is performing his duties, broadly conceived, as well as can be expected, the union member may have a valid complaint about the performance of 'his lawyer.' Such a complaint, filed by the member who initiated the entire enforcement proceeding, should be regarded as sufficient to warrant relief in the form of intervention under Rule 24(a)(2)."

The Court also observed at 538 n. 10:

"The requirement of the Rule [24(a)(2)] is satisfied if the applicant shows that representation of his interest 'may be' inadequate; and the burden of making that showing should be treated as minimal. See 3B J. Moore, Federal Practice § 24.09–1[4] (1969)."

41. If the application was untimely, intervention must be denied. N.A.A.C.P. v. New York, 413 U.S. 345, 346 (1973). Moreover, the question of "timeliness" is a matter for the discretion of the trial court and is to be determined from all the circumstances of the case. Id., at 365–366; see also Tesseyman v. Fisher, 231 F.2d 583, 584 (9th Cir.1955); Pellegrino v. Nesbit, 203 F.2d 463, 465–466 (9th Cir.1953).

rights of the original parties." Despite some authority to the contrary,[42] we ordinarily might well conclude, on the facts before us, that the district court acted within its discretion in denying the application as "untimely." However, our disposition today of the related appeals—vacating and remanding the main case below for reconsideration while leaving the injunction in force—substantially reduces any prejudice to the rights of the original parties and thus undercuts the basis of the district court's ruling.

On the peculiar circumstances of this case and in view of our disposition of the related appeals, No. 71–2105 is vacated and remanded with instructions to permit appellants to intervene in accordance with the views here expressed.

. . . . .[43]

———

Wodecki v. Nationwide Ins. Co.

United States District Court, W.D. Pennsylvania, 1985.
107 F.R.D. 118.

■ GERALD J. WEBER, DISTRICT JUDGE.

In this action to recover health insurance benefits from defendant, Nationwide Insurance, plaintiff received a jury verdict in the amount of $8,200. Following the entry of judgment, this court permitted Hamot Medical Center to file a claim for intervention in an order dated March 15,

---

42. In Cascade Natural Gas Co. v. El Paso Natural Gas Co., 386 U.S. 129 (1967), the Supreme Court, without discussing timeliness, permitted Cascade, after entry of a consent judgment, to intervene of right in additional proceedings involving the formulation of a divestiture decree. The Court noted that Rule 24(a)(2) "applies to 'further proceedings' in pending actions." 386 U.S., at 135–136. Similarly, in Hodgson v. United Mine Workers of America, 473 F.2d 118 (D.C.Cir.1972), the court, citing Cascade, observed at 129:

> "Timeliness presents no automatic barrier to intervention in postjudgment proceedings where substantial problems in formulating relief remain to be resolved."

Other courts, however, have refused to treat Cascade as a "carte blanche" for intervention, or accept it as applying except to an extraordinary fact situation. See, e.g., United States v. Blue Chip Stamp Co., 272 F.Supp. 432, 435–436 (C.D.Cal.1967), aff'd, Thrifty Shoppers Scrip Co. v. United States, 389 U.S. 580 (1968); Spangler v. Pasadena City Board of Education, 427 F.2d 1352, 1354 n. 3 (9th Cir.1970), and cases cited therein.

[**43.** See Wright & Kane, Federal Courts § 75 (6th ed.2002); Gardner, Comment, An Attempt to Intervene in the Confusion: Standing Requirements for Rule 24 Intervenors, 69 U.Chi. L.Rev. 681 (2002); Tobias, Standing to Intervene, 1991 Wis.L.Rev. 415; Shreve, Questioning Intervention of Right—Toward a New Methodology of Decisionmaking, 74 Nw.U.L.Rev. 894 (1980); Brunet, A Study in the Allocation of Scarce Judicial Resources: The Efficiency of Federal Intervention Criteria, 12 Ga.L.Rev. 701 (1978).

Is intervention within 30 days after entry of judgment timely by a member of a putative class who wishes to appeal the denial of class certification when the named plaintiff does not intend to appeal? See United Airlines, Inc. v. McDonald, 432 U.S. 385 (1977).

An order denying intervention of right and allowing permissive intervention only under certain conditions is not immediately appealable. Stringfellow v. Concerned Neighbors in Action, 480 U.S. 370 (1987).]

1985. Plaintiff now moves to dismiss Hamot's claim of intervention. Both parties have supplied the court with briefs in support of their respective positions.

Plaintiff first argues that this court lacks subject matter jurisdiction over Hamot's claim for intervention because:

a) the underlying action against Nationwide has been terminated and satisfied of record on March 27, 1985, and

b) Hamot's claim for intervention does not have an independent jurisdictional basis since the parties are not diverse and the amount in controversy does not exceed $10,000.

... Rule 24[(a)] is entitled "Intervention of Right." Although the rule is silent as to jurisdictional requirements, case law supports the conclusion that no independent grounds of jurisdiction are necessary where the court has jurisdiction over the main case and the intervention is of right rather than permissive. Finance Company of America v. Park Holding Corporation, 60 F.R.D. 504 (W.D.Pa.1973); Jet Traders Investment Corp. v. Tekair, Ltd., 89 F.R.D. 560 (D.Del.1981). In intervention of right cases, the court has ancillary jurisdiction over the intervention claim. In permissive intervention situations under Fed.R.Civ.P. 24(b), the court requires independent jurisdictional grounds.

Hamot claims that it is intervening as of right under Fed.R.Civ.P. 24(a)(2) since the disposition of the judgment monies currently in the possession of the court would as a practical matter negate its ability to protect its interest in these monies, and since Hamot's interests are not represented by either of the parties to this suit. Hamot's interest in the "property" or judgment monies is based on its claim of a contractual assignment of any insurance benefits which Mrs. Wodecki, plaintiff, would recover in this action. Hamot recites facts which make obvious Hamot's concern that disposition of the monies in this action by the court could affect Hamot's ability to satisfy any other judgment which Hamot might later achieve against Mrs. Wodecki.

This court has earlier held that the possible inability to satisfy a judgment not yet rendered does not of itself establish a sufficient nexus to support the exercise of ancillary jurisdiction over a claim of intervention. *Finance Company of America,* supra, at 506. Hamot argues that a sufficient nexus exists in this case between Hamot's claim of intervention and Mrs. Wodecki's claim against Nationwide "since Mrs. Wodecki's suit arises out of her admission to Hamot ... [and] Hamot is simply seeking to recover for this admission." Hamot's Brief at 7.

We do not agree with Hamot's characterization of the two claims. Rather the disposition of Mrs. Wodecki's case depended on the terms of her contract with Nationwide. Her admission to a hospital and resulting medical costs were merely conditions precedent which triggered Nationwide's duty to perform under that contract. Hamot's claim for hospital costs and expenses arises inter alia from a subsequent agreement with Mrs. Wodecki assigning health care benefits to Hamot. The fact that Mrs.

Wodecki's inpatient hospitalization costs were a necessary item of proof of damages in this case, as well as in Hamot's state court claim, while possibly sufficient to support permissive intervention under Fed.R.Civ.P. 24(b)(2), if timely filed, do not provide a sufficient nexus to establish intervention of right. Hamot may more expeditiously complete the litigation of its claims in the pending state action.

Since permissive intervention under Fed.R.Civ.P. 24(b)(2) requires independent grounds for jurisdiction which do not exist on Hamot's claim, plaintiff's motion to dismiss Hamot's intervention claim will be granted.[44]

E.   CLASS ACTIONS

McLaughlin v. Liberty Mutual Ins. Co.

United States District Court, District of Massachusetts, 2004.
224 F.R.D. 304.

■ KEETON, SENIOR DISTRICT JUDGE.

I.

At the hearing on October 7, 2004, the court heard arguments on Plaintiffs' motion to certify a class. . . .

II.

This is a civil action brought by two persons who were employed by the defendant Liberty Mutual Insurance Company as Auto Damage Appraisers.

[44. Have the traditional rules, stated in the principal case, on when an independent jurisdictional basis is or is not required for claims by or against an intervenor, survived the 1990 supplemental jurisdiction statute? See 28 U.S.C. § 1367(a), (b), reprinted supra p. 877.

"The vague phrasing of section 1367(b) could also, but need not, be construed to go beyond pre-existing law in limiting the availability of ancillary jurisdiction over nondiverse parties seeking to intervene as of right as plaintiffs to protect their interests in federal litigation brought by others. The House committee report [reprinted supra p. 878] suggests an ill-conceived intent to ward off an imagined threat to the rule of complete diversity. It would be unfortunate if section 1367's overall policy of encouraging efficient joinder and consistent adjudication were thwarted by a construction of section 1367(b) that ruled out supplemental jurisdiction over a nondiverse intervenor in a diversity action whose interest in the action qualifies the intervenor as merely a Rule 19(a) 'necessary' party but not as a Rule 19(b) 'indispensable' party. Intervention of right by such a party has traditionally avoided prejudice to the intervenor from an action destined to continue whether or not intervention is permitted." Oakley, Recent Statutory Changes in the Law of Federal Jurisdiction and Venue: The Judicial Improvements Acts of 1988 and 1990, 24 U.C.Davis L.Rev. 735, 765–766 (1991). The treatment of this "anomaly" in the 1990 statute is sharply debated in the articles by Rowe, Burbank, and Mengler and the articles by Arthur and Freer cited supra pp. 286–287]

Plaintiffs allege that they are owed overtime pay and seek to recover that pay under the Fair Labor Standards Act, 29 U.S.C. §§ 207 et seq. ("FLSA"), and under Massachusetts law. The claim under the FLSA has been aggregated with that of other employees of Liberty Mutual using the opt-in provision under federal law. Plaintiffs now seek to aggregate their Massachusetts law claim by certifying a class action under Fed.R.Civ.P. 23(b)(3).

Plaintiffs propose a class defined as follows:

All persons who were employed by Defendant as Auto Damage Apprais- ers in the Commonwealth of Massachusetts between February 19, 2001 and the date of entry of final judgment in this action.

The requirements for certifying a class are set forth in Federal Rule of Civil Procedure 23. If the four requirements of Rule 23(a) are met, then the court must decide whether the action fits within one of the three categories in Rule 23(b). The defendant challenges the class certification on two grounds: (1) that numerosity has not been satisfied and (2) that a class action is not superior to other available methods. Even though the defen- dant does not challenge the other requirements of Rule 23, "[a] district court must conduct a rigorous analysis of the prerequisites established by Rule 23 before certifying a class." Smilow v. Southwestern Bell Mobile Sys., Inc., 323 F.3d 32, 38 (1st Cir.2003) (citing General Telephone Co. of Southwest v. Falcon, 457 U.S. 147, 161 (1982)). Accordingly, I turn first to the requirements of Rule 23(a).

III.

A.   Rule 23(a) Requirements

Section (a) of Rule 23 requires that a class meet the following criteria:

(1) the class is so numerous that joinder of all members is impractica- ble,

(2) there are questions of law or fact common to the class,

(3) the claims or defenses of the representative parties are typical of the claims or defenses of the class, and

(4) the representative parties will fairly and adequately protect the interests of the class.

I address these requirements in turn.

1.   Numerosity or Impracticability

The first requirement of Rule 23(a)(1) is often referred to as "numer- osity," but it might more properly be called the "impracticability" require- ment, because the inquiry called for by Rule 23(a)(1) often involves more than merely counting noses. See Andrews v. Bechtel Power Corp., 780 F.2d 124, 131 (1st Cir.1985); see generally 7A Charles Alan Wright, Arthur R. Miller, & Mary Kay Kane, Federal Practice & Procedure § 1762 (2004). Indeed, in this case, both parties urge the court to look beyond the numbers. The first step in the inquiry under Rule 23(a)(1) is, however, assessing the size of the putative class. In this case, plaintiffs have identified 51 likely class members, and defendant does not dispute this tally. Other courts in this district have noted that a 40 person class is "generally found to establish numerosity." In re Relafen Antitrust Litigation, 218 F.R.D. 337, 342 (D.Mass.2003) (Young, J.) (citing McAdams v. Massachusetts Mut. Life Ins. Co., 2002 WL 1067449, at (D.Mass.2002) (Freedman, J.)). Finding that the class size here is slightly above the critical mass of 40, I will consider whether there are any contravening factors militating against class certification, noting that, in some cases, courts have decided to certify a class with fewer than 51 members. See 7A Wright, Miller & Kane § 1762 nn. 38–40 (collecting cases). In other cases, courts have decided not to certify a class with more than 51 members. See id. § 1762 nn. 35–36 (collecting cases).

Defendant argues first that a class action should not be certified because the 51 putative class members could have opted in to the FLSA action, but only 13 affirmatively did so. Hence, according to the defendant, the adjusters have already voted with their feet against a class action, and those who want to take part can do so through joinder. Plaintiffs have cited several cases in which an opt-out state claim has been permitted to proceed in parallel to an opt-in FLSA action. See, e.g., Ladegaard v. Hard Rock Concrete Cutters, Inc., 2000 WL 1774091 (N.D.Ill.Dec.1, 2000); Beltran–Benitez v. Sea Safari, Ltd., 180 F.Supp.2d 772 (E.D.N.C.2001). These cases were primarily concerned with whether the opt-out provision of Rule 23(b)(3) and opt-in provision of the FLSA are incompatible, and both cases concluded that they are not. See *Ladegaard*, 2000 WL 1774091, at *7; *Beltran-Benitez,* 180 F.Supp.2d, at 774. Most of the cases cited by the plaintiffs were at a stage in the proceedings before it could have been known whether the class members would opt in or not. The question before this court, however, is whether the court should decline to certify the class given that few class members have opted in to a factually similar claim under the FLSA. The only case cited by plaintiffs that addresses this question concludes that such a class should be certified. See Scott v. Aetna Services, Inc., 210 F.R.D. 261, 267 (D.Conn.2002) (certifying a class where only 22 employees had opted in out of 281 potential class members).

This question must be answered within the analytical framework provided by Fed.R.Civ.P. 23. At this point, I will consider whether this fact implies that the class is not "so numerous that joinder of all members is impracticable." Fed.R.Civ.P. 23(a)(1). At the outset, it should be noted that membership in the proposed class is independent of whether the FLSA action is joined. As other courts have noted, the FLSA action and state law remedies are entirely separate rights that may be pursued by the plaintiffs. See O'Brien v. Encotech Construction Services, Inc., 203 F.R.D. 346, 352 (N.D.Ill.2001). Thus, an employee's failure to opt in to the FLSA litigation should not deprive them of their right to pursue a state law remedy through a single class action. By enacting an opt-in regime for the FLSA, Congress sought to limit the scope of collective actions under federal law. See De Asencio v. Tyson Foods, Inc., 342 F.3d 301, 306 (3d Cir.2003) (describing the concern of Congress over increasing litigation due to an expansive interpretation of liability under FLSA by the Supreme Court). I should not, however, infer from that restriction on *federal* remedies a concomitant restriction on *state* remedies. Nothing in the statute limits available remedies under state law. See 29 U.S.C. § 216(b) (creating the opt-in class action mechanism for FLSA). Nor should I infer from an employee's election not to pursue a federal remedy a forfeiture of that employee's right to pursue a state remedy. Requiring the employees who have not opted in to the FLSA claim to pursue duplicative litigation in state court would be a waste of judicial resources and would increase litigation costs for the parties, perhaps prohibitively so for the remaining putative class members. Thus, the class should be considered to include all 51 employees, and not just the 13 that have joined the FLSA action.

Defendant also argues that the geographic proximity and identifiability of the class members make joinder practicable. In *Andrews,* 780 F.2d, at 132, the Court of Appeals for the First Circuit found no abuse of discretion where the district court denied class certification for numerosity reasons; in that case the plaintiffs "came from the same small geographic area—all living in southeastern Massachusetts." The defendant points out that the putative class members are all identified, and all work at one of three offices in Massachusetts: Danvers, Hingham, or Westborough, all of which lie within a 35–mile radius of this court. The plaintiffs argue that their residence is the more relevant point of reference for geographic concentration because many employees work out of their homes; the employees reside in towns spread throughout the state: Windsor, Haverhill, Fall River, and East Harwich, for example. The plaintiffs are correct to focus on the residence of the putative class members, or where they are "living," as the First Circuit did in *Andrews.* Id. The employees' residency is a better determinant of the practicability of joinder than their work address, and here the geographic concentration of *Andrews* is not present.

The cases upon which defendant relies for its geographic proximity and identifiability arguments do not view those factors as dispositive in considering the overall ability of individual plaintiffs to join the action. See, e.g., Howard's Rexall Stores, Inc. v. Aetna U.S. Healthcare, Inc., 2001 WL 501055, at *6 (D.Me.2001) (noting that several of the pharmacies who were putative class members had already agreed to join the litigation and contribute to litigation costs); Sanft v. Winnebago Industries, Inc., 214 F.R.D. 514, 524 (N.D.Iowa 2003) (considering the financial resources of the putative class members, who were upper-level managers); *Andrews,* 780 F.2d, at 131 (finding joinder practicable where a subclass had a theoretical maximum of 49 members, but only 11 that were likely to be interested in pursuing the action). A close reading of the cases reveals that identifiability and geographic proximity are certainly *necessary* for joinder to be practicable, but the presence of those factors alone is not *sufficient* to render joinder practicable. Unlike the businesses in *Howard's Rexall* or the executives in *Sanft,* the employees of the defendant here do not necessarily have the means or the individual incentive to pursue the litigation of their own accord through joinder. Indeed, the fact that most plaintiffs have not taken even the simple step of opting in to the FLSA litigation in the related

Dooley matter [see Dooley v. Liberty Mutual Ins. Co., 307 F.Supp.2d 234 (D.Mass.2004)] confirms that joinder would not be a practicable means for pursuing their claims.

Defendant also argues that the alleged fear of retaliation of the putative class members does not weigh against using joinder and in favor of a finding of impracticability. The defendant argues that fear of retaliation is not well founded due to the lack of any actual retaliation during the pendency of the related case of Dooley v. Liberty Mutual Insurance Co., 307 F.Supp.2d 234 (D.Mass.2004), and the availability of legal recourse. The lack of actual retaliation, of course, does not refute the existence of a fear of retaliation. Furthermore, the availability of legal recourse for retaliation for asserting a state law claim is in doubt. See Valerio v. Putnam Associates, Inc., 173 F.3d 35, 45 (1st Cir.1999) (finding no such cause of action under Massachusetts law). Defendant also refers to Magistrate Judge Cohen's findings in relation to an emergency motion made by the plaintiffs that the fear of retaliation in this case was, in his words, "sheer poppycock." McLaughlin v. Liberty Mutual Insurance Co., 224 F.R.D. 295, 298 n. 10 (D.Mass.2004). Magistrate Judge Cohen's findings are persuasive, although he may not have had the benefit of the full record before this court, and a different legal standard was at issue in that matter. One fact, apparently not before the Magistrate Judge in his emergency session, is that the named plaintiffs in this case actually waited until after they had left their employer before they brought this action based on state law. Many courts have suggested that the employer-employee relationship is of such a nature that an employee "may feel inhibited to sue making joinder unlikely." *Ladegaard,* 2000 WL 1774091, at *4; accord *O'Brien*, 203 F.R.D., at 351; Scott v. Aetna Services, Inc., 210 F.R.D. 261, 267 (D.Conn.2002). Whether a fear of retaliation makes joinder impracticable in this case, however, need not be decided. Analytically, a fear of retaliation may be established by the plaintiffs in making their affirmative case for meeting the standard of Rule 23(a)(1). Here, however, the plaintiffs have made their case, as was their burden, by establishing the size of the class and insufficient individual incentive to pursue the case through joinder. The defendant has not defeated the plaintiffs' argument by showing that geographic proximity or identifiability render joinder practicable. Accordingly, I find that the plaintiffs have established that the class is so numerous that joinder is impracticable.

2. Commonality

Rule 23(a)(2) requires that questions of law or fact be shared by the prospective class, but does not require that every question be common. See Kirby v. Cullinet Software, Inc., 116 F.R.D. 303, 306 (D.Mass.1987). Plaintiffs suggest that several common questions of law and fact exist. Defendant does not contend otherwise.

I find that the prospective class shares several common questions of law or fact. The putative class members were all employed by the defendant, so any questions of fact regarding the defendant's actions or practices with regard to its employees will be common questions of fact. Common questions of law include whether the Auto Damage Appraisers were properly classified as exempt and whether the defendant acted in bad faith in so classifying. These questions are "illustrative rather than exhaustive, but establish the existence of the commonality required by Rule 23." *Kirby,* 116 F.R.D., at 306.

I find that plaintiffs have satisfied the second prerequisite of Rule 23(a).

3. Typicality

The third prerequisite under Rule 23(a) addresses the certification of the lead plaintiff or plaintiffs. Under Rule 23(a)(3), the lead plaintiffs claims must be typical of the claims of the proposed class. "The central inquiry in determining whether a proposed class has 'typicality' is whether" the class representatives' claims "have the same essential characteristics as the claims of the other members of the class." Cheney v. Cyberguard Corp., 213 F.R.D. 484, 491 (S.D.Fla.2003) (quoting In re Amerifirst Secs. Litig., 139 F.R.D. 423, 428 (S.D.Fla.1991)). The "plaintiffs need not show substantial identity between their claims and those of absent class members, but need only show that their claims arise from the same course of conduct that gave rise to the claims of the absent members." Priest [v. Zayre Corp., 118 F.R.D. 552, 555 (D.Mass.1988)] (internal quotation marks omitted).

Plaintiffs McLaughlin and Carver (the proposed class representatives) contend that "the claims of the Plaintiffs and the Class arise out of the same policies and wrongful conduct of the Defendant, and are based on the same legal theories." Defendant does not contest this assertion.

I am persuaded that the claims of plaintiffs McLaughlin and Carver are typical of the claims of the class. Accordingly, I find that plaintiffs have met the third prerequisite under Rule 23(a).

4. Adequacy of Representation

Rule 23(a)(4) also addresses the certification of the lead plaintiffs. "Inquiries into the adequacy of representation should focus on the named plaintiffs' ability to prosecute the action vigorously through qualified counsel and their lack of conflicting interest with unnamed class members." *Priest,* 118 F.R.D., at 556 (internal quotation marks omitted); see also *Kirby,* 116 F.R.D., at 308–09 ("The two basic guidelines for meeting the adequacy of representation standard of Rule 23(a)(4) are: (1) the absence of potential conflict between the named plaintiffs and the class members and (2) ... assurance of vigorous prosecution." (internal quotation marks omitted)).

Plaintiffs meet the requirement of vigorous prosecution through qualified counsel. Plaintiffs' attorneys have been litigating before this court in the related *Dooley* litigation, and I am satisfied that they will prosecute this action vigorously and will protect the interests of the absent class members. The record demonstrates that plaintiffs are represented by a "law firm which is thoroughly experienced in class action litigation. . . ." (Plaintiffs'

Memorandum, Docket No. 34, at 14.) Defendant does not contend otherwise.

As for whether plaintiffs McLaughlin and Carver have a conflict of interest with the unnamed class members, plaintiffs offer that all class members "have the same interest in being properly compensated for any overtime hours worked during the class period." (Plaintiffs' Memo., Docket No. 34, at 14.) Defendant does not contend that plaintiffs have any conflict of interest. In these circumstances, I find that the plaintiffs have no conflict of interest with the unnamed class members.

Accordingly, I find that the plaintiffs satisfy the fourth prerequisite under Rule 23(a).

B. Rule 23(b) Requirements

As explained earlier, a proposed class must also fit one of the three subdivisions of Rule 23(b). Plaintiffs seek certification under Rule 23(b)(3). I look first, however, to whether the proposed class qualifies under Rule 23(b)(1) or Rule 23(b)(2). I do so because "where the stricter requirements of 23(b)(1) and 23(b)(2) are squarely presented by the plaintiffs' claims Rule 23(b)(3) is not applicable.... To apply 23(b)(3) [in such circumstances] would run the serious risk of negating the very purpose for which [23(b)(1) and 23(b)(2)] were promulgated." Van Gemert v. Boeing Co., 259 F.Supp. 125, 130–31 (S.D.N.Y.1966); see also In re New England Mutual Life Ins. Co. Sales Practices Litig., 183 F.R.D. 33, 40 (D.Mass.1998) (Keeton, J.) ("When the specific facts of a case warrant certification under either 23(b)(1) or 23(b)(3), the general practice is to certify the class under 23(b)(1), whether or not the court also certifies under 23(b)(3).").

1. Rule 23(b)(1)

I turn first to 23(b)(1). Subsection (b)(1) authorizes a class action if

the prosecution of separate actions by or against individual members of the class would create a risk of

(A) inconsistent or varying adjudications with respect to individual members of the class which would establish incompatible standards of conduct for the party opposing the class, or

(B) adjudications with respect to individual members of the class which would as a practical matter be dispositive of the interests of the other members not parties to the adjudications or substantially impair or impede their ability to protect their interests . . . .

Fed.R.Civ.P. 23(b)(1). The present factual situation does not warrant a finding of either of the risks explained above. These risks are premised on the likelihood of multiple individual suits being brought. As mentioned earlier in Part III.A.1., little interest has been shown by the class members to opt in to the related FLSA litigation, for whatever reason. It is unlikely that individual suits would occur, and even less likely that such suits would result in incompatible standards of conduct for the defendant. Also it does not appear that a substantial risk exists that Liberty Mutual will become "judgment proof" as a result of this litigation. Cf. In re New England Mutual Sales Practices Litigation, 183 F.R.D. 33, 42 (D.Mass.1998).

Accordingly, I find 23(b)(1) inapplicable to the case at bar.

2. Rule 23(b)(2)

Subsection (b)(2) authorizes a class action if

> the party opposing the class has acted or refused to act on grounds generally applicable to the class, thereby making appropriate final injunctive relief or corresponding declaratory relief with respect to the class as a whole.

Fed.R.Civ.P. 23(b)(2). "Subsection (b)(2) was never intended to cover cases like the instant one where the primary claim is for damages[. It] is only applicable where the relief sought is exclusively or predominantly injunctive or declaratory." Eisen v. Carlisle & Jacquelin, 391 F.2d 555, 564 (2d Cir.1968) (citing Advisory Committee's Note, Proposed Rules of Civil Procedure, 39 F.R.D. 98, 102 (1965)). Accordingly, I find 23(b)(2) inapplicable to the case at bar.

3. Rule 23(b)(3): Predominance and Superiority

Having found that this case does not meet the requirements of Rule 23(b)(1) or (2), I must consider whether it nonetheless may be certified as a class action under Rule 23(b)(3). In addition to meeting the Rule 23(a) requirements, a case is appropriately certified as a Rule 23(b)(3) class action only if:

> the court finds that the questions of law or fact common to the members of the class predominate over any questions affecting only individual members, and that a class action is superior to other available methods for the fair and efficient adjudication of the controversy.

These requirements are referred to as "predominance" and "superiority." In making this finding, Rule 23(b)(3) directs the court to consider:

> (A) the interest of members of the class in individually controlling the prosecution or defense of separate actions; (B) the extent and nature of any litigation concerning the controversy already commenced by or against members of the class; (C) the desirability or undesirability of concentrating the litigation of the claims in the particular forum; (D) the difficulties likely to be encountered in the management of a class action.

The requirement that common issues of law or fact predominate over individual ones is not challenged by the defendant. Nonetheless, I note the following questions of law and fact that are common among the class members, as identified by the plaintiffs:

> [W]hether Defendant properly classified Massachusetts [Auto Damage Appraisers] as exempt; if not, whether Defendant acted in bad faith in doing so; and, finally, whether Defendant can satisfy its obligations to

them by paying them "half-time" for their overtime hours under the "fluctuating workweek" doctrine.

(Plaintiffs' Memorandum, Docket No. 34, at 15). The amount of damages for each individual class member will ultimately require some individual proof, but administration of these individual claims will be straightforward and these individual questions do not predominate over the common questions identified above. I conclude that common issues of law and fact predominate over individual issues.

Defendant's main contention is that the class action mechanism is not "superior" to other methods. Defendant has noted that the plaintiffs could request the attorney general to bring a claim on their behalf. This argument has been rejected by a Massachusetts Superior Court considering the similar Massachusetts rule on class actions:

> This Court will not deny class certification based on the possibility that the Attorney General will bring an action that he has yet to bring and not represented to this Court that he will bring. Nor can this Court determine whether an action brought by the Attorney General is a more sensible means than this class action to provide a remedy for the fraud alleged here without scrutinizing the Attorney General's complaint or knowing whether it will be filed.

Olson v. Energy North, Inc., 1999 WL 1332362, *6 (Mass.Super.Ct. Jan. 14, 1999). Some federal courts have denied class certification where the state Attorney General had, in fact, brought a claim on behalf of the consumers in the state. See, e.g., Sage v. Appalachian Oil Co., 1994 WL 637443 (E.D.Tenn. Sept.7, 1994); Commonwealth of Pennsylvania v. Budget Fuel Co., 122 F.R.D. 184 (E.D.Pa.1988). These cases, however, do not bear on whether a court should deny certification simply because the plaintiffs *could* petition the Attorney General to bring suit on behalf of all auto damage appraisers in the Commonwealth, but where the Attorney General has not *actually* brought suit. In this situation, no reason exists for us to presume that the Attorney General would take on the plaintiffs' case, nor does any basis exist for us to know that the Attorney General's suit would bring adequate relief to the class. Judicial resources would not be conserved by taking a wait-and-see approach to whether the Attorney General takes up the plaintiffs' case, especially because the defendant has not provided any indication that such a situation is likely to occur.

Also related to the question of superiority is defendant's argument that the plaintiff class has expressed a disfavor with a class action by not taking advantage of the opt-in provision in the FLSA litigation. In Part III.A.1., I noted that defendant's argument does not have a tendency to show that joinder is practicable. In this part of the analysis, I must consider whether the unwillingness of putative class members to join into FLSA litigation suggests a determination that the class action is not a "superior" means of adjudicating this controversy. The alternative would be either individual suits brought as pendent claims in the opt-in FLSA litigation or a class action in state court. The former option would result in no relief in this court for those who have not opted in. As I determined in Part III.A.1., I will not infer a forfeiture of state remedies, including pursuit of a class action, from the failure to join in the pursuit of federal relief. The latter option would not be a superior means of adjudication. Many of the same issues arise here as have arisen in the FLSA litigation. The parties have entered into joint stipulations and the litigation has been proceeding towards settlement of many of the issues. Resolution of the common issues in a single judicial forum will promote judicial economy and uniformity of outcome. Finally, the class members' failure to opt in does not imply that the class members themselves consider individual action to be superior to a class action. Instead, it suggests that many of the class members lack the individual incentive to bring suit, making a class action superior. I conclude that a class action is a superior means of adjudicating this controversy.

Accordingly, I find that the requirements of Rule 23(b)(3) have been satisfied.

IV.

Although it was not raised by the parties, this court must consider an issue of its own jurisdiction over this case. This court has jurisdiction over the FLSA claims under federal question jurisdiction, and the basis for its jurisdiction over the state law claims is supplemental jurisdiction. 28 U.S.C. § 1367. Under § 1367(c), enumerated situations exist where a district court may decline to exercise supplemental jurisdiction:

(1) the claim raises a novel or complex issue of State law,

(2) the claim substantially predominates over the claim or claims over which the district court has original jurisdiction,

(3) the district court has dismissed all claims over which it has original jurisdiction, or

(4) in exceptional circumstances, there are other compelling reasons for declining jurisdiction.

The issue presented in this case is whether I should decline to exercise jurisdiction under § 1367(c)(2), where the state law claim "substantially predominates" over the federal claim.

This question is left to the discretion of the trial court. See Grispino v. New England Mutual Life Ins. Co., 358 F.3d 16, 19 (1st Cir.2004). Two principles of supplemental jurisdiction are at work in this case: first, "the rules of pendent jurisdiction have always been more flexible in federal question cases than in diversity cases, no doubt to facilitate a federal forum for claims under federal law" and second, the concern over "a defending party haled into court against his will." Rosario Ortega v. Star–Kist Foods, Inc., 370 F.3d 124, 138 n. 13, 144 n. 20 (1st Cir.2004) (citations and quotation marks omitted), cert. granted, 543 U.S. 924 (2004). Here, retaining jurisdiction would facilitate a federal forum for federal claims because it would allow the federal court to hear both federal and state law claims, rather than only the state court being able to hear both federal and state law claims. The pendent state law claims are being brought by additional plaintiffs, rather than against additional defendants, so no risk exists of haling an additional defendant into court—the defendant is already properly before this court.

I am mindful, however, of a Third Circuit opinion which found an abuse of discretion when a district court exercised supplemental jurisdiction over a class of state law plaintiffs where only a small number of the class members opted in to the FLSA litigation that was the source of original jurisdiction. See De Asencio v. Tyson Foods, Inc., 342 F.3d 301 (3d Cir.2003). In *De Asencio,* the state law class consisted of approximately 4,100 persons, of which 447 were members of the FLSA class. Id., at 305. The Third Circuit found an abuse of discretion based on "the inordinate size of the state-law class, the different terms of proof required by the implied contract state-law claim, and the general federal interest in opt-in wage actions . . . ." Id., at 312. It concluded that "the federal action is an appendage to the more comprehensive state action." Id. For several reasons, the concerns expressed by the Third Circuit are not present in this case. The state law class in *De Asencio* was orders of magnitude larger than the 51–member class here. Although only 13 of the 51 class members are also bringing FLSA claims, the nationwide class action, also before this court, is larger than the state class. The state law claim in this case, unlike in *De Asencio,* relies on the same set of facts as does the federal claim. The First Circuit has also recently stated that familiarity with a nationwide class action is reason to exercise discretion to retain jurisdiction over a state claim. See *Grispino,* 358 F.3d, at 19 ("The Massachusetts federal court had already handled a large class action involving the same sorts of claims as this case and had continuing jurisdiction. Its familiarity provided a sufficient basis for its decision to retain jurisdiction over the action."). I conclude that in these circumstances it is within my discretion to retain jurisdiction over the state law claims of the class, and sound reasons of judicial economy favor doing so. Accordingly, I conclude that I have subject matter jurisdiction over the claims of the state law class members.

ORDER OF CERTIFICATION

For the foregoing reasons, it is ORDERED:

(1) Plaintiffs' Motion for Class Certification (Docket No. 32) is ALLOWED.

(2) Until further order of this or a higher court, this action may be maintained as a class action under Fed.R.Civ.P. 23(a) and 23(b)(3), subject to the terms and conditions set forth below.

(3) The Class is hereby certified, consisting of:

Persons who were employed by Defendant as Auto Damage Appraisers in the Commonwealth of Massachusetts between February 19, 2001 and the date of entry of final judgment in this action.

(4) Lead plaintiffs Thomas McLaughlin and George Carver are certified as the representatives of the class.

(5) Counsel for plaintiffs are directed to submit to the court a draft of their proposed form of notice within fourteen days of the date

of this Memorandum and Order of Certification. Any objections to the proposed notice must be filed fourteen days after receipt of the proposed form of notice.

(6) Counsel will be prepared to discuss the proposed form of notice, in addition to any other pending matters, at the next hearing in this case, which has been scheduled for Tuesday, November 23, 2004, at 9:30 a.m.[45]

Amchem Products, Inc. v. Windsor

Supreme Court of the United States, 1997.
521 U.S. 591, 117 S.Ct. 2231, 138 L.Ed.2d 689.

■ JUSTICE GINSBURG delivered the opinion of the Court.

This case concerns the legitimacy under Rule 23 of the Federal Rules of Civil Procedure of a class-action certification sought to achieve global settlement of current and future asbestos-related claims. The class proposed for certification potentially encompasses hundreds of thousands, perhaps millions, of individuals tied together by this commonality: each was, or some day may be, adversely affected by past exposure to asbestos products manufactured by one or more of 20 companies. Those companies, defendants in the lower courts, are petitioners here.

The United States District Court for the Eastern District of Pennsylvania certified the class for settlement only, finding that the proposed settlement was fair and that representation and notice had been adequate. That court enjoined class members from separately pursuing asbestos-related personal-injury suits in any court, federal or state, pending the issuance of a final order. The Court of Appeals for the Third Circuit vacated the District Court's orders, holding that the class certification failed to satisfy Rule 23's requirements in several critical respects. We affirm the Court of Appeals' judgment.

I

A

The settlement-class certification we confront evolved in response to an asbestos-litigation crisis. See Georgine v. Amchem Products, Inc., 83 F.3d

---

[45. The Supreme Court explored the prerequisite of commonality pursuant to Rule 23(a)(2) in Wal–Mart Stores, Inc. v. Dukes, 564 U.S. ___, 131 S.Ct. 2541 (2011), stating that commonality "requires the plaintiff to demonstrate that the class members have suffered the same injury," and that each class member's claim "must depend on a common contention—for example, the assertion of discriminatory bias on the part of the same supervisor. That common contention, moreover, must be of such a nature that it is capable of classwide resolution—which means that determination of its truth or falsity will resolve an issue that is central to the validity of each one of the claims in one stroke." Consistent with the *McLaughlin* case above, the Court also held that class certification pursuant to Rule 23(b)(2) was not appropriate for individualized monetary claims—even those involving back pay—and that monetary claims generally are inappropriate for (b)(2) treatment unless, perhaps, such monetary claims are incidental to claims for injunctive or declaratory relief.]

610, 618, and n. 2 (CA3 1996) (citing commentary). A United States Judicial Conference Ad Hoc Committee on Asbestos Litigation, appointed by THE CHIEF JUSTICE in September 1990, described facets of the problem in a 1991 report:

"[This] is a tale of danger known in the 1930s, exposure inflicted upon millions of Americans in the 1940s and 1950s, injuries that began to take their toll in the 1960s, and a flood of lawsuits beginning in the 1970s. On the basis of past and current filing data, and because of a latency period that may last as long as 40 years for some asbestos related diseases, a continuing stream of claims can be expected. The final toll of asbestos related injuries is unknown. Predictions have been made of 200,000 asbestos disease deaths before the year 2000 and as many as 265,000 by the year 2015.

"The most objectionable aspects of asbestos litigation can be briefly summarized: dockets in both federal and state courts continue to grow; long delays are routine; trials are too long; the same issues are litigated over and over; transaction costs exceed the victims' recovery by nearly two to one; exhaustion of assets threatens and distorts the process; and future claimants may lose altogether." Report of The Judicial Conference Ad Hoc Committee on Asbestos Litigation 2–3 (Mar.1991).

Real reform, the report concluded, required federal legislation creating a national asbestos dispute-resolution scheme. See id., at 3, 27–35; see also id., at 42 (dissenting statement of Hogan, J.) (agreeing that "a national solution is the only answer" and suggesting "passage by Congress of an administrative claims procedure similar to the Black Lung legislation"). As recommended by the Ad Hoc Committee, the Judicial Conference of the United States urged Congress to act. See Report of the Proceedings of the Judicial Conference of the United States 33 (Mar. 12, 1991). To this date, no congressional response has emerged.

In the face of legislative inaction, the federal courts—lacking authority to replace state tort systems with a national toxic tort compensation regime—endeavored to work with the procedural tools available to improve management of federal asbestos litigation. Eight federal judges, experienced in the superintendence of asbestos cases, urged the Judicial Panel on Multidistrict Litigation (MDL Panel), to consolidate in a single district all asbestos complaints then pending in federal courts. Accepting the recommendation, the MDL Panel transferred all asbestos cases then filed, but not yet on trial in federal courts to a single district, the United States District Court for the Eastern District of Pennsylvania; pursuant to the transfer order, the collected cases were consolidated for pretrial proceedings before Judge Weiner. See In re Asbestos Products Liability Litigation (No. VI), 771 F.Supp. 415, 422–424 (JPML 1991). The order aggregated pending cases only; no authority resides in the MDL Panel to license for consolidated proceedings claims not yet filed.

B

[Negotiations took place between committees representing plaintiffs and representing defendants. The Center for Claims Resolution (CCR), a consortium of 20 former asbestos manufacturers, promised to pay more than $200 million to gain release of the claims of plaintiffs who had already filed suit. The plaintiffs' lawyers and CCR then launched the present case to resolve the claims of plaintiffs without already pending lawsuits.]

C

The class action thus instituted was not intended to be litigated. Rather, within the space of a single day, January 15, 1993, the settling parties—CCR defendants and the representatives of the plaintiff class described below—presented to the District Court a complaint, an answer, a proposed settlement agreement, and a joint motion for conditional class certification.

The complaint identified nine lead plaintiffs, designating them and members of their families as representatives of a class comprising all persons who had not filed an asbestos-related lawsuit against a CCR defendant as of the date the class action commenced, but who (1) had been exposed—occupationally or through the occupational exposure of a spouse or household member—to asbestos or products containing asbestos attributable to a CCR defendant, or (2) whose spouse or family member had been so exposed. Untold numbers of individuals may fall within this description. All named plaintiffs alleged that they or a member of their family had been exposed to asbestos-containing products of CCR defendants. More than half of the named plaintiffs alleged that they or their family members had already suffered various physical injuries as a result of the exposure. The others alleged that they had not yet manifested any asbestos-related condition. The complaint delineated no subclasses; all named plaintiffs were designated as representatives of the class as a whole.

The complaint invoked the District Court's diversity jurisdiction and asserted various state-law claims for relief, including (1) negligent failure to warn, (2) strict liability, (3) breach of express and implied warranty, (4) negligent infliction of emotional distress, (5) enhanced risk of disease, (6) medical monitoring, and (7) civil conspiracy. Each plaintiff requested unspecified damages in excess of $100,000. CCR defendants' answer denied the principal allegations of the complaint and asserted 11 affirmative defenses.

A stipulation of settlement accompanied the pleadings; it proposed to settle, and to preclude nearly all class members from litigating against CCR companies, all claims not filed before January 15, 1993, involving compensation for present and future asbestos-related personal injury or death. An exhaustive document exceeding 100 pages, the stipulation presents in detail an administrative mechanism and a schedule of payments to compensate class members who meet defined asbestos-exposure and medical requirements. The stipulation describes four categories of compensable disease: mesothelioma; lung cancer; certain "other cancers" (colon-rectal, laryngeal, esophageal, and stomach cancer); and "non-malignant conditions" (asbestosis and bilateral pleural thickening). Persons with "exceptional" medical claims—claims that do not fall within the four described diagnostic categories—may in some instances qualify for compensation, but the settlement caps the number of "exceptional" claims CCR must cover.

For each qualifying disease category, the stipulation specifies the range of damages CCR will pay to qualifying claimants. Payments under the settlement are not adjustable for inflation. Mesothelioma claimants—the most highly compensated category—are scheduled to receive between $20,000 and $200,000. The stipulation provides that CCR is to propose the level of compensation within the prescribed ranges; it also establishes procedures to resolve disputes over medical diagnoses and levels of compensation.

Compensation above the fixed ranges may be obtained for "extraordinary" claims. But the settlement places both numerical caps and dollar limits on such claims. The settlement also imposes "case flow maximums," which cap the number of claims payable for each disease in a given year.

Class members are to receive no compensation for certain kinds of claims, even if otherwise applicable state law recognizes such claims. Claims that garner no compensation under the settlement include claims by family members of asbestos-exposed individuals for loss of consortium, and claims by so-called "exposure-only" plaintiffs for increased risk of cancer, fear of future asbestos-related injury, and medical monitoring. "Pleural" claims, which might be asserted by persons with asbestos-related plaques on their lungs but no accompanying physical impairment, are also excluded. Although not entitled to present compensation, exposure-only claimants and pleural claimants may qualify for benefits when and if they develop a compensable disease and meet the relevant exposure and medical criteria. Defendants forgo defenses to liability, including statute of limitations pleas.

Class members, in the main, are bound by the settlement in perpetuity, while CCR defendants may choose to withdraw from the settlement after ten years. A small number of class members—only a few per year—may reject the settlement and pursue their claims in court. Those permitted to exercise this option, however, may not assert any punitive damages claim or any claim for increased risk of cancer. Aspects of the administration of the settlement are to be monitored by the AFL–CIO and class counsel. Class counsel are to receive attorneys' fees in an amount to be approved by the District Court.

D

On January 29, 1993, as requested by the settling parties, the District Court conditionally certified, under Federal Rule of Civil Procedure 23(b)(3), an encompassing opt-out class. The certified class included persons occupationally exposed to defendants' asbestos products, and members of their families, who had not filed suit as of January 15.... Various class members raised objections to the settlement stipulation, and Judge Weiner granted the objectors full rights to participate in the subsequent proceedings....

In preliminary rulings, Judge Reed held that the District Court had subject-matter jurisdiction, see Carlough v. Amchem Products, Inc., 834 F.Supp. 1437, 1467–1468 (ED Pa.1993), and he approved the settling parties' elaborate plan for giving notice to the class, see Carlough v. Amchem Products, Inc., 158 F.R.D. 314, 336 (ED Pa.1993). The court-approved notice informed recipients that they could exclude themselves from the class, if they so chose, within a three-month opt-out period.

Objectors raised numerous challenges to the settlement.... Rejecting these and all other objections, Judge Reed concluded that the settlement terms were fair and had been negotiated without collusion.... He also found that adequate notice had been given to class members, see id., at 332–334, and that final class certification under Rule 23(b)(3) was appropriate....

As to the specific prerequisites to certification, the District Court observed that the class satisfied Rule 23(a)(1)'s numerosity requirement, ... a matter no one debates. The Rule 23(a)(2) and (b)(3) requirements of commonality and preponderance were also satisfied, the District Court held, in that

> "[t]he members of the class have all been exposed to asbestos products supplied by the defendants and all share an interest in receiving prompt and fair compensation for their claims, while minimizing the risks and transaction costs inherent in the asbestos litigation process as it occurs presently in the tort system. Whether the proposed settlement satisfies this interest and is otherwise a fair, reasonable and adequate compromise of the claims of the class is a predominant issue for purposes of Rule 23(b)(3)." Id., at 316.

The District Court held next that the claims of the class representatives were "typical" of the class as a whole, a requirement of Rule 23(a)(3), and that, as Rule 23(b)(3) demands, the class settlement was "superior" to other methods of adjudication....

Strenuous objections had been asserted regarding the adequacy of representation, a Rule 23(a)(4) requirement. Objectors maintained that class counsel and class representatives had disqualifying conflicts of interests....

Satisfied that class counsel had ably negotiated the settlement in the best interests of all concerned, and that the named parties served as adequate representatives, the District Court rejected these objections.... Declaring class certification appropriate and the settlement fair, the District Court preliminarily enjoined all class members from commencing any asbestos-related suit against the CCR defendants in any state or federal court. See Georgine v. Amchem Products, Inc., 878 F.Supp. 716, 726–727 (ED Pa.1994).

The objectors appealed. The United States Court of Appeals for the Third Circuit vacated the certification, holding that the requirements of Rule 23 had not been satisfied. See Georgine v. Amchem Products, Inc., 83 F.3d 610 (1996).

E

. . . . .

The Third Circuit, after intensive review, ultimately ordered decertification of the class and vacation of the District Court's anti-suit injunction. . . .

We granted certiorari, 519 U.S. 957 (1996), and now affirm.

II

. . . . .

III

To place this controversy in context, we briefly describe the characteristics of class actions for which the Federal Rules provide. Rule 23, governing federal-court class actions, stems from equity practice and gained its current shape in an innovative 1966 revision. See generally Kaplan, Continuing Work of the Civil Committee: 1966 Amendments of the Federal Rules of Civil Procedure (I), 81 Harv.L.Rev. 356, 375–400 (1967) (hereinafter Kaplan, Continuing Work). Rule 23(a) states four threshold requirements applicable to all class actions: (1) numerosity (a "class [so large] that joinder of all members is impracticable"); (2) commonality ("questions of law or fact common to the class"); (3) typicality (named parties' claims or defenses "are typical . . . of the class"); and (4) adequacy of representation (representatives "will fairly and adequately protect the interests of the class").

In addition to satisfying Rule 23(a)'s prerequisites, parties seeking class certification must show that the action is maintainable under Rule 23(b)(1), (2), or (3). Rule 23(b)(1) covers cases in which separate actions by or against individual class members would risk establishing "incompatible standards of conduct for the party opposing the class," Fed. Rule Civ. Proc. 23(b)(1)(A), or would "as a practical matter be dispositive of the interests" of nonparty class members "or substantially impair or impede their ability to protect their interests," Fed. Rule Civ. Proc. 23(b)(1)(B). Rule 23(b)(1)(A) "takes in cases where the party is obliged by law to treat the members of the class alike (a utility acting toward customers; a government imposing a tax), or where the party must treat all alike as a matter of practical necessity (a riparian owner using water as against downriver owners)." Kaplan, Continuing Work 388 (footnotes omitted). Rule 23(b)(1)(B) includes, for example, "limited fund" cases, instances in which numerous persons make claims against a fund insufficient to satisfy all claims. See Advisory Committee's Notes on Fed. Rule Civ. Proc. 23, 28 U.S.C.App., pp. 696–697 (hereinafter Adv. Comm. Notes).

Rule 23(b)(2) permits class actions for declaratory or injunctive relief where "the party opposing the class has acted or refused to act on grounds generally applicable to the class." Civil rights cases against parties charged with unlawful, class-based discrimination are prime examples. Adv. Comm. Notes, 28 U.S.C.App., p. 697; see Kaplan, Continuing Work 389 (subdivision (b)(2) "build[s] on experience mainly, but not exclusively, in the civil rights field").

In the 1966 class-action amendments, Rule 23(b)(3), the category at issue here, was "the most adventuresome" innovation. See Kaplan, A Prefatory Note, 10 B.C. Ind. & Com. L.Rev. 497, 497 (1969) (hereinafter Kaplan, Prefatory Note). Rule 23(b)(3) added to the complex-litigation arsenal class actions for damages designed to secure judgments binding all class members save those who affirmatively elected to be excluded. See 7A Charles Alan Wright, Arthur R. Miller, & Mary Kay Kane, Federal Practice and Procedure § 1777, p. 517 (2d ed.1986) (hereinafter Wright, Miller, & Kane); see generally Kaplan, Continuing Work 379–400. Rule 23(b)(3) "opt out" class actions superseded the former "spurious" class action, so characterized because it generally functioned as a permissive joinder ("opt in") device. See 7A Wright, Miller, & Kane § 1753, at 28–31, 42–44; see also Adv. Comm. Notes, 28 U.S.C.App., p. 695.

Framed for situations in which "class-action treatment is not as clearly called for" as it is in Rule 23(b)(1) and (b)(2) situations, Rule 23(b)(3) permits certification where class suit "may nevertheless be convenient and desirable." Adv. Comm. Notes, 28 U.S.C.App., p. 697. To qualify for certification under Rule 23(b)(3), a class must meet two requirements beyond the Rule 23(a) prerequisites: Common questions must "predominate over any questions affecting only individual members" ; and class resolution must be "superior to other available methods for the fair and efficient adjudication of the controversy." In adding "predominance" and "superiority" to the qualification-for-certification list, the Advisory Committee sought to cover cases "in which a class action would achieve economies of time, effort, and expense, and promote ... uniformity of decision as to persons similarly situated, without sacrificing procedural fairness or bringing about other undesirable results." Ibid. Sensitive to the competing tugs of individual autonomy for those who might prefer to go it alone or in a smaller unit, on the one hand, and systemic efficiency on the other, the Reporter for the 1966 amendments cautioned: "The new provision invites a close look at the case before it is accepted as a class action ...." Kaplan, Continuing Work 390.

Rule 23(b)(3) includes a nonexhaustive list of factors pertinent to a court's "close look" at the predominance and superiority criteria:

> "(A) the interest of members of the class in individually controlling the prosecution or defense of separate actions; (B) the extent and nature of any litigation concerning the controversy already commenced by or against members of the class; (C) the desirability or undesirability of concentrating the litigation of the claims in the particular forum; (D) the difficulties likely to be encountered in the management of a class action."

In setting out these factors, the Advisory Committee for the 1966 reform anticipated that in each case, courts would "consider the interests of individual members of the class in controlling their own litigations and carrying them on as they see fit." Adv. Comm. Notes, 28 U.S.C.App., p. 698. They elaborated:

> "The interests of individuals in conducting separate lawsuits may be so strong as to call for denial of a class action. On the other hand, these interests may be theoretic rather than practical; the class may have a high degree of cohesion and prosecution of the action through representatives would be quite unobjectionable, or the amounts at stake for individuals may be so small that separate suits would be impracticable." Ibid.

> . . . . .

While the text of Rule 23(b)(3) does not exclude from certification cases in which individual damages run high, the Advisory Committee had dominantly in mind vindication of "the rights of groups of people who individually would be without effective strength to bring their opponents into court at all." Kaplan, Prefatory Note 497. As concisely recalled in a recent Seventh Circuit opinion:

> "The policy at the very core of the class action mechanism is to overcome the problem that small recoveries do not provide the incentive for any individual to bring a solo action prosecuting his or her rights. A class action solves this problem by aggregating the relatively paltry potential recoveries into something worth someone's (usually an attorney's) labor." Mace v. Van Ru Credit Corp., 109 F.3d 338, 344 (1997).

To alert class members to their right to "opt out" of a (b)(3) class, Rule 23 instructs the court to "direct to the members of the class the best notice practicable under the circumstances, including individual notice to all members who can be identified through reasonable effort." Fed. Rule Civ. Proc. 23(c)(2); see Eisen v. Carlisle & Jacquelin, 417 U.S. 156, 173–177 (1974) (individual notice to class members identifiable through reasonable effort is mandatory in (b)(3) actions; requirement may not be relaxed based on high cost).

No class action may be "dismissed or compromised without [court] approval," preceded by notice to class members. Fed. Rule Civ. Proc. 23(e). The Advisory Committee's sole comment on this terse final provision of Rule 23 restates the rule's instruction without elaboration: "Subdivision (e) requires approval of the court, after notice, for the dismissal or compromise of any class action." Adv. Comm. Notes, 28 U.S.C.App., p. 699.

In the decades since the 1966 revision of Rule 23, class action practice has become ever more "adventuresome" as a means of coping with claims too numerous to secure their "just, speedy, and inexpensive determination" one by one. See Fed. Rule Civ. Proc. 1. The development reflects concerns about the efficient use of court resources and the conservation of funds to compensate claimants who do not line up early in a litigation queue. See generally J. Weinstein, Individual Justice in Mass Tort Litigation: The Effect of Class Actions, Consolidations, and Other Multiparty Devices

(1995); Schwarzer, Settlement of Mass Tort Class Actions: Order out of Chaos, 80 Cornell L.Rev. 837 (1995).

Among current applications of Rule 23(b)(3), the "settlement only" class has become a stock device. See, e.g., T. Willging, L. Hooper, & R. Niemic, Empirical Study of Class Actions in Four Federal District Courts: Final Report to the Advisory Committee on Civil Rules 61–62 (1996) (noting large number of such cases in districts studied). Although all Federal Circuits recognize the utility of Rule 23(b)(3) settlement classes, courts have divided on the extent to which a proffered settlement affects court surveillance under Rule 23's certification criteria.

. . . . .

IV

We granted review to decide the role settlement may play, under existing Rule 23, in determining the propriety of class certification. The Third Circuit's opinion stated that each of the requirements of Rule 23(a) and (b)(3) "must be satisfied without taking into account the settlement." 83 F.3d, at 626. . . . That statement, petitioners urge, is incorrect.

We agree with petitioners to this limited extent: settlement is relevant to a class certification. The Third Circuit's opinion bears modification in that respect. But, as we earlier observed, . . . the Court of Appeals in fact did not ignore the settlement; instead, that court homed in on settlement terms in explaining why it found the absentees' interests inadequately represented. . . . The Third Circuit's close inspection of the settlement in that regard was altogether proper.

Confronted with a request for settlement-only class certification, a district court need not inquire whether the case, if tried, would present intractable management problems, see Fed. Rule Civ. Proc. 23(b)(3)(D), for the proposal is that there be no trial. But other specifications of the rule—those designed to protect absentees by blocking unwarranted or overbroad class definitions—demand undiluted, even heightened, attention in the settlement context. Such attention is of vital importance, for a court asked to certify a settlement class will lack the opportunity, present when a case is litigated, to adjust the class, informed by the proceedings as they unfold. See Fed. Rule Civ. Proc. 23(c), (d).

And, of overriding importance, courts must be mindful that the rule as now composed sets the requirements they are bound to enforce. Federal Rules take effect after an extensive deliberative process involving many reviewers: a Rules Advisory Committee, public commenters, the Judicial Conference, this Court, the Congress. See 28 U.S.C. §§ 2073, 2074. The text of a rule thus proposed and reviewed limits judicial inventiveness. Courts are not free to amend a rule outside the process Congress ordered, a process properly tuned to the instruction that rules of procedure "shall not abridge . . . any substantive right." § 2072(b).

Rule 23(e), on settlement of class actions, reads in its entirety: "A class action shall not be dismissed or compromised without the approval of the court, and notice of the proposed dismissal or compromise shall be given to all members of the class in such manner as the court directs." This prescription was designed to function as an additional requirement, not a superseding direction, for the "class action" to which Rule 23(e) refers is one qualified for certification under Rule 23(a) and (b). Cf. *Eisen*, 417 U.S., at 176–177 (adequate representation does not eliminate additional requirement to provide notice). Subdivisions (a) and (b) focus court attention on whether a proposed class has sufficient unity so that absent members can fairly be bound by decisions of class representatives. That dominant concern persists when settlement, rather than trial, is proposed.

The safeguards provided by the Rule 23(a) and (b) class-qualifying criteria, we emphasize, are not impractical impediments—checks shorn of utility—in the settlement class context. First, the standards set for the protection of absent class members serve to inhibit appraisals of the chancellor's foot kind—class certifications dependent upon the court's gestalt judgment or overarching impression of the settlement's fairness.

Second, if a fairness inquiry under Rule 23(e) controlled certification, eclipsing Rule 23(a) and (b), and permitting class designation despite the impossibility of litigation, both class counsel and court would be disarmed. Class counsel confined to settlement negotiations could not use the threat of litigation to press for a better offer, see Coffee, Class Wars: The Dilemma of the Mass Tort Class Action, 95 Colum.L.Rev. 1343, 1379–1380 (1995), and the court would face a bargain proffered for its approval without benefit of adversarial investigation, see, e.g., Kamilewicz v. Bank of Boston Corp., 100 F.3d 1348, 1352 (CA7 1996) (Easterbrook, J., dissenting from denial of rehearing en banc) (parties "may even put one over on the court, in a staged performance"), cert. denied, 520 U.S. 1204 (1997).

Federal courts, in any case, lack authority to substitute for Rule 23's certification criteria a standard never adopted—that if a settlement is "fair," then certification is proper. Applying to this case criteria the rulemakers set, we conclude that the Third Circuit's appraisal is essentially correct. Although that court should have acknowledged that settlement is a factor in the calculus, a remand is not warranted on that account. The Court of Appeals' opinion amply demonstrates why—with or without a settlement on the table—the sprawling class the District Court certified does not satisfy Rule 23's requirements.

A

We address first the requirement of Rule 23(b)(3) that "[common] questions of law or fact ... predominate over any questions affecting only individual members." The District Court concluded that predominance was satisfied based on two factors: class members' shared experience of asbestos exposure and their common "interest in receiving prompt and fair compensation for their claims, while minimizing the risks and transaction costs inherent in the asbestos litigation process as it occurs presently in the tort system." 157 F.R.D., at 316. The settling parties also contend that the settlement's fairness is a common question, predominating over disparate legal issues that might be pivotal in litigation but become irrelevant under the settlement.

The predominance requirement stated in Rule 23(b)(3), we hold, is not met by the factors on which the District Court relied. The benefits asbestos-exposed persons might gain from the establishment of a grand-scale compensation scheme is a matter fit for legislative consideration, see supra, . . . but it is not pertinent to the predominance inquiry. That inquiry trains on the legal or factual questions that qualify each class member's case as a genuine controversy, questions that preexist any settlement.[46]

The Rule 23(b)(3) predominance inquiry tests whether proposed classes are sufficiently cohesive to warrant adjudication by representation. See 7A Wright, Miller, & Kane 518–519.[47] The inquiry appropriate under Rule 23(e), on the other hand, protects unnamed class members "from unjust or unfair settlements affecting their rights when the representatives become fainthearted before the action is adjudicated or are able to secure satisfaction of their individual claims by a compromise." See 7B Wright, Miller, & Kane § 1797, at 340–341. But it is not the mission of Rule 23(e) to assure the class cohesion that legitimizes representative action in the first place. If a common interest in a fair compromise could satisfy the predominance requirement of Rule 23(b)(3), that vital prescription would be stripped of any meaning in the settlement context.

The District Court also relied upon this commonality: "The members of the class have all been exposed to asbestos products supplied by the defendants . . . ." 157 F.R.D., at 316. Even if Rule 23(a)'s commonality requirement may be satisfied by that shared experience, the predominance criterion is far more demanding. See 83 F.3d, at 626–627. Given the greater number of questions peculiar to the several categories of class members, and to individuals within each category, and the significance of those uncommon questions, any overarching dispute about the health consequences of asbestos exposure cannot satisfy the Rule 23(b)(3) predominance standard.

. . . Differences in state law, the Court of Appeals observed, compound these disparities. See id., at 627 (citing Phillips Petroleum Co. v. Shutts, 472 U.S. 797, 823 (1985)).

No settlement class called to our attention is as sprawling as this one. Cf. In re Asbestos Litigation, 90 F.3d, at 976, n. 8 ("We would likely agree

---

46. In this respect, the predominance requirement of Rule 23(b)(3) is similar to the requirement of Rule 23(a)(3) that "claims or defenses" of the named representatives must be "typical of the claims or defenses of the class." The words "claims or defenses" in this context—just as in the context of Rule 24(b)(2) governing permissive intervention—"manifestly refer to the kinds of claims or defenses that can be raised in courts of law as part of an actual or impending law suit." Diamond v. Charles, 476 U.S. 54, 76–77 (1986) (O'Connor, J., concurring in part and concurring in judgment).

47. This case, we note, involves no "limited fund" capable of supporting class treatment under Rule 23(b)(1)(B), which does not have a predominance requirement. See Georgine v. Amchem Products, Inc., 157 F.R.D. 246, 318 (E.D. Pa.1994); see also id., at 291, and n. 40. The settling parties sought to proceed exclusively under Rule 23(b)(3).

with the Third Circuit that a class action requesting individual damages for members of a global class of asbestos claimants would not satisfy [Rule 23] requirements due to the huge number of individuals and their varying medical expenses, smoking histories, and family situations."). Predominance is a test readily met in certain cases alleging consumer or securities fraud or violations of the antitrust laws. See Adv. Comm. Notes, 28 U.S.C.App., p. 697 .... Even mass tort cases arising from a common cause or disaster may, depending upon the circumstances, satisfy the predominance requirement. The Advisory Committee for the 1966 revision of Rule 23, it is true, noted that "mass accident" cases are likely to present "significant questions, not only of damages but of liability and defenses of liability, ... affecting the individuals in different ways." Ibid. And the Committee advised that such cases are "ordinarily not appropriate" for class treatment. Ibid. But the text of the rule does not categorically exclude mass tort cases from class certification, and district courts, since the late 1970s, have been certifying such cases in increasing number. See Resnik, From "Cases" to "Litigation," 54 Law & Contemp. Prob. 5, 17–19 (Summer 1991) (describing trend). The Committee's warning, however, continues to call for caution when individual stakes are high and disparities among class members great. As the Third Circuit's opinion makes plain, the certification in this case does not follow the counsel of caution. That certification cannot be upheld, for it rests on a conception of Rule 23(b)(3)'s predominance requirement irreconcilable with the rule's design.

B

Nor can the class approved by the District Court satisfy Rule 23(a)(4)'s requirement that the named parties "will fairly and adequately protect the interests of the class." The adequacy inquiry under Rule 23(a)(4) serves to uncover conflicts of interest between named parties and the class they seek to represent. See General Telephone Co. of Southwest v. Falcon, 457 U.S. 147, 157–158, n. 13 (1982). "[A] class representative must be part of the class and 'possess the same interest and suffer the same injury' as the class members." East Tex. Motor Freight System, Inc. v. Rodriguez, 431 U.S. 395, 403 (1977) (quoting Schlesinger v. Reservists Comm. to Stop the War, 418 U.S. 208, 216 (1974)).[48]

As the Third Circuit pointed out, named parties with diverse medical conditions sought to act on behalf of a single giant class rather than on behalf of discrete subclasses. In significant respects, the interests of those

---

48. The adequacy-of-representation requirement "tend[s] to merge" with the commonality and typicality criteria of Rule 23(a), which "serve as guideposts for determining whether ... maintenance of a class action is economical and whether the named plaintiff's claim and the class claims are so interrelated that the interests of the class members will be fairly and adequately protected in their absence." General Telephone Co. of Southwest v. Falcon, 457 U.S. 147, 157, n. 13 (1982). The adequacy heading also factors in competency and conflicts of class counsel. See id., at 157–158, n. 13. Like the Third Circuit, we decline to address adequacy-of-counsel issues discretely in light of our conclusions that common questions of law or fact do not predominate and that the named plaintiffs cannot adequately represent the interests of this enormous class.

within the single class are not aligned. Most saliently, for the currently injured, the critical goal is generous immediate payments. That goal tugs against the interest of exposure-only plaintiffs in ensuring an ample, inflation-protected fund for the future. Cf. General Telephone Co. of Northwest v. EEOC, 446 U.S. 318, 331 (1980) ("In employment discrimination litigation, conflicts might arise, for example, between employees and applicants who were denied employment and who will, if granted relief, compete with employees for fringe benefits or seniority. Under Rule 23, the same plaintiff could not represent these classes.").

The disparity between the currently injured and exposure-only categories of plaintiffs, and the diversity within each category are not made insignificant by the District Court's finding that petitioners' assets suffice to pay claims under the settlement. See 157 F.R.D., at 291. Although this is not a "limited fund" case certified under Rule 23(b)(1)(B), the terms of the settlement reflect essential allocation decisions designed to confine compensation and to limit defendants' liability. For example, . . . the settlement includes no adjustment for inflation; only a few claimants per year can opt out at the back end; and loss-of-consortium claims are extinguished with no compensation.

The settling parties, in sum, achieved a global compromise with no structural assurance of fair and adequate representation for the diverse groups and individuals affected. Although the named parties alleged a range of complaints, each served generally as representative for the whole, not for a separate constituency. In another asbestos class action, the Second Circuit spoke precisely to this point:

> "[W]here differences among members of a class are such that subclasses must be established, we know of no authority that permits a court to approve a settlement without creating subclasses on the basis of consents by members of a unitary class, some of whom happen to be members of the distinct subgroups. The class representatives may well have thought that the Settlement serves the aggregate interests of the entire class. But the adversity among subgroups requires that the members of each subgroup cannot be bound to a settlement except by consents given by those who understand that their role is to represent solely the members of their respective subgroups." In re Joint Eastern and Southern Dist. Asbestos Litigation, 982 F.2d 721, 742–743 (CA2 1992), modified on reh'g sub nom. In re Findley, 993 F.2d 7 (CA2 1993).

The Third Circuit found no assurance here—either in the terms of the settlement or in the structure of the negotiations—that the named plaintiffs operated under a proper understanding of their representational responsibilities. . . . That assessment, we conclude, is on the mark.

C

. . . . .

Because we have concluded that the class in this case cannot satisfy the requirements of common issue predominance and adequacy of representation, we need not rule, definitively, on the notice given here. In accord with the Third Circuit, however, ... we recognize the gravity of the question whether class action notice sufficient under the Constitution and Rule 23 could ever be given to legions so unselfconscious and amorphous.

V

The argument is sensibly made that a nationwide administrative claims processing regime would provide the most secure, fair, and efficient means of compensating victims of asbestos exposure. Congress, however, has not adopted such a solution. And Rule 23, which must be interpreted with fidelity to the Rules Enabling Act and applied with the interests of absent class members in close view, cannot carry the large load CCR, class counsel, and the District Court heaped upon it. As this case exemplifies, the rulemakers' prescriptions for class actions may be endangered by "those who embrace [Rule 23] too enthusiastically just as [they are by] those who approach [the rule] with distaste." C. Wright, Law of Federal Courts 508 (5th ed. 1994); cf. 83 F.3d, at 634 (suggesting resort to less bold aggregation techniques, including more narrowly defined class certifications).

For the reasons stated, the judgment of the Court of Appeals for the Third Circuit is

Affirmed.

■ JUSTICE O'CONNOR took no part in the consideration or decision of this case.

■ JUSTICE BREYER, with whom JUSTICE STEVENS joins, concurring in part and dissenting in part.

Although I agree with the Court's basic holding that "settlement is relevant to a class certification," ... I find several problems in its approach that lead me to a different conclusion. First, I believe that the need for settlement in this mass tort case, with hundreds of thousands of lawsuits, is greater than the Court's opinion suggests. Second, I would give more weight than would the majority to settlement-related issues for purposes of determining whether common issues predominate. Third, I am uncertain about the Court's determination of adequacy of representation, and do not believe it appropriate for this Court to second-guess the District Court on the matter without first having the Court of Appeals consider it. Fourth, I am uncertain about the tenor of an opinion that seems to suggest the settlement is unfair. And fifth, in the absence of further review by the Court of Appeals, I cannot accept the majority's suggestions that "notice" is inadequate.

. . . . . ⁴⁹

[**49.** For commentary on *Amchem* and related issues, see Bassett, Constructing Class Action Reality, 2006 BYU L. Rev. 1415; Bassett, When Reform Is Not Enough: Assuring More than

Merely "Adequate" Representation in Class Actions, 38 Ga.L.Rev. 927 (2004); Rubenstein, A Transactional Model of Litigation, 8 Geo.L.J. 371 (2001); Issacharoff, Governance and Legitimacy in the Law of Class Actions, 1999 Sup.Ct.Rev. 187; Willging, Mass Torts Problems and Proposals: A Report to the Mass Torts Working Group, 187 F.R.D. 328 (1999); Weber, A Consent–Based Approach to Class Action Settlement: Improving *Amchem Products, Inc. v. Windsor*, 59 Ohio St.L.J. 1155 (1998).

See also Oakley, Green, Issacharoff & Resnik, Program–AALS Section on Civil Procedure–Summing Up Procedural Justice: Exploring the Tension Between Collective Processes and Individual Rights in the Context of Settlement and Litigating Classes, 30 U.C.Davis L.Rev. 619 (1997); Estreicher, Federal Class Actions After 30 Years, 71 N.Y.U.L.Rev. 1 (1996). See generally Wright & Kane, Federal Courts § 72 (6th ed.2002).

It was held in Deposit Guar. Nat. Bank v. Roper, 445 U.S. 326 (1980), that the named plaintiff has a continuing individual interest in the resolution of the class certification question in order to shift part of the costs of litigation to the class, and thus that the plaintiff may appeal the denial of class certification as of right, after final judgment, even though his individual claim has been fully satisfied. The Court said in part:

> The use of the class action procedure for litigation of individual claims may offer substantial advantages for named plaintiffs. It may motivate them to bring cases that for economic reasons may not be brought otherwise. Plainly there has been a growth of litigation stimulated by contingent-fee agreements and an enlargement of the role this type of fee arrangement has played in vindicating the rights of individuals who otherwise might not consider it worth the candle to embark on litigation in which the optimum result might be more than consumed by the cost. The prospect of such fee arrangements offers advantages for litigation by named plaintiffs in class actions as well as for their attorneys. For better or worse, the financial incentive that class actions offer to the legal profession is a natural outgrowth of the increasing reliance on the 'private attorney general' for the vindication of legal rights; obviously this development has been facilitated by Rule 23.

> The aggregation of individual claims in the context of a class-wide suit is an evolutionary response to the existence of injuries unremedied by the regulatory action of government. Where it is not economically feasible to obtain relief within the traditional framework of a multiplicity of small individual suits for damages, aggrieved persons may be without any effective redress unless they may employ the class-action device. That there is a potential for misuse of the class action mechanism is obvious. Its benefits to class members are often nominal and symbolic, with persons other than class members becoming the chief beneficiaries. But the remedy for abuses does not lie in denying the relief sought here, but with re-examination of Rule 23 as to untoward consequences.

> A district court's ruling on the certification issue is often the most significant decision rendered in these class-action proceedings. To deny the right to appeal simply because the defendant has sought to 'buy off' the individual private claims of the named plaintiffs would be contrary to sound judicial administration. Requiring multiple plaintiffs to bring separate actions, which effectively could be 'picked off' by a defendant's tender of judgment before an affirmative ruling on class certification could be obtained, obviously would frustrate the objectives of class actions; moreover it would invite waste of judicial resources by stimulating successive suits brought by others claiming aggrievement. It would be in the interests of a class-action defendant to forestall any appeal of denial of class certification if that could be accomplished by tendering the individual damages claimed by the named plaintiffs. Permitting appeal of the district court's certification ruling—either at once by interlocutory appeal, or after entry of judgment on the merits—also minimizes problems raised by 'forum shopping' by putative class representatives attempting to locate a judge perceived as sympathetic to class actions.

> That small individual claims otherwise might be limited to local and state courts rather than a federal forum does not justify ignoring the overall problem of wise use of judicial resources. . . .

445 U.S., at 338–340.

F. IMPLEADER

Coates v. CTB, Inc.

United States District Court, Middle District of Alabama, 2001.
173 F.Supp.2d 1200.

■ MYRON H. THOMPSON, DISTRICT JUDGE.

Plaintiff Charles Coates brought suit in Alabama state court against defendant Latco, Inc., and others, stating claims for breach of contract, fraud, negligence, wantonness, and intentional interference with business relations, from the allegedly faulty construction of a chicken house. Defendants properly removed this lawsuit to federal court under 28 U.S.C. §§ 1332, 1441. After removal, Latco, as a third-party plaintiff, impleaded

---

The potential for overlap between "typicality" and "adequacy of representation" is explained in Sweet v. Pfizer, 232 F.R.D. 360, 370 (C.D.Cal.2005), in which the court noted that when an "abundance of individual issues ... bars a finding of typicality, adequacy of representation is necessarily lacking as well."

Subdivision (f), added in 1998 to Rule 23, reprinted supra p. 883, at p. 886, vests the courts of appeals with discretionary appellate jurisdiction of orders granting or denying class certification provided an application to appeal is filed within ten days of entry of the order.

The discretionary power of the courts of appeals to hear interlocutory appeals from class-certification rulings under Rule 23(f) is discussed and applied in Blair v. Equifax Check Services, Inc., 181 F.3d 832 (7th Cir.1999). See also Solimine & Hines, Deciding to Decide: Class Action Certification and Interlocutory Review by the United States Courts of Appeals under Rule 23(f), 41 Wm. & Mary L.Rev. 1531 (2000). In Rutstein v. Avis Rent–A–Car Systems, 211 F.3d 1228 (11th Cir.2000), noted 114 Harv.L.Rev. 1793 (2001), it was held that Rule 23(f) gives an appellate court the authority to review and reverse a trial court's grant of class certification based on the appellate court's de novo review of the facts relating to the predominance issue under Rule 23(b)(3).

An unnamed member of a Rule 23(b)(1) class action who has entered a timely objection to the settlement of the class action at the fairness hearing in the district court need not intervene in the action in order to appeal the district court's approval of the settlement. Devlin v. Scardelletti, 536 U.S. 1 (2002), also discussed infra p. 980, n. 1.

The Private Securities Litigation Reform Act of 1995 (PSLRA) imposes a "gauntlet" of procedural restrictions on the prosecution of a securities-law class action. The Securities Litigation Uniform Standards Act of 1998 contains an exceptionally broad removal provision permitting securities-law class actions to be removed from state courts to the federal courts, where they become subject to the restrictive provisions of PSLRA. See Branson, Securities Litigation in State Courts—Something Old, Something New, Something Borrowed ..., 76 Wash.U.L.Q. 509 (1998); Branson, Running the Gauntlet, A Description of the Arduous, and Now Often Fatal, Journey for Plaintiffs in Federal Securities Law Actions, 65 U.Cin.L.Rev. 3 (1996); Branson, Chasing the Rogue Professional After the Private Securities Litigation Reform Act of 1995, 50 SMU L.Rev. 91 (1996). The Class Action Fairness Act of 2005, discussed supra p. 177, n. 11, has the express objective of promoting even more expansive removal of state-court class actions to the federal courts.

It is not a denial of due process for a state, in the equivalent of what in federal court would be a (b)(3) class action, to exercise jurisdiction over a class of plaintiffs, many of whom otherwise lack minimum contacts with the state. Phillips Petroleum Co. v. Shutts, 472 U.S. 797 (1985); Miller & Crump, Jurisdiction and Choice of Law in Multistate Class Actions: Phillips Petroleum Co. v. Shutts, 96 Yale L.J. 1 (1986).]

third-party defendants Illinois Tool Works, Inc. (ITW) and J & S Tool and Fastener (J & S), two corporations which allegedly supplied some of the tools and material used in the construction of the chicken house. In its third-party complaint, Latco alleges that the chicken houses had leaky roofs, which were caused by defective nails and nail guns manufactured by ITW and sold to Latco by J & S. Latco asserts a number of state-law claims, including common-law indemnity, against ITW and J & S.

This lawsuit is now before the court on ITW's motion to dismiss. In the motion, ITW contends, first, that the third-party complaint is improper under Federal Rule of Civil Procedure 14, in that no sustainable allegation of contribution or indemnity has been made, and, second, that the complaint is untimely. For the reasons that follow, the motion will be denied.

I.   MOTION–TO–DISMISS STANDARD

In considering a third-party defendant's motion to dismiss, the court accepts the third-party plaintiff's allegations as true, Fed.R.Civ.P. 12(b); Andreu v. Sapp, 919 F.2d 637, 639 (11th Cir.1990), and construes the complaint liberally in the third-party plaintiff's favor. Scheuer v. Rhodes, 416 U.S. 232, 236 (1974). The lawsuit may not be dismissed unless the third-party plaintiff can prove no set of facts supporting the relief requested.[50] *Scheuer*, 416 U.S., at 236; Duke v. Cleland, 5 F.3d 1399, 1402 (11th Cir.1993).

II.   DISCUSSION

A.

A defendant, as a third-party plaintiff, may implead a third-party defendant who "is or may be liable to the third-party plaintiff for all or part of the plaintiff's claim against the third-party plaintiff." Fed.R.Civ.P. 14(a).[51] The third-party defendant's liability to the third-party plaintiff

---

[50. In 2007, the United States Supreme Court decided several cases addressing federal pleading standards. Many questioned whether the first of those cases had altered the Scheuer v. Rhodes (more commonly known as the Conley v. Gibson) standard. See Bell Atlantic Corp. v. Twombly, 550 U.S. 544 (2007). Initially it had appeared that the Court might merely be imposing a heightened pleading standard where specifically authorized by statute. See *Twombly*, 550 U.S. at 545–546 (antitrust treble-damages cases); see also Tellabs, Inc. v. Makor Issues & Rights, Ltd., 551 U.S. 308 (2007) (Private Securities Litigation Reform Act requires the plaintiff to "state with particularity facts giving rise to a strong inference" that the defendant intended to deceive, manipulate, or defraud). However, in 2009, the Court clarified its intention to modify the federal pleading standard, stating, "pleadings that ... are no more than conclusions, are not entitled to the assumption of truth. While legal conclusions can provide the framework of a complaint, they must be supported by factual allegations." Ashcroft v. Iqbal, 556 U.S. 662 (2009). The *Iqbal* majority further observed: "Determining whether a complaint states a plausible claim for relief will ... be a context-specific task that requires the reviewing court to draw on its judicial experience and common sense." *Iqbal* thus appears to rewrite Federal Rule of Civil Procedure 8 to impose a preliminary substantive review of the complaint's sufficiency using a plausibility standard, thereby permitting the judge to adjust the required level of pleading detail based on the judge's perception of the plausibility of the plaintiff's allegations.]

51. The *Federal* Rules of Civil Procedure apply in this court, notwithstanding Latco's insistence on citing the *Alabama* Rules of Civil Procedure. Hanna v. Plumer, 380 U.S. 460,

must be in some way dependent on the outcome of the main claim. United States v. Olavarrieta, 812 F.2d 640 (11th Cir.1987); United States v. Joe Grasso & Son, Inc., 380 F.2d 749, 751 (11th Cir.1967); 6 Charles A. Wright & Arthur R. Miller, Federal Practice and Procedure § 1446, at 355–69. An entirely separate claim, even one that arises out of the same set of facts, does not allow a third-party defendant to be impleaded. *Joe Grasso & Son*, 380 F.2d, at 751. The impleaded party "must be liable secondarily to the original defendant in the event that the latter is held liable to the plaintiff." Id.

A logical conclusion from Fed.R.Civ.P. 14's requirement that the third-party defendant "be liable to the third-party defendant for all or part of the plaintiff's claim" is that a court, in deciding an impleader question based on state law, must determine whether applicable state law allows contribution or indemnity in the particular case. 6 Charles A. Wright & Arthur R. Miller, Federal Practice and Procedure § 1446, at 369. The application of Rule 14 depends on the existence of a substantive right to indemnity or contribution under Alabama law.

As a general rule under Alabama law, there is no right of indemnity or contribution among joint tortfeasors. Kennedy Engine Co. v. Dog River Marina & Boatworks, Inc., 432 So.2d 1214, 1215 (Ala.1983); Consolidated Pipe & Supply Co. v. Stockham Valves and Fittings, Inc., 365 So.2d 968, 970 (Ala.1978). However, there is an exception to this rule. This exception is "that a joint wrongdoer may claim indemnity where he has not been guilty of any fault, except technically or constructively, or where both parties are at fault, but the fault of the party from whom indemnity is claimed was the efficient cause of the injury. Where an injury results from a violation of a duty which one owes to another, the parties are not in pari delicto." Mallory S.S. Co. v. Druhan, 17 Ala.App. 365, 84 So. 874, 877 (1920); see also J.C. Bradford & Co. v. Calhoun, 612 So.2d 396, 398 (Ala.1992); Crigler v. Salac, 438 So.2d 1375, 1385 (Ala.1983) (both discussing the exception and citing *Mallory*). For example, in the *Mallory* case, an employer, held liable for an injury to his employee caused by defective ship loading equipment, was allowed to bring suit for indemnity against the manufacturer of the defective equipment. 84 So., at 877 ("An employer, against whom recovery has been had for injury to his employee, may, notwithstanding his negligence in not inspecting, enforce indemnity against one who is under obligation to him, as in this case, to furnish suitable appliances, the breach of which obligation caused the injury.").

The breach of implied warranties of merchantability and fitness for a particular purpose supported plaintiff's suit for indemnity. Id.; see also Restatement (Second) of Torts § 886B (indemnity is appropriate where "the indemnitor supplied a defective chattel . . . as a result of which both were liable to the third person, and the indemnitee innocently or negligently failed to discover the defect," or "the indemnitee was induced to act by a

---

473–74 (1965) (holding that the Federal Rules of Civil Procedure, which are presumptively procedural, apply in diversity actions even if comparable state rules conflict). In any event, Ala.R.Civ.P. 14 is identical to Fed.R.Civ.P. 14.

misrepresentation on the part of the indemnitor, on which he justifiably relied'').

Critical to the *Mallory* court's reasoning was that the employer was guilty of only passive negligence, the failure to inspect the faulty equipment, and the manufacturer was guilty of active negligence in breaching its duty to supply safe products.[52] 84 So., at 877; see also Unicore, Inc. v. Tennessee Valley Authority, 768 F.2d 109, 113 (6th Cir.1985) (analyzing the *Mallory* case).

The *Mallory* case is analogous to the instant situation. The employer, responsible for the injury to his employee, can shift liability for that harm to the manufacturer of the defective equipment that caused the harm. In the instant case, the builder, Latco, which is responsible for any injury resulting from his construction of the chicken houses, can shift liability for that harm to the manufacturer of the defective equipment used in construction, ITW. For the portion of the harm resulting from the use of the nails and nail guns, Latco could be found to be merely passively liable, in that it negligently failed to determine independently whether those items were properly used for the construction, while ITW could be actively negligent by supplying improper items to Latco in breach of implied warranties.

Therefore, a common-law action against ITW for indemnity exists and may be pursued in this court.[53] Because Rule 14 allows Latco to implead

---

52. This requirement means that Latco will *not* be able to recover from ITW if the evidence reveals that Latco was *actively* negligent in the construction of the chicken houses, at least with respect to the use of the nails and nail guns. If such is the case, the *Mallory* exception does not apply, and the general rule barring indemnification or contribution between joint tortfeasors will prevail. However, because Rule 14 requires simply that the party impleaded may be liable for contribution, ITW is properly included in this case.

53. As noted by Judge Ira DeMent in a recent opinion concerning another civil case by a chicken farmer against CTB, impleader may also be proper in this circumstance under the notion of an implied contractual right of indemnity. Price v. CTB, Inc., 168 F.Supp.2d 1299 (M.D.Ala.2001) (order denying motion to dismiss third-party complaint). Under Alabama law, a manufacturer of a product impliedly agrees to indemnify the seller when (1) the seller is without fault, (2) the manufacturer is responsible, and (3) the seller has been required to pay a monetary judgment. Allstate Ins. Co. v. Amerisure Ins. Co., 603 So.2d 961, 963 (Ala.1992); see also Maxfield v. Simmons, 96 Ill.2d 81, 449 N.E.2d 110 (1983) (applying implied contractual indemnity against the manufacturer of roofing materials in a suit charging the builder with shoddy work). The difference between the exception to the general joint-tortfeasor rule and the theory of implied-contractual indemnity is as follows: ITW would be liable under implied-contractual indemnity only if Latco were entirely without fault in the construction; ITW would be liable under common-law indemnity principles, according to the exception, even if Latco were at fault, as long as Latco was only *passively* negligent.

The *Allstate* court noted the similarity between the elements of common-law indemnity and implied-contractual indemnity. 603 So.2d, at 963. It seems reasonable that the exception discussed in *Mallory* should apply to both. Therefore, this court agrees with Judge DeMent in *Price* although this court takes a different tack: ITW may be liable to Latco for contribution or indemnification either because (1) Latco is entirely without fault or (2) Latco has a lesser degree of fault than ITW or is not *in pari delicto* with ITW.

ITW into this case, Latco's other state-law claims against ITW are also properly before this court. Fed.R.Civ.P. 18.

B.

The equitable doctrine of laches does not avail ITW in this case, as ITW has not shown prejudice resulting from any unreasonable delay. Ex parte Sasser, 730 So.2d 604, 605–06 (Ala.1999). Although Latco received the complaint in this case on August 8, 2000, no discovery, excepting only the initial required disclosures by the parties, was conducted prior to February 2001, nor was a scheduling conference held until that time. Latco asserts that ITW has been involved in "every deposition taken in these cases" and had notice of this case as early as March 2001, a month after the scheduling conference. The court also notes that ITW has recently been impleaded into a multitude of civil cases by CTB involving substantially similar facts. There was no unreasonable delay in filing the third-party complaint against ITW, and no prejudice inhered as a result of any delay that may have accrued.

III.   CONCLUSION

For the foregoing reasons, it is ORDERED that third-party defendant Illinois Tool Works, Inc.'s motion to dismiss the third-party complaint, filed August 30, 2001 (Doc. no. 64), is denied.[54]

SECTION 3. TRIAL

A.   THE RIGHT TO TRIAL BY JURY

Dairy Queen, Inc. v. Wood

Supreme Court of the United States, 1962.
369 U.S. 469, 82 S.Ct. 894, 8 L.Ed.2d 44.

■ MR. JUSTICE BLACK delivered the opinion of the Court.

The United States District Court for the Eastern District of Pennsylvania granted a motion to strike petitioner's demand for a trial by jury in an action now pending before it on the alternative grounds that either the action was "purely equitable" or, if not purely equitable, whatever legal issues that were raised were "incidental" to equitable issues, and, in either

---

[54.   See also Owen Equipment & Erection Co. v. Kroger, 437 U.S. 365 (1978) [reprinted supra p. 269].

case, no right to trial by jury existed. The petitioner then sought mandamus in the Court of Appeals for the Third Circuit to compel the district judge to vacate this order. When that court denied this request without opinion, we granted certiorari because the action of the Court of Appeals seemed inconsistent with protections already clearly recognized for the important constitutional right to trial by jury in our previous decisions.

At the outset, we may dispose of one of the grounds upon which the trial court acted in striking the demand for trial by jury—that based upon the view that the right to trial by jury may be lost as to legal issues where those issues are characterized as "incidental" to equitable issues—for our previous decisions make it plain that no such rule may be applied in the federal courts. In *Scott v. Neely*, decided in 1891, this Court held that a court of equity could not even take jurisdiction of a suit "in which a claim properly cognizable only at law is united in the same pleadings with a claim for equitable relief." [55] That holding, which was based upon both the historical separation between law and equity and the duty of the Court to insure "that the right to a trial by a jury in the legal action may be preserved intact," [56] created considerable inconvenience in that it necessitated two separate trials in the same case whenever that case contained both legal and equitable claims. Consequently, when the procedure in the federal courts was modernized by the adoption of the Federal Rules of Civil Procedure in 1938, 28 U.S.C., it was deemed advisable to abandon that part of the holding of *Scott v. Neely* which rested upon the separation of law and equity and to permit the joinder of legal and equitable claims in a single action. . . .

The Federal Rules did not, however, purport to change the basic holding of *Scott v. Neely* that the right to trial by jury of legal claims must be preserved. Quite the contrary, Rule 38(a) expressly reaffirms that constitutional principle, declaring: "The right of trial by jury as declared by the Seventh Amendment to the Constitution or as given by a statute of the United States shall be preserved to the parties inviolate." Nonetheless, after the adoption of the Federal Rules, attempts were made indirectly to undercut that right by having federal courts in which cases involving both legal and equitable claims were filed decide the equitable claim first. The result of this procedure in those cases in which it was followed was that any issue common to both the legal and equitable claims was finally determined by the court and the party seeking trial by jury on the legal claim was deprived of that right as to these common issues. This procedure finally came before us in *Beacon Theatres, Inc. v. Westover*,[57] a case which, like this one arose from the denial of a petition for mandamus to compel a district judge to vacate his order striking a demand for trial by jury.

---

55. 140 U.S. 106, 117. See also Cates v. Allen, 149 U.S. 451, in which the principles expressed and applied in *Scott v. Neely* were explicitly reaffirmed.

56. Id., at 110.

57. 359 U.S. 500.

Our decision reversing that case not only emphasizes the responsibility of the Federal Courts of Appeals to grant mandamus where necessary to protect the constitutional right to trial by jury but also limits the issues open for determination here by defining the protection to which that right is entitled in cases involving both legal and equitable claims. The holding in *Beacon Theatres* was that where both legal and equitable issues are presented in a single case, "only under the most imperative circumstances, circumstances which in view of the flexible procedures of the Federal Rules we cannot now anticipate, can the right to a jury trial of legal issues be lost through prior determination of equitable claims."[58] That holding, of course, applies whether the trial judge chooses to characterize the legal issues presented as "incidental" to equitable issues or not.[58] Consequently, in a case such as this where there cannot even be a contention of such "imperative circumstances," *Beacon Theatres* requires that any legal issues for which a trial by jury is timely and properly demanded be submitted to a jury. There being no question of the timeliness or correctness of the demand involved here, the sole question which we must decide is whether the action now pending before the District Court contains legal issues.

[Defendant, petitioner in the Supreme Court, had been licensed to use the plaintiff's trademark. It continued to use the mark after it had been advised by plaintiff that it had committed a material breach of contract and that the right to use the mark was being terminated. Plaintiff sued to enjoin defendant from future use of the mark and asked also for an accounting to determine the exact amount of money owed by defendant to plaintiff. Defendant made a timely demand for jury trial.]

Petitioner's contention, as set forth in its petition for mandamus to the Court of Appeals and reiterated in its briefs before this Court, is that insofar as the complaint requests a money judgment it presents a claim which is unquestionably legal. We agree with that contention. The most natural construction of the respondents' claim for a money judgment would seem to be that it is a claim that they are entitled to recover whatever was owed them under the contract as of the date of its purported termination plus damages for infringement of their trademark since that date. Alterna-

---

58. Id., at 510–511. [In *Beacon Theatres* the complaint sought equitable relief under the antitrust laws. A counterclaim asked for legal relief, claiming that plaintiff had violated the antitrust laws. An issue common to both the complaint and the counterclaim was the existence of competition between the two parties. The lower courts held that the issues raised in the complaint should be tried first to the court before jury determination of the validity of the charges in the counterclaim. The Supreme Court reversed, holding that if there is an issue common to a claim on which there is a right to jury trial and to another claim on which there is no such right, that issue must be tried to the jury before disposing of other issues in the case. Justice Black wrote the opinion of the court. Justices Stewart, Harlan, and Whitaker dissented. Justice Frankfurter took no part in the case.]

58. "It is therefore immaterial that the case at bar contains a stronger basis for equitable relief than was present in *Beacon Theatres*. It would make no difference if the equitable cause clearly outweighed the legal cause so that the basic issue of the case taken as a whole is equitable. As long as any legal cause is involved the jury rights it creates control. This is the teaching of *Beacon Theatres*, as we construe it." Thermo–Stitch, Inc. v. Chemi–Cord Processing Corp., 5 Cir., 294 F.2d 486, 491.

tively, the complaint could be construed to set forth a full claim based upon both of these theories—that is, a claim that the respondents were entitled to recover both the debt due under the contract and damages for trademark infringement for the entire period of the alleged breach including that before the termination of the contract. Or it might possibly be construed to set forth a claim for recovery based completely on either one of these two theories—that is, a claim based solely upon the contract for the entire period both before and after the attempted termination on the theory that the termination, having been ignored, was of no consequence, or a claim based solely upon the charge of infringement on the theory that the contract, having been breached, could not be used as a defense to an infringement action even for the period prior to its termination.[60] We find it unnecessary to resolve this ambiguity in the respondents' complaint because we think it plain that their claim for a money judgment is a claim wholly legal in its nature however the complaint is construed. As an action on a debt allegedly due under a contract, it would be difficult to conceive of an action of a more traditionally legal character. And as an action for damages based upon a charge of trademark infringement, it would be no less subject to cognizance by a court of law.

The respondents' contention that this money claim is "purely equitable" is based primarily upon the fact that their complaint is cast in terms of an "accounting," rather than in terms of an action for "debt" or "damages." But the constitutional right to trial by jury cannot be made to depend upon the choice of words used in the pleadings. The necessary prerequisite to the right to maintain a suit for an equitable accounting, like all other equitable remedies, is, as we pointed out in *Beacon Theatres*, the absence of an adequate remedy at law. Consequently, in order to maintain such a suit on a cause of action cognizable at law, as this one is, the plaintiff must be able to show that the "accounts between the parties" are of such a "complicated nature" that only a court of equity can satisfactorily unravel them. In view of the powers given to District Courts by Federal Rule of Civil Procedure 53(b) to appoint masters to assist the jury in those exceptional cases where the legal issues are too complicated for the jury adequately to handle alone, the burden of such a showing is considerably increased and it will indeed be a rare case in which it can be met.[61] But be

---

60. This last possible construction of the complaint, though accepted as the correct one in the concurring opinion, actually seems the least likely of all. For it seems plain that irrespective of whatever else the complaint sought, it did seek a judgment for the some $60,000 allegedly owing under the contract. Certainly, the district judge had no doubt that this was the case: "Incidental to this relief, the complaint also demands the $60,000 now allegedly due and owing plaintiffs under the aforesaid contract." 194 F.Supp., at 687.

61. It was settled in *Beacon Theatres* that procedural changes which remove the inadequacy of a remedy at law may sharply diminish the scope of traditional equitable remedies by making them unnecessary in many cases. "Thus, the justification for equity's deciding legal issues once it obtains jurisdiction, and refusing to dismiss a case, merely because subsequently a legal remedy becomes available, must be re-evaluated in the light of the liberal joinder provisions of the Federal Rules which allow legal and equitable causes to be brought and resolved in one civil action. Similarly the need for, and therefore, the availability of such equitable remedies as Bills of Peace, Quia Timet and Injunction must be reconsidered in

that as it may, this is certainly not such a case. A jury, under proper instructions from the court, could readily determine the recovery, if any, to be had here, whether the theory finally settled upon is that of breach of contract, that of trademark infringement, or any combination of the two. The legal remedy cannot be characterized as inadequate merely because the measure of damages may necessitate a look into petitioner's business records.

Nor is the legal claim here rendered "purely equitable" by the nature of the defenses interposed by petitioner. Petitioner's primary defense to the charge of breach of contract—that is, that the contract was modified by a subsequent oral agreement—presents a purely legal question having nothing whatever to do either with novation, as the district judge suggested, or reformation, as suggested by the respondents here. Such a defense goes to the question of just what, under the law, the contract between the respondents and petitioner is and, in an action to collect a debt for breach of a contract between these parties, petitioner has a right to have the jury determine not only whether the contract has been breached and the extent of the damages if any but also just what the contract is.

We conclude therefore that the district judge erred in refusing to grant petitioner's demand for a trial by jury on the factual issues related to the question of whether there has been a breach of contract. Since these issues are common with those upon which respondents' claim to equitable relief is based, the legal claims involved in the action must be determined prior to any final court determination of respondents' equitable claims.[62] The Court of Appeals should have corrected the error of the district judge by granting the petition for mandamus. The judgment is therefore reversed and the cause remanded for further proceedings consistent with this opinion.

Reversed and remanded.

■ MR. JUSTICE STEWART concurs in the result.

■ MR. JUSTICE FRANKFURTER took no part in the decision of this case.

■ MR. JUSTICE WHITE took no part in the consideration or decision of this case.

■ MR. JUSTICE HARLAN, whom MR. JUSTICE DOUGLAS joins, concurring.

I am disposed to accept the view, strongly pressed at the bar, that this complaint seeks an accounting for alleged trademark infringement, rather than contract damages. Even though this leaves the complaint as formally asking only for equitable relief, this does not end the inquiry. The fact that an "accounting" is sought is not of itself dispositive of the jury trial issue. To render this aspect of the complaint truly "equitable" it must appear

---

view of the existence of the Declaratory Judgment Act as well as the liberal joinder provision of the Rules." 359 U.S., at 509.

62. This does not, of course, interfere with the District Court's power to grant temporary relief pending a final adjudication on the merits. Such temporary relief has already been granted in this case (see McCullough v. Dairy Queen, Inc., 290 F.2d 871) and is no part of the issues before this Court.

that the substantive claim is one cognizable only in equity or that the "accounts between the parties" are of such a "complicated nature" that they can be satisfactorily unraveled only by a court of equity. Kirby v. Lake Shore & Michigan Southern R. Co., 120 U.S. 130, 134. See 5 Moore, Federal Practice (1951), 198–202. It is manifest from the face of the complaint that the "accounting" sought in this instance is not of either variety. A jury, under proper instructions from the court, could readily calculate the damages flowing from this alleged trademark infringement, just as courts of law often do in copyright and patent cases. Cf., e.g., Hartell v. Tilghman, 99 U.S. 547, 555; Arnstein v. Porter, 154 F.2d 464; Bruckman v. Hollzer, 152 F.2d 730.

Consequently what is involved in this case is nothing more than a joinder in one complaint of prayers for both legal and equitable relief. In such circumstances, under principles long since established, Scott v. Neely, 140 U.S. 106, 110, the petitioner cannot be deprived of his constitutional right to a jury trial on the "legal" claim contained in the complaint.

On this basis I concur in the judgment of the Court.[63]

[63. See Wright & Kane, Federal Courts § 92 (6th ed.2002); Rendleman, Chapters of the Civil Jury, 65 Ky.L.J. 769 (1977); Redish, Seventh Amendment Right to Jury Trial: A Study in the Irrationality of Rational Decision Making, 70 Nw.U.L.Rev. 486 (1975); McCoid, Procedural Reform and the Right to Jury Trial: A Study of *Beacon Theatres, Inc. v. Westover*, 116 U.Pa.L.Rev. 1 (1967).

"In the end, unless we are prepared for the major re-definition of the role of juries that might come from a re-drafting of the constitutional guarantees, it would seem that the rule of *Beacon Theatres* is the best, or least worst available solution to the problem of preserving the role of jury trials in modern litigation." Gelfand, *Smith v. University of Detroit*: Is There a Viable Alternative to *Beacon Theatres*?, 45 Wash. & Lee L.Rev. 159 (1988). The case referred to in the title of Professor Gelfand's article is Smith v. University of Detroit, 145 Mich.App. 468, 378 N.W.2d 511 (1985).

In Simler v. Conner, 372 U.S. 221 (1963), it was held that the right to a jury trial is governed by federal law, not state law, in a diversity case, and that there is a federal right to jury trial in a suit to determine the amount of fees owing to a lawyer by a client under a contingent fee retainer contract, which the client contended was the product of fraud and overreaching.

The Seventh Amendment does not prevent Congress from creating new statutory public rights and allowing an administrative agency to enforce them by civil penalties without jury trial. Atlas Roofing Co., Inc. v. Occupational Safety and Health Review Commission, 430 U.S. 442 (1977). See Kirst, Administrative Penalties and the Civil Jury: The Supreme Court's Assault on the Seventh Amendment, 126 U.Pa.L.Rev. 1281 (1978).

The Seventh Amendment guarantees jury trial to determine liability in actions by the United States seeking civil penalties and injunctive relief under the Clean Water Act, but the Seventh Amendment does not require that the jury must determine the remedy in a trial in which it must determine liability. Tull v. United States, 481 U.S. 412 (1987).

The precedential value of *Tull* has been greatly reduced by Feltner v. Columbia Pictures Television, Inc., 523 U.S. 340 (1998), which held that the Seventh Amendment's right of jury trial extends to the amount of "statutory damages" for which an infringer is liable under § 504(c) of the Copyright Act, 17 U.S.C. § 504(c). "In *Tull*, we held that the Seventh Amendment grants a right to a jury trial of all issues relating to liability for civil penalties under the Clean Water Act ..., but then went on to decide that Congress could authorize

Ross v. Bernhard

Supreme Court of the United States, 1970.
396 U.S. 531, 90 S.Ct. 733, 24 L.Ed.2d 729.

■ MR. JUSTICE WHITE delivered the opinion of the Court.

The Seventh Amendment to the Constitution provides that in "[s]uits at common law, where the value in controversy shall exceed twenty dollars, the right of trial by jury shall be preserved." Whether the Amendment guarantees the right to a jury trial in stockholders' derivative actions is the issue now before us.

Petitioners brought this derivative suit in federal court against the directors of their closed-end investment company, the Lehman Corporation and the corporation's brokers, Lehman Brothers. They contended that Lehman Brothers controlled the corporation through an illegally large representation on the corporation's board of directors, in violation of the Investment Company Act of 1940, 54 Stat. 789, 15 U.S.C. § 80a–1 et seq., and used this control to extract excessive brokerage fees from the corporation. The directors of the corporation were accused of converting corporate assets and of "gross abuse of trust, gross misconduct, willful misfeasance, bad faith, [and] gross negligence." Both the individual defendants and Lehman Brothers were accused of breaches of fiduciary duty. It was alleged that the payments to Lehman Brothers constituted waste and spoliation, and that the contract between the corporation and Lehman Brothers had been violated. Petitioners requested that the defendants "account for and pay to the Corporation for their profits and gains and its losses." Petitioners also demanded a jury trial on the corporation's claims.

. . . . .

We reverse the holding of the Court of Appeals that in no event does the right to a jury trial preserved by the Seventh Amendment extend to derivative actions brought by the stockholders of a corporation. We hold that the right to jury trial attaches to those issues in derivative actions as to which the corporation, if it had been suing in its own right, would have been entitled to a jury.

---

trial judges to assess the amount of the civil penalties...." 523 U.S., at 354. Noting that "[t]his portion of our opinion [in *Tull*] was arguably dicta," and that "*Tull* is at least in tension with" two precedents decided in 1829 and 1935, 523 U.S., at 354–355, nn. 8–9, the *Feltner* Court continued: "In *Tull*, however, we were presented with no evidence that juries historically had determined the amount of civil penalties to be paid to the Government. Moreover, the awarding of civil penalties to the Government could be viewed as analogous to sentencing in a criminal proceeding.... Here ... there is no similar analogy, and there is clear and direct historical evidence that juries, both as a general matter and in copyright cases, set the amount of damages awarded to a successful plaintiff. *Tull* is thus inapposite." 523 U.S., at 355.

In Hetzel v. Prince William County, 523 U.S. 208 (1998) (per curiam), the Supreme Court unanimously reaffirmed the rule that if a verdict is found to be excessive, plaintiff cannot be required to accept a lesser amount. Instead plaintiff must be given the option of either accepting a remittitur to a lower amount or having a new trial.]

The Seventh Amendment preserves to litigants the right to jury trial in suits at common law—

"not merely suits, which the *common* law recognized among its old and settled proceedings, but suits in which *legal* rights were to be ascertained and determined, in contradistinction to those where equitable rights alone were recognized, and equitable remedies were administered.... In a just sense, the amendment then may well be construed to embrace all suits, which are not of equity and admiralty jurisdiction, whatever may be the peculiar form which they may assume to settle legal rights." Parsons v. Bedford, Breedlove & Robeson, 3 Pet. [28 U.S.] 433, 447 (1830).

However difficult it may have been to define with precision the line between actions at law dealing with legal rights and suits in equity dealing with equitable matters, Whitehead v. Shattuck, 138 U.S. 146, 151 (1891), some proceedings were unmistakably actions at law triable to a jury. The Seventh Amendment, for example, entitled the parties to a jury trial in actions for damages to a person or property, for libel and slander, for recovery of land, and for conversion of personal property. Just as clearly, a corporation, although an artificial being, was commonly entitled to sue and be sued in the usual forms of action, at least in its own State. See Paul v. Virginia, 8 Wall. [75 U.S.] 168 (1869). Whether the corporation was viewed as an entity separate from its stockholders or as a device permitting its stockholders to carry on their business and to sue and be sued, a corporation's suit to enforce a legal right was an action at common law carrying the right to jury trial at the time the Seventh Amendment was adopted.

The common law refused, however, to permit stockholders to call corporate managers to account in actions at law. The possibilities for abuse, thus presented, were not ignored by corporate officers and directors. Early in the 19th century, equity provided relief both in this country and in England. Without detailing these developments, it suffices to say that the remedy in this country, first dealt with by this Court in Dodge v. Woolsey, 18 How. [59 U.S.] 331 (1856), provided redress not only against faithless officers and directors but also against third parties who had damaged or threatened the corporate properties and whom the corporation through its managers refused to pursue. The remedy made available in equity was the derivative suit, viewed in this country as a suit to enforce a *corporate* cause of action against officers, directors, and third parties. As elaborated in the cases, one precondition for the suit was a valid claim on which the corporation could have sued; another was that the corporation itself had refused to proceed after suitable demand, unless excused by extraordinary conditions. Thus the dual nature of the stockholder's action: first, the plaintiff's right to sue on behalf of the corporation and, second, the merits of the corporation claim itself.

Derivative suits posed no Seventh Amendment problems where the action against the directors and third parties would have been by a bill in equity had the corporation brought the suit. Our concern is with cases based upon a legal claim of the corporation against directors or third parties. Does the trial of such claims at the suit of a stockholder and without a jury violate the Seventh Amendment?

The question arose in this Court in the context of a derivative suit for treble damages under the antitrust laws. Fleitmann v. Welsbach Street Lighting Co., 240 U.S. 27 (1916). Noting that the bill in equity set up a claim of the corporation alone, Mr. Justice Holmes observed that if the corporation were the plaintiff, "no one can doubt that its only remedy would be at law," and inquired "why the defendants' right to a jury trial should be taken away because the present plaintiff cannot persuade the only party having a cause of action to sue,—how the liability which is the principal matter can be converted into an incident of the plaintiff's domestic difficulties with the company that has been wronged" ? Id., at 28. His answer was that the bill did not state a good cause of action in equity. Agreeing that there were "cases in which the nature of the right asserted for the company, or the failure of the defendants concerned to insist upon their rights, or a different state system, has led to the whole matter being disposed of in equity," he concluded that when the penalty of triple damages is sought, the antitrust statute plainly anticipated a jury trial and should not be read as "attempting to authorize liability to be enforced otherwise than through the verdict of a jury in a court of common law." Id., at 28–29. Although the decision had obvious Seventh Amendment overtones, its ultimate rationale was grounded in the antitrust laws.

Where penal damages were not involved, however, there was no authoritative parallel to *Fleitmann* in the federal system squarely passing on the applicability of the Seventh Amendment to the trial of a legal claim presented in a pre-merger derivative suit. What can be gleaned from this Court's opinions is not inconsistent with the general understanding, reflected by the state court decisions and secondary sources, that equity could properly resolve corporate claims of any kind without a jury when properly pleaded in derivative suits complying with the equity rules.

Such was the prevailing opinion when the Federal Rules of Civil Procedure were adopted in 1938. It continued until 1963 when the Court of Appeals for the Ninth Circuit, relying on the Federal Rules as construed and applied in Beacon Theatres Inc. v. Westover, 359 U.S. 500 (1959), and Dairy Queen Inc. v. Wood, 369 U.S. 469 (1962), required the legal issues in a derivative suit to be tried to a jury. DePinto v. Provident Security Life Ins. Co., 323 F.2d 826. It was this decision that the District Court followed in the case before us and that the Court of Appeals rejected.

Beacon and *Dairy Queen* presaged *DePinto*. Under those cases, where equitable and legal claims are joined in the same action, there is a right to jury trial on the legal claims which must not be infringed either by trying the legal issues as incidental to the equitable ones or by a court trial of a common issue existing between the claims. The Seventh Amendment question depends on the nature of the issue to be tried rather than the character of the overall action.[64] See Simler v. Conner, 372 U.S. 221 (1963). The principle of these cases bears heavily on derivative actions.

---

64. As our cases indicate, the "legal" nature of an issue is determined by considering, first, the pre-merger custom with reference to such questions; second, the remedy sought; and,

We have noted that the derivative suit has dual aspects: first, the stockholder's right to sue on behalf of the corporation, historically an equitable matter; second, the claim of the corporation against directors or third parties on which, if the corporation had sued and the claim presented legal issues, the company could demand a jury trial. As implied by Mr. Justice Holmes in *Fleitmann,* legal claims are not magically converted into equitable issues by their presentation to a court of equity in a derivative suit. The claim pressed by the stockholder against directors or third parties "is not his own but the corporation's." Koster v. Lumbermens Mut. Cas. Co., 330 U.S. 518, 522 (1947). The corporation is a necessary party to the action; without it the case cannot proceed. Although named a defendant, it is the real party in interest, the stockholder being at best the nominal plaintiff. The proceeds of the action belong to the corporation and it is bound by the result of the suit. The heart of the action is the corporate claim. If it presents a legal issue, one entitling the corporation to a jury trial under the Seventh Amendment, the right to a jury is not forfeited merely because the stockholder's right to sue must first be adjudicated as an equitable issue triable to the court. *Beacon* and *Dairy Queen* require no less.

If under older procedures, now discarded, a court of equity could properly try the legal claims of the corporation presented in a derivative suit, it was because irreparable injury was threatened and no remedy at law existed as long as the stockholder was without standing to sue and the corporation itself refused to pursue its own remedies. Indeed, from 1789 until 1933, the judicial code expressly forbade courts of equity from entertaining any suit for which there was an adequate remedy at law. This provision served "to guard the right of trial by jury preserved by the Seventh Amendment and to that end it should be liberally construed." Schoenthal v. Irving Trust Co., 287 U.S. 92, 94 (1932). If, before 1938, the law had borrowed from equity, as it borrowed other things, the idea that stockholders could litigate for their recalcitrant corporation, the corporate claim, if legal, would undoubtedly have been tried to a jury.

Of course, this did not occur, but the Federal Rules had a similar impact. Actions are no longer brought as actions at law or suits in equity. Under the Rules there is only one action—a "civil action" —in which all claims may be joined and all remedies are available. Purely procedural impediments to the presentation of any issue by any party, based on the difference between law and equity, were destroyed. In a civil action presenting a stockholder's derivative claim, the court after passing upon the plaintiff's right to sue on behalf of the corporation is now able to try the corporate claim for damages with the aid of a jury.[65] Separable claims may

third the practical abilities and limitations of juries. Of these factors, the first, requiring extensive and possibly abstruse historical inquiry, is obviously the most difficult to apply. See James, Right to a Jury Trial in Civil Actions, 72 Yale L.J. 655 (1963).

65. It would appear that the same conclusions could have been reached under Equity Rule 23 and the Law and Equity Act of 1915, Act of March 3, 1915, 38 Stat. 956. See Southern R.

be tried separately. Fed.Rule Civ.Proc. 42(b), or legal and equitable issues may be handled in the same trial. Fanchon & Marco, Inc. v. Paramount Pictures, Inc., 202 F.2d 731 (C.A. 2d Cir.1953). The historical rule preventing a court of law from entertaining a shareholder's suit on behalf of the corporation is obsolete; it is no longer tenable for a district court, administering both law and equity in the same action, to deny legal remedies to a corporation, merely because the corporation's spokesmen are its shareholders rather than its directors. Under the rules, law and equity are procedurally combined; nothing turns now upon the form of the action or the procedural devices by which the parties happen to come before the court. The "expansion of adequate legal remedies provided by . . . the Federal Rules necessarily affects the scope of equity." *Beacon Theatres, Inc. v. Westover*, 359 U.S., at 509.

Thus, for example, before-merger class actions were largely a device of equity, and there was no right to a jury even on issues that might, under other circumstances, have been tried to a jury. 5 J. Moore, Federal Practice ¶ 38.38[2] (2d ed.1969); 3B id., ¶ 23.02[1]. Although at least one post-merger court held that the device was not available to try legal issues, it now seems settled in the lower federal courts that class action plaintiffs may obtain a jury trial on any legal issues they present. Montgomery Ward & Co. v. Langer, 168 F.2d 182 (C.A. 8th Cir.1948); see Oskoian v. Canuel, 269 F.2d 311 (C.A. 1st Cir.1959), aff'g 23 F.R.D. 307; Syres v. Oil Workers Int'l Union, Local 23, 257 F.2d 479 (C.A. 5th Cir.1958), cert. denied, 358 U.S. 929 (1959). 2 W. Barron & A. Holtzoff, Federal Practice and Procedure § 571 (Wright ed.1961).

Derivative suits have been described as one kind of "true" class action. Id., § 562.1. We are inclined to agree with the description, at least to the extent it recognizes that the derivative suit and the class action were both ways of allowing parties to be heard in equity who could not speak at law.[66]

Co. v. City of Greenwood, 40 F.2d 679 (D.C.W.D.S.C.1928); 2 J. Moore, Federal Practice ¶ 2.05 (2d ed.1967). Rule 23 provided:

> "If in a suit in equity a matter ordinarily determinable at law arises, such matters shall be determined in that suit according to the principles applicable, without sending the case or question to the law side of the court."

66. Other equitable devices are used under the rules without depriving the parties employing them of the right to a jury trial on legal issues. For example, although the right to intervene may in some cases be limited, United States for Use and Benefit of Browne & Bryan Lumber Co. v. Massachusetts Bonding & Ins. Co., 303 F.2d 823 (C.A. 2d Cir.1962); Dickinson v. Burnham, 197 F.2d 973 (C.A. 2d Cir.), cert. denied 344 U.S. 875 (1952), when intervention is permitted generally, the intervenor has a right to a jury trial on any legal issues he presents. See 3B J. Moore, Federal Practice ¶ 24.16[7] (2d ed.1969); 5 id., ¶ 38.38[3]. A similar development seems to be taking place in the lower courts in interpleader actions. Before merger interpleader actions lay only in equity, and there was no right to a jury even on issues that might, under other circumstances, have been tried, to a jury. Liberty Oil Co. v. Condon Nat. Bank, 260 U.S. 235 (1922). This view continued for some time after merger, see Bynum v. Prudential Life Ins. Co., 7 F.R.D. 585 (D.C.E.D.S.C.1947), but numerous courts and commentators have now come to the conclusion that the right to a jury should not turn on how the parties happen to be brought into court. See Pan American Fire & Cas. Co. v. Revere, 188 F.Supp. 474 (D.C.E.D.La.1960); Savannah Bank & Trust Co. v. Block, 175

3B J. Moore, Federal Practice ¶¶ 23.02[1], 23.1.16[1] (2d ed.1969). After adoption of the rules there is no longer any procedural obstacle to the assertion of legal rights before juries, however the party may have acquired standing to assert those rights. Given the availability in a derivative action of both legal and equitable remedies, we think the Seventh Amendment preserves to the parties in a stockholder's suit the same right to a jury trial that historically belonged to the corporation and to those against whom the corporation pressed its legal claims.

In the instant case we have no doubt that the corporation's claim is, at least in part, a legal one. The relief sought is money damages. There are allegations in the complaint of a breach of fiduciary duty, but there are also allegations of ordinary breach of contract and gross negligence. The corporation, had it sued on its own behalf, would have been entitled to a jury's determination, at a minimum, of its damages against its broker under the brokerage contract and of its rights against its own directors because of their negligence. Under these circumstances it is unnecessary to decide whether the corporation's other claims are also properly triable to a jury. Dairy Queen, Inc. v. Wood, 369 U.S. 469 (1962). The decision of the Court of Appeals is reversed.

It is so ordered.

■ MR. JUSTICE STEWART, with whom THE CHIEF JUSTICE and MR. JUSTICE HARLAN join, dissenting.

In holding as it does that the plaintiff in a shareholder's derivative suit is constitutionally entitled to a jury trial, the Court today seems to rely upon some sort of ill-defined combination of the Seventh Amendment and the Federal Rules of Civil Procedure. Somehow the Amendment and the Rules magically interact to do what each separately was expressly intended not to do, namely, to enlarge the right to a jury trial in civil actions brought in the courts of the United States.

The Seventh Amendment, by its terms, does not extend, but merely *preserves* the right to a jury trial "[i]n Suits at common law." All agree that this means the reach of the Amendment is limited to those actions that were tried to the jury in 1791 when the Amendment was adopted. Suits in equity, which were historically tried to the court, were therefore unaffected by it. Similarly, Rule 38 of the Federal Rules has no bearing on the right to a jury trial in suits in equity, for it simply preserves inviolate "[t]he right of trial by jury as declared by the Seventh Amendment." Thus this Rule, like the Amendment itself, neither restricts nor enlarges the right to jury trial. Indeed nothing in the Federal Rules can rightly be construed to enlarge the right of jury trial, for in the legislation authorizing the Rules, Congress expressly provided that they "shall neither abridge, enlarge, nor

F.Supp. 798 (D.C.S.D.Ga.1959); Westinghouse Elec. Corp. v. United Elec. Radio & Mach. Workers of America, 99 F.Supp. 597 (D.C.W.D.Pa.1951); John Hancock Mut. Life Ins. Co. v. Yarrow, 95 F.Supp. 185 (D.C.E.D.Pa.1951); 2 W. Barron & A. Holtzoff, Federal Practice and Procedure § 556 (Wright ed.1961); 3A J. Moore, Federal Practice ¶ 22.14[4] (2d ed.1969). But see Pennsylvania Fire Ins. Co. v. American Airlines, Inc., 180 F.Supp. 239 (D.C.E.D.N.Y. 1960); Liberty Nat. Life Ins. Co. v. Brown, 119 F.Supp. 920 (D.C.M.D.Ala.1954).

modify the substantive rights of any litigant." 48 Stat. 1064. See 28 U.S.C. § 2072. I take this plain, simple, and straightforward language to mean that after the promulgation of the Federal Rules, as before, the constitutional right to a jury trial attaches only to suits at common law. So, apparently, has every federal court that has discussed the issue. Since, as the Court concedes, a shareholder's derivative suit could be brought only in equity, it would seem to me to follow by the most elementary logic that in such suits there is no constitutional right to a trial by jury. Today the Court tosses aside history, logic and over 100 years of firm precedent to hold that the plaintiff in a shareholder's derivative suit does indeed have a constitutional right to a trial by jury. This holding has a questionable basis in policy[67] and no basis whatever in the Constitution.

The Court begins by assuming the "dual nature" of the shareholder's action. While the plaintiff's right to get into court at all is conceded to be equitable, once he is there the Court says his claim is to be viewed as though it were the claim of the corporation itself. If the corporation would have been entitled to a jury trial on such a claim, then, it is said, so would the shareholder. This conceptualization is without any historical basis. For the fact is that a shareholder's suit was not originally viewed in this country, or in England, as a suit to enforce a *corporate* cause of action. Rather, the shareholder's suit was initially permitted only against the managers of the corporation—not third parties—and it was conceived of as an equitable action to enforce the right of a beneficiary against his trustee. The shareholder was not, therefore, in court to enforce indirectly the corporate right of action, but to enforce directly his own equitable right of action against an unfaithful fiduciary. Later the rights of the shareholder were enlarged to encompass suits against third parties harming the corporation, but "the postulated 'corporate cause of action' has never been thought to describe an actual historical class of suit which was recognized by courts of law." Indeed the commentators, including those cited by the Court as postulating the analytic duality of the shareholder's derivative suit, recognize that historically the suit has in practice always been treated as a single cause tried exclusively in equity. They agree that there is therefore no constitutional right to a jury trial even where there might have been one had the corporation itself brought the suit.

This has been not simply the "general" or "prevailing" view in the federal courts as the Court says, but the unanimous view with the single exception of the Ninth Circuit's 1963 decision in DePinto v. Provident Security Life Ins. Co., 323 F.2d 826, a decision that has since been followed by no court until the present case.

. . . . .

---

67. See, e.g., Frank, Courts on Trial 110–111 (1949). Certainly there is no consensus among commentators on the desirability of jury trials in civil actions generally. Particularly where the issues in the case are complex—as they are likely to be in a derivative suit—much can be said for allowing the court discretion to try the case itself. See discussion in 5 J. Moore, Federal Practice ¶ 38.02[1].

It is true that in [Beacon Theatres Inc. v. Westover, 359 U.S. 500 (1959),] it was stated that the 1938 Rules did diminish the scope of federal equity jurisdiction in certain particulars. But the Court's effort to force the facts of this case into the mold of *Beacon Theatres* and [Dairy Queen Inc. v. Wood, 369 U.S. 469 (1962),] simply does not succeed. Those cases involved a combination of historically separable suits, one in law and one in equity. Their facts fit the pattern of cases where, before the Rules, the equity court would have disposed of the equitable claim and would then have either retained jurisdiction over the suit, despite the availability of adequate legal remedies, or enjoined a subsequent legal action between the same parties involving the same controversy.

But the present case is not one involving traditionally equitable claims by one party, and traditionally legal claims by the other. Nor is it a suit in which the plaintiff is asserting a combination of legal and equitable claims. For, as we have seen, a derivative suit has always been conceived of as a single, unitary, equitable cause of action. It is for this reason, and not because of "procedural impediments," that the courts of equity did not transfer derivative suits to the law side. In short, the cause of action is wholly a creature of equity. And whatever else can be said of *Beacon Theatres* and *Dairy Queen,* they did not cast aside altogether the historic division between equity and law.

If history is to be so cavalierly dismissed, the derivative suit can, of course, be artificially broken down into separable elements. But so then can any traditionally equitable cause of action, and the logic of the Court's position would lead to the virtual elimination of all equity jurisdiction. An equitable suit for an injunction, for instance, often involves issues of fact which, if damages had been sought, would have been triable to a jury. Does this mean that in a suit asking only for injunctive relief these factual issues *must* be tried to the jury, with the judge left to decide only whether, given the jury's findings, an injunction is the appropriate remedy? Certainly the Federal Rules make it *possible* to try a suit for an injunction in that way, but even more certainly they were not intended to have any such effect. Yet the Court's approach, it seems, would require that if any "legal issue" procedurally *could* be tried to a jury, it constitutionally *must* be tried to a jury.

The fact is, of course, that there are, for the most part, no such things as inherently "legal issues" or inherently "equitable issues." There are only factual issues, and, "like chameleons [they] take their color from surrounding circumstances." Thus the Court's "nature of the issue" approach is hardly meaningful.

As a final ground for its conclusion, the Court points to a supposed analogy to suits involving class actions. It says that before the Federal Rules such suits were considered equitable and not triable to a jury, but that since promulgation of the Rules the federal courts have found that "plaintiffs may obtain a jury trial on any legal issues they present." Of course the plaintiff *may* obtain such a trial even in a derivative suit. Nothing in the Constitution or the Rules precludes the judge from granting a jury trial as a matter of discretion. But even if the Court means that some federal courts have ruled that the class action plaintiff in some situations has a constitutional right to a jury trial, the analogy to derivative suits is wholly unpersuasive. For it is clear that the draftsmen of the Federal Rules intended that Rule 23 as it pertained to class actions should be applicable, like other rules governing joinder of claims and parties, "to all actions, whether formerly denominated legal or equitable." This does not mean that a formerly equitable action is triable to a jury simply *because* it is brought on behalf of a class, but only that a historically legal cause of action can be tried to a jury *even if* it is brought as a class action. Since a derivative suit is historically wholly a creation of equity, the class action "analogy" is in truth no analogy at all.

The Court's decision today can perhaps be explained as a reflection of an unarticulated but apparently overpowering bias in favor of jury trials in civil actions. It certainly cannot be explained in terms of either the Federal Rules or the Constitution.[68]

Parklane Hosiery Co. v. Shore

Supreme Court of the United States, 1979.
439 U.S. 322, 99 S.Ct. 645, 58 L.Ed.2d 552.

■ MR. JUSTICE STEWART delivered the opinion of the Court.

This case presents the question whether a party who has had issues of fact adjudicated adversely to it in an equitable action may be collaterally estopped from relitigating the same issues before a jury in a subsequent legal action brought against it by a new party.

[Stockholders of Parklane Hosiery Company had brought suit claiming it and its officers and directors had issued a false and misleading proxy statement in connection with a merger. Before the suit came to trial the Securities and Exchange Commission brought suit against Parklane and the other defendants. The SEC action was tried, the court found that the proxy statement was false and misleading, and entered a declaratory judgment to that effect. There was no right to jury trial in the SEC action. It was then held in the stockholders' suit that defendants were collaterally estopped from relitigating the issues that had been resolved against them in the suit brought by the SEC. Defendants claimed that to apply collateral estoppel to those issues would defeat their Seventh Amendment right to have a jury determine whether the proxy statement was false and misleading. The Supreme Court first considered whether the stockholders, who

---

[**68.** See Comment, From *Beacon Theatres* to *Dairy Queen* to *Ross*: The Seventh Amendment, The Federal Rules, and a Receding Law–Equity Dichotomy, 48 J.Urban Law 459 (1971). See generally 9 Wright & Miller, Federal Practice and Procedure: Civil 2d §§ 2301– 2307 (1995).

It was held in Colgrove v. Battin, 413 U.S. 149 (1973), that the size of the jury in civil cases may be regulated by local rules of court.]

were not parties to the SEC suit, could use that judgment "offensively" to prevent defendants from relitigating issues resolved in the earlier proceeding.]

I.

. . . . .

C

We have concluded that the preferable approach for dealing with these problems in the federal courts is not to preclude the use of offensive collateral estoppel, but to grant trial courts broad discretion to determine when it should be applied.[69] The general rule should be that in cases where a plaintiff could easily have joined in the earlier action or where, either for the reasons discussed above or for other reasons, the application of offensive estoppel would be unfair to a defendant, a trial judge should not allow the use of offensive collateral estoppel.

In the present case, however, none of the circumstances that might justify reluctance to allow the offensive use of collateral estoppel is present. The application of offensive collateral estoppel will not here reward a private plaintiff who could have joined in the previous action, since the respondent probably could not have joined in the injunctive action brought by the SEC even had he so desired.[70] Similarly, there is no unfairness to the petitioners in applying offensive collateral estoppel in this case. First, in light of the serious allegations made in the SEC's complaint against the petitioners, as well as the foreseeability of subsequent private suits that typically follow a successful government judgment, the petitioners had every incentive to litigate the SEC lawsuit fully and vigorously.[71] Second, the judgment in the Commission action was not inconsistent with any previous decision. Finally, there will in the respondent's action be no procedural opportunities available to the petitioner that were unavailable in the first action of a kind that might be likely to cause a different result.[72]

---

69. This is essentially the approach of [the Restatement (Second) of Judgments (Tent. Draft No. 2, 1975)] § 88, which recognizes that "the distinct trend if not the clear weight of recent authority is to the effect that there is no intrinsic difference between 'offensive' as distinct from 'defensive' issue preclusion, although a stronger showing that the prior opportunity was adequate may be required in the former situation than the later." Reporter's Note, at 99. [The draft Restatement section referred to by the Court became § 29 in Restatement (Second) of Judgments (1982).]

70. SEC v. Everest Management Corp., 475 F.2d 1236, 1240 (CA2) ("[T]he complicating effect of the additional issues and the additional parties outweighs any advantage of a single disposition of the common issues"). Moreover, consolidation of a private action with one brought by the SEC without its consent is prohibited by statute. 15 U.S.C. § 78u(g).

71. After a four-day trial in which the petitioners had every opportunity to present evidence and call witnesses, the District Court held for the SEC. The petitioners then appealed to the Court of Appeals for the Second Circuit, which affirmed the judgment against them. Moreover, the petitioners were already aware of the action brought by the respondent, since it had commenced before the filing of the SEC action.

72. It is true, of course, that the petitioners in the present action would be entitled to a jury trial of the issues bearing on whether the proxy statement was materially false and

We conclude, therefore, that none of the considerations that would justify a refusal to allow the use of offensive collateral estoppel is present in this case. Since the petitioners received a "full and fair" opportunity to litigate their claims in the SEC action, the contemporary law of collateral estoppel leads inescapably to the conclusion that the petitioners are collaterally estopped from relitigating the question of whether the proxy statements were materially false and misleading.

II

The question that remains is whether, notwithstanding the law of collateral estoppel, the use of offensive collateral estoppel in this case would violate the petitioners' Seventh Amendment right to a jury trial.

A

"[T]he thrust of the [Seventh] Amendment was to preserve the right to jury trial as it existed in 1791." Curtis v. Loether, 415 U.S. 189, 193. At common law, a litigant was not entitled to have a jury determine issues that had been previously adjudicated by a chancellor in equity. Hopkins v. Lee, 6 Wheat. [19 U.S.] 109, 112; Smith v. Kernochen, 7 How. [48 U.S.] 198, 217–218; Brady v. Daly, 175 U.S. 148, 158–159; Shapiro & Coquillette, The Fetish of Jury Trials in Civil Cases: A Comment on *Rachal v. Hill,* 85 Harv.L.Rev. 441, 448–458 (1971).

Recognition that an equitable determination could have collateral estoppel effect in a subsequent legal action was the major premise of this Court's decision in Beacon Theatres v. Westover, 359 U.S. 500. . . .

. . . To avoid this result, the Court held that when legal and equitable claims are joined in the same action, the trial judge has only limited discretion in determining the sequence of trial and "that discretion . . . must, wherever possible, be exercised to preserve jury trial." Id., at 510.

Both the premise of *Beacon Theatres,* and the fact that it enunciated no more than a general prudential rule were confirmed by this Court's decision in Katchen v. Landy, 382 U.S. 323. In that case the Court held that a bankruptcy court, sitting as a statutory court of equity, is empowered to adjudicate equitable claims prior to legal claims, even though the factual issues decided in the equity action would have been triable by a jury under the Seventh Amendment if the legal claims had been adjudicated first. The Court stated:

> "Both *Beacon Theatres* and [Dairy Queen, Inc. v. Wood, 369 U.S. 469 (1962),] recognized that there might be situations in which the Court would proceed to resolve the equitable claim first even though the results might be dispositive of the issues involved in the legal claim." 382 U.S., at 339.

---

misleading had the SEC action never been brought—a matter to be discussed in Part II of this opinion. But the presence or absence of a jury as factfinder is basically neutral, quite unlike, for example, the necessity of defending the first lawsuit in an inconvenient forum.

Thus the Court in *Katchen v. Landy*, recognized that an equitable determination can have collateral estoppel effect in a subsequent legal action, and that this estoppel does not violate the Seventh Amendment.

B

Despite the strong support to be found both in history and in the recent decisional law of this Court for the proposition that an equitable determination can have collateral estoppel effect in a subsequent legal action, the petitioners argue that application of collateral estoppel in this case would nevertheless violate their Seventh Amendment right to a jury trial. The petitioners contend that since the scope of the Amendment must be determined by reference to the common law as it existed in 1791, and since the common law permitted collateral estoppel only where there was mutuality of parties, collateral estoppel cannot constitutionally be applied when such mutuality is absent.

The petitioners have advanced no persuasive reason, however, why the meaning of the Seventh Amendment should depend on whether or not mutuality of parties is present. A litigant who has lost because of adverse factual findings in an equity action is equally deprived of a jury trial whether he is estopped from relitigating the factual issues against the same party or a new party. In either case, the party against whom estoppel is asserted has litigated questions of fact, and has had the facts determined against him in an earlier proceeding. In either case there is no further factfinding function for the jury to perform, since the common factual issues have been resolved in the previous action. Cf. Ex parte Peterson, 253 U.S. 300, 310 ("No one is entitled in a civil case to trial by jury, unless and except so far as there are issues of fact to be determined.").

The Seventh Amendment has never been interpreted in the rigid manner advocated by the petitioners. On the contrary, many procedural devices developed since 1791 that have diminished the civil jury's historic domain have been found not to be inconsistent with the Seventh Amendment. See Galloway v. United States, 319 U.S. 372, 388–393 (a directed verdict does not violate the Seventh Amendment); Gasoline Products Co. v. Champlin Refining Co., 283 U.S. 494, 497–498 (retrial limited to question of damages does not violate the Seventh Amendment even though there was no practice at common law for setting aside a verdict in part); Fidelity & Deposit Co. v. United States, 187 U.S. 315, 319–321 (summary judgment does not violate the Seventh Amendment).[73]

---

73. The petitioners' reliance on Dimick v. Schiedt, 293 U.S. 474, is misplaced. In the *Dimick* case the Court held that an increase by the trial judge of the amount of money damages awarded by the jury violated the *second* clause of the Seventh Amendment, which provides that "no fact tried by a jury, shall be otherwise reexamined in any Court of the United States, than according to the rules of the common law." Collateral estoppel does not involve the "re-examination" of any fact decided by a jury. On the contrary, the whole premise of collateral estoppel is that once an issue has been resolved in a prior proceeding, there is no further factfinding function to be performed.

The *Galloway* case is particularly instructive. There the party against whom a directed verdict had been entered argued that the procedure was unconstitutional under the Seventh Amendment. In rejecting this claim, the Court said:

"The Amendment did not bind the federal courts to the exact procedural incidents or details of jury trial according to the common law in 1791, any more than it tied them to the common-law system of pleading or the specific rules of evidence then prevailing. Nor were 'the rules of the common law' then prevalent, including those relating to the procedure by which the judge regulated the jury's role on questions of fact, crystalized in a fixed and immutable system. . . .

"The more logical conclusion, we think, and the one which both history and the previous decisions here support, is that the Amendment was designed to preserve the basic institution of jury trial in only its most fundamental elements, not the great mass of procedural forms and details varying even then so widely among common-law jurisdictions." 319 U.S., at 390, 392 (footnote omitted).

The law of collateral estoppel, like the law in other procedural areas defining the scope of the jury's function, has evolved since 1791. Under the rationale of the *Galloway* case, these developments are not repugnant to the Seventh Amendment simply for the reason that they did not exist in 1791. Thus if, as we have held, the law of collateral estoppel forecloses the petitioners from relitigating the factual issues determined against them in the SEC action, nothing in the Seventh Amendment dictates a different result, even though because of lack of mutuality there would have been no collateral estoppel in 1791.[74]

The judgment of the Court of Appeals is

Affirmed.

■ Mr. Justice Rehnquist, dissenting.

---

74. In reaching this conclusion, the Court of Appeals went on to state:

"Were there any doubt about the [question whether the petitioners were entitled to a jury redetermination of the issues otherwise subject to collateral estoppel] it should in any event be resolved against the defendants in this case for the reason that, although they were fully aware of the pendency of the present suit throughout the non-jury trial of the SEC case, they made no effort to protect their right to a jury trial of the damage claims asserted by plaintiffs, either by seeking to expedite trial of the present action or by requesting Judge Duffy, in the exercise of his discretion pursuant to Rule 39(b), (c) F.R.Civ.P., to order that the issues in the SEC case be tried by a jury or before an advisory jury." 565 F.2d, at 821. (Footnote omitted.)

The Court of Appeals was mistaken in these suggestions. The petitioners did not have a right to a jury trial in the equitable injunctive action brought by the SEC. Moreover, an advisory jury, which might have only delayed and complicated that proceeding, would not in any event have been a Seventh Amendment jury. And the petitioners were not in a position to expedite the private action and stay the SEC action. The Securities Act of 1934 provides for prompt enforcement actions by the SEC unhindered by parallel private actions. 15 U.S.C. § 78u(g).

It is admittedly difficult to be outraged about the treatment accorded by the federal judiciary to petitioners' demand for a jury trial in this lawsuit. Outrage is an emotion all but impossible to generate with respect to a corporate defendant in a securities fraud action, and this case is no exception. But the nagging sense of unfairness as to the way petitioners have been treated, engendered by the imprimatur placed by the Court of Appeals on respondent's "heads I win, tails you lose" theory of this litigation, is not dispelled by this Court's antiseptic analysis of the issues in the case. It may be that if this Nation were to adopt a new Constitution today, the Seventh Amendment guaranteeing the right of jury trial in civil cases in federal courts would not be included among its provisions. But any present sentiment to that effect cannot obscure or dilute our obligation to enforce the Seventh Amendment, which *was* included in the Bill of Rights in 1791 and which has not since been repealed in the only manner provided by the Constitution for repeal of its provisions.

The right of trial by jury in civil cases at common law is fundamental to our history and jurisprudence. Today, however, the Court reduces this valued right, which Blackstone praised as "the glory of English law," to a mere "neutral" factor and in the name of procedural reform denies the right of jury trial to defendants in a vast number of cases in which defendants, heretofore, have enjoyed jury trials. Over 35 years ago, Mr. Justice Black lamented the "gradual process of judicial erosion which in one hundred fifty years has slowly worn away a major portion of the essential guarantee of the Seventh Amendment." Galloway v. United States, 319 U.S. 372, 397 (1943) (Black, J., dissenting). Regrettably, the erosive process continues apace with today's decision.

I

. . . . .

B

The Seventh Amendment requires that the right of trial by jury be "preserved." Because the Seventh Amendment demands preservation of the jury trial right, our cases have uniformly held that the content of the right must be judged by historical standards. E.g., Curtis v. Loether, 415 U.S. 189, 193 (1974); Colgrove v. Battin, 413 U.S. 149, 155–156 (1973); Ross v. Bernhard, 396 U.S. 531, 533 (1970); Capital Traction Co. v. Hof, 174 U.S. 1, 8–9 (1899); Parsons v. Bedford, [28 U.S. (3 Pet.) 433, 446 (1830)]. Thus, in Baltimore & Carolina Line, Inc. v. Redman, 295 U.S. 654, 657 (1935), the Court stated that "[t]he right of trial by jury thus preserved is the right which existed under the English common law when the amendment was adopted." And in Dimick v. Schiedt, 293 U.S. 474, 476 (1935), the Court held, "In order to ascertain the scope and meaning of the Seventh Amendment, resort must be had to the appropriate rules of the common law established at the time of the adoption of that constitutional provision in 1791." [75] If a jury would have been impaneled in a particular

---

75. The majority suggests that Dimick v. Schiedt, 293 U.S. 474 (1935), is not relevant to the decision in this case because it dealt with the second clause of the Seventh Amendment. I

kind of case in 1791, then the Seventh Amendment requires a jury trial today, if either party so desires.

To be sure, it is the substance of the right of jury trial that is preserved, not the incidental or collateral effects of common-law practice in 1791. Walker v. New Mexico & S.P.R. Co., 165 U.S. 593, 596 (1897)....

To say that the Seventh Amendment does not tie federal courts to the exact procedure of the common law in 1791 does not imply, however, that any nominally "procedural" change can be implemented, regardless of its impact on the functions of the jury. For to sanction creation of procedural devices which limit the province of the jury to a greater degree than permitted at common law in 1791 is in direct contravention of the Seventh Amendment. See Neely v. Martin K. Eby Construction Co., 386 U.S. 317, 322 (1967); *Galloway v. United States*, 319 U.S., at 395; *Dimick v. Schiedt*, 293 U.S., at 487; Ex parte Peterson, 253 U.S. [300, 309–310 (1920)]. And since we deal here not with the common law qua common law but with the Constitution, no amount of argument that the device provides for more efficiency or more accuracy or is fairer will save it if the degree of invasion of the jury's province is greater than allowed in 1791. To rule otherwise would effectively permit judicial repeal of the Seventh Amendment because nearly any change in the province of the jury, no matter how drastic the diminution of its functions, can always be denominated "procedural re-form."

The guarantees of the Seventh Amendment will prove burdensome in some instances; the civil jury surely was a burden to the English governors who, in its stead, substituted the vice-admiralty court. But, as with other provisions of the Bill of Rights, the onerous nature of the protection is no license for contracting the rights secured by the Amendment. Because "[m]aintenance of the jury as a fact-finding body is of such importance and occupies so firm a place in our history and jurisprudence ... any seeming curtailment of the right to a jury trial should be scrutinized with the utmost care." *Dimick v. Schiedt*, 293 U.S., at 486, quoted in Beacon Theatres, Inc. v. Westover, 359 U.S. 500, 501 (1959).

C

Judged by the foregoing principles, I think it is clear that petitioners were denied their Seventh Amendment right to a jury trial in this case. Neither respondents nor the Court doubt that at common law as it existed in 1791, petitioners would have been entitled in the private action to have a jury determine whether the proxy statement was false and misleading in the respects alleged. The reason is that at common law in 1791, collateral estoppel was permitted only where the parties in the first action were identical to, or in privity with, the parties to the subsequent action. It was not until 1971 that the doctrine of mutuality was abrogated by this Court in certain limited circumstances. Blonder–Tongue Laboratories, Inc. v.

---

disagree. There is no intimation in that opinion that the first clause should be treated any differently than the second. The *Dimick* Court's respect for the guarantees of the Seventh Amendment applies equally to the first clause as to the second.

University of Illinois Foundation, 402 U.S. 313 (1971). But developments in the judge-made doctrine of collateral estoppel, however salutary, cannot, consistent with the Seventh Amendment, contract in any material fashion the right to a jury trial that a defendant would have enjoyed in 1791. In the instant case, resort to the doctrine of collateral estoppel does more than merely contract the right to a jury trial: It eliminates the right entirely and therefore contravenes the Seventh Amendment.

. . . . .

Relying on *Galloway v. United States*, supra, Gasoline Products Co. v. Champlin Refinery Co., [283 U.S. 494 (1931)], and Fidelity & Deposit Co. v. United States, 187 U.S. 315 (1902), the Court seems to suggest that the offensive use of collateral estoppel in this case is permissible under the limited principle set forth above that a mere procedural change that does not invade the province of the jury and a defendant's right thereto to a greater extent than authorized by the common law is permissible. But the Court's actions today constitute a far greater infringement of the defendant's rights than it ever before has sanctioned. In *Galloway,* the Court upheld the modern form of directed verdict against a Seventh Amendment challenge, but it is clear that a similar form of directed verdict existed at common law in 1791. E.g., Beauchamp v. Borret, Peake 148, 170 Eng.Rep. 110 (K.B.1792); Coupey v. Henley, 2 Esp. 540, 542, 170 Eng.Rep. 448, 449 (C.P.1797). The modern form did not materially alter the function of the jury. Similarly, the modern device of summary judgment was found not to violate the Seventh Amendment because in 1791 a demurrer to the evidence, a procedural device substantially similar to summary judgment, was a common practice. E.g., Pawling v. United States, 4 Cranch. [8 U.S.] 219, 221–222 (1808). The procedural devices of summary judgment and directed verdict are direct descendants of their common-law antecedents. They accomplish nothing more than could have been done at common law, albeit by a more cumbersome procedure. See also Montgomery Ward & Co. v. Duncan, 311 U.S. 243, 250 (1940). And while at common law there apparently was no practice of setting aside a verdict in part, the Court in *Gasoline Products* permitted a partial retrial of "distinct and separable" issues because the change in procedure would not impair the substance of the right to jury trial. 283 U.S., at 498. The parties in *Gasoline Products* still enjoyed the right to have a jury determine all issues of fact.

By contrast, the development of nonmutual estoppel is a substantial departure from the common law and its use in this case completely deprives petitioners of their right to have a jury determine contested issues of fact. I am simply unwilling to accept the Court's presumption that the complete extinguishment of petitioners' right to trial by jury can be justified as a mere change in "procedural incident or detail." Over 40 years ago, Mr. Justice Sutherland observed in a not dissimilar case, "[T]his court in a very special sense is charged with the duty of construing and upholding the Constitution; and in the discharge of that important duty, it ever must be alert to see that a doubtful precedent be not extended by mere analogy to a different case if the result will be to weaken or subvert what it conceives to be a principle of the fundamental law of the land.'' *Dimick v. Schiedt*, 293 U.S., at 485.

II

Even accepting, *arguendo,* the majority's position that there is no violation of the Seventh Amendment here, I nonetheless would not sanction the use of collateral estoppel in this case. The Court today holds:

> "The general rule should be that in cases where a plaintiff could easily have joined in the earlier action or where, either for the reasons discussed above or for other reasons, the application of offensive collateral estoppel would be unfair to a defendant, a trial judge should not allow the use of offensive collateral estoppel.'' . . . .

In my view, it is "unfair'' to apply offensive collateral estoppel where the party who is sought to be estopped has not had an opportunity to have the facts of his case determined by a jury. Since in this case petitioners were not entitled to a jury trial in the Securities and Exchange Commission (SEC) lawsuit. I would not estop them from relitigating the issues determined in the SEC suit before a jury in the private action. I believe that several factors militate in favor of this result.

First, the use of offensive collateral estoppel in this case runs counter to the strong federal policy favoring jury trials, even if it does not, as the majority holds, violate the Seventh Amendment. . . .

Second, I believe that the opportunity for a jury trial in the second action could easily lead to a different result from that obtained in the first action before the court and therefore that it is unfair to estop petitioners from relitigating the issues before a jury. This is the position adopted in the Restatement (Second) of Judgments, which disapproves of the application of offensive collateral estoppel where the defendant has an opportunity for a jury trial in the second lawsuit that was not available in the first action.[76] The Court accepts the proposition that it is unfair to apply offensive collateral estoppel "where the second action affords the defendant procedural opportunities unavailable in the first action that could [easily] cause a different result.'' Differences in discovery opportunities between the two actions are cited as examples of situations where it would be unfair to permit offensive collateral estoppel. . . . But in the Court's view, the fact that petitioners would have been entitled to a jury trial in the present action is not such a "procedural opportunit[y]'' because "the presence or absence of a jury as factfinder is basically *neutral*, quite unlike, for

---

76. Restatement (Second) of Judgments § 88(2), Comment d, p. 92 (Tent. Draft No. 2 1975). Citing Rachal v. Hill, 435 F.2d 59 (CA5 1970), cert. denied, 403 U.S. 904 (1971), the Reporter's Note states, "The differences between the procedures available in the first and second actions, while not sufficient to deny issue preclusion between the same parties, may warrant a refusal to carry over preclusion to an action involving another party.'' Restatement, supra, at 100. [The material referred to is now in Restatement (Second) of Judgments § 29(2) (1982).]

example, the necessity of defending the first lawsuit in an inconvenient forum."

As is evident from the prior brief discussion of the development of the civil jury trial guarantee in this country, those who drafted the Declaration of Independence and debated so passionately the proposed Constitution during the ratification period, would indeed be astounded to learn that the presence or absence of a jury is merely "neutral," whereas the availability of discovery, a device unmentioned in the Constitution, may be controlling. It is precisely because the Framers believed that they might receive a different result at the hands of a jury of their peers than at the mercy of the sovereign's judges, that the Seventh Amendment was adopted. And I suspect that anyone who litigates cases before juries in the 1970's would be equally amazed to hear of the supposed lack of distinction between trial by court and trial by jury. The Court can cite no authority in support of this curious proposition. The merits of civil juries have been long debated, but I suspect that juries have never been accused of being merely "neutral" factors.

Contrary to the majority's supposition, juries can make a difference, and our cases have, before today at least, recognized this obvious fact. Thus, in *Colgrove v. Battin*, 413 U.S., at 157, we stated that "the purpose of the jury trial in . . . civil cases [is] to assure a fair and equitable resolution of factual issues, Gasoline Products Co. v. Champlin Co., 283 U.S. 494, 498 (1931) . . . ." And in Byrd v. Blue Ridge Rural Electrical Cooperative[, Inc., 356 U.S. 525, 537 (1958)], the Court conceded that "the nature of the tribunal which tries issues may be important in the enforcement of the parcel of rights making up a cause of action or defense. . . . It may well be that in the instant personal-injury case the outcome would be substantially affected by whether the issue of immunity is decided by a judge or a jury." See *Curtis v. Loether*, 415 U.S., at 198; cf. Duncan v. Louisiana, 391 U.S. 145, 156 (1968). Jurors bring to a case their commonsense and community's values; their "very inexperience is an asset because it secures a fresh perception of each trial, avoiding the stereotypes said to infect the judicial eye." H. Kalven & H. Zeisel, The American Jury 8 (1966).

The ultimate irony of today's decision is that its potential for significantly conserving the resources of either the litigants or the judiciary is doubtful at best. That being the case, I see absolutely no reason to frustrate so cavalierly the important federal policy favoring jury decisions of disputed fact questions. The instant case is an apt example of the minimal savings that will be accomplished by the Court's decision. As the Court admits, even if petitioners are collaterally estopped from relitigating whether the proxy was materially false and misleading, they are still entitled to have a jury determine whether respondents were injured by the alleged misstatements and the amount of damages, if any, sustained by respondents. . . . Thus, a jury must be impaneled in this case in any event. The time saved by not trying the issue of whether the proxy was materially false and misleading before the jury is likely to be insubstantial. It is just as probable that today's decision will have the result of coercing defendants to agree to consent orders or settlements in agency enforcement action in order to preserve their right to jury trial in the private actions. In that event, the Court, for no compelling reason, will have simply added a powerful club to the administrative agencies' arsenals that even Congress was unwilling to provide them.[77]

———

[77. See Callen & Kadue, To Bury Mutuality Not to Praise It: An Analysis of Collateral Estoppel After *Parklane Hosiery Co. v. Shore*, 31 Hastings L.J. 755 (1980).

Both lower courts and commentators have differed on whether there is a "complexity exception" to the Seventh Amendment. See In re U.S. Financial Securities Litigation, 609 F.2d 411 (9th Cir.1979), certiorari denied 446 U.S. 929 (1980); In re Japanese Electronic Products Antitrust Litigation, 631 F.2d 1069 (3d Cir.1980); Cotten v. Witco Chemical Corp., 651 F.2d 274 (5th Cir.1981), certiorari denied 455 U.S. 909 (1982); SRI Intern. v. Matsushita Elec. Corp. of America, 775 F.2d 1107, 1126–1132 (Fed.Cir.1985). Compare Devlin, Jury Trial of Complex Cases, English Practice at the Time of the Seventh Amendment, 80 Colum.L.Rev. 43 (1980), with Arnold, A Historical Inquiry into the Right to Trial by Jury in Complex Civil Litigation, 128 U.Pa.L.Rev. 829 (1980). See also Campbell, The Current Understanding of the Seventh Amendment Jury Trials in Modern Complex Litigation, 66 Wash.U.L.Q. 63 (1988); Note, The Constitutionality of a Complexity Exception to the Seventh Amendment, 73 Chi.-Kent L.Rev. 865 (1998); Comment, Complex Civil Litigation and the Seventh Amendment Right to a Jury Trial, 51 U.Chi.L.Rev. 581 (1984).

Suppose plaintiff joins a legal claim with an equitable claim. The court erroneously dismisses the legal claim. The equitable claim is tried to the court, which finds in favor of defendant. If the appellate court agrees that dismissal of the legal claim is error, should it order a new trial or is that remedy not available since the court's findings on the equitable claim bar the legal claim as a matter of issue preclusion? Lytle v. Household Mfg., Inc., 494 U.S. 545 (1990).

As previously discussed in connection with "federal officer" removal under 28 U.S.C. § 1442(a)(1), see supra p. 331, n. 8, in Winters v. Diamond Shamrock Chemical Co., 149 F.3d 387 (5th Cir.1998), the court permitted the manufacturers of Agent Orange to remove state-court litigation against them by invoking their status as government contractors. Judge Weinstein had ruled to the contrary in previously remanding similar litigation brought against the same defendants after it had been removed to his court. Ryan v. Dow Chemical Co., 781 F.Supp. 934 (E.D.N.Y.1992). Because Judge Weinstein's ruling resulted in *granting* rather than denying a motion to remand, however, it was unreviewable by dint of 28 U.S.C. § 1447(d). In the *Winters* case the plaintiff sought nonetheless to invoke offensive collateral estoppel against the defendants to deny them the opportunity to relitigate whether they had a right of removal under § 1442(a)(1). The Fifth Circuit held that under *Parklane Hosiery* it would be procedurally unfair to give such preclusive effect to an unappealable order.

In Markman v. Westview Instruments, Inc., 517 U.S. 370 (1996), a unanimous Court held that the construction of a patent, including terms of art by which the claimed invention is described, is exclusively within the province of the court. Since claim construction was not a feature of patent litigation at the time of the adoption of the Seventh Amendment, the allocation as between judge and jury of the power to determine the meaning of a patent claim was decided by reference to existing precedent, the relative interpretive skills of judges and juries, and statutory policy considerations.]

B. EVIDENCE

Conway v. Chemical Leaman Tank Lines, Inc.

United States Court of Appeals, Fifth Circuit, 1976.
540 F.2d 837.

ON PETITION FOR REHEARING

■ Before BROWN, CHIEF JUDGE, and RIVES and GEE, CIRCUIT JUDGES.

■ GEE, CIRCUIT JUDGE:

[This was a Texas diversity case for wrongful death filed by the widow, sons, and employer of Robert E. Conway. On the original hearing, 525 F.2d 927, the court affirmed judgments for the other appellees but reversed because of the improper refusal to allow reference to be made at the trial to Mrs. Conway's remarriage after the death of Conway. The court held that the exclusion of this evidence was error under Civil Rule 43(a) as it stood at the time of trial, in view of Tex.Rev.Civ.Stat.Ann., art. 4675a, which provided: "In an action under this title, evidence of the actual ceremonial remarriage of the surviving spouse is admissible, if such is true, but the defense is prohibited from directly or indirectly mentioning or alluding to any common-law marriage, extramarital relationship, or marital prospects of the surviving spouse." Since the Federal Rules of Evidence had become effective and would govern a retrial, the court considered how to reconcile the new rules and the mandate of Erie R. Co. v. Tompkins, 304 U.S. 64 (1938), reprinted infra p. 733: "The admissibility of evidence, including the particular kind of evidence involved in this case, is now governed by the Rules rather than by state law. See Fed.R.Evid. 402. The policy of the new Rules is one of broad admissibility, and the generous definition of 'relevant evidence' in Rule 401 was specifically intended to provide that background evidence (the fact of remarriage is a part of Mrs. Conway's background) is admissible.... However, we note that the Texas courts continue to hold, despite Article 4675a, that evidence of a widow's remarriage is not admissible in mitigation of damages.... Since under *Erie* state law governs the measure of damages, including admissibility and jury consideration of particular issues, the evidence of Mrs. Conway's remarriage is not admissible on remand for the purpose of mitigating damages, and the jury should be so instructed." 525 F.2d, at 930.]

On rehearing we conclude that we erred in limiting reversal and remand to Mrs. Conway's judgment and affirming those of the other plaintiffs. All judgments are before us for review, and the erroneous refusal of the district court to permit impeachment of Mrs. Conway's testimony appears to us, on reconsideration, to infect all recoveries equally. She was a material witness on both liability and all damages issues, those material to the awards recovered by the other plaintiffs as well as her own. As to these, then, her veracity was quite as material as to her own judgment, and the court's erroneous refusal to permit its testing by cross-examination of her misleading response to the "only marriage" question put by her counsel as damaging to the defense.

Appellees argue vigorously that the answer was not misleading at all.[78] The argument proceeds that in context the question and answer are most fairly interpreted as referring to marriages prior to hers to Mr. Conway, the decedent. Aside from the utter irrelevance of such an inquiry, it is exactly the *context* of the question which renders it so potentially misleading. That context is one of a trial strategy not neutral as to her current marital status but calculated to indicate to the jury that she continued Mr. Conway's unremarried widow. The action was prosecuted in the Conway name despite her remarriage. Trial court rulings were obtained forbidding defendant to refer to her remarriage. And in this context, that of a defendant muzzled as to such matters, came the colloquy set out at n. [78] above. At this point, she made her marital status a sword, not a shield. The effect of such a strategy can only have been to press upon the jury a condition contrary to fact and to seek to derive benefits from the misleading impression so created, rather than merely to let the matter lie as irrelevant.

Finally, appellees contend stoutly that we should view the error as harmless, though the Supreme Court of Texas has ruled squarely that in the state courts of Texas it is reversible and never harmless.[79] And it is true, as noted in our original opinion, that whether or not an error is harmless is a matter of federal law.

But as a matter of policy, it would be unfortunate indeed for us to reach a conclusion having the effect of creating an alternate forum in which beneficiaries of the Texas wrongful death statutory scheme could proceed, knowing that though in state court the fact of a ceremonial remarriage was sure to be admitted, in federal court a refusal to admit it might be deemed harmless "in a given instance." Federal jurisdiction of such matters may often be intentionally created by the assignment of claims or the appointment of nonresident administrators, though the practices are dubious and the trend seems to be away from them. So long as evidence of remarriage is admitted or excluded on a balancing test in federal court[80] and its admission reviewed under Rule 61's harmless-error rubric, the federal forum can only be far more attractive to the remarried widow than the Texas courts, where such evidence is invariably admitted, and the consequences of suit in the former system significantly different.

More importantly, on an analytical plane we recognize in article 4675a one of those rare evidentiary rules which is so bound up with state substantive law that federal courts sitting in Texas should accord it the same treatment as state courts in order to give full effect to Texas'

---

78. On direct, she testified:

Q: Was this your only marriage?

A: Yes, sir.

79. Exxon Corp. v. Brecheen, 526 S.W.2d 519, 525 (Tex.1975): "Article 4675a [making the fact of ceremonial remarriage admissible] would be rendered ineffectual by an independent judicial determination that disregard of its terms in a given instance was harmless error."

80. Fed.R.Evid. 403.

substantive policy. Actions for wrongful death did not exist at common law, and in Texas, as elsewhere, they are entirely the creation of statute. See Marmon v. Mustang Aviation, Inc., 430 S.W.2d 182 (Tex.1968) (Norvell, J.). The Texas version of Lord Campbell's Act is short, consisting of nine statutory provisions, articles 4671–4678, Vernon's Annotated Texas Statutes. These remained constant for almost fifty years, until 1973, when the Texas Legislature, doubtless to forestall further use of the tactics employed here to create a misleading impression of continuing widowhood, enacted article 4675a and no other amendment to the act at that session. Such a course of action evidences clearly that the legislators considered the amendment a matter of significance and one necessary to substantive policy in an area peculiarly within their control. As such, article 4675a represents more than a mere rule of evidence; it is a declaration of policy by the creators of the Texas wrongful death action that the sort of palming off theretofore practiced would no longer be tolerated.

In such and similar circumstances, federal courts have long recognized an exception to the inapplicability of *Erie* to evidentiary questions:

> Although, as has been indicated, the courts have held the *Erie* doctrine inapplicable on questions of evidence, other than those of privilege, it must be remembered that some matters often thought of as part of the law of evidence are not governed by Rule 43(a). Burden of proof is an issue of substance, controlled in diversity cases by state law. The misnamed "parol evidence rule" is not a rule of evidence at all but of substantive law, and state law must be applied. Finally there are circumstances in which a question of admissibility of evidence is so intertwined with a state substantive rule that the state rule excluding the evidence will be followed in order to give full effect to the state's substantive policy.

9 C. Wright & A. Miller, Federal Practice and Procedure: Civil § 2405, at 326–27 (1971). As then Judge Brown observed for our court in a similar situation:

> For all practical purposes, we think the underlying theory of a history of driving while intoxicated presented in the Compton [Compton v. Jay, 1965, Tex., 389 S.W.2d 639] case is substantially the equivalent of a negligent entrustment claim. As the Texas claim and the method of establishing it are so intertwined, we think the same ruling ought to be made by the Federal Court insofar as admissibility is concerned whether it is *Erie*-bound or not. F.R.Civ.P. 43(a); cf. Monarch Ins. Co. of Ohio v. Spach, 5 Cir., 1960, 281 F.2d 401.

E.L. Cheeney Co. v. Gates, 346 F.2d 197, 206 (5th Cir.1965). See also Fry v. Lamb Rental Tools, Inc., 275 F.Supp. 283 (W.D.La.1967).

For these reasons we reject the suggestion that refusal by a federal court to admit evidence of ceremonial remarriage in a Texas wrongful death action may sometimes be harmless error. The constituent statute requires its admission; the Texas Supreme Court has interpreted the statute as mandatory. These determinations, though in a sense matters of evidence-law, are embedded in Texas substantive law and policy, and we adopt them as part of the Texas wrongful death act for application in federal trials of actions brought thereunder.

All judgments herein are reversed, and the cause is remanded for a trial at which the evidence of Mrs. Conway's remarriage, if offered, will be received.

Reversed and remanded.[81]

FEDERAL RULE OF EVIDENCE

Rule 501. General Rule [of Privileges]

Except as otherwise required by the Constitution of the United States or provided by Act of Congress or in rules prescribed by the Supreme Court pursuant to statutory authority, the privilege of a witness, person, government, State, or political subdivision thereof shall be governed by the principles of the common law as they may be interpreted by the courts of the United States in the light of reason and experience. However, in civil actions and proceedings, with respect to an element of a claim or defense as to which State law supplies the rule of decision, the privilege of a witness, person, government, State, or political subdivision thereof shall be determined in accordance with State law.[82]

[81. See generally Wellborn, The Federal Rules of Evidence and the Application of State Law in Federal Courts, 55 Texas L.Rev. 371 (1977).

Compare with the principal case Flaminio v. Honda Motor Co., Ltd., 733 F.2d 463 (7th Cir.1984). Although the circuits are split on the question, the Seventh Circuit construed Evidence Rule 407 as applicable in strict-liability cases and applied this construction in a diversity case in which Wisconsin law governed, even though the Wisconsin Supreme Court had interpreted its identical rule as not applicable to those cases.

The Virginia rule of evidence excluding evidence of the private internal rules of a party when offered to prove negligence or to set the standard against which the party's duties are to be measured is sufficiently bound up with the state's substantive policy to require its application in a diversity action despite the broad mandate of Evidence Rule 402 that all relevant evidence should be allowed. Hottle v. Beech Aircraft Corp., 47 F.3d 106 (4th Cir.1995).]

[82. How will this work in a case in which a state claim within federal supplemental jurisdiction is being heard together with a federal claim and there is evidence, which would be privileged under state law, that is relevant to both claims? The final sentence in the Senate's version of the bill would have read: "However, in civil actions and proceedings arising under 28 U.S.C. § 1332 or 28 U.S.C. § 1335, or between citizens of different states and removed under 28 U.S.C. § 1441(b) the privilege of a witness, person, government, State or political subdivision thereof is determined in accordance with State law, unless with respect to the particular claim or defense, Federal law supplies the rule of decision." See Federal Judicial Center, Federal Rules of Evidence Annotated 41–46 (1975), for the committee reports explaining the two versions of that sentence and the reasons why the conference committee chose the House version, which appears in the rule as finally enacted.

In Miller v. Transamerican Press, Inc., 621 F.2d 721 (5th Cir.1980), Samuelson v. Susen, 576 F.2d 546 (3d Cir.1978), Hansen v. Allen Mem. Hosp., 141 F.R.D. 115 (S.D.Iowa 1992), and

Wratchford v. S.J. Groves & Sons Co.

United States Court of Appeals, Fourth Circuit, 1969.
405 F.2d 1061.

■ Before HAYNSWORTH, CHIEF JUDGE, and BOREMAN and CRAVEN, CIRCUIT JUDGES.

■ HAYNSWORTH, CHIEF JUDGE. The principal question presented is whether, in the diversity jurisdiction, federal or state standards are to be applied by the Court in determining the sufficiency of the evidence to go to the jury. We hold that the federal standard applies, and that there was sufficient evidence on the question of proximate causation to go to the jury.

Preliminarily we are met with the objection that the point is not properly before us, because at the time of the trial everyone assumed that the Maryland standard applied. This was understood by the District Court to require that when the evidence shows that the injury could have occurred with equal probability in each of two ways, only one of which would be laid to the defendants' responsibility, it is the duty of the Court to direct a verdict for the defendants. It was on that basis that the District Court directed a verdict in this case, over the protestations of counsel for the plaintiffs that, within the framework of the Maryland rule, the testimony showed that the injury more probably was the result of the defendants' want of due care. There was no suggestion that a federal standard was applicable.

. . . . .

Ordinarily, of course, a party should not be allowed to change the theory of his case after trial, but when fundamental rights are involved

---

Walker v. Lewis, 127 F.R.D. 466 (W.D.N.C.1989), it is held that on issues for which state law provides the rule of decision, the federal court must apply whichever state's rules of privilege the courts of the forum state would apply.

In Wm. T. Thompson Co. v. General Nutrition Corp., 671 F.2d 100, 104 (3d Cir.1982), the court held that "when there are federal law claims in a case also presenting state law claims, the federal rule favoring admissibility, rather than any state law privilege, is the controlling rule. . . . [O]ur holding is consistent with the legislative history of Rule 501 and the decisions of a number of trial courts." In support of its reference to legislative history, the court quoted the Senate Report, apparently overlooking the fact that the Conference Committee deliberately rejected the Senate version of Rule 501. This is followed in von Bulow by Auersperg v. von Bulow, 811 F.2d 136, 141 (2d Cir.1987) and in Hancock v. Dodson, 958 F.2d 1367, 1373 (6th Cir.1992)

See 23 Wright & Graham, Federal Practice and Procedure: Evidence § 5435 (1980).

The Supreme Court exercised its common-law powers under the first sentence of Rule 501 to hold that confidential communications between a psychotherapist and a patient are privileged. Jaffee v. Redmond, 518 U.S. 1 (1996). The issue arose in a civil rights suit under 42 U.S.C. § 1983 to which had been joined a supplemental claim seeking damages for wrongful death under state law. The Court expressly acknowledged the "disagreement concerning the proper rule in cases such as this in which both federal and state claims are asserted in federal court and relevant evidence would be privileged under state law but not under federal law," 518 U.S., at 15 n. 15, but had no occasion to resolve that disagreement because the privilege it held applicable to the § 1983 claim under the first sentence of Rule 501 was essentially the same as the privilege applicable under state law and the second sentence of Rule 501 to the supplemental wrongful-death claim.]

appellate consideration is appropriate, despite inconsistency in the appellant's position.[83] The right to a jury trial and our traditional faith in the jury's capacity to resolve factual disputes is basic to our federal system of judicial administration.

Because of the nature of the question, in light of the post trial proceedings and the District Court's memorandum, we are constrained to reach the merits.

On a cold winter morning Richard P. Wratchford, the plaintiff's conservatee, was found at the bottom of an open highway drainage hole. His skull had been fractured and his body was almost frozen. The cold did not aggravate the injury, however, because it tended to minimize the brain damage. Nevertheless, the brain damage was so extensive that Wratchford suffers from retrograde amnesia, recalls nothing of the circumstances of the injury, and is apparently totally incapacitated.

Wratchford had left a union meeting in Cumberland, Maryland, at approximately 10:30 o'clock the night before. Apparently, he proceeded eastward on U.S. Route 40 in the direction of his home, for his car was observed by a patrolman at approximately 11:00 o'clock P.M. parked on the right hand shoulder of the east bound lanes of that road, some five hundred feet west of Wratchford's home. His wife testified that she had requested him to pick up some groceries on his way home, and the articles he wished could be purchased in the office of a motel on the north side of Route 40, opposite where Wratchford's automobile was found. The drainage hole in which he was discovered the next morning and its extended flume were approximately on a line between the motel office and his parked automobile. After his removal from the hole, his car keys were discovered lying at the bottom of the hole. It is, therefore, clearly inferable that Wratchford parked where he did on the shoulder of the east bound lanes and left his car with the purpose of walking across the east bound lanes, the median strip and the west bound lanes to the motel in order to make his purchases, and that he sustained his injury while in that endeavor.

Extensive construction work had been underway on Route 40 to convert it from an old two-lane road, one lane in each direction, to a four-lane road, with two lanes in each direction, the east and west lanes being separated by a median strip. The defendant, S.J. Groves & Sons Company, was the general contractor, while the defendant, Miller, was responsible for the construction of the drainage inlets. At the scene of Wratchford's injury, Miller had constructed a "J" inlet in the median strip. It consisted of a concrete flume some twenty-five feet long to carry water into a drainage hole approximately four feet long in an east-west direction parallel to the lanes of traffic, two feet wide and approximately four feet deep. Angle braces had been installed near the top of the hole to form a channel to support a grate. The grate, which, under the contract, was to have been supplied by Groves and installed by Miller, had not been placed. The grate

---

83. 5 Moore's Federal Practice ¶ 46.02, p. 1904; Sibbach v. Wilson & Co., Inc., 312 U.S. 1; Chagas v. Berry, 5 Cir., 369 F.2d 637.

described by the specifications was not one designed for pedestrian traffic, for the bars were placed so widely that a man's foot could pass between them, but, had it been in place, it would not have permitted the leg of a normal adult male to pass into the space between the bars much beyond the knee.

The plaintiffs' theory, of course, is that the defendants were negligent in not having placed the grating, which their contract required, or barricaded the hole to warn potential pedestrians of the presence of the open, unprotected hole.

On the question of causation, the plaintiffs' theory was that Wratchford stepped into the unprotected hole and sustained the fracture of the left, rear portion of his skull in the resulting fall.

The defendants contended that the circumstances gave rise to an inference of equal probability that Wratchford was crossing the median strip at a point somewhat east of the hole, slipped on accumulated ice and snow, which was present in the flume, and slid, slipped or crawled, after his injury, into the hole. Since the District Judge was of the opinion that the injury could have been sustained either way, the one being no more probable than the other, and since, if he sustained his injury on the flume before getting into the hole, the absence of the grate would not have been a proximate cause of the injury, he directed a verdict for the defendants under his understanding of the Maryland rule.

Now, as is generally recognized, the question of the applicability of the *Erie* principle cannot always be resolved by discursive analysis of the rule in question in terms of its being "substantive" or "procedural." Nor is [the] "outcome-determinative" test [of Guaranty Trust Co. v. York, 326 U.S. 99,] the appropriate one in selecting the governing rule for the distribution of functions between court and jury.[84] The general approach in Byrd v. Blue Ridge Rural Electric Corp.[, 356 U.S. 525,] points to the appropriateness of the use of the federal standard.

The Supreme Court has left undecided the question of the standard to determine the sufficiency of the evidence to go to the jury in a diversity case brought in the federal court.[85] What was said in footnote 15 of the *Byrd* opinion[86] was not a final decision of this question. This is indicated by an analysis of Stoner v. New York Life Ins. Co., 311 U.S. 464, which was distinguished in that footnote, for in *Stoner* the trial was to the court without a jury. It is made clear by the Supreme Court's later explicit reservations of the question in Dick v. New York Life Ins. Co., 359 U.S. 437, and Mercer v. Theriot, 377 U.S. 152. The Courts of Appeals are in conflict on the question, but this Court has consistently held that a federal standard is to be applied.

---

84. See Byrd v. Blue Ridge Rural Electric Corp., 356 U.S. 525; Hanna v. Plumer, 380 U.S. 460.

85. See Dick v. New York Life Ins. Co., 359 U.S. 437, 444–445; Mercer v. Theriot, 377 U.S. 152, 156.

[86. That note appears supra p. 752, n. 21.]

In *Byrd,* the Supreme Court held that in a diversity case in which the defendant claimed the bar of the state's workmen's compensation act, the question of whether the plaintiff was the defendant's employee within the meaning of the compensation act was for the jury, notwithstanding the state rule that the question of employment relationship was for the court. Mr. Justice Brennan said for the Court:

> The federal system is an independent system for administering justice to litigants who properly invoke its jurisdiction. An essential character- istic of that system is the manner in which, in civil common-law actions, it distributes trial functions between judge and jury and, under the influence—if not the command—of the Seventh Amendment, as- signs the decisions of disputed questions of fact to the jury [citation omitted]. The policy of uniform enforcement of state-created rights and obligations, see, e.g., *Guaranty Trust Co. of New York v. York,* supra, cannot in every case exact compliance with a state rule—not bound up with rights and obligations—which disrupts the federal system of allocating functions between judge and jury.[87]

An equally grave disruption of the federal system would result from the application of state law rules as to the sufficiency of evidence to go to the jury. Indeed, it has been suggested, not without reason, that the Seventh Amendment commands application of federal rather than state law here.[88] Faith in the ability of a jury, selected from a cross-section of the community, to choose wisely among competing rational inferences in the resolution of factual questions lies at the heart of the federal judicial system. That faith requires consistency within the system and does not permit the accommodation of more restrictive state laws.

As in *Byrd,* the rule as to the sufficiency of the evidence is not bound up with the primary rights and obligations of the parties. In a diversity case, state law defining and limiting those primary rights and obligations must be applied under the *Erie* doctrine, enabling members of society prudently to plan and conduct their affairs, whether their conduct will later be called into question in a state or a federal court. A choice of a rule as to the quantum of proof necessary to support the submission of a case to a jury plays no role in the ordering of the affairs of anyone. It is not the kind of rule which must inexorably find its governance in a diversity case in the corpus of state law. Indeed, unless one accepts the "outcome-determina- tive" test as both inflexible and universal, there is little in this situation to support the choice of the state rule as opposed to the federal.

For such reasons and in keeping with *Byrd'*s concern for the perpetua- tion of an independent federal judicial system through maintenance of those rules fundamental to it, we adhere to our earlier holdings that the federal standard was the appropriate one for application here.

---

87.   356 U.S. 525, 537–538.

88.   See Wright, Federal Courts, pp. 351, 352.

The federal standard may once have been the same as that which the District Court understood was applicable in the state courts of Maryland,[89] but it no longer is.[90] In Ford Motor Co. v. McDavid, 4 Cir., 259 F.2d 261, 266, we expressed it in the following language:

> The old notion that a jury should not be allowed to draw any inference from circumstantial evidence, if the one is as probable as the other, has fallen into discard and has been replaced by the more sensible rule that it is the province of the jury to resolve conflicting inferences from circumstantial evidence. Permissible inferences must still be within the range of reasonable probability, however, and it is the duty of the court to withdraw the case from the jury when the necessary inference is so tenuous that it rests merely upon speculation and conjecture.

The relevant question, therefore, is not whether the judge is of the opinion that the evidence did not make it more probable than not that Wratchford stepped into the hole before his skull was fractured, but whether a jury might reasonably conclude from the evidence that that inference was more probable than the inference of an earlier injury as a result of a slip on ice in the flume. It is true, of course, that somewhere lines must be drawn by a federal judge, for if the inference sought to be drawn lacks substantial probability, any attempted resolution of the question may well lie within the area of surmise and conjecture. Had Wratchford's body and car keys not been found in the hole, had there been no stains on the side of the hole near where his head was, stains believed to have been blood, the probability that he received his injury as a result of a step into the hole may have been so slight as to require the direction of a verdict for the defendants. The probability that he received his injury as a result of a step into the hole is here, at least, equally as great as the probability that he was injured before entering the hole and the situation is not complicated by a multitude of other competing inferences, the existence of which would diminish the probability of the injury's having been sustained in the manner the plaintiffs' theory suggests.

The jury, of course, should be instructed that in order to carry the burden of proof the plaintiffs must persuade them by the preponderance of the evidence that the injury was sustained as a result of a step into the hole rather than in an earlier fall on the ice, but that simply leaves, under appropriate instructions as to the burden of proof, the choice of the two competing inferences to the jury. Termination of the case by the court upon its appraisal of the two conflicting inferences as equally probable was a violation, we think, of the federal standard and the province of the jury, for

---

89.   See Pennsylvania R.R. v. Chamberlain, 288 U.S. 333, 339.

90.   See Lavender v. Kurn, 327 U.S. 645, a F.E.L.A. case, which without expressly overruling *Chamberlain* prescribes a very different standard. It has been accepted as establishing the standard for use in diversity cases. See Planters Mfg. Co. v. Protection Mut. Ins. Co., 5 Cir., 380 F.2d 869; NLRB v. Marcus Trucking Co., 2 Cir., 286 F.2d 583; Baltimore & O.R.R. v. Postom, D.C.Cir., 177 F.2d 53; Preston v. Safeway Stores, Inc., D.D.C., 163 F.Supp. 749, aff'd on other grounds, D.C.Cir., 269 F.2d 781. See also, Moore v. Guthrie Hospital, Inc., 4 Cir., 403 F.2d 366. But see Jellison v. Kroger Co., 6 Cir., 290 F.2d 183.

either inference is not so tenuous that reasonable men might not embrace it. Indeed, when a district judge is confronted with only two conflicting inferences, each of which he regards as equally probable, and there is no other possible explanation of the event, that, itself, strongly indicates that other judges and other reasonable men might rationally regard the one inference as more probable than the other.

We conclude that the case should have been submitted to a jury under appropriate instructions as to the defendants' negligence and its proximate relation to the injury.

. . . . .

Reversed and remanded.[91]

[91. "There is a split among the federal circuits regarding which standard of review should be applied in this context. The Fourth, Fifth, and Tenth Circuits clearly apply the federal standard for sufficiency of the evidence to uphold a jury verdict. . . . The Sixth Circuit looks to state law for the standard. . . . The standards of the Eighth Circuit are somewhat unclear: there are cases which apply only the federal standard, . . . and both the federal and state standard when they are essentially identical." Jones v. Wal–Mart Stores, Inc., 870 F.2d 982, 986 n. 2 (5th Cir.1989). See also 9A Wright & Miller, Federal Practice and Procedure: Civil 2d § 2525 n. 13 (1995); 17 Moore's Federal Practice ¶ 124.07[7][c] (3d ed.1998).

The Fifth Circuit agrees with the principal case in holding that a federal standard governs but rejects the notion that the FELA cases define the federal standard. Boeing Co. v. Shipman, 411 F.2d 365 (5th Cir.1969).

The standard for entry of summary judgment is considered in Celotex Corp. v. Catrett, 477 U.S. 317 (1986), and Anderson v. Liberty Lobby, Inc., 477 U.S. 242 (1986). See Nelken, One Step Forward, Two Steps Back: Summary Judgment After *Celotex*, 40 Hastings L.J. 53 (1988).

See also Schnapper, Judges Against Juries—Appellate Review of Federal Civil Jury Verdicts, 1989 Wis.L.Rev. 237. The author argues that for the last 20 years there had been a de facto suspension of the Seventh Amendment. The Supreme Court has taken no cases on scope of review of jury verdicts and the courts of appeals have been free to do what they want. "[L]eft to their own devices, a large number of appellate judges simply cannot resist acting like superjurors, reviewing and revising civil verdicts to assure that the result is precisely the verdict they would have returned had they been in the jury box." 1989 Wis.L.Rev., at 354.]

CHAPTER XII

APPELLATE JURISDICTION AND PROCEDURE

SECTION 1. THE COURTS OF APPEALS

STATUTES

28 U.S.C. § 1291. Final decisions of district courts

The courts of appeals shall have jurisdiction of appeals from all final decisions of the district courts of the United States, the United States District Court for the District of the Canal Zone, the District Court of Guam, and the District Court of the Virgin Islands, except where a direct review may be had in the Supreme Court.[1]

[1. See 15A–15B Wright, Miller & Cooper, Federal Practice and Procedure: Jurisdiction 2d §§ 3905–3917 (1992); 19 Moore's Federal Practice ch. 202 (3d ed.1998); 3 Moore's Manual: Federal Practice and Procedure § 27.01 (1998); Wright & Kane, Federal Courts § 101 (6th ed.2002). See also Baker, A Primer on the Jurisdiction of the U.S. Courts of Appeals (2d ed.2009) (available for download at the Federal Judicial Center website, www.fjc.gov).

The historic federal rule, always subject to some exceptions, has been to require finality as a basis for appeal. For varying appraisals of the finality rule, see Crick, The Final Judgment as a Basis for Appeal, 41 Yale L.J. 539 (1932); Frank, Requiem for the Final Judgment Rule, 45 Tex.L.Rev. 292 (1966); Redish, The Pragmatic Approach to Appealability in the Federal Courts, 75 Colum.L.Rev. 89 (1975). See generally 16 Wright, Miller & Cooper, Federal Practice and Procedure: Jurisdiction 2d §§ 3920–3931 (1996); 19 Moore's Federal Practice ch. 203 (3d ed.1998); Wright & Kane, Federal Courts § 102 (6th ed.2002).

The finality of a judgment under 28 U.S.C. § 1291 is wholly a question of federal law and state law is irrelevant. Budinich v. Becton Dickinson & Co., 486 U.S. 196 (1988).

The procedure for taking an appeal to the court of appeals is governed by the Federal Rules of Appellate Procedure, adopted in 1968. See 20 Moore's Federal Practice (3d ed.1998); Wright & Kane, Federal Courts § 104 (6th ed.2002).

Both the practical and legal aspects of appellate practice are usefully discussed in Tigar, Federal Appeals: Jurisdiction and Practice (2d ed.1993).

The general rulemaking statute, 28 U.S.C. § 2072, was amended in 1990 by adding a new subsection (c): "Such rules may define when a ruling of a district court is final for the purposes of appeal under section 1291 of this title." This was in response to Recommendation 5.B.4 of the Federal Courts Study Committee, contained at page 95 of its Report of April 2, 1990. No rules of this kind have yet been adopted. The Study Committee also recommended legislation allowing the Supreme Court to adopt rules "to define circum-

28 U.S.C. § 1292. Interlocutory decisions

(a) Except as provided in subsections (c) and (d) of this section, the courts of appeals shall have jurisdiction of appeals from:

(1) Interlocutory orders of the district courts of the United States, the United States District Court for the District of the Canal Zone, the District Court of Guam, and the District Court of the Virgin Islands, or of the judges thereof, granting, continuing, modifying, refusing or dissolving injunctions, or refusing to dissolve or modify injunctions, except where a direct review may be had in the Supreme Court;[2]

----

stances in which orders and actions of district courts not otherwise subject to appeal under acts of Congress may be appealed to the courts of appeals." A statute to that effect was adopted in 1992 as 28 U.S.C. § 1292(e), reprinted infra p. 982.

A member of a school board who dissented from the board's decision not to appeal a decision adverse to it had no standing himself to appeal the decision. His status as a board member did not permit him to "step into the shoes of the board" and invoke its right to appeal, nor could he appeal in his capacity as a parent of a student attending the school involved, since he was not sued as a parent and thus was not a party in that capacity in the district court. Bender v. Williamsport Area School Dist., 475 U.S. 534 (1986). Nor may a private citizen who has intervened in the district court appeal a decision holding a state statute unconstitutional if the state has decided not to appeal. Diamond v. Charles, 476 U.S. 54 (1986).

In Devlin v. Scardelletti, 536 U.S. 1 (2002), also discussed supra p. 940, n. 49, the Court held that a nonnamed member of a Rule 23(b)(1) class, who entered a timely but unsuccessful objection to the fairness of a proposed settlement of the class action, has the right under 28 U.S.C. § 1291 to appeal the approval of the settlement. Justice O'Connor wrote for a divided Court that "[t]he label 'party' does not indicate an absolute characteristic, but rather a conclusion about the applicability of various procedures that may differ based on context." 536 U.S., at 10. Justice Scalia dissented, joined by Justices Kennedy and Thomas. The dissenters would have preferred maintaining a bright-line test for party status by requiring the objecting nonnamed class member formally to intervene in order to have the right to appeal. The entire Court evidently agreed that a nonnamed class member who had lodged a timely but unsuccessful objection to a personally binding settlement, would be entitled to intervene as of right under Federal Rule of Civil Procedure 24(a) in order to gain unquestioned "party" status for purposes of appeal. But the majority refused to tie the right to appeal to intervenor status, deeming a requirement of prior intervention to be an unnecessary complication in tension with the "statutory basis" under § 1291 of "the right to appeal from an action that finally disposes of one's rights." 536 U.S., at 14.

Of particular note, the Supreme Court has held that once the district court has reopened the filing period, the time limit for filing an appeal is jurisdictional. See Bowles v. Russell, 551 U.S. 205 (2007). Accordingly, an appeal cannot be filed outside the prescribed period, even if the district court mistakenly informed the litigant that he had a specific (and longer) period of time in which to file his appeal.]

[2. In an action for a permanent injunction plaintiff's motion for summary judgment is denied. Is this appealable under 28 U.S.C. § 1292(a)(1)? The Supreme Court's answer was "no" in Switzerland Cheese Assn., Inc. v. E. Horne's Market, Inc., 385 U.S. 23 (1966).

A district court's refusal to enter a consent decree containing injunctive relief is appealable under § 1292(a)(1) as the denial of an injunction. Carson v. American Brands, Inc., 450 U.S. 79 (1981). In that case the Court said that for an interlocutory order to be immediately appealable under § 1292(a)(1), "a litigant must show more than that the order has the practical effect of refusing an injunction.... Unless a litigant can show that an interlocutory order of the district court might have a 'serious, perhaps irreparable, consequence,' and that the order can be 'effectually challenged' only by immediate appeal, the general congressional policy against piecemeal review will preclude interlocutory appeal." 450 U.S., at 84.]

(2) Interlocutory orders appointing receivers, or refusing orders to wind up receiverships or to take steps to accomplish the purposes thereof, such as directing sales or other disposals of property;

(3) Interlocutory decrees of such district courts or the judges thereof determining the rights and liabilities of the parties to admiralty cases in which appeals from final decrees are allowed;

(b) When a district judge, in making in a civil action an order not otherwise appealable under this section, shall be of the opinion that such order involves a controlling question of law as to which there is substantial ground for difference of opinion and that an immediate appeal from the order may materially advance the ultimate termination of the litigation, he shall so state in writing in such order. The Court of Appeals which would have jurisdiction of an appeal of such action may thereupon, in its discretion, permit an appeal to be taken from such order, if application is made to it within ten days after the entry of the order: *Provided, however*, That application for an appeal hereunder shall not stay proceedings in the district court unless the district judge or the Court of Appeals or a judge thereof shall so order.[3]

. . . . . [4]

[3. In Yamaha Motor Corporation, U.S.A. v. Calhoun, 516 U.S. 199, 205 (1996), it was held that when an appellate court exercises jurisdiction over an interlocutory order that has been certified for immediate review under 28 U.S.C. § 1292(b), "the appellate court may address any issue fairly included within the certified order" and is not confined to review only of "the particular question formulated by the district court."]

[4. Subsections (c) and (d) relate to the jurisdiction of the Court of Appeals for the Federal Circuit. See also 28 U.S.C. § 1295, defining generally the jurisdiction of the Federal Circuit. That court is unusual. It has the appellate jurisdiction that was formerly in the Court of Claims and the Court of Customs and Patent Appeals, but it also has exclusive jurisdiction of appeals from district courts throughout the country in cases arising under the laws relating to patents or plant variety protection and in cases against the United States, except for Tort Claims Act cases and internal revenue cases. See Adam, The Court of Appeals for the Federal Circuit: More Than A National Patent Court, 49 Mo.L.Rev. 43 (1984); Hale, The "Arising Under" Jurisdiction of the Federal Circuit: An Opportunity for Uniformity in Patent Law, 14 Fla.St.U.L.Rev. 229 (1986).

In Cardinal Chemical Co. v. Morton Int'l, Inc., 508 U.S. 83 (1993), the Supreme Court disapproved of the Federal Circuit's practice of routinely vacating a declaratory judgment determining the validity or invalidity of a patent when the declaratory-judgment claim had been raised by a patent-infringement defendant whose defense of noninfringement prevailed on appeal. The Supreme Court held that there was no constitutional basis for vacating declaratory judgments on the validity issue as moot if the parties continued to dispute that issue, since the Federal Circuit's judgment on the patent-infringement issue remained subject to review by the Supreme Court, whose appellate jurisdiction would extend as well to the validity issue. While the Federal Circuit's discretionary powers of judicial administration might in a rare case justify a refusal to decide the validity issue, as a general matter that would be contrary to sound judicial administration, since it would disserve the "strong public interest in the finality of judgments in patent litigation." Moreover, since the Federal Circuit has exclusive jurisdiction over appeals in patent cases, the disapproved practice left the holder of a patent declared invalid by the trial court with no appellate review as of right of a possibly erroneous trial-court decision that, although vacated, would as a practical matter render the patent worthless.

In U.S. Bancorp Mortgage Co. v. Bonner Mall Partnership, 513 U.S. 18 (1994), the Court unanimously disapproved of the practice of granting vacatur of a judgment under review

(e) The Supreme Court may prescribe rules, in accordance with section 2072 of this title, to provide for an appeal of an interlocutory decision to the courts of appeals that is not otherwise provided for under subsection (a), (b), (c), or (d).[5]

28 U.S.C. § 2105. Scope of review; abatement

There shall be no reversal in the Supreme Court or a court of appeals for error in ruling upon matters in abatement which do not involve jurisdiction.

28 U.S.C. § 2106. Determination

The Supreme Court or any other court of appellate jurisdiction may affirm, modify, vacate, set aside or reverse any judgment, decree, or order of a court lawfully brought before it for review, and may remand the cause and direct the entry of such appropriate judgment, decree, or order, or require such further proceedings to be had as may be just under the circumstances.

---

when the losing party below persuades the prevailing party to settle prior to the determination of the appeal. Although 28 U.S.C. § 2106 broadly authorizes vacatur, traditional principles of equity prohibit granting vacatur incident to settlement in the absence of exceptional circumstances.

In Holmes Group, Inc. v. Vornado Air Circulation Systems, Inc., 535 U.S. 826 (2002), the Court extended the well-pleaded complaint rule to hold that the Federal Circuit lacks appellate jurisdiction of a case in which the defendant asserts a patent-infringement claim as a compulsory counterclaim. Under 28 U.S.C. § 1295(a)(1), the Federal Circuit's appellate jurisdiction is defined in terms of cases in which the district court's jurisdiction "was based, in whole or in part, on section 1338 ...," with further qualifications that restrict the Federal Circuit's jurisdiction to patent rather copyright, mask-work, and trademark cases. In Christianson v. Colt Industries Operating Corp., 486 U.S. 800, 808 (1988), the Court had held that the same test determines whether a case "arises under" the patent laws for purposes of § 1338 as applies under the general federal-question statute, § 1331. Resolving a surprisingly open question under its general "arising under" jurisprudence, the Court extended the core principle of the well-pleaded complaint rule—that statutory "arising under" jurisdiction cannot be based on a federal defense—to also foreclose "arising under" status based on any federal issue presented in the answer as opposed to the complaint. Since a counterclaim is asserted in the answer, a patent-infringement counterclaim does not confer § 1338 jurisdiction on the district court, and hence cannot make a case otherwise within the jurisdiction of the district court into one that is within the appellate jurisdiction of the Federal Circuit. See Note, *Holmes Group, Inc. v. Vornado Air Circulation Systems, Inc.*: Necromancy, Judicial Activism, and the Well–Pleaded Complaint Rule, 84 B.U.L.Rev. 1103 (2004).]

[5. Subsection (e) was added by the Act of October 29, 1992, Pub.L. 102–572, § 101, 106 Stat. 4506. To date it has been used only once, in 1998, to add subdivision (f) to Civil Rule 23. See supra p. 886.

Compare Martineau, Defining Finality and Appealability by Court Rule: Right Problem, Wrong Solution, 54 U.Pitt.L.Rev. 718 (1993), with Rowe, Defining Finality and Appealability by Court Rule: A Comment on Martineau's "Right Problem, Wrong Solution", 54 U.Pitt. L.Rev. 795 (1993).]

28 U.S.C. § 2111. Harmless error

On the hearing of any appeal or writ of certiorari in any case, the court shall give judgment after an examination of the record without regard to errors or defects which do not affect the substantial rights of the parties.

Gulfstream Aerospace Corp. v. Mayacamas Corp.

Supreme Court of the United States, 1988.
485 U.S. 271, 108 S.Ct. 1133, 99 L.Ed.2d 296.

■ JUSTICE MARSHALL delivered the opinion of the Court.

The primary issue in this case is whether a district court order denying a motion to stay or dismiss an action when a similar suit is pending in state court is immediately appealable.

I

Petitioner Gulfstream Aerospace Corporation and respondent Mayacamas Corporation entered into a contract under which respondent agreed to purchase an aircraft manufactured by petitioner. Respondent subsequently refused to make payments due, claiming that petitioner, by increasing the production and availability of its aircrafts [sic], had frustrated respondent's purpose in the transaction, which was to sell the aircraft when demand was high. Petitioner thereupon filed suit against respondent for breach of contract in the Superior Court of Chatham County, Georgia. Respondent, declining to remove this action to federal court, filed both an answer and a counterclaim. In addition, approximately one month after the commencement of petitioner's state-court suit, respondent filed a diversity action against petitioner in the United States District Court for the Northern District of California. This action alleged breach of the same contract that formed the basis of petitioner's state-court suit.

Petitioner promptly moved for a stay or dismissal of the federal-court action pursuant to the doctrine of Colorado River Water Conservation Dist. v. United States, 424 U.S. 800 (1976). In *Colorado River*, we held that in "exceptional" circumstances, a federal district court may stay or dismiss an action solely because of the pendency of similar litigation in state court. Id., at 818; see Moses H. Cone Memorial Hospital v. Mercury Construction Corp., 460 U.S. 1, 13–19 (1983).[6] Petitioner argued that the circumstances of this case supported a stay or dismissal of the federal-court action under *Colorado River*. The District Court disagreed. Finding that "the facts of this case fall short of those necessary to justify" the discontinuance of a federal-court proceeding under *Colorado River*, the District Court denied petitioner's motion. . . .

---

6. The factors to be considered in determining whether any exceptional circumstances exist include the relative comprehensiveness, convenience, and progress of the state-court and federal-court actions. See, e.g., Arizona v. San Carlos Apache Tribe, 463 U.S. 545, 570 (1983).

Petitioner filed a notice of appeal with the United States Court of Appeals for the Ninth Circuit, alleging that the Court of Appeals had jurisdiction over the appeal under either 28 U.S.C. § 1291 or 28 U.S.C. § 1292(a)(1). Petitioner also requested the Court of Appeals, in the event it found that neither of these sections provided appellate jurisdiction, to treat the notice of appeal as an application for a writ of mandamus, brought pursuant to the All Writs Act, 28 U.S.C. § 1651, and to grant the application. The Court of Appeals dismissed the appeal for lack of jurisdiction, holding that neither § 1291 nor § 1292(a)(1) allowed an immediate appeal from the District Court's order.... The Court of Appeals then declined to treat petitioner's notice of appeal as an application for mandamus on the ground that the District Court's order would not cause "serious hardship or prejudice" to petitioner.... Finally, the Court of Appeals stated that even if the notice of appeal were to be treated as an application for mandamus, petitioner did not have a right to the writ because "[i]t was well within the district court's discretion to deny" petitioner's motion....

. . . . .

II

Petitioner's principal contention in this case is that the District Court's order denying the motion to stay or dismiss the federal-court litigation is immediately appealable under § 1291. That section provides for appellate review of "final decisions" of the district courts. This Court long has stated that as a general rule a district court's decision is appealable under this section only when the decision "ends the litigation on the merits and leaves nothing for the court to do but execute the judgment." Catlin v. United States, 324 U.S. 229, 233 (1945).[7] The order at issue in this case has no such effect: indeed, the order ensures that litigation will continue in the District Court. In Cohen v. Beneficial Industrial Loan Corp., 337 U.S. 541 (1949), however, we recognized a "small class" of decisions that are appealable under § 1291 even though they do not terminate the underlying litigation. Id., at 546. We stated in *Cohen* that a district court's decision is appealable under § 1291 if it "finally determine[s] claims of right separable from, and collateral to, rights asserted in the action, too important to be denied review and too independent of the cause itself to require that appellate consideration be deferred until the whole case is adjudicated."

---

7. Justice Frankfurter, speaking for a unanimous court, explained the rationale for this rule in Cobbledick v. United States, 309 U.S. 323, 325 (1940):

"Since the right to a judgment from more than one court is a matter of grace and not a necessary ingredient of justice, Congress from the very beginning has, by forbidding piecemeal disposition on appeal of what for practical purposes is a single controversy, set itself against enfeebling judicial administration. Thereby is avoided the obstruction to just claims that would come from permitting the harassment and cost of a succession of separate appeals from the various rulings to which a litigation may give rise, from its initiation to entry of judgment. To be effective, judicial administration must not be leaden-footed. Its momentum would be arrested by permitting separate reviews of the component elements in a unified cause."

Ibid. Petitioner asserts that the District Court's decision in this case falls within *Cohen*'s "collateral order" doctrine.

Since *Cohen,* we have had many occasions to revisit and refine the collateral-order exception to the final-judgment rule. We have articulated a three-pronged test to determine whether an order that does not finally resolve a litigation is nonetheless appealable under § 1291. See Coopers & Lybrand v. Livesay, 437 U.S. 463 (1978); see also, e.g., Richardson–Merrell Inc. v. Koller, 472 U.S. 424, 431 (1985); Firestone Tire & Rubber Co. v. Risjord, 449 U.S. 368, 375 (1981). First, the order must "conclusively determine the disputed question." *Coopers & Lybrand v. Livesay*, supra, 437 U.S., at 468. Second, the order must "resolve an important issue completely separate from the merits of the action." Ibid. Third and finally, the order must be "effectively unreviewable on appeal from a final judgment." Ibid. (footnote omitted). If the order at issue fails to satisfy any one of these requirements, it is not appealable under the collateral-order exception to § 1291.

This Court held in Moses H. Cone Memorial Hospital v. Mercury Construction Corp., 460 U.S. 1 (1983), that a district court order granting a stay of litigation pursuant to *Colorado River* meets each of the three requirements of the collateral-order doctrine and therefore is appealable under § 1291. . . . In applying the collateral-order doctrine, we found that an order refusing to proceed with litigation because of the pendency of a similar action in state court satisfies the second and third prongs of the test. We stated that such an order "plainly presents an important issue separate from the merits" and that it would be "unreviewable if not appealed now" because once the state court has decided the issues in the litigation, the federal court must give that determination res judicata effect. . . . The Court gave more extended treatment to the first requirement of the collateral-order doctrine that the order "conclusively determine the disputed question." We contrasted two kinds of nonfinal orders: those that are " 'inherently tentative,' " . . . and those that, although technically amendable, are "made with the expectation that they will be the final word on the subject addressed" . . . . We used the order challenged in *Coopers & Lybrand v. Livesay*, supra, which denied certification of a class, as an example of the kind of order that is inherently tentative because a district court ordinarily would expect to reassess and revise such an order in response to events occurring "in the ordinary course of litigation." *Moses H. Cone Memorial Hospital v. Mercury Construction Corp.*, supra, at 13, n. 14. We then stated that an order granting a stay of litigation in federal court pursuant to the doctrine of *Colorado River* was not of this tentative nature. An order granting a *Colorado River* stay, we noted, "necessarily contemplates that the federal court will have nothing further to do in resolving any substantive part of the case" because a district court may enter such an order only if it has full confidence that the parallel state proceeding will "be an adequate vehicle for the complete and prompt resolution of the issues between the parties." . . . Given that a district court normally would expect the order granting the stay to settle the matter for all time, the "conclusiveness" prong of the collateral-order doctrine is satisfied and the order is appealable under § 1291.

Application of the collateral-order test to an order denying a motion to stay or dismiss an action pursuant to *Colorado River,* however, leads to a different result. We need not decide whether the denial of such a motion satisfies the second and third prongs of the collateral-order test—the separability of the decision from the merits of the action and the reviewability of the decision on appeal from final judgment—because the order fails to meet the initial requirement of a conclusive determination of the disputed question. A district court that denies a *Colorado River* motion does not "necessarily contemplate" that the decision will close the matter for all time. In denying such a motion, the district court may well have determined only that it should await further developments before concluding that the balance of factors to be considered under *Colorado River,* see n. [32], supra, warrants a dismissal or stay. The district court, for example, may wish to see whether the state-court proceeding becomes more comprehensive than the federal-court action or whether the former begins to proceed at a more rapid pace. Thus, whereas the granting of a *Colorado River* motion necessarily implies an expectation that the state court will resolve the dispute, the denial of such a motion may indicate nothing more than that the district court is not completely confident of the propriety of a stay or dismissal at that time. Indeed, given both the nature of the factors to be considered under *Colorado River* and the natural tendency of courts to attempt to eliminate matters that need not be decided from their dockets, a district court usually will expect to revisit and reassess an order denying a stay in light of events occurring in the normal course of litigation. Because an order denying a *Colorado River* motion is "inherently tentative" in this critical sense—because it is not "made with the expectation that it will be the final word on the subject addressed"—the order is not a conclusive determination within the meaning of the collateral-order doctrine and therefore is not appealable under § 1291.

III

Petitioner argues in the alternative that the District Court's order in this case is immediately appealable under § 1292(a)(1), which gives the courts of appeals jurisdiction of appeals from interlocutory orders granting or denying injunctions. An order by a federal court that relates only to the conduct or progress of litigation before that court ordinarily is not considered an injunction and therefore is not appealable under § 1292(a)(1). See Switzerland Cheese Assn., Inc. v. E. Horne's Market, Inc., 385 U.S. 23, 25 (1966); International Products Corp. v. Koons, 325 F.2d 403, 406 (CA2 1963) (Friendly, J.). Under the *Enelow–Ettelson* doctrine, however, certain orders that stay or refuse to stay judicial proceedings are considered injunctions and therefore are immediately appealable. Petitioner asserts that the order in this case, which denied a motion for a stay of a federal-court action pending the resolution of a concurrent state-court proceeding, is appealable under § 1292(a)(1) pursuant to the *Enelow-Ettelson* doctrine.

The line of cases we must examine to resolve this claim began some fifty years ago, when this Court decided Enelow v. New York Life Ins. Co., 293 U.S. 379 (1935). At the time of that decision, law and equity remained separate jurisprudential systems in the federal courts. The same judges administered both these systems, however, so that a federal district judge was both a chancellor in equity and a judge at law. In *Enelow,* the plaintiff sued at law to recover on a life insurance policy. The insurance company raised the affirmative defense that the policy had been obtained by fraud and moved the District Court to stay the trial of the law action pending resolution of this equitable defense. The District Court granted this motion, and the plaintiff appealed. This Court likened the stay to an injunction issued by an equity court to restrain an action at law. The Court stated:

> "[T]he grant or refusal of . . . a stay by a court of equity of proceedings at law is a grant or refusal of an injunction within the meaning of [the statute.] And, in this aspect, it makes no difference that the two cases, the suit in equity for an injunction and the action at law in which proceedings are stayed, are both pending in the same court, in view of the established distinction between 'proceedings at law and proceedings in equity in the national courts. . . .'

> . . . . .

> "It is thus apparent that when an order or decree is made . . . requiring, or refusing to require, that an equitable defense shall first be tried, the court, exercising what is essentially an equitable jurisdiction, in effect grants or refuses an injunction restraining proceedings at law precisely as if the court had acted upon a bill of complaint in a separate suit for the same purpose." Id., at 382–383.

The Court thus concluded that the District Court's order was appealable under § 1292(a)(1).

In Ettelson v. Metropolitan Life Ins. Co., 317 U.S. 188 (1942), the Court reaffirmed the rule of *Enelow,* notwithstanding that the Federal Rules of Civil Procedure had fully merged law and equity in the interim. The relevant facts of *Ettelson* were identical to those of *Enelow,* and the Court responded to them in the same fashion. In response to the argument that the fusion of law and equity had destroyed the analogy between the stay ordered in the action and an injunction issued by a chancellor of a separate proceeding at law, the Court stated only that the plaintiffs were "in no different position than if a state equity court had restrained them from proceeding in the law action." 317 U.S., at 192. Thus, the order granting the stay was held to be immediately appealable as an injunction.

The historical analysis underlying the results in *Enelow* and *Ettelson* has bred a doctrine of curious contours. Under the *Enelow–Ettelson* rule, most recently restated in Baltimore Contractors, Inc. v. Bodinger, 348 U.S. 176 (1955), an order by a federal court staying or refusing to stay its own proceedings is appealable under § 1292(a)(1) as the grant or denial of an injunction if two conditions are met. First, the action in which the order is entered must be an action that, before the merger of law and equity, was by its nature an action at law. Second, the order must arise from or be based on some matter that would then have been considered an equitable defense or counterclaim. If both conditions are satisfied, the historical equivalent of the modern order would have been an injunction, issued by a separate equity court, to restrain proceedings in an action at law. If either condition is not met, however, the historical analogy fails. When the underlying suit is historically equitable and the stay is based on a defense or counterclaim that is historically legal, the analogy fails because a law judge had no power to issue an injunction restraining equitable proceedings. And when both the underlying suit and the defense or counterclaim on which the stay is based are historically equitable, or when both are historically legal, the analogy fails because when a chancellor or a law judge stayed an action in his own court, he was not issuing an injunction, but merely arranging matters on his docket. Thus, unless a stay order is made in a historically legal action on the basis of a historically equitable defense or counterclaim, the order cannot be analogized to a pre-merger injunction and therefore cannot be appealed under § 1292(a)(1) pursuant to the *Enelow–Ettelson* doctrine.

The parties in this case dispute whether the *Enelow-Ettelson* rule makes the District Court's decision to deny a stay immediately appealable under § 1292(a)(1). Both parties agree that an action for breach of contract was an action at law prior to the merger of law and equity. They vigorously contest, however, whether the stay of an action pending the resolution of similar proceedings in a state court is equitable in the requisite sense. . . .

We decline to address the issue of appealability in these terms; indeed, the sterility of the debate between the parties illustrates the need for a more fundamental consideration of the precedents in this area. This Court long has understood that the *Enelow–Ettelson* rule is deficient in utility and sense. In the two cases we have decided since *Ettelson* relating to the rule, we criticized its perpetuation of "outmoded procedural differentiations" and its consequent tendency to produce incongruous results. *Baltimore Contractors, Inc. v. Bodinger*, supra, at 184; see Morgantown v. Royal Ins. Co., 337 U.S. 254, 257–258 (1949). We refrained then from overruling the *Enelow* and *Ettelson* decisions, but today we take that step. A half century's experience has persuaded us, as it has persuaded an impressive array of judges and commentators, that the rule is unsound in theory, unworkable and arbitrary in practice, and unnecessary to achieve any legitimate goals.

As an initial matter, the *Enelow–Ettelson* doctrine is, in the modern world of litigation, a total fiction. Even when the rule was announced, it was artificial. Although at that time law and equity remained two separate systems, they were administered by the same judges. When a single official was both chancellor and law judge, a stay of an action at law on equitable grounds required nothing more than an order issued by the official regulating the progress of the litigation before him, and the decision to call this order an injunction just because it would have been an injunction in a system with separate law and equity judges had little justification. With the merger of law and equity, which was accomplished by the Federal Rules of Civil Procedure, the practice of describing these stays as injunctions lost all connection with the reality of the federal courts' procedural system. As Judge Charles Clark, the principal draftsman of the Rules, wrote:

> "[W]e lack any rationale to explain the concept of a judge enjoining himself when he merely decides upon the method he will follow in trying the case. The metamorphosis of a law judge into a hostile chancellor on the other 'side' of the court could not have been over-clear to the lay litigant under the divided procedure; but if now without even that fictitious sea change one judge in one form of action may split his judicial self at one instant into two mutually antagonistic parts, the litigant surely will think himself in Alice's Wonderland." Beaunit Mills, Inc. v. Eday Fabric Sales Corp., 124 F.2d 563, 565 (CA2 1942).

The *Enelow* rule had presupposed two different systems of justice administered by separate tribunals, even if these tribunals were no more than two "sides" to the same court; with the abandonment of that separation, the premise of the rule disappeared. The doctrine, and the distinctions it drew between equitable and legal actions and defenses, lost all moorings to the actual practice of the federal courts.

The artificiality of the *Enelow–Ettelson* doctrine is not merely an intellectual infelicity; the gulf between the historical procedures underlying the rule and the modern procedures of federal courts renders the rule hopelessly unworkable in operation. The decisions in *Enelow* and *Ettelson* treated as straightforward the questions whether the underlying suit, on the one hand, and the motion for a stay, on the other, would properly have been brought in a court of equity or in a court of law. Experience since the merger of law and equity, however, has shown that both questions are frequently difficult and sometimes insoluble. Suits that involve diverse claims and request diverse forms of relief often are not easily categorized as equitable or legal. . . .

. . . Under the rule, appellate jurisdiction of orders granting or denying stays depends upon a set of considerations that in no way reflects or relates to the need for interlocutory review. There is no reason to think that appeal of a stay order is more suitable in cases in which the underlying action is at law and the stay is based on equitable grounds than in cases in which one of these conditions is not satisfied. The rule's focus on historical distinctions thus produces arbitrary and anomolous results. . . .

For these reasons, the lower federal courts repeatedly have lambasted the *Enelow–Ettelson* doctrine. . . . With the exception of the Federal Circuit, which apparently has not yet confronted an *Enelow–Ettelson* appeal, every Circuit is on record with criticism of the doctrine. . . .

Commentators have been no less scathing in their evaluations of the *Enelow–Ettelson* rule. Professor Moore and his collaborators have noted the difficulty of applying archaic labels to modern actions and defenses and expressed the wish that "the Supreme Court will accept the first opportunity offered to decide that the reason for the *Enelow–Ettelson* rule having ceased, the rule is no more." 9 J. Moore, B. Ward, & J. Lucas, Moore's

Federal Practice ¶ 110.20[3], p. 245 (1987). Professor Wright and his collaborators have gone further, arguing that the extensive experience that the courts of appeals have had in attempting to rationalize and apply the rule would justify them in rejecting it. 16 C. Wright, A. Miller, E. Cooper, & E. Gressman, Federal Practice and Procedure § 3923, p. 65 (1977).

The case against perpetuation of this sterile and antiquated doctrine seems to us conclusive. We therefore overturn the cases establishing the *Enelow–Ettelson* rule and hold that orders granting or denying stays of "legal" proceedings on "equitable" grounds are not automatically appealable under § 1292(a)(1). This holding will not prevent interlocutory review of district court orders when such review is truly needed. Section 1292(a)(1) will, of course, continue to provide appellate jurisdiction over orders that grant or deny injunctions and orders that have the practical effect of granting or denying injunctions and have " 'serious, perhaps irreparable, consequence.' " Carson v. American Brands, Inc., 450 U.S. 79, 84 (1981), quoting *Baltimore Contractors, Inc. v. Bodinger*, supra, at 181. As for orders that were appealable under § 1292(a)(1) solely by virtue of the *Enelow–Ettelson* doctrine, they may, in appropriate circumstances, be reviewed under the collateral-order doctrine of § 1291, see Moses H. Cone Memorial Hospital v. Mercury Construction Corp., 460 U.S. 1 (1983), and the permissive appeal provision of § 1292(b), as well as by application for writ of mandamus.[8] Our holding today merely prevents interlocutory review of district court orders on the basis of historical circumstances that have no relevance to modern litigation. Because we repudiate the *Enelow–Ettelson* doctrine, we reject petitioner's claim that the District Court's order in this case is appealable under § 1292(a)(1) pursuant to that doctrine.

IV

Petitioner finally contends that if the order denying the motion for a stay or dismissal is not appealable, the Court of Appeals should have issued a writ of mandamus directing the District Court to vacate the order and grant the motion. In making this argument, petitioner points primarily to respondent's decision to eschew removal of the state-court action in favor of bringing a separate suit in federal court. Petitioner asserts that in the absence of "imperative circumstances" not present in this case, a district court must respond to this kind of conduct by staying or dismissing the action brought in that court. Brief for Petitioner 23. Refusal to do so, petitioner concludes, is a "demonstrable abuse of discretion" warranting the issuance of a writ of mandamus. Id., at 5.

This Court repeatedly has observed that the writ of mandamus is an extraordinary remedy, to be reserved for extraordinary situations. See, e.g., Kerr v. United States District Court, 426 U.S. 394, 402 (1976). The federal

---

8. Issuance of a writ of mandamus will be appropriate in exceptional cases involving stay orders. This Court has made clear, for example, that a stay order that deprives a party of the right to trial by jury is reversible by mandamus. See Beacon Theatres, Inc. v. Westover, 359 U.S. 500, 510–511 (1959).

courts traditionally have used the writ only "to confine an inferior court to a lawful exercise of its prescribed jurisdiction or to compel it to exercise its authority when it is its duty to do so." Roche v. Evaporated Milk Assn., 319 U.S. 21, 26 (1943). In accord with this historic practice, we have held that only "exceptional circumstances amounting to a judicial 'usurpation of power' " will justify issuance of the writ. Will v. United States, 390 U.S. 90, 95 (1967), quoting De Beers Consol. Mines, Ltd. v. United States, 325 U.S. 212 (1945). Moreover, we have held that the party seeking mandamus has the "burden of showing that its right to issuance of the writ is 'clear and indisputable.' " Bankers Life & Cas. Co. v. Holland, 346 U.S. 379, 384 (1953), quoting United States v. Duell, 172 U.S. 576, 582 (1899).

Petitioner has failed to satisfy this stringent standard. This Court held in *Colorado River* that a federal court should stay or dismiss an action because of the pendency of a concurrent state-court proceeding only in "exceptional" circumstances, 424 U.S., at 818, and with "the clearest of justifications," id., at 819. Petitioner has failed to show that the District Court clearly overstepped its authority in holding that the circumstances of this case were not so exceptional as to warrant a stay or dismissal under *Colorado River*. This Court never has intimated acceptance of petitioner's view that the decision of a party to spurn removal and bring a separate suit in federal court invariably warrants the stay or dismissal of the suit under the *Colorado River* doctrine.... Moreover, petitioner has pointed to no other circumstance in this case that would require a federal court to stay the litigation. Petitioner therefore has failed to show that the District Court's order denying a stay or dismissal of the federal-court suit warranted the issuance of a writ of mandamus.

V

The District Court's order denying petitioner's motion to stay or dismiss respondent's suit because of the pendency of similar litigation in state court was not immediately appealable under § 1291 or § 1292(a)(1). In addition, the District Court's order did not call for the issuance of a writ of mandamus. Accordingly, the judgment of the Court of Appeals is affirmed.

It is so ordered.

■ JUSTICE KENNEDY took no part in the consideration or decision of this case.

■ JUSTICE SCALIA, concurring.

I join the Court's opinion, but write separately principally to express what seems to me a necessary addition to the analysis in Part II. While I agree that the present order does not come within the *Cohen* exception to the final-judgment rule under § 1291, I think it over-simplifies somewhat to assign as the reason merely that the order is "inherently tentative." A categorical order otherwise qualifying for *Cohen* treatment does not necessarily lose that status, and become "nonfinal," merely because the court may contemplate—or even, for that matter, invite—renewal of the aggrieved party's request for relief at a later date. The claim to *immediate* relief (in this case, the right to be free of the obstruction of a parallel federal proceeding) is categorically and irretrievably denied. The court's decision *is* "the final word on the subject" insofar as the time period between the court's initial denial and its subsequent reconsideration of the renewed motion is concerned. Thus, it is inconceivable that we would hold denial of a motion to dismiss an indictment on grounds of absolute immunity (an order that is normally appealable at once, see Nixon v. Fitzgerald, 457 U.S. 731 (1982)), to be nonfinal and unappealable, simply because the court announces that it will reconsider the motion at the conclusion of the prosecution's case.

In my view, invocation of the *Cohen* exception makes little sense in the present case because not only (1) the motion is likely to be renewed and reconsidered, but also (2) the relief will be just as effective, or nearly as effective, if accorded at a later date—that is, the harm caused during the interval between initial denial and reconsideration will not be severe. Moreover, since these two conditions will almost always be met when the asserted basis for an initial stay motion is the pendency of state proceedings, the more general conclusion that initial orders denying *Colorado River* motions are never immediately appealable is justified.

I note that today's result could also be reached by application of the rule adopted by the First Circuit, that to come within the *Cohen* exception the issue on appeal must involve "an important and unsettled question of controlling law, not merely a question of the proper exercise of the trial court's discretion." Boreri v. Fiat S. P. A., 763 F.2d 17, 21 (1985), quoting United States v. Sorren, 605 F.2d 1211, 1213 (1979).... This rationale has not been argued here, and we should not embrace it without full adversarial exploration of its consequences. I do think, however, that our finality jurisprudence is sorely in need of further limiting principles, so that *Cohen* appeals will be, as we originally announced they would be, a "small class [of decisions] ... too important to be denied review." ...[9]

[9. On the use of mandamus as a means for escape from the final judgment rule, see Allied Chemical Corp. v. Daiflon, Inc., 449 U.S. 33 (1980); Berger, The Mandamus Power of the United States Courts of Appeals: A Complex and Confused Means of Appellate Control, 31 Buffalo L.Rev. 37 (1982); Note, Supervisory and Advisory Mandamus Under the All Writs Act, 86 Harv.L.Rev. 595 (1973); 16 Wright, Miller & Cooper, Federal Practice and Procedure: Jurisdiction 2d §§ 3932–3935 (1996); 19 Moore's Federal Practice ch. 204 (3d ed.1998).

In Cheney v. United States District Court for the District of Columbia, 542 U.S. 367 (2004), the Court nominally remanded the case to the court of appeals to reconsider whether it should issue a writ of mandamus to block a discovery order resisted by the Vice President on separation-of-powers grounds. The Court made unmistakably clear, however, that despite its extraordinary nature, a writ of mandamus would here be an appropriate means to review a constitutionally questionable order that the district court had refused to certify for interlocutory review under 28 U.S.C. § 1292(b).

As discussed supra p. 388, n. 49, Quackenbush v. Allstate Insurance Co., 517 U.S. 706 (1996), has clarified that appeal under § 1291 rather than petition for a writ of mandamus is the

In re Lorazepam & Clorazepate Antitrust Litigation

United States Court of Appeals, District of Columbia Circuit, 2002.
289 F.3d 98.

■ Before: GINSBURG, CHIEF JUDGE, ROGERS and GARLAND, CIRCUIT JUDGES.

■ ROGERS, CIRCUIT JUDGE:

This appeal presents for the first time in this circuit the threshold question of when interlocutory review of a class certification decision is

---

proper means to review an order remanding a case for some reason other than the grounds for remand specified in 28 U.S.C. § 1447(c).

Rejecting the argument that "the Eleventh Amendment does not confer immunity from suit, but merely a defense to liability," the Supreme Court held in Puerto Rico Aqueduct & Sewer Authority v. Metcalf & Eddy, 506 U.S. 139 (1993), that a district court's order denying a motion by a state or a state entity to dismiss on Eleventh Amendment grounds is a collateral order that may be appealed forthwith under 28 U.S.C. § 1291. But the collateral-order doctrine does not permit immediate appeal of a district court's order rescinding a settlement agreement and granting a motion to vacate a stipulated dismissal. In Digital Equipment Corp. v. Desktop Direct, Inc., 511 U.S. 863 (1994), the Court held that the protection from suit of such a settlement agreement and stipulated dismissal is not equivalent to a qualified immunity from suit.

The denial of a police officer's summary-judgment motion asserting a qualified-immunity defense to a "constitutional tort" action arising from the beating of a suspect is not appealable as a collateral order when the district court's ruling turns on the existence of a triable issue of fact about the conduct of the officer rather than on the officer's entitlement to immunity as a matter of law. Johnson v. Jones, 515 U.S. 304 (1995). But an immediate appeal does lie from the denial of summary judgment on qualified-immunity grounds, despite the existence of a genuine dispute of fact, if the denial of summary judgment is rooted in an abstract proposition of law, such as whether the federal right allegedly infringed by the defendant was "clearly established." Behrens v. Pelletier, 516 U.S. 299, 311 (1996). Indeed, in *Behrens* the Court held that successive "collateral order" appeals may be taken when the defense of qualified immunity is rejected first on motion to dismiss, and later on summary judgment. Justice Breyer, joined by Justice Stevens, filed a vigorous dissent on the successive-appeal issue, characterizing the collateral-order doctrine as an essentially discretionary, judicially created "nonstatutory exception" to § 1291 which should be invoked only for strong reasons of policy, and no more than once per case on qualified-immunity grounds.

In Cunningham v. Hamilton County, Ohio, 527 U.S. 198 (1999), the collateral order doctrine was held inapplicable to permit interlocutory review of an order imposing sanctions on an attorney even though the attorney no longer represented any party in the continuing litigation. But a pretrial order in a criminal case, requiring the defendant involuntarily to receive medication in order to render him competent to stand trial, qualified for review as a collateral order in Sell v. United States, 539 U.S. 166, 175–177 (2003).

An order under 28 U.S.C. § 1367(c) declining to exercise supplemental jurisdiction and thus dismissing state-law claims in federal-question litigation is not a collateral order, and thus is not immediately appealable under § 1291 absent entry of final judgment as to the dismissed claims under Fed.R.Civ.P. 54(b). See Kaufman v. Checkers Drive–In Restaurants, Inc., 122 F.3d 892, 894–895 & n. 3 (11th Cir.1997).

Resolving a circuit split, the Supreme Court held that a party may not appeal an order denying summary judgment based on qualified immunity after a full trial on the merits. Instead, the full record developed at trial supersedes the record as it existed at the time of the summary judgment motion, and thus the qualified immunity defense "must be evaluated in light of the character and quality of the evidence received" at the full trial. Ortiz v. Jordan, 562 U.S. ___, 131 S.Ct. 884 (2011).

The Supreme Court has held that the collateral order doctrine does not authorize an interlocutory appeal of an order finding waiver of attorney-client privilege resulting in mandating the production of those materials. Mohawk Industries, Inc. v. Carpenter, 558 U.S. ___, 130 S.Ct. 599 (2009).]

appropriate under Federal Rule of Civil Procedure 23(f). We take the opportunity to offer general guidance on the scope of our discretion under Rule 23(f) in considering the petition for Rule 23(f) review by Mylan Laboratories, Inc. [and several related defendants] (collectively "Mylan"), of the district court's certification of a class of direct purchasers of the generic anti-anxiety drugs lorazepam and clorazepate from Mylan or UDL. Mylan contends that the district court erred in ruling that despite the Federal Trade Commission's ("FTC") procurement of a settlement against Mylan on behalf of a class of indirect purchasers, a class of direct purchasers had antitrust standing under Illinois Brick Co. v. Illinois, 431 U.S. 720 (1977), and, in the alternative that the certified class consists of both direct and indirect purchasers in violation of *Illinois Brick*. We conclude that interlocutory appeal pursuant to Rule 23(f) typically is appropriate in three circumstances: (1) when there is a death-knell situation for either the plaintiff or defendant that is independent of the merits of the underlying claims, coupled with a class certification decision by the district court that is questionable, taking into account the district court's discretion over class certification; (2) when the certification decision presents an unsettled and fundamental issue of law relating to class actions, important both to the specific litigation and generally, that is likely to evade end-of-the-case review; and (3) when the district court's class certification decision is manifestly erroneous. Applying these standards we deny Mylan's petition for interlocutory review.

I.

The class action now pending in the district court was preceded by two lawsuits brought by the FTC and several States' Attorneys General against Mylan that were ultimately consolidated and ended in a settlement.... The settlement agreement provided, in part, that Mylan would pay disgorgement in the amount of $71,782,017 to satisfy the consumer claims in the States' lawsuit and $28,217,983 to satisfy the States' agency claims. The settlement agreement also provided that the FTC, States, State agencies, and consumers who did not exclude themselves from the settlement, would release their claims against the defendants.

On August 16, 1999, the Judicial Panel on Multidistrict Litigation transferred to the United States District Court for the District of Columbia a Northern District of Illinois lawsuit pending against Mylan. This lawsuit was consolidated, on March 9, 2000, with a lawsuit brought by St. Charles Rehabilitation Center against Mylan. The named plaintiffs in the consolidated action were Advocate Health Care, St. Charles Hospital and Rehabilitation Center, Dik Drug Company, and Harvard Pilgrim Health Care, and they sought class certification as direct purchasers of lorazepam and clorazepate. The amended complaint alleged that Mylan had engaged in price fixing and monopolization in violation of §§ 1 and 2 of the Sherman

Act, and the plaintiffs sought treble damages pursuant to § 4 of the Clayton Act. Mylan moved to dismiss the complaint pursuant to Federal Rules of Civil Procedure 12(b)(1) and 12(b)(6), on the ground that the plaintiffs' proposed class of direct purchasers lacked antitrust standing to assert their claims. In *Illinois Brick,* the Supreme Court held that, with narrow exceptions, only direct purchasers may recover damages for illegal overcharges under § 4 of the Clayton Act. *Illinois Brick,* 431 U.S., at 746–47. Essentially, Mylan argued that the usual direct purchaser rule of *Illinois Brick* should not apply because the FTC had won a monetary recovery for the benefit of a class of indirect consumer purchasers pursuant to § 13(b) of the FTC Act for alleged antitrust violations, and to allow both purchaser classes to obtain relief would undermine the policy rationales behind *Illinois Brick.* In the alternative, Mylan opposed the class certification arguing, inter alia, that the class consisted of direct and indirect purchasers in violation of *Illinois Brick*'s direct purchaser rule. On July 2, 2001, the district court denied the motion to dismiss, and, in accord with the plaintiffs' request, certified the following class:

> All persons and entities in the United States who purchased generic lorazepam tablets and/or generic clorazepate tablets directly from Defendants Mylan and UDL during the period January 12, 1998 through the present, excluding Defendants, their respective parents, subsidiaries and affiliates, any co-conspirators of Defendants, and all governmental entities.

In re Lorazepam & Clorazepate Antitrust Litig., 202 F.R.D. 12, 21 (D.D.C.2001). The district court appointed Advocate Health Care, St. Charles Hospital, Dik Drug, and Harvard Pilgrim as class representatives.

Mylan now petitions for interlocutory review of the district court's denial of its Rule 12(b)(6) motion to dismiss and the district court's certification of a class of direct purchasers. Asserting that "[t]his is not the typical case," Petitioners' Br. at 16, Mylan contends that, in light of the flexible standards for review developed in the circuits, appellate review of its petition under Rule 23(f) is warranted: not only does Mylan's petition raise the novel issue of law of "how properly to calibrate antitrust standing where two antitrust cases collide," id., at 20, the outcome of which is potentially dispositive of the case, but also the district court's decision is particularly susceptible to challenge and there may be no further opportunity to review its decision. Reviving its Rule 12(b)(6) contention, Mylan challenges the district court's certification decision by contending first that under *Illinois Brick,* the FTC's § 13(b) enforcement action on behalf of the ultimate consumers of lorazepam and clorazepate precludes suit by a direct purchaser class. Allowing a direct purchaser class to sue the same defendants for antitrust damages following the FTC's suit and settlement would, in Mylan's view, "topple every rationale" supporting *Illinois Brick*'s rule confining potential antitrust plaintiffs to one level of purchasers. Id., at 17. In "these uncommon circumstances," Mylan concludes, "the direct purchaser class should be denied recovery." Id. Second, as to the certified class, Mylan maintains that, even if direct purchasers may sue for antitrust damages in addition to the consumer class, the district court erred in ruling that the class had antitrust standing under the direct purchaser rule and its narrow exceptions. According to Mylan, many members of the class, including three of the four class representatives, bought lorazepam and clorazepate, not from Mylan, but from pharmaceutical wholesalers, who also purport to be members of the direct purchaser class. Mylan asserts that this purchasing chain makes these class members who purchased from intermediaries "quintessential indirect purchasers," who, under *Illinois Brick,* cannot sue for antitrust damages. Hence, Mylan maintains, the district court erred in not determining, prior to certifying the class, whether the class and its representatives had antitrust standing under *Illinois Brick*.

We first set forth the standards that we will ordinarily apply in exercising our discretion under Rule 23(f), and then we address the contentions in Mylan's petition.

II.

Rule 23(f), added by amendment in 1998, provides that "[a] court of appeals may in its discretion permit an appeal from an order of a district court granting or denying class action certification under this rule if application is made to it within ten days after entry of the order." Fed.R.Civ.P. 23(f). Although other circuit courts of appeals have addressed the scope of Rule 23(f) review, this is a question of first impression for this court. The advisory committee's note to Rule 23(f) states that "[a]ppeal from an order granting or denying class certification is permitted in the sole discretion of the court of appeals" and is "akin to the discretion exercised by the Supreme Court in acting on a petition for certiorari." Fed.R.Civ.P. 23(f) advisory committee's note. The advisory committee's note also indicates that not all class certification issues warrant review, noting that "many suits with class-action allegations present familiar and almost routine issues that are no more worthy of immediate appeal than many other interlocutory rulings" and accordingly directs the "courts of appeals [to] develop standards for granting review that reflect the changing areas of uncertainty in class litigation." Id. The advisory committee's note offers this further guidance:

> Permission to appeal may be granted or denied on the basis of any consideration that the court of appeals finds persuasive. Permission is most likely to be granted when the certification decision turns on a novel or unsettled question of law, or when, as a practical matter, the decision on certification is likely dispositive of the litigation.

Id. Thus, the advisory committee's note identifies two instances in which Rule 23(f) review would likely be appropriate: (1) when a class certification decision as a practical matter terminates the litigation; and (2) when a class certification decision raises a novel issue of law. Relying on this guidance, other circuits have examined the appropriate scope of Rule 23(f).

First among the circuits to address the scope of appellate review pursuant to Rule 23(f), was the Seventh Circuit in Blair v. Equifax Check

Services, Inc., 181 F.3d 832 (7th Cir.1999). In *Blair,* the Seventh Circuit rejected the adoption of a bright-line rule as imprudent and, looking to the reasons for the addition of Rule 23(f), identified three categories of cases in which appellate review would be appropriate. Id., at 834. First, for some cases, denial of class status would sound the "death knell" of the litigation because the "representative plaintiff's claim is too small to justify the expense of litigation." Id. Second, the grant of class status can put substantial pressure on the defendant to settle independent of the merits of the plaintiffs' claims. Id. Third, an appeal may facilitate the development of the law of class actions. Id., at 835. Regarding the first two categories, the Seventh Circuit added that the petitioner must demonstrate that the district court's certification decision was "questionable" and "must do this taking into account the discretion the district judge possesses in implementing Rule 23, and the correspondingly deferential standard of appellate review." Id. It explained, if the district court's decision is "impervious to revision," there is no point to an interlocutory appeal no matter how "dramatic the effect of the grant or denial of class status [is] in undercutting the plaintiff's claim or inducing the defendant to capitulate." Id. Regarding the third category of cases, which it noted is likely to include fundamental issues about class actions that have been poorly developed because so many class actions settle or are resolved in a manner that overtakes procedural matters, id., the Seventh Circuit observed that it is less important to show that the district court's certification decision is questionable, explaining that law can be advanced through affirmances as well as reversals; rather, the more important the question under the second factor is and the "greater the likelihood that it will escape effective disposition at the end of the case," the more appropriate the appeal. Id.

The First Circuit in Waste Management Holdings, Inc. v. Mowbray, 208 F.3d 288 (1st Cir.2000), agreed that *Blair* "captured the essential principles on which Rule 23(f) rests." Id., at 293. However, because of the ease with which issues of law can be characterized as "fundamental," id., at 294, and because so many class certification decisions turn on "familiar and almost routine issues," id. (quoting Fed.R.Civ.P. 23(f) advisory committee's note), the First Circuit narrowed the third category to include only "those instances in which an appeal will permit the resolution of an unsettled legal issue that is important to the particular litigation as well as important in itself and likely to escape effective review if left hanging until the end of the case." Id. At the same time, however, the First Circuit duly noted the broad discretion ceded to the appellate courts by the rule, and cautioned that:

> While we hope that these general comments will be helpful to parties deciding whether to pursue applications under Rule 23(f), we do not foreclose the possibility that special circumstances may lead us either to deny leave to appeal in cases that seem superficially to fit into one of these three pigeonholes, or conversely, to grant leave to appeal in cases that do not match any of the three described categories.

Id. Stating as well that it "intend[s] to exercise [its] discretion judiciously," however, the First Circuit observed that "[b]y their nature, interlocutory appeals are disruptive, time-consuming, and expensive," and that notwithstanding the access to the appellate courts provided by Rule 23(f), the court "should err, if at all, on the side of allowing the district court an opportunity to fine-tune its class certification order, rather than opening the door too widely to interlocutory appellate review." Id. (citing Fed.R.Civ.P. 23(c)(1)). The Second Circuit, in In re Sumitomo Copper Litigation, 262 F.3d 134 (2d Cir.2001), appears to have adopted the approach set forth in *Mowbray*. Id., at 139–40. It stated that Rule 23(f) petitioners ordinarily must show either that the certification order (1) "will effectively terminate the litigation and there has been a substantial showing that the district court's decision is questionable," or (2) "implicates a legal question about which there is a compelling need for immediate resolution." Id., at 139.

Other circuits have elaborated on the *Mowbray* approach. The Eleventh Circuit, in Prado–Steiman v. Bush, 221 F.3d 1266 (11th Cir.2000), adopted five guideposts for Rule 23(f) review: (1) whether the certification ruling is likely to sound the death knell of the litigation; (2) whether the district court's certification decision contains a substantial weakness, such that it likely was an abuse of discretion; (3) whether the appeal presents an unsettled legal question that is of specific and general importance, e.g., issues likely to evade review, issues that are involved in related actions, and interests that affect the public interest; (4) the nature and status of the litigation before the district court, e.g., the status of discovery, the pendency of relevant motions, and how long the matter has been pending; and (5) the likelihood that future events will make immediate appellate review more appropriate, e.g., a change in financial status of a party or ongoing settlement negotiations. Id., at 1274–76. The second factor serves as a sliding scale: the more questionable the district court's decision, the less the remaining four factors need weigh in. Id., at 1274–75 & n. 10. The Eleventh Circuit recognized the possibility that when the district court's certification decision is clearly wrong, Rule 23(f) review "may be warranted even if none of the other factors supports granting the Rule 23(f) petition." Id., at 1275. The Fourth Circuit, in Lienhart v. Dryvit Systems, Inc., 255 F.3d 138 (4th Cir.2001), adopted the Eleventh Circuit's approach with the sliding scale, but firmly stated that when a class certification decision is manifestly erroneous, review is warranted regardless of the remaining factors. Id., at 145–46. The court explained that stringent standards for review are inappropriate as "Rule 23(f)'s purpose [was] to eliminate the unduly restrictive review practices which obtained when mandamus was the only available means to review a class certification prior to final judgment in the absence of a district court's decision to voluntarily certify the issue for immediate review...." Id., at 145. Hence, the Fourth Circuit observed that "[i]n addition to addressing 'death knell' situations and promoting the resolution of legal questions of general importance, a careful and sparing use of Rule 23(f) may promote judicial economy by enabling the correction of certain manifestly flawed class certifications prior to trial and final judgment." Id., at 145. Following the Eleventh and Fourth

Circuits' decisions, the Third Circuit, in Newton v. Merrill Lynch, Pierce, Fenner & Smith, 259 F.3d 154 (3d Cir.2001), identified four categories of cases in which Rule 23(f) would be appropriate: the three set forth by the Seventh Circuit in *Blair* and the advisory committee's note plus the Eleventh and Fourth Circuits' inclusion of a category of likely erroneous class certification decisions. Id., at 165.

The differences among the circuits, which are subtle, are of three types. First, two circuits permit appeal if the district court's decision is erroneous, regardless whether the other factors governing appeal under Rule 23(f) are present. Compare *Newton,* 259 F.3d, at 165; and *Lienhart,* 255 F.3d, at 145–46; with *Mowbray,* 208 F.3d, at 293–94; and *Blair,* 181 F.3d, at 834–35. Second, two circuits allow appeal when a petition raises an unsettled and fundamental question of law, regardless whether the district court likely erred. See *Mowbray,* 208 F.3d, at 293; *Blair,* 181 F.3d, at 835. Third, those same circuits caution that interlocutory appeal of an unsettled question of law is appropriate only when that question may evade effective appellate review at the end of the trial court proceedings. See *Mowbray,* 208 F.3d, at 293–94; *Blair,* 181 F.3d, at 835.

In our view, interlocutory appellate review under Rule 23(f) is properly directed by the guidance set forth in the advisory committee's note. The note reflects, on balance, a reluctance to depart from the traditional procedure in which claimed errors by the district court are reviewed on appeal only upon the conclusion of the proceedings in the district court. Although the rule ceded broad discretion to the appellate courts, it is understood, if not presumed, that appellate courts will act with cognizance of both the concerns underlying interlocutory appeals generally and the specific purposes for the allowance of interlocutory appeals of class certification decisions in Rule 23(f). Delay caused by interlocutory appeals under Rule 23(f) may be less of a concern because filing a petition does not automatically stay the litigation, see *Blair,* 181 F.3d, at 835; in the instant case, the docket indicates that the case proceeded until the district court granted Mylan's motion for a stay on April 15, 2002. Still, interlocutory appeals are generally disfavored as "disruptive, timeconsuming, and expensive" for both the parties and the courts, *Mowbray,* 208 F.3d, at 294, and the more so in a complex class action where the district court may reconsider and modify the class as the case progresses. *Prado-Steiman,* 221 F.3d, at 1276–77; Fed.R.Civ.P. 23(c)(1). As the Eleventh Circuit aptly commented, the exception provided by Rule 23(f) should be exercised in a manner that avoids both micromanagement of complex class actions as they evolve in the district court and inhibition of the district court's willingness to revise the class certification for fear of triggering another round of appellate review. See *Prado-Steiman,* 221 F.3d, at 1273–74. Thus, petitions for Rule 23(f) review are likely to be granted sparingly in cases that fall within neither the guidelines in the advisory committee's note nor the standards we adopt today. Nonetheless, the circuit courts addressing Rule 23(f) are in agreement that restrictions on review should not preclude review in special circumstances that neither the advisory committee's note nor the courts foresaw. See, e.g., *Mowbray,* 208 F.3d, at 294; *Blair,* 181 F.3d, at 834.

With these considerations in mind, we offer the following guidance. Rule 23(f) review will ordinarily be appropriate in three circumstances: (1) when there is a death-knell situation for either the plaintiff or defendant that is independent of the merits of the underlying claims, coupled with a class certification decision by the district court that is questionable, taking into account the district court's discretion over class certification; (2) when the certification decision presents an unsettled and fundamental issue of law relating to class actions, important both to the specific litigation and generally, that is likely to evade end-of-the-case review; and (3) when the district court's class certification decision is manifestly erroneous. Whether the district court's decision is questionable need not affect the appropriateness of Rule 23(f) review in the second category, as issues of law can be advanced through affirmances as well as reversals. *Blair,* 181 F.3d, at 835. But we conclude, unlike *Mowbray* and *Blair,* that error in certifying a class should not entirely be ignored outside the first category. Where a district court class certification decision is manifestly erroneous, for example, Rule 23(f) review would be warranted even in the absence of a death-knell situation if for no other reason than to avoid a lengthy and costly trial that is for naught once the final judgment is appealed. Although these standards are meant as guidance on when Rule 23(f) review ordinarily will be granted, we caution that the standards represent guidance, not a rigid test.

As is true for all the circuits, we are of the view that Rule 23(f) review should be granted rarely where a case does not fall within one of these three categories. The sheer number of class actions, the district court's authority to modify its class certification decision, see Fed.R.Civ.P. 23(c)(1), and the ease with which litigants can characterize legal issues as novel, all militate in favor of narrowing the scope of Rule 23(f) review. See *Prado-Steiman,* 221 F.3d, at 1273–74; see also *Mowbray,* 208 F.3d, at 294. At the same time, there necessarily should be some hesitancy in creating a rigid test for the exercise of an appellate court's discretion to grant a Rule 23(f) petition for review because circumstances may arise that cannot now be anticipated in which review would be appropriate, and conversely, in which review would be inappropriate notwithstanding the fact that a petition falls within the categories of cases in which review would ordinarily be appropriate. As the advisory committee's note indicates, the circuit court standards should "reflect the changing areas of uncertainty in class litigation." Fed.R.Civ.P. 23(f) advisory committee's note. Each circuit, thus, has reserved some leeway in its standards. See, e.g., *Newton,* 259 F.3d, at 165; *Prado-Steiman,* 221 F.3d, at 1276; *Mowbray,* 208 F.3d, at 294; *Blair,* 181 F.3d, at 834. So do we. That said, we nevertheless conclude that, absent special circumstances, this court's consideration of petitions for interlocutory review under Rule 23(f) should ordinarily fall within the three circumstances that we have identified.

III.

Mylan contends in its Rule 23(f) petition for review that, although certification of a class of direct purchasers is consistent with the direct purchaser rule of *Illinois Brick,* it conflicts with what Mylan regards as the underlying policy of *Illinois Brick*—that only one purchaser class has antitrust standing to sue under § 4 of the Clayton Act—when, as here, the FTC has brought suit and obtained a settlement on behalf of a class of consumer indirect purchasers. Mylan also contends that the certified class consists of both direct and indirect purchasers in contravention of *Illinois Brick* and Rule 23's class certification requirements. Seeking to bring itself within the flexible standards for Rule 23(f) adopted by the circuit courts, Mylan maintains that its petition for review should be granted because "important issues of antitrust standing [are] raised by the District Court's class certification ruling" that are novel, significant, and potentially dispositive, and because the class as certified is particularly suspect and may avoid later review given the potential liability Mylan faces. We conclude that Rule 23(f) review is inappropriate because Mylan's arguments in support of its Rule 12(b)(6) motion to dismiss are unrelated to class certification, and because Mylan's only challenge to the class certification decision falls outside the categories for Rule 23(f) review set forth in Part II.

A.

Rule 23(f) interlocutory review is limited to issues that relate to class certification. See Fed.R.Civ.P. 23(f); Bertulli v. Indep. Ass'n of Cont'l Pilots, 242 F.3d 290, 294 (5th Cir.2001); Carter v. W. Publ'g Co., 225 F.3d 1258, 1262 (11th Cir.2000). Thus, under Rule 23(f), this court can review the merits of an appeal only insofar as they bear upon the propriety of class certification, that is, whether the proposed class satisfies the prerequisites of Rule 23. The threshold requirements of class certification under Rule 23(a) are: (1) numerosity (a large enough class such that "joinder of all members is impractical"); (2) commonality ("questions of law or fact common to the class"); (3) typicality ("claims or defenses of the representative parties are typical of the claims or defenses of the class"); and (4) adequacy of representation ("representative parties will fairly and adequately protect the interests of the class"). Fed.R.Civ.P. 23(a); Amchem Prods., Inc. v. Windsor, 521 U.S. 591, 613 (1997). The rule also limits class actions to cases where: (1) separate actions would risk "establish[ing] incompatible standards of conduct for the party opposing the class" or individual adjudications "which would as a practical matter be dispositive of the interests" of nonparty members or "substantially impair or impede their ability to protect their interests"; (2) injunctive or declaratory relief is sought and "the party opposing the class has acted or refused to act on grounds generally applicable to the class"; or (3) "the court finds that the questions of law or fact common to the members of the class predominate over any questions affecting only individual members, and that a class action is superior to other available methods for the fair and efficient adjudication of the controversy." Fed.R.Civ.P. 23(b)(1), (2), & (3); *Amchem,* 521 U.S., at 614–16.

Although Mylan is correct that whether a class of direct purchasers has antitrust standing under the particular circumstances at issue is a novel question of law, the question is unrelated to class certification under Rule 23. As Mylan styled its filing in the district court, its novel question of law is properly raised in a Rule 12(b)(6) motion to dismiss; the denial of a motion to dismiss is generally not subject to interlocutory review under Rule 23(f) because whether the plaintiffs state a cause of action is only relevant to class certification to the extent the inquiry relates to the requirements of Rule 23. See Gen. Tel. Co. of the Southwest v. Falcon, 457 U.S. 147, 160 (1982); Eisen v. Carlisle & Jacquelin, 417 U.S. 156, 177–78 (1974). Mylan's effort to recast its Rule 12(b)(6) arguments as a challenge to class certification on the ground that a class of direct purchasers lacks antitrust standing, is to no avail. That Mylan's argument as to antitrust standing may dispose of the class as a whole and thereby preclude a lawsuit by direct purchasers goes well beyond the purpose of Rule 23(f) review because it is unrelated to the Rule 23 requirements. The fact that Mylan's challenge would be dispositive of the class action is not unlike a variety of issues of law on the merits of a class action because of the very nature of commonality, see Fed.R.Civ.P. 23(a)(2); review of such issues would expand Rule 23(f) interlocutory review to include review of any question raised in a motion to dismiss that may potentially dispose of a lawsuit as to the class as a whole. This result would inappropriately mix the issue of class certification with the merits of a case, which do not warrant interlocutory review pursuant to Rule 23(f). What matters for purposes of Rule 23(f) is whether the issue is related to class certification itself, and Mylan makes no showing that its antitrust standing claim is so related.

. . . . .

B.

Mylan's challenge to the composition of the certified class as assertedly, and improperly, consisting of both direct and indirect purchasers also is inappropriate for Rule 23(f) review.

First, Mylan has not shown that certification of the class would sound the death knell of the litigation. Other than mere assertions, Mylan makes no showing that it will be unduly pressured to settle because of the class's certification. Mylan failed to submit any evidence that the damages claimed would force a company of its size to settle without relation to the merits of the class's claims. See *Prado-Steiman,* 221 F.3d, at 1274; *Mowbray,* 208 F.3d, at 294–95.

Second, Mylan's challenge presents no unsettled question of fundamental importance to the law of class actions. Mylan argues that the district court erred in applying the standards of Rule 23 to the facts of this case, but Mylan does not aver that the district court lacked established law to guide it in that task. Insofar as Mylan's objection is based upon the district court's conclusion that the class representatives are direct purchasers, the law guiding that decision also is well settled. See *Illinois Brick,* 431 U.S., at 735–36.

Third, Mylan has not made a showing that, in light of the district court's discretion, see Hartman v. Duffey, 19 F.3d 1459, 1471 (D.C.Cir.

1994), the class certification was manifestly erroneous. Mylan contends the certified class does not meet the requirements of Rule 23(a)(2–4), namely, predominance, typicality, and adequacy of representation, because members of the class occupy different levels of a distribution relationship with Mylan. Upon the record before us, however, we can not conclude that there is manifest error in the district court's determination that the class representatives have standing under *Illinois Brick* or in the findings of fact underlying that conclusion. As the district court comes to know more about the relationships among Mylan, the pharmaceutical wholesalers, and the class plaintiffs, it may further refine the class, see Fed.R.Civ.P. 23(c)(1)—a possibility that supports our conclusion that immediate appeal is not warranted here.

Accordingly, we hold, upon applying the standards that we have outlined in defining when Rule 23(f) review is ordinarily appropriate, that Mylan's challenges to the class certification do not warrant interlocutory review pursuant to Rule 23(f). Although Mylan would nonetheless have the court reach the merits of the district court's certification decision as well as the merits of its Rule 12(b)(6) motion to dismiss because the issues have been carefully briefed, review under Rule 23(f) is not warranted. Therefore, we deny the petition for review.[10]

----

10. In Coopers & Lybrand v. Livesay, 437 U.S. 463 (1978), the Court rejected the "death knell" doctrine and held that neither the grant nor denial of class certification is appealable as of right under 28 U.S.C. § 1291 as a "collateral order." It has also held that the denial of class certification in a case in which injunctive relief is sought cannot be appealed under 28 U.S.C. § 1292(a)(1) as the denial of an injunction. Gardner v. Westinghouse Broadcasting Co., 437 U.S. 478 (1978).

In Deposit Guar. Nat. Bank v. Roper, 445 U.S. 326, 336 n. 8 (1980), the Court said: "In Coopers & Lybrand v. Livesay, 437 U.S. 463 (1978), we held that the class certification ruling did not fall within that narrow category of circumstances where appeal was allowed prior to final judgment as a matter of right under 28 U.S.C. § 1291. However, our ruling in *Livesay* was not intended to preclude motions under 28 U.S.C. § 1292(b) seeking discretionary interlocutory appeal for review of the certification ruling. See 437 U.S., at 474–475. In some cases such an appeal would promise substantial savings of time and resources or for other reasons should be viewed hospitably." For the holding of the *Deposit Guaranty* case itself, see supra p. 938, n. 49.

Civil Rule 54(b) allows a district court dealing with multiple claims or multiple parties to direct the entry of final judgment as to fewer than all of the claims or parties. To do so, the court must make an express determination that there is no just reason for delay. If a judgment is entered pursuant to such a direction, it is appealable as a final judgment under 28 U.S.C. § 1291. The appellate court may refuse to hear the appeal if it finds that Rule 54(b) was not properly invoked or if it finds that the trial court abused its discretion in finding that there was no just reason for delay, but the discretionary judgment of the trial court must be given substantial deference. Curtiss–Wright Corp. v. General Elec. Co., 446 U.S. 1 (1980). See 10 Wright, Miller & Kane, Federal Practice and Procedure: Civil 3d § 2659 (1998); 19 Moore's Federal Practice § 202.06 (3d ed.1998). The Supreme Court has also restricted the power of an appellate court to compel the entry of a Rule 54(b) certification that the district court has denied. See Reiter v. Cooper, 507 U.S. 258, 269 (1993).

In a civil-rights action the district court held that individual officers who were named as defendants did not have qualified immunity. It also denied a motion for summary judgment

SECTION 2.   THE SUPREME COURT[11]

Ex parte McCardle

Supreme Court of the United States, 1869.
7 Wall. (74 U.S.) 506, 19 L.Ed. 264.

Appeal from the Circuit Court for the Southern District of Mississippi.

by the County, which had argued that it could not be held liable because the sheriff, who authorized the police raids that gave rise to the suit, was not a policymaker for the County. Denial of qualified immunity is appealable before trial, and the court of appeals properly heard the appeals of the individual officers. That court erred, however, in holding that it had discretion to exercise "pendent appellate jurisdiction" and pass on an appeal by the County at the same time. "We need not definitively or preemptively settle here whether or when it may be proper for a court of appeals with jurisdiction over one ruling to review, conjunctively, related rulings that are not themselves independently appealable.... The parties do not contend that the District Court's decision to deny the Chambers County Commission's summary judgment motion was inextricably intertwined with that court's decision to deny the individual defendants' qualified immunity motions, or that review of the former decision was necessary to ensure meaningful review of the latter.... The District Court's preliminary ruling regarding the County did not qualify as a 'collateral order,' and there is no 'pendent party' appellate jurisdiction of the kind the Eleventh Circuit purported to exercise." Swint v. Chambers County Commission, 514 U.S. 35, 48 (1995).

It was held in Hill v. Henderson, 195 F.3d 671 (D.C.Cir.1999), that a district court's order dismissing one count of a complaint was not rendered a "final decision" appealable under 28 U.S.C. § 1291 by virtue of the court's transfer of the remaining counts to another district. Absent certification of the dismissal order for immediate appeal pursuant to Rule 54(b), appeal of the dismissal order must await the transferee court's resolution of the other counts, and must then be appealed in the transferee circuit. The circuits are divided, however. See, e.g., McGeorge v. Continental Airlines, 871 F.2d 952 (10th Cir.1989), which the District of Columbia Circuit expressly declined to follow. See generally Technosteel, L.L.C. v. Beers Construction Co., 271 F.3d 151 (4th Cir.2001).

A circuit split has developed as to whether the prohibition of an appeal from an interlocutory order compelling arbitration under the Federal Arbitration Act, 9 U.S.C. § 16(b)(2), bars appellate review of such an interlocutory order in the exercise of pendent appellate jurisdiction. Compare IDS Life Ins. Co. v. SunAmerica, Inc., 103 F.3d 524, 528 (7th Cir.1996) (Federal Arbitration Act bars pendent appellate jurisdiction) with Freeman v. Complex Computing Co., Inc., 119 F.3d 1044, 1050 (2d Cir.1997) (contra).

Difficult issues of appealability arise in connection with the Federal Arbitration Act, which permits interlocutory appeal of an order denying arbitration but requires a "final decision" before an order compelling arbitration is appealable. This led many circuits to classify arbitration proceedings as either "independent" or "embedded." The first category involves litigation in which the only issue is the duty to arbitrate. An order compelling arbitration leaves nothing left to be determined by the district court, and is therefore immediately appealable. The second category involves litigation that includes a claim that arbitration should be compelled along with other non-arbitral claims. An order compelling arbitration in an embedded proceeding was generally held not subject to immediate appeal until the Supreme Court ruled to the contrary in Green Tree Financial Corp.-Alabama v. Randolph, 531 U.S. 79 (2000).]

[**11.** See generally 16B Wright, Miller & Cooper, Federal Practice and Procedure: Jurisdiction 2d §§ 4001–4033 (1996), and 17 id. §§ 4034–4041 (1988); Stern, Gressman, Shapiro & Geller, Supreme Court Practice (7th ed.1993); Symposium, The Supreme Court Workload, 11 Hastings Const.L.Q. 353 (1984).

The case was this:

The Constitution of the United States ordains as follows:

"§ 1. The judicial power of the United States shall be vested *in one Supreme Court,* and in such inferior courts as the Congress may from time to time ordain and establish."

"§ 2. The judicial power shall extend to all cases in law or equity arising *under this Constitution, the laws of the United States,*" & c.

And in these last cases the Constitution ordains that,

"The Supreme Court shall have appellate jurisdiction, both as to law and fact, *with such exceptions, and under such regulations, as the Congress shall make.*"

With these constitutional provisions in existence, Congress, on the 5th February, 1867, by "An act to amend an act to establish the judicial courts of the United States, approved September 24, 1789," provided that the several courts of the United States, and the several justices and judges of such courts, within their respective jurisdiction, in addition to the authority already conferred by law, should have power to grant writs of habeas corpus in all cases where any person may be restrained of his or her liberty in violation of the Constitution, or of any treaty or law of the United States. And that, from the final decision of any judge, justice, or court inferior to the Circuit Court, appeal might be taken to the Circuit Court of the United States for the district in which the cause was heard, and *from the judgment of the said Circuit Court to the Supreme Court of the United States.*

This statute being in force, one McCardle, alleging unlawful restraint by military force, preferred a petition in the court below, for the writ of habeas corpus.

The writ was issued, and a return was made by the military commander, admitting the restraint, but denying that it was unlawful.

It appeared that the petitioner was not in the military service of the United States, but was held in custody by military authority for trial before a military commission, upon charges founded upon the publication of articles alleged to be incendiary and libellous, in a newspaper of which he was editor. The custody was alleged to be under the authority of certain acts of Congress.

Upon the hearing, the petitioner was remanded to the military custody, but, upon his prayer, an appeal was allowed him to this court, and upon

There is an instructive Symposium on Supreme Court Advocacy, 33 Cath.U.L.Rev. 525 (1984).]

filing the usual appeal-bond, for costs, he was admitted to bail upon recognizance, with sureties, conditioned for his future appearance in the Circuit Court, to abide by and perform the final judgment of this court. The appeal was taken under the above-mentioned act of February 5, 1867.

A motion to dismiss this appeal was made at the last term, and, after argument, was denied.[12]

Subsequently, on the 2d, 3d, 4th, and 9th March, the case was argued very thoroughly and ably upon the merits, and was taken under advisement. While it was thus held, and before conference in regard to the decision proper to be made, an act was passed by Congress,[13] returned with objections by the President, and, on the 27th March, repassed by the constitutional majority, the second section of which was as follows:

> "*And be it further enacted,* That so much of the act approved February 5, 1867, entitled 'An act to amend an act to establish the judicial courts of the United States, approved September 24, 1789', as authorized an appeal from the judgment of the Circuit Court to the Supreme Court of the United States, or the exercise of any such jurisdiction by said Supreme Court, on appeals which have been, or may hereafter be taken, be, and the same is hereby repealed."

The attention of the court was directed to this statute at the last term, but counsel having expressed a desire to be heard in argument upon its effect, and the Chief Justice being detained from his place here, by his duties in the Court of Impeachment, the cause was continued under advisement. Argument was now heard upon the effect of the repealing act.

■ THE CHIEF JUSTICE delivered the opinion of the court.

The first question necessarily is that of jurisdiction; for, if the act of March, 1868, takes away the jurisdiction defined by the act of February, 1867, it is useless, if not improper, to enter into any discussion of other questions.

It is quite true, as was argued by the counsel for the petitioner, that the appellate jurisdiction of this court is not derived from acts of Congress. It is strictly speaking, conferred by the Constitution. But it is conferred "with such exceptions and under such regulations as Congress shall make."

It is unnecessary to consider whether, if Congress had made no exceptions and no regulations, this court might not have exercised general appellate jurisdiction under rules prescribed by itself. For among the earliest acts of the first Congress, at its first session, was the act of September 24th, 1789, to establish the judicial courts of the United States. That act provided for the organization of this court, and prescribed regulations for the exercise of its jurisdiction.

---

12.   See Ex parte McCardle, 6 Wallace [73 U.S.] 318.

13.   Act of March 27, 1868, 15 Stat. at Large 44.

The source of that jurisdiction, and the limitations of it by the Constitution and by statute, have been on several occasions subjects of consideration here. In the case of Durousseau v. The United States,[14] particularly, the whole matter was carefully examined, and the court held, that while "the appellate powers of this court are not given by the judicial act, but are given by the Constitution," they are, nevertheless, "limited and regulated by that act, and by such other acts as have been passed on the subject." The court said, further, that the judicial act was an exercise of the power given by the Constitution to Congress "of making exceptions to the appellate jurisdiction of the Supreme Court." "They have described affirmatively," said the court, "its jurisdiction, and this affirmative description has been understood to imply a negation of the exercise of such appellate power as is not comprehended within it."

The principle that the affirmation of appellate jurisdiction implies the negation of all such jurisdiction not affirmed having been thus established, it was an almost necessary consequence that acts of Congress, providing for the exercise of jurisdiction, should come to be spoken of as acts granting jurisdiction, and not as acts making exceptions to the constitutional grant of it.

The exception to appellate jurisdiction in the case before us, however, is not an inference from the affirmation of other appellate jurisdiction. It is made in terms. The provision of the act of 1867, affirming the appellate jurisdiction of this court in cases of habeas corpus is expressly repealed. It is hardly possible to imagine a plainer instance of positive exception.

We are not at liberty to inquire into the motives[15] of the legislature. We can only examine into its power under the constitution; and the power to make exceptions to the appellate jurisdiction of this court is given by express words.

What, then, is the effect of the repealing act upon the case before us? We cannot doubt as to this. Without jurisdiction the court cannot proceed at all in any cause. Jurisdiction is power to declare the law, and when it ceases to exist, the only function remaining to the court is that of announcing the fact and dismissing the cause. And this is not less clear upon authority than upon principle.

Several cases were cited by the counsel for the petitioner in support of the position that jurisdiction of this case is not affected by the repealing act. But none of them, in our judgment, afford any support to it. They are all cases of the exercise of judicial power by the legislature, or of legislative interference with courts in the exercising of continuing jurisdiction.[16]

---

14. 6 Cranch [10 U.S.] 312; Wiscart v. Dauchy, 3 Dallas [3 U.S.] 321.

[15. The motives were to prevent the Court from passing upon the constitutionality of the Reconstruction Acts. The climate of the case was therefore created by the dramatic intragovernmental strife of the period. Warren recreates the atmosphere in 3 Supreme Court in United States History ch. 30 (1922). See also Fairman, Reconstruction and Reunion, 1964, 413–601 (1971).]

16. Lanier v. Gallatas, 13 Louisiana Annual 175; De Chastellux v. Fairchild, 15 Pennsylvania State 18; The State v. Fleming, 7 Humphreys 152; Lewis v. Webb, 3 Greenleaf 326.

On the other hand, the general rule, supported by the best elementary writers,[17] is, that "when an act of the legislature is repealed, it must be considered, except as to transactions past and closed, as if it never existed." And the effect of repealing acts upon suits under acts repealed, has been determined by the adjudications of this court. The subject was fully considered in *Norris v. Crocker*,[18] and more recently in *Insurance Company v. Ritchie*.[19] In both of these cases it was held that no judgment could be rendered in a suit after the repeal of the act under which it was brought and prosecuted.

It is quite clear, therefore, that this court cannot proceed to pronounce judgment in this case, for it has no longer jurisdiction of the appeal; and judicial duty is not less fitly performed by declining ungranted jurisdiction than in exercising firmly that which the Constitution and the laws confer.

Counsel seem to have supposed, if effect be given to the repealing act in question, that the whole appellate power of the court, in cases of habeas corpus is denied. But this is an error. The act of 1868 does not except from that jurisdiction any cases but appeals from Circuit Courts under the act of 1867. It does not affect the jurisdiction which was previously exercised.[20]

The appeal of the petitioner in this case must be

Dismissed For Want of Jurisdiction.[21]

---

17.   Dwarris on Statutes, 538.

18.   13 Howard [54 U.S.] 429.

19.   5 Wallace [76 U.S.] 541.

20.   Ex parte McCardle, 6 Wallace [73 U.S.] 318, 324.

[21.   See Van Alstyne, A Critical Guide to *Ex Parte McCardle*, 15 Ariz.L.Rev. 229 (1973).

In their dissenting opinion in Glidden Co. v. Zdanok, 370 U.S. 530, 605 n. 11 (1962), Justices Black and Douglas say: "There is a serious question whether the *McCardle* case could command a majority view today."

One year after *McCardle* the Supreme Court held that the 1868 repeal of the statute giving it appellate jurisdiction in habeas corpus cases did not affect another statute under which it could issue original writs of habeas corpus and certiorari. Ex parte Yerger, 8 Wall. [75 U.S.] 85 (1869).

Whatever the power of Congress to accelerate the finality of a judgment by withdrawing appellate jurisdiction while an appeal is sub judice, Congress has no converse power to alter a judgment that has become final by compelling the reopening of litigation. Plaut v. Spendthrift Farm, Inc., 514 U.S. 211 (1995).

See also Hart, The Power of Congress to Limit the Jurisdiction of Federal Courts: An Exercise in Dialectic, 66 Harv.L.Rev. 1362 (1953); Levy, Congressional Power Over the Appellate Jurisdiction of the Supreme Court: A Reappraisal, 22 N.Y.U.Intra.L.Rev. 178 (1969); Brant, Appellate Jurisdiction: Congressional Abuse of the Exceptions Clause, 53 Or.L.Rev. 3 (1973); Anderson, The Power of Congress to Limit the Appellate Jurisdiction of the Supreme Court, 1981 Det.C.L.L.Rev. 753; Sager, Foreword: Constitutional Limitations on Congress' Authority to Regulate the Jurisdiction of the Federal Courts, 95 Harv.L.Rev. 17 (1981); Symposium, Limiting Federal Court Jurisdiction, 65 Judicature 177 (1981).]

STATUTES[22]

28 U.S.C. § 1253. Direct appeals from decisions of three-judge courts

Except as otherwise provided by law, any party may appeal to the Supreme Court from an order granting or denying, after notice and hearing, an interlocutory or permanent injunction in any civil action, suit or proceeding required by any Act of Congress to be heard and determined by a district court of three judges.[23]

28 U.S.C. § 1254. Courts of appeals; certiorari; certified questions

Cases in the courts of appeals may be reviewed by the Supreme Court by the following methods:

(1) By writ of certiorari granted upon the petition of any party to any civil or criminal case, before[24] or after rendition of judgment or decree;[25]

[22. The statutes as they are set out here reflect the changes made by Act of June 27, 1988, Pub.L. 100–352, 102 Stat. 662. This was the first major change in the jurisdictional structure of the Supreme Court since the "Judges' Bill" of 1925 for the first time gave the court control, through the discretionary writ of certiorari, over part of its docket. Now except for appeals from three-judge courts under 28 U.S.C. § 1253, and certified questions from courts of appeals under 28 U.S.C. § 1254(2) (a practice now obsolete—see infra p. 1010, n. 26), review in the Supreme Court is always by certiorari. See Stern, Gressman & Shapiro, Epitaph for Mandatory Jurisdiction, A.B.A.J., Dec. 1, 1988, p. 66.]

[23. See Wright & Kane, Federal Courts § 105 (6th ed.2002); 3 Moore's Manual: Federal Practice and Procedure § 29.03 (1998).]

[24. See United States v. United Mine Workers of America, 330 U.S. 258, 269 (1947), reprinted supra p. 440.

For a colorful description of a dramatic case in which this procedure was belatedly invoked, see Bittker, The World War II German Saboteurs' Case and Writs of Certiorari Before Judgment by the Court of Appeals: A Tale of Nunc Pro Tunc Jurisdiction, 14 Const. Comm. 431 (1997).]

[25. The considerations governing review on certiorari are set out in Rule 10 of the 1997 Revised Rules of the Supreme Court. See Rogers v. Missouri Pac. R. Co., 352 U.S. 500 (1957); Leiman, The Rule of Four, 57 Colum.L.Rev. 975 (1957); Linzer, The Meaning of Certiorari Denials, 79 Colum.L.Rev. 1227 (1979); Stevens, The Life Span of a Judge–Made Rule, 58 N.Y.U.L.Rev. 1 (1983).

See Prettyman, Petitioning the United States Supreme Court—A Primer for Hopeful Neophytes, 51 Va.L.Rev. 582 (1965) and Prettyman, Opposing Certiorari in the United States Supreme Court, 61 Va.L.Rev. 197 (1975).

For an interesting discussion of the Court's prudential policies under Rule 14.1(a) regarding the scope of the issues presented by a petition for certiorari, see Kaisha v. U.S. Philips Corp., 510 U.S. 27, 31–33 (1993) (per curiam; certiorari dismissed as improvidently granted).

Rule 39 of the Rules of the Supreme Court of the United States authorizes petitions for certiorari to be filed in forma pauperis, which is routinely granted upon the filing of simple form and an affidavit of indigency. In reaction to the repeated filing of frivolous i.f.p. petitions by vexatious litigants, the Court amended Rule 39 in 1991 to add Rule 39.8, authorizing the denial of i.f.p. status if the proposed petition is frivolous or malicious. See Zatko v. California, 502 U.S. 16 (1991). The Court has since taken the further step of prospectively barring the Clerk of the Court from accepting any further civil petitions for certiorari from several particularly vexatious i.f.p. litigants unless the normal docketing fee

(2) By certification at any time by a court of appeals of any question of law in any civil or criminal case as to which instructions are desired, and upon such certification the Supreme Court may give binding instructions or require the entire record to be sent up for decision of the entire matter in controversy.[26]

28 U.S.C. § 1257. State courts; certiorari

(a) Final judgments or decrees rendered by the highest court of a State in which a decision could be had,[27] may be reviewed by the Supreme Court by writ of certiorari, where the validity of a treaty or statute of the United States is drawn in question or where the validity of a State statute is drawn in question on the ground of its being repugnant to the Constitution, treaties or laws of the United States, or where any title, right, privilege or

---

($300) is paid and the other normal requirements are met (i.e., 40 printed copies of the petition are presented for filing). See, e.g., Day v. Day, 510 U.S. 1 (1993).

Under 28 U.S.C. § 2101(c), a petition for a writ of certiorari to review "any judgment or decree in a civil action" must be filed "within ninety days after the entry of such judgment or decree." Supreme Court Rule 13(3) provides in its first sentence that the 90–day period for filing a petition for a writ of certiorari runs "from the date of entry of the judgment or order sought to be reviewed," but adds in its second sentence that this period is extended by the filing of a petition for rehearing. In deference to the objectives of § 2101(c), the Court has held that the 90–day filing period is also extended when the court below recalls its mandate, sua sponte, and invites the parties to brief the question whether the case should be reheard en banc. See Hibbs v. Winn, 542 U.S. 88 (2004).

A federal defendant denied postconviction relief under 28 U.S.C. § 2255 may not appeal the ruling under 28 U.S.C. § 1291 without first obtaining the certificate of appealability required by the Antiterrorism and Effective Death Penalty Act of 1996, as codified at 28 U.S.C. § 2253(c)(1)(B). But does § 2253(c)(1)(B) also limit the appellate jurisdiction of the Supreme Court? A sharply divided Court held not in Hohn v. United States, 524 U.S. 236 (1998), after overruling the contrary reasoning of its per curiam opinion in House v. Mayo, 324 U.S. 42 (1945).]

[**26.**   The use of certified questions is now obsolete. The Court has many grounds on which to dismiss certificates, see, e.g., National Labor Relations Board v. White Swan Co., 313 U.S. 23 (1941); Busby v. Electric Utilities Employees Union, 323 U.S. 72 (1944). See also Moore and Vestal, Present and Potential Role of Certification in Federal Appellate Procedure, 35 Va.L.Rev. 1 (1949); Wiener, The Supreme Court's New Rules, 68 Harv.L.Rev. 20, 66–67 (1954). But see Bernard, Certified Questions in the Supreme Court: In Defense of an Option, 83 Dick.L.Rev. 31 (1978).

United States v. Barnett, 376 U.S. 681 (1964), was decided on certificate but it is the exceptional case that proves the rule. The Supreme Court also decided a question certified to it by a court of appeals in exceptional circumstances in Moody v. Albemarle Paper Co., 417 U.S. 622 (1974). See also Iran National Airlines Corp. v. Marschalk Co., 453 U.S. 919 (1981).

The thirteen active judges of the Second Circuit, acting unanimously, invoked § 1254(2) for the first time in 23 years in United States v. Penaranda, 375 F.3d 238 (2d Cir.2004) (en banc), certified questions dismissed, 543 U.S. 1117 (2005). The Second Circuit's extraordinary action was prompted by widespread doubt over the effect of Blakely v. Washington, 542 U.S. 296 (2004), on the validity and administration of the federal Sentencing Guidelines. The Supreme Court chose to address this issue in another case, United States v. Booker, 543 U.S. 220 (2005).]

[**27.**   As to "highest court" see Thompson v. City of Louisville, 362 U.S. 199 (1960) (certiorari to Police Court of Louisville, Ky.); Costarelli v. Massachusetts, 421 U.S. 193 (1975) (Municipal Court of City of Boston).]

immunity is specially set up or claimed under the Constitution, treaties or statutes of, or commission held or authority exercised under, the United States.

(b) For the purposes of this section, the term "highest court of a State" includes the District of Columbia Court of Appeals.

28 U.S.C. § 1651. Writs

(a) The Supreme Court and all courts established by Act of Congress may issue all writs necessary or appropriate in aid of their respective jurisdictions and agreeable to the usages and principles of law.

(b) An alternative writ or rule nisi may be issued by a justice or judge of a court which has jurisdiction.[28]

BUNN, JURISDICTION AND PRACTICE OF THE COURTS OF THE UNITED STATES 237–240 (5th ed.1949)[29]

§ 6. Appellate Jurisdiction over State Courts

This is of course another place where the supremacy of the Federal authority is shown in action. But it was not achieved without a struggle.

The Constitution says that "the Supreme Court shall have appellate Jurisdiction" in "the other Cases before mentioned," which include "all Cases ... arising under this Constitution, the Laws of the United States, and Treaties made, or which shall be made, under their Authority." [30] But it does not say appellate jurisdiction *from what courts*. Therefore, and of course for much weightier reasons than the verbal one, it was repeatedly asserted by lawyers and by politicians, North as well as South, that the State courts were not subject to the appellate jurisdiction of the Supreme Court of the United States.

The first Congress considered the question and decided in favor of the jurisdiction. Section 25 of the Judiciary Act of 1789[31] provided that final judgments of the highest courts of the States in the cases described in the

---

[28. For an illuminating review of the Court's jurisdiction under 28 U.S.C. § 1651, see United States Alkali Export Assn. v. United States, 325 U.S. 196 (1945). A vigorous conflict of opinion as to the propriety of exercising this jurisdiction arose in De Beers Consol. Mines v. United States, 325 U.S. 212 (1945) decided the same day. See also Wolfson, Extraordinary Writs in the Supreme Court Since *Ex parte Peru*, 51 Colum.L.Rev. 977 (1951).

As to the power of an individual justice to stay execution and the power of the Court to vacate the stay, see Rosenberg v. United States, 346 U.S. 273 (1953), noted 32 Tex.L.Rev. 459 (1954).

See also Note, The Powers of the Supreme Court Justice Acting in an Individual Capacity, 112 U.Pa.L.Rev. 981 (1964); Boner, Index to Chambers Opinions of Supreme Court Justices, 65 Law Library J. 213 (1972).]

[29.   Reprinted by permission.]

30.   Article III, § 2.

31.   1 Stat. 85.

section "may be re-examined and reversed or affirmed in the Supreme Court of the United States upon a writ of error." The jurisdiction so conferred was exercised, at first without objection.[32] But the time came when it was challenged, twice by the Supreme Court of Virginia and once by the Supreme Court of Wisconsin. The opinions of the Supreme Court of the United States in the three cases, by Justice Story, Chief Justice Marshall, and Chief Justice Taney,[33] are an eloquent and convincing statement of the proposition that the federal *judicial* power, like other federal powers, is necessarily supreme within its field. The proposition has not been seriously doubted since the civil war. The jurisdiction exists, and is conceded by State courts. The remaining question is: What are its limits?

————

Cox Broadcasting Corp. v. Cohn

Supreme Court of the United States, 1975.
420 U.S. 469, 95 S.Ct. 1029, 43 L.Ed.2d 328.

■ Mr. Justice White delivered the opinion of the Court.

The issue before us in this case is whether consistently with the First and Fourteenth Amendments a State may extend a cause of action for damages for invasion of privacy caused by the publication of the name of a deceased rape victim which was publicly revealed in connection with the prosecution of the crime.

I

[A television station, reporting on court proceedings in a prosecution for rape of a 17–year–old girl, who had died as a result of the rape, gave the name of the victim, which it had learned from the indictments, public records available for inspection. The victim's father sued the station for money damages, relying on Ga.Code Ann. § 26–9901, which makes it a misdemeanor to publish or broadcast the name or identity of a rape victim. Defendant claimed that its broadcast of the name was privileged under the First and Fourteenth Amendments. The trial court gave summary judgment for plaintiff on liability, with a determination of damages to be made later by a jury. On appeal from the judgment of liability, the Georgia Supreme Court initially held that it need not pass on the constitutionality of § 26–9901, since that statute does not create a civil cause of action, but held that the father had a common-law tort claim for the invasion of his privacy through the publication of his daughter's name. It reversed the summary judgment, holding that the trier of fact must determine whether

---

32. By the time of Martin v. Hunter's Lessee (1815) seventeen cases from State courts had been before the Supreme Court. John P. Frank, Historical Basis of the Federal Judicial System, in [13] Law and Contemporary Problems, Winter, 1969, at p. 16.

33. Martin v. Hunter's Lessee, 1 Wheat. [14 U.S.] 304 (1815); Cohens v. Virginia, 6 Wheat. [19 U.S.] 264 (1821); Ableman v. Booth, 21 How. [62 U.S.] 506 (1859). See Charles Warren, The Supreme Court in United States History, Vol. I, p. 442 et seq. (*Martin v. Hunter's Lessee*), Vol. II, p. 7 et seq. (*Cohens v. Virginia*), Vol. III, p. 58 et seq. (*Ableman v. Booth*).

the public disclosure of the name actually invaded the father's zone of privacy. On rehearing the Georgia court met the argument that the victim's name was a matter of public interest and could be published with impunity by relying on § 26–9901 as an authoritative declaration of state policy that the name of a rape victim is not a matter of public concern. It then held that the statute was a "legitimate limitation on the right of freedom of expression contained in the First Amendment."]

II

Appellants invoke the appellate jurisdiction of this Court under 28 U.S.C. § 1257(2) and, if that jurisdictional basis is found to be absent, through a petition for certiorari under 28 U.S.C. § 2103. Two questions concerning our jurisdiction must be resolved: (1) whether the constitutional validity of § 26–9901 was "drawn in question," with the Georgia Supreme Court upholding its validity, and (2) whether the decision from which this appeal has been taken is a "final judgment or decree."

A

Appellants clearly raised the issue of the constitutionality of § 26–9901 in their motion for rehearing in the Georgia Supreme Court. In denying that motion that court held: "A majority of this court does not consider this statute to be in conflict with the First Amendment." 231 Ga., at 68, 200 S.E.2d, at 134. Since the Court relied upon the statute as a declaration of the public policy of Georgia that the disclosure of a rape victim's name was not to be protected expression, the statute was drawn in question in a manner directly bearing upon the merits of the action, and the decision in favor of its constitutional validity invokes this Court's appellate jurisdiction. Cf. Garrity v. New Jersey, 385 U.S. 493, 495–496 (1967).

B

Since 1789, Congress has granted this Court appellate jurisdiction with respect to state litigation only after the highest state court in which judgment could be had has rendered a "[f]inal judgment or decree." 28 U.S.C. § 1257 retains this limitation on our power to review cases coming from state courts. The Court has noted that "[c]onsiderations of English usage as well as those of judicial policy" would justify an interpretation of the final judgment rule to preclude review "where anything further remains to be determined by a State court, no matter how dissociated from the only federal issue that has finally been adjudicated by the highest court of the State." Radio Station WOW, Inc. v. Johnson, 326 U.S. 120, 124 (1945). But the Court there observed that the rule had not been administered in such a mechanical fashion and that there were circumstances in which there has been "a departure from this requirement of finality for federal appellate jurisdiction." Ibid.

These circumstances were said to be "very few," ibid.; but as the cases have unfolded, the Court has recurringly encountered situations in which the highest court of a State has finally determined the federal issue present in a particular case, but in which there are further proceedings in the lower state courts to come. There are now at least four categories of such cases in which the Court has treated the decision on the federal issue as a final judgment for the purposes of 28 U.S.C. § 1257 and has taken jurisdiction without awaiting the completion of the additional proceedings anticipated in the lower state courts. In most, if not all, of the cases in these categories, these additional proceedings would not require the decision of other federal questions that might also require review by the Court at a later date,[34] and immediate rather than delayed review would be the best way to avoid "the mischief or economic waste and of delayed justice," *Radio Station WOW, Inc. v. Johnson*, supra, at 124, as well as precipitous interference with state litigation.[35] In the cases in the first two categories considered below, the federal issue would not be mooted or otherwise affected by the proceedings yet to be had because those proceedings have little substance, their outcome is certain, or they are wholly unrelated to the federal question. In the other two categories, however, the federal issue would be mooted if the petitioner or appellant seeking to bring the action here prevailed on the merits in the later state-court proceedings, but there is nevertheless sufficient justification for immediate review of the federal question finally determined in the state courts.

In the first category are those cases in which there are further proceedings—even entire trials—yet to occur in the state courts but where for one reason or another the federal issue is conclusive or the outcome of further proceedings preordained. In these circumstances, because the case is for all practical purposes concluded, the judgment of the state court on the federal issue is deemed final. In Mills v. Alabama, 384 U.S. 214, for example, a demurrer to a criminal complaint was sustained on federal constitutional grounds by a state trial court. The State Supreme Court

---

34. Eminent domain proceedings are of the type that may involve an interlocutory decision as to a federal question with another federal question to be decided later. "For in those cases the federal constitutional question embraces not only a taking but a taking on payment of just compensation. A state judgment is not final unless it covers both aspects of that integral problem." North Dakota State Board of Pharmacy v. Snyder's Drug Stores, 414 U.S. 156, 163 (1973). See also Grays Harbor Logging Co. v. Coats–Fordney Logging Co., 243 U.S. 251, 256 (1917); Radio Station WOW, Inc. v. Johnson, 326 U.S. 120, 127 1945).

35. Gillespie v. United States Steel Corp., 379 U.S. 148 (1964), arose in the federal courts and involved the requirement of 28 U.S.C. § 1291 that judgments of district courts be final if they are to be appealed to the courts of appeals. In the course of deciding that the judgment of the District Court in the case had been final, the Court indicated its approach to finality requirements: "And our cases long have recognized that whether a ruling is 'final' within the meaning of § 1291 is frequently so close a question that decision of that issue either way can be supported with equally forceful arguments, and that it is impossible to devise a formula to resolve all marginal cases coming within what might well be called the 'twilight zone' of finality. Because of this difficulty this Court has held that the requirement of finality is to be given a 'practical rather than a technical construction.' Cohen v. Beneficial Industrial Loan Corp., [337 U.S. 541, 546]. See also Brown Shoe Co. v. United States, 370 U.S. 294, 306; Bronson v. Railroad Co., 2 Black [67 U.S.] 524, 531; Forgay v. Conrad, 6 How. [47 U.S.] 201, 203. Dickinson v. Petroleum Conversion Corp., 338 U.S. 507, 511, pointed out that in deciding the question of finality the most important competing considerations are 'the inconvenience and costs of piecemeal review on the one hand and the danger of denying justice by delay on the other.' " 379 U.S., at 152–153.

reversed, remanding for jury trial. This Court took jurisdiction on the reasoning that the appellant had no defense other than his federal claim and could not prevail at trial on the facts or any non-federal ground. To dismiss the appeal "would not only be an inexcusable delay of the benefits Congress intended to grant by providing for appeal to this Court, but it would also result in a completely unnecessary waste of time and energy in judicial systems already troubled by delays due to congested dockets." Id., at 217–218 (footnote omitted.)

Second, there are cases such as *Radio Station WOW,* supra, and Brady v. Maryland, 373 U.S. 83 (1963), in which the federal issue, finally decided by the highest court in the State, will survive and require decision regardless of the outcome of future state-court proceedings. In *Radio Station WOW,* the Nebraska Supreme Court directed the transfer of the properties of a federally licensed radio station and ordered an accounting, rejecting the claim that the transfer order would interfere with the federal license. The federal issue was held reviewable here despite the pending accounting on the "presupposition . . . that the federal questions that could come here have been adjudicated by the State court, and that the accounting which remains to be taken could not remotely give rise to a federal question . . . that may later come here . . . ." Id., 326 U.S., at 127. The judgment rejecting the federal claim and directing the transfer was deemed "dissociated from a provision for an accounting even though that is decreed in the same order." Id., at 126. Nothing that could happen in the course of the accounting, short of settlement of the case, would foreclose or make unnecessary decision on the federal question. Older cases in the Court had reached the same result on similar facts. Carondelet Canal & Nav. Co. v. Louisiana, 233 U.S. 362 [1914]; Forgay v. Conrad, 6 How. [47 U.S.] 201 (1848). In the latter case, the Court, in an opinion by Chief Justice Taney, stated that the Court had not understood the final judgment rule "in this strict and technical sense, but has given [it] a more liberal, and, as we think, a more reasonable construction, and one more consonant to the intention of the Legislature." Id., at 203.[36]

In the third category are those situations where the federal claim has been finally decided, with further proceedings on the merits in the state courts to come, but in which later review of the federal issue cannot be had, whatever the ultimate outcome of the case. Thus, in these cases, if the party seeking interim review ultimately prevails on the merits, the federal issue will be mooted; if he were to lose on the merits, however, the governing state law would not permit him again to present his federal claims for review. The Court has taken jurisdiction in these circumstances prior to completion of the case in the state courts. California v. Stewart, 384 U.S. 436 (1966) (decided with Miranda v. Arizona [, 384 U.S. 436

---

36. In *Brady,* supra, the Maryland courts had ordered a new trial in a criminal case but on punishment only, and the petitioner asserted here that he was entitled to a new trial on guilt as well. We entertained the case, saying that the federal issue was separable and would not be mooted by the new trial on punishment ordered in the state courts. 373 U.S., at 85, n. 1.

(1966)]), epitomizes this category. There the state court reversed a conviction on federal constitutional grounds and remanded for a new trial. Although the State might have prevailed at trial, we granted its petition for certiorari and affirmed, explaining that the state judgment was "final" since an acquittal of the defendant at trial would preclude, under state law, an appeal by the State. Id., at 498, n. 71.

A recent decision in this category is North Dakota State Board of Pharmacy v. Snyder's Drug Stores, 414 U.S. 156 (1973), in which the Pharmacy Board rejected an application for a pharmacy operating permit relying on a state statute specifying ownership requirements which the applicant did not meet. The State Supreme Court held the statute unconstitutional and remanded the matter to the Board for further consideration of the application, freed from the constraints of the ownership statute. The Board brought the case here, claiming that the statute was constitutionally acceptable under modern cases. After reviewing the various circumstances under which the finality requirement has been deemed satisfied despite the fact that litigation had not terminated in the state courts, we entertained the case over claims that we had no jurisdiction. The federal issue would not survive the remand, whatever the result of the state administrative proceedings. The Board might deny the license on state law grounds, thus foreclosing the federal issue, and the Court also ascertained that under state law the Board could not bring the federal issue here in the event the applicant satisfied the requirements of state law except for the invalidated ownership statute. Under these circumstances, the issue was ripe for review.[37]

Lastly, there are those situations where the federal issue has been finally decided in the state courts with further proceedings pending in which the party seeking review here might prevail on the merits on nonfederal grounds, thus rendering unnecessary review of the federal issue by this Court, and where reversal of the state court on the federal issue would be preclusive of any further litigation on the relevant cause of action rather than merely controlling the nature and character of, or determining the admissibility of evidence in, the state proceedings still to come. In these circumstances, if a refusal immediately to review the state court decision might seriously erode federal policy, the Court has entertained and decided the federal issue, which itself has been finally determined by the state courts for purposes of the state litigation.

In Construction Laborers v. Curry, 371 U.S. 542 (1963), the state courts temporarily enjoined the labor-union picketing over claims that the

---

37.   Cohen v. Beneficial Industrial Loan Corp., 337 U.S. 541 (1949), was a diversity action in the federal courts in the course of which there arose the question of the validity of a state statute requiring plaintiffs in stockholder suits to post security for costs as a prerequisite to bringing the action. The District Court held the state law inapplicable, the Court of Appeals reversed, and this Court granted certiorari, holding that the issue of security for costs was separable from and independent of the merits and that if review were to be postponed until the termination of the litigation, "it will be too late effectively to review the present order and the rights conferred by the statute, if it is applicable, will have been lost, probably irreparably." Id., at 546.

National Labor Relations Board had exclusive jurisdiction of the controversy. The Court took jurisdiction for two independent reasons. First, the power of the state court to proceed in the face of the preemption claim was deemed an issue separable from the merits and ripe for review in this Court, particularly "when postponing review would seriously erode the national labor policy requiring the subject matter of respondent's cause to be heard by the . . . Board, not by the state courts." Id., at 550. Second, the Court was convinced that in any event the union had no defense to the entry of a permanent injunction other than the preemption claim that it had already been ruled on in the state courts. Hence the case was for all practical purposes concluded in the state tribunals.

In Mercantile National Bank v. Langdeau, 371 U.S. 555 (1963), the two national banks were sued, along with others, in the courts of Travis County, Tex. The claim asserted was conspiracy to defraud an insurance company. The banks as a preliminary matter asserted that a special federal venue statute immunized them from suit in Travis County and that they could properly be sued only in another county. Although trial was still to be had and the banks might well prevail on the merits, the Court, relying on *Curry,* entertained the issue as a "separate and independent matter, anterior to the merits and not enmeshed in the factual and legal issues comprising the plaintiff's cause of action." Id., at 558. Moreover, it would serve the policy of the federal statute "to determine now in which state court appellants may be tried rather than to subject them . . . to long and complex litigation which may all be for naught if consideration of the preliminary question of venue is postponed until the conclusion of the proceedings." Ibid.

Miami Herald Publishing Company v. Tornillo, 418 U.S. 241 (1974), is the latest case in this category.[38] There a candidate for public office sued a newspaper for refusing, allegedly contrary to a state statute, to carry his reply to the paper's editorial critical of his qualifications. The trial court held the act unconstitutional, denying both injunctive relief and damages. The State Supreme Court reversed, sustaining the statute against the challenge based upon the First and Fourteenth Amendments and remanding the case for a trial and appropriate relief, including damages. The newspaper brought the case here. We sustained our jurisdiction, relying on the principles elaborated in the *North Dakota* case and observing:

> "Whichever way we were to decide on the merits, it would be intolerable to leave unanswered, under these circumstances, an important

---

38. Meanwhile Hudson Distributors v. Eli Lilly, 377 U.S. 386 (1964), another case of this genre, had been decided. There a retailer sued to invalidate a state fair trade act as inconsistent with the federal antitrust laws and not saved by a federal statute authorizing state fair trade legislation under certain conditions. The defendant manufacturer cross-petitioned for enforcement of the state act against the plaintiff-retailer. The trial court struck down the statute, but a state appellate court reversed and remanded for trial on the cross-petition. The Ohio Supreme Court affirmed that decision. Relying on *Curry* and Mercantile National Bank v. Langdeau, 371 U.S. 555 (1963), this Court found the state court judgment to be ripe for review, although the retailer might prevail at the trial. 377 U.S., at 389, n. 4.

question of freedom of the press under the First Amendment; an uneasy and unsettled constitutional posture of § 104.38 could only further harm the operation of a free press. Mills v. Alabama, 384 U.S. 214, 221–222 (1966) (Douglas, J., concurring). See also Organization for a Better Austin v. Keefe, 402 U.S. 415, 418, n., (1971)." 418 U.S., at 247, n. 6.[39]

In light of the prior cases, we conclude that we have jurisdiction to review the judgment of the Georgia Supreme Court rejecting the challenge under the First and Fourteenth Amendments to the state law authorizing damage suits against the press for publishing the name of a rape victim whose identity is revealed in the course of a public prosecution. The Georgia Supreme Court's judgment is plainly final on the federal issue and is not subject to further review in the state courts. Appellants will be liable for damages if the elements of the State cause of action are proved. They may prevail at trial on nonfederal grounds, it is true, but if the Georgia court erroneously upheld the statute, there should be no trial at all. Moreover, even if appellants prevailed at trial and made unnecessary further consideration of the constitutional question, there would remain in effect the unreviewed decision of the State Supreme Court that a civil action for publishing the name of a rape victim disclosed in a public judicial proceeding may go forward despite the First and Fourteenth Amendments. Delaying final decision of the First Amendment claim until after trial will "leave unanswered . . . an important question of freedom of the press under the First Amendment," "an uneasy and unsettled constitutional posture [that] could only further harm the operation of a free press." *Tornillo,* supra. On the other hand, if we now hold that the First and Fourteenth Amendments bar civil liability for broadcasting the victim's name, this litigation ends. Given these factors—that the litigation could be terminated by our decision on the merits[40] and that a failure to decide the

---

39. The import of the Court's holding in *Tornillo* is underlined by its citation of the concurring opinion in Mills v. Alabama. There, MR. JUSTICE DOUGLAS, joined by MR. JUSTICE BRENNAN, stated that even if the appellant had a defense and might prevail at trial, jurisdiction was properly noted in order to foreclose unwarranted restrictions on the press should the state court's constitutional judgment prove to be in error.

40. MR. JUSTICE REHNQUIST . . . is correct in saying that this factor involves consideration of the merits in determining jurisdiction. But it does so only to the extent of determining that the issue is substantial and only in the context that if the state court's final decision on the federal issue is incorrect, federal law forecloses further proceedings in the state court. That the petitioner who protests against the state court's decision on the federal question might prevail on the merits on nonfederal grounds in the course of further proceedings anticipated in the state court and hence obviate later review of the federal issue here is not preclusive of our jurisdiction. *Curry, Langdeau, North Dakota State Board of Pharmacy,* California v. Stewart, 384 U.S. 436 (1966) (decided with *Miranda v. Arizona*), and Miami Herald Publishing Co. v. Tornillo, 418 U.S. 241 (1974), make this clear. In those cases, the federal issue having been decided, arguably wrongly, and being determinative of the litigation if decided the other way, the finality rule was satisfied.

The author of the dissent, a member of the majority in *Tornillo,* does not disavow that decision. He seeks only to distinguish it by indicating that the First Amendment issue at stake there was more important and pressing than the one here. This seems to embrace the

question now will leave the press in Georgia operating in the shadow of the civil and criminal sanctions of a rule of law and a statute the constitutionality of which is in serious doubt—we find that reaching the merits is consistent with the pragmatic approach that we have followed in the past in determining finality. See Gillespie v. United States Steel Corp., 379 U.S. 148 (1964); *Radio Station WOW, Inc. v. Johnson*, 326 U.S., at 124; *Mills v. Alabama*, 384 U.S., at 221–222 (DOUGLAS, J., concurring).

III

. . . . .

[On the merits the Court held that the Constitution bars a civil action against the press for publishing true information disclosed in public court documents open to public inspection.]

Reversed.

■ MR. CHIEF JUSTICE BURGER concurs in the judgment.

■ MR. JUSTICE POWELL, concurring.

I join in the Court's opinion, as I agree with the holding and most of its supporting rationale.[41]

. . . . .

■ MR. JUSTICE DOUGLAS, concurring in the judgment.

I agree that the state judgment is "final," and I also agree in the reversal of the Georgia court. . . .

■ MR. JUSTICE REHNQUIST, dissenting.

Because I am of the opinion that the decision which is the subject of this appeal is not a "final" judgment or decree, as that term is used in 28 U.S.C. § 1257, I would dismiss this appeal for want of jurisdiction.

Radio Station WOW, Inc. v. Johnson, 326 U.S. 120 (1945), established that in a "very few" circumstances review of state court decisions could be had in this Court even though something "further remain[ed] to be determined by a State court." Id., at 124. Over the years, however, and despite vigorous dissents by Mr. Justice Harlan, this Court has steadily discovered new exceptions to the finality requirement, such that they can hardly any longer be described as "very few." Whatever may be the unexpressed reasons for this process of expansion, see, e.g., Hudson Distributors, Inc. v. Eli Lilly & Co., 377 U.S. 386, 401 (1964) (HARLAN, J., dissenting), it has frequently been the subject of no more formal an express explanation than cursory citations to preceding cases in the line. Especially is this true of cases in which the Court, as it does today, relies on

---

thesis of that case and of this one as far as the approach to finality is concerned, even though the merits and the avoidance doctrine are to some extent involved.

41.   At the outset, I note my agreement that Miami Herald Publishing Co. v. Tornillo, 418 U.S. 241 (1974), supports the conclusion that the issue presented in this appeal is final for review. 28 U.S.C. § 1257.

Construction Laborers v. Curry, 371 U.S. 542 (1963). Although the Court's opinion today does accord detailed consideration to this problem, I do not believe that the reasons it expresses can support its result.

I

The Court has taken what it terms a "pragmatic" approach to the finality problem presented in this case. In so doing, it has relied heavily on Gillespie v. United States Steel Corp., 379 U.S. 148 (1964). As the Court acknowledges, *Gillespie* involved 28 U.S.C. § 1291, which restricts the appellate jurisdiction of the federal courts of appeals to "final decisions of the district courts." Although acknowledging this distinction, the Court accords it no importance and adopts *Gillespie*'s approach without any consideration of whether the finality requirement for this Court's jurisdiction over a "judgment or decree" of a state court is grounded on more serious concerns than is the limitation of court of appeals jurisdiction to final "decisions" of the district courts.[42] I believe that the underlying concerns are different, and that the difference counsels a more restrictive approach when § 1257 finality is at issue.

According to *Gillespie,* the finality requirement is imposed as a matter of minimizing "the inconvenience and costs of piecemeal review." This proposition is undoubtedly sound so long as one is considering the administration of the federal court system. Were judicial efficiency the only interest at stake there would be less inclination to challenge the Court's resolution in this case, although, as discussed below, I have serious reservations that the standards the Court has formulated are effective for achieving even this single goal. The case before us, however, is an appeal from a state court, and this fact introduces additional interests which must be accommodated in fashioning any exception to the literal application of the finality requirement. I consider § 1257 finality to be but one of a number of congressional provisions reflecting concern that uncontrolled federal judicial interference with state administrative and judicial functions would have untoward consequences for our federal system.[43] This is by no means a novel view of

---

42. The textual distinction between §§ 1291 and 1257, the former referring to "final decisions," while the latter refers to "final judgments or decrees," first appeared in the Evarts Act, Act of March 3, 1891, 26 Stat. 826, which created the courts of appeals. Section 6 of that Act provided that courts of appeals should exercise appellate jurisdiction over "final decisions" of the federal trial courts. The House version of the Act had referred to "final judgments or decrees," 21 Cong.Rec., pt. 4, 3402 (51st Cong., 1st Sess., Apr. 15, 1890), but the Senate Judiciary Committee changed the wording without formal explanation. See 21 Cong.Rec., pt. 10, 10218 (51st Cong., 1st Sess., Sept. 19, 1890). Perhaps significance can be attached to the fact that under the House bill the courts of appeals would have been independent of the federal trial courts, being manned by full-time appellate judges; the Senate version, on the other hand, generally provided that court of appeals duties would be performed by the trial judges within each circuit. See Act of March 3, 1891, § 3, 26 Stat. 826, 827.

The first judiciary act, Act of Sept. 24, 1789, 1 Stat. 73, used the terms "judgment" and "decree" in defining the appellate jurisdiction of both the Supreme Court, id., § 25, 1 Stat., at 85, and the original circuit courts. Id., § 22, 1 Stat., at 84.

43. See, e.g., 28 U.S.C. § 1341 (limitation on power of district courts to enjoin state taxing systems); 28 U.S.C. § 1739 (that state judicial proceedings shall be accorded full faith and

the § 1257 finality requirement. In *Radio Station WOW, Inc. v. Johnson*, supra, 326 U.S., at 124, Mr. Justice Frankfurter's opinion for the Court explained the finality requirement as follows:

"This requirement has the support of considerations generally applicable to good judicial administration. It avoids the mischief of economic waste and of delayed justice. Only in very few situations, where intermediate rulings may carry serious public consequences, has there been a departure from this requirement of finality for federal appellate jurisdiction. *This prerequisite to review derives added force when the jurisdiction of this Court is invoked to upset the decision of a State court.* Here we are in the realm of potential conflict between the courts of two different governments. And so, ever since 1789, Congress has granted this Court the power to intervene in State litigation only after 'the highest court of a State in which a decision in the suit could be had' has rendered a 'final judgment or decree.' Section 237(a) of the Judicial Code, 28 U.S.C. § 344(a), 28 U.S.C. § 344(a). *This requirement is not one of those technicalities to be easily scorned. It is an important factor in the smooth working of our federal system.*" (Emphasis added.)

. . . . .

That comity and federalism are significant elements of § 1257 finality has been recognized by other members of the Court as well, perhaps most notably by Mr. Justice Harlan. See, e.g., *Hudson Distributors v. Eli Lilly*, supra, 377 U.S., at 397–398 (dissenting opinion of Mr. Justice Harlan); Mercantile National Bank v. Langdeau, 371 U.S. 555, 572 (1963) (dissenting opinion of Mr. Justice Harlan). In the latter dissent, he argued that one basis of the finality rule was that it foreclosed "this Court from passing on constitutional issues that may be dissipated by the final outcome of a case, thus helping to keep to a minimum undesirable federal-state conflicts." One need cast no doubt on the Court's decision in such cases as *Langdeau* to recognize that Mr. Justice Harlan was focusing on a consideration which should be of significance in the Court's disposition of this case.

"Harmonious state-federal relations" are no less important today than when Mr. Justice Frankfurter penned *Radio Station WOW* and Republic Gas Co. [v. Oklahoma, 334 U.S. 62 (1948)]. Indeed, we have in recent years emphasized and re-emphasized the importance of comity and federalism in dealing with a related problem, that of district court interference with ongoing state judicial proceedings. See Younger v. Harris, 401 U.S. 37 (1971); Samuels v. Mackell, 401 U.S. 66 (1971). Because these concerns are important, and because they provide "added force" to § 1257's finality requirement, I believe that the Court has erred by simply importing the approach of cases in which the only concern is efficient judicial administration.

---

credit in federal courts); 28 U.S.C. §§ 2253–2254 (prescribing various restrictions on federal habeas corpus for state prisoners); 28 U.S.C. § 2281 (three-judge District Court requirement); 28 U.S.C. § 2283 (restricting power of federal courts to enjoin state court proceedings).

II

But quite apart from the considerations of federalism which counsel against an expansive reading of our jurisdiction under § 1257, the Court's holding today enunciates a virtually formless exception to the finality requirement, one which differs in kind from those previously carved out. By contrast, *Construction Laborers v. Curry* and *Mercantile National Bank v. Langdeau*, are based on the understandable principle that where the proper forum for trying the issue joined in the state courts depends on the resolution of the federal question raised on appeal, sound judicial administration requires that such a question be decided by this Court, if it is to be decided at all, sooner rather than later in the course of the litigation. Organization for a Better Austin v. Keefe, 402 U.S. 415 (1971), and Mills v. Alabama, 384 U.S. 214 (1966), rest on the premise that where as a practical matter the state litigation has been concluded by the decision of the State's highest court, the fact that in terms of state procedure the ruling is interlocutory should not bar a determination by this Court of the merits of the federal question.

Still other exceptions, as noted in the Court's opinion, have been made where the federal question decided by the highest court of the State is bound to survive and be presented for decision here regardless of the outcome of future state court proceedings, *Radio Station WOW,* supra; Brady v. Maryland, 373 U.S. 83 (1963), and for the situation in which later review of the federal issue cannot be had, whatever the ultimate outcome of the subsequent proceedings directed by the highest court of the State. California v. Stewart, 384 U.S. 436 (1966); North Dakota State Board of Pharmacy v. Snyder's Drug Stores, 414 U.S. 156 (1973). While the totality of these exceptions certainly indicates that the Court has been willing to impart to the language "final judgment or decree" a great deal of flexibility, each of them is arguably consistent with the intent of Congress in enacting § 1257, if not with the language it used, and each of them is relatively workable in practice.

To those established exceptions is now added one so formless that it cannot be paraphrased, but instead must be quoted:

> "Given these factors—that the litigation could be terminated by our decision on the merits and that a failure to decide the question now will leave the press in Georgia operating in the shadow of the civil and criminal sanctions of a rule of law and a statute the constitutionality of which is in serious doubt—we find that reaching the merits is consistent with the pragmatic approach that we have followed in the past in determining finality." ...

There are a number of difficulties with this test. One of them is the Court's willingness to look to the merits. It is not clear from the Court's opinion, however, exactly how great a look at the merits we are to take. On the one hand, the Court emphasizes that if we reverse the Supreme Court of Georgia the litigation will end, ante, ... and it refers to cases in which the federal issue has been decided "arguably wrongly." On the other hand, it claims to look to the merits "only to the extent of determining that the issue is substantial." Ibid. If the latter is all the Court means, then the inquiry is no more extensive than is involved when we determine whether a case is appropriate for plenary consideration; but if no more is meant, our decision is just as likely to be a costly intermediate step in the litigation as it is to be the concluding event. If, on the other hand, the Court really intends its doctrine to reach only so far as cases in which our decision in all probability will terminate the litigation, then the Court is reversing the traditional sequence of judicial decisionmaking. Heretofore, it has generally been thought that a court first assumed jurisdiction of a case, and then went on to decide the merits of the questions it presented. But henceforth in determining our own jurisdiction we may be obliged to determine whether or not we agree with the merits of the decision of the highest court of a State.

Yet another difficulty with the Court's formulation is the problem of transposing to any other case the requirement that "failure to decide the question now will leave the press in Georgia operating in the shadow of the civil and criminal sanctions of a rule of law and a statute the constitutionality of which is in serious doubt." ... Assuming that we are to make this determination of "serious doubt" at the time we note probable jurisdiction of such an appeal, is it enough that the highest court of the State has ruled against any federal constitutional claim? If that is the case, then because § 1257 by other language imposes that requirement, we will have completely read out of the statute the limitation of our jurisdiction to a "final judgment or decree." Perhaps the Court's new standard for finality is limited to cases in which a First Amendment freedom is at issue. The language used by Congress, however, certainly provides no basis for preferring the First Amendment, as incorporated by the Fourteenth Amendment, to the various other Amendments which are likewise "incorporated," or indeed for preferring any of the "incorporated" Amendments over the due process and equal protection provisions which are embodied literally in the Fourteenth Amendment.

Another problem is that in applying the second prong of its test, the Court has not engaged in any independent inquiry as to the consequences of permitting the decision of the Supreme Court of Georgia to remain undisturbed pending final state court resolution of the case. This suggests that in order to invoke the benefit of today's rule, the "shadow" in which an appellant must stand need be neither deep nor wide. In this case nothing more is at issue than the right to report the name of the victim of a rape. No hindrance of any sort has been imposed on reporting the fact of a rape or the circumstances surrounding it. Yet the Court unquestioningly places this issue on a par with the core First Amendment interest involved in Miami Herald Publishing Co. v. Tornillo, 418 U.S. 241 (1974), and *Mills v. Alabama,* supra, that of protecting the press in its role of providing uninhibited political discourse.[44]

---

44. As pointed out in *Tornillo,* 418 U.S., at 247 n. 6, not only did uncertainty about Florida's "right of reply" statute interfere with this important press function, but delay by this Court would have left the matter unresolved during the impending 1974 elections. In *Mills,* the

But the greatest difficulty with the test enunciated today is that it totally abandons the principle that constitutional issues are too important to be decided save when absolutely necessary, and are to be avoided if there are grounds for decision of lesser dimension.[45] The long line of cases which established this rule makes clear that it is a principle primarily designed not to benefit the lower courts, or state-federal relations, but rather to safeguard this Court's own process of constitutional adjudication.... In this case there has yet to be an adjudication of liability against appellants, and unlike the appellant in *Mills v. Alabama*, they do not concede that they have no non-federal defenses. Nonetheless, the Court rules on their constitutional defense. Far from eschewing a constitutional holding in advance of the necessity for one, the Court construes § 1257 so that it may virtually rush out and meet the prospective constitutional litigant as he approaches our doors.

III

This Court is obliged to make preliminary determinations of its jurisdiction at the time it votes to note probable jurisdiction. At that stage of the proceedings, prior to briefing on the merits or oral argument, such determinations must of necessity be based on relatively cursory acquaintance with the record of the proceedings below. The need for an understandable and workable application of a jurisdictional provision such as § 1257 is therefore far greater than for a similar interpretation of statutes dealing with substantive law. We of course retain the authority to dismiss a case for want of a final judgment after having studied briefs on the merits and having heard oral argument, but I can recall not a single instance of such a disposition during the last three Terms of the Court. While in theory this may be explained by saying that during these Terms we have never accorded plenary consideration to a § 1257 case which was not a "final judgment or decree," I would guess it just as accurate to say that after the Court has studied briefs and heard oral argument, it has an understandable tendency to proceed to a decision on the merits in preference to dismissing for want of jurisdiction. It is thus especially disturbing that the rule of this case, unlike the more workable and straightforward exceptions which the Court has previously formulated, will seriously compound the already difficult task of accurately determining, at a preliminary stage, whether an appeal from a state court judgment is a "final judgment or decree."

A further aspect of the difficulties which the Court is generating is illustrated by a petition for certiorari recently filed in this Court, Time Inc. v. Firestone, No. 74–944. The case was twice before the Florida Supreme Court. That court's first decision was rendered in December 1972; it rejected Time's First Amendment defense to a libel action, and remanded

---

Court observed that "there is practically universal agreement that a major purpose of [the First] Amendment was to protect the free discussion of governmental affairs." 384 U.S., at 218.

45. One important distinction between this case and *Construction Laborers v. Curry* has already been discussed.... Another is that the federal issue here is constitutional, whereas that in *Curry* was statutory.

for further proceedings on state law issues. The second decision was rendered in 1974, and dealt with the state law issues litigated on remand. Before this Court, Time seeks review of the First Amendment defense rejected by the Florida Supreme Court in December 1972. Under the Court's decision today, one could conclude that the 1972 judgment was itself a final decision from which review might have been had. If it was, then petitioner Time is confronted by 28 U.S.C. § 2101(c), which restricts this Court's jurisdiction over state civil cases to those in which review is sought within 90 days of the entry of a reviewable judgment.

I in no way suggest either my own or the Court's views on our jurisdiction over *Time Inc. v. Firestone.* This example is simply illustrative of the difficulties which today's decision poses not only for this Court, but also for a prudent counsel who is faced with an adverse interlocutory ruling by a State's highest court on a federal issue asserted as a dispositive bar to further litigation. I suppose that such counsel would be unwilling to presume that this Court would flout both the meaning of words and the command of Congress by employing loose standards of finality to obtain jurisdiction, but strict ones to prevent its loss. He thus would be compelled to judge his situation in light of today's formless, unworkable exception to the finality requirement. I would expect him frequently to choose to seek immediate review in this Court, solely as a matter of assuring that his federal contentions are not lost for want of timely filing. The inevitable result will be totally unnecessary additions to our docket and serious interruptions and delays of the state adjudicatory process.

Although unable to persuade my Brethren that we do not have in this case a final judgment or decree of the Supreme Court of Georgia, I nonetheless take heart from the fact that we are concerned here with an area in which "stare decisis has historically been accorded considerably less than its usual weight." Gonzalez v. Automatic Employees Credit Union, 419 U.S. 90 (1974). I would dismiss for want of jurisdiction.[46]

Johnson v. California

Supreme Court of the United States, 2004.
541 U.S. 428, 124 S.Ct. 1833, 158 L.Ed.2d 696.

■ Per Curiam.

We granted certiorari in this case to review a decision of the Supreme Court of California interpreting Batson v. Kentucky, 476 U.S. 79 (1986).

[46. The highest court of a state held, on an interlocutory appeal, that leave to amend should be granted so that plaintiff's wife could be added as a plaintiff to state a claim for loss of society. The Supreme Court granted certiorari. It subsequently held that the decision of the highest state court it had agreed to review was "not 'final' in the strict sense," but that since the case had been tried in the interim and the wife had prevailed on her claim, as "a practical matter" the tenability under federal law of the wife's claim fell "within a categorical exception to strict finality." American Export Lines, Inc. v. Alvez, 446 U.S. 274 (1980).]

540 U.S. 1045 (2003). The case was briefed and argued, but we now conclude that we are without jurisdiction in the matter.

The California Supreme Court reversed the California Court of Appeal's decision reversing petitioner's conviction. 30 Cal.4th 1302, 71 P.3d 270 (2003). The Court of Appeal held that petitioner was entitled to relief under California v. Wheeler, 22 Cal.3d 258, 583 P.2d 748 (1978), and *Batson v. Kentucky*, supra. 88 Cal.App.4th 318, 105 Cal.Rptr.2d 727 (2001). It also noted petitioner's separate evidentiary and prosecutorial misconduct claims, but did not determine whether those claims would independently support reversal of petitioner's conviction. The California Supreme Court addressed only the *Wheeler/Batson* claim, and, after reversing on that ground, remanded "for further proceedings consistent with [its] opinion." 30 Cal.4th., at 1328, 71 P.3d, at 287.

Under 28 U.S.C. § 1257, our jurisdiction is limited to review of "[f]inal judgments or decrees rendered by the highest court of a State in which a decision could be had." In Cox Broadcasting Corp. v. Cohn, 420 U.S. 469 (1975), we described four exceptional categories of cases to be regarded as "final" on the federal issue despite the ordering of further proceedings in the lower state courts. In a post-oral-argument supplemental brief, petitioner argues that the fourth of these categories fits this case. That category involves situations:

> "where the federal issue has been finally decided in the state courts with further proceedings pending in which the party seeking review here might prevail on the merits on nonfederal grounds, thus rendering unnecessary review of the federal issue by this Court, and where reversal of the state court on the federal issue would be preclusive of any further litigation on the relevant cause of action rather than merely controlling the nature and character of, or determining the admissibility of evidence in, the state proceedings still to come. In these circumstances, if a refusal immediately to review the state-court decision might seriously erode federal policy, the Court has entertained and decided the federal issue, which itself has been finally determined by the state courts for purposes of the state litigation." Id., at 482–483.

Here, petitioner can make no convincing claim of erosion of federal policy that is not common to all decisions rejecting a defendant's *Batson* claim. The fourth category therefore does not apply. See Florida v. Thomas, 532 U.S. 774, 780 (2001). "A contrary conclusion would permit the fourth exception to swallow the rule." See Flynt v. Ohio, 451 U.S. 619, 622 (1981) (per curiam).

The present case comes closest to fitting in the third *Cox* category, but ultimately falls outside of it. That category involves "those situations where the federal claim has been finally decided, with further proceedings on the merits in the state courts to come, but in which later review of the federal issue cannot be had, whatever the ultimate outcome of the case." *Cox Broadcasting Corp.*, supra, at 481. In the event that the California Court of Appeal on remand affirms the judgment of conviction, petitioner could once more seek review of his *Batson* claim in the Supreme Court of

California—albeit unsuccessfully—and then seek certiorari on that claim from this Court.

Compliance with the provisions of § 1257 is an essential prerequisite to our deciding the merits of a case brought here under that section. It is our obligation to raise any question of such compliance on our own motion, even though counsel has not called our attention to it. See, e.g., Mansfield, C. & L.M.R. Co. v. Swan, 111 U.S. 379, 384 (1884). But as the present case illustrates, we are not always successful in policing this gatekeeping function without the aid of counsel.

Part of the problem was that the California Court of Appeal's decision was certified by that court for partial publication. It addressed the *Wheeler/Batson* claim in the published portion. 88 Cal.App.4th 318, 105 Cal. Rptr.2d 727 (2001). In the unpublished portion, the court briefly addressed petitioner's evidentiary claims to provide guidance for the trial court on retrial, and noted that it would not address whether petitioner's objections were properly preserved or consider petitioner's prosecutorial misconduct claim. Petitioner appended only the published portion of the California Court of Appeal's decision to his petition for a writ of certiorari. This Court's Rule 14.1(i) instructs petitioners to include, *inter alia*, any "relevant opinions ... entered in the case" in the appendix to the petition for certiorari. The full opinion of the California Court of Appeal was not filed in this Court until the joint appendix to the briefs on the merits was filed. Had the full opinion been brought to this Court's attention, it might have been more evident to us that the Supreme Court of California's decision was not final for the purposes of § 1257.

A petition for certiorari must demonstrate to this Court that it has jurisdiction to review the judgment. This Court's Rule 14.1(g). And a respondent has a duty to "address any perceived misstatement of fact or law in the petition that bears on what issues properly would be before the Court if certiorari were granted." Rule 15.2. Our Rules also require that each party provide a statement for the basis of our jurisdiction in its brief on the merits. Rule 24.1(e). At all stages in this case, both parties represented that our jurisdiction was proper pursuant to § 1257(a).

It behooves counsel for both petitioner and respondent to assure themselves that the decision for which review is sought is indeed a "[f]inal judgmen[t]" under § 1257. Such attention is mandated by our Rules and will avoid the expenditure of resources of both counsel and of this Court on an abortive proceeding such as the present one.

We dismiss the case for want of jurisdiction.

It is so ordered.[47]

[47. See 16B Wright, Miller & Cooper, Federal Practice and Procedure: Jurisdiction § 4010 (1996); 22 Moore's Federal Practice § 406.03[d][v] (3d ed.1998).

Howell v. Mississippi

Supreme Court of the United States, 2005.
543 U.S. 440, 125 S.Ct. 856, 160 L.Ed.2d 873.

■ PER CURIAM.

Petitioner Marlon Howell contends that the Mississippi courts violated his rights under the Eighth and Fourteenth Amendments to the United States Constitution by refusing to require a jury instruction about a lesser included offense in his capital case. He did not, however, raise this claim in the Supreme Court of Mississippi, which unsurprisingly did not address it. As a result, we dismiss the writ of certiorari as improvidently granted.

Petitioner was convicted and sentenced to death for killing Hugh David Pernell. Shortly after 5 a.m. on May 15, 2000, Pernell was delivering newspapers from his car when the occupants of another car motioned for him to stop. The evidence at trial indicated that, when both cars had pulled over, petitioner got out of the trailing car and approached the driver's side of Pernell's car. After a brief conversation and perhaps some kind of scuffle, petitioner pulled out a pistol, shot Pernell through the heart, got back in the other car, and fled the scene. See 860 So.2d 704, 712–715, 738–739 (Miss.2003). At trial, petitioner argued both that he was in another city at the time of the killing and that the evidence was insufficient to prove

---

The fourth of the *Cox* exceptions was held not applicable in Flynt v. Ohio, 451 U.S. 619 (1981). The publisher of *Hustler* was charged in state court with disseminating obscenity. Defendant moved to dismiss on the ground that he had been subjected to selective and discriminatory prosecution in violation of the Equal Protection Clause. The state appellate courts rejected this argument and remanded the case for trial. The Supreme Court, over three dissents, dismissed the writ of certiorari for want of jurisdiction. The majority said, at 622: "Here there is no identifiable federal policy that will suffer if the state criminal proceeding goes forward. The question presented for review is whether on this record the decision to prosecute petitioners was selective or discriminatory in violation of the Equal Protection Clause. The resolution of this question can await final judgment without any adverse effect upon important federal interests. A contrary conclusion would permit the fourth exception to swallow the rule." The fourth exception was held to apply in Fort Wayne Books, Inc. v. Indiana, 489 U.S. 46 (1989), since the case involved a First Amendment challenge to the facial validity of the Indiana RICO statute. The Court distinguished the *Flynt* case on the ground that "[t]he claim before us in *Flynt* was not a First Amendment claim, but rather an Equal Protection claim (albeit one in the context of a trial raising First Amendment issues)." 489 U.S., at 56.

In Goodyear Atomic Corp. v. Miller, 486 U.S. 174 (1988), a state court had held that federal preemption did not bar a particular kind of claim under the state workers' compensation law and ordered the state commission to consider a claim by an employee at a nuclear-production facility owned by the United States. This was held to come within the fourth category recognized in the *Cox* case and thus to be "final" within the meaning of 28 U.S.C. § 1257. The federal question had been finally determined by the state court and a reversal of its holding would preclude any further proceedings. Even if the employer prevailed before the state commission on nonfederal grounds, the unreviewed decision of the state court might seriously erode federal policy in the area of nuclear production.

In Pierce County, Washington v. Guillen, 537 U.S. 129 (2003), the Court applied the second *Cox* exception to hold a state-court order relating to a discovery dispute to be sufficiently final to permit review under § 1257, on the ground that the outcome of further proceedings in the trial court was preordained.]

that Pernell was killed during an attempted robbery (which would deprive the State of an element of capital murder). As part of his non-alibi defense, petitioner sought to supplement the State's proposed jury instruction on capital murder with instructions on manslaughter and simple murder. The trial court refused the additional instructions. The jury found petitioner guilty of capital murder and separately concluded that he should be sentenced to death.

On appeal to the State Supreme Court, one of petitioner's 28 claims of error was the trial court's failure "to give the defendant an instruction on the offense of simple murder or manslaughter." In that argument, petitioner cited three cases from the State Supreme Court about lesser-included-offense instructions, and the only opinion whose original language he quoted was a noncapital case. Ibid.... Petitioner argued that, because the jury "could have found and returned the lesser included offense of simple murder or manslaughter," the failure to give instructions on those offenses was "error" that left the jury no "choice but either to turn [him] loose or convict him of [c]apital [m]urder." In the course of affirming petitioner's conviction and death sentence, the State Supreme Court found that "[t]he facts of this case clearly do not support or warrant" the instruction for manslaughter or simple murder. 860 So.2d, at 744. The court cited and quoted a prior noncapital decision, which construed a state statute and concluded that an instruction should be refused if it would cause the jury to " 'ignore the primary charge' " or " 'if the evidence does not justify submission of a lesser-included offense.' " Ibid. (quoting Presley v. State, 321 So.2d 309, 310–311 (Miss.1975)). The court also cited Grace v. State, 375 So.2d 419 (Miss.1979), an aggravated-assault case rejecting an instruction for simple assault.

Petitioner sought certiorari from this Court, arguing that his death sentence is unconstitutional under that rule of our capital jurisprudence set forth in Beck v. Alabama, 447 U.S. 625, 638 (1980) ("[I]f the unavailability of a lesser included offense instruction enhances the risk of an unwarranted conviction, [the State] is constitutionally prohibited from withdrawing that option from the jury in a capital case"). We granted certiorari, but asked the parties to address the following additional question: " 'Was petitioner's federal constitutional claim properly raised before the Mississippi Supreme Court for purposes of 28 U.S.C. § 1257?' " 542 U.S. 936 (2004). Our answer to that question prevents us from reaching petitioner's constitutional claim.

Congress has given this Court the power to review "[f]inal judgments or decrees rendered by the highest court of a State in which a decision could be had ... where any ... right ... is *specially set up or claimed* under the Constitution or the treaties or statutes of ... the United States." 28 U.S.C. § 1257(a) (emphasis added). Under that statute and its predecessors, this Court has almost unfailingly refused to consider any federal-law challenge to a state-court decision unless the federal claim "was either addressed by or properly presented to the state court that rendered the decision we have been asked to review." Adams v. Robertson, 520 U.S. 83,

86 (1997) (per curiam); see also Illinois v. Gates, 462 U.S. 213, 218 (1983) (tracing this principle back to Crowell v. Randell, 10 Pet. [35 U.S.] 368, 391 (1836), and Owings v. Norwood's Lessee, 5 Cranch [9 U.S.] 344 (1809)).

Petitioner's brief in the State Supreme Court did not properly present his claim as one arising under federal law.[48] In the relevant argument, he did not cite the Constitution or even any cases directly construing it, much less any of this Court's cases. Instead, he argues that he presented his federal claim by citing Harveston v. State, 493 So.2d 365 (Miss.1986), which cited (among other cases) Fairchild v. State, 459 So.2d 793 (Miss. 1984), which in turn cited *Beck,* but only by way of acknowledging that Mississippi's general rule requiring lesser-included-offense instructions "takes on constitutional proportions" in capital cases. 459 So.2d, at 800. Assuming it constituted adequate briefing of the federal question under state-law standards, petitioner's daisy chain—which depends upon a case that was cited by one of the cases that was cited by one of the cases that petitioner cited—is too lengthy to meet this Court's standards for proper presentation of a federal claim.[49] As we recently explained in a slightly different context, "[a] litigant wishing to raise a federal issue can easily indicate the federal law basis for his claim in a state-court petition or brief ... by citing in conjunction with the claim the federal source of law on which he relies or a case deciding such a claim on federal grounds, or by simply labeling the claim 'federal.' " Baldwin v. Reese, 541 U.S. 27, 32 (2004). In the context of § 1257, the same steps toward clarity are just as easy to take and are generally necessary to establish that a federal question was properly presented to a state court. Petitioner did none of these things.

Petitioner also contends that he raised his federal claim by implication because the state-law rule on which he relied was "identical," Tr. of Oral Arg. 17, or "virtually identical," Brief for Petitioner 17–18, to the constitutional rule articulated in *Beck.* Assuming, without deciding, that identical standards might overcome a petitioner's failure to identify his claim as federal, Mississippi's rule regarding lesser-included-offense instructions is not identical to *Beck*—or at least not identical to the Mississippi Supreme Court's interpretation of *Beck.* Mississippi's rule applies even when the jury is not choosing only between acquittal and death. The Mississippi Supreme Court's interpretation of *Beck,* on the other hand, holds that case inapplica-

---

48. Petitioner argues not that the State Supreme Court actually addressed his federal claim, but rather that it "had an adequate opportunity to address" it.

49. See, e.g., Adams v. Robertson, 520 U.S. 83, 89, n. 3 (1997) (per curiam) (concluding that "passing invocations of 'due process' " that "fail to cite the Federal Constitution or any cases relying on the Fourteenth Amendment" do not "meet our minimal requirement that it must be clear that a *federal* claim was presented"); Webb v. Webb, 451 U.S. 493, 496 (1981) (finding a reference to "full faith and credit" insufficient to raise a federal claim without a reference to the U.S. Constitution or to any cases relying on it); New York Central R. Co. v. New York, 186 U.S. 269, 273 (1902) ("[I]t is well settled in this court that it must be made to appear that some provision of the Federal, as distinguished from the state, Constitution was relied upon, and that such provision must be set forth"); Oxley Stave Co. v. Butler County, 166 U.S. 648, 655 (1897) (a party's intent to invoke the Federal Constitution must be "unmistakably" declared, and the statutory requirement is not met if "the purpose of the party to assert a Federal right is left to mere inference").

ble where the jury has the additional option of life imprisonment, see Jackson v. State, 684 So.2d 1213, 1228 (1996)—a conclusion that finds some support in our cases, see Hopkins v. Reeves, 524 U.S. 88, 98 (1998) ("In *Beck,* the death penalty was automatically tied to conviction, and Beck's jury was told that if it convicted the defendant of the charged offense, it was required to impose the death penalty"); Schad v. Arizona, 501 U.S. 624, 646 (1991) ("Our fundamental concern in *Beck* was that a jury ... might ... vote for a capital conviction if the only alternative was to set the defendant free with no punishment at all"). Moreover, unlike *Beck,* see 447 U.S., at 638, n. 14, Mississippi's rule on lesser-included-offense instructions applies in *noncapital* cases (as shown by the cases petitioner did cite). Thus, one opinion of the Mississippi Supreme Court appears to have treated a claim under *Beck* as distinct from one arising under the Mississippi rule. See Goodin v. State, 787 So.2d 639, 656 (2001) ("Having found no [federal] constitutional flaws in the jury instruction given, we must now determine whether our practice entitles Goodin to a manslaughter instruction. We have held that there must be some evidentiary support to grant an instruction for manslaughter").

Petitioner suggests that we need not treat his failure to present his federal claim in state court as jurisdictional. Notwithstanding the long line of cases clearly stating that the presentation requirement is jurisdictional, see, e.g., Exxon Corp. v. Eagerton, 462 U.S. 176, 181, n. 3 (1983); Cardinale v. Louisiana, 394 U.S. 437, 438–439 (1969) (citing cases), a handful of exceptions (discussed in *Gates,* 462 U.S., at 219) have previously led us to conclude that this is "an unsettled question." Bankers Life & Casualty Co. v. Crenshaw, 486 U.S. 71, 79 (1988). As in prior cases, however, we need not decide today "whether our requirement that a federal claim be addressed or properly presented in state court is jurisdictional or prudential, because even treating the rule as purely prudential, the circumstances here justify no exception." *Adams,* 520 U.S., at 90 (citations omitted); accord, Yee v. Escondido, 503 U.S. 519, 533 (1992); *Bankers Life,* supra, at 79; Heath v. Alabama, 474 U.S. 82, 87 (1985); *Gates,* supra, at 222.[50]

Accordingly, we dismiss the writ of certiorari as improvidently granted.

It is so ordered.[51]

---

50. In Three Affiliated Tribes of Fort Berthold Reservation v. Wold Engineering, P. C., 476 U.S. 877, 883 (1986), the Court chose to reach a question that had not been presented in state court for two reasons that are inapplicable here: because the other party had no objection to reaching the question, and because the case had previously been remanded to the state court on other grounds.

[51. But the Court has jurisdiction to review plain error unchallenged in the state court when necessary to prevent fundamental unfairness. Wood v. Georgia, 450 U.S. 261, 265 n. 5 (1981).

A Florida court awarded custody of a child to its mother. Subsequently a Georgia court awarded custody to the father. The Supreme Court held that it lacked jurisdiction to review the Georgia decision. Nowhere in the opinion of the Georgia Supreme Court was any federal

Walker v. Martin

Supreme Court of the United States, 2011.
562 U.S. ___, 131 S.Ct. 1120, 179 L.Ed.2d 62.

■ Justice Ginsburg delivered the opinion of the Court.

This case concerns California's time limitation on applications for postconviction (habeas corpus) relief. The question presented: Does California's timeliness requirement qualify as an independent state ground adequate to bar habeas corpus relief in federal court?

California does not employ fixed statutory deadlines to determine the timeliness of a state prisoner's petition for habeas corpus. Instead, California directs petitioners to file known claims "as promptly as the circumstances allow." In re Clark, 855 P.2d 729, 738, n. 5 (Cal.1993). Petitioners are further instructed to state when they first learned of the asserted claims and to explain why they did not seek postconviction relief sooner. In re Robbins, 959 P.2d 311, 317–318 (Cal.1998). Claims substantially delayed without justification may be denied as untimely. Ibid.; *Clark*, 855 P.2d, at 738, n.5.

California courts signal that a habeas petition is denied as untimely by citing the controlling decisions, i.e., *Clark* and *Robbins*. A spare order denying a petition without explanation or citation ordinarily ranks as a disposition on the merits. Tr. of Oral Arg. 7; see Harrington v. Richter, [562 U.S. ___, 131 S.Ct. 770, 784–785 (2011)]. California courts may elect to pretermit the question whether a petition is timely and simply deny the petition, thereby signaling that the petition lacks merit.

Petitioner below, respondent here, Charles W. Martin, presented the claims at issue—all alleging ineffective assistance of counsel—in a habeas petition filed in the California Supreme Court nearly five years after his conviction became final. He stated no reason for the long delay. Citing *Clark* and *Robbins*, the court denied Martin's petition. In turn, the U.S. District Court for the Eastern District of California dismissed Martin's federal habeas petition raising the same ineffective assistance claims. Denial of Martin's state-court petition as untimely, the District Court held, rested on an adequate and independent state ground, i.e., Martin's failure to seek relief in state court "without substantial delay." See *Robbins*, 959 P.2d, at 322.

---

question mentioned, let alone expressly passed upon, and while the mother used the phrase "full faith and credit" at several points in the state court proceeding, nowhere did she cite to the Federal Constitution or to any cases construing its Full Faith and Credit Clause. Webb v. Webb, 451 U.S. 493 (1981).

Defendant's request that the jury be given an "admonition" that no adverse inference could be drawn from his failure to testify, rather than an "instruction" to that effect, adequately invoked his federal substantive right to jury guidance, since the state's distinction between admonitions and instructions was not the sort of firmly established and regularly followed state practice that can prevent implementation of federal constitutional rights. James v. Kentucky, 466 U.S. 341 (1984).]

The U.S. Court of Appeals for the Ninth Circuit reversed the District Court's decision. Contrasting the precision of "fixed statutory deadlines" with California's proscription of "substantial delay," the appeals court held that California's standard lacked the clarity and certainty necessary to constitute an adequate state bar. 357 Fed.Appx. 793, 794 (2009) (relying on Townsend v. Knowles, 562 F.3d 1200 (CA9 2009)).

In a recent decision, Beard v. Kindler, 558 U.S. ___, 130 S.Ct. 612 (2009), this Court clarified that a state procedural bar may count as an adequate and independent ground for denying a federal habeas petition even if the state court had discretion to reach the merits despite the default. Guided by that decision, we hold that California is not put to the choice of imposing a specific deadline for habeas petitions (which would almost certainly rule out Martin's nearly five-year delay) or preserving the flexibility of current practice, "but only at the cost of undermining the finality of state court judgments." Id., at ___, 130 S.Ct. at 618. In so ruling, we stress that Martin has not alleged that California's time bar, either by design or in operation, discriminates against federal claims or claimants.

I

A

While most States set determinate time limits for collateral relief applications, in California, neither statute nor rule of court does so. Instead, California courts "appl[y] a general 'reasonableness' standard" to judge whether a habeas petition is timely filed. Carey v. Saffold, 536 U.S. 214, 222 (2002). The basic instruction provided by the California Supreme Court is simply that "a [habeas] petition should be filed as promptly as the circumstances allow.... " Clark, 855 P.2d, at 738, n. 5.

Three leading decisions describe California's timeliness requirement: Robbins, Clark, and In re Gallego, 959 P.2d 290 (Cal.1998). A prisoner must seek habeas relief without "substantial delay," Robbins, 959 P.2d, at 317; Gallego, 959 P.2d, at 296; Clark, 855 P.2d, at 750, as "measured from the time the petitioner or counsel knew, or reasonably should have known, of the information offered in support of the claim and the legal basis for the claim," Robbins, 959 P.2d, at 322. Petitioners in noncapital cases have "the burden of establishing (i) absence of substantial delay, (ii) good cause for the delay, or (iii) that the claim falls within an exception to the bar of untimeliness." Id., at 317.[21]

California's collateral review regime differs from that of other States in a second notable respect: All California courts "have original jurisdiction in habeas corpus proceedings," Cal. Const., Art. VI, § 10, thus "no appeal lies from the denial of a petition for writ of habeas corpus," Clark, 855 P.2d, at 740, n. 7. "[A] prisoner whose petition has been denied by the superior

---

21. A petition for habeas relief in a capital case is "presumed to be filed without substantial delay if it is filed within 180 days after the final due date for the filing of [an] appellant's reply brief on the direct appeal.... " California Supreme Court Policies Regarding Cases Arising From Judgments of Death, Policy 3, Standard 1–1.1 (2010).

court can obtain review of his claims only by the filing of a new petition in the Court of Appeal." Ibid. The new petition, however, must be confined to claims raised in the initial petition. See In re Martinez, 209 P.3d 908, 915 (Cal.2009).

Because a habeas petitioner may skip over the lower courts and file directly in the California Supreme Court, In re Kler, 188 Cal.App.4th 1399, 1403, 115 Cal.Rptr.3d 889, 891–892 (2010), that court rules on a staggering number of habeas petitions each year.[22] The court issues generally unelaborated "summary denials" of petitions that "d[o] not state a prima facie case for relief" or that contain "claims [that] are all procedurally barred." People v. Romero, 883 P.2d 388, 391 (Cal.1994) (internal quotation marks omitted). A summary denial citing *Clark* and *Robbins* means that the petition is rejected as untimely. See, e.g., Brief for Habeas Corpus Resource Center as Amicus Curiae 20, and n. 23. California courts have discretion, however, to bypass a timeliness issue and, instead, summarily reject the petition for want of merit. See *Robbins*, 959 P.2d, at 316, n. 1. See also *Saffold*, 536 U.S., at 225–226.

B

In December 1986, Charles Martin participated in a robbery and murder in California. Martin fled the State, but eight years later he was extradited to California to stand trial. Convicted in state court of murder and robbery, Martin was sentenced to life in prison without the possibility of parole. In 1997, the California Court of Appeal affirmed his conviction and sentence, and the California Supreme Court denied review.

Martin initiated his first round of state habeas proceedings in 1998, and the next year, the California Supreme Court denied his petition. He then filed a habeas petition in the appropriate U.S. District Court. Finding that Martin's federal petition included ineffective-assistance-of-counsel claims he had not aired in state court, the District Court stayed the federal proceedings pending Martin's return to state court to exhaust his remedies there.[23]

In March 2002, Martin filed his second habeas petition in the California Supreme Court, raising the federal ineffective assistance claims his earlier filing omitted. He gave no reason for his failure to assert the additional claims until nearly five years after his sentence and conviction became final. Tr. of Oral Arg. 36, 39. In September 2002, the California

---

22. In fiscal year 2008–2009, the California Supreme Court issued dispositions in 3,258 original habeas actions. Judicial Council of California, 2010 Court Statistics Report, State-wide Caseload Trends, 1999–2000 Through 2008–2009, p. 6, http:// www. courtinfo. ca. gov/ reference/ documents/csr2010.pdf (as visited Feb. 15, 2011, and in Clerk of Court's case file). During a similar time period, a total of 2,210 habeas cases were on this Court's docket. See October Term 2008 Filings by Case Type (available in Clerk of Court's case file).

23. Rather than dismiss a petition containing both exhausted and unexhausted claims, "a district court might stay the petition and hold it in abeyance while the petitioner returns to state court to exhaust his previously unexhausted claims. Once the petitioner exhausts his state remedies, the district court will lift the stay and allow the petitioner to proceed in federal court." Rhines v. Weber, 544 U.S. 269, 275–276 (2005).

Supreme Court denied Martin's petition in an order typical of that court's summary dispositions for failure to file "as promptly as the circumstances allow." *Clark*, 855 P.2d, at 738, n. 5. The order read in its entirety: "Petition for writ of habeas corpus is DENIED. (See In re Clark (1993) 855 P.2d 729, In re Robbins (1998) 959 P.2d 311.)." ...

Having exhausted state postconviction remedies, Martin returned to federal court and filed an amended petition. Based upon the California Supreme Court's time-bar disposition, the District Court dismissed Martin's belatedly asserted claims as procedurally precluded. Id., at 27, 57. The Ninth Circuit vacated the dismissal order and remanded the case, directing the District Court to determine the "adequacy" of the State's time bar. *Martin v. Hubbard*, 192 Fed.Appx. 616, 618 (2006). The District Court again rejected Martin's petition, stating that "[t]he California timeliness bar as set forth in ... *Clark/Robbins* is clearly defined, well established and consistently applied." ...

The Ninth Circuit again disagreed. Controlled by its prior decision in *Townsend*, 562 F.3d, at 1207–1208, the Court of Appeals held that California's time bar "has yet to be firmly defined" and was not shown by the State to be "consistently applied." 357 Fed.Appx., at 794. The remand order directed the District Court to determine the merits of the claims Martin asserted in his second petition to the California Supreme Court.

We granted certiorari to determine the "adequacy" of California's practice under which a prisoner may be barred from collaterally attacking his conviction when he has "substantially delayed" filing his habeas petition. Martin does not here dispute that the time limitation is an "independent" state ground. See Brief in Opposition 5–6. See also Bennett v. Mueller, 322 F.3d 573, 582–583 (CA9 2003). Nor does he contend that he established "cause" and "prejudice," i.e., cause for the delay in asserting his claims and actual prejudice resulting from the State's alleged violation of his constitutional rights. See Wainwright v. Sykes, 433 U.S. 72, 87–91 (1977).

II

A

"A federal habeas court will not review a claim rejected by a state court 'if the decision of [the state] court rests on a state law ground that is independent of the federal question and adequate to support the judgment.'" *Kindler*, 558 U.S., at ___, 130 S.Ct., at 615 (quoting Coleman v. Thompson, 501 U.S. 722, 729 (1991)). The state-law ground may be a substantive rule dispositive of the case, or a procedural barrier to adjudication of the claim on the merits. See *Sykes*, 433 U.S., at 81–82.

Ordinarily, a state prisoner seeking federal habeas relief must first "exhaus[t] the remedies available in the courts of the State," 28 U.S.C. § 2254(b)(1)(A), thereby affording those courts "the first opportunity to address and correct alleged violations of [the] prisoner's federal rights," *Coleman*, 501 U.S., at 731. The adequate and independent state ground doctrine furthers that objective, for without it, "habeas petitioners would be able to avoid the exhaustion requirement by defaulting their federal claims in state court." Id., at 732. Accordingly, absent showings of "cause" and "prejudice," see *Sykes*, 433 U.S., at 84–85, federal habeas relief will be unavailable when (1) "a state court [has] declined to address a prisoner's federal claims because the prisoner had failed to meet a state procedural requirement," and (2) "the state judgment rests on independent and adequate state procedural grounds." *Coleman*, 501 U.S., at 729–730.

B

To qualify as an "adequate" procedural ground, a state rule must be "firmly established and regularly followed." *Kindler*, 558 U.S., at ___, 130 S.Ct., at 618 (internal quotation marks omitted).[24] "[A] discretionary state procedural rule," we held in *Kindler*, "can serve as an adequate ground to bar federal habeas review." Ibid. A "rule can be 'firmly established' and 'regularly followed,' " *Kindler* observed, "even if the appropriate exercise of discretion may permit consideration of a federal claim in some cases but not others." Ibid.

California's time rule, although discretionary, meets the "firmly established" criterion, as *Kindler* comprehended that requirement. The California Supreme Court, as earlier noted, framed the timeliness requirement for habeas petitioners in a trilogy of cases. See supra, at 3. Those decisions instruct habeas petitioners to "alleg[e] with specificity" the absence of substantial delay, good cause for delay, or eligibility for one of four exceptions to the time bar. *Gallego*, 959 P.2d, at 299; see *Robbins*, 959 P.2d, at 317.[25] And California's case law made it altogether plain that Martin's delay of nearly five years ranked as "substantial." See *Gallego*, 959 P.2d, at 293–294, 299, and n. 13 (delay of four years barred claim); In re Tsaturyan, No. B156012, 2002 WL 1614107, *3 (Cal.App., July 23, 2002) (delay of 16 months barred claim). See also In re Miller, No. B186447, 2006 WL

---

24. We have also recognized a "limited category" of "exceptional cases in which exorbitant application of a generally sound rule renders the state ground inadequate to stop consideration of a federal question." Lee v. Kemna, 534 U.S. 362, 376 (2002). In *Lee*, for example, the defendant unsuccessfully moved for a continuance when, for reasons unknown to him, his alibi witnesses left the courthouse the day they were scheduled to testify. This Court held inadequate to bar federal review a state court's persnickety application of a rule detailing formal requirements for continuance motions. The defendant had substantially complied with the rule's key requirement and flawless compliance would have been unavailing given the trial court's reason for denying the motion. See id., at 381–382. Martin does not suggest that the application of California's timeliness rule in his case falls within the exceptional category Lee described and illustrated. See Brief for Respondent 28, 29, 54.

25. An untimely petition "will be entertained on the merits if the petitioner demonstrates (i) that error of constitutional magnitude led to a trial that was so fundamentally unfair that absent the error no reasonable judge or jury would have convicted the petitioner; (ii) that the petitioner is actually innocent of the crime or crimes of which he or she was convicted; (iii) that the death penalty was imposed by a sentencing authority that had such a grossly misleading profile of the petitioner before it that, absent the trial error or omission, no reasonable judge or jury would have imposed a sentence of death; or (iv) that the petitioner was convicted or sentenced under an invalid statute." In re Robbins, 959 P.2d 311, 318 (1998).

1980385, *2–3 (Cal.App., July 17, 2006) (delay of two years and six months barred claim).

Martin nevertheless urges that California's rule is too vague to be regarded as "firmly established." "[R]easonable time" period and "substantial delay," he maintains, are "meaningless terms." Brief for Respondent 48 (internal quotation marks omitted). We disagree. Indeterminate language is typical of discretionary rules. Application of those rules in particular circumstances, however, can supply the requisite clarity.

Congressional statutes and this Court's decisions, we note, have employed time limitations that are not stated in precise, numerical terms. Former Federal Habeas Corpus Rule 9(a), for example, set no fixed time limit on submission of habeas petitions. The Rule permitted dismissal of a state prisoner's petition when it appeared that delay in commencing litigation "prejudiced [the State] in its ability to respond." 28 U.S.C. § 2254 Rule 9(a) (1994 ed.). To stave off dismissal, the petitioner had to show that he could not earlier have known, "by the exercise of reasonable diligence," the grounds on which he based the petition. Ibid. In Rhines v. Weber, 544 U.S. 269 (2005), we instructed district courts, when employing stay and abeyance procedure, see supra, at 5, n. 3, to "place reasonable time limits on a petitioner's trip to state court and back." 544 U.S., at 278.

Current federal habeas prescriptions limit the time for filing a petition to one year. The clock runs from "the date on which the [supporting] facts . . . could have been discovered through the exercise of due diligence." 28 U.S.C. § 2255(f)(4) (2006 ed., Supp. III) (applicable to federal prisoners); see § 2244(d)(1)(D) (2006 ed.) (similar provision applicable to state prisoners). "[D]ue diligence," we have observed, "is an inexact measure of how much delay is too much." Johnson v. United States, 544 U.S. 295, 309, n. 7 (2005) (internal quotation marks omitted). But "use of an imprecise standard," we immediately added, "is no justification for depriving [a rule's] language of any meaning." Ibid. "[I]t would seem particularly strange to disregard state procedural rules that are substantially similar to those to which we give full force in our own courts." *Kindler*, 558 U.S., at ___, 130 S.Ct., at 618.

Nor is California's time rule vulnerable on the ground that it is not regularly followed. Each year, the California Supreme Court summarily denies hundreds of habeas petitions by citing *Clark* and *Robbins*. On the same day the court denied Martin's petition, it issued 21 other *Clark/Robbins* summary denials. See Brief for Habeas Corpus Resource Center as Amicus Curiae 20. In reasoned opinions, too, California courts regularly invoke *Clark*, *Robbins*, and *Gallego* to determine whether a habeas petition is time barred. . . .

Martin argued below that California's time bar is not regularly followed in this sense: Use of summary denials makes it "impossible to tell" why the California Supreme Court "decides some delayed petitions on the merits and rejects others as untimely." We see no reason to reject California's time bar simply because a court may opt to bypass the *Clark/Robbins* assessment and summarily dismiss a petition on the merits, if that is the easier path. See, e.g., Strickland v. Washington, 466 U.S. 668, 697 (1984) ("[A] court need not determine whether counsel's performance was deficient ... [i]f it is easier to dispose of an ineffectiveness claim on the ground of lack of sufficient prejudice.... "); cf. Ruhrgas AG v. Marathon Oil Co., 526 U.S. 574, 585 (1999) ("It is hardly novel for a federal court to choose among threshold grounds for denying audience to a case on the merits.").

The Ninth Circuit concluded that California's time bar is not consistently applied because outcomes under the rule vary from case to case. See 357 Fed. Appx., at 794. For example, in People v. Fairbanks, No. C047810, 2006 WL 950267, *2–*3 (Cal.App., Apr.11, 2006), a one-year delay was found substantial, while in In re Little, No. D047468, 2008 WL 142832, *4, n. 6 (Cal.App., Jan.16, 2008), a delay of 14 months was determined to be insubstantial.

A discretionary rule ought not be disregarded automatically upon a showing of seeming inconsistencies.[26] Discretion enables a court to home in on case-specific considerations and to avoid the harsh results that sometimes attend consistent application of an unyielding rule. See Prihoda v. McCaughtry, 910 F.2d 1379, 1385 (CA7 1990) ("Uncertainty is not enough to disqualify a state's procedural ground as one 'adequate' under federal law. If it were, states would be induced to make their rules draconian.... ").

A state ground, no doubt, may be found inadequate when "discretion has been exercised to impose novel and unforeseeable requirements without fair or substantial support in prior state law.... " 16B C. Wright, A. Miller, & E. Cooper, Federal Practice and Procedure § 4026, p. 386 (2d ed.1996) (hereinafter Wright & Miller); see Prihoda, 910 F.2d, at 1383 (state ground "applied infrequently, unexpectedly, or freakishly" may "discriminat[e] against the federal rights asserted" and therefore rank as "inadequate"). Martin does not contend, however, that in his case, the California Supreme Court exercised its discretion in a surprising or unfair manner.

"[S]ound procedure often requires discretion to exact or excuse compliance with strict rules," 16B Wright & Miller § 4028, p. 403, and we have no cause to discourage standards allowing courts to exercise such discretion. As this Court observed in *Kindler*, if forced to choose between mandatory rules certain to be found "adequate," or more supple prescriptions that federal courts may disregard as "inadequate," "many States [might] opt for mandatory rules to avoid the high costs that come with

---

26. Closer inspection may reveal that "seeming 'inconsistencie [s]' ... are not necessarily ... arbitrar[y] or irrationa[l]." Thornburgh v. Abbott, 490 U.S. 401, 417, n. 15 (1989). *Fairbanks* and *Little* are illustrative. In *Fairbanks*, the court found that petitioner did not act diligently when she waited to withdraw her guilty plea until one year after learning that revocation of her driver's license was irreversible. 2006 WL 950267, *2–*3. In *Little*, a pro se prisoner claimed that his trial counsel should have raised a posttraumatic stress disorder defense. Although the filing delay was 14 months, the court entertained it on the merits. 2008 WL 142832, *4, *14. Given the discrete context in which each case arose, the two decisions present no square conflict.

plenary federal review." 558 U.S., at ___, 130 S.Ct., at 618. "Th[at] result would be particularly unfortunate for [habeas petitioners], who would lose the opportunity to argue that a procedural default should be excused through the exercise of judicial discretion." Id., at ___, 130 S.Ct. at 618. . . .

C

Today's decision, trained on California's timeliness rule for habeas petitions, leaves unaltered this Court's repeated recognition that federal courts must carefully examine state procedural requirements to ensure that they do not operate to discriminate against claims of federal rights. See Brown v. Western R. Co. of Ala., 338 U.S. 294, 298–299 (1949); Davis v. Wechsler, 263 U.S. 22, 24–25 (1923); 16B Wright & Miller § 4026, p. 386 (noting "risk that discretionary procedural sanctions may be invoked more harshly against disfavored federal rights, . . . deny[ing] [litigants] a fair opportunity to present federal claims"). See also *Kindler*, 558 U.S., at ___, 130 S.Ct., at 620 (Kennedy, J., concurring) (a state procedural ground would be inadequate if the challenger shows a "purpose or pattern to evade constitutional guarantees"). On the record before us, however, there is no basis for concluding that California's timeliness rule operates to the particular disadvantage of petitioners asserting federal rights.

* * *

For the reasons stated, we find no inadequacy in California's timeliness rule generally or as applied in Martin's case. The judgment of the United States Court of Appeals for the Ninth Circuit is therefore

Reversed.

CHAPTER XIII

ORIGINAL JURISDICTION OF THE SUPREME COURT

STATUTE

---

28 U.S.C. § 1251. Original jurisdiction

(a) The Supreme Court shall have original and exclusive jurisdiction of all controversies between two or more States.

(b) The Supreme Court shall have original but not exclusive jurisdiction of:

(1) All actions or proceedings to which ambassadors, other public ministers, consuls, or vice consuls of foreign states are parties;

(2) All controversies between the United States and a State;

(3) All actions or proceedings by a State against the citizens of another State or against aliens.[1]

United States v. Texas

Supreme Court of the United States, 1892.
143 U.S. 621, 12 S.Ct. 488, 36 L.Ed. 285.

■ MR. JUSTICE HARLAN delivered the opinion of the court.

This suit was brought by original bill in this court pursuant to the act of May 2, 1890, providing a temporary government for the territory of Oklahoma. The 25th section recites the existence of a controversy between

---

[1. See Wright & Kane, Federal Courts §§ 109, 110 (6th ed.2002); 17 Wright, Miller & Cooper, Federal Practice and Procedure: Jurisdiction 2d §§ 4042–4054 (1988); 22 Moore's Federal Practice ch. 402 (3d ed.1998); McKusick, Discretionary Gatekeeping: The Supreme Court's Management of Its Original Jurisdiction Docket Since 1961, 45 Me.L.Rev. 185 (1993).

On the procedure in original actions, see 22 Moore's Federal Practice § 402.05[2] (3d ed.1998); 17 Wright, Miller & Cooper, Federal Practice and Procedure: Jurisdiction 2d § 4054 (1988); Cohen, Wading Through the Procedural Marshes of Original Jurisdiction Guided by the *Tidelands* Case: A Trial Before the United States Supreme Court, 11 Am.J. Trial Advocacy 55 (1987).]

the United States and the state of Texas as to the ownership of what is designated on the map of Texas as "Greer County," and provides that the act shall not be construed to apply to that county until the title to the same has been adjudicated and determined to be in the United States. In order that there might be a speedy and final judicial determination of this controversy the attorney general of the United States was authorized and directed to commence and prosecute on behalf of the United States a proper suit in equity in this court against the state of Texas, setting forth the title of the United States to the country lying between the North and South Forks of the Red river where the Indian Territory and the state of Texas adjoin, east of the 100th degree of longitude, and claimed by the state of Texas as within its boundary. 26 Stat. 81, 92, c. 182, § 25.

The State of Texas appeared and filed a demurrer, and, also, an answer denying the material allegations of the bill. The case is now before the court only upon the demurrer, the principal grounds of which are: That the question presented is political in its nature and character, and not susceptible of judicial determination by this court in the exercise of its jurisdiction as conferred by the Constitution and laws of the United States, that it is not competent for the general government to bring suit against a State of the Union in one of its own courts, especially when the right to be maintained is mutually asserted by the United States and the State, namely, the ownership of certain designated territory; and that the plaintiff's cause of action, being a suit to recover real property, is legal and not equitable, and consequently, so much of the act of May 2, 1890, as authorizes and directs the prosecution of a suit in equity to determine the rights of the United States to the territory in question is unconstitutional and void.

. . . . .

[I]t cannot, with propriety, be said that a question of boundary between a territory of the United States and one of the States of the Union is of a political nature, and not susceptible of judicial determination by a court having jurisdiction of such a controversy. The important question, therefore, is whether this court can, under the Constitution, take cognizance of an original suit brought by the United States against a State to determine the boundary between one of the Territories and such State. Texas insists that no such jurisdiction has been conferred upon this court, and that the only mode in which the present dispute can be peaceably settled is by agreement, in some form, between the United States and that State. Of course, if no such agreement can be reached—and it seems that one is not probable—and if neither party will surrender its claim of authority and jurisdiction over the disputed territory, the result, according to the defendant's theory of the Constitution, must be that the United States, in order to effect a settlement of this vexed question of boundary, must bring its suit in one of the courts of Texas—that State consenting that its courts may be opened for the assertion of claims against it by the United States—or that in the end there must be a trial of physical strength between the government of the Union and Texas. The first alternative is unwarranted both by the letter and spirit of the Constitution. Mr. Justice Story has well said: "It scarcely seems possible to raise a reasonable doubt as to the propriety of giving to the national courts jurisdiction of cases in which the United States are a party. It would be a perfect novelty in the history of national jurisprudence, as well as of public law, that a sovereign had no authority to sue in his own courts. Unless this power were given to the United States, the enforcement of all their rights, powers, contracts, and privileges in their sovereign capacity would be at the mercy of the States. They must be enforced, if at all, in the state tribunals." Story Const. § 1674. The second alternative above mentioned has no place in our constitutional system, and cannot be contemplated by any patriot except with feelings of deep concern.

. . . . .

The Constitution extends the judicial power of the United States "to all cases, in law and equity, arising under this Constitution, the laws of the United States and treaties made, or which shall be made, under their authority; to all cases affecting ambassadors, other public ministers and consuls; to all cases of admiralty and maritime jurisdiction; to controversies to which the United States shall be a party; to controversies between two or more States; between a State and citizens of another State; between citizens of different States; between citizens of the same State claiming lands under grants of different States, and between a State or the citizens thereof and foreign States, citizens, or subjects. In all cases, affecting ambassadors or other public ministers and consuls, and those in which a State shall be a party, the Supreme Court shall have original jurisdiction. In all the other cases before mentioned the Supreme Court shall have appellate jurisdiction, both as to law and fact, with such exceptions and under such regulations as the Congress shall make." Article 3, § 2. "The judicial power of the United States shall not be construed to extend to any suit in law or equity commenced or prosecuted against one of the United States by citizens of another State, or by citizens or subjects of any foreign State." 11th Amend.

It is apparent upon the face of these clauses that in one class of cases the jurisdiction of the courts of the Union depends "on the character of the cause, whoever may be the parties," and in the other, on the character of the parties, whatever may be the subject of controversy. Cohens v. Virginia, 6 Wheat. [19 U.S.] 264, 378, 393. The present suit falls in each class; for it is, plainly, one arising under the Constitution, laws, and treaties of the United States, and, also one in which the United States is a party. It is, therefore, one to which, by the express words of the Constitution, the judicial power of the United States extends. That a Circuit Court of the United States has not jurisdiction, under existing statutes, of a suit by the United States against a State, is clear; for by the Revised Statutes it is declared—as was done by the Judiciary Act of 1789—that "the Supreme Court shall have exclusive jurisdiction of all controversies of a civil nature where a State is a party, except between a State and its citizens, or between a State and citizens of other States, or aliens, in which later cases it shall have original, but not exclusive, jurisdiction." Rev.St. § 687; Act Sept. 24, 1789, c. 20, § 13; 1 Stat. 80. Such exclusive jurisdiction was given to this court because it best comported with the dignity of a State that a case in which it was a party should be determined in the highest, rather than in a subordinate judicial tribunal of the nation. Why then, may not this court take original cognizance of the present suit, involving a question of boundary between a Territory of the United States and a State?

The words, in the Constitution, "in all cases . . . in which a State shall be a party, the Supreme Court shall have original jurisdiction," necessarily refer to all cases mentioned in the preceding clause in which a State may be made, of right, a party defendant, or in which a State may of right be a party plaintiff. It is admitted that these words do not refer to suits brought against a State by its own citizens or by citizens of other States, or by citizens or subjects of foreign States, even where such suits arise under the Constitution, laws, and treaties of the United States, because the judicial power of the United States does not extend to suits of *individuals* against States. Hans v. Louisiana, 134 U.S. 1, and authorities there cited; North Carolina v. Temple, 134 U.S. 22, 30. It is, however, said that the words last quoted refer only to suits in which a State is a party, and in which, also, the opposite party is another State of the Union or a foreign State. This cannot be correct, for it must be conceded that a State can bring an original suit in this court against a citizen of another State. Wisconsin v. Pelican Ins. Co., 127 U.S. 265, 287. Besides, unless a State is exempt altogether from suit by the United States, we do not perceive upon what sound rule of construction suits brought by the United States in this court—especially if they be suits, the correct decision of which depends upon the Constitution, laws, or treaties of the United States—are to be excluded from its original jurisdiction as defined in the Constitution. That instrument extends the judicial power of the United States "to *all* cases," in law and equity, arising under the Constitution, laws, and treaties of the United States, and to controversies in which the United States shall be a party, and confers upon this court original jurisdiction "in *all* cases" "in which a State shall be party;" that is, in all cases mentioned in the preceding clause in which a State may of right be made a party defendant, as well as in all cases in which a State may of right institute a suit in a court of the United States. The present case is of the former class. We cannot assume that the framers of the Constitution, while extending the judicial power of the United States to controversies between two or more States of the Union, and between a State of the Union and foreign States, intended to exempt a State altogether from suit by the General Government. They could not have overlooked the possibility that controversies, capable of judicial solution, might arise between the United States and some of the States, and that the permanence of the Union might be endangered if to some tribunal was not intrusted the power to determine them according to the recognized principles of law. And to what tribunal could a trust so momentous be more appropriately committed than to that which the people of the United States, in order to form a more perfect Union, establish justice, and insure domestic tranquillity, have constituted with authority to speak for all the people and all the States upon questions before it to which the judicial power of the nation extends? It would be difficult to suggest any reason why this court should have jurisdiction to determine questions of boundary between two or more States, but not jurisdiction of controversies of like character between the United States and a State.

. . . . .

... Texas is not called to the bar of this court at the suit of an individual, but at the suit of the government established for the common and equal benefit of the people of all the states. The submission to judicial solution of controversies arising between these two governments, "each sovereign, with respect to the objects committed to it, and neither sovereign with respect to the objects committed to the other," (McCulloch v. State of Maryland, 4 Wheat. [17 U.S.] 316, 400, 410) but both subject to the supreme law of the land, does no violence to the inherent nature of sovereignty. The States of the Union have agreed, in the Constitution, that the judicial power of the United States shall extend to *all* cases arising under the Constitution, laws, and treaties of the United States, without regard to the character of the parties, (excluding, of course, suits against a State by its own citizens or by citizens of other States, or by citizens or subjects of foreign States,) and equally to controversies to which the United States shall be a party, without regard to the subject of such controversies, and that this court may exercise original jurisdiction in all such cases "in which a State shall be party," without excluding those in which the United States may be the opposite party. The exercise therefore, by this court, of such original jurisdiction in a suit brought by one State against another to determine the boundary line between them, or in a suit brought by the United States against a State to determine the boundary between a territory of the United States and that State, so far from infringing in either case upon the sovereignty, is with the consent of the State sued. Such consent was given by Texas when admitted into the Union upon an equal footing in all respects with the other States.

We are of opinion that this court has jurisdiction to determine the disputed question of boundary between the United States and Texas.

. . . . .

Demurrer overruled.

■ MR. CHIEF JUSTICE FULLER, with whom concurred MR. JUSTICE LAMAR, dissenting.

MR. JUSTICE LAMAR and myself are unable to concur in the decision just announced.

This court has original jurisdiction of two classes of cases only, those affecting ambassadors, other public ministers, and consuls, and those in which a State shall be a party.

The judicial power extends to "controversies between two or more States," "between a State and citizens of another State," and "between a State, or the citizens thereof, and foreign States, citizens, or subjects." Our original jurisdiction, which depends wholly upon the character of the parties, is confined to the cases enumerated in which a State may be a party, and this is not one of them.

The judicial power also extends to controversies to which the United States shall be a party, but such controversies are not included in the grant of original jurisdiction. To the controversy here the United States is a party.

We are of opinion, therefore, that this case is not within the original jurisdiction of the court.[2]

Wyoming v. Oklahoma

Supreme Court of the United States, 1992.
502 U.S. 437, 112 S.Ct. 789, 117 L.Ed.2d 1.

■ JUSTICE WHITE delivered the opinion of the Court.

On April 14, 1988, Wyoming submitted a motion for leave to file a complaint under this Court's original jurisdiction provided by Art. III, § 2, of the Constitution. The complaint challenged Okla.Stat., Tit. 45, §§ 939 and 939.1 (Supp.1988) (the Act), which requires Oklahoma coal-fired electric generating plants producing power for sale in Oklahoma to burn a mixture of coal containing at least 10% Oklahoma-mined coal. Wyoming sought a declaration that the Act violates the Commerce Clause, U.S. Const., Art. I, § 8, cl. 3, and an injunction permanently enjoining enforcement of the Act. On June 30, 1988, we granted Wyoming leave to file its bill of complaint over Oklahoma's objections that Wyoming lacked standing to bring this action and, in any event, should not be permitted to invoke this Court's original jurisdiction. 487 U.S. 1231. Oklahoma next filed a motion to dismiss on August 29, 1988, raising these same arguments. We denied the motion to dismiss on October 31, 1988, and ordered Oklahoma to answer Wyoming's complaint within 30 days. 488 U.S. 921. We thereaf-

---

[2. The jurisdiction of the Supreme Court in cases by the United States against a state is concurrent with the district courts. 28 U.S.C. § 1251(b)(2); United States v. California, 328 F.2d 729 (9th Cir.1964).

Although 28 U.S.C. § 1346(f) purports to give federal district courts "exclusive original jurisdiction" of quiet-title actions against the United States, this does not deprive the Supreme Court of its constitutionally conferred original jurisdiction in quiet-title actions brought against the United States by a state. California v. Arizona, 440 U.S. 59 (1979).

As to means of enforcing a judgment against a state, see Virginia v. West Virginia, 246 U.S. 565 (1918), and Powell, Coercing a State to Pay a Judgment: *Virginia v. West Virginia*, 17 Mich.L.Rev. 1 (1918); Fischer, Enforcement of a Money Judgment against a State, 12 St. Louis L.Rev. 57 (1927); Coleman, The State as Defendant under the Federal Constitution; the Virginia—West Virginia Debt Controversy, 31 Harv.L.Rev. 210 (1917); Note, The Original Jurisdiction of the United States Supreme Court, 11 Stan.L.Rev. 665, 690–694 (1959).

As to intervention, see New Jersey v. New York, 345 U.S. 369 (1953) (New Jersey sues New York and New York City. Pennsylvania intervenes. Philadelphia then wishes to intervene); Note 11 Stan.L.Rev. 665, 678–680 (1959).]

ter appointed the Special Master, 489 U.S. 1063 (1989), who ordered the parties to complete discovery and to file a stipulation of uncontested facts, any affidavits believed to be necessary, and a short statement of any disputed issues of material fact that may require a hearing. The parties complied, and each moved for summary judgment. Wyoming argued that the Act is a per se violation of the Commerce Clause. Oklahoma reasserted its arguments on standing and the appropriateness of this Court's exercise of original jurisdiction, submitting as well that the Act was constitutional.

The Report of the Special Master was received and ordered filed on October 1, 1990. 498 U.S. 803. Based on the record before him, the Special Master recommended findings of fact, to which the parties do not object, and conclusions of law generally supporting Wyoming's motion for summary judgment and rejecting Oklahoma's motion for summary judgment. More specifically, the Report recommends that we hold, first, that Wyoming has standing to sue and that this case is appropriate to our original jurisdiction; and second, that the Act discriminates against interstate commerce on its face and in practical effect, that this discrimination is not justified by any purpose advanced by Oklahoma, and that the Act therefore violates the Commerce Clause. The Report also recommends that the Court either dismiss the action as it relates to an Oklahoma-owned utility without prejudice to Wyoming to assert its claim in an appropriate forum, or, alternatively, find the Act severable to the extent it may constitutionally be applied to that utility.

Subsequently, the parties requested the Court to enter a stipulated decree adopting the Special Master's Report and containing conclusions of law. If the decree was to rule on the constitutionality of the Act, however, we preferred to have that issue briefed and argued, and the case was set down for oral argument. 501 U.S. 1215 (1991). We now adopt the Special Master's recommended findings of fact, and with one exception, his recommended conclusions of law.

I

[Wyoming is a major coal-producing state and imposes a severance tax on those who extract coal. From 1981 until 1988 Wyoming provided almost all of the coal to four Oklahoma utilities. Oklahoma then passed a statute requiring coal-fired generating plants in the state to burn a mixture containing at least 10% Oklahoma-mined coal. Wyoming brought suit in the Supreme Court for a declaration that the Oklahoma statute violates the Commerce Clause and for an injunction against its enforcement.]

II

In its motion for summary judgment before the Special Master, Oklahoma again challenged Wyoming's standing and now excepts to the Special Master's recommendation that we reject Oklahoma's submission in this respect....

.   .   .   .   .

... We agree with the Master's conclusion, arrived at after consideration of all the facts submitted to him, that Wyoming clearly had standing to bring this action. The Master observed:

"The effect of the Oklahoma statute has been to deprive Wyoming of severance tax revenues. It is undisputed that since January 1, 1987, the effective date of the Act, purchases by Oklahoma electric utilities of Wyoming-mined coal, as a percentage of their total coal purchases, have declined..... The decline came when, in response to the adoption of the Act, those utilities began purchasing Oklahoma-mined coal. The coal that, in the absence of the Act, would have been sold to Oklahoma utilities by a Wyoming producer would have been subject to the tax when extracted. Wyoming's loss of severance tax revenues 'fairly can be traced' to the Act. See Maryland v. Louisiana, 451 U.S. 725, 736 (1981) (quoting Simon v. Eastern Kentucky Welfare Rights Organization, 426 U.S. 26, 41–42 (1976))." Report of Special Master 11.

The Master recognized that Courts of Appeals have denied standing to States where the claim was that actions taken by United States Government agencies had injured the State's economy and thereby caused a decline in general tax revenues. See, e.g., Pennsylvania v. Kleppe, 174 U.S.App.D.C. 441, 533 F.2d 668, cert. denied, 429 U.S. 977 (1976); State of Iowa ex rel. Miller v. Block, 771 F.2d 347 (CA8 1985), cert. denied, 478 U.S. 1012 (1986). He concluded, however, that none of these cases was analogous to this one because none of them involved a direct injury in the form of a loss of specific tax revenues—an undisputed fact here.... In our view, the Master's conclusion about Wyoming's standing is sound.

Oklahoma argues that Wyoming is not itself engaged in the commerce affected, is not affected as a consumer, and thus has not suffered the type of direct injury cognizable in a Commerce Clause action. The authorities relied on by Oklahoma for this argument, Oklahoma v. Atchison, T., & S.F.R. Co., 220 U.S. 277, 287–289 (1911), and Louisiana v. Texas, 176 U.S. 1, 16–22 (1900), are not helpful, however, for they involved claims of *parens patriae* standing rather than allegations of direct injury to the State itself. Moreover, we have rejected a similar argument in Hunt v. Washington Apple Advertising Comm'n, 432 U.S. 333 (1977). In *Hunt*, the Washington Apple Advertising Commission brought suit to declare as violative of the Commerce Clause a North Carolina statute requiring that all apples sold or shipped into North Carolina in closed containers be identified by no grade other than the applicable federal grade or a designation that the applies were not graded. The Commission was a statutory agency designed for the promotion and protection of the Washington State apple industry and composed of 13 state growers and dealers chosen from electoral districts by their fellow growers and dealers, all of whom by mandatory assessments financed the Commission's operations. The North Carolina officials named in the suit vigorously contested the Commission's standing, either in its own right or on behalf of the apple industry it represented, arguing that it lacked a "personal stake" in the litigation because, as a state agency, it was "not itself engaged in the production and sale of Washington apples or their shipment into North Carolina." Id., at 341. After addressing the Commission's analogues to associational standing, we turned to the Commission's allegations of direct injury:

> "Finally, we note that the interests of the Commission itself may be adversely affected by the outcome of this litigation. The annual assessments paid to the Commission are tied to the volume of apples grown and packaged as 'Washington Apples.' In the event the North Carolina statute results in a contraction of the market for Washington apples or prevents any market expansion that might otherwise occur, it could reduce the amount of the assessments due the Commission and used to support its activities. This financial nexus between the interests of the Commission and its constituents coalesces with the other factors noted above to 'assure that concrete adverseness which sharpens the presentation of issues upon which the court so largely depends for illumination of difficult constitutional questions.' Baker v. Carr, [369 U.S. 186, 204 (1962)]; see also NAACP v. Alabama ex rel. Patterson, 357 U.S. 449, 459–460 (1958)." Id., at 345.

That the Commission was allowed to proceed in *Hunt* necessarily supports Wyoming's standing against Oklahoma, where its severance tax revenues are directly linked to the extraction and sale of coal and have been demonstrably affected by the Act.

Over Oklahoma's objection, which is repeated here, the Special Master also concluded that this case was an appropriate one for the exercise of our original jurisdiction. We agree, and we obviously shared this thought when granting Wyoming leave to file its complaint in the first instance. We have generally observed that the Court's original jurisdiction should be exercised "sparingly," *Maryland v. Louisiana*, 451 U.S., at 739; United States v. Nevada, 412 U.S. 534, 538 (1973), and this Court applies discretion when accepting original cases, even as to actions between States where our jurisdiction is exclusive. As stated not long ago:

> "In recent years, we have consistently interpreted 28 U.S.C. § 1251(a) as providing us with substantial discretion to make case-by-case judgments as to the practical necessity of an original forum in this Court for particular disputes within our constitutional original jurisdiction. See Maryland v. Louisiana, 451 U.S. 725, 743 (1981); Ohio v. Wyandotte Chemicals Corp., 401 U.S. 493, 499 (1971). We exercise that discretion with an eye to promoting the most effective functioning of this Court within the overall federal system." Texas v. New Mexico, 462 U.S. 554, 570 (1983).

Specifically, we have imposed prudential and equitable limitations upon the exercise of our original jurisdiction, and of these limitations we have said:

> " 'We construe 28 U.S.C. § 1251(a)(1), as we do Art. III, § 2, cl. 2, to honor our original jurisdiction but to make it obligatory only in appropriate cases. And the question of what is appropriate concerns, of course, the seriousness and dignity of the claim; yet beyond that it necessarily involves

the availability of another forum where there is jurisdiction over the named parties, where the issues tendered may be litigated, and where appropriate relief may be had.' " Illinois v. City of Milwaukee, 406 U.S. 91, 93 (1972), quoted in California v. Texas, 457 U.S. 164, 168 (1982).

It is beyond peradventure that Wyoming has raised a claim of sufficient "seriousness and dignity." Oklahoma, acting in its sovereign capacity, passed the Act, which directly affects Wyoming's ability to collect severance tax revenues, an action undertaken in its sovereign capacity. As such, Wyoming's challenge under the Commerce Clause precisely "implicates serious and important concerns of federalism fully in accord with the purposes and reach of our original jurisdiction." Maryland v. Louisiana, 451 U.S., at 744. Indeed, we found it not to be a "waste" of this Court's time in *Maryland v. Louisiana* to consider the validity of one State's "first-use tax" which served, in effect, as a severance tax on gas extracted from areas belonging to the people at large, to the detriment of other States on to whose consumers the tax passed. Ibid. Wyoming's claim here is no less substantial, and touches on its direct injury rather than on any interest as parens patriae.

Oklahoma makes much of the fact that the mining companies affected in Wyoming could bring suit raising the Commerce Clause challenge, as private parties aggrieved by state action often do. But cf. *Hunt v. Washington State Apple Advertising Comm'n*, supra. For reasons unknown, however, they have chosen neither to intervene in this action nor to file their own, whether in state or federal court. As such, no pending action exists to which we could defer adjudication on this issue. See, e.g., *Illinois v. City of Milwaukee*, supra, at 98, 108; Washington v. General Motors Corp., 406 U.S. 109, 114 (1972). Even if such action were proceeding, however, Wyoming's interests would not be directly represented. See *Maryland v. Louisiana*, supra, at 743; cf. Arizona v. New Mexico, 425 U.S. 794 (1976). Indeed, Wyoming brings suit as a sovereign seeking declaration from this Court that Oklahoma's Act is unconstitutional. The Constitution provides us original jurisdiction, and Congress has made this provision exclusive as between these parties, two States. It was proper to entertain this case without assurances, notably absent here, that a State's interests under the Constitution will find a forum for appropriate hearing and full relief.

Oklahoma points to the general requirement, reflected in the controlling principles explained above, that "[b]efore this court can be moved to exercise its extraordinary power under the Constitution to control the conduct of one State at the suit of another, the threatened invasion of rights must be of serious magnitude and it must be established by clear and convincing evidence." New York v. New Jersey, 256 U.S. 296, 309 (1921); see also Connecticut v. Massachusetts, 282 U.S. 660, 669 (1931); Missouri v. Illinois, 200 U.S. 496, 521 (1906). On this basis Oklahoma suggests that Wyoming's interest is *de minimis* solely for the reason that loss in severance tax revenues attributable to the Act has generally been less than 1% of total taxes collected. See Affidavit of Richard J. Marble (attached as Exh. B of Appendix to Motion of Wyoming for Summary Judgment). We decline any invitation to key the exercise of this Court's original jurisdiction on the amount in controversy.[3] Oklahoma's argument is, in fact, no different than the situation we faced in Pennsylvania v. West Virginia, 262 U.S. 553 (1923). When Pennsylvania challenged a West Virginia statute designed to keep natural gas within its borders, there was no question but that the issue presented rose to a level suitable to our original jurisdiction:

> "The question is an important one; for what one State may do others may, and there are ten States from which natural gas is exported for consumption in other States. Besides, what may be done with one natural product may be done with others, and there are several States in which the earth yields products of great value which are carried into other States and there used." Id., at 596.

And so it is here. Wyoming coal is a natural resource of great value primarily carried into other States for use, and Wyoming derives significant revenue from this interstate movement. "[T]he practical effect of [Oklahoma's] statute must be evaluated not only by considering the consequences of the statute itself, but also by considering how the challenged statute may interact with the legitimate regulatory regimes of the other States and what effect would arise if not one, but many or every, State adopted similar legislation." Healy v. Beer Institute, 491 U.S. 324, 336 (1989).

Because of the nature of Wyoming's claim, and the absence of any other pending litigation involving the same parties or issues, we find the present case appropriate for the exercise of this Court's original jurisdiction. Accordingly, we accept the recommendation of the Special Master that Wyoming should be permitted to bring this action, and we reject Oklahoma's exceptions to the Special Master's Report.

III

We also agree with the Special Master's ultimate conclusion that the Act is invalid under the Commerce Clause.

.　.　.　.　.

V

... In sum, we hold that the Act is unconstitutional under the Commerce Clause. No portion is severable as to any entity touched by its mandate. A judgment and decree to that effect and enjoining enforcement

---

3. We would not, in any event, readily find the amount here to be de minimis. True, the taxes lost have amounted to less than 1% of revenues received by Wyoming, but even this fractional percentage exceeds $500,000 per year. Wyoming approaches this case viewing such a drain on its tax base year after year, and it aptly paraphrases a famous statement of Senator Everett Dirksen: "[A] half million dollars here and a half million dollars there, and pretty soon real money is involved." Reply Brief for Wyoming 5, n. 3. See Respectfully Quoted: A Dictionary of Quotations Requested from the Congressional Research Service 155 (S.Platt. ed.1989) ("A billion here, a billion there, and pretty soon you're talking about real money").

of the Act will be entered. Jurisdiction over the case is retained in the event that further proceedings are required to implement the judgment.

So ordered.

■ JUSTICE SCALIA, with whom THE CHIEF JUSTICE and JUSTICE THOMAS join, dissenting.

In the almost century and a half since we first entered the business of entertaining "negative Commerce Clause" actions, see Cooley v. Board of Wardens of Port of Philadelphia ex rel Society for Relief of Distress Pilots, 12 How. [53 U.S.] 299 (1852), I think it safe to say that the federal courts have never been plagued by a shortage of these suits brought by private parties, and that the nontextual elements of the Commerce Clause have not gone unenforced for lack of willing litigants. Today, however, when the coal companies with sales allegedly affected by the Oklahoma law have, for whatever reason, chosen not to litigate, the Court sees fit, for the first time, to recognize a *State's* standing to bring a negative Commerce Clause action on the basis of its consequential loss of tax revenue. That is a major step, and I think it is wrong. Even if it were correct, however, summary judgment that Wyoming suffered consequential loss of tax revenue in the present case would be unjustified. I would deny Wyoming's motion for summary judgment and grant Oklahoma's.

. . . . .

■ JUSTICE THOMAS, with whom THE CHIEF JUSTICE and JUSTICE SCALIA join, dissenting.

Even if I believed that Wyoming had standing to challenge the Oklahoma statute (which for the reasons given by JUSTICE SCALIA, I do not) I would decline to exercise the Court's original jurisdiction here.

The Constitution provides that "[i]n all Cases ... in which a State shall be a Party, the Supreme Court shall have original jurisdiction." U.S. Const., Art. III, § 2, cl. 2. Congress, in turn, has provided that "[t]he Supreme Court shall have original and exclusive jurisdiction of all controversies between two or more States." 28 U.S.C. § 1251(a). Given these provisions, one might expect—assuming the existence of a "case" or "controversy" —that we would be required to exercise our original jurisdiction here, for a court having jurisdiction generally must exercise it. "We have no more right to decline the exercise of jurisdiction which is given, than to usurp that which is not given." Cohens v. Virginia, 6 Wheat. [19 U.S.] 264, 404 (1821) (Marshall, C.J.). As the Court observes, however, ... we have exercised discretion in declining to hear cases that fall within the literal terms of our original jurisdiction. See, e.g., United States v. Nevada, 412 U.S. 534, 538 (1973) (per curiam) (controversy between the United States and individual States); Ohio v. Wyandotte Chemicals Corp., 401 U.S. 493, 497–499 (1971) (action by a State against the citizens of other States). We exercise this discretion even with respect to controversies between two or more States, which fall within our original *and exclusive* jurisdiction.[4]

---

4. JUSTICE STEVENS has stated that the Court's explanations for declining to exercise its *nonexclusive* original jurisdiction are "inapplicable" where, as here, its original jurisdiction

See, e.g., Texas v. New Mexico, 462 U.S. 554, 570 (1983); California v. Texas, 457 U.S. 164, 168 (1982) (per curiam); Maryland v. Louisiana, 451 U.S. 725, 739 (1981); Arizona v. New Mexico, 425 U.S. 794, 796–798 (1976) (per curiam). I believe that the Court's decision to accept jurisdiction over this case is a misguided exercise of that discretion.

"It has long been this Court's philosophy that 'our original jurisdiction should be invoked sparingly.' " Illinois v. City of Milwaukee, 406 U.S. 91, 93 (1972) (quoting Utah v. United States, 394 U.S. 89, 95 (1969)). The sound reasons for this approach have been set forth on many occasions, see, e.g., *Ohio v. Wyandotte Chemicals Corp.*, supra, 401 U.S., at 498; *Maryland v. Louisiana*, supra, at 761–763 (1981) (REHNQUIST, J., dissenting), and I need not repeat them here. As Chief Justice Fuller aptly observed almost a century ago, our original jurisdiction "is of so delicate and grave a character that it was not contemplated that it would be exercised save when the necessity was absolute." Louisiana v. Texas, 176 U.S. 1, 15 (1900). In determining which cases merit the exercise of original jurisdiction, the Court typically has focused on two considerations: the nature of the claims involved and the availability of alternate forums where they can be addressed. See, e.g., *Illinois v. City of Milwaukee*, supra, at 93; Massachusetts v. Missouri, 308 U.S. 1, 18–19 (1939).

In my view, both factors cut strongly against exercising original jurisdiction here. Wyoming claims to be injured as follows: the Oklahoma statute decreases coal sales by Wyoming mining companies to Oklahoma buyers, which supposedly decreases the amount of coal those companies extract in Wyoming, which in turn supposedly decreases the tax revenues Wyoming collects from the companies when they extract the coal. Plainly, the primary dispute here is *not* between the States of Wyoming and Oklahoma, but between the private Wyoming mining companies and the State of Oklahoma, whose statute reduced the companies' sales to Oklahoma utilities. It is true, as the Court notes, . . . that Oklahoma passed the statute in its sovereign capacity and that Wyoming collects taxes in its sovereign capacity. That States act qua States is certainly very relevant in assessing the "seriousness and dignity" of a claim. See *Maryland v. Louisiana*, supra, at 764–766 (REHNQUIST, J., dissenting). But it is also critical to examine the extent to which the sovereigns actually have clashed. Cf. *Arizona v. New Mexico*, supra, at 797–798 ("In denying the

---

is *exclusive* under 28 U.S.C. § 1251(a). California v. West Virginia, 454 U.S. 1027, 1027–1028 (1981) (opinion dissenting from denial of motion to file bill of complaint). Similarly, commentators have suggested that the Court's statement that " 'the congressional grant of exclusive jurisdiction under § 1251(a) . . . requir[es] resort to our obligatory jurisdiction only in appropriate cases' " is "an oxymoron." P. Bator, D. Meltzer, P. Mishkin & D. Shapiro, Hart and Wechsler's The Federal Courts and the Federal System 344 (3d ed.1988) (quoting Maryland v. Louisiana, 451 U.S. 725, 739 (1981) (internal quotation omitted)). See also Shapiro, Jurisdiction and Discretion, 60 N.Y.U.L.Rev. 543, 561 (1985) (calling "unanswerable" criticism of the Court's discretionary approach to cases within its exclusive original jurisdiction).

As noted in text, the Court has held otherwise and those precedents have not been challenged here. The exercise of discretion is probably inevitable as long as the Court's approach to standing is as relaxed as it is today.

State of Arizona leave to file, we are not unmindful that the legal incidence of [the challenged action by New Mexico] is upon the utilities''). In my view, an entirely derivative injury of the type alleged by Wyoming here—even if it met minimal standing requirements—would not justify the exercise of discretionary original jurisdiction. Additionally, of course, Wyoming has advanced no reason why the affected mining companies (hardly bashful litigants) did not or could not themselves challenge the Oklahoma statute in another, more convenient, forum. The lower federal courts and the state courts are readily available as appropriate forums "in which the *issues* tendered here may be litigated." Id., at 797 (emphasis in original).

The implications of the Court's novel theory that tax-collection injury alone justifies exercise of original jurisdiction are, in my view, both sweeping and troubling. An economic burden imposed by one State on another State's taxpayers will frequently affect the other State's fisc. (That will virtually always be the case, for example, with respect to income taxes; if State A takes actions that reduce the income of the taxpayers of State B, State B will collect less income-tax revenue.) Under today's opinion, a State that can show *any* loss in tax revenue—even a *de minimis* loss . . . that can be traced (albeit loosely) to the action of another State can apparently proceed directly to this Court to challenge that action. Perhaps the Court is not concerned about that possibility because of its "discretion" in managing its original docket. But, having extended the original jurisdiction to one State's claim based on its tax-collector status, the Court cannot, in the exercise of discretion, refuse to entertain future disputes based on the same theory. That would be the exercise not of discretion, but of caprice.

I respectfully dissent.[5]

[5. See Barnes, Suits Between States in the Supreme Court, 7 Vand.L.Rev. 494, 500–505 (1954). Note, Exclusive Original Jurisdiction of the United States Supreme Court: Does It Still Exist?, 1982 B.Y.U.L.Rev. 727.

In Delaware v. New York, 507 U.S. 490 (1993), the Supreme Court repeatedly referred to the need for "efficiency" in resolving disputes between states that, because of the exclusive jurisdiction provided by 28 U.S.C. § 1251(a), are subject to adjudication only by exercise of the Supreme Court's original jurisdiction. The issue was the power to escheat cash and securities owed by financial institutions to customers who have abandoned their accounts. New York had sought to escheat over $360 million in abandoned securities and dividends held on a "street name" basis by banks and brokerage houses doing business in New York. Most of these firms were Delaware corporations that maintained their principal executive offices in New York. Delaware sued New York, claiming that its right of escheat as the state of incorporation of the account custodians was prior to New York's right as the state in which the accounts were held. All parties agreed that the primary rule of escheat awarded the funds to the state in which the creditor/account holder's last known address was located. But for lack of such an address or because the state of last address had no law of escheat, the bulk of the funds were not covered by the primary rule. The Special Master recommended that the issuer of the securities and dividends be considered the "debtor," and that the right of escheat be granted to the state in which the issuer had its principal executive office. The Supreme Court rejected both prongs of this recommendation: the relevant "debtor" was the bank or brokerage house that held "in street name" the abandoned securities and dividends; the right of escheat belonged to the state of incorporation of these institutions. The hard-and-fast rule giving priority to the state of incorporation rather than the state of principal executive office was deemed imperative lest the Court be compelled to "craft different rules for the novel facts of each case."

In Mississippi v. Louisiana, 506 U.S. 73 (1992), the Supreme Court discussed the standards governing its discretionary power to decline to exercise its exclusive jurisdiction over suits between states. At issue in that suit was a boundary dispute between the two states over an island in the Mississippi River. The Supreme Court had earlier refused to give Louisiana leave to sue Mississippi by bill of complaint within the original jurisdiction of the Supreme Court. After being rebuffed by the Supreme Court, Louisiana had intervened in private litigation involving competing claims of title to land under the laws of the two states and had filed a third-party complaint against Mississippi to determine the boundary of the two states with respect to the disputed land. Because its original jurisdiction in suits between states is made exclusive by 28 U.S.C. § 1251(a), the Supreme Court held that the district court erred by failing to dismiss Louisiana's third-party complaint for lack of subject-matter jurisdiction. The exclusivity of jurisdiction under § 1251(a) did not divest the district court of jurisdiction to determine the boundary issue as between the private parties, however, "because that section speaks not in terms of claims or issues, but in terms of parties."

The Supreme Court dryly noted that "of course" the states would not be bound "by any decision as to the boundary between them which was rendered in a lawsuit between private litigants," but what is the practical significance of this so long as the Supreme Court refuses to exercise its original jurisdiction? In fact after the decision just discussed Louisiana did commence a new action within the Supreme Court's original jurisdiction and the Court granted leave to file its bill of complaint. Louisiana v. Mississippi, 510 U.S. 941 (1993). In its subsequent decision on the merits, the Court began by saying: "Like the shifting river channel near the property in dispute, this litigation has traversed from one side of our docket to the other." Louisiana v. Mississippi, 516 U.S. 22, 23 (1995). The Court found that the land was in Mississippi.

In Virginia v. Maryland, 540 U.S. 56 (2003), the Court exercised its original jurisdiction to resolve in Virginia's favor a dispute over riparian rights in the Potomac River, which lies almost entirely within Maryland. Applying a 1785 compact between the states regarding mutual use of the river, an 1877 arbitral award establishing the Virginia shore as the boundary between the states, and federal common law, the Court held that Virginia and Maryland each has the sovereign right to use the water of the river and to construct improvements into the river in order to withdraw water, subject to a duty of mutual non-interference.]

INDEX

†